THE OXFORD HANDBOOK OF

HOBBES

THE OXFORD HANDBOOK OF

HOBBES

Edited by

A. P. MARTINICH

and

KINCH HOEKSTRA

OXFORD

UNIVERSITY PRESS

OXFORD
UNIVERSITY PRESS

Oxford University Press is a department of the University of Oxford. It furthers
the University's objective of excellence in research, scholarship, and education
by publishing worldwide. Oxford is a registered trade mark of Oxford University
Press in the UK and certain other countries.

Published in the United States of America by Oxford University Press
198 Madison Avenue, New York, NY 10016, United States of America.

Library of Congress Cataloging-in-Publication Data
Names: Martinich, Aloysius, editor. | Hoekstra, Kinch, editor.
Title: The Oxford handbook of Hobbes / edited by A.P. Martinich and Kinch
Hoekstra.
Description: New York, NY : Oxford University Press, 2016. | Series: Oxford
handbooks | Includes index.
Identifiers: LCCN 2015027839 | ISBN 978–0–19–979194–1 (hardcover : alk. paper)
Subjects: LCSH: Hobbes, Thomas, 1588–1679.
Classification: LCC B1247 .O94 2016 | DDC 192—dc23 LC record
available at http://lccn.loc.gov/2015027839

3 5 7 9 8 6 4 2
Printed by Sheridan, USA

Contents

PART III POLITICAL PHILOSOPHY

PART IV RELIGION

PART V HISTORY, POETRY, AND PARADOX

ACKNOWLEDGMENTS

WE first want to thank our editor Peter Ohlin for suggesting this volume and for being as supportive as he has been patient. A variety of other people at or connected with Oxford University Press have been enormously helpful, first for the version online and now for the print edition, in particular: Janish Ashwin, Molly Davis, and Lauren Konopko. Finally, we extend our thanks to Leslie Martinich for her supererogatory and meticulous editorial help.

Contributors

Arash Abizadeh is Associate Professor of Political Science at McGill University. He is currently completing a book titled *Hobbes and the Two Dimensions of Normativity*.

Adrian Blau is Senior Lecturer in Politics, in the Department of Political Economy, King's College London. He has published "Hobbes on Corruption" (in *History of Political Thought*, 2009) and is writing a monograph called *Hobbes's Failed Science of Politics and Ethics*. He is currently editing a methodological textbook called *Methods in Analytical Political Theory*.

Jeffrey Collins is Associate Professor of History at Queen's University in Kingston, Ontario. He is the author of *The Allegiance of Thomas Hobbes* (Oxford University Press, 2005).

John Deigh is Professor of Law and Philosophy at the University of Texas at Austin. He is the author of *The Sources of Moral Agency* (1996), *Emotions, Values and the Law* (2008), and *An Introduction to Ethics* (2010). He was the editor of *Ethics* from 1997 to 2008.

Stewart Duncan is Associate Professor of Philosophy at the University of Florida. He is the author of several articles on Hobbes, Leibniz, and other seventeenth-century philosophers.

Katherine Dunlop is Associate Professor of Philosophy at the University of Texas at Austin. She specializes in the history and philosophy of mathematics and theories of knowledge in early modern philosophy.

Ioannis D. Evrigenis is Professor of Political Science and Chair of the Department of Classics at Tufts University. He is the author of *Fear of Enemies and Collective Action* (2008) and *Images of Anarchy: The Rhetoric and Science in Hobbes's State of Nature* (2014).

Daniel Garber is Stuart Professor of Philosophy at Princeton University. He is the author of *Descartes' Metaphysical Physics*, *Descartes Embodied*, and *Leibniz: Body, Substance, Monad*, as well as numerous articles and edited volumes on the history of early modern philosophy and science.

Franco Giudice is Associate Professor in the History of Science at the University of Bergamo (Italy). His work concerns theories of light and vision in the seventeenth century. He is the author of *Luce e Visione: Thomas Hobbes e la scienza dell'ottica* (1999), *Lo spettro di Newton: La rivelazione della luce e dei colori* (2009), and (with Massimo Bucciantini and Michele Camerota) *Galileo's Telescope: A European Story* (2015). He is currently working on an edition of Hobbes's *Optical Works* with Elaine Stroud for the Clarendon Edition of the Works of Thomas Hobbes.

Nancy J. Hirschmann is Professor of Political Science and Director of the Program on Gender, Sexuality, and Women's Studies at the University of Pennsylvania. She has written broadly on the concept of freedom in contemporary feminism and the history of political thought, including *The Subject of Liberty: Toward a Feminist Theory of Freedom*, which won the Victoria Schuck Award from the American Political Science Association, and *Gender, Class, and Freedom in Modern Political Theory*.

Kinch Hoekstra is Chancellor's Professor of Political Science and Law at the University of California, Berkeley, and an affiliated professor in Philosophy and Classics. He was previously a member of the Faculties of Philosophy and Classics at the University of Oxford, where he was the Leveson Gower Fellow and Tutor of Ancient and Modern Philosophy at Balliol College. Current work includes contributions to *The Oxford Handbook of Thucydides* and *The Cambridge Companion to Thucydides*.

Douglas M. Jesseph is Professor of Philosophy at the University of South Florida. He is the author of *Berkeley's Philosophy of Mathematics* and *Squaring the Circle: The War Between Hobbes and Wallis*, as well as a number of articles on mathematics and methodology in the early modern period.

S. A. Lloyd is Professor of Philosophy, Law, and Political Science at the University of Southern California. She is author of *Ideals as Interests in Hobbes's Leviathan: the Power of Mind over Matter* and *Morality in the Philosophy of Thomas Hobbes: Cases in the Law of Nature*, and she is editor of the *Bloomsbury Companion to Hobbes* and *Hobbes Today*.

Agostino Lupoli is former Professor of History of Modern Philosophy at the University of Milan and Pavia. He has published on epistemological theories from the Renaissance to Kant and on ethical and political thought from Machiavelli to Kant. His publications on Hobbes include the book, *Nei limiti della materia. Hobbes e Boyle: materialismo epistemologico, filosofia corpuscolare e "dio corporeo"* (2006), and the essays "Hobbes e Sanchez"; "La nozione di 'popolo corrotto' (corrupted people) in Hobbes e Machiavelli"; "Teoria scettica della politica e statuto civile dell'ateo: Hobbes e Bayle"; "On Hobbes's Distinction of Accidents"; and "Skinner, Hobbes e il governo misto."

A. P. Martinich is Roy Allison Vaughan Centennial Professor in Philosophy, and Professor of History and Government at the University of Texas at Austin. He is the author of *The Two Gods of Leviathan* (1992), *Hobbes: A Biography* (1999), and *Hobbes* (2005), and co-editor with David Sosa of *The Philosophy of Language* 6th edition (Oxford University Press, 2013).

Tomaž Mastnak is Director of Research at the Institute of Philosophy in the Research Centre of the Slovenian Academy of Sciences and Arts in Ljubljana and a Research Fellow at the University of California at Irvine.

Sarah Mortimer is University Lecturer and Official Student and Tutor in Modern History at Christ Church, University of Oxford. She is the author of *Reason and Religion in the English Revolution* (2010).

Mark C. Murphy is McDevitt Professor of Religious Philosophy at Georgetown University. He works in moral, political, and legal philosophy and is the author of *Natural Law and Practical Rationality* (2001), *An Essay on Divine Authority* (2002), *Philosophy of Law* (2006), *Natural Law in Jurisprudence and Politics* (2006), and *God and Moral Law* (Oxford University Press, 2011).

Jon Parkin, Fellow and Tutor in Modern History at St. Hugh's College, Oxford, works on the reading and reception of political thought and is author of *Taming the Leviathan: The Reception of the Political and Religious Ideas of Thomas Hobbes in England 1640–1700* (2007).

Martine Pécharman is Senior Research Fellow in Philosophy at the Centre National de la Recherche Scientifique (CNRS). She specializes in early modern metaphysics, epistemology, and logic, especially the logic of Port-Royal, John Wallis, and John Locke.

Thomas Pink, Professor of Philosophy at King's College, London, works on the history and metaphysics of ethics, political philosophy, and philosophy of law. He is editing the *Questions Concerning Liberty, Necessity, and Chance* for the Clarendon Edition of the Works of Thomas Hobbes.

Timothy Raylor is Professor of English at Carleton College, Minnesota. With Stephen Clucas, he is editing *De corpore* and its related manuscripts for the Clarendon Hobbes.

David Runciman is Professor of Politics and Chair of the Department of Politics and International Studies at the University of Cambridge. He is the author of *Politics: Ideas in Profile* (2014), *Political Hypocrisy* (2008), *Representation* (2008, with Mónica Brito Vieira), and *The Politics of Good Intentions* (2006).

Quentin Skinner is Barber Beaumont Professor of the Humanities at Queen Mary, University of London. Among his books are *Reason and Rhetoric in the Philosophy of Hobbes* (1996), *Hobbes and Civil Science* (2002), and *Hobbes and Republican Liberty* (2008). *From Humanism to Hobbes* is due to be published in 2017.

Johann Sommerville is Professor of History at the University of Wisconsin, Madison, and the author of a number of works on Hobbes and on early modern politics and thought, including *Thomas Hobbes: Political Ideas in Historical Context* (1992). He is editing *The Elements of Law* for the Clarendon Edition of the Works of Thomas Hobbes.

Richard Tuck is the Frank G. Thomson Professor of Government at Harvard University, where he has been since 1995. Prior to that he had been a University Lecturer in History at Cambridge and Fellow of Jesus College since 1973; he is still an Honorary Fellow of Jesus College. He is the author of many articles and books on political thought and its history, including *Natural Rights Theories* (1979), *Hobbes* (Oxford University Press, 1989), *Philosophy and Government 1572–1651* (1993), *The Rights of War and Peace: Political Thought and the International Order from Grotius to Kant* (Oxford University Press, 1999), and *Free Riding* (2008). He has also produced editions of Hobbes's *Leviathan* (1991), Hobbes's *On the Citizen* (with Michael Silverthorne, 1998), and Hugo Grotius's *The Rights of War and Peace* (2005).

CHAPTER 1

....

INTRODUCTION

....

A. P. MARTINICH

THE *Oxford Handbook of Hobbes* consists of twenty-six original chapters by distinguished philosophers, political theorists, historians, and literary scholars from six countries. The coverage of topics is not comprehensive because no book of a manageable size can discuss all the interesting aspects of Hobbes's thought in detail. The chapters are not reviews of the secondary literature, although they are informed by it. Rather, the goal is to advance the study of Hobbes's thought.

In the first section of this introduction, Hobbes's life is briefly described. In the second section, major themes in Hobbes's philosophy will be discussed. Because it would be redundant to report what the contributors so ably present, most of the chapters are only alluded to. The main points of the other contributors are often stated either for their intrinsic interest or to illuminate the themes further.

1 LIFE

....

Thomas Hobbes (1588–1679) lived through the reigns of four monarchs, through a decade-long civil war (1642–1649), another decade of unstable rule during the Commonwealth (1649–1660), and almost two decades of Charles II's restored monarchy, which was troubled from 1666 on.[1] When he was born, the Church of England was relatively stable and dominated religious life, but, by the time of his death, it competed with Presbyterianism and several other Protestant denominations. During his youth, the monarchy was settled, and King James I's rule could comfortably claim to be absolute, even though most in parliament disagreed. A decade after Hobbes's death, the government was a limited, constitutional monarchy. During Hobbes's youth, Galileo had not yet made his important discoveries, but when Hobbes died, Isaac Newton was

---

[1] The biographies by Malcolm 1996, Martinich 1999, and Skinner 2002: 1–37 are recommended. The most engaging one was written by Aubrey 1898.

the Lucasian Professor of Mathematics. Hobbes had been born in one cultural world and died in another.

In his prose autobiography,[2] Hobbes said that he was born a twin with fear because his mother's fear of the expected invasion of England by the Spanish Armada made her give birth to him prematurely on Good Friday, April 5, 1588. The story cannot be dismissed simply because the Armada was blown off course, since she could not have known that this would happen. His mother carried on as best she could after her husband, a poorly educated and quarrelsome minister of the Elizabethan Church, abandoned them during Hobbes's adolescence after a fight with another clergyman. Hobbes was fortunate to have been taught Latin and Greek by Robert Latimer, who graduated from Magdalen Hall, Oxford, which Hobbes would later attend thanks to the financial support provided by his paternal uncle, a successful glover.

After Hobbes received his bachelor of arts degree, he was hired by William Cavendish, the first earl of Devonshire, to tutor his son, also named William. Since Hobbes was only a couple of years older than William, he became more of a friend to William than a tutor. In his verse autobiography, he said that in his old age he had pleasant dreams about this happiest time of his life. A few years after William died (1628), he became tutor to his son, a third William and the third earl of Devonshire. Hobbes had the new earl study "the three basic elements of the *studia humanitatis*: grammar, rhetoric, and poetry," as well as logic, arithmetic, and geography.[3] During this time, Hobbes prepared a Latin version of Aristotle's *Rhetoric* and, notwithstanding his disdain for central parts of Aristotle's philosophy, adapted the part of it about the passions for his use in some later works.[4]

Hobbes's obvious intelligence and connections to nobility gave him access to some of the most talented people in science and mathematics from the 1630s onward, including Galileo during his third tour of Europe. In England, Hobbes was connected to a group of intellectuals supported by a cousin of the second earl of Devonshire. Their interests centered on mathematics and optics. The expertise Hobbes developed during this period served him well when he came to write *De homine*, a large part of which is devoted to optics. Franco Giudice in his chapter explains the importance of Hobbes's work, which influenced Isaac Barrow and was the only major contender to Descartes's own views until Newton's superseded it. Hobbes's mathematical ability is typically denigrated. Perhaps he should be recognized more as a philosopher of mathematics. Like Barrow, he took geometry to be more basic than arithmetic. In her chapter, Katherine Dunlop shows that Hobbes's "program for enriching geometry" contributed to the development of a calculus. For example, Hobbes's idea that mathematical objects are generated by motion was shared by Newton, who "used it to justify consideration of

---

[2] Hobbes wrote two autobiographies. The verse autobiography was written about 1672 when he was eighty-four. The substantially prose autobiography was drafted initially in the 1650s but completed only a few months before he died. See Skinner 2002: 2, n. 14 for details.

[3] Skinner 2002, 3.

[4] Strauss (1963) first showed the importance of Aristotle's rhetoric for Hobbes's philosophy.

infinitely small quantities (as given by instantaneous rates of change)." (This is not to say that Hobbes was the source of Newton's idea.) She also explains that what seventeenth-century mathematicians demanded was not simply a solution to a problem, such as the squaring of a circle, but a solution that "made intelligible the square's relationship to the circle." And that is what Hobbes attempted to do. Any judgment about Hobbes's success or failure in the foundations of mathematics must recognize the problems in Descartes's own flawed achievements and what was realistically possible given the beliefs of the time. By the end of the 1630s, Hobbes had acquired a good reputation for mathematics and philosophy. Marin Mersenne, the head of an important French circle of philosophers and scientists, sent Hobbes the manuscript of Descartes's *Meditations on First Philosophy*. His comments on that groundbreaking work were published along with five others and Descartes's replies.[5]

Sensing the total breakdown of the English government, Hobbes went into voluntary exile at the end of 1640 and spent the decade in France. By reworking the second part of his *Elements of Law, Natural and Politic*, he produced *De cive*, which Mersenne arranged to have printed in 1642. The presentation of his politics in that work is tighter than that in *The Elements of Law*, but the doctrine is virtually the same. Comments by some of its readers led Hobbes to add a series of clarifying footnotes to the text, and this expanded edition was then printed in 1647. *De cive* was written in Latin partly because it was for European intellectuals and partly because it was supposed to be a section of a formal scientific system, Latin still being the language of philosophy and science.[6]

De cive was the third part of his envisioned three-part work. The first two parts, *De corpore* and *De homine*, were much slower in coming. *De corpore*, the first part of the trilogy, caused Hobbes the most trouble. He had his basic ideas fairly well worked out in 1640, and he had little trouble writing about his own views about physics in a long commentary on the book *De mundo* by Thomas White, a Catholic priest also in exile.[7] A large part of Hobbes's commentary contains the same doctrine as would appear in *De corpore* and, to some extent, is an early draft of that book. What hindered Hobbes's progress were some of the proofs he needed for the third part of *De corpore*. His slow progress on this book was exacerbated by and may have contributed to the debilitation of an illness that kept him at death's door for several months in 1647. *De corpore* was eventually published in England in 1655; an English translation of it followed in 1656. The remaining section, the second in logical ordering, *De homine*, was published in 1658. Although his treatment of emotion is excellent, about half of it is about optics and the book as a whole seems perfunctory.

Hobbes's scientific theory was materialistic and mechanistic. The fundamental objects of reality are bodies in motion, and all change occurs by contact of one body

---

[5] Important and excellent accounts of the reception of Hobbes's philosophy are Goldie 1991, Parkin 2007, and Skinner 2002, 287–345.

[6] *Leviathan* is arguably the first great work of philosophy published in English.

[7] This manuscript, often referred to as *Anti-White*, was discovered in the second half of the twentieth century and published in 1973; Hobbes 1976 is a translation.

against another. Although he may have arrived at the idea of mechanism independently of Galileo, he certainly owed some of his ideas to Galileo, the most important of which may have been the idea of treating nature mathematically. As much as Hobbes admired Galileo, his scientific views were closer to those of Descartes. This closeness, combined with the competitiveness of both men, may explain their antipathy for each other.[8] Hobbes's views about nature were to a surprising extent picked up by Spinoza and then Leibniz. For Hobbes and Spinoza, the physical laws of nature approach the status of truths of geometry, and Leibniz conceived of these laws as hypothetical in form. (Daniel Garber's chapter contains much information on this topic and its significance.)

In addition to the studies in Paris already described, Hobbes served as mathematics tutor to Charles, Prince of Wales, the future Charles II. Hobbes was disconcerted by the title page of *De cive* (1647) because it described him as "tutor" to the Prince of Wales. Many of the royalists in exile considered the low-born Hobbes a mountebank and were irritated by this apparent effrontery.[9] In fact, the description "tutor" had been supplied by Hobbes's friend, Samuel Sorbière. Hobbes did his best to deny the title was his own doing, but people who did not like him were disposed not to believe him.

In his prose autobiography, Hobbes indicates that he began *Leviathan* sometime in 1646, after the Prince of Wales escaped to France. He could hardly have been working on *Leviathan* full time between 1646 and 1651 because he was working on the second edition of *De cive* and then on *De corpore* until at least June 1648. Other evidence points to his working on *De corpore* in 1648–1649. He could have been working on *Leviathan* in 1646 to the extent that some things written at that time later appeared in the final version of the book.[10] The best example of this is chapter 42, "Of Power Ecclesiastical." It is by far the longest chapter, comprises about 12 percent of the book, and deals with the views of the Counter-Reformation theologian Robert Bellarmine, among other things.[11] Since *Leviathan* was intended for an English audience, there was no need for Hobbes to argue against Roman Catholicism at length. It makes sense for him to have written it in Roman Catholic France and would account to a large extent for the hostility of the French clergy toward him. Most of part IV, "Of the Kingdome of Darkness," could also have originally been separate documents. That would explain why Hobbes's anticlimactic definition of "philosophy" appears in chapter 46, after more than 365 pages of philosophizing.

It is more plausible that Hobbes began serious work on *Leviathan* after the beheading of Charles I in January, 1649, by a kangaroo court of the Rump Parliament. It would have been the last of "so many crimes attributed to the commands of God."[12] In *Leviathan*, Hobbes lays out what he perceived to be abuses of power and distortions of

---

[8] See Martinich 1999, 163–171.

[9] Most low-born Englishmen who rose to wealth or prominence did their best to acquire the mannerisms of the better-born or did not make themselves conspicuous among them. In contrast, Hobbes spoke with a distinctly West Country accent and never lost the chip on his shoulder.

[10] Cf. Malcolm 2012, 4–12.

[11] Curley 1994, 549.

[12] Cf. Skinner 2002, 15–16 and 19–20.

Christianity by Roman Catholicism, the Church of England (with a supposedly *jure divino* episcopacy), and presbyterianism. In Hobbes's view, Roman Catholicism was superstitious and unjustifiably claimed to have authority independent of the civil sovereign. Many of the clergy of the episcopal Church of England in exile also thought that the Church had some authority independent of the sovereign, and presbyterianism made the independence of the Church a principle. Despite his attacks on all three religions, Hobbes had many Roman Catholic friends and some in the Church of England, but no Presbyterians to my knowledge.

Hobbes returned to England in the winter of 1650–1651 because the war had ended: he was *persona non grata* at the English court in exile and at the court of Charles I's queen, Henrietta Maria, and he was disliked by the French clergy, except for the few who were his friends; as he allegedly said, he had "a mind to go home."[13] Back in England, he became a controversial figure because of the political and religious doctrines presented in *Leviathan*. Not only did his absolutism clash with the ideology of the Commonwealth, but most royalists also interpreted it as being pro-Cromwell. As for religion, his peculiar blend of old and new views about the Bible and Christianity offended almost everyone. Ironically, his enemies used parts of Hobbes's philosophy when it served their purposes. A notable example was its use in the early 1670s by Samuel Parker to support the rights of the Anglican Church, just when Hobbes's reputation as an atheist was becoming common.

Hobbes's reputation in mathematics and natural science also began to unravel during the 1650s over various classical problems such as squaring the circle.[14] He unwisely began to attack better mathematicians such as John Wallis, whose work contributed to the development of the infinitesimal calculus. It did not help the tone of the debate that Wallis was a Presbyterian and Hobbes a son of the episcopal Church of England.[15]

At the Restoration, Hobbes broadened his attacks to include the experimental science of the Royal Society. He thought its members overvalued fact collection and scientific experiments. He was especially critical of the experiments of Robert Boyle, who claimed to have created a vacuum by extracting air from a glass bulb with the use of a pump. In *Dialogus Physicus* (1661), Hobbes pointed out that it was not obvious that the integrity of the seal between the pump and the bulb was preserved. And even if gross air were extracted, more fine-grained air may have penetrated the glass.[16] Hobbes's criticisms were astute but mistaken.

Hobbes could not understand why the Royal Society did not see that physical science should be a priori. In a letter to the Royal Society, Hobbes wrote that its members would make more progress if they continued his work of deducing from the definitions in *De corpore*. Boyle effectively responded to Hobbes in *New Experiments Physico-Mechanical Touching the Air* (1662).

---

[13] Hyde 1676, 7.
[14] Skinner 2002, 308–323.
[15] Jesseph 1999 and Martinich 1999, 278–283.
[16] Shapin and Schaffer 1985.

The re-established episcopal Church of England was even more uncongenial to Hobbes than was the Royal Society. In general, the Church was bent on revenge for the humiliation inflicted on it by Presbyterians, Independents, nonroyalists, and those who did not support its claim to authority *juro divino*. Although Hobbes belonged only to the last group, he was a special target because of his stinging—and largely justified—criticisms of the Church and his novel attempt to reconcile revealed religion with the new science. In 1666, a parliamentary committee was formed to investigate the supposed atheism and heretical content in *Leviathan*, but the committee never reported. Hobbes sensibly took the potential charges against himself seriously. He burned some of his papers and wrote about the nature and history of heresy. Each work had the satisfying consequence that *Leviathan* was not heretical and that, if it were heretical, there would be no civil punishment for it because heresy was not a crime. Only one of these treatises about heresy was published during his life, specifically, one part of the appendix to the Latin translation of *Leviathan*, which was published in Amsterdam in 1668. According to Hobbes, heresy is a nonstandard belief, and beliefs are not or at least should not be crimes since the law should deal only with physical behavior.

In the 1670s, Hobbes split his time between London and the houses of the third earl of Devonshire in Derbyshire. During this time, he translated both the *Iliad* and *Odyssey*. At least part of his explanation for translating Homer in the 1670s was the one he gave, "Because I thought it might take off my Adversaries from shewing their folly upon my more serious Writings, and set them upon my Verses to shew their wisdom."[17] On the broader issue of Hobbes's views on poetry in general, see Timothy Raylor's chapter.

Hobbes maintained the absoluteness of the sovereign and, in particular, the absoluteness of the English monarch, to the end. In 1679, the Exclusion Crisis was threatening the monarchy. A bill had been introduced to exclude Charles's brother, James, the future King James II, from the line of succession. The third earl of Devonshire (another William Cavendish) was trying to sort out the position he should take, and he seems to have put several questions about the matter to Hobbes. The key one is whether a reigning monarch is "oblig'd to put him"—a person who would not be able to protect the people if he were to ascend the throne—"by, upon the request of his subjects."[18] Hobbes skirts the question at first: he holds that sovereigns reign by "divine right." A king ought to defend his people, and he cannot do that "except his Subjects furnish him with so much money as he shall judge sufficient to doe it," as if Ship Money or a forced loan were the issue. The essence of Hobbes's position is that no one has the right to "force" a king to do anything. If a king's death were to result in a dissolution of the civil state, perhaps because people would not accept his successor, "then the people is a Multitude of lawlesse men relapsed into a condition of warr of every man against every man. Which by making a King they intended to avoid."[19] It seems to me that Hobbes did

---

[17] *Homers Odysses,* "To the Reader."
[18] See Skinner 2002, 34.
[19] Quoted from Skinner 2002, 35.

not favor the exclusion of Charles's brother even though he was a Roman Catholic and would presumably make extensive accommodations for Roman Catholics. For Hobbes, peace trumped personal preference. Hobbes died later that year, on December 4, and was buried within the parish church of St. John the Baptist.

A contrast is sometimes drawn between an early humanistic phase of Hobbes's life and a later scientific one. Although he tended to concentrate on humanistic works earlier in his adult life and at the end of it—with philosophical, mathematical, and scientific ones predominating during the middle part—I think he was interested in both areas for most of his adult life.[20] The purpose of his *De Mirabilibus Pecci* (1627), written during his so-called humanistic period and commemorating a trip, was "to learn the causes of things" ("*rerum perdiscere causas*").[21] He wrote a significant work on poetry while he was struggling over *De corpore* in the 1640s, during his supposed scientific phase. And he published mathematical, scientific, and literary works in the 1670s. Quentin Skinner shows how the humanistic topic of "civil conversation" in Renaissance writers is relevant to Hobbes's treatment of unsociable and arrogant behavior by citizens in *Leviathan*.

2 Hobbes's Views

Hobbes had a comprehensive philosophy of logic and language, physics, philosophy of mathematics and science, metaphysics, ethics, political philosophy, and philosophy of religion. His complete system, notwithstanding the modifications he occasionally made in later works, was presented in three parts, *De corpore* (1655), *De homine* (1658), and *De cive* (1642, 1647).

2.1 Logic, Language, and Science

Hobbes often expressed his dissatisfaction with the Aristotelian metaphysics that he was taught at Oxford. In her chapter, Martine Pécharman makes the important point that when Hobbes wrote about philosophy seriously in the 1640s and later, he did not criticize Aristotle's logic, and he adopted a simplified version of it in *De corpore*. She also insightfully points out that the first part of *De corpore* should be seen as consisting of two noncontiguous sections. Logic proper is laid out in chapters II–V, and philosophical method is laid out in chapters I and VI. Once this organizational discontinuity is laid out, the question of what is the absolute foundation of Hobbes's philosophy has several possibilities. Is it language, with an emphasis on definition, as set out in

[20] See also Evrigenis 2014; cf. Skinner 2002, 5.
[21] Hobbes 1627, [4]. See also Martinich 1998, 69–76.

chapters II, III, and V? Or is it philosophical method, as set out in chapters I and VI? Or is it logic, as set out in chapter IV? Still another possibility is that logic, language, and method are equally primary and that each overlaps to some extent with the others. Language has to observe logic; logic cannot be expressed without language; and scientific discovery and expression require the proper method. If overlapping equality is correct, Hobbes's system is less neat, but perhaps closer to the truth. (For Hobbes's views on language, see Stewart Duncan's chapter. For the foundations of Hobbes's natural philosophy, see Douglas Jesseph's chapter.)

Some distinctive aspects of Hobbes's views about method and logic may be illuminated by beginning with his views concerning scientific method and working backward to his definition of philosophy. There are two methods of science: analytic and synthetic. The analytic method, which is to identify possible causes of some phenomena, applies primarily to specific physical phenomena. The synthetic method, which begins with definitions and generates new propositions as theorems, applies primarily to geometry and politics. In each case, valid reasoning must be employed. For Hobbes, this consists of syllogistic argument. Syllogisms consist of propositions, and the proper form of scientific syllogisms is not that of irreducible categorical assertions but of hypothetical or conditional ones. The most basic of these propositions are definitions, and definitions depend on the meaning of words. This brings us to the definition of philosophy, which does not seem to comport with the analytic/synthetic distinction. Philosophy is knowledge acquired through correct reasoning from causes to effects or from effects to causes. But Hobbes's paradigmatic example of a definition, that a human being is a rational animate body, does not explain the physical causes of a human being. Similarly, his definitions or analyses in chapter 6 of *Leviathan*, such as that desire is a small motion toward a body, do not specify causes. Hobbes aspired to what twenty-first-century natural science has largely achieved through powerful mathematics, observation dependent on sophisticated methods, and cooperative projects. All Hobbes had was Euclidean geometry and an armchair.

2.2 Reason, Appetite, and Will

Part of Hobbes's mechanism and materialism is the analysis of human psychology in terms of motions toward objects and motions away from objects—that is, appetites and aversions. In his chapter, Thomas Pink provides valuable information about the background to the debate between John Bramhall and Hobbes, including their radically different conceptions of human action. Another part of the background is Hobbes's adoption of the Calvinism of late Elizabethan and early Stuart England. The Calvinists emphasized the omnipotence of God in contrast with their Arminian opponents who emphasized God's goodness. The Calvinists had at least these three powerful facts on their side: (1) the Bible first describes God as a creator, and creation was understood to require omnipotence; (2) "Lord God Almighty" is a standard way of referring to God in the Old Testament and suggests that God's lordship is grounded in his omnipotence[22]; and (3) the first four ecumenical creeds all begin with a reference to "God the Father Almighty" and none mentions his goodness. A philosophical inference drawn from these facts, sometimes combined with some principles of ancient Greek philosophy, led to the conclusion that God is the cause of everything. Arminians argued that these views entailed that human beings are not the authors of their own actions, that hence they are not responsible for their sins, and that God is the author of sin. They then claimed that these blasphemies made Calvinism irreparably false. A standard Calvinist reply was to say that whereas God was the cause of the behavior, which is judged by God to be a sin, God himself is not the cause of sin. Hobbes was among the few who bit the bullet and accepted that God is the cause of sin, although he was loathe to say it.[23] Hobbes then went on to explain that God was not culpable for sin because God as sovereign is not subject to law.

He also pointed out that Arminians had their own problems with the Christian principle that God is the cause of all things. They distinguished between the good things that God wills and the bad things that God merely permits. Hobbes retorts, "Such distinctions as these dazzle my understanding; I find no difference between the *will* to have a thing done, and the *permission* to do it, when he that permitteth can hinder it, and knows that it will be done unless he hinder it."[24]

Every action is caused by the last desire a person has before acting. Often, this desire is the last link of a chain of deliberation, which consists of alternating desires. The standard account that reason is a "slave to the passions" in the chain is refuted by Adrian Blau. Reasoning often precedes deliberation and "improves it by altering the images and opinions to which our passions respond," as he says.

2.3 Laws of Nature, the Civil State, and Sovereignty

In broad outline and absent all nuance, Hobbes's political theory can be described as follows. The goal is to justify the existence of a civil state and to give a scientific account of its origin. So the starting point has to be the pre-political condition, in which human beings live without civil laws or any laws at all. This initial condition is a war of all against all in part because, in order to satisfy their natural desire for life, people need to protect themselves from attack and will have to take the initiative and attack others preemptively whenever circumstances allow it. The other part of the reason that the natural condition of human beings is a state of war is that some people desire glory, which is achieved by conquering or dominating others; and since there is no way to

---

[22] For Hobbes "the *power* of God alone without other helps is sufficient justification of any action he doth" and "*Power irresistible justifies all actions, really and properly,* in whomsoever it be found. Less power does not. And because such power is in God only, he must needs be just in all actions" ("Of Liberty and Necessity," 22, and "Questions Concerning Liberty, Necessity, and Chance," 89 and 98, 101–2; see also Martinich 2012).

[23] *Questions Concerning Liberty, Necessity, and Chance,* 297.

[24] *Of Liberty and Necessity,* 23.

know who those people may be, a person needs to suspect everyone, to view everyone as an enemy. This condition of universal war is horrific but fortunately can be escaped by people who hope that human life can be better and can discover by reason the laws of nature, which explain how to end the war. These laws dictate that people should seek peace, that seeking peace requires laying down one's rights to all things, and that one should keep one's covenants.

Among the many nuanced theories about the exact character of the laws of nature are those that hold that the laws of nature are prudential precepts, that is, action-guiding propositions but not genuine laws because no one commands the laws of nature. John Deigh's defense of this interpretation in his chapter explains correctly, I believe, that reason is purely instrumental in deriving the laws. A central aspect of Deigh's interpretation is the reason he thinks that the *laws* of nature are not actual laws. He points out that since that term is a technical one, laws of nature are not laws if the definition says or entails that they are not literally laws. And he thinks the definition does entail that they are not laws. He points out that a parallel case is Hobbes's definition of "civil liberty." Since Hobbes says that only natural liberty is "properly called liberty,"[25] civil liberty is not liberty. Deigh provides the strongest attack on the divine command interpretation of Hobbes's laws of nature. His central premise is that when a phrase of two words is being defined, the term should be understood as a fused expression, with the consequence that the definition gives the meaning of the phrase and that definition need not preserve the literal meaning of the inessentially occurring component words. So the definition of "law of nature" is in effect a definition of "law-of-nature" (or lawofnature). Deigh confirms this practice of Hobbes by giving the example, "liberty of subjects." According to him, "liberty," standing alone, means "without external impediments." In contrast, the term, "liberty of subjects" does not indicate an absence of external impediments but the absence of laws forbidding certain actions. Because laws are not actual external impediments, it is absurd to say that laws deprive one of liberty.

Let's now consider Hobbes's definition of "laws of nature." They are precepts, just as civil laws are precepts, commanded by something—I shall say what in a moment—just as civil laws are commanded by civil sovereigns. Natural laws and civil laws belong to the same genus. The specific difference between them is that civil laws are promulgated through the words of a civil sovereign, whereas the laws of nature are promulgated through reason, the "undoubted word of God."[26] That the laws of nature are a species of law is entailed by Hobbes's division of laws into natural and positive and his elaboration on that distinction.[27] If "laws" in "laws of nature" does not have the same meaning it has in "civil laws," then Hobbes's saying, "Another division of laws is into *natural* and *positive*" is analogous to saying, "Another division of banks is into financial institutions and edges of rivers."

[25] *Leviathan* 21.4, 108.
[26] *Leviathan* 32.2, 195. See also Hobbes 2008, 351.
[27] *Leviathan* 26.36, 147–148.

In the 1670s, he published translations of both the *Iliad* and the *Odyssey*. Although these translations have been criticized for some inaccuracies, their readability stands up well against other translations within a century of his.[28]

He also worked on and published books on natural philosophy and mathematics. Criticism of his philosophy continued through the rest of the century. Among the most notorious propositions attributed to him were these:

1. The foundation of God's authority is his omnipotence rather than his goodness or the fact that he is the creator.
2. The natural condition of human beings is a war of all against all.
3. Self-preservation is the first and most important law of nature.

Although Hobbes did hold (1) and (2), they did not have the adverse consequences that his critics thought they had. Concerning (1), God's omnipotence is integral to the creation story of Genesis chapter 1 (as understood by Christian theologians), the sentiments of some of the Psalms, and other works. Hobbes thought that other traditional properties of God, such as goodness and justice, could be attributed to God as honorifics befitting an omnipotent being. To think that God is an object of which serious study would yield true descriptions is to make of God an object of science and not an object of worship.[29] Concerning (2), his critics thought that Hobbes was making a historical statement about Adam and Eve, even though he made clear that it was a nonhistorical proposition that follows from definitions about the nature of human beings.

As for (3), he did not hold it. Self-preservation, although mentioned in the definition of "law of nature," is the basic desire that motivates human action but is not a law of nature.[30] In *Leviathan*, the first law of nature is to make peace. What is sometimes mistaken to be part of the law of nature, "*and when he cannot obtain it, that he may seek, and use, all helps, and advantages of Warre*," is a fallback position when the law cannot be followed.[31]

In her wide-ranging and illuminating chapter, Sharon Lloyd argues that reciprocity is the key principle in deducing the laws of nature. (However, the principle of reciprocity itself depends on reason: it goes against reason to require other people to treat you in a way that you are not willing to treat them. What reciprocity provides is a rule of thumb by which people can figure out whether a particular action is moral or not.[32]) Lloyd also thinks that grounding normativity in God's command cannot be right because the command of God "does *not* of course suffice to prove that their *normativity consists in their being God's laws.*" That may be the philosophical truth. But Hobbes thinks that the normativity of the laws of nature is grounded in God's omnipotence: "The right of

---

[28] Cf. Nelson 2008, xii–xxii.
[29] Martinich 2012.
[30] Martinich 2013b.
[31] *Leviathan* 1651: 14.4, 64.
[32] Cf. Martinich 2010.

nature whereby God reigneth over men and punisheth those that break his laws is to be derived . . . from his *irresistible power*."[33]

What is the exact relation between the state of nature and the laws of nature? It is helpful for interpretive purposes to distinguish between a primary state of nature, in which there are no laws at all, and a secondary state of nature, in which there are laws of nature.[34] Without this distinction, Hobbes has no plausible way to explain how one could institute a civil state, for if the laws of nature must be taken account of when the state of nature is first considered and the state of nature is a condition of war, then the laws of nature are not the principal nonpolitical causes of peace. One might object that the laws of nature, plus the hope of getting out of the miserable condition of war, are the principal causes, as indicated at the end of chapter 13 of *Leviathan*. However, the text itself introduces both hope and the laws of nature at the same time. The best explanation is that the laws are not in play in chapter 13. Another reason to distinguish between a primary and secondary state of nature is that it provides the resources for a simple explanation and dissolution of a contradiction in Hobbes's text. Near the end of chapter 13, which is devoted to the primary state of nature, the condition of human beings without any laws of any kind, he says that "consequent" to "this war of every man against every man, . . . nothing can be just or unjust."[35] But, in chapter 14, he explains that laying down rights in the state of nature creates obligations, and if a person hinders "those to whom such right is granted, or abandoned, from the benefit of it," then "such hindrance is INJUSTICE and INJURY."[36] Supposing that someone transfers his right to a person by gift and then hinders that person from enjoying the benefit of it, then the person is unjust in the state of nature, the "secondary state of nature." The contradiction is resolved and provides the occasion for repeating that science for Hobbes is generative. He begins with the simplest elements and then builds increasing complex entities. Corresponding to the geometrical construction of points, lines, and a closed plane figure is the construction of the primary state of nature, the secondary state of nature (the primary one plus the laws of nature), and then the civil state and sovereign. (Ioannis Evrigenis gives a searching treatment of the state of nature in his chapter, which examines the various appearances it assumes in Hobbes's different books.)

Perhaps the most substantive change in Hobbes's political philosophy from *De cive* to *Leviathan* involves the precise action that potential subjects perform in instituting a civil state. In *Elements of Law* and *De cive*, it is an act of alienating of rights. In *Leviathan*, a new concept does the heavy lifting. Potential subjects mutually authorize a sovereign to represent them. Considering that fact, combined with the principle that whoever wills the end wills the means (necessary) to that end, it follows that the subjects transfer or alienate all of their rights of governing themselves except for the right to defend themselves from imminent danger. (See Martinich's chapter.)

---

[33] *Leviathan* 31.5, 187; see also *Questions Concerning Liberty, Necessity, and Chance*, 175 and 234.
[34] Martinich 1992.
[35] *Leviathan* 13.13, 63.
[36] *Leviathan* 14.7, 65.

Hobbes's concept of absolute sovereignty is approached from three perspectives. Johann Sommerville describes the similarities and differences between Hobbes's view of absolutism or unlimited power under a united government and that of several of his contemporaries. David Runciman discusses the ill fit between these two elements of Hobbes's theory: (1) anyone can be a sovereign because competence is not a job requirement, and (2) the scope of a sovereign's authority is practically unlimited. Element (1) suggests that limits should be put on authority, and (2) suggests that at least competence should be required of a sovereign. Arash Abizadeh explains how Hobbes handles two other dimensions of sovereignty. On the one hand, as an artificial person, the sovereign's authority is first of all over its subjects, but control over a territory is essential to the sovereign's effectiveness.

A large-scale difference between Hobbes's project in *De cive* and in *Leviathan* is that the latter work does not pretend to be an exclusively scientific work.[37] So *Leviathan* contains empirical examples to illustrate his scientifically demonstrated points, with allusions to events in the English Civil War being the most salient examples.[38] I think he occasionally feels compelled to deal with an issue that he could have avoided—in particular, the family, which his scientific account does not have a place for. His proof of the legitimacy of the state goes from individuals in a state of war to a civil state. However, many of his contemporaries compared what they believed the father's role in a family was to the sovereign's role in the state, and his readers probably would have felt he had left something out if he had not talked about it. In her chapter, Nancy Hirschmann insightfully shows the complexity of his discussion and draws out the consequences of various plausible interpretations.

Although Hobbes has often been understood as either the forerunner of legal positivism or the first legal positivist, Mark Murphy argues in his chapter that the similarities between Hobbes's view and John Austin's are superficial and that at a deeper level Hobbes's theory is more like that of Thomas Aquinas.

2.4 History, Poetry, and Paradox

Kinch Hoekstra's placement of Hobbes's translation of Thucydides' *History of the Peloponnesian War* (1629) into its appropriate historical and thematic context is the foundation for a brilliant explanation for why Hobbes did it, why he did not publish it immediately, and then why he published it when he did. It is not fear of civil war in England, but international relations with Spain that moved Hobbes to translate. In 1623–1624, when the translation was done, the issue was whether England should go to war against Spain. Hobbes thought not; and the Peloponnesian War was supposed to illustrate why. But his view was at odds with the view of the court, and so he thought

---

[37] It is a rhetorically rich work, as Quentin Skinner has shown (1996). Hobbes may have thought that a less rigorous presentation of his theory would increase its influence.

[38] *Leviathan* 13.10, 62.

it inappropriate to publish it. By 1627, the court view had changed to Hobbes's own, so Hobbes would have felt comfortable publishing it. Advocating peace in practice fits with Hobbes's anti-war theory.

In the 1660s and '70s, he returned to history in large part because of circumstances arising from the Restoration. *Behemoth*, his history of the English Civil War, was written to vindicate the cause of King Charles I and to illustrate the horrible consequences of rebellion and the mistake of trying to appease rebels. The first part of *Behemoth* is an impressive analytical account of the causes of the Civil War: the King's lack of direct control over the county militias; his lack of money; the subversion of ministers, Roman Catholics, and Presbyterians; a belief in freedom of religion; seditious doctrines in the universities; the excessive influence of London and the unemployed; and the people's ignorance of their duty. Most of these causes were long-standing conditions. Hobbes says little to nothing about Charles's imprudent and high-handed policies. Parts II through IV are a narrative of the Civil War ending with the Restoration. Charles II would not let the history be published because he did not want to further incite the critics of his reign. (Tomaž Mastnak incisively discusses *Behemoth* in his chapter.)

Behemoth also contains brief versions of the history of heresy and the history of the pope's ascendancy over kings and emperors, histories that he presented at greater length in other works such as the Appendix to the Latin *Leviathan* and *Historia ecclesiastica*. I conjecture that, in this latter work, Hobbes was trying to emulate his friend John Selden, whose *Titles of Honor* (1614 and 1631), one of the few books mentioned in *Leviathan*, gives genealogies of all major titles of honor, from king and emperor to earls and barons. Finding the earliest uses of these titles, sometimes in the ancient Middle East, sometimes in Europe, and sometimes in England, Selden shows how the offices and honors connected with them changed over the centuries. The significance of some title in the seventeenth century might be quite different from its original significance. In general, Selden's histories are deflating. Similarly deflating is Hobbes's argument that the title "heretic" simply meant someone who had nonstandard or novel beliefs. Heretical beliefs are inherently neither true nor false, neither good nor evil. If one goes back to the origins of Christianity, as Hobbes did, and as any good Protestant would, then heresy is no crime.

According to Hobbes's theory of poetry, *Historia ecclesiastica* is not a poem. Whenever a philosopher or literary critic says that something that looks and sounds like poetry and is generally said to be poetry is not poetry, then the theorist often means, "I don't like this kind of poetry." They often have a theory that illuminates not all poetry, but only the kind of poetry that they like. "Poetry" is used in a normative, not a descriptive sense. Hobbes is such an example. One of the great merits of Timothy Raylor's chapter is that he explains precisely what Hobbes's normative sense is—only epic and heroic poetry is poetry—how it differs from philosophy, and how he adhered to this view.

In addition to heresies being called paradoxes, any novel doctrine is often called a "paradox." Although there may have been something in Hobbes's psychology that drove him to novelty, I do not think he consciously tried to be paradoxical. Hobbes simply went where he thought the evidence and arguments led. For politics and society, he thought the old ways were the best ways: what James I thought the English monarchy was and what the Elizabethan episcopal Calvinists thought religion was. Jon Parkin has a different view. He vigorously defends the nonstandard view that Hobbes's use of paradox was tactical.

2.5 Religion

Some of the historical remarks presented earlier invite the substantive question of what Hobbes's honest views about religion were. Agostino Lupoli begins his contribution by noting that there are two major interpretations. According to the dominant one, Hobbes was a debunker of revealed religion, in particular Christianity, and probably an atheist or agnostic. The other interpretation is that Hobbes was genuinely a theist and some of those beliefs—in particular, the belief that the laws of nature are not laws unless commanded by God—are important to his moral and political philosophy.[39] Agostino Lupoli aims to avoid this controversy by beginning not with the question of Hobbes's theological views but with his views about religion, especially those expressed in chapter 12 of *Leviathan*. Lupoli points out that, according to Hobbes, both the true religion and gentile religions have the purpose of getting subjects to be obedient and that propositions about God, other than that he exists, can never be objects of knowledge but of opinion or faith. Consequently, theology cannot be part of science. This does not make Hobbes an atheist or agnostic. Lupoli in effect thinks that Hobbes is a deist. It might also be urged that circumstances made Hobbes a cultural-Anglican deist for most of his life because the sovereign dictates the religion of its subjects. Sarah Mortimer offers a different perspective on Hobbes and religion. Christianity, she says, was "too important, in Hobbes's view, to be ignored." A commonwealth that practiced what Hobbes thought was "true Christianity" would be "stronger and more peaceful than any other." She discusses Hobbes's relation with several "Anglican" leaders (cf. Martinich 1992, 1999, 2012).

Jeffrey Collins discusses the increasing importance of religion in Hobbes's later thought, especially in his *Ecclesiastical History*. Hobbes was able to circumvent censorship, according to Collins, by conveying his anticlericalism and anti-Trinitarianism through rhetorical devices.

Richard Tuck examines Hobbes's treatment of Judaism and Christianity with respect to Hobbes's doctrine of conscience. Tuck argues that, according to Hobbes, Christians under Christian sovereigns have a liberty with respect to conscience that non-Christians do not; the same is true for Jews *mutatis mutandis*. This liberty depends on the fact that Jews constitute God's peculiar kingdom, and Christians, too, will be part of a peculiar kingdom.

---

[39] Martinich 1992, 1999, and 2009. Cf. Collins 2009.

For Hobbes, an absolute monarch is the head of every aspect of state and religion. Each subject is to adopt the conscience of the monarch as his own. The subjects have a public conscience because the sovereign is a public person. They abandon their private consciences (i.e., the judgment they would have made if they had no sovereign). Shared conscience is a kind of positive liberty because it means that one's freedom is used to do the right thing; that is, maintaining peace by following the sovereign.

An open question, it seems to me, is how adopting the conscience of the sovereign fits Independency, which conceives of each congregation as a church. Is Independency compatible with public worship, that is, a unified worship that is a practice of the civil state?

3 CONCLUSION

The chapters of this volume demonstrate at least two things. One is that exciting new research continues to reveal aspects of Hobbes that have not been known or appropriately appreciated for at least a century and that these and older issues will continue to be debated by historians, philosophers, political theorists, and others.

ACKNOWLEDGMENTS

I want to thank J. P. Andrew, Adrian Blau, Kinch Hoekstra, and Leslie Martinich for their comments on this Introduction.

BIBLIOGRAPHY

Aubrey, John. 1898. *Brief Lives*. Oxford: Clarendon Press.
Collins, Jeffrey. 2009. "Interpreting Thomas Hobbes in Competing Contexts." *Journal of the History of Ideas* 70: 165–180.
Curley, Edwin. 1994. "A Note Regarding Chapter XLII," in Thomas Hobbes, *Leviathan*, 549. Indianapolis: Hackett.
Evrigenis, Ioannis. 2014. *Images of Anarchy*. Cambridge: Cambridge University Press.
Goldie, Mark. 1991. "The Reception of Hobbes," in *The Cambridge History of Political Thought, 1450-1700*, edited by J. H. Burns, 589–615. Cambridge: Cambridge University Press.
Hobbes, Thomas. 1627. *De mirabilibus pecci*. [n.p.]
Hobbes, Thomas. 1651. *Leviathan*. London.
Hobbes, Thomas. 1654. *Of Liberty and Necessity*. London.
Hobbes, Thomas. 1655. *Questions Concerning Liberty, Necessity and Chance*. London.
Hobbes, Thomas. 1675. *Homers Odysses*. London.
Hobbes, Thomas. 1839. "Vita, Carmina Expressa," in *Opera Latine*, edited by William Molesworth, lxxxv–xcix. London: Bohm.

Hobbes, Thomas. 1976. *Anti-White. [Thomas White's De Mundo Examined]*, tr. Harold Whitmore Jones. London: Bradford University Press.

Hobbes, Thomas. 2008. *Historia ecclesiastica*, edited by Patricia Springborg, Patricia Stablein, and Paul Wilson. Paris: Honoré Champion Éditeur.

Hyde, Edward. 1676. *Brief View and Survey of the Dangerous and Pernicious Errors to Church and State*. London.

Jesseph, Douglas. 1999. *Squaring the Circle*. Chicago: University of Chicago Press.

Malcolm, Noel. 1996. "A Summary Biography of Hobbes," in *Cambridge Companion to Hobbes*, ed. Tom Sorell, 13–44. Cambridge: Cambridge University Press.

Malcolm, Noel. 2002. *Aspects of Hobbes*. Oxford: Clarendon Press.

Malcolm, Noel. 2012. *Thomas Hobbes, Leviathan, 1. Introduction*. Oxford: Clarendon Press.

Martinich, A. P. 1984. *Communication and Reference*. New York: De Gruyter.

Martinich, A. P. 1992. *The Two Gods of Leviathan*. Cambridge: Cambridge University Press.

Martinich, A. P. 1998. "Francis Andrewes's Account of Thomas Hobbes's Trip to the Peak." *Notes and Queries* 45(4): 436–440.

Martinich, A. P. 1999. *Hobbes: A Biography*. Cambridge: Cambridge University Press.

Martinich, A. P. 2009. "Hobbes's Erastianism and Interpretation." *Journal of the History of Ideas* 70: 143–163.

Martinich, A. P. 2010. "Reason and Reciprocity in Hobbes's Political Philosophy." *Hobbes Studies* 23: 158–169.

Martinich, A. P. 2012. "On Thomas Hobbes's English Calvinism: Necessity, Omnipotence, and Goodness." *Philosophical Readings* 4(1): 18–30.

Martinich, A. P. 2013a. "L'Auteur Du Péché et les Démoniaques," in *Jean Calvin et Thomas Hobbes*, edited by Olivier Abel, Pierre-François Moureau, and Dominique Weber, 43–71. Geneva: Editions Labor et Fides.

Martinich, A. P. 2013b. "Law and Self-Preservation in *Leviathan: On Misinterpreting Hobbes 1650–1700*," in *The Persistence of the Sacred*, edited by Chris Firestone and Nathan Jacobs, 38–65. South Bend, IN: University of Notre Dame Press.

Nelson, Eric. 2008. "General Introduction," in Thomas Hobbes, *Translations of Homer*, xii–lxxxi. Oxford: Clarendon Press.

Parkin, Jon. 1999. *Science, Religion, and Politics in Restoration England: Richard Cumberland's De Legibus Naturae*. Woodbridge: Boydell & Brewer.

Parkin, Jon. 2007. "The Reception of Hobbes's *Leviathan*," in *The Cambridge Companion to Leviathan*, edited by Patricia Springborg, 441–459. Cambridge: Cambridge University Press.

Searle, John. 1969. *Speech Acts*. Cambridge: Cambridge University Press.

Searle, John. 1979. *Expression and Meaning in Speech Acts*. Cambridge: Cambridge University Press.

Shapin, Steven, and Simon Schaffer. 1985. *Leviathan and the Air-Pump*. Princeton, NJ: Princeton University Press.

Skinner, Quentin. 1996. *Reason and Rhetoric in Hobbes's* Leviathan. Cambridge: Cambridge University Press.

Skinner, Quentin. 2002. *Visions of Politics, vol. 3: Hobbes and Civil Science*. Cambridge: Cambridge University Press.

Springborg, Patricia, ed. 2007. *The Cambridge Companion to* Leviathan. Cambridge: Cambridge University Press.

Strauss, Leo. 1963. *The Political Philosophy of Hobbes: Its Basis and Genesis*, translated by Elsa M. Sinclair. Chicago: University of Chicago Press.

PART I

LOGIC AND NATURAL PHILOSOPHY

CHAPTER 2

....

HOBBES ON LOGIC, OR HOW TO DEAL WITH ARISTOTLE'S LEGACY

....

MARTINE PÉCHARMAN

1 HOBBES ON TRADITIONAL LOGIC

....

1.1 "Vain Logic and Philosophy"

Hobbes's Latin prose autobiography indicates that he spent five years studying Aristotelian logic and physics at Magdalen Hall in Oxford.[1] In his *Brief Lives*, John Aubrey writes about this period: "He did not much care for logick, yet he learnd it, and thought himselfe a good disputant."[2] Hobbes adds in his autobiography that a few years later, during a tour of France and Italy,[3] he realized that the philosophy and logic in which, to his judgment, he had made fine progress were "treated with derision by wise people"; for this reason, he threw away this "vain logic and philosophy."[4]

Hobbes's autobiography does not mention that he was engaged as amanuensis to Francis Bacon, presumably by the end of the 1610s. Bacon complained that the untimely teaching of logic in colleges was responsible for a corruption of what should be the "art of arts": Far from providing a method of invention of scientific axioms, useful for any

---

[1] *Tho. Hobbes Malmesburiensis Vita* [1677–9], posthumously published by Richard Blackburne in 1681 (OL I, XIII). Cf. the excerpt from Antony a Wood's *Historia et Antiquitates Universitatis Oxoniensis* (OL I, XLIV–XLV).

[2] Aubrey 1898: 329.

[3] The tour's dates are Summer 1614 to Summer 1615.

[4] OL I, XIII–XIV.

judgment, logic degenerated at the university into something superficial and sterile, thus making it an object of derision.

1.2 The Right Context

Bacon and Hobbes focus their critique on the confinement of the study of logic at the university to a set of formal schemata for the fabric of valid arguments. Even though, in the late sixteenth and early seventeenth centuries booklets on *sophismata, insolubilia,* and *obligationes* were no longer the most ordinary textbooks for the acquisition of logical skills,[5] logic taught at the university was denounced both by Bacon and Hobbes as a merely abstract logic, a vain logic heiress to scholastic logic.

The background at Oxford by the end of the Tudor period is indeed that of an official restoration of Aristotelian logic in as strong a position as its medieval one. Decrees promulgated in 1586 prescribe that Aristotle and the authors faithful to Aristotle are to be defended.[6] Yet, thanks to Charles Schmitt's research on late sixteenth- and early seventeenth-century Aristotelianism in England, two key points have been clarified: (1) Aristotle's revival indicates that the scholastic Aristotelian legacy had been formerly weakened, and (2) Aristotle's revival is not to be viewed as retrograde, but as a reassertion of Aristotelianism on new grounds.[7] E. J. Ashworth has noted that "syllogistic represented the main focus of logic" in this "renewed Aristotelian tradition,"[8] but this does not mean that the dominance of Aristotelianism can be identified with the dominance of scholasticism. The truth was that a bifurcation in the Aristotelian tradition in logic had been introduced by the humanist charge against the barbaric technicalities of analytical discourse and the abuse of formal reasoning in medieval sophisticated and artificialized Aristotelian logic. Humanists like Rudolph Agricola had developed an antischolastic Aristotelianism insisting on the tradition of the *Topics*.[9] Now, although this humanist tradition does not receive recognition in

---

[5] Medieval highly technical logic was not altogether banished out of Oxford panorama during the Tudor period, which was quite eclectic. James McConica notes: "Works of scholastic logic continue to turn up in inventories through the century"; he mentions an early seventeenth-century inventory giving evidence that the *Libellus sophistarum ad usum Oxoniensium* could be found side by side with humanist dialectic treatises and Ramus's logic (McConica 1979, 296–297). One of the most popular logic textbooks in seventeenth century, the *Logicae artis compendium* published anonymously by Robert Sanderson in 1615 and composed from his lectures as a reader in logic at Lincoln College from 1608 onward, also testifies to a significant "medieval heritage," "although in a very abbreviated form" (Ashworth 1985, XLII).

[6] From the *Nova Statuta* promulgated in 1564/5, the works to be studied in logic (designated as "dialectic") already were Porphyry's *Institutiones* and any book in Aristotle's whole *Organon*. Similarly, a 1576 decree stipulated that "eyther in Logick or Philosophy, nothing be defended against Aristotle" (quoted by Sgarbi 2013, 41). The cumulative Aristotelian renewal in Oxford will be confirmed in 1636 by the Laudian statutes.

[7] Schmitt 1983.

[8] Ashworth 1985, XLV. Cf. Ashworth 1988.

[9] On this specific form of Renaissance Aristotelianism, see Spranzi 2011. Rudolph Agricola's logical reform in *De inventione dialectica libri tres* (through a Ciceronian interpretation of dialectic

the new statutes of the university, booklists and student notebooks in early modern Oxford colleges reveal a practice of logic teaching different from the official restrictive recommendations. James McConica and Mordechai Feingold[10] have shown that tutors usually omitted the late medieval accretions to Aristotelian dialectic. Preference was given to the humanist reform of Aristotle's dialectic. Aristotelianism was officially reasserted in resistance to the diffusion of Ramism,[11] without this anti-Ramism entailing that the university "clung to sterile Aristotelian logic."[12] The target was rather, in the context of increasing interest in logical method, the function of dialectic for the organization of knowledge. Ramus's logical reform, by contrast with Agricola's, had gone far beyond criticizing scholastic logic. In the complex matrix studied by Walter Ong, in which Peter Ramus's new dialectic was formed,[13] the Agricolan tradition was coupled with a critique of Aristotle's dialectic as failing to preserve the requirements of the natural logic of human reasoning. In this context, the Oxford 1586 decrees were not a return to scholastic Aristotelianism, but an opposition to Ramist refurbishing of dialectic. Eclecticism, not monolithic scholastic Aristotelianism, was the real background[14] of Hobbes's personal formation in logic.

1.3 Just "Vain Philosophy"

In his history of the humanities in seventeenth-century Oxford, Feingold writes that, like Bacon, Hobbes was "prone to malign the verbalism and emptiness of Aristotelian and scholastic logic."[15] When Feingold emphasizes Hobbes's deriding of specialized logic, his point is that there is discrepancy between that about which "the heralds of the new philosophy" complained—namely, that the sterile Aristotelian logic at the university was moribund—and the true status of logic in early-modern Oxford curriculum. Now, it seems to me that in Hobbes's censure of scholasticism, the case of logic is not reducible to the maligning to which Feingold points.

---

as a method of argumentative invention) is to be viewed as a reform undergone by one of Aristotle's "offshoots" (Spranzi 2011, 96).

[10] McConica 1979; Feingold 1997.

[11] Ramism spread after the publication in London in 1574 of an edition, with the English translation, of the 1572 version of the *Dialecticae libri duo*.

[12] Feingold 1997, 289. For these decrees, sterility and emptiness are on the side of discussions deviating from "ancient and true philosophy" (Aristotle's *Organon* and its commentators); Ramus's followers, not Aristotle's interpreters, are guilty of promoting a useless logic. McConica has argued that the university decision excluded not directly Ramists, but those who distanced themselves from "the 'recovered' humanistic Aristotle, without scholastic comment" (McConica 1979, 301, note). For a different interpretation, see Sgarbi 2013, 41–42.

[13] Ong 1958, 171.

[14] Robert Sanderson's *Logicae artis compendium*, which went through ten editions before 1700, was the perfect illustration of this prevailing eclecticism. See Ashworth 1985, XXXV–LIV for the diverse influences (even a medieval one, with "the doctrines of supposition, exponibilia and consequences") integrated in Sanderson's textbook.

[15] Feingold 1997, 278.

Hobbes's famous charge against the universities is that they had become completely vassal to "the Authority of Aristotle," so that the philosophy taught there "is not properly Philosophy, (the nature whereof dependeth not on Authors), but Aristotelity."[16] In chapter 46 of *Leviathan*, Hobbes denounces the "insignificant Traines of strange and barbarous words, or words otherwise used, then in the common use of the Latine tongue," of which "Vain Philosophy" makes use.[17] And he critiques the theological perversion of religion when the interpretation of Holy Scriptures is left to Aristotelian metaphysics. Yet Hobbes's dark history of philosophy as breeding the monster of scholastic theology does not accuse scholastic logic of being "insignificant speech."[18] This logic plays no role in the "particular Tenets of Vain Philosophy, derived to the Universities, and thence into the Church, partly from Aristotle, partly from Blindnesse of understanding."[19] Meaningless words such as "*Entity, Intentionality, Quiddity*, and other insignificant words of the School" are contrasted in chapter 4 of *Leviathan* with words used about words and speech: the words "*Generall, Speciall, Affirmative, Negative, Interrogative, Optative, Infinitive*." The latter words are not parasitic, but necessary for distinguishing modes of speaking: They belong to a meta-language whose formation is inseparable from human language itself. Words of this natural meta-language are said to be as "usefull" as words for "Figures, Numbers, Measures, Colours, Sounds, Fancies, Relations" whose invention already goes beyond the Adamic model of the use of words

---

[16] *Leviathan*, XLVI.13, 1074. (Page references to *Leviathan* are to the 2012 edition, edited by Noel Malcolm.). Hobbes's blame accuses *expressis verbis* Catholic universities, where "the study of Philosophy . . . had no otherwise place, then as a handmaid to the Romane Religion." Yet the attack is actually directed, whatever the religion concerned, against the application of philosophy to theological matters (such an application is made impossible from the outset by Hobbes's definition of philosophy as the rational knowledge of effects from their mode of generation and, conversely, of possible modes of generation from effects). As it is said even more ironically in the 1668 Latin *Leviathan*'s version of the same chapter: "The logic, physics, metaphysics, ethics, and politics of Aristotle were taught in the universities as if the universe [*universitas*] of the sciences were contained in one man, Aristotle (at that time the greatest Father of the Church)" (Hobbes 2012, 1075). For the presentation of Aristotle as a "one-man band"-philosopher (if I may say so), at the same time metaphysician, physician, logician and rhetorician, see *Historia ecclesiastica*, *Opera Latina* (hereafter OL) V, 359.

[17] *Leviathan*, IV, XLVI. 40, 1098). On the possible misuse of Latin language for building false distinctions upon "Words . . . insignificant" (the example is *Circumscriptive/Definitive*), see XLVI.19, 1082.

[18] See *Leviathan* I, I.5, 24; I, II.9, 36; I, III.12, 46; I, IV.1, 48; 13, 56-57; 20-21, 60; I, V.5, 68; 15, 72; I, VIII.27, 122; IV, XLVI.17, 1080; 19, 1082; 29, 1088; 40, 1098; IV, XLVII.16, 1110. *Leviathan* I, VIII.27 contains an explicit attack against Suarez: see also *The Questions Concerning Liberty, Necessity and Chance* (1656—hereafter abbreviated LNC, EW V, 18). Suarez is presented by Hobbes as the Schoolman *par excellence* on account of his unintelligible verbal artifacts (see *An Answer to Bishop Bramhall*, EW IV, 330: "Suarez and the Schoolmen . . . are not understood"). The neo-scholastic doctrine of freedom is a chief adversary in Hobbes's attack against scholastic theology.

[19] *Leviathan*, IV, XLVI. 14, 1076. Hobbes often quotes the Paulinian passage from *Colossians*, II.8 against the "vain deceits" produced by the attempt to submit religion to natural reason and philosophy. With regard to theological controversies, Hobbes suggests that Paul should have said "pernicious" when he said "vain" for the philosophy mixed with the Holy Scriptures (*De corpore, Ep. Ded.*, 5. Page references are to the 1999 edition of *De corpore*, edited by Schuhmann.).

just for naming things offered to sense perception.[20] The "names of Words and Speech" are only those which are necessarily generated by the use of language. They are needed even by ordinary language as an ultimate kind of words, distinguished from three previous sets of names (for things, for the properties of things, and for their conceptions). Interestingly, abstract words dealing in medieval logic with the distinct properties of terms (e.g., categoremata/syncategoremata) are not contrasted by Hobbes with legitimate names for names. Later, although "Aristotelity" is blamed for the absurdities of Aristotle's whole "naturall Philosophy" ("Metaphysiques" and "Physiques") and for those of his "Morall, and Civill Philosophy" ("Ethiques" and "Politiques"),[21] the *Organon* is not mentioned: "the frivolous Distinctions, barbarous Terms, and obscure language of the Schoolmen, taught in the Universities" are condemned only with respect to "the Metaphysiques, Ethiques, and Politiques of Aristotle."[22] Cees Leijenhorst has provided an insightful study of Hobbes's depreciation of scholastic metaphysics and theology as "vain philosophy," but he does not differentiate Hobbes's critique of scholastic "nonsensical jargon" from the traditional humanist critique of "barbarous" terms in medieval formal logic.[23] It seems to me that, for Hobbes, the case of first philosophy and the case of logic ("dialectic" in the humanist critique) should be distinguished.[24]

The only logic that Hobbes denounces in Part IV of 1651 *Leviathan* is the one vaguely attributed to "the Schoole of the Graecians": "Their *Logique* which should be the Method of Reasoning, is nothing else but Captions of words, and Inventions how to puzzle such as should goe about to pose them."[25] Hobbes is probably thinking of the pseudologic of "Sophists and Sceptics," which is criticized later for their clever paradoxes, which

---

[20] *Leviathan*, I, IV.1, 48. The *De corpore*, I, II.4, 21 makes a different use of the argument from Adamic speech (see also *De homine*, X.2), jointly with the episode of the Babel Tower, to emphasize the voluntary origin of words, which entails the historicity of languages and the caducity of ancient words, progressively replaced with others. Hobbes also emphasizes that the invention of new names, so long as their meaning is unambiguous, is necessary for the communication of science: for instance, analytical geometry has invented names for curves generated through a certain process of construction (the conic sections named "*paraboles, hyperboles*" and the curves named "*cissoeides, quadratices*"). There is a scientific right to invent new names, and even a scientific duty to do so, if the transmission of knowledge requires it. In *De corpore* I, VI.15-5, 69-70, Hobbes insists that this invention can consist in different definitions of the same words for their distinct uses in distinct parts of philosophy: geometry and rhetoric, for instance, propose different definitions of the words "hyperbol" and "parabol," which are, in both cases, technical words appropriate to a certain "doctrine" or teaching.

[21] See *Leviathan*, IV, XLVI, 1060, 1076–1090.

[22] *Leviathan*, IV, XLVII.16, 1110.

[23] See Leijenhorst 2002, 27–34 and 38–39.

[24] Significantly, Hobbes writes in LNC, no. IV: "It troubles him [Bramhall] much that I style School-learning jargon. I do not call all School-learning so, but such as is so; that is, that which they say in defending of untruths, and especially in the maintenance of free-will, when they talk of *liberty of exercise, specification, contrariety, contradiction, acts elicite and exercite*, and the like; which, though he go over again in this place, endeavouring to explain them, are still both here and there but jargon, or that (if he like it better) which the Scripture in the first chaos calleth *Tohu* and *Bohu*" (EW V, 63).

[25] *Leviathan*, IV, XLVI.11, 1060—Malcolm suggests "examine" as a meaning for "pose".

the *De corpore* features as intending deception but mostly begetting self-deception.[26] A good example is Zeno's "sophistical argument" against motion,[27] which, according to Hobbes, violates syllogistic truth-conditions and constitutes therefore a mere paralogism. Hobbes argues that "Sophistical captions are more often faulty in the matter than in the form of the syllogism."[28]

The 1668 Latin *Leviathan*, however, makes room for a specific critique against the Peripatetic school. Hobbes denounces the radical uselessness of the "sect" of Aristotelians with respect to the end of philosophy, the knowledge of the causes of natural phenomena, because it has offered nothing "apart from the subtleties of dialectic and rhetoric."[29] Also, "some" scholastic followers of Aristotle's philosophy are described as having "ambitiously showed off their Aristotelianism" in their "logical and physical treatises."[30] Yet, Hobbes's main objection is that "the majority of them" adopted "Aristotle's doctrine of 'separated forms.'"[31] Although Aristotle's mistaking of the merely connective function of the copula for the denotation of some underlying self-subsisting thing is denounced as the source from which the doctrine of separate essences was derived,[32] the fault is not in Aristotle's logic, which is not denounced itself for contributing to this nonsensical doctrine. What is clear about Aristotle's metaphysics—Hobbes constantly alleges that Aristotle, by his identification *ousia/on*, has defended the separate existence of abstract essences—is not so clear about his logic. The expressions "*Abstract Essences*" and "*Substantiall Formes*" are for Hobbes representative of the "jargon" of metaphysics, but he does not give any example of jargon taken from Aristotelian logic.[33] When the *Appendix ad Leviathan* criticizes the theologians explaining the dogma of Trinity for having made use of "definitions borrowed from Aristotle's logic and metaphysics" instead of grounding their demonstrations only in the Holy Scripture,[34] Hobbes does not blame directly technical words, "*verba artis*,"[35]

---

[26] See *De corpore*, I, V.13, 55. About the distinction between true logic and the "art of Sophists," namely, the technique called "eristics," which means "art of dispute," see *Anti-White* (hereafter abbreviated AW), I.4, 107.

[27] This paradox is known from *Physics* VI and commentaries on Aristotle. Hobbes's *Principia et problemata aliquot geometrica* (1673) testifies of his mistaking Zeno of Citium for Zeno of Elea: the argument about swift-footed Achilles and the tortoise is itself presented as an exemplification within the Stoic school of the so-called *dichotomy argument* against motion, which Hobbes attributes to the "master" of Stoics, Zeno (see OL V, 207–209). Therefore, the "*Logique*" depreciated as merely captious in chapter 46 of *Leviathan*, if its identification with the example of Zeno's argument in *De corpore* is correct, would be eventually for Hobbes the Stoic logic!

[28] *De corpore*, I, V.13, 55 and 50 for the subtitle which I quote here—all translations from the *De corpore* are mine, since, unfortunately, I did not have access while writing this to the translation provided by Aloysius Martinich. This paragraph was absent in MS A.10 and Cavendish's notes, it was added to chapter 5 for the final version.

[29] Latin *Leviathan*, IV, XLVI, 1059.

[30] Latin *Leviathan*, IV, XLVI, 1071.

[31] Ibid.

[32] Latin *Leviathan*, IV, XLVI, 1081.

[33] *Leviathan*, IV, XLVI.15, 1076.

[34] *Appendix ad Leviathan*, ch. I, 1184–1185.

[35] *Appendix ad Leviathan*, ch. I, 1185—the facing English translation drops "*artis*".

but their misuse or misapplication in theological explications. The main charge is not against Aristotelian logic itself, but against its theological abuse when combined with Aristotle's metaphysical doctrine.

1.4 What Is Technical in Traditional Logic?

In his Latin verse autobiography, Hobbes cannot resist an opportunity to play on words. After learning the names of all the syllogistic figures in all the valid moods,[36] he says that finally he was allowed to make every proof "in [his] own mood."[37] Natural reasoning, he means, can achieve demonstration by itself, without the constraint of an artificial logic.

Yet, as is shown by Hobbes's considerations about the logical doctrine of definition on the occasion of his controversy with John Bramhall, the terminology of Aristotelian and medieval logic is not for him a repertory of terms that would have to be ranked in the technical jargon of the Schools. In his *Defence of True Liberty against Necessity* (1655), Bramhall objects that Hobbes's definition of liberty ("the absence of all the impediments to action that are not contained in the nature of the agent") violates "all the rules of right reason": Insofar as it is not by genus and difference, or by matter and form, it is not a definition but merely a description of the accidental "marks and tokens" of liberty, and, moreover, it involves a negation or absence, whereas "[n]egatives cannot explicate the nature of things defined."[38] Hobbes replies by substituting Bramhall's rules on definition with just one rule or "measure of the definition": To define must be to determine the signification of a word in order to use it "without equivocation" in a discourse.[39] Bramhall's argument that negatives are not definitional is easily defeated, merely by assuming the nominal nature of the *definiendum*: "if the word defined signify an absence or negation, I hope he would not have me define it by a presence or affirmation."[40] The right viewpoint on "definition" is that it is only a necessary meta-name for qualifying the meta-name "proposition" when the predicate of a proposition consists in names of decreasing universality dividing a compound name-subject into its different parts. In this regard, even the traditional notion of definition by genus and difference based on Porphyry's doctrine of predicables can be maintained; it only needs to be given a nominalist extensionalist interpretation ("genus" and "difference" are names more and less general). When traditional logic uses the notion of definition by genus and difference, although this notion is grounded on the thesis that the

---

[36] OL I, LXXXVI. Hobbes's enumeration does not include the valid moods of the so-called *fourth figure* (those other moods that had been taken in consideration by Aristotle in *Prior Analytics*, I.7, 29 a 19–29).

[37] OL I, LXXXVII (my translation).

[38] Excerpts from Bramhall's *Defence* are included in Hobbes's LNC. See no. XXIX, EW V, 368, for that objection.

[39] LNC, no. XXIX (EW V, 370).

[40] LNC, no. XXIX (EW V, 371–372).

definition is the essence of the thing defined, this does not amount for Hobbes to the creation of a fictitious logical terminology comparable to metaphysical artifacts such as "separate/abstract essence." As long as genus and difference are not identified (as Bramhall does) with matter and form,[41] Hobbes admits the traditional notion of definition by genus and difference. Thus, once it has been stated that definition is nothing other than the explication of a name by a series of other names, it is quite legitimate to reword Bramhall's requirement of a definition by genus and difference while leaving room for another kind of definition, when names are too universal to be defined in that way: "I confess the rule is good, that we ought to define, when it can be done, by using first some more general term, and then by restraining the signification of that general term, till it be the same with that of the word defined. And this general term the School calls *genus*, and the restraint *difference*. This, I say, is a good rule where it can be done; for some words are so general, that they cannot admit a more general in their definition."[42] By contrast, it is impossible to admit in logic the notion of a definition by matter and form: "Matter is body, that is to say, corporeal substance. . . . But it is impossible that matter should be part of a definition, whose parts are only words."[43]

Thus, through a nominalist reductionist reinterpretation, even scholastic realist terminology can find a place within Hobbes's logic. This is a point that Bramhall misses by making Hobbes's reception of scholastic logic homogeneous with his reception of scholastic philosophy. In *Of Liberty and Necessity* (1646), Hobbes objected to the use of such scholastic distinctions as "liberty of specification/liberty of exercise," which are technical terms in moral philosophy and which belong to a deliberately obscure vocabulary made for "the tyrannizing over men's reason and understanding."[44] Accordingly, for Bramhall, Hobbes is also committed to extend his "invective" indistinctly to all arts and sciences.[45] Traditional logic would be the primordial victim: "What then, must the logicians lay aside their first and second intentions, their abstracts and concretes, their subjects and predicates, their modes and figures, their method synthetic and analytic, their fallacies of composition and division, &c.?"[46] Indeed, Bramhall is doubly mistaken in thinking that Hobbes is opposed to all these terms as so many "terms of art." Actually, for Hobbes, first, not one of the terms enumerated by Bramhall is a technical logical term, but only "Barbara, Celarent, Darii, Ferio, &c. are terms of art."[47] And, second, logical terms of art are not unintelligible: "Barbara, Celarent, and the rest that follow, are terms of art,

[41] Bramhall's equivalence is in accordance with Porphyry's *Isagoge*, VIII, 7: genus is like matter [*hylè*], difference like form [*morphè*].

[42] LNC, no. XXIX (EW V, 370–371).

[43] LNC, no. XXIX (EW V, 371).

[44] *Of Liberty and Necessity*, EW IV, 263–264—reproduced in LNC, no. XIX, EW V, 249–250.

[45] Bramhall (see LNC, no. XIX, EW V, 258) successively reviews terms used by "logicians," "the moral philosopher," "the natural philosopher," "the astrologer and the geographer." The technical terms of "the mathematician," "the metaphysician," and "the divine" are mentioned, too, yet without any examples.

[46] LNC, no. XIX (EW V, 258).

[47] LNC, no. XIX (EW V, 266).

invented for the easier apprehension of young men, and are by young men understood."[48] In the series of logical idiomatic expressions alleged by Bramhall—*first and second inten-tion, abstract/concrete, subject/predicate*, and the like—terms are not for Hobbes, by contrast with the Bishop, items of a technical lexicon: "these are no more terms of art in logic, than *lines, figures, squares, triangles*, &c. in the mathematics."[49] And, with regard to terms that are really technical in logic (*Barbara, Celarent*, etc.), they are not fictional terms, but pedagogi-cal devices that escape confusion with "the enchantment of words not understood."[50]

So, finally, there is nothing common between scholastic jargon, obscure and vain terms "invented to blind the understanding,"[51] and the technical terms of scholastic syllogistic. Unlike the terms forged by scholastic natural and moral philosophy, the late medieval logi-cal neologisms are not presented as terms whose invention is caused by the incapacity to face theoretical difficulties. Barbarous words are for Hobbes words fabricated by "puzzled" philosophers:[52] the "deceiving masters" also are "deceived masters."[53] They are self-deceived by a mistaken use of words and by incorrect modes of reasoning. Significantly, moreover, in the litany of terms that Bramhall considers as the "terms of art and proper idiotisms" of logicians, the distinction *sense divided/sense compounded* is quite well accepted by Hobbes precisely so long as it consists only in a logical distinction. What is faulty, for Hobbes, is indeed Bramhall's use of this distinction in the debate on free will. Bramhall diverts the distinction from its unique right use, which is its use concerning propositions. When denouncing the thesis of the "patrons of necessity"—that an agent is free, who can do if she wills—Bramhall applies the difference *in sensu diviso/in sensu composito* for character-izing the relationship between the power or faculty and the act with regard to freedom and determination.[54] It is this misuse of the logical distinction, not the distinction itself, that

---

[48] LNC, no. XIX (EW V, 267).

[49] Ibid.

[50] LNC, no. XXXIII (EW V, 399). For the topic of insignificant names in the controversy with Bramhall, see (not exhaustive list) LNC, no. I (EW V, 35); no. III (EW V, 47); no. IV (EW V, 63); no. VII (EW V, 77–78); no. XI (EW V, 113); no. XIV (EW V, 182, 195); no. XIX (EW V, 264–265 and 267); no. XXIII (EW V, 326–327); no. XXIV (EW V, 342); no. XXV (EW V, 353); no. XXVI (EW V, 359); no. XXVIII (EW V, 367); no. XXIX (EW V, 370); no. XXXI (EW V, 384); no. XXXII (388); no. XXXIII (EW V, 397); no. XXXVII (EW V, 435).

[51] For such examples in natural philosophy as "*intentional* species," "*qualities infusae or influxae*," etc., see LNC, no. XIX (EW V, 267).

[52] LNC, no. XXXIII (EW V, 397): "some puzzled divine or philosopher, that to decline a difficulty speaks in such manner as not to be understood." See LNC, no. 359: "puzzled Schoolmen" EW V, 359); cf. no. XXXI (EW V, 384). See also *De homine*, X. 3 (OL II, 92).

[53] LNC, no. XXXIII (EW V, 399).

[54] See Chappell 1999, 8 note 23 to the corresponding passage in Bramhall's *Discourse of Liberty and Necessity* (1646): "In their standard use by medieval logicians, the terms *in sensu diviso* and *in sensu composito* refer to two ways of construing conditional sentences containing modal operators, i.e. such sentences as 'If God knows that Adam sinned then necessarily Adam sinned'. Understood in the composite sense, this means, 'It is a necessary truth that if God knows that Adam sinned then Adam sinned ' [. . .]. Understood in the divided sense, however, the sentence means 'If God knows that Adam sinned, then it is a necessary truth that Adam sinned.'" Chappell underlines (1) that for Bramhall (and medieval logicians), the conditional would be true *in sensu composito*, false *in sensu diviso*, whereas for Hobbes it is true in both senses; and (2) that Bramhall's use of the distinction "is not the standard one"

Hobbes rejects when he writes that, in the same way as the expression "hypothetical necessity" is but "jargon" when it is used for something other than a propositional property, Bramhall's "divided sense" and "compounded sense" are "nonsense."[55]

2   HOBBES ON THE NATURE OF LOGIC

2.1 Anthropology and Logic

In *The Questions Concerning Liberty, Necessity and Chance*, when he amends Bramhall's presentation of the rules of logic concerning definition, Hobbes makes a remark expressing his ambivalent relation to the tradition of Aristotelian logic: "I should advise him [Bramhall] to read some other logic than he hath yet read, or consider better those he did read when he was a young man and could less understand them [the rules of logic]."[56] A few lines earlier, Hobbes had asked Bramhall to refer to the *De corpore*, chapter 6, articles 14–15 (namely, the definition of definition and the properties of definition) in order to understand the reason why the law of definition by genus and difference must be reworded as stating only a relation between names. Apparently, the reference to chapter 6 is compatible with keeping traditional logic. Hobbes's aim is not (as Ramus's aim was) to introduce a new anti-Aristotelian logical lexicon, but rather to redefine the available scholastic terminology. Now, in Hobbes's mind, this end may be achieved otherwise than by composing a separate logical treatise; it may be achieved in the anthropology leading to the description of man's natural condition. Wherever man's epistemic ability is affirmed, there is place for introducing nominal definitions that are sufficient to transform the most ordinary technical vocabulary of traditional logic ("proposition," "subject," "predicate," "syllogism") into Hobbes's own logical lexicon. For Hobbes, insofar as human nature is human because of man's linguistic power, the integration of some logical analysis into the anthropological analysis is from this viewpoint performed as quite natural. *The Elements of Law* give, in my view, a fine illustration of such a strategy for combining, in the "no-justification-needed" kind of way, unexpected logical elements with the anatomy of the mental capacities of man.

The Elements of Law's "Epistle dedicatory," dated May 9, 1640, declares that the author's ambition is to "reduce [civil] doctrine to the rules and infallibility of reason."[57] However, the demonstration intended to put an end to "doubts and controversies" in political philosophy is not grounded in the argumentative procedures of traditional logic.[58] In

---

because it does not deal with a conditional proposition, but with a conjunctive proposition ("the cause is necessitated and the effect is free").

[55] LNC, no. XXVIII (EW V, 367).
[56] LNC, no. XXX (EW V, 372).
[57] *Elements of Law*, Ep. Dedic., XV. (Page references are to the 1969 edition, edited by Tönnies.)
[58] *Elements of Law*, I, I.1, 1.

order to generate "the knowledge of what is human nature,"[59] a simple definitional procedure is enough. Definitions stating the meaning of the words applied to man's different cognitive powers constitute a sufficient condition for "reasoning aright."[60] Now, interestingly, at some point in the anthropological analysis, the definitions making it possible for the explication of human nature to proceed are connected with something other than a merely anthropological approach. Although Hobbes refuses a formal presentation of technical logic, the chapter on language includes a piece of logic. In other words, this chapter is bipolarized. In a first stage, man is described as that incomparable animal who is dissatisfied with the indeterminacy of his thoughts: No imaginative sequence belonging to past experience can return unless an external cause at some moment produces the first image from which this "discourse of the mind" is restored. The desire to reduce this random way of thinking issues in the invention of language. The human mind is taken beyond its native condition by the establishment of names: Thanks to their serving as marks, the mind can recall past thoughts to itself. But, in a second stage, once the invention of names is gained, Hobbes introduces the definitions of different sorts of names (positive/privative; universal/singular), and additional considerations, principally on the status of universality, are developed, too. The analysis turns out to be less and less anthropological. It allows the definition of only one form of verbal discourse, which could be integrated better in a rudimentary logic textbook: "Of two appellations, by the help of this little verb is, or something equivalent, we make an affirmation or negation, AFFIRMATION and NEGATION, either of which in the Schools we call also a proposition, and consisteth of two appellations joined together by the said verb is."[61] Thus, in this section of The Elements of Law, the exposition is not as continuous as it should have been: Propositional speech substitutes for human language, logic substitutes for anthropology. In traditional logic, the next step after proposition is syllogism. Yet, in The Elements of Law, Hobbes restricts the definition of syllogism to a minimum. He writes:

> In what manner of two propositions, whether both affirmative, or one affirmative, the other negative, is made a SYLLOGISM, I forbear to write. All this that hath been said of names or propositions, though necessary, is but dry discourse: and this place is not for the whole art of logic, which if I enter further into, I ought to pursue: besides, it is not needful; for there be few men which have not so much natural logic, as thereby to discern well enough, whether any conclusion I shall hereafter make, in this discourse, be well or ill collected: only thus much I say in this place, that making of syllogisms is that we call RATIOCINATION or reasoning.[62]

This passage makes clear that the fragmentary logic introduced in the anthropological analysis is not there for logic's sake, and that, more generally, technical logic

---

[59] Ibid.
[60] Elements of Law, I, I.3, 1.
[61] Elements of Law, I, V.9, 21.
[62] Elements of Law, I, V.11, 22. This paragraph is quite a rhetorical bijou.

is not necessary for distinguishing correct and incorrect forms of reasoning.[63] Yet, for Hobbes, the "dry discourse" providing the definitions of terms proper to the "art of logic" is not sterile. It is a convenient way to convey what is really aimed at by its means: The definition of "ratiocination" as a propositional composition.[64] The same approach appears in 1642–1643 in the *Anti-White*. Having stated that the difference between human nature and animal nature consists in the use of names and that names are imposed to things through a comparison between their singular properties, Hobbes similarly quits the merely anthropological register of analysis and adopts the style of a logician. After defining the property *universal* strictly relative to common names (or names imposed on all things severally which have a similar property), the explication becomes logical: "With two names copulated by a verb, we make a *proposition* by which we note that the second name, or name consequent, is appropriate to the same thing to which the first name, or name antecedent, is appropriate. . . . Again, with two connected propositions having a name common to both which is medium between the names which are not common, we make a *syllogism*."[65]

In the *Leviathan*, by contrast, the anthropological exposition remains anthropological. Chapter 4, "Of Speech," does not substitute logic for the anthropological issue of the use of language. Unless I am mistaken, Hobbes never makes use of the term "proposition" in his analysis of human language and the following analysis of reason/science with the exception of the opening paragraph of the chapter on reason.[66] The terms used instead are "affirmation," "saying," and "assertion."[67] Similarly, the term "*Syllogisme*" is introduced not as a technical term for a combination of propositions that is made possible by a middle term, but merely as the most ordinary Greek word for "the act of reasoning." And this "act of reasoning" itself is explained as consisting of the "summing up of the consequences of one saying to another."[68] As such, Hobbes simply relies on an etymological justification for a strict "computational" approach of reasoning. The continued use of the term "syllogism" is detached from any Aristotelian logical ground.

---

[63] Hobbes's confidence in the reader's "natural logic" is lower in *De cive. See* for instance I.X, note [1647], 95 (page references are to the 1983 edition edited by Warrender): the truth of the conclusion *in the mere state of nature, everyone has a right to everything* is held to be so "hard" for the reader that the link with its premises might be lost, so that Hobbes collects into a unique abridged argument, understandable *uno intuitu*, all the propositions involved in this inference.

[64] In 1655 (*De corpore*, I, I.2), the definition of *ratiocinatio* will be other (see De corpore, 12).

[65] AW, XXX.17–18, 357.

[66] In 1651 *Leviathan*, I, V.1, 64, the subject-matter attributed to professional logicians is "affirmation" rather than "proposition"; correspondingly, "*Syllogisme*" is defined as an addition of two affirmations. Yet, the term "proposition" is present in the description of the technique used by logicians to recover one of the premises of a syllogism from its conclusion by subtracting "one *Proposition*" from "the *summe*." In 1668 Latin *Leviathan*, however, Hobbes plainly attributes to logicians proposition-making by the addition of two names, syllogism-making by the addition of two propositions and demonstration-making by the addition of syllogisms (Hobbes 2012, 65).

[67] *Leviathan*, I, IV.11, 54l; 14, 58l; 21, 60; I, V.4, 64; 5, 66; 10, 68; 17, 70, 72. See also I, II.10, 36; I, VII.4, 98; 5, 100; 7, 102; I, IX.1, 3, 124; III, XXXVI.1, 650.

[68] *Leviathan*, I, IV.14, 58.

It is also remarkable that in his analysis of belief in *Leviathan* Hobbes states only that belief is "both *of* the man, and *of* the truth of what he sayes."[69] In contrast, in *De cive*, the comprehensive treatment of the diverse acts by which the mind gives its assent to a speech begins with the statement: "*that which is believed* is always a *proposition* (that is to say, a speech affirmative or negative), which we grant to be true."[70] The act of knowing consists in mental assent to a proposition received for true because of the significations of the names it copulates. When the reason for assenting to a proposition is derived not from the proposition itself, but from the person who makes this proposition, the mental act is only an act of believing. The *Third Objections* had already shown the difference between affirming (or denying) and assenting. Hobbes had rejected the voluntaristic approach of belief in Descartes's theory of error. His argument was that affirmation and negation (which only deal with names) are indeed acts of our will but that the different kinds of internal assent to a speech, namely, the mental acts of knowing and believing, are not voluntary. Assent is given whether we will it to or not.[71] The *De cive* emphasizes the logical background of this thesis. Whereas the object of assent remained logically imprecise in the *Third Objections*, now the classification of the diverse forms of internal assent makes them correspond without exception to a "proposition." Moreover, the definition of belief is not restrained to isolate it from the definitions of other mental acts about the reception of a proposition in the mind. This also gives Hobbes an opportunity for introducing incidentally a reductionist theory of truth as being the same as a true proposition. The *De cive* supports this theory by stressing the logical status of the names that are the elements of a proposition: "[I]s *true* a *proposition* in which the *name consequent*, which is called by logicians the *predicate*, comprehends in its extent the *name antecedent*, which they call the *subject*."[72] The analysis of belief in *Leviathan* is far removed from that insistence on a connection with logic: The object of belief is not called a "proposition" any longer, it is "the saying of [a] man."[73]

In my view, in *Leviathan*, Hobbes wants to emphasize that affirmation/negation (i.e., assertive speech) belongs to a typology of the diverse "kinds of Speeches" or "formes of Speech."[74] He is careful about proposing at once a division of the "speciall uses of Speech."[75] The framework for a typology of discursive forms ranging from the assertive

---

[69] *Leviathan*, I, VII.5, 100.

[70] *De cive*, III, XVIII.4, 282. However, in the *Anti-White*, XXVI.4, 309, when Hobbes distinguishes "natural knowledge" (the assent given to the truth of a proposition because of its demonstration) from "belief," he does not use for the object of this latter kind of assent the term "proposition," but the circumlocution "that which is said." As for the *Elements of Law*, it says little about belief.

[71] See Objection XIII, in Descartes 1984, 134 (cf. Objection VI, in Descartes 1984, 128).

[72] *De cive*, III, XVIII.4, 284.

[73] *Leviathan*, I, VII.5, 100.

[74] For these notions (in Latin "*formulae loquendi/formulae sermonis*" and "*orationum genera*"), see *Leviathan*, II.10, 36; IV.23, 62; VI.55–56, 94.

[75] *Leviathan*, IV.3, 50. Cf. *The Elements of Law*, where only the expression of conceptions is immediately deduced from the invention of language; other forms of linguistic expression, for other mental contents (passions, volitions), are described in XIII 5–7, 64, 67–68.

form to the forms that "signifie the Appetites, Aversions, and Passions of mans mind"[76] is immediately settled. The science of politics requires an account of how the various modes of thinking get expressed by the various modes of speaking. In particular, "assertion" has to be understood as a kind of verbal discourse, not, like "proposition," as an item of the "art of logic." This is why "proposition" disappears from the anthropology of *Leviathan*. The proper place for "proposition" is in *De corpore*, where it reappears.

2.2 Logic as a Science

Some 1637 letters from Kenelm Digby to Hobbes show that, already in the 1630s, Hobbes was planning a "Logike." The correspondence evoking this book project makes it obvious that Digby would have difficulty understanding Hobbes's approach.[77] Anyway, Digby was too optimistic in expecting at once a manuscript of Hobbes's "Logike." The composition of Hobbes's *Logica* required uninterrupted reworking during the 1640s.

What is clear, in any event, is that Hobbes did not intend to take an explicit position on the long-debated issue of the nature of logic.[78] Instead, he discusses in *Leviathan* the nature of reason. To reason is "nothing else but conceive a summe totall, from *Addition* of parcels; or conceive a Remainder, from *Substraction* of one summe from another."[79] The act or operation of reasoning consists either in the addition of parts into a total or, conversely, in the removal of some subtotal of parts from the total. For instance, in logic, addition and subtraction deal with names, affirmations, and syllogisms. Now, insofar as calculation on any matter is able to go further and better if it is "done by

---

[76] *Leviathan*, I, IV.24 (Hobbes 2012–2, 62).

[77] See *Letter of Sir Kenelm Digby to Hobbes, 17 [/27] January 1637* (Hobbes 1994, I, 42–43): "In your Logike, before you can manage men's conceptions, you must shew a way how to apprehend them rightly; and herein I would gladly know whither you work upon the general notions and apprehensions that all men (the vulgar as well as the learned) frame of all things that occurre unto them; or whither you make your ground to be definitions collected out of a deep insight into the things themselves. Methought you bent this way when we talked hereof; & still I am of opinion it is too learned a one for that which ought to be the instrument of other sciences." Also see *Letter of Sir Kenelm Digby to Hobbes, 11 [/21] September 1637* (Hobbes 1994, I, 50), where Digby, whose interest was to get from Hobbes instruction about the way particulars are known, presented his question in form of a doctrinal dilemma: either the soul is a spirit which "hath within itself the knowledg of all things, & so delivereth over to the fantasie a misty notion of what occurreth to some particular that it (the fansy) is continually beating upon," or the soul has "a power to deduce all knowledg concerning any particular object, out of the species that are administred to it by the senses, when she speculates intensely upon them." Digby conceived the latter possibility "to be the way that seperated soules know all that is done in this world by joining & diving into the species they carry from hence." Reading this, no doubt Hobbes got the feeling that he would have to work hard in order to make Digby change the parameters of his question!

[78] See, for example, Jacopo Zabarella, *De natura logicae* (in his *Opera logica*, 1594 and Martinus Smiglecius *Logica selectis disputationibus et quaestionibus illustrata* (1618 this book was many times reprinted in Oxford and used as a textbook), *Disputatio II, Quaestio V.*

[79] *Leviathan*, I, V.1, 64.

Words,"[80] the very object of logic as a science is also the instrument of all other sciences. That is to say, *qua* specific science, logic is the knowledge of the *organon* for all sciences. Hobbes says that "in what matter soever there is place for *addition* and *substraction*, there also is place for *Reason*,"[81] but he might have said: "there also is place for *logic*," since arithmetic, geometry, and the like would not be able to be sciences if they applied the act of reasoning about their distinct subject matters without combining names in propositions, propositions in syllogisms, and syllogisms in demonstrations. Thus, reason is "nothing but *Reckoning* (that is, Adding and Substracting) of the Consequences of general names."[82]

In 1651 *Leviathan*'s table of the diverse kinds of science or parts of philosophy, "LOGIQUE" appears as a subdivision of "PHYSIQUES," which is itself a subdivision of natural philosophy differentiating the knowledge of the "Consequences from *Qualities*" from the knowledge of the "consequences from the accidents common to all bodies natural."[83] Speech is among "the Qualities of *Men in speciall*"; so, as a subsection of physics, logic constitutes an ultimate division, together with poetry, rhetoric, and the science of just and unjust, of the knowledge of the "Consequences from *Speech*." It is the specific science of the consequences of speech "In *Reasoning*."[84] However, logic plays a second role. Hobbes says that the table classifies the diverse genera of "*Demonstrations* of Consequences of one Affirmation, to another." Logic is thus necessary to the whole classification, in all its divisions; its specific matter, reasoning with words, is necessary to any part of philosophy in order to be a science.

2.3 Logic as an Art

Although the conception of logic as a science distinct by its subject matter (reasoning) from other sciences again makes an occasional appearance in 1660, in the *Examinatio et Emendatio Mathematiae hodiernae*,[85] Hobbes takes it for granted in 1671, in his *Censura brevis* of Wallis's *De motu*, that the word *logica* stands for *logica ars*.[86] Logic is an art; yet, the art of what? *Anti-White*'s first chapter[87] had been entirely devoted to clarifying this point in order to refute a concise marginal statement in Dialogue I of White's *De mundo* that claimed that "philosophy must not be treated logically." For White, this meant that when it is treated logically, philosophy merely attains conclusions whose higher probability may be shortly outweighed by the opposite propositions. Hobbes's

---

[80] Ibid.
[81] Ibid.
[82] Ibid.
[83] *Leviathan*, I, IX, 130–131.
[84] *Leviathan*, 131.
[85] Dialogus I (OL IV, 29). See also *Six Lessons to the Professors of Mathematics* (1656), Lesson II (EW VII, 225).
[86] OL V, 51.
[87] AW I.1–4, 105–107.

comment is based on a definition of philosophy as "the science of general theorems, that is, of all universal propositions, whatever the subject-matter, whose truth can be demonstrated by natural reason." He considers then the different ends of speech: to teach (*docere*), to relate (*narrare*), to rouse emotion (*commovere*), to glorify (*nobilitare*). Logic is, accordingly, an art of speaking, distinct from history, rhetoric, and poetry. However, Hobbes's concern in the opening pages of the *Anti-White* is not to substitute the Renaissance's five-part syllabus of *studia humanitatis* (grammar, rhetoric, poetry, history, moral philosophy)[88] with a new one. His argument is that, among the diverse arts of speaking, the only one convenient for philosophy is logic because the end of philosophy is certainty of knowledge. Now, the only way for delivering certain knowledge on natural and moral matters is to proceed from definitions of names to their composition into "necessary consequences": namely, to demonstrate. Hobbes reduces White's exclusion of logic to the utterly ridiculous statement that "philosophy must not be treated logically because rhetoric teaches nothing certain."[89] Indeed, White confused logic with the art of arguing pro and con about any matter, which begets merely probable conclusions. According to Hobbes, White would have done better if he had stressed that many parts of philosophy (e.g., metaphysics, physics, ethics) have not yet been treated logically,[90] rather than to mistake logic with rhetoric. The rhetorical art of speaking aims to have the hearer act in a certain way, whereas the logical art of speaking demonstrates universally true propositions.

That philosophy "must be treated so that the truth of conclusions is known by a necessary inference"[91] and cannot be dissociated from logic supposes, in the *Anti-White*, an identity between "to demonstrate" and "to teach." The same point is reaffirmed in the *Examinatio et Emendatio Mathematicae hodiernae*: The question "what is it, *to demonstrate?*" is no other than the question "what is it, *to teach?*"[92] Logic, when it is defined as the *ars docendi*, is ipso facto defined as the *ars demonstrandi*. The *Anti-White* emphasizes that philosophy is divided into parts that are de jure methodologically equal despite their heterogeneous subjects and that mathematics is this part that perfectly instantiates the method that might be common to all of them. Geometry and arithmetic are called "mathematical sciences" because both prove general conclusions by beginning with definitions of names that are used univocally. If ambiguity of names is eliminated in advance,[93] then each doctrine can get a mathematical status, independently of the nature of its object. By contrast with geometry and arithmetic, the other parts of philosophy are, so to speak, only provisionally philosophy. They will become

---

[88] Skinner 1996, 23.

[89] AW I.4, 107.

[90] See on this point AW I.1, 105–106.

[91] AW, I.3, 107.

[92] Dialogus I (OL IV, 40).

[93] This entails the exclusion, considered by Hobbes as primordial for producing certainty, of metaphors, which are per se ambiguous and equivocal: *Elements of Law*, I, V.7, 20; see Pécharman 1988b.

sciences and parts of philosophy when their conclusions are demonstrated as true universal propositions.

To be a science and to be a "mathematical" science is the same in the *Anti-White*. Geometry and arithmetic are "mathematics" because of their method, not their objects. And their method is not peculiarly theirs; it is the method of logic. The method of proving general truths is, as it were, a *mathesis universalis*. Hobbes insists in the *Anti-White* that writers boasting of their "physical, theological, geometrical, or metaphysical demonstrations" only make it evident that they misuse the term "demonstration." It is impossible, Hobbes says, to know "what demonstration is" without being aware that "there is no other demonstration than logical."[94]

2.4 Natural Logic

Interestingly, the *Anti-White* attributes to logic understood as the *ars docendi/demonstrandi* that which belongs in *The Elements of Law* to the last mental operation among "the acts of our power cognitive, or conceptive,"[95] namely, "science or knowledge of the truth of propositions, and how things are called."[96] The *Anti-White* shows how the natural functioning of the human mind becomes a universal method for the communication of philosophy through language. *The Elements of Law* made it clear that reason is natural to man, even though it is a second nature and dependent on the use of words. From this viewpoint, the sciences that are, for the *Anti-White*, parts of philosophy on the condition of their conformity with logical method are merely, for *The Elements of Law*, diverse "registers" of a kind of cognitive experience different from the memory of sensible things: The "experience men have of the proper use of names in language" provides the mnemonic capability of recovering *ad libitum* the conceptions associated with the names.[97] The ability of these names to combine into true general propositions makes science possible.[98]

In Hobbes's view, therefore, philosophy as a science merely develops reason as the postlinguistic faculty of universal knowledge. The anthropological ability for science is possible "by the advantage of names."[99] As is highlighted in the *De cive*'s dedicatory epistle, by the mediation of "certain and definite appellations," philosophy is the method conducing from the knowledge—provided by those unambiguous names—of definite properties of singular things to "universal precepts."[100] The "unique way to science" is "the way *by definitions*."[101]

---

[94] AW, XXXIX.7, 433.
[95] *Elements of Law*, I, VI.9, 27.
[96] *Elements of Law*, I, VI.1, 24.
[97] *Elements of Law*, I, VI.1, 24–25. Cf. II, VIII.13, 176.
[98] *Elements of Law*, I, VI.4, 26.
[99] *Elements of Law*, I, V.4, 19.
[100] *De cive, Ep. dedic.*, 74.
[101] *De cive*, XVIII.IV, 284–285.

Demonstration does not differ for the *Anti-White* from natural reason's "right reasoning," *recta ratiocinatio*.[102] Therefore, to infer indisputable theorems in other parts of philosophy than geometry alone only requires that reasoning begins with "assured principles"; that is to say, with definitions of names ensuring by their precision the intellection of their significations. On this condition, all parts of philosophy can be "equally certain": Certitude is not a property "of geometers" but "of method,"[103] and method itself is not geometrical method, but logical method, whose way is no other than the mind's natural syllogizing from definitions of names. For Hobbes, even though the method founding demonstration on initial explications of names has been specific of geometers only, this does not entail a *more geometrico* demonstration. Demonstration is *more logico*, geometers are simply the first to have applied logical method.[104]

Thus, the way to be followed to deliver true universal conclusions indifferently on any matter strictly reflects for Hobbes the progression described in *The Elements of Law* as the mind's four "steps" of science.[105] First step: Knowledge is ultimately grounded in the conceptions of the "qualities, or natures" of the individual objects of sense.[106] Second step: From those singular conceptions, the mind goes to the imposition of general names. For every individual thing, the mind has many conceptions, which are so many causes for which "for one and the same thing, we have many names or attributes," and the many individual things about which we have similar conceptions necessarily "have the same appellation."[107] The qualities of individual things involve no universality, and the correspondent conceptions in the mind involve no universality either; every conception is an individual image of an individual quality of an individual thing.[108] Third step: The formation of true propositions is respectful of the coherence between the significations of general names.[109] And, finally, the progression reaches an end, or last step, with the inference of true conclusions from the combinations between those propositions. Even though the conclusions attained are not about the natures of things (because there are not universal natures of things), but about universal names,

---

[102] AW XXIII.1, 270. Also AW XXX.22, 359, for the description of "right reasoning."

[103] AW XXIII.1, 270. Cf. *De Principiis et ratiocinatione geometrarum* (OL IV, 390): "The certainty of all the sciences is equal. Else they would not be sciences indeed, since *to know* does not admit of *more* and *less*. If physics, ethics, politics were well demonstrated, they would not be less certain than mathematical propositions; and similarly, mathematics would not be more certain than the other sciences, if its propositions were not demonstrated correctly."

[104] When Leibniz in 1682 praises Hobbes for his "having written some excellent things in morals, metaphysics and physics by keeping a mathematical form" (*Ad praefationem Elementorum veritatis aeternae*, in Leibniz 1999, N. 113, 447), his appraisal is quite ambiguous from Hobbes's standpoint because it may mean that Hobbes has universalized *geometrical* demonstrative method in philosophy, whereas Hobbes's intent was to universalize *de facto* the *logical* demonstrative method which is universal *de jure*.

[105] *Elements of Law*, I, VI.4, 26; cf. I, XIII.3, 66.

[106] *Elements of Law*, I, VI.4, 26.

[107] *Elements of Law*, I, V.5, 19.

[108] See on this point AW, XXX.15–16, 355–357.

[109] *Elements of Law*, I, V.13, 22.

their content is not merely nominal. Their conceptual content is indexed to individuals. Science progresses because the "conclusions of most difficult and profound specula- tion" are traceable to the simplest imposition of names.[110]

Accordingly, the dependence of reason on the use of language makes logic insepa- rable from human nature. Designated in the *Anti-White* as the only art of speaking cor- responding to the definition of philosophy, logic achieves the natural functioning of the mind when the mind is, as it were, made human by the control over the occurrence of its thoughts allowed by the use of linguistic marks. It is "natural reason" that concludes truths from the significations of the names.[111] And this way of proving constitutes the only *ars docendi*. From this viewpoint, Hobbes may even consider logic as an art of eloquence without affecting its natural status. A notable change from *The Elements of Law* to the *De cive* concerning the status of logic in relation to eloquence makes this point evident. For the definition of "wisdom" versus "eloquence,"[112] Hobbes restates in *The Elements of Law* his thesis that science consists in a semantic knowledge, the "remembrance of the names or appellations of things, and how every thing is called."[113] But, by contrast, in *De cive*, Hobbes says there are two kinds of eloquence. One aims at exciting passions. The other gives a clear explication of the conceptions of the mind based on the relation between the things named and the "proper and definite significa- tion" of their names.[114] Logic, whose end is truth, can therefore be viewed as a kind of eloquence opposed to rhetoric.

This argument in *De cive* departs from what is found in Hobbes's digest of Aristotle's *Rhetoric*, *A Briefe of the Art of Rhetorique* (1637). According to the digest, for Aristotle, the art of rhetoric "consisteth ... chiefly in *Proofes*; which are *Inferences*," now "all *Inferences* [are] *Syllogismes*;" therefore, "all *Syllogismes*, and *Inferences* belong properly to *Logicke*; Whether they inferre truth, or probability."[115] Hobbes renders this double ability as follows: "a *Logician*, if he would observe the difference betweene a plain *Syllogisme* and an *Enthymeme*, (which is a *Rhetoricall Syllogisme*), would make the best *Rhetorician*."[116] The attribution in *De cive* of a kind of eloquence to logic is quite differ- ent. Its correlate is that logic does not include rhetoric under its jurisdiction. Syllogism is only the matter of logic. Rhetoric merely deals with the arousing of passions. For Aristotle, rhetoric and logic are jointly the office of dialectic, which is the knowledge of all syllogisms.[117] But Hobbes does not endorse that position. When dialectic is

---

[110] *Elements of Law*, I, XIII.3, 66.

[111] See AW XXVI.7, 310.

[112] *Elements of Law*, II, VIII.13, 175.

[113] *Elements of Law*, II, VIII.13, 176.

[114] *De cive*, XII.XII, 192.

[115] Hobbes 1637, 3. The Aristotelian definition of rhetoric says in Hobbes's translation that it is "that Faculty, by which wee understand what will serve our turne, concerning any subject, to winne beleefe in the Hearer" (Hobbes 1637, 4). Aristotle says simply; "Rhetoric may be defined as the faculty of observing in any given case the available means of persuasion."

[116] Hobbes 1637, 3.

[117] Early-modern logicians who define logic as a faculty (not as a science, nor as an art) usually refer to this statement in Aristotle's *Rhetoric*.

mentioned in 1668, in the Appendix to Latin *Leviathan*, Hobbes's meaning forbids that it might function as a common foundation for logic and rhetoric. Hobbes writes: "What is it to reason, if not to impose names on things, join names into statements [*dicta*], and link statements in syllogisms? From these comes dialectic."[118] Dialectic is just the same as logic, the method for deducing truths from definitions; it cannot be divided into two kinds of demonstration, the method for knowing what is certain and the method for knowing what is merely probable.

3 Hobbes's *Computatio sive Logica*

3.1 Puzzles

As investigated earlier, Hobbes's views on the nature of logic before the publication of the *Computatio sive Logica* (1655) are crucial for understanding that book. Its very title is revelatory: Logic is computation.[119] Some of Hobbes's contemporaries particularly derided this identification. John Eachard, Master of Catherine's Hall in Cambridge, published in the 1670s the following pastiche:

> *I do*, in your name, *decree, that in all following Ages* Logick *shall not be called* Logick, *but* Computation; *because that* ratiocinor *signifies not only to* reason, *but to* count *or* reckon; *and* rationes *the same with* computa: *And therefore let the art of* reasoning *be called the art of* computation *or* counting: *of which there be two parts*; addition *and* substraction; *to* add *being all one as to* affirm, *and to* substract *all one as to* deny: *from whence also I do establish a* Syllogisme *to be nothing else but the collection of a* Summ, *or* aggregate: *the* major *and* minor Propositions *being the* Particulars, *and the* Conclusion, *the* summ *or* aggregate *of those particulars.*[120]

---

[118] *Appendix ad Leviathan*, I, 1168.

[119] The original title was simply *Logica* in MS.A.10. Significantly, in his examination of Part I of *De corpore*, Seth Ward changes the title *Computatio sive Logica* into *De dialecticis* (Ward 1656, 14). Ward insists that the novelty of Hobbes's title is adverse to any logical tradition because, so far, writers of logic have used either the word *Logica* or the word *Dialectica* for the *ars ratiocinandi* (*id.*, 15). For him, were the word *Computatio* maintained as a title, its equivalent should not be *Logica*, but *Logistica* because computation and logistic are held by mathematicians to be equivalent. Now, Ward stresses that Hobbes utterly fails to comply with the mathematical meaning of computation, which must be referred to analytic geometry. Ward's comments (*id.*, 16–17) are particularly biased. Despite Hobbes's denial (*De corpore*, I, I.3) of any tribute paid in his definition of ratiocination as computation to the Pythagorean doctrine that numbers are the principles of all things, for Ward, Hobbes confuses the *methodus disserendi* with the *methodus numerandi* and is in full agreement with Pythagoras. Ward's interpretation of the *Computatio* makes it an occultist manifesto, Hobbes being even changed into a Cabalist for whom the knowledge of numbers leads to the possession of omniscience.

[120] Eachard 1672, 20.

In another satiric record, Eachard said:

> By his Logick I profited wonderfully: for it was there (and I must ever acknowledge
> it) that I first was instructed to call Logick Computation: and there I learnt how to
> add and substract Logically: also how to make use of Triangles, Circles, Parabola's,
> and other Mathematical instances; instead of *homo, lapis* or *canis*; and that's upon
> my word, all that I found there.[121]

For Eachard, it was enough to allege that Hobbes was "the first that ever call'd *Logick Computation*" to justify denying that the *Computatio sive Logica* really constituted a treatise on logic.[122] In particular, Eachard did not understand what Hobbes meant by addition and subtraction. For Hobbes, each is grounded in a specific mental act that can be called "consideration." The different properties co-present in one and the same thing conceived by the mind can be successively looked at separately from each other, whether the unity they form in the concept of this thing is the *terminus ad quem* (addition) or the *terminus a quo* (subtraction) of the process. This act of isolating in the mind the diverse aspects represented in the whole concept of a thing constitutes accordingly a precondition of ratiocination. Every object of the mental act of consideration is ipso facto made a possible object within some reasoning: It can be brought into a certain "account" and become an item for the operation of computation. Correlatively, thus, addition and subtraction are not identified with affirmation and negation, as Eachard mistakenly believed. Their status is prepropositional or extrapropositional. *A fortiori*, Hobbes does not confuse them with those operations on the major and minor propositions in a syllogism that lead to the conclusion. They fundamentally deal with the composition or decomposition of any idea of an individual thing: The parts of this singular idea can be alternately objects for mental consideration in either a cumulative or a diminutive way.[123]

Seth Ward, Savilian Professor of Astronomy at Oxford University, had already misunderstood Hobbes in the same way Eachard would. Ward contends that the only thing new in Hobbes's logic are the words "*addition*" and "*subtraction*," which correspond respectively to the composition and division of ordinary dialectics. He writes that Hobbes has just "changed the ancient notation of dialecticians into the new of computation": In his eyes, the definition of computation in *De corpore*'s Part I simply follows the Aristotelian doctrine in *De Interpretatione* that not the single words expressing simple concepts, but rather the two forms of statement making, combination/affirmation and separation/negation, ensure that a speech bears a truth-value.[124]

---

[121] Eachard 1673, *The Author to the Reader*, sp. Later in the book, Eachard particularly mocks the application of the computational model to political matters: let the example of punishment by death sentence be taken; then, hanging is "the *concluding or summing up of a man from the premises*": "to be hang'd is to be *summ'd* or *cast up*" (*id.*, 120–121).

[122] Eachard 1673, 232.

[123] *De corpore*, I, I.3, 13. Cf. MS A.10, 463–464.

[124] Ward 1656, 20 (see *De interpretatione*, 16 a 9).

According to a twentieth-century interpretation by Gabriel Nuchelmans, Hobbes's identification of reasoning with the operations of addition/subtraction might be held to show a kind of allegiance to Ramism: "long before Hobbes wrote his *Computation or Logic*, the view that reasoning is a kind of calculation was a well-established element of the Ramist tradition."[125] Nuchelmans equates Ramus's doctrine of the syllogism "as a form of calculation" and Hobbes's identification of *computare* and *ratiocinari* as suggested by the Greek word *sullogizesthai*.[126] Yet, for Hobbes, this lexical confirmation means instead that the mental operation of syllogizing is more extensive than the formation of a syllogism strictly speaking. Moreover, the very text in the *Dialecticae Institutiones* from which Nuchelmans draws his suggestion undermines the equivalence he alleges.[127] Ramus's goal in this passage is to improve upon the definition of syllogism and its parts in the *Prior Analytics*. When a dubious "question" is examined (e.g., to know whether *A is B*), he says, it can be solved through a "disposition" of its two terms (the antecedent *A* and the consequent *B*) with some "argument" (the middle term *C*). It is only in this context that Ramus insists that the proper meaning of the word "*syllogismus*" is *ratio* or *calculus* and that this word has been transferred from mathematics to dialectic. He cites many passages in Aristotle's works (*Analytics, Topics, Physics*, and *Metaphysics*) that state a synonymy between *logismos* and *syllogismos*: Both mean arithmetic calculation done by addition and subtraction. He concludes that this is the reason why arithmetic is called *logistica*, the art and science of computation. Ramus is concerned only with the similarity between arithmetic computation and the disposition of a question with an argument into a syllogism. Again, this concern is very different from Hobbes's description of the operations of addition and subtraction with respect to a series of mental considerations about a thing's properties.

Nuchelmans suggests that Leibniz should have attributed the originality of reasoning as computation not to Hobbes, but to Ramus.[128] Leibniz writes in *Of the Art of Combination*: "Thomas Hobbes, everywhere a profound examiner of principles, rightly stated that everything done by our mind is a *computation*, by which is to be understood either the addition of a sum or the subtraction of a difference...."[129] However, this early work by Leibniz mainly reveals still another way of misunderstanding Hobbes's conception of computation. Indeed, in the passage just quoted, Leibniz goes on to say:

> So just as there are two primary signs of algebra and analytics, + and –, in the same way there are as it were two copulas, "is" and "is not"; in the former case the mind

---

[125] Nuchelmans 1980, 169 (note to the chapter on Peter Ramus). Cf. Nuchelmans 1983, 131.

[126] See *De corpore*, I, I.3, 13.

[127] Nuchelmans quotes a passage from the Second Part (about *iudicium*) of the *Dialecticae institutiones* (1543): "quemadmodum boni ratiocinatores addendo deducendoque vident, quae reliqui summa fiat: ita hic dialectici partibus addendis subducendisque summam quandam rationis explicant et complectionem conclusionis efficiunt."

[128] Nuchelmans (1980, 169) writes about the definition of *ratiocinatio* as computation: "That this idea is so often regarded as originating with Hobbes is perhaps partly due to the fact that Leibniz refers to him in his *De arte combinatoria*."

[129] Leibniz 1966, 3.

compounds, in the latter it divides. In that sense, the "is" is not properly a copula, but part of the predicate; there are two copulas, one of which, "not", is named, while the other is unnamed, but is included in "is" as long as "not" is not added to it. This has been the cause of the fact that "is" has been regarded as a copula. We could use as an auxiliary the word "really": *e.g.* "Man is *really* an animal", "Man is *not* a stone".'[130]

Obviously, Leibniz's agreement with the thesis that "everything done by our mind is a computation" distorts Hobbes's view. Leibniz's project of "plus-minus-calculus" does not suit the definition of computation in Hobbes's *De corpore*. Leibniz's aim is to base propositional logic on logical calculus, not to claim that computation is the natural functioning of the mind.

Contributing to the misunderstanding of *Computatio sive Logica* is the fact that, in contrast with almost all early modern logic textbooks,[131] initially Hobbes defines philosophy and defines computation[132] but does not define logic itself. *Computatio sive Logica* does not begin by saying what logic is. Rather, philosophy constitutes the *definiendum* at the end of the introductory paragraph in *Computatio sive Logica*: "I come to my design, and I shall begin with the very definition of Philosophy."[133] Hobbes proceeds as if the nature of logic is clear from the equivalence indicated by the title *Computatio sive Logica*. Because philosophy has been defined as discovering by reasoning causes of effects and effects of causes and reasoning as computation,[134] the

---

[130] Leibniz 1966, 3–4. In this text, addition and subtraction are not so much mental operations as formal operators.

[131] The definition of logic is sometimes lacking (e.g., in Edward Brerewood's *Elementa logicae*, 1614, or in Philippe du Trieu's *Manuductio ad Logicam*, 1651). Yet, broadly, in logic textbooks (some of them gaining many editions throughout the seventeenth century), two main definitions are found, which I distinguish as "Def:Argument" and "Def:Conduct." "Def:Argument" says that logic/dialectic is the art of discussing/discoursing/disputing probably on any proposed matter, or on both sides of any doubtful question, or simply the *ars bene disserendi* (John Case, *Summa veterum interpretum in universam dialecticam Aristotelis*, 1584; John Argall, *Ad artem dialecticam introductio brevis et perspicua*, 1605; Samuel Smith, *Aditus ad logicam*, 1613; John Alsted, *Compendium logicae harmonicae* 1615; Thomas Blundeville, *The Arte of Logick*, 1617; Christoph Scheibler, *Philosophia compendiosa*, 1628; Thomas Spencer, *The Art of Logick, delivered in the Precepts of Aristotle and Ramus*, 1638). "Def:Conduct" says that logic is the art of directing human understanding in the knowledge of things (Bartholomew Keckermann, *Systema logicae*, 1600; Franciscus Burgersdijck, *Institutionum logicarum libri duo*, 1637; Adrianus Heereboord, *Ermeneia Logica sive Synopseos logicae Burgersdicianae explicatio* 1651; Zachary Coke, *The Art of Logicke* 1654; Christopher Airay, *Fasciculus praeceptorum logicorum*, 1660). "Def:Conduct" is often followed by the remark that, respective to the double meaning of *logos* in Greek, *reason* is the primary object of logic and *oration* only a secondary object because oration comes from reason (e.g., Keckermann, Burgersdick, Airay). Yet, sometimes, the same remark is linked to "Def:Argument" (e.g., Alsted). It is also to be noted that, although the label "dialectic" is ordinarily given to logic according to "Def:Argument" (for instance by Spencer), also "Def:Conduct" accepts the possibility to say "dialectic" as a synonym for "logic" (e.g., Burgersdick, producing a reversal of Ramus, who first defined dialectic as the *ars bene disserendi* and then added that according to this meaning, dialectic is also called logic).

[132] In MS A.10 (Hobbes 1973, 463), this definitional duet was immediately brought forward; the *Computatio sive Logica* just delays it with a rhetorical "Introduction" about the seeds of true philosophy.

[133] *De corpore*, I, I.1, 12.

[134] *De corpore*, I, I.2, 12.

reader should be able to conclude that logic is essential for rational knowledge of causes and effects. Right reasoning simply consists in "two operations of the mind, *addition* and *subtraction*."[135] Method in philosophy can be mastered only if computation is acknowledged to be immanent logic in the mind. For Hobbes, the identity of logic with the very nature of reasoning makes it available to the human mind from within. No artificial tool external to the mind's operations is required. As the author writes to the reader of *De corpore*: "Philosophy, the daughter of your mind . . ., is within yourself."[136] The mind's internal ability to put into an account its diverse considerations about any thing is enough to allow planning a common subordination of all parts of philosophy to the additive and subtractive operations involved in this computation.

It is striking that the definition of philosophy as a certain method of reasoning, of reasoning as computation, and the division of philosophy into its main parts (natural and politic) seems to be a direct prelude to chapter 6 on methodology, as if the intermediary chapters 2–5, on words, proposition, syllogism, and fallacies, did not belong to the same project. The "epilogue" of chapter 1 on philosophy announces that the project in *De corpore* is to "propose the elements of this science that investigates effects from the known generation of a thing, or on the contrary the generation of a thing from a known effect,"[137] and the introduction to chapter 6 on method starts with stating again the same definition of philosophy.[138] Conceptually, chapters 1 and 6 form one unit, and chapters 2–5 form a different unit on a different topic. So the question is: Why is a seemingly traditional logic inserted between considerations on philosophy and method that might have been placed directly next to each other? If the aim was to provide an introduction to natural philosophy and more generally to the different parts of philosophy forming the whole *Elementa philosophiae*, why was it necessary to include something other than the description of the method answering the definition of philosophy?[139] Presumably, the final chapter on method was responsible for the reworking of the *Computatio* over many years because its content is much different in 1655 than in the early drafts. Noel Malcolm, for instance, writes that, in the period of the *Anti-White*, "one of the topics that was giving [Hobbes] the most difficulty was the nature of scientific method itself."[140] "Two different models of scientific knowledge jostle for position: the knowledge of causes, and the knowledge of definitional meanings."[141] In any

---

[135] Ibid.

[136] Hobbes 1999, 7. Cf. *De corpore*, I, II.8, 23, which does not distinguish between "reasoning," *ratiocinatio*, and "philosophy".

[137] *De corpore*, I, I.10, 18.

[138] *De corpore*, I, VI.1, 57: "*Philosophy is the knowledge, acquired through right reasoning, of phenomena or apparent effects from the conception of some possible production or generation, and of a production that has existed or that has been possible, from the conception of an apparent effect.*" The same continuity between the conclusion of chapter 1 and the beginning of chapter 6 can be observed in MS A.10, 472, and Cavendish's notes.

[139] *De corpore* I, VI.1 defines method as "the investigation as short as possible of effects by means of known causes or of causes by means of known effects."[140] Malcolm 2002–1, 17.

[141] Ibid.

case, Hobbes had planned from the outset that his *Logica* should not be limited to an epistemological treatise on the method required for his new philosophy of nature, man, and political body. It also had to be a reworking of the content of traditional treatises on terms, propositions, and syllogisms.

In those *entre-deux* (if I may say so) standard chapters of the *Computatio sive Logica*, Hobbes is careful, however, to emphasize repeatedly that he forbears addressing for their own sake the logical topics he is dealing with. Only that which is necessary for philosophy must be included in the *Computatio*. He gives natural reasoning priority over artificial and constraining tools of argumentation. That the exercise of the mind is more profitable for learning true logic than the formal rules of syllogistic has a touch of leitmotif. Notably, chapters 4 on syllogism and 5 on fallacies both finish similarly, with the declaration that technical developments can be omitted. "And indeed the foregoing seem to be sufficient for giving the knowledge of the nature of syllogisms, since all that is useful in the extensive treatises others have written on the modes and figures is clearly enclosed in what I have said";[142] "[a]nd that should be sufficient concerning syllogism, which is as it were the first step towards philosophy, since . . . I have said as much as is necessary to make known from whence every legitimate argumentation gets its force."[143] Traditional syllogistic is not useful for demonstrations in philosophy because what is needed for a "legitimate reasoning" is not so much formal rules as "praxis." To "amass all that can be said" on the topic of the rules of syllogism "would be as superfluous as if . . . one wanted give a young child precepts for taking steps."[144] A child will "learn how to step not by precepts, but by taking steps many times."[145] Therefore, "those who spend time reading the demonstrations of mathematicians will learn true logic much more quickly than those who waste it reading the precepts of logicians for syllogiz- ing."[146] The *Epistola dedicatoria* of *De corpore* stresses that the geometry transmitted to us by the Ancients is "the best exemplar of the true logic by which [ancient geometers] were able to discover and demonstrate so excellent theorems."[147] Similarly, according to his Latin prose autobiography, Hobbes's instant intellectual love for Euclidean method

---

[142] *De corpore*, I, IV.13, 49.

[143] *De corpore*, I, V.13, 56.

[144] Ibid.

[145] *De corpore*, I, IV.13, 49. Cf. *Principia et problemata aliquot geometrica* (1673), XII, *OL* V, 205.

[146] *De corpore*, I, IV.13, 49. See the same passage in Cavendish's notes as well (Hobbes 1973, 470). Also *De corpore*, I, V.13, 56: "the art of reasoning is acquired not by precepts, but by the use and reading of those books in which all conclusions are carried through strict demonstrations."

[147] *De corpore*, *Epist. Dedic.*, 3. Aubrey confirms this when he says that to teach geometry "is the best way of teaching logic to Mr Hobbes' way of thinking. It makes [children] reason without making a false step; it fixes their thoughts and cures bird-wittedness; teaches to reason geometrically and analytically in other things" (Aubrey 1972, 61; partially mentioned in Malcolm 2002, 4). Aubrey reports that Hobbes's pedagogical precept was that the study of geometry should be approached as soon as the mastery of Latin is acquired. This linguistic mastery is no longer propedeutic to the *studia humanitatis*: in Hobbes's view of education, mathematics take the central place devoted to the liberal arts in the humanist curriculum of Renaissance England (see Skinner 1996, 19 sq).

when encountering the *Elements* in 1630 for the first time consisted in a great delight with the "art of reasoning" (*ars ratiocinandi*) in geometry, not with the theorems actually deduced through it.[148] Any demonstration of a proposition in the *Elements* refers back to another proposition, and this one in turn refers back to another, and so on, until eventually the reader is "demonstratively convinced of that truth": Only this regressive process to the ultimate principles of any proposition fascinated Hobbes.[149]

Hobbes's long-matured chapter on methodology[150] probably was a source of disappointment for Baconian readers of the *Computatio sive Logica*. Considered by Hobbes's adversaries[151] as a fellow fighter against the obsolete "Aristotelity" taught according to *Leviathan* in English universities, John Webster, the author of *Academiarum Examen, or the Examination of Academies* (1654), surely felt frustrated if he read the *Computatio*. Webster had argued that, given that the knowledge of natural phenomena can be only "*a posteriore*," proceeding from the known properties of things to their causes, "the best part of *Logick* for that purpose is *Induction*" not "verbal and formal *Syllogisms*."[152] What is required, as Bacon indicated, is to find "infallible rules ... for the adaequation of notions and things."[153] Hobbes's chapter on method does not attempt to promote a positive and constructive meaning for induction and is not about the Baconian method for forming notions. So, for Webster, who had praised Bacon's accusation that the old logic failed to explain how truths are reached, the *Computatio* would seem to be concerned only with the demonstration of truths already known, instead of describing a new method of invention. Insofar as Hobbes maintains syllogism as a core logical instrument, he might be subject to Webster's verdict about traditional logic: "that which we know not, *Logick* cannot find out."[154]

No kind of induction finds a place in Hobbes's doctrine of method. In particular, although the *De corpore* states that "it is common to all methods to proceed from what is known to what is unknown,"[155] Hobbes does not evoke Bacon's inductive procedure of invention—the mind's "rising by a gradual and unbroken ascent, so that it arrives at the most general axioms last of all"[156]—as the only right logical method for

---

148 OL I, XIV.

149 See also Aubrey's *Brief Lives* (I, 332).

150 The chapter on scientific method finalizing the *Computatio sive Logica* is totally new in 1655, respective to its fragmentary draft in MS A.10; nor do Cavendish's notes from another early draft help to find in 1645–6 something comparable to its content.

151 Namely, Seth Ward and John Wilkins, in their anonymous publication *Vindiciae Academiarum* (1654).

152 Webster 1654, 34. The inadequacy of syllogism to natural philosophy is emphasized by means of quotations from Bacon's *Novum organum*, Book I, Aphorisms 13 and 14.

153 Webster 1654, 34.

154 Webster 1654, 38.

155 *De corpore*, I, VI.2, 58. For Seth Ward (see Ward 1656, 58), Hobbes's assertion excludes the *analytica* of geometers, which leads from the unknown to things better known, so that by the *regressus* or retrograde way of synthesis it is possible to demonstrate and conclude the unknown from that which is better known.

156 Bacon, *Novum Organum*, Book I, Aphorism 19.

proceeding from particulars to general truths. He adopts quite another standpoint, that of the mind's directing its attention to the ideas that are parts of the whole idea of some individual in sense perception.[157] Actually, even when Hobbes could have praised Bacon's conception of induction, he does not.[158] Moreover, in his negative verdict about the inevitable imperfection of enumerative induction, Hobbes considers it only as an illegitimate process of demonstration. He denounces as "vicious" John Wallis's use of induction instead of syllogism.[159] For Wallis, induction is a method for truth-inquiry, but Hobbes condemns it as an invalid argument.[160]

Interestingly, when in his "Note sulla logica di Hobbes" Mario dal Pra has traced Hobbes's views on logic to several early modern traditions,[161] he has rejected Neal Gilbert's suggestion that Hobbes's conception of method might be indebted to the discussions on method and order by "Italian Aristotelians" (principally, Jacopo Zabarella).[162] Since then, however, Charles Schmitt has emphasized that Zabarella's work on scientific demonstration, together with Giulio Pace's edition of Aristotle's *Organon*, "was increasingly recognized" from the end of the sixteenth century to the mid-seventeenth century.[163] This might appear to confirm the approach privileged by John Watkins and recently reasserted by Marco Sgarbi: The argument that Hobbes's methodology was influenced by Zabarella's resolutive-compositive method.[164] Watkins, who holds that Zabarella and Galileo shared the same methodology, alleges that Hobbes "saw himself as the junior member of a little band of scientific pioneers; and these pioneers belonged to a common methodological tradition."[165] But, in earnest, Hobbes's method

---

[157] See *De corpore*, I, VI.2, 58.

[158] See *Elements of Law*, I, IV.10, 16: "though a man hath always seen the day and night to follow one another hitherto; yet can he not thence conclude they shall do so, or that they have done so eternally. Experience concludeth nothing universally." Hobbes does not seek to oppose Baconian induction to that imperfect induction.

[159] See *Lux mathematica, Controversia I* (OL V, 99).

[160] See *Examinatio et emendatio mathematicae hodiernae, Dialogus I* (OL IV, 53, 137) and *Dialogus V* (OL IV, 179).

[161] Dal Pra 1962, 418–427.

[162] Dal Pra 1962, 431–432 (cf. Gilbert 1960, 211). For a later refutation of the attribution to Hobbes of an Italian Aristotelianism legacy, see Jan Prins (1990), who defends instead the thesis of a Philippo-Ramist or even of a "Systematicist" influence (that of Bartholomew Keckermann) on Hobbes's methodology. In an earlier article, Prins had already argued that "all the characteristics shared by humanist aristotelians can also be found in [Hobbes's] own work" (Prins 1988, 297–298).

[163] Schmitt 1983, 35–37. Chief representatives of this trend are Griffin Powel's *Analysis Analyticorum posteriorum sive Librorum Aristotelis de Demonstratione* (Oxford, 1594), John Flavel's *Tractatus de demonstratione methodicus & polemicus, quatuor libris absolutus* (Oxford, 1619), and William Harvey's *Exercitationes de generatione animalium* (London, 1651).

[164] Sgarbi has recently argued that Hobbes's *Computatio* had been influenced by Paduan Aristotelianism "through the mediation of British Aristotelianism" (Sgarbi 2013, 185). The same argument was already made by Watkins in *Hobbes's System of Ideas*. Also Watkins's approach was based on the importance of Harvey's Preface to his 1651 *Exercitationes*, particularly the section on "The Manner and Order of Acquiring Knowledge," where Harvey says that "we proceed from things more known to things less known, from matters more manifest to matters more obscure" (Watkins 1965, 41).

[165] Watkins 1965, 51.

of knowledge does not need to get its content from Paduan Aristotelianism; the definition of ratiocination as computation is enough for its constitution.

3.2 Innovations

3.2.1 *Compound Idea, Compound Name*

For Hobbes, the end of philosophy is "to establish universal rules about the properties
of things."[166] The originality of the *Computatio* with this respect is that it states that
the mental foundation of the deduction of general theorems merely consists of *ideas of
individuals*. This is possible from the particular status acknowledged for those ideas. An
idea of an individual is not a mental atom nor is it a motley collection of all the manifold
sensible qualities of this individual. It is a *compound* or *complex* idea. Hobbes illustrates
this in chapter 1.3 by the passage of the perception of "something" from obscure distant
vision to clear near vision. The mind finally *composes into one idea of one thing* three distinct ideas previously conceived separately. Together with a first idea of a body, caused
by the mere apparition of "something" from a distance,[167] ideas caused by the two properties of self-motion and rationality additively result in the "whole idea" (or "whole
phenomenon," as reads chapter 6.2) of a man as one "whole thing," a body-animate-
rational.[168] The idea of an individual man is the whole of those properties that allow in
sense perception the identification of its determined *nature*, the nature of *a man*.

The parts of the compound idea of a man are summed up in the mind in the same
sequence as would be in speech the separate common names *body, animate, rational*
to compose the many-words name *body animate rational* equivalent to the one-word
name *man*. A series of one-word names corresponds term-to-term to the sum of conceptions collected by the mind's "internal reasoning without words."[169] This parallel
order must not be mistaken. The decreasing universality of the common names *body,
animate, rational* is not mirrored into a hierarchic relation of ideas in the mind. Each
idea is "both one and of one thing,"[170] yet there is an order between the singular ideas
of singular things. Sense, for Hobbes, involves at the very time of the apparition of a
phantasm to the mind a comparison with, and distinction from, other phantasms.[171]
Recurring similar and dissimilar sensible sequences are retained in the memory so
that a conceptual hierarchy corresponding to the higher or lower repetition of the

---

[166] *De corpore*, I, IV.7, 45.

[167] Cf. *De corpore*, I, III.3, 33: something *visible* is necessarily conceived as *not-in one point*, but as
occupying some space/being extended.

[168] *De corpore*, I, I. 3, 13. Conversely, it is possible to subtract gradually from the compound
idea of a man its component ideas, until the computation reaches back its absolute limit, the mere
undifferentiating (otherwise than spatially or numerically) idea of a body, beyond which the whole idea
of a man is disintegrated. See Pécharman 1989, 1995a, about Hobbes's strata of individuality.

[169] *De corpore*, I, I.3, 13.

[170] *De corpore*, I, V.8, 53.

[171] See *De corpore*, IV, XXV.5, 271.

properties perceived is involved in sense experience itself. The orderly composition of the idea of a man is empirically founded on the constancy of extension and a higher frequency of the property of self-motion over that of rationality in sense perception.[172] The composition of universal names into a less universal name transposes or translates this conceptual order, and not the reverse.

In connection with that, the Aristotelian definition that calls *universal* that which is of such a nature as it can be predicated of many things[173] is turned over against Aristotle. For Hobbes, only a common name, given its divided or distributive reference, is able to answer Aristotle's notion of *katholou* and to meet the double requirement of unicity and predicability of many.[174] A universal is nothing more than one and the same name attributed to many individuals for a similar quality in them causing in the mind a similar image. Nominalistic reductionism, thus, goes hand in hand with the thesis that imagination suffices to ensure that universal names have a conceptual correlate.[175]

3.2.2 *Two-Names Proposition*

Man is actually, despite its grammatical aspect, a name logically as compound as the circumlocution *body animate rational*. Reciprocally, the latter is as much one name as *man*. In the proposition *man is a body animate rational*—that is, in the definition of *man*[176]—the sequence of names that the predicate consists of unveils that the subject is already an addition of names. Its one-word form is merely an abbreviated form.[177] Therefore, the properties that cause, when conjunct, the idea of an individual man also are the reason why the definition of *man*, and the propositions predicating of *man* a part of its definition, are primary and necessary propositions.[178] The compound idea of an individual is a sufficient conceptual foundation to provide the principle of a demonstration. Its structure "whole-parts" constitutes a conceptual rule for predication.[179]

---

[172] *De corpore*, I, I.4, 14. The *Anti-White*, the "laboratory" of *De corpore* (to quote Gianni Paganini's remarkable Introduction to his Italian translation, 48), offers an interesting analysis of comparison of individuals. See AW, XXX.14–19, 355–357; Pécharman 1992b, 2007, 2009, concerning sense perception and mental discourse.

[173] See *De interpretatione*, 7, 17a40–41.

[174] *De corpore*, I, II.9, 23: "a *common name*, insofar as it is the name of many things taken severally, not the name collectively of all of them together . . ., is called for that reason *universal*."

[175] *De corpore*, I, II.9, 24: "to understand the import of a universal, we need no other faculty than the imaginative one, by which we remember that vocal sounds of this kind brought to the mind sometimes one thing, sometimes another one."

[176] As it were, the traditional definition *man is an animal rational* is less philosophical (meaning a weaker principle of demonstration) than the one displaying the compound name *body animate*, to which *animal* is equivalent. See *De corpore*, I, II.14, 26.

[177] *De corpore*, I, II.14, 26; III.10, 37.

[178] *De corpore*, I, III.10, 37.

[179] Hobbes, consequently, does not make truth arbitrary when he claims that a truth is nothing other than a true proposition, "in which two names of the same thing are joined together," so that any "first truth" is born from a human decision about the names imposed on the same thing (*De corpore*, I, V.2, 51; III.7–8, 35–36). He is not the "super-nominalist" Leibniz's *Preface to an Edition of Nizolius* (1670) contends he is (Leibniz 1989a, 128; cf. *Dialogue* (August 1677), in Leibniz 1989b, 270; *New Essays*, IV, V.2, in Leibniz 1996, 396).

If not for the constraint of brevity, the deduction of theorems about the properties of a square, for instance, could be done by using throughout the demonstration the sequence *quadrilateral equilateral rectangular*.[180]

A proposition such as the universal statement *a man is an animal*[181] must be viewed as signifying *the conception-that* the two names are copulated, which is the same as *the conception-that* they are names of the same thing. Again, the latter *conception-that* is the same as *the conception-that* the predicate contains the subject.[182] Thus, this second-rank conception or *conception-that*, which is the reason of the assertion, applies to the comparative extension of the two universal names *man* and *animal* insofar as the consequence relation from the less universal to the more universal is inseparable from the resolutive conceptual order between the ideas parts of the whole idea of a man. To assert the extensional inclusion of the name-subject *man* in the name-predicate *animal* is nothing other than to assert that the idea expressed by the name more universal/less compound *animal* is a part of the idea expressed by the name less universal/more compound *man*. The mental criterion provided by the compound idea of an individual allows reconciling an extensional approach of the predicate with an intensional approach free from any commitment to real essences.[183] Accordingly, to connect into a proposition two names conceived of as both names of the same thing does not make the proposition *a man is an animal* comparable to the proposition *Tully is Cicero*. A critique such as that of John Stuart Mill, who holds that the only propositions that the definition of the *Computatio* is able to account for are "that limited and unimportant class in which both the predicate and the subject are proper names"[184] is unfair. So is Peter Geach's judgment that the *Computatio* belongs to a central stage in the degeneration of logic from Aristotle's "*two-term* theory" in the *Prior Analytics*, the stage of the "*two-name* theory" leading to the "*two-class* theory."[185] A *two-namer* like Hobbes, Geach argues, confounds the relations *to be predicable of X* and *to be a name of X* and

---

[180] See *De corpore*, I, I.3, 13; VI.14–4, 69.

[181] Strictly speaking, *a man is an animal* is an indefinite proposition, not a universal one, since the quantifier *every* is not annexed to the subject. But in reasoning for ourselves *a man is an animal* is just as much universal as *every man is an animal*. The quantifier is required for demonstration to others (*De corpore*, I, III.5, 35; and I, II.11, 24–25; Pécharman 2004, 222–226).

[182] *De corpore*, I, III.2–3, 32. The *Computatio*, I, III.1, still mentions the traditional notion of proposition as a speech affirming or denying, or a mark of truth and falsity. However, since composition and division are no longer the affirmative and negative modes of apophantic speech, but two mental processes about the ideas of individuals, the game has completely changed.

[183] That is, it does not jeopardize Hobbes's principle that predication is a merely internominal relation—against Aristotle's ontological conception of the pre-predicamental relation "to be said-of" (Pécharman 1992a and 1995b).

[184] Mill 1906, 58. In Mill's eyes, Hobbes only produces "a full explanation of such predications as these: Hyde was Clarendon, or, Tully is Cicero." Mill's main argument is that (I quote Prior 1976, 77) "by concentrating on the denotation of names and ignoring their connotation, [Hobbes's theory] takes no account of *why* the names are applicable to the objects in question."

[185] Geach 1981, 51–53, 289. Geach views Aristotle's thesis that a term in the syllogism has interchangeable positions and shifts from subject-position in a proposition to predicate-position in another as the equivalent of "the Fall of Adam."

builds only on the copula the intelligibility of the proposition—otherwise a mere list or catalogue.[186] But, actually, the asymmetry between the two logical relations of attribution and reference is not absent from the *Computatio*. The two-names predication must be viewed as the conjunction of two atomic propositions. *S is P* is to be developed into *This/That is S and This/That is P*, where *This* or *That* designates twice the same individual thing as the extrapropositional subject of the two attributions. So, although the definition of proposition as the affirmation or denial of something about something is not that of the *Computatio*, the two-names proposition is not reducible to referentiality. The two names are rather two distinct "attributes" of the same extrapropositional subject for two distinct modes of conceiving it.

The compound idea of an individual, formed from sense experience, is therefore a sufficient conceptual correlate for a reasoning on universal names. The *Computatio* condemns those (namely, Descartes)[187] who, for one and the same thing, make a distinction between its idea from the imagination and its idea from the intellect. Hobbes attributes this fault to the wrong belief that one idea only cannot answer both a name and a proposition. He argues instead that the idea conceived when understanding the proposition *a man is an animal* is one with the composite image conceived from the name *man*. The proposition *a man is an animal* merely signifies an order of succession between two diverse considerations about the idea-image of a man.[188]

3.2.3 *The Fate of the Middle Term*

Syllogism, as it is defined in the *Computatio*, definitively allows that the compound idea of an individual provides a sufficient mental guarantee for deducing conclusions about the properties of things. The definition of a syllogism as "a speech consisting of three propositions, from two of which the third follows"[189] is for Hobbes an application of his definition of the consequence relation between propositions, the "*follows from*" relation: "a proposition is said to follow from two other propositions, when it is impossible to suppose it is not true, if we suppose that these are true."[190] This latter definition emphasizes that the necessary inference of a conclusion from two premises is irreducible to a formal deduction. The reason why a conclusion *immediately follows from* two premises is that these *are understood to be true*. Everything rests on an epistemological relation holding between the mind and the premises; namely, the thought that the names they connect are names of the same individual. The principle that only another truth follows from true propositions is thus reworded as a principle of efficient causality from a *conception-that* to another. The traditional thesis in syllogistic that "*the*

---

[186] Geach 1981, 48: "Only a name can be a logical subject; and a name cannot retain the role of a name if it becomes a logical predicate; for a predicate purports to give us what holds good or does not hold good of an individual, but a name just serves to name or refer to an individual." Cf. Geach 1980, 60.

[187] See *Third Meditation* about the "two different ideas of the sun" (Descartes 1984, 27).

[188] *De corpore*, I, V.9, 53–54.

[189] *De corpore*, I, IV.1, 42.

[190] *De corpore*, I, III.18, 40.

premises are the causes of the conclusion" is to be corrected: Strictly speaking, knowledge is cause of knowledge, not propositions of another proposition.[191]

Unsurprisingly, the aforementioned definition of a syllogism ignores the essential final part of its definition in the *Prior Analytics*: "a discourse in which, certain things being posited, something different from the posits follows of necessity *from their being so*."[192] Hobbes removes that which, for Aristotle, means that it is *because of* the premises that the conclusion follows. When he insists that, without a common term in the premises, no conclusion would follow from them, and, as a corollary, that only three terms can be in the premises, his main concern is not to affirm (like Aristotle) that a syllogism can include only one middle term, no more, but that this single middle term must be "determined in either premise to one and the same individual thing."[193] From there, the stage is set for a strictly Hobbesian redefinition of syllogism. The mediation is given by the conversion of the "*follows from*" relation into a *computation*. "To compute is *to collect the sum of many things added together*."[194] This perfectly applies to the immediate inference of a conclusion from two premises: "a syllogism is a collection of two propositions into one sum."[195] Hobbes can then substitute for the traditional definition of syllogism a definition in accordance with his conception of logic as the same as computation. The new right definition reads: "a *syllogism* is an addition of three names."[196]

Hobbes's focus is on the first mood of the first figure, consisting of propositions universal and affirmative. It is the only one appropriate for establishing "universal rules about the properties of things."[197] Now, this restriction covers an amendment to the canonical pattern of "Barbara" in traditional logic. That terms are ordered according to their comparative extension[198] entails for Hobbes that the term that is least universal, the *minor term* subject of the conclusion, also comes first in the premises. The term with the widest extension, the *major term* predicate of the conclusion, occurs last. The middle term, more universal than the minor and less universal than the major, gets the middle position: It occurs first as a predicate and then as a subject. Thus, the minor proposition must be the first premise and the major proposition the second. This permutation might be considered as not relevant: The standard order of the premises does not import for the validity of the inference. It could in addition be suggested that, in some respect, the *Computatio*'s juxtaposition of the two occurrences of the middle term conforms to their adjacency in Aristotle's predication *kata pantos*: "if A is predicated

[191] See *De corpore*, I, III.20, 40.

[192] *Prior Analytics*, I, I, 24b18–20 (emphasis added).

[193] *De corpore*, I, IV.4, 43.

[194] *De corpore*, I, I.2, 12.

[195] *De corpore*, I, IV.6, title, 42. The section reads: "a syllogism is nothing other than a collection of a sum made from two propositions connected with each other by a common term."

[196] *De corpore*, I, IV.6, 44.

[197] *De corpore*, I, IV.7, 45 (applying Hobbes's principle that the so-called *negative propositions* actually affirm negative names) and *De corpore*, I, IV.12, 48.

[198] *De corpore*, I, IV.7, 45: *secundum latitudinem significationum*.

of all B, and B of all C, A must necessarily be predicated of all C."[199] Yet, this would be an overstatement because, in the *Prior Analytics*, this principle of transitivity requires that the middle term occurs as a subject before occurring as a predicate; namely, that it is the first term in the syllogism.

The thesis that the syllogistic disposition of terms abides by their "direct order"[200] actually renders the traditional "*middle term*" obsolete in the *Computatio*. The first-figure pattern may even consist of a merely additive schema; for instance, *a man is an animal is a body* because the order of universal names in a syllogism is the correlate of a natural subtractive process of the mind from the compound idea of a man. The mind first conceives the image that is the reason of the name-subject *man* in the minor premise. The image of the same individual as self-moving, which is the cause of the predicate *animal* (more universal) in the minor premise, follows. The mind conceives then the same individual with the property that is the reason of the predicate *body* (still more universal) in the major premise. Last, it conceives that one and the same thing has been the permanent subject of the distinct accidents causing its successive conceptions and that therefore the corresponding three names are names of the same thing. This meta-conception is itself the cause of the understanding that the proposition *a man is a body*—namely, the conclusion—is true.[201] Thus, the middle term loses its traditional function. It is no longer a term that must occur twice to ensure the combination of the premises. The conception causing the name-predicate of the minor premise does not reoccur to cause the name-subject of the major premise. Aristotle's *meson* consists now of a mere *second name*.[202]

3.2.4 *Concrete and Abstract*

Yet Hobbes would make it unachievable to provide in the *Computatio* the organon for deducing universally true propositions in all parts of philosophy if he did not admit other two-names propositions than those copulating two "concrete" names; that is, two names of an individual body. Individual bodies are not the only "things named."[203]

---

[199] *Prior Analytics*, I, IV, 25b37–9.

[200] *De corpore*, I, IV.7, 45.

[201] *De corpore*, I, IV.8, 46.

[202] In 1805, Destutt de Tracy published a French translation of the *Computatio* as an "Appendix" to his *Logique* (Tracy 1805, Appendice no. II, *Calcul, ou Logique*, 589–667). Tracy affirms: "mon ouvrage en sera le commentaire" (*Discours préliminaire*, 118, no. 1. See Pécharman 1988a). For Tracy, Hobbes's description of the "operation of the mind" in a syllogism is a groundbreaking legacy of the *Computatio*, opening the way to a reduction of *reasoning* to the mental act of *judgment*, which discloses the attributes inclosed in the "comprehension" of an *idea*. The only note in Tracy's translation is about IV.7: "je ne puis m'empêcher de faire remarquer que cette première figure du syllogisme, appelée avec raison figure directe, . . . est un véritable *sorite* qui peut se prolonger indéfiniment; et que la justesse de sa conclusion ne vient point de ce que le prétendu terme majeur renferme le moyen et le mineur, ou leur est égal; mais au contraire, de ce que le mineur, le premier sujet, renferme un premier attribut, celui-là un second, un troisième, un quatrième si l'on veut; et enfin celui de la conclusion. De cette réflexion développée et bien entendue, naîtra la rénovation totale de la science logique, et par suite l'anéantissement complet de l'ancien art logique qui est entièrement faux et illusoire" (*Logique*, 633).

[203] *De corpore*, I, V.2, 51. Cf. MS A.10, 470–471; and *Leviathan*, I, IV.14sq, 58–60; V.9sq, 70; IV.XLVI.16–17, 1078–1080; see also *Elements of Law*, I.V.3, 18.

Their "concrete names" are not the whole of language; they form merely a first class of names. The accidents of bodies, either inherent in external bodies ("accidents" *tout court*) or inherent in the percipient ("phantasms"), are denoted by two other classes in which names are "abstract"; that is to say, formed after propositions connecting concrete names.[204] Without those abstract names, Hobbes claims, it would be impossible "to compute the properties of bodies,"[205] which is the purpose in philosophy. A last class of names is that of names qualifying the names in the three first classes: The distinction metalanguage–language makes the classification a finite system. The *Computatio* applies to all four classes the criterion of truth defined about "concrete" propositions: Propositions are true when two names of the same "thing" are copulated.[206]

Hobbes points out, however, that a predication of "coherent" names is not ipso facto known as a true proposition. The *knowledge-that* a proposition is true, required for any inference from it, is not immediate. It would be unattainable without the precept of *reiterated definition* or "continued resolution"[207] of compound names in their parts more universal. Through a series of definitions, first of the names connected in the proposition, then of the names composing those first definitions, and so on, the subordination of the copulated names to the name that is the most universal in a certain class, is made explicit. The proposition is *understood as true*.

This precept of systematic definition cannot be disassociated from a concern for the logical tradition of "categorialism." Hobbes does not endorse the traditional conception of categories as *incomplexa* (uncombined terms) contrasted with *complexa* (propositions).[208] Names in a predicament, apart from the most universal (the only one "simple)," are all of them compound names whose degrees of universality can be represented on a diagram.[209] Interestingly, the way the reference to an individual supports the presentation of the categorial table is changed in the *Computatio* in comparison to the *Anti-White*. The *Computatio* abandons the "image-interrogative criterion" used in the *Anti-White* for enumerating the common names that are appropriate answers

---

[204] *De corpore*, I, III.3, 32–33. Cf. AW, XXVII.1, 312–314; XXVIII.4, 333–334.

[205] *De corpore*, I, III.4, 34. Concerning Leibniz's critique of Hobbes on this topic, see Stefano Di Bella, *The Science of the Individual: Leibniz's Ontology of Individual Substance*, Dordrecht, Springer, 2005, chapter 3.

[206] Correspondingly, a classification of all the modes of "incoherence of names" (*De corpore*, I, V.2, title, 50), as it were the finite system also of false predications, can be set up to prevent any category-mistake. The ban on predications of names from heterogeneous classes is not enough, however, to preserve reasoning in philosophy from "material" falsity (i.e., from "errors . . . in syllogizing" due to false premises) because names from the same class can be contradictory. For Hobbes, any name whatsoever divides with its negative (e.g., *"man"/"not-man"*) the whole field of predication, so that contradiction is due, not to the affirmation and denial of the same predicate of the same subject ("X *is* Y"/"X *is not* Y"), but to the predication of a name and of its negative of the same subject ("X *is* Y"/"X *is* not-Y.") To assert, for instance, *"a man is a rock"* is false, because it amounts to the contradiction *"a man is a not-man."*

[207] *De corpore*, I, V.10, 54.

[208] For the source of this distinction, see i.a. *Categoriae*, 4, 1b25 and 2a4–10.

[209] *De corpore*, I, II.14, 26.

to irreducibly heterogeneous questions arising from the image of some individual.[210] This criterion is indeed doubly flawed. On the one hand, it lists concrete names not only in the first category of substance, but also in others (*"two cubits long"* in the category of quantity,*"white"* in that of quality). On the other hand, the names enumerated in a category are not ordered and even less according to degrees of universality. By contrast, the "predicament of bodies" in the *Computatio*, inspired by Porphyry's tree, disposes the names of bodies on a "scale."[211]

What matters in the *Computatio* is to make the degrees of universality between concrete names in the first category the model, or the source, of the arrangement of names in the other categories. Also abstract names must be ordered according to their extension, with their decreasing universality corresponding to the higher or lesser frequency of that which they denote. The category of relation, which deals with the contents of the categories of quantity and quality, applies the same rule of subordination. By ranging its names from the most to the least universal, each predicamental "formula" figurates the definition of a less universal name on the diagram by an addition of names more universal on the same diagram. The predicaments, in other words, figurate the right status of names for philosophy: Definitions are better than their abbreviations.[212]

4 CONCLUSION

Eventually, the double-way method of computation of the properties of bodies echoing in the *Computatio* the definition of philosophy is not at odds with the central treatise on names, proposition, and syllogism. Their solidarity is made possible from the outset by the criterion status allowed to the compound idea of an individual. The ending chapter on methodology does not assimilate the Aristotelian distinction between *tou hoti* and *tou dioti* to two kinds of demonstration, but to two kinds of knowledge, sense knowledge and rational knowledge. Some sense knowledge is always "the beginning of the investigation,"[213] but the *method of investigation*, also called method of "invention" or discovery of causes,[214] pertains to rational knowledge. The rational knowledge *tou dioti* consists of a double mode of computation about the two relatives, *properties* and *generations*. Either reasoning goes from a property/effect/phenomenon to the "universal" causes of its generation or reasoning describes the generation of a property/effect/phenomenon from "universal" causes. In both cases, the complementarity of abstract names to concrete ones, and their equal submission to definition, are most useful because a cause consists

---

[210] The questions *"what is this, of which I have the image?," "this, of which I have the image, of what quantity is it?," "this, of which I have the image, of what quality is it?,"* and similarly within the comparison of this image with another one—see AW, V.2, 129.

[211] *De corpore*, I, II.15, 27. Cf. AW, VII.5, 148.

[212] *De corpore*, I, VI.14–4, 69.

[213] *De corpore*, I, VI.2, 58. Cf. MS A.10, 472.

[214] See *De corpore*, I, VI.1–10, 57–66.

of "an aggregate or sum of accidents,"[215] all of them denoted by abstract names. From the factual knowledge "*tou hoti*," "*quod est*," or conception of a "whole phenomenon," an analytical reasoning can conduct the resolution of this "whole idea" into its different parts, signified by names more universal than the name denoting the thing perceived.[216] Any one of the accidents involved in the nature of this thing can be itself a new starting point for investigating accidents denoted by names still more universal. Following this ascending way, sense knowledge of a mere *fact* is replaced with rational knowledge of the *cause* or *generation* of the differentiating properties contained in the "whole idea" of an individual.[217] Symmetrically, the rational knowledge of the nature of an individual by its cause, "*tou dioti*," can follow a descending way from original knowledge *tou hoti*. For instance, from some generation known by sense, it is possible to conduct a syn-thetical reasoning until this computation makes it coincident with the generation of the *nature* of an individual.[218] In this second way of reasoning from a cause or generation to a property that is its effect or phenomenon, the causes of more universal accidents (namely, of accidents "which have more universal names")[219] are composed into the causes generating less universal properties.[220] In both ways of the computation, thus, the whole cause of a phenomenon is itself the addition of many aggregates of accidents, a sum of sums, as it were,[221] and the knowledge *tou dioti* of a phenomenon is inseparable from the consideration of the degrees of universality of abstract names. Hobbes's new mechanicist natural philosophy got the logic it needed, because any analysis regresses to and any synthesis proceeds from, universals of which *motion* is the universal cause.[222] Hence, the one-way method of demonstration, which is only synthetical and supposes that universal principles are known per se,[223] is able to unify all the parts of philosophy.

Bibliography

Ashworth, Earline Jennifer. 1985. "Introduction" to *Logicae artis compendium* [Robert Sanderson, 1615], IX-LV. Bologna: Editrice CLUEB.

Ashworth, Earline Jennifer. 1988. "Traditional Logic," in *The Cambridge History of Renaissance Philosophy*, edited by Charles Bernard Schmitt, Quentin Skinner, Eckhard Kessler, Jill Kraye, 143–172. Cambridge: Cambridge University Press.

---

[215] *De corpore*, I, VI.10, 64.

[216] *De corpore*, I, VI.2, 58.

[217] *De corpore*, I, VI.2; cf. VI.4, 58–59.

[218] I take this example from *De corpore*, I, I.5, 14.

[219] *De corpore*, I, VI.2, 59.

[220] Concerning the necessity of universal names for the "method of invention" of a property, see *De corpore*, I, VI.11, 66.

[221] *De corpore*, I, VI.10, 65: the cause can be considered as the "entire cause" of the effect when the aggregate of aggregates is such that, on the supposition of their concurrence, it is impossible to think that the effect is not produced.

[222] *De corpore*, I, VI.5, 60.

[223] *De corpore*, I, VI.5, 60; 12, 66.

Aubrey, John. 1898. '*Brief Lives*', *chiefly of Contemporaries, set down by John Aubrey, between the Years 1669 & 1696*, edited by Andrew Clark, vol. I (A–H). Oxford: Clarendon Press.

Chappell, Vere. 1999. *Hobbes and Bramhall on Liberty and Necessity*. Cambridge. Cambridge University Press.

Dal Pra, Mario. 1962. "Note sulla logica di Hobbes." *Rivista critica di storia della filosofia* (4): 411–433.

Descartes, René. 1984. *The Philosophical Writings of Descartes*, vol. II, translated by John Cottingham, Robert Stoothoff, Dugald Murdoch. Cambridge: Cambridge University Press.

Di Bella, Stefano. 2005. *The Science of the Individual: Leibniz's Ontology of Individual Substance*. Dordrecht: Springer.

Eachard, John. 1672. *Mr Hobbs's State of Nature Considered; In a Dialogue between Philautus and Timothy*. London.

Eachard, John. 1673. *Some Opinions of Mr Hobbs Considered in a Second Dialogue between Philautus and Timothy*. London.

Feingold, Mordechai. 1997. "The Humanities," in *The History of the University of Oxford. Volume IV: Seventeenth-Century Oxford*, edited by Nicholas Tyacke, 211–358. Oxford: Clarendon Press.

Geach, Peter Thomas. 1980. *Reference and Generality. An Examination of Some Medieval and Modern Theories*. 3rd edition. Ithaca: Cornell University Press.

Geach, Peter Thomas. 1981. *Logic Matters*. 2nd edition. Oxford.

Gilbert, Neal Ward. 1960. *Renaissance Concepts of Method*. New York: Columbia University Press.

Hobbes, Thomas. 1637. *A Briefe of the Art of Rhetorique. Containing in substance all that ARISTOTLE hath written in his Three Books of that subject*. London.

Hobbes, Thomas. 1839–45 [*Opera Latina*]. *Thomae Hobbes Malmesburiensis Opera philosophica quae Latine scripsit omnia*, edited by William Molesworth. London: Bohm.

Hobbes, Thomas. 1840–1845. *The English Works of Thomas Hobbes of Malmesbury*, edited by William Molesworth. London: Bohm.

Hobbes, Thomas. 1969. *The Elements of Law, Natural and Politic*, edited by Ferdinand Tönnies [1889], new edition by Maurice Goldsmith. London: Routledge.

Hobbes, Thomas. 1973. *Critique du 'De Mundo' de Thomas White* [=*Anti-White*], edited by Jean Jacquot and Harold Whitmore Jones. Paris: Librairie Philosophique, J. Vrin.

Hobbes, Thomas. 1983. *De Cive. The Latin Version*, edited by Howard Warrender. Oxford. Clarendon Press.

Hobbes, Thomas. 1994. *The Correspondence of Thomas Hobbes*, edited by Noel Malcolm. 2 vols. Oxford: Clarendon Press.

Hobbes, Thomas. 1999. *De Corpore. Elementorum philosophiae sectio prima*, edited by Karl Schuhmann. Paris: J. Vrin.

Hobbes, Thomas. 2012. *Leviathan*, edited by Noel Malcolm. 3 vols. Oxford: Clarendon Press.

Leibniz, Gottfried Wilhelm. 1966. *Logical Papers*, translated and edited by George Henry Radcliffe Parkinson. Oxford: Clarendon Press.

Leibniz, Gottfried Wilhelm. 1989a. *Philosophical Papers and Letters* [1969], a selection translated and edited by Leroy Earl Loemker. Dordrecht: Reidel.

Leibniz, Gottfried Wilhelm. 1989b. *Philosophical Essays*, edited and translated by Roger Ariew and Daniel Garber. Indianapolis: Hackett Publishing Co.

Leibniz, Gottfried Wilhelm. 1996. *New Essays on Human Understanding*, edited by Peter Remnant and Jonathan Bennett. Cambridge: Cambridge University Press.

Leibniz, Gottfried Wilhelm. 1999. *Sämtliche Schriften und Briefe. VI. Philosophische Schriften. 4. 1677-June 1690*, edited by the German Academy of Science. Berlin: Berlin, Akademie-Verlag.

Leijenhorst, Cees. 2002. *The Mechanisation of Aristotelianism. The Late Aristotelian Setting of Thomas Hobbes' Natural Philosophy*. Leiden: Brill.

Malcolm, Noel. 2002. *Aspects of Hobbes*. 2 vols. Oxford: Clarendon Press.

McConica, James. 1979. "Humanism and Aristotle in Tudor Oxford." *The English Historical Review* 94: 291–317.

Mill, John Stuart. 1906. *A System of Logic Ratiocinative and Inductive* [1843], new impression. London: Longmans.

Nuchelmans, Gabriel. 1980. *Late-Scholastic and Humanist Theories of the Proposition*. Amsterdam: North Holland Publishing Co.

Nuchelmans, Gabriel. 1983. *Judgment and Proposition from Descartes to Kant*. Amsterdam: North Holland Publishing Co.

Ong, Walter Jackson. 1958. *Ramus, Method, and the Decay of Dialogue: From the Art of Discourse to the Art of Reason*. Cambridge, MA: Harvard University Press.

Paganini, Gianni. 2010. "Introduction," *Moto, luogo e tempo di Thomas Hobbes*, 9–104. Torino: UTET.

Pécharman, Martine. 1988a. "Une marginalité équivoque: Destutt de Tracy lecteur de la *Computatio* de Hobbes". In *La Marge*, edited by François Marotin, 169–191. Clermont-Ferrand: Presses universitaires Blaise Pascal.

Pécharman, Martine. 1988b. "Métaphore et théorie des classes de noms chez Hobbes", *Recherches sur la philosophie et le langage* (9): 99–119.

Pécharman, Martine. 1989. "Individu et nom propre selon Thomas Hobbes", *Philosophie* (23): 22–36.

Pécharman, Martine. 1992a. "Le vocabulaire de l'être dans la philosophie première: *ens, esse, essentia*". In *Hobbes et son vocabulaire. Études de lexicographie philosophique*, edited by Yves Charles Zarka, 31–59. Paris: J. Vrin.

Pécharman, Martine. 1992b. "Le discours mental selon Hobbes," *Archives de philosophie*, vol. 55 (4): 552–573.

Pécharman, Martine. 1995a. "Hobbes et la question du principe d'individuation". In *L'individuo nel pensiero moderno*, edited by Gian Maria Cazzaniga and Yves Charles Zarka, 203–222. Pisa: ETS.

Pécharman, Martine. 1995b. "La logique de Hobbes et la tradition aristotélicienne", *Hobbes Studies* (VIII): 105–124.

Pécharman, Martine. 2004. "Sémantique et doctrine de la proposition: Hobbes inconciliable avec la tradition terministe?" in *John Buridan and Beyond. Topics in the Language Sciences 1300-1700*, edited by Russell Friedman and Sten Ebbesen, Copenhagen: Det Kongelige Danske Videnskabernes Selskab.

Pécharman, Martine. 2007. "Le signe selon Hobbes," *Lumières* (10): 45–64.

Pécharman, Martine. 2009. "De quel langage intérieur Hobbes est-il le théoricien ?" in *Le langage mental du Moyen Âge à l'Âge classique*, edited by Joël Biard, 265–291. Leuven.

Prins, Jan. 1988. "The Influence of Agricola and Melanchthon on Hobbes' Early Philosophy of Science," in *Rodolphus Agricola Phrisius (1444-1485)*, edited by Fokke Akkerman and Arie Johan Vanderjagt, 293–301. Leiden: E. J. Brill.

Prins, Jan. 1990. "Hobbes and the School of Padua: Two Incompatible Approaches of Science," *Archiv für Geschichte der Philosophie* 72 (1): 26–46.

Prior, Arthur Norman. 1976. *The Doctrine of Propositions and Terms*, edited by Peter Thomas Geach and Anthony John Patrick Kenny. London: Duckworth.

Schmitt, Charles Bernard. 1983. "Aristotelianism in England," in *John Case and Aristotelianism in Renaissance England*, 13–76. Kingston-Montreal: McGill-Queens University Press.

Sgarbi, Marco. 2013. *The Aristotelian Tradition and the Rise of British Empiricism. Logic and Epistemology in the British Isles (1570–1689)*. Dordrecht: Springer.

Skinner, Quentin. 1996. *Reason and Rhetoric in the Philosophy of Hobbes*. Cambridge: Cambridge University Press.

Spranzi, Marta. 2011. *The Art of Dialectic between Dialogue and Rhetoric. The Aristotelian Tradition*. Amsterdam: John Benjamins Publishing Co.

Tracy, Antoine Louis Claude Destutt, marquis de. 1805. *Élémens d'Idéologie. Troisième Partie. Logique*. Paris.

Ward, Seth. 1656. *In Thomæ Hobbii Philosophiam Exercitatio epistolica*. Oxford.

Watkins, John William Nevill. 1965. *Hobbes's System of Ideas: A Study in the Political Significance of Philosophical Theories*. London: Hutchinson.

Webster, John. 1654. *Academiarum Examen, or The Examination of Academies*. London.

CHAPTER 3

···

HOBBES ON LANGUAGE

Propositions, Truth, and Absurdity

···

STEWART DUNCAN

LANGUAGE is important in several ways in Hobbes's philosophy. He regards use of language as a significant feature distinguishing humans from other animals. For instance, in the *Elements of Law*, Hobbes defines a name as a sort of "voice of man,"[1] and argues that "the advantage of names is that we are capable of science, which beasts, for want of them, are not."[2] A similar story in *Leviathan* takes into account the fact that animals do sometimes engage with language. A dog, for instance, will respond to "the call . . . of his master."[3] However, Hobbes maintains, it cannot understand more complex speeches, such as affirmations and negations. As a result, a dog cannot understand someone's "conceptions and thoughts" although perhaps it can understand their "will." The grasp that dogs (and other nonhuman animals) have on language is minimal, Hobbes thinks, and not enough to give them access to the sorts of knowledge that humans can have. Hobbes also argues that—despite humans' superior intellectual abilities—if we correctly understand the workings of language, then we can give an account of human cognitive capacities that refers only to the (corporeal) imagination and not to any further intellectual faculty, such as the sort of intellect that Descartes thought was incorporeal.[4]

The discussion of language also became an important critical tool for Hobbes. This approach is notable in *Leviathan*. There, he criticizes the "insignificant speech," "insignificant words," and "insignificant sounds" of various opponents.[5] Language certainly has its benefits, in Hobbes's account, but it brings with it "the privilege of absurdity; to which no living creature is subject, but man only. And of men, those are of all most

---

[1] *Elements of Law* 5.2.
[2] *Elements of Law* 5.4.
[3] *Leviathan* 2.10, 8.
[4] Language has other roles too, as recently illustrated by Pettit 2008.
[5] *Leviathan* 1.5, 4; 4.1, 12; 4.20, 16.

subject to it, that profess philosophy."[6] Hobbes's particular criticisms of language are often directed at "deceived, or deceiving Schoolmen,"[7] but other philosophers, including Hobbes's contemporary Descartes, are targets at times. Scholastics are particularly singled out, however, for not just using problematic language, but also for intentionally deceiving people with it.[8]

As well as criticizing the errors of other philosophers' language, Hobbes also developed a positive account of the workings of language. One early version is in the *Elements of Law* (1640), a later version is in *Leviathan* (1651), and the lengthiest account is in early chapters of *De corpore* (1655).[9] I consider all three of these accounts in this paper in order to investigate what Hobbes's theoretical views about language are, what his criticisms of others' faulty language are, and how the two relate. This is a broad field.[10] Within it, this chapter focuses on Hobbes's theory of propositions and their truth and its relationship to his criticism of various philosophical claims as absurd and incoherent.[11]

1 Names, Propositions, and Truth

When Hobbes lays out his positive view about the workings of language, he begins with the notion of a *name* and works toward that of a *proposition*. To begin, like Hobbes, with names, we see a basic view in the *Elements of Law* that is revised and elaborated on in the later works. In the *Elements*, Hobbes defines a name as "the voice of a man, arbitrarily imposed, for a mark to bring to his mind some conception concerning the thing on which it is imposed."[12] On this view, a name is a public, external item (thus "voice") but its role, or at least its primary role, is a personal one, that of enabling the speaker to recall thoughts.[13] A great variety of words and phrases count as names. Looking just at the first two paragraphs in which examples occur, we have "one," "two,"

---

[6] *Leviathan* 5.7, 20.

[7] *Leviathan* 3.12, 11.

[8] See, e.g., *Leviathan* 4.21–22, 17 and 46.14–40, 371–79; and Hobbes's claim in *Behemoth* that men in universities "learned to dispute for him [the Pope], and with unintelligible distinctions to blind men's eyes, while they encroached upon the rights of kings" (Hobbes 1990, 41).

[9] The *Elements of Law* circulated as a manuscript soon after its writing but was not published until 1650. On its composition, see Baumgold 2004.

[10] Within this same broad field, Duncan 2011 investigates Hobbes's account of the signification of proper names and how it relates to his criticism of various philosophical terms as insignificant.

[11] Hobbes's views about language were very important to him. Several writers since the middle of the twentieth century have also thought that Hobbes's views have important connections to recent views—see, for example, Martin 1953 and Hungerland and Vick 1981—although this trend has perhaps declined in more recent years.

[12] *Elements of Law* 5.2.

[13] Martinich (2005, 141) translates the equivalent passage in *De corpore* (2.4) as "A name is a human vocal sound."

"three," "just," "valiant," "strong," "comely," "visible," "moveable," "Socrates," "Homer," and "he that writ the Iliad."[14]

The view that names serve as marks is expanded on in *Leviathan*, where names are given two roles. They are again marks for "registering of the consequences of our thoughts."[15] Although not exactly as described in the earlier work, this remains a role that words have for speakers themselves. But names are now also said to be signs. Names function as signs in communication between people, "when many use the same words, to signify (by their connexion and order,) one to another, what they conceive, or think of each matter; and also what they desire, fear, or have any other passion for."[16] This same distinction, between a role of names as personal marks and as signs in communication with others, is also present in *De corpore*.[17]

Names appear to stand in two main semantic relations for Hobbes, naming and signifying. Although one might wonder how the naming relation works, it is relatively clear what, according to Hobbes, is named.[18] Proper names name individuals—thus "Emily" is the name of my cat Emily—whereas general names name several individuals—so "zebra" names each of the zebras, and "red" names each of the red things. It is more puzzling, however, what Hobbes thinks names signify. He repeatedly announces, when presenting his theory, that names signify ideas—so, in the simplest version, when I use "Emily" it signifies my idea of Emily. But outside those theory-stating contexts, he almost always talks as if names signify the very same things they name.[19]

Names alone, however, are not enough for most communication. So one wants to understand what happens when words are combined. Thus, we find the following in the *Elements of Law*:

> Of two appellations, by the help of this little verb IS, or something equivalent, we make an AFFIRMATION or NEGATION, either of which in the Schools we call also a proposition, and consisteth of two appellations joined together by the said verb is: as, for example, this is a proposition: man is a living creature; or this: man is not righteous; wherof the former is called an affirmation, because the affirmation living creature is positive; the latter a negation, because not righteous is privative.[20]

---

[14] *Elements of Law* 5.4–5. Martin (1953, 206) notes that Hobbes's use of "name" is broad but that this "is common in British logical writing," giving several examples. These are all of authors writing some time after Hobbes: J. S. Mill, J. N. Keynes, and Jevons. Mill had read Hobbes's *De corpore* as part of his study of logic and discusses it at several points in his own *System of Logic*.

[15] *Leviathan* 4.3, 12–13.

[16] *Leviathan* 4.3, 13.

[17] *De corpore* 2.1–2. Törnebohm (1960, 54) argues that Hobbes does not give a "proper definition" of "name" and proposes the following as capturing Hobbes's use: "An expression E is a name $=_{def}$ E can be placed before 'is' (or 'are') and/or can be placed after 'is' (or 'are') in the sentence form ' - - - - (is [/] are) - - -' so as to yield a significant sentence."

[18] Watkins (1965, 142) complains that Hobbes does not really explain the name–thing relation.

[19] Here I rely on the arguments of Duncan 2011.

[20] *Elements of Law* 5.9.

In this model, a proposition has the structure "A is B," where "A" and "B" are both names. In the examples given, "man," "a living creature" and "not righteous" are names. They are "joined together" by "is," yielding a proposition. The negations have the same structure as the affirmations: "man is not righteous" is for Hobbes a proposition involving two names, "man" and "not righteous."

After giving this account of propositions, Hobbes goes on to give an account of their truth. This is explained in terms of one name comprehending another.

> In every proposition, be it affirmative or negative, the latter appellation either comprehendeth the former, as in this proposition, charity is a virtue, the name of virtue comprehendeth the name of charity (and many other virtues besides), and then is the proposition said to be TRUE or TRUTH: for, truth, and a true proposition, is all one. Or else the latter appellation comprehendeth not the former; as in this proposition, every man is just, the name of *just* comprehendeth not every man; for *unjust* is the name of the far greater part of men. And then the proposition is said to be FALSE, or falsity: falsity and a false proposition being the same thing.[21]

Hobbes is clear here, as he will be elsewhere, that truth belongs to propositions. But what is comprehension, the key notion in the explanation of truth? The notion is not really explained here, but there is a clue in the way Hobbes talks about "unjust."[22] His treatment of the just/unjust example invokes the things named by the different terms and is suggestive of a view, one that fits well with what Hobbes said in later works. That view is an extensional treatment of comprehension in terms of the objects named. On that view "A" comprehends "B" if and only if the things named by "B" are among the things named by "A."[23]

Chapter 4 of *Leviathan* is the equivalent of chapter 5 of the *Elements of Law*, being the place where Hobbes explains the basics of his view of language. In the *Leviathan* chapter, the term "proposition" is absent, but "affirmation" is still present, and a similar model of how names are combined into affirmations and of how affirmations come to be true is present:

> When two names are joined together into a consequence, or affirmation, as thus, *a man is a living creature*; or thus, *if he be a man, he is a living creature*, if the latter name *living creature*, signify all that the former name *man* signifieth, then

---

[21] *Elements of Law* 5.10.

[22] Talk of comprehension has some verbal resemblance to Leibniz's view that in a true proposition the predicate is contained in the subject. On the relationship between Hobbes's approach and Leibniz's here, see Nuchelmans (1998, 121–22): "It is worthy of note that Hobbes's use of *continens* for the predicate and *contentum* for the subject, which is also found in Geulincx's theory of predication, was reversed by Leibniz." Note too that Hobbes thought about this containment extensionally, but Leibniz did not.

[23] That is admittedly not terribly clear here, and one might want to say it wasn't fully part of Hobbes's view at this point. In taking that line, however, one must acknowledge that there is no other account of comprehension here.

the affirmation, or consequence is *true*; otherwise *false*. For *true* and *false* are attributes of speech, not of things. And where speech is not, there is neither *truth* nor *falsehood*. *Error* there may be, as when we expect that which shall not be, or suspect what has not been: but in neither case can a man be charged with untruth.[24]

Again, truth is a property of propositions—affirmations here, which are said to be a kind of "speech"—which have the basic structure "A is B."[25] Again, too, we have an explanation of when "A is B" is true: just when "B" signifies everything that "A" signifies. Given Hobbes's typical use of "signify" for the relation between a name and the thing it names, "A is B" will then be true if and only if every thing named by "A" is also named by "B." That is, the extensional account of truth that I suggested was present in the *Elements of Law* is more clearly present here.

Some new features of Hobbes's account are introduced here. Generally, the trend is toward discussing more of the phenomena of language, rather than just introducing a basic model. Even in the quote just presented, we see Hobbes talking about the conditional form "if he be a man, he is a living creature," as well as "a man is a living creature." More generally, affirmations are not the only types of speeches acknowledged: "*affirmation, interrogation, commandment, narration, syllogism, sermon, oration*, and many other such, are names of speeches."[26] Thus, the model of affirmations and their truth is explicitly acknowledged to be only a partial story about language.

We have, then, a story about the basic structure of propositions and their truth conditions. This story is repeated and elaborated upon in chapters 2–5 of *De corpore*. Particularly relevant is chapter 3, where Hobbes gives his account of the proposition. As in *Leviathan*, Hobbes acknowledges several types of speech, but focuses on one type, the proposition, which he describes indeed as the only kind of speech that is useful in philosophy.[27] He defines a proposition as

> *speech consisting of two copulated names by which the one who is speaking signifies that he conceives the name which occurs second to be the name of the same thing as the name which occurs first;* or (what is the same) the first name is conceived to be contained by the second name.[28]

---

[24] *Leviathan* 4.11, 14–15.

[25] *Leviathan* 4.18, 16. Nuchelmans (1998, 120) distinguishes two seventeenth-century (and earlier) views of a categorical proposition: the tripartite subject-copula-predicate view and the bipartite subject-verb view. The authors of the Port Royal logic are noted as going the first way, indeed, as holding that "there is only one genuine verb, the copula." This is very much Hobbes's sort of approach, too.

[26] *Leviathan* 4.18, 16.

[27] *De corpore* 3.1.

[28] *De corpore* 3.2. In quoting from the early chapters of *De corpore*, I use Martinich's translation in Hobbes (1981).

This repeats several themes from earlier texts. A proposition is a sort of speech (Latin: *oratio*). It involves two names linked by the copula—in English, "is." So, again, we have the basic structure, "A is B." When are such propositions true?

> The third distinction is that some propositions are *true* and others *false*. A *true* proposition is one in which the *predicate* contains the *subject* within itself, or in which the *predicate* is the name of each and every thing of which the *subject* is the name; as "Man is an animal" is a true proposition, therefore whatever is called "man" is also called "animal." And "Some man is sick" is true since "sick" is the name of a certain man. But what is not true, or a proposition in which the *predicate* does not contain the subject, is called "False," as "Man is a rock."[29]

Again, the truth of propositions is explained in terms of what is named by the subject and what is named by the predicate. A proposition "A is B" is true if and only if every thing named by "A" is also named by "B." Here, this is treated as equivalent to talking of containment.[30]

Another source for Hobbes's views is Chatsworth manuscript A.10. This was published by Jacquot and Jones as a set of Hobbes's own notes for *De corpore*.[31] More recently, Noel Malcolm has argued that the manuscript actually contains Robert Payne's notes on Hobbes's work.[32] Either way, it provides us with some further information (albeit perhaps secondhand) about Hobbes's thought. And it gives us yet more confirmation of Hobbes's consistent basic view about names, propositions, and truth. A true proposition, this text tells us, is one where "the predicate contains the subject."[33]

A certain basic picture is, then, consistently present in Hobbes's thought about language. He starts by thinking about names; thinks about the ways these are used in different kinds of speech; focuses on one of those types, the proposition; explains the basic "A is B" structure of the proposition; and explains the truth of a proposition (and thus all truth) in terms of what is named by the names involved.

2 ABSURDITY AND ITS CAUSES

Having explained his basic model of the workings of language, Hobbes moves on, in both the *Elements of Law* and *Leviathan*, to talk about reason and the passions.

---

[29] *De corpore* 3.7.

[30] The 1656 English translation talks here of comprehension, which was the language used in the *Elements of Law*: "A *True Proposition* is that, whose predicate contains, or comprehends its Subject ... " (*Concerning Body* 3.7, 26).

[31] "Notes pour la 'Logica' et la 'Philosophia prima' du *De corpore*," in Hobbes (1973, 461–513).

[32] Malcolm (2002, 99–101).

[33] "Propositio vera; cujus praedicatum continet in se subjectum; sive cujus praedicatum est uniuscujusque rei, cujus nomen est subjectum" (Hobbes 1973, 466).

Intermingled with the discussion of reason in *Leviathan* chapter 5 is, however, a discussion of absurdity and its causes. *De corpore* has a somewhat different structure, but there chapter 5 is devoted to the discussion of error and absurdity.

In the *Elements of Law*, the absurd is associated with the impossible and the insignificant.[34] Hobbes also makes use of an analogy between absurdity and injustice, in the course of which he presents the view that absurdity is or involves contradiction: "he that is driven to contradict an assertion by him before maintained, is said to be reduced to an absurdity."[35]

In *Leviathan*, the absurd is again associated with the insignificant, with nonsense, with being "without meaning," and with being "senseless."[36] The notion that the absurd is the contradictory, seen in the *Elements of Law*, appears in *Leviathan*, too. We get the same analogy between absurdity and injustice,[37] and, in objecting to some views, Hobbes argues that they are contradictory in order to justify the claim that they are absurd.[38] The absurd is also, in *Leviathan*, associated with the false, as when Hobbes talks of "absurd and false affirmations" and "absurd and false general rules."[39]

In *De corpore*, the absurd is once more associated with the insignificant, as well as with the ridiculous.[40] And an association is again made between the absurd and the false.[41] Meanwhile, the heading of *De corpore* 5.2 talks of a certain "incoherence" (Latin: *incohaerentia*) that is associated with propositions that are always false. Hobbes discusses several ways this can come about. As we will see below, these correspond closely with what Hobbes in *Leviathan* calls causes of absurdity. Thus, the incoherence of *De corpore* appears in *Leviathan* to be the absurdity of the earlier text, and this incoherence is associated with falsity.

There seem to be two main ways one might understand Hobbes's talk of absurdity. The first option is to take the absurd to be the contradictory. This is supported by the passages that use the analogy between absurdity and injustice, among others.[42] The second option is to take the absurd simply to be the false, albeit dramatically described. This is supported by some of the passages and examples discussed later herein. In these, Hobbes discusses the causes of absurdity, but many of his examples appear to involve falsehood without contradiction. One might, given these two supported options, think that Hobbes is simply careless or inconsistent in his talk of absurdity. Thus, Soles (1996, 111) says, discussing one of the passages I consider herein, that "Hobbes is rather cavalier about the distinction between absurdity and falsehood in this context, considering them both to be errors, though he does not in general deny there are meaningful

---

34 *Elements of Law* 6.5, 12.5.
35 *Elements of Law* 16.2.
36 *Leviathan* 4.21, 17; 5.5, 19; 7.4, 31.
37 *Leviathan* 14.7, 65.
38 See, e.g., *Leviathan* 18.18, 93.
39 *Leviathan* 4.22, 17; 5.19, 21.
40 *De corpore* 3.1, 3.12.
41 *De corpore* 1.7, 3.8.
42 *Leviathan* 5.5, 19.

falsehoods."[43] Perhaps we are just left with this slightly unsatisfactory conclusion. Sometimes, for Hobbes, "absurd" is just a dramatic way of saying "false." At other times, it suggests something more: contradictory or inconceivable, perhaps. But there are few or no external markers of which context is which. We just have to work through the claims of absurdity one by one, seeing what is at issue in each case.

In the discussion of absurdity in *Leviathan*, Hobbes provides a list of "causes of absurdity" or of "absurd conclusions."[44] Similarly, in *De corpore* he provides a list of "types of incoherence of names."[45] Each of these is a list of seven ways that language can go wrong. They are not the same list, although there is considerable overlap. There is also a somewhat longer discussion of each of the categories of problem in *De corpore* than in *Leviathan*.[46]

Leviathan lists seven causes of absurd assertions. An eighth, although not included in the numbered list by Hobbes, is provided straight after. They are as follows.[47]

L1 "want of method," i.e., not starting from definitions;

L2 "giving of names of *bodies*, to *accidents*, or of *accidents* to *bodies*";

L3 "giving of the names of the *accidents of bodies without us*, to the *accidents* of our own *bodies*; as they do that say the *colour is in the body*";

L4 "giving of the names of *bodies*, to *names*, or *speeches*";

L5 "giving of the names of *accidents*, to *names*, or *speeches*";

L6 "use of metaphors, tropes, and other rhetorical figures";

L7 "names that signify nothing; but are taken up, and learned by rote from the Schools"; and

L8 "the length of the account; wherein [one] may forget what came before."

We should note that the category "accidents of our own bodies" appears not to include everything one might think of as an accident of one's own body. Height, for example, seems not to be the sort of example Hobbes has in mind. His examples are sound and color, and the error he alleges is giving them names of external bodies by saying things such as "the colour is in the body" and "the sound is in the air." So the color and sound involved are not external color, but internal, experiential color. In the equivalent list in *De corpore*, these are not called any sort of accidents, but *phantasms*, although the parallels between the lists suggest that Hobbes has the same examples in mind in both cases.

Despite considerable overlap between this and the equivalent list in *De corpore*, some items on this list are not on the later one: L1, L6, L7, and L8. These items that are only on the *Leviathan* list appear to be a variety of ways to be led into error. But the other items

---

[43] She is discussing the list of causes of absurdity or incoherence in *De corpore*, which I consider below.

[44] *Leviathan* 5.8, 20.

[45] *De corpore* 5.2.

[46] These lists are discussed at length by Engel (1961) and Martinich (1981, 404–11) and considered more briefly by Peters (1956, 136–37), Soles (1996, 110–11), and Martinich (2005, 143).

[47] *Leviathan* 5.8–16, 20–21.

on the *Leviathan* list, and the overlapping items of the *De corpore* list, are all instances of one particular way to go wrong.

That one way of going wrong, exemplified in L2–L5, lies in giving a name of a thing of one kind to a thing of another kind—giving a name of an accident to a body, or the like. There appear to be five relevant kinds of thing invoked here: bodies, accidents of bodies without us, accidents of our own bodies, names, and speeches. These correspond to the four kinds of things that are said to be "subject to names" in chapter 4 of *Leviathan*, although there names and speeches are grouped together, whereas here they are separated.[48]

Hobbes appears to be using that list of kinds together with a principle that forbids combining two names of different kinds in a proposition of the form "A is B." But what exactly is the role of this principle? Where did it come from, and how does it relate to Hobbes's other views about language?

Moreover, given the way Hobbes is arguing, one might expect him simply to apply the principle "do not apply a name for things of one kind to a thing of another kind" systematically. However, not all the apparently possible cases appear on this list. Why is the giving of names of bodies to names on the list of causes of absurdity, but the giving of names of names to bodies not on the list? Is this second sort of predication not, in Hobbes's view, a cause of absurdity, with the implication that the general principle does not hold? Or is the second sort of predication just not a common enough cause of absurdity to be worth drawing attention to here? An indirect clue as to why the list is incomplete in that way is perhaps provided by the way Hobbes proceeds after giving the list in *De corpore*. He works through each of the listed cases, arguing about particular examples. It is notable that the examples given tend to be of commonly held philosophical positions. Hobbes is not merely examining possible sorts of error. He is also using these views about sorts of error to object to a wide range of philosophical views. Here, his general reflections on language and attacks on others' uses of language come together.

Perhaps, then, there is further illumination to be found in the lengthier argument in *De corpore*. We are presented there with a list of seven sorts of combinations of names that always give rise to a false proposition.[49] If names are "copulated in these ways," the result is "incoherent, and constitute[s] a false proposition." The list is as follows.

D1 "If the name of a Body [is copulated] with the name of an Accident"
D2 "If the name of a Body [is copulated] with the name of a Phantasm"
D3 "If the name of a Body [is copulated] with the name of a Name"
D4 "If the name of an Accident [is copulated] with the name of a Phantasm"
D5 "If the name of an Accident [is copulated] with the name of a Name"
D6 "If the name of a Phantasm [is copulated] with the name of a Name"
D7 "If the name of a Thing [is copulated] with the name of a Speech [Act]"

---

[48] *Leviathan* 4.14-8, 15–16.
[49] *De corpore* 5.2.

One might think that the general reasoning, both here and in *Leviathan*, is as follows. Suppose "A" and "B" are names, and "A is B" a proposition. Hobbes relies on something like the principle (P):

(P)   If "A" and "B" are names for things of different kinds then "A is B" is false.

If "A" and "B" are names of things of the same kind, then the proposition may be true, but may not be: "Socrates is a man" and "Socrates is a giraffe" are both propositions of this sort.

Again, Hobbes applies his apparent principle to only a certain select list of kinds. Here, they are body, accident, phantasm, name, and speech. Allowing that the inclusion of phantasm is a change of terminology but not of content, that is the same list of kinds invoked in the parallel argument in *Leviathan*.[50] Although *De corpore* 2.15–6 shows Hobbes to be rather skeptical about the value of certain traditional lists of predicaments or categories, he seems to have thought his own shorter list had some value.

Some commentators have thought that Hobbes was here discussing what Ryle called category mistakes. Ryle held that the "logical type or category to which a concept belongs is the set of ways in which it is logically legitimate to operate with it" (Ryle 1949, 8). We could perhaps take Hobbes to have such a theory of categories and concepts (or better, in this context, names). For Hobbes on this reading, there are names that fall into four or five types. In any "logically legitimate" sentence of the form "A is B," the type of "B" must be the same as the type of "A." Thus Peters said that Hobbes "tried to show how absurdities are generated by mistakes about the logical behaviour of different classes of terms".[51]

I argue here that Hobbes did not in general think that the mistaken sentences he criticized (those described by D1–D7) fail to be "logically legitimate." His principal criticism is simply that such sentences are false, not that they are in some stronger sense wrongly constructed. In arguing for that, I consider how (P) is related to Hobbes's general theory of propositions and their truth. (P) might appear, especially on a Rylean sort of reading, to be an independent principle about how to construct propositions. In fact, however, if we look at the way that Hobbes uses (P), we see that the employed instances of (P) are derived from a combination of the general theory and some claims about the facts in particular cases. (P) is not, for Hobbes, a fundamental principle about how to structure propositions. It is more like an abbreviated explanation of why certain propositions are false.

[50]   The final item on the list also includes "thing." Martinich (1981, 405) suggests that Hobbes here "lumped together" the four earlier types (body, accident, phantasm, name) "to avoid a needless proliferation of types of absurdity."

[51]   Peters (1956, 136). See also the discussion in Martinich 1981, which is to some extent opposed to that in Engel 1961. Soles (1996, 110) suggests a reading of this sort when she says that "Hobbes restricts semantically the ways in which names can be copulated."

To fill that point out and provide some supporting evidence, I consider three examples, which are of sentence types D1, D2, and D3.

D1. *"If the name of a Body be copulated with the name of an Accident"*

Hobbes's examples here include "essence is a being," "the intellect understands," "A body is extension," and "Whiteness is white." Indeed, his discussion of this sort of incoherence is essentially just a long list of examples. Let us take, as a working example, the Cartesian identification of body with extension, "corpus est extensio."[52] Why, according to Hobbes, is this false, incoherent, and absurd? "For since no subject of an accident, that is, no body, is an accident, no name of an accident should be assigned to a body and no name of a body should be assigned to an accident."

The reasoning seems to be that bodies and accidents are things of different kinds, so saying that something of one kind is something of another kind is a mistake. How, does this fit into the general theory of propositions sketched in Section 1? Surely "body is extension" will be true if the things named by "body" are among the things named by "extension," and this theory makes no reference to kinds. Hobbes might appear to have introduced a new theory of falsity of propositions in presenting these lists.

If we follow out the application of the general theory to the case given, we can see where the problem arises and how it connects to (P). It is reasonably clear what many of the things named by "body" are (leaving various puzzles aside, including puzzles about exactly how to individuate bodies). What, however, is named by "extension"? If "extension" were simply a name of every extended thing, then Hobbes would have to say that "body is extension" was true. Indeed, this is presumably what Hobbes thinks about "body is extended." "Body is extension" works differently, however. "Extended" is, in Hobbes's terminology, a concrete name, but "extension" is an abstract one.[53] Abstract names are said to name the causes of concrete names. For example, "body" is a concrete name, and "corporeity" is the equivalent abstract name. Whereas "extended" names each of the extended things, each of the things that has "parts distant from one another," "extension" is a name for whatever is the cause of something's being extended. Hobbes takes it that none of the things named by "the cause of being extended" is also named by "body." Bodies are not, one might say, the right kind of thing to also be named by that description. Thus, reasoning in terms of the general theory matches up with reasoning that seems to involve (P).

---

[52] See, for instance, the claim in *Principles of Philosophy* 2.21 that "the idea of extension which we conceive to be in a given space is exactly the same as the idea of corporeal substance" (Descartes 1984, 1.232).

[53] *De corpore* 3.3.

D2. If the name of a Body be copulated with the name of a Phantasm.

Turning to this second sort of error, Hobbes again employs philosophically relevant examples, such as "A ghost is a body," and "Sensible species fly through the air and are moved hither and thither."[54] Each of these was, in one way or another, a contentious issue. Hobbes made a point of arguing against ghosts but met with serious opposition on this point, perhaps most famously from Henry More and Joseph Glanvill.[55] The theory of sensible species was a repeated target of Hobbes's attacks. Indeed, it is the one view attacked explicitly in the very first chapter of *Leviathan*, where he identifies it as a view taught by "the philosophy-schools, through all the universities of Christendom, grounded upon certain texts of Aristotle."[56]

What is Hobbes's reasoning here?

> For since ghosts, visible species [...] etc., are no less present to appear to those who are sleeping than to those who are waking, they are not external things, but are phantasms of an imagining mind. Therefore, the names of these things cannot be copulated in a true proposition with the names of bodies.[57]

Thus, we have something like the following argument.

(1) Ghosts and visible species are phantasms (which is to be shown by the sleeping/ waking argument);
(2) Phantasms are not bodies; so
(3) "A is B" cannot be true if is "A" is the name of a ghost or visible species and "B" is the name of a body because nothing named by "B" is also named by "A."

Reconstructing the argument in this way, the general theory about truth and falsity of propositions has a role to play. Much of the work is being done by the arguments for (1), which are supposed to show that ghosts and sensible species are phantasms. The view that phantasms are not bodies is also playing a role. Whatever one thinks of those claims, one thing is clear—this is far from being a case where accepting a principle about predicating names will itself show you that certain sentences are false, incoherent, or otherwise flawed. Hobbes invokes a variety of evidence for his claim, which has little or nothing to do with the logical behavior of different sorts of names and a lot to do with reinforcing his oft-stated view that ghosts are just phantasms.

One could perhaps reconstruct Hobbes's argument as an argument from (P) or at least as an argument from an instance of (P) "if 'A' is the name of a phantasm and 'B' is

---

[54] *De corpore* 5.4.
[55] Glanvill's book on witches went through several versions, and More was responsible for the publication of the final one, *Sadducismus Triumphatus* (Glanvill 1681), after Glanvill's death. On More, Glanvill, and witches, see Jesseph 2005.
[56] *Leviathan* 1.5, 4.
[57] *De corpore* 5.4.

the name of a body, then 'A is B' is false." But that instance is really being supported by Hobbes's views that ghosts are phantasms and phantasms are not bodies rather than by the general truth of (P).

D3. If the name of a Body be copulated with the name of a Name.

Again, we are given several philosophical examples, such as "A universal is a being." Thus, Hobbes appears to be using his claims about language to argue against the view that there are universal things. This would be a partial argument for his particular sort of nominalism, his view that there are neither universal things nor universal ideas. Hobbes's argument is not really explicit. He just tells us that "universal" is the name of a name, not a thing. Can we nevertheless understand this as an argument from his general theory of truth and falsity of propositions, in the manner of the arguments just presented? Modeling our reconstruction on the argument about ghosts and sensible species, we get something like the following:

(1) The things in the examples (universal, etc.) are names;
(2) "Thing" (*ens*) is the name of a body;
(3) "An S is a thing" cannot be true if everything named by S is a name (as nothing named by "S" is also named by "a body"); so
(4) It is false to say that universals, etc., are things.

In the previous case, we were given an argument for the first premise (the sleeping/waking argument that the things mentioned are phantasms). What is the equivalent argument for the first premise here?

Any argument for that premise would be an argument for Hobbes's nominalist view that there are no universal ideas or things, only universal names.[58] So we might think that one of Hobbes's arguments for his nominalism would be an appropriate supporting argument here. But noticing that just draws attention to a problem with the above argument. An argument that there are no universal things or ideas, only names that name many things, is used to support (1), which is then used to support (4)—the claim that there are no universal things. Hobbes's approach appears to be blatantly circular.[59]

---

[58] Hobbes did have other arguments for his nominalism. See *Elements of Law* 5.6 and *De corpore* 2.9.

[59] One might alternatively reconstruct the argument as based on (P) in something like the following way: (1) a proposition that copulates names of two different kinds is absurd; so (2) a proposition that copulates the name of a body with the name of a name is absurd; but (3) in the proposition "A universal is a thing," "a universal" is the name of a name, and "thing" is the name of a body; so (4) the proposition "A universal is a thing" is absurd. Here, again, Hobbes's nominalism would be relied upon (here at 3) in order to argue for it (at 4). Not only is there an absence of explicit appeal to a fundamental principle (P) in the text, but also thinking that there is an implicit one would not remove this oddity.

Meanwhile, Martinich provides another objection to Hobbes's argument: "Nonetheless, there is good reason to doubt that these sentences, taken literally, do involve category mistakes, even when we concede Hobbes his doctrine that universals are names. For on Hobbes's own view, names are themselves objects, typically ink or graphite marks or vocal sounds . . . [But this] should not obliterate

This is not the only case in which one of Hobbes's arguments for one of his fairly fundamental positions appears to be circular or question-begging. Some of his arguments for materialism are like this, too.[60] Moreover, the circular or question-begging status of these arguments is often fairly obvious, such that one suspects that Hobbes himself was probably aware of it. But why give arguments like that?

The answer to that is related, I suspect, to the answer to why Hobbes's table is not systematically complete. Hobbes's aim here was not to put forward a principle about good and bad ways to construct propositions and then to investigate what happened to follow from that principle. Rather, the table allows Hobbes to gather together a big group of positions held by a wide variety of opponents and claim they are all wrong for the same general reason.[61] Now it turns out that to do even that thoroughly, one needs to work through the details of the particular cases and invoke a variety of views and arguments that are unrelated to claims such as (P). Although there is a unity in the cases Hobbes discusses, it is more rhetorical than logical. And, in some cases, he extends this rhetorical unity by subsuming under the general sort of criticism some arguments that are themselves poor, just to be able to say that his opponents in another realm—for instance, with regard to nominalism—make the same mistake as other opponents elsewhere.

Hobbes is talking about mistakes that we might, with caution, call category mistakes, although we would not really be using the phrase in its Rylean sense. The theory of categories and their combination is not a fundamental part of Hobbes's understanding of language, and his arguments are not about logical legitimacy in the Rylean way. Hobbes's claims about particular "category" mistakes can be explained using his theory of propositions and their truth. The "category mistake" falsehoods are false for the same reason that other false sentences are false, not for some new and different reasoning involving a theory of categories. Rather, talk about category mistakes, and the apparent invocation of (P), is a sort of shorthand for explanations of why certain sentences are false. Moreover, although certain category mistake sentences may be contradictory and absurd, they are in general for Hobbes only wrong because false—it's the weaker sense of "absurd" or "incoherent," where it really only means "false," that is in play here—they are not necessarily logically defective in the way Ryle thinks the mistakes he points to are.[62]

---

the point he [Hobbes] wants to make, which, quite simply, is that according to him it is false to assert that universals are nonlinguistic entities" (Martinich 1981, 408–9).

[60] Consider for example the argument of *Leviathan* 34.2, 207.

[61] My view here is similar to Engel's thought that "what Hobbes really wished to do was not to prove some new thesis about language, but rather to lend added strength to a position already established by subsuming it under some general logical linguistic scheme" (Engel 1961, 542).

[62] One might be tempted, perhaps thinking as Peters (1956, 136–37) does about a British philosophical tradition of criticizing other philosophers' language, to speculate that Ryle somehow—directly or indirectly—derived his criticism of category mistakes from Hobbes. Ryle seems, however, to have been inspired by Husserl (see Thomasson 2012, 2.2, citing Ryle 1970, 8).

Hobbes did want to have a theory of language—indeed, he needed one in order to have a theory of minds and of persons. And some of what he says about language is driven by this goal. But at other times—often right next door in the text—his claims and arguments are driven by other goals. Sometimes the point is to defend his other commitments, such as his materialism. Sometimes there's the aim of presenting several of his views as a unified package. And sometimes it seems like he just found he had too good a chance to incorporate another particular criticism under the same general heading. The desire to say "look, my opponents across all these fields all make the same mistake" proved, on occasion, too strong for Hobbes to resist, even when the resulting arguments were poor enough to make the undecided suspicious, never mind the original opponents.

BIBLIOGRAPHY

Baumgold, Deborah. 2004. "The Composition of Hobbes's *Elements of Law.*" *History of Political Thought* 25(1): 16–43.

Descartes, René. 1984. *The Philosophical Writings of Descartes.* Translated by J. Cottingham, R. Stoothof, and D. Murdoch. Cambridge: Cambridge University Press.

Duncan, Stewart. 2011. "Hobbes. Signification, and Insignificant Names." *Hobbes Studies* 24: 158–178.

Engel, S. Morris. 1961. "Hobbes's 'Table of Absurdity.'" *Philosophical Review* 70(4): 533–543.

Glanvill, Joseph. 1681. *Saducismus Triumphatus.* London.

Hobbes, Thomas. 1656. *Concerning Body.* London.

———. 1889. *The Elements of Law.* Edited by Ferdinand Tönnies. London: Simpkin, Marshall, and Co.

———. 1973. *Critique du "De Mundo" de Thomas White.* Edited by J. Jacquot and H. W. Jones. Paris: Vrin-CNRS.

———. 1981. *Part I of De Corpore.* Translated by A. P. Martinich. New York: Abaris Books.

———. 1990. *Behemoth.* Edited by Ferdinand Tönnies. Chicago: University of Chicago Press.

———. 1994. *Leviathan.* Edited by Edwin Curley. Indianapolis: Hackett.

Hungerland, Isabel C., and George R. Vick. 1981. "Hobbes's Theory of Language, Speech, and Reasoning," in Hobbes (1981: 7–169).

Jesseph, Douglas. 2005. "Mechanism, Skepticism, and Witchcraft: More and Glanvill on the Failures of Cartesian Philosophy" in *Receptions of Descartes: Cartesianism and Anti-Cartesianism in Early Modern Europe*, edited by Tad Schmaltz, 199–217. London: Routledge.

Malcolm, Noel. 2002. *Aspects of Hobbes.* Oxford: Clarendon.

Martin, R. M. 1953. "On the Semantics of Hobbes." *Philosophy and Phenomenological Research* 14(2): 205–211.

Martinich, A. P. 1981. "Translator's Commentary" in Hobbes (1981: 333–440).

Martinich, A. P. 2005. *Hobbes.* New York: Routledge.

Nuchelmans, Gabriel. 1998. "Proposition and Judgement," in *The Cambridge History of Seventeenth-Century Philosophy*, edited by Daniel Garber and Michael Ayers, 118–131. Cambridge: Cambridge University Press.

Peters, Richard. 1956. *Hobbes.* Harmondsworth: Penguin.

Pettit, Phillip. 2008. *Made with Words: Hobbes on Language, Mind, and Politics.* Princeton: Princeton University Press.

Ryle, Gilbert. 1949. *The Concept of Mind.* London: Hutchinson's University Library.

Ryle, Gilbert. 1970. "Autobiographical," in *Ryle*, edited by Oscar P. Wood and George Pitcher, 1–15. New York: Doubleday and Co.

Soles, Deborah Hansen. 1996. *Strong Wits and Spider Webs.* Aldershot: Avesbury.

Törnebohm, Håkan. 1960. "A Study in Hobbes's Theory of Denotation and Truth." *Theoria* 26(1), 53–70.

Thomasson, Amie. "Categories," in *The Stanford Encyclopedia of Philosophy (Summer 2012 Edition)*, edited by Edward N. Zalta. http://plato.stanford.edu/archives/sum2012/entries/categories/.

Watkins, J. W. N. 1965. *Hobbes's System of Ideas.* London: Hutchinson. US edition Barnes and Noble, 1968.

CHAPTER 4

HOBBES'S MATHEMATICAL THOUGHT

KATHERINE DUNLOP

HOBBES'S views on mathematics, especially geometry,[1] promise to shed light on his philosophy as a whole. His entire philosophical system is modeled on geometry, which he regards as "the only science that it hath pleased God hitherto to bestow on mankind."[2] But there is less reason to hope that Hobbes's views on mathematics can deepen our understanding of it, for Hobbes is best known for his claim to have "squared the circle" (a problem later shown to have no solution in classical geometry) and his opposition to symbolic methods (which proved vital to mathematics' development). It can easily seem that Hobbes's philosophical preconceptions blinded him to mathematical reality. In particular, his confidence that he could square the circle seems to reflect a conception of "maker's knowledge" as total, on which no property or facet of a constructed object can remain unknown,[3] and his denial that diagrammatic reasoning could be supplanted by algebra seems to rest on his identification of mathematical objects with bodies and a crudely empiricist epistemology.[4]

Contrary to appearances, Hobbes's mathematical program can be understood as a direct, if unsuccessful, response to pressing challenges within the science. A prima facie reason to take his mathematical thought seriously (brought to light by Douglas Jesseph, who sustains a case for its interest and importance) is that his contemporaries did. In the 1640s and early 1650s, Hobbes was considered a preeminent mathematician in Paris and England.[5] In sections 1 and 3, I set out the issues his work promised to address. This period is aptly characterized (following M. S. Mahoney[6]) in terms of a shift in

---

[1] Hobbes's view of computation, as that in which all reasoning consists, is similarly important but will not be discussed here.

[2] *Leviathan*, ed. Waller. 4.17.

[3] See Jesseph 1999a, 221, and 1999b, 427.

[4] So Boyer suggests: 1949, 176.

[5] See Jesseph 1999a, 1–7. Cf. Grant 1996.

[6] See, e.g., Mahoney 1990a.

"canons of intelligibility." The canons widened to include techniques and objects of investigation that were typically not new, but rather recognized as having no place in demonstrative reasoning. In some cases (such as infinitely small elements, regarded as composing a continuous whole), their use had been shown to give rise to paradoxes. While the rationale for excluding others (such as the construction techniques classified as "mechanical") was not formulated as sharply, their use was nonetheless seen as an abandonment of mathematics' special rigor. In this context, would-be innovators had to do more than obtain results; they had to show that their reasoning conferred intelligibility on their solutions. (The urgency of this need is particularly evident in regard to squaring the circle, as I explain in section 3, since from ancient times solutions had been found and rejected solely on grounds of intelligibility.) Hence foundationalist concerns were by no means extraneous to mathematical practice.

In particular, the use of algebraic methods to solve geometrical problems had to be shown to comport with geometry's aims and standards. Section 2 considers how Descartes respects this requirement. For his part, Hobbes denies that it can be met. Granting that "analysis" by algebraic equations is "usefull for . . . finding out" properties of figures, he nonetheless considers it "a way wherein men go round from the Equality of rectangled Plains to the Equality of Proportion, and thence again to the Equality of rectangled Plains," in which "the *Symboles* serve only to make men go faster about, as greater Winde to a Winde-mill." To "add to the Science of Geometry," in contrast, it would be necessary to reason about figures from their "nature and generation."[7] Section 5 explicates the conception of mathematical science that underlies this objection.

Hobbes had his own program for enriching geometry. The views he presses serve to ground methods characteristic of calculus. I show in section 4 that Newton shared his conception of mathematical objects as generated by motion[8] and used it to justify consideration of infinitely small quantities (as given by instantaneous rates of change).[9] Section 6 shows how Hobbes uses this approach to simplify proofs of familiar theorems.

His ambitions to the contrary, Hobbes did not contribute original results to geometry. The publication of *De Corpore* in 1655 was intended to cement his standing as a mathematician. It had the opposite effect, to show what the emperor had for clothes. The book's defects were pointed out with special vigor by the celebrated mathematician John Wallis, beginning a vituperative exchange, which lasted roughly twenty years and ranged over almost the whole of mathematics.[10] In the course of the dispute Hobbes

---

[7] *EW* 7:242.

[8] I do not claim that Newton was influenced by Hobbes; both thinkers may have derived the view from a common source or independently adopted it in response to classical precedents and early modern needs.

[9] Meanwhile Leibniz explicitly appropriated Hobbes's notion of *conatus* for his dynamical theory, and Goldenbaum and Jesseph argue in their contributions to (2008) that it also underwrites fundamental principles of the Leibnizian calculus. Here I consider only Hobbes's connection with Newton, which is more relevant to this paper's overall themes.

[10] The intensity and bitterness of the attacks suggests that their motivation was not purely mathematical. Shapin and Schaffer 1985 opened the field for study of these external factors. Since the entire exchange is covered in excellent fashion by Jesseph 1999a, my remarks are limited to basic disagreements about mathematics.

hardened his views, to the point of denying the Pythagorean Theorem and with it most of classical geometry. In Section 7 I show how Hobbes's position is extreme in comparison with Newton's, and also how it agrees with Kant's. This completes (and clarifies the extent of) my defense of Hobbes's approach, namely that other thinkers succeeded by its means.

Hobbes takes geometry's success to result from acknowledging that reasoning must begin with proper definitions,[11] but finds it necessary to replace many definitions in use. In this way, he claims to have "made the grounds of geometry firm and coherent" for the first time.[12] Hobbes justifies his understandings of the terms by appeal to practices of measurement and calculation. On my view these practices, together with surviving texts from the classical period, comprised the background against which geometrical innovations were assessed. Its importance is clear from the way even self-conscious innovators (like Descartes) respected classical standards of adequacy for solutions to geometrical problems. In section 8 I suggest that this manner of justifying definitions offers Hobbes a way out of the dilemma facing his account of first principles, namely that they must either present themselves as indubitably evident or stand as arbitrary conventions. In this way, Hobbes's account of geometrical definition resolves a problem in his broader views on science.

1 RATIO AND PROPORTION IN CLASSICAL MATHEMATICS

The theory of ratio and proportion gave precise mathematical significance to the notion of intelligibility. In classical mathematics, as formulated by Euclid in the *Elements*, ratios are relationships between numbers (understood as the "natural" or counting numbers—i.e., positive integers) or "magnitudes" (understood as concrete things of definite size; e.g., particular regions of space). Reasoning typically aims to determine ratios rather than exact numerical values or particular spatial configurations. Euclid defines *ratio* only vaguely (as "a sort of relation in respect of size between two magnitudes of the same kind")[13] but makes the notion precise by stating conditions under which two pairs of objects stand in the same ratio. He uses the term "proportional" for such objects. In modern terms, this is to introduce ratios as equivalence classes (of pairs of magnitudes or numbers) determined by the relation of proportionality.

The *Elements* in fact contains two theories of proportion, reflecting stages in the history of Greek mathematics. According to the older theory, two numbers are

---

[11] *Leviathan* 4.17–18.
[12] *EW* 7: 242.
[13] Bk. V Def. 3.

proportional "when the first is the same multiple, or the same part, or same parts, of the second that the third is of the fourth."[14] Here *multiple* means integral multiple and *part* means integral divisor. Since this theory presupposes that any two items standing in a ratio are integral multiples of a common unit, it applies only to numbers. Hobbes and his contemporaries refer to this manner of comparison as "arithmetical proportion."[15] The discovery of incommensurable magnitudes gave rise to another theory, which seventeenth-century writers call "geometrical." According to the newer criterion, a pair of magnitudes A, B is in the same ratio as another pair C, D when any "equimultiples" of A and C "alike exceed, are alike equal to, or alike fall short of" any equimultiples of B and D;[16] that is (in algebraic symbolism), when for all natural numbers m, n, if $mA > nB$ then $mC > nD$; if $mA = nB$ then $mC = nD$; if $mA < nB$ then $mC < nD$. Because this criterion does not presuppose that A and B (likewise C and D) are integral multiples of a common unit, according to it incommensurable magnitudes can be proportional (i.e., stand in the same ratio).

However, the criterion presupposes that A and B (likewise C and D) "can, when multiplied, exceed one another,"[17] which means that their product is defined and is comparable in size with both. In classical mathematics, operations corresponding to multiplication are defined only for certain combinations of magnitudes. A magnitude of whatever dimension (line, plane figure, or solid) can be multiplied by a number (to produce another magnitude of the same dimension); a line can be multiplied by a line (to produce a plane figure); and a plane figure can be multiplied by a line (to produce a solid). Since magnitudes cannot be compared in size with numbers (unless some length is already designated as a unit), neither can the product of any magnitude with a number, so magnitudes cannot stand in ratios with numbers. And since each magnitude in a ratio must be capable (when multiplied by a number) of exceeding the other, it was assumed that a magnitude can have a ratio only to others of the same dimension, because there is no clear sense in which any multiple of, for example, a line, can exceed a surface.

Interestingly, however, Euclid does not speak of these operations on magnitudes as "multiplication."[18] Therefore his treatment does not preclude, but rather is silent on, the application of arithmetical operations and relationships to magnitudes. Nor does he say in general (other than in the definition of *ratio*) when two objects can be compared in respect of size; he indicates only how, in particular cases, lines and planar regions can be compared (namely by arranging them in space). Thus the question of which objects could have a ratio to a given magnitude, according to the geometrical theory of proportion, was to an extent open for early modern writers.

Sometimes Hobbes is directly concerned with conditions on the existence of ratios. For instance, he understands the quantity of "endeavor" as a ratio between the spatial

---

[14] Bk. VII, Def. 20.
[15] *Concerning Body* II.13.1, p. 145; cp. Barrow 1734, ch. XVII.
[16] Bk. V, Def. 5.
[17] Bk. V, Def. 4 states this as a condition on magnitudes' having a ratio.
[18] See Grattan-Guinness 1996 and Palmieri 2001.

distance covered by a moving body and the time in which it moves. In response to Wallis's objection that space cannot stand in a ratio to time, Hobbes appeals to his account (discussed in section 5 below) of spatial extension as the measure of both time and distance.[19] But even when his discussion is not couched in these terms, it often concerns innovations designed to overcome the restrictions on quantitative comparisons.

2 DESCARTES'S GÉOMÉTRIE AND THE ACCEPTABILITY OF CONSTRUCTION TECHNIQUES

In geometry, the rise of "analytic" methods conferred intelligibility on a new manner of expression, which lent itself to powerful techniques of solution. But this change was more gradual than is commonly supposed. In particular, Descartes is supposed to have accomplished the "application of algebra to geometry" at a single stroke[20]; he indeed describes his technique as the basis of a "completely new science"[21] dealing with mathematical objects of every kind. But a closer look at his *Géométrie* shows that he did not count algebraic results as solutions to problems unless they met geometrical standards of intelligibility. This illustrates how the assumptions and practices of classical geometry remained important at the level of foundations.

The *Géométrie* opens with the claim that any geometrical problem can be "reduced to such terms that a knowledge of the lengths of certain straight lines is sufficient for its construction."[22] The basic form of a problem is to find a magnitude or magnitudes—point(s) or line(s)—related in a specified manner to given ones. The procedure is "analytic" in the sense familiar from classical mathematics, which is to

---

[19] Hobbes contends that quantities belonging to distance and to time can stand in a ratio because there can be a ratio between the straight lines by which both are "measured and compared" (*EW* 7:273).

At the same time, Hobbes rejects Wallis's extension of the notion of ratio to algebraically treated relationships in general (see section 7 below). So their dispute concerns how, not whether, to broaden the notion.

[20] Descartes was not the sole inventor of analytic geometry, but he is the most important figure for present purposes. François Viète is among the first to have reformulated algebraic equations as statements of proportionality, so that they could be solved by geometrical techniques. But his work does not raise the same issues as Descartes's. Viète is concerned with geometrical problems that require construction of a line segment or point and admit finitely many solutions, which in algebraic form involve equations in one unknown (see Boyer 1969, 60–61). Only later was it recognized (by Fermat and Descartes) that an equation in two unknowns determines a curve, which raises the issue of constructing the curve. Moreover, while Descartes claims novelty for his method, Viète takes himself to follow the way of the ancients (see Klein 1968, 320–21). Pierre de Fermat is also credited with coinventing analytic geometry. But he says relatively little about foundational issues (cf. Bos 2001, 205), and Hobbes says accordingly little about Fermat (cf. Jesseph 1999a, 33 n.46).

[21] In a famous letter to Isaac Beeckman, quoted in Bos 2001, p. 232.

[22] Descartes 1952, 297.

say that it begins by assuming the existence of a solution.[23] This final configuration is depicted in a diagram, in which the given elements are designated as *a, b, c, . . .* and the lines constituting the solution as *x, y, z. . . .* Next, the magnitudes' relationships are algebraically expressed, and the equations are manipulated to put each in terms of one unknown (*x, y,* etc.). Such a formula is not, in general, a solution to a geometrical problem[24] because the way in which the unknown is designated (say as a term of power > 3 or < ½, or as a negative quantity or root thereof) may have no obvious spatial significance. Thus the final step is to "construct" the solution, and Descartes is as concerned to provide for geometrical treatment of algebraic operations as for the application of algebra to geometry.[25]

His first order of business is to specify operations on line segments corresponding to addition, subtraction, multiplication, division, and the extraction of roots. Descartes's innovation is to interpret arithmetical operations as constructions of segments, so that they result in objects of the same dimension (= 1) however many times they are repeated.

However, Descartes hardly uses his novel operations[26] but typically gives his solutions in terms of figures for which construction procedures were known. He is sensitive to traditional distinctions among constructive procedures, which are important for us to understand. The Greeks classified problems according to the constructions required for their solution, as "plane," "solid," or "linelike."[27] Plane problems can be solved by constructing straight lines and circles, which is to say by extending and rotating line segments (operations that do not leave the plane). A solid problem is solved by constructing an ellipse, hyperbola, or parabola, called a "conic section" because it is found as the intersection of a plane and a cone. The third class of problems is solved by means of certain other curves generated by more complicated procedures. Because their use was seen to yield less insight into the relationship between the given and sought magnitudes, it was regarded as not properly geometrical. The organization of the *Géométrie* respects the distinction between "plane" and "solid" problems, but Descartes widens the second class of curves. He contends that the "exactness of reasoning" that characterizes geometrical solutions pertains not only to the conic sections but also to any curve that "can be conceived of as described by a continuous motion or by several successive motions, each motion being completely determined by those which

---

[23] Hobbes understands "analysis" in this sense when he speaks of it as proceeding from what is merely "supposed" to what is known (*De Corpore* III.20.6, *EW* 1: 309–11).

[24] The formula's adequacy as a geometrical solution is a separate issue from how readily it can be dealt with by algebraic means. Equations of fifth and higher degree were not complete solutions (or, respecting Descartes's terminology, "resolutions") even from the algebraic standpoint, because there were no general algorithms for finding their roots.

[25] As the historian of mathematics Carl Boyer remarks: 1956, 64, and Boyer and Merzbach 2001, 311.

[26] See Bos 2001, 300 *n.*13.

[27] According to the *Collection* of Pappus, which was a main source for early modern writers. The passage in question is translated by Bos, (2001) 38. Hobbes discusses the classification at *De Corpore* III.20.6 (*EW* I: 315–16.)

precede."[28] The idea[29] is that the curve is traced by the intersection point of two lines (themselves either straight or curves whose construction is unproblematic) whose movement is controlled by a single initial motion. Thus it inherits the lines' intelligibility. The *Géométrie* culminates in an account of how curves constructed by such linked motions can be used to construct solutions to equations of fifth and higher degree.

3 SQUARING THE CIRCLE

We can better understand the point of Descartes's restriction by considering what it excludes. Descartes's example of a curve that "must be conceived of as described by two separate motions whose relation does not admit of exact determination" is the quadratrix.[30] Suppose that a square is constructed on the radius of a given circle so that a quadrant of the circle is inscribed in it. The quadratrix is the curve traced by the point of intersection of two segments, one equal in length to the radius and rotating uniformly around the circle's center, so as to sweep from the side of the square to its bottom, and a second of the same length (which is also that of the square's side) and moving uniformly in the same time from the top of the square to its bottom (remaining parallel to both throughout its transit). It can be used to square the circle, that is, to construct a square equal in area to the given circle.[31] But to assign to each segment the velocity required for the motions to take an equal amount of time, the ratio between the radius and the square's side must already be known. Descartes's claim that the relationship of the motions is not "exactly determined" can be taken to mean that it is not given independently of the lines' relationship.[32] Because the construction of the quadratrix in this way presupposes a solution to the problem of squaring the circle, its use was not accepted as a solution.

The case of squaring the circle well illustrates how the adequacy of a solution technique could be a matter for reasoned argument. Some commentators on Hobbes seem to regard the objective as manifestly impossible, like producing a round square.[33] But while it is impossible to construct a square equal in area to a given circle by ruler-and-compass operations, this is far from obvious. To show that the required segment (the square's side) cannot be constructed by this means, one must exhaustively consider all the objects that can, which is done using a notion first introduced in the nineteenth century.[34]

---

[28] Descartes 1952, 43.

[29] As Bos elaborates: 2001, 339.

[30] Descartes 1952, 44.

[31] For details, see Knorr 1986, 226–33.

[32] Descartes apparently held that the relationship between the circle's radius and the square's side not only was not, but could not be, known exactly. See Mancosu 2008, 118–21.

[33] A recent example is George MacDonald Ross 2009, 73.

[34] This is the notion of a field (of algebraic numbers). See the supremely lucid account by Courant and Robbins 1996, Chapter III. In this light, R. S. Peters's comment that "squaring the circle did not

Without the restriction on means of construction, to square the circle is easy. The problem was known from ancient times to be equivalent to that of constructing a square whose perimeter is equal to the circle's circumference. Thus, as Hobbes writes, "any ordinary man may much sooner and more accurately . . . square the circle by winding a small thread about a given cylinder, than any geometrician shall do the same by dividing the radius into 10,000,000 equal parts."[35] The important point, for present purposes, is that this sort of "brute force" yields no mathematical understanding of the relationship between the constructed quantity and the given one.[36] Some such sense of inadequacy is a ground for dismissing "mechanical" methods, among which was counted the use of the quadratrix as well as of curves constructed using taut strings. So, Hobbes writes, "though the length of the circumference were exactly set out, either . . . mechanically, or only by chance, yet this would contribute no help at all towards the section of angles," which refers to trigonometry.[37] On this view, the problem is solved only when lengths along the circumference can be systematically related (as measures of angular size) to lengths of straight-line segments.

In this context, the interesting question was not whether it was possible to square the circle but what status to grant the available means of construction. A ruler-and-compass construction would have fully solved the problem, because these operations were in a sense the most basic terms in which geometrical objects were conceived. Other constructive procedures counted as solutions only insofar as they made intelligible the square's relationship to the circle. Similarly, a symbolic expression of the square's area or boundary length in terms of the circle's was a solution only to the extent that the operations designated by the symbols were well understood. Insofar as they presupposed understanding of the figures' relationship or simply failed to illuminate it, geometric and algebraic techniques were only "approaches" to a solution,[38] or tools or heuristics by which to reach one.

[in the seventeenth century] seem quite such a preposterous project" as now (1979, 40) is a gross understatement: it now "seems preposterous" because it has been proved impossible, by means that lay completely beyond the ken of Hobbes and his contemporaries.

[35] Concerning Body III.20.1, *EW* 1:288.

[36] Compare Davis 1987, 163–64.

[37] Ibid.

[38] I take this term from an account by Leibniz, which nicely illustrates how ways of relating the circle to straight-lined figures could be judged either complete, or lacking. Leibniz explains that "the quadrature, or the turning of the circle into [a] right-lined figure . . . may be understood to be fourfold, to wit, either by calculation, or by linear construction: And each of these again may be either perfectly exact, or else almost, or pretty near." Leibniz classifies his predecessors' attempts as "pretty near," or "approaches." Viète's and Christiaan Huygens's technique, to approximate the value of the circle's circumference by bounding it between inscribed and circumscribed polygons, is "pretty near" construction, which, while "useful in practical geometry, give[s] no satisfaction to the mind which covets the very truth, unless the progression [of increasingly many-sided polygons] could be carried on in infinitum" (1682, 206). The "pretty near calculation" (i.e. numerical approximation of π) by Ludolf van Ceulen likewise fails to satisfy because it involves no rule by which the expansion of the decimal could be infinitely continued. Leibniz distinguishes two kinds of quadratures by "exact calculation" that have been considered. An "algebraical" quadrature would express the ratio in irrational numbers or "the roots of common equations." Leibniz believes this was shown impossible by James Gregory in

As such, they could still be worthy contributions. Since the criteria of adequacy and completeness for solutions were not altogether sharp or fixed, and in any case new efforts often built on previous ones, it made sense to lay claim to approximations and results based on controversial assumptions. This goes some way toward explaining a curious episode that might seem merely to exhibit Hobbes's obstinacy: He retained three solutions in *De Corpore* even after he was persuaded of their failure (by friends who saw the passage in press). Hobbes redescribed the first solution as "false" and "proceeding from a false hypothesis," and claims the second gives only "the finding of a right line as nearly equal to the quadrant of a circle as desired." At the conclusion of the third, he adds that "the reader should take those things that are said to be found exactly of the dimension of the circle and angles as instead said problematically."[39] In the English translation, Hobbes calls each solution an "attempt" and designates steps in them as requiring further investigation.

4 REASONING WITH THE INFINITELY SMALL: NEWTON AND CAVALIERI

The techniques that did most to widen the bounds of intelligibility (and give rise to the calculus) during the seventeenth century were algebraic symbolization and consideration of infinitely small quantities. While Hobbes opposed algebraization, he had a way to bring the infinitely small under consideration that was superficially in agreement with classical conceptions. The approach was not original to Hobbes but was known under the name "method of indivisibles," as the invention of Bonaventura Cavalieri (although few of its practitioners knew his work well).[40] Its elements are also found in Newton, and comparison with Newton and Cavalieri will help us see (in sections 5 and 6) how Hobbes extends the classical framework.

A main application of Cavalieri's method was to problems of "quadrature," that is, finding a rectilinear figure equal in area to a region bounded by a curve (of which

---

1667 (although Gregory's reasoning was disputed by Huygens, and the Royal Society examined the controversy without reaching a conclusion; for details, see Scriba 1983.) An "arithmetical" quadrature "is performed by a certain series exhibiting the quantity of the circle exact by a progression of rational terms" (1682, 207). Leibniz argues that the "error" of the series $1/1 - 1/3 + 1/5 - 1/7 + 1/9, \ldots$, i.e., the difference between the sum of its terms and the area of the circle (with diameter of unit length), decreases with the number of terms, so as to become "less than any assignable quantity." He claims that because the series "consisteth of one regular method of progression," the "whole may sufficiently enough be conceived by the mind" even as the series continues infinitely, so that it delivers the satisfaction missing from van Ceulen's calculation (1682, 208). Leibniz also claims that the rectilinear figure can be constructed "exactly" by means of "transcendental" curves, and calculated "exactly" by "indefinite" equations.

[39] *De Corpore* III.20. Translations by Jesseph 1999a, 127–28.

[40] Diverse techniques were grouped under the name of the method, and the proper interpretation of Cavalieri was one point disputed by Wallis and Hobbes. See Jesseph 1999a, 178ff.

squaring the circle is a special case). What we now recognize as integration took this form in classical mathematics, because its objective was to determine ratios between magnitudes rather than properties of functions. Cavalieri regards every plane figure as enclosed between two parallel "tangents,"[41] such that every line parallel to and between them intersects the figure in a line segment and no other line parallel to them intersects the figure at all. He defines "all the lines" of a figure to mean "the single lines, collected together," that form the intersections of the figure with a plane at an angle to the plane containing the figure, which moves from one tangent to the other.[42] Cavalieri then proceeds to establish ratios between plane figures by comparing "all the lines" of each. In some cases Cavalieri reasons that each line of one figure stands in a certain relation to each line of the other. More typically, he relates the collections comprised of the lines. But Cavalieri is usually careful to make clear that he does not regard the lines as composing the figures[43]; instead, he establishes that the totalities of lines are themselves magnitudes capable of standing in ratios to one another.

That the infinitely small sections produced by the plane's transit are considered only as elements of "all the lines" is one respect in which Cavalieri's way of introducing infinitely small quantities was particularly influential. Infinitely small quantities were excluded from classical mathematics not only on account of conceptual difficulties, but also because by multiplication they cannot be made to exceed finite quantities, and therefore cannot stand in ratios with finite magnitudes. Cavalieri, respecting this restriction, treats as ratios only the relationships of the sections to each other, and even then he compares the sections only as they comprise "all the lines" associated with some figure.

Newton goes further than Cavalieri in conceiving figures to be generated, rather than covered or "retraced," by motion. But he follows the same strategy in using the continuity of motion to make sure of exhausting the elements (in his case points, in Cavalieri's, lines) contained in a higher-dimensional object (for Newton a line, for Cavalieri a plane figure), and also in carefully restricting the contexts in which infinitely small magnitudes are taken into comparison.

Carl Boyer gives a lucid account of how Newton first uses "the idea of an indefinitely small rectangle or 'moment' of area" to find the areas under curves:

> Let the curve be so drawn that for the abscissa x and the ordinate y the area is $z = (n/(m+n))ax^{((m+n)/n)}$. Let the moment or infinitesimal increase in the abscissa ... be o. The new abscissa will then be $x+o$ and the augmented area, $z+oy = (n/(m+n))a(x+o)^{((m+n)/n)}$. If in this expression we apply the binomial theorem, divide throughout by o, and then neglect the terms still containing o, the

---

[41] Cavalieri broadens the usual notion of "tangent," to include lines that intersect vertices formed by rectilinear sides and lines that coincide with boundaries at more than one point. This lets him apply the method to rectilinear figures.

[42] Cavalieri 1635, Def. I of Book II.

[43] Cavalieri once says "plane figures are to be conceived by us as like cloth made up of parallel threads, and also solids as like books composed out of parallel pages" (1647, 3). Despite its lack of fit with Cavalieri's many more careful pronouncements, this passage was taken as the clearest expression of his view. Cf. Jesseph 1999a, 179.

result will be $y = ax^{(m/n)}$. That is, if the area is given by $z = (n/(m+n))ax^{((m+n)/n)}$, the curve will be $y = ax^{(m/n)}$ [and conversely].[44]

In Newton's later presentation, the fundamental role played by rates of change is explicit.[45] He considers the moment o as an indefinitely small interval of time and calculates the increase in length in terms of the "fluxion" of x, that is, the rate at which the one-dimensional spatial quantity is "generated." Newton finds the ratio of the change in the x- and y-coordinates as o "vanishes" (i.e., approaches zero). Thus the momentary increments of x and y are not compared directly with the quantities but occur only in the context of their ratio to each other.

In *Principia Mathematica*, Newton grounds his procedure on the principle that ratios as well as quantities "which in any finite time constantly tend to equality, and which before the end of that time approach so close to one another that their difference is less than any given quantity," become "ultimately equal."[46] The "ultimate ratio" is considered in place of the indefinitely small amounts by which the quantities change as the temporal interval "vanishes."[47] Newton thus sees a clear difference between his procedure and the use of infinitesimals. He emphasizes that he regards "only [the] first proportion when nascent" of "moments" whose magnitude is not considered. Here, *moments* means the "instantaneous increments and decrements" by which a quantity of any kind increases or decreases as a function of a variable.[48] It is essential that "indeterminate and variable" quantities be considered as "increasing or decreasing as if by a continual motion or flux."[49] Newton explicitly appeals to considerations involving motion to justify the supposition of an "ultimate" ratio:

> It may be objected that there is no such thing as an ultimate proportion of vanishing quantities, inasmuch as before vanishing the proportion is not ultimate, and after

[44] Boyer 1949, 191.

[45] Boyer observes that rates of change are in fact fundamental from the beginning: Newton obtains an expression for area "by a consideration of the momentary increase of the area at the point in question. In other words, whereas previous quadratures had been found by means of the equivalent of the definite integral defined as the limit of a sum, Newton here first determined the rate of change of the area, and then from this found the area itself by what we should now call the indefinite integral of the function representing the ordinate. It is to be noted, furthermore, that the process which is made fundamental in this proposition is the determination of rates of change. In other words, what we should now call the derivative is taken as the basic idea and the integral is defined in terms of this" (1949, 191).

[46] Newton 1999, 433.

[47] We could say that because terms in o no longer occur in arithmetical calculations, it is not necessary to drop them. In fact, at this stage Newton typically does not express his reasoning algebraically. But where he does, in the *De Quadratura* of 1704, his justification for neglecting terms in o is that they "come to vanish"; in their place, he considers their "last ratio" (Whiteside 1967–1981, vol. VIII 126–29).

[48] Newton speaks of "every quantity that is, without addition or subtraction, generated from any roots or terms: in arithmetic by multiplication, division, or extraction of the root; in geometry by the finding either of products and roots or of extreme and mean proportionals. Quantities of this sort are products, quotients, roots, rectangles, squares, cubes, square roots, cube roots, and the like" (1999, 647).

[49] Op. cit., 647.

vanishing it does not exist at all. But by the same argument it could equally be contended that there is no ultimate velocity of a body reaching a certain place at which
the motion ceases; for before the body arrives at this place, the velocity is not the
ultimate velocity, and when it arrives there, there is no velocity at all. But the answer
is easy; to understand the ultimate velocity as that with which a body is moving,
neither before it arrives at its ultimate place and the motion ceases, nor after it has
arrived there, but at the very instant when it arrives, that is, the very velocity with
which the body arrives at its ultimate place and with which the motion ceases. And
similarly the ultimate ratio of vanishing quantities is to be understood not as the
ratio of quantities before they vanish or after they have vanished, but the ratio with
which they vanish.[50]

The same reasoning applies to the "first" ratio with which "nascent" quantities begin
to exist. We will now see that Hobbes's mathematics also involves consideration of
"instantaneous" increments in, and rates by, which quantities are generated by motion.
In section 6 I bring out the advantages of this approach, and in section 7 I show how
Hobbes defends it against Wallis's objections.

5 THE FOUNDATIONS OF MATHEMATICS IN HOBBES' *DE CORPORE*

As a materialist, Hobbes regards only bodies and their accidents as real; as a nominalist, he takes the reality of accidents to derive from that of particular bodies. So for the
subject matter of mathematics to be real (as is required of a genuine science), it must
either belong to particular bodies or be caused by them, specifically by their motion.
Furthermore, according to Hobbes, reasoning is not scientific unless it begins from
definitions that incorporate the "cause or generation" (if any) of the things defined.[51]
Hence mathematics should be founded on definitions that involve motions which generate the objects and properties it studies.

Although this requirement on definitions arises from Hobbes's broader philosophical views, he can (and does) argue that it is met by Euclid's definitions of particular
figures, such as solids of revolution (see section 7 below).

Hobbes defines magnitude as extension that is inseparable from any particular
body.[52] He defines dimensions as spaces passed through by moving bodies. Length is
the space traversed by a body whose magnitude "is not at all considered," which body
is itself a point. Surface (or "superficies") is a space consisting of two dimensions, "one

---

[50] Newton 1999, 442.

[51] *Concerning Body* I.6.13, *EW* 1:82.

[52] This is in contrast to place: over time, any one place can be possessed by different bodies, and
different places can be possessed by the same body (*De Corpore* II.8.5).

whereof to every several part of the other is applied whole"; it is traversed by a body "considered as long," whose length is the space "applied whole," in succession, to each part of the other. Solid is, likewise, a space "consisting of three dimensions, any two whereof are applied whole to every part of the third," and is made by the movement of a body "considered as having superficies."[53]

The extension possessed or generated by a body is relevant for mathematics only as it is "determined." As Hobbes explains, mathematics is concerned to answer questions of the form "How much?" When "it is asked, for example, *How long is the journey?* it is not answered indefinitely, *length*"; rather it is "answered determinately, the journey is a hundred miles," or "at least in some such manner, that the magnitude of the thing enquired after may by certain limits be comprehended in the mind."[54] Accordingly, Hobbes understands "determination" as finding (or "making known") the limits within which a portion of extension lies. Extension that is determined is called "quantity." It can be determined in two ways. The first is "by the sense, when some sensible object," such as "a line, a superficies or solid, of a foot or cubit, marked out in some manner," is "set before it"; quantity known in this way is called "exposed." The second is "by comparison with some exposed quantity," as when (in the above example) the journey is compared with a mile, or a pace "or some other measure, determined and made known" through perception. For Hobbes, then, portions of extension whose limits are grasped immediately by sense are the measures to which all quantity is ultimately referred. For an "exposed quantity" to fulfill this role, it must be "some standing or permanent thing, such as is marked out in consistent or durable matter," or at least something that can be "recalled" to sense.[55]

Measurement proceeds by comparing the place filled by the exposed quantity with that of the quantity it measures. Hobbes's criterion for the equality of bodies is that each can fill the place of the other. He notes that two bodies that differ in shape can fill the same place if one's "figure" is "understood to be reducible to" the other's by rearrangement ("flexion or transposition") of its parts. This criterion for equality, together with the part-whole relation, yields definitions of greater and less: a body is greater than another when a part of it fills the same place as the whole of the other and less than another when the whole of it fills the same place as a part of the other.[56]

This account of how extension comes to be considered mathematically matches the procedure of Euclid's *Elements*. We noted above that Euclid does not state general conditions under which magnitudes can be compared in respect of size, but rather presupposes operations by which lines and planar regions can be made to coincide. Hobbes observes, more specifically, that Euclid fails to define equality (sameness of size) or measure (how magnitudes of known size are to be compared with others) but instead

[53] *Concerning Body* II.8.12, *EW* 1:111.
[54] *Concerning Body* II.12.1, *EW* 1:139.
[55] *Concerning Body* II.12.2, *EW* 1:139–40.
[56] *Concerning Body* II.8.13, *EW* 1:112.

takes as an axiom that "those things which lie upon one another all the way are equal."[57] Hobbes assumes that the point of lying magnitudes on one another is to relate them—as equal, greater, or less—to measures whose quantity is known prior to any such operation. His complaint with Euclid is that Euclid's criterion of equality applies only to lines and surfaces, because magnitudes of other kinds cannot literally coincide, i.e. be made to touch in every part.[58] Hobbes's own criterion applies to solids (because the places compared can be three-dimensional) and to portions of extension whose parts cannot be made to coincide all at once but only by rearrangement. While Hobbes uses the homely example of comparing volumes of liquid to motivate his innovation, it serves to ground the techniques of Cavalieri. For in comparing totalities of lines, Cavalieri often takes the lines of a figure in a different order than they are generated by the transit of the plane.[59]

It remains to be explained how magnitudes that are not spatial can be objects of mathematical reasoning. According to Hobbes, time, velocity, and number are "exposed" by relating them to quantities of extension. Number is quantity "in no other sense than as a line is quantity divided into equal parts."[60] Hobbes notes that since it is sensible to ask "How much?" with respect to time, time must have some quantity, which can only be a length; furthermore, "because length cannot be an accident of time, which is itself an accident, it is the accident of a body." We then "determine how much the time is" by "supposing some body to be moved over" this length,[61] and the body must be supposed to move uniformly, "that time may be divided and compounded as often as there shall be need."[62] It is not clear what resources Hobbes can use to define uniformity of motion. For on his account, the measurement of velocity requires a measure of time,[63] and it is thus circular to define uniformity in terms of equality of velocity.[64] Without

[57] EW 7:192.

[58] EW 7:197.

[59] In lectures delivered in the mid-1660s, Isaac Barrow, the first Lucasian Professor of Mathematics, similarly broadens the notion of congruence and explicitly acknowledges Hobbes as a source (1734, 198). Barrow makes explicit that he allows change in the order of parts (that are compared in terms of the places they occupy) in order to accommodate Cavalieri's procedure (op. cit., 196–97). See Mahoney 1990b, 192.

[60] EW 7:194. In Concerning Body, Hobbes grants that number may be exposed either by points or "the names of number, one, two, three, &c." (II.12.5, EW 1:141) and more generally that an exposed magnitude is "either perceived by sense, or so defined by words, that it may be comprehended by the mind" (II.13.1, EW 1:144). He drops this from Six Lessons, presumably because conceding so much autonomy to arithmetic would weaken his case against Wallis, namely that geometrical results cannot be refuted by arithmetical reasoning.

[61] EW 7:194.

[62] Concerning Body II.12.4, EW 1:141.

[63] Specifically, we need one line (CD), traversed by a body in uniform motion, to exhibit the time of the motion, and another (AB) to expose the space traversed "by the body, whose velocity would determine"; setting the bodies at C and A respectively, "we say the velocity of the body [at] A is so great, that it passeth over the line AB in the same time in which the body C passeth over the line CD with uniform motion" (Concerning Body II.12.6, EW 1:142).

[64] Hobbes's definition, "that swiftness by which equal lengths are passed in equal parts of time, is called uniform swiftness of motion" (II.8.17, EW 1:114), manifests the circularity. For the criterion for equality of parts of time requires a prior definition of uniformity. Cf. Jesseph 1999a, 84 n.12.

trying to defend Hobbes, we may note that in general he assumes, as primitive, the motions (and features thereof) that generate magnitudes of particular kinds.

In contrast to measurement and equality, Hobbes more drastically revises the classical conception of lower-dimensional magnitudes (points and lines).[65] By his definition, a body that moves is a point "when [its] magnitude be not at all considered," and "the way it makes is called a *line*, or one single dimension." Although the magnitude of the body is neglected, it must have some, for "there be no body which has" none.[66] Hobbes defines a plane as "that which is described by a strait line so moved, that all the several points thereof describe several strait lines."[67]

From his account of how points, lines, and planes are generated, Hobbes deduces several fundamental propositions of geometry, thus showing them to qualify as knowledge "from causes." That any three points lie in one plane, for instance, follows from the consideration that a plane may be generated by, specifically, rotating a line: "For as any two points, if they are connected by a strait line, are understood to be in the same plane which the strait line is; so, if that plane be circumduced around the same strait line, it will in its revolution take in any third point, no matter how it be situate[d]; and then the three points will be all in that plane."[68]

6 THE ADVANTAGES OF HOBBES'S APPROACH

Hobbes's definition has the consequence that points can be compared with one another with respect to size, which he exploits in his account of "endeavor," or *conatus*. Hobbes defines endeavor as *"motion made through the length of a point, and in an instant or point of time."* It is "to be conceived . . . so as neither the quantity of the time in which, nor of the line in which [the motion] is made, may in demonstration be at all brought into comparison with the quantity of that time, or of that line of which [these are] parts." However, endeavors can be compared to one another as greater and less, just as points

---

[65] Hobbes claims that his definitions express what Euclid must reasonably have meant. The definition of point, as that "which has no part" (Euclid 1956, 153), can be "accurately" or "candidly" taken to mean *"a point is that which is undivided,"* and since division as Hobbes understands it is "an act of the understanding" (cf. *Concerning Body* II.7.5, 95–96), "there is no part where there is no consideration of one." Thus Euclid's definition agrees with Hobbes's. To understand a point instead as incapable of division would be to make it a nonquantity, and "if Euclid had meant it so in his definition, . . . he might have defined it more briefly, but ridiculously, thus, *a point is nothing.*" Similarly, the definition of line, as "length which has no breadth" (loc. cit.), must be taken to mean "a body whose length is considered without its breadth." For it would be "absurd" to understand a line as something that has length and lacks breadth (*EW* 7:201–2).

[66] *Concerning Body* II.8.12, *EW* 1:111.

[67] *Concerning Body* II.14.2, *EW* 1:179.

[68] *Concerning Body* II.14.5, *EW* 1:183.

can.[69] Specifically, the quantity (called *impetus*) of an endeavor is the "swiftness or velocity of" a moving body, "considered" at some instant. While the prospect of points' differing in size is jarring, we can use the notion of endeavor (reversing Hobbes's own order of explanation) to make sense of it. If we think of a point as the increase in "the way made" by a body at an instant, it is clear that its length will depend on the speed with which it is moving then. So for Hobbes "points" play the same role and are subject to the same kind of explanation[70] as "moments" in the Newtonian calculus.

Hobbes claims that "the little that I shall say concerning geometry" in *Concerning Body* "shall be such only as is new, and conducing to natural philosophy."[71] Useful as his approach may be for Newton's theory of motion, he is of course not concerned with it but rather with Galileo's. His notion of quantity of endeavor, in particular, remedies a defect in Galileo's reasoning.[72]

Galileo works in classical proportion theory, in which quantities of different kinds (such as distance and time) cannot have a ratio to one another. Thus he can relate them only indirectly. Specifically, Galileo assumes that distances are as the speeds with which they are covered in uniform motion (in a given time). The ratios of pairs of homogeneous quantities can be compared, however. So Galileo proves, in *Two New Sciences*, that the distance traversed in uniformly accelerated motion is as the square of the time by showing that two lengths of space stand in a ratio "duplicate" to that of the times in which they are traversed. He treats the speed of motion as an "intensive" magnitude, meaning that it increases through the accumulation of "degrees."[73] The main idea of the proof is to relate the distances covered at two times to the degrees of speed then attained. But rather than explaining how (as we would put it) distance and degree of speed increase as functions of a common variable (the time), Galileo uses his "mean speed theorem" to relate the distances to uniform motions that correlate with degrees of speed. (The theorem asserts that a given space is traversed by a uniformly accelerated motion in the same time that it would be traversed by a uniform motion with half the uniformly accelerated motion's final speed.) Because the theorem licenses the substitution of uniform motions for the uniformly accelerated one, the distances can at last be related to the times. But because Galileo understands the quantity of speed in terms of degrees rather than as a relationship between distance and time, a degree of speed cannot simply be equated with the instantaneous rate of a uniform motion, and the justification for this crucial move is never made clear.

[69] *Concerning Body* III.15.2, *EW* 1:206.

[70] Hobbes's account is in fact subtler (or less intelligible, depending on your point of view) than Newton's. For in *De Corpore* II.8.10–11, Hobbes appears to deny that any motion begins (or ends) at a unique place and time, which Newton takes for granted.

[71] III.15.1, *EW* 1:204.

[72] Here I follow Blay 1998, ch. 3. For a different and fuller account of Galileo's importance for Hobbes's mathematical work, see Jesseph 1999a and 2004.

[73] "Intensive" magnitudes were traditionally contrasted with "extensive" ones as those which increase by the addition of degrees rather than of parts.

Hobbes obviates the comparison with uniform motion by asserting that accelerations and distances are related in the way required: "during any time whatsoever, howsoever the impetus [quantity of endeavor] be increased or decreased, the length of the way passed over shall be increased or decreased in the same proportion."[74] His argument is that "in equal times the ways that are passed are as the velocities, and the impetus is the velocity they go withal, reckoned in all the several points of the times."[75] Because each impetus is reckoned in a "point" —that is, a least part—of time, it is not capable of increase or decrease. Therefore the conception of endeavor as motion at an instant builds in, as it were, the uniformity required to conclude that the distances passed in equal times are as the velocities.

Although Hobbes foregrounds the novel results achieved by his method, many of them are false and thus do not show it to best advantage. Its merits are more apparent (together with its defects) in Hobbes's proof of Proposition I.42 of Archimedes's *On the Sphere and Cylinder*. Hobbes gives the proof to illustrate how quantities "are determinable from the knowledge of their causes, namely, from the comparison of the motions by which they are made; and that more easily than from the common elements of geometry."[76]

The proposition, in Hobbes's wording, is that "the superficies of any portion of a sphere is equal to that circle, whose radius is a strait line drawn from the pole [vertex] of the portion to the circumference of [the portion's] base."[77] Archimedes proves the result by "exhaustion," an arduous method that Cavalieri's and other infinitistic techniques were meant to supplant.[78] In a classical exhaustion proof, a surface bounded by curves is supposed to be inscribed and circumscribed by regular polygons, which can (by increasing the number of sides and reducing their length) be made to differ in area by less than any given amount. The aim is to show that the surface is equal in area to some given figure, and the strategy is to suppose them unequal and then derive a contradiction by relating the polygons to the given figure. In this case Archimedes first supposes that the hollow spherical portion exceeds the circle and lets the ratio of the circumscribed to the inscribed polygon be less than that of the surface to the circle. The polygons are related to the circle by comparing each with inscribed and circumscribed conical figures generated by a motion of the circle. Once the contradiction is derived,

---

[74] This simplifies Galileo's reasoning in an obvious manner. In *Two New Sciences*, Galileo represents the increasing degrees of speed as parallels along an axis (representing the time) and represents the distances as segments of a distinct line, without explicitly relating the figures to one another. For Hobbes, "the same line shall represent both the way of the body moved, and the several impetus or degrees of swiftness wherewith the way is passed over" (*Concerning Body* III.15.2, EW 1:207). Hobbes uses this simpler diagram to prove the theorem in *De Corpore* III.16.3.

[75] *Concerning Body* III.15.2, EW 1:207.

[76] *Concerning Body* III.17.13, EW I:265.

[77] *Concerning Body* III.17.13, EW I:265. Hobbes does not make explicit (as Archimedes does) that the portion must be smaller than a hemisphere.

[78] Many practitioners of the techniques claimed they served only to find results (i.e., heuristically), which could then be rigorously proved by exhaustion. See Boyer 1949, 123–24.

the reasoning has to be repeated to show that contradiction follows from supposing that the circle exceeds the portion of the sphere.

In contrast to this double *reductio*, Hobbes's proof is direct and involves only one auxiliary figure. He considers the hollow spherical portion and the circle to be generated by the rotation (around the sphere's axis) of an arc and a straight line, respectively, contained in a single plane. The line that is to be the circle's radius, originally drawn from the vertex to the base, is redrawn tangent to the vertex. The auxiliary figure is the conical surface generated by the rotation of the arc's "subtense" (chord), which is just the original line from vertex to base.

To show that the portion of the sphere is equal to the circle, Hobbes argues that both exceed the conical surface by the same amount. The argument turns on his doctrine that angles "of contingence," formed by the intersection of a straight line and a curve, and angles formed by two straights cannot be compared in respect of quantity. This was a familiar solution to difficulties in applying proportion theory to angles formed by curves, but Hobbes gives it a novel basis, arguing that the two kinds of angles must have different measures because they are generated differently.[79] Angles are generated by "pulling apart or separating" two straight lines, originally supposed to coincide, "in such manner that their concurrence in one point will still remain." The separation is brought about either by rotating one line around this point, in which case the line remains straight, and the "quantity of separation or divergence is an *angle* simply so called" and is measured by the length of the arc produced; or by "continual flexion or curvation in every imaginable point" of one line, in which case the quantity of separation is called an "angle of contingence" and is measured by the degree of bending.[80] Hobbes conceives the separation between the arc and tangent as the result of curving or flexing. He concludes that the surfaces generated by their rotation must exceed the conical surface by the same amount because the angle of contingence between them is "nothing" compared with the angle between the tangent and chord.

The argument lacks rigor. Hobbes does not justify the assumption that the size of the object generated varies as the angle with the axis of rotation.[81] And his application of the incommensurability doctrine appears illegitimate. Hobbes takes it that because the angle between the arc and chord is not comparable with the angle between the tangent and chord, the surfaces created by rotating the arc and tangent are the same in size. But he does not make explicit whether the "continual" bending that produces an angle-bounding curve must have the same degree at every point.[82] Without this

---

[79] *Cf.* Jesseph 1999a, 168.

[80] *Concerning Body* II.14.7, *EW* 1:184.

[81] It holds in this case insofar as (on the usual formula) the surface area of a conical shell is the product of π times the base and hypotenuse of the generating triangle, and the length of the base varies with the angle between hypotenuse and axis. (Notice that the shell and circle will be equal in area if the triangle's base is equal in length to the circle's radius. Thus the restriction Hobbes omits, to portions smaller than a hemisphere, is essential.)

[82] Hobbes indicates in a later work that the quantity of an angle of contingence can be determined only if the curve diverges "uniformly" from the straight line, "as in circles" (*EW* 7:195).

assumption, we can conceive the arc between vertex and base stretched more tautly (as it were) to make a "higher" arch, whose rotation would generate a shape like the top half of an acorn. The angle it forms with the tangent will still be incommensurable with the angle between the tangent and the chord, but (because the bending is greater) it will be greater than the angle formed by the arc that generates the spherical portion. And it is evidently closer to the vertical. So by Hobbes's reasoning, the resulting shape will be larger than the hollow spherical surface. Since not every figure created by rotating a line that makes an angle of contingence with the tangent will be the same in size, we cannot assume that every one will equal the size of the circle.

Yet for all its crudity, Hobbes's proof embodies an important insight. The calculus powerfully proves theorems of geometry by representing quantities in terms of rates of change (what Newton calls "continual motion or flux") in other quantities. For instance, the formula for the volume of a sphere ($4/3\pi r^3$) is found by integrating as the surface area of a disc or sphere increases as a function of distance (from center to periphery). The reasoning is motivated and given significance by conceiving the sphere as an aggregation of (vanishingly thin) discs or spherical shells,[83] but it does not require construction of auxiliary figures. (Compare Euclid's tortuous proof by exhaustion of the result as stated in proportion theory.[84]) To be clear, Hobbes is not yet reasoning in the manner of the calculus when he conceives the spherical portion, circle, and conical surface to be generated by rotation. Little is gained by considering their increase as a function of time, because their increments are in a constant ratio (fixed by the initial configuration of the arc, tangent, and chord) from which their size can be directly computed. But it is distinctive of calculus to suppose that the arc diverges from the tangent at an ever-changing rate, so that the angle between them is negligible compared with that between the tangent and chord, yet the spherical portion remains distinct from the conical surface. (Compare Newton's treatment of infinitesimal increments in the abscissa.)[85] On Hobbes's view this rate has obvious physical significance, because he conceives the process by which lines diverge as a motion (specifically "pulling apart"), and is clearly relevant for mathematics, given his view that objects are understood in terms of their causes.

7 The Clash between Wallis and Hobbes

To this point, I have tried to bring out how Hobbes's view represents an important strain of foundational thought, one that has faded from view as mathematics has become

---

[83]   See Sawyer 1961, Ch. 9, and Priestley 1979, 181–86.

[84]   "Spheres are to one another in triplicate ratio of their respective diameters," *Elements* XII.18.

[85]   It bears noting that Wallis ultimately came to accept Hobbes's view regarding angles of contingence, after having harshly criticized it. See Jesseph 1999a, 184, and Loget 2002.

more abstract and symbolic. But it was not unopposed even in the seventeenth century. Consideration of Wallis's view will round out the contextual picture.

Wallis's most important work, the *Arithmetica Infinitorum* ("Arithmetic of Infinites"), is conceived as a successor to Cavalieri's "geometry of indivisibles."[86] Its overall aim is to find quadratures—for instance (in modern notation), the ratio of the area under the curve $y = x^k$ over the interval $[0, a]$ to that of the rectangle with base a and height a^k. Wallis follows Cavalieri's strategy of considering both figures as collections of infinitely narrow sections perpendicular to the base. His innovation is to use arithmetical reasoning to find sums of infinite series. Thus he finds the limiting value $1:k + 1$ for the ratio in question, which can be expressed[87] as $(0^k + 1^k + 2^k + \ldots n^k) : (n^k + n^k + n^k \ldots n^k)$, by applying what he calls "induction"[88] to series of the form $(0^k + 1^k + 2^k + \ldots n^k) / ((n+1)n^k)$. Wallis claims to "enlarge geometry" by producing "the quadrature not only of the simple parabola, shown by a new method, but also of all higher parabolas."[89] Next, he uses interpolation techniques to find limits for series with fractional, irrational, and negative exponents. The treatise culminates in an expression for the ratio of the areas of a square on a circle's radius and a quadrant of a circle—that is, the value of $4/\pi$—as a "continued fraction," $(3 \times 3 \times 5 \times 5 \times 7 \times 7 \ldots)/(2 \times 4 \times 4 \times 6 \times 6 \ldots)$.[90]

A striking feature of Wallis's reasoning is how freely he symbolizes the results of operations, the possibility of which it was bold to suppose. Wallis was the first to use the symbol ∞ for infinity, specifically for the totality of the "altitudes" (vertical sections) in which a plane figure is supposed to consist. In his derivation of the continued fraction, Wallis introduces the notation "$m\sim: 1 \mid 3/2$" to denote "the term interpolated between the first and second of the series 1, 3/2, 15/8, *etc.* (which are obtained by the continued multiplication of the numbers 1, 3/2, 5/4, *etc.*)." This term is to 1 as the circumscribed square is to the circle.

Wallis expresses his results as ratios.[91] He claims the expression "$1: m\sim: 1 \mid 3/2$" "explains" [*explicare*] the ratio of the circle just as "systematically" as the notation "$1:1\sqrt{2}$," already in use, expresses the ratio of a square's side to its diagonal (Stedall 2004, 163). His assertion of proportionality in the case of quantities found by symbolic means rests on his understanding of ratio and number. First, he identifies ratios with numbers. Although Wallis's techniques are algebraic, he calls his reasoning "arithmetical"

---

[86] 1656a, "*Dedicatio*" (n.p.).

[87] See Ferraro 2008, 10–11.

[88] This is "not mathematical induction in its modern formal sense, but an argument from precedent, an assumption that a pattern or procedure once established could be continued indefinitely" (in the words of Stedall 2001, 3).

[89] Stedall 2004, 3.

[90] Letting R stand for the radius, if the quadrant is considered as a collection of vertical sections, then the length of a section at distance r from the center is $(R^2 - r^2)^{1/2}$. So the ratio of the quadrant's area to the square's is as the sum, as r goes from 0 to R, of terms $(R^2 - r^2)^{1/2}$ to the sum of R taken as many times. Wallis finds the limiting values by a complicated interpolation; see Scott 1938, 47–60.

[91] The first occurrence of ∞, for instance, is the claim that each altitude is related to the totality as 1 to ∞, "or as an aliquot part, infinitely small"; *Treatise on Conic Sections* (published together with the *Arithmetica Infinitorum*), 1656b, 4.

because he conceives of arithmetic as "universal algebra."[92] He thus effectively extends the notion of ratio (now understood as number) to all relationships treated in algebra.

Hobbes vigorously criticizes this aspect of Wallis's reasoning. Just as an object denoted as a result of the square-root operation can stand in a ratio to 1 on Wallis's view, so the object denoted by the lower symbol in a fractional expression can divide the object denoted by the higher. According to the classical tradition, however, *number* means positive integer, so the operations of extracting roots, dividing, and subtracting are in many cases not defined. Assuming that a quotient (the result of division) must be a number in this sense, Hobbes maintains that quotients exist only when there are "aliquot parts." He gives the example of "incommensurable lines" to show that "there [may be] no quotient" even when there exists a proportion, and he concludes that "setting their symbols one above another doth not make a quotient."[93] Thus, on his view, Wallis fails to guarantee the reference of his symbols.

In its general form, the objection has force. The worry that (some of) Wallis's interpolated terms do not correspond to anything in a number family was shared by the great mathematician Pierre de Fermat.[94] But Hobbes does not just criticize Wallis's extension of the number concept; he rejects any extension, even to fractions. This peculiarly restrictive view considerably diminishes arithmetic's interest and importance.

When Hobbes goes on the defensive, he again takes an extreme position on the applicability of arithmetical operations. In 1661, Hobbes published a solution to the duplication of the cube (which ranked alongside squaring the circle as a great unsolved problem). Wallis gave an algebraic argument refuting the solution. In reply, Hobbes maintains that "the examination of geometric problems by algebra is generally useless."[95] Now it was not crazy to deny that solutions to geometrical problems should be evaluated by algebraic criteria. Newton took a similar position, on the basis of which he criticized Descartes. To recap, the initial aim of Descartes's procedure is to express the relationship between the given and sought magnitudes as an algebraic equation. Equations are not considered to define curves until the geometrical stage, in which curves taken as "known" are used to construct solutions. We saw that Descartes seeks to exclude means of construction that are not sufficiently "exact." His criterion of admissibility is formulated algebraically: "All the points of [curves] which we may call 'geometric', that is, which admit of precise and exact measurement, must bear some relation to the points of one straight line which can be expressed by an equation, the same for all points."[96] Descartes also upholds the traditional view that a solution should be constructed using the "simplest" admissible curve. His measure of simplicity is the algebraic degree of the equation expressing the curve, which, he claims, correlates with constructional simplicity (so that, for example, the straight lines and

---

[92] 1657, 73.
[93] *EW* 7: 241.
[94] See Stedall 2004, xxvii.
[95] *OL* 4:294.
[96] Descartes 1952, 48.

circles used to solve "plane" problems have equations of second or lower degree).[97] Newton contends that Descartes's criteria for simplicity give the wrong results in particular cases[98] and are mistaken in principle. For whether a curve should be used for solving a problem depends on the manner of its construction, on which algebraic criteria have no bearing.[99] But Hobbes does not merely hold (with Newton) that solution techniques should be assessed using only geometrical criteria; he rejects the standard geometrical interpretation of (algebraically symbolized) arithmetical operations. Hobbes denies specifically[100] that multiplication can be applied to geometrical magnitudes without raising their dimension. But this is just what Descartes had shown. So Hobbes again condemns a generalizing move that was already accepted in his time and necessary for mathematics to advance.

In contrast, in defending the relevance of constructive procedures for mathematical knowledge, Hobbes takes a position that was to prove viable.

It is central to Wallis's view that arithmetical reasoning is more general than geometry. So, for instance, his justification for regarding proportions in general as numerical relationships is that every number can stand in a ratio with every other; geometrical magnitudes, in contrast, can stand in ratios only with others of the same dimension. Wallis's view of geometrical relationships as special cases of arithmetical ones comes out clearly in his discussion of conic sections. He observes that the curves are so called because the "cutting" of a solid by a plane is the simplest way to construct them. But, Wallis maintains, "beside the supposed construction of a Line or Figure, there is somewhat in the nature of it so constructed, which may be abstractly considered from such construction; and which doth accompany it though otherwise constructed than is supposed." To consider the curves "abstractly" is specifically to represent them by equations.[101] This "abstract mathematics"

> is of great use in all kinds of Mathematical considerations, whereby we separate what is the proper Subject of Inquiry, and upon which the Process proceeds, from the impertinences of the matter (accidental to it), appertaining to the present case or particular construction. For which reason, whereas I find some others (to make it look, I suppose, the more Geometrical) to affect Lines and Figures; I choose rather (where such things are accidental) to demonstrate universally from the nature of Proportions, and regular Progressions; because such Arithmetical

[97] See Descartes 1952, 13.

[98] See Guicciardini 2009, 65–73.

[99] "[I]t is not the equation but its description [i.e., manner of construction] which produces a geometrical curve. A circle is a geometrical line not because it is expressible by means of an equation but because its description (as such) is postulated" (Whiteside (ed.) 1967–1981, vol. V, 425). On the following page, Newton repeats that "It is not the simplicity of its equation, but the ease of its description, which primarily indicates that a line is to be admitted into the construction of problems . . . On the simplicity, indeed, of a construction the algebraic representation has no bearing."

[100] As Jesseph observes in his superb account of the exchange, 1999a, 263.

[101] See Boyer 1956, 110.

Demonstrations are more Abstract, and therefore more universally applicable to particular occasions. Which is one main design that I aimed at in this Arithmetick of Infinites.[102]

On this basis, Wallis argues that Hobbes's definitions involve notions "extrinsic" to mathematics. He charges that not only are they "clogged" with notions that are not necessary for the existence or our understanding of the *definitum* but they are "not reciprocal," meaning that some objects of the kind defined do not have the traits specified in the definition. Accordingly, against the definitions of a line and length (as, respectively, the "way made" and the "space passed through" by a body whose magnitude is not considered), Wallis objects that there can be a point "which is not a *Body*, much lesse *A Body moved*: and a *Line*, or *Length*, through which no body passeth." For instance, the earth's axis is a line that has length, "yet do I not believe that any Body doth, or ever did, passe directly from the one to the other Pole, to describe that Line."[103] Similarly, Hobbes's equality in terms of a comparison of places involves a "wholly extrinsecal" notion, "for Time, Tone, Numbers, Proportions, and many other quantities are capable of Equality, without any connotation of Place."[104]

Hobbes defends his approach by appealing to Euclid's precedent. In Book 11 of the *Elements*, Euclid defines the sphere, cone, and cylinder as products of circular motion by shapes around their own sides.[105] Hobbes asserts that these definitions are "convertible," or reciprocal, "except [unless] you think the globes of the sun and stars cannot be globes, unless they were made by the circumduction of a semicircle."[106] As Hobbes explains, not only are the "proper passions" derivable from these definitions "true of any other cylinder, sphere, or cone, though it were otherwise generated," but we can see their truth by conceiving or imagining that solid to be generated by the process in question.[107] This account generalizes to all geometrical propositions. For instance, we derive the proposition that any three points lie in one plane by supposing the plane in which the third point lies to be generated by the rotation of the line containing the other two.

---

[102] 1685, 292–93.

[103] 1656c, 53.

[104] Op. cit. 54.

[105] Specifically, a sphere is generated by one full revolution of a semicircle around its diameter, which is presumed fixed (Def. 14); a cone, by one full revolution of a right triangle around one side of the right angle, with the other side presumed fixed (Def. 18); and a cylinder, by one full revolution of a rectangular parallelogram around one side of a right angle, with the other side presumed fixed (Def. 21). It is noteworthy that Newton appeals to the same examples to show that a definition may "posit the reason for a mechanical genesis, in that the species of magnitude is best understood from the reason for its genesis" (Whiteside (ed.) 1967–1981, vol. VII, p. 291).

[106] *EW* 7:214.

[107] Hobbes's way of putting it is that "the description of the generation of any one" solid of revolution is "by the imagination applicable to all" figures of that kind (*EW* 7:214).

This account of how the properties of some figure generated by a canonical process can be ascribed to all figures of the same kind matches Kant's account of how
the properties shown to belong to a particular constructed figure can be so ascribed.
Kant claims that while an individual drawn figure "is empirical," it "nevertheless
serves to express the concept without damage to its universality," which is to say that
it represents all objects that "belong under the same concept." For "in the case of this
empirical [intuited object] we have taken account only of the action of constructing
the concept." Kant goes on to say[108] that the individual figure expresses the concept's
"schema," which he defines to mean "a general procedure . . . for supplying for a concept" images of individual objects falling under it.[109] This makes it plausible that by
"the action" of constructing, Kant means the procedure by which the figure is constructed. "Taking account only" of it screens off the figure's distinguishing features,
such as the length of its sides, so as to restrict attention to whatever follows from
the "general conditions of construction," which must hold for any figure of the type.

The position Hobbes takes in the dispute with Wallis remains relevant in another
way. Wallis regards mathematical objects, generally speaking, as an antecedently
existing totality. He claims to follow Euclid in "supposing" that infinite totalities
are given.[110] Hobbes understands this to mean that an infinite sequence of operations has been performed, which he rejects as absurd. On Hobbes's view, to say (for
instance) that space or time is infinitely divisible must not "be so understood, as
if there might be any infinite or eternal division," but rather "taken in this sense,
whatsoever is divided, is divided into such parts as may again be divided."[111] Refusal
to assert a claim that cannot be verified by a finite number of operations marks
constructivist and intuitionist views of mathematics. It leads Hobbes to criticize not
only Wallis,[112] but Euclid himself. According to Hobbes, the criterion for sameness
of ratio in terms of equimultiples requires an impossible "trial in all numbers," that
is, "an infinite time of trial, whether the equimultiples of the first and third, and
of the second and fourth, in all multiplications, do together exceed, together come
short, [or] are together equal."[113] Hence the "arithmetical" theory of ratios had to be
based on a new definition of proportionality, which is given in *De Corpore* 2.11.5.

---

[108] Kant 1998, 630–31.

[109] Op. cit. 273.

[110] Wallis argues that "when Infinites are proposed" in mathematics, it is not meant "that they should
actually Be, or be *possible to be performed*; but only that they be *supposed.*" To suppose, in particular,
that an operation can be infinitely continued is to take the infinitely many objects thus produced as
given. When Euclid claims, for example, that "the same [line segment] AB may be *Bisected* in M and
each of the halves in *m*, and so onwards, *Infinitely*: it is not his meaning when such continual section
is proposed) that it should be *actually done*, (for, who can do it?) but that it be *supposed*. And upon
such (*supposed*) section *infinitely continued*, the parts must be (*supposed*) *infinitely many*; for no *Finite*
number of parts would suffice for *Infinite* sections" (1671, n.p.).

[111] *Concerning Body* II.7.12, *EW* I:100.

[112] See Jesseph 1999a, 185–88.

[113] *EW* 7:242.

8 Hobbes's Account of Definition
and His Views on Science

According to Hobbes, science is attained by a "good and orderly method of proceeding from the elements, which are names, to assertions made by connexion of one of them to another," and thence to syllogisms in which assertions are connected to one another, which culminates in "a knowledge of all the consequences of" the names in question (*Leviathan* 5.25). Science is thus "conditional," as when we know (for example) "that, if the figure shown shall be a circle, then any straight line through the centre shall divide it into two equal parts" (9.52).

Given his emphasis on our prerogative to "impose" names through arbitrary definitions, it is tempting to equate Hobbes's view with the conventionalism of the logical positivists.[114] On the latter, in the classic formulation by A. J. Ayer, mathematics' immunity to empirical refutation is explained by our refusing to apply mathematical terms to putative counterexamples. So mathematical truths are "tautologies" in the sense that their negations contradict the rules for linguistic usage,[115] but these rules (and the definitions that express them) are only conventions. This understanding fits particularly well Hobbes's description of science in *Elements of Law* as "the remembrance of names or appellations of things, and how every thing is called, which is, in matters of common conversation, a remembrance of pacts and covenants of men made amongst themselves, concerning how to be understood of one another."[116]

However, Hobbes also identifies science as knowledge of causes.[117] As he himself argues, this means that "the cause and generation of such things, as have any cause or generation, ought to enter into their definitions":

> The end of science is the demonstration of the causes and generation of things; which if they be not in the definitions, they cannot be found in the conclusion of the first syllogism, that is made from those definitions; and if they be not in the first conclusion, they will not be found in any further conclusion deduced from that; and therefore, by proceeding in this manner, we shall never come to science.[118]

This requirement is obviously in tension with the view that definitions express arbitrary decisions concerning how words are to be used.

Following Jesseph and David Boonin-Vail,[119] I hold that the way to resolve these tensions is to clarify the sense in which definitions are "conventional." Although imposed

---

[114] This identification is made by R. S. Peters in 1979 and Michael Esfeld in 1995. Cf. Sorell 1986, 47–9, and Jesseph 2010, 123.

[115] Ayer 1952, 84.

[116] II.8, xii 176; *cf. De Corpore* IV.25.1.

[117] *De Corpore*, I.6.1–2.

[118] *Concerning Body* I.6.13, *EW* 1:82.

[119] See Boonin-Vail 1994, 31–34.

by our choice, rules for the meaning of words need not be arbitrary. Rather, we may choose to incorporate into a word's definition the cause of the object we wish to name by it, in conformity with our understanding of the object and the exigencies of scientific method. The problem is now to explain how we recognize definitions as appropriate, for the alternative to conventionalism seems to be to attribute to the definitions some kind of "self-evidence." [120] This view is suggested by Hobbes's claim that the nature of definition is to "raise an idea" of the thing defined.[121] But Hobbes lacks resources to explain self-evidence and can hardly claim it for his own first principles.

Careful consideration of how Hobbes lays foundations for geometry shows how experience (in this case, familiarity with mathematical practice) supplies a basis on which definitions can be judged.[122] Hobbes's definition of equality in terms of filling the same place is the linchpin of his account of geometry as scientific knowledge, for it ensures that locating figures at the same place demonstrates their equality by its "cause," and Hobbes regards generation in and movement into places as the main ways in which geometers traditionally introduced and compared objects. But prior to Hobbes's work, equality was not definitionally associated with these procedures; in Euclid's *Elements*, equality is not defined at all. Hobbes claims that where definitions are missing, "every one that will learn geometry must gather [them] from observing how the word to be defined is most constantly used."[123] On his view questions of equality, both in geometrical reasoning and everyday life, are in fact decided by generating figures at or moving bodies to common places. The correctness of his definition need not be immediately apparent to us (from our understanding of equality), because it can be shown by consideration of this practice. The grounding thus conferred on the definition is empirical, since for Hobbes there are two kinds of experience: that "of the effects of things that work upon us from *without*"; and that "men have from the proper use of names in language".[124]

This understanding of how mathematical definitions are assessed fits the strategies used to win acceptance for them. Cavalieri avoids difficulties associated with the composition of a whole from infinitely many parts by defining "all the lines" in terms of the sectioning of a figure by a continuously moving line. But this operation has clear precedent in classical geometry, and Cavalieri takes great care to show that the resulting magnitudes satisfy the criteria for application of the (geometrical) theory of ratios. And while Descartes does not explicitly claim to redefine the notion of exactness, he reconceives the conditions on its application, on close analogy with the traditional classification of solution techniques as plane or solid.

[120] Gauthier 1997 identifies this as the choice facing interpreters and cites F. S. McNeilly as holding the "self-evidence" view.

[121] Underlying this interpretation is the thought that the definition's adequacy is made apparent by its agreement with the idea. See Boonin-Vail 1994, 34.

[122] This extends to geometry Whelan's account of how definitions are justified outside science (1981, 70). This view is also suggested by Sacksteder's remarks in (1981).

[123] EW 7:229.

[124] EW 4:27.

Understanding the relationship between definitions and mathematical practice may also resolve the tension that arises between Hobbes's understanding of science as causal knowledge and his view of scientific propositions as necessary consequences of definitions, taken alone (without regard to the conventionality of definitions). A. P. Martinich argues that a definition cannot establish "something informative," and "any inference drawn from a definition will be similarly uninformative." There need not be "anything constructive," in particular, in such results. Yet science tells us "how things come to be. And if we think of constructive geometry, we see that new things, sometimes very complex, come to be."[125] Hobbes's account of scientific reasoning seems to leave no room for such an advance in knowledge.[126] But if definitions specify constructive procedures, then they contain information that the steps of constructive proof can exploit, while the inferences remain strict in the sense articulated by Hobbes and Kant: Only features that follow from the constructive procedure are considered.[127]

ACKNOWLEDGMENTS

Douglas Jesseph's studies are an indispensable starting point for anyone working on this topic, and my debt to them extends beyond the specific points attributed to him. I am grateful to Al Martinich and Kinch Hoekstra for helpful comments and to the Wissenschaftskolleg zu Berlin for access to research materials.

BIBLIOGRAPHY

Ayer, A. J. 1952. *Language, Truth, and Logic.* New York: Dover.

Barrow, Isaac. 1734. *The Usefulness of Mathematical Learning Explained and Demonstrated,* translated by John Kirkby. Printed for Stephen Austen at the Angel and Bible at St. Paul's Church.

Blay, Michel. 1998. *Reasoning with the Infinite,* translated by M. B. DeBevoise. Chicago: University of Chicago Press.

Boonin-Vail, David. 1994. *Thomas Hobbes and the Science of Moral Virtue.* Cambridge, UK: Cambridge University Press.

Bos, H. J. M. 2001. *Redefining Geometrical Exactness: Sources and Studies in the History of Mathematics and Physical Sciences.* New York: Springer-Verlag, 2001.

---

[125] 2005, 165.

[126] Similar concerns are raised by Philip Pettit (2009, 119).

[127] Martinich is still right to object that by Hobbes's lights the proofs are not strict, because they cannot be expressed as syllogisms (2005, 166–67). For a very clear exposition of the difficulties, see Friedman (1992, ch. 1). But when syllogistic reasoning was all there was to logic, its limitations were hard to appreciate. Even as sophisticated a thinker as Leibniz believed it was adequate for expressing Euclid's proofs. He claimed in a well-known 1684 paper that Christian Herlinus and Conrad Dasypodius successfully put the first books of Euclid's *Elements* into syllogistic form (1989, 27).

Boyer, Carl. 1949. *A History of the Calculus and Its Conceptual Development*. New York: Dover.

Boyer, Carl. 1956. *History of Analytic Geometry*. New York (Yeshiva University): Scripta Mathematica, 1956.

Boyer, Carl, and Uta Merzbach. 2001. *A History of Mathematics*, 3rd ed. Hoboken, NJ: Wiley.

Cavalieri, Bonaventura. 1635. *Geometria indivisibilibus continuorum nova quadam ratione promota*. Bologna: Jacobi Montij.

Cavalieri, Bonaventura. 1647. *Exercitationes geometricae sex*. Bologna: Jacobi Montij.

Courant, Richard, and Herbert Robbins. 1996. *What Is Mathematics?* 2nd ed., edited by Ian Stewart. New York: Oxford University Press.

Davis, Philip J. 1987. "When Mathematics Says No," in *No Way: The Nature of the Impossible*, edited by Philip J. Davis and David Park. New York: Freeman.

Descartes, Rene. 1952. *The Geometry of Rene Descartes*, translated by David Eugene Smith and Marcia Latham. New York: Dover.

Esfeld, Michael. 1995. *Mechanismus und Subjektivität in der Philosophie von Thomas Hobbes*. Stuttgart: Frommann-Holzboog.

Euclid. 1956. *The Thirteen Books of the Elements*, translated and edited by Thomas L. Heath. Vol. 1: Books I and II. New York: Dover.

Ferraro, Giovanni. 2008. *The Rise and Development of the Theory of Series Up to the Early 1820s*. New York: Springer.

Friedman, Michael. 1992. *Kant and the Exact Sciences*. Cambridge, MA: Harvard University Press.

Gauthier, David. 1997. "Hobbes on Demonstration and Construction." *Journal of the History of Philosophy* 35: 509–521.

Goldenbaum, Ursula, and Douglas Jesseph, eds. 2008. *Infinitesimal Differences: Controversies between Leibniz and his Contemporaries*. Berlin: de Gruyter.

Grant, Hardy. 1996. "Hobbes's Mathematics," in *The Cambridge Companion to Hobbes* (pp. 108–128), edited by Tom Sorell. Cambridge, UK: Cambridge University Press.

Grattan-Guinness, Ivor. 1996. "Numbers, Magnitudes, Ratios, and Proportions in Euclid's Elements: How Did He Handle Them?" *Historia Mathematica* 23: 355–375.

Guicciardini, Niccolò. 2009. *Isaac Newton on Mathematical Certainty and Method*. Cambridge, MA: MIT Press.

Hobbes, Thomas. 1904. *Leviathan*, edited by A. R. Waller. Cambridge, UK: Cambridge University Press.

Jesseph, Douglas. 1999a. *Squaring the Circle: The War Between Hobbes and Wallis*. Chicago: University of Chicago Press.

Jesseph, Douglas. 1999b. "The Decline and Fall of Hobbesian Geometry." *Studies in the History and Philosophy of Science* 30: 425–453.

Jesseph, Douglas. 2004. "Galileo, Hobbes, and the Book of Nature." *Perspectives on Science* 12: 191–211.

Jesseph, Douglas. 2010. "Scientia in Hobbes." In *Scientia in Early Modern Philosophy* (pp. 117–127), edited by T. Sorell, G. A. J. Rogers, and Jill Kraye. Dordrecht: Springer Netherlands.

Kant, Immanuel. 1998. *Critique of Pure Reason*, translated by Paul Guyer and Allen Wood. Cambridge, UK: Cambridge University Press.

Klein, Jacob. 1968. *Greek Mathematical Thought and the Origin of Algebra*, translated by Eva Brann. Cambridge, MA: MIT Press. Reprinted by Dover (New York), 1992.

Knorr, Wilbur. 1986. *The Ancient Tradition of Geometric Problems*. Boston: Birkhäuser. Reprinted by Dover (New York), 1993.

Leibniz, G. W. 1682. "The true proportion of the Circle to the Square circumscribed, expressed in Rational numbers ... Englished from the Leipsick Acta Eruditorum Number 11." *Philosophical Collections* 7 (April 1682). London: for Richard Chiswell, at the Rose and Crown in St. Paul's Church-yard.

Leibniz, G. W. 1989. *Philosophical Essays*, edited by, Roger Ariew and Daniel Garber. Indianapolis, IN: Hackett.

Loget, François. 2002. "Wallis entre Hobbes et Newton." *Revue d'histoire des mathématiques* 8: 207–262.

Mahoney, M. S. 1990a. "Infinitesimals and Transcendent Relations: The Mathematics of Motion in the Late Seventeenth Century," in *Reappraisals of the Scientific Revolution* (pp. 461–491), edited by David C. Lindberg and Robert S. Westman. Cambridge, UK: Cambridge University Press.

Mahoney, M. S. 1990b. "Barrow's Mathematics: Between Ancients and Moderns," in *Before Newton: The Life and Times of Isaac Barrow* (pp. 179–249), edited by Mordechai Feingold. Cambridge, UK: Cambridge University Press.

Mancosu, Paolo. 2008. "Descartes and Mathematics," in *A Companion to Descartes* (pp. 103–123), edited by Janet Broughton and John Carriero. Oxford, UK: Blackwell.

Martinich, A. P. 2005. *Hobbes*. New York: Routledge.

Newton, Isaac. 1999. *The Principia: A New Translation and Guide*, translated by I. Bernard Cohen and Anne Whitman. Berkeley and Los Angeles: University of California Press.

Palmieri, Paolo. 2001. "The Obscurity of the Equimultiples: Clavius' and Galileo's Foundational Studies of Euclid's Theory of Proportions." *Archive for History of Exact Sciences*: 555–597.

Pappus of Alexandria. 1986. Book 7 of the Collection, edited and translated by Alexander Jones. New York: Springer.

Peters, R. S. 1979. *Hobbes*. Westport, CT: Greenwood Press.

Pettit, Philip. 2009. *Made with Words: Hobbes on Language, Mind, and Politics*. Princeton, NJ: Princeton University Press.

Priestley, William McGowen. 1979. *Calculus: An Historical Approach*. New York and Berlin: Springer.

Ross, George MacDonald. 2009. *Starting with Hobbes*. London and New York: Continuum.

Sacksteder, William. 1981, "Some Ways of Doing Language Philosophy." *Review of Metaphysics* 34: 459–485.

Sawyer, W. W. 1961. *What Is Calculus About?* New York: Random House.

Scott, J. F. 1938. *The Mathematical Work of John Wallis*. London: Taylor and Francis. Reprinted by Chelsea (New York), 1981.

Scriba, Christoph J. 1983. "Gregory's Converging Double Sequence." *Historia Mathematica* 10: 274–285.

Shapin, Stephen, and Simon Schaffer. 1985. *Leviathan and the Air-Pump*. Princeton, NJ: Princeton University Press.

Sorell, Tom. 1986. *Hobbes*. London: Routledge and Kegan Paul.

Stedall, Jacqueline. 2001. "The Discovery of Wonders: Reading Between the Lines of John Wallis's Arithmetica Infinitorum." *Archive for History of Exact Sciences* 56: 1–28.

Stedall, Jacqueline. 2004. *The Arithmetic of Infinitesimals: John Wallis 1656*. New York: Springer.

Wallis, John. 1656a. *Arithmetica Infinitorum*. Oxford, UK: L. Litchfield for Thomas Robinson.

Wallis, John. 1656b. *De Sectionibus Conicis Tractatus*. Oxford, UK: L. Litchfield for Thomas Robinson.

Wallis, John. 1656c. *Due Correction for Mr. Hobbes: or Schoole Discipline, for not saying his Lessons Right*. Oxford, UK: L. Litchfield for Thomas Robinson.

Wallis, John. 1657. *Mathematica Universalis, in Opera Mathematica Pars Prima*. Oxford, UK: L. Litchfield for Thomas Robinson.

Wallis, John. 1671. *An Answer to Three Papers of Mr. Hobs, Lately Published in the Months of August, and this present September, 1671*. London: s.n., 1671.

Wallis, John. 1685. *A Treatise of Algebra, Both Historical and Practical*. London: John Playford for Richard Davis.

Whelan, Frederick. 1981. "Language and Its Abuses in Hobbes' Political Philosophy." *The American Political Science Review* 75: 59–75.

Whiteside, D. T. 1967–1981. *The Mathematical Papers of Isaac Newton*, 8 vols. Cambridge, UK: Cambridge University Press.

CHAPTER 5

···

NATURAL PHILOSOPHY
IN SEVENTEENTH-CENTURY
CONTEXT

···

DANIEL GARBER

NATURAL philosophy was important to Hobbes. In addition to standing at the foundation of his project of the *Elementa philosophiae*, it was something of independent interest to him, a domain in which he genuinely thought he had made a lasting contribution. Although Hobbes's natural philosophical thought was somewhat idiosyncratic, it is not without context. As a natural philosopher, Hobbes was deeply engaged with the scientific programs of his day. And, even though it is often thought that his natural philosophy was without significant influence, this is not entirely true. Although it may not have generated the intense discussion and debate that his political thought did, it was by no means ignored.

There are many aspects to the larger historical context of Hobbes's natural philosophical thought. There were his relations with English science, for a start. Hobbes was associated with the so-called Welbeck Academy, a group interested in questions of natural philosophy and that included people like Sir Charles Cavendish, Robert Payne, and Walter Warner.[1] And then, of course, there were his interactions with the Royal Society in the 1660s, including the debates with Robert Boyle over the latter's air pump experiments, an issue that has been much studied in recent years, as well as his less well-known exchanges with John Wallis over the theory of motion.[2] In Paris, there was his long association with the Mersenne circle, which included important scientific

---

[1] See Martinich 1999: 98–102; Malcolm 2002a: 10.

[2] On Hobbes's relations with the Royal Society, see Skinner 1969 and Malcolm 2002d. On Hobbes's critique of Wallis's *Mechanica*, see Jesseph 2006, and on their disputes in mathematics, see Jesseph 1999. Hobbes's exchanges with Boyle are central to Shapin and Schaffer 1985. Shapin and Schaffer have many illuminating things to say, but I fear that they may distort Hobbes's views, particularly on the vacuum, to make the dispute more political and theological on Hobbes's part than they were in actuality.

figures like Gassendi, Roberval, and Mersenne himself, as well as his interactions with the English expatriates Thomas White and Sir Kenelm Digby.[3] A complete study of the larger context of Hobbes's natural philosophical thought is far beyond the ambitions of this short chapter. Here, I would like to limit myself to Hobbes's relations with two contemporary figures. As is well known, Hobbes was a great admirer of Galileo, whom he considered as the first real physicist. And, as is also well known, Hobbes was a great rival and antagonist of Descartes. In the chapter that follows, I will try to illuminate Hobbes's natural philosophical thought by discussing it in the context of his two great contemporaries. I will then turn to the legacy of Hobbes's natural philosophy and show the way in which some distinctive features of his thought found their way into the natural philosophical thought of two great later thinkers, Spinoza and Leibniz.

1 HOBBES ON GALILEO: FOUNDER OF NATURAL PHILOSOPHY UNIVERSAL?

Hobbes was a great admirer of Galileo, as were many of his closest associates. Galileo was very much present in the discussions of the Welbeck Academy, with which Hobbes associated from his return to England in 1631.[4] Galileo was also quite central to the thought of Mersenne and his circle, with whom Hobbes was associated during his lengthy stays in Paris. Mersenne, in fact, had translated (or, better, paraphrased) two works of Galileo's for publication in French, the *Meccaniche* and the *Discorsi e dimostrazioni matematiche, intorno à due nuove scienze*, and had boldly presented a summary of the arguments for Copernicanism from the *Dialogo sopra i due massimi sistemi del mondo* in his *Questions Inouyës*.[5] While traveling in Italy in late 1635 or early 1636, Hobbes paid a visit to Galileo, then under house arrest at Arcetri, near Florence.[6] In the so-called *Critique du De mundo*, his extensive but unpublished response to Thomas White's *De mundo*, his first extensive writing on physics, Hobbes referred to Galileo as "not only the greatest [natural] philosopher of our time, but of all time."[7] In the *De corpore*, he praised Galileo as the founder of natural philosophy:

> After him [i.e., Copernicus] the Doctrine of the Motion of the Earth being now received, and a difficult Question thereupon arising concerning the Descent of

---

[3] On Hobbes's relations with Mersenne and the Mersenne circle, see, e.g., Beaulieu 1990, Sarasohn 1985, Paganini 2006, Malcolm 2002c. On some aspects of Hobbes's relations with White, see Gianni Paganini's extensive introduction to Hobbes 2010.

[4] See Jesseph 2004: 193–196.

[5] On Mersenne and Galileo, see Lenoble 1943: 357–360, 391–413, 461–471.

[6] See Martinich 1999: 90–91.

[7] *Critique du De mundo* 10.9: "Galileus, non modò nostri, sed omnium saeculorum philosophus maximus."

Heavy Bodies, *Galileus* in our time striving with that difficulty, was the first that opened to us the gates of Natural Philosophy Universal, which is the knowledge of the Nature of Motion. So that neither can the Age of Natural Philosophy be reckoned higher than to him.[8]

And, in the 1660 dialogue, *Examinatio et Emendatio Mathematicae Hodiernae*, he wrote:

the doctrine of motion is known to very few, notwithstanding the fact that the whole of nature, not merely that which is studied in physics, but also in mathematics, proceeds by motion. Galileo was the first who wrote anything on motion that was worth reading.[9]

There is no question about how important Galileo was for Hobbes.

One might reasonably conclude from this that Hobbes saw his own natural philosophy as continuous with that of Galileo. On one influential line of reasoning, the primary connection is methodological. On this reading, a central feature of Galileo's scientific work is his advocacy of the methodology of resolution and composition, which, on one reading, he, in turn, learned from the School of Padua. The claim, then, is that Galileo's influence on Hobbes was on his ideas of the method of procedure in natural philosophy.[10] Like Galileo, Hobbes thought that method was important for natural philosophy, and, like Galileo, Hobbes understood method in terms of resolution and composition. In the *De corpore*, he wrote:

The first beginnings, therefore, of knowledge, are the phantasms of sense and imagination; and that there be such phantasms we know well enough by nature; but to know why they be, or from what causes they proceed, is the work of ratiocination; which consists . . . in *composition,* and *division* or *resolution.* There is therefore no method, by which we find out the causes of things, but is either *compositive* or *resolutive,* or *partly compositive,* and *partly resolutive.* And the resolutive is commonly called *analytical* method, as the compositive is called *synthetical.*[11]

One can, in fact, argue that the methods of resolution and composition thread their way through all of Hobbes's philosophy, not only his natural philosophy but his political philosophy, and that this shows the deep influence Galileo had on his thought.

There is no question that method was important to Hobbes and that his thought was in many ways shaped by the distinction between resolution and composition. But the idea of method was widespread, as was the conception of method as including, in some sense or another, resolution or analysis and composition or synthesis. It is very difficult

---

[8] *Concerning Body* (London, 1656), Epistle Dedicatory (unpaginated).

[9] *Examinatio et Emendatio* (1660), p. 53, quoted in Jesseph 2004: 203.

[10] This position is argued most forcefully in Watkins 1965. In chapter 3, he gives the scientific background, and, in the succeeding chapters, he works this idea out in more detail.

[11] *Concerning Body* 6.1. For a development of Hobbes's views on method in general, see the chapter on logic in this *Handbook*.

to establish that Hobbes's particular versions of these procedures correspond to those of Galileo or that he derived his methodological ideas from him.[12]

Another temptation is to see the influence of Galileo in Hobbes's materialistic conception of the world in general and in his account of sense perception in particular. In a famous passage in *Il Saggiatore* (1623), Galileo wrote:

> To excite in us tastes, odors, and sounds I believe that nothing is required in external bodies except shapes, numbers, and slow or rapid movements. I think that if ears, tongues, and noses were removed, shapes and numbers and motions would remain, but not odors or tastes or sounds.[13]

This does, indeed, bear a strong resemblance to Hobbes's account of sensation, as given, for example, in the opening chapters of *Leviathan* or in chapter 25 of *De corpore*. But, as with method, I am reluctant to attribute this to an influence of Galileo. Whereas Galileo certainly held the view that what later came to be called "secondary qualities" are subjective states of the perceiver, this is a view that can be found clearly in the ancient Epicurean tradition, also known to Hobbes, and was widespread among Hobbes's corpuscularian and atomist contemporaries. Furthermore, in Galileo, the view is expressed in a somewhat obscure passage in one of his less widely read works. There is no particular reason to see Galileo behind Hobbes's endorsement of a version of this view.[14]

Even so, there are other respects in which Galileo's influence on Hobbes's natural philosophy are undeniable. One can see echoes of Galileo's views on the persistence of motion in Hobbes's own versions of those principles. The idea that a body in motion or rest persists in that state unless interfered with by a body external to itself is fundamental to Galileo's physics, both in the *Dialogo sopra i due massimi sistemi del mondo* (1632) and in the *Discorsi e dimostrazioni matematiche, intorno à due nuove scienze* (1638). In the *Discorsi* the idea that motion is "imprinted" on a body once in motion is central to Galileo's derivation of the behavior of projectiles in Day 4 of the *Discorsi*.[15] And in the *Dialogo*, that same view is central to the way in which Galileo defuses many of the arguments brought against a moving earth.[16] The persistence of motion is also important to Hobbes in the *De corpore*:

> Whatsoever is at Rest, will always be at Rest, unless there be some other Body besides it, which by endeavoring to get into its Place by motion, suffers it no longer

---

[12] This is essentially the point that is made in Jesseph 2004: 199–200. Jesseph also cites Gargani (1971) and Peters (1956) as holding views similar to those argued in Watkins (1965).

[13] Galilei 1890 6: 350, translated in Galilei 1957: 276–277.

[14] Jesseph 2004: 201 defends the view that Galileo was important to Hobbes in this respect. See also Paganini's introduction to Hobbes (2010: 64). But I tend to agree with Brandt (1928: 79 and 150–151) on this question.

[15] See Galilei 1890 8: 243, 272–273. For a translation, see Galilei 1974. Since this edition gives the pagination of Galilei 1890 in the margins, I will not cite the translation separately when quoting or citing the *Discorsi*.

[16] For example, it is claimed that if the Earth were to be moving, then, when we dropped a ball off a tower, it would fall somewhere other than at the base of the tower because the tower would have moved between the time that the ball is released and the time it hits the ground. But because the motion of the

to remain at Rest. . . . In like manner, Whatsoever is Moved, will always be Moved, except there be some other Body besides it, which causeth it to Rest.[17]

One might, in fact, see Hobbes's master principle in physics—"There can be no Cause of Motion, except in a Body Contiguous, and Moved"[18]—as a direct consequence of the persistence of motion and rest.[19] It is quite plausible to see this feature of Hobbes's natural philosophy as deriving from his contact with Galileo, whether directly or through other members of his circle in natural philosophy. One can also see in Hobbes clear echoes—in fact, borrowings—of Galileo's account of the behavior of bodies in uniform acceleration and the behavior of projectiles. In Day 3 of the *Discorsi*, Galileo shows that a body in free-fall will fall a distance in proportion to the square of the time. In Day 4, this is combined with the persistence of horizontal motion to show that a projectile will move in a parabolic path. This account is clearly the basis of chapter 16 of *De corpore*, where Hobbes sets out a more abstract account of the arguments.[20]

More generally, one can see the basic thrust of Hobbes's philosophy as reflecting Galileo's project. In the *Saggiatore*, Galileo presented what was to become a celebrated conception of the new scientific and mathematical world:

> Philosophy is written in this grand book, the universe, which stands continually open to our gaze. But the book cannot be understood unless one first learns to comprehend the language and read the letters in which it is composed. It is written in the language of mathematics, and its characters are triangles, circles, and other geometric figures without which it is humanly impossible to understand a single word of it; without these, one wanders about in a dark labyrinth.[21]

One can argue that this is precisely the kind of program in natural philosophy that Hobbes endorsed. Douglas Jesseph writes:

> In Galileo's writings on the science of motion, Hobbes found what he took to be the key to unlocking a complete account of nature. Hobbes held that all phenomena . . .

earth is "impressed" on the ball, it will continue to rotate along with the tower, even after it has been released. See dialogue 2 of the *Dialogo*, Galilei 1890 7: 164ff, translated in Galilei 1967: 138–141.

[17] *Concerning Body* 8.19.

[18] *Concerning Body* 9.7.

[19] Gianni Paganini emphasizes this connection between Galileo and Hobbes. See his introduction to Hobbes 2010: 32–35.

[20] Note the discussion of this in Jesseph 2004: 204–207. Jesseph, though, notes the very different way in which Galileo and Hobbes discuss this issue. For Galileo, it is an empirical question about how bodies actually behave in the real world; for Hobbes, it is an abstract mathematical question about motions and combinations of motions with different mathematical properties. Brandt sees this as one of the central differences between Galileo and his English follower. See Brandt 1928: 316ff. See also the discussion in Leijenhorst 2004. Leijenhorst puts Hobbes's discussions in the context of discussions about free fall in the 1640s in the Mersenne circle. He emphasizes that, for Hobbes and his French colleagues, the question of the causal explanation of free fall was as important as the mathematical account of the relation between time and distance fallen. This question will be discussed shortly.

[21] Galilei 1890 6: 232; translated in Galileo 1957: 237–238.

must be understood as arising from the motions of material bodies. Galileo's investigations ... offered a starting point and a model of correct procedure ... but he had not pursued the task quite far enough.... It fell to Hobbes to ... fill in the lacunae in Galileo's program. Or so Hobbes would have us believe.[22]

Or, to put it in another way, we can see Hobbes's program as a complete redoing of traditional (i.e., Aristotelian) philosophy, with the categories of Galilean science at its foundation.[23]

All of these ways of seeing Galileo in Hobbes are plausible, and, in their way, right. But, at the same time, they all obscure the fact that, in fundamental ways, Galileo's project for a mathematical physics of motion was fundamentally different from Hobbes's. Galileo and Hobbes share a principle of the persistence of motion and rest: A body in motion will remain in motion or rest, unless caused to change that state. But let us look more carefully at how each articulates and defends that view.

Here is one version of the standard argument that Galileo offers, taken from Day 3 of his *Discorsi*:

> It may also be noted that whatever degree of speed is found in the moveable, this is by its nature indelibly impressed on it when external causes of acceleration or retardation are removed, which occurs only on the horizontal plane: for on declining planes there is cause of more acceleration, and on rising planes, of retardation. From this it likewise follows that motion in the horizontal is also eternal, since if it is indeed equable it is not weakened or remitted, much less removed.[24]

The argument is this. When a body moves toward the center of the Earth, it naturally accelerates; when it moves away, it naturally decelerates, and so, on a horizontal plane, it will always naturally remain the same. It is important to note that what Galileo is talking about here is not rectilinear motion as such but *horizontal* motion: motion on a plane all of whose points remain equidistant from some point toward which the heavy body is attracted. In the *Dialogo*, Galileo makes this assumption explicit:

> Every body constituted in a state of rest but naturally capable of motion will move when set at liberty only if it has a natural tendency toward some particular place; for if it were indifferent to all places it would remain at rest, having no more cause to move one way than another. Having such a tendency, it naturally follows that in its motion it will be continually accelerating.[25]

---

[22] Jesseph 2004: 208.

[23] See Paganini's introduction to Hobbes 2010: 64–67. Cf. Foisneau 2011: 798–802.

[24] Galilei 1890 8: 243.

[25] Galilei 1890 7: 44, translated in Galilei 1967: 20. Cf. Galileo 1890 7: 56, translated in Galilei 1967: 31–32.

That is to say, what persists is circular motion around the point to which a heavy body tends to fall. Galileo is clearly dealing with *heavy* bodies here: bodies near the surface of the Earth that tend to fall to its center.[26] This is also obviously true of the account of "the Descent of Heavy Bodies" that so impressed Hobbes in *De corpore*, the idea that a body in free-fall will fall a distance proportional to the time squared.

But Hobbes's account of the persistence of motion is radically different. For him, the general principles of motion are true of body as such and don't depend on heaviness. Hobbes presents the principle of the persistence of rest as follows:

> Whatsoever is at rest, will always be at rest, unless there be some other body besides it, which, by endeavouring to get into its place by motion, suffers it no longer to remain at rest . . .[27]

The argument here is a kind of Principle of Sufficient Reason argument: If a body at rest were to begin to move, it would have to move in some direction or another, and there is no reason why it should move one way rather than another. And, for a similar reason, Hobbes holds that a body in motion will remain in motion:

> In like manner, *whatsoever is moved, will always be moved, except there be some other body besides it, which causeth it to rest.* For if we suppose nothing to be without it, there will be no reason why it should rest now, rather than at another time; wherefore its motion would cease in every particle of time alike; which is not intelligible.[28]

Here, the argument is very similar and also appeals to a version of the Principle of Sufficient Reason: If a body in motion were to come to rest, there is no reason that it should come to rest in any one moment in preference to in any other moment. These statements (and others like them) are very general: They hold for *body as such* and for *motion as such* and not just for heavy bodies moving near the center to which they are attracted. In this respect, Hobbes is very different from Galileo and his theory of motion.

---

[26] In the *Dialogo*, Galileo attempts to extend this to the cosmological case, but with limited success. What I have in mind here is the so-called Platonic hypothesis about the formation of the planetary system: "Let us suppose that among the decrees of the divine Architect was the thought of creating in the universe those globes which we behold continually revolving, and of establishing a center of their rotations in which the sun was located immovably. Next, suppose all the said globes to have been created in the same place, and there assigned tendencies of motion, descending toward the center until they had acquired those degrees of velocity which originally seemed good to the Divine mind. These velocities being acquired, we lastly suppose that the globes were set in rotation, each retaining in its orbit its predetermined velocity" (Galilei 1890 7: 53, translated in Galilei 1967: 29). This is only partially successful insofar as it extends the account of acceleration to the planets, but it doesn't say how any arbitrary body released in interplanetary space will behave.

[27] *Concerning Body* 8.19.

[28] Ibid.

This signals a fundamental difference between Hobbes and Galileo. Hobbes wants to present a genuine natural philosophy in an almost Aristotelian sense: an explanation of the phenomena of the world that is ultimately grounded in first causes. For Hobbes, this project goes back to his very definition of philosophy:

> PHILOSOPHY is such knowledge of Effects or Appearances, as we acquire by true Ratiocination from the knowledge we have first of their Causes or Generation: And again, of such Causes or Generations as may be from knowing first their Effects.[29]

Hobbes, of course, differs from the schools in seeing the ultimate causes not as matter, form, and privation but as bodies in motion. Hobbes begins his program for natural philosophy in his "First Philosophy" with the very definitions of space, time, body, and motion. General statements, such as the principle of the persistence of motion, are derived not for *heavy* bodies, but for *bodies as such*. For Galileo, on the other hand, the project is different, finding ways, preferably mathematical, of characterizing the behavior of things as we find them. Galileo is not doing natural philosophy in the strict Aristotelian sense, but mixed mathematics. In this way, he is extending the approach that worked so well in domains like optics, mechanics, and observational astronomy to the study of motion.[30]

This central difference between Hobbes and Galileo is reflected in their treatments of gravitation. For Galileo, the problem of the real cause of heaviness—of why heavy bodies tend to fall toward the center of the Earth—is quite beyond our ability to solve. In Day 3 of the *Discorsi*, Sagredo and Simplicio fall into a long discussion on the cause of heaviness, debating about various theories that have been offered. Galileo's spokesman Salviati interrupts them with a stern warning that such questions are not welcome by "the academician," that is, by Galileo.[31] There was a similar moment in Galileo's *Dialogo*. Asked about the cause of why bodies fall, the Aristotelian Simplicio replies with confidence that "everybody is aware that it is gravity." Galileo's spokesman Salviati responds:

> You are wrong, Simplicio; what you ought to say is that everyone knows that it is called "gravity." What I am asking you for is not the name of the thing, but its essence, of which essence you know not a bit more than you know about the essence of whatever moves the stars around. I except the name which has been attached to it and which has been made a familiar household word by the continual experience that we have of it daily. But we do not really understand what principle or what force it is that moves stones downward any more than we understand what moves them upward after they leave the thrower's hand, or what moves the moon around.[32]

---

[29] *Concerning Body* 1.2.

[30] On mixed mathematics or, as it was also known the "middle sciences," see Lennox 1986 and Brown 1991. Recently, Zvi Biener has been arguing that Galileo's work more generally should be understood in terms of the category of mixed mathematics. See Biener 2004.

[31] See Galilei 1890 8: 201–204.

[32] Galilei 1890 7: 260–261; translated in Galilei 1967: 234.

As I pointed out earlier, Galileo is dealing with a physics not of body and motion as such, but of heavy bodies near the surface of the Earth and their characteristic motions.

Hobbes couldn't be more different on this question. For Hobbes, everything is explained in terms of ultimate causes, the motion and collision of bodies: "There can be no cause of motion, except in a body contiguous and moved."[33] And, as a result, the downward fall of heavy bodies must be explained in terms of the interaction of bodies. Heaviness is not a basic property of bodies, but one that needs to be explained in terms of bodies colliding with one another in accordance with principles of motion that pertain to bodies in motion as such. In the *Critique du De mundo*, while discussing a falling stone, Hobbes notes that "it is now sufficiently clear to most philosophers that the stone in question does not move itself; so it has an external mover."[34] This external mover must be the motion of particles in the air around the heavy body. In the *De corpore*, this is taken up in the final chapter, chapter 30, where he offers a properly Hobbesian conjecture about the physical cause of heaviness in bodies, of what pushes heavy bodies near the surface of the Earth toward its center.[35]

In these respects, it is fair to say that, despite his admiration for the Italian scientist, Hobbes's conception of natural philosophy is in a different world from Galileo's project. But, somewhat surprisingly, it turns out to be rather closer to that of his rival, Descartes.

2 HOBBES AND DESCARTES: TOO CLOSE FOR COMFORT?

Although Galileo was clearly a central member of Hobbes's pantheon of important thinkers, Descartes clearly failed to make the cut. It is likely that Hobbes would have first learned about Descartes when he met Mersenne in Paris in the spring of 1636, upon returning there from Italy and a meeting with Galileo.[36] In October 1637, he received a copy of the newly published *Discours* and *Essais* of Descartes, a gift of Sir Kenelm Digby.[37] This initiated Hobbes's first contact with Descartes, a letter to Mersenne, meant for Descartes, concerning the *Discours de la méthode* and the *Dioptrique*, now lost.[38] Mersenne, in turn, sent excerpts of that letter to Descartes, who replied in a letter of January 21, 1641. From the beginning, relations weren't exactly cordial. In his letter, Hobbes seems to have been complimentary to Descartes;

[33] *Concerning Body* 9.7.

[34] *Critique du De mundo*, 10.11.

[35] Leijenhorst (2004) emphasizes the importance to Hobbes of finding a cause for heaviness, unlike Galileo.

[36] Martinich 1999: 92.

[37] Malcolm 1994 1: 51.

[38] Sent November 5, 1640. For a discussion of the possible content of that letter, see Malcolm's note in the textual introduction to Malcolm 1994 1: lii–lv.

Descartes wrote to Mersenne that "[the Englishman] is a man who showed me some respect."[39] But, in his response, Descartes didn't return the favor. In the cover letter of his response, written to Mersenne, Descartes noted that even though Hobbes agreed with him that one should consider only "les figures et les mouvements," still he made many mistakes in what follows from that.[40] In the response written for Mersenne to transmit to Hobbes, Descartes begins in a way that would hardly ingratiate him to the Englishman: "I was very surprised by the fact that, although the style in which it is written makes its author look clever and learned, he seems to stray from the truth in every single claim which he advances as his own."[41] It isn't surprising that the correspondence that followed, which focused mainly on questions in optics, became increasingly unpleasant.[42] This is not the place to go deeply into the exchanges between Descartes and Hobbes over optics, but although they differed in a number of respects, their optics was quite similar. As Richard Tuck suggested, referring specifically to their optical thought, "Hobbes's philosophy gives the impression of having been developed as the next move in a game where Descartes was the previous player."[43]

At roughly the same time as Hobbes was communicating with Descartes over optical questions through Mersenne, Mersenne decided to ask him to write a series of objections to the *Meditationes* for inclusion in the appendix of objections and replies that he was collecting for Descartes.[44] What resulted—Hobbes's objections interleaved with Descartes's replies—was published as the *Objectiones tertiae* to the *Meditationes* in 1641. Although there are no real overt insults, the tone of this exchange isn't much better than the exchanges on optics.[45] It is no surprise that, a few years later, when Samuel Sorbière was in the Netherlands arranging for the publication of a new edition of the *De cive*, Hobbes warned him to be careful of Descartes: "if M. Descartes hears or suspects that a book of mine (this or any other) is being assessed for publication, I know for certain that he will stop it if he can."[46]

At the time Descartes's *Principia philosophiae* appeared in 1644, Hobbes was hard at work on the *De corpore*, which wouldn't appear in print until 1655, after Descartes's death in 1650. Many elements of Hobbes's physics appear in the *Critique du De mundo* (1643?), suggesting that, by 1644, he had already worked out considerable parts of his thought. No letters survive from 1644, and precious few from the years immediately afterward, so we have no direct record of Hobbes's first impressions of Descartes's

---

[39] Descartes 1996 3: 283.

[40] Ibid.

[41] Malcolm 1994 1: 57.

[42] See the accounts of the exchange in Brandt 1928; the contents of the exchange are discussed *passim* in chapters 2 and 3 and the personal animosity in chapter 4. See also the discussion in Tuck 1988.

[43] Tuck 1988: 28.

[44] See Mersenne 1933–88 10: 210–212.

[45] For the details of the exchange, see Sorell 1995 and Curley 1995.

[46] Malcolm 1994 1: 127.

work.[47] And, unlike the *Dioptrique* and the *Meditationes*, there was no direct exchange between Descartes and Hobbes on the *Principia*. But we do have some evidence from letters exchanged between Charles Cavendish and John Pell in late 1644 that he saw it and didn't like it much. In a letter to Pell from September 13/23, 1644, Cavendish wrote: "I beleeue Mr: Hobbes will not like so much of Des Cartes newe booke as is the same with his metaphisickes, but most of the rest I thinke he will."[48] Cavendish seems to have been wrong in thinking that Hobbes would like the nonmetaphysical portions of the book. In a letter to Pell, October 10/20, 1644, Cavendish wrote:

> I receiued yesterday a letter from Mr: Hobbes, who had not seen de Cartes his new booke printed, but had reade some sheets of it in manuscript & seems to receiue little satisfaction from it, & saies a friend of his hath reade it through, & is of the same minde; but by their leaues I esteeme it an excellent booke though I thinke Monsr: des Cartes is not infallible.[49]

The letter from Hobbes to Cavendish is missing, but one can imagine what he said. A letter from two months later, again from Cavendish to Pell, suggests that Hobbes had managed to see the book itself:

> I am of your opinion that Gassendes & de Cartes are of different dispositions; & I perceiue Mr: Hobbes ioines with Gassendes in his dislike of de Cartes his writings, for he vtterlie mislikes de Cartes his last newe booke of philosophie [i.e. the *Principia philosophiae*] which by his leaue I highlie esteem of.[50]

It seems that he didn't like the book as a whole any better than he did the sheets of it that he had read before.

Although he didn't like Descartes's *Principia philosophiae*, Hobbes certainly read it, and read it carefully. From what we know about Hobbes's natural philosophy in the years before the publication of the *Principia* from documents like the *Critique du De*

---

[47] In general, we don't yet have a clear story of the composition of *De corpore*. We have, of course, the *Critique du De mundo*, probably from 1643. For the years immediately following, including probably 1644, the year Descartes's *Principia philosophiae* appeared, we have three manuscript sources that give evidence of drafts in progress after the *Critique*: (1) Chatsworth MS A10; (2) National Library of Wales MS 5297; and (3) Harleian MS 6083, in the possession of Charles Cavendish. The first is now thought to be in the hand of Robert Payne, probably author of the *Short Tract*; see Malcolm 2002b: 140. It is given in an appendix to Hobbes 1973: 461–513, although incorrectly identified as a Hobbes autograph. The second is given in Hobbes 1973: 448–460. The third is given in part in Jacquot 1952. In addition, there is an interesting letter from Charles Cavendish to Joachim Jungius, May 11, 1645, giving some details of Hobbes's thinking about motion at that moment. See Brockdorff 1934. For an account of the three manuscripts, see the editors' introduction to Hobbes 1973, especially chapter 3. For some observations on the composition of the *De corpore*, see the introduction by Schuhmann and Pécharman to Hobbes 1999.

[48] Malcolm and Stedall 2005: 377–378.

[49] Malcolm and Stedall 2005: 382.

[50] Malcolm and Stedall 2005: 395.

mundo, we can also be reasonably confident that the main lines of Hobbes's natural philosophy were not seriously influenced by his reading of Descartes. But when the *De corpore* appeared in print in 1655, it contained a number of passages clearly addressed at Descartes's text, although not by name. In the *De corpore* itself, there are at least three direct references to the *Principia philosophiae*. In *De corpore* 7.2, there is an apparent reference to Descartes's argument in *Principia* 2.21 on the infinity of space. In 7.9, there is a reference to the argument against the possibility of the vacuum found in *Principia* 2.18. Then, in 8.5, there is an apparent reference to Descartes's discussion of space and place in *Principia* 2.10. And then, in 9.7, Hobbes writes: "There is one that has written that things moved are more resisted by things at rest, then by things contrarily moved . . ." That "one" is evidently Descartes, who said something very similar to this in *Principia* 2.44 and 49, paragraphs that deal explicitly with the laws of motion. And finally, in chapter 26, there is a reference to Descartes's account of God and creation in *Principia* 3.[51] There, Hobbes discusses the issues of creation and the infinity of the world. In the *Principia philosophiae*, Descartes had asserted that the world is indefinitely extended (*Principia* 2.21). He begins his account of the structure of the world with a hypothesis about the state of the world at creation (*Principia* 3.46). Hobbes rejects both of these questions as going beyond philosophy. For Hobbes, these questions are not philosophical but theological: "The questions therefore about the Magnitude and Beginning of the World are not to be determined by Philosophers, but by those that are lawfully authorized to order the Worship of God."[52] These passages show that Hobbes had read the *Principia philosophiae* and read it carefully enough to be able to cite particular passages.

Despite these differences that Hobbes emphasized, the similarity between the natural philosophy of the *Principia philosophiae* and the *De corpore* is quite striking. In contrast with Galileo, both Descartes and Hobbes are involved in a kind of Aristotelian *scientia*, an account of nature in terms of its ultimate causes. Both see themselves as giving a very general account of body as such and the explanation of a variety of physical phenomena in terms of the size, shape, and motion of their parts, which they see as the ultimate cause of everything that happens in the physical world. As a consequence, both begin their project with general definitions and general statements about the fundamental elements of the physical world. Part II of Descartes's *Principia philosophiae* begins with a proof for the existence of the external world but is followed quickly by definitions of body, space, internal and external place, the denial of the vacuum, and the definition of motion, followed by the laws of motion. This is parallel to the material Hobbes presents in parts II and III of the *De corpore*. Hobbes begins in chapter 7 with the definitions of space and time. Body follows in chapter 8, as does motion. In chapter 8, Hobbes gives a

---

[51] In the drafts that survive of earlier states of the *De corpore*, though, I could find only one passage that looks as if it may possibly be a reference to the *Principia philosophiae*. In Chatsworth MS A10, Hobbes wrote: "Causa motus nulla esse potest in corpore, nisi contiguo et moto. Motus adversus pugnat cum motu, non quies" (Hobbes 1973: 482). But it is difficult to say whether this is directed at Descartes or not; there is no "est qui . . . scripsit" as there is in the *De corpore*.

[52] *Concerning Body* 26.1.

definition of motion and announces his principle of the persistence of motion, which, in chapter 9 is extended to the principle that all change comes through the direct collision of one body with another. After more general definitions of such things as cause, power, identity, quantity, and the like, Hobbes returns to motion in chapter 15, in the beginning of part III, and introduces his concept of *conatus* or endeavor.

After these general definitions and general propositions, both Descartes and Hobbes turn toward the explanation of specific phenomena. In part III of the *Principia philosophiae*, Descartes treats cosmological phenomena. Beginning with the creation of the world, he offers an account of the planets and how they circle the sun, the light of the sun, and more. It is in this part that Descartes offers his vortex theory of planetary motion, in accordance with which the planets are drawn around a central sun by a swirling vortex of subtle matter. In part IV, then, he discusses terrestrial phenomena, including gravitation, explained in terms of a vortex of fluid surrounding the Earth, the structure of the Earth and how such things as mountains arose, as well as the tides, fire, metals and chemical phenomena, and, most famously, the magnet. Descartes ends with a brief account of sensation, a foretaste of what he had intended to provide in the final parts V and VI of the *Principia philosophiae*, which he never wrote, on the human being. This corresponds to the contents of part IV of Hobbes's *De corpore*, what he calls the "physics proper," the hypothetical explanations of particular phenomena.[53] In chapter 25, Hobbes begins where Descartes ends, with an account of sensation and how it fits into the physical world. This is followed by a discussion of creation and the infinity of the world and why it is not appropriate for philosophical investigation, the world and the stars, light, heat and colors, cold, wind, lightning and thunder, sound, odor, and touch. Hobbes ends with his own account of the cause of gravity, explained, much as Descartes did, in terms of the circulation of subtle matter.

In his classic monograph on Hobbes's natural philosophy, Frithiof Brandt wrote: "No man has so many points of contact with Hobbes as precisely Descartes. The *Principia* and *De Corpore* are as like each other as two drops of water from a natural philosophical point of view."[54] Indeed, it has been suggested that it is precisely the similarity between Hobbes and Descartes that led to their mutual hostility.[55] Given his adulation of Galileo and his extreme dislike of Descartes, it is somewhat ironic how close Hobbes's natural philosophy is to that of Descartes.

Similar as they are, though, there is a crucial difference between the natural philosophies of the two, one that Hobbes fails to mention, interestingly enough. God is

[53] For the distinction between the first philosophy and geometry of parts II and III of *De corpore* and the hypothetical physics of part IV, see above.

[54] Brandt 1928: 375.

[55] "Similarity breeds contempt. Both wanted to give materialistic and mechanistic explanations to the physical world. Both wanted the physical laws of the universe to be formulated mathematically. Both believed that sensations are noniconic; ideas are not similar to the features of the physical objects that cause them. . . . On a personal level, both were vain, glory-seeking, self-absorbed, self-proclaimed geniuses. This statement is purely descriptive. Hobbes, like Descartes, was obsessed with being first" (Martinich 1999: 169). See also Tuck 1988.

absolutely central to Descartes's project for natural philosophy. The centerpiece of part II of Descartes's *Principia philosophiae* is the three laws of motion that he presents:

> [Law 1] Each and every thing, in so far as it can, always continues in the same state; and thus what is once in motion always continues to move.[56]

> [Law 2] All motion is in itself rectilinear; and hence any body moving in a circle always tends to move away from the center of the circle which it describes.[57]

> [Law 3] When a moving body collides with another, if its force [*vis*] of continuing in a straight line is less than the resistance of the other body, it is deflected so that, while the quantity of motion is retained, the direction is altered; but if its force of continuing is greater than the resistance of the other body, it carries that body along with it, and loses a quantity of motion equal to that which it imparts to the other body.[58]

Behind these three laws and, in fact, used in crucial ways to apply the third law to the real world, is the claim that the total quantity of motion, as measured by size times speed, remains constant in the world. Although it isn't called a law, a principle, or anything else, it seems to be the rock on which the rest of his thought about the order in the world is grounded.

For Descartes, these laws are grounded in God and his continued sustenance of the world. Descartes holds that for anything to persist, it must be sustained by God and, as it were, recreated from moment to moment. He writes:

> For the nature of time is such that its parts are not mutually dependent, and never coexist. Thus, from the fact that we now exist, it does not follow that we shall exist a moment from now, unless there is some cause—the same cause which originally produced us—which continually reproduces us, as it were, that is to say, which keeps us in existence.[59]

This, together with the constancy of God, is the basis of his argument for the conservation principle:

> God imparted various motions to the parts of matter when he first created them, and he now preserves all this matter in the same way, and by the same process by which he originally created it; and it follows from what we have said that this fact alone makes it most reasonable to think that God likewise always preserves the same quantity of motion in matter.[60]

---

[56] *Principia* 2.37.
[57] *Principia* 2.39.
[58] *Principia* 2.40.
[59] *Principia* 1.21.
[60] *Principia* 2.36.

In a similar way, Descartes argues that the other laws, too, follow from divine sustenance.[61]

It is a perennial question whether or not Hobbes was really an atheist. But that doesn't matter for the issue at hand because, whatever he may have thought about God and religion, Hobbes doesn't believe that God has any role to play in natural philosophy. In his *De corpore*, Hobbes wrote:

> The *subject* of [natural] Philosophy, or the matter it treats of, is every body of which we can conceive any generation, and which we may, by any consideration thereof, compare with other bodies, or which is capable of composition and resolution; that is to say, every body of whose generation or properties we can have any knowledge. . . . Therefore, where there is no generation or property, there is no philosophy. Therefore it excludes *Theology*, I mean the doctrine of God, eternal, ingenerable, incomprehensible, and in whom there is nothing neither to divide nor compound, nor any generation to be conceived.[62]

In this way, God has no direct role to play in Hobbes's account of the physical world.[63]

Now, Hobbes certainly does advance general propositions about motion that correspond at least roughly to Descartes's laws. But it is very interesting that he does not call them laws, nor does he ground them in God. In the case of the principle of the persistence of motion and rest, for example, we saw that they are grounded in the Principle of Sufficient Reason. More generally, Hobbes sees such principles as consequences of the very definition of body and motion. In chapter 6 of *De corpore*, Hobbes asserts that philosophy begins with definitions. After the definitions, though, "we should first demonstrate those things which are proximate to the most universal definitions (in which consists that part of philosophy which is called 'First Philosophy'), and then those things which can be demonstrated through motion *simpliciter*, in which consists geometry."[64] Which is to say, these facts about motion are taken to be general truths about motion on a par with geometrical theorems—eternal truths of a sort, either things that follow directly from definitions or what he calls geometry.

One possible consequence of the way Hobbes grounds his general propositions about motion may be the lack of a general conservation principle. Even though Hobbes endorsed general propositions that roughly correspond to Descartes's laws of nature, he did not recognize anything like Descartes's conservation law. In Hobbes's universe, the state of the world is determined by individual collisions between individual bodies in motion. He may well have thought that, without a divine guarantor looking out for the

---

[61] For further details about the derivation of the laws of nature in Descartes, see Garber 1992, chapters 7–9.

[62] *Concerning Body* 1.8.

[63] This is not to say that God doesn't play an indirect role. See Pécharman 1997.

[64] *De corpore* 6.17; my translation.

state of things in general, there is no reason to posit that any physical magnitude may be conserved in the world as a whole.

A second possible consequence of Hobbes's rejection of a theological physics may involve force. For both Hobbes and Descartes, the physical world contains just body and motion, where body is understood in terms of extension. This makes it somewhat problematic to understand how there could be genuine physical forces in the world. This is what Descartes has to say about the force a body has to proceed, an element in his account of collision in the third law:

> In this connection we must be careful to note what it is that constitutes the force [*vis*] of any body to act on, or resist the action of, another body. This force consists simply in the fact that everything tends, so far as it can, to persist in the same state, as laid down in our first law. (*Principia* 2.43)

Force, then, derives from the first law of nature, in accordance with which a body in motion or rest will persist in that state of motion or rest: The force "to act on, or resist the action of, another body" is just the tendency a body has to remain in its state of motion or rest. But, as I argued earlier, for Descartes, this first law itself is grounded in God's activity, the way in which an immutable God sustains the world from moment to moment. And so, in a sense, physical force for Descartes is grounded in divine activity.[65] This is certainly not a position open to Hobbes. It is not surprising, then, that for Hobbes the only force a body has to exert on another body or to resist another body is its motion and its motion alone. And so, he writes in *De corpore*, "the Magnitude of Motion ... is that which is commonly called FORCE."[66] Consequently, he holds that "Rest does nothing at all, nor is of any efficacy; and ... nothing but Motion gives Motion to such things as be at Rest, and takes it from things moved."[67] And so, Hobbes writes, "if a point moved come to touch another point which is at rest, how little soever the Impetus or quickness of its motion be, it shall move that other point."[68] Because of this, a body at rest, however large, cannot resist the acquisition of new motion from another body, however small and however slowly it might be moving.

These differences between Descartes and Hobbes will be important in helping us to see how it is that Hobbes's particular vision for natural philosophy is represented in some later thinkers.

---

[65] For a fuller explanation of this claim, see Garber 1992, chapter 9. This remains a somewhat controversial claim. For an alternative reading of Descartes on force, see, e.g., Schmaltz 2008, chapter 3.

[66] *Concerning Body* 8.18; cf. 15.2.

[67] *Concerning Body* 15.3. Cf. 9.9: "Rest cannot be the Cause of any thing; nor can any action proceed from it."

[68] Ibid.

3 Hobbes's Legacy: Spinoza

It is generally thought that Hobbes's natural philosophy was pretty much ignored by later thinkers. Frithiof Brandt, for example, writes: "The years following upon the publication of *De Corpore* were in several respects bitter years to Hobbes. His natural philosophy received but slight recognition."[69] It is certainly true that Hobbes the natural philosopher never attained anything close to the eminence that figures like Galileo, Descartes, or Boyle were to attain. Even so, he was not entirely ignored. In particular, the physics of *De corpore* has an interesting afterlife in the thought of two major figures of the later seventeenth century: Spinoza and Leibniz.

Spinoza is not and was not known as a natural philosopher. But he was interested in questions in natural philosophy, which played a certain role in his thought from fairly early on. His first publication was *Renati Des Cartes Principiorum Philosophiae Pars I, & II . . .*, which appeared in 1663, a commentary and representation in geometrical form of parts I, II, and part of part III of Descartes's *Principia philosophiae*. A considerable part of this work was devoted to a close and detailed discussion of Descartes's natural philosophy, including his laws of nature.

The idea that we live in a world governed by laws of nature was also quite central to Spinoza's vision. In the *Tractatus Theologico-Politicus* (*TTP*), for example, he wrote: "I grant, without reservation, that everything is determined by the universal laws of nature to exist and produce effects in a certain and determinate way."[70] In the *TTP*, this vision of the world is instrumental in his undermining of the idea that God acts specially to the benefit (or detriment) of one or another peoples or that he acts by miracle in the sense of a violation of the laws of nature.[71] Similarly, in the *Ethica*, he wrote:

> Nature is always the same, and its virtue and power of acting are everywhere one and the same, i.e., the laws and rules of nature, according to which all things happen, and change from one form to another, are always and everywhere the same.[72]

---

[69] Brandt 1928: 377. Noel Malcolm makes a similar judgment: "[O]utside the immediate circle of Hobbes's friends and admirers, his reputation as a writer on non-political and non-theological matters was in something of a decline from the mid-1650s onwards [i.e., from the moment of the publication of *De corpore*!]" (Malcolm 2002e: 498).

[70] *TTP* chapter 4, Spinoza 1925 3: 58. Translations from the *TTP* are taken from Edwin Curley's in-progress translation of that work, which he kindly shared with me. See also chapter 6, Spinoza 1925 3: 95: "nature observes a fixed and immutable order, that God has been the same in all ages, both those known to us and those unknown, that the laws of nature are so perfect and fruitful that nothing can be added to them or taken away from them."

[71] See, e.g., *TTP* chapters 4, 6.

[72] E3pref. In referring to the *Ethica*, I use the standard abbreviations. "E" refers to "*Ethica*," followed by the part, "pref." refers to the preface, "p" the proposition, followed by number, "s" a scholium, "app." the appendix, etc. Translations from the *Ethica* are from Curley's version in Spinoza 1985.

The only extended discussion of natural philosophy in Spinoza's writings occurs in part II of the *Ethica*.[73] In the beginning of part II, Spinoza had argued that the mind is the idea of the body. But, of course, there is an idea corresponding to every body; and so, corresponding to every body, there is something of a mind. "And so," Spinoza reasoned, "to determine what is the difference between the human Mind and the others, and how it surpasses them, it is necessary for us, as we have said, to know the nature of its object, i.e., of the human Body."[74] And so Spinoza entered into a brief digression on natural philosophy, what is sometimes called the Short Physical Treatise (SPT). The SPT begins with a characterization of the simplest bodies, presumably the building blocks of the material world.[75] After offering a definition of a complex body, one made up out of smaller parts, Spinoza advances to a more general discussion in which he presents a number of lemmata about complex bodies. The SPT ends with some claims about bodies of increasing complexity—complex bodies in complex bodies making up bodies more complex still—until he reaches the whole of nature, conceived of as an individual.

It is generally held that Spinoza's physics is broadly Cartesian, a variety of Cartesian mechanism.[76] Given the attention that Spinoza paid to Descartes's natural philosophy in his commentary on the *Principia philosophiae*, this is a natural enough assumption to make. But Spinoza was not uncritical of Descartes's natural philosophy. In one of the last letters Spinoza sent, a letter to von Tschirnhaus, he wrote: "the Cartesian principles of natural things are useless, not to say absurd."[77] And when we look more closely at Spinoza's actual statements about natural philosophy, I think we have reason to believe that Spinoza's inspiration is more likely Hobbes than Descartes. Because both Descartes and Hobbes attempt to explain everything in terms of matter and motion in their natural philosophies, it isn't always easy to distinguish between a follower of the one and a follower of the other. But when we look at Spinoza's treatment of the laws of nature, where the two diverge more significantly, the Hobbesian signature becomes clearer.[78]

Although he talks about laws of nature on a number of occasions, Spinoza rarely gives any examples of what he considers laws of nature. There is one example in the *TTP*:

> That all bodies, when they strike against other lesser bodies, lose as much of their motion as they communicate to the other bodies is a universal law of all bodies, which follows from a necessity of nature.[79]

---

[73] I am leaving aside an interesting series of letters about Boyle, written to Oldenburg, along with Oldenburg's responses, which take up certain physical and alchemical questions. See Spinoza, Letters 6, 13. These concern specific questions taken up by Boyle and are occasional reflections connected with specific questions that Oldenburg addressed to Spinoza.

[74] E2p13s.

[75] It isn't at all clear that Spinoza actually believes in such ultimate physical simples or whether this is just a kind of expository convenience.

[76] See, e.g., Rivaud 1924; Lachterman 1978; Savan 1986; Gabbey 1996. Schliesser 2013 is one of the few dissenters to this orthodoxy.

[77] Letter 81, Spinoza 1925 4: 332.

[78] See Gueroult's brief comment in a footnote, Gueroult 1968–74 2: 178–179n.

[79] *TTP*, chapter 4, Spinoza 1925 3: 57–58.

This looks very much like Descartes's third law of nature, the one that covers the collision between two bodies, and, one might argue, it is a kind of local version of Descartes's conservation principle, one that holds between bodies in collision. But Spinoza gives no argument for this principle, which is given only in passing in the *TTP* as an example of a law of nature. In general, in the *TTP*, there is no serious discussion of natural philosophy.

But the SPT presents a somewhat different picture. In the SPT, Spinoza doesn't advance anything that he explicitly labels as a law of nature. But in lemma 3 of the SPT, Spinoza writes:

> L3: A body which moves or is at rest must be determined to motion or rest by another body, which has also been determined to motion or rest by another, and that again by another, and so on, to infinity.[80]

This is very close to what Hobbes argues in *De corpore* 9.7, which we saw above: "There can be no cause of motion, except in a body contiguous and moved."[81] As in Hobbes, Spinoza's proof for this makes no appeal to a transcendent God. The proof, instead, takes L3 to be a direct consequence of E1p28:

> Every singular thing . . . can neither exist nor be determined to produce an effect unless it is determined to exist and produce an effect by another cause, which is also finite and has a determinate existence; and again, this cause also can neither exist nor be determined to produce an effect unless it is determined to exist and produce an effect by another, which is also finite and has a determinate existence, and so on, to infinity.[82]

And as in *De corpore* 9.7, Spinoza connects this with the claim that a body in motion (or rest) will remain in motion (or rest) unless otherwise interfered with:

> Cor.: From this it follows that a body in motion moves until it is determined by another body to rest; and that a body at rest also remains at rest until it is determined to motion by another.

Spinoza's argument for this corollary is as follows:

> This is also known through itself. For when I suppose that body A, say, is at rest, and do not attend to any other body in motion, I can say nothing about body A except

---

[80] Note also Spinoza's Axiom A2, the claim that a body hitting an immovable surface is reflected with the angle of incidence equal to the angle of reflection. The same claim is found in Hobbes, *De corpore* 24.8, and in Descartes's *La Dioptrique*, disc. 2, Descartes 1996 6: 94–96, with very similar arguments. It is significant here that none of the three offers this as a law of nature.

[81] The only commentator who seems to have noticed this is Martial Gueroult. See Gueroult 1968–74 2: 152.

[82] E1p28.

that it is at rest. If afterwards it happens that body A moves, that of course could not have come about from the fact that it was at rest. For from that nothing else could follow but that body A would be at rest.

If, on the other hand, A is supposed to move, then as often as we attend only to A, we shall be able to affirm nothing concerning it except that it moves. If afterwards it happens that A is at rest, that of course also could not have come about from the motion it had. For from the motion nothing else could follow but that A would move. Therefore, it happens by a thing which was not in A, viz. by an external cause, by which it has been determined to rest.

Spinoza's version of the principle of inertia here seems to be stated in terms that put him in direct opposition to Descartes's doctrine of continuous creation. In *Principia* 1.21, Descartes derives the need for God's continuous conservation from the fact that (the parts of time being independent of one another) it does not follow from our existing now that we shall also exist at the next moment (*in tempore proxime sequenti*), unless the same cause that first produced us reproduces us. Spinoza does not make it quite explicit that it follows from A's being at rest at one time that it will be at rest at a later time (unless some cause intervenes to initiate motion) because he puts it negatively—viz. nothing else follows (but cf. III P4–P8 and Gueroult 1, 2: 152, on Spinoza's relation here to Descartes and Hobbes).

Spinoza's argument for the principle of inertia is not the argument from the Principle of Sufficient Reason for the parallel claim that Hobbes makes in *De corpore*. It is, in essence, an elaboration of the first sentence, the claim that the corollary is "known through itself." But it does share with Hobbes's argument the fact that there is no appeal to a transcendent God. Both the way in which the generalizations about bodies in motion are articulated and the avoidance of God in the demonstrations suggest Hobbes as the source of at least these details of Spinoza's physics.

When discussing Descartes earlier, I noted the centrality of the principle of the conservation of quantity of motion in his natural philosophy. But this principle seems to be missing in the brief natural philosophy of the SPT, as it is from Hobbes.[83]

---

[83] There is an aspect of Spinoza's conception of the physical world that one might possibly see as endorsing a conservation principle. For Spinoza, an individual body is defined by a particular "*ratio motus et quietis*," a "*ratio*" of motion and rest, something that remains constant in a given individual and defines that individual as the individual that it is. On this see, e.g., the definition of an individual in the SPT and E4p39s. Spinoza claims that the universe as a whole constitutes an individual and thus has a constant "*ratio*" of motion and rest; see Letter 32, Spinoza to Oldenburg, November 20, 1665, Spinoza 1925 4: 172–173. See Schliesser 2013, who proposes this as evidence that Spinoza endorsed a Cartesian conservation principle. Now, if we interpret "*ratio*" in this phrase as a geometrical proportion of motion and rest, then we may be led to see Spinoza as endorsing a kind of conservation principle here. But I think that this is implausible. First of all, even if a geometrical proportion were at issue, it wouldn't entail a conservation principle of the sort that Descartes held; a proportion could remain constant while the absolute quantity of motion and rest changed quite radically. One might expect this to happen, for example, when an infant grows into a child and then an adult: Even if the proportion of motion and rest remained constant, which it must if the person is to remain the same individual, the

Furthermore, the metaphysical status of these general statements about motion in Spinoza is very close to Hobbes's conception in *De corpore*. In chapter 4 of the *TTP* Spinoza wrote:

> The word *law*, taken without qualification, means that according to which each individual, or all or some members of the same species, act in one and the same certain and determinate manner. This depends either on a necessity of nature or on a decision of men. A law which depends on a necessity of nature is one which follows necessarily from the very nature or definition of a thing.[84]

Laws that follow from the "decision of men" are obviously the positive laws that kings and legislatures make. But the laws of nature are of the other sort, those which "follow necessarily from the very nature or definition of a thing."[85] Like Hobbes, for Spinoza, the laws of nature seem to follow from the nature of matter and motion, and, like Hobbes, he believes that they seem to have something very much like the status of geometrical truths.[86]

It is well known that Hobbes was an important influence on Spinoza's political thought: Hobbes's fingerprints are all over *Ethica* IV, the *TTP*, and the *Tractatus Politicus*. It is quite reasonable to suppose that Spinoza also read Hobbes's *De corpore*, a work written in Latin and easily available in the Low Countries. The natural philosophy of *De corpore* is, in its way, clearly more suited to Spinoza's intellectual project than is Descartes's work. Whereas Descartes makes essential use of a transcendent God in his natural philosophy, particularly in his derivation of the laws of nature, Hobbes, of

---

absolute amount of both could change considerably. But I think that it is implausible to read "*ratio*" in Spinoza's formula as a mathematical proportion of any kind. For a good examination of the problems that arise from any attempt to read "*ratio*" in Spinoza in a mathematical way, see Gabbey 1996: 167–170. I am inclined to read the "*ratio* of motion and rest" in a much broader way, as a mechanical structure of bodies in motion and rest with respect to one another, a structure that defines the individual as the individual that it is. On this see Garber 1994: 53–59.

[84] *TTP*, chapter 4, Spinoza 1925 3: 57.

[85] The remark about impact discussed above ("all bodies, when they strike against other lesser bodies, lose as much of their motion as they communicate to the other bodies") follows almost immediately on this passage, suggesting that it is an example of such a law. On the relation between these two conceptions of law in Spinoza, the human decision versus the necessity of nature, see Rutherford 2010.

[86] Edwin Curley has long argued that the laws of nature in Spinoza must be understood as "inscribed in" (Curley's words, borrowed from Spinoza, *Tractatus de intellectus emendatione* § 101, Spinoza 1925 2: 36–37) the attribute and immediate infinite mode of extension of the divine substance. See Curley 1969, chapter 2 and Curley 1988: 36–48. This is a very interesting and imaginative suggestion that deserves more careful discussion than I can give in this chapter. But whether or not we choose to accept it, it is not obviously inconsistent with the suggestion that I have made about the status of the laws of nature. What is important on my view is that for Spinoza, as for Hobbes, the laws of nature have the same status as the truths of geometry; that is, as eternal truths. So far as I can see, this is fully consistent with the view that the laws of nature are connected with the attribute and immediate infinite mode of extension, so long as one was willing to say that this holds for geometrical truths as well. This, in fact, is close to a reading that is proposed in Yovel 1991: 88–89.

course, does not. Given that he, too, rejected a transcendent God, it would not be surprising for Spinoza to find Hobbes's approach more congenial than Descartes, a better model for his own brief excursus into natural philosophy.

4 HOBBES'S LEGACY: LEIBNIZ

It was in the summer of 1669 that the young Leibniz, then only twenty-three years old, first got interested in physics. He was in Bad Schwalbach with his patron, Baron von Boineburg, when he was shown the laws of impact that had recently been published by Christiaan Huygens and Christopher Wren in the *Philosophical Transactions of the Royal Society*. Leibniz was drawn into the problem and soon started sketching his own approach to the issue and, indeed, his own approach to natural philosophy.[87] These sketches eventually led to two short works: The *Hypothesis physica nova* and the *Theoria motus abstracti*. Both were finished in 1671. The first was dedicated to the Royal Society of London and the second to the Académie Royale des Sciences in Paris. With Boineburg's help, Leibniz made contact with Henry Oldenburg, a German in London who was the secretary of the Royal Society and the editor of the *Philosophical Transactions*, even before the books were finished. Oldenburg, worried about the progress of the sciences in Germany, warmly encouraged his young countryman. As the works were printed, Leibniz sent Oldenburg copies, which he, in turn, circulated among certain members of the Royal Society.[88] Leibniz tried to establish similar contacts with the Académie Royale, but, lacking contacts in Paris at that moment, his attempts were significantly less successful.[89]

Leibniz's fundamental insight in these works is that the Huygens/Wren laws of impact are not basic, but derivative and depend on the physical makeup of the world. As he wrote in a letter to Oldenburg:

> For I have established certain elements of the true laws of motion, demonstrated in the geometrical method from the definitions of terms alone, ... and this has also shown that those rules of motion, which the incomparable Huygens and Wren have established, are not primary, not absolute, not clear but, no less than gravity, follow from a certain state of the ter-aqueous globe, not demonstrable by axiom or theorem, but from experience, phenomena, and observation, however fertile and admirable ... they might be.[90]

So Leibniz's project, then, is in two parts. On the one hand, he attempts to articulate what the basic laws of motion are and then he attempts to work out a hypothetical state

---

[87] See Antognazza 2009: 106–113.
[88] See here Beeley 2004.
[89] See Antognazza 2009: 109.
[90] Leibniz 1923 2.1²: 95. See also *HPN* § 23; Leibniz 1923 6.2: 231–232.

of the world that, together with the basic laws of motion, will yield the phenomena that we observe. The first is the project of the *Theoria motus abstracti*, the second the project of the *Hypothesis physica nova*.

Leibniz's inspiration for the first part of this project was pretty clearly Hobbes. Leibniz wrote a letter to Hobbes on July 13/23, 1670, while working on the project. After some discussion of Hobbes's political and legal thought, Leibniz wrote:

> I have sometimes thought about the abstract principles of motion, a subject in which I greatly admire the foundations you have established. Indeed, I certainly agree with you that no body can be moved by another body unless it is touched by it, and that once it has been moved, the motion it received will continue unless something impedes it.[91]

The young Leibniz's conception of these abstract principles of motion was very Hobbesian. In a preliminary study for the *Theoria motus abstracti*, he wrote:

> [E]xperiments must be eliminated from the science of the abstract reasons for motion, just as they should be eliminated from geometrical reasonings. For they are demonstrated not from fact and sense, but from the definitions of the terms.[92]

As with Hobbes's basic principles of motion in *De corpore*, Leibniz's are to be derived from the definitions of the terms involved. It is not surprising, then, that the principles that Leibniz presents in the *Theoria motus abstracti* are very close to what Hobbes presented. In Leibniz's system, as in Hobbes, there is no force over and above motion: "all power in bodies depends on the speed."[93] And so, from his earliest studies, Leibniz, like Hobbes before him, held that rest cannot be a cause and that a resting body cannot act.[94] And, like Hobbes before him, Leibniz argued that on the abstract principles of motion, a body in motion, no matter how small or how slow, can impose its motion on a body at rest, no matter how large.[95]

This, of course, fits very poorly with what we observe in the world, as Leibniz well knew. And so he framed a set of hypotheses that would reconcile the abstract and a priori laws with the phenomena. The idea of a hypothetical physics grounded in a priori principles of motion is, of course, very Hobbesian: It is the distinction between the a priori first philosophy and geometry of parts II and III of the *De corpore* and the hypothetical and empirical physics of part IV. Leibniz's particular hypothetical physics was quite different from Hobbes's. Unlike Hobbes, but like Descartes in the *Principia philosophiae*, Leibniz began with a creation story and traced the evolution of the world from an initial state to the present state of the world. Ignoring the other planetary

---

[91] Malcolm 1994 2: 718.
[92] Leibniz 1923 6.2: 160. Cf. Beeley 1995.
[93] Leibniz 1923 6.2: 228.
[94] Leibniz 1923 6.2: 161, 169.
[95] See the account of collision, Leibniz 1923 6.2: 268, §§ 20–24.

bodies, he assumed a Sun and an Earth and argued that the pressure of the light against the surface of the Earth results in tiny bubbles ("bullae") in matter. It is in terms of these tiny bubbles that he attempted to explain a wide variety of physical phenomena.[96]

Although the hypothesis wasn't Hobbesian, the inspiration for the project clearly was. In this work of the young Leibniz, we have, perhaps, the last serious echo of Hobbes's *De corpore* program for natural philosophy.

Oldenburg seemed determined to help the young Leibniz establish himself in England. There is good reason to believe that the letter Leibniz sent to Hobbes through Oldenburg never reached its destination.[97] Although we can only speculate about why Hobbes never received it, one can imagine that the politically savvy Oldenburg would have realized that it would not have been wise for the young Leibniz to have been associated with Hobbes, who had been excluded from the Royal Society and who had been feuding with it since its inception. Hobbes had been doing battle with the irascible John Wallis, an influential member of the Society, for even longer, since, at least, the publication of the *De corpore* in 1655.[98] If it were known that Leibniz was on cordial terms with the Monster of Malmesbury, it could only hurt his chances for acceptance in Oldenburg's circles.[99]

At a meeting of the Royal Society on April 2, 1671, Oldenburg gave Leibniz's *Hypothesis physica nova* to Robert Boyle, Robert Hooke, John Wallis, and Christopher Wren.[100] Before receiving any reports, Oldenburg published in the *Philosophical Transactions* a charming and enthusiastic notice of Leibniz's writings:

> The Ingenious Author of this small Tract, though by profession a Civilian, and one of the Privy Counsel of his Electoral Highness of *Maintz*, and upon that Accompt very much taken up with publick affairs, is yet so much pleased with the study and search of Nature, that whatever hours he can redeem from his State-employment, he spends in that which he judgeth incumbent upon him as Man, I mean the Contemplation of the works of God and Improvement of Natural Philosophy. What he hath therein performed, he imparts in this *Hypothesis* to the Learned world, and dedicateth it to the *Royal-Society of England*, and to the *Royal Academy* of *France*, desirous in his Letters to have their thoughts concerning the same.[101]

Evidently, neither Boyle nor Wren took notice of the writing, and Hooke wrote only a short and not altogether positive response. But John Wallis took the task seriously, and, in the next issue of the *Philosophical Transactions*, his very positive review appeared. The often grumpy Wallis began his review by saying that "I found many things that

---

[96] Cf. Garber 2009: 18–20.

[97] See Noel Malcolm's comment on the letter, Malcolm 1994 2: 721.

[98] For two views on why Hobbes had been excluded from the Royal Society, see Skinner 1969 and Malcolm 2002d. For the battles between Hobbes and Wallis, see Jesseph 1999.

[99] See Beeley 2004: 61–62.

[100] Or, at least, the first part of the *Hypothesis*, up to § 48; Leibniz would send the rest later. See Antognazza 2009: 108–109.

[101] Oldenburg 1671: 2213.

are said here quite reasonably, and to which I can clearly assent, since they are plainly consonant with my own opinions."[102] The controversy between Wallis and Hobbes was still raging; in the previous issue of the *Philosophical Transactions*, the one containing Oldenburg's notice of Leibniz, Wallis had published yet another refutation of Hobbes's mathematics.[103] But he didn't seem to notice the connection between Leibniz and Hobbes. The focus of his review was on the non-Hobbesian hypotheses that Leibniz presented; the more Hobbesian *Theoria motus abstracti* received much less attention, and, even there, Wallis concentrated not on the Hobbesian fundamental principles of motion but on the theory of the cohesion of bodies that Leibniz presented. Wallis's very positive report was a great pleasure to Leibniz.[104] Encouraged by that report, Oldenburg arranged for an English publication of Leibniz's two works under the auspices of the Royal Society.[105]

The very positive reception of Leibniz's natural philosophy no doubt played an important role in Leibniz's eventual election as a Fellow of the Royal Society on April 19, 1673, after his first visit to London in January and February of that year.[106] The welcome would sour in later years, particularly in the context of the bitter priority dispute over the discovery of the calculus. Also, by the end of the 1670s, Leibniz abandoned his Hobbesian physics in favor of his new science of dynamics, largely over issues connected with conservation principles.[107] But even so, there is more than a touch of irony in the fact that the young Hobbesian from Germany was welcomed so warmly into the club that had spurned Hobbes himself.

BIBLIOGRAPHY

Antognazza, Maria Rosa. 2009. *Leibniz: An Intellectual Biography*. Cambridge: Cambridge University Press.

Beaulieu, Armand. 1990. "Les relations de Hobbes et de Mersenne," in *Thomas Hobbes: Philosophie première, théorie de la science et politique*, edited by Y.C. Zarka and J. Bernhardt, 81–90. Paris: Presses Universitaires de France.

Beeley, Philip. 1995. "Les sens dissimulants. Phénomènes et réalité dans l'*Hypothesis physica nova*," in *La notion de nature chez Leibniz*, edited by M. de Gaudemar, 17–30. Stuttgart: Steiner.

Beeley, Philip. 2004. "A Philosophical Apprenticeship: Leibniz's Correspondence with the Secretary of the Royal Society, Henry Oldenburg," in *Leibniz and His Correspondents*, edited by P. Lodge, 47–73. Cambridge: Cambridge University Press.

---

[102] Wallis 1671b: 2228.

[103] Wallis 1671a.

[104] See Leibniz to Fogel, October 5, 1671: "Without doubt, the celebrated M. Wallis in his opinion conveyed to me has judged it [i.e., the *Hypothesis physica nova*] in a generous manner and, indeed this opinion having been written by a man so eminently learned in these matters, I could have read none that would have satisfied me more" (Leibniz 1923: 2.1.154); quoted in Beeley 2004: 71.

[105] Antognazza 2009: 109.

[106] Beeley 2004: 69; Antognazza 2009: 150–151.

[107] See Garber 2009, chapter 3.

Biener, Zvi. 2004. "Galileo's First New Science: The Science of Matter." *Perspectives on Science* 12(3): 262–287.

Brandt, Frithiof. 1928. *Thomas Hobbes' Mechanical Conception of Nature.* Copenhagen/ London: Levin & Munksgaard/Librairie Hachette.

Brockdorff, Baron Cay von. 1934. *Des Sir Charles Cavendish Bericht für Joachim Jungius über die Grundzüge der Hobbes'schen Naturphilosophie.* Kiel: K. J. Rössler.

Brown, Gary I. 1991. "The Evolution of the Term 'Mixed Mathematics.'" *Journal of the History of Ideas* 52: 81–102.

Curley, E. M. 1969. *Spinoza's Metaphysics: An Essay in Interpretation.* Cambridge, MA: Harvard University Press.

Curley, E. M. 1988. *Beyond the Geometrical Method: A Reading of Spinoza's Ethics.* Princeton, NJ: Princeton University Press.

Curley, E. M. 1995. "Hobbes versus Descartes," in *Descartes and His Contemporaries: Meditations, Objections, and Replies*, edited by R. Ariew and M. Grene, 97–109. Chicago: University of Chicago Press.

Descartes, René. 1996. *Oeuvres de Descartes.* Edited by C. Adam and P. Tannery. 11 vols. Paris: J. Vrin.

Foisneau, Luc. 2011. "Hobbes's First Philosophy and Galilean Science." *British Journal for the History of Philosophy* 19(4): 795–809.

Gabbey, Alan. 1996. "Spinoza's Natural Science and Methodology," in *The Cambridge Companion to Spinoza*, edited by Don Garrett, 142–191. Cambridge: Cambridge University Press.

Galilei, Galileo. 1890. *Le opere di Galileo Galilei.* Edited by A. Favaro. 20 vols. Florence: Tip. di G. Barbèra.

Galilei, Galileo. 1957. *Discoveries and Opinions of Galileo.* Translated by S. Drake. Garden City, NY: Doubleday.

Galilei, Galileo. 1967. *Dialogue Concerning the Two Chief World Systems, Ptolemaic and Copernican.* Translated by S. Drake. Berkeley: University of California Press.

Galilei, Galileo. 1974. *Two New Sciences.* Translated by S. Drake. Madison: University of Wisconsin Press.

Garber, Daniel. 1992. *Descartes' Metaphysical Physics.* Chicago: University of Chicago Press.

Garber, Daniel. 1994. "Descartes and Spinoza on Persistence and Conatus." *Studia Spinozana* 10: 43–67.

Garber, Daniel. 2009. *Leibniz: Body, Substance, Monad.* Oxford: Oxford University Press.

Gargani, Aldo Giorgio. 1971. *Hobbes e la scienza.* Turin: G. Einaudi.

Gueroult, Martial. 1968–74. *Spinoza.* 2 vols. Paris: Aubier-Montaigne.

Hobbes, Thomas. 1973. *Critique du De mundo de Thomas White.* Edited by J. Jacquot and H. W. Jones. Paris: J. Vrin.

Hobbes, Thomas. 1999. *De corpore: Elementorum philosophiae sectio prima.* Edited by K. Schuhmann. Paris: J. Vrin.

Hobbes, Thomas. 2010. *Moto, Luogo e Tempo.* Edited and translated by Gianni Paganini. Turin: UTET.

Jacquot, Jean. 1952. "Un document inédit: Les notes de Charles Cavendish sur la première version du 'De corpore' de Hobbes." *Thalès* 8: 33–86.

Jesseph, Douglas. 1999. *Squaring the Circle: The War Between Hobbes and Wallis.* Chicago: University of Chicago Press.

Jesseph, Douglas. 2004. "Galileo, Hobbes, and the Book of Nature." *Perspectives on Science* 12(2): 191–211.

Jesseph, Douglas. 2006. "Hobbesian Mechanics." *Oxford Studies in Early Modern Philosophy* 3: 119–152.

Lachterman, David. 1978. "The Physics of Spinoza's *Ethics*," in *Spinoza: New Perspectives*, edited by R. Shahan and J. I. Biro, 71–111. Norman: University of Oklahoma Press.

Leibniz, Gottfried Wilhelm. 1923. *Sämtliche Schriften und Briefe*. Edited by Deutsche Akademie der Wissenschaften zu Berlin, Akademie der Wissenschaften der DDR, Berlin-Brandenburgische Akademie der Wissenschaften, and Akademie der Wissenschaften in Göttingen. Berlin: Akademie Verlag.

Leijenhorst, Cees. 2004. "Hobbes and the Galilean Law of Free Fall," in *The Reception of the Galilean Science of Motion in Seventeenth-Century Europe*, edited by C. R. Palmerino and J. M. M. H. Thijssen, 165–184. Dordrecht: Kluwer.

Lennox, James G. 1986. "Aristotle, Galileo, and 'Mixed Sciences,'" in *Reinterpreting Galileo*, edited by W. A. Wallace, 29–51. Washington, DC: Catholic University of America Press.

Lenoble, Robert. 1943. *Mersenne, ou, La naissance du mécanisme*. Paris: J. Vrin.

Malcolm, Noel. 1994. *Hobbes: The Correspondence*. Oxford: Oxford University Press.

Malcolm, Noel. 2002a. "A Summary Biography of Hobbes," in Noel Malcolm, *Aspects of Hobbes*, 1–26. Oxford: Oxford University Press.

Malcolm, Noel. 2002b. "Robert Payne, the Hobbes Manuscripts, and the 'Short Tract,'" in Noel Malcolm, *Aspects of Hobbes*, 80–145. Oxford: Oxford University Press.

Malcolm, Noel. 2002c. "Hobbes and Roberval," in Noel Malcolm, *Aspects of Hobbes*, 156–199. Oxford: Oxford University Press.

Malcolm, Noel. 2002d. "Hobbes and the Royal Society," in Noel Malcolm, *Aspects of Hobbes*, 317–335. Oxford: Oxford University Press.

Malcolm, Noel. 2002e. "Hobbes and the European Republic of Letters," in Noel Malcolm, *Aspects of Hobbes*, 457–545. Oxford: Oxford University Press.

Malcolm, Noel, and Jacqueline A. Stedall. 2005. *John Pell (1611–1685) and His Correspondence with Sir Charles Cavendish: The Mental World of an Early Modern Mathematician*. Oxford: Oxford University Press.

Martinich, Aloysius. 1999. *Hobbes: A Biography*. Cambridge: Cambridge University Press.

Mersenne, Marin. 1933–88. *Correspondance du P. Marin Mersenne*. Edited by C. de Waard and P. Tannery. 17 vols. Paris: Beauchesne and Éditions du Centre national de la recherche scientifique.

Oldenburg, Henry. 1671. "An Accompt of Some Books." *Philosophical Transactions of the Royal Society* 6(73): 2210–2214.

Paganini, Gianni. 2006. "Hobbes, Gassendi e l'ipotesi annichilitoria." *Giornale Critico della Filosofia Italiana* 85(1): 55–81.

Pécharman, Martine. 1997. "Philosophie première et théologie selon Hobbes," in *Politique, droit et théologie chez Bodin, Grotius et Hobbes* edited by L. Foisneau, 215–241. Paris: Kimé.

Peters, R. S. 1956. *Hobbes*. Harmondsworth, Middlesex: Penguin Books.

Rivaud, Albert. 1924. "La physique de Spinoza." *Chronicon Spinozanum* 4: 24–57.

Rutherford, Donald. 2010. "Spinoza's Conception of Law: Metaphysics and Ethics," in *Spinoza's 'Theological-Political Treatise': A Critical Guide*, edited by Y. Melamed and M. Rosenthal, 143–167. Cambridge: Cambridge University Press.

Sarasohn, Lisa. 1985. "Motion and Morality: Pierre Gassendi, Thomas Hobbes and the Mechanical World-View." *Journal of the History of Ideas* 46: 363–380.

Savan, David. 1986. "Spinoza: Scientist and Theorist of Scientific Method," in *Spinoza and the Sciences*, edited by M. Grene and D. Nails, 95–123. Dordrecht: D. Reidel.

Schliesser, Eric. 2013. "Spinoza and the Philosophy of Science: Mathematics, Motion, and Being," in *The Oxford Handbook of Spinoza*, edited by M. Della Rocca. Oxford: Oxford University Press.

Schmaltz, Tad M. 2008. *Descartes on Causation*. New York: Oxford University Press.

Shapin, Steven, and Simon Schaffer. 1985. *Leviathan and the Air-Pump: Hobbes, Boyle, and the Experimental Life*. Princeton, NJ: Princeton University Press.

Skinner, Quentin. 1969. "Thomas Hobbes and the Nature of the Early Royal Society." *The Historical Journal* 12: 217–239.

Sorell, Tom. 1995. "Hobbes's Objections and Hobbes's System," in *Descartes and His Contemporaries: Meditations, Objections, and Replies*, edited by R. Ariew and M. Grene, 63–96. Chicago: University of Chicago Press.

Spinoza, Benedictus de. 1925. *Spinoza Opera*. Edited by C. Gebhardt. 4 vols. Heidelberg: Carl Winters.

Spinoza, Benedictus de. 1985. *The Collected works of Spinoza*. Edited and translated by E. M. Curley. Princeton, NJ: Princeton University Press.

Tuck, Richard. 1988. "Hobbes and Descartes," in *Perspectives on Thomas Hobbes*, edited by G. A. J. Rogers and A. Ryan, 11–41. Oxford: Oxford University Press.

Wallis, John. 1671a. "An Answer of Dr. Wallis to Mr. Hobbes's Rosetum Geometricum." *Philosophical Transactions of the Royal Society* 6(73): 2202–2209.

Wallis, John. 1671b. "Dr. Wallis's Opinion Concerning the Hypothesis Physica Nova of Dr. Leibnitius." *Philosophical Transactions of the Royal Society* 6(74): 2227–2231.

Watkins, John W. N. 1965. *Hobbes's System of Ideas; A Study in the Political Significance of Philosophical Theories*. London: Hutchinson.

Yovel, Yirmiyahu. 1991. "The Infinite Mode and Natural Laws in Spinoza," in *God and Nature: Spinoza's Metaphysics*, edited by Y. Yovel, 79–96. Leiden and New York: Brill.

CHAPTER 6

<hr>

HOBBES ON THE FOUNDATIONS OF NATURAL PHILOSOPHY

<hr>

DOUGLAS M. JESSEPH

THE natural philosophy of Thomas Hobbes is a curious mixture of abstract first principles and conjectural accounts of the origins of natural phenomena. As set forth in *De corpore*, Hobbes's program for the study of nature begins with very general notions of space, time, body, and motion, together with mechanistic physical principles declaring that all the phenomena of nature arise from the motion and collision of material bodies. This much of the Hobbesian program for natural philosophy appears in Part II of *De corpore* that goes under the title "The First Grounds of Philosophy." By situating his account of the foundations of natural philosophy in this part of his treatise of the body, Hobbes in effect made the foundations of natural philosophy continuous with the foundations of philosophy *simpliciter*. In contrast, the fourth part of *De corpore* is devoted to explicating "the Phænomena of Nature." But in this aspect of his natural philosophy Hobbes constantly stressed our lack of insight into the causes of natural phenomena, with the consequent necessity of relying on conjectured mechanisms that might account for them, rather than deriving explanations demonstratively from mechanistic first principles. Part of what I wish to do here is to see how these two pieces of Hobbes's natural philosophy are related; that is, how the foundations of his program fit together with his explanatory practice.

My procedure will thus fall into two parts: the first examines the accounts of space and time that constitute Hobbes's foundations of his natural philosophy; the second will consider the limitations that Hobbes saw in these foundations; that is, the kinds of questions whose resolution either requires appeal to empirical conjectures or lies beyond the scope of natural philosophy altogether. In the end, Hobbes's program for natural philosophy offers an interesting contrast with other seventeenth-century approaches, notably those of Descartes and Thomas White.

1 HOBBES ON SPACE AND TIME

Hobbes notoriously defined philosophy as "such Knowledge of Effects, or Appearances, as we acquire by true Ratiocination from the knowing we have first their Causes or Generation; And again, of such Causes or Generations as may be from knowing first their Effects."[1] Philosophizing thus requires reasoning about causes and effects. Furthermore, Hobbes held that the great universal cause of all things could only be motion, so that all of philosophy (and specifically natural philosophy) becomes the study of what can be brought about by motion.[2] Indeed, the distinction between first philosophy and natural philosophy can be difficult to draw in Hobbes's system precisely because the fundamental notions in his first philosophy include seemingly physical concepts such as body and motion.[3]

Hobbes instructed his readers that the place to begin "In the Teaching of Naturall Philosophy" is with the thought experiment (as we would now term it) of supposing the world to have been annihilated with the exception of one individual. This solitary thinker would have

> Ideas of the World, and of all such Bodies as he had, before their annihilation, seen with his eies, or perceived by any other Sense: that is to say, the Memory and Imagination of Magnitudes, Motions, Sounds, Colours &c. as also of their order & parts.[4]

This collection of mental contents retained from experience of the world before its annihilation would furnish our solitary thinker with the concept of space because it contains information about the "order and parts" of the phenomenal world. Recollecting the phantasms of things he had once perceived but taking them only to be representations of something external to a perceiving mind, our thinker will "have presently a Conception of that we call *Space*: an Imaginary Space indeed, because a meere Phantasme, yet that very thing which all men call so."[5] From this thought experiment, Hobbes concluded that space is to be defined as "*the Phantasme of a Thing existing without the Mind simply*; that is to say, that Phantasme, in which we consider no other Accident, but onely that it appears without us."[6]

---

[1] *Concerning Body* 1.1.2, 2.

[2] Brandt 1928: 379, notes that the explanatory primacy of motion in Hobbes's system means that, rather than being characterized as a materialist, "Hobbes should more properly be called a motionalist, if we may be permitted to coin such a word."

[3] I discuss the seeming intrusion of physical concepts into Hobbes's first philosophy at greater length in Jesseph 2006.

[4] *Concerning Body* 2.7.1, 67.

[5] *Concerning Body* 2.7.2, 68.

[6] *Concerning Body*, 2.7.2, 69.

At first sight, this definition seems to make space a *phantasm*, or a subjective appearance derived from the experience of bodies rather than an objective or mind-independent framework in which bodies have a determinate location. Some commentators have taken the Hobbesian doctrine of space to foreshadow Kant's conception of space as a form of external intuition.[7] However, the reasons Hobbes offered for adopting his account of space show his doctrine to be far removed from that of Kant. Hobbes did not understand space as a transcendental principle structuring our perception of objects, but rather as the effect of bodies' interactions with the perceptual system. More significantly, Hobbes took the concept of space to be of empirical origin, as something that arises out of the experience of external bodies, whereas Kant understood space as an a priori concept that is presupposed in experience.

Space thus defined is what Hobbes termed "Imaginary Space."[8] If this were all he had to say on the subject, Hobbes would indeed have been some kind of idealist who took space to be a mind-dependent or conceptual entity that arises from the order that perceivers assign to items of experience. But Hobbes did not end his account of space with the definition of imaginary space. Indeed, the main reason for terming something *imaginary* is to mark a contrast between an imaginary thing and its *real* or objective counterpart. In the present case, this contrast requires *real space*, which is an ordering of objects that cannot be reduced to the phantasms of a perceiver and serves as an objective framework in which objects are located. Hobbes's treatment of this distinction in *De corpore* is not as clear or extensive as one might wish. He did remark that

> The Extension of a Body, is the same thing with the MAGNITUDE of it, or that which some call *Real Space*. But this *Magnitude* does not depend upon our Cogitation, as Imaginary Space doth; for this is an Effect of our Imagination, but *Magnitude* is the Cause of it; this is an Accident of the Mind, that of a Body existing out of the Mind.[9]

This passage clearly intends to distinguish between imaginary and real space: imaginary space is the subjective ordering or disposition of perceived objects and is an effect arising from external bodies' interaction with our sensory system; real space, however, is the objective location of the external bodies that are perceived. Hobbes defined body as "*that which having no dependence upon our Thought is coincident or coextended with some part of Space*," so he clearly needed a notion of space that is not entirely mind-dependent.[10]

---

[7] Herbert 1987: 701, declared that "Hobbes's account of space anticipates in many respects the Kantian phenomenology of space that will appear more than a century later," although the basis for this characterization is highly problematic. See Leijenhorst 2002: 107–8, for the difficulties involved in this interpretation.

[8] See Leijenhorst 2002: 105–22, on Hobbes's conception of imaginary space and its background in medieval discussions of the ontology of space. Grant 1969, is a useful summary of medieval and seventeenth-century discussions of imaginary space.

[9] *Concerning Body* 2.8.4, 76.

[10] *Concerning Body* 2.8.1, 75.

An instance of the distinction between imaginary and real space can be taken from the ordering of objects in visual perception. In looking at two chess pieces on a board, a perceiver might see that the white queen is to the left of the white king. This ordering is patently subjective because it varies with the relative positions of the observer and the two pieces. It therefore makes sense to say that the white queen is to the left of the white king in the imaginary space constructed from the phantasms of the perceiver. But the "left of" ordering does not hold absolutely or objectively, since there are vantage points from which it fails. Nevertheless, there remains an objective fact about the relative positions of the two pieces. Furthermore, the pieces' locations in real space (together with the spatial location of our perceiver) cause the ordering in imaginary space.

A clearer and more extensive account of the distinction between imaginary and real space appears in Hobbes's criticisms of Thomas White's *De mundo dialogi tres*. In this work, he defined imaginary space as "the image of a body, insofar as it is a body" so that "the existence of [this] space does not depend on the existence of body but on the existence of the imaginative faculty."[11] However, this imaginary space presupposes a nonimaginary or real space:

> it is impossible that we suppose there to be some body without at the same time thinking it to be endowed with its own dimensions or spaces. Therefore this space, which can be called real, is inherent in a body, as an accident in its subject, and would surely exist even if there were nothing that could imagine it.[12]

Following this line of thought, we should think of imaginary space not as an independent construct of the mind, but rather as an effect of the action of external bodies on the perceptual system.

To see more clearly why this is so, we should recall that Hobbes's ontology recognizes body as the only substance. Therefore, because space cannot be identified with a body, it must be an "accident" of body. However, Hobbes gave a twofold definition of the term "accident," either as "*the Manner by which any Body is conceived*," or as "*that faculty of any Body by which it works in us a Conception of it self*."[13] We can term the first of these the "subjective" definition, whereas the second is an "objective" definition of the term "accident." Defined subjectively, an accident of body is how the body appears to a perceiver; but defined objectively, an accident is the causal mechanism by which a body generates a phantasm in the mind of a perceiver. This distinction corresponds to that between imaginary and real space: imaginary space is the subjective or "fictive"

---

[11] "[D]icemus *spatium esse imaginem corporis, quatenùs corporis*. . . Manifestum hinc est existentiam spatii dependere non ab existentia corporis sed ab existentia imaginativae facultatis" (*Critique du De mundo*, ch. 3, sect. 1, 117).

[12] "Neque possibile est ut corpus aliquod esse existimemus, quin simul putemus ipsum praeditum esse dimensionibus, sive spatiis suis. Hoc spatium igitur quod appellari potest reale inhaerens corpori, ut accidens in subiecto suo, existeret sane, etsi nihil esset quod ipsum imaginari possit" (*Critique du De mundo*, ch. 3, sect. 2, 117).

[13] *Concerning Body* 2.8.2, 75.

location of a body as it appears; real space is the mind-independent *magnitude* of a body, or what Hobbes termed its "true Extension."[14] Real space thus corresponds to the magnitude of a body, whereas imaginary space is the "phantasm" produced by a body as it acts on the senses. As Cees Leijenhorst characterizes the issue, the "relation between *spatium reale* to *spatium imaginarium* exemplifies the cause-effect relation existing between our ideas and external things."[15]

Hobbes's account of time has many similarities to his theory of space, with one very significant difference. Time is defined in *De corpore* as "*the Phantasme of Before and After in Motion*";[16] this is very much like Hobbes's definition of imaginary space as "*the Phantasme of a Thing existing without the Mind simply.*"[17] Time is therefore defined as a mental representation of motion rather than as something objective or independent of perceiving minds and moving bodies. Unlike his treatment of space, Hobbes's account of time has no counterpart to the distinction between imaginary space and real space. The result is that there is no "real time" that orders events independently of the perceiving minds that keep track of its passage. In his words:

> For seeing all men confess a Yeare to be Time, and yet do not think a Year to be the Accident or Affection of any Body, they must needs confesse it to be, not in the things without Us, but only in the Thought of the Mind. . . . What then can Dayes, Moneths and Yeares be, but the Names of such Computations made in our Mind? *Time* therefore is a Phantasme, but a Phantasme of Motion, for if we would know by what Moments Time passes away, we make use of some Motion or other, as of the Sun, of a Clock, or the sand in an Hourglasse.[18]

Interestingly, Hobbes took this theory of time to be consistent with Aristotle's definition, notwithstanding his oft-expressed disdain for Aristotelian metaphysics and natural philosophy. At *Physics* IV, 11 220^a 24–25, Aristotle had defined time as "the number of movement in respect of the before and after"; Hobbes commented on this definition that "Numbring is an act of the mind; and therefore it is all one to say, *Time is the Number of Motion according to Former and Later*; and *Time is a Phantasme of Motion Numbred.*"[19]

Hobbes's natural philosophy therefore defines time as an accident of motion, whereas space is an accident of body. Time, however, is a subjective or mind-dependent accident because it requires an observer to compute or reckon its passage. The accident of space, however, has both an observer-dependent component (imaginary space) and an objective ordering (real space). In the Hobbesian scheme, "MOTION and MAGNITUDE . . . are the most common Accidents of Bodies";[20] furthermore, because "The Extension

---

[14] *Concerning Body* 2.8.5, 77.
[15] Leijenhorst 2002: 107.
[16] *Concerning Body* 2.7.3, 70.
[17] *Concerning Body* 2.7.2, 69.
[18] *Concerning Body* 2.7.3, 69.
[19] *Concerning Body* 2.7.3, 70.
[20] *Concerning Body* 3.15.1, 149.

of a Body, is the same thing with the MAGNITUDE of it,"[21] the two most fundamental properties of body are extension and motion. Space and time derive from these two basic accidents: the accident of extension is the basis for both real and imaginary space, where the one is identified with a body's objective location and the other with the subjective phantasm of its position relative to a perceiver. Time, in contrast, is identified with the measure of a body's motion; but because all measurement requires a measuring mind, time must be an *ens rationis*.

A salient peculiarity of his approach is that, in seeking to define space and time in terms of magnitude (or extension) and motion, Hobbes seems to get the usual order of conceptual dependence backward. One would normally think that such terms as magnitude or motion should be defined in terms of space and time: the magnitude of a body is the amount of space it takes up, whereas its motion is defined as translation from one part of space to another in a given time. Hobbes, however, inverts this traditional order of *definiens* and *definiendum*, evidently thinking that the concepts of magnitude and motion qualify as more perspicuous and primitive than those of space and time.[22] Whatever the limitations of this program, we can now consider how Hobbes employs it in structuring his natural philosophy.

2 FUNDAMENTAL PRINCIPLES OF HOBBESIAN PHYSICS

The picture that emerges shows Hobbes to have a very sparse foundation for his natural philosophy. The world consists of bodies endowed only with magnitude (extension) and motion (or rest). All else is to be accounted for in terms of magnitude and motion, and the only way that anything can be brought about is by the collision of one body with another.[23] Furthermore, our reasoning is confined to those things of which we can have phantasms, and we can have demonstrative certainty only about those things whose causes are fully known to us.

Within this general framework for natural philosophy, Hobbes held that it was possible to have demonstrative knowledge of two fundamental physical principles. In chapter 8 of *De corpore*, which deals with "Body and Accident," he demonstrated (at least to his own satisfaction) a version of the law of inertia that I term the "persistence

---

[21] *Concerning Body* 2.8.4, 76.

[22] Al Martinich has pointed out that this departure from the traditional order of *definiens* and *definiendum* is not an isolated occurrence in Hobbes's work. In *Leviathan*, for instance, he notoriously takes "war" to be the primary term and defines "peace" in terms of it.

[23] Laird 1934 [1968]: 101, sums up the matter by noting "we may say Hobbes's interpretation of Body and Accident, together with his interpretation of Cause, defined his materialism. There was nothing except Body with the ingenerable accident of spatial magnitude and the generable accidents of motion, than which there were no other accidents. Every natural appearance was an *instance* of the motion of bodies."

principle." It asserts "*Whatsoever is at Rest, will always be at Rest, unless there be some other Body besides it, which by endeavouring to get into its Place by motion, suffers it no longer to remain at Rest.*"[24] The second principle Hobbes thought he could demonstrate is what I term that of "action by contact," according to which all alteration in the state of a body derives from impact with another body. In Hobbes's formulation, the principle reads: "There can be no Cause of Motion, except in a Body Contiguous, and Moved."[25] According to Hobbes, both of these principles are capable of a priori demonstration, and it is worthwhile considering his putative demonstrations of them.[26] A demonstration, as defined by Hobbes, is "a Syllogism or Series of Syllogisms derived and continued from the Definitions of Names, to the last Conclusion."[27] Thus, he held that both principles are derivable from nothing beyond definitions of such terms as *space, time, body,* and *motion.*

Hobbes's demonstration of the persistence principle appeals to something like a principle of sufficient reason applied to the case of an isolated body at rest. He writes:

> For suppose that some Finite Body exist, and be at Rest, and that all Space besides be Empty; if now this Body begin to be Moved, it will certainly be Moved some way; Seeing therefore there was nothing in that Body which did not dispose it to Rest, the reason why it is Moved this way is in something out of it; and in like manner, if it had been Moved any other way, the reason of Motion that way had also been in something out of it; but seeing it was supposed that Nothing is out of it, the reason of its Motion one way would be the same with the reason of its Motion every other way; wherefore it would be Moved alike all ways at once; which is impossible.[28]

There is much in this demonstration to criticize, and I have no interest in defending it. It is, however, noteworthy that Hobbes took the persistence principle to be a conceptual truth that follows necessarily from the very definitions of space, body, and motion. Philosophically untutored common sense might well think it possible for a body to move itself spontaneously, but Hobbes took this to be an illusion. He insisted that although we may "feign in our Mind" that such a thing could happen, nevertheless "we cannot comprehend in our Minde how this may possibly be done in nature."[29]

The proof Hobbes offered for the principle of action by contact is sufficiently complex and confusing that I cannot examine it in detail here. In essence, Hobbes employed the persistence principle to argue, first, that a body cannot initiate its own motion; thus, the cause must lie outside of the body. But if a body is surrounded by empty space, there is nothing that could cause it to move; likewise, if the body is surrounded by stationary

---

[24] *Concerning Body* 2.8.19, 83.
[25] *Concerning Body* 2.9.7, 90.
[26] I have discussed these principles and Hobbes's supposed proofs of them at greater length in Jesseph 2006: 129–40.
[27] *Concerning Body* 1.6.16, 62.
[28] *Concerning Body* 2.8.19, 83–84.
[29] *Concerning Body* 2.8.20, 84.

bodies, there is nothing to determine it to motion. Thus, the only cause of a body's initiating motion must be contact with a body in motion.[30]

The point of interest in these two cases is not that Hobbes had solid, convincing arguments for his principles, but rather that he thought they were capable of a priori demonstration. In other words, persistence and action by contact are not simply well-confirmed empirical generalizations or plausible conjectures about how nature works. Instead, they are definitionally true statements that have the status of logical or conceptual truths. One who denies them is guilty not merely of accepting a mistaken physical principle, but of literal self-contradiction and incoherence. As a consequence, anyone who supposes that a body might spontaneously initiate or extinguish its own motion or that anything could arise except from motion and collision of bodies has made an error on a par with supposing that a triangle might have more than three sides or that seventeen might not be a prime number.

3 The Scope of Demonstrative Natural Philosophy

Although Hobbes took twin physical principles of persistence and action by contact to be demonstrable from his foundations for natural philosophy, there are many fundamental questions that were traditionally part of natural philosophy that he took to be either unanswerable or (if answerable at all) only to be resolved empirically. Consider, for instance, questions about the infinitude and uniqueness of the world. At least since Aristotle, natural philosophers had made a habit of attempting to determine whether the world is finite or infinite or whether there could be worlds other than ours. In the medieval era, many natural philosophers in the Aristotelian tradition discussed these issues in considerable depth,[31] and the topics remained the object of natural-philosophical theorizing throughout the seventeenth century. Hobbes, however, threw

---

[30] In his words: "For let there be any two Bodies which are not contiguous, and betwixt which the intermediate Space is empty, or if filled, filled with another Body which is at Rest; and let one of the propounded Bodies be supposed to be at Rest, I say it shall always be at Rest. For if it shall be Moved, the Cause of that Motion (by the 8th. Chapter 19th. Article [i.e., the persistence principle]) will be in some external Body; and therefore if between it and that external Body there be nothing but empty Space, then whatsoever the disposition be of that external Body, or of the Patient it selfe, yet if it be supposed to be now at Rest, we may conceive it will continue so til it be touched by some other body; but seeing Cause (by Definition) is the Aggregate of all such Accidents, which being supposed to be present it cannot be conceived but that the Effect will follow, those Accidents which are either in external Bodies, or in the Patient itself, cannot be the Cause of future Motion; and in like manner, seeing we may conceive, that whatsoever is at Rest, will still be at Rest, though it be touched by some other Body, except that other body be moved, therefore in a contiguous body which is at Rest, there can be no Cause of motion. Wherefore there is no Cause of Motion, in any Body, except it be Contiguous and Moved." (*Concerning Body* 2.9.7, 90)

[31] See Duhem 1985, for an account of medieval debates on these topics.

cold water on such investigations. He remarked that "when we make question whether the World be Finite or Infinite, we have nothing in our Minde answering to the name *World*; for whatsoever we Imagine, is therefore Finite."[32] Since any imagined space is finite, yet we can always imagine it to be further extended, no determinate limit can be assigned to the extent of imaginary space. But we are also in no position to assert that imaginary space is literally infinite because that would require an image or phantasm of the infinite. The question is therefore unanswerable, at least philosophically. In commenting on his treatment of space, Hobbes remarked

> And this is of it selfe so manifest, that I should not thinke it needed any explaining at all, but that I finde Space to be falsely defined by certaine Philosophers, who inferre from thence, One, that the world is Infinite; for taking *Space* to be the Extension of Bodies, and thinking Extension may encrease continually, he inferres that Bodies may be infinitely Extended; and Another from the same Definition concludes rashly, that it is impossible even to God himself to create more Worlds then one; for if another World were to be created, he sayes, that seeing there is nothing without this world, and therefore (according to his Definition) no Space, that new world must be placed in nothing; but in nothing nothing can be placed; which he affirms onely, without shewing any reason for the same; whereas the contrary is the truth: for more cannot be put into a Place allready filled, so much is Empty Space fitter then that which is Full for the receiving of new Bodies.[33]

The two mistaken philosophers here are Descartes and Thomas White. Descartes's error (in the *Principles of Philosophy*, Part II, article 21) was to reason that, since we can imagine any supposed limit to the world to be further extended, there is no limit to space. White's mistake (in the third part of the first dialogue of his *De mundo dialogi tres*) was to ask "what could be clearer than that a thing placed in nothing has no place?"[34] The principle that what is placed in nothing has no place yields the immediate consequence that the world as a whole could not be placed anywhere.

Hobbes's response here shows that he took questions of the infinity and uniqueness of the world to be unanswerable even in principle. There might, for all we know, be no limit to the spatial extent of the universe; likewise, there might be other worlds aside from ours located in alternate spaces. Then again, the universe might be spatially finite and unique. Because no "phantasm" could ever decide the issue, and our spatial concepts cannot resolve such questions a priori, they can be dismissed as pointless and incapable of resolution.

In part IV of *De corpore*, Hobbes returned to these themes and argued that questions about the magnitude and duration of the world must be "inscrutable." In seeking to answer such questions, Hobbes held, we must invariably run up against our cognitive limitations: "Whatsoever we know that are Men, we learn it from our Phantasmes,

---

[32] *Concerning Body* 2.7.12, 73.

[33] *Concerning Body* 1.7.2, 68–69.

[34] "[Q]uid clarius esse potest quam positam in nihilo rem locum nullum habere?" White 1643: 28.

and of *Infinite* (whether Magnitude or Time) there is no Phantasme at all; so that it is impossible either for a man, or any other creature to have any conception of *Infinite.*" Furthermore, "whether we suppose the World to be Finite, or Infinite, no absurdity will follow. For the same things which now appear, might appear, whether the Creator had pleased it should be Finite or Infinite."[35] Such questions are therefore beyond the scope of natural philosophy and "are not to be determined by Philosophers, but by those that are lawfully authorized to order the Worship of God."[36]

A related question in natural philosophy concerns the existence of a vacuum. Aristotle had offered several arguments in the *Physics* (I 7) intended to show that a vacuum is impossible. Likewise, Descartes had declared in part 2, article 16 of his *Principles of Philosophy* that "It is a contradiction to suppose there is such a thing as a vacuum, i.e. that in which there is nothing whatever."[37] Descartes's reasoning on this point was repeated by Thomas White, who argued thus:

> If there were a vacuum, there would be a place without body, that is, a concave body without anything to fill the cavity. . . . So the sides of this concave body will close up because there is no thing between them. But if the sides are closed up, this excludes the vacuum.[38]

Hobbes regarded this sort of a priori argumentation against the vacuum as nonsense more worthy of derision than refutation. Having defined contiguous bodies as those having no space between them, he insisted

> And this is so easie to be understood, that I should wonder at some men, who being otherwise skillful enough in Philosophy, are of a different opinion, but that I finde that most of those that affect Metaphysical subtilties, wander from Truth, as if they were led out of their way by an *Ignis Fatuus*. For can any man that has his natural Senses, think that two Bodies must therefore necessarily Touch one another, because no other Body is between them? Or that there can be no *Vacuum*, because *Vacuum* is nothing, or as they call it, *Non Ens*? Which is as childish, as if one should reason thus; No man can Fast, because to Fast is to eat Nothing; but Nothing cannot be eaten.[39]

The question of a vacuum is, for Hobbes, an empirical one, to be decided on the basis of experimental evidence. This marks an obvious contrast with his attitude toward the

---

[35] *Concerning Body* 4.26.1, 307.

[36] *Concerning Body* 4.26.1, 307. This issue is discussed by Probst 1993, in the context of Hobbes's dispute with Seth Ward and John Wallis.

[37] Descartes, *Oeuvres*, 8: 49.

[38] "Si enim vacuum est locus sine corpore, hoc est, corpus concauum, sine aliquot cauitatem impleat, none vides concauitatem quanta esse sine tertiâ mediante. Vides ergo ex ipsa notione vacui conjuncta esse latera, et si conjuncta sint, iam nullum reliquum esse vacuum" White 1643: dial. 1, §8, 30–31.

[39] *Concerning Body* 2.8.9, 79.

questions of the infinity and uniqueness of the world, which he took to be in principle unanswerable.

The dispute over the vacuum, Hobbes declared, "is carried on with probability enough," but he thought it could be resolved empirically on the basis of "onely one experiment, a common one, but (I think) unanswerable."[40] The experiment Hobbes had in mind involves a vessel with small holes in the bottom and a larger opening at the top. When the vessel is filled with water and the top is stopped shut, water does not flow through the holes; but when the top is opened, water does flow. Hobbes concluded from this that "the Water cannot by its natural endeavor to descend, drive down the air below," because there is no vacuum beneath it. This, Hobbes concludes, is "a sign that all Space is full; for without this the naturall motion of the water . . . downwards, would not be hindered."[41] Opposed to this experimental evidence are "many specious arguments and experiments" that Hobbes considered and rejected. In every case, he argued, the evidence is at best inconclusive and occasionally inconsistent with the a priori principles of persistence and action by contact.[42]

Hobbes's attitude toward questions of the vacuum contrasts with his outright dismissal of the doctrine of rarefaction and condensation. This doctrine has Aristotelian roots and held that the numerically same body might have more or less quantity, acquiring and losing quantity through the contrary processes of rarefaction and condensation.[43] In Hobbes's estimation, this doctrine is incoherent because it violates both the persistence principle and the principle of action by contact. According to Hobbes, "a Body keeps always the same *Magnitude*, both when it is at Rest, and when it is Moved";[44] thus, the change in the magnitude of a body must literally require the destruction of the body. Furthermore, in a case where a body seems to gain magnitude, this change cannot arise spontaneously (by the persistence principle) and must result from the motion and impact of some external bodies (in virtue of the action by contact principle).

[40]   *Concerning Body*, 4.26.2, 309.

[41]   *Concerning Body*, 4.26.2, 309.

[42]   Hobbes considered two principal arguments for a vacuum: an a priori one derived from Lucretius (which held that empty space is necessary for bodies to move) and an empirical one from Torricelli (which interpreted the empty space at the top of the familiar "Torricellian tube" as a true void). Hobbes held that neither argument could definitively rule out the existence of a very subtle fluid filling seemingly empty space, and both tended toward an incoherent metaphysics that attributed spontaneous motion or a tendency toward motion to bodies. For more on Hobbes's case against the vacuum (particularly in the context of his 1661 *Dialogus physicus*), see Shapin and Schaffer 1985: ch. 4.

[43]   The details of the doctrine are obscure enough to be left aside here. An oddity of the doctrine is that a rare body was taken (at least by some) to have *more* quantity in it than a dense one, contrary to our ordinary understanding of density and rarity. This derives from the fact that quantity is, in the words of Kenelm Digby, "nothing else but divisibility; and . . . a thing is bigge, by having a capacity to be divided" 1644: 9. Thus, a highly divisible body contains more quantity than a less divisible body of the same volume.

[44]   *Concerning Body* 2.8.5, 77.

The consequence is that talk of rarefaction and condensation is literally incoherent. In *Leviathan*, Hobbes complained that the doctrine supposes "there could be Matter, that had not some determined Quantity; when Quantity is nothing else but the Determination of Matter" or that there could be a body "made without any Quantity at all, and that afterwards more, or lesse were put into it, according as it is intended the body should be more or less Dense."[45] In either case, the result is that there can be no content assigned to the concepts or (as Hobbes put it in his *Six Lessons*), "nature abhorres even empty words, such as are . . . *Rarefying* and *Condensing*."[46]

4 Hobbes's Program and Its Fate

It should by now be clear that Hobbes's program for natural philosophy is quite a far cry from the dogmatic, antiexperimental, "rationalistic" enterprise that some commentators have claimed it to be.[47] His preference for plenism, for instance, did not arise from an indifference to experimental evidence or his acceptance of some kind of a priori argument against the possibility of a vacuum. Whether or not there is a vacuum is a question left open by the foundational notions in Hobbes's natural philosophy; that is, his account of space, time, body, motion, and causation. Thus, if the question can be resolved at all, it must be resolved on the basis of experiment, and Hobbes held that the experimental evidence was solidly against the hypothesis of a vacuum. Similarly, such phenomena as gravity, the freezing of water, or the propagation of sound cannot be accounted for by deducing them from the first principles of natural philosophy. Hobbes insisted that "where there is place for Demonstration, if the first Principles, that is to say, the Definitions contain not the Generation of the Subject; there can be nothing demonstrated as it ought to be."[48] However, when we lack access to the causes of phenomena (and this is typically the case in the investigation of nature), we must content ourselves with hypothetical causes.[49] The principles of persistence and action by

---

[45] *Leviathan*, ch. 46, 1086.

[46] *Six Lessons*, Lesson 2, 14. It is interesting to note that when he wrote his *Critique of Thomas White*, Hobbes was undecided about the status of rarefaction and condensation. He found White's exposition of the doctrine obscure but did not dismiss the concepts of rarefaction or condensation as incoherent. He declared "I myself affirm nothing concerning the reason for rarity and density, for I prefer ignorance to error. But if someone should demonstrate it clearly, I think he would lay bare the very inner reaches of physics" (*Critique du De mundo*, dial. 3, §10, 123).

[47] Shapin and Schaffer sum up this approach to Hobbes's natural philosophy in declaring that "What Hobbes was claiming . . . was that the systematic doing of experiments was not to be equated with philosophy: going on in the way Boyle recommended for experimentalists was not the same thing as philosophical practice . . . This experimental way and the philosophical way were fundamentally different: they differed in their capacity to secure assent among intellectuals and peace in the polity" 1985: 129.

[48] *Six Lessons*, Epistle.

[49] I deal with the distinction between demonstrative science and the ineradicably hypothetical nature of natural philosophy or "physiques" in Hobbes in Jesseph 1996.

contact rule out certain kinds of natural-philosophical explanations, but they radically underdetermine what sort of mechanisms produce natural phenomena. As Hobbes framed the issue, "all that can be expected" in most cases is the assignment of a possible cause to a phenomenon, because "there is no effect in nature which the Author of Nature cannot bring to pass by more ways than one,"[50] so that "in natural causes all you are to expect is but probability."[51]

This fact accounts for some oddities in the fourth part of *De corpore*, where Hobbes entered into that part of natural philosophy "which is the finding out by the Appearances or Effects of Nature which we know by Sense, some wayes and means by which they may be (I do not say, they are) generated."[52] Rather than deriving the phenomena of nature systematically from a small collection of basic mechanical laws, Hobbes spent this part of *De corpore* introducing a wide variety of mechanistic hypotheses intended to account for them. For instance, his treatment of gravitation in chapter 30 of *De corpore* seeks to explain the accelerated descent of bodies by means of a complex mechanism of air pressure, which in turn arises from the diurnal rotation of the Earth on its axis and the denial of the vacuum. Aside from being hypotheses concerning different sorts of motions, there is nothing to unify the various hypothetical explanations Hobbes assembled in part IV of *De corpore*. As a result, his natural philosophy has a very scattershot aspect that seems more a random walk through a wide variety of topics than a sustained investigation into the workings of the natural world.[53]

Although the Hobbesian foundations of natural philosophy permit a fairly wide range for hypothesis and experiment, there are nevertheless some traditional questions that can be dismissed as incapable of philosophical resolution. No experiment or "phantasm" will settle the question of whether there could be more than one world or whether our world is finite in extent. Furthermore, the foundational concepts of natural philosophy are insufficient to resolve these issues: it does not follow from the definition of space or time that the world is finite or that it is infinite, for example. In this respect, Hobbes's approach to natural philosophy seems far less ambitious than that of Descartes or White. Furthermore, his attitude toward such question seems remarkably less dogmatic that that of other philosophers who held that such questions were capable of definitive resolution.

This is not to say that Hobbes's foundations for natural philosophy leave no effective constraints on what hypotheses the natural philosopher might introduce. Stated most generally, Hobbes's constraints on any putative causal hypotheses are two: "the first, is that it be conceivable, that is, not absurd; the other, that by conceding it, the necessity of the phenomenon may be inferred."[54] More specifically, Hobbes took the persistence

[50] *Decameron Physiologicum*, ch. 2, 22.
[51] *Seven Philosophical Problems*, ch. 1, 7.
[52] *Concerning Body* 4.25.1, 289.
[53] This can be seen in the title of chapter 28 of *De corpore*, which promises to treat "Of Cold, Wind, Hard, Ice, Restitution of Bodies bent, Diaphanous, Lightning and Thunder, and of the Heads of Rivers."
[54] "Hypothesim legitimam faciunt duae res, quarum prima est, Ut sit conceptibilis (id est non absurda) altera, ut ab ea concessa inferri possit Phaenomeni necessitas." *Dialogus Physicus*, 11.

principle and the principle of action by contact as demonstrable a priori constraints on the kinds of hypotheses that are admissible in natural philosophy. These determine a framework within which there is a significant amount of room for hypothesis and experiment. Putative physical principles such as rarefaction and condensation can be eliminated from consideration, Hobbes held, because they are conceptually incoherent. But, for the most part, the explanation of the phenomena of nature will require both empirical investigation and mechanistic hypotheses because such things cannot be settled a priori.

Whatever its limitations (and they are many), Hobbes's foundational program for natural philosophy makes an intriguing contrast with other seventeenth-century approaches to the study of nature. We have seen that Hobbes sought to develop an approach that differs quite significantly from that of Aristotle, Descartes, or White. Furthermore, his frequent recourse to complex mechanistic hypotheses to account for natural phenomena (such as gravitation) set him against the methodology that came to dominate the program of natural-philosophical investigation favored by the Royal Society. It was a commonplace among British natural philosophers of the late seventeenth century to decry the baseless and extravagant hypotheses of their Continental rivals. Indeed, Newton's famous pronouncement in the General Scholium to the *Principia* reflects the Royal Society's disdain for the kind of program pursued by Hobbes. Newton declared that

> I have not as yet been able to deduce from phenomena the reasons for these properties of gravity, and I do not feign hypotheses. For whatever is not deduced from the phenomena must be called a hypothesis; and hypotheses, whether metaphysical or physical, or based on occult qualities, or mechanical, have no place in experimental philosophy.[55]

Despite its failure to gather a following or exert a significant influence on the further development of natural philosophy, Hobbes's approach remains of interest if only as an instance of an alternative conception of how the study of nature should be pursued.

BIBLIOGRAPHY

Brandt, Frithiof. 1928. *Thomas Hobbes' Mechanical Conception of Nature*. Copenhagen/London: Levin & Munksgaard/Librairie Hachette.

Descartes, René, 1897-1913. *Oeuvres*, edited by Charles Adam and Paul Tannery, 13 vols. Paris: J. Vrin.

Digby, Kenelm. 1644. *Two Treatises: In the one of which, The Nature of Bodies; in the other, The Nature of Man's Soule is looked into: In way of discovery, of the Immortality of Reasonable Soules*. Paris: Gilles Blaizot.

---

[55] Newton 1999: 943.

Duhem, Pierre. 1985. *Medieval Cosmology: Theories of Infinity, Place, Time, Void, and the Plurality of Worlds*. Edited and translated by Roger Ariew. Chicago: University of Chicago Press.

Grant, Edward. 1969. "Medieval and Seventeenth-Century Conceptions of an Infinite Void Space beyond the Cosmos." *Isis* 60: 39–60.

Herbert, Gary B. 1987. "Hobbes's Phenomenology of Space." *Journal of the History of Ideas* 48: 709–717.

Hobbes, Thomas. 1656a. *Elements of Philosophy, The First Section, Concerning Body*. London.

Hobbes, Thomas. 1656b. *Six lessons to the professors of the mathematiques*. London.

Hobbes, Thomas. 1661. *Dialogus physicus, sive de natura aeris*. London.

Hobbes, Thomas. 1678. *Decameron Physiologicum*. London.

Hobbes, Thomas. 1682. *Seven philosophical problems*. London.

Hobbes, Thomas. 1973. *Critique du De mundo de Thomas White*. Edited by Jean Jacquot and Harold Whitmore Jones. Paris: J. Vrin.

Jesseph, Douglas. 1996. "Hobbes and the Method of Natural Science," in *The Cambridge Companion to Hobbes*, edited by Tom Sorell, 62–85. Cambridge and New York: Cambridge University Press.

Jesseph, Douglas. 2006. "Hobbesian Mechanics," in *Oxford Studies in Early Modern Philosophy* vol. 3, edited by Daniel Garber and Steven Nadler, 118–152. Oxford: Oxford University Press.

Laird, John. [1934] 1968. *Hobbes*. New York: Russell and Russell.

Leijenhorst, Cees. 2002. *The Mechanisation of Aristotelianism: The Late Aristotelian Setting of Thomas Hobbes' Natural Philosophy*. Leiden, Boston, and Köln: Brill.

Newton, Sir Isaac. 1999. *The Principia: Mathematical Principles of Natural Philosophy*. Edited and translated by I. Bernard Cohen and Anne Whitman. Berkeley: University of California Press.

Probst, Siegmund. 1993. "Infinity and Creation: The Origin of the Controversy Between Thomas Hobbes and the Savilian Professors Seth Ward and John Wallis." *British Journal for the History of Science* 26: 271–279.

Shapin, Steven, and Simon Schaffer. 1985. *Leviathan and the Air-Pump: Hobbes, Boyle, and the Experimental Life*. Princeton, NJ: Princeton University Press.

White, Thomas. 1643. *De mundo dialogi tres*. Paris.

CHAPTER 7

....

THE MOST CURIOUS
OF SCIENCES
Hobbes's Optics

....

FRANCO GIUDICE

1 INTRODUCTION

....

HOBBES had wide-ranging interests in natural sciences and mathematics, but the most important by far for his overall philosophical development was his interest in optics.

The study of light and vision represented a kind of halfway house between epistemology and physics, and this was of vital importance to someone who was trying to give a unified, mechanistic account of the interaction between the physical world and the human mind. In fact, his theory of light and vision served as a model for his explanation of all natural phenomena.[1] And while his study of optical problems was fundamental to the evolution of Hobbes's mechanical philosophy, it can also be said that Hobbes's work in this field was relevant to the development of optical science in the seventeenth century. He was the first person to offer a kinematic explanation of the sine law of refraction, and his work on this topic was a key influence on the work of writers such as Emmanuel Maignan (1601–1676) and Isaac Barrow (1630–1677).[2] Hobbes was not only well aware of having created an original explanation of the sine law of refraction but actually believed that he had laid the foundations of a new science of optics, which had been confirmed by "the authoritie of Experience." So it comes as no surprise that in the last sentence of *A Minute or First Draught of the Optiques*, one of his major works on optics, he would proudly state: "I shall deserve the Reputation of having been the first to lay the ground of two Sciences, this of Opticques, the most curious, and that

---

[1] See Brandt 1928: 204; Alessio 1962: 408–9; Gargani 1971: 219–20.
[2] See Shapiro 1973: 172–81; Giudice 1999: 109–28.

other of natural Justice, which I have done in my booke de Cive, the most profitable of all other."[3]

Although Hobbes dealt with the subject of light and vision in a number of works,[4] the most complete presentation of his theory on optics appears in three treatises: the *Opticae liber septimus* (also known as *Tractatus opticus I*, c. 1640); the *Latin Optical Treatise* (also known as *Tractatus opticus II*),[5] which was probably written in the first or second year after Hobbes's arrival in Paris at the end of 1640[6]; and the above-mentioned *First Draught*, which he completed in 1646, while still in Paris.[7] Only the first of these works was published in a compilation edited by Hobbes's friend Marin Mersenne (1588–1648),[8] while the other two remained unpublished. The second part of the *First Draught* (entitled "On Vision") was, however, eventually published in a revised Latin version as the first part of *De homine* (1658).[9] Although these works were written in the 1640s, Hobbes's interest in optics dated from the early 1630s, when he began to develop the main principles of his theory of light and vision.

2 HOBBES'S EARLY INTERESTS IN OPTICS

Following his initial literary humanistic education,[10] Hobbes made a major change in direction during the 1630s, abandoning his previous studies and devoting himself to natural philosophy and to optics in particular. This change of direction was partly due to his acquaintance with the Earl of Newcastle and his younger brother Sir Charles Cavendish, a talented mathematician who was in correspondence with mathematicians and natural philosophers on the Continent. The Earl of Newcastle and Sir Charles were cousins of the third Earl of Devonshire, who was tutored by Hobbes from early 1631 and had a very strong interest in philosophy and science; as a result of these connections Hobbes was introduced to Robert Payne, who very soon became one of his closest friends. Payne was employed by the Earl of Newcastle nominally as his chaplain but during the mid-1630s devoted much of his time to the study of the phenomenon of refraction, a subject that quickly attracted Hobbes's interest. When in 1634 Payne

---

[3] Hobbes, *First Draught*, ed. Stroud, 622.

[4] See *Elements of Law*, II; *Critique du De mundo*, IX; *Leviathan*, I; *De corpore*, XXIV, XXVII.

[5] Parts of this manuscript (BL MS Harley 6796, fos. 193–266) were included in an appendix to the *Elements of Law* edited by Tönnies in 1889 (*Elements of Law*, 211–26). A complete version of the manuscript was published, without diagrams, by Alessio in 1963 (*Tractatus opticus II*, 147–228).

[6] For this dating, see Raylor 2005: 201–9; Malcolm 2005: 210–35.

[7] The Dedicatory letter and the conclusion to this manuscript (BL MS Harley, 3360, fos. 1–193) have been published in EW, VII, 467–71, and some fragments dealing with Hobbes's view on the vacuum appear in Köhler 1903: 71–72. A critical edition of the manuscript was published by Stroud in 1983.

[8] See Mersenne 1644: 567–89. This work has also been published in OL, V, 215–48.

[9] See Alessio 1962.

[10] On the importance of literary humanistic culture in Hobbes's intellectual development, see Skinner 1996: 215–44.

started a discussion with Walter Warner on the problem of refraction, Hobbes also became involved in the debate. A result of this exchange of ideas was a very short text (with diagrams), handwritten by Hobbes, concerning the angle of refraction. It survives among papers left by Warner, who dubbed it "M^r. Hobbes analogy,"[11] and Warner appears to refer to it in a letter to Payne on October 17, 1634.[12] Even though the kinematic explanation of the law of refraction proposed in this "analogy" follows a standard approach (from Alhazen to Kepler, incident and refracted motion of light had been resolved, as Hobbes does here, into perpendicular and parallel components),[13] the text is nonetheless of great value: it is both Hobbes's first attempt to demonstrate the law of refraction[14] and, most probably, his first work on optics.

There is also another work written in the 1630s where various questions relating to light, color, and vision are discussed and which for a long time was assigned to Hobbes—the so-called *A Short Tract on First Principles*. The *Short Tract* is an anonymous manuscript, with neither date nor title, contained in a body of texts by Sir Charles Cavendish in a volume of Harleian manuscripts in the British Library and published for the first time by Ferninand Tönnies in 1889 as an appendix to his edition of the *Elements of Law*.[15] Tönnies gave the manuscript its present title and confidently identified it as an early work by Hobbes, dating it to 1630. Recently, however, both the attribution of the *Short Tract* to Hobbes and its dating have been matters of intense debate.[16] Although scholars have different opinions about the authorship of this manuscript, they generally agree on two aspects. The first is that the *Short Tract* manuscript is in Payne's handwriting, although this does not necessarily mean that he was also the author of the text. The second is that the theory of light proposed by the author of the *Short Tract* is an Epicurean theory of emission—that is, a theory of emanating species from the light source—which is completely different from the mediumistic theory of

---

[11] BL MS Add. 4395, fos. 131^r, 133^r.

[12] Warner to Payne, October 17, 1634 (in Halliwell 1841: 65): "For the problem of refractions, which you write of, I pray you by any means send it to Mr. Hobbes. . . . For I have found him free with me, and I will not be reserved with him, if it please God I may live to see him again. That analogy which you have, though it be but a particular passion of the subject it concerns, yet it is conductible to the theory and investigation of the cause of refraction."

[13] See Sabra 1967: 93–99.

[14] For a brief analysis of the demonstration which Hobbes offers in the "analogy," see Horstmann 2000: 426–27.

[15] BL MS Harley 6796, fos. 297–308; *Elements of Law*, Appendix I, 193–210.

[16] The first person to seriously challenge Hobbes authorship of the *Short Tract* was Tuck 1988: 16–18, who stressed that since the handwriting in the manuscript is Payne's, it could very well be ascribed to him. Conversely, in his edition of the *Short Tract* Bernhardt 1988: 88–92 argues for Hobbes's authorship, hypothesizing that the text was written in early 1631. This attribution is supported by Zagorin 1993: 505–18 (who places the *Short Tract* in the late fall of 1630), Schuhmann 1995a: 3–36 (who suggested a date of 1632–33), and Leijenhorst 2002: 12–15 (who fully supports Schuhmann). Raylor 2001: 29–58 and Malcolm 2002: 80–145 present convincing arguments against Hobbes's authorship, maintaining that the author of the *Short Tract* is Payne, the former suggesting 1635 or shortly after as the date of its composition, whilst the latter proposes a time between October 1637 and the summer of 1638. I also assumed Hobbes's authorship of the *Short Tract* (see Giudice 1996 and Giudice 1999), but now I agree with Raylor and Malcolm.

light that Hobbes adopted from 1636 and does not require a physical emission but only a motion in the medium caused by the light source. Hobbes wrote about this theory for the first time in a letter to the Earl of Newcastle on October 16, 1636, immediately after his return from the Continent: "But whereas I use the phrases, the light passes, or the coulor passes or diffuseth it selfe, my meaning is that the motion is onely in ye medium, and light and coulor are but the effects of that motion in ye braine."[17] As we shall see, even though he would later develop different solutions in order to explain the precise nature of the motion that constituted light, he never abandoned the idea, stated in October 1636, that light is only pressure or motion in the medium. Thus it can be concluded that if Hobbes had been the author of the *Short Tract*, he would have written it before October 1636.

There is, however, no evidence to suggest that prior to October 1636 Hobbes ever believed in the propagation of the physical species by means of local motion. In fact, his kinematic approach to refraction in 1634 does not indicate any particular adherence to such a theory and even less to the peculiar theory of light transmission in the *Short Tract*. This is also evident from the few surviving letters by Hobbes dating to the time of his third trip to the Continent in 1634–1636. On the contrary, as has been suggested by Noel Malcolm, it is likely that in the last part of this journey in the summer of 1636, in Paris, Hobbes may have already started developing something approaching a mediumistic theory of light.[18]

His two long periods spent in Paris during October 1634 to August 1635 and June to October 1636 would play a crucial role in Hobbes's intellectual life. He met natural philosophers and French mathematicians such as Claude Mydorge (1585–1647), a scholar of geometry and optics and friend of Descartes. Through Mydorge, who was already in contact with Sir Charles Cavendish, Hobbes was introduced to Minim Friar Marin Mersenne, who was also a friend of Descartes. Mersenne's cell in the Convent of the Annunciation in Paris had become a center for a dynamic international scientific community,[19] where Hobbes could also contribute to debates. In 1634 he became involved in a discussion between Mersenne and the mathematician Jean de Beaugrand (c.1595–1640) on the rebound of a bow.[20]

Optics is a very prominent subject in Hobbes's letters from Paris to the Earl of Newcastle. He repeatedly expresses his skepticism about Warner's optical theories, and in his letter on August 15, 1635, to Newcastle Hobbes conveys his perplexity on the validity of Warner's research into the improvement of telescopes[21]: "I understand not how m^r Warner will demonstrate those inventions of the multiplyinge glasse and burning

---

[17]   Hobbes, *Correspondence* I, 38.

[18]   Malcolm 2002: 119–23.

[19]   In his verse *Vita* Hobbes presents a vivid picture of the activities in this community, see OL I, xci.

[20]   Hobbes referred to this event in a letter to Mersenne on March 20, 1641, *Correspondence* I, 102, 108.

[21]   Warner was preparing a tract on the construction of telescopes which he sent to Sir Charles Cavendish at the beginning of 1636, see Sir Charles to Warner on June 2, 1636, and September 2, 1636, in Halliwell 1841: 66–67.

glasse so infinite in vertue as he pretends."[22] Hobbes's criticism was that Warner was following a traditional, merely geometrical approach that did not always prove to be adequate for the explanation of phenomena. This was the case regarding a curious phenomenon of which Sir Charles Cavendish informed Warner in a letter on May 2, 1636. Sir Charles had in fact "latelie" (almost certainly in April) received a "paper" by Hobbes "which is an experiment of the place of the image of a thing contrarie to olde tenet"—that is, not conforming to the "olde" geometrical way. He described the curious phenomenon: "a candle being put into a glasse of a cylindricall forme, the image hangs perpendicularlie over the candle itself . . ., and not at the concourse of the perpendicular from the object with the visual line."[23]

Such phenomena, according to Hobbes, suggested that geometry was inadequate to achieve a right kind of explanation in optics. Consequently, as clearly shown in a letter from Hobbes to the Earl of Newcastle on July 29, 1636, he was suspicious about the geometrical results obtained by Warner and Mydorge, since in Hobbes's opinion those authors did not have a proper understanding of the nature of light: "For the optiques I know Mr Warner and Mr Mydorge are as able men as any in Europe, but they do not well to call their writings demonstrations, for the grounds and suppositions they use, so many of them concerne light, are uncertayne and many of them not true."[24] Hobbes's criticism was even clearer later in his letter, when he commented on a geometric treatise on the location of the image that Warner had sent to the brother of the Earl of Newcastle.[25] In order to demonstrate the inadequacy of Warner's work, Hobbes requested that Warner, via the Earl of Newcastle, explained the appearance of images in two phenomena that had been produced by some alchemists in Paris and witnessed by Hobbes and a number of other people. In the first case, after distilling some fir resin, the images of fir trees could be observed in the glass where the distillation had taken place. In the second, after distilling human blood, human images could be seen in the retort. Hobbes maintained that optics should have been able to explain these phenomena but stressed that even though his explanation might not be sufficient "to make one see how nature workes it," it was certainly better than Warner's old geometrical way:

> M^r warner has sent a tract to Sr Charles concerninge the place of the Image in convexe and concave glasses. I pray yor Lo^p let him see that peece of ye convexe glasse wherein appeare the Images of the firre trees, and see if he can applye his reasons to it, and demonstrate why the Images of those trees wch are long since perhaps burnt a thousand mile hence should be in that place where they are. If the experiment of ye mans image in ye glasse of bloud might be made againe, and shewed him I would have him answer to that also. For my part my opinion of the firre trees is that the same motion by wch the tree it selfe was able to produce the image of a tall tree in

---

[22] *Correspondence* I, 28.

[23] Halliwell 1841: 66.

[24] *Correspondence* I, 33–34.

[25] See Sir Charles Cavendish to Warner on June 2, 1636, and September 2, 1636, in Halliwell 1841: 66–67.

ye ey of a man that looked on it, remayning also in ye rosin and by it moving in the glasse, workes the little image of a tree in the ey of him that looks upon ye glasse, and therefore a little [image of a] tree, because now a little or feynt motion. This reason is not cleare enough to make one see how nature workes it, but the old way by beames and reflection, and refraction leaves a man destitute of any thing to say to it.[26]

What is striking about this passage is the fact that Hobbes makes no comment on Warner's results in relation to the location of the image, but he does seem to suggest implicitly that Warner's results are invalid since they are purely geometrical and as such not helpful in identifying the physical cause of these phenomena.[27] To identify such a cause, it is necessary to adhere to the principle expressed by Newcastle, supported and quoted by Hobbes at the beginning of his letter, "That the variety of thinges is but variety of locall motion in ye spirits or invisible partes of bodies."[28] On the basis of this principle Hobbes hypothesized that trees possessed some sort of motion through which they produced their image in the eye of the observer, and that this motion, still remaining in the resin extracted from the trees, was transmitted to the glass, to be in its turn transmitted to the eye of the observer.

It is difficult to say what kind of role the interpretation of these phenomena played in the process that led Hobbes to develop his mediumistic theory of light. It is, however, clear that it stimulated his attempts to understand how the miniscule motions of an object can be transmitted to the eye of the observer. It is also very possible that, in proposing his mediumistic solution, Hobbes might have been influenced by the first book of Mersenne's *Harmonie Universelle*, which was published in 1636 and which Hobbes could well have read during his stay in Paris in the summer of that year. In his book Mersenne proposed a comparison between sound and light, an analogy that would certainly have been significant for those, like Hobbes, who were researching the question of the transmission of motion from objects to the eye of the observer: "If the nature of light is very carefully considered, perhaps it will be found that it is nothing other than a motion in the air, which carries with it the image of the thing that first moved it, namely the luminous body, to make it sensitive to the eye with the name and appearance of color or light."[29]

3 HOBBES'S THEORY OF LIGHT

As mentioned above, at the time of his return to England in October 1636, Hobbes assumed that light was only motion in the medium, although he was not yet clear

---

[26] *Correspondence* I, 34. For a detailed explanation with references to sources, see ibid., 35 notes 4 and 5.

[27] See Malet 2001: 317.

[28] *Correspondence* I, 33.

[29] Mersenne 1636: I, 45. The very plausible hypothesis that Hobbes had read the first book of Mersenne's *Harmonie Universelle* has been suggested by Malcolm 2002: 123.

about what "kind of motion" was involved.[30] This means that when in 1637 Descartes's *Dioptrique* was published (as one of the *Essais* accompanying his *Discours de la méthode*), Hobbes had at least already developed the central principle of his theory of optics—that the action of light on the eye is determined by a motion of the medium caused by the light source. Hobbes received a copy of the *Essais* from Sir Kenelm Digby (1603–1665) about a year after its publication,[31] but it was only when Mersenne asked for his opinion that Hobbes expressed his thoughts on *Dioptrique*.[32] On November 5, 1640, shortly before leaving England, he wrote a long letter to Mersenne in which he criticized Descartes's optical theories and offered his own demonstration of the law of refraction. This resulted in a brief exchange of letters between Hobbes and Descartes, mediated by Mersenne, which lasted until April 1641 and quickly turned into a bitter dispute, especially on the part of Descartes.[33] Even though Hobbes's letter of November 1640 has been lost, its final part, as it appears from the citations given by Descartes,[34] corresponds to Hobbes's treatise on optics (the so-called *Tractatus opticus I*), which was then published by Mersenne in his *Universae geometriae mixtaeque mathematicae synopsis* in 1644.[35]

The *Tractatus opticus I* was the most comprehensive presentation of Hobbes's theory of light published during his lifetime. At the beginning of the treatise he set out five hypotheses in order to deduce fourteen propositions and a number of definitions and corollaries concerning the nature of light, its refraction, and color.

Hobbes's theory of light—indeed his entire natural philosophy—was based on a mechanistic view of nature that reduced all phenomena to a local motion of material bodies. It is, therefore, not surprising that in the first hypothesis in the *Tractatus opticus I* Hobbes would start with one of the main principles of his natural philosophy, that "Every action is local motion in the agent, just as every passion is local motion in the patient. By the name agent I understand a body by whose motion an effect is produced in another body, and by patient, a body in which some motion is generated by another body."[36]

The other hypotheses state that the sensation of light, namely vision, is the effect produced in the perceiving subject "by the action of the luminous or illuminated object," and that "neither the object nor any of its parts travels from its place to the eye." The action by the luminous body is therefore only a motion propagated to the eye through the contiguous parts of the surrounding medium.[37] Since a luminous source can be seen

---

[30] See *Correspondence* I, 38.

[31] See Digby to Hobbes on October 4, 1637, *Correspondence* I, 51.

[32] See Hobbes to Mersenne on January 28/February 7, 1641, *Correspondence* I, 62.

[33] On this controversy see Brandt 1928: 111–19, 129–42; Shapiro 1973: 155–60; Bernhardt 1979: 432–42; Zarka 1988: 81–98; Giudice 2000: 73–92.

[34] See Descartes to Mersenne for Hobbes on February 8/18, 1641, *Correspondence* I, 86–92.

[35] Brandt 1928: 93–96 was the first to refer to this connection, although he erroneously hypothesized the existence of "two letters" from Hobbes to Mersenne, perhaps confusing the fact that Mersenne sent the letter from Hobbes to Descartes through Constantijn Huygens, who sent it to Descartes in two instances (see Huygens to Descartes January 15, 1641, in AT III, 764–65).

[36] Hobbes, *Tractatus opticus I*, in OL V, 217.

[37] Ibid., 217–18.

simultaneously from all directions, Hobbes concludes that both the luminous source and the medium expand together, acting immediately on the eye to produce vision. He was, however, aware that this motion of expansion could not be limitless, either for the source or for the medium, and assumed that there was a contraction of both the luminous source and the surrounding medium. This would mean that there was an alternating and continuing systolic and diastolic motion similar to the motion of the heart.[38]

To explain how this motion comprising light is propagated to the eye, Hobbes uses a diagram (Figure 7.1) in which *AB* represents a luminous body, such as the sun for example, which is surrounded by a series of concentric circles—*BC, CD, DE*, and so on—whose width decreases in proportion to their distance from the luminous body. When *AB* expands, the part of the medium in the circle *BC* is displaced and pushed into the contiguous circle *CD*. Since each circle pushes the part of the medium that is in front of it into the next circle, the motion spreads until the final one strikes the eye in *E*.[39]

When the motion reaches the eye, it is spread to the retina and through the optic nerve to the brain, where it causes a reaction or counterpressure "whence the motion is propagated back from the brain, through the optic nerve into the retina, and then back towards the sun, through the same line it was previously propagated from the sun to the retina."[40] The entire process takes place instantaneously.

According to Hobbes, light should always be related to vision, since if there were no vision, there would be nothing we could call light. He makes a distinction between *lux*, which refers to the action of a luminous body, and *lumen*, as in a reaction in the perceiving subject.[41] This means that the motion of light (*lux*) is transformed into *lumen* only when such motion is propagated outward by a reactive counterpressure from the brain: "Light [*lumen*], therefore, is the appearance in front of the eyes of that motion which is propagated to the brain by the expansion or swelling of the luminous object, and then back from the eyes into the medium. The light [*lumen*] from the luminous object is therefore a fancy or image conceived in the brain."[42]

As with all other sensible qualities, visual images are not real things existing in the external world; they are only motions in us arising from motions produced by the

---

[38] Ibid., 218: "Every luminous body expands and swells into a greater volume, and then contracts again, having a ceaseless systolic and diastolic motion." In the *Tractatus opticus II*, ed. Alessio, 150, Hobbes gave this analogy with the heart: "We must therefore further suppose that every luminous body not only expands but also contracts, no doubt alternately. The way that the human heart, with its alternating contraction and expansion which we call systole and diastole, constantly pushes and drives the blood through the arteries." It should be noted that Hobbes used the terms systole and diastole in their traditional meaning, where the diastole represents active time and the systole passive, which is opposite to the new concept by William Harvey, see Bernhardt, 1990: 256.

[39] Hobbes also describes this model in *Tractatus opticus II*, ed. Alessio, 148–49; in the *Critique du De mundo*, IX.2, 161–63; and in *First Draught*, ed. Stroud, 94–95.

[40] *Tractatus opticus I*, in OL V, 220. On the subject that in other works Hobbes appears to argue that this reaction takes place in the heart rather than in the brain, see Schuhmann 1995b: 6–7.

[41] On the presence of this terminological and conceptual distinction in Hobbes's optical papers, see Prins 1987: 293–4.

[42] *Tractatus opticus I*, in OL V, 221.

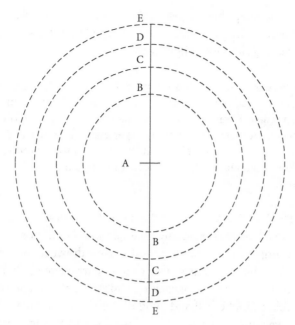

FIGURE 7.1 Hobbes, *Tractatus opticus I*, in OL V, 219.

objects. In this way Hobbes rejected the traditional peripatetic idea that things emanate "species" or "forms" through which their qualities would appear to the perceiving subject.

Although Hobbes considered his model of expansion and contraction to be valid, in order to make it even clearer that a luminous body can be seen simultaneously from all directions, in the *Tractatus opticus II* he introduced another model—the *motus cribrationis*, or motion similar to sievelike motion.[43] As a possible explanation of the propagation of light, this model is presented only in the *Tractatus opticus II* but does not feature in the *Critique du De mundo*, the *First Draught*, or *De corpore*.

In attempting to explain the *motus cribrationis*, Hobbes asks the reader to imagine the miniscule parts of a luminous body as wheat grains in a rotating sieve. They have their own rotating motion inside the sieve in addition to the rotating motion of the sieve itself. This double motion, as in the systole and diastole model, serves to explain the fact that every luminous source, though dilating and contracting, is perceived by the observer as always being at the same distance. It is therefore necessary to reconcile the continuous motion of the advancing and receding of the luminous body with the fact that it stays in the same place. The solution presented in the *motus cribrationis* model is that some parts of the luminous source, like wheat grains in a rotating sieve, move toward the center while others simultaneously move outward. Since the motion would be very fast and the moving parts very small, Hobbes claimed that this

---

[43] *Tractatus opticus II*, ed. Alessio, 150–51, 152–53. See Stroud's analysis of the *motus cribrationis* in *First Draught*, 26–36. A brief mention is also made in Shapiro 1973: 169, and in Bernhardt 1977: 21.

motion would be imperceptible; therefore the luminous source would be seen from all directions at the same time. He later acknowledged that this solution was unsatisfactory and rejected it as a cause of light with this criticism:

> I believe that there is such a motion [*motus cribrationis*] in the sun on account of many other phenomena, but the cause of vision does not consist in that. For the very reason that if an eye were placed in the pole or axis of such a motion, no vision at all would occur. However, we know by experience that other luminous objects around which we can place any eye in all directions, always produce vision uniformly; therefore it remains that vision occurs through the systole and diastole of luminous bodies.[44]

In *De corpore* Hobbes also abandoned the motion of systole and diastole as a cause of light, declaring that light was caused by a "simple circular motion." This is somewhat surprising, in that simple circular motion had the same drawback as *motus cribrationis*, since also in this case the luminous source would be irradiated only in the directions that were perpendicular to the axis of rotation and not in all directions.[45]

Most scholars relate Hobbes's abandoning of the systole and diastole model to the role played by the vacuum in his natural philosophy.[46] In this interpretation, Hobbes would initially have been willing to admit (at least as a hypothesis) to the existence of the vacuum, whereas from May 1648 he would categorically deny its existence.[47] This different position would explain why Hobbes in *De corpore*, published in 1655—being by now an earnest antivacuist—no longer mentions the systole and diastole model but adopts "simple circular motion," which did not need to presuppose the vacuum.

There is no doubt that the vacuum is an integral part of the systole and diastole model. With the sole exception of the *Tractatus opticus I*, every time Hobbes introduces this model he always stresses that it makes the hypothesis of the void plausible.[48] The abandonment of this model could then be due to the fact that admitting the possibility of a vacuum risked compromising the theory of the medium in that it could legitimize the absence of the medium itself. It should be clarified that when Hobbes refers to the vacuum in his theory of light, he refers to the *vacuum disseminatum*—that is, the microscopic void space dispersed or disseminated between the particles, and not to the *vacuum separatum*, an extended or macroscopic space of finite or infinite dimensions in which there are no particles. In other words, when Hobbes describes the expansive action of the luminous body, he uses the concept of the microscopic vacuum. This does not mean that he was a vacuist, since he never accepted the existence of macroscopic empty space.[49]

---

[44] *Tractatus opticus II*, ed. Alessio, 151.

[45] See *De corpore*, XXVII.2, 364–65. See Shapiro 1973: 169.

[46] See Shapiro 1973: 169–70; Pacchi 1978: 61–64; Bernhardt 1990: 265–66; Bernhardt 1993: 225–32.

[47] See Hobbes to Mersenne 15/25 May 1648, *Correspondence* I, 172.

[48] See *Tractatus opticus II*, ed. Alessio, 148; *Critique du De mundo*, IX.2, 161; *First Draught*, ed. Stroud, 96.

[49] For a more detailed analysis of the problem of the vacuum in Hobbes's natural philosophy, see Giudice 1997: 471–85.

4 HOBBES'S THEORY OF REFRACTION
AND COLOR

After describing the nature of light, Hobbes proposed an explanation of refraction based on the definitions of ray and "line of light." In the *Tractatus opticus I* he defined the ray of light as "the path through which the motion from the luminous body is propagated through the medium."[50] Since only bodies can move, a ray occupies space in the same way as a body and therefore has "three dimensions." A ray is therefore "a solid space."[51] At first this definition does not appear to be very different to the traditional medieval concept that every ray of light has some sort of width.[52] Hobbes did, however, add some elements that transformed the traditional view of the ray. He did not agree with the medieval writers' approach to optics, which considered that rays of light could be seen as geometrical lines. He thought that reducing optics to geometry alone carried the risk of ignoring the physical characteristics of a ray of light. Therefore he gave rays not only length but also width, as we can see from his definition of the straight and refracted ray as parallelograms (Figure 7.2).

Hobbes did not consider the motion of the whole parallelogram but only of a specific part of it that he defined as the "line of light": "The line of light which the sides of a ray begin (e.g., line *AB* from which sides *AI, BK* begin) I call simply a line of light. However, any one of the lines which are derived from the line of light by a continual extension (such as *CD, EF*, etc.) I call a propagated line of light" (Figure 7.2). The "propagated line of light," as we can see in the figure, is always perpendicular to the sides of the ray of the propagated pulse front or ray front, which can be thought of as an infinitesimal portion of an expanding wave front.[53]

Hobbes regards the ray as not just a simple geometrical line or the motion of a body but the place of the successive positions of a pulse front that traces out a parallelogram. In order to clarify the concept, in the *Tractatus opticus II* he replaces the term *ray (radius)* with *radiation (radiatio)*: "Therefore, where others use the term 'ray', I shall use the term 'radiation' to avoid ambiguity."[54] This concept of a physical ray was completely new in optics and formed the basis of his explanation of refraction.

Hobbes started his analysis of refraction by stressing that the motion of a ray of light depends on the resistance of the medium and that the speed of each part of the ray has to be considered. In the fifth hypothesis in the *Tractatus opticus I* he had defined a rarer medium as that which offers the least resistance to motion and denser that which offers more resistance, assuming that "air is rarer than water, water rarer than glass, and glass rarer than crystal."[55] When a ray enters perpendicularly from a rarer

---

[50] *Tractatus opticus I*, in OL V, 221.

[51] Ibid., 222.

[52] On the similarities between Hobbes's definition of ray and the medieval definition, see Prins 1987: 296–98.

[53] On the analogy of Hobbes's "line of propagated light" to the front wave concept, see Shapiro 1973: 151.

[54] *Tractatus opticus II*, ed. Alessio, 160.

[55] *Tractatus opticus I*, in OL V, 218.

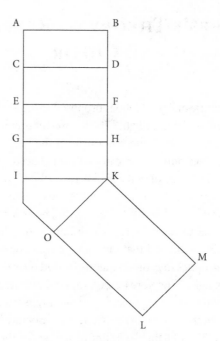

FIGURE 7.2 Hobbes, *Tractatus opticus I*, in OL V, 222.

medium into a denser one, the propagation of light will follow a straight line, as in that case all the parts in the ray in the second medium will meet with the same resistance. When on the other hand a ray enters obliquely from a rarer medium to a denser one, the light will be refracted towards the perpendicular, as the part of the ray which first enters the denser medium will move at a slower velocity than the other part which, still being in the original medium, will continue moving at the same speed. Consequently, in his opinion, in a uniform medium the path is similar to that described by a cylinder, or as if *AB* (Figure 7.3) were the side of a cylinder rolling toward *CD*, and where the front pulse is always perpendicular to the direction of the motion and maintains the same width. When a ray of light enters obliquely in a different medium, the path is similar to that of a "frustum of a cone," and if it rolls, its bases behave "just like two unequal wheels."[56]

With this cone model Hobbes gave a mechanical explanation of the refraction of motion or pulse and showed that the ratio of the sine of the angle of incidence to that of the sine of the angle of refraction is independent of the angle of the incident ray and proportional to the different speeds in the two media. In other words, he was able to demonstrate that his own physical explanation of refraction was completely in line with the geometrical relationship, according to which, when a ray of light moves from one medium to another, the relationship between the sine of the angle of incidence and the sine of the angle of

---

[56] Hobbes presents the cone model not only in the *Tractatus opticus I* (OL V, 223–24), but also in the *Tractatus opticus II*, ed. Alessio, 166–67, and in *First Draught*, ed. Stroud, 122–23.

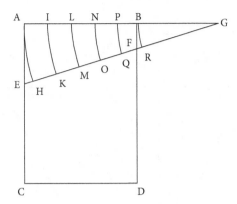

FIGURE 7.3 Hobbes, *Tractatus opticus I*, OL V, 223.

refraction is constant.[57] Hobbes was the first to adopt a mediumistic theory of light where the speed of propagation is greater in a rarer medium than in a denser one.[58]

His theory of refraction, moreover, enabled Hobbes to build a mechanistic model in order to explain the origin of colors. He had already written in his letter of October 16, 1636, to the Earl of Newcastle that color "is not pure light, but light mingled."[59] He returned to the concept using similar terminology in the *Elements of Law*, in which he presumed that light and color differ "only in this, that the one is pure, the other a perturbed light."[60] Color is therefore connected to the idea of a perturbation of pure white light—namely a modification of the motion that comprises the light. In this work he does not actually specify what type of motion is involved in this kind of modification, but in the *Tractatus opticus I* he is more precise, stating that colors are produced by refraction. Using the cone model according to which the sides of a ray of light are propagated with different speeds, he explains that when the ray refracts, it rotates, and therefore the initial straight motion that comprises the incident white light is modified. Sensations of color are no more than the outcome of the combination of the initial rectilinear motion and of the motion of rotation of the sides of the ray of light. The side where the rotating motion is faster produces red and yellow, and the side where the rotating motion is slower produces green and violet. So when we observe a light source through a prism (Figure 7.4), we will see red at one end and blue at the other, and in between yellow, green, and violet.[61]

With his mechanistic explanation of colors Hobbes tried to distance himself from the Aristotelian tradition, which considered the diversity of colors to result from the mixture of black and white. As he stressed in the *First Draught*, "the diversity of other

[57] For a detailed description of how Hobbes developed his derivation of the sine law of refraction, see Shapiro 1973: 258–63; Giudice 1999: 69–74. See also Horstmann 2000: 427–31.

[58] See Shapiro 1973: 134–35.

[59] *Correspondence* I, 37.

[60] *Elements of Law*, 6.

[61] *Tractatus opticus I*, in OL V, 247. See also *Tractatus opticus II*, ed. Alessio, 227, and *First Draught*, ed. Stroud, 318–22. On the minor differences where Hobbes presents his theory of colors in these works, see Blay 1990: 153–68.

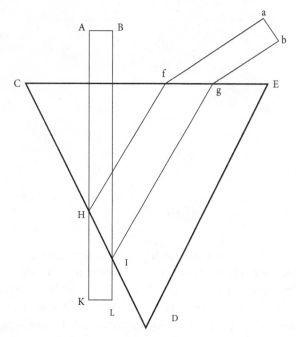

FIGURE 7.4 Hobbes, *Tractatus opticus I*, OL V, 247.

coulors, that are neither white nor black" is not produced from "the mixture of them."[62] Unlike Aristotle, Hobbes did not believe that colors were real entities but only motions in the perceiving subject, with no independent existence. Hobbes believed that the diversity of colors resulted from variations in the motions of light, and, like Descartes, proposed a mechanistic theory of colors with new elements compared with that of Aristotle.[63] Hobbes shared with Descartes the traditional idea that light is pure and uniform and that colors occur from its modification. Therefore, as in all theories prior to Newton, Hobbes considers that colors do not exist independently in the sunlight before some modification.[64]

5 HOBBES VS. DESCARTES

Hobbes's theory of light had much in common with that of Descartes. Both theories fitted into a comprehensive mechanistic view of nature, and both considered light as

[62] *First Draught*, ed. Stroud, 186.

[63] In the *Météores* (AT VI, 325–35) Descartes argued that colors are caused by the modification of light due to the various rotations in the little round corpuscles that form the subtle matter that transmits the light. In the seventeenth century, besides that by Descartes and Hobbes, other theories that varied from the traditional ones were proposed, see Nakajima 1984: 261–78; Giudice 2009: 47–61.

[64] Shapiro 1994: 610–11.

the action of a luminous body that is propagated instantaneously through the medium. Both Hobbes and Descartes rejected the traditional peripatetic idea of species, denying that sensible qualities are inherent in objects, and ultimately they both developed similar theories on the origin of colors. In spite of these similarities, there are fundamental differences between their ideas on the nature of light and the explanation of refraction.[65]

Descartes disagreed with the hypothesis that was the foundation of Hobbes's optics theory—that is, that each phenomenon must be reduced to local motion. In Hobbes's theory the vibratory motion of the luminous source implied an effective, though imperceptible, motion of both the source and the medium. In his reply via Mersenne to Hobbes's lost letter of November 5, 1640, Descartes considered the opening hypothesis of the *Tractatus opticus I* to be unfounded: "in his first hypothesis he makes a false assumption when he says that *all action is local motion*."[66] Descartes's criticism had its raison d'être in the distinction he had made in his *Dioptrique* between "motion and action or inclination to move."[67] According to Descartes, light was not real motion, but an extremely fast action that was propagated instantaneously through the medium. Instantaneous propagation therefore excluded the possibility of identifying light with motion, as there is no motion that extends to any distance in an instant. He considered light as a tendency or inclination to motion which, on the one hand, was connected to local motion in that there was a transfer of action through space and, on the other hand, was different, as this action was not that of a body that moves from one place to another but occurred in an instant without transport of matter, as exemplified by the analogy of the blind man's stick.[68]

Hobbes, however, argued that the concept of inclination to motion, if not transformed into effective motion, made no sense and was unintelligible. Consequently, in order to underline his opposition to Descartes, Hobbes stated in the *Tractatus opticus II*: "what he [Descartes] calls inclination to move, I call motion, and the action, that he differentiates from motion, I . . . understand to be motion."[69]

On the subject of refraction, Hobbes criticized Descartes's analogy with a ball, which he used in his *Dioptrique* to explain this phenomenon, considered a special case of reflection. In Descartes's view there was no significant difference between the motion of a body and the motion of an impulse. He also stated that "as a ball loses much more of its agitation in falling against a soft body than against one that is hard, and as it rolls less on a carpet than on a totally smooth table," so the action by the subtle matter which transmits light "can be much more impeded by the particles of air, which, being soft

---

[65] Hobbes and Descartes had vigorous disputes on various topics such as elasticity, reflection, and the Cartesian concept of "determination," see Prins 1996: 139–41. On the difference of opinion over the concept of "determination," see Gabbey 1980: 254–55.

[66] Descartes to Mersenne for Hobbes, February 8/18, 1641, *Correspondence* I, 90.

[67] See *Dioptrique*, in AT VI, 88. See Martinet 1982: 297–98.

[68] See *Dioptrique*, in AT VI, 85. Descartes returned to this analogy in the letter quoted above from February 8/18, 1641, *Correspondence* I, 90: "For when I press, for example, with a stick against the ground, the action of my hand is communicated to the whole of that stick, and is transmitted as far as the ground, even though we do not suppose in the slightest that the stick is moved."

[69] *Tractatus opticus II*, ed. Alessio, 151.

and badly joined, do not offer it very much resistance, than those of water, which offer it much more."[70]

Hobbes considered such an analogy inadequate, since if in the case of reflection the differences between the motion of a ball and the motion of light are practically negligible, in refraction the physical process is completely different.[71] When light enters a denser medium, it moves toward the normal, while a ball moves away from it. Descartes never understood or made Hobbes's distinction between the refraction of a body and that of an impulse.[72] He interpreted Hobbes's concept of ray of light as a body—as "the successive motion of a sort of imaginary parallelogram," instead of the propagation of an impulse tracing out a parallelogram. Consequently Descartes considered the explanation of the physical cause of refraction by Hobbes to be "completely illusory."[73]

6 HOBBES'S THEORY OF VISION

In Hobbes's optical theory, light is always related to the mechanism of vision. Light and vision constitute complementary aspects, as they represent two necessary stages of the visual process.[74] The first stage implies the propagation of motion from the luminous body to the eye, while the second implies a motion of reaction that reverses the course of the initial motion outward. Thus the observer will perceive the object externally, in the same direction as the luminous body that caused the initial motion.

The most comprehensive analysis of Hobbes's theory of vision can be found in the fourth chapter of the *Tractatus opticus II* and in particular in the second part of the *First Draught*. He begins with a description of the eye, which is extremely similar to what is described in the mainstream literature on the anatomy of the eye in the early seventeenth century.[75] Since the motion of the luminous body affects all parts of the body, Hobbes reasoned that the organ of sight includes not only the eye but also the brain, the vital and animal spirit, and the heart.[76]

In his opinion, when the pressure coming from the object strikes the eye, it passes through the inanimate humors of the eye and reaches to the retina, where the pressure

---

[70] Descartes, *Dioptrique*, in AT VI, 103.

[71] For a detailed analysis of Hobbes's criticism on the derivation of the sine law of refraction by Descartes, see Giudice 1999: 61–69.

[72] See Shapiro 1973: 153.

[73] See Descartes to Mersenne for Hobbes, February 8/18, 1641, *Correspondence* I, 91.

[74] See Stroud 1990: 270.

[75] See *Tractatus opticus II*, ed. Alessio, 199–201; *First Draught*, ed. Stroud, 80–83. Even though Hobbes gave a description of the eye which was widespread in the anatomical literature of the period, this does not imply that he would not take an independent stance. Contrary to the opinion of most of his contemporaries, he believed, for example, that the optical nerve was not hollow, see Giudice 1999: 78.

[76] See *Tractatus opticus II*, ed. Alessio, 199.

continues to the brain through the optic nerve and then through the arteries to the heart. This pressure (or motion of propagation of the impulse) is finally transmitted to all parts of the body that communicate with the brain and heart through the animal spirits. Since each action of the body in the perceiving subject causes a corresponding reaction in the opposite direction, the inward motion will have to follow the same course, but then directed outward. The act of vision therefore consists in this reaction.[77]

The interaction between these different types of motion can be understood only partly by following the pressure of the luminous object through the organs of the senses. To understand how images of the world can be located, it is necessary to examine the geometrical constructions used by Hobbes, the most important of which is the "line of vision."

In the *First Draught* Hobbes defines vision as "the judgment itselfe of the place, where the object appears to bee."[78] The place of visual images is determined only by the motion immediately imposed on the eye, and their location in the world is possible only owing to the ability we have of perceiving the direction of the motion that strikes the eye. Hobbes's view was that this ability is caused by an oriented resistance in the retina produced by the motion of the luminous body, geometrically represented by the "line of vision." This is defined as the line on which every point of the visible object appears, and when it strikes the surface of the eye perpendicularly is called the "optical axis." Even though all the points are seen through the line of vision, we see clearly only those luminous points along the optical axis. In order to have a clear vision it is therefore necessary that the optical axis moves from one end of the object to the other, with a motion similar to that which we use when we read: "Hence it is that in reading wee discerne distinctly but one letter at once and reade no faster than wee can move our eye to the severall letters, thus wee see the whole page at one and the same instant."[79] If we see an extended object, the optical axis sweeps quickly across its surface and the object is perceived by putting together in the memory all the point images produced.

Clear vision, however, also implies psychological attention, in that it depends on the observer's interest, which in turn is based on the motions around the heart. Hobbes considered that the motions of the optical axis follow the will of the perceiving subject.[80] So the visual line, besides being a geometrical construction, also performs a physical and psychological function, and with it Hobbes explained how the observer is able to locate images in space. Visual images are not only different because of the position of the visual line along which they appear in relation to the observer but also for reasons of dimension, distance, motion or rest, color, and also the emotions felt by the observer, since some are connected to pain, and others to pleasure.[81]

---

[77] Ibid., 206.
[78] *First Draught*, ed. Stroud, 341.
[79] Ibid., 348.
[80] *Tractatus opticus II*, ed. Alessio, 213–14.
[81] Ibid., 210. See also Prins 1987: 306–7.

Hobbes's theory of vision was in line with his mechanistic view of natural philosophy, which reduced all natural effects to motion. He reasoned that vision is only "phancie" caused by motion, "phancie being nothing else butt the Judgement concerning the place and force of the lucid or illuminated Agent that worketh on the organ."[82] Because of this mechanistic understanding of vision, Hobbes distanced himself from Kepler's retinal picture theory,[83] which he called "figured light" and not the same as the perceived image we have in vision. Hobbes recognized that the formation of such a picture on the back of the eye had been confirmed experimentally, but he considered it as only a by-product of refraction in ocular humors, which did not give rise to vision. He therefore recommended we "not mistake this image [i.e., the retinal picture] for that which we have in our mind upon sight of the object with our owne eyes. For no man can see the image described in the bottome of his owne eye. . . . Besides the image we see in the bottome of the eye is inverted, butt when wee behold the object, the image wee have of it is nott inverted."[84]

Hobbes's refusal to accept the visual role of Kepler's retinal pictures was closely connected to Descartes's use of it. Descartes had, in fact, made use of Kepler's picture concept to explain how light and colors may enter the eye and reach the nerves and through them the human soul, somehow producing the mental images of objects.[85] Hobbes criticized Descartes's idea that an immaterial soul could be the ultimate center of perception, stating that only the body could receive the motion. The very fact that Descartes argued that light was perceived by the soul through the nerves demonstrated, in Hobbes's opinion, that if that were true, the soul as intended by Descartes was nothing more than a corporeal substance—that is, "the soul is also a body."[86]

Hobbes's theory of vision did not need to resort to the soul, since the mechanism of vision fitted fully into the framework of a mechanistic interpretation of natural phenomena based on concepts of body and local motion, meaning the most universal causes of all phenomena, and thus including the phenomenon of vision.

BIBLIOGRAPHY

Alessio, Franco. 1962. "De homine e A Minute or First Draught of the Optiques di Thomas Hobbes," *Rivista critica di storia della filosofia*, XVII, 4, 393–410.
Bernhardt, Jean. 1977. "Hobbes et le mouvement de la lumière," *Revue d'histoire des sciences*, 30, 1, 3–24.
Bernhardt, Jean. 1979. "La polémique de Hobbes contre Descartes dans le Tractatus opticus II (1644)," *Revue internationale de philosophie*, 129, 432–442.
Bernhardt, Jean. ed. 1988. [Hobbes], *Court traité des premiers principes*. Paris: Presses Universitaires de France.

[82] *First Draught*, ed. Stroud, 398.
[83] See Malet 2001: 305–7.
[84] *First Draught*, ed. Stroud, 268.
[85] Descartes, *Dioptrique*, in AT VI, 115–29.
[86] *Tractatus opticus II*, ed. Alessio, 208.

Bernhardt, Jean. 1990. "L'oeuvre de Hobbes en optique et en theorie de la vision," in *Hobbes oggi*, edited by Andrea Napoli, 245–268. Milano: Franco Angeli.

Bernhardt, Jean, 1993. "La question du vide chez Hobbes," *Revue d'histoire des sciences*, 46, 2–3, 225–232.

Blay, Michel. 1990. "Genèse des couleurs et modèles mécaniques dans l'oeuvre de Hobbes," in *Thomas Hobbes: Philosophie première, théorie de la science et politique*, edited by Jean Bernhardt and Yves Charles Zarka, 153–168. Paris: Presses Universitaires de France.

Brandt, Frithiof. 1928. *Thomas Hobbes's Mechanical Conception of Nature*. Copenhagen/London: Levin & Munksgaard/Librairie Hachette.

Descartes, René, 1897–1913. *Oeuvres* (referred to in the chapter as AT), edited by Charles Adam and Paul Tannery, 13 vols. Paris: Vrin.

Gabbey, Alan. 1980. "Force and Inertia in the Seventeenth Century: Descartes and Newton," in *Descartes: Philosophy, Mathematics and Physics*, edited by Stephen Gaukroger, 230–320. Brighton: The Harvester Press.

Gargani, Aldo. 1971. *Hobbes e la scienza*. Turin: Einaudi.

Giudice, Franco. 1996. "Teoria della luce e struttura della materia nello *Short Tract on First Principles* di Thomas Hobbes," *Nuncius*, 2, 545–561.

Giudice, Franco. 1997. "Thomas Hobbes and Atomism: A Reappraisal," *Nuncius*, 2, 471–485.

Giudice, Franco. 1999. *Luce e visione: Thomas Hobbes e la scienza dell'ottica*. Florence: Olschki.

Giudice, Franco. 2000. "Hobbes e Descartes: la polemica sulla legge di rifrazione," in *Il mestiere di studiare e insegnare filosofia: Saggi in onore di Franco Alessio*, edited by Marco Sbrozi, 73–92. Milan: Wise.

Giudice, Franco. 2009. *Lo spettro di Newton: La rivelazione della luce e dei colori*. Rome: Donzelli.

Halliwell, James O., ed. 1841. *Collection of Letters Illustrative of the Progress of Science in England from the Reign of Queen Elizabeth to that of Charles the Second*. London: Historical Society of Science.

Hobbes, Thomas. 1839–1845a. *The English Works of Thomas Hobbes of Malmesbury* (referred to in the chapter as EW), edited by William Molesworth, 11 vols. London: John Bohn.

Hobbes, Thomas. 1839–1845b. *Thomae Hobbes Malmesburiensis Opera Philosophica quae latine scripsit omnia* (referred to in the chapter as OL), edited by William Molesworth, 5 vols. London: John Bohn.

Hobbes, Thomas. 1889. *The Elements of Law, Natural and Politic*, edited by Ferdinand Tönnies. London: Simpkin and Marshall.

Hobbes, Thomas. 1963. "Tractatus opticus" (referred to in the chapter as Tractatus opticus II), edited by Franco Alessio, *Rivista critica di storia della filosofia*, XVIII, 147–228.

Hobbes, Thomas. 1973. *Critique du De Mundo de Thomas White*, edited by Jean Jacquot and Harold W. Jones, Paris: Vrin.

Hobbes, Thomas. 1983. *A Minute or First Draught of Optiques*, edited by Elaine C. Stroud, Ph. D. dissertation. University of Wisconsin–Madison.

Hobbes, Thomas. 1994. *The Correspondence*, edited by Noel Malcolm, 2 vols. Oxford: Clarendon Press.

Hobbes, Thomas. 2012. *Leviathan*, edited by Noel Malcolm, 3 vols. Oxford: Clarendon Press.

Horstmann, Frank. 2000. "Hobbes und das Sinusgesetz der Refraktion," *Annals of Science*, 57, 415–440.

Köhler, Max. 1903. "Studien zur Naturphilosophie des Th. Hobbes," *Archiv für Geschichte der Philosophie*, 16, 59–96.

Leijenhorst, Cees. 2002. *The Mechanisation of Aristotelianism: The Late Aristotelian Setting of Thomas Hobbes' Natural Philosophy*. Leiden: Brill.

Malcolm, Noel. 2002. *Aspects of Hobbes*. Oxford, UK: Clarendon Press.

Malcolm, Noel. 2005. "Hobbes, the Latin Optical Manuscript, and the Parisian Scribe," *English Manuscript Studies 1100–1700*, 12, 210–232.

Malet, Antoni. 2001. "The Power of Images: Mathematics and Metaphysics in Hobbes's Optics," *Studies in History and Philosophy of Science*, 31, 2, 303–333.

Martinet, Simon. 1982. "Rôle du problème de la lumière dans la construction de la science cartésienne," *XVIIe Siècle*, 34, 285–309.

Mersenne, Marin. 1636. *Harmonie universelle*. Paris: Chez Sebastien Cramoisy.

Mersenne, Marin. 1644. *Universae geometriae, mixtaeque mathematicae synopsis*. Paris: Bertier.

Nakajima, H. 1984. "Two Kinds of Modification Theory of Light: Some New Observations on the Newton-Hooke Controversy of 1672 Concerning the Nature of Light," *Annals of Science*, 41, 261–278.

Pacchi, Arrigo. 1978. "Hobbes e l'epicureismo," *Rivista critica di storia della filosofia*, 33, 54–71.

Prins, Jan. 1987. "Kepler, Hobbes and Medieval Optics," *Philosophia Naturalis*, 24, 3, 287–310.

Prins, Jan. 1996. "Hobbes on Light and Vision," in *The Cambridge Companion to Hobbes*, edited by Tom Sorell, 129–156. Cambridge, UK: Cambridge University Press.

Raylor, Timothy. 2001. "Hobbes, Payne, and a Short Tract on First Principles," *The Historical Journal*, 44, 29–58.

Raylor, Timothy. 2005. "The Date and Script of Hobbes's Latin Optical Manuscript," *English Manuscript Studies 1100–1700*, 12, 201–209.

Sabra, A. I. 1967. *Theories of Light from Descartes to Newton*. London: Oldbourne.

Schuhmann, Karl. 1995a. "Le Short Tract, première oeuvre philosophique de Hobbes," *Hobbes Studies*, 8, 3–36.

Schuhmann, Karl. 1995b. "Hobbes dans les publications de Mersenne en 1644," *Archives de Philosophie*, 58, 2–7.

Shapiro, Alan E. 1973. "Kinematic Optics: A Study of the Wave Theory of Light in the Seventeenth Century," *Archive for History of Exact Sciences*, 11, 2/3, 134–266.

Shapiro, Alan E. 1994. "Artists' Colors and Newton's Colors," *Isis*, 85, 600–630.

Skinner, Quentin. 1996. *Reason and Rhethoric in the Philosophy of Hobbes*. Cambridge, UK: Cambridge University Press.

Stroud, Elaine. 1990. "Light and Vision: Two Complementary Aspects of Optics in Hobbes' Unpublished Manuscript, A Minute or First Draught of the Optiques," in *Hobbes oggi*, edited by Andrea Napoli, 269–277. Milano: Franco Angeli.

Tuck, Richard. 1988. "Hobbes and Descartes," in *Perspectives on Thomas Hobbes*, edited by G. A. J. Rogers and Alan Ryan, 11–41. Oxford, UK: Clarendon Press.

Zagorin, Perez. 1993. "Hobbes's Early Philosophical Development," *Journal of the History of Ideas*, 54, 505–518.

Zarka, Yves Charles. 1988. "La matière et la representation: Hobbes lecteur de la Dioptrique de Descartes," in *Problématique et reception du* Discours de la Méthode *et des* Essais, edited by H. Méchoulan, 81–98. Paris: Vrin.

PART II
....

HUMAN NATURE
AND MORAL
PHILOSOPHY

....

CHAPTER 8

HOBBES ON LIBERTY, ACTION, AND FREE WILL

THOMAS PINK

1 INTRODUCTION

HOBBES's most developed account of action and its liberty is expounded in his controversy with John Bramhall, the exiled Anglican bishop of Derry. Bramhall is the representative, as Hobbes points out, of early modern scholasticism and particularly scholasticism of the Jesuit tradition. Hobbes drily reported that he had found nothing in Bramhall on free will and on free will's relation to God's concurrence that could not have been read earlier in Suarez's *Opuscula*: "It is no great bragging, to say I was not supprised; for whosoever chanceth to read *Suarez* his *Opuscula* where he writeth of *Free-will*, and of the *concourse of God with Mans Will*; shall find the greatest part, if not all that the *Bishop* hath urged in this Question."[1]

Suarez's thought involves a highly developed account of freedom and its ethical significance—what we might term an "ethics of freedom"—that was firmly based on the theological and canonical tradition of the Latin Church. This tradition taught the reality of freedom as a distinctive metaphysical power and developed from a theory of freedom so conceived an account both of the right to liberty and of freedom as a desirable state of liberation. These three kinds of freedom, the power, the right, and the desirable state, were seen as harmoniously related to law, which was taken to be directive of freedom as well as constitutive of it. Within this scholastic tradition, the metaphysical power of freedom took on a dual ethical significance, as the basis equally of right and of obligation: metaphysical freedom variously provided both a normative block to legal coercion of the individual and the normative basis of that very coercion. Underlying this complex theory of freedom and its relation to law and, indeed, essential to the

---

[1] Hobbes in *Questions*, 28.

theory, was a practical reason-based model of action. Human action was conceived as reason taking practical or action-constitutive form: a mode of reason involving special, intellectual, or reason-involving motivations of the will—motivations that constituted a distinctively goal-directed mode of intentionality or of psychological direction at an object of thought. It was as practical reason-based that action could be governed and directed by natural law, conceived as a demanding form taken by practical reason that was specifically directive of the metaphysical power of freedom.

Hobbes denied the existence of distinctively intellectual and action-constitutive motivations of the will. Action was henceforth to come to no more than voluntariness—an effect of nonintellectual passions. Hobbes also denied the very existence of freedom as a metaphysical power. The theory of a right to liberty could no longer be based on any appeal to freedom as a metaphysical power, and nor could natural law be conceived any longer as practical reason in distinctively freedom-directive form. Though the account of liberty and law that resulted was not fully worked out, its outline was clear. Liberty and law would henceforth be opposed phenomena, no longer existing in harmony. And metaphysical freedom could no longer do the work it once did in scholastic jurisprudence to limit legal coercion. Where once the coercion of religious belief was blocked, when it was, by the metaphysical freedom—the free will, or *liberum arbitrium*—of the believer, now a new foundation of liberty of religious belief had to be found: in the supposed privacy and nonvoluntariness of belief.

2 The Ethics of Freedom

2.1 Freedom as a Power

Blame, it seems, is no ordinary criticism. To blame someone for what they do is not just to point out a fault in them. We can do that without blaming them for the fault. Blame adds something more; the thought that not only is there a fault but that also the fault's existence is *their* fault, the responsibility of the person blamed. Blame involves the idea of a special or moral responsibility. In blame we are putting the faulty action down to the person blamed. And if the fault can be put down to them as their fault, that implies that they must have had the power to determine its occurrence for themselves.

Aquinas gave a characterization of moral blame along just these lines. To blame someone is to criticize them rationally—by reference to a standard of reason that they have failed to meet. But to blame someone is not simply to criticize them as foolish or less than sensible. First, moral blame condemns some action or omission not as foolish, but as bad. The criticism then goes further and imputes the fault in their action (or omission) to the agent as their fault, and as their fault because they were in control—they had *dominium* over the act.

Hence a human action is worthy of praise or blame in so far as it is good or bad. For praise and blame is nothing other than for the goodness or badness of his action to be imputed to someone. Now an action is imputed to an agent when it is within his power, so that he has dominion (*dominium*) over the act. But this is the case with all actions involving the will: for it is through the will that man has dominion over his action . . . Hence it follows that good or bad in actions of the will alone justifies praise and blame; for in such actions badness, fault, and blame come to one and the same.[2]

This power to determine things for ourselves is naturally conceived by us as *freedom*. Freedom is a multiway kind of power—a power to do A or to refrain: a power of control that leaves it up to us—within our control—which of these alternatives we do. And this power of control over what we do is one that we definitely do think we possess. Within certain limits provided by our intelligence, knowledge, and physical capacity, it is, we suppose, up to us—within our power—to determine how we act. It is up to us what we do, so that we are free to act otherwise. This multiway power extends to our agency as a whole—and to our decisions to act as well as to the acts decided on. Indeed, there seems to be a dependence of our freedom in general on a freedom specifically of decision making. It is up to me what I do because I can decide for myself what I shall do, and it is up to me how I decide. So we naturally believe in freedom as a power that must be exercisable at the point of decision or choice. This decision-making capacity was traditionally called the will, and so freedom as a natural or metaphysical power to determine for ourselves how we act has traditionally been referred to as freedom of will or free will.

Peter Lombard's discussion of freedom, central to the treatment of this subject in the subsequent school tradition, introduces freedom precisely as a multiway power, that is, a power that by its nature leaves it up to us which actions we perform, one and the same power being exercisable to determine one action or another. Lombard also locates this power in the will, so that it is indeed up to us how we choose or decide. Lombard referred to

free will (*liberum arbitrium*), which the philosophers have defined as the free judgment of the will (*liberum de voluntate iudicium*), because the very power and ability of the will and reason, which I said earlier was free will, is free regarding whichever alternative it pleases because it can be moved freely to this or to that.[3]

How should we understand freedom as a multiway power? In the *Metaphysical Disputations*, Suarez developed an account of two types of efficient cause. An ordinary efficient cause is a necessary cause, with but one effect that it will, of necessity, produce: a brick hurled at a window must break it. But a rational creature, a human or an angel, may be a contingent or free cause. A free cause operates contingently, in that it is antecedently undetermined whether it will produce a given effect. Which of a range of effects will be produced is contingent and up to the free cause to determine. And our

[2] Aquinas 1950, 1a2ae, q.21, a.2, resp, 112.
[3] Lombard 1981, 461.

possession as free agents of this contingent and distinctively multiway causal power is represented and revealed to us in experience: "Second we can argue from experience. For it is evident to us from experience that it is within our power to do a given thing or to refrain from doing it."[4] Bramhall shares this Suarezian conception of freedom as a multiway causal power: "A free Agent is that, which when all things are present, that are needful to produce the effect, can nevertheless not produce it."[5]

2.1.1 Freedom as a Desirable Condition

Besides freedom as free will, there is another kind of freedom. This is freedom not as a power or capacity to determine, but rather as a desirable state or condition that one might seek to attain. This is the idea of freedom as a state of liberation—an ethically desirable state opposed to servitude or enslavement. *Freedom,* or *libertas,* was deployed within the school tradition as the term not just for the multiway power but also for the desirable ethical condition. The medieval theory of freedom was part of a general account of creation, fall, and redemption—a process of corruption and recovery both ethical and metaphysical in which freedom took correspondingly reduced and recovered forms.

Adam's Fall was a fall from an original state of created innocence into a state of ethical degradation—a state that was described as one of servitude. And Christ's redemption was described as a release from the same servitude, bringing ultimate ethical perfection in heaven, a state that was described as one of perfect liberty or freedom, a supernatural condition transcending our original created condition and approaching, as far as the retention of our created human nature could permit, the condition of God.

Peter Lombard gave a highly important kind of theory of freedom as liberation—a theory which built the theory of the ethical condition on a theory of the metaphysical power.[6] For Lombard, as for other thinkers in his tradition, the power of freedom has a proper function. The function of the power of freedom is to take us, through decisions that are right and meritorious or deserving of reward, to the beatitude of heaven. And liberation is the perfection of the power, by the removal of the capacity to use it badly, and the removal of conditions, such as wayward passions, understood as obstructive of or inappropriate to that power as properly used.

As we were originally created, the metaphysical power of freedom was a *libertas minor*—a power both to do good and to do bad. But the final liberation of heaven will involve our enjoyment of the *libertas maior* enjoyed eternally by God—the perfection of our power of freedom through the complete removal of any power to do bad or to sin. The power that is thus perfected is seen not only as perfected but also as increased:

> Indeed a choice (*arbitrium*) that is quite unable to sin will be the freer ... after the confirmation of beatitude there is to be a free will in man by which he will not be

---

[4] *In metaphysicam Aristotelis,* in Suarez 1856–70, vol. 25, 697.
[5] Bramhall in *Questions,* 298.
[6] For his classic discussion, Lombard 1981, 461–9.

able to sin; and this free will is now in the angels and in the saints, who are with the Lord, and certainly it is the more free, as it is the more immune from sin and the more prone to good. For one is further from that servitude of sin, of which it is written: *He who works sin is the slave of sin,* as one's judgment is freer in choosing the good.[7]

The perfection of the power in the *libertas maior* of heaven will involve the power's perfect conformity with reason. Freedom is a power that presupposes our capacity for reason, which is why the power is lacking in the lower, nonrational animals. And the power's perfection will involve the loss of any capacity to use the power in opposition to reason.

2.2 Freedom as a Right

There is a third use for freedom, or *libertas.* If someone tells you what to do, and even threatens you with some sanction if you do not follow their direction, then, if you think they lack the authority to direct you, you may very well protest: "Don't tell me what to do; it's up to me what I do!" And here we find talk of freedom or of what is up to us being used not to assert a power, or a desirable ethical condition, but a right. Here we find another kind of thing called *freedom*: not a capacity to determine for ourselves what we do, but a right to determine for ourselves what we do. This is the idea of freedom as a right to liberty that might comprise various more specific rights. One central such right is the right not to be coerced; that is, the right not to be directed to do something through the threat of penalties if we do not act as directed.

The use of terms such as *up to me* to assert both the power and the right is highly significant. It suggests some intimate connection between the two phenomena. And there is one immediately obvious, indeed almost irresistible, way of understanding the connection between the power and the right: namely, that the right is, fundamentally, a right to exercise the power. Freedom as a right is a right to determine things for oneself, and that is just the right to exercise one's power of freedom—one's capacity to determine things for oneself. How could there be a right to determine things for oneself without the capacity to determine things for oneself? And what else could the right be than the right to exercise the capacity?

This is how Suarez, in particular, understood the right to liberty—as a recognition at the normative level of this power, namely in the form of a right to exercise it. Freedom as a right is, as I suggested earlier, the right to the exercise of freedom as a power. Notice the following passage from Suarez, in which nature equips man both with *libertas* in the form of a power to determine his actions and with the right to exercise that power. The right to liberty is a *dominium libertatis* or right over his own metaphysical freedom.

---

[7] Lombard 1981, 463.

> If, however, we are speaking of the natural law of dominion, it is then true that liberty is a matter of natural law, in a positive, not merely a negative sense, since nature itself confers upon man the true dominion of his liberty (*dominium libertatis*).
>
> For liberty rather than slavery is of natural right, for this reason, namely, that nature has made men free in a positive sense (so to speak) with an intrinsic right to liberty, whereas it has not made them slaves in this positive sense, strictly speaking.[8]

The term *dominium* could be used in scholastic discussions with exactly the same shifting reference as attaches to our *up to us*: either to refer to freedom as a power or to refer to the right to exercise that power.

In basing a right to liberty on metaphysical freedom, Suarez was faithful to a long-standing feature of the canonical tradition of the Latin Church—a canonical tradition of which Suarez was himself a notable and perceptive interpreter. One frequently cited text in early modern Catholic theological discussion is the decree of the fourth provincial council of Toledo of 633, which forbad the use of coercion—legal directives backed up by threats of punishment—to impose the faith on Jews.[9] This ban on coercion was not based on the theory that we might find in the post-Hobbesian English-language tradition—that belief is an internally private and nonvoluntary act that is impossible for humans to coerce. Rather because the act of faith is an act of free will—*liberum arbitrium*—the Church, or the Christian state, lacks the authority to coerce it in Jews. Given free will, any licit coercion would require some adequate juridical grounding—a juridical subjection of the believer to the coercing authority, and in the case of faith that juridical subjection could only occur through baptism, which Jews lack. Once someone is baptized, on the other hand, their free will gives them no protection against coercion. Rather, their free will allows them to be held responsible for their failure to meet an obligation of fidelity which baptism has imposed on them, and so as responsible, they can fairly be threatened with punishment for breach of that obligation.

Metaphysical freedom protects people against coercion. Given free will, coercion is forbidden without special justification, such as justification in the form of obligations of obedience or fidelity incurred to some legitimate coercive authority. But once those obligations have been incurred, the power of freedom then enables people to be bound by those obligations and to be held responsible for meeting them. Metaphysical freedom is thus both a normative barrier to legal coercion and an enabler of it, as a foundation both of liberty and of obligation. In both ways metaphysical freedom is intimately linked to scholastic conceptions of law.

---

[8] *De legibus* in Suarez 1856–70, vol. 5, 141.
[9] Friedberg 1881, vol. 1, 161–2.

3 FREEDOM, LAW, AND ACTION

3.1 Law and Freedom

The primary form of law for Suarez, as for the rest of his tradition, is not the positive law contingently legislated for this or that community, but *natural law*—a law of reason itself that applies to beings capable not only of reason but also of freedom as a metaphysical power. Natural law is a distinctive form of normativity that governs all possessors of human nature—a kind of rational standard that constitutes, at the ethical level, the recognition, not just of human rationality, but of human freedom as well. The scholastic theory of freedom in its various forms is intimately linked, then, to a theory of law. Freedom and law are treated as existing in a complex harmony. Freedom is something that law recognizes and directs; but freedom is something that law also supplies and even something that law directly constitutes—with the freedom so variously related to law taking more than one form.

At the most fundamental level, law presupposes and gives recognition to freedom as a metaphysical power and in two ways. Law provides us with rights, including a right to freedom: freedom as a right is, as I discussed, a right to exercise the power. But freedom also gives direction in the form of obligation. Legal direction, through the imposition of obligations, is needed at all only because freedom exists as a power over alternatives, a power that may be misused in the direction of the bad. Law serves to direct us toward the good, and away from the bad, by constituting the bad as wrong or a breach of obligation. In directing us to the good, law also directs us toward a state of liberation, in which the power of freedom will be perfected.

Fundamental to the late scholastic understanding of the relation between freedom and obligation is blame: moral obligation or obligation under natural law is understood as that standard we can be fairly blamed for breaching. Blame itself is not seen as a mode of punishment or sanction but rather as a distinctive form of rational criticism. The criticism is generally understood just as Aquinas conceived it—a criticism for disregarding reason in a form that governs and addresses not simply some exercise on our part of our capacity for reason, but the exercise by us of a power of freedom.

Practical reason is seen within scholastic ethical theory as containing a variety of kinds of justificatory force. On the one hand, reason may merely recommend through *consilia,* or counsels. Here reason carries the force of mere advice and does not take the force of law. The natural law, by contrast, is reason in preceptive form, a form in which reason does not merely recommend through advisory counsels, or *consilia,* but demands through obligatory precepts, or *praecepta.* In other words, the natural law is a demandingly directive form of reason: reason that with the binding force of obligation serves to direct the proper use of freedom. And this obligatory directive force is communicated by blame—that freedom-presupposing criticism that imputes the badness in our agency to us as our fault, and our fault because of our *dominium,* or freedom to determine for ourselves which action we perform.

Now any directive force of reason must directly address and apply to the will. For it is at the point of the will—the point at which we choose or decide to perform this action rather than that—that we immediately respond to directives of practical reason. Consider what Hobbes would term a *voluntary* action—that is, an action we might perform on the basis of a prior decision or will to perform it. Take a voluntary action such as going to the bank, for example: suppose that going to the bank is advisable because, say, it is a means to getting money. Then if this voluntary action is supported by practical reason with the force of advice or recommendation, so too, in general, will the decision to perform it—the decision to go to the bank. That decision, too, is advisable and can be taken by us just as an advisable decision, motivating us then to go to the bank. The force of recommendation applies not only to voluntary actions but also to decisions to perform those voluntary actions, and that is how the force of recommendation moves us to act as recommended.

As for advisability as a recommendatory justificatory force or mode of justificatory support, so too on this *force model* of obligation, for moral obligatoriness as a parallel but *demanding* justificatory force or mode of justificatory support.[10] Obligations of the natural law are immediate obligations on the will. As Aquinas made clear, under natural law we were bound to will obligatory external actions and bound not to will prohibited ones, so that the existence of an obligation to give alms implied a corresponding obligation to decide and intend to give alms.[11] And Suarez repeated this doctrine. The law of nature speaks to us, he says, as the voice of our reason, and so it must apply to and direct the will itself:

> So teaches Saint Thomas and on this point everyone. And the point is established because the law of nature is placed in reason and immediately directs and governs the will. So it is on the will first and foremost that, as it were, by its very nature the obligation of the law is imposed. So the law is not kept unless through the exercise of the will.[12]

Behind this lies a conception of obligation, not simply as a kind of command, though obligations might be imposed through commands, but as a demanding mode of justificatory support—a preceptive *vis directiva* or justificatory force.

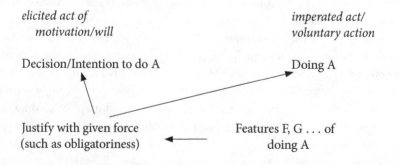

elicited act of motivation/will	*imperated act/ voluntary action*
Decision/Intention to do A	Doing A
Justify with given force (such as obligatoriness)	Features F, G . . . of doing A

---

[10] For further discussion of the force model of obligation and its history, see Pink 2004, 2005, and 2009.

[11] See Aquinas 1950, 1a2ae, q.100, a.9, 463.

[12] *De legibus* in Suarez 1856–70, vol. 5, 123.

Since freedom is exercised in and through the capacity for intentional or deliberate action, this means that both blame and the justificatory force of obligation linked to blame are tied to applying to action. Now, if the force of moral obligation is a justificatory force that is freedom specific and agency specific, this has implications for the capacity for decision or will—the decision-making capacity that any justificatory force within practical reason must address. The capacity for will or decision must itself and in particular be a capacity for free action. The scholastic force of moral obligation, and with it natural law, must address and direct a free will.

3.2 The Practical Reason-Based Model of Action

The *force model* of moral obligation is intimately linked, therefore, to a distinctive model of action that located free action, as required, in the will. This model, general within the school tradition, is *practical reason-based*. For the will can be a locus of free action, as a free will, if the very nature of action is explained as consisting in that mode of exercising reason by which we respond, as agents, to any force of practical reason—as we do at the point of the will when we decide on one voluntary action or another.

Intentional action occurs as the deliberately purposive; it involves goal directedness—intentionally doing something as means to an end, even if in some cases the end at which the action is directed is its own performance and the action is performed only for its own sake. So a central feature of any theory of action will be its account of purposiveness—of the use of means to attain ends.

The scholastic tradition understood purposiveness, and with it intentional action, to consist in a distinctively practice- or agency-constitutive mode of exercising reason. Intentionally to pursue an end is to direct oneself, through the exercise of one's capacity for reason, at an object of thought in a goal-directed and so action-constitutive way. In intentional action one directs oneself at an object of thought, not as something true, nor as something merely good or desirable, but as a goal—something desirable and to be attained through one's exercise of reason. And one exercised reason in this goal-directed way in acts of *electio*: in decisions or intention formations, where what one decided on—the object of the decision—was a goal to be attained through that very decision.

We can look at medieval action theory as locating action as one distinctive form of intentionality or of psychological object direction. For action shares an important characteristic with psychological attitudes such as ordinary beliefs, desires, and emotions—even psychological states which are not, in general, formed by action as the agent's own deliberate or intentional doing. Each of actions and attitudes are directed at an object of thought—an object that makes the action or attitude immediately intelligible as something susceptible of interpretation. The object of a belief or desire or fear tells us what is believed or desired or feared; that is, it gives us the content of the attitude. The object of an action tells us for what purpose the action was performed or at what goal its performance was directed: "Her object in waving like that was to alert her friends."

We may think of the object of an action or attitude as serving to explain that action or attitude by rendering it to some degree intelligible. This explanatory function was identified within the Aristotelian tradition as involving formal causation: the object informs the action or attitude as explanatory form to matter, and makes what it informs the specific action, belief, desire, or fear that it is. Formal causation is not, of course, causation in the modern sense—what Aristotle called causation in efficient form. For the object of thought need not be actual; it need not be realized or instanced in the world as genuine causes in efficient form must be. The object provides intelligibility, but it need not do so as a feature of the world that actually produced the action or attitude made intelligible.

The theory of action was thus developed within a wider account of psychological attitudes and their object direction. Indeed, the primary case of action was taken to occur in psychological attitudes of the will, as choices or decisions, and in the formation of the distinctively goal-directed attitude of intention.

Just as the formation of beliefs is an exercise of theoretical reason directed at objects as truths to be cognized, so intentional actions were supposed to be exercises of practical reason directed at objects as goals, goods to be attained through the action. The locus of such a practical attitude of goal direction was taken to be the will as a faculty of decision and intention—of motivating attitudes that were distinctively rational or reason applying. As Scotus put it:

> Also note that *praxis* or practice is an act of some power or faculty other than intellect, that naturally follows an act of knowledge or intellection, and is suited by nature to be elicited in accord with correct knowledge if it is to be right.[13]

And this capacity is found in the will—a psychological capacity the function of which is precisely to determine action in accordance with deliberation and belief about how to act. The will is the rational appetite—the locus of motivations whose function is to be responsive to and executory of deliberations about how to act:

> From all this it follows that nothing is formally *praxis* except an imperated or elicited act of will, because no act other than that of will is elicited in agreement with a prior act of the intellect.[14]

So the application of practical, action-governing reason is itself practice. We have a theory of action that is *practical reason-based*. Intentional action occurs as a distinctively practical or practice-constitutive mode of exercising reason. The freedom that we exercise in and through action is, therefore, a power exercised over and dependent on the exercise of a capacity for reason: "Reason is the root, the fountain, the original of true liberty, which judgeth and representeth to the will, whether this or that be convenient, whether this or that be more convenient."[15]

---

[13] Wolter 1986, 127.
[14] Wolter 1986, 129.
[15] Bramhall in *Questions*, 30.

In so far as the primary locus of agency is in the will, so freedom is primarily a power of the will—exercised in and through election or choice and decision: "True Liberty consists in the elective power of the rational Will."[16] And, "Certainly all the freedome of the Agent, is from the freedom of the will. If the will have no power over it self, the Agent is no more free than a Staff in a mans hand."[17]

The intellectual nature—the capacity for reason—that humans possess involves a radical psychological distinction between humans and the lower animals, which lack any capacity for reason. This distinction shows up both in the constitution of the mind and in the nature of agency itself.

As reason is above matter and material embodiment, the human capacity to respond to reason, both theoretically in belief and practically, at the point of the will, in action, is exercised independently of any bodily organ. The faculties of intellect and will are immaterial and survive bodily death. So humans possess immaterial capacities or faculties wholly absent from wholly material animal minds. And since the intentional actions that we perform occur as a mode of exercising reason, no such actions are performed by animals. Animal action is only an analogue of fully deliberate or intentional human action, not another case of exactly the same kind.

Human action in fact divides into two elements. There is the primary instance of action, where the practical reason-based model directly applies. These are *actus eliciti* or internal acts of the will itself—acts of choice or decision involving the exercise of reason in action-constitutive form. Then there are the actions decided on that involve capacities outside the will itself, including capacities located in bodily organs such as limb motion. These are *actus imperati,* or external acts—external to the will itself. These latter actions are actions only derivatively, through being motivated objects and effects of the primary cases of action, the elicited actions of the will itself. So the status of imperated actions as actions lies in their being cases of doing something on the basis of a will to do it.

> Voluntariness in the way of an imperated act is nothing else than a certain character or denomination of the imperated act received from an elicited act, of which the imperated act is object and effect. For an imperated act is termed voluntary simply because it proceeds from an elicited act of the will, and is in a measure informed by it, and with it constitutes one morally significant act.[18]

Bramhall faithfully adopts this scholastic model of action:

> This I take to be the clear resolution of the Schools; There is a double act of the will, the one more remote, called *Imperatus*, that is in truth the act of some inferiour faculty, subject to the command of the will, as to open or shut ones eyes; without doubt these actions may be compelled. The other act is neerer, called *actus elicitus*, an act drawn out of the will; as to will, to choose, to elect; this may be stopped or

---

[16] Bramhall in *Questions*, 30.
[17] Bramhall in *Questions*, 32.
[18] *De voluntario* in Suarez 1856–70, vol. 4, 160.

hindered by the intervening impediment of the understanding, as a stone lying on a table is kept from its natural motion, otherwise the will should have a kind of Omnipotence; But the will cannot be compelled to an act repugnant to its inclination, as when a stone is thrown upwards into the air, for that is both to incline, and not to incline to the same object, at the same time, which implies a contradiction.[19]

It might appear that there is very little left in common between imperated actions and the elicited actions of the will that give rise to them. On the one hand, we have a distinctively practical mode of response to an object of thought—an action-constitutive mode of exercising reason that takes immaterial form. On the other hand, we have what is just an efficiently caused effect of the will to perform it—something that, considered in itself, might be the mere motion of a bodily organ. The former is an action because of its mode of direction toward an object internal to it. The latter is contentless and objectless in its own right and is an action simply as an effect of something else. This allowed Hobbes to accuse the scholastics of equivocation in their theory of action.

Animal action, by contrast, involves no immaterial acts of will but simply the motivation of external actions by passions. Passions, which we and the animals share, are motivational or appetitive states that are themselves nonintellectual and—unlike the motivations of the will—are corporeally based. Motivations of the will are responsive to the good in a form that is grasped intellectually. By contrast, the passions are responsive only to sensorily presented goods. While the passions are the only motivations that determine animal action, any influence the passions have on human action (solely through influencing how the will's object appears) is mediated by and subject to the decision of the will—the free exercise of which constitutes the primary form of every deliberate human action. Indeed, it is possible, at least in principle, for human action to occur unmotivated by any passion; though in practice the influence of passions is considerable. For Suarez, the passions cannot act as efficient causes directly on the will, still less determine it,[20] and they will not usually remove freedom. But the passions can make the exercise of freedom in opposition to them very difficult. Disordered passions will therefore require careful discipline through habituation. More than that, with supernatural help, through grace, we may conform to a supernatural law and attain liberation from the weakness of disordered passion and a perfection of our power of freedom beyond anything of which we are naturally capable.

Just as with divine help, we can be raised beyond our human nature, so we can, on occasion, be degraded below it to the level of nonrational creation. It is possible, in cases of madness or extreme emotion even for human passions to motivate action directly, bypassing the will. Then we are reduced to the level of beasts or animals. Our reason is disengaged from our action—and with it freedom or control of what we are doing is lacking too.

[19] Bramhall in *Questions*, 215–16.
[20] *De voluntario* in Suarez 1856–70, vol. 4, 248.

3.3 Summary

The scholastic ethics of freedom that we find in highly developed form in Suarez's ethics thus involves a complex and distinctive theory of normativity, linked to an equally distinctive moral psychology and theory of action—all built on the human possession of freedom as a multiway power over alternatives. The power of freedom is given normative recognition through a distinctive form of normativity within practical reason, which is the normativity of law. And law recognizes the power of freedom both by imposing obligations on us and by affording us rights. First, law provides a mode of rational direction—of justificatory force—that is freedom specific and that addresses a capacity for free action exercised, in practical reason-based form, at the point of the will. This is moral obligatoriness understood as a distinctively demanding mode of justificatory force tied to the direction of free action through its constitutive linkage to moral blame as a freedom-specific mode of rational criticism. Second, law recognizes the power of freedom by providing the right to exercise it—the right to liberty understood as a *dominium libertatis,* or right to determine alternatives. Thus does the normativity of law combine *lex* and *ius,* obligation and liberty, as dual ways of giving ethical recognition to metaphysical freedom. And in directing the power of freedom, law finally serves to liberate us, leading us to that condition in which the power which law directs is perfected.

4 THE IMPACT OF HOBBES

Hobbes challenges every element of this theory both of human self-determination as a multiway power exercised at the point of the will and of the normative recognition of this power in law.

Blame becomes detached from any capacity for self-determination. And such power to determine action that is found in ourselves is not freedom but voluntariness. This is simply a causal power of our appetites to cause their satisfaction—a capacity to do A on the basis of a will or desire to do A. Freedom is no longer the two-way power we ordinarily take it to be. Indeed it is no longer a form of power at all but really an absence of obstacles to power: liberty is now the absence of external obstacles to acting as one wills. And voluntariness and any associated liberty does not extend to our decisions to act—which are simply very powerful appetites and which are themselves inherently nonvoluntary. There is no voluntariness of the will, and so there is no freedom or liberty of the will. Our every action, like every other event, is causally predetermined by prior occurrences. Action is determined to occur by necessity: a necessity with which voluntariness and, on Hobbes's theory of it, liberty are wholly consistent. Since freedom no longer exists as a form of power, so law can no longer exist as giving normative recognition to this power, either by directing its exercise through obligation or by giving a right to its exercise in a form of moral liberty. The relation between law and freedom must take quite another form. And since freedom no longer exists as a power, still less as a power specific to rational creation, so there can be no state of liberation that consists in the rational perfection of the power and its detachment from irrational passions.

On what basis does Hobbes mount his challenge? He mounts his challenge on the basis of what he takes to be well-conceived philosophy that is critical of past forms of linguistic expression. We must carefully consider not just the terms we inherit from past philosophy but also what ideas or conceptions those terms may or may not express. The enemy is school philosophy that uses a jargon to detach us from our own thoughts—from the conceptions we really think with. Hobbes maintains that sound Protestant Christianity supports his view. Philosophy confirms the teachings of Luther and Calvin: there is no freedom of will, and human actions are products of necessity; indeed, they are divinely predetermined. But philosophy can access these truths anyway, independently of any revealed theology: "Questions of free will, of justification, of the way Christ is received in the sacrament, are philosophical."[21]

4.1 Human and Animal

Hobbes's assault on this whole scholastic theory of self-determination centers on the gulf it places between human and animal psychology. To an important extent, Hobbes removes the distinctively reason constitutive, or intellectual part, of scholastic psychology to leave at least in broad outline the part shared with the animals. There are no longer any immaterial faculties of will and intellect. We are left instead with sense, imagination derived from sense, and with passion. The theory of human reason, of human action, and of the capacity to determine action is then reconstructed to fit into this reduced psychology—a psychology that leaves human psychology continuous with, indeed, only a more developed version of the psychology of the lower animals and human action a phenomenon no different from animal action. And with the reason-constitutive faculties of intellect and will goes the distinctive power of freedom that they supported. There are no free causes, operating immaterially, apart from any bodily organ, but only necessary ones operating within a wholly material world.

Hobbes's attack on the idea of a clear psychological gulf between rational humans and nonrational animals involves some continuity, though mainly in rhetoric or expression, between him and the radical Augustinianism of those Protestant authors whom he was so willing to cite in his support. For there is an ancient tradition, going back to the Church Fathers, but deployed with especial emphasis in Calvin, of understanding the consequences of the Fall—the servitude from which freedom as liberation

---

[21] Hobbes, *De cive* 18.14, 293.

releases us—as a kind of degradation, at least in relation to motivation and practice, from humanity to animality.[22] But in Hobbes, of course, it is no longer a question of a degradation from which we might be liberated but of natural condition. And any freedom of will that Calvin supposes us to have lost is supposed by Hobbes to be not lost but strictly unintelligible.

Reason remains peculiarly human. Hobbes does not deny that humans have a distinctive capacity for reason. But it ceases to be a capacity separating the very constitution of our mind from that of animals. Since the psychological states possessed by humans are just those possessed by animals, reason involves something importantly extra-mental—not a further part of the mind, but the use of a tool which some minds, human minds, use to express what they contain. Human reason comes simply to the possession of language, and reasoning is simply a form of thinking with and about language and the ideas expressed in language:

> Out of all which we may define, (that is to say determine,) what that is, which is meant by this word *Reason*, when wee reckon it amongst the Faculties of the mind. For REASON, in this sense, is nothing but *Reckoning* (that is, Adding and Substracting) of the Consequences of generall names agreed upon, for the *marking* and *signifying* of our thoughts; I say *marking* them, when we reckon by our selves; and *signifying*, when we demonstrate, or approve our reckonings to other men.[23]

4.2 Action as Voluntary Action

There are no longer distinctively reason-involving motivations. All motivations are passions. The will is simply the last appetite or passion in deliberating—the passion that finally determines how we act. So action can no longer be understood in terms of some distinctive mode of exercising reason but becomes identified with the only element of scholastic action theory that survives—the category of imperated action. Hobbes's position was clear: imperated acts as effects of the will, are acceptable, allowing for reservations about the term "imperated":

> Wherein letting pass that Metaphoricall speech of attributing command and subjection to the faculties of the Soul, as if they made a Common-wealth or Family among themselves, and could speak one to another, which is very improper in searching the truth of the question; You may observe first that to compell a voluntary act, is nothing else, but to will it; for it is all one to say, my will commands the shutting of mine

---

[22] "But man does not choose by reason and pursue with zeal what is truly good for himself according to the excellence of his immortal nature; nor does he use his reason in deliberation or bend his mind to it. Rather, like an animal he follows the inclination of his nature, without reason, without deliberation." Calvin 1960, vol. 1, 286.

[23] Hobbes, *Leviathan* 5, 18 (references to chapter and 1651 page in Malcolm edn.).

eyes, or the doing of any other action, and to say, I have the will to shut my eyes. So that *actus imperatus* here, might as easily have been said in English, a voluntary action, but that they that invented the tearm, understood not any thing it signified.[24]

The only power that is exercised in action is a power of passive appetites or passions to get us to act as desired. It is a voluntariness that involves motivation, not through a distinctive faculty of will but through passion. And passions are not themselves voluntary. We have no power over will or motivation, since any action-determining power in us is found in our motivations themselves. And this power is not self-determining, since motivations are not themselves voluntary: "I acknowledge this liberty, that I can do if I will, but to say, I can will if I will, I take to be an absurd speech."[25] And, "Can any man but a Schoolman think that the Wil is voluntary? But yet the Wil is the cause of voluntary actions."[26]

Indeed, the very notion of *self*-determination is viewed by Hobbes as viciously regressive: "And if a man determine himself, the Question will still remain what determined him to determine himself in that manner."[27]

The scholastic claim that there are elicited acts of the will itself is confused and even unintelligible. The claim is confused on three counts. First, it involves a distinction of supposedly "rational" or "intellectual" motivations from "nonrational" or "sensitive" motivations or passions—a distinction that Hobbes regards as empty and never satisfactorily explained by its scholastic defenders:

> For I do not fear it will be thought too hot for my fingers, to shew the vanity of such words as these, *Intellectual appetite, Conformity of the appetite to the object, Rational will, Elective power of the Rational will*; nor understand I how Reason can be the root of true Liberty, if the *Bishop* (as he saith in the beginning) had the liberty to write this discourse. I understand how objects, and the Conveniences and the Inconveniences of them, may be represented to a man by the help of his sences; but how *Reason* representeth anything to the *Will*, I [do not] understand.[28]

The idea of a freedom or agency of will is as absurd as the idea of a will or agency of passion, since the former idea reduces to the second: "nor can a man more determine his will than any other appetite; that is, more than he can determine when he shall be hungry and when not."[29]

Second, given the unintelligibility of a practical mode of exercising rationality, the only consistent and intelligible model of agency is that of being the voluntary product

---

[24] Hobbes in *Questions*, 217.
[25] Hobbes in *Questions*, 29.
[26] Hobbes in *Questions*, 256.
[27] Hobbes in *Questions*, 26.
[28] Hobbes in *Questions*, 35–6.
[29] Hobbes in *Questions*, 25.

of a desire to do it. But that model cannot apply to passions or motivations: as we have noted, for Hobbes the will itself cannot be voluntary.

Third, since the will is the locus of a power to act, its role is to explain and give rise to our actions but cannot be supposed to perform actions itself—any more than our power or capacity to dance can be supposed to go in for dancing itself. The very idea of actions of the will is a kind of category mistake:

> Secondly, you may observe, that *actus elicitus*, is exemplified by these words, to Will, to Elect, to Choose, which are all one, and so to will is here made an act of the will; and indeed, as the will is a faculty, or power of a mans soul, so to will is an act of it, according to that power. But as it is absurdly said, that to dance is an act allured or drawn by fair means out of the ability to dance; so it is also to say, that to will, is an act allured or drawn out of the power to will, which power is commonly called, the Will.[30]

And,

> And where he [Bramhall] sayes our Wills are in our power, he sees not that he speaks absurdly; for he ought to say, the Will is the Power.[31]

4.3 Liberty and Power

Freedom survives not as a two-way power over action but as Hobbesian liberty—not itself a power but an absence of obstacles to power, such as to the force of passions or indeed to any force. "As if it were not Freedome enough for a man *to do what he will*; unless his *Will also have power over his Will*, and that his *Will* be not the power it self, but must have another power within it to do all voluntary acts."[32] And, "Liberty is the absence of all impediments to action, that are not contained in the nature, and in the intrinsecal quality of the Agent."[33]

In fact, liberty is no more peculiar to rational humans than is voluntariness—which can as much be found in animal action as in human. Indeed liberty extends even wider—to streams and rivers or to anything with force that might go in for some action. Given a lack of external obstruction to that force, we find liberty:

> How *Reason* representeth any thing to the *Will*, I understand no more than the *Bishop* understands there may be Liberty in Children, in Beasts, and inanimate

---

[30] Hobbes in *Questions*, 217–18.
[31] Hobbes in *Questions*, 40.
[32] Hobbes in *Questions*, 38.
[33] Hobbes in *Questions*, 285.

Creaturs. For he seemeth to wonder how Children may be left at Liberty; how Beasts imprisoned may be set at Liberty; and how a River may have a free course.[34]

In his arguments about causation, Hobbes regularly assumes that where there is power or reason enough for something to happen, then that thing will happen. Thus he argues that all things that begin at some time to exist must have a cause:

> Also the fixt point, that a man cannot imagine any thing to begin without a cause, can no other way be made known but by trying how he can imagine it. But if he try, he shall find as much reason (if there be no cause of the thing) to conceive, it should begin at one time as another, that is, he hath equall reason to think, it should begin at all times, which is impossible. And therefore he must think there was some special cause, why it began then rather than sooner or later, or else, that it began never, but was Eternal.[35]

For Hobbes efficient causes are only Suarezian necessary causes, determining and necessitating but one outcome. In clear contradiction of Suarez, Hobbes denies that the existence of free causal power is ever represented in experience. Experience can reveal no such contingent and multiway form of causal power operating independently of prior necessity. The belief that our actions are not necessitated but free reflects merely our ignorance of their causes—though caused they must be. In fact, this is all that the term "contingent" really means—not uncaused and undetermined, but cause unknown. Hobbes allows that we are sometimes aware of being determined by motivations and then recognize necessity. But when we are not aware of the determination, we mistake this for freedom and genuine lack of determination: "But commonly when we see and know the strength that moves us, we acknowledge Necessity, but when we see not, or mark not the force that moves us, we then think there is none, and that it is not Causes but Liberty that produceth the action."[36]

And indeed it might be unclear how experience could ever do more than fail to represent determination. What would it be not to fail to represent a cause but to represent the lack of a cause?

Against the scholastic postulation of a free cause sufficient for a range of alternative effects, Hobbes puts forward the following a priori argument. All causes must be sufficient to produce their effect. But if they are sufficient the effect must follow. So the idea of a free cause is incoherent: if the free cause is enough for each effect, it must produce each, which is impossible:

> But the *Bishop* defineth Contingents thus, "All things which may be done and may not be done, may happen, or may not happen by reason of the Indetermination, or accidental concurrence of the Causes." By which definition Contingent is nothing, or it is the same that I say it is. For, there is nothing can be done and not be done,

---

[34] Hobbes in *Questions*, 36.
[35] Hobbes in *Questions*, 302.
[36] Hobbes in *Questions*, 217.

nothing can happen and not happen by reason of the Indetermination or accidental concurrence of the causes. It may be done or not done for aught he knowes, and happen or not happen for any determination he perceaveth; and that is my definition. But that the indetermination can make it happen or not happen, is absurd; for indetermination maketh it equally to happen or not to happen; and therefore both; which is a contradiction. Therefore indetermination doth nothing, and whatsoever causes do, is necessary.[37]

4.4 Purposiveness and Explanation

Hobbes, we have seen, reduces action in general to what had previously been the special and secondary case of willed or imperated action—what Hobbes was now to term "voluntary action." Hobbes completely abandoned any theory of purposiveness as consisting in a distinctively practical mode of exercising reason located in the will as a special intellectual or rational appetite.

Instead, Hobbes introduced a new model of purposiveness that could only apply to the case of what had previously been called imperated action. To act purposively was always to do something voluntarily, on the basis of a prior will to do it—a will that, in line with much medieval action theory, Hobbes conceived as an efficient cause of the imperated or voluntary action that it motivated. But now this motivating will was no longer itself a prior case of action but rather a passion.

A central issue in the debate is the explanation of action. Action, it is natural to think, is explained in terms of its motivation—which is given by the goal at which it is directed. Hobbes insists that this goal direction is given through an efficient cause—a prior passion. And in this he is partly adopting the standard scholastic picture of the relation between an imperated action and its elicited cause—only turning that cause into a passion. But he is also rejecting the idea that explanation of an action involves some mode of causation, such as formal causation, other than efficient causation and some form of determination that does not involve an antecedent necessity being imposed on action.

Both Bramhall and Hobbes assume that action is determined. No appeal is made by Bramhall to efficient causation in nondetermining mode. Where the difference lies is in the manner of determination—whether natural or, as Bramhall terms it, moral. The object of the will, for Bramhall, is not an efficient or necessitating cause of its operation—what Bramhall means when he talks simply of a *cause*—but rather a moral determinant of it:

> Secondly, for the manner how the understanding doth determine the Will, it is not naturally but morally. The Will is mooved by the understanding, not as by an efficient, having a causal influence into the effect, but onely by proposing and representing the object. And therefore as it were ridiculous to say, that the object of the sight is

---

[37] Hobbes in *Questions*, 184.

the cause of seeing, so it is to say, that the proposing of the object by the understand-ing to the will, is the cause of willing; and therefore the understanding hath no place in that concourse of causes which according to *T.H.* do necessitate the will.[38]

Bramhall's moral determination, then, is explanation in terms of an object—formal causation as the school tradition termed it. This form of action explanation is avail-able provided we admit the existence of content-bearing actions of the will. Because an action of the will has content or object direction in its own right, the action can be explained, or made intelligible, by that very content and independently of prior effi-cient causes. For the action's object direction or goal direction is internal to the action itself, arising as "form" to the action's "matter."

For Hobbes, the object or content of the motivating will to act still provided the goal at which the action willed was directed. But since the motivating will was not itself a purposive action but merely a passion or passive desire, purposiveness—being delib-erately or intentionally done as a means to an end—was restricted to the action willed. It followed that all explanation in terms of purposes now involved reference to a moti-vating efficient cause. So Hobbes could afford to claim that all explanation of action in terms of the purposes for which it was performed had to be in terms of efficient causes. In fact, Hobbes claimed to find the idea of motivation by objects as opposed to efficient causes completely unintelligible: "Moved not as by an Efficient, is non-sense."[39]

4.5 Liberty, Obligation, and Blame

Scholastic moral theory had restricted to action the application within ethics of "legal" responses and standards, such as blame and obligation, and had based this restric-tion on a conception of action as the locus of a power of multiway self-determination. Hobbes would either remove the restriction to agency or reconstruct the restriction in some other way, such as by appeal to action as a locus of voluntariness.

In scholastic moral theory, whatever disagreements there might have been about the relation of law to divine command, there was generally an essential connection made between something being a wrong or a breach of law and the possibility of blaming the agent—of imputing the badness of the crime to him as his self-determined doing. And that imputation would only be possible in relation to action and its outcomes—in so far as it is these that are up to us or within our control. "If *I* was [determined], then I ought not to be blamed, for no man is justly blamed for doing that which was never in his power to shun."[40] And, "The essence of sin consists in this, that one commit that which he might avoid."[41]

---

[38] Bramhall in *Questions*, 55–56.
[39] Hobbes in *Questions*, 59.
[40] Bramhall in *Questions*, 34.
[41] Bramhall in *Questions*, 185.

But Hobbes rejects the scholastic link of blame to freedom. Blame is no more than a form of disapproval. Why do we blame anyone for anything? "I answer, because they please us not. I might ask him, whether blaming be any thing else but saying the thing blamed is ill or imperfect."[42]

So blame in no way presupposes any power, such as freedom, on the part of the person blamed:

> I answer, they are to be blamed though their Wills be not in their own power. Is not good good, and evill evill though they be not in our power? and shall I not call them so? and is that not Praise and Blame? But it seems that the *Bishop* takes *blame* not for the dispraise of a thing, but for a praetext and colour of malice and revenge against him he blameth ... Here again he [Bramhall] is upon his arguments from Blame, which I have answered before; and we do as much blame them [inanimate things] as we do men; for we say fire hath done hurt, and the poyson hath killed a man, as well as we say the man hath done unjustly; but we do not seek to be revenged of the fire and of poyson, because we cannot make them ask for forgiveness, as we would make men do when they hurt us; so that the blaming of the one and the other, that is, the declaring of the hurt or evill action done by them, is the same in both; but the malice of man is onely against man.[43]

The sinfulness of an action, and its character as a breach of law, does not presuppose freedom as a multiway power but simply the action's voluntariness as a mode of doing what we will: "The nature of sin consisteth in this, that the action done proceed from our will and be against the Law. A Judge in judging whether it be sin or not, which is done against the Law, looks at no higher cause of the action than the will of the doer."[44]

Just as there was no metaphysical power of freedom, there was no room for a normativity of law of the kind that natural law was understood to constitute by Suarez. There was no room for law as Suarez conceived it—as a special directive force of reason that gave normative recognition to the power of freedom both by imposing obligations to direct its exercise (*lex* or *ius*) and by affording rights to protect its exercise (*ius*). There was no longer a kind of normativity that involved both the right and the obligation as twin ways of giving normative recognition to freedom as a power:

> For though they that speak of this subject, use to confound *Jus*, and *Lex, Right* and *Law;* yet they ought to be distinguished; because RIGHT, consisteth in liberty to do, or to forbeare; Whereas LAW, determineth, and bindeth to one of them: so that Law, and Right, differ as much, as Obligation, and Liberty; which in one and the same matter are inconsistent.[45]

---

[42] Hobbes in *Questions*, 39.
[43] Hobbes in *Questions*, 39–40.
[44] Hobbes in *Questions*, 185.
[45] Hobbes, *Leviathan* 14, 64.

The idea of a right to liberty and that of an obligation are for Hobbes just what they might immediately appear to be—simply opposed notions, one marking the provision of alternatives at the level of the normative, the other the denial of them. And if we take law as a source of obligation—which Hobbes proposes to do—then law must be inherently opposed to liberty, and the imposition of law must by its very nature serve to remove liberty: "And Law was brought into the world for nothing else, but to limit the naturall liberty of particular men, in such manner, as they might not hurt, but assist one another, and joyn together against a common Enemy."[46]

In involving obligations, law was not harmonious with freedom, but its essential opposite.

We find Hobbes shifting between a variety of ways of speaking of obligation. Sometimes he gives an account of obligation under natural law that preserves an important element of the force model—the scope of obligation under natural law as binding on nonvoluntary motivation. It is just that motivation is no longer understood as an inner locus of metaphysical freedom, and obligation is no longer understood as a justificatory force linked to blame as a criticism specific to freedom: "The Lawes of Nature oblige *in foro interno*; that is to say, they bind to a desire they should take place: but *in foro externo*; that is, to the putting them in act, not alwayes."[47]

But elsewhere, where civil or human law's relation to the application of sanctions is being emphasized, obligation is treated as governing only the voluntary, so that nonvoluntary thoughts are not subject to obligation. This approach is used to preserve inner religious belief from being bound by coercively enforced human law: "As for the inward *thought*, and *beleef* of men, which humane Governours can take no notice of, (for God onely knoweth the heart) they are not voluntary, nor the effect of the laws, but of the unrevealed will, and of the power of God; and consequently fall not under obligation."[48]

Hobbes appeals to two features of religious belief that supposedly block its legal coercion. First we have its privacy. The human legislator cannot reliably determine what someone's real religious belief might be, so laws on inner belief are unenforceable on that account. Then second, belief is nonvoluntary. Like motivations of the will itself, beliefs cannot be adopted or abandoned at will just in order to avoid sanctions imposed on illegal belief.

This Hobbesian view involved a quite different account of the legal regulation of belief from Suarez. For Suarez, religious belief is not completely private. Religion is a public and social phenomenon, and religious belief, especially, is very liable sooner or later to be expressed. But more crucially, the relative nonvoluntariness of belief is not to the point. For the function of sanction-backed legal coercion is not to motivate people to form or hold beliefs voluntarily, simply on the basis of a will or motivation to avoid sanctions. Rather the function of threatened sanctions is to forcibly direct the

---

[46] *Leviathan*, 26, 138–9.
[47] *Leviathan*, 15, 79.
[48] *Leviathan*, 40, 249–50.

believer's attention to a sound epistemic case, based on evidence or else on authoritative testimony, for the obligatory opinion—a case that the believer had hitherto been willfully and culpably ignoring—so that the required belief is then formed in response to that epistemic case:

> Even a pagan—that is, a non-Christian—king, if he has a knowledge of the true God, may coerce his own subjects into believing that truth, *either by their own reasoning if they are educated, or by putting human faith in more learned men, if they are ignorant*; and consequently, he may compel those same subjects to cease from the worship of idols and from similar superstitions contrary to natural reason.[49]

The punitive imposition of sanctions does not presuppose that belief can be formed at will, irrespective of testimony or evidence. Belief is significantly nonvoluntary precisely because it is dependent on testimony or evidence in its support. But, for Suarez, the subject still has some degree of freedom or control over whether he responds to that evidence. That freedom enables him fairly to be bound by obligations on belief and fairly threatened with punishments for breach of those obligations.

At the same time as helping base religious coercion, we must remember that for Suarez metaphysical freedom also put normative obstacles to such coercion. In particular, as we have seen, the metaphysical freedom of the unbaptized protected them against the coercive authority of the Church or of the Christian state acting on the Church's behalf. Jews and Muslims could not fairly be coerced into believing Christianity, not because the act of faith is nonvoluntary—this does nothing to protect the culpable baptized heretic from canonical penalties on heretical belief—but because the metaphysical freedom of the believer demanded a special justification, which only baptism can provide, for their coercion.

Hobbes's denial of the very existence of metaphysical freedom forced him to limit the authority of the state over religious belief in quite another way—by appeal to novel and, arguably, rather crudely conceived practical limits on the use of punishment in motivating belief. But it is not obvious that these practical limits really apply. Legal coercion does arguably serve to influence belief in exactly the way that Suarez envisaged, by engaging and directing the attention of the believer. The function of penal coercion in the criminal law is often to use the threat of a penalty to engage attention and help communicate a message that there are anyway prior grounds to believe—that the action threatened by punishment really would be seriously wrong. The function of sanction-backed criminal law is in part to drive home an argument and change what people—not nonrational animals but beings equipped with reason—actually believe. [50]

---

[49] *De fide* in Suarez 1856–70, vol. 12, 451.

[50] For an influential defense of a communicative or expressive theory of the function of punishment in recent philosophy see Feinberg (1970). The modern, post-Hobbesian idea that *liberal* punishment cannot seek to change people's thoughts and beliefs—to direct and form their conscience as well as their external actions—is, I would submit, naive both about liberalism and about punishment.

Whatever one thinks of the scholastic commitment to a metaphysics of multiway freedom, that metaphysics at least permitted a substantial conception of a right to liberty—a right that could extend to religious belief. To block the coercion of belief, the schoolmen were not forced to distort the nature of religious belief itself, such as by denying its deeply social and public nature, or the real influence of sanctions as a directive pressure on what people believe.

BIBLIOGRAPHY

Aquinas, Thomas. 1950. *Summa theologiae*. Turin: Marietti.

Calvin, John. 1960. *Institutes of the Christian Religion*, edited by John T. McNeill. 2 vols. Philadelphia: Westminster Press.

Feinberg, Joel. 1970. *Doing and Deserving: Essays in the Theory of Responsibility*. Princeton: Princeton University Press.

Friedberg, Emil. 1881. *Corpus iuris canonici*. 2 vols. Leipzig: Tauchnitz.

Hobbes, Thomas. 1983. *De Cive*, edited by Howard Warrender. Oxford: Clarendon Press.

Hobbes, Thomas. 2012. *Leviathan*, edited by Noel Malcolm. 3 vols. Oxford: Clarendon Press.

Hobbes, Thomas, and Bramhall, John. 1656. *The Questions Concerning Liberty, Necessity and Chance, Clearly Stated Between Dr Bramhall Bishop of Derry, and Thomas Hobbes of Malmesbury*. London.

Lombard, Peter. 1981. *Sententiae in IV Libris Distinctae*. 2 vols. Grottaferrata: Collegii S. Bonaventurae ad Claras Aquas.

Pink, Thomas. 2004. "Suarez, Hobbes and the Scholastic Tradition in Action Theory," in *The Will and Human Action: from Antiquity to the Present Day*, edited by Thomas Pink and Martin Stone, 127–53. London: Routledge.

Pink, Thomas. 2005. "Action, Will and Law in Late Scholasticism," in *Moral Philosophy on the Threshold of Modernity* (New Synthese Historical Library 57), edited by Jill Kraye and Risto Saarinen, 31–50. Dordrecht: Springer.

Pink, Thomas. 2009. "Natural Law and the Theory of Obligation," in *Psychology and Philosophy* (Studies in the History of Philosophy of Mind 8), edited by Sara Heinämaa and Martina Reuter, 97–114. Dordrecht: Springer.

Suarez, Francisco. 1856–70. *Opera Omnia*. 26 vols. Paris: Vives

Wolter, Allan. 1986. *Duns Scotus on the Will and Morality*. Washington, DC: CUA Press.

CHAPTER 9

....

REASON, DELIBERATION, AND THE PASSIONS

....

ADRIAN BLAU

1 INTRODUCTION

....

MANY writers claim that Hobbes saw reason as the slave of the passions. I find this interpretation misleading and suggest that it is often based on misreading. The key contrast is not between reason and the passions but between different passions—the passion for our real good, self-preservation, and passions for apparent goods which undermine self-preservation. By highlighting such clashes, reason can inform our deliberation.

Yet this raises a huge problem: it is not clear whether Hobbes thought we would pick our real or apparent good where they clash. Reason's strength thus remains uncertain. Ultimately, though, we can be confident that Hobbes does not see reason as the slave of the passions and we can cautiously suggest a better summary: reason is the counselor of the passions, at least for those few people who use reason.

Three brief methodological points are worth noting. First, anachronism—using modern words rather than Hobbes's—often leads to misinterpretation. Anachronism is unavoidable, and can help us,[1] but it is dangerous.[2] Misreadings of Hobbes often reflect anachronistic analogies such as reason being enslaved to the passions, or anachronistic viewpoints such as rational choice theory.

To understand what authors meant, then, we should place them in their linguistic and/or political context. But also vital is *textual* context. My second methodological point is that many misinterpretations come from reading comments or passages out of context.

---

[1] Blau 2012b.
[2] Skinner 2002, 49–51, 60–1.

My third methodological point is that we should indicate our uncertainty where firm conclusions are unwarranted. It is tempting to look for evidence which fits our views, then state our conclusions as if they must be right. But that way lies Leo Strauss.[3] It is harder but safer to compare different interpretations and then indicate if the evidence is ambiguous or unconvincing.[4]

This chapter is structured as follows. After describing the deductive nature of Hobbesian reason (section 2) and briefly considering deliberation and the passions (section 3), I reject the view that reason is the slave of the passions (section 4.1). Hobbes is not discussing reason when he writes that "the Thoughts, are to the Desires, as Scouts, and Spies, to range abroad, and find the way to the things desired" (section 4.2). Nor does his account of regulated thoughts involve reason (section 4.3). We should also be careful when describing Hobbesian reason as instrumental (section 4.4). I reject the view that reason enslaves the passions but accept some claims about reason's strength (section 5). After probing reason's place in deliberation (section 6), I present the conflict not as between reason and the passions but between real and apparent goods. Reason highlights our real good—but it is not clear which Hobbes thinks we will pick (section 7). Overall, I cautiously suggest that reason is the counselor of the passions (section 8).

2 REASON

Hobbes talks of reason in four main ways: a set of principles, a faculty, a process, and an outcome. The set of principles is logic, which we apply with the faculty of reason, in a process of reasoning (also called computation, demonstration, ratiocination, and reckoning), producing an outcome called "right reason." The faculty of reason and the process of reasoning happen inside our heads, but the rules of logic and the outcome of right reason are external: an inference is or is not logically valid, objectively speaking. Reason distinguishes humans from animals and reflects our ability to use language. But we often misuse language: we need clear definitions to deduce conclusions that follow necessarily from our premises. Even with clear definitions, though, anyone can fail to reason correctly.

There is much textual support for this highly condensed summary.[5] But the most detailed account, in *De corpore*, is not always helpful.[6] We learn two main things, neither of which can easily be understood from *De corpore* alone. The first is that reasoning

---

[3] See Blau 2012a.

[4] Blau 2011; Blau 2012a, 144, 150–1.

[5] De Mundo *Examined* 37.4, 448; 39.7, 489; *Elements of Law*, ed. Gaskin 6.4, 41; *On the Citizen*, trans. Silverthorne 2.1, 33; 18.4, 236–8; *Leviathan*, ed. Tuck 4.5–14, 13–16; 5, 18–22; 6.51, 28; 46.1–5, 367; *Concerning Body* 1.2, 3; 4.1–4, 44–55; 5.2, 57; 6.15–17, 84–7; 20.6, 312; *Liberty, Necessity and Chance*, ed. Molesworth 95, 191, 365, 450; *Six Lessons* 183–4, 188. (When quoting Hobbes, I remove his italics.)

[6] Barnouw 2008, 43.

is like mathematical "computation," which is the "addition and substraction" of properties.[7] *Leviathan* explains this better. In arithmetic, reason involves adding and subtracting numbers; in geometry, reason involves the same for lines and angles; in logic, it
involves syllogisms and demonstrations; in politics, one adds "Pactions" to calculate
what our duties are; and in law, one adds "Lawes, and facts, to find what is right and
wrong in the actions of private men."[8]

What Hobbes means seems to be as follows. In arithmetic, when you add 2 and 2,
you must get 4. If you don't, your computation is wrong and conflicts with reason.
In geometry, when you have a right-angled triangle whose shortest sides are 3 and 4
units long respectively, the third side must be 5 units long. To suggest otherwise is
against reason. In logic, if your premises are that Socrates is a human and that all
humans are mortal, you must conclude that Socrates is mortal, or your reasoning is
wrong. In politics, if we have a paction (a covenant or contract) to obey the sovereign, and if pactions entail obligations, then we must have an obligation to obey the
sovereign; to conclude otherwise violates reason. In law, if you know that citizens
should pay taxes, and that a particular citizen has not, then you must agree that
his actions are wrong. (The last two conclusions require extra premises, but these
simple examples will suffice for here.) Hobbes often describes distortions of reason
as "corruption."[9]

Hobbes's moral and political philosophy is thus an exercise in logic. For example,
some laws of nature are syllogisms with the following format:

1. Anything that violates peace should be prohibited.
2. X violates peace.
3. X should be prohibited.

I now turn to the second lesson in *De corpore*: Hobbesian deductions are often based
on definitions of words. For example, Hobbes's definitions of liberty and will imply that
natural liberty is consistent with fear.[10] His reasoning is as follows:

1. Every intentional action is the result of the will.
2. Actions performed out of fear are intentional.
3. Therefore, actions performed out of fear are the result of the will.
4. A free man is he who is not stopped from doing what he has a will to do.
5. Therefore, a man can perform actions out of fear and still be free.

Such applications of deductive reason helped Hobbes write stunningly impressive
and highly influential works of moral and political philosophy.

---

[7] *Concerning Body* 1.2–3, 3–5.
[8] *Leviathan* 5.1–2, 18.
[9] Blau 2009.
[10] *Leviathan* 6.53, 28; 21.1–2, 107–8.

3 THE PASSIONS AND DELIBERATION

For Hobbes, everything is matter in motion, with humans motivated by passions—*emotions*, literally. To understand the relationship between reason and the passions, we need say no more about the nature of the passions.[11] We can simply look at their place in deliberation.

Deliberation is the interplay between trains of thoughts and passions, ending with a decision. When we consider doing something, we automatically imagine consequences and undergo an "alternate succession of appetite and fear" about the action and its consequences; the last appetite before decision is called the will.[12] Consider someone thinking about stealing something. He desires the object but fears being caught. If his will is desire, he will try to steal the object; if his will is fear, he will not.

Every intentional action results from deliberation and thus passion. "The passions of man … are the beginning of all his voluntary motions."[13] Passion even underpins the intention to use reason: curiosity is the desire "to know why, and how" and generates "a perseverance of delight in the continuall and indefatigable generation of Knowledge."[14] As Susan James notes, Hobbes's "conviction that passions not only initiate, but also sustain, an interest in reasoning" is quite distinctive.[15] Hobbes himself expressed it well in a 1636 letter: "the extreame pleasure I take in study ouercomes in me all other appetites."[16]

4 IS REASON THE SLAVE OF THE PASSIONS?

Having briefly outlined Hobbes's accounts of reason, passion, and deliberation, I now address the common but incorrect view that Hobbes treats reason as the slave of the passions.

According to Paul Rahe, Hobbes

> suggests that reason is the slave of the passions. Where a man's "Trayne of Imaginations" is not a "wild ranging of the mind" but possesses a certain coherence reflecting guidance or direction, that coherence is rooted in "Passionate Thought" or "Desire." As [Hobbes] puts it, "From Desire, ariseth the Thought of some means we have seen produce the like of that which we ayme at; and from the thought of

---

[11] On the passions, see James 1997, 126–36; James 1998, 26–9; Schmitter 2010; Krom 2011, 66–74.

[12] *Elements of Law* 12.1–9, 70–73; *On the Citizen* 5.1, 69; 13.17, 152; *Leviathan* 6.49–57, 28–9; *On Man*, ed. Gert 11.2, 46; *Concerning Body* 25.13, 408; *Liberty, Necessity and Chance* 357–8, 360, 389, 400–2.

[13] *Elements of Law* 5.14, 39.

[14] *Leviathan* 6.35, 26.

[15] James 1997, 214.

[16] *Correspondence* vol. 1, letter 21, 37.

that, the thought of means to that mean; and so continually, till we come to some beginning within our own power." In short, "the Thoughts, are to the Desires, as Scouts, and Spies to range abroad, and find the way to the things Desired."[17]

Rahe reiterates "reason's enslavement to desire" several times.[18] Such enslavement is also depicted by Hobbes scholars Howard Warrender, Jean Hampton, and Vickie Sullivan; by political theorists Bertrand De Jouvenel and Don Herzog; by moral philosophers J. D. Mabbott and Annette Baier; by legal philosopher Robert George; and in discussions of rational choice theory by political scientist Steven Rhoads, sociologist Dennis Wrong, and economist Ken Binmore.[19]

Other writers describe subservience without mentioning slavery. Michael Oakeshott sees reason as a "servant, revealing . . . the probable means by which desired ends may be attained." For Daniela Coli "reason . . . is nothing but an instrument of calculation at the service of the passions." "The intellect does not integrate with the passions," writes Martin Bertman, but "serves them by attempting to satisfy particular wants or objects of desire." According to Susan James, "reasoning only serves our passions," and when the two conflict, "reason does not struggle against [the passions], but fights, so to speak, on their side." Talcott Parsons states that for Hobbes, "reason is essentially a servant of the passions—it is the faculty of devising ways and means to secure what one desires." According to Stephen Darwall, Hobbes depicts "instrumental reason in the service of the agent's own ends."[20] Janet Coleman and Noel Malcolm depict a similar relationship without mentioning slavery or subservience.[21]

4.1 A Humean Anachronism?

Sixty years after Hobbes died, David Hume described reason as the slave of the passions. Yet Hume has different notions of reason, of the passions, and of their relationship. And he is quite wrong to talk of slavery.

Hobbes and Hume agree that the passions, not reason, directly motivate intentional actions.[22] But this does not enslave reason to the passions. My belly button does not motivate my actions, and I do not think anyone says that my belly button is the slave of my passions, even though it usually goes where my passions tell me to go. (Indeed, even if passion directly motivates action, passion could still serve *reason* if reason tells

---

[17] Rahe 1994, 141–2.

[18] Rahe 1994, 142–4, 388; 2008, 314.

[19] Warrender 1957, 269; Hampton 1986, 34–42; Sullivan 2004, 82, 92–4; De Jouvenel 1957, 234; Herzog 2006, 31; Mabbott 1953, 113; Baier 1986, 42; George 2008, 178–9; Rhoads 1985, 155, 281; Wrong 1997, 73–4; and Binmore 2009, 3–4.

[20] Oakeshott 1975, 27, 94; Coli 2006, 83, 87, 91; Bertman 1976, 535; James 2006, 210–1; Parsons 1982, 88, 96–8; Darwall 1995, 57–79.

[21] Coleman 2000, 154–5; Malcolm 2002, 30.

[22] *Elements of Law* 5.14, 39; Hume 1888, bk. 2, pt, 3, sect. 3, paras. 1–3, 413–4.

us what to do and if we have a consistent passion to follow reason. Neither Hume nor Hobbes says this, of course.)

Much more explicitly than Hobbes, Hume describes two kinds of reason: demonstrative and probabilistic, dealing with logical and empirical matters respectively. "I believe it scarce will be asserted, that the first species of reasoning alone is ever the cause of any action."[23] But probabilistic reason can easily affect our actions. Hume describes what Hobbes had called deliberation but explicitly gives probabilistic reason a role; so, "as our reasoning varies, our actions receive a subsequent variation." Even here, the actual impulse to act "arises not from reason, but is only directed by it."[24] This, though, is not slavery.

Nor do Hume's later comments sound like slavery. "The moment we perceive the falsehood of any supposition, or the insufficiency of any means our passions yield to our reason without any opposition."[25] Similarly, once I see that certain actions are bad means to my ends, "they must become indifferent to me," such that "whenever" I understand that mistake, "my longing ceases."[26] When Hume writes that reason "can never pretend to any other office" than to "serve and obey" the passions,[27] this could include, as Irwin notes, "giving advice or prescriptions in opposition to passion."[28] True, slaves can give masters advice or prescriptions, but masters can do the same for slaves, as can two people who are not in a master-slave relationship.

Hume's slavery metaphor is misleading.[29] He tries so hard to avoid talking about passions and reason conflicting that he depicts a relationship of dominance, but what he describes sounds closer to two compatible faculties: a guide and a motivator. As we will see, this is close to Hobbes's position.

But Hobbes and Hume differ in at least two important ways. First, Hume thinks everyone's reason is the slave of their passions, but Hobbes's narrower notion of reason means he thinks that most people barely use reason at all or use it badly.[30] After all, the civil war happened because less than one in every ten thousand people understood their duties to the sovereign.[31] Usually, reason isn't the slave of the passions, because in most people, reason isn't—it just does not function.

Second, Hume is discussing the passions in general, and many interpreters anachronistically impute the same to Hobbes. Crucially, though, Hobbes never implies that reason serves dangerous passions such as vainglory or ambition.[32] Far from it. If

---

[23] Hume 1888, 2.3.3.2, 413.

[24] Hume 1888, 2.3.3.3, 414.

[25] Hume 1888, 2.3.3.6, 416.

[26] Hume 1888, 2.3.3.6, 417.

[27] Hume 1888, 2.3.3.4, 415.

[28] Irwin 2008, 585.

[29] Karlsson 2006, 249; Allison 2008, 113.

[30] *Concerning Body* 3.8, 36; *Elements of Law* 5.14, 39; *Leviathan* 4.13, 15; 5.18–19, 21; *Dialogue of the Common Law*, ed. Cromartie, 15.

[31] *Behemoth*, ed. Tönnies, 4.

[32] On ambition and vainglory, see especially Baumgold 1988, 71–4, 78, 122–4; Slomp 2000, 35–44, 58–73, 85–96.

reason works properly, it will tell us that following such passions may create a state of nature. Reason is not, and ought not to be, the servant of passions such as vainglory or ambition. Combining these two points, we see that passions such as vainglory and ambition are widespread not because reason is their slave but because reason is so rare.

So, while Hobbes and Hume see reason as motivationally inert, describing this as slavery is highly misleading for Hume and mountainously misleading for Hobbes.

4.2 "Scouts and Spies"

Many scholars who see Hobbesian reason as enslaved to the passions depend at least partly on Hobbes's comment that "the Thoughts, are to the Desires, as Scouts, and Spies, to range abroad, and find the way to the things desired."[33] Even some scholars who do not see the passions enslaving reason read this comment as showing that passions guide the mind.[34]

I believe that the "Scouts and Spies" comment is widely misunderstood due to being quoted out of context. Read in context, it is very mundane. Let us start at the beginning of *Leviathan* chapter 8. Hobbes describes intellectual virtues and defects, like "quicknesse" or "Dullnesse," or whether one has a "steddy direction" in one's thought. Two key ideas are "Fancy," which is the ability to see similarities between objects, and "Judgement," which is the ability to see differences. Hobbes believes that fancy can disguise truth and tends to dominate in rhetorical orations of praise or criticism, where "the designe is not truth, but to Honour and Dishonour ... In Demonstration [i.e., proof], in Councell, and all rigorous search of Truth, Judgement does all."[35] This is part of Hobbes's revisionist approach to rhetoric.[36]

Having discussed these natural wits, Hobbes *briefly* mentions acquired wit—an intellectual faculty "acquired by method and instruction"—of which "there is none but Reason ... But of Reason and Science, I have already spoken in the fifth and sixth Chapters."[37]

It sounds as if Hobbes intends to say no more about reason in chapter 8. Indeed, natural wit is all that he discusses when he turns straight away to the causes of differences in wit. These causes lie "in the Passions," principally "Desire of Power," and its subsidiary desires, "of Riches, of Knowledge, and of Honour." This is because

> a man who has no great Passion for any of these things ... cannot possibly have either a great Fancy, or much Judgement. For the Thoughts, are to the Desires,

---

[33] Baier, Darwall, De Jouvenel, George, Herzog, Mabbott, Malcolm, Rahe, Rhoads, Sullivan, and Wrong.

[34] Pettit 2008, 17; Schmitter 2013, 465–8; see also Murphy 2000, 267.

[35] *Leviathan* 8.1–10, 32–4.

[36] Skinner 1996, 363–75.

[37] *Leviathan* 8.13, 35.

as Scouts, and Spies, to range abroad, and find the way to the things desired: All Stedinesse of the minds motion, and all quicknesse of the same, proceeding from thence. For as to have no Desire, is to be Dead: so to have weak Passions, is Dulnesse.[38]

Recall that "Stedinesse," "quicknesse" and "Dullnesse" were the first things Hobbes discussed under natural wits, and that fancy and judgment too are natural wits.

As I see it, then, the scouts and spies passage says nothing about reason. It is implausible to read this passage as describing how reason finds a way to what the passions desire (a view I too once held). Hobbes never equates reason with "thoughts," so it is odd to interpret this comment as *reason* finding its way to the things desired. The same applies to the comment in chapter 3 that "From Desire, ariseth the Thought of some means we have seen produce the like of that which we ayme at."[39] Rahe treats this as involving reason,[40] but "Thought" is not necessarily reason, and what Hobbes is describing sounds like memory, not reason.

In the context of the whole chapter, then, the scouts and spies comment merely means that passions influence *nonratiocinative* thinking (especially fancy and judgment, and quickness, slowness or steadiness of thinking), and when we desire something we may end up thinking about it even when we start by thinking about something else. *Leviathan* chapter 3 describes a similar process—someone who started by thinking of the civil war and ended by thinking of "the value of a Roman Penny": the thought of civil war led to the thought of betraying the King, which led to the thought of betraying Jesus, which led to the thought of thirty pennies, which led to the thought of the value of a Roman penny. This "wild ranging of the mind" happens "in a moment of time"[41]—in an instant. In *Leviathan* chapter 8, the difference is that the thoughts jump to something which is desired, not merely to something connected almost randomly to another thing.

So, when Hobbes says that the thoughts "find the way" to what we desire, he is not saying that the thoughts find *the way* to what we desire, in other words that they seek and uncover the means by which we can attain our desires. He is only saying that the thoughts find *their* way to what we desire, in other words that they jump to what we desire. If I am desperate to watch a James Bond film and the weekend is coming up, my mind might think: "Will I have time to watch the film this weekend?" If I love playing cricket and I see an area of grass, my mind might think: "Is that a good spot for cricket?" Reading Hobbes's comment in context, then, I believe he is simply saying that our passions lead us to think of James Bond and cricket—or the seventeenth-century equivalents.

---

[38] *Leviathan* 8.16, 35.
[39] *Leviathan* 3.3, 9.
[40] Rahe 1994, 141–2.
[41] *Leviathan* 3.3, 9.

4.3 Regulated Trains of Thought

Hobbes's discussion of regulated thoughts in *Leviathan* chapter 3 also supports my reading of chapter 8. Chapter 3 is, in my view, wrongly used by Rahe and Coleman to justify their interpretation of the passions enslaving reason.[42]

Chapter 3 discusses trains of thought "regulated by some desire," a "Passionate Thought, to govern and direct those [thoughts] that follow, to it self, as the end and scope of some desire, or other passion."[43] There are two kinds of regulated thoughts: looking back from something to its causes, and looking forward from something to its effects. Hobbes's example of regulated thinking about causes is a man who has lost an object: "His mind runs back, from place to place, and time to time, to find where, and when he had it," so as to help him search for it. Hobbes's example of regulated thinking about effects is someone who "desires to know the event [i.e., effect] of an action" and sees a chain of thoughts based on experience. Someone who wants to know what will become of a criminal, for example, may have the following train of thoughts: "The Crime, the Officer, the Prison, the Judge, and the Gallowes."[44] This example was politically salient: crime and punishment were major seventeenth-century concerns.[45] Hobbes gives many examples of crime leading or not leading to punishment: the latter could foster a state of nature.[46] Not coincidentally, his main political texts all exemplify deliberation in terms of crime.[47]

Crucially, Hobbes seems to talk in two different ways about desires regulating thoughts. The man desires to regain the object he has lost, and this desire regulates his train of thoughts about where he might have lost the object. "From Desire, ariseth the Thought of some means we have seen produce the like of that which we ayme at; and from the thought of that, the thought of means to that mean; and so continually, till we come to some beginning within our own power."[48]

But when Hobbes mentions the man who "desires to know . . . what wil become of a Criminal," this does not sound like it is the criminal himself who is thinking: it sounds more like an onlooker, or even a citizen who is simply pondering the effects of crime. Hobbes says something very similar elsewhere: if we often see crimes followed by punishment, when we see a crime we will then expect punishment.[49] Hobbes does seem to deny that this is part of deliberation, which he restricts to thinking about whether to do something.[50] But he probably saw this as part of regulated trains of thoughts more generally.[51]

---

[42] Rahe 1994, 144; Coleman 2000, 154–5.
[43] *Leviathan* 3.3–4, 9; see also 8.3, 33.
[44] *Leviathan* 3.7, 10.
[45] Veall 1970.
[46] Blau 2009, 608–11.
[47] *Elements of Law* 4.7, 32; *On the Citizen* 13.16, 152; *Leviathan* 3.7, 10.
[48] *Leviathan* 3.4, 9.
[49] *Elements of Law* 4.7, 32.
[50] *Liberty, Necessity and Chance* 357; see also 33.
[51] See for example *Leviathan* 7.1–2, 30.

This is akin to my interpretation of the scouts and spies passage, where the thoughts "find their way to the thing desired." In chapter 3, "the thing desired" may be nothing more than a prediction: curiosity about what will happen to a criminal sparks a train of thoughts about the likely consequences. Our own interests need not be at stake. A train of thoughts leading from crime to punishment should arise in the mind of a potential criminal or an onlooker; a train of thoughts leading from the civil war to a Roman penny could arise in the mind of a royalist, a parliamentarian, or a disinterested foreigner. Passion is only relevant here in that the desire to know an answer starts a train of thoughts. This is much less dramatic than the idea that reason is enslaved to the passions. Reason is no more relevant to chapter 3 than to chapter 8.

So, here and in the scouts and spies passage, Hobbes seems to say that desires *effect* thought but do not necessarily *affect* it: they start us thinking but need not change what we think about it (although they could). The desire to see a James Bond film, or to know what happens to criminals, causes new thoughts but may not influence their content. This is a long way from the passions automatically impelling reason to compute means to desired ends, an idea I now consider in more detail.

4.4 Reason as Instrumental

Many writers implicitly or explicitly treat reason as instrumental, finding means to desired ends. Unsurprisingly, these writers often see reason as the slave of the passions.[52] Other writers depict Hobbesian reason as instrumental without mentioning slavery.[53]

Malcolm summarizes the instrumental interpretation of reason well:

> The reduction of "reason" to instrumental reasoning [in *The Elements of Law*] was an important part of [Hobbes's new] psychological picture. Reason, on this view of things, did not intuit values, but found the means to ends that were posited by desire; desires might be various, but reason could also discover general truths about how to achieve the conditions (above all, the absence of anarchic violence) in which desires were least liable to be frustrated.[54]

These writers are all correct that for Hobbes, reason shows us how to avoid what we most dislike—violent death—by following the laws of nature, by adopting monarchy not democracy, and so on. Some writers draw erroneously on *Leviathan* chapters 3 and/

---

[52] Bertman 1976, 535; Binmore 2009, 4; Darwall 1995, 15, 58–79; George 2008, 178–9; Hampton 1986, 34–42; Mabbott 1953, 113; Malcolm 2002, 30; Parsons 1982, 96, see also 88, 97–8; and Rahe 2008, 311, 314.

[53] Airaksinen 1993, 89, 99; Bobbio 1993, 44, 119–21; Irwin 2008, 156; Johnston 1986, 54; Krom 2011, 36, 47, 68–9, 72–3, 77, 101; Larmore 1998, 1164; Martinich 2012, 215–6; Slomp 2000, 42; and Wright 2006, 17–8, 72.

[54] Malcolm 2002, 15.

or 8.[55] But Hobbes is not really discussing reason there. Nonetheless, reason's instrumental component is evident elsewhere.

However, some interpreters emphasize reason's instrumental nature at the expense of its deductive nature. Charles Larmore refers to "the notion of 'right reason,' by which [Hobbes] meant choosing the most efficient means to given ends."[56] George Wright barely mentions ratiocination and writes that "reason for Hobbes is instrumental in essence, scarcely distinguishable from the cunning and skill of the animals."[57] Binmore and Parsons are particularly misleading: anachronistically reading Hobbes through the lens of rational choice theory, they ignore Hobbesian reason's fundamentally deductive nature.

I would say, rather, that reason *is* deductive and *can be* instrumental. This is the position of Airiksanen, Bobbio, Johnston, Malcolm, and Martinich. As Mark Murphy writes, "reasoning, in Hobbes's sense, is not *essentially* an exercise in means-end thinking: all that is essential to reasoning is that it involves the deducing of consequences that follow necessarily from sentences constructed out of well-defined general terms."[58] John Deigh is even more emphatic that reason is not essentially instrumental.[59] Bernard Gert also denies that Hobbesian reason is essentially instrumental, but he bases this on Hobbes's comment about madness,[60] which is an oddly incidental way of reaching a conclusion for which there is ample textual support elsewhere.

Four important qualifications must be added to this view that reason can be instrumental. First, as already noted, Hobbes does not imply that reason finds means to satisfy *all* passions: he never describes people using reason for ambitious or vainglorious ends, say. Such people are not using reason. It is misleading to talk about Hobbesian reason being instrumental to the passions, because reason tells us not to follow some passions. The deductive side of reason can trump its instrumental character, which further shows that reason is not essentially instrumental. Admittedly, Hobbes occasionally depicts geometrical reason as instrumental to our desires.[61] But this is not a necessary relationship.[62]

Second, reason does not *find* means to ends: it *shows* which means are better. Reason does not actually discover new options, as misreading of the scouts and spies passage might imply. Experience—mine or someone else's—tells me what the possible means are, then reason tells me which is best. For example, experience shows that we can tax on the basis of consumption or wealth, and reason supports the former.[63]

---

[55] Rahe 1994, 141–2; Coleman 2000, 154–5; Malcolm 2002, 30; Sullivan 2004, 93–4.
[56] Larmore 1998, 1164.
[57] Wright 2006, 72; see also 17–8.
[58] Murphy 2000, 261; emphasis added.
[59] Deigh 1996, 50, 53–4; 2003, 103–4.
[60] Gert 2001, 244–5, 255.
[61] E.g., *Leviathan* 46.1, 367.
[62] E.g., *Leviathan* 5.1–2, 18; 9.1, 40.
[63] *Elements of Law* 28.5, 174; *On the Citizen* 13.10–11, 147–8; *Leviathan* 30.17, 181.

Third, it is more helpful to think about *consequences* than means. Although Hobbes sometimes describes reason finding "means to ends,"[64] it is more accurate to say that reason reveals the consequences of different actions, especially by showing the undesirable consequences of some things that we like and the desirable consequences of some things that we dislike. Such claims are of course equivalent to means and ends. For example, we may like democracy, but it is a bad means for avoiding a state of nature.[65] Talking about consequences, though, makes clearer what reason is doing and is of course also true to Hobbes's language.

Fourth, reason only works instrumentally in some people. Hobbes believes that most people do not ratiocinate (see section 4.1). They must choose means by deliberation, using experience and prudence. Even for economic or foreign policy decisions, say, Hobbes accepts people deliberating, without reason (see section 8).

So, writers who talk about reason being instrumental are correct that reason does not pick our ultimate ends, as Kant would argue. But we should carefully qualify any claim that reason finds means to ends provided by passions.

4.5 Summary: Is Reason the Slave of the Passions?

Hobbes does not depict reason as the slave of the passions. True, he and Hume see reason as motivationally inert: only passions move us. But this is not slavery. Reason, operating instrumentally, warns us *not* to follow passions such as vainglory and ambition. This is not slavery. Nor is it slavery when "appetite perturbs and impedes the operation of reason." Like other writers at the time, Hobbes describes some appetites as "perturbations" that "frequently obstruct right reasoning."[66] But if P blocks Q, it does not mean that Q serves P. The same applies to the comment that "the Understanding is by the flame of the Passions, never enlightened, but dazled,"[67] and Hobbes's portrayal of passions hindering reason from uncovering the law of nature.[68] I suspect Hobbes means that people rushing to impassioned conclusions do not have time to reason. If P happens so fast that Q cannot happen, though, Q is not enslaved to P.

The basic problem is that the slavery metaphor implies control, which misses Hobbes's point. However, we can describe reason "serving" the passions if we specify this very, very carefully. It does not happen for most people, for most passions, or for some cases of purely logical or mathematical reasoning. And another caveat is crucial: we should use "serving" only to mean "functioning" or "operating." Reason cannot serve the passion for self-preservation as slaves serve their owners but as our senses

---

[64] E.g., *Liberty, Necessity and Chance* 188–9.

[65] *Elements of Law* 24.3–8, 138–41; *On the Citizen* 10.6–19, 119–26; *Leviathan* 19.4–9, 95–7.

[66] *On Man* 12.1, 55; 12.3, 56.

[67] *Leviathan* 19.5, 96.

[68] *Leviathan* 26.21, 143.

serve to tell us what is happening. In other words, some people's reason might function in ways that help certain passions.

Similarly, we should only describe passions "mastering" reason if we mean "overcoming" rather than "controlling" or "commanding." The *Dialogue of the Common Law*, indeed, mentions "the force of an irregular Appetite to Riches, to Power, and to sensual Pleasures," and "how it Masters the strongest Reason."[69] This clearly involves passions overcoming reason, not influencing it. Note how Hobbes specifies a particular passion, not the passions in general.

Of course, we are all driven by our passions. Hobbes seems not to disagree with Thomas White's comment that "All men are addicted to the passions"[70] and accepts that "the affections and passions . . . reign in every one."[71] But this is true by definition: a passion precedes every voluntary action. And even if we follow a passion in conflict with reason, passions are not enslaving reason. If my brother and my sister tell me to do different things, and I do what my brother says, this does not mean my sister serves my brother. At most it means that I serve my brother. It might be valid to say that Hobbes depicts all or most human beings as slaves of their passions, but he does not say—and his writings cannot coherently imply—that reason is the slave of the passions.

5 ARE THE PASSIONS SLAVES OF REASON?

Although I deny that reason serves the passions, I am not arguing that the passions serve reason. I do, however, partly support Gert's and Skinner's views on the force of reason.

Far from reason being enslaved to the passions, writes Gert, "the passions are to be controlled by reason."[72] "Hobbes's view is diametrically opposed to that of Hume": it is not that reason is and ought to be the slave of the passions but that "the passions ought to be subservient to reason"—although generally they are so strong that people often act against reason.[73] So, reason "governs the passions, or tries to, so that its own goal is not threatened."[74]

This is too extreme. Reason cannot "control" the passions. It can show how some passions undermine self-preservation and might thus spark our fear of violent death, but this is not control. In Michael Krom's words, reason's role is to "orient" and "guide" the passions toward the right ends.[75] Gert's overstatement, and

---

[69] *Dialogue of the Common Law* 12.
[70] De Mundo *Examined* 38.14, 472–3.
[71] *Elements of Law* 24.4, 139.
[72] Gert 2001, 253.
[73] Gert 2010, 52.
[74] Gert 2001, 253.
[75] Krom 2011, 36, 68.

his view that reason has a goal, partly reflects his misreading of Hobbes's comments on "natural reason." Gert interprets this as the faculty by which we perceive our real good.[76] But his interpretation is unconvincing.[77] For example, Hobbes often talks of "natural" reason merely to contrast it with supernatural revelation.[78] Nonetheless, Gert is right that Hobbes wants reason to show us that some passions are dangerous.

Quentin Skinner also stresses reason's power over the passions. Skinner is not treating passions as slaves of reason: he would not talk so anachronistically. He merely argues that the *Elements of Law* and *De Cive* are optimistic about reason's power over the passions and that although *Leviathan* is more pessimistic about the power of reason by itself, reason can still triumph when allied with emotive rhetoric.[79]

Skinner's arguments are mostly persuasive, but I believe he overstates reason's power in two ways. First, his claims about *Leviathan*'s alliance between reason and rhetoric depend significantly, though not exclusively, on a questionable view of the first four paragraphs of the Review and Conclusion. In these paragraphs, though, Hobbes is mainly citing other people's opinions.[80] In my opinion, these paragraphs do not support Skinner's thesis as much as he thinks, but nor do they weaken it as much as Schuhmann implies.

Second, I do not find the early texts so positive about reason. For example, the dedication of the *Elements* does not seem as optimistic as Skinner suggests.[81] Moreover, Skinner jumps from Hobbes's comments about the "dictates" of right reason[82] to "its power to order, command *and enforce* particular conclusions upon us," its "inherent capacity to persuade."[83] But "dictates of right reason" could mean two things: (a) reason is a guide, showing us what is good but letting us decide whether to choose it, or (b) reason is a dictator, showing us what is good and making us do it. In Hobbes's day, both meanings were used. Hooker talks of the dictates of right reason in terms of reason "discovering" what is good, right reason being a "guide" whose advice the will may "take or refuse" as it sees fit.[84] But John Donne treats *dictamen rectae rationis* as something which "binds" us as court decrees bind us.[85] Hobbes's comments are ambiguous, but to me they sound more like Hooker than Donne. Overall, though, Skinner offers an important and compelling retort to the view that Hobbesian reason serves the passions.

---

[76] Gert 2001, 248–55; 2010, 49–53.

[77] Martinich 2012, 215–7.

[78] Martinich 2012, 216, n. 26.

[79] Skinner 1996, 298–437.

[80] Schuhmann 1998, 123.

[81] Skinner 1996, 299–300; *Elements of Law* Epistle Dedicatory, 19–20.

[82] *On the Citizen* 2.2, 34; 3.19, 51; 3.27, 53; 15.4, 173; 15.15, 181.

[83] Skinner 1996, 302, 347; emphasis added.

[84] Hooker 1888, bk. 1, ch. 7, sects. 4–6, 222–4.

[85] Donne 1982, pt. 1, distinction 1, sect. 6, 51–2; see also James 1997, 191–5.

6 REASON AND DELIBERATION

To understand reason's influence on the passions, I turn to deliberation. Anachronisms are rife in scholarly discussions of the relationship between reason and deliberation. Consider Hobbes's comment that "in all Deliberations, and in all Pleadings, the faculty of solid Reasoning, is necessary."[86] This may not be Hobbes's view at all,[87] but even if it is, it is not about deliberation. It is misquoted in a small but significant way by Hannah Dawson and by David Van Mill: neither mentions "Pleadings," that is, legal speeches, and Dawson implies that Hobbes talks about deliberation in the singular, not the plural.[88] But "Deliberations, and . . . Pleadings" invokes a standard debate in Hobbes's day, about rhetoric in public assemblies and in law courts respectively.[89] "Deliberations" here means group discussion in parliaments.

John Rawls and David Van Mill sometimes use Hobbes's notion of deliberation.[90] But elsewhere they use anachronistic, modern notions of deliberation—the careful consideration of different options.[91] This makes deliberation sound like ratiocination. But once we work out which comments by Rawls and Van Mill involve their notion of deliberation rather than Hobbes's, such interpretations are legitimate: Hobbes wants citizens to make reflective, peace-abiding decisions, not people recklessly following whatever impulse strikes them.

Anachronisms, however, lead to much more troubling misinterpretations by Martin Hollis and Robert Sugden, Michael Losonsky, and Christopher Tilmouth.[92] Most egregiously, in Hollis and Sugden's rational-choice reading of Hobbes, conflicting appetites lead to deliberation, which Hobbes never says; reason then helps us choose between these conflicting appetites, which Hobbes never says; and this process is called "deliberative reason," a term Hobbes does not and would not use. This is not just anachronistic; it is simply wrong.

So, what does Hobbes believe? My interpretation, which follows Darwall, Gauthier, and Hampton, is that ratiocination occurs *before* deliberation and hence informs and improves it by altering the images and opinions to which our passions respond when we deliberate. According to Hampton, "reason's only role in the deliberative process is to help determine how to achieve a goal set by desire."[93] As Gauthier writes, "reason aids deliberation by showing us the means to obtain, or to avoid, what we will."[94] (This is all compatible with rational choice theory, incidentally. My concern is not with

---

[86] *Leviathan* Review and Conclusion, para. 1, 389.
[87] Schuhmann 1998, 123.
[88] Dawson 2007, 278; Van Mill 2001, 105.
[89] Skinner 1996, 352.
[90] Rawls 2007, 61; Van Mill 2001, 49–55, 89–90.
[91] Rawls 2007, 45, 50, 54, 58–63, 66, 69; Van Mill 2001, 80, 89, 92; see also Zagorin 2007, 255.
[92] Hollis and Sugden 1993, 2; Losonsky 2001, 53–4; Tilmouth 2007, 234–53.
[93] Hampton 1986, 19.
[94] Gauthier 1969, 11.

anachronism itself, or with rational-choice readings of Hobbes, but with anachronistic rational-choice readings which misread Hobbes.)

Gauthier states, rightly, that Hobbes is not clear about the relationship between reason and deliberation, so we should read between the lines.[95] Warrender thinks, wrongly, that the issue is clear-cut and suggests, also wrongly, that the evidence favors deliberation being ratiocinative: Hobbes depicts deliberation as having a reflective element "more often" than he depicts it in purely appetitive terms.[96] In fact, Warrender only gives one reference to support this, and later in this section I will suggest that Hobbes's comment actually supports Gauthier's position, not Warrender's:

1. Because in Deliberation, the Appetites, and Aversions are raised by foresight of the good and evill consequences and sequels of the action whereof we Deliberate; the good or evill effect thereof dependeth on the foresight of a long chain of consequences . . . so that he who hath by Experience, or Reason, the greatest and surest prospect of Consequences, Deliberates best himself; and is able when he will, to give the best counsel unto others.[97]

Without mentioning deliberation, Hobbes makes equivalent points in three other places. One is while discussing taxes:

2. All men are by nature provided of notable multiplying glasses (that is their Passions and Selfe-love,) through which, every little payment appeareth a great grievance; but are destitute of those prospective glasses, (namely, Morall and Civill Science,) to see a farre off the miseries that hang over them.[98]

Another is while discussing the laws of nature:

3. Reason teaches that peace is good; it follows . . . that all necessary means to peace are good, and hence that modesty, fairness, good faith, kindness and mercy . . . [are] virtues. . . . [But m]en cannot divest themselves of the irrational desire to reject future goods for the sake of present goods.[99]

And the last is while discussing emotion:

4. Emotions . . . frequently obstruct right reasoning. . . . They militate against the real good and in favor of the apparent and most immediate good, which turns out frequently to be evil when everything associated with it hath been considered.

[95] Gauthier 1969, 12.
[96] Warrender 1957, 267.
[97] Leviathan 6.57, 29.
[98] Leviathan 18.20, 94.
[99] On the Citizen 3.31–2, 55–6.

For though judgment originates from appetite out of a union of mind and body, it must proceed from reason [*Consilium autem a Ratione sit*]. Therefore, although the real good must be sought in the long term, which is the job of reason, appetite seizeth upon a present good without foreseeing the greater evils that necessarily attach to it.[100]

The Gert edition's translation of passage 4—judgment "must proceed from reason"—is misleading. Hobbes means that judgment starts in deliberation but that reason gives judgment "counsel." The word "must" is also too strong.

Passages 2 to 4 say that reason helps us see further along the chain of consequences. You may desire democracy, but reason proves that monarchy is more stable.[101] You may love giving rhetorically emotive speeches in parliament, but reason demonstrates that they cause discord.[102] You may think that taxation should be proportional to wealth, but according to reason, taxation that is proportional to consumption is less likely to lead to a state of nature.[103] We can read passage 1 along the same lines: reason reveals these consequences (and experience may already have shown the same).

Reasoning about such matters means that when you next deliberate on them, you will see consequences you had not considered before. In the above examples, an image of the state of nature will flash into your mind, and your deliberation may lead you to act in ways more conducive to peace.

In these examples, reason literally alters the imagination. By showing you different consequences, different images arise in your mind. As Darwall puts it, reason can improve deliberation by showing us the consequences of our actions and hence "revis[ing] the appearances that momentary passions produce."[104] A different passion may thus end up as the will. Before using reason, your passion for democracy might spark images in your head of orators debating nobly in public forums; if you deliberate about whether to support parliament or King Charles, you will choose the former. After using reason, thinking of democracy also makes you think of the state of nature. Seeing democracy's dangerous consequences may cause your fear of violent death to overcome your passion for democracy.

These examples involve empirical consequences. Reason can also alter the imagination by showing logical consequences. (Hobbes does not distinguish these two satisfactorily.[105]) For example, if you think that theft can be right, reason shows you that by definition it is not.[106] Recall that according to Hobbes, definitions produce images in the mind.[107]

---

[100] *On Man* 12.1, 55; *De Homine* 12.1, 104.
[101] *Elements of Law* 24.3–8, 138–41; *On the Citizen* 10.6–19, 119–26; *Leviathan* 19.4–9, 95–7.
[102] *On the Citizen* 10.12, 123–4; *Leviathan* 25.15, 135.
[103] *Elements of Law* 28.5, 174; *On the Citizen* 13.10–11, 147–8; *Leviathan* 30.17, 181.
[104] Darwall 2000, 331–2.
[105] Kavka 1986, 8.
[106] *On the Citizen* 18.4, 237.
[107] *Concerning Body* 6.15, 84.

We can also think of reason altering opinions/doctrines, as emphasized by Richard Tuck and Sharon Lloyd. Reason cannot directly alter passions, which are "reason-resistant."[108] But some passions only arise because of preexisting beliefs.[109] Reason can alter beliefs, and different passions will arise. Hobbes thus seeks to educate men by changing their opinions, especially religious ones.[110] He often attacks faulty opinions and urges sovereigns to inculcate favorable ones.[111]

Overall, I see almost no evidence that Hobbes thought deliberation could include ratiocination.[112] There is far more evidence that he saw reason and deliberation as separate processes. I thus read the four quoted passages as implying that reason helps deliberation by supplying images and opinions which the passions then choose between.

7 REAL AND APPARENT GOODS

In my view, to understand the relationship between reason and the passions we must address the distinction between real and apparent goods, which is explicit in passage 4 above, and implicit in passages 1 to 3.

Our real good is self-preservation. Occasionally our real good is directly threatened (e.g., "your money or your life"), and Hobbes expects that we will try to save our life. An apparent good is anything else we desire. Some apparent goods are compatible with our real good, as when someone likes monarchy and enjoys fulfilling his civic duties. But some apparent goods undermine our real good, as with a desire to avoid taxes, which can ultimately lead to a state of nature. Few people, unfortunately, can see which apparent goods undermine their real good, a situation Hobbes wants to correct.

This distinction suggests that "reason versus passion" is less accurate for Hobbes than "passion versus passion." Our passion for our real good struggles with our passions for apparent goods that foster a state of nature. Reason thus supports our passion for our real good, and our passion for apparent goods that do not hinder our real good; reason opposes passions for apparent goods that undermine our real good. True, reason does not want us to act purely on impulse: "reason versus *any* passion," or "reason for some passions and against others," does characterize Hobbes's position correctly, as Gert, Rawls, and Van Mill show. But Hobbes could not coherently say that we should follow our reason rather than our passions: by definition we always follow our passions. We choose not between reason or passion but between passions.

---

[108] Lloyd 1992, 41.

[109] Tuck 1989, 56–7; 1998, 151–5; 2004, 132.

[110] Lloyd 1992, 99–157.

[111] *Elements of Law* 10.8, 62–3; 27.4–10, 164–9; 17.9, 96; 28.8, 176; *On the Citizen* 12.1–8, 131–7; 13.9, 146–7; *Leviathan* 29.6–14, 168–71; 30.3–14, 175–80; 46.12, 370; *Concerning Body* 1.1, 2; *On Man* 13.3, 65; *Behemoth* 3, 16, 56, 62, 64; *Dialogue of the Common Law* 12; *Historia Ecclesiastica* 445–7.

[112] But there are two comments that conflict with my interpretation and which I cannot currently explain: see *Liberty, Necessity and Chance* 79, 234.

So far I have skated over a profoundly important issue: would we pick our real good or an apparent good when the two clash? There are six options:

a. People always pick their apparent good.
b. People always pick their real good.
c. Whether people pick their real or apparent good depends on one or more other factors (e.g., the presence of rhetoric).
d. Hobbes does not have an answer to this question at all.
e. Hobbes's position changes between a, b, c, and/or d in different texts.
f. Hobbes's position changes between a, b, c, and/or d within the same text.

Note that "Hobbes's position" may refer to his conscious intended meaning and/or the implication of what he wrote.

I would confidently reject a. Hobbes believed that reason could lead at least some people to pick their real good at least some of the time (see section 5). I would probably reject b, given Hobbes's comment that some passions can overcome "the strongest Reason."[113] But I am not confident about which of c to f is correct. My uncertainty partly reflects Hobbes's ambiguity. Consider his comment that "the Passions of men, are commonly more potent than their Reason."[114] This could mean that (i) in most but not all men, passions are stronger than reason, or (ii) in all men, passions are usually but not always stronger than reason. These interpretations imply very different things about reason's power. Interpretation (i) could imply that reason, if present, will overcome passion, but that reason is usually absent and passions usually triumph. Interpretation (ii) suggests that even where reason is present it needs another, rarer factor to overcome passions. I suspect that interpretation (i) is right but I am not sure, and I have not rejected Skinner's view that interpretation (ii) applies in *Leviathan* while interpretation (i) applies earlier.

Consider too the comment that "appetite perturbs and impedes the operation of reason" and "frequently obstruct[s] right reasoning."[115] This could mean at least three things: (i) appetite prevents ratiocination from even starting; (ii) appetite allows ratiocination to start but distorts it, preventing it from reaching correct conclusions; or (iii) appetite allows ratiocination to reach correct conclusions but prevents ratiocinators from acting on those conclusions by impelling them to follow short-term goods. Interpretations (i) and (ii) are consistent with reason trumping passion if reason can work properly. Interpretation (iii) is not. I suspect that interpretation (i) is right, but I am not sure.

There are many similar ambiguities. And perhaps Hobbes did not have a definite stance on this matter. The situation is complicated further if we ask: "Whose reason?

---

[113] *Dialogue of the Common Law* 12.
[114] *Leviathan* 19.4, 96.
[115] *On Man* 12.1, 55.

Whose passions?" Is someone more likely to follow reason if it is his own reason than if it is someone else's reason? Hobbes's position here too is unclear.

Fortunately, my chapter does not require a definite stance on how strong Hobbes thinks reason is. I do not need to show how likely it is that we will follow our real good when we can see it clashing with an apparent good, only that reason guides deliberation by highlighting this clash. I now return to this issue and offer a new conceptualization of the relationship between reason and the passions.

8 Reason: Counselor of the Passions

The analogy I offer—cautiously—is that reason counsels the passions. Hobbes talks in similar terms: in section 6, passage 1 describes reason helping us give counsel to others, and passage 4 describes reason counseling judgment.

Counsel gets little emphasis from Hobbes scholars; two valuable exceptions are Skinner and Sommerville.[116] Yet counsel was hugely important in Hobbes's day. Civic humanists advocated the *vita activa* (active civic life) where the *vir civilis* (civic man) advised rulers about the common good.[117] But from the 1620s to the 1640s, there were furious disagreements over who should counsel King James and King Charles. Many parliamentarians wanted this role and attacked the poor guidance offered by counselors such as Buckingham; royalists resented this parliamentary interference.[118]

Hobbes clearly saw counsel as highly important and alludes to these issues from the introduction to his translation of Thucydides onward.[119] He saw civic humanism as politically destabilizing and even says that "the sole cause" of "our land's present civil wars" was that "certain evil men who were not asked for counsel thought that their own wisdom was less fairly valued and counselled the citizens to take up arms against the king."[120] It is no surprise that his main political texts cover counsel so exhaustively.

Interestingly, Hobbes appears to accept counsel based on reason *and* counsel based on experience. *Leviathan* chapter 25, in particular, ideally wants a counselor to use "firme ratiocination" to "deduce the consequences of what he adviseth to be done, and tye himselfe therein to the rigour of true reasoning."[121] But Hobbes is also explicit that

---

[116] Skinner 1996, 69–74, 343–6, 349, 373–4; Sommerville 1996, 248–55, 262, 264–5.

[117] Guy 1993, 13–22; Skinner 1996, 66–87.

[118] Gardiner 1906, xvii–xviii, xxix–xxxii, xxxv, xxxix.

[119] *Thucydides* Introduction, xvi–xvii; De Mundo *Examined* 38.16, 476; *Elements of Law* 13.5, 76; 17.8, 96; 19.5, 105; 21.5, 120; 24.4, 139; 24.8, 140–1; 27.12–15, 169–72; *On the Citizen* 5.5, 71; 6.18, 88; 10.9–15, 122–5; 12.10, 138; *Leviathan* 8.11, 34; 17.9–10, 86–7; 19.4–8, 95–7; 25, 131–6; 30.25–7, 183–5; *Behemoth* 2–3, 23, 82, 109.

[120] De Mundo *Examined* (Latin version) 38.16, 424—my translation, modified from De Mundo *Examined* (English version) 38.16, 476.

[121] *Leviathan* 25.6, 132; 25.12, 134; see also 25.3, 132.

counsel can come from experience,[122] and twice compares counselors to the memory of the body politic[123] —memory being the source of experience.[124]

Hobbes, it seems, permits both sources of counsel: some counselors use experience, others use reason. It may be no coincidence that in passage 1, good counsel requires foresight through experience *or* reason, not experience *and* reason. Experience and reason are different ways of foreseeing the consequences about which we deliberate. (But they are not totally separate: as section 4.4 noted, experience can show us our options, reason then proves which is better.)

Reason and experience involve two kinds of knowledge: reason's deductive knowledge is "the Knowledge required in a Philosopher" and involves ratiocination; experience's knowledge of facts is "Sense and Memory," as in historical writing.[125] *Behemoth*, Hobbes's history of the civil war, can perhaps be seen as experience-based counsel. It is not illegitimate to say that *Behemoth* uses Hobbes's experience, and the experience in the history books on which he drew, to refresh readers' historical memory about the consequences of ignorance of duty.[126]

But *Leviathan* chapter 25 does seem to prefer reason-based counsel, and we can read the *Elements of Law*, *De cive* and *Leviathan* as reason-based counsel for sovereigns. Frederick Whelan notes that in *Leviathan* chapter 30 "Hobbes evidently is offering counsel to the sovereign."[127] Chapter 30 covers the sovereign's duties, and there are equivalent chapters in the *Elements* and *De cive*.[128] Yet Hobbes offers far more counsel than this: the laws of nature show how to avoid violent death, and Hobbes guides sovereigns on education, religion, foreign policy, political institutions, crime, taxation, and so on. Hobbes is rightly prized as a political philosopher abstractly discussing issues such as obligation and rights, but he also gives practical, concrete advice on political and social reform. Many Hobbes scholars focus on how to escape the state of nature, but Hobbes himself wrote far more about how to avoid its return. I explore Hobbes's practical politics elsewhere.[129]

In saying that reason counsels the passions, I am not denying experience's role here. Nor am I implying that this is all reason does: for example, purely deductive reason in mathematics is not counseling the passions. And reason-based counsel works both directly and indirectly. For example, when Hobbes commends consumption taxes, he is both counseling readers' passions by altering the images about which they deliberate, and, for the longer term, showing how to sidestep the dangerous passions which wealth taxes can arouse.

So, I talk cautiously of reason counseling the passions: no short formula accurately captures this complex relationship. We could perhaps describe reason counseling judgment,

---

[122] *Leviathan* 25.11, 134; 25.13, 134–5.
[123] *Leviathan* Introduction paragraph 1, 1; 25.11, 134.
[124] *Leviathan* 3.7, 10.
[125] *Leviathan* 9.1–2, 40; see also *On Man* 10.4, 41.
[126] *Behemoth*, 4.
[127] Whelan 1981, 68.
[128] *Elements of Law* 28, 172–7; *On the Citizen* 13, 142–52; *Leviathan* 30, 175–86.
[129] Blau forthcoming.

as Hobbes himself writes in passage 4. But Hobbes talks of judgment in at least three different ways: the ability to see differences,[130] the last opinion in nonratiocinative thinking about matters of fact,[131] and any kind of decision.[132] So, we cannot be too emphatic about what Hobbes means by reason counseling judgment. We could also talk of reason counseling deliberation, but it surely makes more sense to describe reason counseling the passions by providing the images and opinions on which they work in deliberation.

We should again ask: "Whose reason? Whose passions?" Hobbes's reason counsels the passions of sovereigns, politicians and citizens; it also educates their reason, which will in turn counsel their and others' passions, by showing when self-preservation is endangered and by explaining how to sidestep or control dangerous passions. But reason did not operate in most people, and Hobbes would have seen that many of his readers were unconvinced by his arguments. So, reason can counsel the passions, but it rarely does.

9 CONCLUSION

This chapter's key claims about Hobbes's position are as follows:

1. Reason is essentially deductive. It involves making logically valid inferences from clearly defined concepts.
2. Reason is not the slave of the passions.
3. Reason is not essentially instrumental. It is essentially deductive and can be instrumental, showing us the consequences of different choices.
4. The passions are not the slaves of reason.
5. The key conflict is not between reason and the passions but between our real good and apparent goods. Or to put it another way, the key conflict is between our passion for self-preservation and passions such as vainglory and ambition.
6. Reason, operating before deliberation, can inform deliberation by altering imagination and opinions. Fear of violent death is thus more likely to be the final appetite in deliberation.
7. Reason is, and only could be, the counselor of the passions—or so we might conclude if more people either used their own reason or accepted Hobbes's. Since neither situation is common, I would present Hobbes's position more pessimistically: reason could be the counselor of the passions but usually is not.[133]

---

[130] *Elements of Law* 10.4, 61–2; *Leviathan* 8.3, 33.
[131] *Leviathan* 7.1, 30.
[132] E.g., *Leviathan* 29.6, 168.

[133] Acknowledgements: Earlier versions of this paper were presented at the Hobbes panel at the Sixth Annual Workshops in Political Theory, Manchester Metropolitan University, September 2–4, 2009; and the Second Meeting of the European Hobbes Society," King's College London, May 16–17, 2012. I thank the participants at both conferences for their comments and criticisms, especially Laurens van Apeldoorn, Robin Douglass, Al Martinich, Johan Olsthoorn, and Tom Pink. Special thanks to Robin Douglass for spotting a fundamental flaw in the original argument.

BIBLIOGRAPHY

Airaksinen, Timo. 1993. "Hobbes on the Passions and Powerlessness." *Hobbes Studies* 6: 80–104.

Allison, Henry. 2008. *Custom and Reason in Hume: A Kantian Reading of the First Book of the Treatise*. Oxford: Oxford University Press.

Baier, Annette. 1986. "The Ambiguous Limits of Desire," in *The Ways of Desire: New Essays in Philosophical Psychology of the Concept of Wanting*, edited by Joel Marks, 39–61. New Jersey: Transaction.

Barnouw, Jeffrey. 2008. "Reason as Reckoning: Hobbes's Natural Law as Right Reason." *Hobbes Studies* 21: 38–62.

Baumgold, Deborah. 1988. *Hobbes's Political Theory*. Cambridge: Cambridge University Press.

Bertman, Martin. 1976. "Equality in Hobbes, with Reference to Aristotle." *Review of Politics* 38(4): 534–44.

Binmore, Kenneth. 2009. *Rational Decisions*. Princeton: Princeton University Press.

Blau, Adrian. 2009. "Hobbes on Corruption." *History of Political Thought* 30(4): 596–616.

Blau, Adrian. 2011. "Uncertainty and the History of Ideas." *History and Theory* 50(3): 358–372.

Blau, Adrian. 2012a. "Anti-Strauss." *Journal of Politics* 74(1): 142–155.

Blau, Adrian. 2012b. "Extended Meaning and Understanding in the History of Ideas." Working paper.

Blau, Adrian. Forthcoming. *The Science of Hobbes*.

Bobbio, Norberto. 1993. *Thomas Hobbes and the Natural Law Tradition*. Chicago: University of Chicago Press.

Coleman, Janet. 2000. *A History of Political Thought from the Middle Ages to the Renaissance*. Vol. 2. Oxford: Blackwell.

Coli, Daniela. 2006. "Hobbes's Revolution," in *Politics and the Passions, 1500–1850*, edited by Victoria Kahn, Neil Saccamano, and Daniela Coli, 75–92. Princeton: Princeton University Press.

Darwall, Stephen. 1995. *The British Moralists and the Internal "Ought": 1640–1740*. Cambridge: Cambridge University Press.

Dawson, Hannah. 2007. "The Rebellion of Language Against Reason in Early Modern Philosophy." *Intellectual History Review* 17(3): 277–290.

Deigh, John. 1996. "Reason and Ethics in Hobbes's Leviathan." *Journal of the History of Philosophy* 34(1): 33–60.

Deigh, John. 2003. "Reply to Mark Murphy." *Journal of the History of Philosophy* 41(1): 97–109.

De Jouvenel, Bertrand. 1957. *Sovereignty: An Inquiry into the Political Good*. Cambridge: Cambridge University Press.

Donne, John. 1982. *Biathanatos*, edited by Michael Rudick and Pabst Battin. New York: Garland.

Gardiner, S. R., ed. 1906. *The Constitutional Documents of the Puritan Revolution, 1625–1660*. 3rd rev. ed. Oxford: Clarendon Press.

Gauthier, David. 1969. *The Logic of Leviathan: The Moral and Political Theory of Thomas Hobbes*. Oxford: Oxford University Press.

George, Robert. 2008. "Natural Law." *Harvard Journal of Law & Public Policy* 31(1): 171–196.

Gert, Bernard. 2001. "Hobbes on Reason." *Pacific Philosophical Quarterly* 82(3–4): 243–257.

Gert, Bernard. 2010. *Hobbes: Prince of Peace*. Cambridge: Polity.

Guy, John. 1993. "The Henrician Age," in *The Varieties of British Political Thought, 1500–1800*, edited by J. G. A. Pocock, 13–46. Cambridge: Cambridge University Press.

Hampton, Jean. 1986. *Hobbes and the Social Contract Tradition*. Cambridge: Cambridge University Press.

Herzog, Don. 2006. *Cunning*. Princeton: Princeton University Press.

Hobbes, Thomas. 1839. *De Corpore, in The English Works of Thomas Hobbes of Malmesbury*, vol. 1, edited by William Molesworth. London: John Bohn.

Hobbes, Thomas, 1841. *The Questions Concerning Liberty, Necessity, and Chance*, vol. 5, edited by William Molesworth. London: John Bohn.

Hobbes, Thomas, 1845. Six Lessons to the Professors of the Mathematics, in *The English Works of Thomas Hobbes of Malmesbury*, vol. 7, edited by William Molesworth. London: John Bohn.

Hobbes, Thomas. 1973. *Critique Du De Mundo de Thomas White*, edited by Jean Jacquot and Harold Whitmore Jones. Paris: Librairie Philosophique J. Vrin.

Hobbes, Thomas, 1976. *Anti-White. Thomas White's De Mundo Examined*, translated by Harold Whitmore Jones. London: Bradford University Press.

Hobbes, Thomas. 1990. *Behemoth or the Long Parliament*, edited by Ferdinand Tönnies. Chicago: University of Chicago Press.

Hobbes, Thomas. 1991. *Leviathan*, edited by Richard Tuck. Cambridge: Cambridge University Press. (Page numbers in this chapter are to the 1651 Head edition.)

Hobbes, Thomas. 1991. *Man and Citizen*, edited by Bernard Gert. Indianapolis: Hackett.

Hobbes, Thomas. 1994. *The Elements of Law, in Human Nature and De Corpore Politico*, edited by J. C. A. Gaskin. Oxford: Oxford University Press.

Hobbes, Thomas. 1994. *The Correspondence. Volume I: 1622–1659*, edited by Noel Malcolm. Oxford: Clarendon Press.

Hobbes, Thomas, 1998. *On the Citizen*, edited by Richard Tuck and Michael Silverthorne. Cambridge: Cambridge University Press.

Hobbes, Thomas, 2005. *Writings on Common Law and Hereditary Right*, edited by Alan Cromartie and Quentin Skinner. Oxford: Oxford University Press.

Hobbes, Thomas. 2008. *Historia Ecclesiastica: Critical Edition, Including Text, Translation, Introduction, Commentary and Notes*, edited by Patricia Springborg, Patricia Stablein, and Paul Wilson. Paris: Honoré Champion.

Hollis, Martin, and Robert Sugden. 1993. "Rationality in Action." *Mind*, new series, 102(405): 1–35.

Hooker, Richard. 1888. *The Works of Mr. Richard Hooker: Volume I*, edited by John Keble, R. W. Church, and F. Paget. 7th ed. Oxford: Clarendon Press.

Hume, David. 1888. *A Treatise of Human Nature*, edited by L. A. Selby-Bigge. Oxford: Clarendon.

Irwin, Terence. 2008. *The Development of Ethics: A Historical and Critical Study. Volume II: From Suarez to Rousseau*. Oxford: Oxford University Press.

James, Susan. 1997. *Passion and Action: The Emotions in Seventeenth-Century Philosophy*. Oxford: Oxford University Press.

James, Susan. 1998. "Explaining the Passions: Passions, Desires, and the Explanation of Action," in *The Soft Underbelly of Reason: The Passions in the Seventeenth Century*, edited by Stephen Gaukroger, 17–33. London: Routledge.

James, Susan. 2006. "The Passions and the Good Life," in *The Cambridge Companion to Early Modern Philosophy*, edited by Donald Rutherford, 198–220. Cambridge: Cambridge University Press.

Johnston, David. 1986. *The Rhetoric of Leviathan. Thomas Hobbes and the Politics of Cultural Transformation*. Princeton: Princeton University Press.

Karlsson, Mikael. 2006. "Reason, Passion, and the Influencing Motives of the Will," in *The Blackwell Guide to Hume's Treatise*, edited by Saul Traiger, 235–255. Oxford: Blackwell.

Kavka, Gregory. 1986. *Hobbesian Moral and Political Theory*. Princeton: Princeton University Press.

Krom, Michael. 2011. *The Limits of Reason in Hobbes's Commonwealth*. London: Continuum.

Larmore, Charles. 1998. "Scepticism," in *The Cambridge History of Seventeenth-Century Philosophy: Volume II*, edited by Daniel Garber and Michael Ayers, 1145–1192. Cambridge: Cambridge University Press.

Lloyd, Sharon. 1992. *Ideals as Interests in Hobbes's Leviathan: The Power of Mind over Matter*. Cambridge: Cambridge University Press.

Losonsky, Michael. 2001. *Enlightenment and Action from Descartes to Kant: Passionate Thought*. Cambridge: Cambridge University Press.

Mabbott, J. D. 1953. "Reason and Desire." *Philosophy* 28(105): 113–123.

Malcolm, Noel. 2002. *Aspects of Hobbes*. Oxford: Oxford University Press.

Martinich, A. P. 2012. "Egoism, Reason, and the Social Contract." *Hobbes Studies* 25(2): 209–222.

Murphy, Mark. 2000. "Desire and Ethics in Hobbes's Leviathan: A Response to Professor Deigh." *Journal of the History of Philosophy* 38(2): 259–268.

Oakeshott, Michael. 1975. *Hobbes on Civil Association*. Indianapolis: Liberty Fund.

Parsons, Talcott. 1982. *On Institutions and Social Evolution*. Chicago: University of Chicago Press.

Pettit, Philip. 2008. *Made With Words: Hobbes on Language, Mind, and Politics*. Princeton: Princeton University Press.

Rahe, Paul. 1994. *Republics Ancient and Modern. Volume 2: New Modes & Orders in Early Modern Political Thought*. Chapel Hill: University of North Carolina Press.

Rahe, Paul. 2008. *Against Throne and Altar: Machiavelli and Political Theory Under the English Republic*. Cambridge: Cambridge University Press.

Rawls, John. 2007. *Lectures on the History of Political Philosophy*. Cambridge, MA: Harvard University Press.

Rhoads, Steven. 1985. *The Economist's View of the World: Government, Markets, and Public Policy*. Cambridge: Cambridge University Press.

Schmitter, Amy. 2010. "Hobbes on the Emotions." Supplement to "17th and 18th Century Theories of Emotions," in *The Stanford Encyclopedia of Philosophy* (Winter 2010 ed.), edited by Edward N. Zalta. <http://plato.stanford.edu/archives/win2010/entries/emotions-17th18th/ld3hobbes.html>. Accessed June 18, 2012.

Schmitter, Amy. 2013. "Passions and Affections," in *The Oxford Handbook of British Philosophy in the Seventeenth Century*, edited by Peter Anstey, 442–471. Oxford: Oxford University Press.

Schuhmann, Karl. 1998. "Skinner's Hobbes." *British Journal for the History of Philosophy* 6(1): 115–125.

Skinner, Quentin. 1996. *Reason and Rhetoric in the Philosophy of Hobbes*. Cambridge: Cambridge University Press.

Skinner, Quentin. 2002. *Visions of Politics. Volume I: Regarding Method*. Cambridge: Cambridge University Press.

Slomp, Gabriella. 2000. *Thomas Hobbes and the Political Philosophy of Glory*. Basingstoke: Macmillan.

Sommerville, Johann, 1996. "Lofty Science and Local Politics," in *The Cambridge Companion to Hobbes*, edited by Tom Sorrell, 246–273. Cambridge: Cambridge University Press.

Sullivan, Vickie. 2004. *Machiavelli, Hobbes, and the Formation of a Liberal Republicanism in England*. Cambridge: Cambridge University Press.

Tilmouth, Christopher. 2007. *Passion's Triumph over Reason: A History of the Moral Imagination from Spenser to Rochester*. Oxford: Oxford University Press.

Tuck, Richard. 1989. *Hobbes*. Oxford: Oxford University Press.

Tuck, Richard. 1998. "Hobbes on Education," in *Philosophers on Education: New Historical Perspectives*, edited by Amelié Oksenberg Rorty, 148–156. London: Routledge.

Tuck, Richard, 2004. "The Utopianism of Leviathan," in *Leviathan After 350 Years*, edited by Tom Sorell and Luc Foisneau, 125–38. Oxford: Clarendon Press.

Van Mill, David. 2001. *Liberty, Rationality, and Agency in Hobbes's Leviathan*. Albany: State University of New York Press.

Veall, Donald. 1970. *The Popular Movement for Law Reform 1640–1660*. Oxford: Oxford University Press.

Warrender, Howard. 1957. *The Political Philosophy of Hobbes: His Theory of Obligation*. Oxford: Clarendon Press.

Whelan, Frederick. 1981. "Language and Its Abuses in Hobbes' Political Philosophy." *American Political Science Review* 75(1): 59–75.

Wright, George. 2006. *Religion, Politics and Thomas Hobbes*. Dordrecht: Springer.

Wrong, Dennis, 1978. "Is Rational Choice Humanity's Most Distinctive Trait?" *American Sociologist* 28(2): 73–81.

Zagorin, Perez. 2007. "Hobbes as a Theorist of Natural Law." *Intellectual History Review* 17(3): 239–255.

CHAPTER 10

THE STATE OF NATURE

IOANNIS D. EVRIGENIS

1 INTRODUCTION

IN a striking chapter toward the end of the first part of *Leviathan*, Thomas Hobbes described the natural condition of mankind as a war in which "every man is Enemy to every man," and wherein uncertainty and vulnerability make for a life that is "solitary, poore, nasty, brutish, and short."[1] He was by no means the first to invoke the state of nature in this context. Several years earlier, as Hobbes was working on his translation of Thucydides, rendering into memorable English the famous descriptions of anarchy in the "Archaeology," during the plague in Athens, and throughout the *stasis* in Corcyra, Grotius was making the rather impious suggestion, in *De jure belli ac pacis*, that the state of nature was a condition in which there was no jurisdiction.[2] Shortly thereafter, echoing this idea in *The Elements of Law*, Hobbes offered his readers a first glimpse of "ye Condition of men in meere nature."[3] That depiction marked the start of a series of successive efforts, which culminated in *Leviathan*, to provide a credible and memorable account of the state of nature as the miserable condition that awaited all those who contemplated rebellion.

If the suggestion that one must consider the state of men outside civil society seems somewhat odd, it was all the more so in the context of Hobbes's political treatises, which he presented as attempts to impose order and precision on political philosophy, a realm hitherto marred by inconstancy, absurdity, and vagueness. Even within the confines

---

[1] *Leviathan* 13: 62.
[2] See, e.g., Thucydides 1629: 1.5–6, 2.53, 3.82–83. Grotius 1631: II.vii.xxvii, ". . . in statu naturali, quo nulla erat jurisdictio." The phrase recurs in II.v.ix and II.v.xv. Grotius's English translators were more enthusiastic in their use of the term, which appears several times in their notes, and is even used to mistranslate "ad merum jus naturæ" (II.vi.v).
[3] That is the title given to the section consisting of Chapters 14 and 15 of Part I of *The Elements of Law*, in the table of contents (e.g., Devonshire Mss., Chatsworth, HS/A/2A). All subsequent references to the *Elements* are to the Tönnies edition.

of *Leviathan*, the state of nature stands in stark contrast to the standards Hobbes set for himself and to the material that preceded it. Whereas, for example, the opening chapters of the book take the reader through a series of painstaking definitions of the minutiae of human nature and behavior, Chapter 13 is elusive and even ostensibly self-contradictory. For instance, while he had described the state of nature as a war of all against all, Hobbes also claimed that "there had never been any time, wherein particular men were in a condition of warre one against another."[4] He then presented the state of nature as an "Inference, made from the Passions," but also suggested that it could be confirmed by the reader's experience, and likened it to the conditions one would encounter amid civil war, or in the America of his day. Despite these difficulties, it was this most elusive of Hobbes's images that became the best known and most widely influential element of his political theory. It informed the work of those who found his views congenial, and, as importantly, the positions of his adversaries, and it remains current in a broad range of political discourse to this day.

It seems paradoxical that the most successful element of Hobbes's political thought is the one that falls far short of his stated standards of precision, but it is precisely because it violated those standards that the state of nature became so successful. This appears to be something that Hobbes knew from the start, since he was well aware of the fact that despite certain basic characteristics, human beings are shaped by their experiences and environment in ways that lead them to desire different things, so that an argument that will appeal to one will leave another unaffected.[5] Having expressed the desire to convince all men that they ought to measure the inconveniences of that current state not against unrealistic expectations, but rather against the more terrible alternative of anarchy, Hobbes knew that he had to supply a reminder of that fact that would not only be persuasive and memorable but also appeal to readers with varied beliefs, convictions, and interests.[6] In his discussion of how one mind affects another, in *The Elements of Law*, Hobbes noted that instigation and appeasing work in the same way as persuasion, by increasing or diminishing another's passions. He added,

> as in raising an opinion from passion, any premises are good enough to infer the desired conclusion; so, in raising passion from opinion, it is no matter whether the opinion be true or false, or the narration historical or fabulous. For not truth, but image, maketh passion; and a tragedy affecteth no less than a murder if well acted.[7]

---

[4] *Leviathan* 13: 62, 63.

[5] In the Introduction to *Leviathan*, for instance, Hobbes writes of the "similitude of the thoughts, and Passions of one man, to the thoughts, and Passions of another," but warns that this should not be mistaken to extend to the *objects* of the Passions, . . . for these the constitution individuall, and particular education do so vary, and they are so easie to be kept from our knowledge, that the characters of mans heart, blotted and confounded as they are, with dissembling, lying, counterfeiting, and erroneous doctrines, are legible onely to him that searcheth hearts (2).

[6] In the Epistle Dedicatory to *The Elements of Law*, Hobbes wrote "it would be an incomparable benefit to commonwealth, if every man held the opinions concerning law and policy here delivered (xvi; cf. *Leviathan* 31: 193). On why human beings are poor judges of their circumstances, see *Leviathan* 18: 94. On preference for the lesser evil, see *De Cive* Pref., ∫∫ 20–21; *Leviathan* 14: 70; 20: 106–7.

[7] *The Elements of Law* I.13.7.

The passions that Hobbes was after were the fear of violent death and the desire for commodious living, and the image that would raise them would be a vivid reminder of what life would be like without a power to keep all in awe.

2 THE ROAD TO THE *SUMMUM MALUM*

Despite having characterized it as a state of war, Hobbes explained that the state of nature is not simply a condition of actual fighting but rather one of "perpetual diffidence" arising from the fact that effectively equal individuals all have a natural right to preserve themselves and, hence, the attendant right to everything that might help them do so.[8] Without a sovereign authority that will establish and uphold laws, diffidence will sooner or later lead to conflict.[9] To see how unpleasant life under such circumstances could be, Hobbes encouraged his readers to consider

> the experience of savage nations that live at this day, and ... the histories of our ancestors, the old inhabitants of Germany and other now civil countries, where we find the people few and short lived, and without the ornaments and comforts of life, which by peace and society are usually invented and procured.[10]

This account of the state of nature accords well with the overall tone of the *Elements*, a work Hobbes advertised to the Earl of Newcastle as based on the "rules and infallibility of reason," and which was never intended for publication, but was only circulated in manuscript form among a few friends and acquaintances.[11] The colorless examples in Hobbes's first description of the state of nature fit the tone of the rest of the chapter, wherein equality plays an important role, and the unpleasantness of the natural condition of mankind sounds persuasive but hardly frightening. Faint traces of anarchy can be found in Hobbes's insistence on the various consequences of equality and the right of everyone to all things, to judge for himself, and to use his own discretion when it comes to his own security. Yet the very examples intended to persuade the readers that such a condition exists also told them that it was irrelevant to them.

Hobbes had expressed his repeated frustration with what passed for civil philosophy, alleging that rather than beginning from the right foundations, as proper philosophy should, those who had "written of justice and policy in general, do invade each other, and themselves, with contradiction."[12] To succeed where they had failed, Hobbes proposed

---

[8] On the state of war, see *The Elements of Law* I.14.11. On natural right, I.14.6–10. On effective equality, I.14.2.

[9] *The Elements of Law* II.10.8.

[10] *The Elements of Law* I.14.12.

[11] See *Elements of Law* Ep. Ded. An unauthorized edition violating the original division of the work appeared in 1650, with disastrous results for its subsequent interpretation (see Evrigenis 2014). No edition respecting Hobbes's original division appeared until Tönnies', in 1889.

[12] *The Elements of Law* Ep. Ded.

to put together a system composed of three parts, treating body, man, and citizen. As he began assembling these, "thoughtfully and slowly," the seething debates regarding the rights of dominion and the duties of subjects, *the true forerunners of the approaching War*," caused him to set aside the first two parts and devote his attention to the completion of the third.[13] This was printed in Paris in 1642 as *Elementorum philosophiæ sectio tertia de cive* and was, once again, circulated only among friends and acquaintants. In this version, of which very few copies survive and even fewer are intact, the reader confronts the state of nature from the outset. In the striking frontispiece advertising the three parts of the book (*libertas, imperium, religio*), the condition of liberty is represented by an armed Algonquian warrior with a menacing expression, flanked by scenes of savage cruelty involving a manhunt and cannibalism. The contrast with *imperium*, on the other side of the divide, could not be starker. There, a figure representing justice and sovereignty presides over a landscape bearing all the signs of industry, prosperity, and order.

As the system that Hobbes had been working on would have treated human nature in the preceding section, *De Cive* opened by considering the condition of man without society.[14] Building further on the themes outlined in the *Elements*, Hobbes argued therein that, contrary to those who claim that man is born fit for society, the beginning of civil society lay in men's mutual fear, itself the result of effective equality and of a universal natural right to self-preservation and to the means thereto. Although he did not offer any new examples of the state of nature, Hobbes added some color to the existing ones:

> They of America are Examples hereof, even in this present Age: Other Nations have been in former Ages, which now indeed are become Civill, and Flourishing, but were then few, fierce, short-lived, poor, nasty, and [lack] all that Pleasure, and Beauty of life, which Peace and Society are wont to bring with them.[15]

This work attracted sufficient interest, despite its limited dissemination, to prompt Hobbes to produce a revised version for publication.[16] That version, which was published in Amsterdam by Elzevir in 1647 under the different title *Elementa philosophica de cive*, contained the 1642 text but also a substantial preface to the readers and several explanatory notes, in which Hobbes described his purpose and method and addressed various objections that had been raised by readers of the earlier version.[17] A controversial choice of prefatory material by Samuel Sorbière, who was overseeing the publication on behalf of Hobbes, resulted in the production of two frontispieces for this

---

[13] *De Cive* Pref., ∫ 19.

[14] *De Cive* I. The title, according to the table of contents, is "*De Hominum statu extra societatem.*" The chapter heading is "*De statu Hominum extra societatem.*"

[15] *De Cive* I.13.

[16] See Warrender's introduction to his edition of *De Cive* [*The Latin Version*, pp. 7–8].

[17] See *De Cive* Pref. ∫ 24. The new title was meant to assuage the publisher's concerns that the third part of a system whose previous parts had not been published would discourage potential readers.

edition. While a few copies bore a hasty reproduction of the 1642 frontispiece, which appears to have been the one Hobbes had intended to use, the majority were published with a different and far less striking design.[18]

In the Epistle Dedicatory, Hobbes noted that true wisdom comes from remembrance originating in fixed and precise terms, which allows one to progress from individual observations toward universal precepts.[19] Those who had hitherto claimed the title of moral philosopher had failed precisely because they had been lacking such a suitable starting point, one which Hobbes found in the "*darkness of doubt itself*."[20] There, he discovered two "absolutely certain postulates of human nature, one, the postulate of human greed by which each man insists upon his own private use of common property; the other the postulate of natural reason, by which each man strives to avoid violent death as the supreme evil in nature."[21]

The latter, in particular, marked the starting point of Hobbes's effort to succeed where those before him had failed. The evils that have resulted from their falsehoods and nonsense are the best indication of the potential benefits that one could derive from the application of a proper method.[22] Thus, rather than waste his time in attempting to persuade his readers that they should embrace this or that good as the highest, Hobbes would instead focus on something which interfered with everyone's pursuit of the good, no matter what that might be. The negative focus of this new method is captured nicely in Hobbes's concluding exhortation to the readers, to

> chuse to brooke with patience some inconveniences under government (because human affairs cannot possibly be without some) then ... disturb the quiet of the publique; That weighing the justice of those things you are about, not by the perswasion and advise of private men, but by the Lawes of the Realme, you will no longer suffer ambitious men through the streames of your blood to wade to their owne power; That you will esteeme it better to enjoy your selves in the present state though perhaps not the best, then by waging Warre, indeavour to procure a reformation for other men in another age, your selves in the meane while either kill'd, or consumed with age.[23]

If, as Hobbes would put it later in *Leviathan*, "man by nature chooseth the lesser evil," then to get his readers to accept their present inconveniences would require a much more undesirable alternative.[24] The readers would encounter that alternative upon turning the page, in Hobbes's latest account of the state of nature.

---

[18] See Warrender's introduction to his edition of *De Cive* [*The Latin Version*, Plate III]. On the preparation, production, controversy, and reception of the book, see *The Correspondence of Thomas Hobbes* I, 125–47, 152–64.

[19] *De Cive* Ep. Ded., ∫ 4.

[20] *De Cive* Ep. Ded., ∫ 8.

[21] *On the Citizen*, tr. Silverthorne, Ep. Ded., ∫ 10: [*summum naturæ malum*].

[22] *De Cive* Pref., ∫ 4.

[23] *De Cive* Pref., ∫∫ 20–21.

[24] *Leviathan* 14, 70.

Although based on its predecessor of 1642, the 1647 version diverges in certain important respects. The first difference occurs in the title of Chapter I, which this time around read, "Of the State of Man without Civil Society."[25] The most important changes, however, came in the form of Hobbes's notes to controversial passages, and Chapter I contained two of the most controversial. The first two notes had to do with the venerable notion that "Man is a Creature born fit for Society," and with Hobbes's challenge to it. With regard to the former, Hobbes pointed out, first, that civil societies are more than mere gatherings, and, second, that a *desire* for society is not tantamount to a *capacity* for it. Hobbes did not deny the existence of such a desire, but he noted that the capacity for civil society required both reason and education, and experience shows that many men of mature years lack either or both prerequisites.[26] Men appear to seek society not because of any love for their fellows but because they need help in fulfilling their desire for gain and glory. By their very nature, however, these goods are attained at the expense of others, which makes dominion, rather than society, the best means of achieving them. Hence Hobbes had no doubt that if fear were removed, men would seek dominion rather than society. This is why he reached the equally controversial conclusion that the beginning of all large and lasting societies lay in men's mutual fear.[27] Hobbes's second note was aimed at those who misunderstood him to mean nothing other than fright, when in fact he understood fear in far broader terms:

> a certain foresight of future evill; neither doe I conceive flight the sole property of fear, but to distrust, suspect, take heed, provide so that they may not fear, is also incident to the fearfull. They who go to Sleep, shut their Dores; they who Travell carry their Swords with them, because they fear Theives. Kingdomes guard their Coasts and Frontiers with Forts, and Castles; Cities are compast with Walls, and all for fear of neighbouring Kingdomes and Townes; even the strongest Armies, and most accomplisht for Fight, yet sometimes Parly for peace, as fearing each others power, and lest they might be overcome. It is through fear that men secure themselves.[28]

If this note were intended to appease those who found natural man too fearful in the earlier version, however, then its effect is dubious, for Hobbes's clarification expanded the scope of fear greatly and brought the tone of Chapter I, which was otherwise unchanged, in closer conformity with the original alarming frontispiece of 1642.[29]

The increasing prominence of fear in Hobbes's first three attempts at an account of the state of nature signal his sustained intention to work toward an effective account of the *summum malum*. Yet, these attempts failed precisely for the reasons that Hobbes had identified in *Elements* I.13. The first three accounts of the state of nature tried to persuade the reader that it is an undesirable condition which every sensible individual

---

[25] *De statu Hominum extra Societatem civilem.*

[26] *De Cive* I.2, note to "born fit."

[27] *De Cive* I.2.

[28] *De Cive*, I.2, note to "The mutuall fear."

[29] Hobbes mentions "fear" once in *Elements* I.14, five times in the 1642 version of *De Cive*, and sixteen in that of 1647.

would wish to stay away from, but they gave him no real reason to think that it was a condition that he was likely to find himself in. In those three accounts, Hobbes does not ask explicitly whether the state of nature ever existed, and the examples that he offers to prove that it might have are rather anodyne. The American scene on the frontispiece, the most frightening of Hobbes's examples, was seen only by a very small fraction of his readers and was, in any case, an unlikely prospect for most of them. Even if life among the Indians were as undesirable as Hobbes claimed, it was not sufficiently threatening to cause a broad range of readers to reconsider their political behavior. If anything, the example of the ancient inhabitants of "now civil countries" made the prospect of an unpleasant life more remote still. As Hobbes had noted in the *Elements*, "not truth, but image, maketh passion," and these images had very few of the makings of a lasting fear of violent death.[30]

3 A State of Misery

De Cive was successful enough to require reprinting, at which point Hobbes was offered the opportunity to revisit that text and make changes. He declined, stating that he had nothing to add or subtract.[31] On its own, this detail might appear to be nothing more than evidence that he was satisfied with the book as it was, but that conclusion is complicated by the appearance of a much lengthier and very different English book on more or less the same subject matter, a mere four years later. At first glance, *Leviathan* appears an unlikely locus for the most memorable account of the state of nature. Its famous frontispiece suggests the triumph of *imperium* over *libertas*, depicting a commonwealth under the complete control of a gigantic sovereign whose posture makes commodious living possible. Under his protection, everything functions as it should and where it should, and evidence of order and prosperity abounds. Closer in the structure of its opening section to the *Elements* than to *De Cive*, *Leviathan* does not introduce the reader to the natural condition of mankind until Chapter 13. Prior to encountering the state of nature, the reader making his way through *Leviathan* must once again go through a series of chapters in which Hobbes examines the mind before landing upon some new territory.

Having previously identified the *summum malum* as his own starting point, Hobbes now asserts boldly that "there is no such *Finis ultimus*, (utmost ayme,) nor *Summum Bonum*, (greatest Good,) as is spoken of in the Books of the old Morall Philosophers," for not only do men desire different things, but there is also "a general inclination of all mankind" toward "a perpetuall and restlesse desire of Power after power, that ceaseth only in Death."[32] Competition among men for riches, honor, or any other form

---

[30] *Elements of Law* I.13.7.

[31] See Hobbes to Samuel Sorbière, Saint-Germain, November 17/27, 1647 (*The Correspondence of Thomas Hobbes* I, 163–64).

[32] *Leviathan* 11, 47; cf. *The Elements of Law*, I.9.21. On the *summum malum*, see *De Cive* Ep. Ded., ∫ 10; cf. Evrigenis 2008: 102–9.

of power will lead to conflict, but desire for commodious living and fear of death or wounds dispose men toward obedience of a common power.[33] There is much in human nature, however, that can interfere with such a disposition, and few things can do so as effectively as religion, a phenomenon that also has its roots in man's "perpetuall solicitude for the time to come."[34] Although the title of Chapter 13 promises to consider mankind's felicity and misery in the natural condition, a being concerned with the future can quickly conclude that the state of nature is an undesirable condition that should be avoided at all costs.[35]

Abandoning the controversial opening statement of *De Cive*, according to which the origin of large and lasting societies lay in men's mutual fear, in *Leviathan* Hobbes returned to the model of the *Elements* and began his account of the natural condition by asserting men's effective equality. This time, however, the space devoted to this claim was more significant, and the arguments in its support more pointed. Where physical equality is concerned, and even though some men are clearly stronger than others, even the weakest of them can kill the strongest, "either by secret machination or by confederacy with others, that are in the same danger with himself."[36] When it comes to the faculties of the mind, Hobbes found "yet a greater equality amongst men, than that of strength."[37] It is important to note, however, that whereas Hobbes's pronouncement regarding effective physical equality pertains to man's capacity, the equivalent pronouncement regarding mental equality refers not just to man's mental abilities but also—and more significantly—to one's perception of them. This distinction is crucial, especially in light of the fact that Hobbes described his readers as the children of pride.[38]

In the *Elements*, Hobbes had argued that men "ought to admit amongst themselves equality."[39] In *Leviathan* he knows that they will not, because of

> a vain conceipt of ones owne wisdome, which almost all men think they have in a greater degree, than the Vulgar; that is, than all men but themselves, and a few others, whom by Fame, or for concurring with themselves, they approve. For such is the nature of men, that howsoever they may acknowledge many others to be more witty, or more eloquent, or more learned; Yet they will hardly believe there be many so wise as themselves: For they see their own wit at hand, and other mens at a distance.

---

[33] *Leviathan* 11, 47–48.

[34] *Leviathan* 12, 52. Hobbes lists several human characteristics that contribute to conflict in the remainder of Chapter 11 (pp. 48–51).

[35] In the Latin edition of 1668, the title of Chapter 13 is even more provocative: misery drops out, and what remains is a consideration of mankind's "felicity in the present life" ("*De Conditione generis Humani quantùm attinet ad felicitatem praesentis vitae*").

[36] *Leviathan* 13, 60.

[37] *Leviathan* 13, 60.

[38] High above everything else on the frontispiece hovers a quotation from Job 41.24 (Vulgate). As Hobbes's contemporaries would have known, the line that follows describes Leviathan as "king over all the children of pride" (Job 41.25, Vulgate; 41.34, KJV). Hobbes quotes the full passage at the end of *Leviathan* 28 (pp. 166–67).

[39] *The Elements of Law* I.14.2.

But this proveth rather that men are in that point equall, than unequall. For there is not ordinarily a greater signe of the equall distribution of any thing, than that every man is contented with his share.[40]

Hobbes knows that human beings prefer to govern themselves to being governed by others, and even though they tend to overestimate their abilities, few lack the skills to do so.[41] By presenting his incendiary statement regarding mental equality as he did, Hobbes was able to preserve a space in which any particular reader might see himself as the reasonable exception to the rule and those around him as evidence of its validity. Most men tend to overestimate their capacity to govern themselves but a few can put things in proper perspective and see things for what they are. If the nature of men is such as to cause them to think of themselves as better than they are, then the reader is likely to accept Hobbes's proposition and see himself as the exception to the rule.

An individual who surveys this state of affairs and judges himself to be at least as good as anyone else will like his chances of attaining his ends. However, by being led to the insight that others think the same way, he will come to realize that when he and another similarly minded individual decide to pursue the same end, they will become enemies and "endeavour to destroy, or subdue one an other."[42] One worried about the future will soon discover that it makes little sense, in this setting, to invest in it. So long as he remains on his own, any potential invader will consider him at best an equal match. Worse still, if he "plant, sow, build, or possesse a convenient Seat, others may probably be expected to come prepared with forces united, to dispossesse, and deprive him, not only of the fruit of his labour, but also of his life, or liberty," only to find themselves in his shoes.[43] Thus, paradoxically, a condition that begins in promising terms for the individual quickly becomes one of perpetual diffidence.

In such a condition, the best means of defense is anticipation, namely preemptive action, such as will allow one "by force, or wiles, to master the persons of all men he can, so long till he see no other power great enough to endanger him."[44] The trouble with this strategy, however, is that it too remains vulnerable to the existence of immoderate men. While moderate men would be satisfied with such dominion as would render them secure, there are some who take pleasure in "contemplating their own power in the acts of conquest, which they pursue farther than their security requires."[45] Their existence leaves the moderate with no other option but to continue to pursue even greater dominion so as to secure themselves against them. The conclusion is simple if

---

[40] *Leviathan* 13, 61. Cf. *ibid.*, 27, 154; 30, 176; *De Cive* Pref., § 3; *The Elements of Law* II.8.13: "For generally, not he that hath skill in geometry, or any other science speculative, but only he that understandeth what conduceth to the good and government of the people, is called a wise man."

[41] See *Leviathan* 15, 76–77.

[42] *Leviathan* 13, 61.

[43] *Leviathan* 13, 61.

[44] *Leviathan* 13, 61.

[45] *Leviathan* 13, 61.

regrettable: Since the acquisition by force of dominion is "necessary to a mans conservation, it ought to be allowed him."[46]

Hobbes's distinction between the moderate, who might be content with as much power as is necessary for their conservation, and the proud, who derive pleasure from their dominion over others, might appear as a qualification of his earlier claim regarding vanity as a universal human characteristic. It is important to note, however, that the logic of the argument renders the distinction between the moderate and the proud insignificant. So long as certain individuals are proud and willing to overstep the boundaries of reason, others will be forced to follow them toward preemptive conflict. Hobbes reinforced this conclusion by insisting in the next paragraph that men—without qualification—"have no pleasure, (but on the contrary a great deale of griefe) in keeping company, where there is no power able to over-awe them all," because they all expect that others value them as much as they value themselves.[47] Once again, however, the comparative nature of relative valuation means that not everyone can win this game. Those who feel slighted will thus seek to extract valuation by subduing those who refuse them the honors they think they deserve, thereby teaching everyone else a lesson too.

Human nature, thus, contains "three principall causes of quarrell": (i) competition for goods deemed necessary for one's preservation and commodious living; (ii) diffidence arising from the threat that others pose for one's person, relations, and possessions; and (iii) glory, arising from the need to have others acknowledge one's worth.[48] Without a common power "to keep them all in awe," human beings equipped with these tendencies will find themselves in a condition of war.[49] Dressing up his definition of this condition in the memorable simile of foul weather, Hobbes noted that, like gathering clouds, war consists not simply in fighting but in any manifestation of the desire to fight. Although he concludes his description of the state of war by declaring that "All other time is PEACE," the reader who considers the preceding definition realizes that that promise is an empty one, for Hobbes's definition of war appears all-encompassing.[50]

Without a common power to ensure peace and without the assistance of others, in the state of nature man can rely only on his own powers, which are inadequate. Burdened by a multitude of needs and desires but armed with a very limited capacity to fulfill them, and hampered further by the diffidence that his solicitude for the future and recognition of the perils of equality must engender in him, his life becomes perilous and unpleasant. "In such a condition," argues Hobbes,

> there is no place for Industry; because the fruit thereof is uncertain: and consequently no Culture of the Earth; no Navigation, nor use of the commodities that

---

[46] *Leviathan* 13, 61.

[47] *Leviathan* 13, 61.

[48] *Leviathan* 13, 61.

[49] *Leviathan* 13, 62.

[50] *Leviathan* 13, 62.

may be imported by Sea; no commodious Building; no Instruments of moving, and removing such things as require much force; no Knowledge of the face of the Earth; no account of Time; no Arts; no Letters; no Society; and which is worst of all, continuall feare, and danger of violent death; And the life of man, solitary, poore, nasty, brutish, and short.[51]

4 PROOF

The reception of the state of nature shows that with this "Inference made from the Passions," Hobbes succeeded in capturing the imagination of his readers and imprinting an image of the natural condition in their minds.[52] Difficult though it was, this achievement was but a part of the process. Hobbes still had to convince them that this colorful image was one that ought to matter to them in making their political calculations. Hobbes's references, in the earlier political treatises, to America and the savage ancestors of civilized nations showed that he had been aware from the start of the need to address the status of the state of nature. Chapter 13 of *Leviathan* suggests, however, that Hobbes found those examples inadequate, for he now devoted three paragraphs to this question. Although new to the account of the state of nature, all of this evidence of its validity came from Hobbes's earlier works.

Hobbes began this part of his account by addressing those who, having "not well weighed these things," might find his description of human nature strange.[53] If, despite his invitation to know or read himself, the reader nevertheless found Hobbes's inference from the passions suspicious, he could weigh Hobbes's account of anarchy against his own experience and doubtless conclude that it is valid. Invoking a series of everyday activities that he had listed in the Preface to *De Cive*, Hobbes now asked the reader to consider his own acts of prudence when faced with uncertainty: when he travels, he arms himself and prefers to go accompanied; when he goes to sleep, he locks his doors; in his very house, he locks his chests; and all this despite the fact that there are laws and officers charged with upholding them.[54] Giving voice, for the first time, to the reader's reasonable doubt about whether such a condition ever existed, Hobbes states that he believes that "it was never generally so, over all the world: but there are many places,

---

[51] *Leviathan* 13, 62. Variants of this list occur in *The Elements of Law*, I.13.3, Hobbes's answer to the Preface to Gondibert (Davenant 1650: 143), and *De Corpore* I.i.7.

[52] *Leviathan* 13, 62.

[53] *Leviathan* 13, 62.

[54] *Leviathan* 13, 62. Cf. *De Cive* Pref., ∫ 11. Hobbes's language in both works suggests that he was criticized severely for suggesting, thereby, that human beings are evil (see esp. *De Cive* Pref., ∫ 12). In a doubly bold statement, which has been read as denying the existence of divine law and of any standard of natural justice, Hobbes asserts that neither the passions of man, nor the actions that result from those passions can be considered sins, until there is a law that forbids them (*Leviathan* 13, 62).

where they live so now."[55] His first example is the familiar one of the savage people "in many places of *America*," whose reliance on clans for security accounts for their brutish life.[56] Hobbes's second example strikes closer to home. The reader wishing to imagine what life in anarchy would be like need no more than consider the fate of those who used to live in peace, under a single government, and who have now descended into a civil war.[57] If an encounter with the savages of America was an unlikely prospect for most of Hobbes's readers, the civil war that had occasioned Hobbes's political treatises at home and the Thirty Years' War on the Continent would have left readers in little doubt that the state of nature existed and could manifest itself at any moment.

To those who might object that human beings have never existed outside of groups, Hobbes responded by pointing out that even if a condition of war had never obtained among individuals, in the absence of a superior power, sovereigns would always assume the "state and posture of Gladiators."[58] The crucial difference between them and individuals in the state of nature, however, is that by doing so, they create a sphere of security in which their subjects can engage in all those activities that are imprudent in the state of nature and whose absence renders that condition so miserable. The subjects' ability to do this, in turn, allows the commonwealth to thrive, which explains why commonwealths are not constrained by the effective equality that characterizes the natural condition of human beings.

Returning to his earlier assertion that in the absence of law no action can be a crime, Hobbes spells out the dreadful consequences of anarchy. In a condition in which no common power has legislated, there can be no right or wrong, nor just or unjust, and hence no property, since one can possess things only fleetingly until another seize them from him. Passing his own judgment on the promise of the chapter's title, Hobbes thus writes of the "ill condition, which man by meer Nature is actually placed in," but notes that through a combination of the passions and reason, we are also offered a way out of it.[59] Driven by a fear of death, a desire for commodious living, and a hope to be able to make it possible, reason will provide the means for the attainment of peace in the form of the laws of nature.[60] The fundamental law of nature dictates that men "*seek Peace, and follow it*," while natural right allows that one defend oneself by all means.[61] It has been thought that the cycle of conflict created by the law and right of nature is a vicious one, for the uncertainty that dictates anticipation will always prevent one individual from trusting another. One might argue that this view perhaps takes Hobbes's memorable description of the state of nature as "solitary, poore, nasty, brutish, and

---

[55] Leviathan 13, 63; cf. *The Questions concerning Liberty, Necessity, and Chance* (EW V: 183–84).

[56] *Leviathan* 13, 63.

[57] See *De Cive* Pref., ∫∫ 19–23; 11.6; 13.6.

[58] *Leviathan* 13, 63. The image comes from *De Cive* XVII.27.

[59] *Leviathan* 13: 63.

[60] *Leviathan* 13: 63. In *Leviathan* 8, Hobbes wrote, "For the Thoughts, are to the Desires, as Scouts, and Spies, to range abroad, and find the way to the things Desired" (35).

[61] *Leviathan* 14: 64.

short," too literally.[62] To do so, however, would be to lose sight of the fact that Hobbes wrote consistently of temporary associations in the state of nature, whose transitory successes can teach their participants the value of restraint and the reliable security that can result from inequality.[63]

5 IMAGES HISTORICAL OR FABULOUS

Readers' reactions to Hobbes's account of the state of nature show that rather than dismiss his suggestion that such a story be taken seriously, most merely disputed his version of it, usually by referring to sources considered authoritative. While Hobbes described the natural condition as an inference made from the passions and stated his belief that "it was never generally so, over all the world," some of his examples gave the unmistakable impression that he was describing primitive, presocial man.[64] This sense of temporality was reinforced by the fact that in his own theory the state of nature precedes the establishment of the commonwealth through a contract. One wishing to dispute Hobbes's version of prehistory had several sources to turn to, but those who argued against him in print relied mainly on three categories of sources: (i) Genesis and commentaries on it, (ii) the accounts of the ancient historians and ethnographers, and (iii) the constant stream of information regarding the native inhabitants of the New World and the ethnographic studies of Europe that resulted from the encounter with America.[65]

For Hobbes's contemporaries, one of the most striking features of his depiction of the state of nature was the absence from it of any reference to the Book of Genesis. Hobbes made a point of using Scripture to support his arguments and repeatedly noted its special status in that regard.[66] Yet when it came to this concept whose roots actually lay in Genesis, his accounts were curiously silent. Readers of *Leviathan* would have had every reason to expect to find Genesis alluded to in Chapter 13, for Hobbes had discussed the Creation in the Introduction, and the significance of Adam and Babel in his examination of speech.[67] Moreover, in *De Cive*, Hobbes had pronounced God's dominion over Adam and Eve not simply natural but also by agreement and had held up the serpent's invitation to rebellion as emblematic of the kind of conduct that dissolves a commonwealth.[68] Several among those who responded to him in print noted

---

[62] For a detailed corrective of this common mistake, see Hoekstra forthcoming: Part I.

[63] See, e.g., *De Cive* I.13, where Hobbes writes of allies (*socii*), as well as *Leviathan* 13: 61, where he writes of invaders coming "prepared with forces united." On the mechanism through which individuals can form such temporary associations and leave behind the state of nature, see Evrigenis 2008: 120–26.

[64] *Leviathan* 13: 63.

[65] See Evrigenis 2014.

[66] On the status of Scripture, see *The Elements of Law* I.13.4; *De Cive* Pref., §§ 12, 16–17; *Leviathan* Review & Conclusion, 395.

[67] *Leviathan* Introduction: 1; 4: 12.

[68] Genesis 3:5; *De Cive* XVI.2; XII.1.

the omission and attributed the shortcomings of Hobbes's depiction of the natural condition to his neglect of this obvious source of evidence.[69] Perhaps in response to such objections, a Latin edition of *Leviathan* that appeared in 1668 featured an interesting addition. Just before listing the examples of America and of civil wars, Hobbes wrote, "But (someone will say) there never was a war of all against all. What? Did not Cain kill his own brother Abel out of envy—a misdeed so great that he would not have dared to commit it if there had then existed a common power capable of avenging it?"[70] The English *Leviathan* already contained plenty of statements that were interpreted as evidence of atheism, and this addition—which seems to deny the existence of God, His omnipotence, or His concern for human affairs—would appear to confirm the validity of the charge.[71]

Indeed, writing to Hobbes in 1670, Leibniz expressed his certainty that Hobbes would not deny that such a pure state of nature could not have existed, given God's rule over the world.[72] As Leibniz observed, Genesis as a whole presented a major difficulty for Hobbes's account of the state of nature, since, according to the former, man had never been in an anarchic condition, as Hobbes knew well. In a telling passage, Hobbes described the first human beings as God's "*peculiar* Subjects, whom he commanded by a Voice, as one man speaketh to another."[73] It is remarkable, therefore, that Leibniz's objection was not raised more often.

As we have seen, however, Hobbes was not interested in providing a history of the emergence of civil society. Rather, he sought to convey the dangers inherent in attempting to dismantle it. In this light, his choice of Cain's crime over the Fall is apt, for it not only belonged firmly in man's postlapsarian condition but also symbolized something that would have been plainly apparent to Hobbes's contemporaries, namely that rebellion—Adam's—leads to the worst form of civil war, namely fratricide. But this example also sent a powerful message to rulers by drawing their attention to the fact that even under an omnipotent ruler, man would always be disposed toward rebellion.

Having described the state of nature as the condition of man outside civil society and likened it to the savage ancestors of civilized nations, Hobbes also prompted his readers to compare his exercise to one that they had encountered numerous times in the pages of the ancient historians, poets, and philosophers—such authors as Plato,

---

[69] See, e.g., Clarendon 1676: 26–41, 63–79; Coke 1662: 24–36; [Filmer] 1652: A3ʳ; [Parker] 1670: Ch. IV; Tenison, 1671: 139; Ward 1654: 54; Ward 1656: V.i.

[70] *Leviathan* (Malcolm, ed.) 13: 63, n. 38.

[71] As Templer noted, this statement also disregards Adam's "jure paterno" (1679: 60). This might have posed a problem for Hobbes, who in *De Cive* had declared that "*a Sonne cannot be understood to be at any time in the State of Nature, as being under the power and command of them to whom he owes his protection as soon as ever he is born, namely either his Fathers, or his Mothers, or his that nourisht him*" (I.10, note to "In the meere state of Nature"). Cf. [Filmer] 1652: 1–2. Hobbes, however, had foreseen this objection in his exchange with Bramhall, where he had described it as "no deep consideration" (EW V: 184). Adam's absence from and consequent inaction in Genesis 4 is striking.

[72] Gottfired Wilhelm Leibniz to Thomas Hobbes, Mainz, July 13/23, 1670 (British Library, Add. MS 4294, fol. 64)ᵛ.

[73] *Leviathan* 35: 216.

Polybius, Ovid, and Cicero—as well as Hobbes's own Thucydides. For many of those who saw Hobbes's state of nature as a deviation from Scripture, his views on a variety of matters and his association with Gassendi—who was widely considered an Epicurean—amounted to evidence of Hobbes's Epicureanism, a conclusion that seemed to fit well with his alleged atheism. From there, it was but a short step to detecting the influence of Lucretius over Hobbes's account of the natural condition.[74] This view was so widespread among those who attacked Hobbes in print that in introducing his celebrated translation of *De rerum natura*, in 1682, Thomas Creech noted that "the admirers of Mr. Hobbes may easily discern that his Politicks are but Lucretius enlarg'd; His state of Nature is sung by our Poet; the rise of Laws; the beginning of Societies; the Criteria of Just and Unjust exactly the same, and natural Consequents of the Epicurean Origine of Man; no new Adventures."[75]

Indeed, the reader turning to Book V of Lucretius's poem encounters a world that is not entirely hospitable, in which human beings can only with "great labor" extract meager benefits from the plants and trees, all the while besieged by wild beasts, the elements, and diseases.[76] Things were not very different when human beings first entered this world. Living almost like beasts, though vulnerable to them, and lacking even the most basic protection from the elements and the implements to cultivate the earth, they could depend only on what nature could provide. In such conditions, there was no lasting association and no sense of a common good or law.[77] Gradual attempts to escape the misery of this condition led to the realization that the weak should be protected, a covenant (*foedera*) which was respected by the greatest part of men, even if it did not bring about concord.[78]

For Lucretius civilization is not simply preferable to man's primitive condition, as the commonwealth is to the state of nature for Hobbes. Still, his account of the transition details the gradual acquisition of the makings of what Hobbes would describe as commodious living.[79] There is a famous contrast in *De rerum natura*, however, that corresponds to the one Hobbes wished to draw between the natural condition and civil society. In one of the most famous passages of the poem, Lucretius declares,

> PLEASANT it is, when on the great sea the winds trouble the waters, to gaze from shore upon another's great tribulation: not because any man's troubles are a delectable joy, but because to perceive what ills you are free from yourself is pleasant.

---

[74] Lucretius and Hobbes shared an interest in Thucydides—*De rerum natura* concludes with a famous consideration of the Athenian plague—but there are also numerous similarities to Hobbes's views throughout *De rerum natura*, including Lucretius's attack on prevailing notions regarding life after death (I), his emphasis on sense and the dangers inherent in its deceptions (I, II, III), the rejection of incorporeal beings (I), the relationship between free will and necessity (II), and a mechanical conception of the will (IV).

[75] Lucretius 1682: Preface, b3ᵛ.

[76] Lucretius 1992: V.201–34.

[77] Lucretius 1992: V.933–61.

[78] Lucretius 1992: V.1024–27.

[79] Lucretius 1992: V.1448–57. Cf. *The Elements of Law* I.13.3; *Leviathan* 13: 62.

Pleasant is it also to behold great encounters of warfare arrayed over the plains, with no part of yours in the peril.[80]

In his Preface to *De Cive*, Hobbes had expressed the hope that once his readers had considered the perils of the alternative—the one encapsulated in the state of nature—they would conclude that it made sense for them to submit to the relatively minor inconveniences of life under government, since life can never be without some inconvenience.[81]

Toward the conclusion of the *Elements*, Hobbes offers a clue suggesting that Lucretius was not far from his mind as he was thinking about the state of nature. There, using Lucretius's title as a synonym for the natural condition, Hobbes defends his controversial suggestion that the civil laws are the measure of right and wrong, arguing that there is no such thing as right reason "to be found or known *in rerum naturâ*."[82] Unlike Genesis, the various archaeologies of the Greeks and Romans contained evidence that supported the broad outlines of a story in which man's original condition was nasty and brutish. But was this merely a thing of the past, or a consideration that should matter to Hobbes's readers? By linking it to America, Hobbes suggested that it still mattered.

Even though it was no longer news, the existence of America continued to pose a profound challenge for Hobbes and his contemporaries. The questions occasioned by its discovery—regarding the origin of the natives, their history, and their relationship to Scripture—continued unabated. Not least, the determination of their status—as fully human or something else—had a direct bearing on the legality of attempts to enslave them and seize their land and resources.[83] Hobbes's use of America in his earlier political treatises attests to its symbolic power. Already the main contemporary example of the state of nature in the *Elements*, in *De Cive* America was promoted to the very symbol of the nasty and brutish condition of liberty. None of this is surprising. Hobbes had access to several of the era's major travel accounts and was involved in the Virginia Company, where he represented his employer's interests.[84] In fact, Hobbes was in attendance when the company is likely to have received and discussed a letter in which the Council in Virginia notified it of the 1622 massacre around Jamestown.[85]

Yet, despite his access to all this information about America, Hobbes's references to it are few and rather pedestrian. More important, in *Leviathan*, America was demoted

---

[80] Lucretius 1992: II.1–6.

[81] *De Cive* Pref., §§ 20–21.

[82] *Elements of Law* II.10.8; cf. *A Dialogue between a Philosopher and a Student, of the Common Laws of England*, ed. Cromartie, p. 26/[26–27].

[83] See, e.g., Grotius 1884; Vitoria 1999; Wey Gómez 2008.

[84] A catalogue, in Hobbes's hand, of books held in the Hardwick Library during the 1620s and 1630s contains the most popular travel narratives, including several volumes of Hackluyt and Purchas, but also various other travel accounts and works on geography, as well as an entry for "Virginia and Bermuda businesse bound together" (Devonshire Mss., Chatsworth, HS/E/1A). The records of the Virginia Company show that Cavendish gave Hobbes one of his shares, thereby making him a member (Kingsbury, ed. 1906–35: II, p. 40). As Malcolm notes, Hobbes is listed as in attendance at "no fewer than thirty-seven meetings" (2002: 54).

[85] See Kingsbury, ed. 1906–35: III, pp. 611–15.

to merely one of several examples, with war and civil war now taking pride of place. Occurring as it does in the context of the first explicit treatment of the status of the state of nature, this shift is understandable. Propagandists on behalf of colonization had attempted from the first to portray America as the promised land, but there was plenty of evidence to suggest that it was an inhospitable place fraught with uncertainty and danger. This was the image of America that the *Elements* and *De Cive* referred to, and it was one that could have been expected to resonate with most readers, for even the best informed among them could not deny the dangers that lay on the other side of the ocean. But precisely because of his access to a wealth of information about America, Hobbes would have known all too well that the life of its natives was not simply "solitary, poore, nasty, brutish, and short." The qualification in *Leviathan* reflects this awareness.[86]

Hobbes welcomed feedback from his readers and took it into account as he revised the successive versions of his works.[87] The transformation of the section devoted to persuading his readers that the state of nature was real and should be taken seriously shows that the previous versions had not been effective. If the allusions to well-known sources succeeded in evoking strong associations in his readers' minds, the conclusions that followed from those associations were not clearly favorable to Hobbes's argument. All of these sources were surrounded by controversy, and there was no single interpretation of them that commanded universal agreement. Perhaps more important, they coexisted uneasily, for as the disagreement surrounding each of them had shown, one could interpret the existence of new lands and peoples as evidence against the validity of Scripture, just as one could invoke Scripture to refute the fantastical accounts of the ancient historians and poets. There were certain manifestations of the state of nature, however, the existence and awfulness of which could not be denied by any of Hobbes's contemporaries, and it was these now that carried the weight of the argument, namely war and civil war.

6 CONCLUSION

Following the publication of the English *Leviathan*, the state of nature became a point of reference for pamphleteers and philosophers. Even though he attacked it as a "lamentable foundation," in 1670, Bishop Parker nevertheless recognized that Hobbes's state of nature, "as odd as it is, is become the Standard of our Modern Politicks; by which men that pretend to understand the real Laws of Wisdom and Subtility must square their Actions, and therefore is swallowed down, with as much greediness as an Article of Faith by the Wild and Giddy People of the Age."[88] In fact, the state of nature reached

---

[86] Compare, e.g., the description of the Indians in *Elements* I.13.3 to *Leviathan*, where Hobbes uses the qualifier "many places" twice in two consecutive sentences (13: 63).

[87] See, e.g., the Hobbes's preface to his translation of Thucydides (EW VIII: vii, ix), and his explanation of the changes he made to *De Cive* (Pref., §§ 22–24).

[88] [Parker] 1670: 116, 118.

far beyond Parker's wild and giddy contemporaries and can be encountered in political arguments ranging from seventeenth-century sermons to twenty-first-century textbooks of international relations.[89]

The diversity of the settings in which the state of nature played an important role during this period is but one sign of Hobbes's success in persuading his readers of the undesirability of disorder by evoking a series of images of anarchy. Another is the fact that it was used by those who disagreed with Hobbes as much as by those who agreed with him: even though their accounts of man's natural sociability diverged from his own, they took the state of nature for granted. This body of political thought is too vast and diverse to classify neatly. Nevertheless, there is one rough division that is useful in making sense of it and in appreciating the significance of Hobbes's state of nature in the evolution of modern political discourse. This division results from the two principal attributes of Hobbes's state of nature, anarchy and equality, the consequences of life without a common power. For Hobbes, these two attributes were what made the state of nature a condition steeped in uncertainty and therefore one that any sensible individual would want to leave behind. For his emulators and critics, these characteristics became the foci of a wide range of battles, some with unexpected consequences.

Stemming as they do from a common source, namely the absence of authority, neither of these attributes is exclusive, yet each symbolizes a distinct tendency. Under the heading of anarchy, one finds those for whom the principal manifestation of the state of nature was the domain of international relations, the arena in which sovereigns assume the posture of gladiators. In this area, in which the focus is on sovereignty, war, and international law, one comes across the writings of Pufendorf, Vattel, and Kant, all of whom positioned their theories vis-à-vis Hobbes's state of nature.[90] This line of thought paved the way for the theories of international relations of the twentieth and twenty-first centuries, in which the paradigm of the international system as a state of nature remains alive and well.

Under the heading of the legacy of the state of nature as a condition of equality, one might place those thinkers whose primary concern was with internal arrangements and issues, including rights and obligation. The statures of Locke and Rousseau in this domain give the impression that the role of the state of nature is limited to the conceptual framework of the social contract, an impression that might be reinforced by the fact that the term *state of nature* no longer enjoys the currency that it once did among theories of rights and domestic institutions. Yet despite appearances, the state of nature has been perhaps most influential in this area.[91]

---

[89] See, e.g., Allestree 1667: 7 and Nye 2005: 3.

[90] See Pufendorf 1964: II.ii; Vattel 1797: IV.i; Kant 1983.

[91] The most obvious examples of this tendency are Rawls's description of the original position as an initial situation in which individuals are stripped of advantages and disadvantages caused by "natural fortune or social circumstances" (Rawls 1971: § 4, p. 18) and Nozick's counter (1974: Part I).

For Hobbes's readers, any discussion of the natural condition of mankind would have been expected to include a position on whether natural man was prelapsarian or post-lapsarian.[92] Although he took advantage of this connection, Hobbes never addressed this matter explicitly. Many readers took his description of natural man as the depiction of a sinner. Others saw that it was possible to extract from his state of nature an account of man that was compatible with certain understandings of Christian doctrine but did not *require* a religious foundation. This characteristic, for example, gave Rousseau the opportunity to put equality to use in a vision of the social contract which, though very different from Hobbes's, would have been impossible without him.[93]

The richness of great works such as *Leviathan* opens them up to sometimes wide-ranging interpretations. While there is little disagreement among commentators that Hobbes's vision of civil society should be characterized as authoritarian, his political writings have been credited with having generated or consolidated an impressive array of tendencies, from totalitarianism to democracy and from liberalism to possessive individualism. Hobbes's theory of how one mind affects another, as laid out in *The Elements of Law*, and his subsequent manipulation of the image of the state of nature, help account for this variety of positions and for the longevity of the paradigm that gave rise to them. Long after critics such as Hume and Mill had contested the notion that individuals were bound by a social contract, those concerned with fixing the boundaries of individual rights, demarcating the proper sphere for state intervention, and determining the marks of sovereignty continued to utilize the state of nature as their point of reference.[94]

When invoked, the state of nature is contrasted to life under government.[95] Its manifestations, therefore, are as many as the visions of government that animate those contrasts. Throughout the successive reformulations of his political theory, Hobbes enhanced its structural versatility by offering a multitude of examples and allusions as to the status of the state of nature in order to construct the image that would permit him to persuade individuals who might otherwise disagree widely, that obedience to a single authority was the only way to end conflict.

BIBLIOGRAPHY

Manuscripts

Devonshire

Chatsworth, HS/A/2A [The Elements of Law Natural and Politic]
Chatsworth, HS/E/1A Hardwick Library Catalogue

---

[92] See, e.g., Templer 1673: 55–59.
[93] See, e.g., Rousseau's Letter to Beaumont (Rousseau 2001: 925–1007, esp. 971).
[94] Hume 1987; Mill 1978: 73.
[95] This is true even of Locke's account, in which the state of nature is sometimes preferable to life under government.

London

British Library, Add. MS 4294, fol. 64^v Gottfired Wilhelm Leibniz to Thomas Hobbes, Mainz, July13/23, 1670.

Books

Allestree, Richard. 1667. *A Sermon Preached before the King at White Hall on Sunday Nov. 17, 1667*. London: Printed by J. Flesher for James Allestree at the Rose and Crown in Duck Lane.

Clarendon, Edward Hyde, Earl of. 1676. *A Brief View and Survey of the Dangerous and Pernicious Errors to Church and State in Mr. Hobbes's Book, Entitled Leviathan*. Oxford, UK: s.n.

Coke, Roger. 1662. *A Survey of the Politicks of Mr. Thomas White, Thomas Hobbes, and Hugo Grotius, etc*. London: G. Bedell & T. Collins.

Davenant, Sir William. 1650. *The Preface to Gondibert, an Heroick Poem, etc*. Paris: Matthieu Guillemot.

Evrigenis, Ioannis D. 2014. *Images of Anarchy: The Rhetoric and Science in Hobbes's State of Nature*. Cambridge, UK: Cambridge University Press.

Evrigenis, Ioannis D. 2008. *Fear of Enemies and Collective Action*. Cambridge, UK: Cambridge University Press.

Filmer, Robert. 1652. *Observations concerning the Originall of Government, etc*. London: R. Royston.

Grotius, Hugo. 1631. *De Jure Belli ac Pacis Libri Tres, etc*. 2nd ed. Amsterdam: W. Blaev.

Grotius, Hugo. 1884. *On the Origin of the Native Races of America. A Dissertation*. Translated by Edmund Goldsmid. Edinburgh: privately printed.

Hobbes, Thomas. 1642. *De Cive*. London.

Hobbes, Thomas. 1647. *De Cive*. London.

Hobbes, Thomas. 1651. *Leviathan, or, The Matter, Forme, & Power of a Common-wealth Ecclesiasticall and Civill*. London.

Hobbes, Thomas. 1668. *Leviathan, sive De Materia, Forma, & Potestate Civitatis Ecclesiasticae et Civilis, in Thomae Hobbes Malmesburiensis Opera Philosophica, quae Latine scripsit, omnia*. Amsterdam.

Hobbes, Thomas. 1839–45 [*Opera Latina*]. *Thomae Hobbes Malmesburiensis Opera philosophica quae Latine scripsit omnia*, edited by William Molesworth. London: Bohm.

Hobbes, Thomas. 1840–1845. *The English Works of Thomas Hobbes of Malmesbury*, edited by William Molesworth. London: Bohm.

Hobbes, Thomas. 1969. *The Elements of Law, Natural and Politic*, edited by Ferdinand Tönnies, 2nd edn. London: Frank Cass.

Hobbes, Thomas. 1983. *De Cive: The Latin Version*, edited by Howard Warrender. Oxford: Clarendon Press.

Hobbes, Thomas. 1994. *The Correspondence*, edited by Noel Malcolm, 2 vols. Oxford: Clarendon Press.

Hobbes, Thomas. 1998. *De Cive*. Edited by Richard Tuck and Michael Silverthorne. Cambridge: Cambridge University Press.

Hobbes, Thomas. 2012. *Leviathan*, edited by Noel Malcolm. 3 volumes. Oxford, UK: The Clarendon Press.

Hoekstra, Kinch. Forthcoming. *Thomas Hobbes and the Creation of Order*. Oxford, UK: Oxford University Press.

Hume, David. 1987. "Of the Original Contract," in *Essays Moral, Political, and Literary*, edited by Eugene F. Miller, 645–687. Indianapolis, IN: Liberty Fund.

Kant, Immanuel. 1983. "Idea for a Universal History with a Cosmopolitan Intent," in *Perpetual Peace and Other Essays*, translated by Ted Humphrey, 29–40. Indianapolis, IN: Hackett Publishing Company.

Kingsbury, Susan Myra, ed. 1906–1935. *The Records of the Virginia Company of London*. 4 volumes. Washington, DC: US Government Printing Office.

Lucretius Carus, Titus. 1682. *T. Lucretius Carus the Epicurean Philosopher, His Six Books De natura rerum, etc.*, translated by Thomas Creech. Oxford, UK: L. Lichfield for Anthony Stephens.

Lucretius Carus, Titus. 1992. *De rerum natura*, translated by W.H.D. Rouse and revised by Martin F. Smith. Cambridge, MA: Harvard University Press.

Malcolm, Noel. 2002. *Aspects of Hobbes*. Oxford, UK: Oxford University Press.

Mill, John Stuart. 1978. *On Liberty*, edited by Elizabeth Rapaport. Indianapolis, IN: Hackett Publishing Company.

Nozick, Robert. 1974. *Anarchy, State, and Utopia*. New York: Basic Books.

Nye, Joseph S. 2005. *Understanding International Conflicts: An Introduction to Theory and History*, 5th ed. New York: Pearson/Longman.

[Parker, Samuel]. 1670. *A Discourse of Ecclesiastical Politie, etc.* London: John Martyn.

Pufendorf, Samuel. 1729. *Of the Law of Nature and Nations*. Translated by Basil Kennett. 4th ed. London: Printed for J. Walthoe, et al.

Rawls, John. 1971. *A Theory of Justice*. Cambridge, MA: Belknap Press of Harvard University Press.

Rousseau, Jean-Jacques. 2001. *Letter to Beaumont, Letters Written from the Mountain, and Related Writings*, translated by C. Kelly and J. R. Bush, edited by C. Kelly and E. Grace. Vol. 9, The Collected Writings of Rousseau. Hanover, NH: University Press of New England.

Templer, John. 1679. *Idea theologiæ Leviathanis*. London: E. Flesher for G. Morden.

Tenison, Thomas. 1671. *The Creed of Mr. Hobbes Examined; in a Feigned Conference between Him and a Student in Divinity*, 2nd ed. London: F. Tyton.

Thucydides. 1629. *Eight Bookes of the Peloponnesian Warre Written by Thvcydides the Sonne of Olorvs. Interpreted with Faith and Diligence immediately out of the Greeke by Thomas Hobbes Secretary to ye Late Earle of Deuonshire*, translated by T. Hobbes. London: Imprinted [at Eliot's Court Press] for Hen: Seile.

Vattel, Emer de. 1797. *The Law of Nations, or, Principles of the Law of Nature, applied to the Conduct and Affairs of Nations and Sovereigns*. London: G. G. and J. Robinson, 1797.

Vitoria, Francisco de. 1999. *On the American Indians*. In *Political Writings* (pp. 231–292), edited by Anthony Pagden & Jeremy Lawrance. Cambridge, UK: Cambridge University Press.

Ward, Seth. 1654. *Vindiciæ Academiarum containing, Some Briefe Animadversions upon Mr Websters Book, Stiled The Examination of Academies*. Oxford, UK: Leonard Lichfield for Thomas Robinson.

Ward, Seth. 1656. *In Thomæ Hobbii Philosophiam Exercitatio Epistolica, etc.* Oxford, UK: H. Hall for Richard Davis.

Wey Gómez, Nicolás. 2008. *The Tropics of Empire: Why Columbus Sailed to the Indies*. Cambridge, MA: MIT Press.

CHAPTER 11

··

HOBBES ON THE FAMILY

··

NANCY J. HIRSCHMANN

THE family is a topic that has engaged political theorists and philosophers since ancient times, yet it is frequently treated as a tangent or a "side issue"—or, even more commonly, completely ignored—by twentieth- and twenty-first-century interpreters of canonical political philosophy. Despite Plato's argument that the family had to be abolished in order for the good state to flourish and Aristotle's arguments that a man's performance as a good father was essential to his performance as a good citizen, the family has been seen in the modern era as lying outside of the domain of politics and hence political philosophy. This ideal achieved the status of explicit dogma in eighteenth-century Europe, when the ideology of "the sentimental family" arose to simultaneously acknowledge the social importance of the family and to completely knock it off the stage of legitimate political discourse.[1]

This ignorance of the family among secondary analysts is no less true of readers of Hobbes than it is of other canonical figures. Granted that Hobbes does not devote large sections of his major works to the topic of family relations, the family nevertheless plays a pivotal role in his construction of the state of nature and civil society. Yet *The Cambridge Companion to Hobbes*, for instance, has not a single entry on the family, and indeed the topic cannot even be found in the index. Major secondary analyses of Hobbes by Jean Hampton (1986), Richard Tuck (1989), Richard Flathman (1993), S. A. Lloyd (1992), and Quentin Skinner (2008) hardly mention the family. Others, such as Kavka (1986) and Baumgold (1988), have very brief discussions.[2] This is not to single out any particular theorists, philosophers, or historians for some kind of "sexism" in their treatment of Hobbes but rather to point out the ways in which *not* thinking about

---

[1] Okin 1982.

[2] I do not focus on older sources, such as Warrender (1957), Gauthier (1969), or Spragens (1973), all written before feminist theory had the significant impact that it had by the end of the 1980s. Hampton's book is notable for its section on "the battle of the sexes," but she mainly takes this as an example of the rationality of "giving in" in certain circumstances without applying this to the actual "battle" between men and women in Hobbes's state of nature.

the family is a normalized state for political philosophy. Bringing the family into the analysis of Hobbes requires a conscious effort.

Yet the family is important to Hobbes's political theory; as Joanne Wright suggests, Hobbes is "interested in families, and hence gender relations... insofar as they reveal something important about the nature of political relationships."[3] Family heads have an interest in ruling and controlling the behavior of the family members under them; the sovereign then only has to be concerned with ruling those family heads, teaching them not to rebel, and so forth. But in addition to facilitating the sovereign's ability to maintain order in this direct way, families teach children the values and ideals that they need to become "citizens" as well: law-abiding, security-loving, domesticated individuals. Hobbes says several times that one of the reasons that children owe obligations of gratitude to their parents is the "education" they receive from them. But this education is clearly less formal than university education; rather, it is a mode of instruction through the shaping of personality and understanding. The family is an institution that helps create individuals who want the very order that Hobbes wants citizens to desire.

Feminists, perhaps not surprisingly, have paid a great deal of attention to the family, though admittedly not many of them focus on Hobbes.[4] This is owing to, most logically, not only the historical—and at times sexist—association of women with families but also the more immediate fact that families generally (though not always for Hobbes [5]) entail children, which require women to produce. The question of where women fit into the family and how the family fits into the social contract in modern political thought is something that tends to leap out at feminists but to be ignored by most other commentators. Yet it is a central problem for Hobbes: What the family is, what it looks like, how it is formed, and how it operates all hinge on Hobbes's account of women. But one need not be a feminist in order to be intrigued by the puzzle of logic and history that Hobbes sets forth in his text surrounding the origin, structure, and function of the family.

1 THE NATURAL FAMILY

The puzzle starts in Hobbes's infamous state of nature, in which women are claimed by Hobbes to be profoundly equal to men in both intelligence and strength. As he

---

[3] Wright (2004), 78.

[4] The explosion of feminist theory in the 1970s was focused more on John Stuart Mill (Rossi 1970, Annas 1977), John Locke (Butler 1978, Shanley 1979), and of course Rousseau (Lange 1981). Susan Okin's *Women in Western Political Thought* (1979) considers Plato, Aristotle, Rousseau, and Mill, but ignores Hobbes altogether, as does Clarke and Lange's early anthology of feminist readings of the canon (Clark and Lange 1979). See, however, Elshtain (1981) and Flax (1983). Feminists have recently paid more attention to Hobbes; see Hirschmann and Wright (2013), Hirschmann (2007), Wright (2004), and Kahn (2004) in particular.

[5] One of Hobbes's definitions of a family is "a man and his servants," excluding not only mothers, as I discuss below, but also children.

notes in *De Cive*, "the inequality of their natural forces is not so great, that the man could get the dominion over the woman without war."[6] Similarly, in *Leviathan* he notes "there is not always that difference of strength or prudence between the man and the woman, as that the right [of "Dominion" over each other] can be determined without War."[7] So men and women are relatively equal in both strength and wit, and even if women on the whole are less strong than men, they are not so much weaker that men do not have to worry. Just as the physical or mental inferiority of some men to others is evened out by the fact that no one can dominate another for long, so women, to the extent that they may be physically less strong than most men, are nevertheless strong enough to make dominion an open question. Moreover, they have as much chance at being superior mentally as they do being inferior physically; a man may be stronger, for instance, but a woman may be more prudent. It is this claim of equality that leads Carole Pateman and Teresa Brennan to state that "in Hobbes' state of nature female individuals can be victors in the war of all against all just as often as male individuals."[8]

What this remarkable moment in modern political theory means for the family is that its familiar patriarchal form is not a given; we cannot assume that men automatically and unilaterally dominate women. Indeed, Hobbes seems to have set the stage for the egalitarian marriage that later feminists like John Stuart Mill were to advocate. Technically, of course, in the state of nature there can be no *marriage* of any kind by definition, there being "no Matrimoniall lawes."[9] However, given "the natural inclination of the Sexes, one to another," particularly "lust," men and women will likely have sexual contact, which means that children are likely to be produced.[10] Accordingly, Hobbes notes that "there be always two that are equally parents: the Dominion therefore over the child, should belong equally to both." However, he also claims that this "is impossible; for no man can obey two Masters."[11] Which parent, then, should prevail? In the state of nature, according to Hobbes, before "matrimonial laws" dictate parental rights and duties, dominion does not naturally follow from generation in and of itself. It follows from the work that a parent (or other person) does in caring for the child. Thus dominion over each child is to be determined by contract to determine who gets to (or has to) provide this care and protection; such contracts may grant dominion to the man or to the woman, or evenly divide the children among them, as Hobbes claims the Amazons contracted to keep female babies and send males back to their fathers.[12] Children are something that men and women both desire, according to Hobbes; after all, the "natural inclination" he attributes to humans is not only between men and women but

[6] Hobbes, *De Cive*, 9.10, 209.
[7] Hobbes, *Leviathan*, ch. 20, 253.
[8] Pateman and Brennan 2007, 79.
[9] Hobbes, *Leviathan*, ch. 20, 254.
[10] Ibid., ch. 20, 253.
[11] Ibid., ch. 20, 253.
[12] Ibid. ch. 20, 254.

of men and women "to their children" as well (though obviously such inclination is of a different, nonsexual character).[13] And as Hobbes notes in discussing succession, "men are presumed to be more inclined by nature, to advance their own children, than the children of other men."[14]

But as Hobbes's prominent example of the Amazons suggests, the family is not defined merely by reproduction or "generation." The family form we are familiar with today could be established only by contracts that articulate long-term and ongoing relationships between a man and a woman in relation to the children they share. But even that would be quite tricky, for it is difficult if not impossible to have reliable contracts in the state of nature without a sovereign to back them up: that is the whole point of leaving the state of nature and forming the social contract. Thus, that dominion over children may be determined by contract does not mean that such contracts were always—or even often—made. Hobbes notes that "If there be no Contract, the Dominion is in the Mother," because without matrimonial laws governing the sexual activity of women, paternity is uncertain: A man may want dominion over a child, but there is no way for him to know whether he is the biological father. Indeed, unless he has regular contact with the woman, he is unlikely even to know that a child has been born.[15]

By contrast, pregnancy and parturition give the mother dominion from the moment of birth, "since every man [which obviously here includes women] by law of nature hath right or propriety to his own body, the child ought rather to be the propriety of the mother (of whose body it is part, until the time of separation) than of the father."[16] Once children are born, mothers' dominion is reinforced if they "nourish" the child rather than "expose" it, just as men's dominion would be based on such action; but because the infant was originally part of the woman's body, Hobbes seems to suggest that women have a stronger title to dominion. Certainly, for at least the first six months of life, the infant is entirely dependent on her for sustenance, since in the days before formula, breast milk was the only food that newborns could ingest, thus again indicating that women's bodies are essential to children's lives, and serving as a factor in their obligations of obedience.[17] Moreover, by contrasting "nourish" to "expose," Hobbes seems to be saying that unless a woman actually casts a child aside and abandons it, dominion over it lies with her. Children, once they are born, then owe obedience to the mother for taking care of them and keeping them alive, literally with her body, and so her claim to dominion gains

---

[13] Ibid., ch. 20, 253.

[14] Ibid., ch. 19, 250.

[15] Ibid., ch. 20, 254. Certainly, a man does not need to be the biological father to desire dominion over a child, but the fact that Hobbes stresses the importance of contract over children resulting from sex suggests that he thinks that men will want dominion over their biological offspring.

[16] Hobbes, *Elements*, 2.4.1.

[17] This is another reason why, in order to gain dominion over a child, a man would have to gain dominion over its mother as well—or at least have some other lactating woman under his dominion. It is notable that Hobbes does not argue that women are uniquely vulnerable at the time of parturition and that men conquer them at that moment, thereby securing not only the child but the woman who is best suited to keep it alive. It is precisely the fact that he does not make such an argument that has made possible so much feminist interpretation of women's place in the family.

further strength vis-à-vis the logic of consent: The children want to live; therefore they must consent to obey whoever provides for them. Thus Hobbes says "It is to be presumed that he which giveth sustenance to another, whereby to strengthen him, hath received a promise of obedience in consideration thereof. For else it would be wisdom in men, rather to let their children perish, while they are infants, than to live in their danger or subjection, when they are grown."[18] Similarly, in *De Cive* Hobbes says, "If therefore she [the mother] breed him, because the state of nature is the state of war, she is supposed to bring him up on this condition; that being grown to full age he become not her enemy; which is, that he obey her."[19]

Whether this is an example of the logic of contract for Hobbes—since all infants wish to live, we can infer their consent, which then binds them in perpetuity—or an application of the fourth law of nature, gratitude, is not entirely clear. Schochet suggests that gratitude holds a kind of force in the state of nature that other laws do not hold, particularly in terms of the formation of families.[20] But whether such an argument could apply to a child too young to understand the nature of gratitude (not to mention the nature of contract) might mean that these two possible explanations collapse into one another: The child wants to live as all living humans do; the caretaker, usually the mother (because she can provide breast milk), keeps the child alive; therefore, the child has an obligation to obey the mother. But whatever the reasoning, what this tells us is that the first "families" in the state of nature would seem to be matriarchal, not patriarchal. In order for men to be the heads of patriarchal families, they must convince women to contract with them or defeat women in war—for if they defeat a woman, they get her children. Whether such contracts are obtained by institution or acquisition, however, "universally, if the society of the male and the female be such an union, as the one have subjected himself to the other, the children belong to him or her that commands."[21] But again, men's victory in such war is far from certain, given Hobbes's claims about women's equality, which is why he says "him *or her* that commands." Men who cannot beat women in war would need to work out some other sort of negotiation with women in relation to the children they produce; but such negotiations would not likely result in a patriarchal family.

2 THE PATRIARCHAL FAMILY

So why, then, does Hobbes define "the family" in *Leviathan* as "a man and his children; or ... a man and his servants; or ... a man, and his children, and servants together,"

---

[18]   Hobbes, *Elements* 2.4.3.
[19]   Hobbes, *De Cive*, 9.3.
[20]   Schochet 1990, 60. See also Schochet 1967 and 1975, ch. 12, and Hirschmann 2013.
[21]   Ibid., 9.5.

leaving the mother completely out of the picture?[22] It seems counterintuitive: If Hobbes wanted to claim that the natural family was patriarchal, wouldn't saying "a man, his wife, his children and servants" reinforce, rather than weaken, the patriarch's position? It is possible that by "man" Hobbes means "person" or "human," as he seems to have meant in the above-cited passage regarding the obligations that women's pregnancy and parturition impose upon their children. But in *De Cive*, Hobbes says, "A *father* with his *sons* and *servants*, grown into civil person by virtue of his paternal jurisdiction, is called a *family*," suggesting a specifically patriarchal form.[23] And in *The Elements of Law*, although women are mentioned in the definition of family— "the whole consisting of the father or the mother, or both, and of the children, and of the servants, is called a FAMILY"— even here, he immediately follows this with "wherein the father or master of the family is sovereign of the same and the rest (both children and servants equally) subjects," once again making wives and mothers invisible.[24]

Where do the women fit into this scheme? It is certainly possible—getting even more deeply into Hobbes's transgendering language—that Hobbes subsumed mothers under the title of "father" and "master," just as he used "he" to refer to pregnant women; in fact, the chapter in which women's dominion over children is discussed is titled "*Of Dominion PATERNALL, and DESPOTICAL*,"[25] and throughout that chapter Hobbes includes mother-right under specifically "paternal dominion." But this radically different meaning of the term would apply only in cases where women were the "lords" of their children to begin with. The place of mothers in the *patriarchal* family is the more obvious puzzle, because her unique position in such a family is that she still presumably has duties to care for her—now his—children.

In this capacity, it is most likely that women are subsumed under the category "servant." Historically, the Roman term *familia* refers to "the total number of slaves belonging to one man,"[26] and we know that Hobbes references Roman ideals throughout his work,[27] so it could make sense for Hobbes to consider women within that category. Although Alice Clark may be correct in her general assessment of married women's status in Hobbes's day—that although "the wife was subject to her husband... she was by no means regarded as his servant"—Mendelson and Crawford maintain that by law, women working in their husbands' trades did so precisely as "servants" as opposed to widows or even married women who worked in different trades from their husbands,[28] so there is legal support for such social consideration. Hobbes's texts certainly suggest it as a logical solution to this puzzle. He maintains that when someone is vanquished, in order to avoid death, he or she will contract to be a servant, in which case the victor

---

[22] Hobbes, *Leviathan*, ch. 20, 257.
[23] Hobbes, *De Cive*, 9.10.
[24] Hobbes, *Elements*, 2.4.10.
[25] Hobbes, *Leviathan*, ch. 20, 251.
[26] Engels 1972, 121.
[27] Skinner 2008.
[28] Clark 1968, 12, Mendelson and Crawford 1998, 330.

"shall have the use" of "his life, and the liberty of his body."[29] In this, of course, it is not the conquest itself that produces the right of dominion, Hobbes says, but the covenants that the victor is able to exact from the vanquished under duress. It is in this specific way—not the simple fact of a patriarchal head—that the family is "a little Monarchy."[30] Moreover, Hobbes defines a servant as anyone "who is obliged to obey the commands of any man before he knows what he will command him"—a description that could easily cover wives in patriarchal marriage.[31]

If that is so, it would seem that, rather than equal partners to a reciprocal contract, women are either vanquished, and hence contract with men to be servants, or else they are not vanquished and do not enter into contracts with men at all—that is, they are excluded from families altogether. This might seem to contradict Hobbes's earlier egalitarian views on the ability of women and men to contract equally for dominion of their children, let alone their prior dominion. And given the unlikeliness of women's complete exclusion from the family, the conceptual question of *how* women *became* servants is itself a problem. It is their status as servants—people who consent to the dominion of another and who agree to obey and abide by that other's decisions—that constitutes the crux of feminist debate over the status of women and the constitution of the family in Hobbes's theory.

This odd disjuncture between the "warrior women" that seem to populate Hobbes's state of nature and the subordinate or even invisible wives and mothers that make the family possible is what prompted one of the first feminist analyses of Hobbes, when Carole Pateman and Teresa Brennan asked "why it is that a free and equal female individual should always be assumed to place herself under the authority of a free and equal male individual?" The fact that this had not been addressed prior to their 1979 article made it, in their terms, "a very embarrassing question" for Hobbessian commentators.[32] And indeed, the very few Hobbessian analysts who had commented on the family up to this point did not resolve it, or even acknowledge it in some cases. For instance, Gordon Schochet argued in 1967 that although Hobbes rejected much of Robert Filmer's patriarchal theory of monarchical authority, Hobbes himself nonetheless based his theory of sovereign rule on a different understanding of patriarchal authority. The family, in Schochet's reading, plays a vital role in Hobbes's theory, for it is the primary way in which states get their start, whether by institution (men and women agreeing to unite for the production of children) or acquisition (war resulting in conquest). That is, the way in which human society formed had first to be through

---

[29]   Hobbes, *Leviathan*, ch. 20, 255.

[30]   Ibid., ch. 20, 257.

[31]   Hobbes, *De Cive*, 206. Stanlick (2001) makes a similar point, as does Pateman (1991, 64), in which she says that she has reconsidered the earlier assertion made by Brennan and Pateman that the "possibility. . . that the wife has the same status as a servant. . . . is unlikely. . . for the master-servant relationship, like slavery, originates in force" (Brennan and Pateman 2007, 59. I reference the 2007 reprint of this article, which originally appeared in *Political Studies* in 1979.).

[32]   Brennan and Pateman, 2007, 52.

families, which then formed the foundation for larger associations such as tribes, villages, and eventually states. Thus, the "state of nature" is not populated by "abstract individuals" but rather contains families, on this reading, in which rules of primitive civil society prevail:

> It was as if the state of nature extended only to the door of the household but did not pass over the threshold, for Hobbes claimed that there was private property in the family but not in the state of nature. There can only be private ownership where there is sufficient security, a qualification that precluded the state of nature. But a family, Hobbes wrote, "is a little city."[33]

The logical structure of the state of nature, on this reading, involved a population of heads of families, or patriarchs, who were the individuals engaged in a state of war of all against all and who were the parties to any kind of social contract. Accordingly, "The elemental social unit for Hobbes was not the individual but the family."[34]

The heads of these families were always men, according to Schochet; by the time "man" arrives at the social contract, each contractor is already the ruler of "his" family, and his consent to a sovereign authority binds those family members. Moreover, those family members, because they owe obligations of obedience to their patriarchal family leader, thereby owe similar obedience to the sovereign. The family, accordingly, is inherently political in nature, and the apparent bifurcation of public and private that sits at the heart of liberalism is in fact illusory; their imbrication is instead central to liberalism, its ideological declarations notwithstanding. Indeed, what Schochet identified in particular was the overtly *patriarchal* nature of the family in early modern British thought, and of the state as a direct result. As Brennan and Pateman were later to note, social contract theory and patriarchal theory were not polar opposites of free individuals versus constrained ones; rather, they were being developed at approximately the same time and indeed partly in response to one another. But Schochet failed to address the "very embarrassing question" of why such families had to be patriarchal, dependent on women's freely chosen subordination.

Schochet's argument stimulated a few responses. In the following year R.W.K. Hinton published "Husbands, Fathers, and Conquerors," which highlights Hobbes's granting of equal status to women simply as a means of making their subordination in the family invisible. Hinton posited that Hobbes strategically pays lip service to women's equality in order to make fathers' absolute power the product of consent, thereby asserting that men were the exclusive parties to the social contract on behalf of all family members.[35] Like Schochet, Hinton maintains that the patriarchal family exists in the state of nature, prior to the social contract. But although Hinton

---

[33] Schochet 1967, 440.
[34] Ibid., 443.
[35] Hinton 1968, 55, 57, 64.

discusses the rationale for Hobbes's argument that children consent to "parental" authority[36] and also substitutes *parents* and *parental* for Hobbes's explicit usage of *father* and *paternal* several times,[37] he, like Schochet, never considers why free and equal women in the state of nature would voluntarily consent, through a marriage contract, to subordination to their husbands, brushing away the issue by calling fathers' power in the family "natural."[38]

Several years later, as feminist readings of other canonical theorists were starting to emerge, Richard Chapman argued in the *American Political Science Review* that Hobbes was not a patriarchalist at all: Rather than the family being a model for the state, "the state is the model for the family." The family, moreover, serves the state, particularly as it "performs a vital service in political education."[39] In defense of his rejection of patriarchalism, Chapman corrals some of the arguments I have noted above: He acknowledges that "the mother may govern as well" as the father; he claims that "a man and a woman are equals, according to Hobbes's view, and it is a matter of indifference to him which of them rules."[40] But a few sentences later Chapman notes Hobbes's definition of a family as a man and his children without commenting on the apparent contradiction he has inadvertently identified.[41] Indeed, after noting the logical problem of basing father-right on generation and claiming "there is no theoretical reason why a 'free' woman should confine herself to one man," he oddly comments "If no man is willing to exercise dominion over the child, then the mother is the 'lord' of the child," as if mothers gain dominion only if fathers decline it, completely reversing the logic of what Hobbes has described.[42] He bases this on Hobbes's acknowledgment of the "general practice" of patriarchal families; but he fails to note that Hobbes, when he says with an almost visible shrug that "for the most part Common-wealths have been erected by the Fathers, not by the Mothers of families,"[43] is not *recommending* father-right and patriarchy as much as *observing* it.

Chapman then spends the rest of this section, titled "Consent," explaining children's obligations of obedience to parents with no mention of the wife or mother except to claim that Hobbes follows the Roman model of the *patria potestus*, in which women, even after marriage, remained subject to their fathers' authority unless the marriage occurred "with *manus*, that is, accompanied by a ceremony in which the woman was transferred from the domestic cult of her father's family to that of her husband's."[44] This,

---

[36] Ibid., 56.

[37] Ibid., 56, 57, 64–65.

[38] Ibid., 55.

[39] Chapman 1975, 78–79.

[40] Ibid. 78, note 29; 80.

[41] Ibid., 80.

[42] Ibid.

[43] Hobbes, *Leviathan* ch. 20, 253.

[44] Chapman 1975, 83; see also Grubbs 2002, 20.

however, Brennan and Pateman maintain, seems "hardly plausible" as an account of Hobbes, because "everyone knew in the seventeenth century that wives and husbands were part of one family."[45]

If Chapman is correct that Hobbes's brand of—to invert Eisenstein's term— "anti-patriarchal patriarchalism"[46] is founded on consent, he leaves unanswered, indeed even unasked, Brennan and Pateman's "embarrassing question" of *why* women would consent to such an arrangement in the first place. The closest Chapman comes to an answer is a passage from *The Elements of Law*: "The man, to whom for the most part the woman yieldeth the government, hath for the most part, also, the sole right and dominion over the children."[47] But that begs rather than answers the question of *why* natural women would "yield." Nor do Schochet or Hinton confront the problem that feminists were soon to identify concerning women's place in the family. All of these theorists assumed, without defense or analysis, women's subordination to husbands in the state of nature.

Certainly, one might respond, if the state is to be the model for the family, as Chapman argues, or if the family is the model for the state, as Schochet suggests, then that family has to be authoritarian: Hobbes is best-known for his argument that sovereign authority in any society, regardless of political form, had to be absolute. But why that family must be *patriarchal* is less clear. After all, though Hobbes believes democracy to be more vulnerable to internal strife, the fact that he does allow for the possibility of an absolutist authoritarian democratic government—and certainly an aristocratic one—makes one wonder why Hobbes dismissed the idea that husbands and wives could share equally in dominion over children. Indeed, Hobbes refers repeatedly throughout *Leviathan* to the sovereign as a "man, or assembly of men" suggesting that although the latter may be less stable and convenient than the former, it is a common form of authority. Certainly he favors monarchy over aristocracy or democracy, but the latter are not dismissed with the immediacy with which Hobbes dismisses the possibility of shared parental

---

[45] Brennan and Pateman 2007, 59. Chapman does point out that at the end of Part II of *Leviathan* "Hobbes expresses Platonic disillusionment with his work" because "it differs too widely from contemporary practice" (87), which could support his argument that Hobbes's family in the state of nature coheres to the *patria potestas*; for once the social contract was instigated, the *pater* would not have to wield such powerful authority, letting wives attain the comparatively equal status they held in early- to-mid-seventeenth-century England, particularly in their economic power; some women even voted before 1642, especially leading up to the civil war (Mendelson and Crawford 1998, ch. 7). This situation eroded by the end of the century, when women were more uniformly subordinate to men (although, as Mendelson and Crawford note, even in Hobbes's period married women had somewhat less freedom and power, economically and politically, than did single women and particularly widows). But if that is the case, then Chapman's central thesis, that the authoritarian state must be the model for the family, rather falls apart.

[46] Eisenstein (1981) calls Locke a "patriarchal anti-patriarchalist," which Pateman then takes up in relation to Hobbes, saying "he is a patriarchalist who rejects paternal right" (1989, 446). But Chapman is highlighting the reverse: patriarchal power based on the free consent of individuals under it.

[47] Hobbes, *Elements*, 2.4.7, 133.

dominion.[48] Was it because Hobbes was really concerned with women and wives, and not just children, as the subjects of dominion in the family?[49]

Although, as just noted, Hobbes makes offhand references to the ways in which laws commonly determine father-right over mother-right and seems to accept marriage as a given in civil society, he leaves open, without any direct explanation, the larger and prior question of why patriarchal marriage is necessary in the first place. This may be because the logic of his argument contradicts the institution of marriage, and particularly patriarchal marriage, in which women are subordinate to men. Hobbes's arguments about contracts for dominion over children contain a certain circularity that goes beyond the paradoxical character of contracts in the state of nature. That is, without a sovereign to back up contracts, we cannot rely on others to fill their side of the deal. As Gregory Kavka suggests, the lack of trust in the state of nature creates a negative feedback loop: A and B can promise each other an exchange of goods or services or a promise of behavior, but it is in the interest of neither to perform first, because the danger is that the other will take the goods the one has provided and not fulfill his end of the agreement in turn. Certainly, Kavka notes, Hobbes argues that once A performs first, B has a rational reason to perform in turn, because otherwise he will gain a reputation for unreliability and others will not be willing to contract with him in the future. But that does not change the irrationality of A's performing first.[50]

But contracts over children are not only unenforceable without a sovereign, just like other contracts; they are often unimaginable. That is, if there were no long-term sexual relationships in the state of nature *prior* to marriage, then men and women would have no cause—or even opportunity—to enter into contracts over children in the first place, as a woman would be long gone before she knew she was pregnant, making it impossible for a man to know that he fathered a given child. Hobbes's example of the Amazons is more an exception than the rule. As Susanne Sreedhar maintains, Hobbes likely based his reference to the Amazons on a story related by Quintus Curtius in which the Amazon queen Thalestris seeks out Alexander the Great because she wishes

[48] One possible explanation for Hobbes's dismissal of shared authority in marriage is that aristocratic and democratic assemblies can have an odd number to avoid deadlock, whereas marriage is a dyad. But Hobbes explicitly notes that assembly members can fail to show up some days—so even if there was an odd number to start, one could not guarantee an odd number every time there was a vote (*Leviathan*, ch. 16, 19). Further, he says that one of the disadvantages of an assembly is that it can disagree with itself, even to the point of civil war--the marital analogy being divorce—suggesting the likelihood of deadlock (*Leviathan*, ch. 19). He also mentions that deadlock can result in a decision by default (*Leviathan*, ch. 18). Alternately, one could imagine that in such an assembly, in the case of a tie there could be an agreed default rule for tie-breaking; but again, in the family analogy, a wife could be favored by such a default rule as much as a husband. Finally, even if the above arguments were rejected, one could get around the dyad of husband and wife in the context of the larger extended families that Schochet, for instance, posits in the state of nature, with, say, a council of elders that includes women and specifies an odd number. Thanks to Kinch Hoekstra for raising these possible objections.

[49] Pateman (1989) argues this as well.

[50] Kavka (1986), 137–40. This is not to say that Kavka believe Hobbes is correct, only that this is what Hobbes argues.

to mate with him for reproduction (based on his reputed physique, in which she is disappointed). She offers to let him keep a boy child and will keep it herself if it is a girl (the Amazons did not keep boy children because they grow up to be men, which would threaten their order).[51] Certainly if any woman, Amazon or not, negotiated an agreement prior to copulation, then the man with whom she contracted would know that he was the father (assuming that she kept her end of the agreement and did not have sex with another man in the meantime). But as Sreedhar notes, Thalestris does not do so to subordinate herself to Alexander, nor does she do so because of lust; even though Alexander "serv[es] her passion," that is not Thalestris's primary goal. It is having a female child. Given that she is a queen, presumably news of her pregnancy would travel and it would be difficult to hide, thus making it logical for her to fulfill her end of the bargain (following Kavka's reasoning about second performance affecting reputation); as a queen, she might be concerned for her reputation as someone who does not betray those with whom she makes agreements. But in the state of nature, where it is more likely that a woman and man would have sex for the purpose of satisfying lust alone,[52] pregnancy would be discovered only well after the fact, at which point, unless there was already a society established, the man would be ignorant. And unless the woman is already subordinate to the man, she has no reason to let him know, as that would provide him with a motive to seek dominion over the child. Indeed, in the account of the Amazons found in Justin's epitome of the *Philippic History of Pompeius Trogus*—with which Hobbes would likely have been familiar, as it was commonly included in the seventeenth-century curriculum—their practice was to kill male infants, not send them to their fathers.[53]

So marriage, in order to come into being, requires the pre-existence of the very condition that it creates; and the origin of the family is quite a puzzle for Hobbes's logic. This is something that most commentators have overlooked, even though it is a clear example of the standard Hobbesian problem of first beginnings. That they solve it by positing the patriarchal family as natural assumes what it must prove. Certainly the fact that Hobbes postulates the possibility of such contracts indicates that he must believe that marriage and families, or something resembling them, *can* exist in the state of nature, notwithstanding the absence of matrimonial law. But if commentators are correct that such families are always patriarchal, then Hobbes has defined away

---

[51] Sreedhar 2013, 263–65.

[52] In Herodotus's account of the Amazons, the Scythian men similarly wooed the Amazons because of "their strong desire to obtain children from so notable a race" (Herodotus, *Persian Wars*, "Melpomene" 4.111). These men, however, do not gain any sort of superiority over their female mates and indeed go home to obtain their inheritances and move with the Amazons to a new land, where they live together as a new tribe, the Sauromatae, where the men and women hunt together and wear similar clothing. On Herodotus' *Histories*, see Hazewindus (2004), esp. ch. 5 on his account of the Amazons.

[53] Justinus (1853). Thanks to Kirstie M. McClure for this reference and the Rawlinson edition of Herodotus cited in the previous note. On texts common to the seventeenth-century education, see Watson (1901), 214.

women's contracting abilities before he has even declared them in his text. Claims about Hobbes's abstract individualism notwithstanding, he acknowledges some ability of natural beings to form "confederacies" in the state of nature, for "no man can hope by his own strength, or wit, to defend himselfe from destruction, without the help of Confederates."[54] And in his exchange with Bramhall, Hobbes declares, "It is very likely to be true, that since the creation there never was a time in which mankind was totally without society."[55] He cites this as the major reason why people might want to keep covenants in the state of nature—or at least to perform second once someone else has performed first, as Kavka suggests—for those who do not keep them will be unable to form such alliances. And this could be taken to suggest why people might want to establish marriage contracts and families. After all, "conjugall affection" is one of the three things "that are dearest to a man," second only to "his own life, & limbs," but ranking higher than even "riches and means of living."[56] It is not entirely certain whether the term *conjugal affection* refers specifically to sex; but given that Hobbes is not averse to naming "lust" in conjunction with his remarks about the "natural inclination" of men and women toward their children, this passage could be taken to suggest that Hobbes believed that family is central to human nature. But again, none of this leads directly to *patriarchal* marriage or family. So we are still left with Pateman and Brennan's "embarrassing question."

3 RETHINKING THE ROLE OF THE FAMILY

What about love? Could that explain women's apparent voluntary subordination? In *De Cive* Hobbes says that the fourth way in which a woman may transfer sovereignty over her children is "if a woman for society's sake give herself to a man on this condition, that he shall bear the sway,"[57] implying that women, more than men, seek social relations and perhaps love. In several places Hobbes equates love with desire rather than sympathetic emotion, the difference being only that "by Desire, we always signifie the Absence of the Object; by Love, most commonly the Presence of the same."[58] But Hobbes does seem to believe that people can love each other in the more emotional sense of the word, and especially their children,[59] and he says that "conjugall affection" is important to humans, as just noted. However, why would women be more vulnerable to love than men? Although it makes sense for natural man to propose a contract that denies all other men access to his beloved, natural woman's prudence would cause her

---

[54] Hobbes, *Leviathan* ch. 15, 204. On Hobbes's individualism, see Macpherson (1962) and Flax (1983).

[55] Hobbes, "Questions Concerning Liberty, Necessity, and Chance," 78.

[56] Hobbes, *Leviathan*, ch. 30, 382.

[57] Hobbes, *De Cive*, 9.4–5.

[58] Hobbes, *Leviathan*, ch. 6, 119.

[59] Hobbes, *Elements*, 1.9.17.

to think twice about a commitment that subordinates her and leaves her male partner still free to consort with other women. That is, the contract may stipulate monogamy for both parties, but if the woman is subordinate to the man, she cannot really enforce that term of the contract. Indeed, Patapan maintains that "in his [Hobbes's] view erotic love is generally bad for human beings." [60] More moderately, we can certainly argue that within the framework that Hobbes establishes, love is an emotion that is more likely to *grow out of* families than it is to *found* them. It would be foolish to fall in love—or at least to act on such feelings—in the state of nature, without laws to protect one's dealings with an intimate. Note in Curtius's account of Thalestris that she rationally calculates the desirability of mating and wastes no sentiment, although she clearly has "passion" to satisfy. By contrast, the trust—or at least predictability—that sovereign law, including matrimonial law, fosters for Hobbesian men and women could allow such love to be expressed and even felt more freely.

One common answer to the paradox of women's subordination, Hobbes's references to the powerful Amazons notwithstanding, is that women trade obedience for protection. Pateman herself argues that

> When a woman becomes a mother and decides to become a lord and raise her child, her position changes; she is put at a slight disadvantage against men, since now she has her infant to attend to. Conversely, a man obtains a slight advantage over her and is then able to defeat the woman he had initially to treat with as an equal.

Therefore "mother-right can never be more than fleeting."[61] It is because of this prior subjection, she maintains, that the sexual contract precedes and indeed founds the social contract, which is formed specifically and exclusively by men. Other feminist commentators agree, for similar reasons: Pregnancy makes women vulnerable to attack, as Nancy Stanlick argues; having infants makes women even more vulnerable to attack, as Brennan and Pateman maintain; women want to care for their children even though it makes them vulnerable, as Karen Green maintains, even "limitedly altruistic"; women are simply less strong than men regardless of reproductive status, as Audrey McKinney suggests; and women are less hostile and atomistic than men, precisely because of their role in reproduction, and thus are not as aggressive as men, as both Jane Flax and Christine Di Stefano argue.[62] And certainly that is at least the implied rationale that Schochet, Hinton, and Chapman rely on.

But this reading misses certain features of Hobbes's argument about women and thereby misunderstands his view of the family and how it comes about. The most obvious is the concept of "protection": Why would natural woman trade obedience for protection? After all, Hobbes observes, those who claim that women's physical weakness

---

[60] Patapan 2003, 820.

[61] Pateman 1989, 457.

[62] Stanlick 2001, Brennan and Pateman 2007, Green 1994, McKinney 1993, Flax 1983, DiStefano 1983. Many of these sources argue for several of these various points, in different configurations.

ensures father right "show not, neither can I find out by what coherence, advantage of so much strength... should generally and universally entitle the father to a propriety in the child, and take it away from the mother."[63] As I have already noted, even if women's strength is inferior, Hobbes says: So what? They are not so weak that they could not subdue a man. And even if they could not, they would most likely think they could, as women suffer from "Vainglory, a foolish over-rating of their own worth" as much as men.[64] And at any rate such minor difference in strength has no relationship to their dominion over children, which proceeds not from strength but from preservation.

Furthermore, it would seem irrational for a woman to give over such powers to men without more of a guarantee than a simple reassurance from a single man, her husband. As Hobbes notes,

> the mutual aid of two or three men is of very little security; for the odds on the other side, of a man or two, giveth sufficient encouragement to an assault. And therefore before men have sufficient security in the help of one another, their number must be so great, that the odds of a few which the enemy may have, be no certain and sensible advantage.[65]

One man cannot offer a woman, much less a woman and her children, much protection at all; men would have to institute some sort of allegiance with each other in order to entice multiple women to join their protective society. But then why wouldn't a woman build her own confederacy, indeed one with other women, and have as many children as possible, who will then grow up to be under her command? If the Amazons had any lesson to offer Hobbes, it should have been that.

This would then raise the possibility that women are parties to the social contract, even as heads of their own confederacies or families; and this in turn offers a different reading of the relationship of the family to the state. This reading starts with the notion that mother-right is *not* a disability in Hobbes's state of nature, as most commentators assume, but a power. And indeed it is *because* it is a power that men want to conquer women. There is no reason to assume, as Pateman and others do, that caring for a child makes a woman less able to defend herself unless we radically alter Hobbesian assumptions, according to which a woman would abandon an infant if she found that it jeopardized her security. Or more likely, given that abandoning it would allow someone else to nourish it and thereby claim its allegiance, she would probably kill it. Indeed, Hobbes says that the parent who raises the child and thereby gains dominion over it "may alienate them, that is, assign his or her dominion, by selling or giving them in adoption or servitude to others; or may pawn them for hostages, kill them for rebellion, or sacrifice them for peace, by the law of nature, when he or she, in his or her conscience, think it to be necessary."[66] This is hardly the vision of nurturing motherhood assumed by most

---

[63] Hobbes, *Elements*, 2.4.2.
[64] Hobbes, *Leviathan*, ch. 27, 341.
[65] Hobbes, *Elements*, 1.19.3.
[66] Hobbes, *Elements*, 2.4.8.

readers. The idea proffered by Pateman and others that "when a woman becomes a mother and decides to raise her child," such a decision is irrevocable, is simply unsupported by Hobbes's text. A woman would simply revoke her decision as soon as it put her life in danger.

This is not something that most commentators consider. Indeed, Pateman asserts that having a child is such a liability that if Hobbesian women were truly rational egoists, they would never raise children in the first place—perhaps, even, they would never have them. She says this to point out the illogicality of Hobbes's argument, because the human race would cease to exist.[67] But not only does that ignore the short-term self-interest of Hobbesian men and women, particularly lust, which ensures that children would always be born,[68] it also underplays the instrumental value that children can serve adults in the state of nature. After all, why are children seen as an asset in the first place? Why would men want to secure dominion over women in order to secure dominion over children? The most obvious answer is confederacy and obedience; if children owe obligations of obedience to parents for keeping them alive—obligations that persist into the children's adulthood—such obligations are a rich power resource.

In other words, a more likely scenario than abandoning or killing the child is that, under the power of confederacy, the mother and child would work together to defeat the man. We know that Hobbes believes such confederacy to be superior to those adults form with peers, because children enter the age of consciousness with the regularity of obedience already in place; Hobbes certainly knew enough about children, having tutored them, to understand the ways in which they are psychologically beholden to parents. And in the state of nature, children would not need to be very old to serve as useful confederates; after all, a two-year-old could distract an adult, even serving as "bait," and a five-year-old could steal. The view that infants are burdens pure and simple, placing women at such a disadvantage that it cannot be overcome, reflects romantic visions of childhood and motherhood that did not pertain in Hobbes's day but rather developed in the eighteenth and nineteenth centuries.[69] In Hobbes's formula, rather than being a liability, motherhood provides a natural source of power that would give women a strategic advantage over men. Accordingly, motherhood cannot be the cause of woman's downfall in the way Pateman and other feminists maintain.

But this still does not answer Pateman and Brennan's embarrassing question; it instead rejects Hobbes's apparent acceptance of patriarchy. The answer hinges, I believe, on flipping the standard interpretation on its head. Namely, *the patriarchal family does not precede the social contract but follows from it.* This is true in a literal sense, of course—Hobbes explicitly says that there are no "Matrimoniall Lawes" in the state of

---

[67] Pateman 1988, 49.

[68] Hobbes says that women feel lust as well as men, thus undermining an implicit foundation of Pateman's (1988) thesis that the act of rape underlies the sexual, and hence social, contract. In her view, Hobbesian women would have to never agree to sex because it risks subordination; but, as I have suggested, that seriously underestimates the strength and wit, not to mention desire, of the Hobbesian woman.

[69] Plotz 2001; Heywood 2001.

nature, as I have already noted. But what I mean is that although some patriarchal families might exist in the state of nature, so might many other family forms exist as well, including matriarchies in which men are subordinate, confederacies of women from which men are altogether absent, and even egalitarian relationships between men and women. The heterosexual patriarchal family can exist naturally, but it cannot become a *regularized* norm until *after* the social contract is instigated. The fact that women would never, as Pateman maintains, "agree to create a civil law that secures their permanent subjections as wives" misses a central point: When we consent to the social contract, we consent to everything the sovereign decides, and we do not have a say about what laws the sovereign passes. We have no idea ahead of time whether he or she will decree mother-right or father-right, monogamy or polygamy, or even any family structure at all.[70] All we know is that, as individuals in the state of nature, we are desperate for relief, which can come only through a "confederacy" that is seemingly impossible to maintain without a common authority over us. Even women's "natural" confederacy with children might have a degree of uncertainty; children can always be ungrateful and turn on their caregiver, as wrong as this might be in Hobbes's view. However, having children and experiencing some of the advantages of confederacy could lead women to see the logic of the social contract, just as scholars like Schochet and Hinton maintain that families lead fathers to see the benefits of a sovereign authority.

Given this, it makes sense within Hobbes's theory for women to consent to the social contract, his passages about "fathers" consenting to the social contract notwithstanding. Only then, *after* women have consented to the social contract, could women's wholesale subjugation come into play. It is logical for a sovereign concerned with order and security to command an authoritarian family structure, for in this way the sovereign channels humans' natural desire for dominion into a formal structure that feeds the sovereign's interests: that is, the sovereign need not control everyone directly, but only heads of families, who in turn would keep their respective family members in line. Without an authoritarian family structure, the danger of people's interactions in daily commerce and the like degenerating into civil chaos is much greater; families could provide a structure of discipline, habituating men and women to obedience and curbing their natural hostility and distrust.

Why the sovereign would legislate a *patriarchal* family structure makes less logical sense but has textual support. Hobbes notes in a number of places how disruptive men are over sexual issues in the state of nature; in quarrels of competition in the state of nature, men "use Violence, to make themselves masters of other men's persons, wives, children, and cattell."[71] Similarly, "the ancient Heathen did not think they Dishonoured, but greatly Honoured the Gods, when they introduced them in their Poems, committing Rapes, Thefts, and other great, but unjust, or unclean acts."[72]

---

[70] *Leviathan*, ch. 21, 271.

[71] Hobbes, *Leviathan* ch. 13, 185.

[72] Ibid., ch. 10, 156.

If men, but not women, are so disruptive, it could make sense for the sovereign to write laws establishing father-right in order to secure peace among men. Patriarchal matrimonial law would thus help secure peace by establishing territorial or property rights over women—and perhaps even more important, over the products of women's bodies, namely children—which the sword of Leviathan now upholds.[73] The feminist objection that women would not consent to such subordination—such an obvious problem in the state of nature—dissolves in civil society. Such consent would not have to be "given," since citizens have already authorized all of the sovereign's actions when they consent to the social contract. In this, the family does for women what the social contract does for men; it takes away their ultimate natural powers. That the social contract alone is insufficient to tame women's powers—in that the sovereign must also authorize the patriarchal family—is the only relevant difference between the sexes. For rather than being inferior in the state of nature, women are at least potentially, if not actually, superior via their powers of reproduction and the natural confederacies that result.

Of course, the logical (if somewhat humorous) objection is that if men are so combative, the women should simply sit back and let them kill each other and then step in to subordinate the remainders. But that would assume a level of coordination among women that Hobbes does not grant anyone in the state of nature; women are as caught up in the chaos of the state of nature as men are—although it is interesting to note that in Justin's *Epitome*, when the Scythian men are killed in battle, their wives, who become the Amazons, kill the men who stayed behind so that all of the women will be equal.[74] Indeed, it is puzzling why Hobbes did not recommend matriarchy from the start, because that would remove much of men's motive for dominion over women and hence a major source of conflict. Hobbes's reference to the minor disadvantages women supposedly have compared with men, such as weeping, demonstrates the weakness of his argument when it comes to differentiating among citizens in terms of gender. Although Hobbes can claim men's consent to the sovereign because the state of war unconditionally threatens all, women's consent to men's dominion cannot be rationally deduced in the state of nature because reproduction does not threaten women. Or, to be more precise, to the degree that reproduction does threaten women (e.g. women can die in childbirth), the patriarchal family does not on the whole protect them.

So perhaps it is not men who are so disruptive and dangerous after all: perhaps it is women. That is, perhaps Hobbes defines the family without reference to women, and under a patriarchal authority, in order to suppress its most dangerous and disruptive element. Children are much less of a threat to the rule of the father than wives are to the rule of husbands because children owe a debt to parents for "preserving" and educating them, and once grown they presumably have things to gain in the form of inheritance and succession. But women would seem to have nothing to gain by sticking to a

---

[73] Hirschmann 1992, 42–44.
[74] Justinus 1853.

contract of servitude unless it was backed by the sword of Leviathan. This is especially so when women stop having babies; if we accept the standard view, in which having babies puts women at a physical disadvantage, then when the children grow up, women are back on an equal footing with men. By that time, Hobbes might say, they have consented to the husband's authority, but there is no clear reason why they cannot change the terms of the contract if they are still in the state of nature.

Thus the patriarchal authoritarian family accomplishes a significant task for the sovereign, reducing the danger of differences, particularly those specific kinds of differences pertaining to sex and reproduction that women display. Within the family, children and servants—including wives—are subjected and bound to their master without qualification. And it is this aspect of the family that provides the strongest model for civil society. In *Elements*, in the middle of discussing the family, including "covenants of cohabitation" between men and women and parental dominion over children, Hobbes notes that "the subjection of them who institute a commonwealth amongst themselves, is no less absolute, than the subjection of servants"—like wives—except that they have "greater hope" because they have voluntarily entered the contract, rather than "upon compulsion."[75] He says this to explain that children are "freemen" rather than "servants" not by right but only by the "natural indulgence of parents.... And this was the reason, that the name that signifieth children, in the Latin tongue is *liberi*, which also signifieth freemen."[76] The next paragraph then offers Hobbes's definition of the family, cited earlier, that includes mothers—the only such occurrence in his major texts.

Because Hobbes here explicitly includes mothers in the family, women might seem to be included in the category of "parents" who indulge their children, suggesting women's power in the family. Yet just a few paragraphs earlier, Hobbes denies this by saying that only one person can rule in the family, "and therefore the man, to whom for the most part the woman yieldeth the government, hath for the most part, also, the sole right and dominion over the children."[77] With women thus denied the status of "freemen" that even their (male?) children attain, their servitude might seem to eliminate them from citizenship. Yet at the same time Hobbes is also implying that women are the ultimate model of Hobbesian civil subordination—for what Hobbes does to women, he seeks to do to all men, namely, subordinate them so thoroughly and bind them so effectively to that subordination through their free choice that the sovereign need make active use of force only infrequently.

Thus, although the picture Hobbes seems to draw indicates that the family, and particularly the patriarchal family, predates the social contract—as Schochet, Hinton, and many feminists argue—the logical tenets of his theory do not require it or even assert it with any consistency; indeed, his theory becomes stronger and more consistent if the social contract predates the patriarchal family. But of course such "explanation" is made possible only by virtue of Hobbes's normative framework, wherein he clearly

[75] Hobbes, *Elements*, 2.4.9.
[76] Ibid.
[77] Ibid., 2.4.7.

endorses both men's and women's subjugation to the sovereign as conducive to social order and peace. The family, then, is key to Hobbes's theory, for women "consent" to men's dominion just as men "consent" to their own imprisonment when they break the law; in both cases they freely choose their loss of freedom by virtue of the fact that they have consented to the sovereign's authority to rule them as he or she sees fit. By paying attention to how the family is structured and particularly to how women came to be subordinate wives, we gain some valuable insights into Hobbes's texts.[78]

BIBLIOGRAPHY

Annas, Julia. 1977. "Mill and the Subjection of Women." *Philosophy*, 52 (March): 179–194.

Baumgold, Deborah. 1988. *Hobbes's Political Theory*. New York: Cambridge University Press.

Brennan, Teresa, and Carole Pateman. 2007. "Mere Auxiliaries to the Commonwealth: Women and the Origins of Liberalism," in *Rereading the Canon: Feminist Interpretations of Locke* (pp. 51–73), edited by Nancy J. Hirschmann and Kirstie M. McClure. State College, PA: Pennsylvania State University Press.

Butler, Melissa. 1978. "The Early Liberal Roots of Feminism: John Locke and the Attack on Patriarchy." *American Political Science Review* 72 (1): 135–150.

Chapman, Richard Allen. 1975. "Leviathan Writ Small: Thomas Hobbes on the Family." *The American Political Science Review* 69 (1): 76–90.

Clark, Alice. 1968. *Working Life of Women in the Seventeenth Century*. London: Frank Cass.

Clark, Lorenne M. G., and Lynda Lange, eds. 1979. *The Sexism of Social and Political Theory: Women and Reproduction from Plato to Nietzsche*. Toronto: University of Toronto Press.

DiStefano, Christine. 1983. "Masculinity as Ideology in Political Theory: Hobbesian Man Considered." *Women's Studies International Forum*, 6 (6): 633–644.

Eisenstein, Zillah R. 1981. *The Radical Future of Liberal Feminism*. New York: Longman Publishers.

Elshtain, Jean Bethke. 1981. *Public Man/Private Woman: Women in Social and Political Thought*. Princeton, NJ: Princeton University Press.

Engels, Friedrich. 1972. *The Origin of Family, Private Property, and the State*, edited by Eleanor Burke Leacock. New York: International Publishers.

Flathman, Richard E. 1993. *Thomas Hobbes: Skepticism, Individuality, and Chastened Politics*. Newbury Park, CA: Sage.

Flax, Jane. 1983. "Political Philosophy and the Patriarchal Unconscious," in *Discovering Reality: Feminist Perspectives on Epistemology, Metaphysics, Methodology, and Philosophy of Science*, edited by Sandra Harding and Merrill B. Hintikka. Boston: Reidel.

Gauthier, David P. 1969. *The Logic of Leviathan: The Moral and Political Theory of Thomas Hobbes*. Oxford, UK: Clarendon Press.

Green, Karen. 1994. "Christine De Pisan and Thomas Hobbes." *Philosophical Quarterly* 44 (177): 456–475.

[78] Particular thanks to Kirstie M. McClure for her suggestions on various classical accounts of the Amazons during the writing of this chapter and to the editors of this volume for their many helpful suggestions.

Grubbs, Judith Evans. 2002. *Women and the Law in the Roman Empire: A Sourcebook on Marriage, Divorce and Widowhood*. New York: Routledge.

Hampton, Jean. 1986. *Hobbes and the Social Contract Tradition*. New York: Cambridge University Press.

Hazewindus, Minke W. 2004. *When Women Interfere: Studies in the Role of Women in Herodotus' Histories*. Amsterdam: J. C. Geiben.

Herodotus. 1875. *Histories*: Volume 3. *The Persian Wars*, translated by George Rawlinson. New York: Scribner, Welford and Armstrong. Available at: http://mcadams.posc.mu.edu/txt/ah/Herodotus/Herodotus4.html (Accessed September 17, 2013.)

Heywood, Colin. 2001. *A History of Childhood: Children and Childhood in the West from Medieval to Modern Times*. Cambridge, UK: Polity Press.

Hinton, R.W.K. 1968. "Husbands, Fathers, and Conquerors." *Political Studies* 16 (1): 55–8.

Hirschmann, Nancy J. 1992. *Rethinking Obligation: A Feminist Method for Political Theory*. Ithaca, NY: Cornell University Press.

Hirschmann, Nancy J. 2007. *Gender, Class, and Freedom in Modern Political Theory*. Princeton, NJ: Princeton University Press.

Hirschmann, Nancy J. 2013. "Gordon Schochet on Hobbes, Gratitude, and Women," in *Feminist Interpretations of Thomas Hobbes* (pp. 125–145), edited by Nancy J. Hirschmann and Joanne H. Wright. University Park: Pennsylvania State University Press.

Hirschmann, Nancy J., and Joanne Wright, eds. 2013. *Feminist Interpretations of Thomas Hobbes*. University Park: Pennsylvania State University Press.

Hirschmann, Nancy J., and Kirstie M. McClure, eds. 2007. *Rereading the Canon: Feminist Interpretations of John Locke*. State College: Pennsylvania State University Press.

Hobbes, Thomas. 1985. *Leviathan*, edited by C.B. Mapherson. New York: Penguin.

Hobbes, Thomas. 1991. *Man and Citizen: De Homine and De Cive*, edited by Bernard Gert. Indianapolis, IN: Hackett.

Hobbes, Thomas. 1994. *The Elements of Law, Natural and Politic*, edited by J.C.A. Gaskin. New York: Oxford University Press.

Hobbes, Thomas. 1999. "The Questions Concerning Liberty, Necessity, and Chance," in *Hobbes and Bramhall on Liberty and Necessity*, edited by Vere Chappel. New York: Cambridge University Press.

Justinus, Marcus Junianus. 1853. *Epitome of the Philippic History of Pompeius Trogus*, translated, with notes, by the Rev. John Selby Watson. London: Henry G. Bohn. Available at: http://www.forumromanum.org/literature/justin/english/trans2.html#4 (Accessed online September 17, 2013.)

Kahn, Victoria. 2004. *Wayward Contracts: The Crisis of Political Obligation in England, 1640–1674*. Princeton, NJ: Princeton University Press.

Kavka, Gregory S. 1986. *Hobbesian Moral and Political Theory*. Princeton, NJ: Princeton University Press.

Lloyd, S.A. 1992. *Ideals as Interests in Hobbes's Leviathan: The Power of Mind over Matter*. Cambridge, UK: Cambridge University Press.

Lynda Lange. 1981. "Rousseau and Modern Feminism," *Social Theory and Practice* 7, (3): 245–277.

Macpherson, C.B. 1962. *The Political Theory of Possessive Individualism: Hobbes to Locke*. Oxford: Oxford University Press.

McKinney, Audrey. 1993. "Hobbes and the State of Nature: Where Are the Women?" *Southwest Philosophical Studies* 15: 51–59.

Mendelson, Sara, and Crawford, Patricia. 1998. *Women in Early Modern England, 1550–1720.* Oxford: Clarendon Press.

Okin, Susan Moller. 1979. *Women in Western Political Thought.* Princeton, NJ: Princeton University Press.

Okin, Susan Moller. 1982. "Women and the Making of the Sentimental Family." *Philosophy and Public Affairs* 11 (Winter): 65–88.

Pateman, Carole. 1988. *The Sexual Contract.* Stanford, CA: Stanford University Press.

Pateman, Carole. 1989. "'God Hath Ordained to Man a Helper': Hobbes, Patriarchy and Conjugal Right." *British Journal of Political Science* 19 (4): 445–463.

Pateman, Carole, and Quentin Skinner. 2013. "Hobbes, History, Politics, and Gender: A Conversation with Carole Pateman and Quentin Skinner," conducted by Nancy J. Hirschmann and Joanne H. Wright, in *Feminist Interpretations of Thomas Hobbes* (pp. 18–43), edited by Nancy J. Hirschmann and Joanne H. Wright. University Park: Pennsylvania State University Press.

Pateman, Carole, and Teresa Brennan. 2007. "Afterword: Mere Auxilliaries of the Commonwealth in an Age of Globalization," in *Rereading the Canon: Feminist Interpretations of John Locke* (pp. 75–90), edited by Nancy J. Hirschmann and Kirstie M. McClure. University Park: Pennsylvania State University Press.

Plotz, Judith A. 2001. *Romanticism and the Vocation of Childhood.* New York: Palgrave.

Rossi, Alice S. 1970. "Sentiment and Intellect: The Story of John Stuart Mill and Harriet Taylor Mill," in *Essays on Sex Equality*, edited by Alice S. Rossi. Chicago: University of Chicago Press.

Schochet, Gordon J. 1967. "Thomas Hobbes on the Family and the State of Nature." *Political Science Quarterly* 82 (3, Sept.): 427–445.

Schochet, Gordon J. 1975. *Patriarchalism in Political Thought: The Authoritarian Family and Political Speculation and Attitudes Especially in Seventeenth-Century England.* Oxford, UK: Blackwell.

Schochet, Gordon J. 1990. "Intending (Political) Obligation: Hobbes and the Voluntary Basis of Society," in *Thomas Hobbes and Political Theory*, edited by Mary Dietz. Lawrence: University of Kansas Press.

Shanley, Mary Lyndon. 1979. "Marriage Contract and Social Contract in 17th Century English Political Thought." *Western Political Quarterly* 32 (1): 79–91.

Skinner, Quentin. 2008. *Hobbes and Republican Liberty.* New York: Cambridge University Press.

Spragens, Thomas. 1973. *The Politics of Motion: The World of Thomas Hobbes.* Lexington: University of Kentucky Press.

Sreedhar, Susanne. 2013. "Toward a Hobbesian Theory of Sexuality," in *Feminist Interpretations of Thomas Hobbes* (pp. 260–279), edited by Nancy J. Hirschmann and Joanne H. Wright. University Park: Pennsylvania State University Press.

Stanlick, Nancy A. 2001. "Lords and Mothers: Silent Subjects in Hobbes's Political Theory." *International Journal of Politics and Ethics* 1 (3): 171–182.

Tuck, Richard. 1989. *Hobbes.* New York: Oxford University Press.

Warrender, Howard. 1957. *The Political Philosophy of Hobbes: His Theory of Obligation.* Oxford, UK: Clarendon Press.

Watson, Foster. 1901. "The Curriculum and Text-Books of English Schools in the First Half of the Seventeenth-Century." *Library* TBS6 (part 2): 159–268.

Wright, Joanne H. 2004. *Origin Stories in Political Thought: Discourses on Gender, Power, and Citizenship.* Toronto: University of Toronto Press.

CHAPTER 12

....

NATURAL LAW

....

S. A. LLOYD

"THE laws of nature," Hobbes wrote, "are the sum of moral philosophy."[1] They are eternal and immutable prescriptive precepts, discoverable by unaided natural reason, and "the science of them, is the true and only moral philosophy."[2] These laws, being rules of reason, make a claim on anyone capable of exercising reason, exempting only children and madmen. The laws of nature apply to interactions among individuals, to sovereigns in their treatment of subjects, and to interactions among sovereign nations, for "the law of nations and the law of nature is the same thing."[3] The laws of nature both comprise Hobbes's moral philosophy and ground and tether his entire political philosophy.

I'll begin by showing that reciprocity is the core requirement of the laws of nature and suggest one possible derivation of the reciprocity requirement as a theorem of reason following by Hobbes's philosophical method of definitional derivation from a simple axiom of rational agency. I'll then discuss the duties owed by sovereigns to their subjects under the laws of nature, followed by an explanation of how those laws impose on individuals a duty to submit to sovereign authority and the limits of that duty articulated in Hobbes's account of the "true liberties" of subjects. Building on the ideas so far introduced, I'll show how the laws of nature may usefully, and indeed ought, to guide sovereign policy in the international arena, paying special attention to the constraints they impose in the conduct of war. I'll then briefly sketch a theory of the relationship in Hobbes's system between natural law and civil law, and between both of these and divine positive law. Finally, with all of these applications of reciprocity or "cases in the law of nature"[4] established, I shall discuss the major interpretive question of the source of the laws of nature's normativity or *oughtness*.

---

[1] *De cive* 3.32. References are to chapter and paragraph number.
[2] *Leviathan* 15, 79. References are to Head edition chapter, followed by the page number of that edition.
[3] *Leviathan* 30, 185.
[4] *Elements of Law*, Dedicatory Epistle.

1 RECIPROCITY AS THE LAW OF NATURE

Hobbes famously insisted that all of what he calls the Laws of Nature may be captured "in these words, *quod tibi fieri non vis, alteri ne feceris: do not that to others, you would not have done to yourself*."[5] He consistently presented his Laws of Nature as applications of the Biblical Golden Rule. Because Hobbes's central precept articulates a kind of reciprocity requirement, and because he argues that the laws of nature are theorems of reason, I shall refer to his precept as "the reciprocity theorem."

Hobbes identifies this theorem variously as the "core" or "sum" of the "Law of Nature," and sometimes simply as the Law of Nature itself. He offers various formulations of reciprocity as prohibiting

- doing what one thinks unreasonable to be done by another to oneself,[6]
- doing what one would not have done to oneself,[7]
- doing what one would not approve in another,[8]
- reserving to oneself any right one is not content should be reserved to all the rest,[9]
- allowing to oneself that which one denies to another[10]

and correlatively as commanding that

- whatsoever you require that others should do to you, that do ye to them,[11]

and that

- we love others as ourselves.[12]

---

[5] *De cive* 3.26; also *Leviathan* 15, 79.

[6] "*Do not that to another, which thou thinkest unreasonable to be done by another to thy selfe.*" *Leviathan* 26, 140.

[7] "The laws of nature . . . have been contracted into one easy sum . . . and that is, *Do not to another, which thou wouldest not have done to thy selfe*" *Leviathan* 15, 79.

[8] *Leviathan* 27, 152.

[9] *Leviathan* 15, 77. Cf. *Philosophical Rudiments* 3.14 (chapter and paragraph number), where Hobbes writes that "what rights soever any man challenges to himself, he also grant the same as due to all the rest."

[10] *Leviathan* 42, 272.

[11] *Leviathan* 14, 65. See also *Elements of Law*, I.4.2 for an application of this principle: "*Whatsoever right any man requireth to retain, he allow every other man to retain the same.*"

[12] "*Thou shalt love thy neighbor as thyself* . . . is the natural law, having its beginning with rational nature itself" (*Philosophical Rudiments* 17.8). "[T]he law of nature, which is also the moral law, is the law of the author of nature, God Almighty . . . [f]or the sum of God's law is, *Thou shalt love God above all, and thy neighbour as thyself*; and the same is the sum of the law of nature, as hath been showed" *Elements of Law* II.10.7. Cf. *Philosophical Rudiments* 4.12 and *Elements of Law* I.5.6: "*Thou shalt love thy neighbour as thyself* . . . which is . . . so to be understood, as that a man . . . should esteem his neighbour worthy all rights and privileges that himself enjoyeth; and attribute unto him, whatsoever he looketh

Hobbes identifies the requirement that we love others as ourselves with a fairness requirement that we each apply some or other uniform set of standards to everyone, without exempting ourselves from the rules or judgments we apply to others. He writes,

> [T]hat same equity, which we proved in the ninth place to be a law of nature, which commands every man to allow the same rights to others they would be allowed themselves, and which contains in it all the other laws besides, is the same which Moses sets down (Levit. xix. 18): *Thou shalt love thy neighbour as thyself.* And our Saviour calls it *the sum of the moral law.* . . . But to love our neighbour as ourselves, is nothing else but to grant him all we desire to have granted to ourselves.[13]

Reciprocity suggests a test for discerning whether one's actions comport with the law of nature; namely, that the agent imagine herself on the receiving end of the action she proposes to perform and consider whether from that vantage point she would fault the action as unreasonable:

> [T]here is an easy rule to know upon a sudden, whether the action I be to do, be against the law of nature or not . . . [*viz.*] [*t*]*hat a man imagine himself in the place of the party with whom he hath to do, and reciprocally him in his.*[14]
> [T]he rule by which I said any man might know, whether what he was doing were contrary to the law or not, to wit, what thou wouldst not be done to, do not that to another; is almost in the self-same words delivered by our Saviour.[15]
> [For a man in a quiet mind] there is nothing easier for him to know, though he be never so rude and unlearned, than this only rule, that when he doubts whether what he is now doing to another may be done by the law of nature or not, he conceive himself to be in that other's stead. Here instantly those perturbations which persuaded him to the fact, being now cast into the other scale, dissuade him as much. And this rule is not only easy, but is anciently celebrated in these words, *quod tibi fieri no vis, alteri ne feceris: do not that to others, you would not have done to yourself.*[16]

Reciprocity is a rational constraint on justifiable (i.e., *blameless*) action. The various notions Hobbes uses in the effort to call our attention to the core requirement of natural law—disapproval, judging unreasonable, iniquitous, or unacceptable, being unwilling to allow—differ to some degree. But all these terms convey our judgment of the *unjustifiability* of the actions they characterize. People express this judgment through ascriptions of moral fault or blame. When we behave in a way we fault others for behaving, our action lacks vindication, is unjustifiable, or is, in Hobbes's phrase, "contrary

---

should be attributed unto himself: which is no more, but that he should be humble, meek, and content with equality."

[13] *Philosophical Rudiments* 4.12. Cf. 3.14: The ninth law of nature dictates "that what rights soever any man challenges to himself, he also grant the same as due to all the rest."

[14] *Elements of Law* I.4.9. Cf. *De cive* 3.26: This rule lets us determine whether our actions "may be done by the law of nature or not"; *De cive* 4.23, and the famous formulation from *Leviathan*, 15, 79.

[15] *De cive* 4.23.

[16] *De cive* 3.26.

to reason." Hobbes's notion of contrariety to reason is broad, encompassing unreasonableness as well as mere irrationality. I use the more familiar term "unjustifiability" to express this broad notion of contrariety to reason.[17]

All of the particular laws of nature Hobbes specifies in *Leviathan*'s chapters 14, 15, and review and conclusion are derivable from the reciprocity theorem along with premises about what people would judge unreasonable. For example, because we would think others unreasonable to treat us as their natural inferiors, we must acknowledge them as our equal by nature (Law 9); because we would find others unreasonable to insist on being the judge in their own case, neither may we insist on being the judge in our own (Law 17); if we would fault others for demanding that we surrender a part of our natural right while preserving their entire natural right intact, we must reciprocally surrender that portion of natural right we require them to surrender in order to our safety (Law 2).

Although individuals will differ in many of their judgments of justifiability, those that ground the laws of nature may be expected to be widely, Hobbes thinks universally, shared because they engage our basic human need to secure a social environment in which we can function and flourish. The laws of nature operate to secure peaceful, civilized communities. In *De cive*, Hobbes contrasts life outside of the commonwealth with life within it:

> [O]ut of it, there is a dominion of passions, war, fear, poverty, slovenliness, solitude, barbarism, ignorance, cruelty; in it, the dominion of reason, peace, security, riches, decency, society, elegancy, sciences, and benevolence.[18]

Like traditional conceptions of natural law, Hobbes's understands those laws to preserve a certain character of human community, as distinct from best serving the narrow self-interest of each particular individual. Explaining in *Philosophical Rudiments* why men's natural right to all things had to be given up, Hobbes wrote

> [R]eason, namely, dictating that they must forego that right *for the preservation of mankind*; because the equality of men among themselves . . . was necessarily accompanied with war; and with war joins *the destruction of mankind*.[19]

Michael Silverthorne's translation of the corresponding passage in *De cive* is this:

> [A]t the dictation of reason, that right had to be given up for the preservation *of the human race*. For the inevitable consequence of men's being equal . . . was war, and the consequence of war is *the ruin of mankind*.[20]

---

[17] When Hobbes himself uses the terms "justify" and "justified," he is speaking of vindicating as innocent of wrongdoing, as when he writes of sovereigns that "they will all of them justify the war by which their power was at first gotten, and whereon, as they think, their right dependeth," requiring men's "approbation" of their action (*Leviathan* R&C, 391).

[18] *De cive* 10.2.

[19] *Philosophical Rudiments* 15.5, emphasis added.

[20] *On the Citizen*, 173. In his Introduction to *On the Citizen*, Richard Tuck notes that "Hobbes himself never repudiated the book, despite having published *Leviathan* four years later, and he proudly

Lest we imagine that Hobbes may be using the term "mankind" idiosyncratically as a synonym for the individual, he had already counterposed these: "it is easily judged how disagreeable a thing to the preservation either of mankind, or of each single man, a perpetual war is."[21]

The laws of nature and their corresponding moral virtues aim to establish and preserve communities, rather than individuals: "[G]ood dispositions are those which are suitable for entering into civil society; and good manners (that is, moral virtues) are those whereby what was entered upon can be best preserved."[22]

Yet to say that the laws of nature "come to be praised, as the means of peaceable, sociable, and comfortable living" is not to say that every agent values peace as the best means to satisfying his personal interest. Hobbes recognized that peace may not always be in the rational self-interest—even the long-run rational self-interest—of every agent. Many agents in Hobbes's world *stand to fare better by destabilizing the peace* than by adhering to the laws of nature that promote it: "needy and hardy" men who will benefit from disruption of the prevailing social order, men ambitious of military command or other office, potent or popular men whom others will protect,[23] the wealthy and powerful who can privately command defenses, religious zealots who care more for their cause than they do for peace or their narrow self-interest, and even, on occasions, sovereigns, who may rationally hope to enrich themselves and their people by foreign wars. That the laws of nature are suited to preserve communities but not necessarily individuals is easily seen by considering the final law of nature Hobbes specifies in *Leviathan's* Review and Conclusion: "To the Laws of Nature, declared in Chapter XV. I would have this added, *that every man is bound by nature, as much as in him lieth, to protect in war the authority, by which he is himself protected in time of peace.*"[24]

Here, Hobbes asserts that the laws of nature require everyone to do all they can to defend the sovereign in wartime: "when the defense of the commonwealth, requireth at once the help of all that are able to bear arms, every one is obliged," even though, in less extreme cases, allowance is to be made "for natural timorousness; not only to women . . . but also to men of feminine courage."[25] This law of nature does not say that people are obliged to defend their sovereign in wartime only if they expect to gain personally from doing so, nor does it excuse them from this duty when they stand to fare worse by honoring it. People are to do all that is within their power, no matter their personal

---

reprinted it in his collected works (in Latin) in 1668, alongside a Latin translation of *Leviathan*" (*On the Citizen*, ix). If Tuck is correct, this passage is evidence that Hobbes all along held that the problem with war is its harm to humanity generally, thus implying that the value of the laws of nature in forestalling war is their securing the good of humanity.

[21] *Rudiments* 1.13, emphasis added. Silverthorne translates the parallel passage in *De cive*, "One may easily see how incompatible perpetual *War* is with the preservation of the human race or of individual men," *On the Citizen*, 30.

[22] *On the Citizen*, 69–70.

[23] And who can extort money or preferments from the state as a condition for desisting from their disruptive actions. See *Leviathan* 30, 183.

[24] *Leviathan* R&C, 390.

[25] *Leviathan* 21, 112.

interest, to defend in war the government that has formerly protected them. They are even required to risk death in defending the sovereign, to just the extent they are psychologically able to bring themselves to do so.[26]

It is difficult to see how this requirement of the law of nature could possibly be understood as a dictate of personal prudence. War is dangerous. Obeying the directive of this law of nature will almost certainly compromise the particular interests of many of the individuals who obey it, but it is nonetheless quite plausibly a rule that would help to preserve civil communities, in part through its deterrent effect on would-be attackers.

Hobbes's laws of nature articulate a set of natural duties rather than obligations, meaning that their claim on us does not depend on our having agreed or promised to follow them. One is to be faulted for ingratitude to good parents and other benefactors despite the fact that one has never promised not to be ungrateful. Those who have never agreed to treat others fairly are nonetheless blameworthy for behaving inequitably. Hobbes notes that, even during war, gratuitous cruelty is forbidden by the law of nature; it would certainly be no moral defense to explain that one had never undertaken any obligation to refrain from such cruelty. The third law of nature, requiring the keeping of valid covenants, specifies a natural duty to fulfill our voluntarily undertaken valid obligations.

The laws of nature do not always operate to best secure the narrow self-interest of the agent who follows them because Hobbes concedes that the wicked often prosper. But we are nevertheless to follow them, the only exception being in the extreme case in which doing so would procure our own "certain ruin." In *Leviathan* he writes, "The laws of nature oblige . . . to the putting them in act, not always. For he that should be modest, and tractable, and perform all he promises, in such time, and place, where *no man else* should do so, should but make himself a prey to others, and procure his own certain ruin, contrary to the ground of all laws of nature, which tend to nature's preservation."[27] Notice, though, that Hobbes is willing to excuse people from obedience to the laws of nature only to avoid their own certain destruction and not to procure lesser gains or to avoid lesser harms, including mere risk of death (as required under the final law of nature). In less extreme cases, we are bound to obey the laws of nature even when doing so is not in our narrow self-interest.

2 Derivation of the Reciprocity Theorem

We won't count a person as acting in accordance with reason unless he is willing to offer what he regards as justifying considerations for his actions. But to offer a consideration

---

[26] Once they have been captured, are within the guards and garrisons of the enemy, then they are permitted (although not required) to save their lives by promising allegiance to their captor. But until that happens, the final law of nature requires them to fight for their sovereign to the utmost of their power.

[27] *Leviathan* 15, 79.

as justifying one's action commits one to accepting that same consideration as justifying the like actions of others, *ceteris paribus*. (Nothing counts as a reason for doing a particular action unless it counts as a reason for doing actions of the type of which the particular action is an instance, other things equal.) But we do not count an act as contrary to reason unless we are prepared to fault the agent for doing it. So when one does what one is prepared to fault others for doing, one acts contrary to reason. In compliance with Hobbes's approved method of definitional derivation, we can arrive at the reciprocity theorem as follows:

1. Man is rational.[28]
2. Insofar as a man is rational, his action is not contrary to reason.
3. That which is not contrary to reason is judged to be done with right.[29] But because what is judged to be done without right is not judged to be done with right, it follows (by contraposition) that whatever one judges to be done without right is contrary to reason; and so that
4. To do what one judges to be done without right is to act contrary to reason.
5. If one judges another's doing of an action to be without right, one judges the action done to be done without right.
6. Therefore, *If one judges another's doing of an action to be without right, and yet does that action oneself, one acts contrary to reason* (from 4 and 5). That is, *to do what one condemns in another is contrary to reason.*
7. Therefore, *qua* rational, one must not do to another what one thinks unreasonable for another to do to oneself. QED, the reciprocity theorem.

Premise 3, which takes rightfulness or justifiability to belong to the concept of conformity with reason, is doing the heavy lifting in Hobbes's derivation of the reciprocity theorem. Premises 1 and 2 come into play only when Hobbes seeks to motivate compliance with the reciprocity theorem and with the conclusions he derives using it. People care greatly about how others regard them, desiring to be respected, esteemed, and deemed rationally justified in the eyes of their fellows and of God. To be judged lacking

---

[28] This is a definition. *Leviathan* 4, 13: "The names *man* and *rational*, are of equal extent, comprehending mutually one another." Cf. *Elements of Philosophy* I.2.14; *Human Nature* 1.4: "Man's nature is the *sum of his natural faculties and powers* . . . contained in the definition of man, under these words, *animal* and *rational*"; and *Elements of Philosophy* I.1.3: "compounded into this one name, *body-animated-rational*, or *man*."

[29] "[T]hat which is not contrary to right reason, that all men account to be done justly, and with right" (*Rudiments* 1.7). "[S]ince all do grant, that is done by *right*, which is not done against reason, we ought to judge those actions only *wrong*, which are repugnant to right reason" (*Rudiments* 2.15). Hobbes is here offering to analytically unfold the concept of being done with right. It would be beside the point to complain that some people don't always speak as precisely. Hobbes does not understand his assertion as an empirical generalization because the claim that every individual invariably judges as "done with right" every action "not contrary to reason." Rather, Hobbes holds that applied to actions "not contrary to reason" = "judged to be done with right" = blameless. Mistaken individual judgments do not threaten conceptual connections.

in justification is felt as demeaning, lowering us to the level of madmen, children, or nonhuman animals. Thus, our pride in our possession of reason motivates us to seek to justify our actions. Pride is among the most powerful of motivations in the Hobbesian scheme.

Premise 5 asserts that the identity of the agent performing an action is irrelevant to assessments of the action's conformity to reason, all other things (such as role obligations) equal. Hobbes's argument is to be understood as agreeing with common sense that the differing positions, obligations, and circumstances of agents are properly relevant to our judgments of blame or fault by entering into the description of the action at hand. It may matter greatly to our assessment of an action whether it falls under the description "consensual sexual act," "act of infidelity," "violation of religious vow of celibacy," "rape," or "marriage consummation." What premise 5 asserts is that when we condemn the action of another insofar as it falls under a particular action-type (e.g., the breaking of a vow), it is contrary to reason for us to do any action falling under that very same-action type.

Because people differ to some degree in their ascriptions of blame on account of their differences in bodily constitution, education, experience, and much else, there is no reason to expect that the application of the reciprocity theorem will yield an extensive single set of universal norms or convergence among all competent reasoners on all practical questions, or "cases in the law of nature," that may arise. We may diverge in our readiness to fault others for having nonprocreative relations, or for having abortions, or for eating animals. Such divergence in private judgments will not cause a problem so long as we do converge on the law of nature requirement of submission of disputes to arbitration.

Hobbes does *not* hold that because other people's reasons for wanting things are of the same kind as mine, their reasons are reasons *for me*. The only reasons for me are my reasons. Hobbes's point is merely that I have nothing that counts as a reason at all unless it is a justifying consideration I would be willing not just to give to others, but also to accept from them as justifying their like conduct. It is never the case for Hobbes that just because someone else wants something, I have a reason to provide it. I have reason to do so only if I would fault others in circumstances relevantly similar to mine for failing to provide it to him. For Hobbes, only one's own *judgments of blameworthiness* can provide one with reasons. Even my own wants will not provide me with reasons to act, unless I am prepared to fault others for failing to act on wants of that sort in relevantly similar circumstances. Justifying action by appeal to reasons is an exercise of the faculty of judgment, not of desire; desires do not provide reasons for action, although they do motivate and, concomitant with judgment, cause actions.

Perhaps the most striking implication of this view is that atheists and rebels against God have no reason to obey even an omnipotent and vengeful God because they are not willing to fault others for disobedience. (Here, we ignore the possibility that atheists might, on grounds suggested by Pascal, fault the disobedient for their narrow irrationality given the consequences of wagering wrongly and in light of our epistemological limitations.) The position Hobbes articulates does not aspire to establish the universality or full generality of all moral norms. It provides an intermediate point between that position on the one hand and egoism on the other—a kind of moral minimum that is nonetheless recognizably moral.

Hobbes is describing a *consistency requirement of an individual's evaluative attitude toward an action under a description*. To violate this requirement of reason is, says Hobbes, a form of absurdity. Consistency in the evaluation of actions across persons is a kind of reciprocity. These limited requirements of reciprocity and universality must be observed if an action is to accord with reason because men's courses "not being circumscribed within reasonable bounds, their reason becomes invisible."[30]

What the argument establishing the reciprocity theorem tells us is that it is against reason to do what one faults others for doing, even if doing so would best advance the ends one happens to have. Hobbes goes so far as explicitly to *deny* that for men "those actions are most reasonable that conduce most to their ends."[31] For Hobbes, an action can effectively serve a desired end and still be contrary to reason. But it is also true that, on Hobbes's conception of reason, it may accord with reason to pursue ends that not all men can agree on and to act in ways that not all men can approve.

Moral reasoning then, as we undertake when deriving and using the laws of nature, is inconsistent with partiality, as Hobbes makes plain in his remark that it is ironic that Cato should have such a reputation for wisdom considering that, with him, "animosity should so prevail instead of judgment, and *partiality instead of reason, that the very same thing which he thought just* in his popular state, *he should censure as unjust* in a monarchical."[32] Had earlier moral philosophers properly performed their task of facilitating wisdom, people would already have learned that it is contrary to reason to evaluate one's own actions differently than one evaluates the like actions of others: "that the very same man should . . . esteem his own actions far otherwise in himself than he does in others . . . [is one of] so many signs, so many manifest arguments, that what hath hitherto been written by moral philosophers, hath not made any progress in the knowledge of the truth."[33] Thus, Hobbes's conceptual linkages show that rational people are committed to impartiality and to consistency in their evaluative judgments across settled descriptions of actions, precisely the requirement articulated in premise 5.

---

[30] *Three Discourses*, 106. The behavior Hobbes is here describing as not being circumscribed within reasonable bounds is the measuring of one's actions not "by the rule of Aequum and Justum, but by the square of their own benefit and affections: *and so not being circumscribed within reasonable bounds, their reason becomes invisible*" (emphasis added). This work, initially published anonymously in 1620, is now believed by some, on the basis of word-printing analysis by computer, to have been authored by the young Hobbes.

[31] *Leviathan* 15, 72: In Hobbes's reply to the Foole, where Hobbes condemns the reasoning relying on this claim as "specious" but "false." The Foole passage, because it takes on the challenge posed by the person who rejects all moral norms or requirements of the reasonable, tries to show that even from the vantage point of the merely rational, it is not true that those actions are most reasonable that most conduce to the agent's ends. This principle has already been ruled out as against reason by the reciprocity theorem.

[32] *Rudiments* Epistle Dedicatory, emphases added.

[33] *Rudiments*, Epistle Dedicatory.

3 Duties of Sovereigns Toward Subjects Under the Law of Nature

The duties of sovereigns under the laws of nature comprise Hobbes's art of government. Sovereigns, too, are bound by *all* the laws of nature because, these being divine, no person nor commonwealth can alter or abrogate them. For instance, all are bound by equity "to which, as being a precept of the law of nature, a sovereign is as much subject, as any of the meanest of his people." [34] It is true that the sovereign has final authority to interpret what equity requires of subjects and of himself, but that does not mean that equity simply is whatever the sovereign thinks it is. Hobbes insists that "there is no judge subordinate, *nor sovereign*, but may err in a judgment of equity." [35] Sovereigns may be mistaken, but their interpretations and applications of the laws of nature are nonetheless to be treated as authoritative. Only God may hold them accountable for their errors.[36]

Sovereigns have additional duties under the law of nature that are office-specific. Hobbes writes that

> [t]he office of the sovereign . . . consisteth in . . . the procuration of *the safety of the people*; to which he is obliged by the law of nature, and to render an account thereof to God, the author of that law, and to none but him. But by safety here is not meant a bare preservation, but also all other contentments of life, which every man by lawful industry, without danger, or hurt to the commonwealth, shall acquire to himself. [37]

It is the sovereign's duty to leave people as much liberty as is safely possible, by which Hobbes means the maximum extent of liberty compatible with the maintenance of civil peace. All "harmless liberty" is to be allowed, and it is best that the sovereign's reasons for prohibiting subjects' activities be fairly intuitive so that people do not accidentally violate the laws through ignorance. Harmless liberties include such things as "the liberty to buy, and sell, and otherwise contract with one another; to choose their own abode, their own diet, their own trade of life, and institute their children as they themselves think fit; and the like." [38]

What Hobbes terms the "true liberties of subjects" form a special case. As discussed in chapter 21 of *Leviathan*, these are the rights that cannot be transferred by valid covenant. Because they cannot be transferred, subjects are morally blameless when acting

---

[34] *Leviathan* 30, 180.
[35] *Leviathan* 26, 144.
[36] For elaboration of Hobbes's hierarchy of responsibility, according to which subjects are accountable to God for their obedience to the sovereign, whereas sovereigns are accountable to God for the rightness of their commands, see Lloyd 2009: 281–286.
[37] *Leviathan* 30, 175.
[38] *Leviathan* 21, 109.

in defense of these rights; although sovereigns may legitimately command actions that threaten the interests these rights protect, subjects may legitimately disobey those commands. That does not mean that sovereigns may not legitimately punish them for their disobedience; these are liberty rather than claim rights. Commands to kill, wound, or maim oneself; to abstain from things necessary to preserve one's life; to incriminate oneself or one's loved ones; to do things that would subject oneself to punishment or not to resist punishment may permissibly be disobeyed. It may seem that these sorts of liberties are far from harmless, but Hobbes suggests that acknowledging them does not threaten public safety, for two reasons. First, it is not *necessary* to public safety that subjects obey commands to, say, execute themselves, because there are plenty of others who are bound to carry out the sovereign's execution orders. Second, the improbability that individuals will *reliably obey* such commands would render any presumed obligation on them to do so of no practical importance. Subjects need not, even if they could validly, divest themselves of the true liberties because the sovereign's ability to promote the public good does not depend on their doing so.

The sovereign's duty under the law of nature of procuring the common good further includes the regulation of doctrine and religion so that subjects do not develop false beliefs that pit moral or religious teachings or the claims of private conscience against their duty of civil obedience. Taking educational measures against the "poison of seditious doctrines" is especially important because, as Hobbes insightfully stressed, sovereign power ultimately depends on people's opinions of the sovereign's rights and their own political duties and especially on the opinions of those forces who are supposed to coerce compliance with the sovereign's commands. For "if men know not their duty, what is there that will force them to obey the laws? An army, you shall say. But what shall force the army?" [39] This is why Hobbes writes that "the actions of men proceed from their opinions; and in the well- governing of opinions, consisteth the well-governing of men's actions, in order to their peace, and concord . . . It belongeth therefore to him that hath the sovereign power, to be judge, or constitute all judges of opinions and doctrines, as a thing necessary to peace, thereby to prevent discord and civil war." [40] Hobbes took regulation of doctrine to require the education of ordinary people in their civic and moral duties by preachers trained in correct doctrine in the universities and suggested that his book *Leviathan* would make a suitable university text. We can hardly disagree with his taste in texts.

Finally, the law of nature requires sovereigns to provide for the future good of their subjects both by establishing a mechanism for an orderly succession and, to us controversially, by doing whatever they sincerely think necessary for securing subjects' eternal good. "Forasmuch," Hobbes writes, "as eternal is better than temporal good, it is evident, that they who are in sovereign authority, are by the law of nature obliged to further the establishing of all . . . they believe the true way thereunto. For unless they

---

[39] *Behemoth* ed. Tonnies, 75.
[40] *Leviathan* 18, 91.

do so, it cannot be said truly, that they have done the uttermost of their endeavor [for the good of the people]." [41] It does not necessarily follow from this that sovereigns must dictate the profession and practice of religion to their subjects, for a conscientious belief in the value of free faith would condemn such imposition. Still, sovereigns are required to take whatever measures they think needed to help their subjects toward a happy afterlife.

4 THE NATURAL LAW DUTY TO SUBMIT TO GOVERNMENT

Hobbes, once granted the reciprocity theorem, can argue quite directly for the requirement of civil obedience and its particular elements. Using the reciprocity theorem, he can, for example, derive a requirement of reason that we be willing to submit our disputes with others to binding arbitration, just so long as it is the case that we would fault others for refusing to submit to such arbitration. He can show that our unwillingness to permit others to exempt themselves from laws they judge wrong entails that we must not exempt ourselves from laws we disapprove. He can even support his absolutist stance by arguing that (although we may be willing to permit others to seek to overthrow our common government whenever *we* judge the government to be illegitimate or evil) if we are not willing to allow as legitimate others' acting to overthrow our common government whenever *they* judge it (however wrongly in our view) to be illegitimate or evil, then we must also refrain from seeking to overthrow our government on the basis of our own judgment of its demerits. Most importantly, the reciprocity theorem can establish a moral requirement to submit to government; something that not one of the discrete laws of nature can successfully do. The requirement to seek peace with willing others falls far short of a directive to enter civil society, as does the requirement to reciprocally lay down portions of our natural right or to submit disputes to impartial arbitration. But if we, for reasons of self-interest, insist that others should enter into a coercively empowered system of legal regulation and adjudication, so must we. Indeed, Hobbes answers the question of how we can know who the sovereign is by considering whom we require others to obey in order to secure our safety. It is not true that every single individual fares best by seeking peace, laying down his rights on equal terms, or keeping all his covenants. Without the reciprocity theorem, none of these laws of nature can be derived, let alone a moral requirement to submit to government. With the reciprocity theorem, which rules out all asymmetrical reasoning and free-rider problems, Hobbes can establish all of his laws of nature.

---

[41] *Elements of Law* II.9.2.

5 RECIPROCITY, THE RIGHT OF NATURE, AND THE TRUE LIBERTIES OF SUBJECTS

The reciprocity theorem allows Hobbes to ground the right of nature and its successor rights, the true liberties of subjects, and to delimit their scope nonarbitrarily. This is an important virtue because the liberty right to do whatever we conscientiously judge needful or useful for self-preservation is by no means uncontroversial. There is a large and sophisticated philosophical literature challenging the contention that we enjoy any such right.[42] Some have argued that it would be morally wrong for a person to push another into the grill of an oncoming car in order to prevent the car from hitting himself. Many have argued that traitorous betrayal of a just cause in defense of one's own single life is not morally defensible. The reciprocity theorem can respect the intuitions grounding the judgments just mentioned because our human drives and frailties limit what we will think may be reasonably expected of us while necessitating that we make certain demands on others. It is our judgments of what it would be unreasonable to blame us for doing balanced against our judgments of what harms to us others should be faulted for inflicting that set the limits of justifiable liberty in a principled, determinate way. Because we would judge it unreasonable for others to whom we owe no special obligations to fault us for doing what we sincerely believe necessary to preserve our lives, we must grant them that same right of nature. Hobbes's position that so long as the state can execute offenders we are to be allowed the liberty to disobey orders to execute ourselves can be viewed as *balancing* our readiness to fault others for refusing the state that obedience without which it cannot effectively protect us, against our judgment that it would be wrong of others to fault us for failing to do what we may be unable to bring ourselves to do, especially when others can do it in our stead. Similar balancing between the actions we are prepared to fault in others and those actions of our own for which we are unwilling to be faulted explains Hobbes's positions on the liberties to refuse military service if providing a substitute and against self-incrimination or other actions that might lead to one's own punishment.

Once Hobbes has the reciprocity theorem, he need not be concerned about free-rider problems, or "fooles," for that theorem licenses only *symmetrical* worlds in which (from the individual's point of view) everyone is justified in doing/forbearing certain types of action in the circumstances or no one is justified in doing/forbearing those types of action in the circumstances, but never asymmetrical worlds in which reason approves our doing what cannot be approved in others.

In contrast, the problem of free-riders and fools looms large on more traditional interpretations according to which Hobbes is trying to show that reason approves whatever course of action is expected to best achieve the satisfaction of our individual

---

[42] The works of Jefferson McMahan and Frances Kamm are illustrative.

desires for self-preservation (or more generally for our own good) in the long run. For it may well be true that undetected unilateral defection from beneficial cooperative schemes not infrequently *does* best advance our ends and that men can often reasonably count on being able to unilaterally defect without detection. Because Hobbes has already proved that reason dictates a reciprocity constraint on action that rules out free-riding, his reply to the Foole is better understood as a (successful) rebuttal to the claim that if an action turns out well, it cannot have been against reason to do it. This inference is obviously faulty (e.g., the fact that the holder of a winning lottery ticket chose his winning number by compiling the birthdates of his family members does not allow us to infer that his betting those numbers [or any numbers, for that matter] was rational) and explains why the person who defends it is a fool. Hobbes's thin, deflationary reply is perfectly adequate to answer defenses of immoral behavior defended by appeal to the Foole's principle that "those actions are most reasonable that conduce most to [one's] ends."[43]

6 International Duties Under the Law of Nature

Hobbes tells us that the law of nature is the law of nations.[44] This is sometimes taken for the claim that there is no law of nations, that the international arena is an anomic war of all against all. Rather, reason discovers a set of moral norms that bind even in the absence of any policing authority or set of social conventions, many of which can be applied quite directly to relations among states. Allowing safe conduct to negotiators mediating disputes, submission to arbitration of disputes, and keeping of covenants or treaties are all reasonable means of avoiding international war. In particular, the second law of nature requiring that we be willing to lay down rights whose retention by others threatens our safety along with others who are *also* willing to lay down those rights provides a framework for the design of international treaties and international institutions.

Not just international institutions, but also topical treaties (underwritten by the third law of nature) may also be required under the law of nature. If a nation requires that other nations refrain from some practice or policy, then it must itself observe the same restrictions; these sorts of reciprocal arrangements are usually established by treaty. We can even see how the law of nature justifies international rules of war and constraints on the treatment of prisoners of war because warfare beyond these limits invites visceral hatred, retaliation, and revenge that make the resumption of peaceful relations

---

[43] *Leviathan* 15, 72.

[44] "Concerning the offices of one sovereign to another, which are comprehended in that law which is commonly called the law of nations, I need not say anything in this place, because the law of nations and the law of nature is the same thing" (*Leviathan* 30, 185).

much more difficult; so, by requiring that our enemies observe limits, we must do so as well. Even in a state of nature, treaties are morally binding under the third law of nature requiring the keeping of covenants so long as no new cause for doubting that our partners will perform arises after the treaty is made.

Of course, Hobbes famously held that a covenant without an enforcement mechanism is "mere words"; but enforcement need not require a global super-sovereign. What is needed is assurance that others will fulfill their obligations under treaty, and this assurance may be provided by a system of reciprocal sanctions imposed by varying coalitions of national actors without a centralized sovereign enforcement body.

Taken as a whole, the scheme of international treaties and institutions required under the laws of nature falls far short of constituting a global sovereign. Because Hobbes's normative system aims to secure optimal agency,[45] international treaties can be expected to preserve a large degree of national sovereignty. They would likely license restrictions in the first instance only on actions affecting other states and on not matters internal to foreign states. But, nothing in Hobbes's theory precludes mutually acceptable conventions licensing intervention in the internal affairs of foreign states. Hobbes's eternal and immutable laws of nature, with the requirement of reciprocity at their core, operate to secure peace at every level, domestic and international, among parties willing to observe them.

7 THE LAW OF NATURE APPLIED TO *JUS IN BELLO* AND *JUS AD BELLUM*

Hobbes himself identified some duties in the treatment of foreign entities owed by sovereigns under the laws of nature to their own subjects. These include avoiding unnecessary wars because, as Hobbes writes in the *Elements of Law*, "such commonwealths, or such monarchs, as affect war for itself, that is to say, out of ambition, or of vain-glory, or that make account to revenge every little injury, or disgrace done by their neighbors, if they ruin not themselves, their fortune must be better than they have reason to expect."[46] Yet the primary duty of sovereigns under the law of nature is to do their utmost to secure *salus populi*.

Wars of self-defense are always morally permissible, and each nation is the ultimate judge of whether its preservation is threatened. But the reciprocity requirement of the law of nature implies that wars to *improve* other peoples, when their improvement is not necessary for our defense, will be morally impermissible just insofar as we would judge it unreasonable of them to wage war on our state in order to improve us. Furthermore, Hobbes offers the example of sending religious missionaries abroad to

---

[45] For discussion of Hobbes's system as aimed at securing optimal agency, see Lloyd 2009: chapter 1.
[46] *Elements of Law* 9.9.

convert foreigners to our national religion as the sort of cultural interference prohibited by the reciprocity requirement of the law of nature because we would not approve their doing the same to us.[47]

The fifth law of nature requiring mutual accommodation forbids depriving others of their necessities for the sake of providing ourselves with superfluous goods, with Hobbes writing that because others can be expected to fight for their necessities (and rightfully so) "he that shall oppose himself against it, for things superfluous, is guilty of the war that thereupon is to follow."[48] Notice, too, that a war to gain superfluities is, *by definition*, an unnecessary war. Hobbes insists in *De cive* that increasing national wealth by preying on other nations "is not to be brought into rule and fashion"[49] and, in *Leviathan*, that should the pressure of a growing population compel a nation to colonize foreign territories, it must, under the law of nature, restrain colonial settlements so that they do not extinguish native populations or deprive them of their means of preservation.[50] It is easy to see the reciprocity requirement at work in these constraints on the treatment of foreign peoples.

8 The Liberties of Troops Under Orders

According to Hobbes's view, democratic citizens are no more responsible for their government's wrongful policies than are the subjects of autocracies or authoritarian regimes because *neither is responsible at all* for its government's wrongful policies. Not having any right under the law of nature to act wrongfully, no one can transfer that right to the sovereign. And being *required* under the right of nature to submit to sovereign authority, each would act wrongfully to refuse its commands.[51] A sovereign is the public judgment to which we are required by the law of nature to defer. What we do wrongfully according to our own private judgment is our own responsibility and leaves us open to moral liability to force. But when morality itself requires us to submit our private judgment to a public judgment, the actions we do (not because we want to do them, but only) because the public authority commands them, are actions for which the blame belongs to it, not us.

This is true as well of troops under orders: "[I]f I wage war at the commandment of my prince, conceiving the war to be unjustly undertaken, I do not therefore do unjustly; but rather if I refuse to do it, arrogating to myself the knowledge of what is just and

---

[47] *Leviathan*, 27, 152.

[48] *Leviathan*, 15, 76.

[49] *Philosophical Rudiments*, 13.14.

[50] *Leviathan*, 30, 181.

[51] Excepting, as earlier noted, commands engaging the "true liberties of subjects" that directly and immediately threaten our preservation.

unjust, which pertains only to my prince."[52] This squares with Hobbes's position in *De homine* 15.2 that "If someone sins at another's command, both sin, since neither did right; *unless*, by chance, the *state* commanded it to be done, *so that the actor ought not to refuse.*"

That the subject is not author of actions commanded by his sovereign in violation of natural law is clearly Hobbes's position, but we might wonder how this can be consistent with his view in chapters 17 and 18 of *Leviathan* that subjects "own and authorize" the actions of their sovereigns. Authorization must be *transitive*: If subjects authorize their sovereign to defend them, and their sovereign commands an action as a means to their defence that is unjust, iniquitous, or otherwise contrary to the laws of nature, then surely the subjects must have authorized that unjust or iniquitous action.

This inconsistency is merely apparent for the simple reason that subjects cannot authorize the sovereign to violate the laws of nature because *they have themselves no right* to violate the laws of nature: "they that vow anything contrary to any law of nature, vow in vain; as being a thing unjust to pay such vow."[53] Subjects cannot authorize the sovereign to act iniquitously "[f]or unless he that is the author hath the right of acting himself, the actor hath no authority to act."[54]

Were we to think of a democratic people as sovereign, Hobbes's hierarchy of responsibility would not insulate ordinary citizens from moral liability for the wrongful actions that, in their role as government, they command themselves to undertake. However, Hobbes took the idea that citizens remain sovereign to be *strictly incoherent*, and his argument to that conclusion is plausible. Each individual is self-governing in a state of nature, but in order for many individuals to become a unified entity—"the people"— they must combine themselves into an "artificial person," or commonwealth, which is done by authorizing a representative (which could be an assembly or even a rule-governed system of bodies) to act on their behalf. Once this is done, individuals are members of a commonwealth, which has sovereign authority.[55] Until it is done, groups of individuals, with each individual acting on private judgment, are a mere "concourse of people," each responsible solely for her individual actions. A sovereign is the authorized representative of a commonwealth; a bunch of people is not a commonwealth until they have authorized a common representative. A number of individuals may mutually agree to take the judgment of the majority of themselves on any question as the will of the body and binding on each member of society, but then sovereignty rests in that majority group, which alone is responsible for any wrongful commands or

---

[52] *Philosophical Rudiments*, 12.2. Hobbes speaks here of knowledge, but what he intends is judgment of what is to be counted as just and unjust.

[53] *Leviathan*, 14, 69.

[54] *De homine*, 15.2, emphasis added.

[55] Hobbes defines a commonwealth as "one person, of whose acts a great multitude . . . have made themselves every one the author, to the end he [the representative] may use the strength and means of them all as he shall think expedient for their peace and common defense. And he that carryeth this person is called SOVEREIGN, and said to have *sovereign power*, and everyone besides, his SUBJECT" (*Leviathan* 17, 88).

policies it issues, with no one having any authority to authorize its actions contrary to the law of nature.

Hobbes further argues against the coherence of the idea that citizens retain private authority to judge the justice of, and refuse to comply with what they think to be, the unjust laws or commands of the sovereign. Hobbes held that the only alternatives consistent with the reciprocity requirement of the law of nature are universal submission of all private judgment to authority or universal retention of all private judgment. Although in practice many areas of decision within commonwealths are left to the discretion of citizens, citizens cannot in principle limit the authority of their sovereign representative. Were the authority of the sovereign to be limited, disagreements could well arise as to whether or not the sovereign had overstepped those limits. In such cases, who is entitled to decide whether the limits have been overstepped? If that decision is up to the sovereign, the limits won't justify action against the sovereign's judgment. If the decision belongs to individuals, they effectively remain in a state of nature because a condition in which each judges for him- or herself whether to defer to the judgment of another remains a condition of universal private judgment, which is just what a state of nature is. If the ultimate decision belongs to some other body, that body is actually sovereign, and the issuing authority merely a subordinate functionary.

9 THE RELATIONSHIP AMONG NATURAL, CIVIL, AND DIVINE POSITIVE LAWS

Hobbes describes the relationship between the moral law and positive civil law as one of mutual containment. What it means to say that these types of law are of "equal extent" and contain each other is subject to interpretation. If the laws of nature command submission to all civil laws, and if every civil legal system must include the laws of nature (and their interpretation and enforcement) as elements of itself, then we might see them as of equal extent and containing each other. If each sovereign has ultimate authority to interpret the laws of nature, and the laws of nature themselves require subjects to treat the sovereign's interpretation of their content as authoritative, Hobbes's system will be a "self-effacing" natural law theory[56] rather than a form of legal positivism. That is, the law of nature will direct subjects to treat the civil law as authoritative, even in its interpretations of natural law. Morality itself requires that we treat legal positivism as if it were true. In this, Hobbes innovated a unique and important theory of law that arguably overcame in the seventeenth century the sterile legal debates of the twentieth century over positivism and natural law.

[56] Lloyd 2009: 264–266.

Divine positive laws, such as the Ten Commandments, also require interpretation. Hobbes argues that Judeo-Christian scripture authorized the civil sovereign to be the final earthly interpreter of these laws.

10 Whence the Claim of the Laws of Nature on Us?

We can organize the landscape of Hobbes scholarship on the question of the normativity of the laws of nature into three main camps: those appealing exclusively to the narrow self-interest of individuals, those appealing to God's command, and that appealing to the requirements of effective agency. The strengths of the first sort of interpretation are that it appears to secure the motivational efficacy of the laws of nature by instrumentally linking them to some desire alleged to be necessary and overriding, that they are simple and straightforward in construction, and that they enjoy an easy fit with the tone of many of Hobbes's remarks. These interpretations are, at least for today's post-Humean reader, the most natural construal of Hobbes's theory. Their disadvantages are that they rely on assumptions and arguments that conflict with complex Hobbesian psychology and so are of dubious normativity, they do not reliably track the particular content of the laws of nature, and they ascribe to Hobbes arguments so philosophically and practically implausible as to make us wonder about Hobbes's competence. Considered in the proper context of Hobbes's political project, these interpretations are almost comically perverse. They have Hobbes showing that if men want to preserve their lives, they should submit to government rather than take up arms against it. It cannot have been news to his readers that war may be hazardous to one's health. Those willing to fight the state are clearly willing to risk death in pursuit of their ends, so how could Hobbes have intended to dissuade them by proffering a demonstration that war threatens their preservation?

In order to capture the eternal and immutable claim of the laws of nature on all rational persons, self-interest interpretations must offer arguments of the following general form:

1. All (sane adult) people *most* desire their own temporal bodily self-preservation.
2. Seeking peace is *necessary* for satisfaction of the paramount desire for temporal bodily self-preservation.
3. It is necessary for peace that all people follow the laws of nature.

Therefore, all people must follow the laws of nature.

However, none those these premises is plausible nor supported by Hobbes's texts.[57] People risk death in pursuit of moral or religious ends or in defense of family or cause

---

[57] See Lloyd 2009: 152–165 for arguments supporting this assertion, and pages 165–182 for objections to Kavka's "rule-egoism" variant of desire-based derivation.

or country or reputation. Some find their prospects better when they do not seek peace. And we know from experience that peace can be had even if many people violate laws of nature.

A. E. Taylor, Howard Warrender, F. C. Hood, and, most recently, A. P. Martinich have defended interpretations that, despite their substantial differences, have been jointly classified as divine command interpretations.[58] These views agree in understanding the normativity of Hobbes's laws of nature to be a function of their having been commanded for our observance by God.[59] Some of these views adopt a traditional instrumental account of the derivation of the laws of nature, but append to it an argument from the nature of law to ensure the normativity of the derived laws, *qua* God's commands. Others suggest that knowledge of the laws of nature is innate, written in the heart. Taylor argued, as against traditional narrow self-interest derivations, that Hobbes's moral theory is independent of his psychological theory and is a strict deontology. Warrender, too, understood Hobbes's psychological theory as formulating empirical postulates employed in the application of his moral theory (his theory of obligation), although no part of that theory. Although Martinich does not press their logical independence thesis, he does agree with Taylor and Warrender that God's command grounds the obligatory nature of the laws of nature.

Divine command interpretations deploy wrongly neglected passages in Hobbes's writings, emphasizing his well-documented assertions that

> [t]he only law that obligates in the state of nature is the law of nature. Law is command, not counsel, directed toward one formerly obligated to obey. The only source of natural obligation in the state of nature is God's irresistible power. Therefore, the Law of Nature obligates in virtue of its being commanded by God toward those formerly obligated by God's irresistible power to obey.[60]

On this basis, they assert that the laws of nature are literally laws, binding as such, and in this way they account for the normativity of the laws of nature.

It is true that Hobbes maintained consistently throughout his political writings that the laws of nature track God's laws as revealed through prophesy and that, considered as God's commands in his natural kingdom, the laws of nature are literally laws. This does not of course suffice to prove that their *normativity consists in their being God's laws*, but it would be silly to deny that Hobbes viewed them as God's laws. The main question, however,

---

[58] See Taylor 1965: 35–55, Warrender 1957, Hood 1964, and Martinich 1992. These views hold that the laws of nature are literally laws in virtue of having been commanded by God and that the laws' normativity (although not necessarily men's actual motive for obeying them) depends on that fact.

[59] Warrender thinks God's command makes the laws of nature obligatory, but he is willing to allow that one might just as well think of the laws of nature as free-standing moral imperatives bearing their own authority. However, they are not to be thought of as contingently obligatory depending on their instrumental relation to the satisfaction of any desire.

[60] Martinich offers this variation on the argument: Justice and injustice require a law. Law requires a common power. The only law in the state of nature is the law of nature. The only common power in the state of nature is God. Therefore, justice and injustice exist in the state of nature because God establishes the law of nature. See Martinich 1992: chapter 4.

setting aside familiar worries about how mere power, even God's, could create genuinely moral obligation, is how to continue from here to derive the specific laws of nature Hobbes enumerates. To say with Martinich that "Hobbes takes it as beyond question that what is deducible as the best means to self-preservation must be the command of God"[61] is to lay one's interpretation open to most of the failings of traditional narrow self-interest views while piling on top the further problem of explaining how those not graced by prophetic knowledge can learn what God has commanded. This is a serious epistemological problem, one that, unless resolved, must undermine the normativity of divine command derivations. The laws of nature are known by reason, but *the fact that they are God's laws cannot possibly be known by reason.* Thus, if their claim on us depends on our acknowledging them to be God's commands, they may press a claim on very few of us. That cannot have been what Hobbes intended. The whole point of relying on reason rather than revelation is to avoid such complicated problems in discerning God's will. The alternative of assuming this knowledge to be innate sits poorly with Hobbes's texts and general method and with his unwavering insistence that the laws of nature are *theorems* of reason, rules *found out by reasoning*. As Kavka put this point, "In the end, we must infer the content of God's commands from our knowledge of the contents of the laws of nature, not vice versa."[62]

Bernard Gert made the case in a number of important works over many years that Hobbes actually took reason to have an end of its own, imposing on us a duty of self-preservation, which duty in turn grounds the laws of nature. Gert collected substantial textual support for his interpretation, and it shares the advantage with other duty-based interpretations of offering to give a firm normative support for the laws of nature. One textual difficulty for any view of this sort is that it will conflict with Hobbes's definition of the right of nature as a liberty to use, or *not use*, whatever means one deems needful for preservation. Gert's view departs from traditional desire-based interpretation in its insistence that natural reason is not merely instrumental, but has its own end or goal, namely self-preservation. Although it may not be the case that all men do in fact desire self-preservation, reason imposes on them a requirement to pursue this end and insists that they rationally ought to desire it. Gert suggested that self-preservation, although the most important of the rationally required desires, is not the only such desire; desires for one's own long-term benefit, for health, for security, and to avoid pain and disability are also rationally required. Although some natural desires are not rationally required, all rationally required desires are natural, Gert maintained, which allows Hobbes to use them as a universal basis for his moral and political conclusions.

Gert's argument for the laws of nature proceeds as follows:

1. The desire for (temporal bodily) self-preservation is rationally required.
2. Seeking peace is necessary for satisfaction of the desire for (temporal bodily) self-preservation.
    C1. Therefore, men should seek peace (as being rationally required).

---

[61] Martinich 1992: 335.
[62] Kavka 1986: 362.

3. The laws of nature are a necessary means to peace.

  C2. Therefore, reason requires men to follow the laws of nature.

This argument adopts the instrumental form of traditional self-interest derivations, but would, if successful, evade their failure to correctly describe human psychology, to track what people most care about. The objection to premise (2) of the argument is familiar: Seeking peace is not always and for everyone either necessary or most conducive to self-preservation (let alone to self-interest more broadly defined). The difficulty unique to Gert's sort of view comes with premise (1). There is scant textual evidence that Hobbes believed reason imposes on us a duty, obligation, or demand to desire any particular ends.

Gert offers as evidence the correct observation that Hobbes conceived of madness as passions run amok, overvehement by our ordinary standards, and unguided by reason. But it is not obvious how this could be supposed evidence that reason dictates ends. For to take Gert's own example, asserting that "someone who uses all of his experience, instrumental reasoning, verbal reasoning, and science in order to kill himself in the most painful possible way, [is] not only … mad, but [is] acting irrationally,"[63] his madness (i.e., overvehemence of passion) does not suffice to make his action irrational unless we assume that he does not, for example, most desire to achieve salvation and believe that choosing a painful death of martyrdom will best achieve his end. But, of course, we can assume no such thing. Even in Gert's imagined extreme case, there is no difficulty in understanding how the behavior might be both mad and rational by Hobbes's analysis. So Hobbes's view that madness exists cannot show that he rejected an instrumental conception of rationality.

More importantly, Hobbes explicitly acknowledges that reason may *require* self-sacrifice or risking death when the survival of the commonwealth is at stake—this is the content of his final law of nature—as Gert himself acknowledged. It makes no sense to hold that reason necessarily requires self-preservation and also forbids it on some occasions.

Third, we count actions as against reason only when they are blameworthy, according to Hobbes; what is wrong with actions against reason is that they cannot be justified to others. But the failure to desire one's own preservation is not itself blameworthy in this sense. We might well justify our suicide to others in terms of the pain, shame, comparative dispensability, or pointlessness of our life. Of course, we may blame a person for her suicide or recklessness when her death precludes her fulfilling her obligations to dependent others, say, but the fault in such cases lies in her failure to honor her obligations and not in her failure to desire or to act to secure self-preservation.

Fourth, and crucially, in relying on premise (1), Gert's argument fails to account for the normativity of the laws of nature, even though this ought to have been its

---

[63] Gert 2001: 248.

great advantage. Not only may some people lack any motivation at all to follow those laws, should they not actually desire self-preservation, but by deriving the duty to seek peace from the assertion that one ought to desire self-preservation, the "oughtness" of that fundamental law of nature receives no satisfying explanation. What is the normative force of Hobbes's "oughts" on Gert's interpretation? We ought to seek peace because we ought to desire self-preservation, but we still have no explanation of how the demand that one desire or take self-preservation as one's paramount end is supposed to be normative for actual people just by saying that not to do so is irrational. What, exactly, is the problem Gert sees with irrationality? Is it that irrationality angers God, as divine command interpretations suggest? Is the problem that irrationality gets us less of what we want, as traditional desire-based interpretations maintain? Or is irrationality supposed to be simply bad in itself, for no reason? Notice, too, that the third and fourth of these problems become intensified when Gert expands his list of rationally required desires because it is only more doubtful that we will see it as proper to blame men for failing to desire each of those things—health, security, avoidance of disability or pain—no matter their other desires, in all or even most cases, and that actual men will desire all the things they "ought" to on this view.

Finally, and most significantly, Gert's account cannot accommodate men's *transcendent interests* in any way that is compatible with its suggested derivation of the laws of nature and is, for that reason, sharply incompatible with Hobbes's complex psychology.[64] Gert holds that self-preservation is rationally required. Is this temporal self-preservation preservation of our natural bodily life or is it cosmic self-preservation of the Christian person beyond bodily death? Because Gert holds that all rationally required desires are *natural*, whereas expectations for life eternal cannot be natural but must depend on supernatural revelation, he cannot take as rationally required anything other than preservation of one's present bodily life. Consideration for the preservation of our current bodily selves is thus supposed to dictate the ultimate requirements of reason. Such a view of reason renders it motivationally inefficacious for most of Hobbes's immediate readership. Hobbes himself clearly rejects it in his many statements proclaiming the rationality of our concern for our eternal over our merely temporal prospects, for instance:

> [I]f the command be such as cannot be obeyed, without being damned to eternal death; then it were madness to obey it;[65]

> [E]*ternal life* is a greater reward than the *life present*; and *eternal torment* a greater punishment than the *death of nature*.[66]

---

[64] For a general discussion of transcendent interests, see Lloyd 1992, especially chapters 3 and 8.
[65] *Leviathan* 43, 321.
[66] *Leviathan* 38, 238.

Definitional derivations of the class to which belongs my account of reciprocity as a requirement of rational agency are distinguished from more familiar self-interest, desire-based interpretations by their refusal to allow any synthetic premises into Hobbes's derivation of his laws of nature. Their reasons for doing so are primarily methodological: Because Hobbes viewed moral philosophy as a science—to be precise, as the science of the laws of nature—and insisted that science is a system of demonstrated truths deduced from universal propositions true by virtue of the definitions of their component terms, no synthetic empirical premises could properly appear in the derivation of the precepts that are the theorems of this science. This methodological constraint would appear to rule out as impermissible the two sorts of empirical claims on which desire-based derivations typically depend: (1) the psychological claim that men desire self-preservation above all else and (2) the causal claims that peace is the only (or the best) means for achieving self-preservation and that the actions and prohibitions demanded or prohibited by the second through twentieth laws of nature are the only (or the best) means for achieving peace. Hobbes is articulating a conventionalist view of science as a purely formal system modeled on Euclidean geometry, and he is committed to the view that moral philosophy, *qua* science (as well as the political philosophy it is intended to ground), must conform to these methodological constraints. The superior fit of definitional derivations of the laws of nature with the philosophical method Hobbes explicitly insists he is using constitutes their primary generic advantage over desire-based derivations as interpretations of Hobbes's intended theory.

McNeilly sees peace as what he terms a "necessary" value because, like power, it is something a person who wants anything must also want. But he distinguishes sharply between the reasonableness of seeking peace and the reasonableness of entering a peace. Obtaining peace on simply any terms is not reasonable, for "[p]eace is not to be promoted at the cost of all the values which it is intended to serve ... How this cost is calculated will depend on the particular values of each particular person."[67] So, although the fundamental law of nature requires us to think of peace as desirable and to investigate whether it makes sense for us to do what we'd need to do to secure it, that law does not actually require us to make peace.

The main difficulty in McNeilly's attempted derivation of the laws of nature is that it understands the first and fundamental law to say that we should do what it takes to settle a peace *only if we believe our ends are best promoted by doing so*. Whether and on what terms to settle a peace is entirely up to the individual, according to his own particular values, beliefs, sense of his relative power and bargaining position, and the like. And so long as enough others do seek peace that a general social environment is created that will allow the agent some hope of success in pursuing his ends, there is no need at all for the agent himself to do anything other than perhaps appear to go along with the norms others have obligated themselves to observe or fly below their radar in

---

[67] McNeilly 1968: 195.

pursuing his own ends. Because it is not true at all, least of all true by definition, that others will settle a peace only if *every individual* participates or that others will settle a peace only if *I*, the agent, do so as well, McNeilly's account will not yield Hobbes's intended first law of nature, which directs each and every agent to settle a peace with willing others.

This problem is reproduced in his effort to derive the second law of nature requiring that a man be willing when others are also willing to lay down his right to all things and be contented with as much liberty as he is willing to allow to others. Although it is true that so long as everyone retains his or her right to all things there can be no peace, it does not automatically follow that each must give up this right or that all who do so must do so equally.[68] It is enough to undo the terrible effects of a universal unlimited right that not everyone retains a right to all things. And because, again, it is neither empirically plausible nor true by definition that no one will lay down his right unless each and every person does so equally, McNeilly's considerations will not yield Hobbes's second law of nature. This problem is not confined to McNeilly's definitional interpretation but is endemic to desire-based derivations as well and also to Martinich's divine command account insofar as he takes the content of God's laws of nature to direct necessary means to self-preservation. All of these equally elide the argument from the desirability of peace to the conclusion that any rational agent must do his fair share in securing peace. What is needed is an *analytically defended premise* that shows that *reason dictates reciprocity*. That is precisely what we have in the derivation offered in Section 2 on Hobbes's reciprocity theorem.

References

Gert, Bernard. 2001. "Hobbes on Reason." *Pacific Philosophical Quarterly* 82: 243–257.

Hobbes, Thomas. 1990. Behemoth or The Long Parliament, edited by Ferdinand Tonnies with an introduction by Stephen Holmes. Chicago: University of Chicago Press.

Hobbes, Thomas. 1968. *Leviathan*, ed. C. B. Macpherson. Harmondsworth: Penguin.

Hobbes, Thomas. 1995. *Three Discourses*, edited by Noel B. Reynolds and Arlene W. Saxonhouse. Chicago: University of Chicago Press.

Hobbes, Thomas. 1998. *On the Citizen*, translated by Richard Tuck and Michael Silverthorne. Cambridge: Cambridge University Press.

Hood, Francis C. 1964. *The Divine Politics of Thomas Hobbes*. Oxford: Clarendon Press.

Kavka, Gregory S. 1986. *Hobbesian Moral and Political Theory*. Princeton, NJ: Princeton University Press.

Lloyd, S. A. 1992. *Ideals as Interests: The Power of Mind over Matter*. New York: Cambridge University Press.

Lloyd, S. A. 2009. *Morality in the Philosophy of Thomas Hobbes: Cases in the Law of Nature*. New York: Cambridge University Press.

---

[68] Martinich (2005: chapter 3) argues that it may be rational to settle peace on subequal terms.

Martinich, A. P. 1992. *The Two Gods of Leviathan*. Cambridge: Cambridge University Press.

Martinich, A. P. 2005. *Hobbes*. London: Routledge.

McNeilly, F. S. 1968. *The Anatomy of Leviathan*. New York: Columbia University Press.

Taylor, A. E. 1965. "The Ethical Doctrine of Hobbes," in *Hobbes Studies*, edited by K. C. Brown. Cambridge, MA: Harvard University Press.

Warrender, Howard. 1957. *The Political Philosophy of Hobbes*. Oxford: Oxford University Press.

PART III

POLITICAL PHILOSOPHY

CHAPTER 13

....

POLITICAL OBLIGATION

....

JOHN DEIGH

1 Hobbes and the Modern Theory of Natural Law

THE ideas about political allegiance that prevailed in the West in the seventeenth century derived from Christian thought. Specifically, they derived from the Christian view of human beings as universally subject to laws that God ordains for their good. These laws, according to Christian dogma, are not only divine but also natural in the sense of belonging to nature and thus, with respect to human beings, human nature. And because they are part of human nature, people come to know them through reason as well as revelation. These laws constitute the foundations of morality. They are the fundamental principles of right and wrong in how people live their lives. Morality, therefore, on the Christian understanding of it, is inherent in human nature and not an externally imposed code of conduct. This notion of morality as founded on natural law ordained by God for the benefit of humankind received in the work of Thomas Aquinas its clearest and deepest theoretical exposition.[1] Aquinas's exposition from its publication in the thirteenth century and throughout the rest of the Middle Ages was the standard statement of the theory. The theory then underwent significant change in the seventeenth century. While the change did not affect the identification of universal standards of morality with laws of nature, it did alter the understanding of the relation of these laws to the common good of humankind.

On the Thomistic understanding, the laws of nature were determinants of natural goodness. Accordingly, human goodness corresponded to a good human life, and to live such a life, a happy life, a person's appetites and passions had to be in harmony with his or her reason and judgment. Such harmony consisted in knowledge of the ends it was worth pursuing in life and how to achieve them and in mastery of one's

---

[1] Aquinas 1963.

appetites and passions that ensured their being attuned to those ends and the means one chose to pursue them. A person thus lived in accordance with natural law when he or she achieved such knowledge and self-mastery. On the seventeenth-century understanding, by contrast, the laws of nature were standards of right action in the sense of action incumbent on men and women for their self-preservation and the preservation of their fellows. While living in accordance with the laws of nature was therefore necessary for living well, provided that others too lived in accordance with them, it was not sufficient, let alone definitive, for living a good human life. A person whose conduct conformed to the laws of nature might still be unfortunate in the choices he made of the ends to pursue and could, as a result, live a very unhappy life. Natural law on either understanding brought moral order to human life. But the kind of order it brought on the scholastic understanding differed from the kind it brought on the seventeenth-century understanding. On the former, such order was reflected in a well-ordered soul. On the latter, it was reflected in a peaceful community. The difference represented a radical change in how natural law was theorized.

The chief architect of this change was Hugo Grotius. The modern theory of natural law originates in his writings.[2] Grotius was principally a jurist. The theory he fashioned was the product of a mind trained in the law, and its notion of natural law was a lawyer's notion. Accordingly, just as lawyers understand civil laws as instruments for maintaining peace and resolving conflicts within the societies they regulate, so Grotius understood natural law as serving similar ends in circumstances unregulated by positive law. He first applied this understanding to a dispute between a Dutch shipping company and some of its shareholders over the company's right to distribute as prizes booty that one of its ships acquired through seizure of a Portuguese galleon on the high seas. The shareholders' opposition to the distribution was religiously based and made in view of Portugal's claim to dominion over the waters in which the galleon was seized. As against Portugal's claim, however, Grotius maintained that these waters were international and as such no country's civil law applied within them. At the same time, he denied that such waters were lawless areas. To the contrary, conduct on them was regulated by laws that governed the conduct of every ship and sailor and that, by virtue of their being part of human nature, were knowable by all men. This thesis, moreover, was an instance of the general truth that these laws governed the conduct of men in any area of the world or in such circumstances as war, in which no civil government had jurisdiction. Grotius, then, first in an early work, *De Iure Praedae*, and then in his great work, *De Iure Belli ac Pacis*, expounded the natural law and how it applied in these areas and circumstances.

The main premisses of Grotius's theory are that self-preservation is the dominant end in human life and that human beings are sociable creatures. The two features that these premisses describe combine to generate the core problem of the natural human

---

[2] Grotius 1925 and Grotius 1950. For fuller accounts of Grotius's ideas, see Tuck 1979: 58–81; and Schneewind 1998: 66–81.

condition. The problem arises from these features because individual efforts at self-preservation lead to conflict among people as each competes with others for the goods he or she needs, and these conflicts are sufficiently fierce as to thwart the desires people have for social relations. Moreover, it resists individual resolution, since to pull back from the competition would be to put one's preservation in jeopardy, yet unrestrained competition destroys any hope of a sociable life. To resolve the problem, then, requires collective change in behavior. In particular, it requires reciprocal exercises of self-restraint by all. The laws of nature prescribe the terms of the mutual self-restraint necessary for the members of a society to live together peacefully on conditions that respect the right of each to self-preservation. Accordingly, Grotius held that the laws of nature, which God ordained and people knew by virtue of their reason, established the moral order within human society that diminished human conflict and thereby kept the society from disintegrating. The theory of natural law, as Grotius expounded it, was thus a theory of the moral order by which human beings lived together peacefully. This order included a ruler or ruling body empowered to enact and enforce civil laws necessary for maintaining that order and for defending the society from foreign enemies. It was thus a political order, the society a political society or commonwealth. The theory's explanation of how men formed a commonwealth and empowered one man or a body of men to rule as sovereign over them explained as well the political authority of the ruler or rulers and the political obligation that each subject had to obey them.

Grotius's theory provided the framework within which the major political philosophers of the seventeenth century worked out their theories of political obligation. The most profound of these theories was due to Thomas Hobbes. Unlike Grotius, Hobbes was not a lawyer; he was a man of letters. Soon after graduating from Oxford he was employed by an aristocratic English family as a tutor. That position brought him into contact with important philosophers both in England and abroad. In midlife, Hobbes began writing treatises in philosophy and politics. His philosophical writings covered ontology, physics, psychology, religion, and ethics as well as law and politics, and he worked systematically on all of these topics. To this end he found Grotius's theoretical framework as applied to the latter two topics especially congenial to his program. Throughout his writings in political philosophy he never abandoned this framework. At the same time, the theory of political obligation he developed within the framework materially changed from his earliest work, *The Elements of Law*, which he wrote and privately circulated in 1640, to his masterpiece, *Leviathan*, which he published in 1651.[3] For this reason the common practice among scholars of taking Hobbes's theory to be static and each of the different texts in which he expounded it—*Elements*, *De Cive*, and *Leviathan*—to be presenting the same set of core ideas though expressed somewhat differently is liable to misrepresent Hobbes's thought at these different stages of its development. One should instead treat these texts separately and use the differences

---

[3] Hobbes published a Latin translation in 1668. The translation has attracted scholarly interest because it does not consistently match the English text of 1651.

among them as a guide to the deeper argument in each that supports their common Grotian themes.

In either case, the primary text is *Leviathan*. Those who take Hobbes's theory to be static typically treat this work as the basic text to be interpreted and treat the other works as supplementary. This way of treating Hobbes's works, however, as I said, tends to yield unreliable interpretations. On the alternative, which takes each of the works as deserving separate interpretation, the theory as formulated in *Leviathan* has, in virtue of *Leviathan's* being Hobbes's mature and deepest statement of his political philosophy, a privileged position in relation to the theory's formulations in the other works. It is the one that is properly identified as Hobbes's theory of political obligation, just as the final draft of an essay is the one that is properly identified as the author's view. I favor this alternative way of treating Hobbes's work.

Accordingly, I focus, in the discussion that follows, on the theory's formulation in *Leviathan*.[4] I take this formulation to represent Hobbes's considered view and regard the formulations in the earlier works as representing views whose reworking yielded the view expressed in *Leviathan*. I do not, then, regard the texts of these earlier works as expressing the same ideas as Hobbes advanced in *Leviathan* and therefore do not treat them as sources of alternative formulations that provide evidence of these ideas and so help to resolve problems of interpretation that *Leviathan's* text presents. In a larger project than I can undertake here, they would prove useful as expressions of alternative ideas that Hobbes entertained as he worked out his theory within the Grotian framework. Seeing these alternatives would lead, I believe, to greater appreciation of the theory as Hobbes formulated it in his masterwork.[5]

2 HOBBES'S SCIENTIFIC METHOD

Hobbes saw his theory as a contribution to science. Indeed, his ambition was to expound a science of politics.[6] Its different branches included ethics and politics as well as such physical sciences as mechanics, astronomy, geology, and optics.[7] In *Leviathan*, Hobbes explains the method of science and commends it as the method one applies to achieve knowledge of universal truths in the areas that the different branches cover.

---

[4] I use Hobbes's English text only and ignore the alternative formulations in the Latin translation. The differences raise questions of provenance and purpose that I cannot address here. For discussion of the differences, see Edwin Curley, "Purposes and Features of this Edition," *Leviathan* (Indianapolis: Hackett Publishing Co., 1994), pp. lxxiii–lxxiv.

[5] For relevant differences between Hobbes's exposition in *De Cive* and his exposition in *Leviathan*, see Deigh 2012. For relevant differences between Hobbes's exposition in *The Elements of Law* and these other two works, see Tuck 1979: 119–42.

Hereafter I use DC to abbreviate *De Cive* and L to abbreviate *Leviathan* and will cite page numbers for DC from Hobbes 1998, and page numbers for L from Hobbes 1996.

[6] For Hobbes science is the same as philosophy.

[7] L: 61.

Since his ambition was to develop a science of politics, one can assume that he applied this method in working out, in books I and II of *Leviathan*, the central arguments of his theory. How rigorously he applied it, however, is not always clear. Hobbes, in writing *Leviathan*, had rhetorical as well as philosophical ambitions, and his pursuit of the former sometimes obscures how successful he was in carrying out the latter.[8] Nonetheless, a good working assumption in interpreting the central arguments of the theory is that they conform to the method of science as Hobbes understood it.

Science, in Hobbes's view, is knowledge gained through the proper use of reason. In *Leviathan* he defines reason as the faculty of calculating with words. "This word *Reason*," he writes, "when wee reckon it amongst the Faculties of the mind, . . . is nothing but *Reckoning* (that is, Adding and Subtracting) of the Consequences of the general names agreed upon, for *marking* and *signifying* of our thoughts."[9] The proper use of reason, then, is sound calculation with general names whose denotations are fixed by agreement. Hobbes explains this method in chapter 5 after having laid its groundwork in chapter 4. Scientific knowledge, he declares, consists of propositions that are derived in accordance with logic from true propositions that one forms by using apt definitions of the terms "appertaining to the subject at hand."[10] The method for achieving such knowledge consists in first setting down apt definitions of the general names that pertain to the relevant branch of science and then deriving through reason, that is, through the adding and subtracting of names, the consequences of affirmations formed from these names on the basis of definitions that are the starting points of the science. Definitions are apt only if the *definiendum* and the *definiens* are coextensional. What makes the propositions one forms from apt definitions true, then, is there being in each case a connection between the subject and the predicate such that the extension of the predicate contains that of the subject. The definitions thus figure as premises in a branch of science, and one arrives at knowledge in that branch only if one starts with apt definitions of the relevant terms and understands each subsequent use of those terms as expressing the meaning given in the definitions with which one starts.[11]

This last point, given the assumption that the central arguments of Hobbes's theory conform to the method of science as he understood it, yields an important stricture on interpreting *Leviathan*'s presentation of those arguments. Because conformity to the method requires consistency in the use of the words whose definitions are the arguments' premises, one must assume, in the absence of evidence to the contrary, that Hobbes uses the words he defines consistently. In other words, one must assume, in the absence of contrary evidence, that these words have, in each of their occurrences, the meaning he assigns them with those definitions. Further, one must have strong evidence to justify an interpretation that goes against this assumption. For Hobbes not only implies, in giving an explanation of the method of science as he understands it, that

---

[8] See Skinner 1996: 343–56.
[9] L: 32.
[10] L: 35.
[11] For a more detailed account of Hobbes's view of science, see Deigh 1996.

the central arguments of his theory reflect consistent use of the words he defines but also censures those who ignore the method's requirement that one's words be defined and used consistently with the meanings assigned in those definitions. "Seeing then that *truth* consisteth in the right ordering of names in our affirmations," he observes, "a man that seeketh precise *truth*, had need to remember what every name he uses stands for, and to place it accordingly; or else he will find himselfe entangled in words, as a bird in lime-twiggs; the more he struggles, the more belimed."[12] And thus to avoid such entanglement, Hobbes continues, "men begin at settling the signification of their words; which settling of significations, they call *Definitions*; and place them at the beginning of their reckoning."[13]

The assumption that Hobbes uses the words he defines consistently in accordance with those definitions is particularly important to interpreting the theory of political obligation in *Leviathan*. How to interpret the theory is controversial. The controversy has tended to divide scholars on questions the answers to which depend on whether they accept or reject the assumption. Specifically, the two leading interpretations differ according as Hobbes is read as consistent or inconsistent in his use of words crucial to his formulation of the theory. In the following sections, I will first (section 3), expound Hobbes's theory without broaching this controversy, then (section 4), explain the controversy and present the portions of *Leviathan*'s text that give rise to it, and finally (section 5), adjudicate the competition between the leading interpretations.

3 HOBBES'S EXPLANATION
OF POLITICAL OBLIGATION

Hobbes's theory explains the obligation subjects have to their sovereign. It is a moral obligation. To breach it is to act unjustly. The injustice is the same in every case. It consists in a subject's breaking a promise of obedience to the sovereign. The circumstances of that promise, however, differ according as the subject belongs to the group of people who formed the commonwealth and elected the sovereign or belongs to a people whom the sovereign has conquered or, last, belongs to a generation of people that is younger than the generations who first formed the commonwealth or were conquered and subsequently subjected to the rule of a foreign sovereign. In the first case, which Hobbes calls commonwealth by institution, each subject, through contracts that he or she makes with every other, promises in exchange for a similar promise by each of the others obedience to whomever they elect sovereign. In the second case, which Hobbes calls commonwealth by acquisition, the subjects, being members of a vanquished people, make promises of obedience directly to the victors' representative. In the last case,

---

[12] L: 28.
[13] Ibid.

the subjects make promises of obedience directly to whoever is already sovereign at the time of the promise.

The relation between sovereign and subject in all three cases is nonreciprocal. In none of them does the sovereign have an obligation to any of the subjects, while in all three each subject has an obligation of obedience to the sovereign. The reason is that the sovereign makes no promise to any of the subjects. All the promises are made by the subjects, either to one another or to the sovereign directly. The sovereign, then, in virtue of having no obligation to any of the subjects, has the right to do anything with regard to them. At the same time, the subjects' obligations of obedience to the sovereign are not total. Because, in Hobbes's view, it is common knowledge that no one could voluntarily submit to his own demise. Any promise not to defend oneself against lethal attack, Hobbes argues, is invalid; hence no one could be obligated to forbear from defending himself from such an attack. This generalization is true even and especially when the sovereign is the attacker. Hence subjects do not violate their obligations of obedience to the sovereign if, contrary to the sovereign's commands to submit to lethal force, they resist the sovereign's efforts to kill or torture them. Subjects thus retain, as part of their right of nature, a right to resist the use of lethal force against them. This right of resistance is, on Hobbes's argument, inalienable. Accordingly, he held that the subjects are not subordinate to the sovereign in all manner of action, and their obligation to obey the sovereign does not give the sovereign absolute rule over them.

Hobbes maintained that the relation between sovereign and subject was the same in all three cases. Accordingly, he crafted his theory's explanations of the subjects' obligations to obey the sovereign to sustain this feature. The theory's explanation in the case of commonwealth by institution is the base case. The explanations in the other two cases derive from it. Accordingly, let us start with it.

3.1 Commonwealth by Institution

Hobbes, in keeping with Grotius's theoretical framework, begins with an account of men and women in their natural condition. Self-preservation is the driving end of their actions. Their individual efforts to preserve themselves, when they are in this condition, lead them into conflict with each other, and the conflicts they engage in become increasingly deadly as each seeks more and more power to defeat his or her enemies. At the same time, because no one can make himself or herself invulnerable to lethal attack, none can become so powerful as to be able to achieve permanent dominance over all others. Consequently, the situation is destined to degenerate into a war of each against everyone else unless they all, or at least most of them, collectively take steps to preempt such a war. And because no one in such a war can expect to survive for long, foresight of its likelihood inclines people toward taking those steps. It inclines them, in other words, to form a society whose collective power is sufficient to protect each from the dangers of all-out war. On Hobbes's version of the Grotian paradigm, the desire men and women have for society, which brings them together, derives from their horror of the war that will break out among them, a war of all against all, if each continues to live without lasting ties to others.

Essential to the argument in *Leviathan* for the inevitability of a war of all against all, if men and women were to remain in their natural condition, is the exclusion of reason from this condition. As I noted earlier, Hobbes, in *Leviathan*, defines reason as the faculty of calculating with words. Accordingly, he denies that reason is a natural faculty.[14] On his account of human cognition, reason is a cognitive power men and women acquire by learning language. The cognitive powers they have innately are their senses, memory, and imagination. These natural powers are sufficient for them to be able to anticipate future events on the basis of their past experiences, and as their store of experiences enlarges, their ability to anticipate future events becomes greater. Hobbes defines this ability as prudence. The more experiences a man or woman has, the more prudent he or she becomes. Men and women in their natural condition are more or less prudent, and their prudence explains their seeking more and more power to defeat their enemies. Prudence alone, however, is insufficient to show them what steps they must take to establish peace and thus preempt a war of all against all. Reason is also necessary. Only through reason will they gain knowledge of those steps. It takes reason, in other words, properly used, to gain knowledge of the actions necessary to achieve peace. That knowledge is the science of justice, whose results, or theorems, as Hobbes calls them, are the laws of nature that men and women must follow if they are to avoid conflict that inevitably escalates into a war of all against all.

Specifically, their following the laws of nature is necessary to create the bonds among them through which they can achieve peace. These bonds are artificial in the sense that, unlike, say, bonds of love between parents and their children, they are wholly products of voluntary action. Initially, men and women in their natural condition are free to do what is necessary to preserve themselves. They have, as Hobbes puts it, a right of nature, and in their natural condition, this right is a right to all things. As long as they retain this right, they will be disposed to take from others whatever they need to survive, and likewise they will be disposed to interfere with the actions of others whenever such interference is necessary for their survival. These dispositions undermine their interest in achieving peace. The first law of nature, which Hobbes presents as the fundamental law, is that one seek peace if one has hope of achieving it. Accordingly, the second law, which Hobbes derives from the first, is that one must be willing to give up one's right to all things to the extent necessary to achieve peace so far as others are willing to give up theirs to the same extent. The acts by which one gives up a portion of this right are the acts by which the bonds necessary for peace are created.

In general, one gives up one's right to all things, that is, reduces the amount of freedom one can claim for doing what is necessary to preserve oneself, by committing oneself through declarations or other signs of commitment to forbear from doing certain

---

[14] On this point, see Deigh 1996: 47–52.

actions. One can do this universally by renouncing the right, although such renunciation is not likely to improve one's chances of preserving oneself. Alternatively, one can
do it selectively by making a commitment to another to forbear from doing certain
actions. In that case, Hobbes says, one transfers one's right to do those actions to this
other person, who then stands to benefit from one's commitment insofar as one's forbearances keep one from interfering with his efforts at self-preservation. Let us refer to
him as the beneficiary of one's commitment. In making such a selective commitment
one becomes obligated or bound to its beneficiary. That is, one is under an obligation
to him to forbear doing those actions one signified one is committed not to do. With
respect to others, however, to whom one has made no such commitment, one remains
as free as before. Hence, by making such a commitment and thus becoming obligated
to its beneficiary, one creates an artificial bond to him.

One can create such bonds unilaterally. In that case, Hobbes says, one makes a
free gift to the beneficiary of the right one has transferred to him. The alternative is
the mutual creation of such bonds, which is to say, the mutual transference of rights.
Hobbes calls such mutual transferences contracts. A contract benefits both parties
insofar as the forbearances to which each is committed in making the contract keep
him from interfering with the other's efforts at self-preservation. Indeed, the second
law of nature anticipates the reciprocal benefits that contracts provide, for to follow
the law people must make contracts with each other. Sometimes the commitment
that a party to a contract makes consists in a promise to forbear from doing certain actions at some time in the future. Such a commitment is what Hobbes calls
a covenant. Covenants, because they entail a delay in performing one's part of the
contract, require that the other party trust one to perform. If there is no trust, then
no contract will be made. And if, after making such a contract, one gives the other
party sufficient reason to warrant loss of trust, then the contract is void. In addition,
then, to the second law of nature, which requires that one make contracts, there
must also be, if peace is to be achieved, a law requiring that one keep the promises
implicit in the contracts one makes. In other words, following the first law requires
not only following the second but also following this third law, that one keep one's
covenants.

Hobbes takes the third law to be the foundation of justice. To renege on a commitment is to breach the promise implicit in it. Such a breach, Hobbes says, is the very
definition of injustice. Justice then, as Hobbes defines it, consists in keeping one's
covenants. Once Hobbes introduces this standard of justice into his theory, he puts
himself in position to explain how people can create the artificial bonds by which they
achieve peace. They do so by undertaking obligations to each other to obey a single
individual or an assembly whom they subsequently elect sovereign. These obligations
result from each transferring his or her right to all things to every other member
of the group, and such a transference is brought about by a contract in which each
covenants to obey whoever is elected sovereign. Each then bonds with every other to
form an artificial union of men and women under the rule of the individual or assembly whom they elect sovereign, and as Hobbes observes, they do so "by Covenant of

every man with every man, in such manner, as if every man should say to every man, *I authorise and give up my Right of Governing my selfe, to this Man, or to this Assembly of men, on this condition, that thou give thy Right to him, and Authorise all his Actions in like manner.*"[15] And while men and women in their natural condition cannot be expected to keepsuch covenants, once reason guides their actions, which to say, once they recognizedand follow the laws of nature, these covenants can serve as an instrument for theirachieving peace.

3.2 Commonwealth by Acquisition

Hobbes produced his main works in political philosophy at the time of the English civil war. His sympathies were royalist, and he hoped that his works would aid the royalists' cause. Since England's royal monarchs based their claims to rule on their being descendants of William the Conqueror, Hobbes would have doubtlessly seen the necessity of including in his theory an explanation of the obligation of subjects to sovereigns who had come to power by force. Giving such an explanation within Grotius's theoretical framework, however, presents a problem. Theories that have this framework explain how a commonwealth is formed by supposing that each subject makes a contract with every other to obey whomever they elect sovereign. The obligations of obedience the subjects then have arise from these contracts, and a standard assumption behind this explanation is that the subjects make these contracts voluntarily. When someone or some assembly comes to power by force, by contrast, as happens when a people are conquered, any assumption that vanquished people become obligated by voluntarily promising obedience to the victors would seem absurd. To the contrary, the same force that brought about their defeat is bound to explain their obedience as well. Accordingly, promises they make to obey the victors would be, with few exceptions, coerced. Hence, one apparently cannot assume of any of them that he or she makes such a promise voluntarily. Consequently Grotius's theoretical framework appears to be unsuitable to explaining the obligations of subjects to sovereigns who have come to power by force.

   Hobbes is well aware of this problem. He deals with it directly in *Leviathan* by denying that promises of obedience that the members of a vanquished people make to the victors are any less voluntary than the contracts people would make in forming a commonwealth so as to end the war of all against all. In either case, Hobbes observes, people make these covenants out of fear, and the object of their fear is death and violence at the hands of another or others. In the case of commonwealth by acquisition, they fear death and violence at the hands of the victors. In the case of commonwealth by institution, each fears death and violence at the hands of the others. It follows, then, that though the source of the fear differs in these cases, the emotion's object is the same. Hence, the motive of their action in making these promises is the same. Consequently,

---

[15] L 120.

if their promises give rise to obligations of obedience in one case, they give rise to such obligations in the other.

Of course Hobbes's argument does not show that such promises give rise in either case to obligations. It shows only the biconditional proposition that they give rise to obligations in one case if and only if they do so in the other. Thus if, in either case, the promises were made involuntarily, then promises made out of such fear would not give rise to obligations. Hobbes, though, recognizes this possibility and argues against it.[16] Early in *Leviathan* he distinguishes between voluntary and vital movements.[17] The former are produced when the imagination stimulates appetites and aversions; the latter are those movements, like automatic breathing or blinking, that occur independently of thought or imagination. All movements that spring from fear, which is a type of aversion, are therefore voluntary. Hobbes then applies this result to the covenants by which people found a commonwealth or submit to the rule of a conqueror. He thus brings his theory into conformity with the assumption behind explanations of the sort that fit the Grotian paradigm. At the same time, Hobbes acknowledges the common view that promises extracted by threats do not give rise to obligations. This view, he argues, reflects civil law, which invalidates promises made under threats of death or violence.[18] The reason such promises do not give rise to obligations, Hobbes argues, is not that they are made out of fear but rather that the civil law, which is to say, the sovereign, disallows the transference of the right to what is promised that they would otherwise bring about. When people in their natural condition make promises, as is true of the covenants by which people found a commonwealth or submit to the rule of a conqueror, the motive behind them is irrelevant to their giving rise to obligations, since they are made before the enactment of any civil law that might invalidate them.

Hobbes, having thus shown that the covenants of subjects to a sovereign who has come to power by force are as valid as the covenants by which people found a commonwealth, declares that the covenants in either case consist in the same promise. They differ, he points out, only in the character of the transactions by which they are made.[19] The covenants people make in founding a commonwealth are mutual. Each consists in a promise of obedience to whoever is elected sovereign that a person makes to every other founding member of the commonwealth in exchange for a like promise of obedience from each of them. By contrast, the covenants that people who have been vanquished make to the victors are unilateral. Each consists in a promise of obedience to the victors that a member of the vanquished makes in hopes of receiving in return from them the benefits of life and liberty. Thus, while the motive and content of these promises are the same in either case, the transaction by which the right to all things is transferred in the founding of a commonwealth is different from the transaction by which it is transferred in the submission of vanquished people to the rule of the victors.

---

[16] For a more extensive account of Hobbes's view, see Deigh 2002: 483–506.
[17] L: 37–38.
[18] L: 139.
[19] L: 138.

In the former, the right is transferred through a contract that each subject makes with every other. In the latter, the right is transferred through a free gift that each subject makes to the sovereign.

3.3 Allegiance of the Members of Later Generations

Hobbes does not directly discuss the obligations that subjects who belong to generations whose members were born after the formation of the commonwealth have to their sovereign. Nevertheless his explanation of these obligations is evident from his explanations in the other two cases. Subjects who belong to these later generations recognize that the sovereign has the power of life and death over them. Consequently, their situation is like that of a vanquished people. They too fear death and violence at the hands of their sovereign and accordingly, though only implicitly, promise obedience to the sovereign. "[E]very man," Hobbes writes, "is supposed to promise obedience, to him, in whose power it is to save, or destroy him."[20] Accordingly, their obligations to obey the sovereign, like the obligations of a vanquished people, result from their making a free gift to the sovereign of their right to all things in hopes of receiving in return the benefits of life and liberty.

4 AN EXEGETICAL CONTROVERSY

The issue that has generated the main controversy among scholars over how to interpret Hobbes's theory is the place of the laws of nature, specifically the third law, in the theory's explanations of these obligations. The issue arises with respect to the explanations in all three cases but is most perspicuous in the first case, commonwealth by institution. Accordingly, let us focus exclusively on the explanation in this case. The issue is, to put it succinctly, whether covenants consisting in promises of obedience to whoever is elected sovereign are alone sufficient to explain the subjects' obligations to obey that individual or assembly once the election occurs. Scholars who affirm the sufficiency of these covenants correspondingly hold that no law of nature contributes to the explanation.[21] Obversely, scholars who deny the sufficiency of the covenants hold that the laws of nature, particularly the third law, help to explain the obligation to obey the sovereign. Indeed, they hold that if men and women in their natural condition were not subject to the laws of nature, the covenants each made to every other to obey whomever they elected sovereign would not bring about any obligation to obey that individual or assembly.[22]

---

[20] L: 140.

[21] See, e.g., Watkins 1965, Gauthier 1969, Kavka 1986, and Gert 2010.

[22] See, e.g., Warrender 1957, Hood 1964, Martinich 1992, and Schneewind 1998.

The issue arises because Hobbes, in *Leviathan*, does not clearly accept Grotius's notion of the laws of nature as defining obligations that people have in all circumstances and so in circumstances that lie outside of the jurisdiction of any commonwealth. His definition of a law of nature as "a Precept, or generall Rule, found out by Reason, by which a man is forbidden to do, that, which is destructive of his life" omits the idea of such a law's defining an obligation.[23] Indeed, at the close of chapter 15, he appears explicitly to reject Grotius's notion. There he writes, in reference to the laws of nature whose exposition he has just concluded, "These dictates of Reason, men use to call by the name of Lawes, but improperly: for they are but Conclusions, or Theoremes concerning what conduceth to the conservation and defence of themselves; whereas Law, properly is the word of him, that by Right hath command over others."[24]

And he repeats the point in chapter 26, where he writes, "For the Lawes of Nature . . . in the condition of meer nature (as I have said before in the end of the 15th chapter,) are not properly Lawes."[25] Plainly, if the laws of nature are not properly laws before a commonwealth is formed, then they are not properly laws at the time people make covenants for the purpose of forming a commonwealth. Consequently, none of them can contribute to the explanation of the obligations to obey the sovereign that people undertake through these covenants.

Nevertheless, many scholars have resisted taking these passages as decisive. Hobbes's remarks at the close of chapter 15, in particular, are ambiguous. In the sentence immediately following the one I quoted, he writes, "But yet if we consider the same Theoremes, as delivered in the word of God, that by right commandeth all things; then are they properly called laws."[26] And this sentence has spurred scholars to look for other passages that support interpreting Hobbes as conceiving the laws of nature as universally obligatory by virtue of being commands of God despite his not having defined them as such. One such passage occurs a few paragraphs before chapter 15's closing remarks. In this passage, Hobbes characterizes the laws of nature as binding in conscience but not in practice,[27] and some scholars have taken this characterization as implying that they define obligations that bind conscience while leaving people free to ignore them when making war is necessary for self-preservation. Additional passages occur in chapter 31, which concludes book II and in which Hobbes, through discussion of what he calls the kingdom of God by nature, negotiates the transition from the philosophical treatment of his subject to its theological treatment in books III and IV. For example, Hobbes, who later in the chapter

---

[23] L: 91.

[24] L: 111.

[25] L: 185. Hobbes here qualifies the thesis that the laws of nature are not properly laws by restricting it to the circumstances of "meer nature" because, as he goes on to say, "When a Common-wealth is once settled, then are they actually Lawes, and not before; as being then the commands of the Common-wealth." L: 185.

[26] L, p. 111.

[27] L: 110.

identifies the laws of nature with God's laws,[28] writes, "The Right of Nature, whereby God reigneth over men, and punisheth those that break his Lawes, is to be derived, not from his creating them as if he required obedience, as of Gratitude for his benefits; but from his *Irresistible Power*."[29] And again in the same paragraph, he declares, "To those therefore whose Power is irresistible, the dominion of all men adhaereth naturally by their excellence of Power; and consequently it is from that Power, that the Kingdome over men, and the Right of Afflicting men at his pleasure, belongeth Naturally to God."[30]

Of course interpreting Hobbes as having conceived the laws of nature as universally obligatory by virtue of being commands of God does not alone show that any of the obligations they define is crucial to Hobbes's explanation of the subjects' obligations to obey their sovereign. To make an argument for taking one of them—specifically, the obligation that the third law defines—as crucial to the explanation requires showing that Hobbes did not take the contracts on which a commonwealth is founded to be on their own the source of obligations to obey the sovereign. And the evidence for so interpreting Hobbes is chiefly the passage near the beginning of chapter 15 in which he says as much. That passage is worth quoting at length.

> [B]efore the names of Just and Unjust can have place, there must be some coërcive Power, to compel men equally to the performance of their Covenants, by the terrour of some punishment, greater than the benefit they expect by the breach of their Covenant; and to make good that Propriety, which by mutual Contract men acquire, in recompense of the universal Right they abandon: and such power there is none before the erection of a Common-wealth. . . . And therefore where there is no . . . Propriety, there is no Injustice; and where there is no coërcive Power erected, that is, where there is no Common-wealth, there is no Propriety; all men having Right to all things: Therefore where there is no Common-wealth, there nothing is Unjust. So that the nature of Justice, consisteth in keeping of valid Covenants: but the Validity of Covenants begins not but with the Constitution of a Civill Power, sufficient to compel men to keep them.[31]

Plainly, if no covenant a person makes before a commonwealth is formed can bring about the transference to another of a right, then no such covenant can on its own be the source of an obligation. Hobbes makes this point by first distinguishing, in chapter 14, between valid and invalid covenants and then asserting, in this passage, that no covenant a person makes before a commonwealth is formed is valid. Since only valid covenants bring about the transference of rights, people cannot bring about such a transference prior to their founding a commonwealth. Hence, the obligation to obey whomever they elect sovereign that arises from the contracts they make with each other for the purpose of founding a commonwealth must have its source outside of

---

[28] L: 248.
[29] L: 246.
[30] L: 247.
[31] L: 100–101. See also, L: 90.

these contracts. Accordingly, its source, given the interpretation of Hobbes as conceiving the laws of nature as universally obligatory by virtue of their being commands of God, is a law of nature, specifically the third law. Being universally obligatory, this law binds men and women even before they form a commonwealth. It also applies to covenants regardless of whether they meet the conditions of validity Hobbes expounds in chapter 14. The latter point, to be sure, might seem problematic. Shouldn't the making of a covenant give rise to an obligation only if the covenant is valid? But if the conditions of validity are understood as conditions covenants must meet to bring about on their own a transference of a right, then the point still holds. On this interpretation, one transfers a right through making a covenant only if making the covenant gives rise to an obligation to keep it. In other words, on this interpretation, the right is transferred as a result of the obligation one incurs rather than vice versa.

Unfortunately, Hobbes does not consistently affirm the thesis that covenants people make before they form a commonwealth are invalid. Indeed, he explicitly contradicts it in chapter 14. "Covenants entered into by fear, in the condition of meer Nature," he writes, "are obligatory. For example, if I covenant to pay a ransome, or service for my life, to an enemy; I am bound by it. For it is a Contract, wherein one receiveth the benefit of life; the other is to receive mony, or service for it; and consequently, where no other Law (as in the condition, of meer Nature) forbiddeth the performance, the Covenant is valid."[32] This statement counters the evidence for interpreting Hobbes as holding that the contracts on which a commonwealth is founded are not on their own the source of the obligation to obey the sovereign. Thus, if the controversy is to move past the apparent stalemate that these contradictory passages create, one must introduce as a criterion for evaluating competing interpretations some other measure than how closely the interpretation fits the text. Such measures may differ according to which of the several interests Hobbes had in writing *Leviathan* one assumes was his primary one. Taking as our working assumption, as I suggested in section 2, that Hobbes's philosophical interest was primary, we should then, in evaluating the competing interpretations, use as the measure how closely the theory that an interpretation attributes to Hobbes conforms to his method of science.[33]

5 RESOLUTION OF THE CONTROVERSY

Accordingly, the question is on which of the two competing interpretations of Hobbes's theory we have considered does the theory more closely conform to this method. Let

[32] L: 97–98.

[33] See p. 7 above. It makes sense to use this measure if one is assessing *Leviathan* as a work of philosophy. Clearly if one assumes that, instead of an interest in philosophical truth, some such interest—as advancement of the royalist cause or reduction in the religious hostilities that had in England erupted into civil war—was primary, then one should use a different measure. Examining which interest was in fact primary is beyond the scope of this chapter. The assumption I make is, as I said, a working assumption.

us refer to these interpretations as the contract interpretation and the divine command interpretation. On the former, the contracts on which a commonwealth is founded are on their own the source of the obligation to obey the sovereign. On the latter, the source of the obligation to which those contracts give rise is the third law of nature. Other things equal, an interpretation that attributes to Hobbes consistency in his use of his theory's chief terms more closely conforms to his method than one that does not, for the method requires that these terms be defined and used consistently with the meaning given them in these definitions. This consideration argues for preferring the contract interpretation to the divine command interpretation. Comparing how the two represent Hobbes's use of the term 'obligation' shows that the contract interpretation is the better one.

Hobbes defines 'obligation' in chapter 14. After explaining the two ways in which one can lay down a right—renunciation and transference—he writes, "[W]hen a man hath in either manner abandoned, or granted away his Right; then is he said to be Obliged, or Bound, not to hinder those, to whom such Right is granted, or abandoned, from the benefit of it."[34] Either of these ways of laying down a right consists in an act of speech or its equivalent in deed. On either, one declares one's commitment to forbear doing certain acts or signals that commitment nonverbally. In short, on Hobbes's definition, every obligation has as its source some voluntary act performed by the person who acquires it. Or as Hobbes puts the point later, in chapter 21, "there [is] no obligation on any man which ariseth not from some act of his own."[35] Only the contract interpretation represents Hobbes as consistently using the term with this meaning. The divine command interpretation, by contrast, represents him as sometimes using the term with a different meaning. Specifically, because Hobbes's theory, on this interpretation, holds that every law of nature is universally binding and therefore a source of obligations independently of any voluntary act on the part of those it binds, the interpretation represents Hobbes as using 'obligation' with a different meaning from the one given in his definition.

Because the divine command interpretation attributes to Hobbes this deviation from his method of science, its defenders must justify the attribution. Their justification consists in the passages from chapters 15 and 31 cited earlier as showing that Hobbes conceived the laws of nature as binding in virtue of being commands of God. Yet these passages are not conclusive.

Consider, first, the remark at the close of chapter 15 that the laws of nature are properly called laws even before a commonwealth is formed. It is not a categorical affirmation. What Hobbes affirms is a hypothetical proposition—namely, if one considers the laws of nature as commands issued by God to those over whom he rules, then they are properly called laws even before a commonwealth is formed. This proposition is consistent with his categorically denying that they are properly called laws.

---

[34] L: 93–93.
[35] L: 141.

So, too, Hobbes's statement that the laws of nature bind *in foro interno* is open to an interpretation on which it is consistent with his definition of obligation. The distinction between the laws' binding *in foro interno* and their binding *in foro externo* is, Hobbes points out in a remark following this statement, a distinction between an obligation one breaches by intending to do an act in violation of a law and an obligation one breaches by acting in violation of a law. This distinction anticipates the distinction he later draws, in chapter 27, between sin and crime. To sin, Hobbes says, is to show contempt for a lawgiver by intending to violate his laws, and a crime, as he defines it, is a sin that includes acting in violation of the law that one intended to violate. Thus every crime is a sin, but not every sin is a crime.[36] Accordingly, when Hobbes writes in chapter 15 that the laws of nature bind *in foro interno*, he means to be capturing the idea of sinning against God. The question, then, is how the obligation to God arises such that one can sin against him. And while part of the answer is that it arises in virtue of the obligation to obey God, the full answer requires determining how this latter obligation arises. It begs the question to assume that the obligation arises independently of the voluntary acts of those who have it. That is, it begs the question to assume that when Hobbes describes the laws of nature as binding *in foro interno*, he is using a notion of obligation that is inconsistent with the one he defines in chapter 14. Consequently, although they bind *in foro interno*, whether they bind everyone may be contingent on everyone's performing an act of the kind that gives rise to the obligation.

Hobbes gives the full answer to the question how obligations to God arise near the beginning of his discussion, in chapter 31, of the kingdom of God by nature. Explaining what he means by such a kingdom, he first dismisses as metaphorical the use of the expression 'kingdome of God' to mean God's dominion over all things, humans, animals, plants, and inanimate bodies. Metaphorical speech, Hobbes holds, is unfit for science. It is one of the abuses of speech and causes of absurdity that he canvasses in chapters 4 and 5 when he explains the proper uses of speech in the service of science. The expression when properly used, Hobbes says, refers to God's power to rule over his subjects by verbal instructions to which rewards for compliance and punishment for noncompliance are attached. Thus, he writes,

> For he onely is properly said to Raigne, that governs his Subjects, by his Word, and by promise of Rewards to those that obey it, and by threatning them with Punishment that obey it not. Subjects therefore in the Kingdome of God, are not Bodies Inanimate, nor creatures Irrationall; because they understand no Precepts as his: Nor Atheists; nor they that believe not that God has any care of the actions of mankind; because they acknowledge no Word for his, nor have hope of his rewards, or fear of his threatnings. They therefore that believe there is a God that governeth the world, and hath given Praecepts, and propounded Rewards, and Punishment to Mankind, are Gods Subjects; all the rest, are to be understood as Enemies.[37]

---

[36] L: 201.
[37] L: 245–46.

The model Hobbes appears to be applying to explain what he means by 'the king-dome of God by nature' is that of a commonwealth in which God is the sovereign. Not every man or woman, however, is a subject in this commonwealth. To the contrary, Hobbes excludes atheists and believers who deny God's providence. They are not, in their natural condition, bound by the laws of nature. They are, Hobbes says, to be understood as enemies of God rather than sinners against him.[38] Only those, then, who believe in God and that he rewards those who obey him and punishes those who do not are his subjects.[39] And while Hobbes does not explain why, the answer would appear to be that, like the relation of victors to those they have vanquished, God has the power of life and death over human beings. Accordingly, the same principle that he uses to explain how in the latter case, the case of sovereignty by acquisition, the obligation to obey those who have the power of life and death over one arises applies in the former case as well. When one sees that another has unassailable power over one's life and has hope of receiving from him the benefits of being spared death and violence in return for the promise of obedi-ence, one makes such a promise. Of course such a promise will be made only by people who both recognize that another has such unassailable power over their lives and believe that this all-powerful person will exercise that power to benefit or harm them according as they obey or disobey him. Hence it does not apply to any atheist or any believer who denies God's providence. Atheists and believers who deny God's providence may, through reason, come to know the laws of nature, but in their natural condition they know them only as "Theorems concerning what conduceth to the conservation and defence of themselves."[40]

It remains to consider the passages from chapter 31 that defenders of the divine com-mand interpretation cite to justify their attributing to Hobbes inconsistency in how he uses the term 'obligation'. These passages reflect what I earlier called the nonreciprocal relation between sovereign and subject. Every subject has an obligation of obedience to the sovereign, but the sovereign has no obligation to any of the subjects. In ruling, the sovereign acts as he or she pleases in the case of monarchy and however the supreme assembly wills in the cases aristocracy and democracy. It is as though the sovereign

---

[38] Hobbes subsequently makes clear, by reference to Job and the afflictions he suffers from God, that one may still be subject to God's punishment even though one has not sinned against him. See L: 247.

[39] He reaffirms this point in the next paragraph, "[T]here may be attributed to God a twofold Kingdome, *Naturall* and *Prophetique*: Naturall, wherein he governeth as many of Mankind as acknowledge his Providence." L: 246 (italics in original).

[40] L: 111. Some may question this way of explaining the grounds of Hobbes's restriction on who the subjects in the kingdom of God by nature are because Hobbes, when specifying in ch. 14 the validity conditions on covenants, writes (L, p. 97), "To make Covenant with God, is impossible, but by Mediation of such as God speaketh to, either by Revelation supernaturall, or by his Lieutenants that govern under him, and in his Name." See e.g., Gauthier, *The Logic of the Leviathan*, pp. 194–95. But Hobbes in this passage denies only the validity of covenants made directly with God. He allows that covenants made with God through the mediation of a representative are valid. In this respect, such a covenant would be no different from one made with a conqueror through the mediation of a representative, and the latter possibility is perfectly in order in Hobbes's theory. Nothing in the theory, after all, makes it necessary that a conqueror actually visit a country whose people his or her army has vanquished to be their sovereign.

retained, after the formation of the commonwealth, the right to all things that men and women, in their natural condition, have. Thus, when Hobbes speaks of "the Right of Nature, whereby God reigneth over men, and punisheth those that break his Lawes," he is pointing out this feature of God's position as supreme ruler over humankind. And in going on to trace this position to God's irresistible power, his point is that God, unlike men and women in their natural condition, has no need to negotiate a contract with anybody, since owing to his omnipotence, none is capable of hurting him. Consequently, nothing drives him to give up his right to all things, a right that no man or woman would give up either were it not necessary to do so to avoid death and violence at the hands of others. This point is consistent with no one's ever having an obligation to obey God, for it is consistent with no one's ever promising obedience. That many men and women do is thus the result of their recognition of God's omnipotence and their hope of his benefiting them in return for promises of obedience.[41]

Similarly, when Hobbes subsequently speaks of God's "dominion of all men", he is again referring to God's irresistible power. Thus, elaborating the point, he writes, "[C]onsequently it is from that Power, that the Kingdome over men, and the Right of Afflicting men at his pleasure, belongeth Naturally to God." At the same, he says, in chapter 20, that dominion is either sovereignty as one finds it in a commonwealth by acquisition or analogously the position of parents in relation to their children. In either case, it results from promises of obedience that a vanquished people or children make to those whom they recognize as having the power to save or destroy them. Thus, his description of "those . . . whose Power is irresistible" as having dominion of all men is consistent with his definition of obligation since it implies that all men have promised to obey those with such power. Still, the implication contradicts his earlier observation that atheists and believers who deny his Providence are not subjects in the kingdom of God by nature. His saying in this passage that God has dominion of all men appears, then, to be a slip. In any case, the confusion to which the passage leads makes it inconclusive evidence at best for the divine command interpretation.

Finally, some scholars have suggested that Hobbes would not have used the term 'law of nature' if he did not regard the laws of nature as universal laws that bind men and women as such. After all, they point out, Hobbes takes the meaning of a term that consists of two names joined together, such as 'raw meat' or 'hot meal', as a function of the separate meanings of its component names.[42] One problem with this suggestion, though, is that it requires treating the passages in which Hobbes states that the laws of nature are not properly laws as incoherent asides. But even if one ignores these

[41] The case for interpreting Hobbes as referring in this passage to God's irresistible power without implying that all men and women are obligated to obey him is strengthened by comparison with the corresponding discussion in *De Cive*, ch. 15, of the kingdom of God by nature. In the discussion in *De Cive*, Hobbes introduces the notion of a natural obligation, an obligation that arises from nature and is due to the weakness of human beings as distinct from one that arises from agreement. DC: 173–75. In *Leviathan*, by contrast, he abandons this distinction of two kinds of obligation. On this point, see Brian Barry 1968: 117–37.

[42] See Hoekstra 2003:111–20; and Lloyd 2009: 200–1.

passages, the suggestion does not advance the case for the divine command interpretation. Since Hobbes defines law as a command "addressed to one formerly obliged to obey [its commander],"[43] taking him, as the suggestion implies, to mean by 'law of nature' a law as he here defines it, merely raises anew the question of how obligations to God arise.

More important, though, is the failure implicit in the suggestion to grasp the role of definitions in the method of science as Hobbes understands it. Definitions in this method are the starting points of the reasoning, which is to say, the adding and subtracting of words, that yields the theorems of science. The definitions serve as instructions concerning with what words one can replace other words when one is adding and subtracting them. Recall that apt definitions must be ones in which the *definiendia are coextensive with their definiens*.[44] Otherwise the adding and subtracting of words would not preserve truth. Hence, when a term consisting of two names joined together is defined, the definition preempts the use of the definition of either name whenever that name occurs as a component of the term. Likewise, it preempts the use of either name with some undefined meaning whenever the name occurs as a component of the term. The preemption is necessary to prevent the term from having two distinct extensions and thus being ambiguous. It is necessary, in other words, to prevent the very problem that Hobbes sees definitions as averting.

Hobbes's own practice reflects this understanding of the preemptive role that a definition of a term that consists of two names conjoined together has in the method of science. 'Law of nature' is not the only such term Hobbes defines. In chapter 21, for instance, he defines 'liberty of subjects' after first defining 'liberty'. His definition of 'liberty' is the absence of external impediments to motion. His definition of 'liberty of subjects', is the absence of laws forbidding action. Hobbes, however, also observes that laws in themselves are not external impediments to action and hence that one speaks absurdly in holding that a law deprives one of liberty. 'Liberty', therefore, when it occurs in 'liberty of subjects', does not have the meaning with which Hobbes defines it. As Hobbes puts the point, in such occurrences it is not used with its proper sense.[45]

A successful defense of the divine command interpretation ultimately requires giving convincing evidence that Hobbes, in explaining, in *Leviathan*, the subjects' obligations of obedience to the sovereign, understood 'a law of nature' differently from how he defined it in chapter 14. For the case for taking him to be using the term 'obligation' differently from how he defined it depends on his deviating in his use of 'law of nature' from its definition in chapter 14. Careful examination of the evidence that defenders of this interpretation commonly advance for this deviation shows that it is less than convincing. Consequently, on the assumption that in parts I and II of *Leviathan* Hobbes's philosophical interest is primary, the contract interpretation, being the one that more

[43] L, 183.
[44] L: 28.
[45] See L:145–48.

closely conforms to his method of science, represents his theory better than does the divine command interpretation.

6 Conclusion

The peculiarity of Hobbes's definition of a law of nature is that it omits, in sharp departure from the natural law tradition, attribution of such laws to God's will. The omission is too striking to be inadvertent. Presumably, it reflects Hobbes's interest in expounding theories of ethics and politics that qualify as science. Science, in his view, is the product of natural reason, and knowledge gained through natural reason is importantly different from what he calls prophetic knowledge, knowledge that comes from revelation.[46] As opposed to Descartes, Hobbes denies that science rests on knowledge of God. His assertion that "the Name of God is used, not to make us conceive him; (for he is Incomprehensible; and his greatnesse, and power are unconceivable;) but that we may honour him" implies as much, since if there is no apt definition of God, no branch of science includes theorems about him.[47] Some scholars suggest that Hobbes's omission of any reference to God's will from his definition of a law of nature is evidence of closeted atheism.[48] But this suggestion overreaches. It is evidence only of Hobbes's view of and aspiration for science. This view and this aspiration make him the most farsighted of the seventeenth-century philosophers who adopted Grotius's theoretical framework. They explain, in large part, why *Leviathan* remains a vital work for contemporary moral and political theory.

Bibliography

Aquinas, Thomas. 1963. *Summa Theologica* IaIIae94. London: Blackfriars.

Barry, Brian. 1968. "Warrender and his Critics." *Philosophy* 43: 117–137.

Curley, Edwin. 1994. "Introduction to Hobbes's Leviathan," in *Leviathan*, edited by Edwin Curley. Indianapolis, IN: Hackett.

Deigh, John. 1996. "Reason and Ethics in Hobbes's Leviathan." *Journal of the History of Philosophy*, 34: 33–60.

Deigh, John. 2002. "Promises under Fire." *Ethics*, 112: 483–506.

Deigh, John. 2012. "Hobbes's Philosophy in De Cive and Leviathan." *Hobbes Studies*, 25: 199–208.

Gauthier, David. 1969. *The Logic of Leviathan: The Moral and Political Theory of Thomas Hobbes*. Oxford, UK: Oxford University Press.

---

[46] L: 246.

[47] L: 23. N.B., Hobbes prefaces this assertion with the same point he makes against Descartes's claim to having an intellectual idea of God as independent, infinite, all-powerful, all-knowing, and creator of all things. See Hobbes 1970: 71–72.

[48] See, e.g., Curley 1994: xxxi.

Gert, Bernard. 2010. *Hobbes: Prince of Peace*. Cambridge, UK: Polity Press.

Grotius, Hugo. 1950. *Commentary on the Law of Prize and Booty (De Iure Praedae Commentarius)*, translated by Gwladys L. Williams and Walter H. Zeydel. Oxford, UK: Clarendon Press.

Grotius, Hugo. 1925. *On the Law of War and Peace (De Iure Belli ac Pacis)*, translated by Francis W. Kelsey. Oxford, UK: Clarendon Press.

Hobbes, Thomas. 1969. *The Elements of Law*, 2nd ed. Edited by M. M. Goldsmith. New York: Barnes & Noble.

Hobbes, Thomas. 1970. "The Third Set of Objections, with the Author's Reply." *The Philosophical Works of Descartes*, reprint ed., vol. II, translated by Elizabeth S. Haldane and G.R.T. Ross. Cambridge, UK: Cambridge University Press.

Hobbes, Thomas. 1996. *Leviathan*, edited by Richard Tuck. Cambridge, UK: Cambridge University Press.

Hobbes, Thomas. 1998. *On the Citizen*, edited by Richard Tuck and Michael Silverthorne. Cambridge, UK: Cambridge University Press.

Hoekstra, Kinch. 2003. "Hobbes on Law, Nature, and Reason." *Journal of the History of Philosophy* 41: 111–120.

Hood, F. C. 1964. *The Divine Politics of Thomas Hobbes: An Interpretation of Leviathan*. Oxford, UK: Oxford University Press.

Kavka, Gregory. 1986. *Hobbesian Moral and Political Theory*. Princeton, NJ: Princeton University Press.

Lloyd, Sharon. 2009. *Morality in the Philosophy of Thomas Hobbes*. Cambridge, UK: Cambridge University Press.

Martinich, A. P. 1992. *The Two Gods of Leviathan: Thomas Hobbes on Religion and Politics*. Cambridge, UK: Cambridge University Press.

Schneewind, J. B. 1998. *The Invention of Autonomy: A History of Modern Moral Philosophy*. Cambridge, UK: Cambridge University Press.

Skinner, Quentin. 1996. *Reason and Rhetoric in the Philosophy of Hobbes*. Cambridge, UK: Cambridge University Press.

Tuck, Richard. 1979. *Natural Rights Theories: Their Origin and Development*. Cambridge, UK: Cambridge University Press.

Warrender, Howard. 1957. *The Political Philosophy of Hobbes: His Theory of Obligation*. Oxford, UK: Oxford University Press.

Watkins, J.W.N. 1965. *Hobbes's System of Ideas: A Study of the Political Significance of Philosophical Theories*. London: Hutchinson.

....

CHAPTER 14

AUTHORIZATION
AND REPRESENTATION
IN HOBBES'S *LEVIATHAN*

....

A. P. MARTINICH

IN *Leviathan*, Thomas Hobbes holds that prospective subjects[1] authorize a sovereign to represent them. Authorization and representation, the two key concepts in Hobbes's political theory in *Leviathan* are, of course, closely related to other significant concepts. Representatives are persons, and giving up or alienating some rights to the sovereign typically follows upon authorization. In this chapter, I explicate Hobbes's distinctive view of these concepts. The project is difficult because he seems to have changed his view and his terminology, and he sometimes did not write clearly, whether by accident or design.

1 AUTHORIZATION AND ALIENATION

....

The theory of the origin of sovereignty that appears in chapter 21 of *Leviathan* was preceded by those in *The Elements of Law, Natural and Politic* (1640), *De cive* (1642, 1647), and chapter 17 of *Leviathan* (1651). Hobbes's last statement of the origin of sovereignty by institution is in the Latin *Leviathan* and will be discussed last of all. The earliest two books rely on the concept of alienation alone to explain the relation between the sovereign and the subjects. According to those books, when a group of people decides to institute a government, each member of the group alienates her rights "to the will of one man or one council."[2] If the rights are alienated to some one person, the result is a

---

[1] Hereafter I'll use "subject" to denote both subjects and prospective subjects.
[2] *De cive* 5.6; see also *Elements of Law* 19.7. *De cive* and the *Elements of Law, Natural and Politic* will be referred to by chapter and section.

monarchy; if they are alienated to an assembly of a few people, the result is an aristocracy; and if they are alienated to an assembly of all the people, the result is a democracy.

One apparent problem with Hobbes's theory of alienation is that it does not indicate the limits of the rights that are alienated. Although the rights given up by one person are equal to the rights given up by every other person, neither the precise rights nor the number of them given up is specified. Let's consider only the number of them. If all of one's rights were alienated, then the subject would not have the right to resist the sovereign. If the right of self-preservation is retained, then it is arguable that Hobbes is logically committed to the subjects' retaining a substantial number of other rights because of his "right-to-the-means-to-an-end" principle: "Whoever has a right to the end has a right to the means to that end."[3]

It seems sensible that subjects would judge that the means necessary to that end included disobeying the sovereign in some situations. Furthermore, subjects cannot reasonably give up the right to judge when their lives are in immediate danger because that is tantamount to giving up the right of self-preservation.[4] And this is something that human beings cannot do, according to Hobbes's understanding of human beings.

Another problem with the "pure alienation" theory is that it is plausible that the alienation of rights may be unacceptable to citizens. This was particularly true of those English in the seventeenth century who prided themselves on being free and believed the myth of the Norman yoke, according to which the English were free until William conquered England, when the native Anglo-Saxons lost that freedom. If, in alienation, the subjects give up their rights, then they have no personal stake in the government, and it would be easy for them to complain about what the government does with the rights that it possesses. When subjects do not personally participate in a government, they may become psychologically alienated from it and that alienation leads to political instability.

Even though he never explicitly rejected the pure alienation theory of *The Elements of Law* and *De cive*, at some point, he must have seen that a better theory was available because he gave a substantially different and more attractive theory in chapter 17 of *Leviathan*, "the theory of authorization-cum-alienation." The key passage expressing this theory is the first part of what I call "the sovereign-making formula":

> I Authorise and give up my Right of Governing my selfe, to this Man, or to this Assembly of men.[5]

---

[3] See *Leviathan* 18.8, 90; also 14.21, 68. References to *Leviathan* give the page in a copy of the 1651 Head edition preceded by the number of the chapter and paragraph, where appropriate. See Hobbes 2011.

[4] I think that the suggested argument, considered as an objection to Hobbes's theory, is cogent. Sreedhar (2010) argues that Hobbes actually held this doctrine. I think he does not acknowledge the objection and would not want to because it would frustrate his desire to make the sovereign absolute.

[5] *Leviathan* 17.13, 87.

There is a problem with this passage. It is contradictory or incoherent. The incoherence results from the different grammatical requirements of "authorize" and "give up." The verb "authorize" takes a name or description of a person as its direct object (and perhaps an infinitive phrase).[6] But the verb "give up" takes a name or description of some right or rights as its direct object and a prepositional phrase that says to whom the rights are given up. Hobbes tries to make the phrase "this Man, or to this Assembly of men" fulfill both requirements and it cannot. If the direct object of "authorize" is the phrase "this man or assembly of men," then that phrase cannot be the object of the preposition "to" in the phrase "give up my right *to* this Man or Assembly of men" (emphasis added). And if that phrase is not the object of the preposition "to," then that preposition does not have an object. A noun cannot simultaneously be a direct object and the object of a preposition. This grammatical defect points to the existence of a difference between authorization and alienation about which Hobbes was not yet clear. His lack of clarity about the two concepts results in a contradictory thought.

He tries to make the same right to be both alienated and the object of authorization even though it is impossible to authorize a person to exercise some right R if one has given up or alienated R.[7] Suppose Soma sells or gives her bicycle to Boris. She thereby gives up or alienates her right to it, and this alienation includes the right of telling Boris how he may use it. Authorization is different. If a person P authorizes someone to exercise some right on P's behalf, P retains the right and hence can instruct the recipient about how to exercise it. Alternatively, if Soma rents her bicycle to Boris, she alienates some use of her bicycle to Boris in exchange for money while she retains the right of ownership.

One might object that I have not considered another sense of "authorization" that is compatible with the alienation of rights. According to this sense, the person P bestowing authorization continues to take responsibility for the exercise of the alienated right by the person authorized. So, in this sense, P alienates P's rights to the sovereign S, and S represents P in the exercise of P's now lost rights. This concept is highly counterintuitive. Alienating a right and representing someone are logically independent actions.

---

[6] The phrase, "I authorize" is grammatically incomplete. One must say who is authorized to do what. Whenever Detective Joe Fontana, played by Dennis Farina in *Law and Order*, wanted to get a citizen to allow him and his partner to do something they were not legally permitted to do, he said to the citizen, "It's okay; we're authorized." Authorized by whom to do what?

[7] It may seem that the sovereign does not receive any rights that he did not have before the alienation because of Hobbes's remark, "For he that renounceth or passeth away his right giveth not to any other man a right which he had not before [because there is nothing to which every man had not right by nature], but only standeth out of his way, that he [the 'recipient'] may enjoy his own original right without hindrance from him" (*Leviathan* 14.2). However, there's a difference between A's right to, say, eat an apple and B's right to, say, eat an apple. A's right is for A to eat an apple and B's right is for B to eat an apple, and these are different rights. Virtually every sovereign depends on subjects' positively contributing to the sovereign's work. So, the right of the sovereign S to defend B, is not the same as the right of B to defend B. If subjects did not transfer their particular rights to the sovereign, they would be hindering it. See further Martinich 2005: 150–154. Johan Olsthoorn raised the issue in this footnote and helped me formulate my response.

One can alienate a right without any person representing another, for example, in giving a gift. And one can represent someone without there being any alienation, as, for example, in a friend being the proxy of another gratis. The fact that Hobbes used two terms, "authorize" and "give up," suggests that he had some sense that two things are involved. Also, we will see that when he presents his theory in chapter 21, he separates the two concepts of authorization and alienation. Although it is not contradictory to coin a word to designate two very different actions, the conjunction of a person's giving up a right R to a sovereign S and that person's being responsible for S's exercise of R does not fit Hobbes's conception of authorization.

Also, the suggested interpretation of authorization would remove the attraction of authorization. Authorization is supposed to immunize the sovereign from criticism. Subjects cannot reasonably criticize their sovereign for doing something if the action is actually owned by them. If they don't like the behavior of the sovereign, they should criticize themselves. The other side of the attractiveness of authorization is that it gives subjects a reason to identify with their sovereign. In seeing him act, they are seeing their own actions.

So far, I have not considered the entire sovereign-making formula. A person authorizes the sovereign to govern and gives up some rights: "on the condition that thou give up thy right of governing yourself and authorize all of his actions." It may well seem that this passage provides a clue as to how the entire formula can be interpreted in a consistent and politically defensible way. This interpretation—the "government-alienation" interpretation—does not save "the [grammar] of the passage but does preserve its sense."[8] All persons alienate their right to govern themselves and authorize all the actions of the sovereign. This interpretation does remove the contradiction I described. But it has a serious problem as an interpretation of Hobbes's political philosophy. If subjects give up their rights of governing themselves, then they end up with virtually no rights that they may authorize the sovereign to exercise. There is not much left if subjects give up their right of governing themselves. And the remaining rights are not even the right ones—the right ones being precisely the ones they gave up, the rights of governing themselves and all that are entailed by doing so, such as the right to judge what rights the subjects need to give up in order for the sovereign to do its job. In a word, the government-alienation interpretation of the sovereign-making formula trivializes authorization.

My objection to the government-alienation interpretation is obviously connected with the scope of government. Alienating fewer rights is better than alienating more rights, and alienating trivial rights is better than alienating dearly held rights, ceteris paribus. If the number and costliness of the rights actually or potentially given up did not greatly affect the contentment of citizens, alienation of them would be acceptable. So the question arises: Exactly which rights are given up, and which are immune from alienation? Hobbes had given a relatively detailed answer to this question in *De cive*.

---

[8] I am grateful to Robin Douglass for offering this interpretation; the quoted phrase is his.

The sovereign must have the right to punish, the right to raise and keep armed forces, the right to judge when the armed forces should be deployed, the right to determine the rules of property, and the right to immunity from all laws.[9]

This relatively detailed answer is far from a complete description and not detailed in the way a subject should want it detailed. Despotism is in the details. There is no a priori way to know what the sovereign will command its subjects to do. Giving the sovereign the right to defend subjects from internal and external enemies and the right to make all political judgments leaves open the possibility that everyone will be required to do two years of service in the armed forces, or fourteen, or forty, and to have to practice Reformed Protestantism or Roman Catholicism or Islam, et cetera. The specific possibilities are limitless and cannot be exhaustively described. The phrase "et cetera," rather than being shorthand for a possible, complete description, in fact indicates that subjects are open to almost unlimited restrictions on their freedom. What the sovereign will in fact command will be determined by what the sovereign thinks the circumstances are and his attitude about responding to them. We might say that the sovereign has an "et cetera" right.

It is no good to hold that the "et cetera" right is innocuous because, as Hobbes pointed out, the sovereign's commands cannot cover most activities in life. But Hobbes is wrong about how oppressive laws can be. He underestimates the abilities of rulers from Caligula to Kim Jong-Il to make life miserable for people. The serious problem is not the number of rights that a sovereign may require one to give up. Being commanded not to play tiddlywinks at 2:00 AM on Wednesday, not to eat cactus needles, not to use incandescent light bulbs, and ten million other things would not involve any diminution in one's contentment. The problem is losing dearly held rights, such as those listed in the Universal Rights of Man; that leads to misery. The danger in granting an et cetera right to an authority was recognized in the events leading to the English Civil War. The Convocation of 1640 passed Canon 6, which required all officials of the Church to take the following oath:

> I, A. B. do swear that I approve the doctrine and discipline, or government established in the Church of England, as containing all the things necessary to salvation: and that I will not endeavour by myself or any other, directly indirectly, to bring in any popish doctrine . . .; nor will I ever give my consent to alter the government of this Church by archbishops, bishops, . . . *et cetera*.

Opponents of the Laudian Church understandably resisted taking what they called the "et cetera" oath because they realized that the "et cetera" exposed them to being required to approve of all sorts of doctrines and disciplines abhorrent to them. Hobbes in effect endorsed the content of an et cetera clause when he wrote that the sovereign has "*the chief authority in the city, for direction of future actions of his citizens.*"[10] The

---

[9] *De cive* 6.3–10.
[10] *De cive* 6.9.

right to make future, unspecified laws, unrestricted except by such weak considerations as the threat of immediate death, indicates that Hobbes would be comfortable replacing his sovereign-making formula with a paraphrase of the et cetera oath:

> I, A. B. swear to give to the sovereign my rights to defend myself against external and internal enemies, my rights to what the sovereign needs to defend myself against them, my right to judge what the sovereign needs to defend myself against them; *et cetera*.

Only a reckless or naïve person would accept an et cetera clause or anything equivalent in a sovereign-making formula. The et cetera clause would undermine the freedom of Englishmen and the principle that neo-Roman republicans believed was key to liberty—namely, the right not to live under the possibility of oppression.[11]

The general problem with the government-alienation interpretation of the sovereign-making covenant is that it minimizes the attractiveness of authorization. The attractiveness, as Hobbes intended it, is that acceptance of the government, and thereby responsibility for its actions, is written into the terms of establishing it. The actions of the sovereign are owned by and properly attributed to the subjects.

It did not take Hobbes long to see that authorization and alienation are conceptually separate. Whereas government, according to Hobbes, needs both authorization of a sovereign and alienation of rights, authorization logically precedes alienation. This difference between authorization and alienation, and the way that the first theoretically does not need the second, is explained in chapter 21 of *Leviathan*, "Of the Liberty of Subjects,"[12] his best account of the institution of sovereignty.[13]

This is not to say either that Hobbes did not struggle with the relationship between the two concepts or that he wanted to do without alienation. Alienation is a practical necessity in almost every case of absolute sovereignty. This may explain why, in the early part of chapter 21, he says that political liberty is what remains after the sovereign has laid down all the laws:

> The liberty of a subject lieth therefore only in those things which, in regulating their actions, the sovereign hath pretermitted, such as is the liberty to buy, and sell, and

---

[11] Pettit 1997 and Skinner 2008.

[12] It is possible that Hobbes began to see the light as early as his writing of chapter 18. In the first paragraph, he wrote that a sovereign is created when "a *Multitude* of men do agree and *Covenant*, *every one, with every one*, that to whatsoever *Man* or *Assembly of Men*, shall be given by the major part, the *Right* to *Present* the Person of them all . . . shall *Authorise* all the Actions and Judgements of that Man, or Assembly of men . . ." (*Leviathan* 18, 88). Although Hobbes used a form of "give," he did not say that men give *up* their rights. Rather something is given *to* the sovereign. So there is no mention of alienation here. In effect, the sovereign is given a right that consists of the power to govern. This is another way of saying that the sovereign is authorized.

[13] If it seems strange that Hobbes would improve his theory between chapters 17 and 21, a plausible explanation is that theorists often do not immediately see how a new theory ought to be worked out. Also, Hobbes's thought in chapter 21 was motivated by his attempt to attack republicanism, which arguably puts a high premium on authorization.

otherwise to contract with one another, to choose their own abode, their own diet, their own trade of life, and institute their children as they themselves think fit, and the like.

There is nothing here about freedom of speech, religion, or political assembly, nor even nonpolitical assembly. Pretty bleak, I think. And, in the next sentence, he recommits himself to absolute sovereignty. By the limited liberty of subjects "we are not to understand that ... the Soveraign Power of life, and death, is either abolished, or limited."[14] However, Hobbes's justification of absolute sovereignty differs from those he had given in his earlier political writings. The foundation of absolute sovereignty is not the near total alienation of rights by the subjects, but solely their authorization of the sovereign. The sovereign is absolute because "every Subject is Author of every act the Soveraign doth."[15] And this authorship itself involves no restriction on the subject's liberty.[16] The idea of giving up rights disappears from the revised sovereign-making formula: "I authorize all his [the sovereign's] action."[17] Shortly later Hobbes repeats almost the same words verbatim, "I authorize, or take upon me, all his [the sovereign's] actions"[18] and glosses them by saying that in them "there is no restriction at all, of his own [the subject's] former naturall Liberty."[19] This is the theory of pure authorization. Hobbes's point that "no man is bound by the words [of authorization] themselves either to kill himself or any other man" depends on this fact.[20] The discrepancy between the sovereign-making formula in chapter 17 and chapter 21 was noted by Robert Filmer:

> I cannot but wonder Mr Hobbes should say [in chapter 21] "the consent of a subject to sovereign power is contained in these words, 'I authorize and do take upon me all his actions.'" In which there is no restriction at all of his own former natural liberty. Surely here Mr Hobbes forgot himself, for before, he makes the resignation to go in these words [from chapter 17] also, I "give up my right of governing myself to this man." This is a restriction certainly of his own former natural liberty when he gives it away.[21]

In short, Hobbes's theory in chapter 17 is not consistent with the theory in chapter 21.

---

[14] *Leviathan* 21.7, 109.

[15] *Leviathan* 21.7, 109.

[16] Skinner 2008: 128–130, 133, emphasizes that Hobbes changed his view about liberty between *The Elements of Law* and *Leviathan*.

[17] *Leviathan* 21.10, 111. The corresponding passage in the Latin Leviathan is: "actionum omnium ejus hominis cui summam tribuimus potestatem authorem me facio" (Latin *Leviathan* 21.13).

[18] The corresponding passage in the Latin Leviathan is: "author sum omnium actionum ejus cui summam tribuimus potestatem" (Latin *Leviathan* 21.13). Hobbes apparently did not look at his earlier translation of the authorization formula when he translated this passage.[19] *Leviathan* 21.14, 112.

[20] *Leviathan* 21.15, 112.

[21] Filmer 1991: 193.

So far, in chapter 21, all of the political lifting has been done by authorization. Alienation has not been mentioned.[22] A person could authorize a well-to-do individual to represent her in some transaction without transferring any right to that individual. In relatively informal organizations, one member often allows another member to represent her in meetings without remuneration. A lawyer or real estate agent may represent a client gratis. If subjects authorized an omnipotent human being, then they would not need to alienate any rights. The acceptance of Yahweh by the Israelites to be their particular sovereign can be interpreted as authorization without alienation. In medieval England, a monarch was supposed to "live of his own;" he was supposed to govern England from his personal resources and revenues and not to require subjects to alienate rights through taxes. William I could do this, in fact, because he owned a large part of England. During the Tudor and early Stuart period, the ideology of "living of his own" survived even though the Stuarts depended on taxation and other special sources of revenue. Alienation of some rights is usually a practical necessity for accomplishing the "end for which sovereignty was ordained."[23]

Hobbes justifies the alienation of rights as a practical necessity in two ways. The first approaches the issue from the perspective of the subject. Whoever wills the end wills the means to the end. The subject wills the end of being governed or having his life protected by the sovereign. The means necessary to achieving that end is the alienation of certain rights. Therefore, whoever wills the end of being governed is rationally obliged to alienate certain rights.

Let's again ask how extensive these rights are. The crucial limit is specified by the necessity of giving up to the sovereign one's right to judge which rights are to be given up. The argument is that if the subject retained the right to judge which rights were to be given up, then the sovereign's ability to govern would be frustrated.[24] So the force of an et cetera phrase is implicit in the means necessary for a sovereign to govern. Hobbes's derivation of the sovereign's right to decide what the limits are on alienation can also be related to the second law of nature, by which a person gives up her right to all things. The natural reading of this law entails that a person gives up some of her rights, not all of her rights. But the argument that concludes that a subject gives up her right to judge which rights she has to give up has the effect that a subject gives up potentially all of her rights except those relating directly to self-protection. What at first seemed to be a reasonably limited alienation of rights ends up being a potentially oppressive alienation of rights.

Hobbes's second justification for the alienation of rights takes the perspective of the sovereign. The principle that Hobbes appeals to is that whoever has a right to the end has a right to the means.[25] He illustrates this crucial principle when he explains why a

---

[22] Cf. Skinner 2002: 206, and Skinner 2008: 173.
[23] *Leviathan* 21.15, 112.
[24] *Leviathan* 21.15, 112.
[25] *Leviathan* 18.8, 90; see also 18.20, 94; 30.3, 175; and 38.13, 237–238.

subject has an obligation not to interfere with the sovereign when the sovereign arrests a person other than the subject herself: because doing so would take "away from the sovereign the means of protecting us and is therefore destructive of the very essence of government."[26] Of course, a subject always retains the liberty to defend herself against the force of the sovereign because not doing so would frustrate that same end of government, the preservation of one's own life.

The discussion in the last two paragraphs may suggest that subjects have a great deal of liberty, and Hobbes does say that subjects of a monarchy have as much liberty as subjects have under republican governments. But we have already seen that these rights are greatly limited because in willing the means necessary to the end of government, subjects transfer and hence alienate their right to judge which rights are necessary to the end of government. Without that alienation, the sovereign would be liable to being second-guessed by his subjects. And so Hobbes returns to the "leftovers" view of liberty: "other liberties . . . depend on the silence of the law."[27]

What is significantly new about the "pure authorization theory" is that authorization can stand alone and explain the origin of government. Alienation comes by way of authorization, plus the principle that whoever has a right to the end has a right to the means to that end and a premise about what the sovereign needs to do his job. It should also be noted that this theory is superior to the pure alienation theory because it promotes political stability. The subjects are committed to accepting the actions of the sovereign as their own actions. It is superior to the authorization-cum-alienation theory because it is consistent.[28] According to the pure authorization theory, the sovereign is authorized to govern, and certain rights are given up, as necessary, to achieve the goal of a commonwealth.[29]

One might have expected that Hobbes would have carried over his best theory into the Latin *Leviathan*, which was prepared about 1667 or 1668.[30] Unfortunately, he does not. He may not have appreciated how much better the theory of pure alienation is over his earlier theories even while he was presenting it in chapter 21. The Latin *Leviathan*

---

[26] *Leviathan* 21.17, 112.

[27] *Leviathan* 21.18, 113.

[28] One might argue that the authorization-cum-alienation theory should be understood as the same as the pure authorization theory. My problem with this suggestion is that the text of chapter 18 does not support this reading. Also, what rights a sovereign commands to be transferred to him cannot be initially specified because the sovereign is not a party to the covenant and because the rights that are transferred change depending upon the sovereign's changing judgment of what's necessary. See Green (2015) for an alternative way of resolving the inconsistency.

[29] One might criticize the philosophical cogency of the pure alienation theory on the grounds that, by the principle that whoever has a right to the end has the right to the means, each subject has to alienate this right to govern himself, and so that right is both authorized and alienated. I cannot explore that objection here.

[30] Rogers and Schuhmann claim that the Latin *Leviathan*, published by Blaeu in 1668, was largely translated from a manuscript owned and corrected by Hobbes. However, the Latin *Leviathan* sometimes abbreviates the English text and contains grammatical errors. Most of these errors were corrected for the 1670 edition, probably by an accomplished Latinist who did not consult with Hobbes or have a copy of one of the English editions (Rogers and Schuhmann 2003: 241–258).

is usually philosophically no better than, and is sometimes inferior to, the English *Leviathan*. There may be several explanations for this. He was in his late seventies when he was translating *Leviathan* into Latin. He had lost interest in political theory in the 1650s, although not the practical application of it. And it is possible that some parts of the Latin *Leviathan* had been written before the English version when his theory was inferior to the one in the English *Leviathan*.

One of the best examples of the inferiority of the Latin *Leviathan* is the passage in which Hobbes should have been expressing the authorization-cum-alienation theory. In this passage, instead of using two verbs to distinguish authorization from alienation, he uses one verb, "*concedere*,"[31] and gives it two direct objects, "*authoritas*" and "*jus meum regendi meipsum*":

> *Ego huic homini (vel huic coetui) Authoritatem et Ius meum regendi meipsum con-cedo, ea conditione, ut tu quoque tuam Authoritatem et Ius tuum tui regendi in eun-dem transferas.*[32]

"*Concedere*" usually means something like *giving up, giving in to* someone, *submitting to power*; and so, by extension, it can also mean *to agree* or *to comply with* someone's wishes. Hobbes probably wanted to convey simultaneously both the giving up sense and the agreeing sense in order to capture the conflation of alienation and authorization in the English *Leviathan*. But "*concedere*" cannot simultaneously mean both "give up" and "authorize." So the passage above is philosophically defective. Also, since what the speaker "concedes" ought to be the same as what his co-covenanters concede, he should have used "*concedere*" in the second half of the formula. Instead, he switches to the verb "*transfero*," which unambiguously indicates an alienation of rights, and authorization is not mentioned at all. Instead of repairing the defects of the English version, he gives a translation that makes the theory worse. It appears to be a reversion to the pure alienation theory. A related problem about the inferiority of the Latin *Leviathan* is discussed in Section 2.

2 PERSONS AND REPRESENTATION

My second major goal in this chapter is to show that for Hobbes the primary relation of representation is between the person of the sovereign and its individual subjects. The kind of representation in which Hobbes is primarily interested requires a person. So we need to understand his theory (or theories) of persons. In *Leviathan*, Hobbes's

---

[31] Individual words and short phrases in Latin are placed in italics. Longer segments are in the typeface of the original publication.

[32] Latin *Leviathan* 17.13, 85.

dominant view is that all persons, both natural and otherwise, are representatives: "to *personate* is to . . . *represent* himself or another."[33]

In addition to the English *Leviathan,* I will also discuss the corresponding passages in *De homine* and the Latin *Leviathan* because scholars think they may shed some light on his views in *Leviathan* or show that he changed his view once or possibly twice. However, I think that his views in the later two works are more problematic than the ones in the English *Leviathan,* and I care primarily about that latter text. Sufficient for my purposes is what the English *Leviathan* shows, namely, that sovereigns are non-natural persons and representatives. We shall also see that although commonwealths are also non-natural persons, they are not representatives in the first instance. I will emphasize their difference from sovereigns in Section 3.

Hobbes's first characterization of persons is found at the beginning of chapter 16 of *Leviathan:*

> A PERSON, is he, whose words or actions are considered, either as his own, or as representing the words or actions of an other man, or of any other thing to whom they are attributed, whether Truly or by Fiction.
> When they are considered as his owne, then is he₁ called a Naturall Person: and when they are considered as representing the words and actions of an other, then is he₂ a Feigned or Artificiall person.[34] [subscripts added]

In the first sentence, Hobbes is defining a person as one whose verbal or nonverbal actions represent someone, either himself or another. Often the representative is a human being. Each normal human adult usually represents himself and hence is a natural person. But sometimes a representative is a sovereign and then it always represents someone other than itself. This is not to say that the human being who is the sovereign never acts as a natural person. He does.[35] The human being who is the sovereign is not identical with the sovereign because, if he were, then every action of the private person would be the action of the sovereign. Hobbes admits that a sovereign can enter into contracts as a private person. More importantly, although sovereigns have an "artificial eternity of life," humans do not.[36] Whereas the natural person who is sovereign dies, the sovereign never dies according to English law. Also, human beings who constitute sovereigns are not identical with the sovereign because the individual human beings of the assembly of an aristocracy and democracy are not sovereigns. This lack of identity is what Hobbes's official theory ought to dictate. Unfortunately, because of his affection

---

[33] *Leviathan* 16.3, 80; cf. Skinner 2002. See also Pettit 1997, Pitkin 1967, Runciman 1997, 2000, 2010, Tricauld 1982.

[34] *Leviathan* 16.1, 80.The phrase "feigned or artificial persons" does not necessarily indicate two subclasses of persons. The word "or" could have an appositive use as in "man or rational animal." Hobbes likes to use this construction, and it appears in his definition of a person in the Latin *Leviathan,* "*persona propria, sive naturalis,*" as we shall see later.

[35] *Leviathan* 19.4, 95–96; 23.2, 123; and 28.25, 166.

[36] *Leviathan* 19.14, 99.

for monarchy, I think he sometimes identifies the monarch with the man instead of the office. Even if one believed that monarchs are identical with natural human beings, it would not be possible for sovereigns that are democratic or aristocratic assemblies to be identical with their constituent members because then an aristocracy of, say, four human beings would have four sovereigns, and a democratic assembly of one hundred human beings would have one hundred sovereigns. It would be ad hoc to intentionally identify a monarch with the human being holding that office. That sovereigns are not natural persons is shown by the claim that the actions of a natural person "are considered as his own." Because a sovereign's actions are not considered to be his own, he does not own or author them.[37]

This much, I believe, is uncontroversial. Almost everything else about his view of persons is: For example, the correct interpretation of the next clauses—"when they are considered the words and actions of an other, then is he a feigned or artificial person." Quentin Skinner says that, as a matter of strict grammar, "he$_2$," should have "an other" as its antecedent.[38] On that construal of the text, the feigned or artificial person is the thing to whom the words and actions of someone are attributed. In other words, the non-natural person ("the feigned or artificial person") would be the thing represented and not, as the first sentence asserts, the representative. If this is the correct way to understand these clauses, then Hobbes has introduced three kinds of persons: (1) generic persons, who represent themselves or others (paragraph 1); (2) natural persons, who represent themselves (first half of second paragraph); and (3) persons who are represented by others (second half of second paragraph).

Skinner gave a good reason not to understand the last clauses of the second paragraph in this way: "the flow of the sentence" suggests that "he$_2$," probably does not have "an other" as its antecedent.[39] He says that the antecedent is the natural person referred to at the beginning of the first paragraph of the block quotation just presented. However, a "natural person" is not mentioned at the beginning of the first paragraph. "Natural person" makes its appearance in the second paragraph. The person mentioned in the first paragraph is the generic person whose words or actions are considered "either as his own or as representing those of another man." Because the definition of the first paragraph is generic, I do not think that "A PERSON" refers only to natural persons. If "he$_2$," referred to a natural person, then it would follow that a natural person would be a "feigned or artificial person" (a non-natural person). This view yields a contradiction or paradoxical result that can be avoided. On the interpretation I suggest, a human being who is a monarch is or "bears" two persons: His own natural person and a non-natural person in virtue of his office.

It is more plausible to construe "he$_2$," as part of a parallel syntactic structure in the second paragraph. Both "he$_2$," and "he$_1$," of the preceding clause have the same antecedent: "A PERSON." This antecedent refers to persons generically. This use of "person" allows

---

[37] *Leviathan* 17.13, 87.
[38] Skinner 2002: 188.
[39] Skinner 2002: 187.

Hobbes to talk later about, say, "persons by fiction" or "fictitious persons," in analogy perhaps with "accused murderer" or "alleged document." So he might have said that fictional characters like Agamemnon are feigned persons, if he had wished to, in contrast with sovereigns who are artificial persons. (Whether he wished to do this is a vexed question.) Whatever the correct interpretation of these two paragraphs of *Leviathan*, it is certain that Hobbes held that some persons represent other persons. A sovereign represents subjects, and the judges and ministers appointed by a sovereign represent the sovereign.

One might have hoped that the corresponding passages about persons in *De homine* (1658) and the Latin *Leviathan* (1668) would be obviously consistent with that of the English *Leviathan*. Unfortunately, it is not obvious. Each poses problems of its own. The corresponding passage in *De homine* occurs in its last chapter, "*De homine fictitio*."[40] My guess is that Hobbes used "*homo*" in the title rather than "*persona*" in order to justify its inclusion in *De homine*.[41] This is confirmed by the chapter's title in the book's table of contents.[42] It may initially seem that a discussion of *homo fictitio* does not strictly belong in *De homine* because *homines* are naturally occurring entities, and non-natural persons seem to depend of something non-natural. However, Hobbes was justified in discussing persons in *De homine* because the ideas of both natural and fictive or fictional or feigned persons outside a civil state are intelligible.[43] In fact, Hobbes introduces his discussion of persons in a nonpolitical context. Agamemnon is a *persona fictitia*; the words of the actor are attributed to the fictional character. The example of Agamemnon leads to Hobbes's definition of "person":

> Persona est cui Verba & Actiones hominum attribuuntur vel suae vel alienae. Si suae, Persona naturalis est; si alienae, Fictitia est.[44]

The first sentence says that a person is the thing to which the words and actions of men are attributed, either their own or those of others. This is clear. The sense of the first half of the second sentence also seems clear. If the words or actions are attributed to the thing that produced them, then it is a natural person. The precise meaning of the rest of the sentence is unclear. I believe a correct translation is: "if [the words and actions are attributed] to some other, he is fictional [or: feigned, or: artificial]." That is, if the words or actions are attributed to something other than the thing that produced them,

---

[40] The phrase "*homo fictitio*" is not quite correct because Hobbes distinguishes between a man and a person.

[41] It seems to me that, strictly speaking, artificial persons are not human beings. But if one thinks that monarchs are artificial persons and identical with human beings, then human beings can be artificial human beings.

[42] *De homine* 87.

[43] Also, the discussion of persons in *Leviathan* occurs appropriately in Part I, "Of Man," as Johan Olsthoorn reminded me.

[44] *De homine* 15.1, 84: "A person is he to whom the words and actions of men are attributed, either to himself or to another. If [the words and actions are attributed] to himself, he is a natural person; if [the words and actions are attributed] to some other, he is fictional [or feigned, or artificial]."

then that other thing is the person. On this interpretation, the words and actions of an actor playing Agamemnon are attributed to Agamemnon, and Agamemnon is the person. So the person is the thing represented and not the representative. This view, the opposite of the one in the English *Leviathan*,[45] is consonant with Hobbes's remark shortly thereafter that even bridges and hospitals and inanimate things can be persons. In *Leviathan*, Hobbes holds that these things can be personated but not that they are persons.

This interpretation has several considerations in its favor. One is that the language of representation in *De homine* is introduced, not in the context of giving an explanation of the way a sovereign represents or even of representation in general, but in the limited context of a person exceeding his authority: "some bear the person of the one commanding; and others do something not by the one commanding."[46] The latter representatives are exceeding their authority.

The interrelations between persons, representation, authors, and actors that worked so well in *Leviathan* do not work well in *De homine*. Hobbes's author/actor distinction, which is inspired by theater, ill fits that phenomenon. When one looks to the author of stage actors, one looks for the playwright. But Hobbes conflates the stage actor, say, Nikos Sedaris, with the fictional character, Agamemnon. Whereas the stage actor remains the actor for Hobbes, the words and actions of the stage actor are attributed to the fictional character; for example, Agamemnon. Hobbes does not, and could not plausibly, say that Agamemnon is the author of the words and actions because Agamemnon could hardly authorize any actor or other human being to represent him on the stage. Aeschylus, the author of *Agamemnon*, is not mentioned at all for good reason. Agamemnon's return to Argos is not owned by Aeschylus.[47]

The oddities attaching to *persona fictitia* may have been the result of his changing his primary perspective from politics in *Leviathan* to nonpolitical human behavior in *De homine*.[48] Even if man and person do not come apart for a natural person, they do come apart when nonnatural persons are at issue. In the political case of *Leviathan*, the words and actions of the sovereign get attributed to his subjects. In the nonpolitical case of *De homine*, the words of the actor get attributed to the fictional character. The interpretation of *De homine* being considered is also consonant with the fact that Hobbes applies only one term to the class of non-natural persons, the postclassical word *fictitia*, much closer to English "fictional" than the classical terms "*ficta*" or "*artificiosa*." Because Hobbes uses only the word *fictitia* for non-natural persons, when he

---

[45] Cf. Skinner 2002: 189.

[46] "[A]lii jubente eo cujus Personam gerunt, alii non jubente id faciunt" (*De homine* 15.2, 84).

[47] Complications such as the fact that repressive governments often hold authors responsible for what their characters say and do are not relevant here.

[48] Hobbes is no clearer about whether a person is the representative or the thing represented when he writes, "one Person, [is one] that can speak, command, or do any act of a Person" (*An Answer to a Book Published by Dr. Bramhall*, 71). Whether a bridge, a thing represented, is a person or not depends on whether we say that it can speak or command through a representative.

previews the content of *De cive* at the end of chapter 15 of *De homine*, he has to allude to sovereigns as "fictions of this kind" ("Hujus modi . . . Fictionum").[49]

Hobbes's comment that the verbal and nonverbal actions of many men are attributed to one thing straightforwardly fits fictional characters. There are many theatrical productions in which different human actors have their actions attributed to something different from them—say, Agamemnon. And it is certainly apposite to say that Agamemnon is *fictitia*:[50] "loqui non ipse Histrio, sed aliquis alius, puta, Agamemnon, nimirum Faciem Fictitiam Agamemnonis induente Histrione, qui pro illo tempore erat Agamemnon."[51] Hobbes's difficulty in talking about the relation between stage actor and fictional character is indicated by the contradiction within the last quoted passage: The actor does not speak; Agamemnon speaks, and Agamemnon is identical with the actor ("qui . . . erat Agamemnon").

The idea of the words and actions of many successive men being attributed to one person does not neatly fit Hobbes's political theory. In the political case, he is primarily interested in the relationship between the words and actions of one sovereign and many subjects. This is not to say that there is no Hobbesian political relation that satisfies the many-one relation of being "attributed to." In an aristocracy and democracy, the words and actions of the many individual people who constitute the sovereign are attributed to the sovereign, which in turn are attributed to the many subjects. Hobbes's clearest statement of the relationship of one sovereign to many subjects occurs when he is preparing to talk about the fact that sovereigns can represent the person of God.

> For if many men agree that whatever some one [man] or some assembly from the many does, they themselves will hold it to be the action of each one of them; each will be the author of the actions which the man or assembly does.[52]

In short, Hobbes's account of sovereigns as persons in *De homine* is subordinated in chapter 15 and is of little value to his political theory. It is possible that he did not care because *De homine* is not supposed to be a work of politics and seems to have been cobbled together simply to complete his promised trilogy. For example, of the fifteen chapters, two through nine are about optics, and the last six about a hodgepodge of topics, including desire, speech, and religion. It does not approach being a complete anthropology.

---

[49] *De homine* 15.4, 85.

[50] In *Leviathan*, Hobbes begins the chapter with his definitions of various persons and only briefly uses the example of the theater to illustrate what a person is.

[51] *De homine* 15.1 84: "the actor himself did not speak, but some other [did], for example, Agamemnon, namely, the actor putting on the false face of Agamemnon, who was for that time Agamemnon."

[52] Hobbes *De homine*: 15.4, 85: "Si enim consentiant Homines plures ut quicquid fecerit unus aliquis, vel coetus ex pluribus, id se pro actione uniuscujusque ipsorum habituros esse, erit unusquisque, Actionum quas homo vel coetus faciet, Author."

About a decade later, Hobbes returned to the issue of personhood in his Latin translation of *Leviathan*.[53] Chapter 16 of the Latin *Leviathan* is briefer than the English text, and the brevity begins with the title. The English title, "Of Persons, Authors, and Things Personated," becomes "Of Persons and Authors" ("*De Personis & Authoribus*"). Here is Hobbes's definition of persons:

> Persona est *is qui suo vel alieno nomine res agit.* Si suo, Persona *Propria*, sive Naturalis est; si alieno, Persona est ejus, cujus Nomine agit *Repraesentativa*.[54]

The translation of the first sentence and the definition of a natural person is again unproblematic: "A person is he who does things in his own name or that of another. If in his own [name], he is a proper or natural [person] . . ." In other words, the generic person represents either himself or something other than himself. If he acts in his own name, then he is a natural person.

The translation of the rest of the passage is problematic, and several Latinists have given two different translations. The first of these is:

> and if in [the name of] another, the person is Representative of him in whose name he acts.

According to this translation, the non-natural person is the representative, not the thing represented. This translation fits the doctrine of the English *Leviathan,* as one would expect of the translation. It is not necessary to say that he *returned* to his earlier theory of persons because his account in *De homine* may have been different simply because it had a different purpose. Also the typography of the Latin largely fits Hobbes's practice of putting the names of the things being defined in italics: Persona . . . Persona *Propria*, . . . Persona . . . *Repraesentativa*.

Nonetheless, Hobbes's translation of the English *Leviathan* is somewhat odd. The original, "represented truly or by fiction," is replaced by Latin words that literally mean "representative of him in whose name he acts." The distinction in the English *Leviathan* between representing truly and by fiction disappears in the Latin translation, even though the distinction is sensible because a sovereign truly represents people, according to Hobbes's account, and representing a fictional character or even a bridge or hospital does involve some kind of fiction. The concept of representation that appears in the definition of a generic person is transferred in the Latin *Leviathan* to the definition of a non-natural person. Finally, the presence of "*suo vel alieno*" in the Latin *Leviathan* is a kind of echo of *De homine*'s "*suae . . . alienae.*" But why should the former echo the latter, instead of adhering to the English words? Of course, it is possible that the definition of non-natural persons in the Latin *Leviathan* is supposed to be the same as

---

[53] Published in 1668 at the end of *Opera Omnia* and then separately, in an edition with some of the grammar corrected by a Latinist, in 1670 (Rogers and Schuhmann 2003), and 1676 in London.
[54] Latin *Leviathan* 1676: 79.

the one in *De homine*. There is an alternative translation of the Latin *Leviathan* that is consonant with that view:

> If in [the name of] another, the person belongs to him, in whose name he acts as representative.

According to this translation, the (non-natural) person is not the representative but the thing represented, the thing in whose name the representative is acting. So the doctrine of persons would be like that in *De homine* and not in the English *Leviathan*. This translation would, in effect, explain why Hobbes departed from the syntax and vocabulary of the English in the way he did. It is certainly odd to translate a passage so as to say the opposite of the passage translated. But one cannot put that past Hobbes.

A proponent of the alternative translation may reason that if Hobbes had wanted to say the same thing as he said in *Leviathan*, he would have given a straightforward Latin equivalent of the phrase "feigned or artificial," perhaps, "*ficta vel artificiosa*," and he would have retained the parallel structure of the second paragraph of *Leviathan*. But he does neither. Although "*Repraesentativa*" could be used to denote what "feigned or artificial person" had denoted in *Leviathan*, it is not a translation of that phrase. As for the parallel structure, he could have written the "*si alieno*" clause as "*si alieno, Persona Repraesentativa*." Instead, he goes out of his way to destroy the parallel structure by omitting a name for the relevant kind of person between "*Persona*" and "*est*" and inserting "*cujus Nomine agit* Repraesentativa." What the last clause of the just-quoted passage literally says, according to this alternative translation, is "If (he acts in the name) of another thing, the person belongs to him in whose name the representative acts." "*Repraesentativa*" is not the name of the non-natural person. No name is given for this nonnatural person. On this interpretation, the definitions of a natural and a nonnatural person are not actually species of a so-called generic definition of "person," just as religion, as defined in chapter 6, may not be the genus of superstition.[55] So the term "generic" would be a misnomer if it were applied to the definition of person in the Latin *Leviathan* as someone who acts in someone's name.

Whether Hobbes thought of the representative or the represented as the person in the Latin *Leviathan*, he needed to introduce the idea of representation in the definition of a non-natural person because he had not included it in his definition of "person" at the beginning of the text we are considering.

The meaning of "*si alieno, Persona est ejus, cujus Nomine agit Repraesentativa*" has a duck/rabbit quality; its meaning seems to shift as one's focal point on the text does. Over a stretch of three years, I have alternated between the two translations discussed. And, just as I had determined that a large majority of competent readers of Latin favored the first translation, two additional Latinists opted for the latter. At that point, I considered

---

[55] Cf. Martinich 1992: 50–59.

the possibility that Hobbes had intended his definition to be ambiguous between the two translations. I conjecture that he intended both of them.

Each translation gives him something reasonable and perhaps at least part of what he intended. Like the definition in the English *Leviathan*, non-natural persons are representatives. And, like the definition in *De homine,* non-natural persons are things represented. A complete theory of persons should make both sovereigns and subjects, playwrights and state actors, stage actors and fictional characters persons. My last word on this topic is anticlimactic: Because my concern is the doctrine of the English *Leviathan*, the inconclusive results of the Latin *Leviathan* are not a problem for my view.

3 Sovereigns as the Primary Political Representatives

The goal of this section is to show that the primary political relation in *Leviathan* is the one between the sovereign and the subject. The sovereign directly represents each subject individually. One consequence of this is that the existence of the commonwealth is logically consequent upon the existence of the sovereign. A second is that the sovereign represents the commonwealth, too. Theoretically, Hobbes could have done without the commonwealth altogether because it itself cannot act. The essential political entities for Hobbes are the sovereign and the subjects. The commonwealth is epiphenomenal; it acts only in virtue of the actions of the sovereign, so to say that the commonwealth acts is metonymy.

The key passage for my interpretation is the same as the one that prepares for the introduction of authorization-cum-alienation. In order to escape the state of nature, people "confer all their power and strength upon one man or upon one assembly of men, ... which is as much as to say, to appoint one man or assembly of men to bear their person."[56] This conferral of power is upon the sovereign, not upon the commonwealth because, as Hobbes often says, it is the sovereign's actions that are owned by each subject.[57] He does not say that subjects own the actions of the commonwealth, and, indeed, in the sovereign-making formula, the commonwealth is not mentioned at all. The commonwealth is introduced after the words "This done." That is, the commonwealth follows upon the creation of the sovereign: "This done, the Multitude so united in one Person, is called a COMMON-WEALTH; in latine CIVITAS."[58] Syntactically,

---

[56] *Leviathan* 17.13, 87.

[57] For example, Hobbes 115; cf. Newey 2008: 106. I do not agree with Skinner when he says, "our sovereigns . . . should not be regarded as their own but rather as those of the person whom they are representing, that is, the person of the state" (Skinner 2002: 200). Sovereigns are persons because they represent other things.

[58] *Leviathan* 17.13, 87. Cf. "the Person in whose name the sovereign acquires the right to speak and act will be the Person engendered by the multitude out of its agreement to be represented" (Skinner

Hobbes is indicating that the creation of the commonwealth is either temporally posterior to the creation of the sovereign ("done") or the cause of it. This interpretation is confirmed by the text of the Latin *Leviathan*, which uses a past construction for "this done," namely, "*quo facto*." The priority of the sovereign is confirmed in the next chapter, chapter 18. Hobbes says that by instituting the commonwealth, "the Rights of the Sovereign" are created, not the rights of the commonwealth.

The sovereign has "the right to present the person" of all his subjects.[59] It has "all the rights and faculties on whom the sovereign power is conferred." It, not the commonwealth, has the sovereign power. Subjects are "Subjects to the Soveraign" and not to the commonwealth.[60] Because the sovereign represents each individual subject, and the subjects come to be united in the commonwealth, Hobbes also says that the sovereign is the "Representative of the Commonwealth."[61]

It would be misleading or mistaken to infer that the commonwealth is the author of the actions of the sovereign. The literal truth is that the individual subjects are the authors of what the sovereign does, and they own those actions. Skinner takes a different view:

> whenever our sovereigns exercise their powers to procure our safety and contentment, the acts they perform should not be regarded as their own but rather as those of the person whom they are representing, that is, the person of the state.[62]

However, if the actions were attributed to the commonwealth, as Skinner thinks they are, then individual subjects could distance themselves from responsibility for those actions: "The commonwealth is the author of the actions, not me."[63] That is precisely what Hobbes wants to avoid, I believe. Hobbes ensures that the individual subjects are responsible for the sovereign's behavior by making the sovereign the direct representative of the individual.[64] Indeed, Hobbes wants to reduce the commonwealth to as close to nothing as he can.[65] That is why he is happy to say that "the commonwealth is no person," has "no capacity to do anything but by the representative, that is, the

---

2007: 171, also 200). I believe Hobbes's text shows that the agreement to be represented is each individual's agreement to be represented individually. The commonwealth is not yet in play.

[59] Some editors think that "present" is a mistake for "represent." However, it is plausible that Hobbes was using "present" as a synonym for "bear" because he uses "*gerendi*" when he translated the passage into the Latin *Leviathan*: "Personam omnium gerendi Ius" (Latin *Leviathan* 18.1, 86).

[60] *Leviathan* 23.8, 88.

[61] *Leviathan* 7.37, 159–160; 28.12, 163; 28.13, 163; and 29.6, 168; cf. Skinner 2002: 200.

[62] Skinner 2002: 200.

[63] In fact, in my opinion, subjects are not culpable for the actions of their government although they may be culpable for not trying hard enough to prevent their government from acting badly.

[64] By the same token, the sovereign cannot be unjust to any individual subject because each individual directly authorizes the sovereign, and subjects have an obligation directly to the sovereign. Also, because the sovereign's behavior is the subjects' actions and no one can injure themselves, the same conclusion follows. *Leviathan* 21.21, 114, and 18.6, 90.

[65] Skinner (2008: 188–189) thinks that the sovereign is a person "by Fiction" and denies that he is "real or substantial." He thinks that the commonwealth is the more important object.

sovereign," and "a commonwealth without a sovereign power is but a word without substance and cannot stand."[66]

The unity of the sovereign is logically prior to the unity of the commonwealth, and its unity is not the same as the unity of the commonwealth. The unity of the monarch is the unity of the human being who constitutes the monarch. The unity of the aristocracy and the democracy is presumably the unity of the human beings who constitute the aristocratic and democratic assemblies, respectively.[67] That the sovereign and the commonwealth are logically separate is evident from Hobbes's comment that "the Soveraign in every Commonwealth, is the absolute Representative of all the subjects."[68] Substituting "sovereign" for "commonwealth" would result in nonsense: "the sovereign in every sovereign is the absolute representative of all the subjects." The subjects in a commonwealth constitute the commonwealth but are subject to the sovereign and typically do not constitute part of the sovereign: "And he that carryeth this person is called SOVEREIGN, and said to have sovereign power, and every one besides, his SUBJECT."[69] However, these statements cannot be precisely true because a sovereign and a commonwealth have different properties, as we have already shown. The sovereign can be constituted by a single human being, but a commonwealth is never constituted by a single human being. Hobbes also indicates a difference in his principal analogy of the commonwealth. The commonwealth is a living body, and the sovereign is its soul.[70]

That the primary and direct political relationship holds between the sovereign and the subjects also emerges from considering the first part of the sovereign-making formula of chapter 17, "I authorize and give up my right of governing myself, to this man or to this assembly of men."[71] The man or assembly of men is the sovereign, not the commonwealth. The category of a commonwealth is determined by the type of sovereign it has, and the sovereign, of whatever type, is the representative of "every one of the multitude," each individual, not an artificially unified object.[72] It is in virtue of the unity of the sovereign, of whatever type, that subjects have a unity in the commonwealth: "A multitude of men are made one person when they are by one man, or one person, represented . . . For it is the unity of the representer or representative, not the unity of the represented, that maketh the person one."[73] In other words, the subjects have to rely on the unity of some logically prior entity in order for them to be united. This other entity

---

[66] *Leviathan* 31.1, 186.

[67] Perhaps the unity of a democracy is identical with the unity of all the subjects, if the latter can be said to be a unity at all.

[68] *Leviathan* 22.5, 115.

[69] *Leviathan* 17.14, 88. There are other passages in which Hobbes muddies the waters and either conflates or gives the impression of conflating sovereign and commonwealth.

[70] *Leviathan* 21.21, 114; Latin *Leviathan*: "*Is qui summam habet Potestatem, pro Anima est, corpus totum vivificante & movente*" (1668: bbb^r).

[71] *Leviathan* 17.13, 87.

[72] *Leviathan* 19.1, 94; cf. Skinner 2002: 200.

[73] *Leviathan* 16.13, 82; see also 17.13, 87.

cannot be the commonwealth because then its unity would exist before it was created, a logical impossibility.[74]

Hobbes would not want the sovereign to be the creation of the commonwealth because if the sovereign were, then the sovereign would directly represent the commonwealth, not each individual subject. The danger, as far as Hobbes is concerned, is that the authority of the sovereign would be mediated by the authority of the commonwealth, and this would open the door to some theorist to argue that the sovereign may fail to represent the commonwealth correctly and that the constituents of the commonwealth, the subjects, could make this judgment. The sovereign could not be the judge in this circumstance because no one can be a judge in his own case.[75] The distance being considered here between the sovereign and the subjects is logical in the sense that to go from a proposition about the sovereign to one about his subjects one would need a mediating premise about the commonwealth such that one could argue as follows: "The sovereign (directly) represents the commonwealth; the commonwealth (directly) represents the subjects; therefore, the sovereign (indirectly or mediately) represents the subjects." The distance is also psychological because a person going through the logical calculation would feel more removed from the proposition that appears higher in the proof. English law in the first half of the seventeenth century countenanced an analog of this distance. The monarch directly represented or ruled the people and could do no wrong, although the ministers of the king could do wrong because they did not represent the subjects—as Lord Strafford and the Archbishop William Laud knew only too well because they were executed for obeying Charles I. In other words, if the sovereign or the king represents the subjects indirectly, then he may be open to the same vulnerability as the king's ministers had been, and Hobbes did not want that. I am not saying that the alternative theory being considered is cogent but rather that Hobbes would not want to say anything to inspire anyone to adopt it on the basis of his own theory. In fact, the alternative theory is similar to a central part of John Locke's theory.[76] Locke uses the words "society" and "community" where we have used "commonwealth." Society or the community selects a sovereign, who is given limited powers; the sovereign may be removed by the society, and, in general, the sovereign may perish without the society perishing.[77]

Sometimes Hobbes wants to give the impression that the commonwealth is at least equiprimordial with the sovereign. So he says that to the "COMMON-WEALTH ... [OR]

---

[74] This problem of a prior-existing unity may apply equally to sovereigns as to commonwealths. The sovereign does not exist prior to the sovereign-making action. Hobbes gives the impression that he has a solution to this problem for monarchy. The multitude is made "one person when they are by one man ... represented." The unity of monarchy is guaranteed by the preexisting unity of the human being who is the monarch. But the person of an assembly does not exist prior to the unity-making action of authorization.

[75] *Leviathan* 15.30, 78.

[76] See also Skinner 2007.

[77] Quentin Skinner once said in conversation that the problem with Hobbes's theory is that "he has no theory of society." I think that this is what he meant.

that great LEVIATHAN . . . wee owe . . . our peace and defence."[78] But in the next sentence, he confuses the issue by saying "by this authority, given *him* by every particular man in the commonwealth, *he* hath the use of so much power and strength conferred on *him* that, by terror thereof, *he* is able to conform the will of them all" [emphasis added].[79] Grammatically, the italicized pronouns refer to the commonwealth, and we may say that, by metonymy, what Hobbes is saying is true. But, according to Hobbes's express doctrine, the pronouns should refer to the sovereign because the commonwealth only acts in virtue of the sovereign acting. This interpretation is confirmed when he explains that the person he is speaking of is "the essence of the commonwealth." The essence of the commonwealth is not the commonwealth, according to the doctrine of essence.[80]

And if the essence is identified with the soul, it is again not identical with commonwealth.[81] Hobbes then again switches the focus of the discussion from the sovereign to the commonwealth, and then back again:

> And in him [the sovereign] consisteth the Essence of the Commonwealth; which, (to define it [commonwealth],) is One Person, of whose Acts a great Multitude, by mutuall Covenants one with another, have made themselves every one the Author.
>
> And he that carryeth this person is called SOVERAIGNE, and said to have *Soveraigne Power*; and every one besides, his SUBJECT.[82]

Reversing the illusion of those who try to "make men see double and mistake their lawful sovereign," Hobbes tries to get men to see single by conflating the commonwealth with the sovereign.[83] The logic of Hobbes's theory cannot support a strict identification of sovereign and commonwealth. In a monarchy, one human being constitutes the monarch. If the subjects constituted part of a monarchy, then they would have a vote in the decisions of the sovereign. But they don't.

4 CONCLUSION

I have tried to show that Hobbes's best theory of the origin of the political sphere is that individual people (through a covenant) authorize some one entity—one human being in the case of monarchy and some assembly of human beings in the case of aristocracy and democracy—to represent them. The action of authorization in itself does not involve alienation of any rights and hence does not limit the liberty of the covenanting individuals. Their liberty comes to be limited either in virtue of the principle

[78] *Leviathan* 17.13, 87.
[79] *Leviathan* 17.13, 87–88.
[80] *De homine* 8.23, 71.
[81] *Leviathan* Introduction, 1.
[82] *Leviathan* 17.13, 88.
[83] *Leviathan* 39.5, 248.

that whoever wills the end wills the means and the fact that human sovereigns almost always lack sufficient resources of their own to govern or in virtue of the fact that whoever has a right to an end has a right to the means to that end.

The action of authorization creates the relation of representation between the sovereign, who has some preexisting unity, and the covenanting individuals. A consequence of this relation is the creation of the commonwealth and thereby a unity of the individuals themselves. In addition to representing individual citizens, the sovereign represents the commonwealth because the commonwealth lacks the power to act on its own. Hobbes's theory of authorization and representation, then, is his attempt to defend the priority and privileges of the sovereign, not the commonwealth.[84]

REFERENCES

Filmer, Robert. 1991. *Patriarcha and Other Writings* Cambridge: Cambridge University Press.

Green, Michael J. 2015. "Authority and Political Authorization," *Journal of the History of Philosophy* 53(1): 25–47.

Hobbes, Thomas. 1658. *De homine*. London.

Hobbes, Thomas. 1676. *Leviathan*, in *Opera philosophica*. London.

Hobbes, Thomas. 2011. *Leviathan*, revised edition, edited by A. P. Martinich and Brian Battiste. London/Peterborough: Broadview Editions.

Martinich, A. P. 1992. *The Two Gods of Leviathan*. Cambridge: Cambridge University Press.

Martinich, A. P. 2005. *Hobbes*. London: Routledge.

Newey, Glen. 2008. *Routledge Philosophy Guidebook to Hobbes and Leviathan*. London: Routledge.

Pettit, Philip. 1997. *Republicanism*. Oxford: Oxford University Press.

Pitkin, Hanna. 1967. *The Concept of Representation*. Berkeley: University of California Press.

Rogers, G. A. J. and Schuhmann, K. 2003. *Introduction to Thomas Hobbes LEVIATHAN*. Bristol: Thoemmes and Continuum.

Runciman, David. 1997. *Pluralism and the Personality of the State*. Cambridge: Cambridge University Press.

Runciman, David. 2000. "What Kind of Person is Hobbes's State? A Reply to Skinner." *The Journal of Political Philosophy* 8: 268–278.

Runciman, David. 2010. "Hobbes's Theory of Representation: Anti-Democratic or Proto-Democratic?," in *Political Representation*, edited by Ian Shapiro et al., 15–34 Cambridge: Cambridge University Press.

[84] I want to thank Michael LeBuffe, Kinch Hoekstra, all the members of "Hobbes: Politics and Philosophy Workshop," King's College, London, May 2012, especially Adrian Blau, Robin Douglass, and Johan Olsthoorn, and the audience at Emory University, especially Ursula Goldenbaum, for their illuminating comments on this chapter. Leslie Martinich and J. P. Andrew also graciously helped with the editing. Finally, I want to thank Dean Randy Diehl for awarding me a Dean's Fellowship from the University of Texas at Austin, which gave me additional time to work on this chapter.

Skinner, Quentin. 2002. "Hobbes and the Purely Artificial Person of the State," in *Visions of Politics, Volume 3*, 177–208. Cambridge: Cambridge University Press.

Skinner, Quentin. 2007. "Hobbes on Persons, Authors, and Representatives," in *The Cambridge Companion to Hobbes's Leviathan*, edited by Patricia Springborg, 157–180. Cambridge: Cambridge University Press.

Skinner, Quentin. 2008. *Hobbes and Republican Liberty*. Cambridge: Cambridge University Press.

Sreedhar, Susanne. 2010. *Hobbes on Resistance: Defying the Leviathan*. Cambridge University Press.

Tricaud, François. 1982. "An Investigation Concerning the Usage of the Words 'Person' and 'Persona' in the Political Treatises of Hobbes," in *Thomas Hobbes: His View of Man*, edited by J. G. van der Bend, 89–98. Amsterdam: Rodopi.

···

CHAPTER 15

HOBBES (AND AUSTIN, AND AQUINAS) ON LAW AS COMMAND OF THE SOVEREIGN

···

MARK C. MURPHY

WHAT is uncontroversial about Hobbes's theory of the nature of human law—because Hobbes includes it in his explicit definition of law[1] —is that it consists in commands laid down by the sovereign. Once we begin to ask about its precise meaning, its further implications, or its justification, though, we find ourselves immediately in areas of disagreement and dispute. Whether Hobbes's view is aptly characterized as a variety of natural law theory,[2] legal positivism,[3] or some third view[4]; whether Hobbes's theory entails substantive normative restrictions on the sovereign's lawmaking capacities[5]; and whether Hobbes is attempting to capture a certain concept or recommending a certain way of responding to the law—these are unsettled issues regarding Hobbes's jurisprudence.

I want to address some of these questions in this essay. The way that I will do so is by focusing on the role of these key concepts, *command* and *sovereign*, in Hobbes's theory. John Austin, whose 1832 *Province of Jurisprudence Determined*[6] set the standard for English jurisprudence until supplanted by H.L.A. Hart's mid-twentieth-century *The Concept of Law*,[7] also defended a "command-of-the-sovereign" account of the law's nature. I will

---

[1] *Leviathan*, ed. Curley, 26.3, 137 (citation to chapter, paragraph, and 1651 page). See also *De Cive*, ed. Warrender, 14.1, 168, and *Dialogue of the Common Law*, ed. Cromartie and Skinner, 31.

[2] See Murphy 1995, Dyzenhaus 2001, and Dyzenhaus 2012.

[3] See Hart 1961 [1994]: 63; Watkins 1973: 114; Ladenson 1980; Hampton 1986: 107–110; Kavka 1986: 248–250; Lloyd 1992: 15; Gardner 2001: 200.

[4] See Gauthier 1990, Lloyd 2001, and Finkelstein 2006.

[5] See Dyzenhaus 2001.

[6] Austin 1832 [1995].

[7] Hart 1961 [1994].

use an extended comparison between Hobbes's views and Austin's as a way of addressing these various unsettled questions regarding Hobbes's position. I am going to emphasize the great gulf between Hobbes's command theory and Austin's. I will try to show not only that many of the surface similarities are illusory but also that where the similarities are genuine they bespeak not Hobbesian innovations that come to full flower in Austin's positivism but rather Hobbes's endorsement of more traditional ideas about the nature of law.

1 HOBBES AND AUSTIN ON COMMANDS AND SOVEREIGNTY: WHAT ARE COMMANDS, AND WHAT IS SOVEREIGNTY?

It is perfectly natural to elide the differences between Hobbes's and Austin's accounts of the nature of law. Here is Hobbes's account, from *Leviathan*:

> It is manifest that law in general is not counsel, but command; nor a command of any man to any man, but only of him whose command is addressed to one formerly obliged to obey him. And as for the civil law, it addeth only the name of the person commanding, which is *persona civitatis*, the person of the commonwealth.[8]

Thus for Hobbes the civil law consists in commands laid down by the sovereign for that sovereign's subjects.

Similarly, Austin writes that "Every law, or rule, is a command"[9]; this is, on Austin's view, the "key to the sciences of jurisprudence and morals."[10] In order to distinguish civil law from other rules, Austin claims that it is the commands given by political superiors—sovereigns—to political inferiors—subjects—that make for civil law.[11] Thus Austin holds that civil law consists in commands laid down by the sovereign for that sovereign's subjects.

It is a commonplace of legal theory to treat Hobbes's theory as a positivist account of the law's nature, a positivism that reaches full maturity in Austin's account.[12] But the imputed alliance between Hobbes and Austin is supposed to go deeper than that, not only to their common positivism but to the particular "command of the sovereign" form of positivism that both of them endorse.[13] And this is all understandable, given

---

[8] *Leviathan*, ed. Curley, 26.2, 137.

[9] Austin 1832 [1995]: I, 21.

[10] Austin 1832 [1995]: I, 21.

[11] Austin 1832 [1995]: I, 19.

[12] Lloyd writes that it is anachronistic to ask whether Hobbes is a positivist (Lloyd 2001: 187). This is a bizarre claim. To be a legal positivist is to affirm a certain thesis about law. Hobbes had in his possession all of the conceptual resources needed to affirm or deny the thesis. Therefore it makes sense to ask whether he did affirm that thesis—that is, to ask whether Hobbes was a legal positivist.

[13] See, e.g., the opening passages of Carnes 1960.

their official formulations of their positions. But once we see what Hobbes and Austin mean by *command* and *sovereign*, it becomes clear that there are very important differences between their positions.

For Austin, a command is an expression of a person's desire that some other person perform some action. This is not sufficient to distinguish commands from other directives—requests, pleas, and the like. On Austin's view, what marks the difference between commands and other directives is that the person expressing the desire vis-à-vis the other's conduct also expresses the intention to visit upon the commanded party an evil of some sort—a "sanction"—if he or she fails to comply. It is this liability to a sanction's being imposed on the commanded by the commander that makes it true, on Austin's view, that one who is commanded to do something is "bound" or "obliged" to perform, and why the performance counts as a "duty."[14] Austin places no constraints on the size of the sanction or on the chance of its actually being imposed; even the slightest chance of the slightest threatened evil is sufficient to make such an expression of will a command.[15]

One immediate point to be noted is that it is a necessary feature of commands as Austin characterizes them that they are binding, obliging, duty-imposing. To hold that a command was issued but no duty imposed is, on Austin's view, a contradiction in terms. Hobbes, however, does not assert this necessary connection between commands and sanctions or between commands and duties. Like Austin, Hobbes takes commands to be directives, marked as such by the "imperative manner of speaking" that is characteristically employed in giving them.[16] The mark of a command is that in commands (as opposed to in counsels) one gives a directive "without expecting[17] other reason than the will of him that says it."[18] (Hobbes immediately goes on to draw an inference from this necessary feature of commands, that is, that they always are for the good of the commander.[19] This somewhat peculiar inference is available only by drawing upon distinctive Hobbesian metaethics and action theory, and elaborating upon these is not to the point here.) But Hobbes does not say that there must actually be such a reason; fools, impudent children, and political pretenders can give commands that fail to obligate, fail to give any reason for compliance.

One might find puzzling Hobbes's claim that the commander gives a directive "without expecting other reason" than the commander's own will. One thing that Hobbes cannot mean is that the commander does not take any facts other than the commander's say-so to be relevant to whether the commanded has a good reason to go along. Hobbes himself supplies almost immediately an account of what extra conditions might have to be in place—that, for example, the commanded has covenanted to obey the commander.[20] More plausible is to read Hobbes's remark in this way: when one

[14] Austin 1832 [1995]: I, 22.
[15] Austin 1832 [1995]: I, 23.
[16] *Leviathan*, ed. Curley, 25.1, 131.
[17] That is, "calling for" or "needing."
[18] *Leviathan*, ed. Curley, 25.2, 131.
[19] *Leviathan*, ed. Curley, 25.2, 131–132.
[20] *Leviathan*, ed. Curley, 25.4, 132.

gives a command, one expects that the commanded may take the fact of the command as itself part of the reason to do what is commanded; therefore, because of that, it will be appropriate to give as grounds for doing x that the commander said to do x, even if there are other facts (like the preexisting covenant) that would have to be brought forward to explain why the command is reason-giving in the way that it is. As I noted above, though, this is all to be framed in terms of what the commander *suggests* or *implies* in commanding; it is not to be thought that Hobbes holds that there is no command unless the commanded really does have reason to go along.

Because Hobbes is here trying to distinguish between counsel and command, he does not reflect on the fact that there are cases in which directives given in the imperative form fit Hobbes's conditions thus far stated but are not commands. Beggars, for example, may put their directives in the imperative form, and expect nothing but their say-so to give a reason, without thereby becoming commanders of alms rather than beggars of alms. I take it that, pressed on this point, Hobbes would appeal to the *mandatory* character of commands: that commands do not pretend to be optional for the commanded, unlike pleas or begs. So the kind of reason one's say-so is put forward as giving is, in Hobbes's case, one that leaves no option for noncompliance.

We have identified two key differences between Hobbes's and Austin's views of commands thus far. One of them is about the connection between obligation/duty and commanding. On Hobbes's view, commands are not necessarily obligating; although one pretends to one's say-so being reason-giving in commanding, one's pretense may be deceitful or confused or may otherwise fall short. On Austin's view, by contrast, to fail to impose a duty is to fail to command. The other is about the sort of reason that commands give. Commands, on Hobbes's view, can give reasons; when they give reasons in the way that they are put forward as giving reasons, the command itself is part of the reason to do what is commanded. On Austin's view, the reason to go along is not the say-so of the commander but the prospect of the unhappy consequence resulting from failure to comply.

These are major differences on the character of commanding. But I want to delay commenting on how important these differences are from the point of view of legal theory until we have before us the other crucial, apparently common element of Austin's and Hobbes's views: that the relevant commands be issued by a *sovereign*.

Austin notes that we must say that, to count as law, commands are issued by a superior of some sort. But one way that one might be tempted to characterize the relevant superiority—in terms of an ability to impose sanctions—cannot be the right way. Given that anyone who manages to give a command is superior to the commanded at least insofar as he or she is able to impose sanctions on the commanded—that is just what is involved in giving a command, on Austin's view—it is simply "tautological" to say that laws are made by superiors.[21] To make the definition informative, we need to characterize a sense of superiority that is not simply given with the concept of a command and

---

[21] Austin 1832 [1995]: I, 31.

that can do the work of distinguishing properly between commands that make for law and those that do not.

Austin's solution is to define law in terms of *political* superiority, and political superiority in terms of *habits of obedience*. Suppose that in some population there is some party to whom the bulk of the populace has a habit of obedience. This party seems eligible to be thought of as the source of the law of that populace, although we would need some way to distinguish between the true source of law and subordinate officials; it may be that the bulk of the populace has a habit of obedience toward the chief of police, say, without it being at all plausible to think of the law of that community as what the chief of police commands. Austin tries to handle this by adding that the relevant party must be in a habit of obedience toward no one else. So the sovereign is the party within a political community to whom the bulk of the members of that community have a habit of obedience and who has a habit of obedience to no one else.[22]

Hobbes's conception of sovereignty, in terms of which he characterizes human law, is massively at odds with Austin's. For Austin, sovereignty is simply a matter of social fact; to characterize some party as a sovereign is not to commit oneself to any views about the desirability of that sovereign or the moral entitlement of that sovereign to rule or to be obeyed.[23] But this is not Hobbes's conception: His account of sovereignty is normative through and through. As Hobbes argues, law is not just command but command of one party to another *who is obligated to obey one's commands,* and in the civil law, the relevant parties are sovereign and subject.[24] Hobbes is plain in his characterization of sovereignty that it is a *normative* relation of obligation, brought about by covenanting.[25] Hobbes often emphasizes that sovereigns have their actions owned by the subjects, who count as authors in virtue of the covenant made; but authorship is cashed out by Hobbes in normative terms, in terms of what various actors are obligated to do.[26]

So Hobbes and Austin offer command-of-the-sovereign theories of the law's nature, but their conceptions of *command* and *sovereignty* are deeply at odds with each other. This is certainly true with respect to their accounts of commands, but the contrast in the case of sovereignty is much more salient. Austin's place in the history of jurisprudence

---

[22] Austin 1832 [1995]: VI, 167–170.

[23] "The existence of law is one thing; its merit or demerit another. Whether it be or not is one enquiry; whether it be or be not conformable to an assumed standard, is a different enquiry" (Austin 1832 [1995]: V, 157).

[24] Ladenson 1980 purports to defend a Hobbesian concept of law, and rightly notes that a Hobbesian view contrasts with an Austinian view in ways that allow a Hobbesian view to escape certain criticisms to which an Austinian view is subject. But Ladenson treats the authority of law as simply the right to coerce in accordance with its demands and holds that it "entails no correlative duties," including no "duties of allegiance" by subjects toward sovereigns (Ladenson 1980: 141). This is clearly at odds with Hobbes's own account of law, which emphasizes the obligation to obey. Ladenson does note that the view he is defending in that paper is "Hobbesian" rather than Hobbes's. But I think that the centrality of obligation in Hobbes's account of law makes clear that Ladenson's account, whatever its virtues, is not "consistent with, and based upon, [Hobbes's] fundamental ideas" (Ladenson 1980: 134).

[25] *Leviathan,* ed. Curley, 17.13–14, 87–88.

[26] *Leviathan,* ed. Curley, 17.13, 87–88.

as the paradigmatic positivist is due to his scrupulous rejection of theories of law that appeal to normative facts, facts of the very sort that Hobbes appeals to in giving an account of sovereignty.[27]

To bring out how important these differences between Hobbes and Austin are, I will note two advantages for the Hobbesian view, one arising from his conception of commands and one arising from his conception of sovereignty.[28]

One thing that turns on the difference between Austinian and Hobbesian analyses of command is whether command views can survive a particular challenge posed to such views as a class in Hart's *The Concept of Law*. Hart notes that it is an adequacy criterion for any legal theory that it accommodate the datum that those living under a legal system can take what Hart calls "the internal point of view" with respect to it. While there are in any legal system those who are concerned with the law only to the extent that it offers evidence to make predictions about how officials will respond to their own actions, it is also true that there are in any legal system those who are concerned to take the law as a standard for conduct because they judge there to be good reason to do so. This latter perspective Hart calls the "internal point of view." Hart levels against Austin's theory the criticism that this theory is unable to accommodate the datum that some people take the internal point of view toward the law: On Austin's view, the relevance of commands is just their inclusion of sanctions, and such a view does not make room for the existence of people who take the law's say-so to be a rule for their behavior regardless of whether official displeasure will be incurred if one fails to go along.[29] By contrast, Hobbes's view does seem to accommodate the internal point of view. For on the Hobbesian view, commands are at least put forward as reasons to perform the action commanded; to take the internal point of view with respect to law as Hobbes characterizes it is to take the law just as it presents itself to be.[30]

Here is a second issue in legal theory affected by the gap between Hobbes's and Austin's views. It is a platitude about law that it is authoritative; thus one criterion on which legal theories are rightly assessed is how well they capture this platitude.[31] Austin's view, with its characterization of the obliging, duty-imposing character of

---

[27]   This point is discussed in Gauthier 1990: 7–8, and Murphy 1995: 39.

[28]   This fact that Austin's view is to be distinguished from Hobbes's, and that the proper distinctions enable Hobbes to avoid some troublesome objections, is also noted by Barry: "Hobbes, as everybody knows, was an early exponent of the 'command theory of law' which received its classic statement from Austin. However, if I am right, Hobbes's version is free of the most fundamental logical objections to Austin's theory" (Barry 1968: 131). As I argue below, though, it is false to think that Hobbes is an "early" exponent of a command theory of law.

[29]   Hart 1961 [1994]: 56–57.

[30]   For a discussion of the internal point of view in relation to Austin's and especially Hobbes's theory, see Finkelstein 2006. Finkelstein focuses on the kind of reasons given by the covenant to obey that makes law binding; I focus here on a thinner point, that Hobbesian, unlike Austinian, commands are the sort of thing to which one could take the internal point of view.

[31]   See Murphy 2006b: 6–9 and Shapiro 2011: 15.

law as simply constituted by the sanction element, does very poorly in accommodating this commonplace about law. That the smallest chance of the smallest evil makes for a duty seems to have no anchor in any of our ordinary thought about duty, legal or otherwise. By contrast, the Hobbesian view takes being genuinely binding to be an essential feature of legality, so much so that there is no law at all unless there exists an obligation to obey between the lawgiver and the subject. The conception of legal obligation offered by a Hobbesian account of law is thus what Scott Shapiro has recently classified as "adjectival" (rather than "perspectival"): legal obligation, for Hobbes, is just obligation that arises from the imposition of law.[32]

If there is any worry here about Hobbes's view, it is that by characterizing law and legal obligation in this way, insufficient heed is given to the fact that legal systems can exist while utterly failing to obligate. One might argue, then, that Austin's view at least captures the fact that even if law always manages to produce legal obligations understood in an Austinian way—actions that are backed by sanctions for noncompliance—nevertheless there is no commitment to the position that law will always be obligatory in a richer way,[33] which seems to be what Hobbes is committed to. I am not sure whether Hobbes should be bothered by this worry, for it is plausible that given Hobbes's account of the conditions under which commonwealths count as minimally functional[34] and the conditions under which one tacitly consents to obey the sovereigns of such commonwealths,[35] so long as there are at least minimal provisions for human survival and comfort, the conditions under which residence constitute tacit consent will be triggered and there will be a genuine obligation—as Hobbes understands obligation—to obey. So Hobbes might well deny that such legal systems count as counterexamples to Hobbes's thesis that law exists only where subjects are obligated to obey. If one wishes to attack the implications of Hobbes's legal theory here, it may be that the only way to do so is by way of an attack on Hobbes's political theory as a whole. (It is true, though, that those who wish to abstract a Hobbesian legal theory from its context in a Hobbesian political theory may well find the objection much more troubling.)

[32] See Shapiro 2011: 184–186. To ascribe legal obligation adjectivally is to ascribe obligation that exists in virtue of being required by law; to ascribe it perspectivally is to say that, from the point of view of the law, some norm is obligatory. Only from the former does *being obligatory* follow from *being legally obligatory*.

[33] What is this "richer" way? Unfortunately how Hobbes understands obligation is itself a vexed issue. I discuss some of the possibilities, and offer an explanation for Hobbes's unclarity, in Murphy 1994. Suffice it to say that none of the interpretive possibilities reduces obligation to the threat of a sanction of some size being imposed. I discuss below the connection in Hobbes's view between obligation and reason.

[34] See Hart on the "minimal content of natural law," which is explicitly drawn from Hobbes (Hart 1961 [1964], 187–195).

[35] See *Leviathan*, ed. Curley, Review and Conclusion 7, 391 for Hobbes's clearest statement of the conditions under which one has tacitly covenanted to obey existing sovereigns.

2 HOBBES AND AUSTIN ON COMMANDS AND SOVEREIGNTY: WHY OFFER AN ACCOUNT OF LAW IN TERMS OF THE COMMANDS OF A SOVEREIGN?

I have thus far emphasized the deep differences between Austin's and Hobbes's accounts of the law's nature, differences masked by their common "command of the sovereign" formulation. I want to consider now another deep difference, a difference regarding the *rationales* for their legal theories.

We can approach this difference by considering a challenge to my characterization of the gap between Austin's and Hobbes's views. "For all you have said," the challenger might point out,

> the plain truth is that the commonality between these views far outstrips the differences. This is not just a verbal matter, a matter of their both using the terms *command* and *sovereign* in their accounts of law. The commonality can be exhibited by noting that both views are subject in equal measure to most of the major criticisms that Hart levels against command theories as a class in *The Concept of Law*. If they are thus equally subject, it is plain that what has been noted thus far, even if true, is not indicative of a great gulf between Hobbes's and Austin's theories of law.

There is an important truth to this challenge. One thing that Austin's and Hobbes's accounts of commands have in common is that they both satisfy some fairly minimal constraints on what an account of commands should look like. The issuing of a command is a *datable event*, and commands take as their objects *some future action* by someone *other than the commander*. If there is a command, there is some time at which that command was given. If there is a command, then it is a command that someone do such and such. And while metaphorical self-commanding is possible, literal self-commanding is not. Hobbes's account of commanding satisfies these constraints; so does Austin's. And it is of course unsurprising that there is agreement here, given how uncontroversial these elements of commanding are.

But it is just these elements that Hart seizes upon to criticize Austin's command theory of law. As Hart points out, not all laws come into existence in this time-stamped way; under some legal systems, custom is a source of law, and the existence of law that holds on account of custom need not have some determinate time at which it comes into existence. Further, not all laws are laws that direct agents to perform some future action. Some do—Hart calls these "duty-imposing" rules and concedes that the command view has its greatest plausibility as an account of such norms—but some do not. Some rules are "power-conferring" rules, rules that give people ability to alter the rules or their applications. Further, not all laws bind only parties other than the lawmaker; it is a common phenomenon for legal systems to include norms that bind the lawmakers themselves.[36]

Hart's claim is that these obvious features of paradigmatic legal systems make plain the inadequacy of command theories of law. These are not criticisms directed against command views that take on board eccentric analyses of commands, like Austin's; they apply against *any* recognizable command view, for any plausible account of commands would have to ascribe to commands the features that Hart relies upon in his argument.

Now, one could deny that command views lack the resources to deal with these objections. While Hart thinks that dealing with these objections within the constraints set by the command view results in an implausible and inelegant account, it is open to these authors to push back by emphasizing the merits of the command view as a reason for accepting some complications. Both Hobbes and Austin deny that custom is genuinely a source of law in the sense of something that itself is sufficient to confer legal status; on both views, custom's role in making law holds only with the approval of the sovereign, whose command to take custom as binding is required to make it so.[37] (Contra Hart,[38] this need not involve the sovereign's having any detailed knowledge of the customs in that community in order for the sovereign's command to incorporate it into law.) Hobbes and Austin may well take power-conferring laws to be defined wholly in terms of duty-imposing laws: What is relevant about a law conferring a power to make a will is that the sovereign imposes duties on parties to respond to what the law counts as "a will." Even if the pragmatics of power-conferring norms differ from those of duty-imposing norms, still the former is fully reducible, *legally*, to the latter. As to the alleged ability of a sovereign to self-bind by law, Hobbes and Austin have arguments—arguments we will consider below—that this phenomenon is illusory.

So there are some maneuvers that Hobbes and Austin can make to enable their command theories of law to blunt Hart's criticisms. But it is true that these maneuvers are costly.

I raise these Hartian criticisms of Hobbes and Austin obviously not to settle any dispute between defenders of command formulations and their critics but to set the stage to make a point about the different rationales behind Hobbes's and Austin's views. Suppose that we grant that, *as formulated*, Hobbes's and Austin's views are equally subject to Hart's criticisms. Nevertheless, it could be true that Hobbes's view and Austin's view are nevertheless to be distinguished because they are not equally threatened by those criticisms. How could it be that, as formulated, both are equally subject to these criticisms yet not equally threatened by those criticisms?

The idea is this: Philosophical views, when subjected to admittedly damaging criticism, often respond to that criticism via revision—by transforming the view so that they are no longer open to the damaging objections. Whether it is appropriate to

---

[36] Hart 1961 [1994]: 26–49.

[37] *Leviathan*, ed. Curley, 26.7, 138. See also *Dialogue of the Common Law*, ed. Cromartie and Skinner, 63.

[38] Hart 1961 [1994]: 47–48.

respond by revision rather than by abandoning the position or absorbing the criticism (that is, conceding its force and inescapability while holding that nevertheless the view is still defensible) depends in large part on the rationale for the current formulation. If the rationale for the current formulation treats certain aspects of that formulation as dispensable because of subordinate importance, there can be good reason to revise the view in a way that is not ad hoc (because it is still supported by the view's rationale) and enables the avoidance of the criticism. This is just a description of a phenomenon that every theorist in any field will recognize. Some revisions of a theory are acceptable because they preserve the proposed theory's key insights while giving up some inessential thesis; some revisions are unacceptable because they give up something so central to the theory in question that such revisions would be tantamount to abandoning the position.

To be explicit, then, one way in which Hobbes's and Austin's theories, though equally subject to Hart's criticisms, could be unequally threatened by them would be if Hobbes's view permits revision of the theory in a way that escapes the force of these criticisms while Austin's view does not. If this is true, then it is one further way in which we can see how deep are the differences between Hobbes's and Austin's theories of law. So here are the questions we need to answer: Could one make sense of a Hobbesian theory of law that discards the idea that laws are commands? Could one make sense of an Austinian theory of law that discards the idea that laws are commands? I think that the fact that we should reach different conclusions here—there is room for a noncommand Hobbesian theory of law but not for a noncommand Austinian theory—further illustrates the gulf between these two accounts.

It seems plain that for an Austinian there is no prospect of reasonable revision in the face of Hart's criticisms: One must either absorb or deflect those criticisms or give up on Austinianism as a theory of the law's nature. The central point is this: For Austin, commands are the key to jurisprudence—or indeed to any science of binding norms. It is a conceptual truth that to be a law is to be a command of some sort. But I do not think that the same holds true of Hobbes's view. On Hobbes's view, the key to jurisprudence is not *command*. The key to jurisprudence is *obligation*. Thus there is some room for a Hobbesian theory of law to be revised in the face of a criticism like Hart's.

What is nonnegotiable in Hobbes's legal theory is that law has to *obligate*. That this is *not* the linchpin of Austin's view is clear from the fact that duty is, on Austin's view, so cheaply had; anybody with a desire regarding someone else and any ability to make that other's life somewhat less pleasant has the capacity to impose a duty by commanding. For Hobbes, though, obligation is *not* cheap; to obligate someone to some course of action is to bind him or her in such a way that it rules out as unreasonable any incompatible option. Hobbes *never* treats obligation as something that one could violate without falling into a rational error of some sort; indeed, the whole point of the celebrated "Reply to the Fool" is to ensure that what is putatively obligatory (keeping one's covenants) is rationally required[39]; and indeed, the whole point of distinguishing

[39] *Leviathan,* ed. Curley, 15.4–7, 72–74.

between the *in foro externo* and *in foro interno* binding power of the laws of nature is to ensure that what is binding is nothing that it would be foolish to do, nothing that would make one, against all reason, a target of opportunity for others.[40]

All of the different sorts of law that Hobbes considers—divine and human, natural and positive—are taken by Hobbes to be obligating. It is because law is obligating that Hobbes sees fit to characterize law in terms of command. It cannot be counsel, for counsel is not the right sort of thing to be obligatory. Commands may obligate or fail to obligate, but in either case they are the right sort of thing to be law.

Hobbes is also plain that it is law's character as obligating that explains why we must place its source in the sovereign. Note, again, that this is not a move available to Austin; it is not because of law's obligating character that Austin places the sovereign at its source, for obligating is easy to do on Austin's view, and the sovereign is not particularly privileged as a source of obligation. But for Hobbes, the only plausible place to locate the source of civil law is in the person whose say-so is authoritative for the members of the commonwealth: that is, the sovereign.

We can add to the force of Hobbes's argument here by adding a reflection on the systematic character of law. It would not be sufficient for Hobbes's account of law to meet the desideratum that law be obligating by holding that for each rule of every legal system there is *something* that makes that rule obligatory. Such a view would be compatible with some norms being part of law because they are implications of the law of nature, and thus obligatory, and others being part of the law only because given by the sovereign, whom the subjects have covenanted to obey. We would lack, under this scenario, any sense of why the various rules of the civil law constitute *one* system of rules. But the systematic character of law is accommodated by holding that civil law consists in those rules the obligatory character of which arises from the obligation to obey the sovereign power.[41] Unlike on Austin's view, where it looks as though we have two independent conditions cobbled together—the fact of sovereignty and the facts of commanding—on Hobbes's view both the command element and sovereignty element have their place in virtue of their role in capturing the obligating character of civil law.

What would this revised Hobbesian view look like? It might still want to take law to be rooted in illocutionary acts without committing itself to the view that the sort of illocutionary act at stake is one of commanding. It is constitutive of commanding that it concern future actions by parties other than the commander. Perhaps instead one could appeal to a (neologizing) illocutionary act of "rule imposition"—of laying down standards of conduct for some specifiable group of agents. Because there is no constraint on what the objects of such rules can be, they might be able to confer powers as well as make conduct mandatory, and they might be able to bind the lawgiver as well as the subject. (No doubt Hobbes would be unhappy with the idea of the sovereign's being bound

---

[40] *Leviathan*, ed. Curley, 15.36–37, 79; see also *Dialogue of the Common Law*, ed. Cromartie and Skinner, 32.

[41] Thus the Hobbesian covenant plays the role that a Hartian rule of recognition plays, as truthmaker for the claim that certain social facts' holding counts as certain laws' being valid.

by law. But Hobbes has the resources to distinguish between the various ways in which a sovereign can be bound by law—more on this below—and Hobbes could feel free to make a normative point about law, that even if it is *possible* for the sovereign to place itself under a legal rule, that does not mean that it is *desirable* for the sovereign to do so.)

This is just a sketch of a possibility for Hobbes. It does not help with the problem of custom, if that is indeed a problem. And it still leaves Hobbes with a *personal* account of law—that law is always the product of a person (albeit an artificial one), making law through the performance of speech acts. Such views are sometimes taken to be hopelessly obscuring of how law functions in modern, impersonal legal systems, but there are some grounds for thinking these assessments less than obvious.[42]

3 Hobbes's Theory of Law as Innovative?

My aim has been to lay out the structure and rationale of Hobbes's account of the nature of civil law. My entry point into this question was the surface similarity between Hobbes's view and Austin's. I have argued that although Hobbes and Austin both offer accounts of the law's nature in terms of the commands laid down by a sovereign, the substance and rationales for these views are deeply at odds. The common notion that Hobbes and Austin are natural jurisprudential allies should be, I think, abandoned.

Yet one might accept the argument thus far while still suspecting that I have not done justice to the Hobbes-Austin connection. True, Hobbes is no positivist, while Austin is a paradigmatic positivist. True, Hobbes's key to jurisprudence is real, unqualified obligation, while Austin's key is command understood as a sort of threat. But surely Hobbes's legal theory, in its appeal to the say-so of an ultimate authority as the essence of law, represents a decisive break from the natural law tradition that precedes him and thus paves the way for Austin's jurisprudence.

It is hard to evaluate claims like this, that Hobbes "paved the way" for Austin. What is easier to evaluate is the claim that Hobbes's jurisprudence represents a decisive break from the natural law jurisprudence of the scholastics. And that seems to me to be an error. The notion that human law consists in the commands of a sovereign is, in concept if not in terminology, familiar from the jurisprudence of Aquinas, who is the paradigmatic natural law theorist. The idea that law consists fundamentally in commands and that these commands have to be identified as coming from some ultimately authoritative party is not an innovation in Hobbes but a commonplace of the predecessor natural law theory.[43]

---

[42] See Murphy 2006a: 43.

[43] For an extended discussion of the commonalities between Aquinas's and Hobbes's approaches to law, see Martinich 1992: 115–116.

Aquinas declares that laws are precepts, but he identifies precepts with commands.[44] On his view, all acts of law are commands or defined in terms of commands.[45] (The possible exception to this is punishment, which Aquinas calls an act of law without suggesting that what it is for law to punish someone can be analyzed in terms of commanding; nevertheless, this characterization of punishment as an act of law, though not a matter of command, is not well integrated with the rest of Aquinas's account.)

And it is not surprising that Aquinas understands law in terms of commands. The idea that law is always laid down by a *personal* source—a person, or group of persons—is absolutely central to his thought about law. Aquinas conceives of law primarily in terms of its *ordering* role, its ordering disparate elements so that they act toward a single good.[46] This is true not only for human law but for the eternal and natural law as well.[47] And Aquinas thinks that such ordering would require the work of an ordering intelligence to direct diverse things to a common end.[48] While this of course does not entail that Aquinas must affirm a command conception of law—Aquinas could have appealed to some other way in which the intentional interventions of intelligent persons order the actions of agents within a community—it does make clear why he would be inclined toward such an account. And this understanding of the role of law is manifest in Aquinas's general definition of law as an "ordinance for the common good, laid down by one having care of the community, and promulgated."[49]

The other aspect of the nature of Hobbes's theory of law that is also present in Aquinas's view is the idea that the commands that make for human law come from the highest authority within a particular political community.[50] This is Aquinas's view as well, as the just-quoted definition makes clear: It is the person who has "care of the community" whose say-so makes for law. On the face of things, then, there is no basis for holding that Aquinas affirms a command-of-the-sovereign view of the nature of law any less than Hobbes affirms it. To hold that Hobbes's command view counts as a move away from natural law jurisprudence would be just a mistake.

Now arguments of this sort are always open to the objection that in abstracting away from some of the details of their positions, interesting differences have been lost. I want to consider two such differences that might seem to count as important moves Hobbes makes away from Aquinas and toward Austin. One of them concerns custom as a source of law; the other concerns the possibility of a limitation on sovereignty.

One might think the fact that Aquinas allows custom to be a source of law in its own right—whereas Hobbes (along with Austin) denies it this status—shows that there is

---

[44] Aquinas, *Summa Theologiae*, IaIIae 92, 2 obj. 1 (not denied).

[45] Aquinas, *Summa Theologiae*, IaIIae 92, 2.

[46] Aquinas, *Summa Theologiae*, IaIIae 91, 1 ad 3.

[47] Aquinas, *Summa Theologiae*, IaIIae 91, 1–2.

[48] Aquinas, *Summa Theologiae*, Ia 2,3; 22, 1.

[49] Aquinas, *Summa Theologiae*, IaIIae 90, 4.

[50] But on Aquinas's view isn't the highest authority in a political community *God*, since God is the ultimate authority over all human beings? Yes (Aquinas, *Summa Theologiae*, IaIIae 93, 3; IIaIIae 102, 4); but this is Hobbes's view as well: see, e.g., *Leviathan*, ed. Curley, 43.1, 321.

a deeper divide between them than I have let on, or that somehow Aquinas's commitment to a personal conception of authority and a command conception of law is less deep than Hobbes's. I think this would be a mistake, though; the divide between Aquinas and Hobbes here is not the result of some difference in their theories of the nature of the law but in their theories about the conditions under which some speech act can be ascribed to a collective.

Aquinas asks whether custom can make or abrogate law, and he answers in the affirmative:

> All law proceeds from the reason and will of the lawgiver; the Divine and natural laws from the reasonable will of God; the human law from the will of man, regulated by reason. Now just as human reason and will, in practical matters, may be made manifest by speech, so may they be made known by deeds: since seemingly a man chooses as good that which he carries into execution. But it is evident that by human speech, law can be both changed and expounded, in so far as it manifests the interior movement and thought of human reason. Wherefore by actions also, especially if they be repeated, so as to make a custom, law can be changed and expounded; and also something can be established which obtains force of law, in so far as by repeated external actions, the inward movement of the will, and concepts of reason are most effectually declared; for when a thing is done again and again, it seems to proceed from a deliberate judgment of reason. Accordingly, custom has the force of a law, abolishes law, and is the interpreter of law.[51]

I am not interested here in the merits of Aquinas's argument.[52] What is important here is that Aquinas is taking the standard case of law, something like a statute laid down by an authoritative lawgiver, and attempting to assimilate customary law to that paradigm case: Because political authority resides fundamentally in the community as a whole—as Aquinas argues, to direct to an end "belongs to the one to whom the end belongs,"[53] and so a sovereign "has not the power to frame laws, except as representing the people"[54]—the people as a whole can issue a command that some course of action be adopted or refrained from.

Now Hobbes will of course have none of this. But note that what is in dispute between Hobbes and Aquinas here is not whether sovereignty is essential to lawgiving or whether it must be exercised in commanding for a law to be present. What is at issue between them is whether it makes any sense for a multitude to speak unless it is represented in some way. As noted, Aquinas unqualifiedly says that the directing of something to an end "concerns him to whom the end belongs"[55]; therefore the direction of individuals to the common good must belong to the community as a whole. The direction of

---

[51] Aquinas, *Summa Theologiae*, IaIIae 97, 3.

[52] The argument does seem strained in its attempt to assimilate deeds to illocutionary acts, though. See also Murphy 2005: 66.

[53] Aquinas, *Summa Theologiae*, IaIIae 90, 3.

[54] Aquinas, *Summa Theologiae*, IaIIae 97, 3 ad 3.

[55] Aquinas, *Summa Theologiae*, IaIIae 90, 3.

individuals to the common good, though, is the work of law, hence there must be some sense in which the community can act as lawgiver: "The making of law belongs either to the whole people or to a public personage who has care of the whole people."[56] The sovereign, then, can make law only insofar as this power has been bestowed on him or her by the whole people; the people is the primary legislator. Hobbes would reject the idea that prior to the institution of political authority the people can act as lawgiver, for before the institution of political authority, there is really no people at all. He puts the point clearly in *De cive*:

> [M]en distinguish not enough between a *People* and a *Multitude*. The *People* is somewhat that is *one*, having *one will*, and to whom one action may be attributed; none of these can properly be said of a Multitude. The *People* rules in all governments. . . . In a *Democraty*, and *Aristocraty*, the Citizens are the *Multitude*, but the *Court* is the *People*. And in a *Monarchy*, the Subjects are the *Multitude*, and (however it seeme a Paradox) the King is the *People*.[57]

Any number of humans can make up a multitude, on Hobbes's view, but a people only comes into being with a covenant to set up a sovereign; it is this sovereign that is the people.[58] Aquinas's account, by which a people can make law apart from the activity of an instituted sovereign, is quite impossible, for "a Multitude cannot promise, contract, acquire right, conveigh Right, act, have, possesse, and the like."[59] So it is true, then, that Hobbes and Aquinas disagree about the role of custom in making and abrogating law. But it is a mistake to see this as rooted in a differing level of commitment to a command-of-the-sovereign conception of law.

One might think that the key difference between Aquinas and Hobbes is that Hobbes thought that a legal limitation on the sovereign is not merely undesirable but impossible. The argument is simple: Because law is the command of a sovereign and the sovereign is not bound by its own commands (either because commands are other-directed or because the sovereign may free himself or herself from those commands at will), the sovereign cannot be bound by law.[60] (This idea is, unsurprisingly, also endorsed by Austin.[61])

The question here is whether Aquinas disagrees. Aquinas explicitly considers whether all are subject to the law, and with pointed reference to the sovereign of the political community:

> [1] The sovereign is said to be exempt from the law, as to its coercive power; since, properly speaking, no man is coerced by himself, and law has no coercive power save

[56] Aquinas, *Summa Theologiae*, IaIIae 90, 3.
[57] *De Cive*, ed. Warrender, 12.8, 151.
[58] *De Cive*, ed. Warrender, 6.1, 91–92; see also *Leviathan*, ed. Curley, 16, and 17.13, 87.
[59] *De Cive*, ed. Warrender, 6.1, 92.
[60] *Leviathan*, ed. Curley, 26.6, 137–138.
[61] Austin 1832 [1995]:VI, 212.

from the authority of the sovereign. Thus then is the sovereign said to be exempt from the law, because none is competent to pass sentence on him, if he acts against the law. Wherefore on Psalm 50:6, "To Thee only have I sinned," a gloss says that "there is no man who can judge the deeds of a king." [2] But as to the directive force of law, the sovereign is subject to the law by his own will, according to the statement (*Extra, De Constitutionibus,* chapter beginning "Since everyone") that "whatever law a man makes for another, he should keep himself." And a wise authority says: "Obey the law that thou makest thyself." Moreover the Lord reproaches those who "say and do not"; and who "bind heavy burdens and lay them on men's shoulders, but with a finger of their own they will not move them" (Matthew 23:3–4). Hence, in the judgment of God, the sovereign is not exempt from the law, as to its directive force; but he should fulfill it of his own free will and not of constraint. [3] Again the sovereign is above the law, insofar as, when it is expedient, he can change the law, and dispense in it according to time and place.[62]

There are three distinct points here. One point, which is defended in the passage marked [1], is that with respect to law's coercive power, the sovereign is clearly above the law. This is pretty clearly not interestingly different from the view offered by Hobbes and Austin. Another point, defended in the passage I have marked [3], is that the sovereign is above the law in the sense that the sovereign has the power to add, change, and dispense from the law. Again, this is no different from Hobbes's and Austin's position (except for one qualification, noted below).

The key passage, then, if one wants to find an illuminating difference between Hobbes and Aquinas, is [2], and it is unfortunately ambiguous. Is Aquinas saying that there is indeed law that applies to and binds the sovereign and the sovereign should thus follow it, even though uncompelled by coercion? That is a simple and plausible reading. But here is another reading, better supported by the arguments that Aquinas offers in the passage: Perhaps Aquinas is saying that even though no human law strictly speaking applies to the sovereign, nevertheless a moral principle (a principle of the natural law, as Aquinas would put it) binds the sovereign to act in a certain way because of the existence of that law. Here is an illustration of this second way of being bound *because of* a rule, though not *by* that rule: If I have laid a rule on my children not to use profanity and the relevant circumstances that make this a good rule for my children to follow also apply to me, then I should not use profanity either—not because the rule binds me but because it is a good idea not to exempt myself from this directive, especially once I have laid that norm upon my children. But it would be false to say that, strictly speaking, I am bound by the antiprofanity rule: I am not within its scope and so cannot be bound by it.

The former reading is simple, but it requires us to think of commands as not being essentially other-directed. The latter reading allows all commands to be other-directed but nevertheless takes the law to provide some guidance—natural law guidance—to the

---

[62] Aquinas, *Summa Theologiae,* IaIIae 96, 5 ad 3.

sovereign, as the human law can be a relevant circumstance that makes it the case that the sovereign ought to act one way rather than another.

The latter reading generates no real tension between Aquinas and Hobbes. Hobbes is perfectly happy to say that there are norms of equity that apply to sovereigns,[63] and there is nothing that need bar him from saying that sovereigns should honor norms of conduct similar to those imposed on subjects, at least when their circumstances are relevantly similar.

The former reading produces some tension between Aquinas's and Hobbes's views. There are passages in Hobbes where he *seems* to say that the sovereign can make laws applying to its own conduct, but Hobbes's (dubious) master argument against legal limitation entails that this is no real legal limitation given the sovereign's ability to change or dispense from the law.[64] If Aquinas were to hold that a legal rule applies directly in this way, he could not adopt Hobbes's argument that this is no real limitation given the sovereign's ability to dispense itself from the requirements of the law, for Aquinas thinks that there are substantive natural law limitations on the legal effects that the lawmaker can bring about. It may be that just as on Aquinas's view a lawmaker cannot make a law requiring blasphemy—this will not be a real law, but a perversion of it, as much a law as a counterfeit dollar is a dollar[65] —a lawmaker cannot issue a dispensation allowing him-, her-, or itself to act viciously, if that dispensation itself would count as a perversion of law. The tension between Aquinas and Hobbes, on this reading, is not so much about whether the sovereign can be guided by law but whether there are limitations on the sovereign's lawmaking and law-changing activity from a nonlegal source.

I find, then, that there is nothing dramatically different between Hobbes's command-of-the-sovereign account of law and Aquinas's that could serve as a basis for the claim that Hobbes's view counts as innovative in the direction of Austin's position. If there is anything innovative in the direction of Austin's position, it is simply that posited in the standard view that Hobbes, unlike Aquinas, does not take there to be moral constraints on the norms that the sovereign can command into law.

This is not quite the claim that Aquinas is not a positivist and Hobbes is. As we have seen, because Hobbes makes certain merits—the fact that law proceeds from a source that subjects are genuinely obligated to obey—essential to legality, his view is not a positivist one. But one could say that there is an *aspect* of positivism that Hobbes affirms yet Aquinas rejects—the view that the merits of a sovereign's commands cannot make a difference to whether those commands constitute law.

I think that this reading of Hobbes is mistaken. Although I cannot make a full argument on behalf of this view here, I want to sketch a couple of different ways for making the case for Hobbes's antipositivism even in terms of the content of law.

One way to make this argument is to liken Hobbes's views on law to those of Lon Fuller. Fuller argued that there are normative constraints on law—an "internal

---

[63] *Leviathan*, ed. Curley, 30.15, 180.
[64] *Leviathan*, ed. Curley, 29.9, 169.
[65] Aquinas, *Summa Theologiae*, IaIIae 95, 2; for discussion, see Murphy 2006: 13–14.

morality"—such that, although law can exist with some failures with respect to such constraints, law cannot exist when the failure with respect to them is egregious. Fuller illustrates this with a fable of Rex, who though nominally the lawmaker within a community fails ever to make law because he fails ever to make a rule that counts as law.[66] Fuller's claim is that the massive failure to produce law that is general, public, prospective, comprehensible, consistent, possible to follow, stable, and applied as given results not only in bad law but in no law at all. What makes this an *internal* morality of law is that such norms of lawgiving are constitutive of the sort of relationship that legality is: a sort of respectful reciprocity between the makers and followers of law. A comparison between Hobbes's views of law and Fuller's is central to David Dyzenhaus's recent reading of Hobbes as antipositivist. On his reading of Hobbes, the laws of nature—particularly the neglected final two thirds of Hobbes's list—specify a Hobbesian account of the internal morality of law such that a sovereign's flagrant flouting of these requirements counts as a sovereign's not really acting as sovereign at all. This tension comes out most dramatically with respect to the role of subordinate judges. On Hobbes's view, judges should interpret the sovereign's will through the lens of the laws of nature.[67] But the more the sovereign's directives run contrary to those norms, the less sense a judge will be able to make of this task. There are certain ways for a Hobbesian sovereign to try to rule that are at odds with that sovereign's ruling through law, and Hobbes's theory of the laws of nature tries to make out what those ways are.[68]

An alternative argument appeals immediately to the *substance* of law, to what a would-be law requires of subjects. Recall that Hobbes's key idea is that the law obligates. This is the basis for Hobbes's view that the law has to proceed from the sovereign, whose subjects are obligated to obey. But it might well be wondered whether this key idea would have implications for the possible content of law as well.

Hobbes thinks that there are a variety of things that we cannot be obligated to do, even with full awareness and willingness to bind ourselves.[69] And thus Hobbes reaches the conclusion that there are some things that the sovereign can tell us to do that we cannot be obligated to do.[70] When Hobbes is specific about these constraints, they revolve around the goods of self-preservation, which the laws of nature require us to pursue and with respect to which not to act stupidly. So if Hobbes is serious when he says that the limits of obligation are the limits of law,[71] then Hobbes commits himself

---

[66] Fuller 1964: 33–38.
[67] *Leviathan*, ed. Curley, 26.26, 145.
[68] See Dyzenhaus 2001 and Dyzenhaus 2012.
[69] See, e.g., *Leviathan*, ed. Curley, 14.29, 69–70.
[70] *Leviathan*, ed. Curley, 21.11–15, 111–112.
[71] Hobbes affirms a number of connections between law and other normative concepts that provide further support for the point that I am making here: if one has a right to φ, then there is no law prohibiting one from φ-ing (*Leviathan*, ed. Curley, 14.3, 64 and 26.44, 150); if one has the liberty to φ, then there is no law prohibiting one from φ-ing (21.18, 113); if one does not act unjustly in φ-ing, then there is no law prohibiting one from φ-ing (26.4, 137). It follows, then, that if the sovereign commands a subject to φ, and the subject has the right not to φ, has the liberty not to φ, and does not act unjustly in not φ-ing, then the sovereign's command is not law over one. For Hobbes, though, anything that one is not obligated to do, even if the sovereign commands it, is such that one may do it without

to the very same position that Aquinas defends: that the human good, which sets the limits of reasonable conduct, also sets the limits to the sorts of norms that can become law by being commanded by the sovereign authority.[72]

4 Conclusion

It is most tempting to treat Hobbes as a mere forerunner to Austin if one thinks of Hobbes's command-of-the-sovereign view as substantially similar to Austin's own view and itself a radical break from earlier jurisprudence. But as I have argued, Hobbes's and Austin's views exhibit deep differences, and the conception of law as command of the sovereign was a familiar idea even in the work of Aquinas. So the temptation to elide the differences between Hobbes's and Austin's jurisprudence, natural as it is, is nonetheless to be resisted.[73]

Bibliography

Aquinas, Thomas. *Summa Theologiae*, translated by Fathers of the English Dominican Province. Westminster, UK: Christian Classics.

Austin, John. 1832 [1995]. *Province of Jurisprudence Determined*, edited by Wilfrid Rumble. Cambridge, UK: Cambridge University Press.

Barry, Brian. 1968. "Warrender and his Critics." *Philosophy* 43: 117–137.

Carnes, John. 1960. " 'Why Should I Obey the Law?'" *Ethics* 71: 14–26.

Dyzenhaus, David. 2001. "Hobbes and the Legitimacy of Law." *Law and Philosophy* 20: 461–498.

Dyzenhaus, David. 2012. "Hobbes on the Authority of Law," in *Hobbes and the Law*, edited by David Dyzenhaus and Thomas Poole, 186–209. Cambridge, UK: Cambridge University Press.

Finkelstein, Claire. 2006. "Hobbes and the Internal Point of View." *Fordham Law Review* 75: 1211–1228.

Fuller, Lon. 1964. *The Morality of Law*. New Haven, CT: Yale University Press.

Gardner, John. 2001. "Legal Positivism: 5½ Myths." *American Journal of Jurisprudence* 46: 199–227.

Gauthier, David. 1990. "Thomas Hobbes and the Contractarian Theory of Law." *Canadian Journal of Philosophy* 16: 5–34.

Hampton, Jean. 1986. *Hobbes and the Social Contract Tradition*. Cambridge, UK: Cambridge University Press.

Hart, H.L.A. 1961 [1994]. *The Concept of Law*, 2nd ed. Oxford, UK: Oxford University Press.

injustice, within one's rights, and at one's liberty (21.10-16, 111–112). For further discussion, see Murphy 1995: 38–41.

[72] No doubt Hobbes offers a thinner account of the human good than Aquinas does. For discussion of the irrelevance of this fact to the questions of legal theory discussed here, see Murphy 1995: 49–62.

[73] I owe thanks to David Dyzenhaus and Al Martinich for helpful criticisms and suggestions.

Hobbes, Thomas. 1983. *De Cive: The Latin Version*, edited by Howard Warrender. Oxford: Clarendon Press.

Hobbes, Thomas. 1994. *Leviathan: With Selected Variants from the Latin Edition of 1668*. Edited by Edwin Curley. Indianapolis: Hackett Pub. Co.

Hobbes, Thomas. 2005. *A dialogue between a philosopher and a student, of the common laws of England, in Thomas Hobbes: Writings on Common Law and Hereditary Right*, edited by Alan Cromartie and Quentin Skinner. Oxford: Clarendon Press.

Kavka, Gregory S. 1986. *Hobbesian Moral and Political Theory*. Princeton, NJ: Princeton University Press.

Ladenson, Robert. 1980. "In Defense of a Hobbesian Conception of Law." *Philosophy and Public Affairs* 9: 134–159.

Lloyd, S. A. 1992. *Ideals as Interests in Hobbes's Leviathan: The Power of Mind over Matter*. Cambridge, UK: Cambridge University Press.

Lloyd, S. A. 2001. "Hobbes's Self-Effacing Natural Law Theory." *Pacific Philosophical Quarterly* 82: 285–308.

Martinich, A. P. 1992. *The Two Gods of Leviathan: Thomas Hobbes on Religion and Politics*. Cambridge, UK: Cambridge University Press.

Murphy, James Bernard. 2005. *The Philosophy of Positive Law: Foundations of Jurisprudence*. New Haven, CT: Yale University Press.

Murphy, Mark C. 1994. "Deviant Uses of 'Obligation' in Hobbes's *Leviathan*." *History of Philosophy Quarterly* 11: 281–294.

Murphy, Mark C. 1995. "Was Hobbes a Legal Positivist?" *Ethics* 105: 846–873.

Murphy, Mark C. 2006a. *Natural Law in Jurisprudence and Politics*. Cambridge, UK: Cambridge University Press.

Murphy, Mark C. 2006b. *Philosophy of Law: The Fundamentals*. Malden, MA: Blackwell.

Shapiro, Scott J. 2011. *Legality*. Cambridge, MA: Harvard University Press.

Watkins, J. W. N. 1973. *Hobbes's System of Ideas*, 2nd ed. London: Hutchinson.

CHAPTER 16

....

THE SOVEREIGN

....

DAVID RUNCIMAN

1 INTRODUCTION

....

THE true radicalism of Hobbes's conception of politics comes out in his account of what it means to be sovereign. There are two basic elements to this account. The first is that there are no meaningful limitations on *who* can be sovereign. Anyone can do it. That is, anyone or anything possessed of a will has the capacity needed to exercise sovereign power. So all arguments to the effect that some people are disqualified—whether by aptitude or origin or "form"—are invalid. Second, there are no meaningful limitations on *what* sovereigns are entitled to do. They can do anything. Sovereign power is effectively unconstrained by rules external to the sovereign's own will, which means that any constraints are ones that the sovereign can overturn by an act of will. There are, of course, practical limits on what sovereigns can do: they do not have supernatural powers and so are constrained by the realms of natural possibility. But no one is allowed to impose these limits on a sovereign. Kings cannot turn back the tide, but subjects cannot stop them from trying.

Anyone can be sovereign; sovereigns can do anything. Each of these claims on its own is fairly radical: one in its uncompromising insistence on natural equality (the sovereign is no different from anyone else in the state of nature, having no special gifts or qualities) and the other in its uncompromising insistence on political inequality (the sovereign is entirely different from everyone else in the civil state). But it is their conjunction that makes Hobbes a unique figure in the history of political thought.

Moreover, it is their conjunction that has consistently done most to alarm Hobbes's critics. It seems almost absurd to believe that an insistence on absolute power should go along with total nondiscrimination about who should wield it (indeed, some modern critics have been explicit in calling it "absurd, " in the sense that it contradicts some of our most basic political instincts[1]). If anyone can be sovereign, then surely you need

[1] See Pitkin 1967, Okin 1982.

some limitations on what a sovereign can do. Otherwise you might find yourself being governed by fools or monsters with no means of stopping them from doing their worst. Equally, if the sovereign can do anything, then surely you need some limitations on who can be sovereign. The grant of absolute power seems to make it imperative that there be some means of determining who is qualified to exercise it. As a result, ever since Hobbes wrote, attempts have been made to modify one or other aspect of his account of sovereignty in the light of the other.

For instance, many commentators have highlighted Hobbes's insistence that the sovereign still has to abide by the laws of nature. In this respect, it can be argued that sovereigns are subject to some sort of external constraint in the form of moral rules. (On this account natural equality generates a kind of political equality: These rules apply to everyone, even sovereigns.) Alternatively, attempts have been made to find in Hobbes an argument that sovereign power is at root democratic, implying that Hobbes did prioritize between different possible holders of it. This argument rests on the idea that Hobbes saw democracy as the default condition of politics: Other forms of government (monarchy, aristocracy) are the consequence of democratic decisions. Identifying the "deontological Hobbes" and the "democratic Hobbes" are different ways of trying to make his account of sovereignty more conventionally acceptable or at least less obviously ridiculous. They also mean prioritizing some of Hobbes's texts over others. In the case of the "democratic" Hobbes, it means finding the essence of Hobbes's theory of sovereignty in his earlier writings, particularly *De Cive*, rather than in *Leviathan*.[2]

The problem is that there is no evidence across Hobbes's oeuvre that he ever saw the need to modify his account of sovereignty. This is most clearly indicated by the fact that the final thing Hobbes wrote, his short note of 1679, titled "Questions Relative to Hereditary Right," gives an unequivocal restatement of the two basic principles: No one can force the current sovereign to choose a particular successor, and the sovereign can choose anyone.[3] Hobbes always thought that if the two parts were to go together at all they had to go together uncompromisingly. However, although he was many things, Hobbes was not crazy. He knew that the idea of giving absolute power to absolutely anyone is difficult to accept and seems obviously flawed. The challenge was not to modify one or other part of his theory but to reconcile them—to show how and why they had to go together. As Tom Sorell has written of *Leviathan*, Hobbes needed to remind his audience that he meant what he said: He had to provide "confirmation, in the face of the incredulity he expects from some readers, that nothing less than all the rights of sovereignty are needed in practice."[4] For many of his contemporaries, it was precisely the all-or-nothing quality of Hobbes's account of sovereignty that made it so alarming. Either you bought into the whole package or you were left with nothing: For some, this seemed to open the door to revolutionary chaos rather than closing it down.[5]

---

[2] See Tuck 2006. For the counterview, see Hoekstra 2006.
[3] See Skinner 2002a.
[4] Sorell 2004, 190.
[5] See Parkin 2010.

However, *Leviathan* is not the only place where Hobbes made his all-or-nothing case, and the account given there cannot be taken as a proxy for Hobbes's views in general. His views did change as to the best way to confirm his uncompromising theory of sovereignty, and across his writings there are various different attempts to reconcile the elements of the theory. In particular, there is a shift in what Hobbes sought to accommodate within the theory without in any way compromising it. In this chapter I want to highlight some of these differences and illustrate the fundamental shift in Hobbes's approach when he wrote *Leviathan*. That book contains what is in some ways the most radical version of the theory but also the most accommodating. I will conclude by suggesting that it is here, rather than in *The Elements of Law* or *De Cive*, that we see a foreshadowing of the distinctive character of modern democracy.

I will focus on the three individual chapters in each of his main political philosophical works devoted to the question of how the sovereign should behave, in each case tied into the wider theory of sovereignty that connects the three books. The chapters are respectively: Part II, Chapter IX of *The Elements of Law*, "Of the Duty of Them that have the Sovereign Power"; Chapter XIII of *De Cive*, "On the Duties of those who Exercise the Sovereign Power"; Chapter XXX of *Leviathan*, "Of the Office of the Soveraign Representative." I will say something about the differences in these titles later on. The three chapters serve roughly the same purpose in each book—to show that it is possible to talk about how sovereigns should behave without calling into question the underlying premise that there are no meaningful limitations on either the *who* or the *what* of sovereign power—yet they are strikingly different in their emphasis. Those differences reveal a lot about how Hobbes viewed the ongoing challenge of justifying sovereign power as he understood it.

2 THE ELEMENTS OF LAW

In *Elements of Law* Hobbes makes it clear that sovereigns have "duties" as well as "rights," but he never suggests that the duties are any limitation on their rights. The duties simply follow from the rights. If you have that sort of power, Hobbes is saying, then these are the ways in which you ought to behave. But if you do not behave in that way, your right to exercise the power is unaffected. Sovereigns who act in such an irresponsible way as to foment disobedience or rebellion will of course lose their power. But they will not do so because they have breached their duties; it will be because they have effectively abdicated their rights. Hobbes never deviates from this position throughout his writings: No one can ever claim that dutiful behavior on the part of sovereigns is a precondition of their right to rule.

That given, Hobbes provides two different ways of understanding how the idea of duty might still apply to sovereigns. The first is that sovereigns must obey the laws of nature and will be answerable to God for any failure to do so. The basic rule of nature is to seek peace ("reason dictateth peace"), but there are many other laws of nature consequent on that, including the ones that require that we behave equitably toward one another, show gratitude, bestow mercy, reciprocate sociability, and so on. So in these terms a sovereign is answerable to God for any failure to behave in a way that anyone could understand as reasonable. It looks like a significant constraint. But it is politically nugatory. No one can enforce these rules except God, which means that no one can use these rules to limit what sovereigns are entitled to do. Subjects might hope that undutiful sovereigns will eventually get their punishment. But they can neither anticipate when this might happen nor prejudge what form it might take. The basic problem for anyone hoping that God might step in to punish sovereigns is that Hobbes leaves it up to the sovereign to interpret what counts as divine intervention (it is up to sovereigns, for instance, to decide what constitutes a miracle). Sovereigns may not be able to escape divine judgment in the end, but they can always evade it in the eyes of their subjects because it is their fundamental right to tell their subjects what counts as punishment.

The fact that the sovereign remains subject to the laws of nature emphasizes the fundamental political inequality of the civil state rather than any underlying equality. All other inhabitants of that state are subject to those laws only on the terms set down by the sovereign, who determines what they mean and when they apply. The sovereign, by contrast, is subject to the laws of nature simply as a matter of "conscience." It is a consistent theme of Hobbes's political philosophy that "conscience" has no political weight. Subjects must obey the civil laws regardless of conscience. Sovereigns are free to disobey those laws regardless of conscience. To say something is a matter of conscience is, in Hobbes's terms, tantamount to saying that it is politically irrelevant.

The other reason Hobbes gives for thinking that sovereigns will do their duty is more substantial: it is that the duty of sovereigns coincides with "their profit." In other words, what is good for the people is good for the sovereign, so that sovereigns who wish to pursue their own good will be obliged to act in such a way as to benefit their subjects. This is a relatively conventional argument, summed up by the ultrafamiliar line *Salus populi suprema lex* ("by which must be understood not the mere preservation of their lives but generally their benefit and good").[6] Hobbes then goes on to elaborate a series of areas in which it will be to the advantage of the sovereign to achieve this benefit: in matters of "multitude," "commodity of living," "peace amongst ourselves," and "defence against a common power." It will be no good to any sovereign, whoever it happens to be, to have absolute power over a state that is depopulated, poor, fractious, or vulnerable to attack.

What is most striking about this list of areas where the interests of sovereign and subject coincide is the first item: "multitude" (or population). In none of Hobbes's other accounts of how sovereigns should behave does he make explicit what he says here, that sovereigns are obliged to regulate sexual behavior in specific ways. In *Elements of Law* he says sovereigns must forbid "any copulations as are against nature" (i.e., nonprocreative acts) as well as "promiscuous use of women," "one woman [having] many husbands," and "marriages within certain degrees of kindred and affinity."[7] It is the duty of

---

[6] *Elements of Law* ed. Gaskin, XXVIII.1, 172.
[7] Ibid.

sovereigns to ensure the healthy reproduction of the species because, as Hobbes says, to do otherwise "is against the law of natural reason in him that hath taken into his hands any portion of mankind to improve."[8]

This is an interesting argument for a number of reasons. First, it goes further to specify the content (rather than the form) of the civil law than Hobbes does anywhere else on any other subject. Hobbes does elsewhere (particularly in *Leviathan*) emphasize that sovereigns must control their subjects in particular ways, and he is often very specific about how this should be done (certain doctrines should be taught in universities, for instance, and others should be banned). But these rules are about ensuring that people obey the law and refrain from activities that might encourage sedition. Nonprocreative sexual behavior does not in itself predispose people to disobey the law: it is not a seditious act. Hobbes concedes as much when he also says that "a private man living under the law of natural reason only" does not break the law of nature by performing any of the above listed acts. I take this to mean that Hobbes sees sex for pleasure as not wrong in itself.[9] Indeed, the laws of nature, in the state of nature, are silent on these matters: Hobbes says nothing about them in his lists of natural laws. It is only in civil society, where the improvement of a "portion" of mankind has become the imperative, that they hold. So there are some rules that apply to sovereigns only *after* they have exited the state of nature rather than because they are the only people who still live in it. These rules apply because the good of collective entities sometimes trumps the good of individuals.

Is this a significant concession? On the one hand, no. Hobbes is not saying that the sovereign has to behave in the manner prescribed for everyone else—in fact, I take it as implicit in this argument that promiscuity on the part of sovereigns is not against the laws of nature (and, doubly implicit in Hobbesian terms, that if sovereigns are to be promiscuous it is better that it should be nonprocreative, since it is incumbent on sovereigns to do nothing that might muddy the question of succession or raise issues of favoritism). But, on the other hand, this passage does suggest that there are some areas in which sovereigns have strict obligations that are not directly derivable from the laws of nature but rather from the conditions of civil existence and the requirement to improve it. The rules of equity, for instance, which Hobbes also insists are part of the duties of sovereigns and include the specific injunction that sovereigns should tax on the basis of consumption, not wealth, do derive directly from the laws of nature. This is not an altogether comfortable position for Hobbes: It has the potential to open up a can of worms (has a sovereign who judges that the prosperity of the state is consistent with lax rules about sexual morality done anything wrong?). That may be why he dropped it.

It could be argued that underlying the general account of the duties of sovereigns in *Elements of Law*, both in relation to conscience and benefit, is an implicit claim about the unique capacity of sovereigns to exercise their reason. To be sovereign is to be provided with a space to think coherently about the demands of justice. Passion might still

---

[8] Ibid.
[9] For a fuller discussion of Hobbes's views of sex, see Hillger 2009.

lead sovereigns astray. But if they are thinking clearly, sovereigns are in a position to guide their own behavior according to the laws of nature without the need for external constraint. Anyone can do this in theory: That is the basic postulate of Hobbes's idea of natural equality. But in practice no one else is in this position. Individuals in the state of nature are able to recognize the laws of nature as abstract theorems, but they cannot turn them into guides for conduct because the condition of mutual fear that exists between individuals makes it possible to justify any sort of behavior in the name of personal safety. All that individuals in the state of nature can agree to is that they would be better off leaving it, and they must therefore abide by the covenant that makes this possible. Their "duties" are reduced to a single act of escape. Meanwhile, once they have left the state of nature behind, subjects are bound to treat the sovereign's judgments about how they should behave as final. In the state of nature anything can be justified. In civil society nothing is justified except on the sovereign's terms.

So the basic question about sovereigns and their duties—why would they do their duty, given their unlimited power—could be turned on its head. Why would sovereigns *not* do their duty? What good reason would they have? Having absolute power and presiding over a civil society that ought to be in a state of peace, sovereigns would find it very hard to justify treating their subjects with injustice. Individuals in the state of nature can justify anything by their being afraid. If a sovereign said his actions were motivated by his fear of his subjects, then that sovereign would be effectively admitting that the whole project of civil society had failed: It is an inherently unreasonable answer in Hobbes's terms. The power that sovereigns possess means that they do not need to be afraid. They need to be vigilant, of course, including against the threat of violence from disgruntled subjects, but that is different from existing in the fearful state of nature: There vigilance is no security because no one has the power to make it effective. Sovereigns have that power. Existing in a state of perpetual fear is incompatible with equitable behavior. But being vigilant does not stop you treating people fairly. In fact, in Hobbes's terms, perpetual vigilance is the sine qua non of justice.

Sovereigns have no good reason not to do their duty. This double negative is perhaps the simplest way of explaining why sovereign right coincides with sovereign duty. Yet it is striking that Hobbes does not make the case explicitly in these terms. Why not? The answer is that it is not entirely consistent with his wider project. First, Hobbes does not want to imply that being reasonable is one of the preconditions of sovereignty. Sovereigns are sovereign whether they are reasonable or not. All they need is a will. The clearest evidence of this is that sovereigns can be large assemblies ("democracies") as well as small groups or individuals. In such assemblies the majority decides, but the majority does not have to be a reasonable body (indeed, Hobbes supplies plenty of grounds for thinking that majorities in large assemblies will not be reasonable, but will be erratic, inconsistent, and swayed by passion). The duties of sovereignty hold whether the sovereign is reasonable or not; it is up to the sovereign whether or not to abide by them. A clear-thinking sovereign will have no reason not to abide by the laws of nature. But whether the sovereign is clear-thinking or not is not for anyone to judge.

Second, Hobbes does not actually say that individuals in the state of nature have good reasons to breach the laws of nature. They still have every reason to abide by them. The problem is that the primary injunction to secure their own safety means that they are free to interpret those laws as they see fit. So strictly speaking, it is not that individuals in the state of nature are free to act unjustly towards people they fear may threaten their safety. Instead, they are free to decide what counts as injustice. Hobbes never suggests that anyone in the state of nature can ever justify ingratitude, no matter how dangerous the situation they find themselves in. What they can do is refuse to call it ingratitude. (In the same way, no one in the state of nature is entitled to murder; what they are entitled to do is call any killing they perform self-defense, even if it is done with malice and without provocation.) An argument that says sovereigns have uniquely good reasons to obey the laws of nature does not fit with Hobbes insistence that uncertainty is the primary cause of the war of all against all. Sovereigns have the same good reasons to obey the laws of nature as everyone else: they are what reason prescribes. What sovereigns can uniquely do is decide for everyone else what counts as a breach of the laws of nature. They can end the uncertainty. But that means that the distinguishing characteristic of sovereigns Hobbes wants to emphasize in this context is their continuing ability to interpret the laws of nature as they see fit rather than their having greater capacity to abide by them.

What is clear in *Elements of Law* is that Hobbes does not modify either of his basic claims about sovereignty: Anyone can do it and anything can be done. He creates a space for the dutiful sovereign, but he provides no means of confining a sovereign to that space. The duties of sovereigns do not limit sovereign power. Equally, they do not make some people better qualified to be sovereign than others. It is true that he does spend quite a lot of time pointing up the differences between the three "sorts of commonwealth" (monarchy, aristocracy, democracy).[10] Some of these differences are temporal: Hobbes insists that democracy is "prior" to the other forms of government because no sovereign can be chosen except by the consent of the majority. But this is a formal requirement, consistent with the idea that the minimal condition for sovereignty is the exercise of will (or, as he puts it elsewhere, the ability to assent or dissent from any proposition). Groups can do this, even in the state of nature, because the majority view is at least a decision: a yes or a no. This is therefore something (perhaps the only thing) on which it is hypothetically possible to secure unanimous agreement: People will agree that if the group is to be capable of taking a decision, then the majority view must count as the decision.

But if you want more than that—concord, rationality, the "right" decision—you are asking too much. Democracies can be sovereign; however, in practice, Hobbes suggests that democracies will almost inevitably turn into a form of aristocracy, because in any large assembly decision making will be dominated by a few orators. Yet by naming it aristocracy Hobbes is adamant that he is not making any qualitative judgment: He

[10] *Elements of Law*, XXI.

insists here, as he does throughout his writings, that there is no difference between aristocracy and oligarchy. The only meaningful distinction between the different forms of government is simply a question of number. A sovereign can be many, few, or one. Judging whether the few are the "good" few is as redundant as judging whether the many have made the "right" decision.

In part II, chapter V of *Elements of Law*, Hobbes sets out what he calls "the incommodities of several sorts of government compared." This implies that he does discriminate between better and worse types of sovereign. But in fact, his basic point is a general one: that the incommodities of government are never as bad as the incommodities of having no government, and that the incommodities of the different sorts of government are all variants on the incommodity of government per se (which is the basic inconvenience of being subject to another's will). Where he does distinguish between the different forms of sovereign power is by listing the things that can go wrong in a monarchy (avarice, nepotism, caprice) and then arguing repeatedly that these things are worse under an aristocracy or democracy simply because there will be more scope for them (the greater the number of people who make up the sovereign power, the greater the number who can be avaricious, nepotistic, etc.) This argument is entirely consistent with the anyone/anything view of sovereignty. Hobbes is saying there is nothing you can do about the things that might go wrong, so better to think in terms of worst-case contingencies than best-case scenarios. It is also consistent with the practical purpose of *Elements of Law*: It was a privately circulated manuscript for an elite group of readers to dissuade them from the idea that the grass might be greener and to provide them with arguments to persuade others likewise. The basic argument was this: Whatever you dislike about the present arrangement would not be remedied under any alternative; likely it would be worse.

Elements of Law does not make the case that democracy is prior to the other forms in anything but a formal and nonnormative sense. It does make the case that monarchy is better than the alternatives, but only because of the degree to which things can go wrong, not because monarchs are "better" at doing their duty as sovereign. Monarchs may be as bad as anyone else. The best that can be said for them is that when things go bad, they are liable to do less damage. The further claim, that monarchs have a greater capacity for doing good than any assembly because they are less liable to be distracted from their duties by specious arguments and oratorical flummery, is never made explicit. The most Hobbes will say is that there are more things that can go wrong in a democracy than in a monarchy. He does not want to dilute the core of his argument: Sovereigns of all kinds retain their rights regardless of how they perform their duties.

3   DE CIVE

De Cive, a book completed soon after *Elements of Law* but as part of a wider philosophical project and intended for a wider readership, repeats many of these arguments and does not deviate from the core account of sovereignty. Indeed, Hobbes provides an excellent summary of it in one of his notes to the text, in the chapter titled "Three Kinds of Commonwealth."

> Most say that power should not be divided; but they do want it to be constrained and kept within limits. That is fair enough. But if, when they say restrained and limited, they understand the term to mean "divided," then their distinction will not hold. I myself would wish that not only kings but also assemblies that have sovereign power would want to refrain from wrongdoing, remember their duties, and stay within the limits of the natural and divine laws. But those who make this distinction want sovereigns to be limited and constrained by others. And as this cannot occur without the limiters having to have some share in power by which to limit them, it is a division of power, not restraint.[11]

This suggests quite clearly that Hobbes knew what he was up against in persuading people of his view of sovereignty. However, the chapter in *De Cive* on the duties of sovereigns is different from *Elements of Law*, starting with its title. It is called "On the Duties of Those Who Exercise Sovereign Power." Hobbes begins with a distinction between the "right" and the "exercise" of sovereign power, and insists "they can be separated." He then goes on, in an arresting analogy:

> When *right* and *exercise* are separated, the government of the commonwealth is like the ordinary government of the world, in which God the first mover of all things, produces natural effects through the order of secondary causes. But when he who has the right to reign wishes to participate himself in all judgments, consultations and public actions, it is a way of running things comparable to God's attending directly to every thing himself, contrary to the order of nature.[12]

This passage appears to imply two things: that it is more ordinary for the right and exercise of sovereignty to be separated (it is more "natural") and that in those circumstances the sovereign is like "God the first mover of all things." That is, God is there in the background but essentially noninterventionist. God the first mover still has the power to intervene and suspend the laws of physical nature, just as the holder of sovereign right retains the power to intervene and suspend the regular working of the state. But the assumption must be in both cases that in the normal run of things, that power will not be exercised.

Richard Tuck has taken this passage to be evidence of the "democratic" side of Hobbes's argument when read in conjunction with an earlier passage in the book that highlights the possibility of a "sleeping sovereign," meaning a democratic assembly that meets only rarely and delegates its powers in the interim.[13] Hobbes says: "The intervals between meetings of the citizens may be compared to the times when a Monarch is

---

[11] *On the Citizen*, ed. Tuck and Silverthorne, VII.4, 93–94.
[12] Ibid., XIII.1, 142–43.
[13] See Tuck 2006.

asleep; for the power is retained though there are no acts of commanding."[14] This would mean a democratic assembly handing the administration of the state over to a nondemocratic body while retaining its sovereign right (the only condition being that the people must decide for themselves when they wish to be awoken, since anyone "who gives the exercise of his power to another person while he sleeps, and can wake up again only with the consent of that person, has lost his life and his power together").[15] As Tuck sees it, this "sleeping" variety is for Hobbes the preferable kind of democracy: an assembly with the power to take the ultimate decisions but without the disadvantages of debating over the details, with all the scope for oratorical grandstanding that this brings.

There is certainly something to be said for the idea that Hobbes allows for this possibility, but that is hardly surprising, since his theory of sovereignty allows for all the logically coherent possibilities. What is striking about the chapter on the duties of sovereigns—in which the distinction between right and exercise is formulated—is that it discusses duties only in the context of those who exercise the sovereign power, not those who have the right but not the exercise. (Hobbes says he is interested only in those "who exercise sovereign power whether in their own right or by someone else's.")[16] Perhaps it would be odd for Hobbes to talk about the duties of sleeping sovereigns: Who can have duties if he or she is asleep? But Hobbes also says nothing about the duties of those who exercise sovereign power *toward* those who have the right: No one is ever to think that their duty in exercising sovereign power refers back to the sleeping sovereign (they never, for instance, think about what the sleeping sovereign might want, might approve, or might like to discover has happened upon waking up). They only refer to their duties under the laws of nature. And this may be why in *De Cive*, unlike in *Elements of Law*, Hobbes says nothing in this chapter about the sovereign being answerable to God. That might confuse things: Is the sovereign answerable to the "first mover" of sovereign power, or the originator of the laws of nature?

So the curious consequence of Hobbes beginning with this distinction in *De Cive* is that he actually offers a more pared down account of the hold that duties have on those who exercise sovereign power. In this chapter everything depends on the idea that "the safety of the people is the supreme law," and nothing on the idea that sovereigns are ultimately answerable for their actions to their "God." Why does Hobbes begin with this distinction? I would think it is not to justify or make possible a democratic reading but to do what he is usually doing when he employs an idea that is conventionally assumed to carry some political weight (like "conscience," or indeed "democracy" itself): showing that it makes no difference. If sovereign right is separated from the exercise, then every question about what it means to be sovereign applies to those who exercise the power, up to the point that those who have the right resume the exercise of it when it will apply to them. This is a neutralizing argument, not a substantive one.

---

[14] *On the Citizen*, VII.16, 99.
[15] Ibid., 100.
[16] Ibid., XIII.1, 143.

When sovereigns are asleep, their political significance is the same as the political significance of a noninterventionist god: nil.

Having said that *De Cive* offers a more pared down account of sovereign duties by making everything depend on the coincidence of the interests of the people and the interests of the exerciser of sovereign power, it offers a much fuller account of what those duties are. Hobbes goes into some detail about what sovereigns will need to do to maintain the public benefit, which is also their own benefit. He lists four areas, as in *Elements of Law*, but the list is different: "Multitude" is dropped, and "commodity of living" is separated out into two separate categories, "acquisition of wealth" and "full enjoyment of innocent liberty."[17] By this last Hobbes means that sovereigns must not make too many laws or try to control too much: Subjects must be free, where possible, to use their own "initiative." Of course it is up to the sovereign to decide what counts as too many, and what laws there are will have to be properly enforced. But Hobbes believes it is the duty of those who exercise sovereign power to strike a balance between doing too little and doing too much. There is also an implication that if in doubt, it is better to do too little than too much. When there are too many laws—"more laws than we can easily remember"—the whole system of justice is liable to be discredited, because men find they have broken the law without knowing it.[18] This will be harder to remedy than having too few laws, since sovereigns can always respond to excessive license by adding more. It is also worth remembering that *De Cive*, like *Elements of Law*, was a work written with a view to defusing civil conflict, not rebuilding in its aftermath. An accommodating conception of civil law, which might provide the basis for a settlement between monarchists and parliamentarians, is consistent with such an aim.

Hobbes gives more details in *De Cive* about what is involved in securing "defence from external enemies," which he now lists as the first duty of sovereigns. He divides the task here in two: Sovereigns must be "forewarned" and "forearmed."[19] The second requires having sufficient resources to meet any threat, while the first requires being alert to any possible danger, even when it is barely perceptible. This requires an extensive network of spies and informers. The image Hobbes uses here is "the analogy of the spider's webs, whose incredibly fine threads spread out in all directions and convey outside movements to the spiders sitting in their little cavities inside."[20] The idea conveyed by this image is different from that of the sovereign as the "first mover." In some ways it is the opposite. Now the sovereign is the nerve center of the state, not the originator of its workings.

In this passage Hobbes calls those who exercise sovereign power the "soul" of the commonwealth. There is a noticeable contrast in the use of this image here and its later deployment in *Leviathan*, where Hobbes also calls the sovereign the "publique Soule."

[17] Ibid., XIII.6, 144.
[18] Ibid., XIII.15, 151.
[19] Ibid., XIII.7, 144
[20] Ibid., 145.

In the later work Hobbes explicitly interprets this to mean that the sovereign "animates" the commonwealth ("giving [it] Life and Motion").[21] This idea is closer to the idea of the sovereign as "first mover." In *De Cive* he uses it to mean that the sovereign responds to motion as the soul responds to light. Thus the job of those who exercise sovereign power in regard to defense from foreign enemies is to respond to the littlest things and judge their significance. This idea stands in contrast to the picture of the sovereign painted by the imperative to preserve innocent liberty. In that case, it is better to err on the side of inactivity; here clearly it is better to err on the side of doing too much. In dealing with enemies of the state, it is harder to undo the damage caused by inattention than the damage caused by an excess of attention.

In fleshing out the range of sovereign duties implied by *Salus populi suprema lex*, Hobbes gives a picture in *De Cive* of a kind of divided sovereign. This does not mean a division of powers—always anathema to Hobbes—and it is not consequent on the potential division between right and exercise of sovereignty, which, as I have suggested, makes no real difference in this context. Rather, it is something more like a divided personality. Sovereigns have to be both hypersensitive and also somewhat reserved: They must be alert to every danger but careful not to make too many demands of their subjects. They must be vigilant but also tolerant. In *De Cive* much more than in *Elements of Law*, there is an indication that it might be quite difficult to do your duty as sovereign, not because of all the temptations to go astray but simply because it is a very demanding role. However, Hobbes does not want to go too far with this thought in *De Cive*, in part because he does not want to suggest that some people might not be up to it (to repeat: Sovereigns are still sovereign even when they fail in their duties) but also because he has not fleshed out the idea that sovereignty is a "role." That is the shift that comes in *Leviathan*.

4 LEVIATHAN

In *Leviathan* the chapter on the duties of sovereign has a somewhat different name: It is called "Of the Office of the Sovereign Representative." In fact, Hobbes drops the language of duty almost entirely (that is, in the English version of the book; the term remains the same in Latin, *officium*, as used for "duty" in *De Cive*). At a couple points he uses *office* and *duty* interchangeably in *Leviathan*, but for the most part the argument of this chapter is couched exclusively in terms of "office" and "right": Whoever has the right of sovereign power thereby holds or performs a particular office. To have this right is to be required to play a role consistent with the possession of that right. In that sense the most significant change is that sovereignty is reduced to a single role—"office"—rather than a range of "offices" or "duties." Hobbes spends most of this chapter elaborating on what sovereigns need to do to ensure that the role is a meaningful one:

---

[21] *Leviathan*, ed. Malcolm, XXIX, 518.

The duty of sovereigns is primarily to make sure that everyone recognizes that they are the holders of the right. So the emphasis in this chapter is different. Its first half is devoted to establishing all the things that sovereigns must do to ensure that their subjects are not confused about who holds the rights of sovereignty, starting with an insistence that "it is the Office of the Soveraign to maintain those rights entire; and consequently against his duty, First, to transferre to another, or lay from himself any of them."[22]

The idea that sovereignty is a kind of role that must be played properly is consistent with the big shift in *Leviathan*, which is toward a theory of "authorization" as the foundation of sovereign power. In *Elements of Law* and *De Cive*, sovereigns acquire their rights by a form of alienation of right: Individuals agree to let sovereigns take over their right to interpret the law of nature as they see fit and hence become subject to their will. This might happen on an individual-by-individual basis (when sovereignty is acquired by conquest) or by an agreement among individuals (when sovereignty is "instituted"). In *Leviathan* Hobbes makes a different sort of argument: Individuals agree to be the authors of the actions of sovereigns, so that they will all treat the sovereign's will as though it were their own. Hobbes makes this case in the language of "personation" and "representation." Sovereigns are persons who speak and act for other persons, who then own the actions and must behave as though they had performed the actions themselves. Sovereigns therefore do not simply speak for themselves: They speak for all the individuals who have authorized them. In this way, sovereigns may be said to represent the entire commonwealth.

There are many things to be said about this argument and it has been extensively discussed elsewhere.[23] I just want to make two comments here. First, in formal terms there is one truly radical interpretation of this account: Not only can anyone be sovereign but it is possible for someone to be sovereign without even knowing it. Sovereigns who are authorized in this way—that is, whose actions will be taken as the actions of their subjects—need only continue acting as they have always acted in order to be sovereign; in that sense, they may be oblivious. In cases of sovereignty by acquisition, this is irrelevant, since these sovereigns compel people to authorize them; they will hardly be oblivious to what they are doing. But when it is by institution, Hobbes's account in *Leviathan* is at least formally consistent with the sovereign being ignorant of what is going on. All the subjects of sovereign power have to do is take another's will as their own. What the person whose will they have taken as their own thinks about the matter is irrelevant.

In some ways, this sounds absurd. Why would you bind yourself to do what someone else does without even telling that person that that is what you are doing? Yet the point of Hobbes's account is to make clear that "authorization" does not depend on what is communicated to the sovereign. It depends on what individuals communicate to each other in the act of authorization. What they actually say is: "*I Authorize and give up my Right of Governing my selfe, to this Man, or to this Assembly of men, on this condition,*

---

[22] Ibid., XXX, 520.
[23] See the chapter by Martinich in this volume.

that thou give up thy Right to him, and Authorise all his Actions, in like manner."[24] It might sound as though something were being transferred to the sovereign, but really the transfer is with each other. The result is that nothing about the act of authorization in this case constrains the person who is authorized. It is, as Hobbes puts it, "authority without stint."[25] When authority is given to someone for a particular purpose, then that purpose must be communicated to the person who is authorized (as in any formulation along the lines of "I authorize you to do x on my behalf"). Sovereign power is certainly authorized for a purpose: to achieve peace. But, crucially, that purpose is not communicated to the sovereign in the act of authorization. The authors do not say: "I authorize you to bring peace." In fact, they do not say "I authorize you" at all. They say "I will authorize that person if you will."

Putting it like this emphasizes two things. First, for the formal structure of Hobbes's argument, it really does not matter who is sovereign: Anyone or anything possessed of a will could do it. Second, however, the reason it sounds slightly absurd when expressed in these terms is that Hobbes is clearly not thinking like this. He is thinking entirely differently. This is not simply a formal account. Hobbes conceives of the sovereign as having to act in such a way as to make the idea of his having been authorized plausible through his actions. He must continually remind people that his actions are their actions. He has two resources for doing this. One is the power he now has to compel people to accept his actions as their actions: He can make them obey, using fear of his power as a weapon. The other is by playing his part in such a way as to make it clear that he speaks for them. He must be a good actor.

Hobbes's theory of representation thus opens up a whole new set of possibilities about how a sovereign might conceive his duty: not just to uphold the laws of nature, not just to interpret the laws of nature, but to act in such a way as to make that interpretation plausibly the interpretation of his subjects. This is consistent with Hobbes's ideas of natural equality: As he says in the introduction to *Leviathan*, "He that is to govern a whole Nation, must read in himself, not this, or that particular man: but Man-kind."[26] But it also creates a new world of artifice. In *Leviathan* Hobbes deploys the full range of idioms for conceiving of representation—including the legal, aesthetic, theatrical, and theological ones—to describe the different ways in which sovereigns may be said to speak and act for others.[27] None of these constrain the ability of the sovereign to decide what actions to undertake, but they do make the "office" of sovereign a more creative or expressive role than it is in the earlier versions of the theory. Sovereigns, as described in *Leviathan*, "perform" their duties. They have what Hobbes now explicitly calls a "public persona."

The other point I want to make is that the distinction that Hobbes draws in *De Cive* between the right and the exercise of sovereign power shifts in *Leviathan* to a

---

[24] Leviathan, XVII, 260.

[25] Ibid., XVI, 250.

[26] Ibid., "Introduction," 20.

[27] The best account of this is in Brito Vieira 2009; see also Malcolm 2002.

new location—it is no longer in the chapter on sovereign duties—and is given a very different form. It comes in chapter XXIII entitled "Of the Publique Ministers of the Soveraign Power." Here Hobbes describes the relationship between the sovereign and those who are charged with "the administration of the Publique Business" in the language of representation. "A Publique Minister is he, that by the Soveraign (whether a Monarch or an Assembly), is employed in any affaires, with Authority to represent in that employment, the Person of the Common-wealth."[28] That this is equivalent to the distinction between right and exercise given in *De Cive* is shown by the fact that Hobbes uses the same primary example of what he has in mind: "to a Protector, or Regent, may bee committed by the Predecessor of an Infant King, during his minority, the whole Administration of his Kingdome."[29]

One of Hobbes's purposes in this chapter is to distinguish between those who serve the state and those who serve the sovereign in a private capacity (or, as Hobbes puts it, those who serve his "natural person," which would include all the officers of his household). He also makes a distinction, which is not there in *De Cive*, between those who are given the "general Administration, either of the whole Dominion, or of a part thereof," and those who "have a special Administration, that is to say, charges of some special business, either at home or abroad."[30] The former are comparable to those who have the exercise of sovereign power; the latter are more like special officers, whose power only extends as far as their remit. For the second category it would not make sense to talk about their having the duties of a sovereign (duties referential only to the laws of nature) because their primary duty is clearly to stay within the terms of their remit.

But the big difference is what is allowed by the language of authority and representation. Although it is doing the work of the right/exercise distinction, it is much more flexible and open ended. Public ministers are authorized by the sovereign, and in that way they represent the state (or "the person of the commonwealth"). There are two ways in which this might be understood: First, as a transitive relationship—the sovereign speaks for the person of the state, the ministers speak for the person of the sovereign, so the ministers speak for the person of the state. The alternative is to see it as a triangular relationship—sovereign and ministers both speak for the person of the state. The sovereign has not authorized his or her ministers to speak for him or her but has authorized them to speak for the thing that the sovereign also represents: the public person of the commonwealth.

Which reading is closest to what Hobbes had in mind? The reason for preferring a transitive account is that it keeps the lines of authority clear: Power comes from the sovereign. However, the problem with a transitive account is that it appears to confuse two different kinds of authority. The sovereign has been authorized without stint, yet the sovereign does not authorize his or her ministers without stint, even in cases where a minister has been given the power to administer the whole state. Hobbes is adamant

---

[28] *Leviathan*, XXIII, 376.
[29] Ibid.
[30] Ibid., 376, 378.

that sovereigns must set limits for ministerial power, even if only temporal ones, if they are to remain sovereign. So sovereigns are not bound by what their ministers do in the way that subjects are bound by what their sovereigns do. In both cases the relationship is founded on authorization, but of different kinds. The reason for preferring a triangular account is that it keeps separate the different forms of authorization that underpin the workings of the state.

This is a significant difference because the sovereign who authorizes is not the person who bears responsibility for the actions of the minister. The sovereign, by authorizing, gives the minister power to act. The minister, by acting, binds the members of the state to action, but not the sovereign. So, for instance, when the sovereign gives someone the power to levy taxes, the people who are bound are the subjects, who have to pay the taxes. The sovereign remains effectively unbound. Hobbes needs this structure of argument so as to make it possible to act on behalf of the sovereign without limiting the sovereign's own freedom of action. This is a more dynamic setup than the one in *De Cive*. Now sovereigns and their ministers can exercise power more or less coterminously, one as the authorizer and the others as the representative of the state. There is no suggestion, either in this chapter or anywhere else in *Leviathan*, that sovereigns must be asleep when others are acting on their behalf. Instead, what is made explicit is that sovereigns have a kind of double personality: There is the natural person or persons (in the case of an assembly) whose will gives life to the state, and there is the public persona of the state that lives as a result. That public person can be represented in many different ways for many different purposes by many different representatives without diminishing the authority of the sovereign. It remains an uncompromising theory: The sovereign must abdicate no rights if he or she (or it) is to remain sovereign. But the concepts of representation and authorization make the theory a more flexible one.

5 CONCLUSION

The striking differences between the three books in their accounts of the duties of sovereigns do not significantly change the terms of Hobbes's basic argument, which remain the same in each case. The reasons that readers have always had for being alarmed about the implications of this argument are there in all three books. What does change is the way Hobbes opens up the argument to allow for different ways of conceiving the role of sovereigns, given their distinctive rights and duties.

The biggest differences are between *Leviathan* and the earlier two books. First, *Leviathan* makes explicit the idea that to be sovereign is to play a part and therefore includes an element of public performance as well as simply the performance of moral or prudential duty. Second, *Leviathan* deploys the language of authorization and representation in place of the binary distinction between right and exercise. That binary, by focusing on the basic contrast between action and inaction (being awake and being asleep), leaves little room for ideas of coterminous authority. Third, in *Leviathan*

Hobbes provides a way of thinking about the divided character of the sovereign without diminishing his or her unified authority. Here the key idea is that of "persona." Sovereigns have a natural and a political persona: The political persona of the state can be represented by different people in different ways, so that the sovereign can still exercise power without having to be the center of everything. In *Leviathan* the sovereign is no longer the spider at the heart of the web but neither is he or she simply god, the first mover of things. The sovereign is both a more ambivalent and a more flexible figure, capable of moving in and out of political life as he or she sees fit and as circumstances allow.

These differences suggest an alternative route from Hobbes to modern conceptions of democracy than the one argued for by Tuck, which focuses on *De Cive* and more or less ignores *Leviathan*. Tuck places Hobbes in a tradition that runs through to Rousseau and more radical modern conceptions of democracy, in which the sovereign right of the people underpins all the constitutional arrangements of the state. In this account the distinction between the right and exercise of sovereignty is crucial because it is what allows the people to retain their sovereign rights even when they are not involved in the administration of the state. The problem is that in Hobbes's version, the retention of that right is effectively meaningless. To give it a meaningful democratic form it would be necessary for those who exercise power in the state to refer back to the people who possess the right in order to consider how they might want the right to be exercised. Hobbes does not require this. Yet without it there is no difference between monarchy and democracy, since monarchs, even if only exercising rights on behalf of a sovereign people, can do whatever they want. And that, I take it, was Hobbes's point in *De Cive*: not to argue that all states are at bottom democratic but that the idea that all states are at bottom democratic makes no difference to the exercise of power in a state.

Leviathan stands at the basis of a different tradition, which runs through to authors like Sieyes and other theorists of representative democracy.[31] This tradition rests on the idea that the person of the state never acts in its own right; it is always represented either by the sovereign power within the state or by various representatives of that sovereign power. Hobbes still wants to insist on a fundamental distinction between the sovereign power and all other political representatives. No one can act for the state except on the sovereign's say-so. But when they do act for the state, they can do so in ways that go beyond merely acting for the sovereign. In that way the state can have multiple representatives yet retain its sovereign identity.

The view that *De Cive* gives us the "democratic" Hobbes rests on an idea of democracy that sees the people as sovereign in right but having given others the exercise of the power. The Hobbesian version of this idea seems to me too pared down an account to be a plausible basis for any modern conception of democracy. *Leviathan* suggests a different possibility: of various agents of the state, authorized by a single sovereign representative, each able to represent the state in their own way. Hobbes would insist that

---

[31] See Manin 1997; Hont 2005.

the line between the sovereign representative and all other representatives should never be blurred. Yet in practice that is precisely the line that has become blurred in modern democracies. Sovereign states have multiple different representatives who derive their power from the authority of the people; yet the people rarely if ever exercise that power. Sovereign right is not asleep in contemporary democracies. More often it is not there at all. Instead, we have political representatives who exercise power, sovereign states in whose name they exercise it, and democratic peoples who judge, through elections and public opinion, how the representatives are doing.[32]

There is no possibility of a separation of powers in Hobbes's account: The sovereign representative must still be the final judge of the terms of this multiple representation. Hobbes is insistent that the sovereign should face no competition. Democracy is meaningless unless there is competition to represent the state. Nonetheless, Hobbes's theory of representation marks the point where sovereign power may begin to open up in ways that go beyond the uncompromising nature of Hobbes's own theory of sovereignty.

BIBLIOGRAPHY

Brito Vieira, Monica. 2009. *The Elements of Representation in Hobbes. Aesthetics, Theatre, Law, and Theology in the Construction of Hobbes's Theory of the State.* Leiden: Brill Academic Publishers.

Hillger, Richard. 2009. "Hobbes and sex." *Hobbes Studies* 22: 29–48.

Hobbes, Thomas. 1996. *On the Citizen*, edited by R. Tuck and M. Silverthorne. Cambridge, UK: Cambridge University Press.

Hobbes, Thomas. 1999. *The Elements of Law, Natural and Politic*, edited by J.C.A. Gaskin. Oxford, UK: Oxford University Press.

Hobbes, Thomas. 2012. *Leviathan*, edited by Noel Malcolm (3 vols.). Oxford, UK: Oxford University Press.

Hoekstra, Kinch. 2006. "A Lion in the House: Hobbes and Democracy," in *Rethinking the Foundations of Modern Political Thought*, edited by A. Brett & J. Tully. Cambridge, UK: Cambridge University Press.

Hont, Istvan. 2005. "The Permanent Crisis of a Divided Mankind: 'Nation-State' and 'Nationalism' in Historical Perspective," in *Jealousy of Trade*. Cambridge, MA: Belknap Press.

Malcolm, Noel. 2002. "The Title Page of Leviathan," in *Aspects of Hobbes*. Oxford, UK: Clarendon Press.

Manin, Bernard. 1997. *The Principles of Representative Government*. Cambridge, UK: Cambridge University Press.

Okin, Susan Moller. 1982. " 'The Soveraign and His Counsellours': Hobbes's Re-evaluation of Parliament." *Political Theory* 10: 49–75.

Parkin, Jon. 2010. *Taming the Leviathan: The Reception of the Political and Religious Ideas of Thomas Hobbes in England 1640–1700*. Cambridge, UK: Cambridge University Press.

---

[32] For a full account of this conception of modern democracy, see Runciman 2010.

Pitkin, Hanna. 1967. *The Concept of Representation.* Berkeley: University of California Press.

Runciman, David, 2010. "Hobbes's Theory of Representation: Anti-democratic or Proto-democratic?" in *Political Representation,* edited by I. Shapiro et al. Cambridge, UK: Cambridge University Press.

Skinner, Quentin. 2002a. "Hobbes's Life in Philosophy," in *Visions of Politics,* vol. 3. Cambridge, UK: Cambridge University Press.

Skinner, Quentin. 2002b. "The Context of Hobbes's Theory of Political Obligation," in *Visions of Politics,* vol. 3. Cambridge, UK: Cambridge University Press.

Sorell, Tom. 2004. "The Burdensome Freedom of Sovereigns," in *Leviathan after 350 Years,* edited by Tom Sorell and Luc Foisneau. Oxford, UK: Clarendon Press.

Tuck, Richard. 2006. "Hobbes and Democracy," in *Rethinking the Foundations of Modern Political Thought,* edited by A. Brett and J. Tully. Cambridge, UK: Cambridge University Press.

CHAPTER 17

···

HOBBES AND ABSOLUTISM

···

JOHANN SOMMERVILLE

THERE is wide agreement among Hobbes scholars that one of the philosopher's main intentions in *Leviathan*, and in his earlier political writings, was to defend the absolute power of sovereigns—and most of all of monarchs. It is also commonly recognized that he was in some ways an odd absolutist.[1] This chapter is about Hobbes's absolutism and how it relates to the ideas of other absolutists.

A number of Hobbes's contemporaries saw his political theory as an example of doctrines that were supported in the writings of other thinkers. The Whig martyr Algernon Sidney contended that the ideas of "Laud, Manwaring, Sybthorpe, Hobbes, Filmer, and Heylin" were false and pernicious. Their writings were a curse, he said, which completed "the shame and misery of our age and country."[2] The lawyer John Whitehall declared that the aim of Hobbes's account of the origins of government was "to give the property of the People to the Prince, (like a dear Son of *Sibthorpe* and *Manwaring*)." Indeed, he argued, Hobbes's ideas were in some respects worse than theirs.[3] Writing against the theories of Filmer, John Locke argued that his adversary's doctrine that monarchy is by divine right was a recent novelty. Locke concentrated on refuting Filmer's version of the case while leaving the story of the theory's creation and propagation "to historians to relate, or to the memory of those who were contemporaries with Sibthorp and Manwaring to recollect."[4] Although Locke wrote especially against Filmer's *Patriarcha*—first published in 1680—he also took a number of side swipes at Hobbes and profoundly disagreed with much of his political thinking—and not least with his notion that subjects hold no rights of property against their sovereigns. Peter Heylin, the friend and biographer of Laud, was also a friend of Filmer. In

---

[1] An excellent discussion of absolutism that compares and contrasts Hobbes's ideas with those of other absolutists is Mark Goldie 2011, especially at 288, 290–91, 293.

[2] Sidney 1990, 11.

[3] Whitehall 1679, 7 (quotation); Whitehall 1680, 58: "And thus far he is worse than *Sibthorpe* or *Manwaring*." A fine account of the reception of Hobbes's ideas by his contemporaries is Parkin 2007.

[4] Locke 1988, 143 (first treatise, ch. 1, sect. 5).

1659—six years after Filmer's death—he lamented that Sir Robert had not "suffered his Excellent Discourse called *Patriarcha* to appear in publick" arguing that "it would have given such satisfaction to all our great Masters" in political thinking "that all other Tractates in that kind, had been found unnecessary."[5] Filmer held that political and fatherly authority are essentially the same and that neither is derived from the consent of subjects, and he disagreed with Hobbes's account of the origins of government. But he wholeheartedly endorsed Hobbes's views on the nature of political authority: "With no small content I read Mr Hobbes's book *De Cive*, and his *Leviathan*, about the rights of sovereignty, which no man, that I know, hath so amply and judiciously handled. I consent with him about the rights of exercising government."[6] Filmer derived many of his arguments from the writings of the French theorist Jean Bodin. Bodin was one of the few contemporary political thinkers cited in Hobbes's *Elements of Law*. Hobbes approvingly referred to Bodin in support of the key principle that sovereignty is indivisible.[7]

Hobbes graduated from Oxford University in February 1608. So, too, did Roger Maynwaring.[8] Maynwaring became a clergyman and, in 1627, he delivered two notorious sermons defending the imposition by the King of an extraparliamentary tax known as the Forced Loan. Hobbes helped to collect the Loan in Derbyshire. The Loan was widely regarded as illegal and unconstitutional. When parliament met in 1628, it condemned the Loan. It also impeached Maynwaring. The Lords sentenced him to imprisonment during the House's pleasure and permanently disabled him from holding any office in church or state. Once parliament had voted the King taxes, he pardoned Maynwaring and later promoted him to the Bishopric of St. David's.[9] Hobbes told his friend and biographer John Aubrey that "Bishop Maynwaring (of St David's) preached his doctrine."[10] Maynwaring drew on the thinking of Hadrian (or Adrian) Saravia, whose *De Imperandi Authoritate* (On the Authority of Commanding), published at London by the royal printer in 1593, combined Bodinian sovereignty with patriarchalism of a strikingly Filmerian variety.[11]

As Deborah Baumgold remarks, "The defense of absolutism, preferably monarchic absolutism" is central to Hobbes's "theory of politics."[12] In the modern literature on Hobbes, the terms "absolutism" and "absolutist" are used frequently and unapologetically. In scholarly discussions of how early modern European states were in fact governed, by contrast, there has been much debate on whether such terms are useful, and

---

[5] Peter Heylin to Sir Edward Filmer, April 20, 1659, in Heylin 1659, "387" = 207.

[6] Filmer 1991, 184.

[7] *Elements of Law* 2:8:7, 172.

[8] Foster 1891–2 gives the date of Hobbes's B.A. degree as February 5, 1607/8 (2:721) and that of Maynwaring (Mainwaring) as February 1607/8 (3:960.)

[9] Sommerville 2000.

[10] Aubrey 1898, 1:334. A discussion of the material in this and the previous paragraph is in Sommerville 1992, 9–19. There is a good treatment of the links between Hobbes and Maynwaring in Martinich 1999, 13–14, 59–60.

[11] Maynwaring 1627, 1:11; 2:19.

[12] Baumgold 1988, 3.

the point is sometimes made that they are anachronisms that were not current before the nineteenth century.[13] It is true that Hobbes nowhere speaks of absolutism, but arguably this is unimportant. He did talk repeatedly about absolute power. Discussing commonwealths by conquest and by institution, he remarked that "the sovereign is absolute over both alike; or else there is no sovereignty at all." Speaking of subordinate representative institutions, he declared that in bodies politic the power of the representative is always limited "and that which prescribeth the limits thereof is the power sovereign. For power unlimited is absolute sovereignty. And the sovereign, in every Commonwealth, is the absolute representative of all the subjects." Hobbes claimed he had proved that "all governments, which men are bound to obey, are simple and absolute." In "monarchy there is but one man supreme," he said, whereas aristocracies and democracies were governed by "one supreme assembly, with the same power that in monarchy belongeth to the monarch, which is not a mixed, but an absolute sovereignty."[14] Filmer compiled a pamphlet entitled *The Necessity of the Absolute Power of All Kings: and in particular, of the King of England*, lifting its contents from Bodin. He contrasted absolute monarchy with limited or mixed monarchy, arguing that nonabsolute monarchy was anarchic. In the parliament of 1628, Maynwaring was accused of going "about to infuse into his Majesty that which was most unfit for his royal breast—an absolute power not bounded by law."[15] Hobbes and his contemporaries talked about absolute power, and some of them defended it. It makes sense to call them absolutists despite the anachronism.

The next section deals with points on which there was broad agreement between Hobbes and other absolutists, including the key idea that political authority in every state should be held by a single person or assembly. Section 2 concerns differences between Hobbes and other thinkers on the origins and nature of government and on the relationships between states and families and between political and paternal or fatherly power. Section 3 is about moral theory and ideas on justice, equity, and property. Section 4 discusses issues connected with religious authority and church–state relations, whereas Section 5 is about resistance and self-defense.

1 ABSOLUTE AND INDIVISIBLE SOVEREIGNTY: IN THE *ELEMENTS OF LAW*

Hobbes listed the things that dispose people to rebellion. One was the idea "that the sovereign is in such sort obliged to his own laws, as the subject is." Hobbes rejected this, arguing that sovereigns cannot "be said to be subject to the laws which they may abrogate at their pleasure, or break without fear of punishment." The law, he held, was the

---

[13] Sommerville 2012.
[14] *Leviathan* 20/105, 22/115, 42/300–1 (references to 1651 chapter and page).
[15] Johnson and Keeler, 1977–83, 3:408.

command of the sovereign, who has the right to punish disobedience. Sovereigns "have all punishments in their own disposing" and therefore "cannot be so commanded, as to receive hurt for disobeying, and consequently no command can be a law unto them." So it is an error to suppose that the sovereign "can be subject to any law but that of God Almighty."[16] Equally false, according to Hobbes, was the view "that the sovereign power may be divided," and it was on this point that he cited Bodin, endorsing his claim that if there were a commonwealth wherein the rights of sovereignty were divided, we must confess "that they are not rightly to be called commonwealths, but the corruption of commonwealths. For if one part should have power to make the laws for all, they would by their laws, at their pleasure, forbid others to make peace or war, to levy taxes, or to yield fealty and homage without their leave; and they that had the right to make peace and war, and command the militia, would forbid the making of other laws, than what themselves liked."[17] Hobbes continued to emphasize the need to have a single sovereign authority in every state in his later political and historical writings, sometimes presenting the claim as a logically necessary feature of what a state is and on other occasions implying that a state with a divided sovereign would be ill-governed rather than impossible.[18] In *Behemoth*, he blamed the defeat of the royalists in the English Civil War in part on the love of some of their leaders "for Mixarchy, which they vsed to praise by the name of Mixt Monarchy, though it were indeed nothing else but pure Anarchy."[19]

These ideas also featured in the writings of Bodin, Filmer, and many others. "To majesty or sovereignty belongeth an absolute power not subject to any law," said Bodin, in words that Filmer copied into his *Necessity of the Absolute Power of All Kings*. "It behoveth him that is a sovereign," Bodin proceeded, "not to be in any sort subject to the command of another; whose office it is to give laws unto his subjects, to abrogate laws unprofitable, and in their stead to establish other; which he cannot do, that is himself subject unto laws." As Hobbes noted, Bodin declared that such "states, wherein the rights of sovereignty are divided, are not rightly to be called commonweals, but rather the corruption of commonweals."[20] In 1648, Filmer published a pamphlet entitled *The Anarchy of a Limited or Mixed Monarchy*. Its title summarized its contents. Although Bodin thought it impossible to divide sovereignty, he argued that it is perfectly feasible for a sovereign monarch to institute a day-to-day administration that incorporates non-monarchical elements. Indeed, he held that this was a good idea, and he recommended that kings temper the monarchical nature of their governments by augmenting it with aristocratic and democratic institutions.[21] Hobbes adopted much the same position in

[16] *Elements of Law* 2:8:6, 172.

[17] *Elements of Law* 2:8:7, 172–73.

[18] Hobbes's use of analytical and prescriptive versions of the theory of indivisible sovereignty are discussed and documented in Baumgold 1988, 56–66.

[19] *Behemoth*, 263; cf. 275. Cf. *Leviathan* 18/92–3, 29/170.

[20] Filmer 1991, 173, 179, quoting from Bodin 1962, 88, "73" = 91, 194 (1:8; 1:9). A comparison of Bodin's ideas with those of Hobbes is in King 1974. There is interesting material on the links between Hobbes's ideas and those of Bodin and other absolutists in Foisneau 2007.

[21] Bodin 1583, 272 (2:2): "Car il y a bien difference de l'estat, & du gouuernement"; 1013 (6:6): in a royal monarchy "l'estat Royal . . . doit estre temperé par le gouuernement Aristocratique & Populaire."

the *Elements of Law*, claiming that "though the sovereignty be not mixed, but be always either simple democracy, or simple aristocracy, or pure monarchy; nevertheless in the administration thereof, all those sorts of government may have place subordinate." He gave the example of republican Rome, claiming that it was a sovereign democracy but that its ordinary administration included nondemocratic elements—with monarchical dictators and an aristocratic senate whose powers were, however, wholly subordinate to those of the people.[22]

The theory of indivisible sovereignty had significant corollaries on which there was broad agreement among absolutists including Hobbes. Since the sovereign held all political authority, anyone else who had such authority necessarily possessed it on license from the sovereign who could withdraw it. No one could call the sovereign to account. Normally, no one could actively resist the sovereign (as we shall see in the final section, there could be exceptions to this important rule). Institutions such as the English Parliament or the French Estates General had no share in sovereignty, which was held by the King alone in monarchies like England and France. Sovereigns appointed public officials and could remove them. They might choose to consult others—such as Parliament—in legislating, but it was the sovereign who made the laws and who interpreted them. On all these points, Hobbes and other absolutists agreed.

Hobbes's approach to political philosophizing is sometimes contrasted with that of most other absolutists who are said to have adopted the theory of "the divine right of kings." There is something in this. Many absolutists revered Aristotle and drew heavily on the scholastics, unlike Hobbes. Many absolutists paid scant attention to geometry or to scientific changes. Hobbes self-consciously developed a new and systematic philosophy, of which his politics was only one part. His principles were based on rigorous argument from first principles. However, although most absolutists were rather more respectful than Hobbes of earlier writers, they did attempt to base key claims on rational argument, and sometimes their arguments were not that different from those of Hobbes. The treatment of indivisible sovereignty by Bodin and Filmer is a case in point. Moreover, Hobbes was perfectly capable of using language characteristic of divine right thinkers and of pressing some of their favorite texts into service. Divine right theorists contended that sovereigns derive their authority from God alone and not from any human. They concluded that sovereigns are accountable only to God for how they govern. In *Leviathan*, Hobbes stated that "The Monarch, or the Soveraign Assembly only hath immediate Authority from God, to teach and instruct the people; and no man but the Soveraign, receiveth his power *Dei gratia* [by the grace of God] simply." The office of the sovereign, he declared, is to procure the safety of the people, "to which he is obliged by the Law of Nature, and to render an account thereof to God, the Author of that Law, and to none but him."[23]

A biblical text that was much debated by Hobbes's contemporaries was 1 Samuel 8, in which the prophet Samuel warns the children of Israel that if they insist on having

---

[22] *Elements of Law* 2:1:17, 115–16.
[23] *Leviathan* 23/125; 30/175.

a king, he might act oppressively, for instance by taxing them heavily and enslaving their children. Opponents of absolutism argued that Samuel was warning them against absolute monarchy and perhaps any kind of monarchy. Absolutists, on the other hand, commonly interpreted the passage as meaning that subjects have a divinely ordained duty to put up with the actions of their sovereigns, even if they are oppressive. In the opinion of the German thinker Henning Arnisaeus, Samuel had described what kings have the power to do although not what they ought to do. According to William Barclay (a Scottish/French legal and political theorist whom Locke described as "that great assertor of the power and sacredness of kings"), the text underlined the "supreme dominion" and "impunity" of kings. Jacques-Bénigne Bossuet—the most famous defender of absolute monarchy in Louis XIV's France—similarly remarked that the prophet had been referring to things that kings "have the right" to do "with impunity with respect to human justice." That, he observed, is why King David said to the Lord "To thee only have I sinned" (or, as the King James version puts it, "Against thee, thee only, have I sinned": Psalms 51:4), although he had committed adultery and murdered Uriah the Hittite. Arnisaeus interpreted David's words in the same way. Filmer declared that the passage was about the "unlimited jurisdiction of kings." "Isn't power of this kind absolute?" asked Hobbes rhetorically in De cive. In Leviathan, he bluntly stated that "This is absolute power." He also cited the case of David and Uriah to confirm the claim that sovereigns cannot do injury to their subjects, although they can do actions that are "against the law of nature, as being contrary to equity" and so do injury "to God."[24]

Hobbes argued that in a monarchy the right of appointing a successor is held by the current monarch: "the disposing of the Successor, is alwaies left to the Judgment and Will of the present Possessor."[25] He also insisted that a ruler lost power if he ceased to protect his subjects, stressing "the mutuall Relation between Protection and Obedience." A rebel could become a legitimate sovereign if his rebellion succeeded and he established power by conquest. A man who was subject to one sovereign has the liberty to submit to another when "the means of his life is within the Guards and Garrisons of the Enemy," for, at that point, he "hath no longer Protection" from his old ruler.[26] This claim had immediate practical implications at the time Leviathan was published because it licensed former royalists to make their peace with England's recently victorious republic, and this understandably offended die-hard supporters of the exiled Charles II. In claiming that hereditary right is not indefeasible—since kings can appoint their successors, and usurping governments can become legitimate—Hobbes was not, however, straying from mainstream absolutist thinking. In the earliest times, said Saravia, succession had been by primogeniture "unless the father, in whom supreme power resided,

---

[24] Arnisaeus 1610, 216–17 (on Samuel and David); Barclay 1600, 141 ("suprema haec dominatio, & impunitas tributa Regibus"); Locke 1988, 419 (second treatise, ch. 19, sect. 232); Bossuet 1990, 83; Filmer 1991, 35; De cive 11:6, 184; Leviathan 20/105; 21/109 (David and Uriah).

[25] Leviathan 19/100.

[26] Leviathan, Review and Conclusion 395–96 (protection and obedience); 390 (guards and garrisons); cf. Elements of Law 2:2:15, 126, and De cive 7:18, 159.

decided otherwise."[27] In 1606, the convocation of Canterbury—the representative body of most of England's clergy—agreed on canons concerning government, and these included one that asserted that a government that began in rebellion becomes legitimate once it is "throughly settled."[28] In his *Patriarcha*, written before the Civil War, Filmer contended that a king could "come to the crown by usurpation" and argued that God could most justly "suffer princes to be removed and others placed in their rooms" "for the correction of the prince or punishment of the people." He listed donation along with election and succession as ways by which sovereignty could be transmitted. It was only after the execution of Charles I and the establishment of the English republic that Filmer moved to the position that "an usurper can never gain a right from the true superior." This claim was intended to show that Charles II was the true sovereign in England, but it had the implication, when taken with the rest of Filmer's theory, that if we could find Adam's one true heir, he or she would have the right to govern the whole world. Locke was quick to note the contradictions and absurdities that followed.[29] On the question of indefeasibly hereditary right, it was the postwar Filmer rather than Hobbes who was the innovator.

Hobbes took the same line as other absolutists on many matters, and it is unsurprising that he was sometimes grouped with them. On a number of points, however, he diverged from all or most of them, although sometimes the extent of the divergence turns out on closer inspection to be less than it looks at first. An example is his account of the origins of government.

2 THE ORIGINS AND NATURE OF GOVERNMENT AND THE POWERS OF FATHERS AND SOVEREIGNS

Absolutists commonly claimed that sovereigns derive their power from God alone. They were sometimes willing to admit that on occasion in the past the people had appointed someone to be their king, but they contended that if the king in question is a genuine sovereign (and not a subordinate magistrate in what is in fact a democracy), then he is not accountable to the people but only to God. The people, they argued, might designate or nominate the person of the sovereign, but his authority comes from God alone. One argument used to support this contention was that when a group of people at first met together to form a state, none of them had the power to judge and

---

[27] Saravia 1611, 167: "nisi parens, penes quem summa erat potestas, aliud statuisset."
[28] *The Convocation Book* 1844, 51.
[29] Filmer 1991, 11 (usurpation and punishment), 44 (donation etc.), 285 (usurper and true superior); in *Directions for Obedience to Government in Dangerous or Doubtfull Times*, 1652.

punish others and that the sovereign—who does have this power—therefore cannot derive it from the people.

Hobbes argued rather differently, claiming that in the state of nature individuals have the right of nature, empowering "each man" to do "anything which, in his own Judgement, and reason, hee shall conceive to be the aptest means thereunto."[30] He claimed that we establish the commonwealth by covenanting together to lay aside the right of nature in favor of a sovereign. In the *Elements of Law* and *De cive*, he argued that the first form of government must necessarily be democracy. Of the three possible forms—monarchy, aristocracy, and democracy—"the first in order of time of these three sorts," said Hobbes in the *Elements*, "is democracy, and it must be so of necessity, because an aristocracy and a monarchy, require nomination of persons agreed upon," and he repeated the point in *De cive*.[31] He claimed that the original democracy may later transfer power to an aristocracy or to a monarch. If it establishes a monarch, then it transfers sovereignty to him, and "if this sovereignty be truly and indeed transferred, the estate or commonwealth is an absolute monarchy."[32] In England in the course of the civil wars between the king and parliament (1642–6, 1648), many had serious doubts about whether the people had transferred all their powers to the king and about whether the state was an absolute monarchy. Parliamentarians commonly contended that the people had at first been sovereign and drew the conclusions that they (or their representatives in Parliament) still shared sovereignty with the king and that since the king's authority was derived from the people it was subject to conditions imposed on him by them. In *Leviathan*, Hobbes revised his account of the origins of government, this time arguing that the sovereign is instituted when individuals covenanted with each other "to conferre all their power and strength upon one Man, or upon one Assembly of men, that may reduce all their Wills, by plurality of voices, unto one Will."[33] The sovereign does not enter into the covenant and so cannot breach it. Nor does he lay down the right of nature.[34] Since the sovereign agreed on by individuals as they exit the state of nature can be one man, democracy is no longer the necessary first form of government, and monarchies (and aristocracies) do not need to arise from an act of transference by the people. Arguably, this new account of the institution of states brought Hobbes closer into line with usual absolutist theory than he had earlier been. The right of nature, in accordance with which the sovereign is empowered to act, is, of course, a natural right and so is derived from God, the author of nature. It is notable that Bossuet, an utterly mainstream absolutist, followed *Leviathan*'s account closely, contending that if we examine people as "they are naturally and before any government is established," we will find "nothing but anarchy" where all are "in continual

---

[30] *Leviathan* 14/64. An excellent discussion of Hobbes's account of the state of nature is Hoekstra 2007.

[31] *Elements of Law* 2:2:1, 118; cf. *De cive* 7:5, 152.

[32] *Elements of Law* 2:2:9, 121–23.

[33] *Leviathan* 17/88.

[34] *Leviathan* 18/89; 28/161–62.

war against all." In such a state there could be no property or security. The way out of this situation of total liberty and confusion, he claimed, was for each individual to renounce the right of nature in favor of an agreed government.[35]

Hobbes's—and Bossuet's—account of the institution of commonwealths was based on the premise that, by nature, people are free and equal. Some absolutists strongly rejected that premise on the grounds that we are, in fact, born into subjection to our parents and especially to our father (since the father was almost universally regarded as the senior partner of the parents). This was the position of Filmer, who criticized Hobbes for building his political system on a nonexistent state of nature, rather than on "the principles of *regnum patrimoniale* a paternal kingdom, as he calls it." Moreover, he argued that Hobbes's account of the origins of government was "full of contradiction."[36] Hobbes held that, in addition to commonwealths by institution—established by covenants between individuals—there were commonwealths by conquest and paternal dominion. It was commonplace to argue that many states arose by conquest: "Yea Reason, and the verie light of nature, leadeth us to beleeve very force and violence to have given course and beginning unto Commonweals."[37] That states could grow from families or amalgamations of families was also widely recognized. Hobbes's discussion of the family included what were (for his contemporaries, at least) some striking paradoxes, but, as often, the position he finally settled on was not dramatically unorthodox.

The standard view of authority in the family was that it belongs to the father. Filmer was typical in asserting that "God at the creation gave the sovereignty to the man over the woman, as being the nobler and principal agent in generation."[38] So, within the family, it was the father who held dominion over the wife and children. A second point on which there was almost universal agreement was that the father possesses authority over the children *by nature* and not as a consequence of the children's consent. Filmer was again typical in observing "How a child can express consent, or by other sufficient arguments declare it before it comes to the age of discretion I understand not," and he went on to insist that "all men grant" that children have a duty of obedience to their parents "before consent can be given."[39] Hobbes innovated on both these points. He argued that, in the state of nature, the parents could "dispose of the dominion over the

[35] Bossuet, from *Cinquième avertissement aux Protestants*, 1690, in Bossuet 1966, 83–84: "Car à regarder les hommes comme ils sont naturellement et avant tout gouvernement établi, on ne trouve que l'anarchie . . . où tous sont en garde, et par conséquent en guerre continuelle contre tous"; "la souveraineté ou la puissance publique . . . se forme et résulte de la cession des particuliers, lorsque fatigués de l'état où tout le monde est le maître et où personne ne l'est, ils se sont laissés persuader de renoncer à ce droit qui met tout en confusion, et à cette liberté qui fait tout craindre à tout le monde, en faveur d'un gouvernement dont on convient." Bossuet's use of Hobbes's ideas is discussed in Malcolm 2002, 506–7.

[36] Filmer 1991, 185.

[37] Bodin 1962, 47 (1:6). Bodin 1583, 69: "La raison & lumiere naturelle nous conduit à cela, de croire que la force & violence a donné source & origine aux Republiques."

[38] Filmer 1991, 192. Early-modern ideas on the natural subjection of women are discussed in Sommerville 1995, especially at 16–39.

[39] Filmer 1991, 192.

Child by Contract" but that if "there be no Contract, the Dominion is in the Mother" since "it cannot be known who is the Father, unless it be declared by the Mother" and since "the Infant is first in the power of the Mother" to whom the child therefore owes its life if she chooses to nourish it. Second, he denied that the dominion of parents over their children stems "from the Generation" insisting that it is derived "from the Childs Consent, either expresse, or by other sufficient arguments declared." Hobbes did, however, acknowledge that if "the Mother be the Fathers subject, the Child, is in the Fathers power."[40] He seems to have believed that, in the state of nature, mothers would normally become subject to fathers, for he argued that "a great Family" is "as to the Rights of Sovereignty, a little Monarchy ... wherein the Father or Master is the Sovereign."[41] Before "the Institution of Common-wealth," he declared, "the Father, and Master" were "absolute Soveraigns in their own Families."[42] Once sovereigns had been established, he argued, they had a duty to teach the young to honor their parents, to "which end" children "are to be taught, that originally the Father of every man was also his Soveraign Lord, with power over him of life and death; and that the Fathers of families, when by instituting a Common-wealth, they resigned that absolute Power, yet it was never intended, they should lose the honour due unto them for their education." Here, the dominion of mothers and the consent of children have dropped out of the picture. It also seemingly turns out that the commonwealth was instituted not by the consent of every individual but only by that of fathers of families. Moreover, it turns out, too, that among the rights that subjects retained when they entered political society was the right to be honored by their children and, more generally, any right the resignation of which was "not necessary to the Institution of Sovereign Power."[43] Despite Hobbes's paradoxes, his final position quite conventionally portrays a commonwealth by institution as an amalgamation of families. In Bodin's theory, a state had to consist of "at least three families."[44] In Hobbes's, as in Filmer's, it could be a single family, provided that it was large enough to defend itself.[45]

Absolutists sometimes distinguished between absolute and arbitrary monarchy and also between royal and lordly (or seigneurial or despotic) monarchy. Bossuet, for instance, noted that there "is among men a kind of government which is called arbitrary." "It is one thing," he said, "for a government to be absolute, and another for it to be arbitrary." In an arbitrary government, he declared, "the prince has the right to dispose as he wishes, not only of the goods, but also of the lives of his subjects" and "there is no law but his will." Such government, he insisted, was "barbarous and odious."[46] Bodin distinguished between royal monarchy, seigneurial monarchy, and tyranny. In the first kind of monarchy, the king governed his subjects by laws, and they held rights

---

[40] *Leviathan* 20/103 (dominion in mother; mother as father's subject); 20/102 (child's consent).
[41] *Leviathan* 20/105.
[42] *Leviathan* 22/121.
[43] *Leviathan* 30/178.
[44] Bodin 1962, 9 (1:2). Bodin 1583, 11–12.
[45] *Leviathan* 20/105.
[46] Bossuet 1990, 263 (bk. 8, article 2, proposition 1).

of property. In the second, the king ruled by right of conquest and governed as a master over slaves. In a tyranny, the monarch scorns the law of nature and abuses the persons and goods of his free subjects as though they were slaves. Bodin made clear his abhorrence of tyranny and his strong preference for royal over seigneurial monarchy.[47]

Hobbes argued that "Dominion acquired by Conquest, or Victory in war, is that which some Writers call DESPOTICALL" and noted that this "is the Dominion of the Master over his Servant." He dismissed tyranny as simply a term of abuse used by those "that are discontented under *Monarchy*." Toward the end of *Leviathan*, Hobbes spoke approvingly of "Arbitrary government" and of "Absolute and Arbitrary Legislative Power."[48] Passages like these have helped to support the modern myth that identifies Hobbism "with arbitrary despotism, even with twentieth-century totalitarianism."[49] In fact, there is little justification for this. Like Hobbes, Filmer argued for arbitrary power, and, like Hobbes, he did not advocate despotism or totalitarianism. He did not construe arbitrary power as meaning the authority to act on mere caprice or without reason. According to Filmer, "the supreme power is always arbitrary" because "that is arbitrary which hath no superior on earth to control it." "The legislative power," he declared, "is an arbitrary power, for they are *termini convertibiles* [convertible terms]."[50] Hobbes emphatically did *not* recommend that the sovereign govern oppressively or give commands on a whim, without regard to the public interest. When Bishop John Bramhall maintained that, in Hobbes's opinion, it was not a sin for the king to have a servant hanged for negligent attendance or similar random reasons not covered by law, Hobbes responded that this was "wilful slander."[51] Hobbes's point in equating the powers of sovereigns in commonwealths by institution with those in despotical ones was not to show that all sovereigns may rightly oppress their subjects, but that in all commonwealths, whatever their origins, the rights and duties of the sovereign are the same. The duties included "the procuration of *the safety of the people*" and Hobbes spelled out that "by Safety here, is not meant a bare Preservation, but also all other Contentments of life, which every man by lawfull Industry, without danger, or hurt to the Common-wealth, shall acquire to himself."[52] He declared that "the duty of a sovereign consisteth in the good government of the people." When the sovereign's acts "tend to the hurt of the people in general, they be breaches of the law of nature, and of the divine Law." He rejected the idea that some forms of government are geared to the interests of the people and others to those of the ruler on the grounds that both had the same interests: "governing to the profit of the subjects, is governing to the profit of the sovereign."[53] Filmer made a similar point.[54] The king, said Hobbes, has no incentive to take the lands, goods, liberties,

---

[47] Bodin 1583, 270–79 (2:2).

[48] *Leviathan* 20/103 (dominion by conquest); 19/95 (tyranny); 46/377 (arbitrary government); Review and Conclusion, 391.

[49] Baumgold 1988, 101.

[50] Filmer 1991, 100.

[51] Hobbes 1839–45, 4:371.

[52] *Leviathan* 30/175.

[53] *Elements of Law* 2:9:1, 179.

[54] Filmer 1991, 253.

and lives of the people, for "what becomes of his power when his Subjects are destroyed, or weakned, by whose multitude, and strength he enjoys his power, and every one of his Subjects his Fortune?"[55]

Hobbes's account of the origins and nature of government includes some distinctive twists and emphases but can nevertheless reasonably be seen as belonging to the mainstream of absolutist thinking. It is much harder to maintain that his broader moral theory and his thinking on religious and ecclesiastical matters belong to that mainstream.

3 MORAL THEORY, JUSTICE, EQUITY, AND PROPERTY

According to most absolutists and most early modern writers of all political persuasions, people are perpetually bound by natural laws—or laws of nature—defining what is right and wrong and discoverable by reason.[56] The laws of nature, it was commonly agreed, were moral laws, made by God, the author of nature. Hobbes innovated by arguing that although the "Lawes of Nature are Immutable and Eternall," we are not always bound to act on them. They do indeed always "oblige *in foro eterno*; that is to say, they bind to a desire they should take place; but *in foro externo*; that is, to the putting them in act, not always." For if other people are not abiding by natural law, I will put myself at a disadvantage if I do so, since "he that should be modest, and tractable, and performe all promises, in such time, and place where no man els should do so, should but make himself a prey to others, and procure his own certain ruine." This would be "contrary to the ground of all Lawes of Nature, which tend to Natures preservation." So, in the state of nature, which was a state of war of all against all, the laws of nature did not oblige to action, for "Force, and Fraud, are in warre the two Cardinall vertues."[57] Others held that the laws of nature oblige to action even in the state of nature. But Hobbes agreed with the rest in claiming that we must abide by natural law once the commonwealth is established.

An important implication of Hobbes's account of the state of nature is that the notions of "Justice and Injustice have there no place." Moreover, he added, it "is consequent also to the same condition, that there be no Propriety, no Dominion, no *Mine* and *Thine* distinct; but onely that to be every mans, that he can get; and for so long, as he can keep it." Justice and rights of property began only when sovereigns were instituted. Because subjects authorized the acts of the sovereign, "whatsoever he doth, it can be no injury to any of his Subjects; nor ought he to be by any of them accused of Injustice." Hobbes admitted that sovereigns "may commit Iniquity" toward their subjects but

---

55 *Dialogue of the Common Laws*, 38.
56 Two important recent works on Hobbes's moral theory are Lloyd 2009 and Zagorin 2009.
57 *Leviathan* 15/79 (laws of nature); 13/63 (force and fraud).

denied that they could do "Injustice, or Injury in the proper signification."[58] Similarly, he denied that subjects have rights of property against the sovereign. "Every man has indeed a Propriety that excludes the Right of every other Subject," but this stems "from the Soveraign Power" because, without the sovereign's protection, no one would have a greater right to anything than anyone else. So "the Propriety of Subjects" does not exclude "the Right of the Soveraign Representative to their Goods."[59]

Most absolutists contended that subjects do have rights of property even against their sovereigns and that kings can commit injustice against their subjects. Bodin was typical in arguing that sovereigns ought normally to obtain the consent of their subjects to taxation, although he admitted that rulers could tax without consent in a case of "urgent necessity."[60] In justifying the Forced Loan, Maynwaring pointed to "the vrgent and pressing *Necessities* of State" especially in foreign affairs.[61] Bossuet castigated injustice in rulers, remarking that it was "a profanation" for "unjust kings" "to be seated on the throne of God."[62] But Maynwaring approached the position on justice that Hobbes was later to adopt when he declared that "*Iustice* (properly so called) intercedes not between *God* and *Man*; nor betweene the *Prince*, being a *Father*; and the *People*, as *Children*; (for *Iustice* is betweene *Equals*)."[63] Like Hobbes, Filmer argued that property did not predate the institution of the commonwealth, although he built his case not on ideas about the state of nature but on the thesis that "the natural and private dominion of Adam" was "the fountain of all government and property."[64]

Arguably, the differences between Hobbes and other absolutists on justice and property were verbal rather than substantial. Although he claimed that sovereigns cannot commit injustice to their subjects, he conceded that they can act iniquitously toward them and, by doing so, break the law of nature that requires us to deal equitably with others. "Equity," he insisted, "is a Law of Nature," and he noted that equity was also called "(though improperly) Distributive Justice."[65] So sovereigns cannot do injustice to their subjects if we use the term strictly, but they can if we employ a broader sense of it. Again, Hobbes claimed that subjects do not have absolute rights of property that exclude the rights of the sovereign. But this does not mean that he encouraged rulers to despoil their subjects whenever they pleased. The sovereign had a duty to promote the interests of the people. Hobbes noted that the principle that the subject has rights of property "exclusive of the Soveraigns Right" had the harmful practical effect of making it difficult for the government to raise money "for the necessary uses of the Common-wealth; especially in the approach of warre." The "Kings word," he said, "is

---

[58] *Leviathan* 13/63 (no justice or property in the state of nature); 18/90 (injury, injustice, and iniquity). A discussion of Hobbes's views on injustice and iniquity is in Pettit 2008, 127.

[59] *Leviathan* 29/169–70.

[60] Bodin 1583, 157 (1:8); 863 (6:2): "necessité vrgente."

[61] Maynwaring 1627, 1:27; cf. 20.

[62] Bossuet 1990, 62 (bk. 3, article 2, fourth proposition).

[63] Maynwaring 1627, 2:25.

[64] Filmer 1991, 225.

[65] *Leviathan* 15/77 (equity the eleventh law of nature); 15/75 (equity and distributive justice).

sufficient to take anything from any Subject, when there is need; and the King is judge of that need."[66] True, Hobbes did not claim that taxation ordinarily requires consent, as Bodin did. But Hobbes agreed with other absolutists that need or necessity justified taxation without consent.

A standard doctrine among absolutists was passive obedience (passive disobedience might be a better term). They claimed that the laws of nature bind us all perpetually and that Christians are also bound by laws that God has revealed in the Bible. If the king commands acts that infringed these laws, subjects had a duty to disobey him but meekly to accept the penalties meted out for such disobedience or perhaps to resort to flight. So if the sovereign orders us to do things that are not forbidden by God or nature, we should actively obey him. But if his orders contravene the higher laws of God or nature, we must disobey. Hobbes rejected the distinction between active and passive obedience, insisting that all "Transgression of a Law" is sin.[67] Passive obedience was no kind of obedience at all, and suffering a penalty was not obeying: "Every Law is a command *to do*, or *to forbeare*, neither of these is fulfilled by suffering." The Bible requires obedience to the sovereign. Hobbes expressed amazement that "when the Laws" and clerics disagreed, people so often followed the clergyman's interpretation of Scripture, although he was generally "an ignorant, though a ready tongued Schollar, rather than the Laws that were made by the King with the consent of the Peers and Commons of the Land."[68] Many absolutists thought that the clergy had authority to interpret Scripture and that individuals should follow either the clergy or their own consciences in deciding what God's laws said. Hobbes held that both of these positions threatened to undermine the state.

4 RELIGIOUS AUTHORITY AND CHURCH–STATE RELATIONS

"*Temporall* and *Spirituall* Government," declared Hobbes, "are but two words brought into the world, to make men see double, and mistake their *Lawfull Soveraign*."[69] He claimed that clerics have no powers or functions that are independent of the sovereign. Few other absolutists went so far in depriving the clergy of power. Gallicans such as Bossuet denied that the Pope could depose the King of France, but granted the church a range of powers that were independent of the state. The Anglican clergy acknowledged that the monarch was Supreme Governor of the English church, but argued that bishops and other clergy have powers that are derived directly from God

---

[66] *Leviathan* 29/173; 20/106.
[67] *De cive* 14:23, 218; *Leviathan* 27/151.
[68] *Behemoth*, 172–73 (suffering and obedience; ignorant clergyman); 177 (Bible requires obedience).
[69] *Leviathan* 39/248.

and not from the monarch. The powers include performing the sacraments and judging and excommunicating sinners. Hobbes denied that the clergy held any powers from God rather than from the sovereign. Because absolutist ideas were especially prevalent among the Anglican clergy rather than the laity in Hobbes's lifetime, it is clear that he differed from many absolutists on questions of church–state relations. Possibly they did not include Filmer or Bodin, both of whom were rather quiet about the rights of the clergy. Although Filmer married a bishop's daughter, he said little about the authority of bishops and did not mention excommunication in his political writings. Filmer declared that he approved of what Hobbes had to say "about the rights of sovereignty,"[70] and he did not except the philosopher's remarks on the sovereign's power over clerics.

An important point to note in assessing just how much Hobbes differed from conventional Anglican thinking on the question of church and state is that although Anglicans held that the clergy derive some powers directly from God, they argued that in any particular state the clergy can *exercise* those powers only on the authority of the sovereign. As William Laud, Archbishop of Canterbury, put it in 1637, "though our *Office* be from *God* and *Christ immediately*, yet may wee not *exercise* that *power*" "but as *God* hath *appointed* us, that is, not in his *Majesties*, or any *Christian Kings Kingdomes*, but by and under the power of the *King* given us soe to doe."[71] Hobbes was well aware of this argument, which he addressed in the course of his controversy with Bramhall over liberty and necessity. The bishops, he observed, claim that they have the power to ordain ministers:

> They derive not, say they, the right of ordination from the civil sovereign, but from Christ immediately. And yet they acknowledge that it is unlawful for them to ordain, if the civil power do forbid them. But how have they right to ordain, when they cannot do it lawfully? Their answer is, they have the right, though they may not exercise it; as if the right to ordain, and the right to exercise ordination, were not the same thing.[72]

If Hobbes is correct, and the right to ordain—or to perform other ecclesiastical acts— is the same as the right to exercise ordination (or whatever), then the Anglican position on this point collapses into Hobbes's own. There are nevertheless large divergences between them on other issues, including the question of whether the sovereign can, in person, perform all the functions of clerics. In *Leviathan*, he resoundingly answered this question in the affirmative, asserting that Christian sovereigns are empowered "to Preach," "to Baptize, and to Administer the Sacrament of the Lords Supper; and to Consecrate both Temples, and Pastors to Gods service."[73] In *De cive*, Hobbes said things

[70] Filmer 1991, 184.
[71] Laud 1637, 7.
[72] Hobbes 1839–45, 5:142–43.
[73] *Leviathan* 42/297.

that sounded more like conventional Anglicanism, but arguably there, too, and in the *Elements of Law*, his hyper-Erastian position is incompatible with the teachings of the Anglican clergy.[74]

On questions of religious authority and church–state relations, Hobbes parted company with many conventional Anglicans and royalists whose sympathies lay with absolutism. The same goes for Hobbes's arguments concerning the right of self-defense, which led a number of royalists to criticize him sharply and, indeed, to see *Leviathan* as a "*Rebells catechism.*"[75]

5 Resistance and Self-Defense

Most absolutists granted subjects no rights of resistance or self-defense against the sovereign. Bossuet firmly rejected the contention that individuals have the right to defend themselves against unjust life-threatening attacks by people in public authority, contending that to grant them such a right would lead to the overthrow of the state. He insisted that subjects must generally obey the ruler, arguing that "there is only one exception to the obedience due to the prince, which is when his commands run contrary to God's." Even in this case, he stressed, active resistance is not licit. "Subjects have nothing to oppose to the violence of princes but respectful remonstrances, without mutiny and without murmurings, together with prayers for their conversion."[76] Bodin similarly denied that subjects can ever employ violence against an absolute monarch.[77] According to Filmer, the claims that no one can give up the right to defend himself from force by force and that we cannot validly covenant not to defend our lives and means of living are "doctrines destructive to all government whatsoever," since they license "any rogue or villain" to "murder his sovereign" if the sovereign "but offer by force to whip or lay him in the stocks."[78]

Hobbes, by contrast, held that people cannot lay down the right of self-defense, and arguably this notion flows naturally from his account of self-preservation. When individuals—or individual fathers—first established the commonwealth, he said in the *Elements of Law*, it was necessary that each "man should not retain his right to everything," but it was also necessary that "he should retain his right to some things: to his own body (for example) the right of defending, whereof he could not transfer; to the

---

[74] The question of whether Hobbes shifted from a conventionally Anglican position to a much more Erastian one is discussed in Tuck 1989, 85–86; Nauta 2002, 592; Sommerville 1992, 119–27; and Sommerville 2007, 369–70.

[75] Bramhall 1658, 515.

[76] Bossuet 1966, 90; Bossuet 1990, 173, 174, 181 (bk. 6, article 2, propositions 1, 2, and 6).

[77] Bodin 1583, 302 (2:5).

[78] Filmer 1991, 195.

use of fire, water, free air, and place to live in, and to all things necessary for life."[79] "It is manifest," he said in *Leviathan*, "that every Subject has Liberty in all those things, the right whereof cannot by Covenant be transferred." So a covenant "not to defend a mans own body" would be void, as would an agreement to kill himself "or not to resist those that assault him." This applied even in the case of a criminal who had been "justly condemned to death." Hobbes argued that no one is bound to confess a crime when interrogated on the sovereign's authority or to obey the sovereign's command to execute "any dangerous, or dishonourable Office" unless failure to do so "frustrates the End for which the Sovereignty was ordained," namely, peace and security. If you were commanded to serve as a soldier, you could often refuse "without Injustice" if, for example, you were a man "of feminine courage."[80] Nor were you obliged to accuse or act as a witness against a father, wife, or benefactor whose condemnation would bring you into misery.[81]

In the 1640s, it was parliamentarians who stressed the right of self-defense, which they used to justify resisting the king (or his wicked advisors) in the Civil War. Hobbes's doctrine was seen by some royalists as undermining the king's cause and providing polemical ammunition for his enemies.[82] The charge has been repeated more recently by Jean Hampton who argued that *Leviathan* was indeed a "'Rebel's Catechism'" and that Hobbes's discussion of the right of self-defense creates problems so serious as to render "the entire Hobbesian justification for absolute sovereignty invalid."[83] More recently, Susanne Sreedhar has convincingly challenged Hampton's interpretation, arguing that "Hobbes carefully circumscribes the rights to resist such that none can pose a threat to the absolute right or power of the sovereign."[84] So his case is arguably consistent. But for an absolutist, it was most unusual. Just occasionally, a writer in the absolutist tradition allowed a whole community to defend itself against a king who threatened it with destruction. Barclay did this, as Locke noted.[85] But for an absolutist to argue for individual rights of self-defense against kings was exceedingly odd.

In sum, Hobbes was an absolutist, and, despite his love of paradox and his belief in his own originality, he agreed on many key questions with the mainstream of absolutist tradition. But he diverged from it on some points and especially on church–state relations and the right of self-defense.

---

[79] Hobbes, *Elements of Law* 1:17:2, 88–89; cf. 2:1:7, 111. A different interpretation of Hobbes's position in the *Elements of Law* is in Tuck 1979, 121–25; Tuck (124–25) argues that in *De cive* and *Leviathan* Hobbes rejected the idea that we can renounce our right of self-defense, but (121–23) that he is more ambiguous in the *Elements*. At 122, he contends that a key passage in EL 2:1:7 is in only two of the manuscripts of the work, but this is incorrect. See also Sommerville 1992, 177–78, n.19.

[80] *Leviathan* 21/111–12.

[81] *Leviathan* 14/70.

[82] The use of self-defense and self-preservation in the thinking of Hobbes's contemporaries is discussed in Sommerville 1992, 33–37.

[83] Hampton 1986, 197. Pettit 2008, 129, inclines toward Hampton's position.

[84] Sreedhar 2010, 123.

[85] Barclay 1600, 159; Locke 1988, 419–21 (second treatise, ch. 19, sect. 232–33, quoting the relevant passage in Latin and English translation).

Bibliography

Arnisaeus, Henning. 1610. *De jure majestatis libri tres*. Frankfurt: J. Thymius.

Aubrey, John. 1898. *"Brief Lives," Chiefly of Contemporaries*, edited by Andrew Clark, 2 vols., Oxford: Clarendon Press.

Barclay, William. 1600. *De regno et regali potestate adversus Buchananum, Brutum, Boucherium, & reliquos Monarchomachos, libri sex*. Paris: Guillaume Chaudière.

Baumgold, Deborah. 1988. *Hobbes's Political Theory*. Cambridge: Cambridge University Press.

Bodin, Jean. 1583. *Les Six Livres de la Republique de I. Bodin Angeuin. Ensemble une Apologie de Rene Herpin*. Paris: Jacques du Puis.

Bodin, Jean. 1962. *The Six Bookes of a Commonweale*, translated by Richard Knolles (1606) and edited by Kenneth Douglas McRae. Cambridge: Harvard University Press.

Bossuet, Jacques-Bénigne. 1966. *Politique de Bossuet: texts choises et presentés par Jacques Truchet*. Paris: Armand Colin.

Bossuet, Jacques-Bénigne. 1990. *Politics Drawn from the Very Words of Holy Scripture*, translated and edited by Patrick Riley. Cambridge: Cambridge University Press.

Bramhall, John. 1658. *The Catching of Leviathan*, appended to *Castigations of Mr. Hobbes*. London: E. T. for J. Crook.

The Convocation Book. 1844. *The Convocation Book of M DC VI. Commonly called, Bishop Overall's Convocation Book*. Oxford: John Henry Parker.

Filmer, Sir Robert. 1991. *Patriarcha and Other Writings*, edited by Johann P. Sommerville. Cambridge: Cambridge University Press.

Foisneau, Luc. 2007. "Omnipotence, Necessity and Sovereignty: Hobbes and the Absolute and Ordinary Powers of God and King," in *The Cambridge Companion to Hobbes's Leviathan*, edited by Patricia Springborg, 271–290. Cambridge: Cambridge University Press.

Foster, Joseph. 1891-2. *Alumni Oxonienses: The Members of the University of Oxford 1500-1714*. 4 vols., Oxford: James Parker & Co.

Goldie, Mark. 2011. "Absolutism," in *The Oxford Handbook of the History of Political Philosophy*, edited by George Klosko, 282–295. Oxford: Oxford University Press.

Hampton, Jean. 1986. *Hobbes and the Social Contract Tradition*. Cambridge: Cambridge University Press.

Heylin, Peter. 1659. *Certamen Epistolare, or, the Letter-Combate*. London: J. M. for H. Twyford and others.

Hobbes, Thomas. 1839-45. *English Works*, edited by Sir William Molesworth. 11 vols. London: Bohn and Longman.

Hobbes, Thomas. 1969. *Elements of Law*, edited by Ferdinand Tönnies. Second edition. London: Frank Cass and Co. (References are to the pages of this edition and also to part, chapter, and section.)

Hobbes, Thomas. 1983. *De Cive. The Latin Version*, edited by Howard Warrender. Oxford: Clarendon Press.

Hobbes, Thomas. 2005. *A Dialogue Between a Philosopher and a Student, of the Common Laws of England*, edited by Alan Cromartie, in Hobbes, *Writings on Common Law and Hereditary Right*, edited by Cromartie and Quentin Skinner. Oxford: Clarendon Press, 1–146.

Hobbes, Thomas. 2010. *Behemoth*, edited by Paul Seaward. Oxford: Clarendon Press.

Hoekstra, Kinch. 2007. "Hobbes on the Natural Condition of Mankind," in *The Cambridge Companion to Hobbes's Leviathan*, edited by Patricia Springborg, 109–127. Cambridge: Cambridge University Press.

Johnson, R. C., and M. F. Keeler, eds., 1977–83. *Proceedings in Parliament 1628*. 6 vols. New Haven: Yale University Press.

King, Preston. 1974. *The Ideology of Order: A Comparative Analysis of Jean Bodin and Thomas Hobbes*. New York: Barnes and Noble.

Laud, William. 1637. *A Speech Delivered in the Starr-Chamber*. London: Richard Badger.

Lloyd, S. A. 2009. *Morality in the Philosophy of Thomas Hobbes: Cases in the Law of Nature*. Cambridge: Cambridge University Press.

Locke, John. 1988. *Two Treatises of Government*, edited by Peter Laslett. Cambridge: Cambridge University Press.

Malcolm, Noel. 2002. *Aspects of Hobbes*. Oxford: Clarendon Press.

Martinich, A. P. 1999. *Hobbes: A Biography*. Cambridge: Cambridge University Press.

Maynwaring, Roger. 1627. *Religion and Alegiance: In Two Sermons*. London: I. H. for Richard Badger, 1627.

Nauta, Lodi. 2002. "Hobbes on Religion Between *The Elements of Law* and *Leviathan*: A Dramatic Change of Direction?" *Journal of the History of Ideas* 63.4: 577–598.

Parkin, Jon. 2007. *Taming the Leviathan: The Reception of the Political and Religious Ideas of Thomas Hobbes in England 1640–1700*. Cambridge: Cambridge University Press.

Pettit, Philip. 2008. *Made with Words: Hobbes on Language, Mind, and Politics*. Princeton: Princeton University Press.

Saravia, Hadrian. 1611. *De Imperandi Authoritate, in Diversi Tractatus Theologici*. London: The Company of Stationers.

Sidney, Algernon. 1990. *Discourses Concerning Government*, edited by Thomas G. West. Indianapolis: Liberty Classics.

Sommerville, Johann. 1992. *Thomas Hobbes: Political Ideas in Historical Context*. Houndmills: Macmillan.

Sommerville, Johann. 2000. "Maynwaring, Roger (1590–1653)," in *The Dictionary of Seventeenth-Century British Philosophers*, edited by Andrew Pyle, 2 vols. 2:562–563. Bristol: Thoemmes Press.

Sommerville, Johann. 2007. "*Leviathan* and Its Anglican Context," in *The Cambridge Companion to Hobbes's Leviathan*, edited by Patricia Springborg, 358–374. Cambridge: Cambridge University Press.

Sommerville, Johann. 2012. "Early Modern Absolutism in Practice and Theory," in *Monarchism and Absolutism in Early Modern Europe*, edited by Cesare Cuttica and Glenn Burgess. London: Pickering and Chatto, 2012, 117–130.

Sommerville, Margaret R. 1995. *Sex and Subjection: Attitudes to Women in Early-Modern Society*. London: Arnold.

Sreedhar, Susanne. 2010. *Hobbes on Resistance: Defying the Leviathan*. Cambridge: Cambridge University Press.

Tuck, Richard. 1979. *Natural Rights Theories: Their Origin and Development*. Cambridge: Cambridge University Press.

Tuck, Richard. 1989. *Hobbes*. Oxford: Oxford University Press.

Whitehall, John. 1679. *The Leviathan Found Out*. London: A. Godbid and J. Playford.

Whitehall, John. 1680. *Behemoth Arraign'd*. London: for Thomas Fox, 1680.

Zagorin, Perez. 2009. *Hobbes and the Law of Nature*. Princeton: Princeton University Press.

CHAPTER 18

....

SOVEREIGN JURISDICTION, TERRITORIAL RIGHTS, AND MEMBERSHIP IN HOBBES

....

ARASH ABIZADEH

THE modern ideology of the sovereign state joins together two fundamentally distinct currents.[1] On the one hand, the state is supposed to be an essentially *artificial person*, a nonphysical entity whose juridical personality transcends any particular place, whereas, on the other hand, it is supposed to be an intrinsically *territorial entity* located in a specifically prescribed, physical place.[2] As a juridical entity, it metaphorically embodies the union of all the individuals who are its members and in whose name it claims sovereign power; as a territorial entity, it comprises the geographical space over which it claims sovereign jurisdictional authority. These two components of sovereign-state ideology are directly reflected in the dual transformation incurred by the rise of the modern state in Western Europe. On the one hand, the modern state arose in tandem with a process of *nationalization*, whereby the differential class privileges of the *ancien régime* were eroded by a new category of national citizenship, one that fused together membership of the polity with a uniform set of civil, social, and political rights and obligations.[3] Here, the *civic boundaries* of membership mark the key divide: between citizens, in whose name the state claims sovereign power and to whom it attributes a distinct bundle of rights and obligations, and noncitizens. On the other hand, the modern state was consolidated via a process of *territorialization*, whereby the primarily personal jurisdiction of feudal rulers was displaced by the state's fundamentally territorial

---

[1] References to Hobbes's works (chapter.paragraph, page) are given as follows: *Elements of Law* = Hobbes 1994, *Philosophical Rudiments* = Hobbes 1983a, *Leviathan* = Hobbes 2012. Page numbers following a / for *Philosophical Rudiments* are to *De cive*'s Latin original = Hobbes 1983b; page numbers following a / for *Leviathan* are to the Head edition.

[2] For the pre- and early-modern European background to these two dimensions, see Brett 2011.

[3] Brubaker 1992, cf. Marshall 1950.

jurisdiction.[4] The modern state claims sovereign jurisdictional authority—and in theory imposes a uniform set of laws—over all things and persons located within its territory. Here, the key divide is marked by *territorial boundaries*: between what is located inside and what is outside.

An account of how these two currents can be united is the required background for any theory of the sovereign state's purported territorial rights: an account of how an essentially nonphysical, artificial entity acquires a physical location and, concomitantly, sovereign jurisdiction over geographical space and of what shape jurisdiction takes when civic and territorial boundaries diverge, such as when nonmembers are present inside or members outside.[5] A second requirement for any such theory is that it not collapse sovereign jurisdictional authority into ownership: The modern state's jurisdiction over persons does not amount to a kind of property right; its citizens are its subjects, not its slaves.

If theorists have often turned to the social contract tradition to grapple with the central normative problems associated with the modern state, historians have frequently turned to one of the tradition's central figures to locate the origins of sovereign-state ideology—namely, Thomas Hobbes, widely hailed as one of the paramount ideological founts of the sovereign state.[6] Indeed, the answer to whether and how Hobbes could account for the territorial rights claimed by states is important not only for shedding light on the genealogy of sovereign-state ideology, but also because it is central for understanding many aspects of Hobbes's own political philosophy: his account of the nature of sovereignty, property rights, political obligation, the status of foreigners within a state, and colonialism.

The fact is, however, that Hobbes fully embraced neither of the two currents in question: He located sovereignty not in the juridical person of the state itself, but in the ruling monarch or assembly who has proprietary ownership of sovereign power, and he refrained from conceiving the state as an intrinsically territorial entity. He did nevertheless anticipate central elements of each current. It is rather easy to see how the social-contract tradition could feed into the first, juridical current of sovereign-state ideology: After all, the social contract is typically supposed to comprise the agreements of individuals to unite as co-members and jointly to obey the authoritative directives issued in the name of a polity *qua* juridical person. Indeed, Hobbes himself gave powerful articulation to the idea of the state as an artificial person, and although he portrayed sovereignty as the *object* of a private-property right, he did distinguish it in *kind* from property.

It is rather more difficult, by contrast, to see precisely how the social-contract tradition could feed into the second current; social-contract theory is set up primarily to explain the grounds of political membership, political obligations, and jurisdiction over persons—not territorial jurisdiction. It is true that John Locke did at least

---

[4] Pangalangan 2001.

[5] On the potential problems facing any such account, again see Brett 2011.

[6] See, e.g., Skinner 2002b: chapter 14.

implicitly furnish an account of a commonwealth's territorial rights. But he could do so only by supposing a kind of prepolitical, private dominion. Individuals in the state of nature acquire private dominion over land prior to the establishment of political society and independently of any social conventions by "mixing their labour" with it; a political society is formed and acquires territorial rights when individuals unite in a social contract by which they confer upon the commonwealth their rights of dominion—at least the jurisdictional incidents of such rights.[7] To explain territorial rights, in other words, Locke had to eschew the social-contract account of the origin of authority and jurisdiction: He had to assume that individuals acquire, independently of any social contract, private dominion not just in the sense of property or *ownership* of land, but also in the sense of *jurisdiction* over land (which they could then confer on the commonwealth). Locke's "solution" was of course wholly at odds with Hobbes's own philosophy. According to Hobbes, sovereign authority is presupposed by, and is not consequent to, private dominion over things; private dominion can arise only once sovereign power has already been constituted. On Hobbes's official account, jurisdiction is, in the first place, over persons, not over territory or things. It is grounded in a series of sovereignty-covenants by which individuals each give up their right to act on their own private judgment and agree instead to obey the commands of a common sovereign. There is no mention, in any of Hobbes's descriptions of sovereignty-covenants, of territory or territorial jurisdiction; for someone widely regarded as an ideological founder of the modern territorial state, Hobbes wrote surprisingly little about territory in any context at all.[8]

Yet, crucially, when readers turn to Hobbes's account of political obligation, territorial boundaries loom very large indeed. Hobbes's discussion of messengers, travelers, and residents seems to suggest that an individual's physical exit from the state's territory is sufficient to annul the obligation to obey his or her sovereign, and entry practically sufficient to establish it.[9] The question is how Hobbes was able to move from a social-contract account of political authority and obligation, with its emphasis on consent and hence personal jurisdiction, to such strongly territorial conclusions.

The answer, I argue, lies in two features of Hobbes's theory: first, the twofold character of his account of political obligation, which requires not just consent (a juridical relation) but also the sovereign's willingness and ability to protect the individual's life and its bare essentials (a partly physical relation); and second, the constitutive role of protective power in his account of tacit consent. The result in practice is very nearly the inverse of Hobbes's official, social-contract theory: Rather than beginning with consent, which then establishes political jurisdiction over persons, the sovereign

---

[7] For Locke on territorial rights, see Stilz 2009, Miller 2011a. For an exploration of a "Lockean" theory of territorial rights, see Nine 2008.

[8] See Baldwin 1992: 212. In a representative statement that, as we shall see, is also an exaggeration, Brett (2011: 212) goes so far as to say that in Hobbes "the silence about territory is almost total."

[9] E.g., *Leviathan* 21.24, 346/115: "whosoever entreth into anothers dominion, is Subject to all the Laws thereof."

begins with effective power over persons within a geographical space and over whom he claims jurisdiction, from which power the consent of persons, in a vast array of cases, is then inferred. We have here not quite an instance, but a prominent ancestor of the nonconsent theories that contemporary philosophers adorn with the deceptive rhetoric of consent, as well as an ancestor of more fully blown theories of intrinsically territorial jurisdiction and rights. The fact that, ultimately, the Hobbesian state and its jurisdictional authority are territorial only in a derivate and instrumental rather than foundational and intrinsic sense, however, suggests that it is a mistake to think that the modern ideology of the state univocally posits it as an intrinsically territorial entity. There are two traditions here: the Lockean one that, in grounding jurisdictional authority in private dominion over things, portrays the state as intrinsically territorial, and the Hobbesian one that, in deriving property rights from jurisdictional authority, does not.

1 Dominion vs. Sovereignty, Property vs. Jurisdiction

The birth of the ideology of state sovereignty has been associated with at least three transformations in the early-modern period: first, the disentangling of a private-law concept of property from a public-law concept of political jurisdiction (said to be conflated under feudalism);[10] second, the replacement of the feudal regime of overlapping political jurisdictions with an undivided, exclusive notion recovered from classical Roman law;[11] and third, the emergence of the state as a juridical person to whom sovereignty is attributed, a person distinct from both the rulers or government and the governed people.[12] Hobbes's role in these transformations, and his view of the relationship between private property and sovereign jurisdiction, are most precisely pinpointed in the light of the Roman and medieval background of his thought.

To have *property* in something is typically to have a set of relatively secure rights including the right to control, use, consume, transfer, and enjoy the fruits and income of the thing; by contrast, to have *jurisdictional authority* is to have a set of rights to make, adjudicate, and/or enforce the legal rules—including the legal rules governing property in things or by persons—within a particular domain (whether defined territorially or not).[13] The Romans recognized this conceptual distinction: Property was

---

[10] Gilmore 1941.

[11] Ruggie 1983, 1993, Lee 2012, (forthcoming).

[12] Skinner 2002b: chapter 14, 2002a: chapter 6.

[13] For an analysis of the standard incidents of property ownership, see Honoré 1961. For the conceptual distinction between property and jurisdictional authority, see Buchanan 2003, Nine 2008, Stilz 2009. I avoid describing property as an "absolute" right because in all legal systems, including the classical Roman one, property rights face certain restrictions and the possibility of being stripped. See Honoré for the general point and, in the case of limits in Roman law, Borkowski 1997: 160–162.

captured by Roman private-law terms such as *dominium* and *proprietas*, jurisdictional authority by public-law terms such as *imperium* and, to some extent, *jurisdictio*.[14] Thus, although, as the *Digest* made clear, it was deemed impossible to have private property in the sea, it was perfectly possible for the republic to claim political jurisdiction over it; moreover, the republic and its jurisdictional authority were not themselves viewed as the private property of any individuals or group (who could thereby dispose of it at their own discretion).[15]

In Roman private law, to have *dominium* over something was to have the full and exclusive rights of ownership to it, including the right to control, use, take proceeds from, and dispose; above all, the *dominus* (lord, master) was entitled to a legal proprietary remedy or *vindicatio* to secure and/or recover, if need be, his property against invasion. Some things (such as the sea, owned commonly by all people, or provincial lands, public roads, and the sea shore, owned publicly by the republic) could not be owned privately; and other things (such as sacred objects) could not be owned at all, whether in common, publicly, or privately; but both corporeal and noncorporeal things, including human beings and abstract things akin to legal rights (such as servitudes), could be owned privately. Under classical Roman law, *dominium* was undivided and exclusive: A thing could only have one (even if joint) *dominus*. Nonowners could have rights or servitudes to use another's property, such as a *usufructus* to use the thing and enjoy its fruits for some period of time, but these rights were sharply distinguished from *dominium*.[16] In Roman public law, by contrast, *imperium* referred, in its broadest sense, to the highest forms of public power (the right to give enforceable orders and commands), whereas *jurisdictio* referred to the magisterial power and activity of settling legal principles to administer justice in civil matters (*jus dicere*, to declare what the law is, to declare judgment and to give a legal remedy).[17]

By the feudal period in Europe, the conceptual distinction between property and jurisdictional authority had become considerably blurred. Even at the terminological level, the strictly private-law Roman term *dominium* had, by the twelfth century, come to be used for both property ownership and political jurisdictional authority.[18] This, of course, was the terminological legacy inherited by Hobbes's century, which is why Hobbes in *De cive*, in addition to using *dominium* to refer to property, could also

---

[14] See Berger 1953. The term *potestas* was used in both public-law and private-law contexts: In the former context, it referred to the power of a magistrate, in the latter to the power of a *paterfamilias* over the things and members of his household.

[15] Tuck 2003: 144, 147. There is some evidence from the *Digest*, however, that the republic was sometimes viewed as the public property of the Roman people.

[16] Borkowski 1997. The holder of usufructuary rights, for example, was obligated to return the property to its *dominus* in its original condition.

[17] *Imperium* was divided, moreover, into *imperium merum* (pure) and *imperium mixtum* (mixed). The former appears to have referred to full, coercive magisterial power in criminal matters, whereas the latter may have referred to the point where *imperium* and *jurisdictio* overlapped; that is, magisterial power in both criminal and civil matters (mixed because it was delegable from the magistrate to nonmagistrate). See Berger 1953, Gilmore 1941: 21–24, Lee (forthcoming).

[18] Coleman 1983.

use *dominium* and *imperium* interchangeably to refer to the authority of the supreme magistrate.[19] The terminological fluidity did not necessarily imply conceptual confusion: As J. H. Burns has argued, the two senses of *dominium* could be, and often were, marked by writers of the feudal period as distinct in principle. But the two senses of *dominium* were indeed conflated in practice: What came to be called, with the appropriation of Roman legal terminology, the *dominium* of the feudal lord in his land was not simply a property holding, but also involved a quasi-political, legal authority to administer justice within his domain—to settle disputes, exact penalties, and, indeed, even a nearly legislative power to establish rules of conduct.[20] Jurisdictional authority itself, moreover, frequently came to be seen not just as a *kind* of private property under feudalism, in the sense that property in land included jurisdictional authority over it, but also as an *object* of a private-property right, in the sense that it was securely held and heritable just as other objects of private property.[21]

There were, of course, important countercurrents in the medieval period,[22] and what they make clear is that if we want to see whether Hobbes thought of sovereignty as privately owned, we should above all ask about his views on royal succession. In France, as early as the first quarter of the fourteenth century, the conception of public office as something like the office holder's private property was challenged by the Franciscan monk François de Meyronnes (d. 1328) who, wanting to argue against women's right of royal succession, drew a sharp distinction between women's capacity to receive a private inheritance and their incapacity to inherit the *dignitas* of the crown.[23] The lawyer Jean de Terrevermeille (c. 1370–1430), in turn, sharply distinguished private *dominium* over goods such as a dwelling house from the monarch's public *dominium* over his realm—where private dominion can, but royal dominion cannot, be held *patrimonialiter*. The key difference was, again, that in patrimonial possessions succession is by hereditary right, and the heir is free to sell or alienate his inheritance as he sees fit, whereas the successor to the crown is not an "heir" at all: Although the first-born son normally succeeds, the king has no say in the succession; neither he nor his successor can dispose of the realm via bequest as he sees fit.[24]

---

[19] See, e.g., *Philosophical Rudiments* 5.11, 89/134. *De Cive*'s contemporary translator—Charles Cotton, according to Malcolm (2002)—also frequently translated Hobbes's *imperium* as "dominion."

[20] Burns 1992: chapter 2.

[21] Bloch 1938. See, e.g., Bloch's discussion of how the office itself came to be called a fief or benefit (*beneficium*) (p. 275).

[22] As Maiolo (2007) argues, the patrimonial theory of political authority was only one theory among others.

[23] A string of fourteenth-century commentators followed suit: In 1371, the jurist Raoul de Presles (1316–1382) argued that kingship is not strictly hereditary like a private patrimony but is a *dignité* "touching on the administration of the public thing," and so not heritable by women. The philosopher Nicole Oresme (c. 1320–1382) drew the same anti-female conclusion, distinguishing between "pure succession" to the king's private patrimony, on the one hand, and succession to the *dignité royale*, on the other—the latter requiring the successor not only to be of proper lineage, but also to have the qualifications appropriate for royal office. See Krynen 1993: 127–130.

[24] Burns 1992: 44–45.

Yet, despite these important countercurrents, the view of jurisdictional authority as a kind and/or object of private-property rights extended well into the late-medieval and early-modern period in Europe. It is implicitly found, among other places, in the account of public dominion given by the English lawyer John Fortescue (c. 1394–c. 1476). Fortescue famously distinguished between *dominium politicum* and *dominium regale*: In a political dominion, which originates in consent, the ruler or rulers govern according to laws established by citizens; in a royal dominion, which originates in force, the ruler governs according to laws established by himself. Moreover, in a *dominium regale*, the king possesses the realm in hereditary right: The kingdom is the king's *dominium reale*—quite literally his real property—and both the kingdom and the public office of kingship are properly inherited in the same way that the king's private patrimony is.[25] And, moving beyond theory to practice, in fifteenth- and sixteenth-century France, public office itself was often open for purchase (despite attempts to outlaw the practice in some cases), and in 1604 ownership of office became heritable as well.[26]

Under feudalism, moreover, *dominium* came to be seen as multiple and overlapping. Although the Romans had insisted that a thing could only have one *dominus*, by the twelfth century, *dominium* was regarded as divisible: A lord's vassal or subtenant was not merely deemed to have usufructuary rights, but rather a kind of *dominium—dominium utile*—in the land, even while the overlord had *dominium directum* in it.[27] A similar pattern of overlapping right was imputed to jurisdictional authority. In the late twelfth-century dispute attributed to Lothair and Azo, and canonized in the medieval study of law, Lothair had asserted that *imperium merum* is held only by the supreme magistrate—the Holy Roman Emperor—whereas Azo had asserted that it is also held by lesser magistrates with the right of the sword. That Azo's view reigned supreme among medieval jurists reflects the practical reality of overlapping jurisdictional authorities under feudalism—not just a mix of civil and ecclesiastical, but also of local, regional, countrywide, and even universal authorities, not to mention multiple personal fealties. Just as vassals held against their lord a kind of *dominium* in the land—which could not be extinguished at the lord's discretion—lords and lesser magistrates in a prince's realm also held against their prince a kind of dominion in their estate and/or public office—of which they could not be stripped by their prince.[28] This is in part why aristocrats could inherit public office: It was part of their patrimony. The supreme magistrate was not the only proprietary owner of public office or jurisdictional authority.

If *imperium* or jurisdictional authority could be an object of proprietary ownership, the owner of jurisdictional authority was typically deemed to be the individual office holder himself: Kingship was owned by the king, lordship by the lord, and so on. This

---

[25] Chrimes 1936: 9–15, 309–312; Burns 1985: 780; 1992: 60–61. Similarly, the Scottish philosopher John Mair (1467–1550) portrayed a monarch's *dominium* over his kingdom as differing only in degree, not kind, from a private individual's *dominium* over his property (Burns 1985: 23).

[26] Mousnier 1971, Giesey 1977.

[27] Burns 1992: 18.

[28] Gilmore 1941: chapter 1.

contrasts with the older, Roman idea of the *respublica* and its offices as a public thing incapable of being owned by any individual. Again, rival ideas of public office still had currency in the medieval period: Even Fortescue recognized the possibility of a republican regime—a *dominium politicum*—in which the jurisdictional authority exercised by magistrates ultimately resides with the citizens.[29] What did not register in the medieval period, however, was the idea that jurisdictional authority belongs neither to rulers nor to those whom they rule, but to the distinct juridical person of the state.

All of this, according to some of the most prominent histories on offer, is supposed to have changed with the early-modern theories of absolute sovereignty culminating in Hobbes: (1) public-law and private-law concepts are supposed to have been disentangled, so that sovereignty was neither a kind nor an object of private property; (2) overlapping jurisdictional authorities were replaced by an indivisible, centrally unified notion of sovereignty; (3) and sovereignty, rather than being the property of any particular individual or group, is supposed to have become the public property of the state itself *qua* juridical person.[30] In fact, I argue, although Hobbes did indeed ultimately portray sovereign jurisdictional authority as different in *kind* from property, sovereignty as unified and indivisible, and the state as a distinct juridical person, he nevertheless continued to view jurisdictional authority as the *object* of the sovereign's (not the state's) proprietary right.

It is true that much of what Hobbes wrote may suggest that he even thought of sovereignty as a kind of property right in persons and things, appearing to conflate jurisdictional authority with ownership. In the *Elements* and *De cive*, he asserted that a "despotical" king acquires "property or dominion, over the person" of his subjects such that he may say "that he is *his*."[31] By the time he wrote *Leviathan*, however, Hobbes's language had evolved: The equivalent passages pair political "Dominion" with "Soveraignty" rather than with property, drop the proprietary language about subjects, and explicitly contrast subjects to slaves.[32] It is also true that Hobbes explicitly asserted, in all three political works, that a subject's property rights are only against other subjects, never against the sovereign[33]—which might suggest that the sovereign's "dominion" in the realm comprises a property right to all things in it. Hobbes's point here, however, across his three political works, was that sovereignty intrinsically comprises *absolute* jurisdictional authority and that sovereign power is the *precondition* for property rights

---

[29] In the early thirteenth century, Azo had argued that the people considered as a corporate entity (*universitas*) possess—both originally and perpetually—the power to make laws: rulers, including the emperor, are mere *rectores* to whom authority is lent, not donated, and the people retain the right to recall their power if their rulers fail in their duties of office (Skinner 2002b: 13–17). This thought was powerfully reiterated in the early-modern period, against established royalist doctrine, by the monarchomachs (Lee 2008).

[30] See citations in notes 10–12.

[31] *Elements of Law* 22.1; 22.4, 216–127; cf. *Philosophical Rudiments* 8.5,119.

[32] *Leviathan* 20.2, 306/102; 20.10, 312/103–104.

[33] *Elements of Law* 24.2, 137; 27.8, 168; *Philosophical Rudiments* 6.15, 100–101; 8.5, 119; *Leviathan* 24.7, 390/128; 29.10, 504/169–170.

(i.e., that there are no prepolitical property rights constraining the sovereign's jurisdictional authority). Indeed, the distinction between jurisdictional authority and property comes out rather starkly in Hobbes's parallel assertion that a subject may sue the sovereign in a court of law to recover his property—which, if the subject could literally have no property rights against the sovereign, would have been impossible:

> If a Subject have a controversie with his Soveraigne, of debt, or of right of possession of lands or goods, or concerning any service required at his hands, or concerning any penalty corporall, or pecuniary, grounded on a precedent Law; he hath the same Liberty to sue for his right, as if it were against a Subject; and before such Judges, as are appointed by the Soveraign. For <u>seeing the Soveraign demandeth by force of a former Law</u>, and not by vertue of his Power; he declareth thereby, that he requireth no more, than shall appear to be due by that Law. The sute therefore is not contrary to the will of the Soveraign; and consequently the Subject hath the Liberty to demand the hearing of his Cause; and sentence, according to that Law. But if he demand, or take any thing <u>by pretence of his Power</u>; there lyeth, in that case, no action of Law: for all that is done by him in Vertue of his Power, is done by the Authority of every subject, and consequently, he that brings an action against the Soveraign, brings it against himselfe.[34]

There is no property, Hobbes claimed, in a pure state of nature prior to covenants. "*Propriety* is an effect of Common-wealth . . . the act onely of the Soveraign; and consisteth in the Lawes."[35] Since it is via *laws* that the sovereign, in the exercise of his jurisdictional authority, establishes rights of property, he may exercise his legislative authority in such a way as to grant his subjects property rights to things—rights that they may legally hold against him. Hobbes's real point was thus to deny that subjects could have "absolute" property rights against their sovereign,[36] and this in two senses. First, since the sovereign's authority is absolute, he is above the law;[37] that is, his jurisdictional authority is not confined to legislative authority: He may "take any thing by pretence of his Power," even if it is not his property, and still act according to his sovereign jurisdictional "Authority." Second, the sovereign could, even in virtue of his specifically *legislative* authority (by which property rights are assigned), simply change the law: His jurisdictional authority allows him to legislate anything to be, as

---

[34] *Leviathan* 21.19, 342/113, emphasis added. See also *Philosophical Rudiments* 6.15, 100–101 (which discusses the possibility of an action of law against the sovereign in the context of having asserted that citizens have no property right against the sovereign) and 12.4, 149.

[35] *Leviathan* 24.5, 388/128. It is true that Hobbes argued that, prior to the establishment of a full-fledged commonwealth, a mother typically has "Dominion" over her offspring, unless she has contracted away such dominion to the father (*Leviathan* 20.4–5, 308–310/102–103). But the proprietary right in one's children arises because a family is a proto-commonwealth: It is like "a little Monarchy," save for the fact that it may yet be too small in numbers to offer its members security against external attack (*Leviathan* 20.15, 314/105).

[36] Hobbes provided this more precise formulation at *Leviathan* 29.10: 504/169, denying "*That every private man has an absolute Propriety in his Goods; such, as excludeth the Right of the Soveraign Power*."

[37] *Leviathan* 29.9, 504/169.

far as his subjects are concerned, his own property. What the subject's property hold-ing does not include, in other words, is a relatively secure immunity against expro-priation by the sovereign.[38] Thus, although Hobbes did indeed fuse the vocabulary of property and jurisdictional authority, the two were distinct for him conceptually: He was using the language of property/dominion to express a point about the sovereign's absolute jurisdictional authority over property rights. The case of Hobbes therefore shows us something very important about the structural relation between jurisdic-tional authority and property: The jurisdictional authority to regulate property rights in things may indeed be used to establish property in things, but an authority's prop-erty in things remains a contingent effect, not intrinsic part, of his or her jurisdic-tional authority.[39]

Hobbes did, however, hold that jurisdictional authority could be the *object* of a natu-ral person's proprietary rights. It is true that Hobbes denied that magistrates in general could have an absolute, private-property right in public office. Acknowledging that "in these parts of *Europe*, it hath been taken for a Right of certain persons, to have place in the highest Councell of State by Inheritance," Hobbes argued that this aristocratic presumption was an artifact of the history of ancient German conquests, "wherein many absolute Lords joining together to conquer other Nations, would not enter in to the Confederacy, without such Priviledges." In reality, however, considered as rights against the sovereign, such privileges are "inconsistent with the Sovereign Power" and are held only conditionally "by the favour of the Sovereign," so that aristocrats cannot, once sovereign power has been established, continue "contending for them as their Right."[40] In sum, "if the Propriety of Subjects, exclude not the Right of the Sovereign Representative to their Goods; muche lesse [does it exclude his right] to their offices of Judicature, or Execution."[41]

---

[38] Honoré (1961: 119), noting that a "right to security" is one of the standard incidents of ownership, also notes that, on the one hand, security is "consistent with the existence of a power to expropriate or divest in the state," while, on the other hand, "a general power to expropriate . . . would be fatal to the institution of ownership." The final point helps to make sense of Hobbes's claim that subjects do not have property rights against the sovereign: The Hobbesian sovereign does have a general power to expropriate.

[39] This is why it is somewhat misleading when, under the rubric of territorial rights, contemporary political philosophers include, in addition to territorial jurisdiction, the right to control and use the resources within the territory and the right to regulate the movement of persons and things across territorial boundaries (Stilz 2011, Miller 2011b)—as if territorial jurisdiction is of the same order as the other two kinds of rights. Both the state's putative resource rights (which are essentially property rights) and rights of border control are parasitic on its putative jurisdictional authority: The state may indeed exercise its jurisdictional authority so as to grant itself property rights over the resources in its territory, but that is a contingent outcome. The state may, alternatively, grant another entity resource rights in its territory—which does not, of course, amount to transferring territorial jurisdiction. It is possible to treat jurisdiction itself as an object of property rights too, so that the holder of jurisdictional authority could sell it, but transferring territorial jurisdiction remains conceptually distinct from transferring property in land.

[40] *Leviathan* 30.25, 546–548/184.

[41] *Leviathan* 29.11, 504/170.

Yet if early-modern authoritarian writers such as Hobbes directly attacked the patrimonial claims of magistrates who treated their offices as their private property, these writers conspicuously exempted one office from their attack: the office of *summum imperium* or sovereignty itself. Their point, in other words, was not to deny that public office could be the object of private-property rights per se, but to centralize the ownership of *imperium* in the exclusive hands of the sovereign. Although feudal theories did conceive of public office as its holder's property, their conception of property permitted diffuse, multiple, and overlapping ownership. By contrast, Alciato (1492–1550) starkly asserted—indeed, he was perhaps the first to do so—that the office of kingship is the private property of the king in the full and exclusive sense of ownership found in classical Roman law. He did this by first distinguishing between two senses of "having" or holding *imperium*: having a veritable *right in* the power of *imperium*, as one's property, and having the mere right to administer, exercise, or *use* that power as a kind of usufructuary or even merely usuary right. He then proceeded to rehabilitate Lothair, against the dominant verdict of medieval jurists, by arguing that only the prince could have a private proprietary right in his *imperium merum*; lesser magistrates only have the exercise of *imperium merum*, not ownership of it (and so could not redelegate it, as its owner could). Charles Dumoulin (1500–1566) applied Alciato's distinction to French law, similarly arguing that only the king rightly has an absolute proprietary title in jurisdictional authority, while lesser magistrates merely have a right of use.[42]

Hobbes, like Grotius before him, transparently followed this tradition established by Alciato: the tradition that, rather than abandoning the idea of property in one's office, intensified it by rehabilitating the Roman notion of full and exclusive property, distinguishing a property right in *imperium* from its exercise or use, and monopolizing the ownership of *imperium* in the hands of a supreme magistrate. Not surprisingly, Hobbes's view emerges most starkly in his discussion of succession: The true sovereign has the right to determine his own successor—indeed, the right to transfer sovereign power whenever and to whomever he wishes—precisely in virtue of his proprietary right in the sovereign power. As he put it in the *Elements of Law*, because the sovereign monarch "hath the dominion in his own right, he may dispose thereof at his own will."[43] If, by contrast, a democratic assembly of the people retains the right to choose a monarch's successor—and to do so effectively it must retain the power to assemble itself independently of the monarch's will—then the people is the true sovereign, and the *summum imperium*, as Hobbes put it in *De cive*, remains the people's *dominium*: The nominal monarch only has *usus* or *exercitium* of sovereign power as *usufructuarius*. He repeated the point in *Leviathan*: In contrast to true, unlimited monarchs,

[42] Gilmore 1941: 50–69. See Lee (forthcoming) for Bodin's attack on Alciato's rehabilitation of Lothair and its implication that lesser magistrates to whom *imperium* had been delegated could not redelegate it.

[43] *Elements of Law* 23.11, 134. A true sovereign "is at liberty to dispose as well of the succession, as of the possession." *Elements of Law* 21.9, 121. Cf. *Philosophical Rudiments* 7.15, 113; *Leviathan* 19.14–23, 298–304/99–101.

"Elective Kings and Princes have not the Soveraign Power in propriety, but in use only."[44] Thus, on the one hand, sovereignty could take one of three forms: monarchy, where the sovereign is one individual; aristocracy, where the sovereign is an assembly governed by majority rule, but in which only some subjects have the right to participate; or democracy, where the sovereign is an assembly governed by majority rule and open to all subjects.[45] On the other hand, whatever form sovereignty takes, sovereign power may either be exercised directly by the sovereign, in which case the sovereign and the administration or government are the same, or be lent to public officers to exercise or administer, in which case sovereign and administration or government are distinct. The crucial point in the latter case is that the sovereign reserves the right to *recall* the sovereign power, because it remains his (or her or its) property. Hobbes was perfectly clear about the potentially unwelcome implications of his proprietary view, conceding that since a true sovereign owns the sovereign power by a proprietary right, and since it is therefore "lawfull for a Monarch to dispose of the Succession by words of Contract, or Testament," a sovereign may (even while alive) "sell, or give his Right of governing to a stranger . . . not used to live under the same government, nor speaking the same language."[46]

Hobbes thus repeatedly claimed, throughout all three of his political works, that it is the sovereign who owns the sovereign power.[47] The sovereign is the supreme *dominus* (a term Hobbes explicitly used in his Latin treatise as a title for the sovereign[48]) both in the political sense of having supreme jurisdictional authority and in the proprietary sense of owning that authority. Yet Quentin Skinner has argued that one of Hobbes's great contributions to the modern ideology of state sovereignty is that, in *Leviathan*, he finally came to attribute the ownership of sovereignty to the person of the state itself rather than to "the official person of the sovereign."[49] In fact, Hobbes did no such thing. Skinner is, of course, quite right that Hobbes conceived of the state as an "artificial person" with a juridical "personality." With a new doctrine of "authorization" and "representation" in hand, moreover, Hobbes in *Leviathan* depicted the commonwealth as constituted via a series of covenants in which a multitude of previously unobligated individuals each promise to do two things: (a) give up their right of nature to do whatever they individually judge necessary to preserve themselves and instead obey the commands of a sovereign individual or assembly and (b) "authorize" the sovereign to "represent" them as a unified body and as individual members of that

---

[44] *Philosophical Rudiments* 7.15–16, 113–115/156; *Leviathan* 19.18, 300/100. Cf. *Elements of Law* 21.9, 121–122.

[45] *Elements of Law* 20.3, 110–111; *Philosophical Rudiments* 7.1, 106–117; *Leviathan* 19.1, 284/94.

[46] *Leviathan* 19.23, 304/101. Cf. *Philosophical Rudiments* 9.13, 127/169: "what a man may transferre on another by Testament, that by the same Right may he yet living, give, or sell away; To whomsoever therefore he shall make over the *summum imperium*, whether by gift, or sale, it is rightly made."

[47] In *De cive*, Hobbes frequently used the expression *qui habet imperium summum* as a Latin equivalent for "the sovereign."

[48] E.g. *Philosophical Rudiments* 5.12, 90/135.

[49] Skinner 2002b: 402–404. Elsewhere, Skinner (2002a: 200) likewise asserts that Hobbes "is always careful to insist . . . that sovereigns are not the proprietors of their sovereignty."

body.[50] This unified corporate body is what Hobbes equivalently called the "people," "state," or "Common-wealth"—although in the case of a democracy he also used the term "people" in a second, more active sense, to denote the *sovereign* assembly (i.e., the assembled people who represents the "people" in the first, more passive sense equivalent to the "state").[51] (Hobbes was aware that the term "people" was also used by some to denote an array of individuals without corporate unity, but for Hobbes such an array is, strictly speaking, a mere "multitude," not truly a people.[52])

Although the represented people/state is not itself the sovereign, it is nevertheless an artificial person and, as such, has a juridical personality capable of owning things in law.[53] It may therefore seem that because, according to the doctrine of *Leviathan*, the sovereign "representeth" or, as Hobbes also put it, "beareth the Person of the people"[54] or state, the *dominus* of sovereign power must be the person of the state itself, and that the sovereign has or possesses the sovereign power merely in the sense of having a usufructuary right to exercise it (on behalf of the people/state whom the sovereign represents).[55] This follows naturally from a commonsensical way of thinking about the represented/representer relation, but the conclusion is precisely the one that Hobbes was keen to avoid. He avoided it by reversing the commonsense view that the represented is ontologically prior to its representer. Beginning with the premise that the people/state *qua* corporate body does not exist by nature, he argued that it paradoxically comes into existence only once its members have a common "Representer."[56] And because the people/state does not come into being until the sovereign representer is authorized to represent it, it is itself incapable of authorizing its representer to represent it: It is not the people/state collectively, but its members each individually who authorize the sovereign to represent the state, "Every man giving their common Representer, Authority from himselfe in particular." As a consequence, subjects are each *individually*

---

[50] For the *Leviathan*'s new doctrine of authorization and representation, see Chapter 14 of this volume. For discussion, see Skinner 2005. The locutions in *Leviathan* 19.1, 284/94 ("representative of all and everyone of the Multitude") and *Leviathan* 19.3, 286/95 ("represent them every one" and "every man to have his person represented") speak against Runciman's (2009) claim that the sovereign represents the people collectively only and not also individually. Hobbes's statement that the sovereign "representeth two Persons, . . . one Naturall, and another Politique" (*Leviathan* 23.2, 376/123) would speak against my reading only if "*only* two persons" were implied, but that is ruled out by Hobbes's contention that the sovereign represents God, too (*Leviathan* 45.17, 1032/359).

[51] See also *De cive*, where Hobbes declared that in a monarchy "the King is the People." *Philosophical Rudiments* 12.8, 151.

[52] On the significance for Hobbes of the distinction between an array of individuals and a united, corporate body, see Tuck 2006.

[53] Hobbes had already made this last point clear in *Philosophical Rudiments* 5.9, 89. See also the characterization of the commonwealth as a "person in law" in *Elements of Law* 27.7. 167. *Leviathan* 16.11, 248/82 notes that even an imaginary entity represented by fiction may have "Possessions, and other Goods, and Rights" in law.

[54] *Leviathan* 19.4, 288/95.

[55] This is the conclusion that Lee (2012) has felt forced to concede in his work in progress.

[56] *Leviathan* 16.13, 248/82.

the "Authors" of, and so responsible for and obligated by, "all the actions the Representer doth."[57]

Yet the sovereign's subjects clearly do not own the sovereign's jurisdictional *authority* in any proprietary sense: Jurisdictional right over themselves is precisely what they each bestow on the sovereign consequent to their covenant to obey the sovereign and authorize his actions. They own this authority neither individually, nor—and this was the conclusion that Hobbes was most keen to draw—collectively as a people/state.[58] The jurisdictional authority of the sovereign, Hobbes insisted, is the *precondition* of the people/state's existence and hence its juridical capacity to own things; that authority itself is not the *object* of the state's ownership rights. To put this more starkly: For Hobbes, the sovereign constitutes, is prior to, and is above the state and its laws; the state, by contrast, is constituted by, consequent to, and subject to the sovereign. This is precisely why the people/state, even should its members be unanimous in their desire, cannot justly reclaim sovereignty from their sovereign representative: "they have also every man given the Soveraignty to him that beareth their Person; and therefore if they depose him, they take from him that which <u>is his own</u>."[59] The represented people cannot justly reclaim sovereignty because the people does not have any proprietary right in sovereignty. Concomitantly, even if (unlike how Hobbes himself used the term) the state is thought of as comprising the legally constituted institutions of public office, sovereignty is not owned by the office of the sovereign but by the sovereign himself: The sovereign is master of the law, not vice versa. The sovereign owns sovereignty in the precise sense that he can control it, use it, lend its use or exercise to others, and even sell or transfer it as he sees fit. The people, in the passive sense that is equivalent to the state, can itself do no such thing.[60] Ultimately, Hobbes's theory is not of state sovereignty but—depending on the form—of royal, aristocratic, or popular sovereignty.[61] The sovereign representer is *dominus*: He owns sovereignty, whereas other

---

[57] *Leviathan* 16.14, 250/82. Hobbes used the vocabulary of ownership to describe the relation between an author and its representer (the author "owns" its representer's actions), but here he was using this vocabulary in an extended, nonproprietary sense that implies being responsible for (as in the expression "owning up to"). This "responsibility" sense of ownership is, of course, different from the proprietary sense at stake in my discussion (e.g., the author who "owns" his representer's actions, in the responsibility sense, cannot sell those actions). On Hobbes's account of authorization and representation, see Runciman 2000, Abizadeh 2013.

[58] Again, "people" here is to be understood in the first, more passive sense specified earlier, as the person represented, rather than—as can also occur in a democracy—as the person of the sovereign representative assembly. In a democracy, the people in the second, more active sense of the term (i.e., the democratic assembly whose will is governed by majority rule and who represents the people/state) is precisely who "owns" sovereignty.

[59] *Leviathan* 18.3, 264/89, emphasis added. Hobbes indicated on numerous occasions that the state's capacity to act (and, by extension, to own things) is parasitic on the sovereign's capacity to do so. See, e.g., *Leviathan* 26.5, 416/137–138.

[60] It is true that the office of the sovereign representative imposes on him, according to Hobbes, a series of "duties" of office (*Leviathan* 30). But these natural duties merely comprise the instrumentally and constitutively necessary conditions for maintaining sovereign power itself.

[61] Skinner's (2002b: 402–404) cited textual evidence does not support his thesis. Although he paraphrases Hobbes as saying that the state rather than the sovereign is "the person possessed of sovereign power," at no point is he able to quote Hobbes himself using such language (to say, for

magistrates merely administer it.[62] Or, more precisely, even if a lesser magistrate does have private-property rights in his office, he has them only at the pleasure of his sovereign.

2 TERRITORIALITY AND MEMBERSHIP

According to the modern ideology of the sovereign territorial state, (1) sovereignty is possessed by the state itself, and (2) sovereign jurisdiction is not only over members but also directly over a particular territory—meaning that the state's territorial rights are held *in rem* against *all* persons. We have seen that the first thesis was not embraced by Hobbes; the question is how he relates to the second. If supreme jurisdictional authority is owned by the sovereign, then what is the nature of that authority? What territorial rights does a sovereign have against foreigners—including other sovereigns or states? And what are the membership status and the obligations of travelers or persons who, like Hobbes himself in the 1640s, live abroad in the territory of a foreign sovereign?

The sovereignty-covenants by which subjects obligate themselves to obey very clearly establish the sovereign's *personal* jurisdiction over them. Hobbes depicted two ways in which sovereign power over persons could be established: Individuals could "agree amongst themselves, to submit to some Man, or Assembly of men, voluntarily, on confidence to be protected by him against all others," in which case each subject covenants with every other, and the sovereign is not party to any of the covenants; or individuals could "submit themselves" to one who might otherwise destroy or enslave them, promising obedience in return for "giving them their lives," in which case subjects covenant directly with the sovereign. Sovereignty established in the first way is "Politicall" or "by *Institution*," its genesis motivated by individuals' "fear of one another"; sovereignty

---

instance, that the state—or commonwealth or people, for that matter—"owns," "possesses," or has "dominion" in sovereignty, language that Hobbes *did* use for the sovereign). The only passage that Skinner cites as evidence for his thesis that "the true legislator is the state or commonwealth itself" rather than the sovereign is *Leviathan* 26.5, 416/137. But the paragraph in question pulls in the opposite direction: It begins, first, with the claim that "The Legislator in all Common-wealths, is only the Soveraign"; it pauses, second, to note that, in one sense, "the Common-wealth is the Legislator"; but, third, noting that since "the Common-wealth is no Person, nor has capacity to doe any thing, but by the Representative," it concludes that "therefore the Soveraign is the sole Legislator." Skinner distorts the passage's message by quoting the third point first and quoting the second point—the formulation Hobbes was provisionally considering—last, as if it were Hobbes's final analysis. My own reading is that Hobbes was not so much trying to decide between two opposing assertions (that the commonwealth is legislator versus the sovereign is legislator) as trying to reconcile the two formulations: In reality, the sovereign is the true and "sole Legislator," but the commonwealth can be said to legislate as well, albeit only in the secondary sense that the sovereign legislates in its name.

[62] *Leviathan* 19.9, 292/97, 23.2, 376/123–124. In *Leviathan* 23.2, 376/123, Hobbes characterized public ministers as representing "the Person of the Common-wealth." But in *Leviathan* 23.12, 382/126, he wrote that they "represent their Soveraign in that office," and in *Leviathan* 29.11, 504/170, he characterized officers of "Judicature, or Execution" as representing "the Soveraign himselfe." Cf. *Leviathan* 23.11, 382/126.

established in the second way is "by Naturall force" or "by *Acquisition*," its genesis motivated by fear of the one to whom they submit.[63] Hobbes divided sovereignty by acquisition, in turn, between "PATERNALL," where the "right of Dominion" is initially acquired over one's family, and "DESPOTICALL," where it is acquired over those whom one has conquered in war.[64]

The relation between a commonwealth's genesis (instituted vs. acquired) and form (monarchy, aristocracy, or democracy) is somewhat complicated in Hobbes. Fortescue, we have seen, had fused together genesis and form in his distinction between *dominium politicum* and *dominium regale*. In the *Elements* and *De cive*, Hobbes echoed this tradition, tightly linking political or instituted commonwealths to democracy and natural or acquired commonwealths to monarchy. Instituted commonwealths, he explicitly asserted in both works, must always begin as a democracy. This is, in part, because forming a commonwealth by institution requires many individuals first to *assemble* together in order to constitute themselves as a commonwealth.[65] Hobbes began by suggesting, in chapter 20 of the *Elements*, that *in principle* it is conceivable that such an array of individuals could assemble and directly establish an aristocracy or monarchy by unanimously consenting to be ruled by "some certain number of men by them determined and named" or, alternatively, by a single named individual.[66] But he then went on in chapter 21 to argue that this in-principle possibility is a practical impossibility: Unanimity on such particulars cannot be expected in a "great multitude of men," so that, in order to settle on any aristocrats or monarch in particular, they "must" first commit themselves to a majority-rule decision-making procedure—which commitment, Hobbes claimed, already constitutes the multitude as a democratic sovereign assembly.[67]

In the *Elements*, Hobbes asserted that each of the assembled individuals must, as the multitude's first order of business, *expressly* consent to a decision rule.[68] This assertion, of course, left him open to the objection that, in a "great multitude of men," express, unanimous agreement on a particular decision rule might be as practically unfeasible as unanimity on particular individuals. In *De cive*, he closed up this potential gap by subtly amending his argument for why all regimes must first pass through a democracy. The reason, he argued in his Latin treatise, is that the very act of assembling to form a commonwealth already *tacitly* commits each to abide by majority rule, which ipso facto constitutes the assembly as a democratic sovereign:

> Those who met together (*coïerunt*) with intention to erect a City, were almost in the very act of meeting (*coïerunt*) a Democraty; for in that they willingly met, they are

---

[63] *Leviathan* 17.15, 262/88; 18.4, 266/89; 20.1–2, 306/101–102. Hobbes used the equivalent language in *De cive*, referring to a *civitas* that is "*politicum*" or "*institutivum*" versus one that is "*naturali*" or "*Acquisita*." *Philosophical Rudiments* 5.12, 90/135; 8.1, 117/160. See also *Elements of Law* 19.11, 108.

[64] *Leviathan* 20.4, 308/102; 20.10–11, 312/103–104. Cf. *Elements of Law* 19.11, 108; *Philosophical Rudiments* 5.12, 90/135; 8.1, 117/160; 9.1, 121–122/164.

[65] See, e.g., Hobbes's reference to "many men assembled together" (*Elements of Law* 20.1, 107).

[66] *Elements of Law* 20.3, 110.

[67] *Elements of Law* 21.1, 118–119.

[68] *Elements of Law* 20.3, 110.

suppos'd oblig'd (*intelliguntur obligati*) to the observation of what shall be determin'd by the major part: which, while that *conuentus* lasts, or is adjourn'd to some certain dayes, and places, is a clear Democraty; for that *conuentus*, whose will is the will of the Citizens, hath the *summum imperium*.[69]

The reason that assembling to form a commonwealth is itself implicitly to consent to abide by majority rule and, therefore, to constitute a sovereign democratic assembly is that, otherwise, given practical realities, the intention to form a commonwealth would be in vain.[70] The conclusion in both works is therefore the same: In an instituted commonwealth, a monarch or aristocratic assembly can become sovereign only after an already-constituted democratic sovereign assembly transfers its sovereignty to a monarch or aristocratic assembly by majority vote.[71]

With respect to acquired commonwealths, by contrast, in the *Elements* and *De cive* Hobbes portrayed the paternal or "patrimonial" kind as originating in dominion over one's family, which is itself the start of a "little kingdom" that gradually, through procreation and acquiring servants by conquest, becomes a genuine (monarchical) commonwealth—a "REGNVM PATRIMONIALE."[72] Only a purely despotic commonwealth is left, in these two works, with no explicit relation to one of the three forms, although Hobbes's language strongly implies that the despotic *dominus* is also a single man.[73] Indeed, in the *Elements* and *De cive*, Hobbes suggested that even the nonmonarchical forms that arise by institution ultimately originate in the attempt to reconstitute a commonwealth out of the ashes of a kingdom destroyed by civil war.[74]

In *Leviathan*, however, although Hobbes implicitly persisted in the view that instituted commonwealths must begin as democracies, he explicitly granted that acquired commonwealths may begin in any form. It is true that it might even seem that Hobbes

---

[69] *Philosophical Rudiments* 7.5, 109/152.

[70] "[T]hat single Persons doe contract each with other may be inferred from hence, that in vain sure would the City have been constituted, if the Citizens had been engaged by no contracts to doe, or omit what the City should command . . . it followes, that they must be made between single Citizens, namely that each man contract to submit his will to the will of the major part." *Philosophical Rudiments* 7.7, 110.

[71] *Elements of Law* 21.1, 6, 9: 119–121; *Philosophical Rudiments* 7.8: 110; 7.11: 111.

[72] *Elements of Law* 12.1, 126; *Philosophical Rudiments* 8.1, 117; 9.10: 126/168.

[73] Whereas, when describing an instituted commonwealth, Hobbes referred to the sovereign as "some man, or Councel of Men," he invariably referred to a paternal sovereign as a single *dominus* (*Philosophical Rudiments* 8, 117–121). Cf. the discussion in *Elements of Law* 22, 126–129, which describes a commonwealth "by acquisition" as a "kingdom" and invariably refers to the master as "one man." Hobbes did refer to "paternal, and despotic" dominion in *Elements of Law* 19.11: 108, but, in that work, he did not clearly distinguish paternal/patrimonial from despotic commonwealths (e.g., chapter 22).

[74] All "other governments (*regimina*) were compacted (*conglutinata*) by the artifice of men (*artificio hominum*) out of the ashes of Monarchy, after it had been ruined with seditions." *Philosophical Rudiments* 10.3: 131/172. The passage does not explicitly say that Hobbes was referring to instituted commonwealths, but the inference is warranted by the reference to *artificio hominum*, which contrasts with *civitate naturali* or *acquisita*, and in light of the fact that no passage in *De Cive* entertains the possibility of an acquired democracy or aristocracy. Cf. the equivalent passage in *Elements of Law* 24.3: 138.

abandoned his thesis that instituted commonwealths must begin as democracies: The explicit claim, found in the earlier works, that instituted aristocracies and monarchies must first pass through a democracy is no longer found in *Leviathan*,[75] and Hobbes's initial formulation of institutive sovereignty-covenants in chapter 17 suggests that persons might each *individually* (rather than collectively, as an already-constituted democratic assembly) authorize a particular man as their sovereign, "as if every man should say to every man, *I Authorise and give up my Right of Governing my selfe, to this Man, or to this Assembly of men.*"[76] A number of commentators have concluded that Hobbes did change his mind about the genesis of institutive commonwealths—such that a monarch could be unanimously and directly authorized by each individual—and some have explained the purported change as the natural outcome of his new doctrine of authorization and representation.[77]

The *Leviathan's* apparent shift is merely apparent, however. The ostensible positive textual evidence from chapter 17 merely restates the position Hobbes had already advanced in the *Elements*: It is in principle conceivable that a multitude could unanimously and directly consent to a particular monarch or aristocratic assembly. But, once again, as Hobbes's fuller treatment in chapter 18 of *Leviathan* makes clear, in practice this is not a feasible way to institute a commonwealth. Hobbes opened chapter 18 with the claim that a commonwealth by institution is established as soon as the members of a multitude have covenanted to abide by majority rule:

> A *Common-wealth* is said to be *Instituted*, when a *Multitude* of men do Agree, and *Covenant, every one, with every one*, that to whatsoever *Man*, or *Assembly Of Men*, <u>shall be given by the major part</u>, the *Right* to *Present* the Person of them all, (that is to say, to be their *Representative*;) every one, as well he that *Voted for it*, as he that *Voted against it*, shall *Authorise* all the Actions and Judgements, of that Man, or Assembly of men.[78]

And, in the very next paragraph, Hobbes once again depicted a multitude wishing to institute a commonwealth as *assembling* together and, in so doing, already constituting itself as a "People": It is "by the consent of the People assembled" that "the Soveraigne Power is conferred" on "him, or them" who is subsequently instituted sovereign.[79] That this is the consent of the people *collectively* rather than of each individual is clear from the reference to the people's assembly and from the previous paragraph's explicit reference to majority rule. But the fact that "the People assembled" can collectively *confer* sovereign power implies that the assembly is itself an already-instituted democratic sovereign. Indeed, those who have traditionally read the first paragraph to say that a sovereign is established for the first time only *after*

---

[75] For speculation as to why, see Hoekstra 2006: 212.
[76] *Leviathan* 17.13, 260/87.
[77] Goldsmith 1966: 159–161.
[78] *Leviathan* 18.1, 264/88, underlining added.
[79] *Leviathan* 18.2, 264/88.

the majority has voted face an insurmountable problem: Hobbes had clearly implied, earlier in chapter 16, that there can be no commonwealth instituted until it has a sovereign to represent it. The answer, of course, is that as soon as "a *Multitude* of men" covenant to abide by majority rule, they have already constituted their majority-rule-governed assembly as their sovereign.[80] The sovereign assembly of the people may, if it chooses, collectively transfer sovereignty to a monarch or aristocratic assembly, but it may also retain its sovereignty. If there were any doubt that assembling together with the intention of establishing a commonwealth in itself constitutes a multitude as a democratic sovereign assembly, Hobbes dispelled it in chapter 18's fifth paragraph. He did so by repeating the argument he had given in *De cive* for why an instituted commonwealth always begins as a democracy, namely, that merely to assemble with the intention of establishing a commonwealth is tacitly to covenant to abide by majority rule: If an individual "voluntarily entered into the Congregation of them that were assembled, he sufficiently declared thereby his will (and therefore tacitely covenanted) to stand to what the major part should ordayne"—including with respect to "<u>any</u> of their Decrees."[81]

In the case of acquired sovereignty, however, Hobbes's view did evolve: He now envisioned the possibility of a nonmonarchical origin for acquired sovereignty and this in two respects. First, he envisioned that sovereign power could be acquired not only on an individual but also on a collective basis: The sovereign could either be authorized by each subject *individually* or be authorized by individuals who, having already constituted themselves as a democratic body governed by majority rule, *collectively* covenant with a new (postdemocratic) sovereign. Second, Hobbes envisioned that sovereignty could itself be acquired by an assembly rather than a king:

> A *Common-wealth by Acquisition*, is that, where the Soveraign Power is acquired by Force . . . when men <u>singly, or many together by plurality of voyces</u>, for fear of death, or bonds, do authorise all the actions of that <u>Man, or Assembly</u>, that hath their lives and liberty in his Power.[82]

As we shall see, the possibilities of collective submission *by* and *to* an assembly are both rather important for Hobbes's account of colonialism, and it may be that the shift in *Leviathan* is explained (not by his new account of authorization but) by his virgin treatment of the colonial experience. Indeed, in *Leviathan*, Hobbes considerably complicated his account to allow for commonwealths of mixed origin: He envisioned a "Monarch of diverse Nations, whereof he hath, in one the Soveraignty by Institution of the people assembled, and in another by Conquest, that is by Submission of each

---

[80] The fact that *Leviathan* 18.1 deploys the new language of authorization and representation in the course of giving this collective account (which passes through a democratic sovereignty stage) is further evidence against the view that his new authorization view led Hobbes to abandon the collective account found in the *Elements* and *De Cive*.

[81] *Leviathan* 18.5, 268/90, emphasis added.

[82] *Leviathan* 20.1, 306/101–102, underlining added.

particular"; he also imagined instituted sovereignty in which not each individual but instead the "Fathers of families" who already have dominion by acquisition over their own household assemble to institute a commonwealth.[83]

It is a striking fact that territory is wholly absent from any of these accounts: Hobbes portrayed the constitution of sovereign power exclusively as a matter of how "ius Dominij" may be obtained "in personas hominum."[84] Even more strikingly, once we ask how the artificial person of the state is supposed to relate to material existence and objects, it turns out that, on Hobbes's account, the state's artificial personality is physically embodied not in a particular geographical terrain, but in the bodies of its subjects.[85] Thus, for Hobbes, unlike Locke, there is no intrinsic relationship between the state and territory, which is why it is possible to have a properly constituted commonwealth without any fixed territory, a wandering "Common-wealth in the Wildernesse," such as were the "Children of Israel,"[86] or such as sailors whose supreme commander is their admiral at sea. This is not to say, of course, that the members of a commonwealth do not need the fruits of the earth;[87] it is just to say that a commonwealth is intrinsically constituted as a *people*, not territory. This is why colonial settlers or traveling armies are not, simply by virtue of having left their sovereign's territories, free to form a new commonwealth or pledge allegiance to a new sovereign. It is true that Hobbes allowed that there exist two types of "*Plantations*, or *Colonies*": namely, those that "remain united to their Metropolis" as "Provinces" and those that become "a Common-wealth of themselves, discharged of their subjection to their Soveraign that sent them." But the latter kind of colony is discharged of its subjection only in virtue of the "Licence, or Letters" granted by their former sovereign and not in virtue of having quit the sovereign's territories.[88]

The clear implication of Hobbes's account of sovereignty-covenants is that the sovereign gains complete jurisdictional authority over persons who submit by covenant but fails to acquire any territorial rights *in rem* against those who do not: All other persons are simply "enemies"[89] against whom the sovereign retains an original right of nature, but without any political authority over or claim against them. Jurisdictional authority, for Hobbes, can be acquired only over persons who have covenanted to join the commonwealth and to obey its sovereign representative. It might therefore appear that, strictly speaking, Hobbes's account implies that the commonwealth has no territorial boundaries at all: With respect to its members, the sovereign has jurisdictional

---

[83] *Leviathan* 20.14, 314/104–105; 30.11, 528/178.

[84] *Philosophical Rudiments* 8.1, 117/160.

[85] The "*Matter*" from which "the Nature of this Artificiall man" is composed "is *Man*" in the ordinary, natural sense. *Leviathan* Introduction.2, 16–18/1–2.

[86] *Leviathan* 24.6, 388/128.

[87] *Leviathan* 24.1–3, 386/127.

[88] *Leviathan* 24.14, 396/131.

[89] At best, they are members of a foreign commonwealth that is disposed to offer the sovereign's commonwealth "Honour, and Friendship" or that is party to a temporary, private alliance or "League." *Leviathan* 24.14, 396/131, 22.29, 370/121.

authority over all of them wherever they are, and, with respect to nonmembers, the sovereign has no jurisdictional authority anywhere, even in the territory claimed by the sovereign.

Yet that stark conclusion faces an important puzzle: It is seemingly belied by a number of cases of jurisdictional authority that Hobbes discussed and in which territory seems to play a crucial and even foundational role. One such case is that of the subject banished or exiled from the sovereign's territory. Hobbes asserted that "If the Soveraign Banish his Subject," causing him to "depart out of the dominion of the Common-wealth," then "during the Banishment, he is not Subject." This suggests that jurisdictional authority is inherently territorial: that merely being outside the territorial dominion of the sovereign is sufficient to end the sovereign's authority and the subject's political obligations. The case of exile is ambiguous, however, and the suggestion is to be resisted: Hobbes also said that "a Banished man, is a lawfull enemy of the Commonwealth that banished him; as being no more a Member of the same," indicating that banishment comprises two simultaneous but distinct acts: the subject's physical expulsion from the sovereign's territory and his civic expulsion from membership of the commonwealth.[90] Indeed, Hobbes did not even deem expulsion from the sovereign's territories as necessary for exile: He contemplated the case of an exile banished only "out of a certaine part" of the dominion but nevertheless stripped of membership and hence placed in the precarious position of "enemy of the Common-wealth" resident in its territory.[91]

The cases of the messenger and traveler who leave with the sovereign's blessing are more instructive and challenging, however. It is true that Hobbes claimed that "he that is sent on a message, or hath leave to travel, is still Subject," seemingly suggesting again that territorial presence and absence do not play a determinative role in jurisdictional authority. But the *reason* given by Hobbes serves to underline the relationship between territory and jurisdiction: The authorized traveler remains subject only because of a "Contract between Soveraigns, not by vertue of the [subject's own] covenant of Subjection" to his original sovereign.[92] Exit from the sovereign's territory, in other words, actually would release the traveler from his sovereignty-covenant to obey his sovereign; he remains subject only because he has somehow become obligated to the sovereign whose territory he has entered, and *that* sovereign has, by "Contract between Soveraigns," delegated the exercise of jurisdictional authority over the traveler back to the original sovereign. (Presumably, as part of that contract, the sovereign who claims jurisdiction over the territory a traveler has entered may still require that he abide by [some of] his laws). But this suggests that where there is no contract between sovereigns, or where the traveler enters land not controlled by any sovereign, then the

---

[90] *Leviathan* 21.24, 346/114; 28.21, 492/164–165. This interpretation is strengthened by Hobbes's discussion in *De Cive*, where he described banishment as a case of a subject being "freed from his subjection by the will of him who hath the Supreme Power." *Philosophical Rudiments* 7.18, 116.

[91] *Leviathan* 38.21, 492/164–165.

[92] *Leviathan* 21.24, 346/114.

traveler, simply in virtue of exiting his sovereign's territory, has also escaped his former sovereign's jurisdictional authority.

So the puzzle is this: On the one hand, Hobbes's official account of how sovereignty is established fails even to mention territory, grounds a foundationally personal juris-diction, and implies that whatever territorial jurisdiction the sovereign has is parasitic on his jurisdiction over subjects; on the other hand, his discussion of the cases of mes-sengers and travelers suggests that the sovereign's jurisdiction over persons is parasitic on his foundationally territorial jurisdiction.

Resolving the puzzle requires paying attention to two complicating features of Hobbes's theory of political authority and obligation. The first is its twofold character. It is a fundamental premise of Hobbes's political philosophy that the very purpose of joining a commonwealth is to preserve one's life and the bare essentials of a "contented life" (including a minimum level of corporal liberty).[93] This premise led Hobbes to conclude that a sovereign's political authority to command, and a subject's political obligation to obey, persist only if the sovereign, through his own natural strength and/ or the organized power of the state apparatus, is willing and able to protect the subject's life and its bare essentials: "The Obligation of Subjects to the Soveraign, is understood to last as long, and no longer, than the power lasteth, by which he is able to protect them."[94] Hobbes was keen to insist that this does not mean that actual protective power is *sufficient* for political authority and obligation: A covenant is also necessary, so that, even in the case of "Dominion acquired by Conquest, or Victory in war," dominion and obligation do not arise until "the Vanquished, to avoyd the present stroke of death, covenanteth either in expresse words, or by other sufficient signes of the Will" to obey the victor. In short, Hobbes advanced a twofold theory according to which (1) consent (covenant) and (2) protective power are individually necessary and jointly sufficient conditions of political authority and obligation.

The latter, *de factoist* element of Hobbes's theory is relevant because it directly links jurisdictional authority and political obligation to the physicality of the subject's body. The body has a physical location, and its protection requires being able to control events in the physical space around the subject's body; this is precisely what provides the link to territory. The complication is that the *de factoist* element does not intrinsi-cally link jurisdictional authority to any fixed geographical space in particular: The subject's body can move about in space and so, too, can the sovereign's apparatuses of state protection. This is why for Hobbes, unlike Locke, jurisdictional authority has no intrinsic link to a fixed territory and is not parasitic on any intrinsically sedentary notion of statehood. The issue for Hobbes is simply the geographical reach of the state-organized capacity to protect.

This is why, even if the subject *remains* in the sovereign's territory, but the territory is overrun by a conqueror or the sovereign otherwise loses the capacity to protect in

---

[93] See, e.g., *Leviathan* 14.8, 202/65–66; 17.1, 254/85; 30.1, 520/175. Cf. *Leviathan* 15.22, 234/77, and the discussion in Sreedhar 2010: 68.

[94] *Leviathan* 21.21, 344/114.

his territory, the subject is released from political obligation.[95] At bottom, in addition to being *consensual*, the grounds of jurisdictional authority are *protectional*, not territorial, and what they ground is jurisdiction over persons. The "mutuall Relation between Protection and Obedience"[96] is also what explains the difference between the individual traveler and a party of colonists or troops abroad. In normal circumstances, the individual traveler who enters the territory of a foreign sovereign is, in principle, discharged of his former political obligations because he can no longer reasonably expect the state-organized protection of his sovereign. (The exception is someone, such as an ambassador, who, although alone, enjoys the *virtual* protection of his sovereign because it is known that any harm to him will be interpreted as a sign of and pretext for war.) Colonists, whom Hobbes considered to be obligated even outside of the sovereign's territory, are different from individual travelers because "*Plantations*, or *Colonies*" are, by definition, "numbers of men sent out from the Common-wealth, under a Conductor, or Governour, to inhabit a Forraign Country."[97] The fact that colonists proceed under a "Governour" means that their protection, both against foreign enemies and against each other, still depends on the political command structure organized under their sovereign.[98] But, like any other subject, the moment that a colonist is "taken prisoner in war; or his person, or his means of life be within the Guards of the enemy," he is freed of his political obligations, "for it is then, that he hath no longer Protection from" his "former Soveraign."[99] Hobbes was explicit that territorial location is essentially irrelevant here: "The case is the same" for a subject who loses his sovereign's protection at home as it is for one "deteined . . . in a foreign country."[100] The case of the soldier, whether at home or abroad, is also essentially the same: "as long as" his sovereign "keeps the field, and giveth him means of subsistence, either in his Armies, or Garrisons," he remains under obligation; but as soon as he suffers from "want of Protection, and means to live as a Souldier," he is freed.[101]

[95] *Leviathan* 29.23, 518/174.

[96] *Leviathan* R&C.17, 1141/395–396.

[97] *Leviathan* 24.14, 396/131.

[98] The traveling merchant's status depends on the circumstances. Hobbes seems to have suggested that the sovereign retains jurisdictional authority over merchants even when they are abroad: "to assigne in what places, and for what commodities, the Subject shall traffique abroad, belongeth to the Soveraign . . . it belongeth to the Common-wealth, (that is, to the Soveraign only,) to approve, or disapprove both of the places, and matter of forraign Traffique." *Leviathan* 24.9, 392/129. (I say "seems" because the passage may also be referring to the traffic of the merchant's goods, not his person, abroad.) Presumably if the merchant travels in such a way that he continues to enjoy his sovereign's protection (e.g., he is accompanied by actual or virtual military protection), then, like the ambassador, colonist, or soldier, he remains bound by his original covenant to obey. If not, then, like other individual travelers, he remains bound to his sovereign only in virtue of a "Contract between Soveraigns." *Leviathan* 21.24, 346/114. In the *Elements of Law* 17.12, 92, Hobbes claimed that it is a law of nature that "*men allow commerce and traffic indifferently to one another.*"

[99] *Leviathan* 21.22, 344/114; R&C.6, 1134/390.

[100] *Leviathan* 21.22, 344/114. Cf. 27.24, 468/156, which primarily concerns a person in the territory of the sovereign.

[101] *Leviathan* R&C.6, 1134/390–391. This passage shows why (Sreedhar 2010: 38–39, 84–85) is mistaken to think that the "soldier contract" somehow alienates the inalienable right to self-defence

In sum, the Hobbesian commonwealth has no essentially territorial jurisdictional boundaries: Whatever jurisdictional authority the sovereign has is entirely parasitic on or derivative of his essentially contractual and protectional jurisdiction over persons. This is because, first, the sovereign has jurisdictional authority over members (who have covenanted to obey) wherever they are, as long as the sovereign is willing and able to protect them, and, second, the sovereign has no jurisdictional authority over nonmembers (who have not covenanted) regardless of where they are—they remain "enemies" against whom the sovereign only possesses a right of nature. It is true, of course, that there remains a weaker, derivative, and nonjurisdictional sense in which the commonwealth can still be said to have territorial boundaries. This is because sometimes the sovereign is able to protect his subjects (in the sense relevant to personal jurisdiction) in a particular geographical space without being able to enforce or protect the property rights that he assigns to them there. The British sovereign's troops, for example, may be able to protect colonists' lives and bare essentials in the Americas without being able to protect (against nonsubject enemies) their claim to all the American lands over which the British sovereign has nominally granted them ownership. One can sensibly speak here of the commonwealth's territorial boundaries as encompassing the area in which the sovereign is, as a matter of fact, able effectively to enforce his subjects' property rights as he defines them. But there is no question of territorially circumscribed jurisdictional boundaries here: The sovereign still enjoys (extraterritorial) jurisdiction over his own colonist-subjects, even with respect to property; he is just not able to protect effectively their property rights against foreigners in all parts of the earth.[102]

and obligates the soldier to await, in the face of certain death, his captain's permission to surrender or flee (cf. Baumgold 1983). (Hobbes was frequently explicit about the inalienability of the right of self-defence: "no Law can oblige a man to abandon his own preservation" when faced with "present death." *Leviathan* 27.24, 468/157.) It is true that, at *Leviathan* 21.16, 338–340/112, Hobbes asserted that a soldier who enlists is "obliged, not onely to go to the battell, but also not to run from it, without his Captaines leave," but Hobbes here had in mind cases in which a soldier is merely cowardly or afraid, not circumstances in which (the soldier himself judges that) survival in battle is hopeless. For all subjects, including soldiers who enlist, the obligation to obey ends, even prior to being captured, whenever one's cause is "manifestly" hopeless: "For where a number of men are manifestly too weak to defend themselves united, every one may . . . save his own life, either by flight, or by submission to the enemy . . . as hee shall think best; in the same manner as a very small company of souldiers, surprised by an army, may cast down their armes, and demand quarter." *Leviathan* 20.15, 314/105. It is true that a "company" is led by a captain, but Hobbes's phrasing implies that each soldier may proceed "in the same manner" as other subjects (i.e., by his own judgement) "as hee shall think best." Hobbes's distinction between when a regular subject and a soldier is released from political obligation is a function of the different circumstances under which each can reasonably expect protection: If the sovereign's territory is overrun by a conqueror, a regular subject in a nonmilitary zone may not be able reasonably to expect protection, even if the sovereign's army still "keeps the field," but a solider within the "Garrisons" of his own army can. Contrary to Sommerville's (1992: 185, note 3) suspicion, in other words, Hobbes's distinction does "flow very naturally" from his premises.

[102] It is also true that sovereigns may covenant with one another (*Leviathan* 22.29, 370/122); it might consequently be thought that there could be intersovereign covenants about the division of territorial jurisdiction (just as Hobbes suggested there could be intersovereign covenants about *personal* jurisdiction over travelers). But beyond the fact that such covenants are extremely precarious, they would not in any case establish essentially territorial jurisdiction. A Hobbesian

This stark conclusion about the lack of essentially territorial jurisdictional boundaries might still be challenged, however, in light of the second complicating feature of Hobbes's theory of political authority and obligation. Hobbes's theory not only has a twofold aspect, appealing to both consent and actual protective power; it also incorporates an element of *de factoism* into the very notion of consent itself. This is because consent is a communicative act, and communicative meaning for Hobbes is not necessarily determined by an agent's actual intentions (whether expressed or not). Sometimes it is determined by the intentions that can be reasonably imputed to an agent in light of known general facts about human nature, the purpose of language, canons of rationality, sociolinguistic (e.g., semantic and syntactic) conventions that govern the use of communicative expressions, specific facts about the (e.g., pragmatic) circumstances, and the specific actions of the agent.[103] This is why, for example, regardless of what one actually intends to say, one can never be reasonably understood to intend to give up the right of defending one's own life.[104] The upshot is that, for Hobbes (unlike contemporary liberals), the act of actually intending to consent is not a necessary condition of actually consenting: Actually consenting is sometimes constituted not by one's *actual* intention to consent but, rather, by the intentions that can reasonably be *imputed* to one by observers/hearers, even when the imputed intentions fail to correspond to any actual mental states of the agent.[105] One's consent is "expresse" when others reasonably take, as a sign of one's will, "words spoken with [the speaker's] understanding of what they signifie," but it is "tacite" or "by Inference" when others reasonably take, as a sign of one's will, "the consequence" of one's words, one's silence, one's actions, or even one's inaction, independently of one's actual intentions.[106] And one tacit sign of consenting

---

sovereign does not, in virtue of such a covenant, actually *transfer* his sovereignty over his own subjects in relation to the lands claimed by the foreign sovereign; nor does he somehow acquire sovereignty over foreigners in relation to the lands he claims. Consider a covenant about territorial jurisdiction between the English and French sovereigns. From the perspective of English subjects, French territories are still under the jurisdictional authority of the English sovereign; it is just that the English sovereign (who is the one who provides, for English subjects, the security guarantees of valid covenants) has delegated (in virtue of the intersovereign covenant) the *exercise* of his sovereignty over them, with respect to French land, to the French sovereign (who effectively becomes, from the perspective of English law, the English sovereign's magistrate); and vice versa for the French sovereign. There is no territorial right *in rem* against all persons as such, moreover; and whatever claims one sovereign has over a foreign sovereign's subjects depends on the latter's *personal* jurisdiction over his own subjects.

[103] For an analysis of Hobbes's philosophy of language in this regard, see chapter 3 of Abizadeh (in progress).

[104] *Leviathan* 14.8, 202/66.

[105] On the one hand, this means that in an extremely important sense Hobbes is not a forerunner of modern liberalism: For liberals, actual consent is constituted by the actual intention to consent. (This fact is the basis for Simmons's [1979: 88] distinction between acts that are "signs" of tacit [i.e., actual] consent and acts that merely "imply" consent but are not evidence for consent.) On the other hand, Hobbes is a forerunner of modern liberals' attempt to use the vocabulary of consent to describe the absence of consent (e.g., hypothetical consent) in order surreptitiously to draw on the normative significance that liberals attribute to an individual's *actual intentions*.

[106] *Leviathan* 14.14, 204/66–67; R&C.7, 1134–1135/391. Again, it must be emphasized that this is not the way that modern liberals define tacit consent: Because tacit consent is a type of actual consent,

to obey, according to Hobbes, simply is being under a sovereign's protective power, so that should a person merely "live under their Protection openly, hee is understood to submit himselfe."[107]

This is in part why Kinch Hoekstra has argued that, in the final analysis for Hobbes, being under the protective power of a sovereign is not merely necessary for political authority and obligation, but is also sufficient to establish so-called consent and, therefore, effectively *sufficient* for political authority and obligation.[108] And because Hobbes associated "living under their Protection" above all with being present in the sovereign's territory, then it might seem that Hobbes was a theorist of foundationally territorial jurisdiction after all. Indeed, Hobbes did not merely suggest that exiting territory in principle *releases* the traveler from a sovereign's jurisdiction; he also suggested, conversely, that merely *entering* a sovereign's territory *establishes* jurisdictional authority over a person: "whosoever entreth into anothers dominion, is Subject to all the Laws thereof" (again, unless there is an intersovereign contract or the territory's sovereign specifically exempts the traveler).[109] Hobbes's discussion of the offspring of two independent monarchs seemingly reiterates the claim that territorial presence is itself sufficient to establish jurisdictional authority (unless it is contractually given up by the sovereign): "If a man and a woman, Monarches of two severall Kingdomes, have a Child," and they have no "contract concerning who shall have the Dominion of him," then "the Dominion followeth the Dominion of the place of his residence. For the Soveraign of each Country hath Dominion over all that reside therein."[110]

Lea Brilmayer has argued that any theory of consent that purports to ground sovereign jurisdictional authority must fail because it ultimately *presupposes* a prior account of territorial sovereignty. If she is right, then not only did Hobbes's consent theory of personal jurisdiction *in fact* collapse into a theory of territorial jurisdiction, it also had to do so *in principle*. Brilmayer presents two general arguments for her thesis. First, for an act of consent actually to obligate an individual to a would-be sovereign, the latter must already have the right legitimately to demand the former's consent, for example as a condition of entry into (or of remaining in) its territory. Brilmayer concludes that this, in turn, presupposes that the would-be sovereign is *already* the legitimate sovereign over the territory in question: Consent is superfluous. Second, for a would-be sovereign to have the right to interpret certain actions or omissions as a sign of consent (i.e., to determine what counts as an act of consent that obligates the individual), it must already have jurisdictional authority over the person. If the would-be sovereign of a state has the authority to take the individual's entry into (or presence in) its own territory as an instance of consenting to its jurisdictional authority, then that is because

---

for modern liberals, it must still be accompanied by an agent's actual intention to consent (Simmons 1979: 79–83).

[107] *Leviathan* R&C.7, 1135/391.

[108] Hoekstra 2004: 67–69.

[109] That is, unless travelers "have a privilege by the amity of the Soveraigns, or by speciall licence." *Leviathan* 21.24, 346/114.

[110] *Leviathan* 20.6, 310/103.

it already enjoys jurisdictional authority over the individual in virtue of its *prior*, sovereign territorial jurisdiction: Consent is again superfluous. This prior, territorial basis of sovereign authority is precisely why, conversely, the sovereign of a state does not have the authority to take the individual's entry into (or presence in) the territory of *another* state as consent to its own putative jurisdictional authority. (The reason that the English sovereign cannot take an individual's entry into Chinese territory to be a sign of consent to English rule is because it has no prior jurisdiction over Chinese territory.) Consent, therefore, does not establish territorial sovereignty; it presupposes it.[111]

The problem with Brilmayer's first argument is that its premise (that one must have a right to demand consent) does not support her conclusion (that one must have sovereign authority). For the conclusion to follow the premise, the right that one must have to demand consent must include a claim-right; but Hobbes assumed that it is sufficient to have a liberty-right to demand consent. That is to say, a potential sovereign in a state-of-nature relation with a potential subject already has, Hobbes assumed, a right of nature to demand consent in exchange for allowing entry (or, in the case of a conqueror, for sparing the subject's life). But the mere liberty to coerce others does not amount to the authority to rule them. The problem with Brilmayer's second argument is that it ignores the possibility that there may be conditions that qualify an action (or omission) as consent independently of any authoritative declaration to that effect. And, indeed, when Hobbes suggested that one's presence in a sovereign's territory may establish political authority over one, he took himself to be specifying the conditions under which one's actions actually count as tacit signs of consent (rather than specifying who has the authority to interpret one's actions as signs of consent).[112] So consent may very well be incapable of establishing territorial sovereignty, but it does not of necessity presuppose it.

Nor do the examples of the traveler entering and the monarchs' offspring residing in a territory show that Hobbes attributed an inherently territorial jurisdictional authority to the sovereign. First, recall that, according to Hobbes's twofold theory of political obligation, it is the sovereign's actual power to protect, and not a person's territorial presence per se, that grounds political obligation. These two cases, like the case of a traveler who departs from the sovereign's territory, are fully explained by the *protectional*, rather than territorial, grounds of sovereign authority: A traveler who enters

---

[111] Brilmayer 1989.

[112] That there could be a fact of the matter about whether one has consented or not in the absence of a prior sovereign to make an authoritative declaration, is made possible by the fact that Hobbes believed that intersubjective meaning is possible prior to the establishment of sovereign authority: Even if conventional meanings are precarious in the state of nature, the conventions that make intersubjective communication possible are still normative. It might, of course, be objected that shared conventions could not arise in the first place unless they had already been consented to, but that consent itself, since it is an act of communication, presupposes an already existing set of shared linguistic conventions—which is viciously circular. (See Parry 1967, and, more generally, Russell 1921: 90.) But Hobbes believed that communication has a preconventional foundation: "not all Actions are signes by Constitution; but some are Naturally signes." *Leviathan* 31.39, 572/192; cf. 14.7, 202/66 and *Philosophical Rudiments* 15.16, 194–195.

or a child who resides in a sovereign's territory will normally be under the sovereign's protective power. This is why, by contrast, an enslaved captive present in the territory controlled by a sovereign is nevertheless under no political obligation: His life and its bare essentials remain unprotected.

Second, even being under the protective power of a putative sovereign is not a sufficient sign of consent, nor, consequently, of political obligation. The suggestion to the contrary fails adequately to account for the case of those who, like some foreign spies, are *secretly* present in the territory controlled by the sovereign, enjoying the general protections of social order afforded by him.[113] The passage in question does not state that, should a person live under a sovereign's protection, he is thereby understood to submit himself. It states that should a person "live under their Protection <u>openly</u>, hee is understood to submit himselfe to the Government: But if he live there secretly," then he remains a nonconsenting nonmember, free of political obligation, although "lyable to any thing that may bee done to a Spie, and Enemy of the State."[114] Indeed, even someone who *openly* enjoys the general protections afforded by a sovereign in a territory, but has always openly denied the sovereign's authority, is a subversive enemy who has not submitted himself as a member of the commonwealth: As Hobbes put it in the preface to *De cive*, "those who will not acknowledge themselves subject to the civill Magistrate, and will be exempt from all publique burthens, and yet will live under his Jurisdiction (*in civitate tamen esse*), and look for protection from the violence and injuries of others" should not be counted as among one's "fellow Subjects (*cives*)" but as "enemies, and spies."[115] Like the exile banished within some confined part of the sovereign's dominions, they are in the sovereign's territory, enjoy the general protections of social order afforded by the sovereign, but remain in a state-of-nature relation to the constituted commonwealth and its sovereign. Presence within the territories controlled by a sovereign is insufficient to establish political obligation: The sovereign's jurisdictional authority is fundamentally over persons and only derivatively over territory.

---

[113] Hoekstra (2004: 68) appears to collapse consent into protective power when he writes that since for Hobbes "the mere fact of their being alive counts for assent (whenever there exists a power that can destroy them)," "we may conclude that all of the living have consented to the power over them," such that "The only people free of obligation to the present power are the dead (and slaves in shackles)." He does go on to say that "In the ordinary case of *de facto* rule, we can justifiably presume consent" (2004: 69), which leaves the door open to extraordinary cases; in a later piece, Hoekstra (2006: 211) specifies cases of explicit refusal as such an exception. But the spy eludes Hoekstra's account. For a fuller analysis of Hobbes's theory of political authority and obligation and criticism of Hoekstra's argument, see chapter 6 of Abizadeh (in progress).

[114] *Leviathan* R&C.7, 1135/391, emphasis added. Hobbes also discusses spies at *Leviathan* 23.12, 382/126: "if a man be sent into another country, secretly to explore their counsels, and strength . . . because there is none to take notice of any Person in him, but his own; he is but a Private Minister; but yet a Minister of the Common-wealth." That the comma appears before "secretly" and that the spy's "own" private person is taken notice of suggest that Hobbes was here contemplating a spy whose presence (although not mission) is known to his hosts. Such a spy presumably remains obligated to his prior sovereign in virtue of the intersovereign covenant that covers other travelers in general.

[115] *Philosophical Rudiments* Preface, 36/83.

The case of colonial rule complicates Hobbes's theory of jurisdictional authority, however, in a way that might seem to introduce an intrinsically territorial element. Recall that, for Hobbes, sovereignty takes the form of a democracy when the sovereign is an assembly and all of the commonwealth's subjects have the right to participate in it; if only some subjects have the right to participate, then it is an aristocracy. The clear implication is that if the sovereign is an assembly in which all the subjects in the commonwealth's metropolis have the right to participate, but the subjects residing in its colonies do not, then sovereignty takes the form of an aristocracy. But Hobbes explicitly asserted, apparently to the contrary, that colonial rule of this kind amounts to *monarchical* rule of one people—or commonwealth—over another:

> If a Popular, or Aristocraticall Common-wealth, subdue an Enemies Countrie, and govern the same, by a President, Procurator, or other Magistrate; this may seeme perhaps at first sight, to be a Democraticall, or Aristocraticall Government. But it is not so . . . Nor are those Provinces which are in subjection to a Democracie, or Aristocracie of another Common-wealth, Democratically, or Aristocratically governed, but Monarchically.[116]

The puzzle is why Hobbes would count the colonial province, which clearly has the same sovereign as the metropolis, a separate commonwealth. One possibility is that Hobbes was tacitly assuming that a commonwealth is *constitutively* territorial: That although the colonials are subject to the same sovereign, they nevertheless inhabit a distinct territory and ipso facto constitute a separate people/state. The thought that this was Hobbes's tacit assumption is encouraged by his discussion of the example he used to illustrate the point. The example, worth quoting in full, begins by reference to the land of Judea:

> whereas heretofore the Roman People, governed the land of *Judea* (for example) by a President; yet was not *Judea* therefore a Democracy; because they were not governed by any Assembly, into which, any of them, had right to enter; nor by an Aristocracy; because they were not governed by any Assembly, into which, any man could enter by their Election: but they were governed by one Person, which though as to the people of *Rome* was an Assembly of the people, or Democracy; yet as to the people of *Judea*, which had no right at all of participating in the government, was a Monarch. For though where the people are governed by an Assembly, chosen by themselves out of their own number, the government is called a Democracy, or Aristocracy; yet when they are governed by an Assembly, not of their own choosing, 'tis a Monarchy; not of *One* man, over another man; but of one people, over another people.[117]

---

[116] *Leviathan* 19.10, 294/98.
[117] *Leviathan* 19.13, 298/99. Cf. the Latin version's reference to "the rule of many commonwealths by one commonwealth." *Leviathan* 19, 299, translated in note 56, p. 298.

The entire discussion presumes, of course, that Romans and Jews, although subject to the same sovereign, constitute two distinct peoples. There are at least two possibilities that could account for the apparent departure from his official doctrine that a people/state's boundaries are *civic* and encompass all individuals who have covenanted to submit to (and are protected by) the same sovereign: first, that the people/state is defined *territorially*, as all those residing within a particular area; or second, that the people/state is defined *socio-culturally*, as all those who share a particular history or culture.[118] If the reference to the "land of *Judea*" weakly suggests the former, Hobbes's later reference to government by "strangers" who are "not used to live under the same government, nor speaking the same language" suggests the latter.[119]

The difficulty with these passages is not just that they seem to cut against Hobbes's official theory, but that Hobbes explicitly acknowledged the existence of distinct provinces, even distinct colonial provinces, within a single commonwealth under the same sovereign: "when in one Common-wealth there be divers Countries, that have their Lawes distinct one from another, or are farre distant in place, the Administration of the Government being committed to divers persons, those Countries where the Soveraign is not resident, but governs by Commission, are called Provinces." Indeed, to illustrate his point, Hobbes produced, in addition to the English colonies of "*Virginia*, and *Sommer-Ilands*" (Bermuda), the very same example he had used to illustrate the case of apparently distinct commonwealths, namely, "The Romans who had the Soveraignty of many Provinces."[120]

The key to resolving the difficulty lies in noticing the constant use, in these passages, of the terms related to *administration* and *government*. Recall that Hobbes made a critical distinction between the sovereign, who *owns* sovereign authority, and the government officials or magistrates, who merely *administer* or exercise sovereign authority.[121] In *Leviathan*, the term "government" can refer either (1) to the sovereign who represents the commonwealth or (2) to the sovereign's subordinate representatives who are given the administration "of the whole Dominion, or of a part thereof," such as when a sovereign appoints a subordinate "Gouvernor" or assembly to administer "a Province, Colony, or Town."[122] In the colonial context, Hobbes tended to use the terms related to "government" in the latter, subordinate sense. Thus, whereas earlier Hobbes had used the terms "monarchy," "aristocracy," and "democracy" as names for the form of *sovereignty* or the commonwealth, here,

[118] A third possibility, that boundaries are still civic but distinguish rights-bearing citizens from noncitizen subjects, can be immediately ruled out because Hobbes famously equated citizen and subject.

[119] *Leviathan* 19.23, 304/101.

[120] *Leviathan* 22.16, 358/118, underlining added.

[121] On Hobbes's debt to Bodin in making this distinction, see Hoekstra 2006: 198. See also Hoekstra 2013.

[122] *Leviathan* 23.3, 376/123–124; 22.16, 358/117, quoting marginal heading. The sovereign powers may be delegated to a subordinate government that administers the entire commonwealth in the case of "an Infant King," for example. *Leviathan* 23.3, 376/124; 19.9, 292/97.

in the passages on colonialism under question, he was evidently using them as names for the form of the administration or subordinate government. To take the very first passage I cited in this regard: Hobbes denied that colonial rule by an exclusively metropolitan assembly could amount to "a Democraticall, or Aristocraticall Government," asserting that the colonial provinces are not "Democratically, or Aristocratically governed, but Monarchically." Similarly, when Hobbes was analyzing the tendency of the Romans and the English to entrust the administration of their colonies to the hands of a single praetor or "Governour," he concluded that this is simply because of the natural tendency "to commit the Government of their common Interest rather to a Monarchicall, then a Popular form of Government."[123] The terms "democracy," "aristocracy," and "monarchy," therefore, can refer either to the form of sovereignty or commonwealth, or to the form of administration or subordinate government.[124]

Thus, when Hobbes referred to distinct "peoples" or "commonwealths" within the same colonial empire, he is best understood to be using the words in a looser sense than his usual one, to denote subunits within the same commonwealth (in the strict sense) defined in terms of distinct administrative units with their own "Lawes distinct" and their own territorial jurisdiction "farre distant in place." In other words, whereas territorial boundaries play no intrinsic role in constituting a commonwealth and sovereign jurisdiction as such, they may very well be used *legally*, within a commonwealth, to constitute subordinate *domestic* jurisdictional boundaries. And this is precisely what Hobbes claimed, suggesting, for example, that although a subordinate governing assembly may have legislative jurisdiction over colonial persons outside its substate territorial unit, its *executive* jurisdiction over persons is territorially circumscribed:

> an Assembly residing out of the bounds of that Colony whereof they have the government, cannot execute any power over the persons, or goods of any of the Colonie, to seize on them for debt, or other duty, in any place without the Colony it selfe, as having no Jurisdiction, nor Authoritie elsewhere, but are left to the remedie, which the Law of the place alloweth them. And though the Assembly have right, to impose a Mulct [i.e., fine] upon any of their members, that shall break the Lawes they make; yet out of the Colonie it selfe, they have no right to execute the same. And that which is said here, of the Rights of an Assembly, for the government of a Province, or a Colony, is appliable also to an Assembly for the Government of a Town, or University, or a College, or a Church, or for any other Government over the persons of men.[125]

---

[123] *Leviathan* 19.10, 294/98; 22.16, 358–360/118.

[124] In *Elements of Law* 21.5, 120, Hobbes asserted that, although the form of sovereignty may be democratic, when "the right of sovereignty be in the assembly . . . yet the use thereof is always in one, or a few particular men," suggesting that the effective form of administration can never be democratic.

[125] *Leviathan* 22.16, 360/118.

3 CONCLUSION

The Hobbesian sovereign's territorial rights are entirely parasitic on his personal juris-diction over his own subjects; the sovereign has no territorial rights *in rem* against nonsubjects. Nevertheless, territorial control is, as a matter of fact, an *instrumentally* crucial way in which the state is able to secure protection, and protection is a neces-sary condition for jurisdictional authority over persons. And although, as the case of the spy and its analogues demonstrate, protection is not wholly sufficient to establish consent, Hobbes did nevertheless take it be a sufficient sign of consent in a vast array of cases: For Hobbes, consent is not nullified—as it is for contemporary liberals—simply because it is motivated by the fear of exile or even death. So although in principle terri-tory plays no role in *grounding* or constituting jurisdictional authority, in practice it is extremely important for Hobbes, and, in the vast majority of cases of *individual* politi-cal obligation, Hobbes's theory mirrors theories of inherently territorial jurisdiction. With respect to organized groups, by contrast, and above all with respect to foreign sovereigns and their commonwealths, the sovereign enjoys no territorial jurisdiction at all, not even over the territory the sovereign controls: Foreign invaders commit no injustice in virtue of their invasion.

The reasons for the in-practice convergence of Hobbes's theory, in the case of iso-lated individuals, with intrinsically territorial theories of jurisdiction are instructive. For Hobbes, consent, whether express or tacit, is supposed to be a form of *actual* con-sent, but, as we have seen, his notion of actual consent is not equivalent to the con-temporary liberal one: Actual Hobbesian consent is possible even when an agent does not actually intend to consent (and it is not nullified by fear of extreme harm). It is a precursor, in other words, to what we now call *hypothetical consent*, and it is on this ter-rain that contemporary theories of territorial rights come into their own. But Hobbes stands as a warning to such theories: His theory of sovereign jurisdiction shows why it is so difficult for any theory in the social-contract (actual consent) or contractual-ist (hypothetical consent) tradition to justify the territorial rights that contemporary states claim against *foreigners*. Hobbes did, of course, think that the sovereign has the right to enforce his will against foreigners on the territory he controls, but unless they become his subjects, the sovereign does so in principle without any authority: He has a right of nature, a mere liberty-right, not a claim against them. Yet asserting even this more minimal right depends on the thesis that persons in the state of nature have the liberty-right to do to others whatever they will—a thesis that may already be too much for contemporary theorists to swallow.

Hobbes's political philosophy also has rather uncomfortable implications for contemporary democratic societies that host interstate migrants. Recall that, for Hobbes, a democratic commonwealth is defined as one in which all its sub-jects have the right of political participation. If some subjects are denied rights of political participation—and Hobbes was certainly not opposed to this—the state is aristocratic, not democratic. The upshot is that, on Hobbes's analysis, a democratic state has three options when migrants enter the territory it controls and submit themselves to its jurisdiction. If the state recognizes the migrants as subjects and grants them full rights of political participation, it remains a democracy. If it denies its new subjects such rights, it automatically ceases to be a democracy, metamorphosing into an aristocracy. And if it treats the migrants as enemies, not subjects, by incarcerating them—as is done today by many self-styled liberal democracies—it becomes a slave-holding democracy.[126]

ACKNOWLEDGMENTS

For valuable comments, I am grateful to Teresa Bejan, Helge Dedek, Evan Fox-Decent, Bryan Garsten, Kinch Hoekstra, Daniel Lee, Jacob Levy, Matthew Longo, Catherine Lu, Al Martinich, Rob Sparling, Anna Stilz, Yves Winter, and participants at the workshop of the McGill Research Group on Constitutional Government, January 2013, and the Yale Political Theory Workshop, April 2013. I also thank SSHRCC for funding.

BIBLIOGRAPHY

Abizadeh, Arash. 2013. "Leviathan as Mythology: The Representation of Hobbesian Sovereignty," in *Hobbes Today: Insights for the 21st Century*, edited by S. A. Lloyd, 113–152. Cambridge: Cambridge University Press.

Abizadeh, Arash. In progress. *The Oscillations of Thomas Hobbes: Between Insight and the Will.*

Baldwin, Thomas. 1992. "The Territorial State," in *Jurisprudence: Cambridge Essays*, edited by Hyman Gross and Ross Harrison, 207–230. Oxford: Oxford University Press.

Baumgold, Deborah. 1983. "Subjects and Soldiers: Hobbes on Military Service." *History of Political Thought* 4(1): 43–64.

Berger, Adolf. 1953. *Encyclopedic Dictionary of Roman Law*. Philadelphia: American Philosophical Society.

Bloch, Marc. 1938. *La société féodale*. Paris: Éditions Albin Michel.

Borkowski, Andrew. 1997. *Textbook on Roman Law*, 2nd ed. Oxford: Oxford University Press.

Brett, Annabel S. 2011. *Changes of State: Nature and the Limits of the City in Early Modern Natural Law*. Princeton: Princeton University Press.

Brilmayer, Lea. 1989. "Consent, Contract, and Territory." *Minnesota Law Review* 74(1): 1–35.

Brubaker, Rogers. 1992. *Citizenship and Nationhood in France and Germany*. Cambridge: Harvard University Press.

---

[126] If the host society incarcerates only some migrants but denies others political rights, then, technically speaking, it becomes a slave-holding aristocracy. The mere fact of incarceration does not, for Hobbes, signify slavery: Criminals are punished as member subjects, not enemies. (See Yates 2014.) The slave or captive is denied membership *and* incarcerated.

Buchanan, Allen. 2003. "Boundaries: What Liberalism Has to Say," in *States, Nations, and Borders: The Ethics of Making Boundaries*, edited by Allen Buchanan and Margaret Moore, 231–261. Cambridge: Cambridge University Press.

Burns, J. H. 1985. "Fortescue and the Political Theory of *Dominium*." *The Historical Journal* 28(4): 777–797.

Burns, J. H. 1992. *Lordship, Kingship, and Empire: The Idea of Monarchy, 1400–1525*. Oxford: Clarendon Press.

Chrimes, S. B. 1936. *English Constitutional Ideas in the Fifteenth Century*. Cambridge: Cambridge University Press.

Coleman, Janet. 1983. "Medieval Discussions of Property: *Ratio* and *Dominium* According to John of Paris and Marsilius of Padua." *History of Political Thought* 4(2): 209–228.

Giesey, Ralph E. 1977. "Rules of Inheritance and Strategies of Mobility in Prerevolutionary France." *The American Historical Review* 82(2): 271–289.

Gilmore, Myron Piper. 1941. *Argument from Roman Law in Political Thought, 1200–1600*. Cambridge, MA: Harvard University Press.

Goldsmith, M. M. 1966. *Hobbes's Science of Politics*. New York: Columbia University Press.

Hobbes, Thomas. 1983a. *De Cive: The English Version*, edited by Howard Warrender. Oxford: Clarendon Press.

Hobbes, Thomas. 1983b. *De Cive: The Latin Version*, edited by Howard Warrender. Oxford: Clarendon Press.

Hobbes, Thomas. 1994. *The Elements of Law, Natural and Politic: Part I, Human Nature, Part II, De Corpore Politico, with Three Lives*, edited by J. C. A. Gaskin. Oxford: Oxford University Press.

Hobbes, Thomas. 2012. *Leviathan: The English and Latin Texts*, edited by Noel Malcolm. Oxford: Clarendon Press.

Hoekstra, Kinch. 2004. "The *de facto* Turn in Hobbes's Political Philosophy," in *Leviathan After 350 Years*, edited by Tom Sorell and Luc Foisneau, 33–73. Oxford: Clarendon Press.

Hoekstra, Kinch. 2006. "A Lion in the House: Hobbes and Democracy," in *Rethinking the Foundations of Modern Political Thought*, edited by Annabel S. Brett, James Tully, and Holly Hamilton-Bleakley, 191–218. Cambridge: Cambridge University Press.

Hoekstra, Kinch. 2013. "Early Modern Absolutism and Constitutionalism." *Cordozo Law Review* 34(3): 1079–1098.

Honoré, A. M. 1961. "Ownership," in *Oxford Essays in Jurisprudence*, edited by A. G. Guest, 107–147. Oxford: Oxford University Press.

Krynen, Jacques. 1993. *L'empire du roi: Idées et croyances politiques en France XIIIe-XVe siècle*. Paris: Éditions Gallimard.

Lee, Daniel. 2008. "Private Law Models for Public Law Concepts: The Roman Law Theory of Dominium in the Monarchomach Doctrine of Popular Sovereignty." *The Review of Politics* 70(3): 370–399.

Lee, Daniel. 2012. "The Rights of Sovereignty and Its Exercise: Civil Law Origins of a Public Law Distinction." In *Political Thought and Intellectual History Research Seminar 2011–12*. Cambridge: University of Cambridge.

Lee, Daniel. Forthcoming. *Popular Sovereignty in Early Modern Constitutional Thought*. Oxford: Oxford University Press.

Maiolo, Francesco. 2007. *Medieval Sovereignty: Marsilius of Padua and Bartolus of Saxoferrato*. Delft: Eburon.

Malcolm, Noel. 2002. *Aspects of Hobbes*. Oxford: Clarendon Press.

Marshall, T. H. 1950. "Citizenship and Social Class," in *Citizenship and Social Class and Other Essays*, 1–85. Cambridge: Cambridge University Press.

Miller, David. 2011a. "Property and Territory: Locke, Kant, and Steiner." *Journal of Political Philosophy* 19(1): 90–109.

Miller, David. 2011b. "Territorial Rights: Concept and Justification." *Political Studies* 60(2): 252–268.

Mousnier, Roland. 1971. *La vénalité des offices sous Henri IV et Louis XIII*. Paris: Presses Universitaires de France.

Nine, Cara. 2008. "A Lockean Theory of Territory." *Political Studies* 56(4): 148–165.

Pangalangan, Raul C. 2001. "Territorial Sovereignty: Command, Title, and the Expanding Claims of the Commons," in *Boundaries and Justice: Diverse Ethical Perspectives*, 164–182, edited by David Miller and Sohail H. Hashmi. Princeton: Princeton University Press.

Parry, Geraint. 1967. "Performative Utterances and Obligation in Hobbes." *The Philosophical Quarterly* 17(68): 246–252.

Ruggie, John Gerard. 1983. "Continuity and Transformation in the World Polity: Toward a Neorealist Synthesis." *World Politics* 35(2): 261–285.

Ruggie, John Gerard. 1993. "Territoriality and Beyond: Problematizing Modernity in International Relations." *International Organization* 47(1): 139–174.

Runciman, David. 2000. "What Kind of Person Is Hobbes's State? A Reply to Skinner." *The Journal of Political Philosophy* 8(2): 268–278.

Runciman, David. 2009. "Hobbes's Theory of Representation: Anti-democratic or Proto-democratic?," in *Political Representation*, edited by Ian Shapiro, Susan C. Stokes, Elisabeth Jean Wood, and Alexander S. Kirshner, 15–34. Cambridge: Cambridge University Press.

Russell, Bertrand. 1921. *The Analysis of Mind*. London: George Allen & Unwin.

Simmons, A. John. 1979. *Moral Principles and Political Obligation*. Princeton: Princeton University Press.

Skinner, Quentin. 2002a. *Visions of Politics: Hobbes and Civil Science*, vol. III. Cambridge: Cambridge University Press.

Skinner, Quentin. 2002b. *Visions of Politics: Renaissance Virtues*, vol. II. Cambridge: Cambridge University Press.

Skinner, Quentin. 2005. "Hobbes on Representation." *European Journal of Philosophy* 13(2): 155–184.

Sommerville, Johann. 1992. *Thomas Hobbes: Political Ideas in Historical Context*. New York: St. Martin's Press.

Sreedhar, Susanne. 2010. *Hobbes on Resistance: Defying the Leviathan*. Cambridge: Cambridge University Press.

Stilz, Anna. 2009. "Why Do States Have Territorial Rights?" *International Theory* 1(2): 185–213.

Stilz, Anna. 2011. "Nations, States, and Territory." *Ethics* 121(3): 572–601.

Tuck, Richard. 2003. "The Making and Unmaking of Boundaries from the Natural Law Perspective," in *States, Nations, and Borders: The Ethics of Making Boundaries*, edited by Allen Buchanan and Margaret Moore, 143–170. Cambridge: Cambridge University Press.

Tuck, Richard. 2006. "Hobbes and Democracy," in *Rethinking the Foundations of Modern Political Thought*, edited by Annabel S. Brett, James Tully, and Holly Hamilton-Bleakley, 171–190. Cambridge: Cambridge University Press.

Yates, Arthur. 2014. "The Right to Punish in Thomas Hobbes's *Leviathan*." *Journal of the History of Philosophy* 52(2): 233–254.

CHAPTER 19

HOBBES AND THE SOCIAL CONTROL OF UNSOCIABILITY

QUENTIN SKINNER

HOBBES warns us in chapter 13 of *Leviathan* that there are three principal elements in our nature that cannot fail to engender quarrels and war. The first is our competitiveness, which makes us try to master the persons and property of others. The second is our associated lack of trust, which prompts us to anticipate and respond to any threatened assaults. The third is our thirst for glory, which leads us to react with hostility toward any apparent signs of being undervalued.[1] These propensities render us "dissociate" from one other, as a result of which "men have no pleasure, (but on the contrary a great deale of grief) in keeping company."[2] Still worse, we are "apt to invade, and destroy one another," whether in the name of making gains or protecting ourselves or upholding our elevated sense of our value and worth.[3] Cumulatively these invasions give rise to a war "of every man, against every man" in which everyone is equally condemned to living "without other security, than what their own strength, and their own invention shall furnish them withall."[4]

If any form of social life is to be possible, these destructive tendencies will obviously have to be curbed and controlled. Hobbes turns in chapter 17 of *Leviathan* to consider how we can hope to introduce the necessary methods of restraint. He concludes that the only means by which men can hope to win security from their common enemies and the injuries of one another will be to erect a "visible Power to keep them in awe, and tye them by feare of punishment" from engaging in acts of violence.[5] More specifically, he argues, the one and only route to security lies in covenanting, every man with every man, to "conferre all their power and strength upon one Man, or upon one Assembly of men," thereby agreeing to "submit their Wills, every one to his Will, and their Judgements, to his Judgment."[6]

---

[1] On this theme, see Slomp 2000.
[2] Hobbes 2012, ch. 13, vol. 2, 190.
[3] Hobbes 2012, ch. 13, vol. 2, 190, 194.
[4] Hobbes 2012, ch. 13, vol. 2, 192.
[5] Hobbes 2012, ch. 17, vol. 2, 254.
[6] Hobbes 2012, ch. 17, vol. 2, 260.

Hobbes's analysis in chapter 13 of the unsociable qualities that dictate this drastic solution appears at first sight to be complete. If we turn to chapter 15, however, we find that he has more to say. There are various other passions, he now maintains, that are common to mankind and are no less capable—although in a more indirect way—of giving rise to conflicts and war. Some people are "*Stubborn, Insociable, Froward, Intractable*," and these failures of civility are "contrary to the fundamentall Law of Nature, which commandeth *to seek Peace*."[7] Others are prey to vengeful feelings of vainglory, which provoke them into "glorying in the hurt of another" and thereby "tendeth to the introduction of Warre."[8] Still others are prideful, thinking themselves better than other men and refusing in consequence to "enter into conditions of Peace."[9] Finally, there are those who suffer from overweening arrogance, who "require for themselves, that which they would not have to be granted to others" and likewise undermine the prospects of peaceful life.[10]

At the beginning of chapter 17 Hobbes argues that these more indirect threats to human security will similarly have to be controlled by coercive force. He even suggests, rather strangely, that the requirement of modesty will have to be enforced by "the terror of some Power."[11] But he never enlarges on this suggestion, nor does he ever explain how the use of legal means to compel men to follow the social virtues would be practicable. Even if we cannot hope, however, to use the force of law to impose modesty upon the arrogant, or tractability upon the "froward," it remains obvious that these unsociable and potentially contentious forms of behavior will somehow have to be resisted and controlled—or at least managed and coped with—if any tolerable social life is to be sustained. How, then, can this be done?

The question of how to cope with the unsociable had been widely canvassed in Renaissance moral theory and especially in the genre of Italian writings on the topic of *la civil conversazione*.[12] Among numerous treatises on this subject, those which enjoyed the widest circulation in England were Baldassare Castiglione's *Libro del cortegiano* of 1528, Giovanni della Casa's *Galateo* of 1558, and Stefano Guazzo's *Civil conversazione* of 1574.[13] All these texts were soon translated into English,[14] and Castiglione's *Courtier* was reprinted at least six times in London

---

[7] Hobbes 2012, ch. 15, vol. 2, 232.

[8] Hobbes 2012, ch. 15, vol. 2, 232. For Hobbes on vainglory see Cooper 2010.

[9] Hobbes 2012, ch. 15, vol. 2, 234.

[10] Hobbes 2012, ch. 15, vol. 2, 234. Hoekstra 2013 powerfully argues that Hobbes's anxiety about our disposition to view others with contempt grounds his theory of human equality. If we are to live a secure and comfortable life, we must do everything to uphold the cause of peace. But if we give in to pride and arrogance, we are sure to provoke conflict and war. We must therefore be willing to acknowledge human equality in the name of peace.

[11] Hobbes 2012, ch. 17, vol. 2, 254. For Hobbes on modesty, see Cooper 2010.

[12] In this section and in section 3 I draw extensively on Skinner 2013, esp. 2–15.

[13] These writers are considered together in Whigham 1984, Panichi 1994, and Borrelli 2000, 67–92. See also Burke 1993, 98–102; Ménager 1995, 149–85, and (on della Casa) Farneti 2000, esp. 494–504. For the reception of the genre in Tudor England, see Richards 2003, 29-33, 44–47, 63–64.

[14] See Castiglione 1561; della Casa 1576; Guazzo 1581.

before the end of the sixteenth century.[15] A number of imitations also appeared, including Simon Robson's *Courte of civill courtesie* of 1577, which purported to be a translation of an Italian text,[16] and Lodowick Bryskett's dialogue of 1606, entitled *A discourse of civill life*, the avowed aim of which was "to frame a gentleman fit for civill conversation."[17]

When these writers speak about what Castiglione (in Thomas Hoby's translation of 1561) describes as "manerlye conversation,"[18] they are not referring merely or even principally to habits and styles of speech. As Guazzo makes clear in criticizing those who refuse to take part in conversation, he does not mean that they are unwilling to talk; he means that that they are unwilling to come together in social life. The contrast he draws throughout *The Civile Conversation*, as George Pettie expresses it in his translation of 1581, is always between "solitarinesse and Conversation."[19] Guazzo's basic aspiration is to show that "solitarinesse ought to be taken altogether out of the world, & company & conversation to be chosen."[20] "Too be shorte," he concludes, "my meaning is, that civile conversation is an honest commendable and vertuous kinde of living in the world."[21]

Castiglione similarly speaks in *The Courtier* about how a man should conduct himself "in hys lyving and conversation."[22] When the respected figure of Federico Fregoso turns to this question in book II, he expresses himself largely in negative terms. The courtier must never be "stubborne and full of contencion," thereby stirring men to argument, and he must be "no lyer, no boaster, nor fonde flatterer."[23] Later Federico adds that, besides taking care not to "bragg and boast of them selves," courtiers should never act vainly and pridefully, never show "a proude and haughtye stomake."[24] A good courtier will always behave with reverence and respect, and will never stray beyond the recognized boundaries of social life.[25]

The underlying suggestion that the ideal of civil conversation can best be grasped by reflecting on what it means to fail in civility is taken up at greater length by Guazzo in the opening book of *The Civile Conversation*. He begins by distinguishing between those whose lack of sociability debars them from civil conversation and those who cannot easily be excluded in spite of the fact that their conduct leaves much to be desired.[26] Turning to the latter group, Guazzo proceeds to itemize a number of social vices that undermine the conditions of civilized social life. First he speaks of the

[15] The British Library catalogue records two printings in English (1561, 1588) and four in Latin (1571, 1577, 1585, 1593).
[16] Richards 2003, 13.
[17] Bryskett 1606, 5.
[18] Castiglione 1994, 102.
[19] Guazzo 1581, bk. 1, fo. 18^r.
[20] Guazzo 1581, bk. 1, fo. 17^v.
[21] Guazzo 1581, bk. 1, fos. 22^{r-v}.
[22] Castiglione 1994, 149.
[23] Castiglione 1994, 121.
[24] Castiglione 1994, 155.
[25] Castiglione 1994, 121.
[26] For this distinction see Guazzo 1581, bk. 1, fo. 27^r.

slanderous, who "with the falsenesse of their tongues, seeke to blemishe the bright-
nesse of others names."[27] Then he turns to the contentious and the obstinate,[28] who
are ready "even for very trifles" to engage in "dyre debate and strife."[29] These are the
people whom della Casa had already described (in Robert Peterson's translation of
1576) as the "froward," whose conversation "consisteth in overtwharting other mens
desiers," and whose testiness turns friends into foes.[30] Next Guazzo criticizes the
boasters and the vainglorious,[31] together with those whom he describes as the ambitious,[32] who "seeke in companie to goe before others"[33] and are proud, haughty, and
contemptuous.[34] Here too he echoes della Casa, who had spoken with similar distaste
of those who "make a vaine glorious boasting of them selves: vaunting and telling in a
bravery, what wonderfull exploits they have doone."[35] Finally Guazzo rounds on those
who suffer from "presumpteous arrogancy" and are blinded by love of themselves.[36]

Given that all these vices are inimical to social life, they will somehow have to be
managed and controlled. But this brings us back to our original question: how can this
be done? Here the writers on civil conversation may be said to draw an implicit distinction between those types of behavior which are likely to strike us as merely embarrassing or irritating and those which may appear, in addition, to be seriously insulting or
offensive. They all agree that in the latter case, where a gentleman's standing or reputation may be in question, there is only one proper response, and that is to issue a challenge to a duel.[37] When the count in book I of Castiglione's *Courtier* lists the attributes
of the ideal courtier, he simply assumes that one reason why courtiers need "to be skil-
ful on those weapons that are used ordinarily emong gentlemen" is that "there happen
often times variaunces betwene one gentleman and an other, wherepon ensueth a combat."[38] He warns us that we must "have a foresight in the quarelles and controversies
that may happen," but he is insistent that a courtier must stand ready to fight whenever
"he muste needs to save his estimation withall."[39] Guazzo likewise observes that dueling
is not merely a frequent occurrence but that men of honor can hardly avoid such com-
bats if they are to ensure that their reputations remain intact. As the figure of Annibale
remarks, he has known many occasions on which "certaine Gentlemen have convayed
themselves into some close place, where because the one would not live with the name

27 Guazzo 1581, bk. 1, fo. 27^r.
28 Guazzo 1581, bk. 1, fo. 39^v.
29 Guazzo 1581, bk. 1, fo. 40^v.
30 della Casa 1576, 25.
31 Guazzo 1581, bk. 1, fo. 41^v.
32 Guazzo 1581, bk. 1, fo. 43^v.
33 Guazzo 1581, bk. 1, fo. 44^r.
34 Guazzo 1581, bk. 1, fo. 44^v.
35 della Casa 1576, 36.
36 Guazzo 1581, bk. 2, fo. 2^v.
37 On the place of the duel in writings on civil conversation, see Peltonen 2003, 44–58.
38 Castiglione 1994, 47.
39 Castiglione 1994, 47.

of an evil speaker, & the other of a false accuser, they have made an ende of their lives and their quarrels both together."[40]

Simon Robson in his *Courte of civill courtesie* of 1577 speaks yet more emphatically about the need to stand ready to exact private revenge. If someone impugns my honor with "reprochefull names," there can be no question of allowing such an insult to pass. I must "either offer the first blowe (if the place serve for it) or els chalenge him into the feild."[41] If, Robson later repeats, "the other give mee the first lie, or like disgrace, it is not inough to say hee lieth againe: but I must needs offer a blow, or chalenge the feeild."[42] Robson is even willing to provide advice on precisely how such challenges should be phrased. You should declare that, "if any body have any quarell to mee, I have businesse into sutche a place, sutche a day, at sutche an hower: I wil have but my selfe and my man, or but my selfe and my freinde, there hee may finde mee if hee dare."[43] By these means the civilities will be upheld, but your lethal purpose will nevertheless be made clear.

If, however, we are confronted not with insults but merely with the ill-mannered and condescending behavior of the prideful, the arrogant, and the vainglorious, then our aim should be to respond condescendingly in turn. More specifically, as the figure of Annibale proposes in book II of Guazzo's *Civile Conversation*, we should seek to shame such persons, bringing them into line by means of satirizing and ridiculing them "in manner of mockerie, or of scorn" until they "are driven to amende their manners and life."[44] Guazzo is proposing, in other words, that "laughing to scorn" may be one of the most effective means of curbing and controlling the most prevalent forms of unsociability.

Guazzo's advice derives from a number of more general beliefs that he shares with other writers on civil conversation about the nature of laughter and the range of emotions it may be said to express. The accounts they offer owe an obvious debt to various classical writers, especially Aristotle in his *Rhetoric* and the Roman rhetoricians influenced by his analysis, above all Cicero and Quintilian.[45] Hobbes is no less indebted to the same authorities, and it is important in this connection to remember that he was not only a deep admirer of Aristotle's *Rhetoric*—which he characterized to John Aubrey as "rare"[46] —but also the author of the earliest English translation of Aristotle's text, which he published anonymously as *A Briefe of the Art of Rhetorique* in 1637.[47]

---

[40] Guazzo, 1581, bk. 1, fo. 29ᵛ.
[41] Robson 1577, 24.
[42] Robson 1577, 24.
[43] Robson 1577, 21.
[44] Guazzo 1581, bk. 2, fo. 4ᵛ.
[45] My discussion of the classical sources draws on (but also corrects) Skinner 2004.
[46] Aubrey 1898, vol. 1, 357.
[47] Hobbes began by making a Latin paraphrase of Aristotle's text, which he seems to have produced in the early 1630s; the English translation, which he published in 1637, is based on this text. Hobbes's Latin paraphrase is preserved at Chatsworth as Hobbes MS D.1: *Latin Exercises* (bound MS volume with *Ex Artistot: Rhet.* at 1–143).

Aristotle examines the phenomenon of laughter in the passage from book II of the *Rhetoric* in which he reflects on the manners of youth. One characteristic of young people is said to be that (in the words of Hobbes's translation) they are "Lovers of Mirth, and by consequence love to jest at others."[48] Inquiring into the feelings expressed by their mirth, Aristotle suggests that "*Jesting* is witty Contumely," having previously explained that contumely "is the disgracing of another for his own pastime."[49] Aristotle's basic idea is thus that the laughter induced by jesting is generally an expression of scorn, a suggestion already present in his earlier observation that among the sources of pleasure are "ridiculous Actions, Sayings and Persons."[50] As he points out himself,[51] he had already pursued these implications in his *Poetics*, especially in his brief section on comedy.[52] Comedy deals in the risible, and the risible is an aspect of the shameful, the ugly, or the base. If we find ourselves laughing at others, it will be because they exhibit some fault or mark of shame that, while not painful, makes them seem appropriate objects of contempt.[53]

These assumptions are more fully explored in Roman antiquity[54] and may even be said to be reflected in the Latin language itself, in which the verb to laugh, *ridere*, is scarcely distinct from the verb to mock, *deridere*. The fullest exploration is provided by Cicero in book II of his *De oratore*, in which the figure of Caesar is persuaded to discourse about the concept of the laughable. He begins by offering a restatement and elaboration of Aristotle's argument. "The place or region," he lays down, "in which laughable matters may be said to be found is occupied by *turpitudo* and *deformitas*."[55] Caesar speaks of *deformitas* only at the end of his introductory remarks, where he brutally observes that "in physical deformity and weaknesses of the body there is a lot of good material for making jokes."[56] He mainly concentrates on the potential for derisive laughter to be found in those whose conduct is *turpis*, that is, base or foul, shameful or ignoble. As he summarizes, "the things that chiefly and even solely provoke laughter are the sorts of remarks that note and call attention to something shameful, although without doing so in a shameful way."[57] We do not laugh at serious improbity, for this

---

[48] [Hobbes] 1986, 86.

[49] [Hobbes] 1986, 70, 86.

[50] [Hobbes] 1986, 57.

[51] Aristotle 1926, I. 11. 28, 128, and III. 18. 7, 466.

[52] It may be, however, that Aristotle is referring to a fuller discussion in the now lost book II of his *Poetics*.

[53] Aristotle 1995, 1449a, 44.

[54] In quoting from Cicero and Quintilian I have used the Loeb editions but supplied my own translations.

[55] Cicero 1942, II. 58. 236, vol. 1, 372: "Locus autem, et regio quasi ridiculi . . . turpitudine et deformitate quadam continetur."

[56] Cicero 1942, II. 59. 238, vol. 1, 374: "Est etiam deformitatis et corporis vitiorum satis bella materies ad iocandum."

[57] Cicero 1942, II. 58. 236, vol. 1, 372: "haec enim ridentur vel sola, vel maxime, quae notant et designant turpitudinem aliquam non turpiter." On Cicero and laughter as ridicule, see O'Callaghan 2007, 38–41.

deserves punishment as opposed to mockery; nor should we laugh at people's misery, for no one likes to see the wretched taunted. We should recognize that "the materials for producing ridicule are to be found in the vices of those who neither enjoy esteem nor have suffered calamity."[58] It is here that we come upon the base and the shameful, whose vices are deserving of mockery and whose manners "if elegantly touched on, give rise to laughter." [59]

The other leading rhetorician who examines the connections between laughter and scorn is Quintilian in book 6 of his *Institutio oratoria*. He quotes Cicero's contention that laughter "has its source in a certain kind of *deformitas* or *turpitudo*,"[60] and he adds that "those sayings which excite laughter are often false (which is always ignoble), often cleverly distorted, always base and never honorable."[61] He concludes that "laughter is never very far removed from derision," and thus that the overriding emotion expressed by it will generally be one of disdainful superiority.[62] As he later summarizes, "the most ambitious way of glorying over others is to speak derisively."[63]

It was essentially this view of laughter that the Renaissance writers on civil conversation inherited.[64] We find it most fully restated and developed by Castiglione in book II of *The Courtier*, in which the figure of Bernardo Bibbiena responds at length to Lady Emilia's request that he should explain the value of jests and "howe we should use them."[65] What passion of the soul, Bernardo begins by asking, can be so powerful as to make us burst out in an almost uncontrollable way, as we do when we laugh? One of the feelings involved must always be some form of joy or happiness. As Bernardo puts it, laughing "alwaies is a token of a certein jocundenesse and merrie moode that he feeleth inwardlie in his minde."[66] But this joy is of a peculiar kind, appearing as it does to be connected with feelings of contempt. Whenever we laugh we are "mockinge and scorninge," seeking "to scoff and mocke at vices."[67] Later in the discussion he repeats that most jesting is "grounded upon scoffing," and involves "deceit, or dissimulacion, or mockinge, or rebukinge" of others.[68]

This understanding of the emotions expressed by laughter is strongly endorsed by the English writers on civil conversation. Simon Robson in his *Courte of ciuill courtesie* treats it as obvious that to laugh is to mock or deride.[69] To say that someone's behavior

---

[58] Cicero 1942, II. 59. 238, vol. 1, 374: "materies omnis ridiculorum est in istis vitiis quae sunt in vita hominum neque carorum neque calamitosorum."

[59] Cicero 1942, II. 59. 238, vol. 1, 374: "eaque belle agitata ridentur."

[60] Quintilian 2001, VI. 3. 8, vol. 3, 66, referring to Cicero *De oratore*, II. 58. 236, vol. 1, 372: "[Risus habet] sedem in deformitate aliqua et turpitudine."

[61] Quintilian 2001, VI. 3. 6, vol. 3, 66: "ridiculum dictum plerumque falsum est [hoc semper humile], saepe ex industria depravatum, praeterea <semper humile,> numquam honorificum."

[62] Quintilian 2001, VI. 3. 8, vol. 3, 66: "A derisu non procul abest risus."

[63] Quintilian 2001, XI. 1. 22, vol. 5, 20: "Ambitiosissimum gloriandi genus est etiam deridere."

[64] Herrick 1964, 36–57.

[65] Castiglione 1994, 153.

[66] Castiglione 1994, 154.

[67] Castiglione 1994, 155–56.

[68] Castiglione 1994, 179, 188.

[69] Robson 1577, 10–11.

is "worthy the laughyng at" is to claim that it deserves "disprayse, or mockyng" by those who know how to comport themselves.[70] Lodowick Bryskett writes in similar terms in his *Discourse of civill life*. He acknowledges that urbanity requires our jesting to be "sharpe and wittie, and yet not bitter or overbiting," but he adds that "a discreet or wittie jest cannot be much worth, or move men to laugh, unles it have a certaine deceit or offence intended."[71]

We encounter a comparable line of argument among the neo-Ciceronian rhetoricians of the same period, who are no less interested in the power of words to affect people's behavior and hence to regulate social life. Among the English vernacular rhetoricians by far the most influential was Thomas Wilson, whose *Arte of rhetorique* was first published in 1553 and went through at least seven printings before the end of the century.[72] Wilson includes in his treatise an extensive section entitled "Of delitying the hearers, and stirryng them to laughter." "We laugh alwaies," he agrees, "at those thynges, whiche either onely or chiefly touche handsomely, and wittely some especiall fault, or fonde behavior in some one body, or some one thing."[73] Our aim in provoking laughter will generally be to elicit "scorne out right."[74]

What specific actions or attributes particularly deserve to be laughed to scorn? The Renaissance writers reiterate that physical deformity provides an excellent subject for jokes. Castiglione goes so far as to suggest that "the hedspring that laughing matters arise of, consisteth in a certain deformitie or ill favourednesse."[75] It is true that he warns us to "take heed of too much taunting in touching a man, especially in the ill favourednesse of visage or yll shape of bodye." But he nevertheless accepts without demur that "the misshapes and vices of the bodie minister manie times ample matter to laughe at, if a man can discreatly handle it."[76]

If we shift, however, from physical to moral deformity, we come upon a contrast between the Renaissance writers and their classical authorities. Cicero had argued that neither tragic miseries nor grave improbities are fit subjects for laughter; our mockery should be limited to those who are *turpis*, foul, or base in some way. The figure of Bernardo in Castiglione's *Courtier* agrees that we ought not to "scoff and mocke" at serious wickedness nor at persons "of such miserye that it should move compassion."[77] But when he turns to those who deserve to be laughed at, he prefers to speak of using ridicule not against those who are foul and base but rather against those who display the specific vices of incivility. The sort of people who rightly "much provoke laughter,"[78]

---

[70] Robson 1577, 10.
[71] Bryskett 1606, 246.
[72] Baumlin 2001, 283, 289–90. On Wilson see Mack 2002, 76–78, 83–84, 96–99; Shrank 2004, 182–219.
[73] Wilson 1553, sig. T, 2^v.
[74] Wilson 1553, sig. T, 3^r.
[75] Castiglione 1994, 155.
[76] Castiglione 1994, 159.
[77] Castiglione 1994, 156.
[78] Castiglione 1994, 163.

he maintains, are those who "bragg and boast of themselves," who are "proude and haughtye,"[79] and who "passe the degree" in speaking of themselves with affectation and vaingloriousness.[80] Guazzo writes in close agreement with this sense of priorities. He too speaks of proud and haughty "halfe Gentlemen" who "make boast of the woorthinesse of their auncestours," dismissing them as contemptible and therefore "to bee laughed at."[81] He also speaks of those who suffer from "vaineglorie" and like to "put difference betweene themselves and other," concluding once again that these are among the people who particularly deserve "to bee laughed at."[82] It is chiefly against unsociability, they agree, that scornful laughter should be deployed.

We can now see how the writers on civil conversation reach the conclusion that laughter can serve as a potent means of social control. They have laid it down that to laugh is generally to express contempt. If, then, we can manage to direct our laughter, as they suggest, against the boastful, the vainglorious, and the proud—in a word, against the uncivil—we can perhaps hope to cure them of their incivility. Since they will not wish to be viewed with contempt, we can expect them to take considerable pains to change their behavior, if only in the hope of avoiding further ridicule. Laughter can thus be used as a means of discouraging people from acting "oute of measure" and of keeping them firmly within the established bounds of civil conversation and sociability.[83]

Castiglione accordingly concludes that "the kinde of jesting that is somewhat grounded upon scoffing seemeth verie meete for great men," who can use it to shame and humiliate those who "go beyond bounds" and need to be disciplined.[84] Thomas Wilson likewise emphasizes the controlling power enjoyed by those who, "when time serveth, can geve a mery answere, or use a nippyng taunte." Confronted with some socially unacceptable form of behavior, such people have the ability to "abash" the person who has failed in civility and "make hym at his wittes ende, through the sodein quip & unloked frumpe geven." Wilson assures us that "I haue knowen some so hit of the thumbes" by the rebuking and reforming power of laughter that they have been unsure "whether it were beste to fighte, chide, or to go their waie." Nor is their discomfiture surprising, for "wher the jest is aptly applied, the hearers laugh immediatly, & who would gladly be laughed to scorne?"[85] The clear implication is that once you have been "abashed, and putte out of countenaunce" in this way, you will take considerable pains to ensure that it does not happen again.[86]

It is true that some scruples are occasionally expressed at this stage in the argument. If, as Guazzo puts it, we find a companion on the brink of "committing some absurditie either in wordes or in matter," we might think it more magnanimous to attempt "discreetely to prevent him." We ought perhaps to "take holde of him" and "staye him

---

[79] Castiglione 1994, 155.
[80] Castiglione 1994, 163–64.
[81] Guazzo 1581, bk. 2, fo. 37^r.
[82] Guazzo 1581, bk. 2, fo. 39^r.
[83] Castiglione 1994, 163.
[84] Castiglione 1994, 179.
[85] Wilson 1553, sig. T, 2^r.
[86] Wilson 1553, sig. T, 2^v and 3^v.

up: not staying till hee fall, to make the companie fall a laughing, and him selfe to bee ashamed." We should be ready to demonstrate in a friendly manner "the good account wee make of him," and "give him to understande howe jealous wee are of his honour," thereby preventing him from having reason "to thinke him selfe had in contempt."[87]

Much more emphatically, Giovanni della Casa wholly rejects the idea of using derisive laughter as a means of imposing civility. Della Casa's *Galateo* is an attempt, very much in the spirit of Castiglione's *Courtier*, to explain how best to conduct ourselves in our "familiar conversation, and behaviour with men."[88] As a papal Nuncio, however, and a firm believer in the principles of the Counter-Reformation, della Casa writes in tones of considerable moral earnestness.[89] He warns us that under no circumstances should we allow "that a man should scorne or scoffe at any man, what so ever he be: no not his very enimy, what displeasure so ever he beare him."[90] Anyone who has "a sporte and a pleasure to make a man blush" is guilty of "spitefull behaviours" of a kind that make him "unworthy to beare the name of an honest gentleman." If we wish to follow "good maner & honesty," we must make sure that we "scorne no man in any case."[91]

Della Casa is unusual, however, in placing so much emphasis on these scruples. Generally, the writers on civil conversation are not merely willing but eager to show us how to deploy the restraining power of laughter to hold the social vices at bay. First we need to deal with the contentious and the obstinate,[92] those whom della Casa had described as the "froward," whose conversation "consisteth in ouertwharting other mens desiers," and whose testiness turns friends into foes.[93] Castiglione tells the following anecdote about how to cope with such frowardness:

> A worthie Gentlewoman in a noble assembly spake pleasauntly unto one, that shall be namelesse for this tyme, whome she to shewe hym a good countenance, desired to daunce with her, and he refusing both that, and to heare musick and many other entertainmentes offred him, alwaies affirming suche trifles not to be his profession, at last the Gentlewoman demaundyng him, What is then your profession? He aunswered with a frowning looke: To fight.
>
> Then saide the Gentlewoman: Seing you are not nowe at the warre nor in place to fight, I woulde thinke it beste for you to bee well besmered and set up in an armorie with other implementes of warre till time wer that you should be occupied, least you waxe more rustier then you are.[94]

The lady's mockery, Castiglione assures us, produced exactly the desired effect. Her response gave rise to "muche laughinge of the standers by," thereby turning the froward

[87] Guazzo 1581, bk. 2, fo. 28^{v}.
[88] della Casa 1576, 4.
[89] As noted in Burke 1993, 98–102.
[90] della Casa 1576, 62.
[91] della Casa 1576, 63.
[92] Guazzo 1581, bk. 1, fo. 39^{v}.
[93] della Casa 1576, 25.
[94] Castiglione 1994, 43.

warrior into an object of general contempt.[95] As Castiglione summarizes, "she left him with a mock" in such a way that his "foolishe presumpcion" was laughed to scorn.[96]

We also need to know how to deal with the boastful and the vainglorious. Here Guazzo sets aside his earlier anxieties about the potential dangers of ridicule. Not only does he speak with particular contempt of boastful ignorance, but he offers several examples to illustrate how the power of laughter can be used to expose this failing to well-deserved scorn. One case he cites is that of a visit paid by Alexander the Great to the house of the celebrated painter Apelles. Alexander began "reasoning of painting" to his host and proceeded to speak in a manner "impertinent and contrarie to that art." Whereupon "the wise Painter whispered him in the eare, that hee shoulde speake no more of that matter, or els that he shoulde speake softly, for that his prentices laught him to scorne."[97] A second and, as Guazzo puts it, a more odious example is that of the "poore feeble Sophist" who came before King Cleomenes and "reasoned in his presence of valour and force." The king immediately "fell a laughing," and replied that, if an eagle were to speak to him of strength he would listen, but if a swallow were to do so "I shoulde not forebeare laughing" at such vaingloriousness.[98]

Finally, we need to be able to control the pride and haughtiness of those who, in Guazzo's words, "seeke in company to goe before others" and treat their supposed inferiors with disdain.[99] Wilson tells the story of "a gentleman of great landes & small witte" who "talked largely at a supper, and spake wordes scant worth the hearyng." One of his hearers, "muche greeved with his foolie, saied to hym: Sir I haue taken you for a plaine meanyng gentleman, but I know nowe, there is not a more deceiptfull bodie in al Englande." When another guest remonstrated, he retorted that "I must nedes say he is deceiptful, for I toke hym heretofore for a sober wittie young man, but now I perceive, he is a foolish bablyng felowe." The power of this kind of ridicule to impose control is explicitly underlined. Wilson ends by telling us that "they al laughed, and the gentleman was muche abashed."[100]

Hobbes's civil philosophy has rarely been considered in relation to the genre of writing on civil conversation, and we have even been urged to see in *Leviathan* an aspiration to transcend any trivial concerns with what Hobbes describes in chapter 11 as "Decency of behaviour" and "such other points of the *Small moralls*."[101] But in fact Hobbes was intimately acquainted with, and much preoccupied by, Renaissance traditions of writing on precisely these themes. There can be no doubt in the first place that he made a close study of several leading Italian texts on *la civil conversazione*. While he was serving as tutor to the Earl of Devonshire in the 1620s he compiled a catalogue of the

---

[95] Castiglione 1994, 43.
[96] Castiglione 1994, 43.
[97] Guazzo 1581, bk. 2, fo. 22ʳ. A different version of the story can be found in Brathwait 1630, 276.
[98] Guazzo 1581, bk. 2, fo. 23ᵛ.
[99] Guazzo 1581, bk. 1, fo. 44ʳ.
[100] Wilson 1553, sig Aa, 4ᵛ.
[101] Hobbes 2012, ch. 11, vol. 2, 150. Cf. Farneti 2000, 489, 498.

earl's library in which he recorded copies of Castiglione's *Courtier* in English, French, Italian, and Latin[102]; della Casa's *Galateo* in Latin[103]; and Guazzo's *Civile Conversation* in English, Italian, and Latin.[104] Hobbes and the young earl studied Castiglione's *Courtier* together, and Hobbes even required his pupil to produce a Latin translation of the opening book.[105]

It is clear, moreover, that Hobbes was much indebted to these writers in formulating his own account of sociable life. He closely follows their anatomy of incivility, focusing as they had done on the froward and obstinate, the boastful and vainglorious, and those who are marked by arrogance and pride. More generally, he is in basic agreement with the principles of civil conversation as laid down by Castiglione, Guazzo, and their followers. First and most basically, he fully endorses their broad understanding of the concept of conversation itself. When he summarizes the laws of nature at the start of chapter 18 of *The Elements of Law*, he explains that they are described as laws because "they are dictates of natural reason" and are specifically described as moral laws "because they concern men's manners and conversation one towards another."[106] When he turns in chapter 3 of *De cive* to examine the injustice involved in failing to honor our contracts and promises, he describes this failure to observe the laws of nature as inimical to our *conversatio* with our fellow citizens.[107] And when he offers his further summary of the laws of nature at the end of chapter 15 of *Leviathan*, he goes so far as to proclaim that "Morall Philosophy is nothing else but the Science of what is *Good*, and *Evill*, in the conversation, and Society of man-kind."[108]

Hobbes's aim, in other words, is not merely to show men how they can be brought to live in obedient subjection to the laws of the state; it is also to show them how they can hope to follow a "peaceable, sociable, and comfortable" way of life.[109] He wants, in short, to make men fit for what he calls "Civill Society."[110] As he puts it in summary in the Review and Conclusion of *Leviathan*, the question is not merely how to impose obedience but also how to produce "a constant Civill Amity" among men.[111]

When Hobbes goes on to consider how such a code of sociability might be imposed, he similarly draws on a number of classical arguments that the writers on civil conversation had already invoked. These intellectual allegiances are most clearly revealed in Hobbes's analysis of laughter and the range of passions it may be said to express. It is true that, in his first and fullest analysis in chapter 9 of *The Elements*, he begins with a noisy proclamation of his own originality: "There is a passion which hath no name, but

[102] Hobbes MSS (Chatsworth), MS E. 1. A, 69, 70, 126.
[103] Hobbes MSS (Chatsworth), MS E. 1. A, 84. The work is listed as "Galataeus de moribus."
[104] Hobbes MSS (Chatsworth), MS E. 1. A, 83, 84, 128.
[105] Malcolm 2007, 4.
[106] Hobbes 1969, 18. 1, 95.
[107] Hobbes 1983, III. III, 109.
[108] Hobbes 2012, ch. 15, vol. 2, 242.
[109] Hobbes 2012, ch. 15, vol. 2, 242.
[110] Hobbes 2012, ch. 15, vol. 2, 238.
[111] Hobbes 2012, vol. 3, 1132.

the sign of it is that distortion of the countenance we call LAUGHTER, which is always joy; but what joy, what we think, and wherein we triumph when we laugh, hath not hitherto been declared by any."[112]

After this self-congratulating flourish, however, the analysis that Hobbes offers is very similar to the one already developed by Castiglione on the basis of his classical authorities.[113] Hobbes agrees that what generally provokes us to laugh is a sense of our own superiority over other people's incapacities or absurdities.[114] As he phrases it in his formal definition: "the passion of laughter is nothing else but a sudden glory arising from sudden conception of some eminency in ourselves, by comparison with the infirmities of others, or with our own formerly."[115] He also agrees that the laughter in which we express our joy at this "sudden imagination of our own odds and eminence"[116] cannot fail to embody an element of condescension and contempt. "Men laugh at the infirmities of others, by comparison of which their own abilities are set off and illustrated," and at jests in which "the wit whereof always consisteth in the elegant discovering and conveying to our minds some absurdity of another."[117] To laugh is to glory over others, and is thus to dishonor them.[118] "To be laughed at" is consequently to be "derided, that is, triumphed over"[119] and viewed with scorn.[120]

For Hobbes, accordingly, laughter can hardly fail to be seriously offensive, and he explicitly insists in *The Elements* that there is only one way in which it can be indulged "without offence."[121] This is when we laugh together in company at the follies of the world. When this happens, we pour scorn upon "absurdities and infirmities abstracted from persons" and "all the company may laugh together."[122] But in all other instances our laughter takes the form of "recommending ourselves to our own good opinion, by comparison with another man's infirmities or absurdity."[123] The possibility that we might sometimes laugh self-deprecatingly at our own absurdity is explicitly ruled out. Hobbes goes so far as to assert that "when a jest is broken upon ourselves . . . we never laugh thereat."[124] So it is hardly surprising, he concludes, "that men take it heinously to be laughed at," for in fact they are being treated as worthy only of contempt.[125] Summarizing in a harsh passage at

---

[112] Hobbes 1969, 9. 13, 41.

[113] This is perhaps surprising, for in the intervening period the classical theory had been extensively criticized. For details see Skinner 2004, 149–53.

[114] See Morreall 1983, 4–14 on Hobbes as the strongest defender of the "superiority theory" of laughter.

[115] Hobbes 1969, 9. 13, 42. See also Hobbes 1983, I. II, 90, where he adds in still more classical vein that we laugh at *turpitudo* as well as *infirmitas*.

[116] Hobbes 1969, 9. 13, 41.

[117] Hobbes 1969, 9. 13, 41-2.

[118] Hobbes twice equates laughing at people with dishonoring them. See Hobbes 1969, 9. 13, 41.

[119] Hobbes 1969, 9. 13, 42.

[120] Hobbes connects laughter specifically with scorn in *Leviathan*: see Hobbes 2012, ch. 6, vol. 2, 88.

[121] Hobbes 1969, 9. 13, 42.

[122] Hobbes 1969, 9. 13, 42.

[123] Hobbes 1969, 9. 13, 42.

[124] Hobbes 1969, 9. 13, 42.

[125] Hobbes 1969, 9. 13, 42. For laughter as a means specifically of expressing and soliciting contempt (*contemptus*) see Hobbes 1983, I. VII, 94.

the end of chapter 9, in which he compares human life with a race, he ends by declaring that it is when we "see another fall" that our "disposition to laugh" comes into play.[126]

A similar analysis reappears in chapter 6 of *Leviathan*. Laughter, Hobbes again affirms, is almost invariably an expression of superiority and a means of glorying over others: "*Sudden Glory*, is the passion which maketh those *Grimaces* called LAUGHTER; and is caused either by some sudden act of their own, that pleaseth them; or by the apprehension of some deformed thing in another, by comparison whereof they suddenly applaud themselves."[127]

Hobbes had spoken in *The Elements* about the *infirmities* of others as a cause of laughter, but here he echoes still more strongly the classical and Renaissance view that *deformity* is likewise an appropriate object of mirth. As he intimates, however, he is chiefly interested in moral rather than physical deformity, and this emphasis is brought out still more clearly in his final attempt to supply a definition of laughter, which he puts forward in his *De homine* of 1658. Here he rounds off his observations by aligning himself yet more closely with the writers on civil conversation, claiming that "invariably, the passion of laughter is a sudden commendation of oneself prompted by the *indecorousness* of someone else."[128]

Hobbes endorses so many of the arguments originally deployed by the writers on civil conversation that, when it comes to the question of how to impose sociability, one might expect him once more to follow their lead. But at this stage he suddenly takes a very different tack. Not only does he part company with their line of argument, but it would scarcely be an exaggeration to say that much of what he goes on to suggest is framed as a direct response to, and repudiation of, what they had earlier proposed.

First of all, Hobbes is utterly dismissive of the idea that we should seek to enforce civility by means of private revenge. He refuses even to permit the state to treat vengeance as a possible justification for punishment. "The aym of Punishment," he roundly declares, "is not a revenge."[129] As for avenging incivilities by dueling to the death, he denounces this practice as nothing better than an upstart and vainglorious custom "not many years since begun, amongst young and vain men."[130] He objects that the alleged hurts assuaged by duels are "not Corporeall, but Phantasticall," and are therefore not worth the attention of anyone "that is assured of his own courage."[131] He expresses bewilderment that men are prepared to use such lethal violence merely to uphold their sense of self-worth and are consequently ready to fight "for trifles, as a word, a smile, a different opinion, and any other signe of undervalue."[132] He praises "the Lawes of the Greeks, Romans, and other both antient, and moderne Common-wealths" for refusing

[126] Hobbes 1969, 9. 21, 48.
[127] Hobbes 2012, ch. 6, vol. 2, 88.
[128] Hobbes 1839, XII. 7, 108: "universaliter passio ridentium, est sui sibi ex indecoro alieno subita commendatio."
[129] Hobbes 2012, ch. 28, vol. 2, 486.
[130] Hobbes 2012, ch. 27, vol. 2, 466.
[131] Hobbes 2012, ch. 27, vol. 2, 466.
[132] Hobbes 2012, ch. 13, vol. 2, 192.

to pay any heed to "the offence men take, from contumely, in words, or gesture, when they produce no other harme, than the present griefe of him that is reproached."[133] Most dismissively of all, he maintains that the real reason why vainglorious young men are prone to engage in such murderous acts of vengeance is that, paradoxically, they lack courage and magnanimity. As wise legislators recognize, "the true cause of such griefe" consists "not in the contumely, (which takes no hold upon men conscious of their own virtue,) but in the Pusillanimity of him that is offended by it."[134]

Hobbes is no less vehemently opposed to the further suggestion that incivility may be controlled by derision and ridicule. He first announces his dissent in chapter 16 of *The Elements of Law*. It is one of the laws of nature, he declares, "*That no man reproach, revile, deride, or any otherwise declare his hatred, contempt, or disesteem of any other.*"[135] The same contention recurs in chapter 3 of *De cive*, in which he explicitly insists that laughter amounts to just such an expression of disesteem and contempt. "It is prescribed by the law of nature," he repeats, "that no one should exhibit hatred or contempt of other people by what they do, or by what they say, or by how they look at them, or by laughing at them."[136] Finally, he makes the same point with no less emphasis in chapter 15 of *Leviathan*, in which he again declares that it is a precept of the law of nature "That no man by deed, word, countenance, or gesture, declare Hatred, or Contempt of another."[137]

Here Hobbes is directly opposing the generally accepted view among the writers on civil conversation about how to control unsociability. But at the same time he is closely aligning himself with earlier critics, notably Giovanni della Casa, who had already voiced similar doubts. It is true that Hobbes's reasons for forbidding scornful laughter are at first rather different from those of della Casa. As we have seen, della Casa's objection had been that such mockery is an instance of dishonorable incivility in itself. By contrast, Hobbes's initial argument is at least as much prudential as moral in character. As he explains in *The Elements*, his reason for outlawing laughter is that "all signs which we shew to one another of hatred and contempt, provoke in the highest degree to quarrel and battle" and consequently serve to undermine civil peace.[138] The same argument is more expansively developed in the opening chapter of *De cive*. Hobbes now explains that "because all pleasure and exaltation of the mind consists in being able to think highly of oneself by comparison with others, it is impossible for people to avoid exhibiting some mutual contempt, whether they express it by laughter, or by words, or by some gesture or other sign."[139] As he warns us, however, "nothing gives

---

[133] Hobbes 2012, ch. 27, vol. 2, 480.

[134] Hobbes 2012, ch. 27, vol. 2, 480.

[135] Hobbes 1969, 16. 11, 86.

[136] Hobbes 1983, III. XII, 113: "lege naturali praescriptum esse, nequis vel factis, vel verbis, vel vultu, vel risu, alteri ostendat se illum vel odisse, vel contemnere."

[137] Hobbes 2012 ch. 15, vol. 2, 234.

[138] Hobbes 1969, 16. 11, 86.

[139] Hobbes 1983, I. V, 94: "Cumque omnis animi voluptas omnisque alacritas in eo sita sit, quod quis habeat, quibuscum conferens se, possit magnifice sentire de se ipso, impossibile est quin odium & contemptum mutuum ostendant aliquando, vel risu, vel verbis, vel gestu, vel aliquo signo."

greater offence to the mind than such behavior, and nothing is more likely to give rise to a desire to hurt" and a consequent relapse into violence and the state of war.[140] A similar argument reappears in chapter 15 of *Leviathan*, in which Hobbes warns us yet again that the reason why we must never behave contemptuously is that "all signes of hatred, or contempt, provoke to fight, insomuch as most men choose rather to hazard their life, than not to be revenged," with the result that they fall not merely into breaches of the peace but eventually into a condition of war.[141]

If we turn, however, to Hobbes's final remarks about laughter in *Leviathan*, we encounter a wholly different argument. He now aligns himself with the most irenic of the writers on civil conversation and denounces scornful laughter in the same moralistic tones. He had already spoken with disapproval in *The Elements*, declaring that "it is vain glory, and an argument of little worth, to think the infirmities of another sufficient matter for his triumph."[142] But in *Leviathan* he goes much further. Closely echoing della Casa, he now maintains that scornful laughter is a sign of cowardice, and is therefore dishonorable. It is "incident most to them, that are conscious of the fewest abilities in themselves; who are forced to keep themselves in their own favour, by observing the imperfections of other men. And therefore much Laughter at the defects of others, is a signe of Pusillanimity."[143] To which he adds, echoing Guazzo, that such laughter also embodies a failure of magnanimity. "For of great minds, one of the proper workes is, to help and free others from scorn; and compare themselves onely with the most able."[144] Hobbes's final reason for rejecting scornful laughter is thus the same as his reason for condemning duels: both appear to reflect high confidence, but both are in truth expressions of cowardice.

The conclusion at which Hobbes finally arrives, however, merely raises once again the question from which we started out. He forbids us to control the unsociable by means of any form of physical or even verbal violence. But he agrees that the froward, the vainglorious, the prideful, and the arrogant are prone to act in violation of the laws of nature, and are liable in consequence to generate conflict and war. If there is to be any prospect of leading a "peaceable, sociable, and comfortable" way of life, they will somehow have to be coped with or controlled.[145] But how?

Hobbes is by no means bereft of answers and has three different suggestions to make. The first carries us back to Guazzo's distinction between those who, while lacking civility, will nevertheless have to be admitted to civil conversation, and those whose behavior is so unsociable that they will have to be excluded. Hobbes agrees that, in the case of those who are irredeemably untrustworthy or intractable, the only solution will be

---

[140] Hobbes 1983, I. V, 94: "qua quidem nulla maior animi est molestia, neque ex qua laedendi libido maior oriri solet."

[141] Hobbes 2012, ch. 15, vol. 2, 234.

[142] Hobbes 1969, 9. 13, 42; cf. also Hobbes 1983, I. II, 90.

[143] See Hobbes 2012, ch. 6, vol. 2, 88 and the reiteration of the argument in the Latin version at 89.

[144] See Hobbes 2012, ch. 6, vol. 2, 88 and the reiteration of the argument in the Latin version at 89.

[145] Hobbes 2012, ch. 15, vol. 2, 242.

to prevent them at the outset from taking any part in civil life. Turning first to the untrustworthy, he argues that anyone who "breaketh his Covenant, and consequently declareth that he thinks he may with reason do so, cannot be received into any Society, that unite themselves for Peace and Defence."[146] Later he adds that anyone who is so intractable that, "for the stubbornness of his Passions, cannot be corrected" will like-wise have to be "left, or cast out of Society, as combersome thereunto."[147]

Hobbes briefly mentions a second possibility in chapter 18 of *Leviathan*, although he scarcely develops it. He suggests that, once a civil association has been instituted, it may be possible for the sovereign to deter men, by means other than the imposition of coercive force, from doing disservice to the commonwealth and thereby jeopardiz-ing the peaceful conversation of mankind. Specifically, he suggests, the sovereign may be able to penalize such unsociable subjects with some form of ignominy while at the same time honoring and rewarding good citizenship, thereby harnessing men's inher-ent competitiveness and encouraging habits of civility in others.[148]

Hobbes's principal suggestion, however, simply takes the form of a plea for forbear-ance. He sees little prospect of being able actively to control the behavior of froward, vainglorious, prideful, and arrogant men. Although their conduct is inimical to peace, the only effect of trying to control them will be to jeopardize peace itself. His final word is thus that such people will simply have to be tolerated. As he puts it at the outset of his discussion in chapter 15 of *Leviathan*, the watchword has to be *"That every man strive to accommodate himselfe to the rest."*[149] This injunction is one of the pathways to peace and is consequently one of the laws of nature. It is also the very definition of sociability, for "the observers of this Law, may be called SOCIABLE."[150] If peace is to be preserved, what will somehow have to be mustered in the face of incivility is "an unfeigned and constant endeavour" to act in a manner that remains "modest, and tractable" and truly sociable at all times.[151]

Hobbes is usually thought of as the political writer par excellence who insists that the key to peace lies in subjecting ourselves to the laws of an absolute sovereign whose duty is to keep us all in awe. But this is only one half of his argument. If peace is to be preserved, we also need to maintain a high and unremitting level of self-control, even in the face of unsociable people whose conduct is all too likely to prompt us to react toward them with hatred and contempt. At the heart of Hobbes's civil philosophy lies the demanding insistence that, since the unsociability of such people cannot be restrained either by the state or by the disciplining forces of civil society, the only way to prevent their behavior from leading to war will be to control ourselves. Self-control,

---

[146] Hobbes 2012, ch. 15, vol. 2, 224.
[147] Hobbes 2012, ch. 15, vol. 2, 232.
[148] Hobbes 2012, ch. 18, vol. 2, 276; cf. ch. 28, vol. 2, 490.
[149] Hobbes 2012, ch. 15, vol. 2, 232.
[150] Hobbes 2012, ch. 15, vol. 2, 232.
[151] Hobbes 2012, ch. 15, vol. 2, 240.

as much as the coercive force of law, is the key to peace.

ACKNOWLEDGMENTS

For commenting on drafts I am deeply indebted to the two editors of this volume and to Susan James, Noel Malcolm, Tim Raylor, Raffaella Santi, Keith Thomas, and Phil Withington.

BIBLIOGRAPHY

Aristotle. 1926. *The "Art" of Rhetoric,* edited and translated by J. H. Freese. London: Heinemann.

Aristotle. 1995. *Poetics,* edited and translated by Stephen Halliwell. London: Heinemann.

Aubrey, John. 1898. *"Brief Lives," Chiefly of Contemporaries, Set Down by John Aubrey, Between the Years 1669 & 1696,* edited by Andrew Clark, 2 vols. Oxford, UK: Clarendon Press.

Baumlin, Tita French. 2001. "Thomas Wilson (1523 or 1524–16 June 1581)," in *British Rhetoricians and Logicians 1500–1650* (pp. 282–306), first series, edited by Edward A. Malone. Detroit: Gale Group.

Borrelli, Gianfranco. 2000. *Non Far Novità: Alle radici della cultura italiana della conservazione politica.* Naples: Bibliopolis.

Brathwait, Richard. 1630. *The English Gentleman.* London.

Bryskett, Lodowick. 1606. *A discourse of ciuill life containing the ethike part of morall philosophie.* London.

Burke, Peter. 1993. *The Art of Conversation,* Cambridge, UK: Polity Press.

Castiglione, Baldassare. 1561. *The courtyer of Count Baldessar Castilio . . . done into English by Thomas Hoby.* London.

Castiglione, Baldassare. 1994. *The Book of the Courtier,* translated by Thomas Hoby, edited by Virginia Cox. London: Everyman.

Cicero, Marcus Tullius. 1942. *De oratore,* edited and translated by E. W. Sutton and H. Rackham, 2 vols. London: Heinemann.

Cooper, Julie E. 2010. "Vainglory, Modesty, and Political Agency in the Political Theory of Thomas Hobbes." *Review of Politics* 72: 241–269.

Della Casa, Giovanni. 1576. *Galateo . . . A treatise of the maners and behauiours, it behoueth a man to vse and eschewe, in his familiar conuersation,* translated by Robert Peterson. London.

Farneti, Roberto. 2000. "Una civile conversazione. Una proposta di etica italiana." *Iride* 3: 489–508.

Guazzo, Stefano. 1581. *The Civile Conversation,* translated by George Pettie. London.

Herrick, Marvin J. 1964. *Comic Theory in the Sixteenth Century.* Urbana: University of Illinois Press.

Heyd, David. 1982. "The Place of Laughter in Hobbes's Theory of the Emotions." *Journal of the History of Ideas* 43: 285–295.

Hobbes, Thomas. 1839. *Elementorum philosophiae sectio secunda de homine* in *Thomae Hobbes Malmesburiensis opera philosophica quae Latine scripsit omnia* (vol. 2, pp. 1–132), edited by William Molesworth. London: Bohn.

Hobbes, Thomas. 1969. *The Elements of Law Natural and Politic,* 2nd ed., introduction by M. M. Goldsmith, edited by Ferdinand Tönnies. London: Frank Cass & Co.

Hobbes, Thomas. 1983. *De Cive: The Latin Version*, edited by Howard Warrender. Oxford: Clarendon Press.

Hobbes, Thomas. 1986. *A Briefe of the Art of Rhetorique* in *the Rhetorics of Thomas Hobbes and Bernard Lamy* (pp. 33–128), edited by John T. Harwood. Carbondale and Edwardsville: Southern Illinois University Press.

Hobbes, Thomas. 2012. *Leviathan*, edited by Noel Malcolm, 3 vols. Oxford, UK: Clarendon Press.

Hoekstra, Kinch. 2013. "Hobbesian Equality," in *Hobbes Today: Insights for the 21st Century* (pp. 76–112), edited by S. A. Lloyd. Cambridge, UK: Cambridge University Press.

Malcolm, Noel. 2007. *Reason of State, Propaganda, and the Thirty Years' War: An Unknown Translation by Thomas Hobbes*. Oxford, UK: Clarendon Press.

Ménager, Daniel. 1995. *La Renaissance et le rire*. Paris: Presses Universitaires de France.

Morreall, John. 1983. *Taking Laughter Seriously*. Albany, NY: State University of New York Press.

O'Callaghan, Michelle. 2007. *The English Wits: Literature and Sociability in Early Modern England*. Cambridge, UK: Cambridge University Press.

Panichi, Nicola. 1994. *La virtù eloquente: La "civil conversazione" nel Rinascimento*. Urbino: Montefeltro.

Peltonen, Markku. 2003. *The Duel in Early Modern England: Civility, Politeness and Honour*. Cambridge, UK: Cambridge University Press.

Quintilian. 2001. *Institutio oratoria*, edited and translated by Donald Russell, 5 vols. Cambridge, MA: Harvard University Press.

Richards, Jennifer. 2003. *Rhetoric and Courtliness in Early Modern Literature*. Cambridge, UK: Cambridge University Press.

Robson, Simon. 1577. *The courte of ciuill courtesie*. London.

Shrank, Cathy. 2004. *Writing the Nation in Reformation England 1530–1580*. Oxford, UK: Oxford University Press.

Skinner, Quentin. 2004. "Hobbes and the Classical Theory of Laughter," in *Leviathan After 350 Years* (pp. 139–166), edited by Tom Sorell and Luc Foisneau. Oxford, UK: Clarendon Press.

Skinner, Quentin. 2013. "Hobbes, Laughter and Civil Conversation," in *L'antidoto di Mercuri: La "civil conversazione" tra Rinascimento ed età moderna* (pp. 1–22), edited by Nicola Panichi. Florence: Olschki.

Slomp, Gabriella. 2000. *Thomas Hobbes and the Political Philosophy of Glory*. Basingstoke, UK: St. Martin's Press.

Whigham, Frank. 1984. *Ambition and Privilege: The Social Tropes of Elizabethan Courtesy Theory*. Berkeley: University of California Press.

Wilson, Thomas. 1553. *The Arte of Rhetorique, for the use of all suche as are studious of Eloquence*. London.

PART IV

....

RELIGION

....

....

CHAPTER 20

HOBBES AND RELIGION WITHOUT THEOLOGY

....

AGOSTINO LUPOLI

1 INTRODUCTION

....

ALTHOUGH discussion of Hobbes's theology dates from the appearance of *Leviathan*, it is noteworthy that no professional theologians of the time considered Hobbes one of their number, and none endeavored a serious rebuttal on properly theological terrain. When theologians polemicized against him, as bishop Bramhall[1] did, it was fundamentally to denounce his atheism, and, as an atheist, Hobbes was an opponent but not a worthy interlocutor in a theological controversy. From this point of view, his theology was not even entitled to be defined as a wrong one: it was a "mad divinity," as Henry Hammond, an important biblical scholar who was a friend of Hobbes's, characteristically defined it.[2] Objectively justifiable or not, made in good or bad faith, this kind of judgment prevailed among scholars until some twentieth-century revisionist interpretations proposed, from different point of views and with different intentions, a reappraisal of Hobbes's theology.

An erudite and all-embracing examination of the extensive recent literature commenting on the problem of Hobbes's theology (including his consideration of religion) is beyond the scope of this chapter. However, Frank Lessay's division of it into classes according to three different critical approaches (historical, theological, and philosophical; respectively represented by Arrigo Pacchi, A. P. Martinich, and Luc Foisneau) deserves to be mentioned.[3] Perhaps Lessay's tripartite classification can be simplified

---

[1] Bramhall 1658.

[2] "A farrago of all the maddest divinity that ever was read, and having destroyed Trinity, Heaven, Hell, may be allowed to compare ecclesiastical authority to the kingdom of fairies," quoted in Tuck 1992, 111.

[3] Lessay 2004, 265–294: see Pacchi 1998; Martinich 1992; Foisneau 2000.

by distinguishing only two more comprehensive arrays of scholars. On the one hand, those who claim that Hobbes had a merely opportunistic purpose while treating theological topics; on the other hand, those who assert that Hobbes's philosophy contains a real theological contribution or that the political philosophy rests on theological assumptions and concepts and/or that he is not an irreligious philosopher.[4] Even scholars, like Pacchi, who try to refuse this choice and to adopt a neutral and conciliatory position do not really escape it because even establishing the importance of Hobbes's theological commitments does not amount to excluding their instrumental nature.

This interpretative division can be well illustrated by the two classical studies by Leo Strauss[5] and Howard Warrender.[6] Strauss finds in Hobbes the paradigm of the modern theoretical approach to politics, one characterized by the complete desacralization of the political dimension, and well represents those whose interest is concentrated on the big historical and theoretical theme of the relationship between politics and religion. Warrender makes the consistency of Hobbes's political philosophy depend on the religious foundations of obligation, and he can represent those who aim to recover a genuine conceptual structure of a theological type at the core of Hobbes's political philosophy.

The truth is that it is very difficult to come to a neutral appraisal of Hobbes's theological commitment because no philosopher or historian of modern political thought tackles the matter totally free from biases or general assumptions. Furthermore, Hobbes's "theology" is situated in a complex frame of relationships to the other "elements" of his philosophy—not only to politics, but also to the doctrine of science (logic) and physics. Consequently, its appraisal depends on the way these relationships are understood (or ignored).

Strauss's essay is particularly instructive because it deals with the subject in the context of an overall view of Hobbes's philosophy—a view according to which Hobbes's whole philosophy is subservient to his *Religionskritik*. This amounts to nothing less than an inversion of Hobbes's *ordre des raisons*, for Hobbes clearly places the treatment of theological issues on a terrain entirely determined (both as it concerns the method and the content), in the first place, by the doctrine of science or logic (*Logic*) and, in the second place, by physics and civil philosophy. Although there is no room here to develop a detailed criticism of Strauss's construal, two general points are worth noting. First, the claim that Hobbes's system is an ad hoc theoretical construction oriented to sustaining a *Religionskritik* rests on a hypothesis admittedly arising from a general metaphysical perspective of Strauss's own. Second, it does not take seriously the fundamental and incontrovertible difference between medieval and modern thought (including Hobbes's); namely, the methodological assumption of the autonomy of philosophy from religion and theology.

According to the modern assumption of autonomy, philosophy is not subservient to a pre-established picture of religious beliefs and problems, and theological themes

---

[4] Martinich 2009; Collins 2009.

[5] Strauss 2005.

[6] Warrender 1957.

arise from—and can have cognitive legitimacy within—a merely philosophical and rational terrain (although this does not rule out that concepts and schemes of theological origin can operate covertly in philosophical thought). It is known that this attitude becomes more radical in those philosophers (such as Descartes and Hobbes) who articulated a strong riposte to the skeptics' challenge on the terrain of method or doctrine of science.

The interpretative assumption of the present inquiry is that there is no valid reason not to take seriously Hobbes's own line of argument; that is, to start from Hobbes's decisive argument in his *Logic* concerning the cognitive status of theology.

2 The Cognitive Status of Theology

The *De corpore* deploys a complex and thorough theory of science that rigorously restricts the objects of science to those that can be subjected to inferential procedures stated in the definition of philosophy, which, in brief, means objects liable to (kinetic) generation.[7] Therefore, says Hobbes, the *subject* of Philosophy "excludes *Theology*, I mean the doctrine of God, Eternal, Ingenerable, Incomprehensible, and in whom there is nothing neither to divide nor compound, nor Generation to be conceived." And "it excludes," he also explicitly adds, "the doctrine of *Angels . . . History*, as well *Naturall* as *Politicall*" and "lastly the doctrine of *God's Worship*."[8] Theology is excluded not only from the domain of knowledge τοῦ διότι, but also from that of knowledge τοῦ 'ότι[9] because none of its objects is in the domain of experience; therefore, there is no basis for inductive theological knowledge or theological prudence.

Even though Hobbes expounds his complete doctrine of science only in the *De corpore* (1655), in *The Elements* he had clearly delineated "the acts of our *power cognitive*,"[10] that is, "*Sense, Imagination, Discursion, Ratiocination,* and *Knowledge*." And he had also defined *Truth* (which "is all one" with "*true proposition*"),[11] *Evidence* (the "concomitant of a mans *conception* with the *Words* that signifie such conception"),[12] *Knowledge* "which we call *Science*" ("*evidence of Truth*"),[13] *supposed* and *probable* proposition, *Opinion, Belief, Faith,* and *Conscience*.

Only *true* propositions can be said to be *known* in the proper sense; to know a proposition is the same as to know it is true. But the fact that "what is not truth, can be never known"[14] implies neither that what is not known is not true, nor that what is not true cannot be "thought," "supposed," or "admitted for" true. As for the propositions

---

[7] *De corpore*, 1.8, 16 (Hobbes 1999, ed. K. Schuhmann; hereinafter ed. Schuhmann).
[8] *Concerning Body*, 1.8, 7–8.
[9] *De corpore*, ed. Schuhmann, 6.2, 58.
[10] *Human Nature*, 6.9, 68. Cf. *Philosophicall Rudiments* 18.4, 345–348.
[11] *Human Nature*, 5.10, 52.
[12] Ibid., 6.3, 62.
[13] Ibid., 6.4, 63.
[14] Ibid., 6.2, 61.

that are *not known*, Hobbes considers the domain composed by them and divides it in progressively more restrictive subsets. Subtracting the set of propositions surely false, there remains the large domain of propositions "we think probable," which is composed of two subsets: one is that of propositions *not known* (for true) but nevertheless *supposed* to be true because they were not demonstrated to be false and the other that of propositions "we *admit* for truth by errour of reasoning, or from trusting to other men."[15] The "admittance" of the former is "supposition" and that of the latter "is called *Opinion*." Opinion "is called *Belief*, and sometimes *Faith*" when the admittance of propositions derives from "trust to other men"; therefore, Faith is a particular case of opinion.

This distinction is very important because it corresponds to a profound difference between the "conscience" (i.e., what we would call the *psychological status*) of him who *supposes the truth* and that of him who has the *opinion of the truth* of a proposition. Whereas the *supposition of truth* entails the awareness that probable propositions may be false, the *opinion of truth* excludes this awareness. As the "errour of reasoning" embedded in the demonstration of a proposition is accompanied by the false conscience of *knowledge*, thus the *belief* or *faith* is characterized by the (*psychological* not *logical*) exclusion of falsity.

In other words, Hobbes points out that certainty (or the impossibility not to assent to a proposition) is not only the necessary effect of true knowledge, but is also a psychological status that accompanies *opinion* and brings about the psychological impossibility of doubting either the truth of a proposition erroneously thought to be demonstrated or the words of those we trust. The use of the word "conscience" makes good his case because, Hobbes observes, by it "we commonly mean" not *supposition* but only "either *Science* or *Opinion*"; that is, "men say that such and such a thing is true upon their Conscience" only when "they *know* or *think* they know it to be true." As a result of this, when men "say things upon their Conscience, are not therefore presumed certainly to know the truth of what they say";[16] therefore the mental status of certainty, *pace* Descartes, accompanies both opinion and science and so cannot be relied on as a standard to discriminate between true and false propositions. Conscience, Hobbes concludes, may be defined as *"opinion of evidence"* because it entails not only the opinion of the truth of what is said, but also the opinion of the possession of the *knowledge* of it. In a sense, Hobbes's position contains in embryo Hume's radical criticism of rational knowledge,[17] even if it is intended less for a skeptical purpose than to claim toleration in philosophical and theological controversies.

Hobbes does not at all intend to equate science and opinion: they share the same psychological status of subjective certainty but are objectively and definitely distinguished by the fundamental epistemological fact that, whereas the former is subjected to the

---

[15] Ibid., 6.6, 65–66. "Errour of reasoning" obviously includes both noncorrect reasoning (fallacious deductions) and nonreasoning (inductions).

[16] Ibid. 6.8, 66.

[17] Hume 1968, bk. 1, pt. 4, sect. 1, 180–187.

rules of demonstration and therefore open to rational examination, control, and discussion, the latter exclusively depends on processes of deliberation that are out of our power.[18] Thanks to philosophy (i.e., reason) we become aware of the nature of opinion (which includes faith) and of the nature our passions, and thus we understand how by them men can be induced to behavior contrary to natural reason (i.e., to natural law and to peace). In fact, civil philosophy is nothing more than the knowledge of "the causes of peace" with the purpose to neutralize the causes of war, which, for the most part, consist in opinion (i.e., "errour of reasoning" and "faith").

Hobbes does recognize that men cannot conduct their lives solely according to theorems and that they often must rely on opinion and faith,[19] but only reason can determine their reliability. Nor did Hobbes ever think that reason and knowledge by themselves were enough to modify opinion and faith or conduct. It is beyond the compass of this chapter to explain how his science of human nature could change human conduct; we need to say that Hobbes distinguishes the "Truth of Speculation" from "Practice" and assigns to the intervention of the absolute sovereign the possibility to "convert" the former into the latter.[20]

Reason (i.e., philosophy) teaches us that the limits of opinion in general are those of induction, but Hobbes allows that, for all its uncertain cognitive status, "there be many things which we receive from *report* of *others*, of which it is impossible to imagine any cause of *doubt*."[21] Thus, we can distinguish when our trust is confirmed by reason and when it is a mere psychological subjection to *authority*. Because faith or belief is "admitting of Propositions upon *trust*"[22] of those who utter them, we can distinguish between, so to say, a *rational* trust and a *rhetorical* trust.

What Hobbes says about *opinion* concerns religion because the two domains of *opinion* contain the two sources of religion: the "errour of reasoning" ("erroneous collection"[23] concerning the invisible spirits) and the "*report* of *others*" (i.e., persons presenting themselves as capable of revealing things concerning God/gods and its/their will). Even though Hobbes says nothing in the sixth chapter of *The Elements* about *religious* opinion and faith, the implicit question is to which category religious opinion and faith belong. We will see that Hobbes substitutes opinion or faith as "erroneous collection" concerning invisible spirits with a correct demonstration of the existence of God and replaces faith as merely psychological subjection to authority with faith as a trust demanded by reason itself. As a result of these substitutions, religion will undergo a metamorphosis that delivers it from any jurisdiction of theology, at least conceived of as a speculative or scholastic construction.

---

[18] "Sense, Memory, Understanding, Reason, and Opinion are not in our power to change . . . and therefore are not effects of our Will, but our Will of them" (*Leviathan*, 31, 198).

[19] Lupoli 2006, 44–50.

[20] *Leviathan* 31, 193.

[21] *Human Nature*, 6.9, 67.

[22] Ibid.

[23] Ibid., 11.6, 139.

2.1 Real God and "Invisible Spirits"

Does the epistemological exclusion of theology from knowledge contradict Hobbes's demonstration of God's existence? No, because when the demonstration is fully deployed in *De corpore*, it clearly appears to be a fundamental postulate of mechanistic physics that necessarily demands a First Mover.[24] For all its possible religious use, this notion is a physical one peculiar to Hobbes's mechanism.

Given his merely kinetic notion of cause and his anti-Aristotelian position that matter is adynamic, it is necessary for Hobbes to hypothesize that, following the chains of causes backward, the primary status of matter must have been (before the acquisition of any properties or motions) devoid of any power (i.e., motion). This amounts to conceiving of matter as an absolutely inactive primary fluid (*primum fluidum*).[25] Consequently, the infusion and conservation of motion in a *primum fluidum*, which is to be conceived of as devoid of any cohesion and resistance, demands the existence of a First Mover endowed with extraordinary functions beyond physical conceivability (i.e., above reason).[26] To claim its existence means to depict it as a body. Moreover, all the functions and powers necessary to produce the mechanistic "generations" that constitute the physical world have to be attributed to it and, first of all, those necessary to "create"[27] in the primary fluid a number of coherent corpuscles (in practice, "atoms")[28] capable of receiving and conveying motion. This operation can be equated by Hobbes with "creation" because it brings forth the physical world as it is the object of experience, since only starting from the existence of atoms can it be agitated by motion and "generations." Hobbes dares to put forward some hypotheses concerning the "bodily God" or First Mover, although only in his advanced age, and in particular in the posthumously published *Answer to Bramhall*.

Armed with his physical demonstration of a First Mover's existence, he firmly refuses the accusation of atheism and denounces the insubstantiality and the logical (and juridical) fallacy of the charge of "atheism by consequence." He claims that an indictment for atheism could be maintained only if supported by an explicit "affirmation uttered or written, and not by any other way: precisely if the indictee has directly denied that God exists."[29] The reason is that "*verborum consequentiae difficillimae judicatu sunt*" ("the consequences of words are very difficult to judge"). Thus, someone who does not realize that the denial of God's existence is a consequence of propositions he affirmed is at most guilty of "the ignorance of well reasoning." Therefore, Hobbes concludes, it is against equity "that the life of a man is demanded on the basis

---

[24] *De corpore*, ed. Schuhmann, 9.7, 97; Ibid. 26.1, 281–283. See also: *Objectiones tertiae* 5, 180; *Critique du De mundo*, 26.6–7, 310; *Human Nature* 11.2, 132–133.

[25] Lupoli 2006, 537–554; Gorham 2012.

[26] *Leviathan* 31, 195; and *Answer to Dr. Bramhall*, 36–37.

[27] *Decameron physiologicum*, 77–78.

[28] *Dialogus physicus*, 29.

[29] *Appendix ad Leviathan*, 548: "Dicto igitur aliquo, sive prolato sive scripto, reus fieri, neque ullo alio modo, potest: nempe, si directe negaverit Deum esse."

of logical niceties concerning consequences or is put in jeopardy by his adversaries' skil-fulness in the art of logic."[30] But what he said in the *Appendix ad Leviathan* to defend himself is used as a weapon against his adversaries in the *Answer to Brahmall*. He says that those who say that "God is an *incorporeal substance*" are the ones who ignore "well reasoning."[31] Those who hold this doctrine "do absolutely make God to be nothing at all," although Hobbes refrains from calling them atheists because it is "by ignorance of the consequence they said that which is equivalent to atheism . . . and this *atheism by conse-quence* is a very easy thing to be fallen into."[32]

Although self-interested, Hobbes's willingness to excuse "the ignorance of well reason-ing" represents a proposal of a kind of tolerance,[33] at least among philosophers, and is entirely in line with his view of "*opinion of truth*" or "*opinion of evidence*," that is, what "we *admit* for truth by errour of reasoning" and yet is not in our power to doubt.

The Great Mystification of scholastic theology and spiritualistic ontologies, which Hobbes denounces, makes men believe they can conceive something both existing and incorporeal.[34] I struggled elsewhere to demonstrate that Hobbes's materialism has an epistemological and not metaphysical basis.[35] What is worth observing here is that his materialistic assumption holds whatever the source from which the mind comes to think something real: whether it is the rational calculation by which the existence of the First Mover is necessarily postulated or the deceptive pull of the passions to objectify the fear of the unknown in order to render it more controllable.[36] The two notions are the outcome

---

[30] "Nam si dictum vel factum sit id quod lege prohibetur, et proinde punire possit, illud definiri ita debet, ut illi omnes, qui lege illa obligandi sunt, cognoscant hoc et illud factum, prout lege cum circumstantiis definitum est, vel haec vel illa verba, quae in lege ipsa scribuntur, punienda esse. *Nam verborum consequentiae difficillimae judicatu sunt.* Itaque si reus, *ignoratione bene ratiocinandi,* contra literam legis loqutus sit, nullo cuiquam damno facto, excusabit illum ignorantia" (*Appendix ad Leviathan*, 548–549, emphasis added). And thereafter: "Ex quo intelligitur, quoties verba fiunt crimen, juxta Concilii Niceni sententiam, verba illa in formulam debere redigi; ut unusquisque quae verba crimen habent, quae non habent, sine pluribus syllogismis certus esse possit" (Ibid., 554).

[31] *Answer to Dr. Bramhall*, 129.

[32] Ibid., 130.

[33] Christ himself will adopt this principle of tolerance on the Day of Judgment (*Leviathan* 43, 327 and 328: "they that have built false Consequences on the true Foundation, shall see their Doctrines condemned; nevertheless they themselves shall be saved").

[34] "*Substance incorporeall* are words, which when they are joined together, destroy one another, as if a man should say, an *Incorporeall Body*" (*Leviathan* 34, 207). See, also *Critique du "De mundo"* 27.1, 312: "Ex qua definitione apparet idem esse *ens & corpus;* nam corporis quoque eadem ab omnibus definitio recipitur; pro *ente* igitur de quo loquimur dicemus semper *corpus,* nimirum utentes vocabulo Latino." Cf. also *Leviathan* 12, 53: "But the opinion that such Spirits were Incorporeal, or Immaterial, could never enter into the mind of any man by nature; because, though men may put together words of contradictory signification, as *Spirit,* and *Incorporeall*; yet they can never have the imagination of any thing answering to them."

[35] Lupoli 2006, ch. 1.

[36] "This perpetuall feare, alwayes accompanying mankind in the ignorance of causes, as it were in the Dark, must needs have for object something. And therefore when there is nothing to be seen, there is nothing to accuse, either of their good, or evil fortune, but some *Power*, or Agent *Invisible*: In which sense perhaps it was, that some of the old Poets said, that the Gods were at first created by humane Feare: which spoken of the Gods, (that is to say, of the many Gods of the Gentiles) is very true. But the acknowledging of one God Eternall, Infinite, and Omnipotent, may more easily be derived, from the

of completely different *inferences* (from which it follows, first of all, that the spiritualistic mystification cannot work with the notion of First Mover). Although the "ignorance of causes"[37] is at the origin both of the belief in "invisible spirits" and of the "acknowledgement of one God Eternall, Infinite, and Omnipotent," the idea of God as "invisible spirit" is the outcome of a fallacious inference, whereas the idea of God as "one First Mover, that is a First and Eternal Cause" is the outcome of a correct one.

In *Leviathan*, Hobbes limits the origin of religion from "perpetuall feare, always accompanying mankind in the ignorance of causes" to "the many Gods of the Gentiles," whereas he admits that "the acknowledging of one God Eternall, Infinite, and Omnipotent" (that is the true God) "may more easily be derived, from the desire men have to know the causes of naturall bodies, and their severall vertues." Does this mean that the Biblical God, too, originates from this desire? The rest of chapter 12 of *Leviathan* does indicate that the Biblical religion shares much with other (false) religions.

In this chapter, Hobbes allows for the identification (i.e., substitution) of the God of Christian religion with the real corporeal First Mover while suggesting that Christian religion had the same origin as other religions. After all, it could not be maintained that Christian religion originated only from a rational conclusion reached by "men . . . by *their own meditation*." The fallacy of the conclusion of "invisible spirits"[38] has two aspects: its inductive nature[39] and the irrational conception of cause as an obscure (i.e., not kinetic and mechanical) "invisible power." By contrast, the reasoning about the First Mover is a correct inference starting from the true concept of cause.

The idea of God as the "invisible power" is either "feigned" by men's fancy or "imagined from tales" of others (i.e., true or false prophets), whereas the existence of the First Mover as an inconceivable and "incomprehensible"[40] Agent of whom there is no

---

desire men have to know the causes of naturall bodies, and their severall vertues, and operations; than from the fear of what was to befal them in time to come. For he that from any effect he seeth come to passe, should reason to the next and immediate cause thereof, and from thence to the cause of that cause, and plonge himselfe profoundly into the pursuit of causes; shall at last come to this, that there must be (as even the Heathen Philosophers confessed) one First Mover; that is, a First, and an Eternall cause of all things; which is that which men mean by the name of God" (*Leviathan* 12, 52–53).

[37] Cf. *Leviathan* 11, 50.

[38] The philosophical "one First Mover" can be defined a "spirit" (*Answer to Dr. Bramhall*, 31: "a most pure, and most simple Corporeal Spirit"); in *Leviathan* (12, 53) Hobbes even admits the use of the words "Spirit Incorporeall" (although "not *Dogmatically*, with intention to make the Divine Nature understood; but *Piously*, to honour him with attributes, of significations, as remote as they can from the grossenesse of Bodies Visible"). For simplicity's sake, however, I will use "invisible spirit" or "power" only for the God of religion.

[39] *Leviathan* 12, 53: "For the way by which they think these Invisible Agents wrought their effects . . . men that know not what it is that we call *causing*, (that is, almost all men) have no other rule to guess by, but by observing, and remembring what they have seen to precede the like effect at some other time, or times before, without seeing between the antecedent and subsequent Event, any dependance or connexion at all: And therefore from the like things past, they expect the like things to come; and hope for good or evil luck, superstitiously, from things that have no part at all in the causing of it."

[40] "Incomprehensible, and above their understanding" (Ibid.). See, also *De corpore politico* 2, 6.9, 134; *Critique du De mundo* 35.16, 395–396; *Leviathan* 31, 191; Ibid. 34, 208; Ibid. 46, 371 and 374; Ibid. "A Rev., and Concl.," 394.

adequate image at all in the mind[41] is deduced from the general idea of a Cause necessarily to be acknowledged *existing*.

Hobbes goes further in stressing that the necessary inference concerning the "one First Mover" is drawn by men "without thought of their fortune; the solicitude whereof, both enclines to fear, and hinders them from the search of the causes of other things; and thereby gives occasion of feigning of as many Gods, as there be men that feign them."[42] In saying this, Hobbes reveals that the "First Mover" is not intrinsically connected with man's natural and "perpetual solicitude of the time to come"[43] that is the "anxiety" and "care" of his "fortune," which is the essence of historical religion. Moreover, he suggests that the "belief in invisible spirit" is incompatible with the "acknowledgement" of a First Mover. It is from the idea of "invisible spirits" or "powers" that historical and natural worship originated, whereas the acknowledgment of the bodily First Mover instead leads only to the declaration of its unintelligibility and omnipotence (as the Cause of all).[44]

That the natural origin of all historical religions is shared by Biblical religion is clear both from Hobbes's affirmation that the founders of true religion ("*Abraham, Moses, and our Blessed Saviour*") *cultivated* the same natural seeds of religion as the founders of false religion[45] and from his explicit statement that "*all* formed Religion, is founded at first, upon the faith which a multitude hath in some one person, whom they believe not only to be a wise man, and to labour to procure their happiness, but also to be a holy man, to whom God himselfe vouchsafeth to declare his will supernaturally."[46] That the nature of *all* formed religions, be they true or false, is the same (i.e., "*Feare* of power invisible") is implied in the definition in chapter 6, where Hobbes says that the true religion differs from the false ones only in the content of the mental representations of the invisible power (or powers):

> *Feare* of power invisible, feigned by the mind, or imagined from tales publiquely allowed, RELIGION; not allowed, SUPERSTITION. And when the power imagined, is truly such as we imagine, TRUE RELIGION.[47]

[41] "They cannot have any Idea of him in their mind, answerable to his nature" (*Leviathan* 11, 51). The similitude follows of the "man that is born blind" who "may easily conceive . . . there is somewhat there, which men call *Fire*, . . . but cannot imagine what it is like, nor have an Idea of it in his mind." Cf. *Objectiones tertiae*, 11, 189: "quoniam ergo non est demonstratum nos ideam Dei habere, et christiana religio nos obligat credere Deum esse inconceptibilem, hoc est, ut ego opinor, cujus idea non habetur, sequitur existentiam Dei non esse demonstratam, multo minùs creationem." See also *Human Nature* 11.2, 132.

[42] *Leviathan* 12, 53.

[43] Ibid., 12, 52. "For as Prometheus, (which, interpreted, is, *The prudent man*,) was bound to the hill *Caucasus*, a place of large prospect, where, an eagle, feeding on his liver, devoured in the day, as much as was repaired in the night: So that man, which looks too far before him, in the care of future time, hath his heart all the day long, gnawed on by fear of death, poverty, or other calamity; and has no repose, nor pause of his anxiety, but in sleep."

[44] Ibid., 12, 54.

[45] Ibid.

[46] Ibid., 12, 58 (emphasis added).

[47] *Leviathan* 6, 26.

All this suggests that Hobbes's approach to religion presupposes the following four assumptions: first, that the notion of God shared by historical religions is clearly different from the rational notion of philosophy; second, that belief in something immaterial is the outcome of the self-interested mystification of deceiving theologians and philosophers; third, that the Biblical religion historically shared with the false religions the same "cultivation" (i.e., exploitation) of the natural seeds of any religion; and fourth, that the Christian religion can be differentiated from others "when the power imagined, is truly such as we imagine." Because this would mean having an image of God as an inconceivable, infinite, and omnipotent body that is the cause of all causes (i.e., the First Mover), assimilating the emotionally neutral First Mover and the much-feared God of religion will be problematic.

Hobbes is aware that the mere criticism of the "erroneous doctrine" of the invisible spirits as the objectification of fear will not necessarily affect the *belief* in them. Rather, "the Dark" of "the ignorance of causes"[48] can be dispelled only if the faith in invisible spirits is substituted by the rational acknowledgment of the bodily First Mover (if this ever happens). He holds the doctrine of the bodily God in letters dated from 1640[49] and, even though the argument was explicitly formulated only in the first Latin edition of *Leviathan* (1668), the logical premises were already clear in the English edition of 1651. It is very likely that when Pierre Bayle attributes to Hobbes "une hardiesse, ou une intrépidité d'esprit"[50] ("a boldness, or intrepidity of mind"), he refers to his capacity to follow the conclusions of reason without self-censorship even in such a delicate case as the assertion of God's corporeity. And there can be no doubt that Hobbes was completely aware of the consequences of this assertion.

The four stated assumptions also show that, whereas theology disappears from the compass of the sciences, inquiry into religion remains because it is an important natural human phenomenon that is open to observation. Although many of the objects of such an inquiry are shared with speculative theology, they are considered therein only insofar as they are anthropological and political. This political and anthropological reduction of religion does not prevent Hobbes from referring to *true* religion and *true* prophets, and yet this does not entail any logical necessity for him to acknowledge that there is a proper knowledge of the truth of a religion or of the reliability of those who claim that God has spoken to them "supernaturally, and immediately."[51]

The human condition from which religion arises is perfectly integrated with the description of the "state of meer Nature" and the making of the commonwealth. Like the state, religion is exclusively a human fact[52] because it is the outcome of

---

[48] Cf. *supra* note 38.

[49] Cf. *Correspondance du P. Marin Mersenne* 10, 427. See Lupoli 2006, 521.

[50] Bayle, Art. *Charron*, 310a.

[51] *Leviathan* 32, 196.

[52] "Seeing there are no signes, nor fruit of *Religion*, but in Man onely; there is no cause to doubt, but that the seed of *Religion*, is also onely in Man" (Ibid. 12, 52).

psychological dynamics that, unlike that of animals, is all directed toward the future. The "Anxiety of the time to come" and the "search of the causes of their own good and evill fortune" have the same root in human nature; that is, in that natural condition of the ignorance of causes. In this state, a man's deliberations are based on mere inductions (and not on sound knowledge of causes) conditioned by objects that are but figments of "his own Fancy"[53] or "imagined from tales" *admitted* for true by his trust in "the Authority of other men, such as he thinks to be his friends, and wiser than himself."[54] In brief, in order to exorcize and control his "perpetual solicitude of the time to come," man *objectifies* it in "Invisible Agents" whose favors he struggles to win by "the Worship, which naturally men conceived fit to bee used towards their Gods."[55]

Hobbes alludes to two stages of religion. A first primitive stage is characterized by the practice of natural *personal* worship and private beliefs, different "by reason of the different Fancies, Judgements, and Passions of several men."[56] Then, a second *social* stage follows, in which religion turns into a body of beliefs, laws, and ceremonies common to a whole society, which constitutes the cement of a society. This happens, as we have seen, when some men "nourished and ordered" the seeds of religion "with a purpose to make those men that relied on them, the more apt to Obedience, Lawes, Peace, Charity, and civil Society."[57] In other words, when some men succeed in being recognized as the mediators with the invisible spirits and their exclusive spokesmen[58] (i.e., prophets), then they gain the obedience of others. Whether they cultivate the seeds of religion instrumentally, falsely asserting their relationship with the deity, or do it really "by Gods commandement and direction,"[59] religion is used alike in both cases as an instrument of power (even though Hobbes is unrivaled in expressing this in a less frank way).

Thus, religion is the first historical foundation of political power and either constitutes "part of humane Politiques" or coincides *tout court* with "Divine Politiques." Hence, there is no religion as a collective, organized, and institutionalized phenomenon without a state. Likewise, it may seem that there can have been no state without the "cultivation" of the "natural seeds of Religion." The distinction between "human" and "divine" politics, which seems a prelude to the acknowledgment of two qualitatively different foundations of civil power, on the contrary develops into an entirely opposite theory; that is, to a confirmation of the artificial nature of the state, even when it is founded by a "Divine Politiques."

---

[53] Cf. supra, n. 41.

[54] *Leviathan* 12, 52.

[55] Ibid. 12, 55.

[56] Ibid. 12, 54.

[57] Ibid. Hobbes alludes to an initial mythical period of this stage, "a golden age" of humanity (*Philosophicall Rudiments*, "Preface to the Reader"), characterized by a complete harmony due to the full coincidence between civil and religious power (cf. Giargia 2012).

[58] *Leviathan* 36, 225.

[59] Ibid. 12, 54.

3 THE PARADOX OF "THE GREATER POWER" WITHOUT "THE GREATER FEAR"

It is well known that Hobbes's political doctrine is based on a deterministic theory of the passions that assigns the primary role in motivating human actions to the fear of violent death. Power over other humans is a function of this fear, and, if there is no natural human sovereignty, it is due to the fact that nobody possesses such a power of deterrence that is stronger or greater than that of others. Because of the natural equality of human beings, someone who cultivates the dangerous and illusory passion of vain-glory is sooner or later destined to a painful and mortal disillusion. The equality of humans in the state of nature is the core assumption in the genetic model of Hobbes's politics. And equality means that, in the state of nature, no one has a "greater power" (of deterrence) than others. Therefore, an obvious theoretical problem arises from the fact that Hobbes claims that, in the state of nature (and not only in this state), there is an entity that is *thought* to be endowed with a "greater power" than all others.

Now, first, it seems that, according to Hobbes's psychological and anthropological account, "greater power" must be defined as greater power *of deterrence* (i.e., whoever holds "the greater power" is the one who produces the greater fear that disposes others to submit). Second, Hobbes not only admits that humans "naturally" (i.e., unavoidably) believe in the existence of such an entity (leaving aside its reality), but also explains that the fear raised by it is the main component of the "natural seed of Religion" and what both "all the founders of Common-wealths and the Law-givers of Gentiles" and "*Abraham, Moses,* and our *Blessed Saviour*" depended on "to make those men that relied on them, the more apt to Obedience." This suggests that religion is the necessary origin of all commonwealths, both those of Gentiles and of Hebrews (and that the coherent development of Hobbes's anthropology would be a doctrine *à la* Vico).

However, although Hobbes does admit the historical function of religion in the making of states and societies, he is very far from giving to it the role of the essential, natural, and providential factor in the humanization and civilization of human beings. Why is this so, given that nothing would seem more consonant with Hobbes's anthropology than to assign the decisive function in the making of the state to a fear that (1) "hath place in the nature of man before Civill Society," (2) is natural, and (3) is provoked by a "greater power" that thus must be the most terrifying? Hobbes answers that, in this case "the greater power" does *not* correspond with the "greater fear":

> The Passion to be reckoned upon, is Fear; whereof there be two very generall Objects: one, The Power of Spirits Invisible; the other, The Power of those men they shall therein Offend. Of these two, though the former be the greater Power, yet the fear of the latter is commonly the greater Feare. The Feare of the former is in every man, his own Religion: which hath place in the nature of man before Civil Society.[60]

---

[60] *Leviathan* 14, 70.

The adverb "commonly" seems to reduce the general significance of the affirmation, but our perplexity is not resolved. Why is the fear of the lesser power "commonly the greater," when it should be the opposite? Why are men able to exert a greater deterrence through a lesser power than the greater power of invisible spirits? In a sense, these questions explain all of Hobbes's theological concern.

We have to consider the peculiarity of the "object" of the fear and how it can exert its deterrence. The deterrence of "Spirits Invisible" does not have the strength of the "natural necessity" that, according to Hobbes, does not leave a person any other possibility of action than that which is immediately necessary to escape imminent death, whatever punishments he or she may incur in consequence of performing the action in question.[61] That deterrence will never be such as to free (*de facto* and *de jure*) men from every prior bond.

It is only *this* deterrence capacity that prevails over all other possible deterrents, and, normally, only the human sovereign possesses it. The threat of spirits or God/gods must be *future* (either dealing with a natural phenomenon to come or with the afterlife), whereas only the threat of a man can compel us to neglect any future threat and face the immediate present one. The "invisible spirits" or "powers" (albeit thought to hold the civil sovereignty) cannot exert a deterrence directly, but only mediately through a representative—that is, through a visible man.

That political sovereignty can be really and directly exercised only by agents capable of an immediate and irresistible physical deterrence with "a sufficient and clear Promulgation" of their commands[62] is a fundamental theorem of political science. And if these requisites can belong only to men of flesh and blood, then not only did there never exist, but there could not exist a political dominion of God over human beings except through representatives, such as his "prophetical" kingdom over the Jews. Whatever the subjects may think, sovereignty would belong to God's representatives on the strength of the subjects' obligation by their consent (i.e., by the covenant). After all, if an invisible agent endowed with the "greater power" wishes to exercise his dominion through representatives, then he also wants his "Soveraign Right" to arise not "from Nature" but "from Pact";[63] that is, from the pact by which the subjects oblige themselves to (those they believe are) his representatives.

---

[61] *Philosophicall Rudiments* 2.18–19, 21–32 ("There is in every man a certain high degree of fear, through which he apprehends that evill which is done to him to be the greatest, and therefore by naturall necessity he shuns it all he can, and 'tis suppos'd he can doe no otherwise"). Cf., also, Ibid., 6.4, 88:"For all men, by a necessity of nature, chuse that which to them appear to be the lesse evill." And *Leviathan* 27, 157: "If a man by the terrour of present death, be compelled to do a fact against the Law, he is totally Excused; because no Law can oblige a man to abandon his own preservation. And supposing such a Law were obligatory; yet a man would reason thus, *If I do it not, I die presently; if I do it, I die afterwards; therefore by doing it, there is time of life gained.*" And yet, what is "done or omitted" "contrary to the Lawes" by "fear of Spirits . . . is a Crime" (Ibid. 27, 156). Also Ibid. 15, 76.

[62] *Leviathan* 31, 187.

[63] *Leviathan* 31, 187.

In addition, if the hypothesis about the human prerogative of the requisites of sovereignty were true, then the political use of religion would turn out to be double-edged. Although religion can help make men obedient, this political use of religion involves the false opinion that sovereignty depends on subjects' acknowledgment that their sovereign embodies the particular nature of God's representative. Consequently, sovereigns who would allow their subjects to hold this opinion—apart from the fact that they would fail in their function of teaching their subjects the true causes of obedience[64]—would jeopardize their own states by making others arbiters of their sovereignty.

This error is quite similar to those concerning the acquisition of dominion "by generation and by conquest." In fact, since "all the founders of Common-wealths" relied on religion, Hobbes in effect theorizes a third way of historical acquisition of dominion—by religion[65]—and, as in the other cases, what gives the right of sovereignty is consent (i.e., the covenant).[66]

That in the twentieth chapter of *Leviathan*[67] there is no mention of a *religious* dominion (in addition to the other two) is easy to understand: religion does not characterize one particular historical way of founding the state, but instead is involved in the origin and life of all states where it has been variously structured in churches, congregations, assemblies. Moreover, as we have seen, religion has its roots in human nature, and the "feare of power invisible" is so strong as to drive men to submit themselves despite their natural love for liberty[68] (at the time of the foundation of the state) and to alter the natural emotional dynamics conducive to the preservation of life (once the state has been founded). Thus, to dispute the erroneous doctrines concerning religion, whether regarded as "part of humane Politiques" or "Divine Politiques," involves many more themes and problems than to correct the errors concerning the dominions "by generation and by conquest." For the latter refutation, one chapter is enough, whereas the criticisms concerning the religious origin of the commonwealth take about half of *Leviathan*.

4 THE WORD OF GOD

Despite Hobbes's intention to consider religion only as "part of humane Politiques" or "Divine Politiques," it is precisely this approach that, as we have seen, leads to the question whether direct sovereignty belongs only to men. It is thus necessary to deal with the concept of God's representatives.

[64] See *Philosophicall Rudiments* 13, and *Leviathan* 30.

[65] "Dominion is acquired two wayes; By Generation and by Conquest" (*Leviathan* 20, 102).

[66] "The Rights and consequences of both *Paternal* and *Despotical* Dominion, are the very same with those of a Soveraign by Institution" (*Leviathan* 20, 104).

[67] And also in *The Elements* (*De corpore politico* 2, ch. 3 and 4), and the eighth and ninth chapters of *De cive*.

[68] Cf. *Leviathan* 17, 85.

In chapter 31 of *Leviathan*, Hobbes discusses the question of the meaning of "Word of God" in the restricted political sense (relevant for the earlier posed question) of the word of him who "rules by words"; that is, who uses words to make known his commands or laws (which demands a "Proclamation, or Promulgation by the voyce of man"). From the three ways "God declareth his Laws"—"by the Dictates of *Naturall Reason*, by *Revelation*, and by the *voyce* of some *man*, to whom by the operation of Miracles, he procureth credit with the rest"—"there ariseth a triple Word of God, *Rational, Sensible* and *Prophetique*: to which Correspondeth a triple Hearing; *Right Reason, Sense Supernaturall*, and *Faith*."[69] We will see how all these distinctions answer to the purpose of demonstrating that there can be no knowledge of the existence of prophets, but only faith, and how Hobbes uses this idea to play a complex (and somewhat baroque) conceptual game.

Hobbes's references in chapters 31 and 32 to revelation, miracles attesting the "credit" of the prophet, and the "holy Prophets" by whose mouth God gave positive laws to his "peculiar Nation (the Jews)" give Hobbes's assertions an orthodox tone. Even the exclusion of the "Sense Supernaturall, which consisteth in Revelation or Inspiration" from the ways God communicates is prudently justified not by openly denying its existence, but by the fact that "Revelation or Inspiration" is not an appropriate way of receiving "Universal Laws" "because God Speaketh not in that manner, but to particular persons, and to divers men divers things." Moreover, "how God speaketh to a man immediately," he says with a certain sarcasm, "may be understood by those well enough, to whom he hath so spoken; but how the same should be understood by another, is hard, if not impossible to know. For if a man pretend to me, that God hath spoken to him supernaturally, and immediately, and I make doubt of it, I can not easily perceive what argument he can produce, to oblige me to beleeve it."[70]

He who claims that God spoke to him can say God did it only in one of the following ways: "in the Holy Scripture," in a dream, by a vision, by a voice, and, finally, "by supernaturall Inspiration." Hobbes does not deny the existence of prophets but any possible rational demonstration of it, and he relies on this fact to draw the conclusion that "though God Almighty can speak to a man, by Dream, Visions, Voice, and Inspiration; yet he obliges no man to beleeve he hath so done to him that pretends it; who (being a man) may erre, and (which is more) may lie."[71] In short, no divine obligation exists to *believe* him.

The "sensible word" of God and the correlate "sense supernatural" having been excluded, there remain the "rational" and the "prophetique" words of God, to which two "hearings" are correlated, "right reason" and "faith," and two kingdoms of God correspond, the "natural" and "prophetique." Given what we have just seen about the prophet, in which sense can Hobbes speak of a "prophetique" word of God—that is, a divine word through prophets? The answer is very important for understanding what

---

[69] *Leviathan* 31, 187.
[70] Ibid. 32, 196.
[71] Ibid.

we called his "conceptual game," and it is to be found, first, in the fact that the "hearing" corresponding to God's prophetic word is "faith" and, second, that this "prophetic" word is limited to God's direct kingdom over the Jews. From this, a chain of consequences follows: the existence of prophets is only an object of faith (not of knowledge), this faith (since no Old Testament prophets live) is reduced to faith in the Scripture, which in turn is nothing else than faith in the man whom we trust in when we admit the Scripture for true (i.e., in a prophet). We may suspect that Hobbes is making fun of us, but it is not so because the prophet who is standing surety for Scripture has a completely different legitimization—the political covenant—as we shall see.

Hobbes's argumentative strategy evidently aims to avoid any accusation that he denies the Scripture. But how to reconcile the admission of the Scripture with the denial of any divine obligation to believe in any prophet and, in consequence, in any supernatural communication of the Scripture? Revealingly, in the course of his discussion touching "How God speaketh to men" in chapter 32, Hobbes twice professes that reason is not subject (and cannot be subjected) to the power or will of any man (ourselves included). The first time he states that we can only "captivate our Understanding" but not "submit" it "to the Opinion of any other man" and that "to captivate" is only "to forbear contradiction," that is "to speak" and "live" "as (by lawfull Authority) we are commanded."[72] The second time he refers more explicitly to the sovereign and concludes that "he may oblige me to obedience, so, *as not by act or word to declare I beleeve him not; but not to think any otherwise then my reason perswades me.*"[73]

Obviously, Hobbes is referring to his own situation, and, through this twofold profession of the independence of reason and submission to "lawfull Authority," he is giving us the key to read his doctrine of prophecy and his general stance concerning religion. He will respect at any cost two bonds: that of reason (which demands first and foremost a full and clear correspondence between notions and words[74]) and that of his sovereign's law. Do these two bonds conflict? No. The dictates of natural reason oblige me to obey the sovereign and "not by any act or word to declare I beleeve him not." When reason dictates that I obey my sovereign's commands to speak and behave according to the Scripture,[75] he *de facto* acts for me *as a prophet*. To obey him "in sum, is Trust, and Faith reposed in him" (the sovereign).[76] So we do not go against our reason in professing the Scripture is true because we do it neither on the basis of any knowledge, nor of any divine obligation, but at the order of the sovereign, whom we (obliged by our reason) virtually accept as our true prophet (even if an officiating prophet and not a supernatural prophet). In this way, he has overturned the religious relationship we saw earlier between being God's representative and being sovereign: the latter is no longer

---

[72] *Leviathan* 32, 196.

[73] Ibid. (emphasis added).

[74] *Human Nature*, 6.3.

[75] "The Scriptures themselves were made Law to us here, by the Authority of the Common-wealth, and are therefore part of the Law Civil" (*Answer to Dr. Bramhall*, 112).

[76] *Leviathan* 32, 196.

to be derived from the former, but vice versa. We can have no prophet before having a human sovereign; not only did there never exist a civil sovereignty of God over men except through human beings of flesh and blood, but one cannot exist.

In this way, Hobbes achieved a complete subordination of religion to reason because its two components are radically changed. As we have observed, historical religion contains the two components of opinion: (1) "errour of reasoning" (God as "invisible spirit") and (2) "trusting to other men."[77] Hobbes denounces the first erroneous inference and replaces it with the correct reasoning leading to the existence of the "First Cause" or "Mover." He then replaces what we called the *rhetorical* faith, as mere psychological subjection to authority, with the *rational* trust in our Christian sovereign whose command to speak and behave according to the Scripture reason obliges us not to contradict. If this does not amount to a complete repudiation of the dogmatic bases of Christian religion, it entails at least a metamorphosis of it, which was undoubtedly unacceptable to all Christian churches, including the reformed ones.

One observation is worth making on Hobbes's way of deploying his argument, particularly in chapter 32 where, after all the rational premises we have seen on the word of God, he seems to end by dogmatically leaning on the Scripture to find the "marks whereby . . . a true Prophet" is "to be acknowledged." Obviously, this is blatantly incongruous because it inverts the stated logical dependence between prophet and Scripture. Yet he immediately looks in the Scripture and finds that "the teaching of the Religion which God hath established, and the shewing of a *present* Miracle joined together, were the only marks whereby the Scripture would have a true Prophet, that is to say, immediate Revelation to be acknowledged."[78] "Seeing Miracles now cease," only the first requirement remains, and the question of who teaches "the Religion which God hath established" can be decided only by him who judges the conformity to Scripture, namely, the sovereign. But, instead of saying this, Hobbes affirms that only the Holy Scriptures (*sola scriptura*) "since the time of our Saviour, supply the place, and sufficiently recompense the want of all other Prophecy."[79]

It is clear enough that Hobbes adopts a rhetorical maneuver that combines two distinct arguments. On the one hand, he suggests that the acknowledgment of the authenticity of Scripture depends only on *rational* trust in the "lawfull Authority," but, according to the safeguard or tolerance principle we have seen above, he prudently omits asserting it until after he has given it a scriptural foundation.[80] On the other hand, he develops an argument *ad hominem* that starts from the assumption of the truth and authenticity of Scripture in order to look in it for the "marks" of "a true

---

[77] See note 15.

[78] *Leviathan* 32, 198.

[79] Ibid.

[80] Another example of important omission in *Leviathan* is the conclusion concerning the bodily nature of God.

Prophet" and, on the basis of these marks, to achieve a self-legitimation of Scripture as the only source of prophecy:

> from which, by wise and learned interpretation, and carefull ratiocination, all rules and precepts necessary to the knowledge of our duty both to God and man, without Enthusiasme, or supernaturall Inspiration, may easily be deduced. And this Scripture is it, out of which I am to take the Principles of my Discourse, concerning the Rights of those that are the Supream Govenors on earth, of Christian Common-wealths; and of the duty of Christian Subjects towards their Soveraigns.[81]

So he moves to the long exegesis that makes up the twelve chapters of the third part of *Leviathan* (and many other places) and by which he will find confirmation of his doctrines on prophets and prophecy.

5 HOBBES'S EXEGESIS: THE "UNUM NECESSARIUM"

When considering Hobbes's exegesis, we have to remember the rationale of his approach to Scripture. In his argumentative architecture, the extrinsic necessity, dictated by the historical context, of demonstrating the compatibility of his civil philosophy with Scripture turns into an intrinsic epistemological need demanded by the rationality of political obedience. At this point, the interpretation of Scripture constitutes an internal theoretical task of Hobbes's philosophy itself, and, particularly in *Leviathan*, he accomplishes it with the greatest earnestness and efficacy.

The focus of Hobbes's interpretation is that both the Old and the New Testaments exclude any continuity in the transfer of the capacity of a prophet or God's representative. The only sources of this transfer could be, in the Old Testament, the prophets directly invested by God, that is—in addition to Abraham—Moses and the continuous succession of high priests, and, in the New Testament, Christ and the Apostles directly chosen by him.

As for the Old Testament, the question concerns only the kingdom of which God wanted to be civil sovereign. Every high priest was sovereign as God's "Viceregent"[82] who transferred his office to the person that he appointed as his successor. Therefore the right of sovereignty goes back to Moses. But this continuity was broken when the Jews wanted and obtained "with the consent of God himselfe"[83] a human king like other peoples. At this point, the high priests became subordinate to the king who also exercised absolute jurisdiction in religious matters.

As for the New Testament, Christ did not take on himself any civil sovereignty; moreover, he did not bequeath to the apostles chosen by him any prerogative of designating

---

[81] *Leviathan* 32, 198.
[82] *Leviathan* 40, 254.
[83] Ibid.

or ordaining those who would exercise the magisterium after them. The evidence for this is the fact that this prerogative was autonomously exercised by the assemblies of the early Christians[84] who, from the time of Christian kingdoms, coincide with the people that can express its will exclusively by its sovereign representative.

In sum, the Old Testament assigns to the human sovereign of the Jews religious juris-diction, thereby supplying a general political paradigm of the rights of sovereignty; the New Testament assigns to the sovereign the appointment of teachers and makes him the arbiter of the conformity of their teaching to Scripture and thereby confers on him full religious magisterium.

Hobbes's exegesis is impeccable except that it tends to emphasize the passages that are useful to confirm his thesis and to understate those that could contradict it, as in II Chronicles 26:16–21, where Azariah orders King Uzziah to leave the sanctuary. That Azariah's prerogative was real is indicated by the fact that God punishes Uzziah by making leprosy break out on his forehead.

Hobbes's long exegesis also contains a series of important "theological" conclusions all aiming to minimize any possible deterrence to civic obedience based on threats concerning the afterlife: for example, his interpretations of Christian eschatology, sin, redemption, salvation, the sacraments, and heresy, as well as his detailed refutation of Bellarmine and his reconstruction of the history of Christianity.

The hermeneutic principles adopted by Hobbes provide for the use of mere nat-ural reason ("carefull ratiocination" and "easy deductions") and strictly exclude "Enthusiasme" or "supernaturall Inspiration."[85] Hobbes cannot deny that, in Scripture, "there be many things in God's word above reason; that is to say, which cannot by natu-ral reason be either demonstrated, or confuted," but he peremptorily affirms that "there is nothing contrary to it."[86] This means that Hobbes, like Spinoza after him, rejects any hermeneutic key deriving from any theological tradition or authority and relies only on his own reason. The exception, of course, is the authority of the one who has the exclusive right over and responsibility for the interpretation of Scripture. So, as for his own interpretation, Hobbes declares in *Leviathan* that he does "but *propound* it; main-taining nothing in this, or any other paradox of Religion; but attending the end of that dispute of sword, concerning the Authority . . . by which all sorts of doctrine are to bee approved, or rejected."[87] Obviously, Hobbes intends to address his proposal first of all

---

[84] *Leviathan* 42, 288–292.

[85] *Leviathan* 32, 198.

[86] *Leviathan* 32, 195.

[87] *Leviathan* 38, 241 (emphasis added). Here, Hobbes refers in particular to his interpretation of the nature and place of the Kingdom of God after Judgment. In the *Appendix ad Leviathan*, Hobbes prudently affirms that "Ego vero nemini Scripturam Sacram praeterquam mihi interpretari soleo" (517). See also *Leviathan* "Review and Conclusion," 394; and *Answer to Dr. Bramhall*, 104–107. Cf., also, *Leviathan* 26, 143: "The Authority of writers, without the Authority of the Common-wealth, maketh not their opinions Law, be they never so true. That which I have written in this Treatise, concerning the Morall Vertues, and of their necessity, for the procuring, and maintaining peace, though it bee evident Truth, is not therefore presently Law; but because in all Common-wealths in the world, it is part of the Civil Law: For though it be naturally reasonable; yet it is by the Soveraigne Power that it is Law."

to the sovereign,[88] and the proposal concerns how to carry out the extremely delicate and crucial role of interpreter of the Scripture.

On the crucial role of interpreters, *De cive* and *Leviathan* seem to diverge. But the differences are only due to the different historical contexts in which the two works were written. In the early forties in England, there was still a "lawfull Church"[89] that claimed to perform its duties *jure divino*.[90] So, on the one hand, Hobbes could not ignore that its rights were granted by the sovereign, and, therefore, he must affirm that he "who hath the Soveraign power in the City, is oblig'd as a Christian, where there is any question concerning *the Mysteries of Faith,* to interpret the Holy Scriptures by *Clergy-men* lawfully ordain'd."[91] But, on the other hand, since the ordaining is exclusively the sovereign's business, he can conclude that "in Christian Cities the judgment both of *spirituall* and *temporary matters* belongs unto the civill authority: And that man, or councell who hath the Supreme power, is head both of *the City,* and *of the Church*; for a *Church,* and a *Christian City* is but one thing."[92] Consequently, whereas the right of interpreting Scripture is formally granted to the church, its performance depends on the sovereign's authorization and on the existence of "mysteries." As for "mysteries" and "obscure places of Scripture," Hobbes cannot deny them because of the obedience he is, at that time, obliged to. But in chapter 18, he says quite clearly that reason obliges us to conclude that they are completely useless and unnecessary for salvation. In chapter 17, in a climax of conceptual density and expressive efficacy, he says that: "they who doe judge that any thing can be determin'd, (contrary to this common consent of men concerning the appellations of things) out of obscure places of Scripture, doe also judge that the use of speech, and at once all humane society, is to be taken away."[93] That is to say, "the obscure places of Scripture" cannot really supply the mind with meanings of words (i.e., ideas) different from those coming from experience; those who pretend this actually abuse the words by introducing nonexistent meanings and (apart from the legitimate suspicion that they do it with the concealed purpose of acquiring the greatest power over men) undermine the use of language (i.e., of reason[94]) that is indispensable to the peaceful and civil life of men.

In the following chapter of *De cive,* Hobbes virtually empties the domain of the truths necessary to salvation deriving from the interpretation of "obscure places of Scripture" and, consequently, strongly retrenches the role of the interpreter. He argues that "to a Christian there is no other article of Faith requisite as *necessary* to Salvation, but only this, THAT JESUS IS THE CHRIST."[95] On the one hand, this "one article" implies

---

[88] "I recover some hope, that one time or other, this writing of mine, may fall into the hands of a Soveraign, who wil consider it" (*Leviathan* 31, 193).

[89] *Philosophicall Rudiments* 18.11, 358.

[90] *Leviathan* 47, 385. *Behemoth* 3, 222.

[91] *Philosophicall Rudiments* 17.28, 339.

[92] Ibid.

[93] Ibid. 17.28, 338.

[94] "Imo ipsam tollit rationem, quae nihil aliud est praeter veritatis per talem consensum factae investigatio" (*De cive* 17.28, 255).

[95] *Philosophicall Rudiments* 18.6, 349.

many revealed truths (none of them contrary to reason) because "the whole Symbol of the Apostles is contained in this one Article"; on the other hand, it is by itself enough for salvation because "many men for this alone, without the rest, were admitted into the Kingdome of God."[96] For salvation, faith alone is not enough because it also requires obedience to civil laws;[97] therefore "seeing then it is Necessary that Faith, and Obedience (implyed in the word Repentance) do both concur to our Salvation, the question by which of the two we are Justified, is impertinently disputed."[98] So Hobbes dismisses in two words the crucial theological problem of justification. Finally, since no other article is necessary for faith, any interpretation of Scripture introducing further "mysterious" truths is superfluous.

Hobbes's latitudinarian stance is on this point absolutely steadfast: "If any man be displeased," he exclaims, "that I doe not judge all those eternally damned, who doe not inwardly assent to every article defined by the Church (and yet doe not contradict, but if they be commanded, doe submit) I know not what I shall say to them, for the most evident Testimonies of Holy Writ which doe follow, doe withold me from altering my opinion."[99] A subject is obliged, however, both on the strength of compact and for salvation (which requires civil obedience), to "profess" any article, however useless for salvation or meaningless according to reason, which the sovereign may be pleased to command. "Profession" does not require "faith" because it is not "an inward perswasion of the minde" (which, moreover, is not in our power), but only "outward obedience."[100]

So, there is no contradiction between Hobbes's doctrine that the interpretation of the Holy Scriptures, "where there is any question concerning *the Mysteries of Faith*," belongs to "*Clergy-men* lawfully ordain'd," and the doctrine that such interpretation is pointless. So long as there are people who believe that "we are oblig'd to a supernatural Doctrine which therefore it is impossible for us to understand," it will be "repugnant to aequity" to leave us "so destitute as that we can be deceiv'd in necessary points."[101] This characterizes the English society of the time of *De cive*, in which the subjects, disconcerted and perplexed by contending religious sects, "as it were sailing between *Scilla* and *Carybdis*," cannot "distinguish betweene the things necessary to Salvation, and those which are not necessary."[102] Beyond this, Hobbes says that, in a state where natural law and Scripture are respected by the subjects and the sovereign, the former reserve their "inward faith" to the sole article that Jesus is the Christ, and the latter does not command the "profession" of any other article and restricts his own role of legislator in spiritual matters to safeguarding the internal peace and independence of the state.

Hobbes more explicitly "propounds" all this in *Leviathan*, where the radically changed historical situation allows him to denounce[103] the "knots" that bound the consciences

---

[96]   Ibid., 352.

[97]   Ibid. 18.2–6.

[98]   *Leviathan* 43, 329.

[99]   *Philosophicall Rudiments* 18.6, 352–353.

[100]   Ibid. 18.4, 348.

[101]   *Philosophicall Rudiments* 17.28, 338–339.

[102]   Ibid., 341.

[103]   "In that part which treateth of a Christian Common-wealth, there are some new Doctrines, which, it may be, in a State where the contrary were already fully determined, were a fault for a Subject

of the citizens and that the recent political events have all "untyed" at last.[104] So Hobbes can depict the new English commonwealth as better suiting his political philosophy because it had put an end to the "praeterpolitical Church Government in England," thus restoring the citizens

> to the Independency of the Primitive Christians to follow, Paul or Cephas, or Apollos, every man as he liketh best: Which, if it be without contention, and without measuring the Doctrine of Christ, by our affection to the Person of his Minister, (the fault which the Apostle reprehended in the Corinthians) is perhaps the best.[105]

By stringing together Paul's admonishments to the Corinthians about the divisions of Christians[106] and his own civil doctrines, Hobbes makes them convertible.

Hobbes concludes his exegesis with an equation between the freedom of conscience of citizens (the Protestant "liberty of Christians") and their subjection only in "words and actions" to the state. Thus, he supplies a modern political version of the theological Pauline split between "carnal" and "spiritual men," a split that acknowledges a neat separation between the private and public dimensions of the life of citizens.

6 "Truth of Speculation" and "Utility of Practice"

What perhaps makes Hobbes's consideration of religion—and his denunciation of its interested and deceptive metaphysical systematization by theologians—difficult to understand is the fact that it does not have the historically codified outcome we would expect: neither the abstract Enlightenment outcome nor the pessimistic skeptical one. He was too close to Renaissance skeptical and naturalistic thought to think that humanity would ever get rid of superstition while, at the same time, being philosophically far enough from it to reject the aristocratic detachment of the philosopher, like Montaigne. His philosophical project is intended less for a private intellectual satisfaction than for a

---

without leave to divulge, as being an usurpation of the place of a Teacher. But in this time, that men call not onely for Peace, but also for Truth, to offer such Doctrines as I think True, and that manifestly tend to Peace and Loyalty, to the consideration of those that are yet in deliberation, is no more, but to offer New Wine, to be put into New Cask, that both may be preserved together" (*Leviathan*, "Review and Conclusion," 394).

[104] "First, the Power of the Popes was dissolved totally by Queen *Elizabeth*; and the Bishops, who before exercised their Functions in Right of the Pope, did afterwards exercise the same in Right of the Queen and her Successors; though by retaining the phrase of *Iure Divino*, they were thought to demand it by immediate Right from God; And so was untyed the first knot. After this, the Presbyterians lately in England obtained the putting down of Episcopacy: And so was the second knot dissolved: And almost at the same time, the Power was taken also from the Presbyterians" (*Leviathan* 47, 385).

[105] Ibid.

[106] I Corinthians 3:4–7.

sovereign who "may . . . convert this Truth of Speculation, into the Utility of Practice."[107] In a sense, like Kant, Hobbes addresses himself "respectfully to the state,"[108] ruling out any disobedience, and he has no illusions about the betterment of human nature but sees in reason (however different their conceptions of reason may be) the sole means of achieving mankind's universally shared aim of peace.

Man's fundamental dysfunctions are love of glory, which drives him to deceive himself about his own power, and the fear of invisible spirits, which drives him to be deceived by others about this privileged relationship with invisible agents endowed with a "greater power." Man's dysfunctions are ineliminable because they belong to his nature. Religion, in particular, derives from an "anxiety" congenital to life, one that can only be held back by absolute sovereignty.

As the state will never be constituted entirely by just[109] citizens (i.e., by citizens causally determined not by fear of punishments but only by the covenant; i.e., by natural laws; i.e., by the fear of returning to the state of nature), so it will never be constituted by purely rational men who simply acknowledge God as First Cause and his commands as the simple natural laws. It is up to the philosopher (i.e., Hobbes) to teach the truth and to expose the "erroneous doctrines," but it is up to the state to "convert" it into practice according to the historical circumstances.

As we have seen, all controversies and questions about "spiritual matters"[110] conceal words devoid of meaning (and thus there is no theological science); they are not raised by reason but by the ambition of theologians and the interest of the clergy.[111] What scholarship has called Hobbes's "theology" is nothing more than his commitment to free religion and worship from all theological "superstructions"[112]—the means by which churches and clerics justified their conflicts, ambitions, and claims to power—and from all aspects incompatible with the concept of the infinite bodily First Cause.

As we have seen, in De cive, Hobbes envisions a tolerant society, freed from all theological conflicts and marked by a latitudinarian public worship.[113] In Leviathan, Hobbes's proposal to the sovereign concerning religion and worship expands to biblical exegesis and the limits and characteristics of worship. Given the anthropological ineliminability of religion and worship arising from men's anxiety, what the philosopher living in a Christian Commonwealth can propose to his sovereign is to fight not religion but theology. Two needs of human nature must be reconciled: the rational one driving to the philosophical God and the passional one demanding worship of a God regarded as sensitive to men's manifestations of honor and submissiveness.

Hobbes's solution consists in fusing the philosophical and the religious God in the concept of God as King by nature. This means that the terrain where both needs of

---

[107] *Leviathan* 31, 193.

[108] Kant 1917, 89.

[109] Cf. *Philosophicall Rudiments* 3.5, 39–40; Ibid. 4.21, 68–69; *Leviathan* 15, 74.

[110] *Philosophicall Rudiments* 17.28, p. 337.

[111] This is the main theme of *Historia Ecclesiastica*. Cf. the conclusion of *Concerning Heresie*.

[112] *De corpore politico* 2, 6.9, 120.

[113] Rousseau will share this perspective: see *Du Contract Social*, bk. 4, ch. 8.

human nature may be reconciled, according to Hobbes, is that of politics, thanks to the ready political application of the concept of infinite causal power. Transposed to a political dimension, this concept immediately becomes that of an *"Irresistible Power,"*[114] which brings in a relationship of subjection for men who believe in the existence of a being endowed with it. And the belief in his irresistible power excites an "internal Honour, consisting in the opinion of Power and Goodenesse," from which "arise three Passions; *Love,* which hath reference to Goodnesse; and *Hope,* and *Fear,* that relate to Power: And three Parts of externall worship; *Praise, Magnifying,* and *Blessing."*[115]

Thus, whereas Hobbes outlines a phenomenology of worship that fully confirms its passional origin, he also describes natural worship as "dictated to men by their Natural Reason onely"[116]:

> The End of Worship amongst men, is Power. For where a man seeth another wor-shipped, he supposeth him powerful, and is the readier to obey him; which makes his Power greater. *But God has no Ends*: the worship we do him, proceeds from our duty, and is directed according to our capacity, by those rules of Honour, that Reason dictateth to be done by the weak to the more potent men, in hope of benefit, for fear of dammage, or in thankfulness for good already received from them.[117]

This is not a properly rational apprehension of God as First Cause. Reason here only restricts worship within the bounds of the analogy with honoring "potent men," yet this is enough to purge the worship of all supernatural, metaphysical, and mysterious aspects required by the clergy and churches and to liberate it from the irrational aspects introduced by their theologies.

No problem arises from the attribute of *existence* or from any others that, despite the absolute unknowableness of God,[118] are consequences of the general assumption that he must be absolutely distinguished from anything we can conceive of as caused, finite, and imaginable. Hobbes thus rejects any form of Renaissance pantheism that identi-fies God with the world or with its soul.[119] Nothing is attributable to God that may be predicated of finite things, such as having "figure," our having "an *Idea* of him," his hav-ing "Parts"[120] or being a "Totality" or "in this, or that *Place*" or being something that is "*Moved,* or *Resteth,*" or has any "Passive faculty."

There are also attributes—such as providence, goodness, care of mankind—specifically belonging to God as object of "*Love, Hope,* and *Fear,*" although Hobbes affirms that these are "taught" by reason; they do not appear to be easily reconcilable with the

---

[114] *Leviathan* 31, 187.

[115] Ibid. 31, 189.

[116] Ibid. 31, 188.

[117] Ibid. 31, 189–190 (emphasis added).

[118] Ibid. 31, 191.

[119] Ibid. 31, 190.

[120] This does not mean that God cannot be defined as a "part" of the universe (*Answer to Dr. Bramhall,* 86).

general characterizations that the Almighty King by nature shares with God as First Cause. Their meaning seems to depend on the attribution of will and "ends" to God, whereas Hobbes claims that "God has no Ends" and that "when we ascribe to God a *Will*, it is not to be understood, as that of a Man, for a *Rationall Appetite*; but as the Power, by which he effecteth every thing."[121] This is a puzzling affirmation because of the use of the scholastic definition of will as *appetitus rationalis*, which for Hobbes is devoid of any meaning. Because Hobbes's doctrine is that will is a passion, not ascribing will to God implicitly follows from the fact that passions cannot be attributed to him. The identification between God's will and power has the theological implication of the denial of the difference between the *potentia absoluta* and the *potentia ordinata* of God.[122] And the more Hobbes insists on saying that the attributes of providence, goodness, and care of mankind are "taught by reason," the more he reveals a slippage of the sense of *reason* in reference to worship.

The fact is that the attribution to God of providence, goodness, and care of mankind depends exclusively on the existence of worship and vice versa. However purged of all irrational and interested rituals of historical religions, worship answers a passional need of man and does not arise from pure reason and knowledge of God. The attributes specifically connected to worship appear to be, if not irrational, at least arational.

First, men's obedience and gratitude have no relationship with the "right of Gods Sovereignty" because this "is to be derived, not from his Creating them as if he requireth obedience, as of Gratitude for his benefits; but from his *Irresistible Power*."

Second, sin has no necessary relationship with the "fortune" of men (either in this world or the next) because it is not the cause of God's afflictions, and "the Right of Afflicting, is not always derived from mens Sin, but from Gods Power."[123] Hobbes considers the problem of evil and concludes that the sufferings of innocent creatures are rationally irreconcilable with "Divine Providence." Therefore, in the Kingdom of God, by nature there is no rationally definable difference between a God who cares for mankind and a God who does not care; consequently, the attribute of providence loses any meaning when referred to the infinite causal power, denoting only a human expectation and desire to honor him.

Third, in the Kingdom of God by nature the condition of those who refuse any worship—that is, of atheists and of those who do not believe "that God has any care of the actions of mankind"[124]—is not rationally distinguishable from those of the believers. It is true that atheists and deniers of God's providence expose themselves to his afflictions as his "enemies," but, in that Kingdom, this does not worsen their condition compared to the believers because of the nature of God's right to afflict or to spare his

---

[121] Ibid.

[122] Therefore Hobbes's incidental distinctions between "operations ordinary" and "extraordinary" of God are to be interpreted as lip-service (cf. *Leviathan* 26, 149 and *Philosophicall Rudiments* 13.1, 191–192).

[123] *Leviathan* 31, 187–188.

[124] Ibid. 31, 186.

tribulations.[125] What, then, actually differentiates those who recognize the existence of a Kingdom of God by nature and those who do not? Only this: the correct conception of the relation between cause and effect; thereby the former *know* and the latter are *ignorant*[126] of the fact that the natural and human world constitutionally lacks a causal self-sufficiency and must be absolutely distinguished from its cause.

It is a general logical requirement never to confuse God as the first infinite cause with any of his effects, and this finally explains why Hobbes never admits that God can be conceived as a king ruling by a direct "sensible word." All acts and sensible words by which a sovereign by pact rules are caused, whereas God's actions are uncaused and his speech can be understood as consisting only in the series of secondary causes necessarily deriving from his infinite power. Steadfast in this point, Hobbes denies that, even in his prophetical kingdom where he ruled as a civil sovereign, God spoke by a sensible word to his "viceregents," the "holy Prophets" of the Old Testament, and to Moses—although the Bible says that God spoke to him "mouth to mouth" and "face to face, as a man speaketh to his friend."[127]

The only way to conceive a "sensible word" of God is to attribute it to a representative of his; this is confirmed by Hobbes's interpretation of the doctrine of Trinity and by his affirmation that, even in the "world to come," God will exercise his civil sovereignty over the elect through Christ; that is, it will be a "Kingdome of God by Christ."[128]

What essentially characterizes Hobbes's concept of God is its correlation with the constitutional lack of causal self-sufficiency of the world; this radically differentiates Hobbes's materialism from both classical atomistic materialism and from all Renaissance materialisms. Whether this conception arises exclusively from the terrain of a radical anti-Aristotelian criticism or conceals also a secret religious origin is a question that Hobbes's texts do not allow us to solve. How the bodily God operates on the natural world is above reason; the physical metaphor of the two fluids Hobbes uses in his *Answer to Bramhall* alludes to a continuous action of God as an omnipresent and all-pervasive cause.[129] This is also confirmed by what Hobbes says about the human world, where he affirms that any action of man can be traced back to God.

God operates in all the infinite chains of human and natural events, and every aspect and every moment of human life is to be ascribed to his infinite power.[130] The fact that this God is to be conceived, *qua* First Cause, as an unknowable body

---

[125] "He that renounceth the mercy of God obligeth himeselfe not to any punishment, because it is ever lawfull to deprecate the punishment however provok'd, and to enjoy Gods Pardon if it be granted" (*Philosophicall Rudiments* 2.22, 33).

[126] This is the reason why atheism is a sin "to be numbered among those of imprudence or ignorance" (*Philosophicall Rudiments*, 14.19, pp. 226; cf. *Appendix ad Leviathan*, 548–549).

[127] Cf. *Leviathan* 36, 226–227. However Hobbes, for obvious reasons, allows that "in what manner God spake unto them, is not manifest" (ibid., 228; see also "Review and Conclusion," 393).

[128] *Leviathan* 44, 345. Cf. 35, 219.

[129] *Answer to Dr. Bramhall*, 36.

[130] *Leviathan* 21, 108.

ontologically distinct (and not only rationally distinguishable) from the world (or from the domain of things *caused*) implies that Hobbes cannot be defined as an atheist. It is also evident that Hobbes tries to make his conception of God appear as close as possible to Calvin's,[131] but, rather than the God of Calvin, Hobbes's God evokes that of Spinoza.

References

Bayle, Pierre. 1982. *Oeuvres diverses, Volumes supplementaires*, v. I, 1 (repr. of 1740 ed.), edited by É. Labrousse. New York: Hildesheim.

Bramhall, John. 1658. *Castigations of Mr. Hobbes His Last Animadversions, in the Case Concerning Liberty, and Universal Necessity. With an Appendix Concerning The Catching of Leviathan or, The Great Whale*. London: J. Crook.

Collins, Jeffrey R. 2009. "Interpreting Thomas Hobbes in Competing Contexts." *Journal of the History of Ideas* 70, 1.

Foisneau, Luc. 2000. *Hobbes et la toute-puissance de Dieu*. Paris: PUF.

Giargia, Myriam. 2012. "Verità, potere e miti in Hobbes," in *Verità del potere, potere della verità*, edited by Alberto Pirni, 177–186. Pisa: Edizioni ETS.

Gorham, Geoffrey. 2012. "The Theological Foundation of Hobbesian Physics: A Defence of Corporeal God." *British Journal for the History of Philosophy*. doi: 10.1080/09608788.2012.692663.

Hobbes, Thomas. 1964 [1974]. *Objectiones tertiae ad Cartesii Meditationes de prima philosophia*, in *Œuvres de Descartes* vol. VII, edited by Charles Adam and Paul Tannery, 171–196. Paris: Librairie Philosophique J. Vrin.

Hobbes, Thomas. 1642. *Elementorum philosophiae Sectio tertia De cive*. Paris.

Hobbes, Thomas. 1649 [1650]. *Humane Nature: Or, The Fundamental Elements of Policie. Being a Discoverie of the Faculties, Acts, and Passions, of the Soul of Man, From their Original Causes, According to Such Philosophical Principles as Are not Commonly Known or Asserted*. Oxford.

Hobbes, Thomas. 1650. *De corpore politico. Or The Elements of Law, Moral & Politick*. London.

Hobbes, Thomas. 1651a. *Philosophicall Rudiments Concerning Government and Society*. London.

Hobbes, Thomas. 1651b. *Leviathan, or The Matter, Form, and Power of a Common-wealth Ecclesiastical and Civil. By Thomas Hobbes of Malmesbury*. London.

Hobbes, Thomas. 1841. *Appendix ad Leviathan*, in *Thomae Hobbes Malmesburiensis opera philosophica quae latine scripsit omnia*, edited by William Molesworth. 5 vv. vol. III, 511–569. London.

Hobbes, Thomas. 1656. *Elements of Philosophy the First Section, Concerning Body Written in Latine by Thomas Hobbes of Malmesbury; and now Translated into English; to Which Are Added Six lessons to the Professors of Mathematicks of the Institution of Sr. Henry Savile, in the University of Oxford*. London.

Hobbes, Thomas. 1661. *Dialogus physicus, sive, De natura aeris conjectura sumpta ab experimentis nuper Londini habitis in Collegio Greshamensi, item de duplicatione cubi*. London.

---

[131] Overhoff 2000, 155.

Hobbes, Thomas. 1678. *Decameron Physiologicum, or, Ten Dialogues of Natural Philosophy by Thomas Hobbes; to which is Added The Proportion of a Straight Line to Half the Arc of a Quadrant, by the Same Author.* London.

Hobbes, Thomas. 1682. *An Answer to a Book Published by Dr. Bramhall, Late Bishop of Derry; Called the Catching of the Leviathan. Together with an Historical Narration Concerning Heresie, and the Punishment thereof.* London.

Hobbes, Thomas. 1682. *Behemoth, the History of the Causes of the Civil Wars of England, from 1640 to 1660,* in *Tracts of Mr. Thomas Hobbs of Malmsbury.* London.

Hobbes, Thomas. 1688. *Historia Ecclesiastica carmine elegiaco concinnata,* in *Opera philosophica quae latine scripsit omnia,* vol. V, 341–408. London.

Hobbes, Thomas. 1973. *Critique du "De mundo" de Thomas White,* edited by Jean Jacquot and Harold Whitmore Jones. Paris: Vrin-CNRS.

Hobbes, Thomas. 1999. *De corpore. Elementorum Philosophiae Sectio Prima,* edited by Karl Schuhmann, with Martine Pécharman. Paris: Librairie Philosophique J. Vrin.

Hume, David. 1968. *A Treatise of Human Nature,* edited by L. A. Selby-Bigge. Oxford: Clarendon Press.

Kant, Immanuel. 1917. *Der Streit der Fakultäten, Zweiter Abschnitt. Erneuerte Frage: Ob das menschliche Geschlecht im beständigen Fortschreiten zum Bessen sei* (1798), in *Kants Gesammelte Schriften,* Königlich Preußischen Akademie der Wissenschaften, Berlin-Leipzig, 1900 Abt. 1, bd. VII, 1–115. Berlin: Reimer.

Lessay, Frank. 2004. "Hobbes's Protestantism," in *Leviathan After 350 Years,* edited by Tom Sorell and Luc Foisneau, 265–294. New York/Oxford: Clarendon.

Lupoli, Agostino. 2006. *Nei limiti della materia. Hobbes e Boyle: materialismo epistemologico, filosofia corpuscolare e "dio corporeo."* Milano: Baldini Castoldi Dalai.

Martinich, A. P. 1992. *The Two Gods of Leviathan: Hobbes on Religion and Politics.* Cambridge: Cambridge University Press.

Martinich, A. P. 2009. "Interpreting the Religion of Thomas Hobbes: An Exchange." *Journal of the History of Ideas* 70, 1.

Mersenne, P. Marin. 1932–88. *Correspondance du P. Marin Mersenne, religieux minime,* edited by Cornelis De Waard and Armand Beaulieu, 17 vv. Paris: Éditions du CNRS.

Overhoff, Jürgen. 2000. *Hobbes's Theory of the Will. Ideological Reasons and Historical Circumstances.* Lanham, MD: Rowman & Littlefield.

Pacchi, Arrigo. 1998. *Scritti Hobbesiani (1978–1990),* edited by Agostino Lupoli. Milano: Angeli.

Rousseau, Jean-Jacques. 1762. *Du Contract Social; ou, Principes du Droit Politique.* Amsterdam: M.M. Rey.

Strauss, Leo. 2005. *La critique de la religion chez Hobbes: une contribution à la compréhension des Lumières (1933–1934),* translated by Corinne Pelluchon. Paris: PUF.

Tuck, Richard. 1992. "The 'Christian Atheism' of Thomas Hobbes," in *Atheism from the Reformation to the Enlightenment,* edited by Michael Hunter and D. Wootton, 111–130. Oxford: Clarendon.

Warrender, Howard. 1957. *The Political Philosophy of Hobbes: His Theory of Obligation.* Oxford: Clarendon Press.

CHAPTER 21

....

HOBBES, CONSCIENCE, AND CHRISTIANITY

....

RICHARD TUCK

THE question of how far Hobbes thought that a sovereign's judgments should refashion the inner life of his subjects has remained one of the most difficult issues in Hobbes scholarship. Thirty years ago, Alan Ryan set out the alternatives clearly in what is still the best discussion of the topic. Either "somehow or other the sovereign could and should exercise complete control over our opinions, and render dissidence literally unthinkable" (what Ryan called "a totalitarian ambition," similar (he said) to that of Rousseau or Hegel), or there should merely be "uniformity of *profession* in matters of religion and jurisprudence" (the "usual" view), or "Hobbes had more positive concern for freedom of speech and for the exercise of individual conscientiousness than is generally thought."[1] Ryan himself concluded that the usual view was the correct one, but he was aware of the attractions of both the other alternatives—although it is fair to say that he was rather swiftly dismissive of the first and more sympathetic to the third while insisting that freedom of thought in Hobbes was always defended on purely pragmatic grounds.[2] Since then, rather few people have defended the first alternative, although I have expressed more sympathy for it than most.[3] But there is one way of approaching the question that has, I think, not hitherto been considered. In general,

---

[1] Ryan (1983: 200, 215) for the comparison with Rousseau and Hegel. The volume was a collection of essays in memory of John Plamenatz. Two recent discussions of Hobbes on the conscience, which include full bibliographies, are Tralau (2011) and Hanin (2012). Tralau argues that Hobbes's account of the "public" conscience is inconsistent with his account of the "private" conscience, and the inconsistency is an indication of an intent to deceive; Hanin is closer to my own view, that Hobbes genuinely wished his citizens to live according to their consciences and to align them with the sovereign's decrees, although he, too, thinks (following Ryan) that "it is far from clear that Hobbes's combination of external submission and internal dissent forms a sustainable model" (81).

[2] See his further discussion of the question in Ryan 1988.

[3] See in particular Tuck 2003. I was more in agreement with Ryan when I wrote the Introduction to my edition of Leviathan; see *Leviathan* ed. Tuck: xviii.

people have written on Hobbes's ideas about toleration and public profession as if he thought that all religions—and religion has always been for obvious reasons the key instance—raised the same issues for the relationship between the sovereign and the citizen. But a striking feature of Hobbes's work is the amount of intellectual effort he put into distinguishing between Judaeo-Christianity and other religions and the different place he accorded it in the inner life of the citizen. If we think hard about the reason why Hobbes chose to do this, we might begin to get a clearer sense of what he thought about the sovereign's power over our innermost thoughts.

As always, we have to begin with Hobbes's basic political and moral ideas. In many respects, they were put forward most clearly in the first work he wrote on the subject, the manuscript *Elements of Law* of 1640 (which was largely the basis for his first published work in the area, *De cive* of 1642). Only the *Elements of Law* contains the full account of the passions and of man's emotional life that he promised to provide in *De homine* but failed to deliver and that he only sketched in *Leviathan*. The central claim is expressed most vividly in a summary of his ideas, which he provided in the concluding chapter:

> In the state of nature, where every man is his own judge, and differeth from other concerning the names and appellations of things, and from those differences arise quarrels, and breach of peace; it was necessary there should be a common measure of all things that might fall in controversy; as for example: of what is to be called right, what good, what virtue, what much, what little, what *meum* and *tuum*, what a pound, what a quart, &c. For in these things private judgements may differ, and beget controversy. This common measure, some say, is right reason: with whom I should consent, if there were any such thing to be found or known *in rerum naturâ*. But commonly they that call for right reason to decide any controversy, do mean their own. But this is certain, seeing right reason is not existent, the reason of some man, or men, must supply the place thereof; and that man, or men, is he or they, that have the sovereign power ... and consequently the civil laws are to all subjects the measures of their actions, whereby to determine, whether they be right or wrong, profitable or unprofitable, virtuous or vicious; and by them the use and definition of all names not agreed upon, and tending to controversy, shall be established. As for example, upon the occasion of some strange and deformed birth, it shall not be decided by Aristotle, or the philosophers, whether the same be a man or no, but by the laws.[4]

The essential thought here, as I have emphasized on many occasions,[5] is that moral conflicts arise from epistemic conflict: it is the fact that we disagree even about what

---

[4] *Elements of Law* 2.10.8. The last part of this passage (on the "strange and deformed birth") is found in *De cive* at 17.12, and the first part at 6.9. The remark that right reason is "non-existent" does not appear in those words in *De cive*, although a related sentiment is to be found (e.g., at 14.17). *De cive* treats "right reason" throughout as the reason of each individual—see, e.g., Hobbes's note to 2.1—and therefore did not need to declare that in its traditional acceptation it is nonexistent.

[5] For instance *Leviathan*: xvii.

is "profitable" as well as about what is "right" or "good" that gives rise to the struggles of the state of nature. In principle, as Hobbes always emphasized, men did not in fact disagree about the fundamentals of morality at all: everyone would concede to another man the right to defend himself against attack, and everyone would accept that they were not entitled unnecessarily or wantonly to attack other people. This last thought may be less familiar to followers of the standard accounts of Hobbes, but it is expressed, for example, in the ban even in the state of nature on revenge; as Hobbes said about revenge in the *Elements*, it is "directed to no end," and "to hurt one another without reason, is contrary to that, which by supposition is every man's benefit, namely peace."[6] A similar account of a universal core morality had been advanced earlier by Hugo Grotius as part of an attempt to show that all societies could share a minimal set of moral principles and negotiate among themselves on its basis. But Hobbes's central political idea was that a universal morality of this kind was not enough because there would still be radical disagreement among men—not over the general character of the principles, but over the relevant conditions for their implementation. When am I at risk? Who is my enemy? When *is* violence unnecessary? Unless these factual questions can be answered, agreement on the minimal morality is of little practical utility, and Hobbes was fully aware that they could not be answered; indeed, a great deal of recent English politics (such as the Ship Money case) had turned precisely on the impossibility of deciding these questions objectively. The role of the sovereign was to decide these issues, not, of course, by seeing the truth more clearly than his subjects (for there was no truth here), but simply by determining one answer to be canonical for his (or its) subjects.

As a consequence, his power had to be (in one sense) unlimited, for almost anything could in theory count as an answer to these kinds of question; but, in another sense, his power was restricted because he was entitled to answer *only* these kinds of question. We can grasp Hobbes's theory in this area best by considering precisely what the rights and duties of an agent in the state of nature were—for, as is well known, Hobbes consistently treated the sovereign as an agent still in the state of nature, morally speaking. An individual in the state of nature has the "right to all things" because any thing *may* count as necessary to his preservation; as long as he acts in good faith toward this end, he is morally justified. But this is not the same as saying that his right is unlimited because if he does not conscientiously believe that something is necessary for his preservation, he is not entitled to cause harm to anyone in order to secure it:

> [T]hus much the law of nature commandeth in war: that men satiate not the cruelty of their present passions, whereby in their own conscience they foresee no benefit to come. For that betrayeth not a necessity, but a disposition of the mind to war, which is against the law of nature.[7]

---

[6] *Elements of Law* 1.16.10.
[7] *Elements of Law* 1.19.2.

And even if we were to follow a correct interpretation of the law of nature but inwardly to dissent, we would be breaking the law of nature by doing so:

> seeing the laws of nature concern the conscience, not he only breaketh them that doth any action contrary, but also he whose action is conformable to them, in case he think it contrary. For though the action chance to be right, yet in his judgment he despiseth the law.[8]

And going against our conscience matters because we "fear the penalties of the life to come"[9] and understand that God knows our inward beliefs. In a note to the 1647 edition of *De cive* intended to clarify his ideas, Hobbes put these thoughts quite plainly. "Briefly, in a state of nature, Just and Unjust should be judged not from actions but from the intention and conscience of the agents. What is done of necessity, or in pursuit of peace, or for self-preservation is done rightly. Apart from this, all infliction of harm on men is a violation of natural Law and a wrong against God."[10]

Just the same is true of the sovereign; he (or it), too, can break the law of nature by acting insincerely or against conscience. In a particularly striking passage of *De cive*, Hobbes used the example of laws concerning religion to make this point:

> [O]ne may question whether sovereigns and the ministers of sovereign power in a commonwealth (whoever they may be, whether one man or several) are not offending against the law of nature, if they do not ensure instruction in the doctrine and practice of the worship which they themselves believe is indispensable to the citizens' *eternal salvation*, or if they permit a contrary teaching or practice. It is evident that they are acting against conscience and, so far as they can, are intending the citizens' eternal damnation. For if that was not their intention, I do not see why (being sovereign and uncompellable) they would allow teachings and practices among their citizens which they believe will damn them.[11]

And he said the same about a sovereign choosing his successor:

> if he did not make his wishes about his *successor* known, by Will or otherwise, while he was still alive, one makes a first assumption that he did not wish the commonwealth to revert to Anarchy or a state of war, that is, to the ruination of the citizens. One makes this assumption . . . because he could not do that without breaking the natural laws by which he was bound in the court of conscience to do everything that necessarily contributes to peace.[12]

But if the sovereign does sincerely decree that a particular course of conduct is "just" or "good" or "honourable," then a loyal citizen will take the decree as deciding the matter for him.

---

[8] *Elements of Law* 1.17.13.
[9] *On the Citizen* 12.2.
[10] *On the Citizen* 13.27 n.
[11] *On the Citizen* 13.5.
[12] *On the Citizen* 9.14.

However, as Alan Ryan emphasized, there are two ways in which we might understand this. One is the familiar modern liberal thought that, in public discourse, we bracket our own convictions and agree to go along with the opinions of our fellow citizens as represented by the sovereign's pronouncements, although inwardly we continue to dissent from them. This would, as Ryan said, be the standard view, and it seems on the face of it to make a great deal of sense. But it does imply that in a Hobbesian commonwealth the citizens will be continually resisting mentally the determinations of their sovereign, so that, in effect, the struggles and enmities of the state of nature continue into civil society, although internally. Apart from anything else, this does not look like the recipe for a very stable commonwealth, nor does it correspond to the general tenor of Hobbes's argument, in which the well-founded commonwealth is to be a place of thorough-going peace. The other is the more remarkable thought: that we *actually* take the decree as determinative, both externally *and* internally. On this account, the sovereign's judgment genuinely becomes *our* judgment. As I said at the beginning of this chapter, this has rarely been put forward except as a possibility to be dismissed, but there are many passages in Hobbes's writings that suggest this way of interpreting the situation is indeed the correct one.

For example,

> The conscience being nothing else but a man's settled judgement and opinion, when he hath once transferred his right of judging to another, that which shall be commanded, is no less his judgement, than the judgement of that other; so that in obedience to laws, a man doth still according to his conscience, but not his private conscience. And whatsoever is done contrary to private conscience, is then a sin, when the laws have left him to his own liberty, and never else. And then whatsoever a man doth, not only believing it is ill done, but doubting whether it be ill or not, is done ill.[13]

Or, as he said two chapters later,

> [the] Christian religion not only forbiddeth not, but also commandeth, that in every commonwealth, every subject should in all things to the uttermost of his power obey the commands of him or them that is the sovereign thereof; and that a man in so obeying, doth according to his conscience and judgment, as having deposited his judgment in all controversies in the hands of the sovereign power; . . .[14]

He used the same kind of language to make the same point in *Leviathan*:

> [A] mans Conscience, and his Judgement is the same thing; and as the Judgement, so also the Conscience may be erroneous. Therefore, though he that is subject to no Civill Law, sinneth in all he does against his Conscience, because he has no other rule to follow but his own reason; yet it is not so with him that lives in a Common-wealth;

---

[13] *Elements of Law* 2.6.12.
[14] *Elements of Law* 2.8.5.

because the Law is the publique Conscience, by which he hath already undertaken to be guided.[15]

And in *De cive* (which is, in this respect as in some others, actually a much less sober work than *Leviathan*), he even described the private exercise of judgment in moral matters as the fundamental sin:

> What is *just* or *unjust* derives from the law of the ruler. Legitimate kings therefore make what they order just by ordering it, and make what they forbid unjust by forbidding it. When private men claim for themselves a knowledge of *good* and *evil*, they are aspiring to be as Kings. When this happens the commonwealth cannot stand. The oldest of God's commands is (Gen. 2.17): *Do not eat of the tree of the knowledge of good and evil,* and the oldest of the devil's temptations is (3.5): *You will be as gods knowing good and evil.* The first reproach God made to men is (v. 11): *Who told you that you were naked, unless you have eaten of the tree of which I told you not to eat?* as if he were saying, how did you decide that the nakedness in which it seemed good to me to create you, was dishonourable, except by usurping for yourselves a *knowledge* of good and evil?[16]

A couple of paragraphs later, he added, about tyrannicide, that

> the divine question applies: *Who told you that he was a Tyrant, unless you have eaten of the tree of which I told you not to eat?* For why do you call him a *Tyrant* whom God made a *King,* unless you, a private person, are claiming for yourself a knowledge of *good* and *evil?*

The ideal in *De cive* of a pre-lapsarian state, in which individuals had no beliefs of a conventional kind about the matters that had come into contention after the Fall, found expression using another myth in the Preface, where Hobbes (in a remarkable passage) depicted a remote era of "peace . . . and a golden age, which did not end until Saturn was expelled and the doctrine started up that one could take up arms against kings" and in which the "ancients" had

> preferred that the knowledge of Justice be wrapped up in fables rather than exposed to discussion. Before questions of that kind began to be debated, Princes did not lay claim to sovereign power, they simply exercised it. They did not defend their power by arguments but by punishing the wicked and defending the good. In return the citizens did not measure Justice by the comments of private men but by the laws of the commonwealth; and were kept at Peace not by discussions but by the power of Government. In fact, they revered sovereign power, whether it resided in a man or in an Assembly, as a kind of visible divinity.[17]

---

[15] *Leviathan* chapter 29, original ed. pp. 168–169.
[16] *Of the Citizen* 12.1
[17] *Of the Citizen* Preface 6.

Against these passages, there are others in which Hobbes appears to be endorsing something more like what I have termed the "liberal" view—as for example *Elements* 2.6.3:

> To take away this scruple of conscience concerning obedience to human laws, amongst those that interpret to themselves the word of God in the Holy Scriptures; I propound to their consideration, first: that no human law is intended to oblige the conscience of a man, but the actions only. For seeing no man (but God alone) knoweth the heart or conscience of a man, unless it break out into action, either of the tongue, or other part of the body; the law made thereupon would be of none effect, because no man is able to discern, but by word or other action whether such law be kept or broken.

Or the eloquent remarks toward the end of *Leviathan* assailing the scholastics:

> There is another Errour in their Civill Philosophy (which they never learned of Aristotle, nor Cicero, nor any other of the Heathen,) to extend the power of the Law, which is the Rule of Actions onely, to the very Thoughts, and Consciences of men, by Examination, and *Inquisition* of what they Hold, notwithstanding the Conformity of their Speech and Actions: By which, men are either punished for answering the truth of their thoughts, or constrained to answer an untruth for fear of punishment . . . [T]o force him to accuse himselfe of Opinions, when his Actions are not by Law forbidden, is against the Law of Nature; and especially in them, who teach, that a man shall bee damned to Eternall and extream torments, if he die in a false opinion concerning an Article of the Christian Faith.[18]

And, perhaps most clearly, in his discussion in the same work about belief in miracles:

> [I]n these times, I do not know one man, that ever saw any such wondrous work . . .: and the question is no more, whether what wee see done, be a Miracle; whether the Miracle we hear, or read of, were a reall work, and not the Act of a tongue, or pen; but in plain terms, whether the report be true, or a lye. In which question we are not every one, to make our own private Reason, or Conscience, but the Publique Reason, that is, the reason of Gods Supreme Lieutenant, Judge; and indeed we have made him Judge already, if wee have given him a Soveraign power, to doe all that is necessary for our peace and defence. A private man has alwaies the liberty, (because thought is free,) to beleeve, or not beleeve in his heart, those acts that have been given out for Miracles, according as he shall see, what benefit can accrew by mens belief, to those that pretend, or countenance them, and thereby conjecture, whether they be Miracles, or Lies. But when it comes to confession of that faith, the Private Reason must submit to the Publique, that is to say, to Gods Lieutenant.[19]

[18] *Leviathan* chapter 46, original ed. p. 378.
[19] *Leviathan* chapter 37, original ed. pp. 237–238.

However, although Hobbes said in these passages (and a few other similar ones) that human law does not oblige the conscience, this claim cannot be taken quite at its face value. It is true that it cannot do so directly, for the reasons he gave—the legal system cannot apply sanctions to a purely internal commitment, nor should it purport to do so. In this sense, indeed, "thought is free." But Hobbes's general account of our moral life makes this a trickier issue than it seems at first sight. If I believe in the truth of Hobbes's arguments, I must believe that (as he said in many of the passages quoted earlier as examples of what we may call the "internalist" view) it is a *sin* to follow my own conscience in situations where my sovereign has pronounced to the contrary. So, although I might freely think something other than what the sovereign says, it is hard to see how I can believe that I ought morally to do anything other than he prescribes. Consequently, I cannot straightforwardly have any internal *moral* dissent from my sovereign's commands; the "liberal" picture according to which I can internally disagree but externally must obey does not seem to correspond very accurately to what Hobbes thought about the most important range of possible disagreements in which a modern liberal would be interested. It may be relevant, on this view, that the clearest statement in Hobbes about freedom of thought in the face of the sovereign's commands, the passage on miracles in *Leviathan* just quoted, is not directly concerned with *moral* disagreement, nor with the meaning of the terms "just" or "good," the knowledge of which was the fruit of the forbidden tree, but is concerned with a factual question (although it must be acknowledged, a factual question with considerable moral significance).

Like many components of Hobbes's thought in this area, this was a familiar piece of contemporary theology. Calvinists had long argued that human law does not in itself oblige the conscience.[20] Some civil laws, they thought, simply prescribe punishment for breach of a moral law (such as that against murder), and those laws do oblige the conscience in the sense that we are obliged to refrain from performing the proscribed act. But others do not oblige in the same way (a favorite example was dietary or sumptuary laws): in these cases, the sovereign in effect offers the citizen a choice between performing the act and being punished and not performing the act, and the citizen is free to choose which he wishes to do. Punishment, in these cases, becomes like a tax, and only if the citizen refuses to make the choice has he sinned; the judgment by the sovereign that one should not (say) eat meat on a Friday was not authoritative for the citizen. Only God can put human beings under a specific moral obligation, and the essence of "Christian liberty" was that there should be few such obligations; as the English Calvinist Andrew Willett said, "If everie law did binde the conscience, then by reason of such a multitude of lawes, which are impossible to be kept, mens consciences should be so snared and entangled, as none should be free."[21]

---

[20] For Calvin himself, see his discussion in the *Institutes* (book 4 chapter 10) structured round the familiar distinction between the *forum internum* and the *forum externum* that Hobbes himself, of course, used. I provided a brief discussion of the issue in Tuck 1974: 46–47.

[21] Willet 1611: 618.

Willet specifically named the "Romanists" as the opponents of this position, and, indeed, many Catholic theologians were hostile to it—but so were many anti-Calvinist Protestants. Hugo Grotius put their case particularly clearly in his *De Imperio Summarum Potestatum circa Sacra* of 1647:[22]

> External actions are the primary object of human authority; internal actions are a secondary object, not on their own account, but on account of external actions; and therefore human commands do not occupy themselves with internal actions which are completely separate from and do not concern external actions.... This is also a common saying in law: *No-one is punished for thinking.* The reason is that authority needs the kind of object which can become known to the commanding body [*in imperantis notitiam cadat*]. But only God *knows the hearts of all men* and therefore is the only one to have authority over them....
>
> [But] internal acts too are subject to authority, in a secondary manner. This can happen in two ways: either because it is the ruler's intention or indirectly. The former occurs when an internal act is joined to an external one and as it were flows into it, for example when intentions are taken into account in the judgment of offences, committed or begun. The latter occurs when the ruler has pronounced a certain act illegal (*therefore one must be subject, not only to avoid his wrath, but also for the sake of conscience* [Rom. 13:5]), thereby making it also illegal to think of undertaking such an action; not because human law in itself deals with thought, but because no one can in honesty wish to do what it is dishonest to do.[23]

Grotius's position here seems to me to be very close to Hobbes's general view of the subject, although, of course, Hobbes greatly widened the scope of what the sovereign can legitimately demand of his subjects to include actions that, for Grotius (as for most of his contemporaries), would have been against the laws of God or nature.

That might have appeared to be the end of the matter, with Hobbes indeed the alarming theorist of sovereign authority penetrating right into our inner selves—Ryan's "totalitarian." But, as I said at the beginning of this chapter, what has been overlooked by most people who have written on these topics is that within Hobbes's general theory of internal alignment with the sovereign's pronouncements there is a special exemption, not for religion in general, but specifically for the Christian and Jewish religions. Their exemption is possible within Hobbes's theory because of their unique *political* history, which has not been shared by any other religions; Hobbes's restlessly returning to the subject of Christianity in his writings was, I believe, in large part motivated by his concern to clarify and delineate its exceptional status in his theory. But, correspondingly, the importance he accorded to the special political history of the religions

---

[22] Hobbes had presumably read it by the time he wrote *Leviathan*; in addition, manuscripts of the work had been circulating in England since 1617 (by the time of his death, John Selden possessed two copies), and Hobbes could in principle have known it before it appeared in print. See van Dam 2001: vol. 1, 39–44, 58–64.

[23] van Dam 2001: vol. 1, 207 (chapter 3.1). For the Catholic viewpoint, see Bellarmine 1601: volume 2, 644–652 (*De laicis* chapters 9–10).

is evidence—and perhaps the best evidence—that without such an exemption the sovereign's determinations do indeed control our inner life. This is because (as he repeatedly made clear) the Christian, like the pagan, was obliged in his outward professions to follow the directions of his sovereign, so it could only be at the level of the *inner* life that there was scope for a special freedom for the Christian—and, by implication, no freedom for the non-Christian.

To understand this, we have first to distinguish between what Hobbes said about the "religion of the gentiles," in particular the religions of the ancient world, and what he said about Judaism or Christianity. On the subject of what we might call non-Abrahamic religion, Hobbes was always clear: there are no true propositions about God as such except for the proposition that "he" brought the world into being. Consequently, all descriptions of God are merely ways of doing honor to this unknown creator and therefore are to be regulated by the civil sovereign in the same way as all other titles of honor:

> The attributes therefore given unto the Deity, are such as signify either our incapacity, or our reverence; our incapacity, when we say: incomprehensible and infinite; our reverence, when we give him those names, which amongst us are the names of those things we most magnify and commend, as omnipotent, omniscient, just, merciful, &c.[24]

In the manuscript *Critique of Thomas White* [aka *Anti-White*]of 1643 (which contains many of his most interesting remarks on religion), Hobbes used this argument to dissolve the problem of evil, which he took to be a pagan as much as a Christian problem. Because the names that we give God are (as he said) "oblations" and not "propositions," there is no inconsistency between calling him "omnipotent" and denying him the description "source of evil": "omnipotent" is a name of great honor, and "source of evil" is a name of great dishonor, and there is no conflict between them since neither of the names possesses a determinate truth content. We have no more right to exercise our own judgment over propositions within a religion of the gentiles than we have to exercise it over the use of terms such as "good" or "just" or "human."[25]

But this theory, which handed the sovereign complete control over theology and religion, did not cover the Abrahamic religions because they had a special status. Hobbes began to explore this issue in *De cive*, in a discussion of the Kingdom of God. The *Elements of Law* contains nothing about the Kingdom of God; *De cive*, on the other hand, has three chapters expressly devoted to it (chapter 16, "On the Kingdom of God by Nature"; chapter 17, "On the Kingdom of God by the Old Agreement [Covenant]"; and chapter 18, "On the Kingdom of God by the New Agreement [Covenant]").[26] The

---

[24] *Elements of Law* 1.11.3

[25] *Critique du De Mundo*: 395–396 (chapter 35.16); *De Mundo Examined*: 434.

[26] Although we used the word "Agreement" to translate Hobbes's *Pactum*, I now think that this was a mistake and that the traditional "Covenant" would be more appropriate, and my quotations from our edition are emended accordingly. While *foedus* became the standard Latin term for the Covenant, *pactum* is used both in the Vulgate and among early Protestants. See Musculus 1560: 178.

themes developed in these chapters are those which later filled much of *Leviathan*: that God can be seen as a Hobbesian sovereign, first ruling in the natural world by virtue of his absolute power and then ruling in specific kingdoms by virtue of agreements. The account of God's natural kingdom was an extension of the brief remarks in *The Elements* about the honor naturally due to God; Hobbes took this thought and developed it into a full-scale account of worship, in which men are depicted as worshipping the inscrutable but omnipotent God, according him such descriptions as most honored and treating as his sovereign commands whatever they felt themselves naturally bound by but, in all such activities, mediating their worship through their sovereign.

But Hobbes now added to this an account of two other Kingdoms of God: the special or "peculiar" kingdoms. These were, first, the Kingdom of Israel or, more precisely, the kingdom created when the Jews agreed with God through Moses, and, second, the Kingdom that Christ promised in the future for those who believed in him. The obvious theological puzzle in Hobbes, as in covenant theology generally, was that, given the "natural" kingdom, why were special kingdoms needed at all? After all, God already ruled all mankind. The conventional answer was that by the special covenant or covenants God promised his grace to those who believed in him, but Hobbes, who raised this question expressly at *De cive* 16.4, produced an unexpected answer: *the special kingdoms had the effect of conferring on the citizens some liberty that they would otherwise not possess.* The covenant of God with Abraham merely committed Abraham to the worship of God, and Abraham and his descendants were simply the sovereigns of the Jews, determining their religion in the way any sovereign could determine religion under the natural law. But the covenant of God with the Jewish people at the time of Moses was different and reflected their keen concern with liberty:

[W]hen that people had halted in the desert near Mount Sinai, and was not only wholly free but also totally hostile to human subjection because of their recent experience of Egyptian slavery, it was proposed that they should all renew the *old Covenant* in these terms (Exodus 19.5): *If therefore you hear my voice and keep my Covenant* (i.e. the *Covenant* made with *Abraham, Isaaac* and *Jacob*), *you shall be my particular property out of all the peoples, for the whole earth is mine, and you shall be to me a priestly kingdom, and a holy people.* And the whole people answered together (v.8): *We will do all that the Lord has spoken.* . . . In this covenant, note, among other things, the term *Kingdom*, not previously used. For although God was their king both by *nature* and by the *Covenant* with *Abraham*, they nevertheless owed him only natural obedience and natural worship, as his subjects, but the religious worship which *Abraham* had instituted they owed him as subjects of *Abraham, Isaac* or *Jacob*, their natural Princes. For the only *Word of God* that they had received was the natural word of right reason, and there was no *covenant* between God and themselves except in so far as their wills were included in the will of *Abraham*, as their Prince. But now, by the *covenant* made at Mount *Sinai*, a *kingdom of God by design* [*institutivum*] comes into being over them, as each individual gave his consent. This is the point at which that *Kingdom of God* which is so famous in holy scripture and in the writings of Theologians comes into being.[27]

---

[27] *Of the Citizen* 16.8,9.

Hobbes reiterated the connection with liberty shortly afterward, when he explained this idea by reference to the teachings of

> Judas of Galilee mentioned at Josephus, Jewish Antiquities 18.2 in these words: *Judas of Galilee was the founder of the fourth sect of seekers of wisdom They agree with the Pharisees in everything except that they burn with a constant passion for liberty, believing that God alone is to be regarded as Lord and Prince, and they will more readily bear the most exquisite forms of punishment, together with their families and loved ones, than call any mortal man Lord.*[28]

The point of this stress on *liberty* is that, under a special kingdom (and only there), the civil or terrene sovereign is no longer entirely free to determine the religion of his citizens. They have a covenant with *God* as their sovereign, and their *prince* is a viceroy. Hobbes expressed this thought at the conclusion of chapter 16:

> just as in merely human Kingdoms one must obey the subordinate magistrates in everything, except when their orders entail the crime of treason, so in God's Kingdom obedience had to be given to the princes *Abraham, Isaac, Jacob, Moses,* and the *Priest* and the *King,* each in his time, except when their orders entailed the *crime of treason against God.* The crime of treason against God comprised, first, *denial of divine providence;* for this was to deny that *God is King by nature;* and, second, *Idolatry,* or the worship not of *other* gods (for there is only one God) but of the gods *of other peoples,* that is, the worship of the one God, but under other *names, attributes* and *rites* than those instituted by *Abraham* and *Moses.* For this was to *deny that the God of Abraham* was their King by the *covenant* which they, like *Abraham,* had entered into. In all other matters obedience was due; and if the King or Priest who held sovereign power ordered any other thing that was contrary to the *laws,* that was an offence by the holder of sovereign power, not by the subject; whose duty is to carry out the orders of his superiors, not to dispute them.[29]

So the special kingdom of God was the one exception to the general rule about the scope of obedience due to a human sovereign. This was not just true of the Kingdom of the Jews: Christians, too, are in this position, for although the Kingdom promised by Christ has not yet come, the covenant has been taken by all Christians, and

> we must not therefore think that those who entered into that Covenant with faith in Christ would not need also to be governed on earth, so that they would persevere in the faith and obedience which they promised in the agreement. For the Heavenly Kingdom and the promised country would be irrelevant unless we were to be guided to it.[30]

---

[28] *Of the Citizen* 16.9.
[29] *Of the Citizen* 16.18.
[30] *Of the Citizen* 17.6.

Consequently, a Christian magistrate, like a Jewish one, cannot decree that his subjects should be of a different religion (at least as far as fundamentals are concerned). Hobbes made this entirely clear when he discussed (as he did in all three of his political works) the question of the obedience owed by a Christian to an infidel ruler. As we have just seen, non-Abrahamists were obliged to obey their sovereign in religious matters, in the full sense; that is, their sovereign's pronouncement on religion was as authoritative for them as his pronouncements on "what is to be called right, what good, what virtue, what much, what little, what *meum* and *tuum*, what a pound, what a quart, &c." But that was not true for Christians (and by implication for Jews). As Hobbes said at 2.6 of the *Elements*,

> The difficulty therefore of obeying both God and man, in a Christian commonwealth is none: all the difficulty resteth in this point, whether he that hath received the faith of Christ, having before subjected himself to the authority of an infidel, be discharged of his obedience thereby, or not, in matters of religion. In which case it seemeth reasonable to think, since all covenants of obedience are entered into for the preservation of a man's life, if a man be content, without resistance to lay down his life, rather than to obey the commands of an infidel; in so hard a case he hath sufficiently discharged himself thereof. For no covenant bindeth farther than to endeavour; and if a man cannot assure himself to perform a just duty, when thereby he is assured of present death, much less can it be expected that a man should perform that, for which he believeth in his heart he shall be damned eternally. And thus much concerning the scruple of conscience that may arise concerning obedience to human laws, in them that interpret the law of God to themselves.[31]

Among other things, this passage emphasizes how mistaken it is to suppose that Hobbes's theory rests on the psychological impossibility of suicide. It cannot be thought an isolated aberration of Hobbes's, for he made it even clearer in *De cive*, where he said of a Christian under an infidel sovereign that

> in *spiritual matters*, i.e. in things relating to the mode of worshipping God, he must follow some *Church of Christians*. For it is a Presumption of Christian faith that in supernatural matters God speaks only through Christian interpreters of holy scripture. But what follows? Are princes to be resisted when they are not to be obeyed? Of course not! This is contrary to the civil agreement. What then must one do? Go to Christ through Martyrdom. If anyone thinks this a harsh thing to say, it is very certain that he does not believe with his whole heart that JESUS IS THE CHRIST, *the Son of the living God* (for he would long to be dissolved and to be with Christ), but is using a pretence of Christian *faith* to try to slip out of his Agreement to obey the commonwealth.[32]

---

[31] *Elements of Law* 2.6.14.
[32] *Of the Citizen* 18.13.

Even in *Leviathan*, he was still saying the same kind of thing, although he now emphasized that Christians were not *obliged* to suffer martyrdom for their faith:

> They have the licence that Naaman had,[33] and need not put themselves into danger for it. But if they do, they ought to expect their reward in Heaven, and not complain of their lawful Soveraign; much lesse make warre upon him. For he that is not glad of any just occasion of Martyrdome, has not the faith he professeth, but pretends it onely, to set some colour upon his own contumacy.[34]

It is worth observing that this is more or less orthodox Protestantism, that one should passively resist a sovereign who attacks one's religion but not actively seek to overthrow him.

To be a Christian, as Hobbes repeatedly said, was to have faith that Jesus is the Christ, that is, the Messiah. Faith is not founded on philosophical analysis but on "the trust we have in other men," that is, trust that they reported something accurately. Like all other contentious beliefs, in principle, faith in a historical record was controllable by the sovereign (this is a point he made at greater length in the chapter on *Religio* in the *De homine* of 1658); but in the special kingdoms of God, the civil sovereign did not determine the content of faith, at least not as straightforwardly as he did among the gentiles. When Hobbes wrote the *Elements* and *De cive*, he argued that, in the special kingdom of the New Covenant, the men whose account we have to trust "are the holy men of God's church succeeding one another from the time of those that saw the wondrous works of God Almighty in the flesh."[35] Furthermore,

> seeing our faith, that the Scriptures are the word of God, began from the confidence and trust we repose in the church; there can be no doubt but that their interpretation of the same Scriptures, when any doubt or controversy shall arise, by which this fundamental point, that Jesus Christ is come in the flesh, is not called in question, is safer for any man to trust to, than his own, whether reasoning, or spirit; that is to say his own opinion.[36]

Or, as he said in the passage from *De cive* just quoted, citizens must "follow some *Church of Christians*" because

> to decide questions of faith, i.e. questions *about God*, which are beyond human understanding, one needs God's blessing (so that we may not err, at least on essential questions) and this comes from CHRIST himself by *laying on of hands*. For our eternal salvation we are obliged to accept a supernatural doctrine, which because

---

[33] Hobbes discussed this fully in chap. 42, 344–345 Tuck ed. (pp. 271–273 original). The reference is to Naaman bowing down in the House of Rimmon (2 Kings 5.17).

[34] *Leviathan* chapter 43, original ed. p. 331.

[35] *Elements of Law* 1.11.9.

[36] *Elements of Law* 1.11.10.

it is supernatural, is impossible to understand. It would go against equity if we were left alone to err by ourselves on such essential matters. Our Saviour promised this Infallibility (in matters essential to salvation) to the *Apostles* until the day of judgement, i.e. to the *Apostles* and to the *Pastors* who were to be consecrated by the *Apostles* in succession by the *laying on of hands*.[37]

Hobbes's theory in *De cive* thus exempted the Jew and the Christian from the usual authority of the gentile sovereign over religion. But—and this is a very important point—it did not exempt them from the authority of a Jewish or Christian sovereign. For a citizen, his Christianity is *represented* by his sovereign's Christianity, just as his judgment in all other respects is represented by his sovereign's judgment: the sovereign, it cannot be emphasized enough, *is* the citizen. If one has a Christian sovereign—a sovereign who acknowledges the foundation of Christianity, that Jesus is the Christ—then one has to accept his judgment about the interpretation of Scripture; but, as a Christian, the sovereign has in turn to accept the interpretation of the Church and mediate it to his subjects.

Hobbes was arguing the same as he had done about the sovereign as interpreter of God's *natural* laws; that is, the laws of nature taken as the commands of God. There, too, as we have seen, the sovereign's interpretation was canonical for his subjects' consciences, but the sovereign was obliged to consult his own conscience in coming to his interpretation, and, if he failed to do so, he would be thought of as sinning against God (although not, of course, against man).[38] In matters of Christianity, the Christian sovereign (in the argument of *De cive*) consulted not his conscience but the Church; otherwise, the structure of the argument was the same, and, indeed, the passage about the conscience in *The Elements* that I have already quoted comes from the discussion in 2.6 about submitting to the judgment of the Christian sovereign in religious matters.[39] But if a Christian was living under a gentile or "infidel" sovereign, he did not have to submit internally to his judgment about Christianity, although he might externally; instead, he had to turn to the Church as an interpretative authority.

The practical implication of this theory was, unsurprisingly, to give a new and systematic foundation to the institutions of the Church of England. The King was Supreme Governor of the Church, and the King (in Parliament) promulgated the laws of the Church; on the other hand, the King consulted the leaders of the ordained clergy in order to determine what kind of doctrine he should dictate to his subjects. This

---

[37] *Of the Citizen* 17.28.

[38] See, e.g., *Of the Citizen* 6.13. n.

[39] This is, I think, the explanation of the "anomaly" to which Noel Malcolm has drawn attention in his edition of *Leviathan* (1: 40–41). The question is not (in a Christian commonwealth) whether the *subject* is entitled to consult the Church independently of the sovereign, but whether the *sovereign* is entitled to make doctrine without consulting the Church. It is true that the sovereign can select those who are to be ordained (just as the King of England selected the bishops), but the ordination comes via the Apostolic succession, and, once ordained, the pastors (or some of them) have to be consulted by the sovereign.

was, after all, exactly what had happened in both the Henrician Reformation and the Elizabethan Church Settlement—the monarch decided which theological doctrines urged on him by members of the Church ought to be inscribed in law. In *The Elements*, Hobbes also stated that the government of the Church by bishops "hath a divine pattern" and that the apostles had ordained bishops (although not under that name) to govern priests, with the implication that it was the bishops whom the King should consult.[40] In *De cive*, he was more evasive about the rule of bishops but still concluded that "as a Christian, therefore, the holder of sovereign power in the commonwealth is obliged to interpret holy scripture, when it is a question about the *mysteries of faith*, by means of duly ordained *Ecclesiastics*."[41] The greater degree of evasiveness about bishops is presumably connected to the fact that, during 1641, Hobbes had begun to sympathize with those in Parliament who wished to destroy episcopacy in order to divert hostility from the royal government.[42] But it should be stressed that in *The Elements* and *De cive*, Hobbes was still expressing loyalty to a Church as the source of the sovereign's judgments and that this loyalty was still being expressed in the *Critique of White* in 1643 [aka *Anti-White*], when he went so far as to say that the principal reason for human unhappiness was a refusal to follow the Church's teachings.

Although Hobbes modified it in some of its details, this account remained the basis of his theology from 1642 onward. In *Leviathan*, it is still the case that Christianity and Judaism possess a special character and that adherence to them gives the citizen a different set of rights from those enjoyed by citizens in the Kingdom of God by nature. But Hobbes did introduce one major change in *Leviathan*, and doing so may well have been the point of the book. In *The Elements* and *De cive*, as we have seen, Hobbes had treated the Church as authoritative for Christians and therefore for the representative Christian, the sovereign; but in *Leviathan*, he in effect destroyed the Church. I quoted earlier the well-known passage in part 4 of *Leviathan* praising religious toleration. but what has been less commented on is that this defense of Independency is linked to a piece of ecclesiastical history earlier in the book, in which Hobbes argued that there had been no authoritative interpreters of Scripture in the early church:

> When a difficulty arose, the Apostles and Elders of the Church assembled themselves together, and determined what should be preached, and taught, and how they should Interpret the Scriptures to the People; but took not from the People the liberty to read, and Interpret them to themselves. The Apostles sent divers Letters to the Churches, and other Writings for their instruction; which had been in vain, if they had not allowed them to Interpret, that is, to consider the meaning of them. And as it was in the Apostles time, so it must be till such time as there should be Pastors, that could authorise an Interpreter, whose Interpretation should generally be stood to: But that could not be till Kings were Pastors, or Pastors Kings.[43]

---

[40] *Elements of Law* 2.7.8.
[41] *Of the Citizen* 17.28, immediately after the passage just quoted.
[42] See his letter to the Third Earl of Devonshire in Malcolm 1994: vol. 1, 120.
[43] *Leviathan* chapter 42, original ed. p. 281.

This new idea, that there had never been an authoritative Church and that, in the absence of a Christian sovereign, Christians are free to make their own religious truth, led Hobbes to a new history of Christianity, which he presented in support of the Independents' regime of religious toleration. The whole history of Christianity was now one of steadily increasing checks on liberty:

> The web begins at the first Elements of Power, which are Wisdom, Humility, Sincerity, and other vertues of the Apostles, whom the people converted, obeyed, out of Reverence, not by Obligation: Their Consciences were free, and their Words and Actions subject to none but the Civill Power. Afterwards the Presbyters (as the Flocks of Christ encreased) assembling to consider what they should teach, and thereby obliging themselves to teach nothing against the Decrees of their Assemblies, made it to be thought the people were thereby obliged to follow their Doctrine, and when they refused, refused to keep them company, (that was then called Excommunication,) not as being Infidels, but as being disobedient: And this was the first knot upon their Liberty. And the numbers of Presbyters encreasing, the Presbyters of the chief City of a Province, got themselves an authority over the Parochiall Presbyters, and appropriated to themselves the names of Bishops: And this was a second knot on Christian Liberty. Lastly, the Bishop of Rome, in regard of the Imperiall City, took upon him an Authority . . . over all other Bishops of the Empire: Which was the third and last knot, and the whole *Synthesis* and *Construction* of the Pontificiall Power.[44]

The knots were then untied in reverse order, culminating in the freedom from priestly power enjoyed by Englishmen after 1649.

We can summarize the change from Hobbes's earlier position to his later one by saying that, whereas at the time of *The Elements* Hobbes had believed that if Christians were independent of a state, they would still need to consult the Church, now he had come to believe that in such a situation Christians could interpret Scriptures by themselves. And just as in *The Elements* he had argued that a Christian sovereign would represent his subjects by consulting the Church over doctrine, so now he argued that he would represent his subjects by interpreting the Scriptures himself.[45] Furthermore, just as in *The Elements* he had accepted that where the sovereign did not choose to act on behalf of his subjects vis-à-vis the Church, the subjects would continue to be free to do so themselves, so now he accepted that if the sovereign did not choose to interpret Scripture himself, the subjects would continue to be free to interpret it themselves. This seems to me to express in an extremely simple form Hobbes's theology in *Leviathan* because it captures both the interest in religious pluralism and toleration that he displayed in the last chapter and the disconcerting claim that a Christian sovereign could be the sole authoritative interpreter of Christianity for his subjects. Seen as the logical

---

[44] *Leviathan* chapter 47, original ed. pp. 384–385.
[45] For confirmation of this, see, e.g., his remarks on Abraham, *Leviathan* chapter 40, original ed. p. 250.

working out of the theory of the representative sovereign, once the necessity of the Church for Christianity had been called into question, these two apparently contradictory principles make perfectly good sense together. They also help to explain Hobbes's own sense of freedom in *Leviathan* to construct a new version of Christianity himself, one based on a denial of Hell—a Christianity (I have argued elsewhere) designed to free people from unnecessary fear because it offered them either a natural death, which all men must fear anyway, or the hope of eternal life, and no prospect of eternal torment.

Hobbes had thus become, as his angry friends recognized, a kind of sectary, or at least a supporter of the religious program of the sectaries.[46] Moreover, he never fully disavowed this. It is true that when he translated *Leviathan* into Latin after the Restoration he cut out the passage from chapter 47 in blatant support of religious toleration, but he left untouched the equally striking passage about the absence of authoritative teaching in the time of the Apostles—a passage the meaning of which would have been entirely clear to contemporaries, all of whom were fully aware of the modern significance that the history of the early Church possessed.[47] His writings against a law of heresy at this time carry the same message: that a wise sovereign may well leave his citizens free to interpret their Christianity in the way that seems best to themselves.

It is customary among those who have recognized the tolerationist side to Hobbes to explain it by his involvement in the politics of the 1640s and 1650s and by his personal hostility to the Anglicans in exile; this was indeed the first explanation suggested by his friends.[48] But given the kind of story I have been telling in this chapter, another explanation is possible. From the beginning, Hobbes's religion offered a counterweight to his politics. Scriptural religion was always an area in which the sovereign's powers were limited, and Hobbes may simply have continued to think through the implications of this and to have worked out how religion could be seen as an arena of personal liberty for the citizen. Moreover, the consistency with which he accorded a special area of freedom to the Christian or Jew—who alone of all the peoples of the world are entitled to ignore the determination made by their civil sovereign of a contentious set of beliefs (if their sovereign does not share their religion)—suggests very strongly that Hobbes was not the atheist of his popular reputation.[49] But religious freedom of this kind (if

---

[46] And maybe the political program of some of them—it is noteworthy that, unlike everyone else except the Levellers, Hobbes argued in *Leviathan* that jurors are judges of law as well as of fact.

[47] *Ad omnem, quae oriebatur difficultatem, Apostoli & Presbyteri solebant convenire, & quidem quid praedicarent, & docerent, & quomodo ad populum Scripturas interpretarentur, determinarunt; libertatem autem illas legendi, & interpretandi, nemini ademerunt. Leviathan* ed. Malcolm: 813.

[48] For a full discussion of this issue, see Collins 2005.

[49] This is, of course, a very difficult question. In an article from 1992 entitled "The 'Christian Atheism' of Thomas Hobbes," I argued that "in *Leviathan* he had indeed effectively become an atheist, at least of a kind. The natural religion to which Hobbes subscribed all his life, and which we might reasonably term 'deism', was very far from an orthodox theism. God, on his account, was like the modern 'big bang' at the start of the universe . . . " (Tuck 1992: 128). At that time, I thought that "this view of religion was kept from overwhelming Hobbes's orthodox Christianity in the *Elements of Law* and *De cive* by a continued insistence on the special character of the doctrines propounded by the Christian Church; but in *Leviathan* this insistence faltered, and Christianity became in effect the civil religion of modern England" (Tuck 1992: 129). I would still say that Hobbes's natural religion, the

my argument has been correct) is not easily generalizable to intellectual freedom of a modern, liberal kind. The peculiarity of the Jews and Christians was that they lived in a different kind of kingdom from that of the gentiles and had (ultimately) a different kind of sovereign, one whose orders they had to follow (internally, although not necessarily externally) against the orders of his viceroy on earth. We are prone to extrapolating from early-modern defenses of toleration to modern ones, as if religious freedom in the seventeenth century is equivalent to the freedom of thought in the twenty-first century; but, in Hobbes's case, at least, such an extrapolation is difficult because even a theist today cannot believe that he lives in a special kingdom under a different sovereign from the one that governs his actual state, and a non-theist certainly cannot do so. Politics, for Hobbes, suffused everything, even religion, and the only way out of our common-wealth's psychic hold on us was for us to enter into a different commonwealth and not to look for something other than politics as a source of principles by which to live.

References

Bellarmine, Robert. 1601. *Disputationum ... de controversiis Christianae fidel, adversus huius temporis haereticos*. Ingoldstadt: Adam Sartorius.

Collins, Jeffrey. 2005. *The Allegiance of Thomas Hobbes*. Cambridge: Cambridge University Press.

Hanin, Mark. 2012. "Thomas Hobbes's Theory of Conscience." *History of Political Thought* 33: 55–85.

Hobbes, Thomas. 1973. *Critique du De Mundo de Thomas White*. ed Jean Jacquot et Harold Whitmore Jones. Paris: Librairie Philosophique de J. Vrin.

Hobbes, Thomas. 1976. *Thomas White's 'De Mundo' Examined*, tr. Harold Whitmore Jones. London: Bradford University Press.

Hobbes, Thomas. 1994. *Elements of Law, Natural and Politic*, ed. J. C. A. Gaskin. Oxford: Oxford University Press.

Hobbes, Thomas. 1998. *On the Citizen*, edd. Richard Tuck and Michael Silverthorne. Cambridge: Cambridge University Press.

Malcolm, Noel, ed. 1994. *The Correspondence of Thomas Hobbes*. Oxford: Oxford University Press.

religion of the gentiles, was very far from orthodox theism; the difficulty lies in characterizing his distinctive attitude to Christianity. For the reasons I have given in this chapter, I no longer think it is quite true that for Hobbes Christianity was *simply* the civil religion of modern England, in the sense that the religions of the gentiles were their civil religions; the Christian in *any* state could hold on to his faith irrespective of the public religion promulgated by his sovereign, but the gentile could not. Hobbes keeps telling us that the authority of Judaism and Christianity rests on their historical status, and in particular the historical act of the covenants, and we should take him at his word: outside an acceptance of that history, we have no grounds for a conventional idea of God at all, but within it we do. It is hard to say whether this is exactly "atheism" or not, but it is at least not *straightforward* atheism of the kind popularly attributed to Hobbes; and the fact that Hobbes cared so much about establishing this distinction suggests that it meant more to him than would have been the case if it was merely a move in a campaign against (say) clerical power.

Musculus, Wolfgang. 1560. *Loci communes in usus S. Theologiae Candidatorum parati*. Basle: Officina Hervagiana.

Ryan, Alan. 1983. "Hobbes, Toleration, and the Inner Life," in *The Nature of Political Theory*, edited by David Miller and Larry Siedentop, 197–218. Oxford: Oxford University Press.

Ryan, Alan. 1988. "A More Tolerant Hobbes?" in *Justifying Toleration*, edited by Susan Mendus, 37–59. Cambridge: Cambridge University Press.

Tralau, Johan. 2011. "Hobbes contra Liberty of Conscience." *Political Theory* 39: 58–84.

Tuck, Richard. 1974. "*Power* and *Authority* in Seventeenth-Century England." *The Historical Journal* 17: 43–61.

Tuck, Richard. 1992. "The 'Christian Atheism' of Thomas Hobbes," in *Atheism from the Reformation to the Enlightenment*, edited by Michael Hunter and David Wootton, 111–130. Oxford: Oxford University Press.

Tuck, Richard. 2003. "The Utopianism of *Leviathan*" in *Leviathan After 350 Years*, edited by Tom Sorell and Luc Foisneau, 125–138. Oxford: Oxford University Press.

van Dam, Harm-Jan, ed. 2001. *Hugo Grotius, De Imperio Summarum Potestatum*. Leiden: Brill.

Willet, Andrew 1611. *Hexapla, that is, A six-fold commentarie vpon the most divine epistle of the holy apostle S. Paul to the Romanes*. Cambridge: Cantrell Legge.

....

CHAPTER 22

CHRISTIANITY AND CIVIL RELIGION IN HOBBES'S *LEVIATHAN*

....

SARAH MORTIMER

HOBBES was a most unusual Christian, so unusual that some have doubted whether he deserved to be counted as a Christian at all.[1] His works contained scathing critiques of the Christian clergy, at times pouring scorn on doctrines which his contemporaries considered central to the Christian religion. One acquaintance, the Earl of Clarendon, noted drily that "he hath not that reverence to the Scripture, or adoration of the Author of it, that would become him to have"; other readers of his work were less polite, denouncing him as a heretic or even an atheist.[2] And yet, Hobbes certainly recognized the potential power of the Christian story, and his works of civil philosophy were designed to establish not merely a commonwealth but a Christian Commonwealth. To Hobbes, a commonwealth that embraced "true" (or Hobbesian) Christianity would be stronger and more peaceful than any other—it would surpass the republics of antiquity and the monarchies of contemporary Europe. Christianity, once interpreted correctly, could successfully fulfill the natural human desire for religion and could do so in a way that united the commonwealth. Indeed, Hobbes believed that Christianity was uniquely able to complement and strengthen the civil philosophy to which he was committed. Hobbes's high regard for "true" Christianity should not be underestimated. Moreover, its sources and its implications are worth unraveling if we are to understand Hobbes's broader intellectual project.

Christianity was too important, in Hobbes's view, to be ignored—especially in the 1640s and early 1650s, when the episcopal Church of England had been abolished and a new settlement seemed elusive. Parliament had agreed to dismantle the old church

---

[1] Strauss 1953, esp. 195–9; Curley 1992 and 1998, Jesseph 2002. Others have insisted on the Christian character of Hobbes's philosophy, especially Martinich 2002.

[2] Clarendon, 1676, 202; for criticism see Mintz 1962, esp. 55–6.

when it voted down bishops in 1643, but agreeing on what should replace it proved extremely difficult. Numerous schemes were floated, from the strict Presbyterianism endorsed by the Scots to the wide-ranging toleration set out in the Levellers' Agreements of the People.[3] In effect, therefore, a wide space had been opened up in the late 1640s for theological discussion, and English and Scottish writers were eager to fill this space with their own views and ideas. Although Hobbes was one of these writers, seizing this unprecedented opportunity for heterodox speculation, he was also extremely uncomfortable with the unregulated religious discussion he saw around him. He feared that the main beneficiaries of such a situation would be the power-hungry clerics, men who habitually took advantage of the credulity of the people to advance their own aims. In his *Leviathan*, therefore, he wanted to close this theological space once and for all, by explaining to his contemporaries—and especially to the next sovereign—just what true Christianity looked like. Hobbes had written about theology before, especially in *De Cive* and *Critique of De Mundo*. But *Leviathan* contains the fullest account of Hobbes's theology, and for this reason it will be my focus in this chapter.

Although Hobbes was, I will argue, committed to a certain form of Christianity, the theology which Hobbes set out in *Leviathan* was both unusual and highly polemical. Indeed, throughout his life he was stridently critical of Presbyterianism, of Roman Catholicism, and of the kind of *jure divino* episcopalianism he saw in contemporary Anglicanism. His relationship with Anglicans was especially complex, however, and cannot simply be reduced to mutual hostility—especially when we recall the positive dimension to Hobbes's theological speculations. Recent scholarship has shown the many personal connections between Hobbes and the defenders of the old episcopal church and stressed the extreme anxiety of the latter over the Erastian doctrines they found in Hobbes's writing.[4] It is becoming increasingly clear that Anglican thought from at least the 1650s was shaped in part by the need to respond to Hobbes. But the traffic may not have been all one way. Anglican theology was in flux in the 1640s and 1650s, and its leading exponents were drawing on new and even heterodox sources in their efforts to strengthen the doctrine and discipline of their church.[5] I will suggest in the second half of this chapter that Hobbes exploited some of these Anglican ideas for his own purposes, and that we need to see his theology within the context of a divided but dynamic response to the failure of the old Church of England.

1 NATURAL RELIGION AND HUMAN BEINGS

Hobbes's approach to religion, like his political thought, took human beings as its starting point—and it is with Hobbes's understanding of the human experience of religion

---

[3] Morrill 2008, 67–80.

[4] E.g., Collins 2005, esp. ch. 7; Parkin 2007, 62–8; Jackson 2007.

[5] See section 3.

that we must begin. Religious belief was, for Hobbes, one of the central features of human life; it was one of the crucial characteristics that differentiated men from animals. The cause of religion was clear to him: it arose because the human desire for power and control could never be fully satisfied, and men would always feel, at least to some extent, at the mercy of forces beyond their control. In a marginal comment in *Leviathan* he put this most clearly, writing, "The naturall Cause of religion, [is] the Anxiety of the time to come." Men's ability to reason, to use language, and to consider the future, made them "inquisitive into the Causes of the Events they see."[6] And yet their curiosity could never be satisfied fully, and the causal chain could never be made complete; "the knowledge of Consequence"—which for Hobbes is the true meaning of science—"is not Absolute but Conditionall."[7] Where our understanding of consequences ends, religion may begin, filling the imaginative space beyond the known causal chain.

Even where we have true scientific or philosophical knowledge, there will still be space for religious belief. Philosophy, for Hobbes, is only possible where we know how an effect follows from a cause, and where we can analyze events and objects by examining the ways in which they were made.[8] Such knowledge is of limited scope, and in *Leviathan* Hobbes argues that those who make a full and profound inquiry into causes will, in the end, be forced to acknowledge a first cause. However much of the causal chain the scientist understands, he will never be able to explain how it first began or how it will end. Of course, this does not mean the scientist has knowledge of God, only that in realizing the limits of his understanding he makes space for the existence of a divine being. Those, on the other hand, who do not make such an effort will be even more willing to believe in gods, for their ignorance of causes will lead them to fear "Powers Invisible" and to seek to placate them. But however much we study, there will always be gaps in the causal chain, not only in the distant past, but also in the future. Men know that their knowledge of causes is incomplete, and the unease that this brings leads them to imagine unseen powers which control their fate.[9]

The causes of natural religion are, therefore, common to all, for they are deeply rooted in the human characteristics of anxiety and unease. But the practices and customs through which men seek to allay this fear have proved very diverse. In *Leviathan*, Hobbes initially argues that each individual develops his own ritual practices, but his discussion of religion quickly moves away from the individual and portrays religion as a social practice. Religious practices depend on language and on a common understanding of signs and rituals. Like language itself, religious worship develops through social interaction, and the seed of natural religion (that is, fear) grows into particular ceremonies and rituals through cultivation by men within particular societies. On

---

[6] Hobbes 1996, 76.

[7] Ibid., 47.

[8] Ibid., 47, 458.

[9] Ibid., 74–5; see also the discussion in Martinich 2002, 193–5. Hobbes does not, however, deploy this argument consistently; see Curley 1992 and 1998.

first glance this diversity is striking, for men in different times and places have come to honor and worship all kinds of things, everything from the mighty ocean and the roaring winds to humble vegetables, like onions and leeks. But the difference between these practices is not as great as it might seem, Hobbes argues, because the purpose of all religious practices is similar. They exist to make human beings feel less fearful and to make them "more apt to Obedience, Lawes, Peace, Charity and civill Society." It is crucial for Hobbes that religion must be directed toward social ends, assuaging our fear and enabling us to live more peacefully.[10]

Human religiosity is, then, a fact of life no less true or important than the human desire for glory or to protect oneself. Fear of things unknown gives rise to religion, and for human beings this fearfulness is closely related to our anxieties over hostile forces here on earth. In the state of nature we are troubled by our inability, on our own, to secure ourselves for the future, and only through establishing a sovereign and obeying the laws of nature can we dispel our anxieties. Given Hobbes's analysis of religion, it is perhaps not surprising that his remedy for our fear of the gods is no different than his remedy for our fear of other people. In both cases we need to create the context in which we can follow the laws of nature by transferring our natural right to the sovereign. And, just as the sovereign can regulate language so that communication is possible, so he can regulate worship so that public religion is possible.[11] Without special revelation, men cannot have access to anything beyond the natural causal chain; the officers of the commonwealth cannot mediate between men and God or channel divine grace. But the sovereign can satisfy the natural religious impulses of human beings by assuaging their fears and prolonging their lives.

It is clear that, for Hobbes, religious practices are primarily social, and they must be geared toward the preservation of peace and order. But this does not mean that they are purely human, or that their connection to God or to anything beyond the human realm is irrelevant. As we have seen, Hobbes argues (at least in *Leviathan*) that reason tells us there is a first cause beyond our reason, on which our reason itself depends. We can therefore view the dictates of reason, or the laws of nature, as the commands of God and the misfortunes which befall us when we disobey these commands as divine punishments. When we do so, we are part of the natural kingdom of God, recognizing his laws, acting as his subjects, and accepting the consequences of our actions as the working out of his providence. For Hobbes this is a valid course of action; to stand outside God's kingdom (as the atheists do) is to be his enemy.[12] Even as subjects, Hobbes adds, we cannot tame God's power or his rights over us; his power is irresistible and he retains the right to afflict us and make us suffer even when we have not sinned. Hobbes needs to leave this possibility open in order to explain Jesus's death, but the overall thrust of his discussion of the natural kingdom of God is that God generally operates through natural punishments for the breach of natural laws. Natural religion, in so far

---

[10] Hobbes 1996, 76–9.

[11] Ibid., 252–3. See also 255 for Hobbes's claim that reason is "the undoubted word of God."

[12] Ibid., 111; 253–4; Hobbes 1998, 164.

as it reinforces the natural laws, should bring society the natural rewards of peace and security—all within the natural kingdom of God.[13]

Hobbes's insistence that it is the commonwealth that provides the conditions for natural religious worship left no space for separate spiritual power and no role for priests. He stressed that the best kinds of natural practices were those which enabled us to live together, and that societies were far more successful if power were not divided. Hobbes acknowledged that religion, like other social practices, provides many opportunities for domination, and that people can use religion to win the power over others that they naturally seek. This is paradigmatically true in the Church of Rome, where the pope and his priests have made the laity subservient to them, but it stems from the very nature of religion. "So easie are men to be drawn to believe anything," Hobbes argued, from those who "can with gentlenesse, and dexterity, take hold of their fear, and ignorance." It is crucially important therefore, for the sake of peace and stability, to make sure that men are drawn to believe doctrines that will preserve their unity and life in society; any religious principles that simply increase the power of particular people, the clergy, must be suppressed.[14]

We have seen that the limited capacity of human reason and human science gives rise to natural religion, but Hobbes also argues that there are other sources for our beliefs about God. God has given positive laws to some human beings, whom he rules in a "Prophetique" kingdom. Here, humans covenant with God to obey his laws. What we learn of God through prophesy is, for Hobbes, a different kind of knowledge from that we gain by reason. It is not science, for that is knowledge of causes; rather, it is history, based on knowledge of fact, in this case the historical accounts of God's revelations given to human beings in the past.[15] The correct response to historical information is belief, at least where the person from whom we receive this information is someone that we trust, or that stands in authority over us. For Hobbes, the most important source of information about God's laws is, of course, the Bible, but for us to believe this we need someone to make it authoritative to us, so that it is not simply just another text. For this reason Hobbes is keen to make clear that our faith in the scriptures depends on our faith in the church (that is, the sovereign) who provides us with this text. Our ideas about God come from the account we have of his dealings with human beings, and we accept that account on the authority of the church. Because our faith in God's word is based on our faith in the sovereign, all power within the commonwealth must be united and the true prophet is he who upholds, rather than subverts, the established order.[16]

There are two sources for our understanding of God, reason (or its limits) and scripture, but Hobbes is keen to argue that they complement each other. In Hobbes's account, the prophetic word and the word of reason enable us to live more peacefully

---

[13] Ibid., 253–4 (cf. 333 for Hobbes's reading of the atonement).
[14] Ibid., 79–86 (quotation from p. 82); 233–5.
[15] Ibid., 246. See also Pocock 1972.
[16] Ibid., 48–9; 321.

and happily here on earth, for they help us to order our relationships with others and to obey the laws of nature. This is, perhaps, especially clear with regard to natural religion and the religion of the Old Testament; I will consider the case of Christianity in the next section. At least in the case of non-Christians, the religious needs of human beings can, it seems, be satisfied in the same way as any other desires: through the creation of sovereign power.

2 CHRISTIANITY

The account given so far may explain the religions of the ancient world, but Hobbes knew that it would not satisfy a Christian. Indeed, it was vitally important for him to take account of the doctrines of the New Testament and of the distinctive ideas that can be found there. Christianity is different in one crucial respect from the other religions Hobbes discussed, for it offers the hope of life beyond death. Pagan religions, and even Judaism, had not been especially concerned about personal immortality, but Christianity certainly was—with obvious consequences for political and social life. Hobbes needed to show how the Christian conception of an afterlife could in fact strengthen, rather than diminish, the power of the sovereign. For this reason, he devoted books three and four of *Leviathan* to showing how Christianity, properly understood, would reinforce, and not undermine, the commonwealth—even when the concept of personal immortality was taken seriously. Hobbes therefore offered in *Leviathan* his own, new, account of Christianity, which is the subject of this section. But few of Hobbes's ideas were entirely unprecedented, and in the third part of the chapter I turn to consider some of the sources he may have used.

Religion is fueled by anxiety, as we have seen, and perhaps the greatest source of anxiety for human beings is death. Humans cannot predict what will happen to them after they die; for them, death is the end of a chain of causes, and they have no natural knowledge of anything beyond death. Moreover, death is centrally important for Hobbes because it marks the limits of the sovereign's power. Not only is the sovereign unable to protect people from their own mortality, but he is also unable to punish them with anything worse than death. As a result, the most effective challenge to the sovereign's power will also be a challenge to the finality of death. Hobbes recognized this problem clearly, acknowledging that no commonwealth can stand "where any other than the sovereign hath a power of giving greater rewards than Life."[17] Where men have only natural reason or even natural religion, the issue will not arise, for the fate of human beings after death falls outside the scope of the knowledge we derive from reason or experience. We simply do not and cannot know about what will happen to us. Christianity changes this picture dramatically, however, for the scriptures provide a

---

[17] Ibid., 306–7.

history and an eschatology in which death is overcome through resurrection. The New Testament holds out to Christians the promise of eternal life, and the message of Christ and the Apostles found there is clear: it is better to obey God than man.[18]

With the circulation of ideas about personal immortality, and with the development of a cult of martyrs, the potential for civil discord was greatly intensified. This was true in early Christianity, but by the seventeenth century, after a century of religious violence, contemporaries were more aware of it than ever. The need for correct interpretation had now become urgent—and Hobbes was anxious to address this. For him, the only way to avoid "the calamities of Confusion and civil war" is through a proper understanding of "what is meant in holy Scripture, by *Life Eternall* and *Torment Eternall*."[19] These are terms which Hobbes prioritizes in his interpretation, emphasizing their powerful and contested nature. But he argues that in reading the scripture and making sense of its message, we "are not to renounce our Senses . . . [nor] our naturall Reason," insisting that there is nothing within the scripture that is contrary to reason.[20] On the contrary: a true interpretation will show how the Christian scriptures, rightly understood, complement natural religion and civil society rather than undermining either. Here it is important to be clear that the issue is not, for Hobbes, whether religion is "true" in any sense that his contemporaries would have recognized. Unlike them, he simply does not believe that we have direct access to anything beyond this earthly world, unless by a direct revelation from God himself. Instead, the question for him is whether Christianity can fulfill the purposes of all religion, namely to make people obedient and to assuage their anxiety. Fortunately for Hobbes, a true understanding of the scriptures, supported by reason, will do this.

The central human problem, for Hobbes, is death, and he suggested that Christianity was uniquely able to resolve this problem through the promise of eternal life. The purpose of Christ's mission, on Hobbes's reading, is to tell people about the future kingdom of God, in which they will live forever. All people are invited to enter this kingdom, and the conditions for entry are not onerous. Almost all that is required is for a person to accept Jesus Christ as the messiah, that is the person through whom God will rule in the future, and to obey the laws of nature. Hobbes accepts that human beings will not always obey these laws, and he argues that Christ also makes satisfaction to God for men's sins. (It is for this reason that Hobbes needs to argue that God's right to punish is not dependent on personal guilt, and that God has a perfect right to afflict the innocent Jesus.) With this nod toward the doctrine of the atonement Hobbes moves on, and the role of Christ in satisfying for human sin plays a very small part in Hobbes's theology.[21] Instead, the focus is elsewhere, on the possibility of eternal life for Christians. Cast like this, Christianity shares its basic features with natural religion and the religion of the Israelites, but—and crucially—it also deals with the anxiety created by the prospect of

[18] See esp. Acts 5:29.
[19] Hobbes 1996, 307.
[20] Ibid., 255.
[21] Ibid., 403–4, 333.

death. Christians are told that they need not be fearful on this score, so long as they follow the laws of nature. In this way, Hobbes can show how Christianity fulfills the deepest human need, but it is worth underlining at this point how far he has moved from mainstream Christian teaching. For the majority of his contemporaries, it was original sin—not death—that was the source of human misery, and redemption from that sin was the central message of Christianity.

Hobbes's new and unusual reading of the scriptures was thoroughgoing, and it is worth spelling out in more detail. According to him, Adam became mortal when he ate from the tree of knowledge and was banished from the garden of Eden—he lost the access to the tree of life that would have kept his body in being. All Adam's descendants are similarly mortal, but the eternal life that was lost with Adam was made possible again through Jesus Christ. Hobbes found support for his ideas in St Paul's well-known words to the Corinthians, "For as in Adam all die, even so in Christ shall all be made alive" (1 Cor 15:22), but Hobbes differed from his contemporaries in his account of what Adam's death and the Fall actually meant. For him, all that was lost at the Fall was the ability to continue in life forever; Adam's capacity to reason or to act was not affected in any way. By the same token, for Hobbes what is gained for the Christian through the work of Christ is the ability to live forever; there is no other "damage" to human beings caused by the Fall which needs to be repaired.[22] Such a theology fits well with Hobbes's evaluation of human beings as, like everything else in the universe, matter in motion—and his insistence that what is good for them is to remain in motion for as long as they can. There is no space for original sin in Hobbes's psychology and nor is there in his biblical interpretation.

Alongside this Pauline story, in which Christ is the second Adam, Hobbes also offers another, slightly different, story in which Christ is the second Moses. The first Moses had communicated with God on behalf of the people of Israel; indeed, God had been represented to the people by Moses, in Hobbes's idiosyncratic Trinitarian scheme. Moses had provided a single, unified channel of communication between God and the people, ensuring that there were no conflicts of interpretation and dealing with all matters both civil and religious. Christ, as the second Moses, will also rule his people as sole sovereign under God, but this kingdom lies in the future, not in the present. Just as Moses enabled the people of Israel to become God's "Peculiar Kingdome," so Christ offers people the opportunity to enter the future kingdom of God. The crucial difference between Moses and Christ is, of course, the kingdom of the latter lies in the future, and we cannot enter it in the present.[23]

Hobbes's decision to cast Christ as both Adam and Moses, and to do so in this unusual way, had important consequences for his discussion of the Church. Under Adam and Moses (at least on Hobbes's reading) there had been no distinction between civil and spiritual power, and nor would there be in the future kingdom of God. Christ had not set up a church or given his followers any special powers; all they had been

---

[22] Ibid., 307–9.
[23] Ibid., 336–8.

commanded to do was to preach the future kingdom and encourage men to prepare for it by obeying the laws of nature. Priests who claimed that Christ had established a new kingdom, which was represented on earth by the Church, were highly pernicious in Hobbes's view, and he proclaimed, "The greatest and main abuse of Scripture . . . is the wresting of it, to prove that Kingdome of God, mentioned so often in the Scripture, is the present church."[24] As this suggests, there is no room in Hobbes's thought for the suggestion that the Church might mediate between men and God or that it might channel God's grace in any way. Grace is just the free gift of God, which means his willingness to accept people into the kingdom in the future; it is not a supernatural quality infused into men by the Holy Spirit or by the sacraments.[25] Hobbes does argue that if we want to live a "religious" life, a life pleasing to God, then we need to do this within the framework of an institution under a sovereign lawgiver. But that institution is the commonwealth, which itself is the only legitimate church.

In Hobbes's view, then, the Christian message was superior to any natural religion, for it provided the most effective means of dealing with anxiety for the future. The power of the Christian message was immense, and Hobbes recognized that it needed to be harnessed to the commonwealth in order to stabilize it. Of course, Hobbes argued that the interpretation of scripture should be left to the sovereign, whose reading of the text we must take as our own. And yet Hobbes also held that all authority (except God's irresistible power) is based on consent, and so the sovereign's power to make scripture law for his subjects comes from their own consent. This point is not so obvious in *Leviathan*, but Hobbes was quite explicit about it in his debate with Bishop Bramhall, where he insisted that since the Bible "cannot be a law of itself without special and supernatural revelation," it is "made law by the assent of the subjects," acting through the sovereign.[26] The sovereign, and through him the people, can accept or reject the message found in the scriptures; God's future kingdom will only contain those who have consented to his authority. The purpose of Hobbes's lengthy discussion of the scriptures is to encourage people to provide this consent: to show to the sovereign, and indeed to all his readers, the great advantages of accepting the true message of the Bible. Hobbes's version of Christianity was, to him, compelling; not only was it compatible with reason, but it also filled the space beyond reason in the best possible way, from a Hobbesian point of view.

3 HOBBES AND THE ANGLICANS

It is easy to see why this version of Christianity seemed so attractive to Hobbes, but very few of his contemporaries felt the same way. Indeed, their reaction was more often one

---

[24] Ibid., 419.

[25] Ibid., 94, 330. Of course, Hobbes's insistence that the Church cannot mediate between humans and God was shared by many early Reformers.

[26] Hobbes 1839–45 vol. V, 179.

of disgust than admiration. Certainly his ideas were unorthodox, idiosyncratic, and at times bordering on the heretical; they have bewildered and troubled readers ever since their publication. But we should not be too hasty in assuming that Hobbes's ideas were all his own; he may well have drawn on the ideas that were current in Anglican circles, particularly among the churchmen with whom he was acquainted. Hobbes's links to the Anglican clergy are well documented; we know he wrote to Robert Payne, canon of Christ Church until his ejection in 1648, for example, and that he spent long hours locking horns with Bishop Bramhall.[27] *Leviathan* was, at least in part, a contribution to the royalist cause, written during the ongoing debates in Paris over how best to restore royal power and authority—and the future of the Church of England was very much a part of these debates. To understand Hobbes's theological agenda, and its relationship to contemporary debates, therefore, we need first to consider what his Anglican acquaintances were doing. Certainly there are some striking parallels.

The Anglican clergy were a disparate group, but Hobbes's ties were to a particular circle of men. This was a circle that extended across the channel, including exiled clerics like John Bramhall and John Cosin, as well as those who, like Gilbert Sheldon and Henry Hammond, had remained in England. All were academic theologians with a strong commitment to an episcopal church and to an ethical interpretation of Christianity that stressed the need for good works and rejected Calvinist predestination. In response to the crisis of the 1640s, they were especially concerned about upholding the necessity and authority of bishops, but they were also seeking to reshape the theology of the Church of England. They wanted to distance it from the continental Reformed churches and (in the eyes of their enemies at least) bring it closer to Catholicism.[28] Moreover, several of the clergy who remained in England began to believe that the only way to preserve the Church of England was to emphasize its independence from the state and even from the monarchy. They argued that its bishops held their authority by divine right, acting as successors to the Apostles, and they played down the role of the king in the church. Perhaps the first to make this case was Jeremy Taylor, in 1642, but it grew more common in the late 1640s, when Charles I seemed all too willing to abandon episcopacy in order to obtain Scottish support. Under the leadership of Hammond and, to a lesser extent, Sheldon, the necessity of episcopacy was forcefully asserted.[29] This "dualist" model of church and state was obviously unacceptable to Hobbes, but its theological foundations were closer to his own than either side cared to acknowledge.

To trace the connections between Hobbes and the Anglicans we need to begin by recognizing that the most significant influence upon the latter—and especially upon Hammond—was Hugo Grotius, the Dutch jurist, historian, and theologian. They found in Grotius the intellectual basis for an ethical Christianity and for an episcopal church whose basis lay in revelation and not in nature. Grotius thought that Christianity must be based in the message and ministry of Christ, rather than in human nature or

[27] Collins 2000; Tuck 1992 and 1993; Jackson 2007.
[28] The classic statement of this new, ethical Christianity is Hammond 1643; for the ways in which it departed from earlier English theology see Allison 1966.
[29] Taylor 1642; Mortimer 2010b, 99–103.

natural law, and his Anglican readers used this idea in the service of their church.[30] But Grotius's legacy, in theology as well as in politics, was double edged, not least because his opinions shifted significantly after his imprisonment and exile in 1619. Prior to this, Grotius's views can fairly be described as Erastian, and Hobbes may have drawn upon Grotius's earlier writings.[31] Far better known, though, in the 1640s, were the works Grotius wrote in exile; these were especially important to the members of this Anglican circle. It is these works to which we must turn next, therefore.

The starting point for Grotius was the distinction between Christianity, which was based on history and revelation, and natural laws and rights, based on observation and reasoning. He made this clear in his celebrated *On the Rights of War and Peace* (1625), writing that the

> Truth of the Christian Religion, in those Particulars which are additional to natural and primitive Religion, cannot be evidenced by mere natural Arguments, but depends upon the History we have of CHRIST's Resurrection, and the Miracles performed by him and his Apostles.[32]

For Grotius, as the quote makes clear, the reason why the historical story found in Christianity is crucial is because it tells us about the afterlife. The scope of "natural Arguments" is this mortal world, and the natural laws and rights that reason can lay down do not depend on eternal rewards or punishments. To this extent, Grotius can be seen as a precursor to Hobbes. But the consequences Grotius then went on to draw were rather different from those of Hobbes. For Grotius, it was important to maintain the distinction between natural laws and the duties of a Christian, for he believed that church membership must be voluntary and that Christian faith could not be imposed by any human authority. Although the basic tenets of natural religion could be upheld by force, because they were necessary for social life, Christianity could not.[33] Indeed, it was because Christianity was based on historical testimony, and not part of nature, that men and women were free to choose or reject it.

In a slightly later work, *Of the Truth of the Christian Religion* (1627), Grotius provided a fuller account of the relationship between Christianity and nature. Here he insisted that while we have natural knowledge of the existence of God, it is only through revelation that we know of God's will for us and of the ways in which he will reward or punish us. The central revelation, the one which mattered to Grotius and his readers, is the message brought by Christ, who commands us to obey his laws in order to receive his rewards. Christianity is, on this account, based on an historical narrative that is quite separate from the natural course of human affairs and cannot be known or understood through nature alone. Here Grotius was following the argument of the Italian anti-Trinitarian Faustus Socinus, as J-P Heering has shown, although Socinus

[30] Mortimer 2010a, chs. 3 and 4.
[31] Tuck notes parallels between Grotius and Hobbes in 1991a and b, but my reading of Grotius's theology is rather different from his.
[32] Grotius 2005, 1041.
[33] Grotius 2005, 977, and 1137; 1037–42.

himself actually went further than this. Indeed, Socinus held that men were naturally mortal and that by nature they had no knowledge of God at all. Thus Socinus was able to preserve a very clear distinction between an ethics based on human nature and the duties of a Christian that were known through revelation.[34]

Underpinning this separation between Christianity and natural law was a strong claim about human freedom. Grotius and Socinus both believed that Christianity had to be chosen by human beings, and that it was the act of choice which made religious faith valuable in God's sight. Socinus even suggested that if religion were part of human nature then this would compromise our ability to choose it freely.[35] Christianity must therefore stand above and apart from the natural world, based as it is on the revelation brought by Christ, a revelation that took place in time and is known to us through historical accounts. Christianity does not affect the laws of nature, which apply to all human beings, but it supplements them with the laws of Christ, which apply to those who choose to become Christians. These two sets of laws have separate sets of sanctions and are built on fundamentally different foundations. Socinus was not especially interested in natural law, but Grotius was, and his account of natural law was different, at least in some ways, from his predecessors. Whereas they tended to see natural and divine law as part of the same overarching edifice, an edifice which was of course Christian, Grotius was beginning to separate these laws and to dismantle the edifice.[36] Most important, he was even suggesting that natural law and Christianity were conceptually distinct and independent of each other.

This Grotian (and Socinian) theology stood right at the outer limit of Christianity, but elements of it were proving attractive to some of the Anglican clergy in the 1640s and 1650s. Some of the correspondence between Hammond and Sheldon has been preserved, and what is perhaps most striking is how frequently they refer to Grotius as the leading authority on theological matters. They dismissed Grotius's occasional Erastian lapses and used him to make their case for the apostolic foundations of their church.[37] Hammond, who was the most prolific of the episcopalians, claimed that the church was established by Christ, through the Apostles, and that it could not be altered or abolished by the civil magistrate. This appeal to the historical, rather than the natural, foundations of their church was unusual, but he and his friends believed it could help explain the continuing existence of the Church of England in the face of state persecution. And, by insisting that individual human beings were free to choose or to reject Christianity, Hammond and his friends sought to strengthen the resolve of their flocks while simultaneously criticizing the Roman Catholic Church for tyrannizing over

---

[34] Heering 2004, 116, 118–20; Leo Strauss noted the several parallels between Hobbes's theology and the Socinians: see Strauss 2011, 69–72.

[35] Socinus 1666 vol. I, 537; free will is assumed in Grotius 2012 but stated explicitly in Grotius 1988, 106.

[36] Haakonsen 1998, 1327–30.

[37] See e.g., Pocock 1849, 127; Pocock 1852, 325–6, 329.

conscience.[38] Indeed, in the 1640s and 1650s, these Anglican clergy moved decisively and explicitly away from predestination (to the discomfort of many of their friends), realizing that an independent episcopal church required a theology of free will.[39] They were calling on English men and women to reject the state church and to follow instead the outlawed Church of England; they needed to demonstrate that such a choice was both reasonable and meritorious.

During the 1640s and 1650s, therefore, these Anglicans were engaged in a delicate and highly controversial effort to rewrite the theology of their church—and Hobbes must have seen this. One way to read the second half of *Leviathan* is as an attempt to exploit the theological space opened up by recent Anglican writing and to sabotage their project by destroying its foundations. Certainly Hobbes shared some of their ideas, but he used them for his own purposes and he was highly selective. Moreover, on some subjects, particularly free will, but also the role of Christ, Hobbes was even able to suggest that his ideas were authentically Protestant—much more so than those of his Anglican critics. His purpose was not to restore orthodoxy to Anglican thought, of course, but rather to emasculate it. He did not succeed, but his Anglican acquaintances recognized the force of his challenge and made a vigorous effort to oppose him.[40]

The similarities between Grotius and Hobbes can be traced to their understanding of Christianity as a historical story that was distinct from the laws and rights of nature. Both men believed that human beings (and human nature) could be understood without reference to the Christian story, with its account of man's Fall; they both saw Christianity as part of history, distinct from natural knowledge or philosophy. Moreover, both men believed that human beings could recognize the laws of nature through reason and both saw these laws as primarily designed to enable life here on earth, rather than spiritual fulfillment. But, whereas Grotius and the Anglicans downplayed nature in order to emphasize the duties of a Christian, Hobbes took a very different course. Instead, he reduced Christian ethics to a natural law which was now much thinner and less demanding. And yet Hobbes was quite traditional in denying that there could be tension between natural law and Christianity. Instead of arguing, as Grotius did, that Christ had revealed a new set of laws and a new set of sanctions, Hobbes took what was in many ways a much more standard line. He argued, as we have seen, that Christ came to satisfy for the sins of men and to proclaim a future kingdom; he insisted strongly (and in line with the vast majority of his contemporaries) that Christ had not brought any new laws. He then drew the corollary that Christ had not set up a church while on earth. Again this was a mainstream view since it was usually argued that the church could be traced back to Adam and that Christ had not brought new commands or precepts.[41]

---

[38] Mortimer 2010a, ch. 5; Mortimer 2011.

[39] For this discomfort see for example Robert Sanderson's correspondence with Hammond in Hammond 1660.

[40] Parkin 2007; Collins 2005, ch. 7; Mortimer 2010a, ch. 5.

[41] E.g., Overall 1844, 74–8; Calvin 1961, 373–4.

If Christ had not set up a church, with its own distinctive laws, then it followed for Hobbes that people could not choose to place themselves within that church. But Hobbes was not content to leave it there, and he mounted a fierce attack on the doctrine of free will which, as we have seen, was central to the Anglican endeavor. Hobbes would have been particularly aware of the importance of free will, for he had spent much time and effort arguing with Bramhall on this issue, and he was sharply critical of the bishop's position. As Hobbes realized, a successful attack upon his opponents' theology of the will would render their entire system of Christianity incoherent and, as Hobbes saw very clearly, such an attack could be carried out in the name of orthodox Protestantism. Aligning himself with the Protestant theology of the bondage of the will, Hobbes insisted that faith was a gift of God that could not be earned.[42] His determinist philosophy ruled out any space for the kind of choice that might be spiritually valuable, and it rendered the Grotian model utterly incoherent, at least in Hobbes's view. His critique of the theology of free will is suggested in *Leviathan*, where the will is defined as "the last appetite in deliberation," but it comes out much more fully in his debate with Bishop Bramhall, whose views about human freedom were roughly in line with Grotius's. Bramhall maintained that God's rewards and punishments must be connected to our choices and our capacity for moral responsibility; against him, Hobbes mounted a relentless attack on the conception of the will that underpinned this model. Unfortunately for Hobbes, the determinism he insisted on against Bramhall stood in tension with his civil philosophy, as Patrick Riley showed particularly clearly.[43] But the great advantage of this critique of free will, for Hobbes, was that it was extremely effective in undermining contemporary Anglican thinking.[44]

In a similar way, Hobbes's understanding of Christian history and indeed of the Christian scriptures was different from, but perhaps in dialogue with, Grotius's. For the Dutch writer, Christianity was based on the testimony of the Apostles, set out in the New Testament and now accessible to all human beings. Indeed, one of the central arguments of *Of the Truth of the Christian Religion* concerned the credibility of the gospel stories; for Grotius, there was no reason to suspect the historical accuracy of the accounts of Jesus's life, death, and resurrection. Every individual reader ought to see the value of following the teaching set out in the gospels. Conversely, however, Grotius could make distinctions between parts of the scripture, seeing some as more useful than others. Commenting on 2 Timothy 3:16, for example, he wrote that the Bible contained much historical and ethical material, as well as the prophetic words that could properly be seen as directly inspired.[45] Hobbes took a different line, insisting that we could know about Christianity only from the scriptural text, but he did not privilege the gospels or suggest that they were any more credible than other parts of the Bible. Indeed, he argued that the authority of the scriptures came

---

[42] Overhoff 2000, ch. 4; Martinich 1992, 273–8. See also Chappel 1999.
[43] Riley 1982, ch. 2.
[44] Collins 2005, 266–7.
[45] Grotius 2012, esp. 142–7; Grotius 1679, 992.

from the sovereign and not from our personal opinions about the intrinsic qualities of the text.[46] Yet, as I have suggested, Hobbes was also keen to persuade people that they have good reasons to assent to the Christian scriptures, just as they have good reasons to assent to sovereign power. And these reasons must suffice, until and unless a person receives a special revelation from God. This was enough, for Hobbes, and his efforts to redefine the meaning of choice or free will may have been designed to lower the stakes involved during a period of religious flux. At any rate, he sought to encourage his readers to accept the kind of theology most likely to yield peace and stability here on earth and to insulate them from the claims made by the episcopalians.

Hobbes's interpretation of Christianity was, therefore, an unusual and eclectic mixture of some of the more interesting ideas of his contemporaries. Its timing is understandable, for the early 1650s must have seemed to Hobbes the ideal time to promote a new and properly reformed Christianity. The Rump was still deciding on the form and doctrine of any new English church, and it was clear that the Parliament itself, rather than the clergy, would have overall control of the new church. Hobbes drew heavily on the Erastian arguments circulating at the time, as Jeffrey Collins has shown,[47] but *Leviathan* also suggests a shrewd engagement with an alternative tradition. This was the theology associated with Grotius, a theology with which Hobbes's Anglican acquaintances were experimenting in their efforts to defend their church. Their ideas, especially the new Anglican emphases on human free will and on *jure divino* episcopacy, made them vulnerable to charges of heterodoxy, and indeed Catholicism—as they were well aware. In such a delicate situation, it is not surprising that they sought to distance themselves from the theology of *Leviathan*, nor that they sought to dismiss it by highlighting Hobbes's scoffing tone and emphasizing his novelty.[48] But Hobbes's ideas were closer to some of his contemporaries than is often realized, and it was the way in which Hobbes could put ideas already circulating to completely different use that caused such contention.

4 RELIGION AND SOCIETY

Hobbes's religious views outraged his contemporaries, but they have also puzzled historians who have long debated whether he was sincere in his professions of Christianity. Certainly, Hobbes's view of the Christian story is unusual; more important, perhaps, is that his version of Christianity does not prioritize the themes of original sin and redemption which stood at the heart of contemporary piety. But what is most striking about Hobbes's Christianity is, as I have suggested, how well it

---

[46] Hobbes 1996, 260.
[47] Collins 2005; a different account can be found in Martinich 2009.
[48] E.g., Hammond 1653, esp. 384; Parkin 2007, 102–3, 116; Mortimer 2010a, 128–37.

is integrated with his account of human beings. Hobbes assumed that human beings were religious, and in *Leviathan* he showed how Christian doctrines could satisfy men's fears in ways which also contributed to peace and stability here on earth. Whether we count Hobbes as "Christian" or not may depend on our own definitions, but his theology was central to his project. He saw the opportunity to adopt some of the arguments current among his acquaintances and integrate them into a comprehensive account of society in which Christianity supported, rather than undermined, the state.

True Christianity was the best religion for a commonwealth, on Hobbes's account, but he thought that every commonwealth would need some kind of public religion. Hobbes's view of human beings made it difficult for him to imagine a society of atheists, and we have little indication that he ever entertained such a proposition. Part of what it is to be human, for Hobbes, is to be afraid and anxious about the unknown—and every society has to take account of that fear and channel it through public religion. Even the most "scientific" society will be unable to explain the origins of life or what happens after death, and it is crucial to make sure that the beliefs which people have about these issues contribute to the stability of the society. Because religious belief is like competition or diffidence, part of the makeup of human beings, no sovereign can ignore it. That is not to say, however, that revelation or Christianity is required for social life, or even that Hobbes believed in any transcendent or divine being. Hobbes may well have found such a being literally incredible, but he recognized clearly the social value of properly directed religious worship.[49] Public religion made possible a common and united response to the anxieties and uncertainties that are bound to afflict any group of people. And while Hobbes was willing to acknowledge that there could be successful commonwealths without Christianity or revelation—the Roman republic was one—he does not seem to have thought that there could be commonwealths without religion.

Although Hobbes recognized that there could be stable commonwealths without Christianity, he insisted that no commonwealth would last if it allowed the kind of Christianity which his contemporaries practiced. True Christianity may have been Hobbes's most favored religion, but he subjected the Christianity espoused by the clerics around him to caustic and biting criticism. There can be no doubt that Hobbes did feel that the Christianity he saw around him, especially in its Roman Catholic and Presbyterian forms, was based on ignorance and pride and had the potential to overturn the commonwealth. But it does not follow from this that he sought to replace Christianity with atheism or that he wanted his readers to eschew all religious belief. Far better, in Hobbes's view, to replace the deficient, destabilizing version of Christianity with one that would promote unity and alleviate anxiety.

---

[49] See Jesseph 2002 for a clear statement of Hobbes's atheism.

It is easy to see Hobbes's intentions in books three and four of *Leviathan* as primarily critical, designed to undercut the claims to power and authority being made in Paris and, to a lesser extent, in Britain by Catholics and Presbyterians. Certainly this was part of Hobbes's plan, but I have suggested that he did not want to throw the Christian baby out with the clerical bathwater. Instead, he wanted to adopt that baby and transform it—for he recognized the power of the Christian story, not only to destroy commonwealths but also to support them. He wanted to show that, given the necessity for a public religion, Christianity could in fact be the most successful and that it could reinforce sovereign power by harnessing to it the sanctions of eternal life. Hobbes took seriously Christ's words that "my Kingdom is not of this world" (John 18:36), and he showed, more forcefully than any of his predecessors, the potential consequences for a Christian commonwealth.

BIBLIOGRAPHY

Primary Sources

Calvin J. 1961. *Institutes of the Christian religion,* edited by J.T. McNeill and translated by F. Lewis. London: S.C.M. Press.

Chappell, V. 1999. *Hobbes and Bramhall on Liberty and Necessity.* Cambridge: Cambridge University Press.

Grotius, H. 1679. *Opera Omnia Theologica.* London.

Grotius, H. 1998. *Meletius, sive, De iis quae inter Christianos conveniunt epistola,* edited by G. H. M. Posthumus Meyjes. Leiden: Brill.

Grotius, H. 2005. *The Rights of War and Peace,* edited by R. Tuck. Indiana: Liberty Fund.

Grotius, H. 2012. *Of the Truth of the Christian Religion,* edited by M.R. Antognazza. Indiana: Liberty Fund.

Hammond, H. 1643. *A Practicall Catechism.* London.

Hammond, H. 1653. *A Letter of Resolution to Six Quaeres.* London.

Hammond, H. 1660. *Charis kai eirene, or, A Pacifick Discourse of Gods Grace and Decrees.* London.

Hobbes, T. 1996. *Leviathan,* edited by R. Tuck. Cambridge: Cambridge University Press.

Hobbes, T. 1998. *On the Citizen,* edited by R. Tuck and translated by M. Silverthorne. Cambridge: Cambridge University Press.

Hobbes, T. 1839–45. *The English Works of Thomas Hobbes,* edited by W. Molesworth. London: John Bohn.

Hyde, Edward, Earl of Clarendon. 1676. *A Brief View and Survey of . . . Leviathan.* London.

Overall, J. 1844. *The Convocation Book of M DC VI, Commonly Called Bishop Overall's Convocation Book.* Oxford: John Henry Parker.

Pocock, N. 1848. "Illustrations of the State of the Church During the Great Rebellion (continued)." *Theologian and Ecclesiastic,* vol. 7.

Pocock, N. 1852. "Illustrations of the State of the Church During the Great Rebellion (continued)." *Theologian and Ecclesiastic,* vol. 13.

Socinus, F. 1666. *Opera Omnia: in duos tomos distincta.* Irenopoli [Amsterdam].

Taylor, J. 1642. *Of the Sacred Order and Offices of Episcopacy.* Oxford.

Secondary Sources

Allison, C. F. 1966. *The Rise of Moralism: The Proclamation of the Gospel from Hooker to Baxter*. London: S.C.M. Press.

Collins, J. 2000. "Christian Ecclesiology and the Composition of *Leviathan*: A Newly Discovered Letter to Thomas Hobbes." *Historical Journal*, 43: 217–231.

Collins, J. 2005. *The Allegiance of Thomas Hobbes*. Oxford: Oxford University Press.

Curley, E. 1992. "'I durst not write so boldly' or How to Read Hobbes's Theological-Political Treatise." In *Hobbes e Spinoza, scienza e politica*, edited by D. Bostrenghi, 497–593. Naples: Bibliopolis.

Curley, E. 1998. "Religion and Morality in Hobbes," In *Rational Commitment and Social Justice: Essays for Gregory Kavka*, edited by J. L. Coleman and C. W. Morris, 90–121. Cambridge: Cambridge University Press.

Haakonssen, K. 1998. "Divine/Natural Law Theories in Ethics," in *The Cambridge History of Seventeenth-Century Philosophy*, edited by D. Garber and Michael Ayers, 1317–1357. Cambridge: Cambridge University Press.

Heering, J.P. 2004. *Hugo Grotius as Apologist for the Christian Religion: A Study of His Work De Veritate Religionis Christianae, 1640*, translated by J.C. Grayson. Leiden: Brill.

Jackson, N. 2007. *Hobbes, Bramhall and the Politics of Liberty and Necessity: A Quarrel of the Civil Wars and Interregnum*. Cambridge: Cambridge University Press.

Jesseph, D. 2002. "Hobbes's Atheism." *Midwest Studies in Philosophy*, 26: 140–166.

Martinich, A. P. 1992. *The Two Gods of Leviathan: Thomas Hobbes on Religion and Politics*. Cambridge: Cambridge University Press.

Martinich, A. P. 2009. "Hobbes's Erastianism and Interpretation." *Journal of the History of Ideas*, 70: 143–163.

Mintz, S. 1962. *The Hunting of Leviathan: Seventeenth-century Reactions to the Materialism and Moral Philosophy of Thomas Hobbes*. Cambridge: Cambridge University Press.

Morrill, J. 2008. "The Puritan Revolution," in *Cambridge Companion to Puritanism*, edited by J. Coffey and P. Lim, 67–88. Cambridge: Cambridge University Press.

Mortimer, S. 2010a. *Reason and Religion in the English Revolution: The Challenge of Socinianism*. Cambridge: Cambridge University Press.

Mortimer, S. 2010b. "Exile, Apostasy and Anglicanism in the English Revolution," in *Literatures of Exile in the English Revolution and Its Aftermath, 1640–1690*, edited by P. Major, 91–104. Aldershot: Ashgate.

Mortimer, S. 2011. "Kingship and the 'Apostolic' Church 1620–1650." *Renaissance and Reformation Review*, 13: 225–246.

Overhoff, J. 2000. *Hobbes's Theory of Will: Ideological Reasons and Historical Circumstances*. Oxford: Rowman and Littlefield.

Parkin, J. 2007. *Taming the Leviathan: The Reception of the Political and Religious Ideas of Thomas Hobbes in England, 1640–1700*. Cambridge: Cambridge University Press.

Pocock, J. G. A. 1972. "Time, History, and Eschatology in the Thought of Thomas Hobbes," in *Politics, Language and Time*, 148–201. London: Methuen.

Riley, P. 1982. *Will and Political Legitimacy: A Critical Exposition of Social Contract Theory in Hobbes, Locke, Rousseau, Kant, and Hegel*. Cambridge: Harvard University Press.

Rose, J. 2011. *Godly Kingship in Restoration England: The Politics of the Royal Supremacy 1660–1688*. Cambridge: Cambridge University Press.

Strauss, L. 1953. *Natural Right and History*. Chicago: University of Chicago Press.

Strauss, L. 2011. *Hobbes's Critique of Religion and Related Writings*, translated by G. Bartlett and S. Minkov. Chicago: University of Chicago Press.

Tuck, R. 1992. "The 'Christian Atheism' of Thomas Hobbes," in *Atheism from the Reformation to the Enlightenment*, edited by M. Hunter and D. Wootton, 111–130. Oxford: Oxford University Press.

Tuck, R. 1993. "The Civil Religion of Thomas Hobbes," in *Political Discourse in Early Modern Britain*, edited by N. Phillipson and Q. Skinner, 120–138. Cambridge: Cambridge University Press.

CHAPTER 23

THOMAS HOBBES'S ECCLESIASTICAL HISTORY

JEFFREY COLLINS

IN *Leviathan* Hobbes defined history as a "register of knowledge of fact," and he distinguished its two branches as "natural history" and "civil history," based upon the latter's unique "dependence on man's will."[1] Both branches relied upon fallible witnesses and neither attained that knowledge of consequences required of a "science." This taxonomy fails to mention what was, in Hobbes's day, the largest historiographical enterprise of all: sacred history. To cite one example well known to him, Francis Bacon's *The Advancement of Learning* categorized history as "natural, civil, ecclesiastical, and literary." Bacon subdivided "ecclesiastical history" into church history, the history of prophecy, and the history of providence.[2] (Moderns more commonly designate the first of these subdivisions as ecclesiastical history and the latter two as divine history.)

Hobbes was very well aware of this conventional historical classification, and on several occasions his writings mention "sacred" or "holy history." Both *De Cive* and *Leviathan* use these terms to reference the narrative of the Old Testament.[3] More intriguingly, *Leviathan* refers to those humans who "wrote the holy history" in distinguishing the actual words of God from the "metaphorical" words of God (such as "let there be light") invented to characterize the divine will.[4] This more deflationary reference to "divine history" implies fallible human origins. In a similar vein, distinguishing scientific knowledge from faith, Hobbes observed that we accept the Scriptures as divine because of our faith in ecclesial authority. "And so it is also with all other history. For if I should not believe all that is written by historians of the glorious acts of Alexander or Caesar, I do not think the ghost of Alexander or Caesar had any just cause to be offended, or anybody else but the historian." Sacred history and profane

---

[1] *Leviathan*, 47.
[2] Bacon 1996, 175, 184–85.
[3] *De Cive*, 188, 194.
[4] *Leviathan*, 280.

history, each a source of secondhand knowledge, were alike potentially deceptive in both effect and design. "If Livy say the Gods made once a cow speak, and we believe it not," Hobbes concluded, "we distrust not God therein, but Livy." What we believe upon the "authority of men only and their writings, whether they be sent from God or not, is faith in men only."[5]

The skeptical flavor of this passage again recalls Bacon, who illustrated the tendency to credit "things weakly authorized or warranted" by noting the

> inconvenience of this error in ecclesiastical history; which hath too easily received and registered reports and narrations of miracles . . . which though they had a passage for a time, by the ignorance of the people, the superstitious simplicity of some, and the politic toleration of others holding them but as divine poesies; yet after a period of time, when the mist began to clear up, they grew to be esteemed but as old wives' fables, impostures of the clergy, illusions of spirits, and badges of antichrist, to the great scandal and detriment of religion.[6]

These are Bacon's words, but Hobbes might well have written them. They are marked by contempt for received tradition, an awareness of the gullibility of the vulgar, deep suspicion of clerical trickery, and a concession to the *politique* requirements of statecraft when faced with entrenched error. They appropriately initiate a discussion of Hobbes's approach to sacred history.

The topic is a neglected one. Amid ever expanding interest in Hobbes's theological and ecclesiological views, his efforts at divine and (particularly) ecclesiastical history have not received the attention they merit. Doubtless this is partly owing to the confinement of these efforts to Hobbes's more minor Restoration writings and to the perceived archaism of sacred history as a genre. But it may also be that the ingenuity of Hobbes's sacred history, which strongly anticipated patterns of Enlightenment historiography, seems unremarkable to us for precisely that reason. Anachronism can often breed a specious familiarity in this manner. Read with fresh attention, Hobbes's extensive efforts at sacred history emerge as original and audacious writings.

1 ECCLESIASTICAL HISTORY AS A HOBBESIAN GENRE

Hobbes's sacred history was extensive in scale. His interest in the subject was dynamic, generally expanding as his career advanced. The manuscript "Elements of Law" contains a great deal of scriptural citation but little sustained sacred history. The ecclesiastical history of the later church is almost entirely missing, and the "divine history"

---

[5] *Leviathan*, 37.
[6] Bacon 1996: 142.

of scripture is not extensively narrated but only episodically mentioned to evidence the unity of divine and civil law among the Jews or the political passivity of the early Christians.[7] A similar pattern of eschewing historical analysis in favor of scripture mining designed to "confirm" Hobbesian doctrine marks *De Cive* (1641). Here, however, somewhat more extensive narration is deployed to establish useful aspects of the ancient Jewish polity, such as the particularity of its "covenant with God" and its subordination of prophetic authority to civil power.[8] Likewise a slightly fuller account of the passive, otherworldly primitive church is offered. But the work contains only gestures toward any sustained ecclesiastical history of the later church as one of decline and corruption.[9] Both "The Elements of Law" and *De Cive* confine themselves to the narrative of scripture, and neither evidences much engagement with the scholarly historiography of the later church.

The situation is transformed in *Leviathan* (1651). Here, in a vastly expanded discussion of religious themes, Hobbes extended himself beyond static and isolated scriptural points and offered a more substantial "sacred history," running from Jewish times through the primitive Christian era into the period of Roman theological and ecclesiology corruption and the Reformation. These themes consume scores of pages in Hobbes's masterpiece and undergird critical argumentative claims within his discussion of the "Christian Commonwealth." *Leviathan* was also the first of Hobbes's major texts that indicates—albeit often obliquely—an engagement with scholarly ecclesiastical history.

After the Restoration, with his civil philosophy banned and with his clerical adversaries emboldened, Hobbes produced writings centrally oriented around sacred history. By now, the "divine history" of scripture no longer diverted him significantly. He was more vitally engaged by the post-Constantinian history of the church, the history of the early church councils, the paganizing corruption of church theology by the late patristics, and the medieval history of clerical corruption and persecution. These topics of "ecclesiastical history" dominated his verse *Historia ecclesiatica*, his various tracts on heresy, and the appendix to his Latin *Leviathan*. More surprisingly, they were also important themes within his *Dialogue between a Philosopher and a Student of the Common Laws of England* and his history of the English civil war, *Behemoth*. Indeed, the relative scholarly neglect of these last two works might be blamed on a modern tendency to treat sacred history as a dead genre.

2   TRADITIONS AND INFLUENCES

Before exploring the specifics of Hobbes's thickened account of ecclesiastical history, we require some indication of the broader scholarly world that would have informed

---

[7] *Elements of Law*, ch. 25.
[8] *De Cive*, 187–202.
[9] *De Cive*, 203–33.

his efforts. The tradition of Christian sacred history was more than a millennium old by the seventeenth century. Its earliest practitioners were informed by the work of the "father of ecclesiastical history," Eusebius of Caesarea. His *Ecclesiastical History* was a narrative of trial and persecution on the one hand and, on the other, an effort to redeem the providential purposes of the Roman Empire by celebrating the Constantinian conversion.[10] Eusebius's fifth- and sixth-century Byzantine heirs—Socrates Scholasticus, Sozomen, Theodoret of Cyrrhus, Evagrius Scholasticus, and John of Ephesus—were animated by continuing that project and (increasingly) chronicling the rise and fall of heresies.[11] The travails of the Western Empire made such heroically imperial church histories less appealing there. Augustine and his colleague Orosius spurned the "historiography of Christian empire as an aspect of ecclesiastical history," and *The City of God* might be read as a rejection of any link between divine and civil history.[12] Nevertheless, Latin Christendom eventually provided new paradigms of sacred history, remarrying civil and ecclesiastical narratives as parallel manifestations of providence. The birth of the Holy Roman Empire made the question of *translatio imperii* a dominant one for chroniclers such as Otto of Freising,[13] and the role of the papacy in that process (clouded by the forged Donation of Constantine) implicated sacred history. More radically, the twelfth-century mystic Joachim of Fiore devised a Trinitarian historical schematic according to which the "age of the father" (the "old law" of the Jews) had given way to the "age of the son" (the Christian era), which would in turn lead to an "age of the spirit" marked by global conversion and a new *ecclesia spiritualis*. The millenarian overtones of Joachimism could be assimilated into a reading of the "four monarchies" of the book of Daniel, and it appealed to chiliastic sects, particularly after the Reformation.[14]

Foundational though they were, by Hobbes's day these works had been superseded by the more methodologically sophisticated and ideologically plural histories of the Reformation era. By then humanism had rendered the *artes historicae* a notably more scholarly discipline, bringing erudition and source criticism to bear on historical practice. Masters of the new historical method from Baudouin to Bodin all insisted that *historia integra* must include critical church history alongside the history of polities, war, and culture.[15] But the capacity of such a source-based approach to produce a common ecclesial narrative had been destroyed by the Reformation. Dueling histories emerged, and alongside these less confessional efforts at ecclesial history (or source criticism) by humanists such as Paolo Sarpi.

The polemic needs of the Reformation thus launched sacred history projects of industrial scale, often collaboratively written and grounded on innovative archival

---

[10] Momigliano 1990: 132–52.
[11] Cross 1997: 574.
[12] Pocock 2003: 71–81.
[13] Pocock 2003, 101–21.
[14] Löwith 1957; Martinich 1992: 286–96.
[15] Grafton 2007: 28, 105.

research (if not always on scrupulous critical judgment). Groundbreaking was Johannes Sleidanus's 1555 *De statu religionis et reipublicae, Carlo V Caesare Commentarii*, a widely translated account of the Reformation from the Ninety-Five Theses through the Diet of Augsburg.[16] The grandest effort on the Protestant side, however, was presided over by the hard-line Lutheran Hebraist Matthias Flacius. Produced between 1559 and 1574, it became known as the "Magdeburg Centuries." Seeking to parry the rhetorical challenge "where was your church before Luther?" the centuriators' *Historia Ecclesiae Christi* presented the pure Christianity of the primitive church, its slow corruption by the Anti-Christ of Rome, and its redemption by Luther. Occasionally lax with sources, it nevertheless enjoyed enormous sway over Protestant historiography. So too did Flacius's own *Catalogus Testium Veritatis* (1556), which arrayed hundreds of witnesses to "Lutheran" truth from across the centuries and did much to redeem figures such as Huss and Wycliffe.[17]

These foundational efforts by Flacius and his cohort were widely mined by Protestants.[18] In England the "Centuries" were used by figures such as John Bale, John Jewel, and John Foxe. Protestant historiography was marked by theological variation and by divergent levels of millenarian intensity but united in its negative case against Roman spiritual and political corruption.[19] It typically preserved the integrity of corporate church authority through the major councils and the period of creedal formation, but deconstructed as clerical trickery everything from clerical celibacy, to the doctrine of transubstantiation, to the political claims of the "papal monarchy." This scholarship exploited the critical tools of the humanists but also shared the humanists' basic historical schematic presenting the "Middle Ages" as a period of darkness and corruption. The new techniques produced critical scholarship on important historical documents, exposing, for instance, the "False Decretals" and several letter of Ignatius of Antioch as spurious.

Protestant efforts did not go unanswered. In 1571 Pope Pius V convened a commission tasked with refuting the Magdeburg Centuries. Chief among the histories of the Counter-Reformation, intent on vindicating the Catholic Church with the new historical techniques, was Cardinal Cesare Baronius's *Annales Ecclesiastici*. Encouraged by Philip Neri as early as the 1560s, these appeared in twelve volumes from 1588 to 1607.[20] Catholic historiography proliferated in the seventeenth century, advanced by Benedictine and Bollandist scholarship. The context of this later work was not merely to riposte Protestant histories but to alternatively buttress or undermine the claimed autonomy of "national" Catholic churches.[21]

Thomas Hobbes's exposure to sacred history would have been decisively mediated by this voluble sixteenth- and early-seventeenth-century scholarship, which was marked

---

[16] Kress 2008.
[17] Olson 2002.
[18] Cameron 1988: 132–36.
[19] Levy 1967: ch. 3.
[20] Pullapilly 1985: 16.
[21] Knowles 1963: ch. 1–2; Momigliano 1990: 132–36.

by improved critical standards but also by intense polemical impulses. Few of the major ecclesiastical historians sought to undermine the basic notion that divine purposes could be read in the history of the visible church. But humanist scholarship exposed the shortcomings of traditional accounts, and Protestant historiography was firmly dedicated to discrediting vast swathes of church history. The Eusebian celebration of ecclesiastical empire no longer commanded uniform assent. That Hobbes was influenced by these historical perspectives can hardly be doubted and is perhaps indicated by the early essay "On Rome," published in the *Horae Subsecivae* (1620) sometimes attributed to his authorship (or to that of William Cavendish, his tutee). Here we read of the conversion of Constantine: "to see the ill effects so good a cause produced cannot but breed admiration. For the Ambition of the Bishops of Rome made this their first step to greatness, and subversion of the Empire." The essay's acid remarks about clerical "encroachment . . . under color of Religion and Saint Peter's Keys," or about the "sumptuousness of the Pope and the pride of his government," are little more than shibboleths of Protestant historical memory.[22] Whether or not Hobbes wrote them, they serve as emblems of the historiographical culture in which he operated. Of Hobbes's deeper immersion in this scholarship he, quite typically, leaves few clues. Always sparing with his references, those of an historical nature tended to be to the classical pagans. We know, for instance, that Hobbes was familiar with the writings of Luther and Calvin, but we can only guess as to whether he knew their more historical writings, such as the former's *On the Councils and the Church* or the latter's *Treatise on Relics*.

Nevertheless there is room for informed supposition. The library at Hardwick Hall, catalogued by Hobbes in the 1620s, was well stocked with works of sacred history. It contained an edition of the Magdeburg Centuries and much else besides. The earliest sacred history was represented by editions of Joachim Camerarius's volumes containing Eusebius, Socrates Scholasticus, Sozomen, and Theodoret. Complete editions of most of the patristic writers were also present, as were medieval works such as Bede's *Historiae ecclesiasticae gentis Anglorum*, an unidentified chronicle of the Franciscans (probably by Angelo Clareno), and the complete writings of Innocent III. The library possessed a great many Reformation era and seventeenth-century ecclesiastical histories (and source collections) as well. Beyond the standard editions of the major reformed theologians, it held most of Cardinal Bellarmine's works, an edition of the canons of the Synod of Dort, Sarpi's *History of the Council of Trent*, Richard Crackenthorpe's 1621 *Defense of Constantine*, several histories of the Jesuit order, historical writings by Bishop James Usher, a translation of Jean Paul Perrin's history of the Waldesians, and John Selden's 1618 *The History of Tithes*. Unsurprisingly, the library was full of hostile attacks on the papal monarchy, including Phillipe de Mornay's *The Mystery of Iniquity*, Pierre du Moulin's *De Monarchia Temporali Pontificis Romani*, and similar works by the English churchmen Robert Abbot and Samuel Harsnett.[23]

[22] Reynolds 1995, 71–72, 92–102.
[23] Springborg 2008, 281–92.

A considerable volume of ecclesiastical history was thus at Hobbes's disposal. It is nevertheless difficult to fix which works most influenced him, and when. His explicit references to this scholarship are rare. Of the early church historians, Hobbes's *Historical Narration Concerning Heresy* mentions Eusebius, and his *Answer to Bramhall* makes a dismissive mention of Sulpicius Severus's fourth-century *Life of Saint Martin* as part of an attack on the "fables of the Roman clergy." *Behemoth* condemned the "progress of the Pope's power" by appealing to Mornay's *Mystery of Iniquity* alongside *The Grand Imposture of the (now) Church of Rome* (1626) by the English bishop Thomas Morton.[24] In a letter of 1636, Hobbes explicitly mentioned his desire to read a history of the Sabbath (probably by Peter Heylyn), though he feared that it would "put" dangerous thoughts into the "Heads of vulgar People."[25] Years later, Hobbes would commend historical writings of the English Independents, including those of John Owen and Louis du Moulin.[26]

But these passing mentions only scratch the surface, and scholars have scarcely begun the monumental task of fixing the local specifics of Hobbes's more extensive but silent appropriation of ecclesiastical history. It seems certain that humanist and Protestant historical writing heavily influenced him. But it can also be said that, as his interest in ecclesiastical history developed, Hobbes's own "church primitivism" pushed him far beyond where most Protestant historians desired to go.

3 FROM DIVINE HISTORY TO ECCLESIASTICAL HISTORY

The broad trajectory of Hobbes's lifelong engagement with sacred history saw him move from a fairly straightforward divine history drawn from the scriptures toward a more extensive ecclesiastical history of the Christian church through the ages, seemingly drawn from a broader array of historiographical sources.[27] Most of the existing scholarship on Hobbesian sacred history has foregrounded the former of these topical foci.[28] All of Hobbes's major political writings mined the scriptures for confirming evidence, often roughly historical in nature, of scientific truths. In this context the lessons of the scriptures often seemed secondary in their evidentiary value. Hobbes distilled a few key points from the holy writ: that the Jews' covenant with God was historically unique and not to be aped by overzealous Christian covenanters; that the Jewish polity was an Erastian one, with both the Hebrew Kings and the Sanhedrin in turn enjoying

---

[24] *Behemoth*, 133–34.
[25] *Correspondence*, 30.
[26] *Correspondence*, 449; Collins 2005: 224–36.
[27] Schumann 2000: 13.
[28] Eisenach 1981: 57–66.

a unified spiritual and temporal authority; and finally that the coming of Christ did not disrupt either of these patterns. Covenants with God and holy kingdoms on earth remained forbidden to Christians, and Christ diminished none of the ecclesiastical authority wielded by civil sovereigns.

In sustaining these points, Hobbes was undoubtedly influenced by modern scholarship of an Erastian stripe. It has been convincingly argued that his interpretation of the Sanhedrin, for instance, owes a great deal to the revival of serious Hebraism among scholars such as Grotius and Selden.[29] That said, aside from a single mention of the first-century Jewish historian Flavius Josephus, Hobbes sustained both his reading of the ancient Jewish polity and his interpretation of the primitive church entirely from the scriptures.[30] Only with *Leviathan* did Hobbes substantially supplement this effort at scriptural hermeneutic with ecclesiastical historical narrative. That new interest, which Hobbes would maintain through the final decades of his life, required a sustained exploration of late antique, medieval, and Reformation Christianity. At this point Hobbes became a full participant in the early modern culture of sacred history writing as it had been shaped by the apologetical requirements of the Reformation.

Hobbes's sacred history would maintain the broad form of Protestant historiography, valorizing the purity of primitive Christianity and condemning, as a long age of papal corruption, the centuries dividing the primitive church from the European Reformation.[31] In crucial respects, however, his history would break from Protestant conventions. Hobbes was considerably less interested than most Protestant historians in celebrating the Reformation.[32] His *Historia Ecclesiastica*, for instance, advanced only to Luther and no further, and in many of his works he heaped scorn on both the Presbyterian and English episcopal churches (which were the major Reformation "options" for a nonsectarian English Protestant). Hobbes's ecclesiastical history often had a decidedly unredeemed tone, and his Protestant partisanship chiefly revealed itself negatively as anti-Catholicism. A second divergence, as we shall see below, involved Hobbes's willingness to pursue the project of debunking ecclesial tradition back into the era of the early church councils. This step, which implicated Trinitarian orthodoxy, was not taken by the major Protestant historians. A third particularity of Hobbes's sacred history was its reliance upon a general account of religious belief and a general historical thesis about the motors of religious change. Such a protosociological "natural" history of religion was not common among Protestant historians, who tended to rely upon a more providential historical framework.

Leviathan broke much of this new ground for Hobbes. The work's twelfth chapter laid out a natural theory of religion, according to which its uniquely human "seed" is the combination of insatiable curiosity about unknowable first causes and a "perpetual fear" of death. These emotions project themselves onto "some power or agent invisible,"

---

[29] Nelson 2010, chapter 3; Malcolm 2004b, 241–64; Sommerville 2000: 169, 171.
[30] *De Cive*, 188.
[31] Martinich 2003: 284–96; Lessay 2004: 267–68; Whittaker 1988: 86; Eisenach 1982: 215–43.
[32] Lessay 2004: 298.

and thus are gods created. Causal powers are attributed to these agents, and honors are paid. Of fear and ignorance, then, "consisteth the natural seed of religion, which by reason of the different fancies, judgments, and passions of several men hath grown up into ceremonies so different that those which are used by one man are for the most part ridiculous to another."[33] The history of religion, for Hobbes, was the history of this process, and he previewed what such a history of fancy might look like, listing some of the "absurd opinions of Gentilism" that deified everything from crocodiles to leeks. The use of specious divinations, images, and so forth allowed the "authors" of these pagan religions to "obtrude on" the ignorance of their subjects, making religion a critical component of civil rule.[34]

Hobbes insulated sacred history from this account of natural religion, which was shot through with skepticism and ridicule, by distinguishing religions created by human "invention" from those born of "God's commandment and direction":

> But both sorts have done it with a purpose to make those men that relied on them the more apt to obedience, laws, peace, charity, and civil society. So that the religion of the former sort is a part of human politics, and teacheth part of the duty which earthly kings require of their subjects. And the religion of the latter sort is divine politics, and containeth precepts to those that have yielded themselves subjects in the kingdom of God. Of the former sorts were the founders of commonwealths and the lawgivers of the Gentiles; of the latter sort were Abraham, Moses, and out blessed Saviour, by whom have been derived unto us the laws of the kingdom of God.[35]

"Divine politics" of course had a history, and we can read this passage as a definition of sacred history in all but name. Leaving aside the skepticism that often seemed to attach to Hobbes's account of whether God truly "directed" men, it should be noted that his sacred history and the natural history of religion generally share the same telos: civil peace. Hobbes's ecclesiastical history would largely structure itself around the question of whether the church had, in its various eras, advanced or hindered this earthly goal. He did not compose his sacred history around soteriological or millenarian narratives. Many of his theological novelties indeed, such as his mortalism, seem designed to short-circuit predictive historical speculations of that kind.[36] Thus, although Hobbes made an effort to particularize the sacred history of Judeo-Christianity, his natural history of religion as such implicates sacred history and tends to privilege the psychological and political dimensions of religion over the providential. In this respect *Leviathan* can be read as an early participant in the broad intellectual revolution that gradually ensured that religions "came to be credited with a natural rather than a sacred history."[37]

---

[33] *Leviathan*, 66–67.
[34] *Leviathan*, 66–69.
[35] *Leviathan*, 67–71.
[36] Johnston 1989: 47–63.
[37] Harrison 1999, 3.

Leviathan's twelfth chapter also offers a general thesis about the "causes of change in religion." Religion defied abolition, Hobbes wrote, but "new religions may again be made to spring out of them by the culture of such men as for such purpose are in reputation." Setting aside—in this context—the distinction between false and true religion, Hobbes wrote that "all formed religion is founded at first upon the faith which a multitude hath in some person" taken to be holy. When the "wisdom," "sincerity," or "love" of these authorities corrodes, or when their "tokens of divine revelation" fail, their authority is "contradicted and rejected." The reputation for wisdom is lost by the folly of requiring "a belief of contradictories." The reputation for sincerity is lost when hypocrisy is exposed. The reputation for love fails when the "private ends" of religious injunctions are revealed. Finally, the credit of prophetic or miraculous power fails when such wonders cease, or are exposed by natural science.[38]

This model of religious revolution had Epicurean overtones.[39] Hobbes did not apply it to paganism alone. Christianity, he wrote, succeeded because of the "contempt into which the priests of the Gentiles of that time had brought themselves." Most Christian historians interpreted the conversion of the ancient world as a providential miracle global in scale, but Hobbes offered a more earthly rationale, emphasizing paganism's internal failures. So too Roman Catholicism:

> was, partly for the same cause, abolished in England and many other parts of Christendom (insomuch as the failing of virtue in the pastors maketh faith fail in the people), and partly from bringing of the philosophy and doctrine of Aristotle into the religion by the Schoolmen, from whence there arose so many contradictions and absurdities as brought the clergy into a reputation both of ignorance and of fraudulent intention, and inclined people to revolt from them, either against the will of their own princes, as in France and Holland, or with their will, as in England. . . . So that I may attribute all the changes of religion in the world to one and the same cause, and that is, unpleasing priests, and those not only amongst Catholics, but even in that church that hath presumed most of reformation.[40]

This passage was a prospectus of the sacred history that Hobbes would pursue in the latter portions of *Leviathan* and even more fully in his Restoration writings. His explicit comparison of Papalism to paganism was a Protestant truism. Not so Hobbes's inclusion of the reformed faith in the cyclical process of religious rot and reinvention. Nor did most Protestant historians embed the providential drama of sacred history within a psychological and political account of natural religion.

The latter half of *Leviathan* contains historical analysis informed by this distinctive perspective. Much of this material would have been familiar to readers of Hobbes's earlier texts, particularly the iteration of an Erastian interpretation of the Jewish polities,

---

[38] *Leviathan*, 71–72.
[39] Harrison 1990, 34; Springborg 2010: 33–39.
[40] *Leviathan*, 73–74.

and a passive, apolitical account of the primitive church.[41] The post-apostolic ecclesial history offered in *Leviathan* was designed to demonstrate the accretion of intellectual and political corruption layered onto the Christian tradition by power-hunting clergy. This, of course, was perfectly compatible with standard Protestant historiography. Hobbes's interest in participating in such a project of debunking was twofold. First, he wished to continue to espouse his view—first formulated in the early 1640s— that "the dispute for precedence between the spirituall and the civill power, has of late more then any other thing in the world, bene the case of civill warres in all places of Christendome."[42] This theory of religious violence would prove a central organizing principle of Hobbes's fully developed ecclesiastical history. Of course, this was a boilerplate political lesson to Protestant historians living through the wars of religion. Often Hobbes sustained his version by crossing swords with Bellarmine over scriptural proof texts, as when he used verses from the Pauline epistles to prove that pastors in the primitive church "lived upon voluntary contributions."[43] There is an historical point here, but it is not embedded in a sustained historical narrative.

In general, *Leviathan* included arguments drawn from ecclesiastical history, but these still tended to be somewhat scattershot historical allusions detached from sustained narration. For instance, the folly of sovereigns attempting to secure peace by strategically surrendering power is illustrated by William the Conqueror's "oath not to infringe the liberty of the church," which resulted eventually in the sedition of Thomas Becket.[44] But this isolated historical reference is not further elaborated and serves primarily as a Protestant catchword.

Leviathan comes closest to sustained ecclesiastical history in part four, "Of the Kingdom of Darkness." Here, Hobbes blamed spiritual darkness partly on widespread scriptural ignorance but also on the introduction of the "demonology of the heathen poets" into theology, on the Christianization of the "vain and erroneous philosophy of the Greeks," and on "false or uncertain traditions, feigned or uncertain history."[45] This declension was an historical process, and Hobbes touched upon the familiar way stations on the road to Babylon. Transubstantiation, for instance, was specifically dated by Hobbes to the time of Innocent III, "when the power of the popes was at the highest."[46] He evidenced the papacy's "wanton insulting" of sovereignty by retailing the legend that Pope Alexander III, reconciling with Frederick Barbarossa, put his foot on the Emperor's neck while haranguing him with scripture.[47]

In general *Leviathan*'s narration of church corruption is informed by a greater level of historical detail than Hobbes had previously offered. Some of this shows itself in his more specific account of the "relics of Gentilism" that had corrupted Christianity. Thus

---

[41] *Leviathan*, chapters 40–42.
[42] *Correspondence*, 120.
[43] *Leviathan*, 365.
[44] *Leviathan*, 211.
[45] *Leviathan*, 412.
[46] *Leviathan*, 417.
[47] *Leviathan*, 423.

is the canonization of saints exposed as a "custom as ancient as the commonwealth of Rome itself," tracing back to the "canonisation" of Romulus.[48] So too are processions and candles traced to the Greeks and Romans, with erudite references to the reception of Caracalla into Alexandria with incense, and to the processions of Priapus and Ambarvalia. Although he references virtually no sources, Hobbes's knowledge of pagan practices was almost certainly drawn from the expanding humanist scholarship on the subject. Gerardus Vossius's *De Theologica gentili et physiologica Christiana* (1641), Philip Clüver's *Germaniae Antiquae Libri Tres* (1636), and John Selden's *De Dis Syris* (1617) were likely sources.[49]

Leviathan's discussion of Christian church history also appears more thickly researched than it had been in Hobbes's earlier writings. Again, specific references are lacking, but likely sources suggest themselves. Hobbes's discussion of the clergy illegitimately assuming their offices *Dei gratia* or *providentia Dei* very closely parallels Selden's critique of the practice in his *Titles of Honor* (1614), a work commended by Hobbes as an "excellent treatise."[50] There are many textual parallels—on issues such as primitive ordination, the definition of *ecclesia*, the nature of early excommunication—between *Leviathan* and works such as Grotius's *De Imperio Summarum Potestatum Circa Sacra* (1647) and Louis du Moulin's *The Power of the Christian Magistrate in Sacred Things* (1650). It would be impossible to trace the many standard Protestant points about papal corruptions found in *Leviathan*, but that they derive from the research efforts of Flacius and his colleagues is overwhelmingly likely. That Hobbes also explored on this own the era's expanding collections of ecclesiastical documents is also likely, and is evidenced at least once by an explicit marginal note to the Decretals of Pope Gregory IX during Hobbes discussion of the fourth Lateran Council.[51]

Leviathan's sacred history was not offered as a comprehensive narrative. Roman "corruptions" were exposed as nonscriptural, but their introduction into church practice was not consistently dated or explained. Exempla drawn from Protestant and humanist ecclesiastical history (and from pagan religious history) appear more regularly in *Leviathan*, but often in a scattered way as required by Hobbes's thematic discussions. Nevertheless, the work suggested a raised level of historiographical erudition on Hobbes's part and presented the broad outline of an assault on papal corruption, according to which the "relics of gentilism" slowly corrupted Christian theology and practice, and papal jurisdiction increasingly encroached upon the just power of sovereignty. All of this was clearly informed by the historical scholarship that had been produced since the Reformation. Hobbes appears to have become increasingly aware of the need to sustain his ecclesiological and theological views with serious historical scholarship. *Leviathan* explicitly condemned the ignorance achieved by the "legends,"

---

[48] *Leviathan*, 451.
[49] Collins 2005: 46–52.
[50] Selden 1614: 116–18, 128–34; *Leviathan*, 368.
[51] *Leviathan*, 414.

"fictitious miracles," and "histories of apparitions and ghosts alleged by the doctors of the Roman church."[52]

If, however, Hobbes's ecclesiastical primitivism was familiar, many readers were affronted by some of its consequences in his work. The first of these was Hobbes's endorsement of the minority view that the divine history of the early church vindicated an Independent (or Congregational) church settlement. *Leviathan* cast both Presbyterian and episcopal ecclesiology in an unfavorable light as species of "praeterpolitical Church government" upheld by "knots on Christian liberty" and "pious frauds."[53] This argument carried explosive political implications in the Interregnum context, and Hobbes would abandon it after the Restoration.

Far more consequentially for the future shape of his ecclesiastical history was a theological implication of *Leviathan*'s primitivism: namely, a heretical account of the Trinity.[54] Hobbes, notoriously, defined the Trinity as a "three part" personation of God, extending from Moses to Christ to the apostles. Such a sequential reading seemed to deny the eternity of the Trinity and was particularly problematic for characterizing the mortal Moses as a representative of divinity. Seemingly designed to uphold his political theory and wildly unconventional, Hobbes's interpretation of the Trinity appears in *Leviathan* largely as a theological point drawn from scripture.[55] It would prove, however, critical to his sacred history after the Restoration, and sustaining it would encourage Hobbes to apply historical criticism not just to the corrupt papal church but to the early church councils themselves.

4 ECCLESIASTICAL HISTORY AS CODED PHILOSOPHY

The conditions of the Restoration political scene elicited from Hobbes his most unalloyed efforts at ecclesiastical history proper. If sacred history both divine and ecclesiastical had grown in importance in *Leviathan*, it nevertheless remained a subordinate genre and rhetorical mode. The work offered a general historical scheme of corruption and decline, but it often relied upon unspecific condemnations of "gentilism" and a mere juxtaposition of the simple primitivism of the scriptures against later neopaganizing tendencies. *Leviathan* thus evidenced Hobbes's growing engagement with sacred history, but had its limitations as a source for any sustained narrative.

In Hobbes's Restoration writings the situation is transformed. Ecclesiastical history—sustained narratives of the post-apostolic church—became a dominant genre within

---

[52] *Leviathan*, 467.
[53] *Leviathan*, 481–2.
[54] Tuck 1993: 133–35; Paganini 2003: 13–15.
[55] *Leviathan*, 103, 327.

Hobbes's later writings. This surprising development was partly forced by circumstance. *Leviathan's* civil science, theological novelties, and abandonment of episcopacy had enraged many royalists. Although he preserved some credit with the king, Hobbes was not permitted to publish as freely as he had during the 1650s. He was targeted, and under this pressure he apparently burned many of his private papers.

But Thomas Hobbes was not one to abandon the field of intellectual combat, and this is where ecclesiastical history performed a crucial function in his writing career. The history of the church became a central theme of a spate of writings produced by Hobbes in the late 1660s. Because they were obsessed with an effort to delegitimize the prosecution of heresy in England, these writings are often taken to be defensive in tone and purpose. But Hobbes's heresy writings, his *Dialogue* on the common law, his Latin *Leviathan*, and *Behemoth* all coincided with the fall of the Earl of Clarendon and the subsequent collapse of episcopal influence at the Caroline court. In this context, if he continued to seek self-protection, Hobbes could afford to again assert himself cautiously in print and in circulated manuscripts.[56] In these finely balanced circumstances, ecclesiastical history became a useful genre to Hobbes. It allowed him to encode ecclesiological and theological arguments that he wished to persist in defending but which remained risky.

Above all Hobbes sought to continue to defend his claim that the civil war which had occasioned *Leviathan* had been the product of seditious clergy undermining unified sovereignty. This claim targeted Presbyterianism above all but also exposed the episcopal Church of England to critique for its arch view of its own authority. The latter implication had been highly impolitic after 1660 and had encouraged Hobbes to make rather thin claims of steadfast allegiance to the bishops. He purged the endorsement of Independency from *Leviathan* when the work appeared in Latin in 1668. Few were fooled, and in truth, particularly as episcopal influence over Charles II temporarily waned, Hobbes was not inclined to retreat.

All of this explains the inclusion of sustained ecclesiastical history in Hobbes's most consequential Restoration work, *Behemoth*. The oft-noted neglect of that book is indeed partly explained by its incongruous (to moderns) obsession with medieval church history. As a political narrative of the civil war, *Behemoth* was little more than a crib sheet from James Heath's 1662 *Brief Chronicle of the Late Intestine Warr in the Three Kingdoms of England, Scotland, and Ireland*.[57] The work's originality as a philosophical history hinged entirely on its extended analysis of the deep religious roots of the war. The book's very title invoked a common Protestant allegory for Rome. Luther repeatedly characterized the papal "beast in the reeds" as "Behemoth," and church historians such as Thomas Fuller and Philip Mornay also referred to the "Behemoth of the Pope's Infallibility."[58] Hobbes's borrowing of the allegory poses few interpretive puzzles. Although *Behemoth* purports to offer a multipronged analysis of those parties who had rebelled against Charles I, Hobbes's early references to London merchants and

---

[56] Parkin 2007: ch. 5.

[57] *Behemoth*, 42–43.

[58] Seaward 2010: 60–65; Springborg 1995: 357–60.

common lawyers are not sustained.[59] Rather, the work offers a reductive account of the civil war, blaming it on the division of sovereignty between the "spiritual and temporal" authorities that had so exercised Hobbes in *Leviathan*.

This thesis is sustained with an extensive narrative of western church history, which consumes a great deal of the first book of *Behemoth*. In this text, Hobbes touches only briefly on the Jewish polity and its primitive Christian successor and instead foregrounds a caustic deconstruction of the so-called papal monarchy of the high Middle Ages.[60] Hobbes first offers a taxonomy of the various papal claims on "spiritual power" independent of sovereignty. Clerical legal exceptions, appeals and payments to Rome, jurisdiction over marital law (a "monopoly on women"), the power of absolving subjects of their secular obedience, the right to formulate canon law, excommunication, the power to define heresy—all were familiar targets for Hobbes's lash.[61] But for the first time he offered a narrative of their career as seditious inventions. Exploiting what had become a very familiar humanist-Protestant claim, Hobbes denied that Pope Sylvester, at the time of the Constantinian conversion, had enjoyed lordship over the emperor. Catholic historians such as Baronius and Bellarmine had by this time dropped reliance on the forged Donation of Constantine and the other False Decretals, but Hobbes did not pause to acknowledge this fact.[62]

Indeed, the extensive narrative of papal usurpation contained in *Behemoth* is marked, it must be said, by a polemical tone and by historical misrepresentations. Hobbes dates the papal monarchy to an early period, the eight century, when the people of Rome are said to have taken an oath of allegiance to the pope. It reached its peak in the centuries between the papacy of Leo III and Innocent III (misdated by Hobbes), during which time the papacy and the Carolingian dynasty—in Hobbes's reductive telling—struck an unhealthy alliance that chiefly empowered Rome. Coronations in "god's name," Hobbes wrote, became a dangerous point of ceremony easily exploited by the popes. The original practice of emperors gifting the papacy thus reversed itself, he argued, badly botching the historical details as he did so. For instance, Hobbes incorrectly asserted that Calixtus I, the third-century pope, allowed the clergy and people of Rome to grant him the papacy in the ninth century.[63] Hobbes's assault on the increasingly powerful papacy of the Gregorian era could be similarly clumsy with detail. Clerical celibacy, with a complex history dating back to the fourth century, is presented as a crude effort by Gregory VII to enlist "many lusty Batchelors at his service." Auricular confession to a priest is cast by Hobbes as an effort to awe men and "spy" on kings, and is cast as a Gregorian innovation based upon the dubious Protestant historical claim that earlier confession was performed in writing.[64] The doctrine of transubstantiantion, formalized by the twelfth century, is characterized by Hobbes as a "wanton . . . insult upon the

[59] *Behemoth*, 108–11.
[60] *Behemoth*, 112–13.
[61] *Behemoth*, 114–18.
[62] *Behemoth*, 119.
[63] *Behemoth*, 123, note 28.
[64] *Behemoth*, 124.

dullness" of the laity, designed to empower clergy with miraculous power.[65] More absurdly still, Hobbes's attack on seditious "ecclesiastical policie" presented the itinerant friars of the Franciscan and Dominican orders as naked efforts to empower Rome against civil powers.[66] Hobbes polemicized against the synthesis of Aristotelian philosophy and Christian theology as a system of intentional absurdity.[67]

Most striking in *Behemoth* is Hobbes's less than heroic account of the Reformation. That Hobbes was uninterested in it as a theological revolution is unsurprising. Perhaps more unexpected is his modest estimation of the Reformation as an assertion of Erastian power. Illustrating the master theory of religious change laid out in *Leviathan*, Hobbes attributed the Reformation to the scandals of priests and monks, to the desire of the laity for church wealth, and to Henry VIII's jealousy of his own power. The "doctrine of Luther" is given only passing mention. The campaign against Roman power was no doubt just, but Hobbes diminished the Reformation's achievement by quickly transitioning into a condemnation of Presbyterian sedition and the sectarian license bred by the Reformation more broadly. The Presbyterians sermonized for rebellion, in England and elsewhere, much "as the preaching Fryers had done." The Roman "cloak of Godlinesse" masking "impious Hypocrites" and rebels had been replaced by one of a Genevan cut.[68] In the Restoration context, however, it was Hobbes's blasts against the residual popery of the English bishops that carried the greatest sting. *Behemoth* blasted not just the pope but "bishops also in their severall Dioceses" for claiming power *jure divino*.[69] The book openly condemned Archbishop Laud's imposition of the Scottish prayer book and his provocative Arminianism.[70] Hobbes characterized the popular *Whole Duty of Man* (by the episcopal cleric Richard Allestree) as a seditious work claiming, like Presbyterianism, a "right from God immediately."[71] He cast aspersions on the loyalism of the episcopal Church of England during the civil war, suggesting that it had been more strategic than conscientious.

These passages offended the Restoration bishops, and when Charles I accordingly prevented the publication of *Behemoth*, Hobbes seems to have suppressed them. Nevertheless, they go some way toward explaining why a vast amount of the original material in *Behemoth* was cast as an ecclesiastical history of clerical usurpation, first papal, then Presbyterian and episcopal (particularly that considerable faction which viewed episcopacy as a matter of divine right and seemed insufficiently deferential to the royal supremacy).[72] Hobbes wished to both strike at his Restoration enemies and to maintain the thesis of his earlier writings, according to which uncontrolled church power generated civil wars across Christendom. His history of the civil war was thus

---

[65] *Behemoth*, 126.
[66] *Behemoth*, 127–28.
[67] *Behemoth*, 28–30, 160–64.
[68] *Behemoth*, 137–41.
[69] *Behemoth*, 113.
[70] *Behemoth*, 187–88.
[71] *Behemoth*, 168–71.
[72] Rose 2011: 148–62.

embedded within a long ecclesiastical history of post-apostolic Christianity. In this regard *Behemoth* certainly struck many Protestant notes, undoubtedly drawn from the confessionally oriented writings of Mornay, Foxe, Fuller, and others, and also from the humanist researches of Selden, Grotius, and their colleagues.[73] But the work was very far from a celebration of the Reformation. It is more accurate to say that it was a study of the failures of the Reformation in England and a cautionary tale on the perpetual dangers of clerical power. The sacred history of *Behemoth* thus extended the traditional Protestant theme of antipopery in radical directions.

Hobbes's most dedicated effort at ecclesiastical history went still further, breaking even more dramatically with standard Protestant historiography. His concerns about the supposed destabilizing effects of orthodox Christianity did not merely concern questions of church authority; they were also theological in nature. *Leviathan*'s inventive theology strove for a minimalism that would staunch public dispute and limit the number of necessary Christian doctrines. Among the theological "mysteries" that Hobbes sought to rationalize was the Trinity, which, as indicated above, was tendentiously interpreted through his understanding of "personisation."[74] Clerical critics of Hobbes, most notable Bishop Bramhall, had reacted with outrage. Denial of the Trinity was a dangerous business, and Hobbes formally, if grudgingly, retreated from his account when *Leviathan* appeared in Latin in 1668, thus ostensibly protecting himself from a charge of "obstinate" heresy.[75]

But again, Hobbes was not inclined to let the matter rest. His *Historia Ecclesiastica*, building on themes treated in Hobbes's heresy writings and in *Dialogue* on the common law, would in fact continue to advance a skeptical account of the Trinity. Instead of theological argument, Hobbes would now offer historical criticism, turning his attentions to the early church councils that had first formulated Trinitarian orthodoxy. This was a step few Protestant were willing to take. Luther had preserved the integrity of the first four church councils. Historical primitivism was useful to a point but could not be permitted to undermine Trinitarian orthodoxy. Hobbes's ecclesiastical history broke these constraints. It did so largely by casting doubt on the intellectual integrity of the Council of Nicaea and by offering a deconstructive account of the notion of heresy itself. This approach had been signaled in *Leviathan*, where "heresy hunting" was in general cast as a malignant pursuit by power-hungry clergy. Hobbes here blamed this on Innocent III, who at the fourth Lateran Council claimed that kings could be stripped of sovereignty if they failed to suppress heresy.[76]

What in *Leviathan* was evidenced with a passing historical allusion became a central focus of Hobbes's sustained historical narratives in the Restoration. Hobbes's "heresy" writings appeared in a rush after the year 1668: in an appendix to the Latin *Leviathan*

---

[73] Seaward 2010, notes at 120, 122–30, 132.
[74] Wright 1997, 497–528.
[75] *Leviathan*, 540–42.
[76] *Leviathan*, 93, 392.

(1668), in *An Historical Narration Concerning Heresy* (denied a license in 1668[77]), and in extended passages of both the *Dialogue on the Common Law* and *Behemoth*.[78] These texts have traditionally been read as defensive efforts on Hobbes's part, designed to shield himself from a heresy prosecution by undermining the statutory foundations of the legal prosecution of heresy in England and by denying heresy its traditional status as a common law offense.[79]

All of these texts, however, offer more than legal analysis. They are works of ecclesiastical history, and as such they build toward Hobbes's verse *Historia Ecclesiastica*. Together they allowed Hobbes to both undermine the very notion of heresy as a tool of clerical power and also to advance his attack on orthodox Trinitarianism by critically examining the history of its formation.[80] The extensive appendix to the Latin *Leviathan* and Hobbes's *Historical Narration Concerning Heresy*, both written by 1668, are in fact sustained narratives of ecclesiastical history. They begin by noting the Greek definition of heresy as "the doctrine of any sect," a neutral definition carrying no taint of falsity, which follows Diogenes Laertius and which Hobbes may have borrowed from the Jesuit Denis Pétau.[81] Hobbes then narrated the process by which that neutral definition was coopted by power-hunting mystery mongers. Heresy began its more insidious career as a marker of dangerous error, according to Hobbes, when sophistical Greek philosophers converted to Christianity and began to corrupt its simple claims. "In the early church down to the time of the Council of Nicaea, the doctrines over which Christians differed for the most part concerned the doctrine of the Trinity." An effort to suppress these quarrels led to the formation of an orthodox "catholic faith," after which "heresy" began to denote dissent from this sanctioned theology. "And so far as I have been able to ascertain from the works of the historians," wrote Hobbes, "this was the origins of the name 'catholic church,' and in every church the terms 'catholic' and 'heretical' are correlatives."

Hobbes then narrated how this process of orthodoxy formation was executed by the early councils. Nicaea was his focus, convened by Constantine to suppress the civil chaos unleashed by Arianism. But Nestorianism and Eutychianism (or monophysitism) are also mentioned, and Hobbes recounted the abuse of heresy hunting by the papacy as its power grew. He incorrectly dated papal infallibility claims to the seventh-century grant of papal primacy over the bishops by the Emperor Phocas. But few Protestants would have been given pause by his account of how Rome used the notion of heresy to persecute and execute pure Christians, from the Waldensians to the early reformers and Anabaptists. Many of them, however, would have dissented from his view that in England, after the Tudors had coopted the power of defining heresy and orthodoxy from Rome, the English Church's authority to punish heresy had lapsed

---

[77] *Correspondence*, 699.
[78] Cromartie 2005: liii–lviii.
[79] Milton 1993: 501–41; Tuck 1990: 153–71.
[80] Lessay 2000: 147–48.
[81] Tuck 1993: 133–34.

after the abolition of the Court of High Commission in 1641. That it was "inequitable that a man whose faith is chosen at his own peril only should be punished on the ground that his faith is erronerous" was an advanced tolerationist position in 1668, even in Protestant circles.[82]

What would really have alarmed Hobbes's Protestant readers, however, was his use of historical criticism to undermine the Council of Nicaea itself and to shred the intellectual coherence of creedal Trinitarianism. The Latin *Leviathan* generally presented Constantine's decision to punish heresy as an effort to ensure civil peace, an effort that was exploited by the clergy and even by Athanasius himself, who is chastized by Hobbes for being as "zealous in opposing the Emperor" as he was in pursuing truth. In his *Dialogue on the Common Laws* and his *Historical Narration Concerning Heresy*, both of which reiterate this ecclesiastical history of heresy and orthodoxy, Hobbes even more boldly suggested that the emperor at Nicaea had been "too indifferent" in the face of clerical efforts to complicate modest Christian theology with "arcane" Greek philosophy.[83] Constantine's implicit exercise of infallible theological judgment was permitted him in Hobbes's account of sovereignty, but Hobbes strongly suggests that the emperor had acted imprudently in deploying his authority on such nonsensical theological minutiae.[84]

These aspersions on the intellectual coherence of Nicaean Trinitarianism and on the seditious spirit of the clergy even during the great councils of the early church were extensions of standard Protestant historical primitivism into new and dangerous territory. Hobbes's defense of primitive church independency had angered episcopal and Presbyterian clergy, who did not appreciate being swept up in a critique of popery.[85] Now Hobbes's ecclesiological radicalism was joined by a theological radicalism, advanced against Trinitarianism and the early councils by way of a historical criticism that bored to uncomfortable depths.

This theological project was the central concern of Hobbes's most extensive effort at ecclesiastical history, the *Historia Ecclesiastica*. Perhaps begun as early as the 1650s (according to Aubrey), this verse history was complete by 1671.[86] It was published only posthumously but circulated as a manuscript and very much belongs to the intellectual context of the 1660s, when Hobbes began to deploy ecclesiastical history to assert, in coded fashion, doctrines that he could no longer argue openly.

The *Historia Ecclesiastica* is an extensive work impossible to fully summarize in the present context, but in broad terms it can be described as a critical and often lacerating reconstruction of the formation of orthodoxy during the primitive church. Ranging freely over pagan, Jewish, and Christian material, the work is reminiscent

---

[82] *Leviathan*, 521–27.

[83] *Dialogue*, 96; *Historical Narration*, 5–7.

[84] For Constantine as the watershed in Christian history, see Martinich 1992: 396.

[85] The significance of this aspect of *Leviathan* has been a matter of interpretive disagreement. See Martinich and Collins, 2009: 143–80.

[86] Springborg 2010: 86.

of the "universal histories" fashionable in the seventeenth century and composed by, among others, Hobbes's associates Edward Herbert (*De Religione Gentilium*, 1663) and John Aubrey (*Remaines of Gentilisim*, 1666).[87] Composed as a humanist dialogue the more easily to convey invective, the poem begins by setting forth the distinction of ancient "pure religion" and the "impossible system" of modern theology. Its theme is the history of these "empty dogmas," which are offensive to wisdom *sola scriptura* and are generated by fractious theologians, "for whom war is useful."[88] The design of such deceivers is to undermine the just spiritual authority of sovereignty.

No reader of *Leviathan* would have been surprised by this Erastianism or by Hobbes's theological minimalism and spite for scholastic theology. But the willingness of *Historia Ecclesiastica* to use these features of the Hobbesian system as weapons against ancient orthodoxy was dangerously new. The poem traced the corruption of truth to the ancient astrologers, who in Egypt learned to exploit "the stupidity of the people" by speaking for divinity and thus set up the perpetual war between priestly superstition and scientific reason.[89] The infection of mysticism worked its way to Assyria and Greece and then to Rome. In Greece emerged the "herd of Aristotle," and the schools of Epicurus, Plato, Zeno, Democritus, and Pyrrho.[90] What original wisdom these masters boasted was soon lost in the squabbling of their followers, which in turn spawned broader social and political divisions.[91]

Historia Ecclesiastica transitions to the Christian era without pausing a moment for pious celebration:

> At the time when the Paul the Evangelist spread the seeds of our salvation in Greek fields,
>   There was throughout the world the greatest abundance of false philosophers; the tide of wickedness was at the full.
>   The Holy Church called more than a few of them to her table.
>   The faith grew as a parasite.[92]

Hobbes argued that the Greek intelligentsia converted to Christianity for mere property and power and imported their squabbling and philosophical hair splitting into the church. The "holy Councils" were corrupted by these men, who struck dumb the "plain-spoken" Church Fathers. Vicious battles marred the councils: "To win was Catholic, to lose was heretical." Hobbes does not present the Constantinian conversion as a providential miracle but as a piece of stagecraft by an emperor aware that "Christians made outstanding soldiers."[93]

[87] Springborg 2010: 139–40.
[88] *Historia Ecclesiastica*, 305–7.
[89] *Historia Ecclesiastica*, 319–27.
[90] *Historia Ecclesiastica*, 345–49.
[91] Springborg 1994, 553–71.
[92] *Historia Ecclesiastica*, 355.
[93] Ibid., 360–63.

The Arian schism marred this *politique* achievement, and in narrating it Hobbes casts scorn upon the creedal formation of Trinitarianism. The dispute became violent, and Constantine wisely attempted to control it at Nicaea. "Amazed at the jealousy and ambition of these holy men," the emperor urged peace and compromise. The council instead suppressed Arianism with the "vain" rhetoric and "philosophical method of the Greeks," which only spread confusion and error.[94] Heresy, denoting punishable error, was thus born, and ages of violent upheaval with it.[95] The paradoxes of the Trinity became dogma, upheld by nonsensical Aristotelian notions of substance and essence, and punishments were devised for those who resisted this new intellectual order. The *Historia Ecclesiastica* was stunningly blunt in condemning Constantine for his failure to prevent this development. The "Nicene Church played the Sphinx" in order to "take sovereign power away from Kings." But it was the emperor's "heedless" mistake to concede the "Fathers rights to which they were not entitled." The insidious use of Hellenistic philosophy to supersede scripture "was the first step toward supremacy for the clergy who, from then on, see the Holy Scripture subordinated to their own opinions."[96] In the middle of a long exploration of the Nicaean Creed that was openly contemptuous of its philosophical coherence, Hobbes wrote: "What is Arius to us, what is Athanasius to us? Full salvation is found in the sacred texts alone."[97] Constantine had failed to see this, and his deference had made the church "double-headed by a double law of God, one law for souls, and another for bodies."[98]

The *Historia Ecclesiastica* thus launched into a history of papal usurpation and tyranny, detailing how the church undermined sovereigns and scourged heretics for centuries. These features of the work require less comment, as they followed in more standard Protestant tracks. The papacy filled the power vacuum created by the disarray of the Western Empire. New heresies arose and were suppressed by new councils. Scholasticism bound primitive religious truth and empowered the growing hierarchical power of Rome. These features of Hobbes's ecclesiastical history, however, are more briefly and vaguely told, covering material that he also narrated in *Behemoth*.[99] The proto-Protestants (Wylliffe particularly) are briefly noted, as is the "righteous Saxon" Luther, but Hobbes did not narrate the Reformation, and he again directs derision at the Presbyterians and episcopal-men.[100] The *Historia Ecclesiastica* was in no way a celebration of the Reformation, and if it shared with Reformation historiography a general model of primitive church purity and medieval church corruption, its critical apparatus cut much more deeply into the common core of an ancient orthodoxy that mainstream Protestantism had struggled mightily to protect.

---

[94] Ibid., 373.
[95] Ibid., 377.
[96] Ibid., 395, 449, 503.
[97] *Historia Ecclesiastica*, 377–81, 419; Springborg 2010: 228–35.
[98] *Historia Ecclesiastica*, 405.
[99] *Historia Ecclesiastica*, 525–63.
[100] Ibid., 571, 573, 577, 579.

With the *Historia Ecclesiastica*, Hobbes had composed a radical theological deconstruction implicitly hostile to Trinitarian orthodoxy. Its account of ancient Egypt and Greece seems to have borrowed heavily from Johann Clüver's 1645 *Historia totius mundi epitome a prima rerum origine usque ad annum Christi MXDCXXX*.[101] This work only briefly touched on the origins of papal corruption, for details of which Hobbes undoubtedly relied upon the standard Protestant historiography. This was not his poem's primary purpose, however, which was chiefly dedicated to exposing the philosophical corruption of Christian theology and the political machinations of the early councils.[102] Here Hobbes clearly relied upon the accounts of Eusebius and his Byzantine successors (Socrates Scholasticus seems to have been an important source).[103] The skeptical overtones of his account, however, owe less to the Eusebian tradition (though Eusebius was often suspected of Arianism) and more to his own broad skepticism of Greek philosophy and scholasticism. For some details of the Council of Nicaea Hobbes also likely relied on John Selden's partial translation of the annals of the Alexandrian Patriarch Eutychius.[104]

As a factual narrative, Hobbes's *Historia Ecclesiastica* is derivative and often unreliable. Its originality rested not on its researches but on its interpretive daring. Like *Behemoth*, it reasserted Hobbes's impolitic critique of "popery" without sparing Protestantism. Like Hobbes's heresy writings, it used historical critical methods to advance an anti-Trinitarian theology from which, in other writings, Hobbes had formally retreated. In both of these ways, ecclesiastical history allowed Hobbes space to assert his political and theological agenda under conditions of censorship. None of these texts was, in the event, licensed for publication. But Hobbes's expectation that they might be encouraged their composition, and the striking originality of the works ensured their circulation and survival.

Arnaldo Momigliano once wrote that it was "impossible to indicate the exact moment in which the history of the Church began to be studied as the history of a human community instead of a divine institution." He proposed the writings of Pietro Gianonne. Others have preferred Johann Lorenz von Mosheim's *Institutionum historiae ecclesiasticae* of 1755.[105] Thomas Hobbes typically does not figure in this discussion. He should. To read the sacred history in *Leviathan* or the *Historia ecclesiastica* is to be thrown into the milieu of the Enlightenment. The narrative arc of Hobbes's ecclesiastical history paralleled the Protestant and humanist historiography dominant in his era, and he shared the negative anti-Catholic agenda of this writing. The polemic purposes of his sacred history, however, more clearly prefigured the deism and anticlericalism of the early Enlightenment and more clearly served *politique* purposes rather than any project of confessional reform. The work was certainly read in this manner by the deist Charles

---

[101] Springborg 1996: 1075–78.
[102] Lessay 2000: 154.
[103] Martinich 1996: 281.
[104] Toomer 2009: 600–13.
[105] Momigliano 1990: 151.

Blount, who, in correspondence with Hobbes, reveled in the subversive account of the Nicene Council found in the *Historical Narration Concerning Heresy.*[106] So too did the German deist Christian Thomasius celebrate *Historia Ecclesiastica*, writing that "with it [Hobbes] has thrust his hand, so to speak, into the heart and bowels of the Pope, and has found out his hiding place better than anyone before him."[107]

Hobbes's ecclesiastical history strongly prefigured what J.G.A. Pocock has called the "Enlightenment narrative," which posited a post-Constantinian "Christian millennium" of "barbarism and religion" as a foil for the Enlightenment's own intellectual revolution.[108] Hobbes wrote sacred history in part to advance his theological innovations. But this history was also designed to provide a usable past that would help to justify the purposes and methods of modern sovereignty. Sovereignty, conceived of as an abstract Leviathan personating the wills of an atomized individuals and thereafter willing on their behalf, found its most powerful foil in the corporate religious culture of medieval Christendom. Disabling corporate religion as a source of either jurisdictional power or moral authority was a major purpose of Hobbes's political theory. As his career and notoriety advanced, that task was increasingly performed through historical writing. Hobbes, with implausible and relentless reductiveness, cast the post-apostolic church as the instrument of cheats at once tyrannical and seditious. A grand conspiracy of the clerics provided him with a theory of religious violence and civil war. This, in turn, served to justify the absolute intellectual and political authority of sovereignty on the one hand and, on the other, the prudence of theological minimalism and a certain degree of religious toleration. The shape of future liberalism can be glimpsed in these projects, and the future of liberal historical mythology in Hobbes's ecclesiastical histories.

BIBLIOGRAPHY

Primary Sources

Bacon, F. 1996. *A Critical Edition of the Major Works*, edited by Brian Vickers. Oxford, UK: Oxford University Press.

Hobbes, T. 1680. *An historical narration concerning heresie and the punishment thereof.* London.

Hobbes, T. 1889. *The Elements of Law Natural and Politic*, edited by Ferdinand Tönnies. London: Simpkin, Marshall and Co.

Hobbes, T. 1994. *Leviathan: With Selected Variants from the Latin Edition of 1688*, edited by Edwin Curley. Indianapolis, IN: Hackett.

Hobbes, T. 1997. *The Correspondence of Thomas Hobbes*, edited by Noel Malcolm. Oxford UK: Oxford University Press.

Hobbes, T. 1998 *On the Citizen*, translated by Richard Tuck and Michael Silverthorne. Cambridge, UK: Cambridge University Press.

---

[106] *Correspondence*, 759–63.
[107] Malcolm 2004: 532.
[108] Pocock 1999: 1–3.

Hobbes, T. 2005. *Writings on Common Law and Hereditary Right*, edited by Alan Cromartie and Quentin Skinner. Oxford, UK: Oxford University Press.

Hobbes, T. 2008. *Historia ecclesiastica:* critical edition, edited by Patricia Springborg, Patricia Stablein, and Paul Wilson. Paris: Honoré Champion.

Hobbes, T. 2010. *Behemoth, or The Long Parliament*, edited by Paul Seaward. Oxford, UK: Oxford University Press.

Reynolds, N., and Arlene Saxonhouse. 1995. *Three Discourses: A Critical Modern Edition of Newly Identified Work of the Young Hobbes.* Chicago: University of Chicago Press.

Selden, J. 1614. *Titles of Honor.* London.

Secondary Sources

Cameron, E. 1998. *Interpreting Christian History: The Challenge of the Churches' Past.* Oxford, UK: Oxford University Press.

Collins, J. 2005. *The Allegiance of Thomas Hobbes.* Oxford, UK: Oxford University Press.

Cross F. L., and Livingston E. A., eds. 1997. *The Oxford Dictionary of the Christian Church.* Oxford, UK: Oxford University Press.

Eisenach, E. 1981. *Two Worlds of Liberalism: Religion and Politics in Hobbes, Locke, and Mill.* Chicago: University of Chicago Press.

Eisenach, E. 1982. "Hobbes on Church, State, and Religion." *History of Political Thought* 2: 215–243.

Fahlbush, E. et al. 2001. *The Encyclopedia of Christianity.* Grand Rapids, MI: Eerdmans.

Grafton, A. 2007. *What Was History: the Art of History in Early Modern Europe.* Cambridge, UK: Cambridge University Press.

Hay, D. 1987. "Scholars and Ecclesiastical History in the Early Modern Period the influence of Ferdinando Ughelli," in *Politics and Culture in Early Modern Europe*, edited by Phyllis Mack and Margaret Jacob. Cambridge, UK: Cambridge University Press.

Johnston, D. 1989 "Hobbes's Mortalism." *History of Political Thought* 10: 647–663.

Kess, A. 2008. *Johann Sleidan and the Protestant View of History.* Hampshire, UK: Ashgate.

Knowles, D. 1963. *Great Historical Enterprises.* London: Thomas Nelson.

Lessay, F. 2000. "Hobbes and Sacred History," in *Hobbes and History*, edited by G. A. John Rogers and Tom Sorell. London: Routledge.

Lessay, F. 2004. "Hobbes's Protestantism," in *Leviathan after 350 Years*, edited by Tom Sorell and Luc Foisneau. Oxford, UK: Oxford University Press.

Levy, F. J. 1967. *Tudor Historical Thought.* San Marino, CA: Huntington Library.

Löwith, K. 1957. *Meaning in History.* Chicago: University of Chicago Press.

Malcolm, N. 2004. *Aspects of Hobbes.* Oxford, UK: Oxford University Press.

Malcolm, N. 2004. "Leviathan, the Pentateuch, and the Origins of Biblical Criticism," in *Leviathan after 350 Years*, edited by Tom Sorell and Luc Foisneau. Oxford, UK: Oxford University Press.

Martinich, A. P. 1996. "On the Proper Interpretation of Hobbes's Philosophy." *Journal of the History of Philosophy* 34: 273–83.

Martinich, A. P. 2003. *The Two Gods of Leviathan: Thomas Hobbes on Religion and Politics.* Cambridge, UK: Cambridge University Press.

Martinich, A. P., and Collins, J. 2009. "Interpreting the Religion of Thomas Hobbes: An Exchange." *Journal of the History of Ideas* 70: 143–180.

Milton, P. 1993. "Hobbes, Heresy, and Lord Arlington." *History of Political Thought* 14: 501–546.

Momigliano, A. 1990. *The Classical Foundations of Modern Historiography*. Berkeley: University of California Press.

Nelson, E. 2010. *The Hebrew Republic: Jewish Sources and the Transformation of European Political Thought*. Cambridge, MA: Harvard University Press.

Olson, O. K. 2002. *Matthias Flacius and the Survival of Luther's Reform*. Wiesbaden: Lutheran Press.

Paganini, G. 2003. "Hobbes, Valla, and the Trinity." *British Journal for the History of Philosophy* 11: 13–15.

Parkin, J. 2007. *Taming the Leviathan: the Reception of the Political and Religious Ideas of Thomas Hobbes in England, 1640–1700*. Cambridge, UK: Cambridge University Press.

Pocock, J.G.A. 1999. *Barbarism and Religion*: Volume 2. *Narratives of Civil Government*. Cambridge, UK: Cambridge University Press.

Pocock, J.G.A., 2003. *Barbarism and Religion*: Volume 3. *The First Decline and Fall*. Cambridge, UK: Cambridge University Press.

Pullapilly, C. K. 1975. *Caesar Baronius: Counter-Reformation Historian*. South Bend, IN: University of Notre Dame Press.

Rose, J. 2011. *Godly Kingship in Restoration England: the Politics of the Royal Supremacy*. Cambridge, UK: Cambridge University Press.

Schumann, K. 2000. "Hobbes's Conception of History," in *Hobbes and History*, edited by G. A. John Rogers and Tom Sorell. London: Taylor & Francis.

Sommerville, J. 2000. "Hobbes, Selden, Erastianism, and the history of the Jews," in *Hobbes and History*, edited by G. A. John Rogers and Tom Sorell. London: Taylor & Francis.

Springborg, P. 1996. "Hobbes and Cluverius." *Historical Journal* 39: 1075–1078.

Springborg, P. 1994. "Hobbes, Heresy, and the Historia Ecclesiastica." *Journal of the History of Ideas* 55: 553–571.

Springborg, P. 1995. "Hobbes's Biblical Beasts: Leviathan and Behemoth." *Political Theory* 23: 357–360.

Toomer, G. J. 2009. *John Selden: A Life in Scholarship*. Volume 1. Oxford, UK: Oxford University Press.

Tuck, R. 1990. "Hobbes and Locke on Toleration," in *Thomas Hobbes and Political Theory*, edited by Mary Dietz. Lawrence: University of Kansas Press.

Tuck, R. 1993. "The Civil Religion of Thomas Hobbes," in *Political Discourse in Early Modern Britain*, edited by Nicholas Phillipson and Quentin Skinner. Cambridge, UK: Cambridge University Press.

Whitaker, M. 1988. "Hobbes's View of the Reformation." *History of Political Thought* 9: 45–58.

Wright, G. 1999. "Hobbes and the Economic Trinity." *British Journal for the History of Philosophy* 7: 397–428.

PART V

HISTORY, POETRY, AND PARADOX

CHAPTER 24

....

HOBBES'S THUCYDIDES

....

KINCH HOEKSTRA

HISTORY, in Hobbes's day, was not primarily about the past.[1] Even ancient history was used to grasp the present and form the future. Scores of prominent figures, from Niccolò Machiavelli (1469–1527) to Justus Lipsius (1547–1606) and beyond, had influentially undertaken to reach the decision-making elites by appealing to the wisdom of the ancient historians. Ideas of the similarity of different eras or of patterns of human actions over time were broadly accepted in renaissance and early modern Europe, and made history an effective lever in contemporary politics. A pattern's applicability through time, and therefore its relevance for the present, was more powerfully confirmed by more ancient sources, which were also imbued with authority by a regard for the exceptional wisdom of the ancients. Yet Hobbes was famously emphatic that reading classical texts generated disastrous effects: rebellions and seditions, including the English Civil War, were provoked by the reception of "these Greek, and Latine Authors."[2] Scrutiny of Hobbes's Thucydides shows that when he undertook the edition

[1] I have presented versions of this account a few times over the course of more than a decade, at the Faculty of Classics at the University of Oxford, the Lorenzo Valla Group at the University of Tokyo School of Law, the Early Modern Sodality at Berkeley, the Political Philosophy Colloquium at Princeton University, the Yale University Political Theory Workshop, and, finally, as a public lecture in Justus Lipsius Zaal, Erasmushuis, at KU Leuven. I am grateful to my hosts on these occasions, including Akira Koba, Kentaro Matsubara, Philip Pettit, Bryan Garsten, and Johan Olsthoorn. Audiences on each occasion provided substantial feedback. I would like to single out for thanks Charles Beitz, Teresa Bejan, Stefan Eich, Daniel Garber, Nicholas Gooding, Victoria Kahn, George Kateb, Melissa Lane, Amy Rabinowitz, Ethan Shagan, Joshua Vandiver, Rosemarie Wagner, and Samuel Zeitlin.

[2] Thomas Hobbes, *Leviathan* (Hobbes 1651), 21.9, 111: "And by reading of these Greek, and Latine Authors, men have from their childhood gotten a habit (under a false shew of Liberty,) of favouring tumults, and of licentious controlling the actions of their Soveraigns . . . with the effusion of so much blood; as I think I may truly say, there was never any thing so deerly bought, as these Western parts have bought the learning of the Greek and Latine tongues." Cf. Hobbes, *The Elements of Law* (Hobbes 1969), 2.8.10, 2.8.13, 2.9.8; *De cive* (Hobbes 1983), 12.3; *Leviathan*, 29.14, 170–171; 31.41, 193; 46.11, 369–370; 46.18, 372–373; 46.31–32, 376; 46.35–36, 377–378; *Behemoth* (Hobbes 2009), 110, 137, 164–166, 179–180, 198, 232, 322.

he nonetheless believed that ancient history could also serve as a weapon *against* war. The present power of the past could be marshaled to promote a more peaceful future.

Hobbes's edition of Thucydides has been seen as the culminating accomplishment of a humanist phase that ended in 1630. Most interpreters thus either set aside the work to focus on Hobbes's later philosophical doctrines or argue for its connections with those ideas. Those of the latter who have focused on the political theory have generally read his Thucydides either in light of Hobbes's later focus on civil war and the state of nature or as undertaken primarily to provide an indictment of democracy.[3] Those who have focused on the theory of (what we have come to call) international relations have most often taken both authors to propound a kind of realism or *Realpolitik*, usually emphasizing Thucydides' Melian Dialogue and Hobbes's claim that commonwealths permissibly act toward one another as individuals do in the natural condition of war. I aim in this chapter to cast light on a few related matters, including Hobbes's concern with the relation between commonwealths and his view of wars of expansion, his analogy between individuals and commonwealths, the evidence for and the nature of his humanism, and why he undertook and published a translation of this ancient historian when he did.[4]

---

[3] His much later autobiographies may seem to say as much, although at least the prose life ties the anti-democratic motivation to why he published it around 1628 rather than why he undertook it years earlier. In his prose life, Hobbes writes: "Of the Greek Historians Thucydides delighted him most, and having translated him into English little by little in his free time . . ., around 1628 he brought it out in public; so that the folly of the Athenian Democrats would be revealed to his fellow citizens." (*Thomae Hobbes Angli Malmesburiensis philosophi vita* (Hobbes 1681), 3: Inter Historicos Graecos Thucydidem prae caeteris dilexit, & vacuis horis in sermonem Anglicum paulatim conversum . . ., circa annum Christi 1628. in publicum edidit; eo fine, ut ineptiae Democraticorum Atheniensium concivibus suis patefierent.) In his verse life, he says: "And then I turn to our Histories, to *Greek*, and to *Latin* ones; I also frequently read Poems. *Horace, Vergil,* and *Homer* I came to know, Euripides, Sophocles, Plautus, Aristophanes, and more, and many Writers of Histories; but *Thucydides* pleased me above the rest. He taught me how foolish Democracy is, and how much wiser one Man is than an Assembly. I brought it about that this Writer would speak to the *English*, so that they would shun the Rhetoricians they were about to consult."

> (*Thomae Hobbesii Malmesburiensis vita* (Hobbes 1679), 4:
> Vertor & ad nostras, ad *Graecas,* atque *Latinas*
> Historias; etiam Carmina saepè lego.
> *Flaccus, Virgilius,* fuit & mihi notus *Homerus,*
> *Euripides, Sophocles, Plautus, Aristophanes,*
> Plures, & multi Scriptores Historiarum;
> Sed mihi prae reliquis *Thucydides* placuit.
> Is Democratiam docuit me quam sit inepta,
> Et quantum Coetu plus sapit unus Homo.
> Hunc ego Scriptorem feci ut loqueretur ad *Anglos,*
> Consultaturi Rhetoras ut fugerent.)

The meaning at the end is uncertain. "Consultaturi" may bear the sense that the English were facing deliberations or decisions, and the specific meaning may be that Parliament was about to meet.

[4] I provide here an interpretation of some elements of Hobbes's prefatory materials and some relevant political contexts in which he undertook his edition; I will lay out elsewhere an interpretation of further factors, including Hobbes's practice of translation and his relation to earlier readings of Thucydides.

We will better understand what Hobbes aimed to do with his edition if we focus on the context of its creation—the 1620s rather than the civil war of the 1640s—and this will in turn encourage us to discern aspects of the later works that have been neglected.

1 Monarchy, Aristocracy, and Democracy

As secretary to one of the most prominent noble families in England, Hobbes would have wanted this edition to establish his name in the front rank of the humanists of the day, which required a demonstration of skill. Translations of Greek and especially Latin classics had proliferated in the previous decades, with a focus on the historians.[5] As a latecomer, Hobbes perceived how to stand out nonetheless: he would translate a classical author never before translated from Greek into English, one renowned for the difficulty of his language and the profundity of his wisdom.

There can be little doubt, however, that Hobbes had further purposes. Given his insistence that the classical works that circulated so widely in his day incited disobedience and war, his participation in the classicizing culture of renaissance translation is remarkable.[6] He evidently believed that Thucydides might provide an ancient antidote to this ancient disorder. Understanding Hobbes's political purposes will help explain why (beyond a claim that he had not yet discovered his scientific interests or deductive method) he chose to intervene through history and translation, and not by philosophy or open precept. It will also clarify why Hobbes would have been content with a full and faithful translation rather than making his Thucydides into a thoroughgoing Hobbesian by selection and construal. We should be careful, however, not to assume that Hobbes himself was a thoroughgoing Hobbesian by the 1620s. Using what we know of Hobbes's later concerns to determine what is of interest in his Thucydides risks distortion, although some degree of corroboration can be gained by demonstrating that an interpretation is consistent with later works.

---

[5] For example, there had been English translations of Caesar by Golding (1565); Polybius by Watson (1568); Appian by W. B. (1578); Plutarch by North (1579); Herodotus by Rich (1584); Tacitus by Savile (1591) and Grenewey (1598); Livy (1600), Pliny (1601), Suetonius (1606), and Ammianus Marcellinus (1609) by Holland; Josephus by Lodge (1602); Sallust by Heywood (1608); Lucan by Gorges (1614); and Florus by Bolton (1618).

[6] Hobbes's indictment seems sweeping but was evidently limited to certain texts or the misuse of others. His own practice indicates that history and classics were and remained particularly worth reading. John Aubrey's section on "*His bookes*" runs as follows: "He had very few bookes. I never sawe (nor Sir William Petty) above halfe a dozen about him in his chamber. Homer and Virgil were commonly on his table; sometimes Xenophon, or some probable historie, and Greek Testament, or so" (Aubrey 1898: 1:349). Hobbes could more readily make do with few books in his own rooms because he could draw on (and order books for) the Cavendish library, which was rich in works of history and classics (see esp. Hardwick MS E1A, a library catalogue compiled by Hobbes around 1630).

Thucydides presents the Peloponnesian War as a struggle between democratic and oligarchic or aristocratic polities, so it is striking that Hobbes reads Thucydides as force-fully rejecting both of the dominant alternatives. "For his opinion touching the gouern-ment of the State," Hobbes says, "it is manifest that he least of all liked the *Democracy*."[7] And yet when "the *Few*" govern, according to Hobbes's Thucydides, "euery one desireth to be chiefe" and bristles at feeling undervalued—"whereupon sedition followeth, and dissolution of the gouernment."[8] Hobbes admits in passing that Thucydides praised the government of Athens "when it was mixt of the *Few* and the *Many*"; but he detects in the text a preference for monarchy, a form of government that is at the most in the background of Thucydides' narration.[9] Interpreters have been tempted to smile at Hobbes's monarchical and anti-democratic Thucydides, as if the monarchist could not help from falling into patent anachronism in his picture of ancient Athens, or as if the classicizing humanist did not notice the absurdity in thinking that democracy was a real threat in 1620s England.

When translating, Hobbes reasonably renders a famous passage about Pericles as the idea that, while Athens was in name a democratic state, it was in fact a government of the principal man. In his prefatory materials he pushes this further, saying that Thucydides particularly commends the government of Athens when it was "in effect *Monarchicall* vnder *Pericles*," so that it appears that "he best approued of the *Regall Gouernment*."[10] For Hobbes to offer a work he interprets as touting monarchy at the expense of aristoc-racy and democracy might seem like a predictable stance, especially under a monarch. But it is not an entirely straightforward move for Hobbes, who undertakes this work while in the employ of the second Earl of Devonshire, a prominent aristocrat, and dedi-cates it to the third Earl of Devonshire after the death of his father (identifying himself as "Secretary to the late Earle of Deuonshire" on the illustrated title page). The opening of the edition, a few short pages after this dedication, may seem an inauspicious place for Hobbes to offer a criticism of aristocracy (or to offer an interpretation of the work being presented as critical of aristocracy). This is one puzzle posed in the early pages of the edition and signals to readers that they should consider the context of monarchy, as well as problems with both aristocracy and democracy. And this setting highlights the potential complexity of someone in Hobbes's position: according to Hobbes's theory (at least in later works), he is required to obey the employer he has agreed to serve, but he must also and above all obey the monarch, ultimate master of both master and servant.

Hobbes's substantive account of Thucydides' criticism of democracy is itself more focused on the destructive effects of competition between political leaders than a dis-missive account of the ignorant rabble. He says that Thucydides "noteth the emula-tion and contention of the Demagogues, for reputation, and glory of wit; with their

---

[7] Thucydides, *Eight Bookes of the Peloponnesian Warre*, translated by Thomas Hobbes (London, 1629), sig. A1v. Citations of this work to signature rather than page are all to Hobbes himself.

[8] Ibid., sig. a2r.

[9] Ibid., sig. a2r.

[10] Ibid., sig. a2r; cf. *Eight Bookes*, 117 (Thucydides 2.65.9).

crossing of each others counsels to the dammage of the Publique" and "the inconstancy of Resolutions, caused by the diuersity of ends, and power of Rhetorique in the Orators; and the desperate actions vndertaken vpon the flattering aduice of such as desired to attaine, or to hold what they had attained of authority and sway amongst the common people."[11] Here, too, the problem is that the leaders compete for glory, pursue their private ends, and advocate inconsistent and reckless policies so long as they can win the people's favor with them. Hobbes presents a Thucydides who is not directly concerned about democracy as mob rule, but about elite competition that leads to sedition and civic dissolution, and especially about leaders who disregard the public good and promote a foolish policy of war that leads to the downfall of the commonwealth.

Such is the primary political problem that Hobbes himself underlines in his prefatory materials. Because the great problem that is the focus of Hobbes's later political philosophy is civil war or sedition, interpreters have been quick to emphasize Thucydides' powerful description of *stasis* or civil war in Corcyra as especially Hobbesian,[12] to wonder whether Hobbes read the entirety of the account of the war itself as a civil war among Greeks, to suppose that he was influenced by the account of the primitive condition of Greece as a kind of natural condition of conflict, or to emphasize the expressions within Thucydides about peace being the greatest good and sedition the greatest evil. Such themes are surely suggestive, and Thucydides may have engaged or influenced Hobbes in one or more of these ways. Yet Hobbes himself does not seem to have underlined these lessons in his edition. Nor should this be surprising when we consider that the English situation in the 1620s, although characterized by fierce partisan debate (especially about whether England should intervene abroad), is not one of sedition or imminent civil war. Nor is democracy an important political program when Hobbes takes up his Thucydides; nor are those rare radicals who might identify their political ideals as democratic a likely audience for his edition.[13] It is, however,

---

[11] Ibid., sigs. a1v-a2r.

[12] So Richard Schlatter in his edition adds just two remarks of his own to his selection of Hobbes's marginal comments: one is to say that the Athenians in the Melian Dialogue "talk as if they had read Hobbes!"; the other is to suggest of the Corcyraean stasis that the passage is "pure Hobbes and might have come from the pages of *Leviathan*" (Schlatter ed. 1975: 582, 580). With the coming of civil war, Hobbes's translation of the Corcyra episode loomed larger than when it first appeared. For example, John Potts, Member of Parliament for Norfolk from 1640 to 1648, is especially taken with the work for its vivid description of stasis, repeatedly marking it out in his copy of the 1634 edition for emphasis (copy offered for sale by Lux & Umbra, South Jordan, Utah; consulted July 24, 2011). I set aside for now the civil war context of Hobbes's Thucydides, for example, the intriguing copy of the 1634 edition signed (and presumably acquired) by the Earl of Strafford sometime between being made earl on January 12, 1640, and being executed on May 12, 1641 (sold at Bonhams, Oxford, September 10, 2013: sale 20706, lot 329). Hobbes lays out his view of the importance of Strafford's trial in *Behemoth*, 191–204.

[13] The criticism of democracy is prominent in the prefatory materials, and is too large a theme to address here in addition to the implicit criticism of unnecessary war. A satisfactory account of what Hobbes's Thucydides says about monarchy, democracy, and aristocracy requires consideration of details about the complex and changing politics of court and parliament in the 1620s, especially as they relate to Hobbes's patrons—including the contexts of the 1620 *Horae Subsecivae*, the Virginia Company,

a situation in which the policies of the British monarch are hotly contested, and given Hobbes's support for the Thucydidean monarch, it may be illuminating to identify those policies. We are used to thinking of Hobbes's context as that of the English Civil War, and this is importantly true even for the works of the Restoration, all written in the shadow of that war. But it should be obvious that this is not the relevant context for his projects in the 1620s, and proceeding as if it were is likely to lead to misconceptions.[14]

2 THE CLASSICS AND PREVENTIVE WAR

Hobbes's edition of Thucydides was registered with the Stationers' Company on March 18, 1628, a process that normally involved submission of a substantially complete manuscript. It bore the date 1629 when published, but was already published by the first day of that year.[15] Before this, at least the translation itself remained in effectively finished but unpublished form for a long time. Some sentences (and maybe much more) in the prefatory materials must have been written later, closer to the time of publication, and a letter from Hobbes of November 6, 1628, shows that the dedicatory epistle was not complete until then.[16] In his epistle to the readers, Hobbes is as vague about the length of the delay as he is about its motivation: "After I had finished it, it lay long by mee, and other reasons taking place, my desire to communicate it ceased."[17] Given the length of normal publication

the Forced Loan, and much else. I will provide a reading of the edition in light of these matters elsewhere.

[14] The one event from the 1620s that several writers have pointed to as a likely stimulus for Hobbes's undertaking is the Petition of Right. The Petition was not proposed in Parliament until May 1628, by which time the protracted process of translation would have been finished. While the Petition and the events directly leading up to it could not have been the motivation for the project, they may help to explain the timing of the eventual publication and some of the prefatory content.

[15] The register for "18° Martij 1627" (i.e., 1628 New Style) records that Henry Seile "Entred for his Copie . . . A booke Called The Historye of THUCIDIDES in English by Master HOBBS" (Arber 1877: 4:161). Noel Malcolm notes that there is a copy of the 1629 edition in Dr Williams's Library, London, which is inscribed by Samuel Harrison as a gift from Hobbes on January 1 of that year (Malcolm 2007: 11 n. 44). January 1, 1629 Old Style would be January 1, 1630 New Style, but Harrison effectively removed this possibility by first writing "1628."

[16] Thomas Hobbes, The Correspondence, ed. Noel Malcolm (Hobbes 1994), 1:6. For examples of what must have been written some time after the work of the translation, presumably close to the time of publication, see the passages from the prefatory materials quoted in the following sentence and in the next note.

[17] Thucydides, Eight Bookes, sig. A4r; see also sig. A4v, where Hobbes says: "[I] haue therefore at length made my Labour publike . . ." (emphasis added). (When quoting from sections of early modern books set in italic type as the default with roman type used for emphasis and proper names (notably "To the Readers" (sigs. A3r–A4v) and the speeches in Eight Bookes), I reverse this convention for clarity and consistency.) Note that Hobbes says in his prose autobiography that he translated Thucydides in his spare time, gradually ("& vacuis horis in sermonem Anglicum paulatim conversum": Thomae Hobbes Angli Malmesburiensis philosophi vita, 3, emphasis added). Note also the distinction there between the process of translating the work and the later date of publication, which reflects the distinction at Eight Bookes, sig. A3r, between the reasons for which he "vndertooke this Worke at first" and those for which he has "since . . . publish[ed] it."

delays, Hobbes must be talking about many months of delay and quite possibly a few years or more. Considering the immensity of the task, there can be little doubt that he must have *undertaken* it several years before 1628.[18] So let us go back five years, dividing that period into the last years of the reign of James I and the first years after the accession of Charles I to the throne.

Before the failure of the Spanish Match between Prince Charles and the Infanta Maria (sister of King Philip IV of Spain) in October of 1623, the plan for such a match had been passionately and popularly denounced, and public opinion ran high for war with Spain. After the failure of the match, Charles and Buckingham, the first minister, took up positions at the head of the anti-Spanish bloc, and the salient political situation of England until the death of James I at the end of March 1625 was one of tension between the King's attempt to keep his policy of peace with Spain broadly in place and the clamorous demands by the Prince and the first minister, most parliamentarians, and the most vocal segments of the citizenry for an all-out attack.

When Protestant rule of the Palatinate crumbled and fell (1622–1624), such an intervention into the European wars was presented in pamphlet after pamphlet as necessary to defend not only the true religion, but also England itself from what was repeatedly portrayed as an otherwise inevitable takeover by Spain. Francis Bacon banged on this drum as loudly as anyone, especially when his primary audience was Charles or Buckingham, and he appealed to a range of classical Greek sources in doing so. In his 1624 *Considerations Touching a Warre With Spaine*, addressed to Charles, Bacon argued that England must wage war with Spain "not for the *Palatinate* onely, but for *England, Scotland, Ireland,* our *King,* our *Prince,* our *Nation,* all that we haue." Bacon says that to show that a war on foreign soil is tantamount to self-defense, he must prove "that a *iust Feare,* (without an Actuall Inuasion or Offence,) is a sufficient Ground of a *War,* and in the Nature of a true *Defensiue*."[19] He thus appeals to authority:

> [I]t is good to heare what time saith. *Thucydides*, in his *Inducement* to his Story of the great *Warre* of *Peloponnesus*, sets downe in plaine termes, that the true Cause of that *Warre* was; *The ouergrowing Greatnesse of the Athenians, and the feare that the Lacedemonians stood in thereby*; And doth not doubt to call it, *A necessity imposed vpon the Lacedemonians of a Warre*: Which are the Words of a meere *Defensiue*.[20]

Also in 1624, John Reynolds, from what he mistakenly thought was the safety of France, exhorts Parliament to tell old King James "that old *Pericles* made the greatnesse of his

---

[18] Noel Malcolm's judgment that Hobbes's translation "was *completed* several years before its publication in 1628" may overstate (Malcolm 2002: 73, emphasis added); but this must be closer to the mark than the suggestion that Hobbes had yet to finish the translation when Cavendish died in 1628 (Malcolm 2002: 8, which is thus best understood as referring to the edition as a whole).

[19] Bacon 1629: 12.

[20] Bacon 1629: 13, referring to Thucydides 1.23.6; Bacon goes on to quote "what time saith" according to a longer excerpt from the Latin translation of book I. For further context for this reading of Thucydides, see Hoekstra 2012: 25–54.

generositie and courage, to reuiue and flourish on his Tombe, when hee caused the *Athenians* to warre vpon the *Pelloponessians*. . . . Tell him that to transport Warre into *Spaine*, is to auoide and preuent it in *England*."[21] Bacon looks to Thucydides' Sparta and concludes that England should go to war with Spain; Reynolds looks to Athens and comes to the same conclusion.

So long as James was still on the throne and the official royal policy was that of a prudent peace, writers used classical texts as a cloak that simultaneously revealed the intention behind their publication and yet provided plausible cover for the person responsible for it.[22] That some such cover as translating another author was required to criticize policy about Spain is underlined by James's repeated proclamations aimed specifically against writing and speech on such policy. In a proclamation of December 24, 1620 (drafted by Francis Bacon), James is moved by the intensity of calls for a war-like stance toward Spain "straitly to command" all of his subjects, "from the highest to the lowest, to take heede, how they intermeddle by Penne, or Speech, with causes of State, and the secrets of Empire, either at home, or abroad," and requiring them to call any such discourse they witness to the attention of an officer of state within 24 hours.[23] Promising that offenders will be "seuerely punished," James gave specific motivation for any such cover to be deep by warning that he will not be fooled by those who use "faire, and specious" language or "fine, and artificiall glosses, the better to give passage to the rest of their imputations, and scandalls."[24] In manifest exasperation, he reissues this proclamation some seven months later, adding language to prohibit "couering, or concealing such unfitting Discourse."[25] James even warned Parliament on multiple occasions not "to meddle with matters of gouernment, or mysteries of State, namely matters of Warre or Peace," and particularly strategy toward Spain.[26]

Consider three translations. A 1623 translation of Demosthenes' First Philippic, entitled *Against Philip of Macedon, the Potent and Politicke enemy of the State of Athens,*

---

[21] [Reynolds] 1624, sig. B1v. According to the ODNB, his 1624 pamphlets so annoyed James that he had Reynolds extradited from France and imprisoned.

[22] Authors who challenged royal policy regarding Spain could be denied publication or punished, and the licensing system could be deployed to discourage or carefully control publication that might be perceived as reflecting on that policy. So, earlier in James's reign, when Adam Islip wished to publish Edward Grimeston's translation and continuation of Louis Turquet de Mayerene's *The generall historie of Spaine* (London, 1612), this was only allowed on condition "that euerye sheete is to be by Master Etkins revised [i.e., reviewed as it was printed] and by Aucthority allowed." The delivery, scrutiny, and retrieval of each of the 354 printing sheets slowed the production process to nearly four years (Williams 2013: 70).

[23] James I 1620. Bacon's role is detailed in Spedding 1874: 7:151–156. The one letter in Hobbes's correspondence that predates that containing the dedicatory epistle to his edition of Thucydides is from Robert Mason, dated December 10, 1622; Mason here suggests both that Hobbes is very interested in England's foreign policy, and that he is very wary about writing in a vein that could be taken to be meddling with *arcana imperii* (Hobbes, *Correspondence* 1:1–4).

[24] James I 1620. See James's warning against treating "mysteries of state" "vnder colour" of "a faire shew of respect": James I 1621b: 7.

[25] James I 1621a (dated July 26).

[26] James I 1621b: 40.

presented Philip, potent and politic enemy of Athens, as stand-in for Philip IV of Spain, potent and politic enemy of England.[27] Demosthenes warns the English that Philip "is not able to hold himselfe satisfied with the quiet enioying of those places hee hath already subdued, but still hee compasseth and reacheth after further matters, and while yee vse delayes, doth encircle you on euery side, and doth as it were spreade his nettes round about you."[28] "And shall we then waite and attend his pleasure?" asks Demosthenes: "Shall we not embarke our selues? Shall we not goe foorth with some part of our owne souldiers now at last . . . shall we not set sayles into his Countrey?"[29]

Also in 1623, John Bingham translated Xenophon's "*Historie*." Bingham addresses his work to the captains and citizens "exercising Armes in the Artillerie Garden of London" and begins with a misleading denial: "I doe not present this Translation unto you, to the end to incite you to Militarie cogitations." This is true, Bingham clarifies, only because "[y]our forwardnesse that way is such alreadie, as rather deserueth commendation, than requireth any mans words of incitement or exhortation."[30] Bingham quickly turns to say that his Xenophon is meant "to present unto you in your owne Language, a Precedent of Warre of another nature, than you have hitherto beene exercised in": in particular so that they may ready themselves for "a long and dangerous March" through the territory of different enemies—presumably through to the Palatinate.[31] To this work, Bingham appends without explanation a translation of the concluding section of *De militia romana*, a commentary on Polybius by Justus

---

[27] Demosthenes 1623. The editor is Thomas Gokin, but he makes clear in his preface that he did not translate the work. A translation of Demosthenes by Thomas Wilson was used for a similar purpose under Elizabeth, as the title makes clear: *The three Orations of Demosthenes chiefe Orator among the Grecians, in fauour of the Olynthians . . .: with those his fower Orations titled expressely & by name against king Philip of Macedonie: most nedefull to be redde in these daungerous dayes, of all them that loue their countries libertie, and desire to take warning for their better auayle, by example of others.* See, e.g., sigs. π4v, *iir, and **iir-v of Demosthenes 1570. On this work as a thinly veiled argument for a more aggressive policy against Philip II, see Strype 1725: 1:619–620; Sullivan 2004; and Blanshard and Sowerby 2005.

[28] Demosthenes 1623: 6. Philip IV had pursued an aggressive policy since taking the throne in 1621, in particular by renewing the war against the Dutch.

[29] Demosthenes 1623: 20. A similar parallel is drawn throughout *An Experimentall Discoverie of Spanish Practises, or The Covnsell of a well-wishing Souldier, for the good of his Prince and State* (1623, reprinted the following year as *A Trve Sovldiers Covncel*), e.g. at 25–27: "Surely, my gracious Soveraign, I am of opinion against *Phillip* of *Spaine*, in the behalfe of my *Countrie*, as that noble Common-wealths man *Demosthenes*, against *Philip* of *Macedon* in behalfe of the *Athenians*; which no doubt hath much affinity with our case at this time . . .And therfore since that like examples, whilst the world doth last, will bring forth like effects, I will be of *Demosthenes* minde; if since we cannot shunne the warres with *Spain*, either at this time, or hereafter, when he hath made himselfe more strong; either by the conquest of his neighbours, or otherwise: that you should begin with him whilst you haue the advantage of him; and then you shall by proofe finde how profitable it will be unto you; when you must needs doe a thing, to doe it with a courage and cheerfulnesse, and forasmuch as there is no man of another minde, but that we shall haue the King of *Spaine*, by so much more our mighty enemy, the greater Princes suffer him to be. Oh why be we so backward, or why linger you oh noble King . . . ?"

[30] Xenophon 1623, sig. [A1?r]. Bingham's dedicatory epistle is dated May 16, 1623.

[31] Ibid., sig. [A1?v].

Lipsius.[32] This might seem an antiquarian curiosity, but in context it is far from it: this work was seen to show the relevance of Roman military discipline and operations for modern armies (the explicit theme of the translated section), and the string of spectacular military victories by Prince Maurice of Orange (Maurits van Oranje-Nassau) against Spain from 1589 until the Twelve Years' Truce in 1609 was attributed in part to his deployment of this Polybian model.[33] The background is the peril of Spanish subjugation, and the implicit but clear promise is of military success despite the preponderance of Spanish power. Despite his earlier claim not to be using ancient history as an exhortation to war, Bingham thus leaves his readers with a practical call to emulate these ancient military examples: "I exhort againe that they be put in practise."[34]

The subtitle of Thomas Barnes's 1624 translation of Isocrates' *Archidamus*, to turn to the third example, was *The Covncell of Warre*. This unmistakably referred to the ten-member Council of War constituted in April 1624 in anticipation of war with Spain, as James began to concede ground to Parliament, Charles, and Buckingham.[35] Barnes explains that "the noise I now heare of preparation for warre, hath made these his Arguments, and whole discourse not only to run in my minde, but also to run out at my pen," but then denies the suggestion that he is "medling in Orations that concerne politique affaires" by claiming that his task "is only . . . construction of Phrases, not application of Histories."[36] Even as he marshals classical authority for a definite and public purpose, the translator wishes to retain plausible deniability. Yet the simple message that Barnes has his Isocrates communicate to an English audience is that the time has come to "prepar[e] for warre" and the choice is simple: "either aduancement or ruine."[37] A famous context for Hobbes's later political thought is the use of the classics to make the anti-monarchical case for a republic and even for revolution or civil war; an important context for Hobbes's translation of Thucydides, however, is that even his

---

[32] Ibid., sigs. V2r–X3v.

[33] See Hahlweg 1987, Oestreich 1953, and Fiedler 1985: 140–153.

[34] Xenophon 1623, sig. X3r. For more on Bingham, see Lawrence 2009.

[35] On this Council, see Young 1989.

[36] Isocrates 1624, sig. A3v-[A4r]. The parallel with the need to take up arms to liberate the Palatinate is obvious, but it is made fully explicit only in a brief marginal indication toward the end of the work (sig. D3r). In the text, Archidamus argues that they should be ready to abandon their city: "not vnlike those armies which consist of mercinary forces whose trade is nothing but warre. Moreouer hauing no certaine Cittie of abode, able to liue without houses in the open field, rouing vp and downe throughout all countries . . . and thinke all places which are fit for warre to bee their habitation and natiue Countrie." The marginal comment here (one of only three in the work, and which may have been added by the printer rather than by Barnes) is: "A discription of Mansfieds Army." This refers to Ernst von Mansfeld, at this point the primary beneficiary of the new war subsidy, who had arrived in England in April with perhaps 7,000 German soldiers and was recruiting and preparing for an ill-fated expedition to fight through to the Palatinate. James insisted that the force should focus solely on the Palatinate rather than getting involved in conflicts in the Spanish Netherlands, while Buckingham had considerably greater ambitions for the mission. Few of the roughly 12,000 English soldiers who joined Mansfeld's expedition ever made it back to England, and the high (and worse than futile) expenditure of Parliamentary funds was blamed on Charles and Buckingham.

[37] Ibid., sig. A3v.

monarchical countrymen were busy weaponizing classical authors and deploying them in favor of foreign war.

In 1624, James began to give way to the more warlike policy favored by the new Parliament, outspoken members of the public, and his son, and this shift in policy was secured by the accession of Charles to the throne in late March 1625. But things changed when Charles and Buckingham had their way, lurching into what were touted as preventive attacks on the Continent that would bolster England's reputation and aid her allies. Two naval expeditions proved especially important both for England's strategic position in Europe and how they were received at home. One was a calamitous attack on Spain in 1625, at Cádiz; the other was a disastrous attack on France in 1627, when Buckingham invaded the Île de Ré. Both were ignominious routs that led to disproportionate loss of life and a precipitous decline in England's international standing.[38] Although activist members of Parliament and the public had been clamoring for such actions for years, Buckingham was held responsible for the failures and was, by the end of 1627, the most reviled man in England. The defeats and Charles's way of trying to mend them swung both people and Parliament against him in an opposition that came to a head only with the advent of civil war.[39] In the nearer term, they led to England's withdrawal from the Thirty Years' War and the signing of peace treaties with both France and Spain. By late 1628, Charles was committed to peace with France, having earlier that year resolved to make peace with Spain.

Five years earlier the situation was different, and Hobbes found himself in an awkward position. Not only were the heir apparent and the royal favorite advocating war with great Continental powers; Hobbes's employer William Cavendish was allied with this war party, as was Francis Bacon, for whom Hobbes was also working during these years.[40] Despite being pushed hard to abandon detente with Spain, however, his sovereign was committed to a policy of peace and security that rejected unnecessary wars (a position we know Hobbes endorsed in his later writings). What to do?

3 SECRET INSTRUCTION

Hobbes claims that Thucydides is the greatest of historians. "For the *principall* and *proper worke* of History, [is] to instruct, and enable men, by the knowledge of Actions

---

[38] The failed second siege of Saint-Martin-de-Ré left some 5,000 dead of the English force of 7,000; losses from the Cádiz Expedition were still higher. Another utter failure was Charles's endeavor from 1625 to assist the efforts of the Danes in northern Germany with 4,000 English troops.

[39] Hobbes observes that in the "Grand Remonstrance" by Parliament in late 1641, the first three complaints against Charles I were that he dissolved earlier parliaments, undertook the "fruitlesse expedition against Cales" (i.e., Cádiz), and abandoned the Palatinate: *Behemoth*, 216.

[40] On Cavendish, see Malcolm 2007: 87–88. Malcolm's perspicacious paragraph constitutes the only discussion I know that plausibly connects the Thucydides edition with the politics of the Thirty Years' War.

past, to beare themselues prudently in the *present*, and prouidently towards the *Future*," and Thucydides does this best: "there is not extant any other . . . that doth more fully and naturally performe it."[41] But in what way does Hobbes think that Thucydides will instruct and enable men to act with prudence?

Hobbes explicitly argues that Thucydides' teaching is implicit. He tells us that in Thucydides "the History it selfe" instructs not by "discourses inserted" but by "the contexture of the Narration."[42] This suggests that Hobbes finds Thucydides' instruction for the present and the future not so much in the author's reflections or in claims made in the speeches—the nearly exclusive sources for those who have ascertained a moral or political teaching in the text—but in Thucydides' account of what *happens* in the course of the history. Thucydides' teaching, according to Hobbes, is to be found in what is "meerely narratiue."[43] It cannot be captured by extracting *sententiae*, for the moral of the story is in the story itself.

Hobbes emphasizes that Thucydides' history has a unity as a whole and should be considered as a single body.[44] Doing so shows that Thucydides criticizes the Athenians "by the necessity of the narration, not by any sought digression. So that no word of his, but their own actions do sometimes reproach them. . . . So cohaerent, perspicuous and perswasiue is the whole Narration."[45] Hobbes approves of Lipsius' commendation of Thucydides for "euery where secretly instructing, and directing a mans life and actions."[46] This echoes Hobbes's own previous judgment: "open conueyances of Precepts (which is the Philosophers part) he neuer vseth, as hauing so cleerely set before mens eyes, the wayes and euents, of good and euill counsels, that the Narration it selfe doth secretly instruct the Reader, and more effectually then possibly can be done by Precept."[47] What, then, is Thucydides' secret instruction? And if Hobbes has discerned it, why does he not tell his readers what it is?

As we have seen, Hobbes believes that attention to Thucydides' unfolding narrative of the actions of the war reveals the folly of the Athenians. Against Dionysius of Halicarnassus, Hobbes argues: "men profit more by looking on aduerse euents, then on prosperity. Therefore by how much mens miseries doe better instruct, then their good successe, by so much was *Thucydides* more happy in taking his Argument, then *Herodotus* was wise in chusing his."[48] That the kernel of instruction is what his readers can learn from the "euents, of good and euill counsels" and the Athenian actions that result in failure and misery suggests that it is precisely the calamity for Athens of

---

[41] Thucydides, *Eight Bookes*, sig. A3r.

[42] Ibid.

[43] Ibid.

[44] Ibid., sig. a4r.

[45] Ibid., sigs. a2v-a3r.

[46] Ibid., sig. b1r. Cf. Lipsius 2004: 732: occulte ubique instruens, actiones vitamque dirigens.

[47] Thucydides, *Eight Bookes*, sig. a3r; see sig. A3v. See also a4v: "*Marcellinus* saith, he was obscure on purpose, that the Common people might not vnderstand him. And not vnlikely; for a wise man should so write (thogh in words vnderstood by all men) that wise men only should be able to commend him."

[48] Ibid., sig. a3v.

the naval expedition to Sicily (and the overall calamity of the war for all of Greece) that makes Thucydides an instructor for human benefit. Hobbes thought that the way that the narrative of Thucydides' history could instruct the readers of his own edition was to call attention to the kind of disaster that must be avoided by a polity that wishes to survive and ensure the well-being of its people. And the cause of such disaster is a kind of ambitious and imprudent overreaching, anatomized in most detail in Thucydides' account of the leaders' desire for personal glory and benefit despite the risks to the public, and the heedless popular fervor for extending the war.[49] Hobbes's reader is presented with a stark existential warning against a naval expedition against a powerful enemy, undertaken with the claimed justification of checking the power of a putative threat, relieving distant allies, and recapturing collective glory. Ashamed to heed "timerous suggestions" in public deliberations about such a matter, people prefer to believe in their invincibility at the outset, and are thus destroyed. Faced with such a prospect, Hobbes puts before his audience the case of Athens' error and downfall and advises them to listen to the counsel of fear.[50]

Hobbes says that he made a mistake, however, when he assumed that those to whom he first presented his Thucydides would approve of what he approved when reading him: "in this errour peraduenture was I, when I thought, that as many of the more iudicious, as I should communicate him to, would affect him as much as I my selfe did."[51] Identifying Hobbes's "errour" here is key to understanding a primary purpose of his edition, the reason he decided not to publish it, and why he later reversed this decision.

In the opening of his edition, Hobbes makes clear that his general purpose in translating the text of Thucydides was to provide "profitable instruction for Noblemen, and such as may come to haue the mannaging of great and waighty actions."[52] The noble and influential are supposed to learn something from this English Thucydides about taking action of great import. Hobbes had served as a tutor to William Cavendish, second Earl of Devonshire, and his tuition of the third earl (also named William Cavendish) suggests that those lessons included a careful study of ancient historians. Using ancient history for didactic purposes would thus have been a straightforward extension of Hobbes's role as tutor in the Cavendish family.

As mentioned earlier, Hobbes writes that after he had finished his edition, "it lay long by" him, and "other reasons taking place," his "desire to communicate it

---

[49] Thucydides 6.8–24.

[50] Thucydides, *Eight Bookes*, sig. a1v: "For a man that reasoneth with himselfe, will not be ashamed to admit of timerous suggestions in his businesse, that he may the stronglyer prouide; but in publique deliberations before a Multitude, Feare, (which for the most part aduiseth well, though it execute not so) seldome or neuer sheweth it selfe, or is admitted. By this meanes it came to passe amongst the Athenians, who thought they were able to doe any thing, that wicked men and flatterers draue them headlong into those actions that were to ruine them."

[51] Ibid., sig. A3v. In the very short list of Hobbes's admitted errors, this seems to be the earliest extant. It may be on his mind when, writing in 1628 about his epistle dedicatory to Thucydides, he expresses concern that "I may faile, through ignorance to do what I entend" (Hobbes, *Correspondence* 1:6).

[52] Ibid., sig. A2r.

ceased." He begins the next sentence with the word "For," signaling that he is providing an explanation for his earlier decision to withhold his Thucydides from the press:

> For I saw, that, for the greatest part, men came to the reading of History, with an affection much like that of the *People*, in *Rome*, who came to the spectacle of the *Gladiators*, with more delight to behold their bloud, then their Skill in Fencing. For they be farre more in number, that loue to read of great Armies, bloudy Battels, and many thousands slaine at once, then that minde the *Art*, by which, the Affaires, both of Armies, and Cities, be conducted to their ends.[53]

This suggests that Hobbes wanted his Thucydides to communicate lessons about accomplishing the proper ends of military and political activities, and that what he wanted to accomplish with his edition was frustrated or undermined by his first audience having reacted with enthusiasm to Thucydides' portrayals of "bloudy Battels, and many thousands slaine at once."[54]

The political situation shifted significantly in these years, which is also relevant to the possibility that Cavendish or other members of Hobbes's target audience failed to understand the point of his Thucydides or indeed reacted in a way contrary to his purposes.[55] This fits well with Hobbes's observation that those he had hoped would be interested in learning political and military prudence instead read the history like people excited by bloodlust. As Isaac Casaubon had remarked in the preface to his 1609 edition of Polybius, "history lights the flame of emulation"[56]; this may have proved true despite Hobbes's self-conscious attempt to use history to extinguish the flame of misguided ambition. Perhaps, that is, the early readers charged with great and weighty actions whom Hobbes hoped to influence did not get the message, but were swept away (as others since have been) by the narrative of the Peloponnesian War despite the arc of that narrative. It seems that their appetite for war was whetted rather than diminished by reading of the ambitions of noble Pericles and his famous fellow Athenians. In that case, Hobbes's desire to communicate his edition any further would have been undercut.

By 1628, however, when Hobbes went forward with the publication process, there was hardly a war party to speak of, and peace with the Continental powers was again

---

[53] Ibid., sig. A4r.

[54] If there is a particular referent of "many thousands slaine at once," it is very likely to be the casualties from the terrible Athenian defeat in Sicily. This would further suggest that Hobbes's error was about how his readers would react to the Sicilian expedition and its aftermath.

[55] Less plausible (especially given Hobbes's account of how his initial readers reacted without minding the arts of war and politics) is that Cavendish or Bacon or others *understood* the point that Hobbes was making with his Thucydides, but, rather than being swayed, they took exception to Hobbes's attempt to inhibit their aims. Such men had great influence and indeed authority over Hobbes and could have required him to suspend the project as contrary to their own aims or judgment.

[56] Polybius 1609, sig. aiiiir: flamma aemulationis accenditur.

the ascendant royal policy.[57] And the reversal of popular feeling and political will in the wake of the calamitous setbacks of Cádiz and the Île de Ré meant that readers were not going to read of the rise and fall of Athens without acute attention to the fall and how that fall was (even according to Thucydides' own judgment) a consequence of foolish military ambition.[58]

England's ambitions were also chastened by the plague that devastated London in 1625–1626. Any English reader of that time would have been gripped by Thucydides' celebrated account of the plague that broke out in Athens at the beginning of the second year of the war.[59] Both calamities turned people's eyes from what they might gain by war to what they had lost or stood to lose by disease. The contrast is drawn sharply in an account from 1625, in which the author writes about England's recent imperial ambitions that "All these Castles were built in the Ayre." "We swallowed vp nothing but the *East* and *West-Indies* in our Imaginations" before the disaster struck: "the Golden-Age was comming in agen: Our English Almanacks seem'd to speake of none but Holy-daies: *Great-Brittaine* stood on the toppe of her white Cliffes triumphing." But then "Heauen saw vs boasting in our owne strengths, and growing angry at it, hath turnd it into weakenesse." "Neuer was such a sudden Ioy changed into so sudden a Lamentation," continues the author, and "those Belles which were ready to cleaue the Ayre with echoes at King *Charles* his Coronation, did nothing presently but ring out Knelles for his Subiects . . . so that in 13 weekes more then 33000. haue falne dead to the ground at their dolefull tunes."[60] This was not a wild figure, for a recent study estimates mortality in London in 1625 at a staggering rate of more than 20 percent.[61]

This author is writing in response to a work by Thomas Dekker, but on the catastrophe of the plague the two are in complete agreement. Dekker vividly describes how "in many Church-yards (for want of roome) they are compelled to dig Graues like little Cellers, piling vp forty or fifty in a Pit."[62] "The Bells euen now toll, and ring out

---

[57] Although there was broad consensus against military adventuring abroad by late 1628 (by which time Bacon, Buckingham, and the second Earl of Devonshire were all dead), an English Thucydides could stand as a warning in the future. Like Thucydides' own text, it could become "a Monument to instruct the Ages to come" (*Eight Bookes*, sig. a2v). And if provided with a suitably monarchical twist, the edition could also count as an intervention in the domestic political situation of 1628, characterized by roiling disputes that threatened the stability to be realized by obedience to the monarch.

[58] There is a hint that even forty years later Hobbes may still associate the disaster of Cádiz with his reading of Thucydides: in *Behemoth* (147), he draws a parallel between the failure of the third Earl of Essex (vice-admiral at the attack on Cádiz in 1625) despite the "fortunate expedition to Cadiz" by his father the second Earl of Essex in 1596, and the failure of Asopius in 428 BCE in commanding the Athenian fleet near Naupactus despite the success of his father Phormio, who had defeated the Spartans at Naupactus the previous year (see Thucydides 2.80.1–2.103.1 with 3.7.1–5). Hobbes takes these cases to illustrate the foolishness of relying on such insubstantial grounds for belief in "successe in Warre."

[59] Thucydides 2.47–59.

[60] *The Run-awyaes Answer, To a Booke called, A Rodde for Runne-awayes* (1625), sigs. [A4?v]-B1r.

[61] Slack 1985, esp. p. 151. This is out of a total London population of 206,000 (a figure that seems to exclude outparishes). Cf. Creighton 2013: 1:660. London accounted for roughly half of the plague deaths. From 1624 to 1625, there was a more than sevenfold increase in burials (Slack 1985: 146).

[62] Dekker 1625, sig. C1v.

in mine eares, so that here againe and againe I could terrifie you with sad Relations," Dekker writes. "Death walkes in euery street: How many step out of their Beds into their Coffins? And albeit no man at any time is assured of life, yet no man (within the memory of man) was euer so neere death as now: because he that breakes his Fast, is dead before Dinner."[63] Dekker, picking up a theme common in the 1625 plague litera-ture, frames the whole of his treatment in terms of this reversal of expectations, England now being the one that is subject to a kind of overwhelming military invasion—by God himself. As the 1620s progressed, a warning against military adventuring abroad was less likely to make a practical difference but more likely to be heard and approved.

There is substantial evidence that Hobbes's views, both when he undertook his edi-tion and later, were at odds with the positions of the war party, which, for a few fer-vent years, was led by Buckingham and Charles and stridently supported by Bacon's pen.[64] Despite close relations with and dependence on prominent members of this party, Hobbes used his edition of Thucydides to caution against its policies. His criti-cism of the leaders who flattered the people's pride in their commonwealth and thereby drove the Athenians "headlong into those actions that were to ruine them" is stoked by present passion: it sets up a parallel between the Athenians' disastrous invasion of Sicily and the new war party's proposals to intervene on the Continent, and particu-larly to venture against Spain. Pericles tells the Athenians early in the war that they may hope for victory so long as "you doe not . . . striue to enlarge your dominion, and vndergoe other voluntary dangers"; Hobbes comments that "*Thucydides* hath his mind here, upon the Defeat in *Sicily*, which fell out many yeares after the death of *Pericles*."[65] Had the Athenians continued to follow the more conservative policy of the leader whom Hobbes characterized as a wise monarch, they would have been saved. They instead chose danger abroad and followed the counsel of Pericles' glory-seeking ward, Alcibiades, which led to their total defeat.[66] So it is that Thucydides presents Hobbes's readers with the "euents, of good and euill counsels."

Another (potentially complementary) explanation for Hobbes's unwillingness to publish his translation once it was finished is that he may have already subscribed to his "doctrine of doctrines," which prohibited publication that contradicted a law or

---

[63] Ibid., sig. C4r.

[64] Bacon reveals that his late efforts were not commissions from Buckingham so much as attempts to curry favor with him when he wryly writes at the end of 1625: "My wants are great; but yet I want not a desire to do your Grace service, and I marvel that your Grace should think to pull down the monarchy of Spain without my good help" (Spedding 1878: 2:617).

[65] Thucydides, *Eight Bookes*, p. 78 (Thucydides 1.144.1).

[66] An echo of Hobbes's audacious use of Thucydides to counsel against the desired course of his patrons may be present in a letter of a decade later, when he writes to the Hon. Charles Cavendish (1620–1643), son of the second Earl of Devonshire and brother of the third, in a moralistic and dehortatory tone: "that I say is rather counsayle for the future then reprehension of any thinge past. Which I shall leaue to your choyce to weigh as the humble aduice of a servant, or to laugh at it, or call me foole or Thucidides for my presumption" (August 22, 1638, *Correspondence* 1:52). It is worth noting that Hobbes was no longer narrowly obliged as a servant to the Devonshires during the last stages of composition, having been dismissed from service after the second Earl's death in June of 1628.

other sovereign pronouncement.[67] Once James I had died—and quite possibly already from the time of the concessions that James made in 1624 under pressure to roll back his pacifist policy—the message of Hobbes's Thucydides was in tension with sovereign policy. That Hobbes again changed his mind about publication by 1628 would be explained by the fact that Charles had by then pulled in his horns. On this account, Hobbes's changes of mind were due to an unchanging commitment to support changing sovereign policy. It is also worth considering how Hobbes's decisions about publication—to produce his Thucydides, then to shelve it rather than publish it, and then to publish it—fit in with the theory articulated in his later works that one has a natural law obligation to promote peace so long as it does not put one's own self-preservation at risk.

4 A HOBBESIAN THUCYDIDES

But is to read Hobbes's Thucydides as discouraging a military expedition abroad to accept that it is inconsistent with his later works? The law of nature means that there are norms even in Hobbes's state of nature, but these allow and even require one to do what one can to preserve oneself, including attacking others preventively. "And from this diffidence of one another, there is no way for any man to secure himselfe, so reasonable, as Anticipation," as he puts it in *Leviathan*; "that is, by force, or wiles, to master the persons of all men he can, so long, till he see no other power great enough to endanger him: And this is no more than his own conservation requireth, and is generally allowed."[68]

Alberico Gentili and Francis Bacon had both cited Lipsius' view that the Belgians are the bulwark of Europe against a Spanish onslaught and that for England to fight with them against the Spanish should thus be construed as a kind of self-defense.[69] They both relied on a range of ancient Greek sources to back up their more general view that there can be no peace so long as another is able to cause us harm, and a similar view is prominent in Hobbes's work. In the words of his 1640 *Elements of Law*:

> For there is little use and benefit of the right a man hath, when another as strong, or stronger than himself, hath right to the same. Seeing then to the offensiveness of man's nature one to another, there is added a right of every man to every thing, whereby one man invadeth with right, and another with right resisteth; and men live thereby in perpetual diffidence, and study how to preoccupate each other; the estate of men in this natural liberty is the estate of war.[70]

---

[67] See Hoekstra 2006, esp. 35–60.
[68] Hobbes, *Leviathan*, 13.4, 61.
[69] Gentili 1598: 127 (1.16); Bacon 1629: 26.
[70] Hobbes, *Elements of Law*, 1.14.10–11.

And Hobbes takes a decisive further step. Whereas Bacon joined Gentili and Grotius in insisting that war cannot legitimately be based on "vmbrages, light Iealousies, [or] Apprehensions a farre off," Hobbes arguably drops all objective criteria, evidently requiring only that the person or commonwealth who anticipates a threat does so in service of his or its own perceived preservation.[71] Even the bellicose Bacon holds that to justify prevention he must spend much of his time showing that an attack on Spain would meet the moral and juridical requirement that the cause of England's fear is of a kind that would constitute compulsion, the (ultimately Aristotelian) test of which is whether the fear would unnerve a person of firm character or a resolute government.[72] Hobbes, by contrast, argues that for a sovereign "to make War upon another like Soveraign Lord, and dispossess him of his Lands . . . is Lawful, or not Lawful according to the intention of him that does it. For, First, being a Soveraign Ruler, he is not subject to any Law of Man; and as to the Law of God, where the intention is justifiable, the action is so also."[73]

Hobbes provides some support for the view that the timorous or rash person, or the sovereign with a wild view of what is needful, attacks with as much right as the courageous or the prudent. In the final words of his *Elements of Law*: "For that which is the law of nature between man and man, before the constitution of commonwealth, is the law of nations between sovereign and sovereign, after."[74]

There can be little doubt that Hobbes drew on Thucydides in setting up what we might call the *problem* of early modern political theory, this "estate of war" characterized by preventive attack and general hostility. Hobbes is helped by the historian, and perhaps by the readings of Gentili and Bacon and others, to go further than they had in proposing that war is the natural condition of interaction between both individuals and commonwealths. There are surely many ways in which Thucydides may have influenced Hobbes, including the development of his scientific approach, a confirmation of the fruitfulness of treating human nature as constant, and an insistence on a hard-headed account of motivations. Furthermore, a number of Hobbes's predecessors

---

[71] Bacon 1629: 13. See Hoekstra 2008. It may mislead, however, to say that for Hobbes there is no objective standard here. On the one hand, he sometimes invokes standards, such as having to be according to reason, without suggesting that they can be met by belief or intention alone (see, e.g., the traditional standards mentioned in n. 73, below). On the other hand, the requirement of a particular belief or intention is itself an objective one (legitimacy depends on the objective truth that there is a kind of subjective perception).

[72] Bacon 1629: 13, 21–30. Cf. Aristotle, *Nicomachean Ethics* 3.6–9; Aquinas, *Scriptum super Sententiis* 4.29.2.

[73] Thomas Hobbes, *Dialogue of the Common Laws* (Hobbes 2005), 135–136. Note that Hobbes deploys terms from the just war tradition in going on to specify what can qualify an intention as lawful, including necessity of subsistence, response to irreparable injuries received, and provision for one's security based on a just cause of fear. (And *salus populi* is another such term.) Hobbes makes clear earlier in this work that preventive war can be justified in some circumstances. "[U]pon the sight, or apprehension of any great danger to his People; as when their Neighbors are born down with the Current of a Conquering Enemy," a sovereign may send soldiers "to help those weak Neighbours by way of prevention, to save his own People and himself from Servitude" (*Dialogue*, 22–23).

[74] Hobbes, *Elements of Law*, 2.10.10; cf. *Leviathan*, 30.30, 185.

were struck by Thucydides' account of primitive lawlessness in which violence was seen to be legitimate,[75] and Hobbes's conception of the state of nature probably owes something to this account of early Greece. And Hobbes's understanding of the logic of the state of nature—the logic of prevention or anticipation that makes it a state of war—itself emerges from a tradition of Thucydides interpretation. Not least, the lesson of "how much mens miseries doe better instruct, then their good successe"[76] may help to explain one of the most striking features of Hobbes's political philosophy, which is that he gives pride of place to the miseries of war in the state of nature rather than the felicity that follows from the peace of commonwealth.

It is thus easy to sketch a realist tradition going back to Hobbes and through him to Thucydides, or to highlight realist passages from Thucydides as Hobbesian.[77] But to do so is misleading. Richard Tuck, for example, has emphasized the passage where Thucydides says that the war was caused by the growth of Athenian power and the fear this caused, and that in which the Mytilenians say that they are entitled to attack Athens in self-defense even without any precedent injury caused them by the Athenians; and he has suggested a related linking of Thucydides, Bacon, and Hobbes.[78] Tuck concludes that, "given the striking resemblance in almost every particular" between Bacon's 1624 piece promoting war with Spain "and the views which Hobbes expressed in his later works, it is hard not to believe that Hobbes actually drafted the treatise for his master," for whom he worked as an amanuensis during this period. He goes on to suggest that the translation of Thucydides itself probably grew out of his association with Bacon and that through this association Hobbes was "involved in the campaign for a war with Spain in the early 1620s."[79]

Hobbes did work for Bacon in or near the period in which the latter wrote his hawkish *Considerations*. But Hobbes's later works, as we shall see, do not match up with Bacon's argument in this piece. And it is consistent with Hobbes's theory of servanthood that, if he had a hand in that work, it was directed by the master, and the guiding purpose is clearly Bacon's.[80] Moreover, it is precisely the deployment of Thucydides

---

[75] For several examples, see Hoekstra 2012: 28.

[76] Thucydides, *Eight Bookes*, sig. a3v.

[77] See note 12 on the Hobbesian Athenians at Melos, and Wootton 1997. A misreading of Hobbes has arisen from a misreading of Hobbes's Thucydides that is based on a misreading of Thucydides. And vice-versa. So Wootton takes Hobbes's engagement with Thucydides as evidence that Hobbes was a Machiavellian because he assumes that the unblinking advocacy of power politics that the Athenians provide in the Melian Dialogue is "Hobbesian" (228) and because he limits Thucydides to that dialogue. (Wootton fixates on the Melian Dialogue and never mentions any other part of Thucydides: see 210, 211, 216, 228, 237, 241.) Reducing Thucydides to 5.84–116 and assimilating Hobbes to the Athenian position therein leads Wootton to the indefensible conclusion that, "[l]ike Machiavelli, Hobbes believes that commonwealths must pursue expansionary foreign policies" (232).

[78] Tuck 1999: 23 (citing Thucydides 1.23 and 3.12.2–3) and 127. Although there are important further elements to his interpretation of Hobbes in this work, Tuck here tries to fit Hobbes into his version of a Weberian thesis that the modern idea of rights developed from the justification of European expansionism (ibid., esp. 14–15, 109–139).

[79] Tuck 1999: 127 (and n. 53), 128. Richard Schlatter similarly suggests in his edition of the work that Hobbes may have turned to Thucydides at Bacon's suggestion (Schlatter ed. 1975, xxvii).

[80] Hobbes's fidelity is what Bacon prizes. Hobbes is surely one of the "good pens which forsake me not" who—as Bacon writes to Tobie Matthew in mid-1623, when Matthew is with Charles and

in the *Considerations* that makes it much *less* likely that Hobbes was meaningfully involved in its composition. For Bacon here quotes Thucydides in and translates him from Latin, not Greek, and the Latin does not come from the edition that Hobbes used.[81] Although Tuck's view that Hobbes drafted this treatise for Bacon is unlikely, it is probable that Hobbes would have read it once it was drafted (whether he would have had it via Cavendish or directly from Bacon). Given the timing, some kind of influence by Bacon on Hobbes's work on Thucydides can be reasonably assumed, but this does not imply agreement or approval.

We can be reasonably sure of Hobbes's involvement in one specific work of Bacon's because John Aubrey reports that Hobbes translated the essay "Of the true Greatnesse of Kingdomes and Estates."[82] And what Hobbes faithfully translated included, in the English, this: "A Civill Warre, indeed, is like the Heat of a Feaver; But a Forraine Warre, is like the Heat of *Exercise*, and serveth to keepe the Body in Health."[83] It is tempting to correlate Hobbes's own ideas with Bacon's, for Hobbes will later state that humans naturally seek ever greater power, and that commonwealths may licitly act toward one another as individuals do in the natural condition. That preservation in the state of nature may require a constant effort to expand dominion has led numerous interpreters to the conclusion that Hobbes is an exceptionally unrestrained imperialist.[84]

Buckingham in Spain—are translating versions of some of his works into Latin (he mentions *The Advancement of Learning, Henry the Seventh*, and the *Essays*: Spedding 1874: 7:429). Hobbes is proud to tell Aubrey that Bacon frequently employed him—along with "his servant Mr. Bushell"—"in this service" of "sett[ing] downe his present notions," and that Bacon "was better pleased with his *minutes*, or notes sett down by him, then by others who did not well understand his lordship" (Aubrey 1898: 1:83; cf. 1:331).

[81] It is doubtful that Hobbes would have drafted the quotations from (the beginning of) Thucydides in the *Considerations* after having begun his translation, given that there are no clear verbal echoes between the English translation of Thucydides in each and no indication that the person who penned the *Considerations* even referred to the Greek. Moreover, although Hobbes is explicit that he relies from the outset of his translation on the 1594 Portus edition of Thucydides as the best available (*Eight Bookes*, sig. A4r), Bacon uses a different edition. The Latin quoted by Bacon (Bacon 1629: 13–14) is very close to Valla's Latin as it is found in most editions through that of the Stephanus edition of 1588 (Thucydides 1588: 17) and markedly different from the revision in the Portus edition of 1594 (Thucydides 1594: 17). Not least, Bacon's essential move here is to gloss Thucydides' account of the cause of the war as "A necessity imposed vpon the Lacedemonians of a Warre: Which are the Words of a meere Defensiue" (cf. at n. 20, above), whereas Hobbes makes nothing of necessity or defense in providing his own gloss (*Eight Bookes*, sig. a4v).

[82] Aubrey (Aubrey 1898: 1:83 and 1:331) remembers this (or perhaps the shorter 1612 version, entitled "Of the greatnesse of Kingdomes") as the essay "of the Greatnesse of Cities," which echoes in the beginning of Hobbes's translation of Thucydides (*Eight Bookes*, 2 re. "greatnesse of Cities") and in turn echoes Botero (whose work is listed by Hobbes in the Hardwick library catalogue of about 1629 (MS E1A) as "of the Greatnesse of Citties"—presumably Botero 1606, *A Treatise, Concerning the causes of the Magnificencie and greatnes of Cities*).

[83] Bacon 1985: 97. See Bacon 1609: 32 and Bacon 1619: 43: "Bella enim generosa, Proditiones degeneres & turpes" or "Warres are gener[ous] and heroicall, but Treasons are base and ignoble." Cf. Bacon 1629: 21–22, where he considers whether a foreign war can be an effective preventive medicine or cure for civil war.

[84] Hans Morgenthau and Hannah Arendt were two of the most influential advocates of this view. See Morgenthau [1948] 2005: 66–67 and 235–239; Arendt [1951] 1968, esp. 17–23. See also note 77, above.

But Hobbes does not share Bacon's enthusiasm for foreign war or the expansion of empire. We must remember that Hobbes lays out the problem of the war of anticipation in order to persuade readers of his solution: the condition of war is what must be overcome by obedience to authority. Parties in the natural condition may seek their own preservation, but natural law forbids them from exercising their power gratuitously at their own or others' expense. Even in the arena of relations between commonwealths, where he sees no prospect of a common authority, Hobbes strikes a cautious note, especially about the pursuit of conquest. Unlike Grotius, his emphasis in doing so is on the threat of such an enterprise to self-preservation, but this warning does have a moral element for Hobbes, too. Although the right of nature allows an individual or a state to do whatever it judges necessary to preserve itself, it does not excuse unnecessary harm. The law of nature, which is the moral law, forbids an individual to engage in wanton cruelty, for example, or a commonwealth to acquire by force anything it does not judge necessary for its proper end.

Hobbes is as wary of expansion and foreign wars as Bacon is keen. In *The Elements of Law*, Hobbes says that the sovereign is required by the "supreme law, *salus populi*" to look after the defense of the subjects, and he insists that this is a twofold mission. On the one hand, defense consists of "the obedience and unity of the subjects," which requires "the means of levying soldiers, and . . . money, arms, ships, and fortified places in readiness." This Hobbes is well-known, although it is worth noting that this militarization is explicitly defensive. On the other hand, defense of the subjects consists "in the avoiding of unnecessary wars." For violating their obligation to look after the safety of the people and for foolishly doing that which is likely to lead to their own destruction, Hobbes condemns "such commonwealths, or such monarchs, as affect war for itself, that is to say, out of ambition, or of vain-glory, or that make account to revenge every little injury, or disgrace done by their neighbours."[85]

The most popular way to characterize Hobbes's theory of international relations is to take as emblematic the analogy he draws between individuals in the natural condition and sovereigns or states in such a condition. Such an interpretation gives short shrift, however, to Hobbes's insistence from at least 1640 that the fundamental duty and the basic self-interest of a sovereign consist in providing for the safety and well-being *of the people*.[86] If Hobbes's earlier view was also that the proper end of the commonwealth, and therefore of the military, is to provide for the preservation of the people rather than the expansion of the commonwealth or the glory of its leaders, then it will be clearer

---

[85] Hobbes, *Elements of Law*, 2.9.9.

[86] Ibid. See how Hobbes distinguishes the virtue and prudence of the citizen from those of the sovereign at *Behemoth*, 165–166. The famous illustration of "Kings, and Persons of Soveraigne authority" being "in the state and posture of Gladiators" has been understood as justifying aggression, but is cast in defensive terms ("their Forts, Garrisons, and Guns" are "upon the Frontiers of their Kingdomes") with the welfare of the people as the proper purpose of this posture ("because they uphold thereby, the Industry of their Subjects; there does not follow from it, that misery, which accompanies the Liberty of particular men": *Leviathan* 13.12, 63).

what Hobbes had hoped his elite readers would realize about how to "minde the *Art*, by which, the Affaires, both of Armies, and Cities, be conducted to their ends."[87]

The prevalent interpretation of the state of nature between commonwealths has led to an understanding of Hobbes as committed to imperialism or at least to an aggressive foreign policy. If Thucydides taught him anything, though, it was to be wary of any such policy. The Hobbesian sovereign is armed and prepared, but is so in order to meet the contingent requirements of the defense of the citizens and to ensure peace. In *De cive*, Hobbes writes:

> Now all the duties of rulers [imperantium] are contained in this one maxim: *The safety of the people is the supreme law....* . And because governments [imperia] are constituted for the sake of peace, and peace is sought on account of safety, one who is placed in authority [imperio] who would use it otherwise than for the safety of the people would act against the reasons of peace, that is, against natural law.... . For sovereigns can confer no greater happiness on the citizens than that, being protected from foreign and civil war, they can enjoy the wealth acquired by their industry.[88]

Sovereigns must procure the safety of their people and thus must protect them from war. War may be necessary, however, to procure that safety. Sovereigns who undertake wars for other purposes so trouble Hobbes that he even endorses deterring such sovereign undertakings by statute. In his *Dialogue of the Common Laws*, Hobbes first targets the imprudence of those kings who strive to gain glory by military means, holding that conquests are difficult to maintain and that the conquerors are unlikely to enjoy the conquest for long.[89] More strikingly, he says that as long as they do not prevent kings from the necessary defense of their people, statutes that inhibit "such Kings as for the Glory of Conquest might spend one part of their Subjects Lives and Estates, in Molesting other Nations, and leave the rest to Destroy themselves at Home by Factions" are to be welcomed as "very good for the King and People."[90] Hobbes does not want this to undermine his fundamental position that the sovereign cannot be legally limited from protecting the people at his discretion, but it is remarkable that he nonetheless commends such laws for "creating some kind of Difficulty for such Kings" who would go to war at their subjects' expense.

In *Leviathan*, Hobbes is especially colorful, characterizing "the insatiable appetite, or *Bulimia*, of enlarging Dominion" as a serious infirmity of the body politic.[91] He goes on to describe the ways in which even putatively successful conquests are imprudent,

---

[87] Thucydides, *Eight Bookes*, sig. A4r.

[88] Hobbes, *De cive*, 13.2, 13.6: Imperantium autem officia omnia hoc vno dicto continentur: *Salus populi suprema lex* ... Quoniam autem imperia pacis causa constituta sunt, & pax propter salutem quaesita, qui in imperio positus, eo aliter quam ad salutem populi vteretur, faceret contra pacis rationes, hoc est, contra legem naturalem ...Amplius enim ad faelicitatem ciuilem, quam vt à bello externo & ciuili tuti, opibus industria partis frui possint, summi imperatores conferre non possunt.

[89] Hobbes, *Dialogue of the Common Laws*, 16.

[90] Ibid., 21.

[91] Hobbes, *Leviathan*, 29.22, 174. Cf. Hobbes, *De cive*, 13.14.

"with lesse danger lost, than kept."[92] Whereas Bacon had put forward Thucydides as a champion of war beyond one's borders, Hobbes in the Latin version of this passage shows that, in 1668, he still has Thucydides' Athens in mind when he writes of such bulimia as a deadly disorder, "from which once perished the Athenian and Carthaginian Commonwealths."[93] Two paragraphs earlier, where in the English version he laments the "dangerous Disease" that is "the Popularity of a potent Subject," Hobbes in the Latin edition illustrates this point with the example of the instigator of the Sicilian expedition, Alcibiades.[94]

Gentili's Thucydides decisively justified preventive attack and ultimately condoned imperial expansion; Bacon's did the same in a way that supported a claim about the situation of international relations in general.[95] Hobbes's Thucydides provided the foundation for an even more abstract claim about the universally bellicose relations between sovereign states and between free individuals. But this abstract principle was the starting point of an argument for peace and the preservation of the people, and Hobbes meant his Thucydides to issue a stark warning to and about those who would imperil that peace and those people.

5 Politic History

Hobbes sees in Thucydides a cautionary or dehortatory history perfectly fitted to the politics of his own times. He also appears to recognize a model for his own actions. As we saw earlier, Hobbes's position in the 1620s is a precarious one, reflected in his description of those who disagreed when the party for war had grown powerful in Athens: "the good men either durst not oppose, or if they did, vndid themselues."[96] He immediately goes on to tell us that Thucydides' own way out of this dilemma was to avoid the usual political arena and focus on the writing of his history (though, as we have seen, Hobbes understands this writing to carry considerable political freight).[97]

---

[92] Ibid.

[93] Hobbes, Latin *Leviathan* (Hobbes 1668), 156: "quo perierunt olim Civitates Atheniensis & Carthaginensis." The Punic Wars began with a dispute over Sicily, reached a pinnacle with Hannibal's invasion of Italy, and ended with Rome's total destruction of Carthage. Hobbes also talks of Rome's conquests in a register that differs from that of many of his predecessors. In the epistle to *De cive*, he characterizes the conquered territories as having been despoiled or robbed (*spoliatis*) by Rome, which like a beast of prey tore nearly the whole world to pieces (*totum ferè orbem terrarum diripuerat*: Hobbes 1983: 73).

[94] Hobbes, *Leviathan*, 29.20, 173; Latin *Leviathan*, 156: cujus exempla habemus . . . in Civitate Atheniensi Alcibiadem, Pisistratum, &c. ("of which [disease] we have the examples . . . in the Athenian Commonwealth of Alcibiades, Peisistratus, etc.").

[95] See Hoekstra 2012: 40–43, 48–54.

[96] Thucydides, *Eight Bookes*, sig. a1v.

[97] Ibid., sig. a1v: Thucydides "forbore to come into the Assemblies, and propounded to himselfe, a priuate life." Hobbes immediately goes on to discuss Thucydides' views about "the gouernment of the State," so a commitment to a private life apparently need not preclude writing about public or political matters.

"It is therefore no maruell, if he meddled as little as he could, in the businesse of the Common-wealth, but gaue himselfe rather to the obseruation and recording of what was done by those that had the mannaging thereof."[98] Hobbes, too, focuses on that history while his patrons are spoiling for a fight that could lead to England's ruin, and his views of human nature, politics, and warfare must have been deeply imprinted by that focus. And Hobbes is also attentive to how Thucydides was able to influence the influential without undoing himself, and how it was by writing his narrative that Thucydides was "euery where secretly instructing, and directing" his readers' lives and actions, even two thousand years later.[99] Along with much else, Thucydides provided Hobbes with an exemplar of wise action and "politic" writing.

Reflecting on the demagogues who drove Athens into intervening abroad—and apparently also on the war-mongering politics of the parliaments of the early 1620s—Hobbes writes: "such men onely swayed the Assemblies, and were esteemed wise and good Common-wealths men, as did put them vpon the most dangerous and desperate enterprizes."[100] Hobbes evidently reflects on his own plight when he ponders the risks faced by those who instead gave "temperate, and discreet aduice."[101] In Thucydides, Hobbes not only found a model of political action through writing, but also an alibi, a way to proceed with discretion. What Hobbes offers to his patrons and proposes to publish is a translation of a work by someone else, about other times, with a helpful apparatus and plenty of encouragement to read the work through and consider the arc of the narrative and what it reveals about the actions of the Athenians that led to their miseries and defeat.

The edition of Thucydides is generally understood to be the summit of Hobbes's humanist phase, shortly after which he took a basic turn (perhaps because of an encounter with Euclid) and became Hobbes the philosopher or scientist. But we may wonder whether we have enough evidence that the translator of Thucydides is a humanist who has not yet been converted to philosophy (or science in Hobbes's sense). A philosophical treatise would not have been adequate to the situation Hobbes faced, which prohibited him from drawing an explicit conclusion or propounding open precepts—whereas history, as Hobbes says again and again, could communicate via a narration of what happened. Hobbes's way of communicating by this history, via the whole of the narrative, met the requirements of the moment that could not have been met by publishing philosophy, by providing wise maxims from ancient sources, or by reducing Thucydides to quotations from the Melian Dialogue or a collection of the speeches for consumption by the powerful. Not least, the lesson to be learned here is a prudential one and thus apt for a historical rather than a philosophical mode of instruction: this point is not that prevention, expansion, or military adventuring abroad never pays (and certainly not that they are absurd given the proper definitions), but that the odds are

---

[98]   Ibid., sig. a2r.
[99]   Ibid., sig. b1r.
[100]   Ibid., sig. a1v.
[101]   Ibid.

such that we would be foolish to bet the realm on it. The coat of history and the cloak of translation allow Hobbes to deliver a lesson without doing so openly or in a manner that would be inappropriate for a servant. The resulting misrecognition has been dramatic, to the point that the most widespread interpretation of Hobbes's endorsement of Thucydides is that it confirms the bellicosity at the core of his thought. Hobbes's lament that his first readers perversely responded to his Thucydides with martial enthusiasm applies in a different way to readers centuries later. When the next war rumbled on the horizon, Hobbes did not again seek to fight fire with fire; he largely eschewed the implicit lessons of history, rhetoric, and prudence, and opted instead for the cold water of philosophy.

In his Thucydides, however, Hobbes imitated not only Thucydides himself, but also scholars like Lipsius, whom he quotes approvingly about Thucydides' secret instruction in concluding his prefatory materials. In Lipsius, Hobbes had a shining example of a scholar who had developed a great cultural reputation and significant political influence by providing a great edition of an ancient historian and by offering political lessons for contemporary political and military figures by drawing heavily on Tacitus, Thucydides, and others—all the while hiding behind the figures he is quoting.[102] As Lipsius said of his *Politica*, in which he spoke through the words of the ancients: all of it is mine, and none of it.[103] Hobbes built on what he learned from Lipsius by putting these two projects together, for he discovered that he could communicate his political lessons *through* a scholarly edition and translation of an ancient historian. Translated into English, Thucydides would be the best possible authority to "instruct, and enable" Hobbes's countrymen, "by the knowledge of Actions past, to beare themselues prudently in the present, and prouidently towards the *Future*."[104] Hobbes's accomplishment was magnificent: he provided an impressively accurate and insightful translation and an elegant edition of the most difficult, austere, and intellectual of the ancient historians. But his aim was higher still, for it was nothing less than to save England from setting sail for its own destruction.

BIBLIOGRAPHY

Primary sources

Aubrey, John. 1898. *"Brief Lives," chiefly of Contemporaries, set down by John Aubrey, between the Years 1669 & 1696*, edited by Andrew Clark, 2 vols. Oxford: Clarendon Press.
Bacon, Francis. 1609. *De Sapientia Vetervm Liber*. London.
Bacon, Francis. 1619. *The Wisedome of the Ancients*, translated by Arthur Gorges. London.

---

[102] For the first, see Tacitus 1574; for the second, see esp. Lipsius 2004.
[103] Lipsius 2004: 232 (omnia nostra esse, et nihil).
[104] Thucydides, *Eight Bookes*, sig. A3r.

Bacon, Francis. 1629. *Considerations Touching a Warre With Spaine*, in *Certaine Miscellany Works of the Right Honovrable, Francis Lo. Verulam, Viscount S. Alban*, edited by William Rawley. London.

Bacon, Francis. 1985. *The Essayes or Counsels, Civill and Morall*, edited by Michael Kiernan. Cambridge, MA: Harvard University Press.

Botero, Giovanni. 1606. *A Treatise, Concerning the causes of the Magnificencie and greatnes of Cities*, translated by Robert Peterson. London.

[Cavendish, William.] 1620. *Horae Subseciuae. Observations and Discovrses*. London.

Dekker, Thomas. 1625. *A Rod for Run-awayes*. London.

Demosthenes. 1570. *The three Orations of Demosthenes chiefe Orator among the Grecians, in fauour of the Olynthians . . .: with those his fower Orations titled expressely & by name against king Philip of Macedonie: most nedefull to be redde in these daungerous dayes, of all them that loue their countries libertie, and desire to take warning for their better auayle, by example of others*, translated by Thomas Wilson. London.

Demosthenes. 1623. *The First and Most Excellent Oration of that Renowned Orator Demosthenes, against Philip of Macedon, the Potent and Politicke enemy of the State of Athens*, edited by T[homas] G[okin]. London.

An Experimentall Discoverie of Spanish Practises, or The Covnsell of a well-wishing Souldier, for the good of his Prince and State. 1623. S.l.

Gentili, Alberico. 1598. *De ivre belli libri III*. Hanau.

Hobbes, Thomas. 1651. *Leviathan, or, The Matter, Forme, & Power of a Common-wealth Ecclesiasticall and Civill*. London.

Hobbes, Thomas. 1668. *Leviathan, sive De Materia, Forma, & Potestate Civitatis Ecclesiasticae et Civilis*, in *Thomae Hobbes Malmesburiensis Opera Philosophica, quae Latine scripsit, omnia*. Amsterdam.

Hobbes, Thomas. 1679. *Thomae Hobbesii Malmesburiensis vita*. London.

Hobbes, Thomas. 1681. *Thomae Hobbes Angli Malmesburiensis philosophi vita*. London.

Hobbes, Thomas. 1969. *The Elements of Law, Natural and Politic*, edited by Ferdinand Tönnies, 2nd edn. London: Frank Cass.

Hobbes, Thomas. 1983. *De Cive: The Latin Version*, edited by Howard Warrender. Oxford: Clarendon Press.

Hobbes, Thomas. 1994. *The Correspondence*, edited by Noel Malcolm, 2 vols. Oxford: Clarendon Press.

Hobbes, Thomas. 2005. *A dialogue between a philosopher and a student, of the common laws of England*, in *Thomas Hobbes: Writings on Common Law and Hereditary Right*, edited by Alan Cromartie and Quentin Skinner. Oxford: Clarendon Press.

Hobbes, Thomas. 2009. *Behemoth, or, The Long Parliament*, edited by Paul Seaward. Oxford: Clarendon Press.

Isocrates. 1624. *Archidamus, or, The Covncell of Warre*, translated by Thomas Barnes. London.

James I. 1620. *A Proclamation against excesse of Lauish and Licentious Speech of matters of State*. London.

James I. 1621a. *A Proclamation against excesse of lauish and licentious speech of matters of State*. London.

James I. 1621b. *His Maiesties Declaration, Touching his proceedings in the late Assemblie and Conuention of Parliament*. London.

Lipsius, Justus. 2004. *Politica: Six Books of Politics or Political Instruction*, edited by Jan Waszink. Assen: Royal Van Gorcum.

Polybius. 1609. *Polybiou tou Lykorta Megalopolitou Historiōn ta sōzomena*, edited by Isaac Casaubon. Paris.

[Reynolds, John]. 1624. *Vox Coeli, or, Newes from Heaven*. [London] ("Elesium").

The Run-awyaes Answer, To a Booke called, A Rodde for Runne-awayes. 1625. *S.l.*

Tacitus, Cornelius. 1574. *Historiarvm et Annalivm libri qvi exstant*, edited by Justus Lipsius. Antwerp.

Thucydides. 1588. *Peri tou Peloponnēsiakou polemou*, edited by Lorenzo Valla and Henri Estienne, 2nd edn. [Geneva].

Thucydides. 1594. *Peri tou Peloponnēsiakou polemou*, edited by Lorenzo Valla, Henri Estienne, Francesco Porto, and Emilio Porto. Frankfurt.

Thucydides. 1629. *Eight Bookes of the Peloponnesian Warre*, translated by Thomas Hobbes. London.

Xenophon. 1623. *The Historie of Xenophon: Containing the Ascent of Cyrvs into the Higher Covntries*, translated by John Bingham. London.

Secondary sources

Arber, Edward. 1877. *A Transcript of the Registers of the Company of Stationers of London; 1554-1640 A.D.*, vol. 4. London.

Arendt, Hannah. [1951] 1968. *Imperialism: Part Two of The Origins of Totalitarianism*. San Diego and New York: Harcourt Brace.

Blanshard, Alastair J. L., and Tracey A. Sowerby. 2005. "Thomas Wilson's Demosthenes and the Politics of Tudor Translation." *International Journal of the Classical Tradition* 12(1): 46–80.

Creighton, Charles. [1891] 2013. *A History of Epidemics in Britain*. Cambridge: Cambridge University Press.

Fiedler, Siegfried. 1985. *Kriegswesen und Kriegführung im Zeitalter der Landsknechte*. Koblenz: Bernard & Graefe.

Hahlweg, Werner. [1941] 1987. *Die Heeresreform der Oranier und die Antike*. Osnabrück: Biblio Verlag.

Hoekstra, Kinch. 2006. "The End of Philosophy (The Case of Hobbes)." *Proceedings of the Aristotelian Society* 106(1): 23–60.

Hoekstra, Kinch. 2008. "A Source of War: Gentili's Thucydides," in *Alberico Gentili: La salvaguardia dei beni culturali nel diritto internazionale*, edited by Diego Panizza and Pepe Ragoni, 113–144. Milan: Giuffrè.

Hoekstra, Kinch. 2012. "Thucydides and the Bellicose Beginnings of Modern Political Theory," in *Thucydides and the Modern World: Reception, Reinterpretation, and Influence from the Renaissance to Today*, edited by Katherine Harloe and Neville Morley, 25–54. Cambridge: Cambridge University Press.

Lawrence, David R. 2009. *The Complete Soldier: Military Books and Military Culture in Early Stuart England, 1603-1645*. Leiden: Brill.

Malcolm, Noel. 2002. *Aspects of Hobbes*. Oxford: Clarendon Press.

Malcolm, Noel. 2007. *Reason of State, Propaganda, and the Thirty Years' War: An Unknown Translation by Thomas Hobbes*. Oxford: Clarendon Press.

Morgenthau, Hans J. [1948] 2005. *Politics Among Nations: The Struggle for Power and Peace*, 7th edn., revised by Kenneth W. Thompson and W. David Clinton. New York: McGraw-Hill/Irwin.

Oestreich, Gerhard. 1953. "Der römische Stoizismus und die oranische Heeresreform." *Historische Zeitschrift* 176(1): 17–43.

Schlatter, Richard, ed. 1975. *Hobbes's Thucydides*. New Brunswick, NJ: Rutgers University Press.

Slack, Paul. 1985. *The Impact of Plague in Tudor and Stuart England*. London: Routledge.

Spedding, James. 1874. *The Letters and the Life of Francis Bacon*, vol. 7. London.

Spedding, James. 1878. *An Account of the Life and Times of Francis Bacon*, 2 vols. London: Trübner.

Strype, John. 1725. *Annals of the Reformation and Establishment of Religion*, vol. 1, 2nd edn. London.

Sullivan, Robert G. 2004. "Demosthenes' Renaissance *Philipics*: Thomas Wilson's 1570 Translation as Anti-Spanish Propaganda." *Advances in the History of Rhetoric* 7(1): 111–137.

Tuck, Richard. 1999. *The Rights of War and Peace: Political Thought and the International Order from Grotius to Kant*. Oxford: Oxford University Press.

Williams, William Proctor. 2013. "'Vnder the Handes of . . . ': Zachariah Pasfield and the Licensing of Playbooks," in *Shakespeare's Stationers: Studies in Cultural Bibliography*, edited by Marta Straznicky, 63–94. Philadelphia: University of Pennsylvania Press.

Wootton, David. 1997. "Thomas Hobbes's Machiavellian Moments," in *The Historical Imagination in Early Modern Britain: History, Rhetoric, and Fiction, 1500–1800*, edited by Donald R. Kelley and David Harris Sacks, 210–242. Cambridge: Woodrow Wilson Center and Cambridge University Press.

Young, Michael B. 1989. "Revisionism and the Council of War, 1624–1626." *Parliamentary History* 8(1): 1–27.

CHAPTER 25

MAKING HISTORY

The Politics of Hobbes's Behemoth

TOMAŽ MASTNAK

IN what appears to be Hobbes's last letter, addressed to his publisher William Crooke, the philosopher mentioned "my Book concerning the Civil Wars of *England*, &c."[1] Hobbes referred to the work we today know as *Behemoth*, which was written in the mid-1660s but was first published in a pirated edition in 1679.[2] It was probably Crooke who had told Hobbes that the book was printed illegally.[3] Hobbes had asked him not to print the book himself because the king had refused to license it.[4] Although Hobbes had misgivings about the title of the pirated edition he heard about, he was apparently less worried about the multitude of "the errors of the presse."[5] The title of the first three printings was *The History of the Civil Wars of England: From the Year 1640, to 1660.*[6] One more pirated edition followed in the last year of Hobbes's life, under the title of *Behemoth* and with the subtitle *An Epitome of the Civil Wars of England, From 1640, to 1660.*[7]

---

[1] To William Crooke, August 18/28, 1679, in *Correspondence*, 2: 774.

[2] For the date of composition, the circulation of manuscripts, and the publication history, see Tönnies 1889; MacGillivray 1970; MacGillivray 1974; Nicastro 1977; Nicastro 1979: xlviii–xlix; Borot 1990; Milton 1993; Schuhmann 1998: 198; Vaughan 2002; Mastnak 2009; Seaward 2010: 6–17, 92–99.

[3] To William Crooke, June 19/29, 1679, and to John Aubrey, August 18/28, 1679, in *Correspondence*, 2: 771, 772, 774.

[4] To William Crooke, June 19/29, 1679; August 18/28, 1679; cf. to John Aubrey, August 28/28, 1679, in *Correspondence*, 2: 771, 772.

[5] See To John Aubrey, August 18/28, 1679, in *Correspondence*, 2: 772.

[6] Macdonald and Hargreaves 1952: 65–66 (nos. 86, 87, 87a). For Seaward 2010: 97, Macdonald and Hargreaves's identification of no. 86 as the first edition "seems warranted."

[7] Macdonald and Hargreaves 1952: 66 (no. 88). Another unauthorized *Behemoth* edition followed in 1680: *Behemoth. The History of the Civil Wars of England, From the Year 1640, to 1660*; Macdonald and Hargreaves 1952: 66 (no. 89). For a detailed description of the first printed editions of *Behemoth*, see now Seaward 2010: 83–92.

One may be tempted to say that just as Hobbes had entered the republic of letters with a book of history, Thucydides' *Peloponnesian War*,[8] Hobbes departed as a historian with *Behemoth*. As the introduction to the only eighteenth-century edition of Hobbes's works stated, the book was "in some Measure Mr. *Hobbes*'s Legacy to the Publick, since it was the last Piece of his that went to the Press during his Life."[9] If one may believe William Crooke, "no Book [was] being more commonly sold by all Booksellers" at the turn of the 1670s and '80s than *Behemoth*, Hobbes's "History of the Causes of the Civil Wars of England."[10] When Hobbes began to be rediscovered after a century of neglect, *Behemoth*[11] and his translation of Thucydides[12] were among the first of his writings to be reprinted.

Hobbes was brought back into public debates as a political thinker by intellectuals who were themselves involved in liberal or radical politics. In their view of Hobbes, history and politics were intertwined, theoretically as well as biographically. They saw Hobbes's political ideas as thoroughly determined by the political circumstances of his life. Adam Smith wrote that "the bigotry of his times" gave Hobbes "occasion to think that the subjection of the consciences of men to ecclesiastic authority was the cause of dissensions and civil wars that happened in England during the times of Charles the 1st and Cromwell," and to formulate his alternative accordingly.[13] Dugald Stewart explained that Hobbes's political ideas were a result of his being "a witness of the disorders which took place in England at the time of the dissolution of the monarchy by the death of Charles the First."[14]

The centrality of the English Civil War for our understanding of Hobbes's political philosophy has often been reaffirmed and only occasionally questioned. But if Hobbes's political philosophy was so thoroughly shaped by his experience of the Civil War, what he wrote of that civil war should be considered of prime importance for understanding his political philosophy. However, *Behemoth* has been one of the more neglected works of Hobbes because it was only a "book of history."[15] I intend to show that it is mistaken, or at least seriously misleading, to think of *Behemoth* as simply a history. The best interpretations of *Behemoth* as a history have established that Hobbes wrote a very unusual history book and led to the conclusion that *Behemoth* was more exactly a book of politics. As such, *Behemoth* has been read as Hobbes's Machiavellian treatise. I aim to

---

[8]   Hobbes 1629.

[9]   Anonymous 1750: xx. Robertson (1910: 233 n.) identified "Dr [John] Campbell of the 'Biographia Britannica'" as the author.

[10]   "The Bookseller to the Reader," prefixed to the publication of *Behemoth* in *Tracts*. Crooke may have been the source of the note in Anonymous (1750: xx) that "[a]t that Time, when Things were fresh in Memory . . . it was much read and admired."

[11]   In Maseres 1815.

[12]   See Hobbes 1812, 1822, 1823, 1824, 1830. Hobbes's translation of Thucydides was one of the very few works of his published in the eighteenth century with a portrait of the translator. See Hobbes 1723; cf. Macdonald and Hargreaves 1952: 3–4 (no. 5).

[13]   Smith 1978: 397.

[14]   Stewart 1854: 280.

[15]   See Mastnak 2009.

show that Hobbes's analysis of English Civil War politics was indeed Machiavellian (or, rather, reason of state), but that his own political position, bearing on his interpretation, was that of his political philosophy as the science of just and unjust. In *Behemoth*, Hobbes is at work as political analyst and political philosopher.

1 "A Work of History"

The first printed judgment on *Behemoth* as a "history" is perhaps the three words in parenthesis in Anthony Wood's entry on *Behemoth*: "containing many faults."[16] Francis Maseres was the first to promote *Behemoth* as a historiographical work, printing it in 1815 in his collection of histories of the "civil wars of England." He considered it a "valuable work," "written in a very clear and lively style," containing "a great deal of curious historical matter," and being "faithful and exact in point of fact."[17] Maseres was moderately critical only where Hobbes's opinions of "the Civil Government in General, and of the Monarchical Government of England in particular"[18] influenced his judgment of the "moral merit" of the "persons" involved in the narrated events.[19] Tönnies in his edition recommended *Behemoth* as of "high interest to the historical student" (but no less to "the philosopher and politician").[20] His contemporary Leslie Stephen was more reserved: Hobbes "too often, like many better historians, finds it enough to explain events by the wickedness of the other side. That agreeable theory is an excuse for not attempting to discover the causes of discontent."[21]

After Maseres, *Behemoth* was not used as a source for the study of the English Civil War. It has, however, sporadically been used to provide insights into or illustrations of historical developments linked to the Civil War, such as the increase in size and influence of big commercial towns, primarily London.[22] The growth of trading towns was part of what came to be called the emergence of "bourgeois society," at the core of which were the new "market-made wealth" and "market morality" embodied in

[16] Wood 1692: 2.481; cf. Wood 1813–20: 3.1213. Wood's judgment on *Behemoth* may have simply reflected his low opinion on James Heath's *Chronicle*, the purported source of *Behemoth*. See Wood 1692: 2.226; Wood 1813–20: 3.664.

[17] Maseres 1815: 1.lxxviii–lxxix. Maseres was reputed for his "conversation," which "abounded in anecdote and information, particularly in the incidents in English history from 1640 to his own date." Courtney 1921–2: 12.1293.

[18] Maseres refuted those "erroneous Opinions" in an appendix to his reprint of *Behemoth*. Maseres 1815: 2.657–671.

[19] Maseres 1815: 1.lxxix.

[20] Tönnies 1889: x.

[21] Stephen 1904: 29. Discovering the "causes" of the Civil War was, as I will show, Hobbes's stated aim in *Behemoth*.

[22] Cf. Corfield 1973: 218; Hill 1990: 48–49; cf. Pearl 1961, 1972; Farnell 1977; Howell 1983: 67, 77; Porter 1996: 1. Coates (2004) did not cite Hobbes but argued that London's wealth was the single most important element in Parliament's victory.

the "possessive individual," according to C. B. Macpherson. He credited *Behemoth* as a lucid analysis of that great social and political transformation, destroying "the old constitution" and replacing it "with one more favourable to the new market interests."[23] *Behemoth* came to figure in debates about the history of English constitutionalism. George Peabody Gooch defined the subject of *Behemoth* as "the constitutional struggle." As a liberal, Gooch was unsympathetic to Hobbes's presentation of that struggle. He called it "superficial and unimaginative" and Hobbes the old "impenitent absolutist" with "measureless contempt" for "continual changes of régime" and for the "principle of representation on which our liberties have been built."[24] More recently, Deborah Baumgold and Quentin Skinner, among others, have read *Behemoth* as an analysis of the "constitutional struggle between Parliament and king."[25] Skinner discusses Hobbes's judgments of the "democraticall Gentlemen," whose "reliance on classical arguments about freedom and servitude eventually pushed them into adopting a standpoint so radical as to be virtually republican in its constitutional allegiances."[26] Skinner's conclusions sound almost like Gooch's: "Hobbes reserves some of his harshest words of contempt for the 'Democraticall Gentlemen' and their 'designe of changing the government from Monarchical to Popular, which they called Liberty,'" and his polemic is marked with "ferocity" and "violence."[27]

Maseres had brought Hobbes as a historian to the attention of the early nineteenth-century public because Hobbes was an "eye-witness" to most of the political "transactions" of the English seventeenth century.[28] Eye-witnessing made historical writing "true and authentick"—a quality Maseres praised in his reprint of Thomas May's history of the Civil War a few years earlier.[29] But for the Victorian James Fitzjames Stephen, that quality of *Behemoth* was a window not into historical events but into the mind of the author who described them. *Behemoth*, Stephen wrote, "is the only contemporary account which shows us what sceptical men of the world thought of the great contest and of its party cries."[30] That opened, as it were, a line of inquiry reaching into our own times. For Leslie Stephen, *Behemoth* was interesting because it threw "some light upon Hobbes's sympathies when the war was actually raging."[31] Tönnies's student and the translator of *Behemoth* into German, Julius Lips, studied the work as the key to Hobbes's political attitudes toward the protagonists of the Civil War.[32] For Hans-Dieter Metzger, *Behemoth* was a testimony to Hobbes's political antipathies, especially to the

[23] Macpherson 1962: 64–66, 94. For a critique of Macpherson that made good use of *Behemoth*, see Thomas 1965; cf. Letwin 1972. Yerby (2008: 265) has recently restated Macpherson's thesis.

[24] Gooch n.d.: 35–38.

[25] Baumgold 1988: 71; Skinner 1965: 156, 159, 170; 1996: 431; 2002a: 13; 2002b: 15 ff.; 2008: 139 ff.

[26] Skinner 2002b: 15.

[27] Skinner 2008: 178–179.

[28] Maseres 1815: 1.lxxviii.

[29] Maseres 1812: xiii. The quoted passage referred to William Temple's history of the Irish rebellion, also reprinted by Maseres.

[30] Stephen 1892: 39.

[31] Stephen 1904: 29.

[32] Lips 1927.

decades-long animosity between Hobbes and Edward Hyde.[33] More recently, Jeffrey Collins read *Behemoth* as providing "retrospective evidence" for Hobbes's positive attitude toward the Independents and Cromwell.[34] More generally, Tönnies read *Behemoth* as a work that helped him understand Hobbes's way of thinking,[35] whereas others have found it relevant for studying particular aspects of Hobbes's thought.[36] MacGillivray's observation in his pioneering study of *Behemoth*, that the book may be seen as telling us "more about Hobbes than about the Civil War,"[37] applies to all these studies.

A number of scholars have shifted the discussion away from the informative value of *Behemoth* to the question of *what kind of history* Hobbes wrote. They answer first that *Behemoth* is a "dialogue-history,"[38] "the masterpiece of Hobbesian dialogue."[39] As MacGillivray pointed out, the dialogue form is "a very uncommon form for a history at any period."[40] Hobbes himself called *Behemoth* "my Dialogue of the Civil Wars of England."[41] More recently, a number of scholars argued that *Behemoth's* dialogue was instrumental in reaching—and instructing—a wider audience.[42] The purpose of the work was understood to have been political education, and the dialogue form was thus of central importance for achieving that purpose.[43]

Even more than its dialogue form, what distinguished *Behemoth* from contemporaneous histories of the Civil War was Hobbes's ambition to explain the causes of and reflect on the events: "the sheer quantity of ideas that Hobbes brings to it."[44] Tönnies, two centuries after the appearance of *Behemoth*, was in a position to appreciate the Hobbesian historiographical anomaly. For him, *Behemoth* was perhaps the first rationalistic interpretation of contemporary history of the type that was to become popular with Voltaire.[45] Tönnies returned to that characterization in a later work of his, when he wrote that the "cunning lawgivers, founders of religion, and shavelings play already in *Hobbes* (especially in 'Leviathan' and 'Behemoth') the same role, which *Voltaire* was later

---

[33] Metzger 1991: 92.

[34] Collins 2007: especially 151 ff. Sommerville 2004: 170–171, cited *Behemoth* to prove the opposite; similar argument: Catlin 1922: 16–17.

[35] "*Behemoth* . . . significatif de le mentalité du philosophe." Tönnies 1936: 80. In the original: "Denkungsart." Tönnies 1998– : 22.544.

[36] E.g., Tuck 1989: 34–36; 1993: 341–344, and, in greater detail, Milton (1993) discussed *Behemoth* in the context of their research on Hobbes's views on heresy. See also Champion 2006: 227–228; Parkin 2007: 240.

[37] MacGillivray 1970: 179.

[38] Malcolm 2002: 24.

[39] Borot 2004: 181–184.

[40] MacGillivray 1970: 180. Among the first to turn attention to the dialogue form was Ranke (1957: 2. 515; this work began to appear in the late 1850s).

[41] To William Crooke, June 19/29, 1679, in *Correspondence*, 2: 771.

[42] Reik 1977: 191–193.

[43] Vaughan 2002: especially 114. Cf. Dietz 1990: 100.

[44] MacGillivray 1970: 180, Brownley 1989: 490; see Levy 1997; Fussner 1962: especially 170; MacGillivray 1974; Richardson 1988: chap. 2; Woolf 1990; Worden 1993; Wootton 1997; Pocock 1999, 2000; essays in Rogers and Sorell 2000, especially Sommerville 2000; Norbrook 2001; Vaughan 2002: especially 92.

[45] Tönnies 1925a: 61.

to elevate to have European currency in the educated circles."[46] Tönnies's loyal friend and collaborator in promoting Hobbes studies, Baron von Brockdorff, put it more simply: as a historian, Hobbes in *Behemoth* "appears as the typical man of the Enlightenment."[47]

More recently, scholars have preferred linking *Behemoth* and its wealth of ideas to the intellectual world in which Hobbes grew up and in which he moved in his younger years and to relating it to intellectual developments that, when Hobbes wrote, lay still in the future. A good example is Fritz Levy's "intellectual biography of *Behemoth*." He linked *Behemoth* to the English debates about the usefulness of history and poetry of the 1620s, in which Hobbes took part. That led Levy to explore Hobbes's relationship with Francis Bacon and Ben Jonson and his circle and possible other influences on Hobbes's understanding of history, including John Selden and Thomas May's transla-tion of Lucan.[48] Levy also discussed *Horae subsecivae* (especially the discourses "Of Reading History" and "Upon the Beginning of Tacitus" as evidence for what Hobbes and Cavendish were thinking about after their return from Italy) and Hobbes's transla-tion of Thucydides. One of his conclusions was that "Hobbes's humanist period did not end in the 1620s, and that *Behemoth* thus should be considered in discussions of Hobbes's humanism."[49] That said, Hobbes's understanding of history had changed from *Horae subsecivae* to the translation of Thucydides and again by the time he wrote *Behemoth*. By then, Hobbes had "lost all faith that a reasonable person might learn very much of value from history" and "come to realize that history could be manipulated by the unscrupulous to serve their own ends, or the ends of their party." *Behemoth* was the result of that *disillusionment*: "a disillusioned discourse on history" providing a way to finding correctives necessary for the public to read histories without being hurt by their venom.[50]

As a "discourse on history," *Behemoth* was a very specific kind of history. Levy found that kind of history in Bacon and plausibly assumed that it must have been familiar to Hobbes, who was often with Bacon in the years when he was writing *History of Henry VII*, revising the *Essays*, and remaking the *Advancement of Learning* into a part of the *Instauratio Magna*.[51] In Levy's view, Hobbes's *Behemoth* "fits into the Baconian catego-ries as principally a discourse on histories or examples, but with enough narrative sur-viving (especially in the third and fourth dialogues) to suggest that the mixed mode of ruminated history may have been lurking at the back of its author's mind."[52]

What Bacon called "*discourse vpon Histories or Examples*" was "the fourme of writ-ing ... which *Machiauel* chose wisely and aptly for Gouermente."[53] Ruminated history

---

[46] Tönnies 1925b; cf. Tönnies 1998– : 15.137.

[47] Brockdorff 1929: 120.

[48] Levy 1997: 250–257.

[49] Levy 1997: 247 n. 13. Levy referred to Skinner 1991, 1993 (revised versions reprinted in Skinner 2002a).

[50] Levy 1997: 261, 262, 266. The "venom" reference is to *Leviathan*, 171.

[51] Levy 1997: 251.

[52] Levy 1997: 250; cf. Borot 1990: 15; Vaughan 2002: 94, 114.

[53] Bacon 2000: 162.

was "a forme of Writing, which some graue and wise men haue vsed, containing a scattered History of those actions, which they haue thought worthy of memorie, with politique discourse and obseruation thereupon; not incorporate into the History, but seperately, and as the more principall in their intention." Bacon mentioned this form under the heading of civil history, but it was a mixture. "But Mixtures, are things irregular, whereof no man can define." And thus "this kind of RVMINATED HISTORY," Bacon thought, belonged more "amongst Bookes of policie . . . than amongst Bookes of History: for it is the true office of History to represent euents themselues, together with the counsels, and to leaue the obseruations, and conclusions thereupon, to the liberty and facultie of euery mans iudgement."[54] Behemoth indeed fits this description quite well, but to the degree that it fits this kind of history, Behemoth falls out of history. What Hobbes wrote thus appears as "discourse of Gouernemente, such as Machyauel handleth," for which "historye of Tymes is the best grounde."[55] The question Levy's argument raises, but does not answer, is thus: why not call Behemoth "a Booke of policie"?

David Wootton, treading much the same terrain as Levy, asserted that Behemoth was "a study in Machiavellian politics" and "a self-consciously Machiavellian text."[56] Hobbes never mentioned Machiavelli. But there is ample evidence in what we know of Hobbes's life to support the claim that studying Machiavellian politics and reason-of-state treatises was of formative importance for his intellectual development.[57] Whereas the formal nature of Leviathan conceals "the extent of Hobbes's debt to a reading of Thucydides, Tacitus, Niccolò Machiavelli, and Justus Lipsius," that indebtedness comes into the open in Behemoth.[58] Behemoth's "fundamental presuppositions are Machiavellian,"[59] as is its politics.[60] Wootton goes so far as to argue that the whole perspective of Behemoth is Machiavellian. Since the English of those times had named the devil Old Nick (after Niccolò Machiavelli), "the diuells mountain" in Behemoth's first paragraph, which opens the view of history, might be seen as "Niccolò's Mountain."[61] For John Cleveland, a lecturer on rhetoric at Cambridge, a poet of royalist allegiance,

---

[54] Bacon 2000: 70.

[55] Bacon 2000: 163. History of times is the form of history that "representeth a TIME," not a person or action, and thus "representeth the magnitude of Actions, & and the publique faces and deportments of persons." Bacon 2000: 66.

[56] Wootton 1997: 217, 228.

[57] Cf. Wootton 1997: 213, 214, 216, 220.

[58] Wootton 1997: 211. On Machiavelli in Leviathan, see now Borrelli 2009.

[59] Wootton 1997: 234.

[60] Wootton 1997: 225–228, 232.

[61] Wootton 1997: 228–229. If one wished to speculate, one could as well find a less direct way to Machiavelli in this opening paragraph. In the first sentence, Hobbes takes the reader "in time" and defines the time "which passed between the years of 1640 and 1660," that is, the subject of his book, as "the highest of time." Behemoth, 107. If Behemoth is thus a "history of time," and if Bacon defined "historye of Tymes" as "the best grounde for discourse of Gouernemente, such as Machyauel handleth" (Bacon 2000: 163), Hobbes did take the interlocutors of his dialogue, and his readers, onto the prime Machiavellian terrain.

and a contemporary of Hobbes's, "Old *Machiavel*" was "great *Behemoth*'s younger Brother."[62]

Having satisfied himself that he had established *Behemoth* as "a study in Machiavellian politics,"[63] Wootton, however, maintained that *Behemoth* was "a book of history," which led him to the question of how the work related to a "tradition of historical writing."[64] Wootton called attention to *Behemoth*'s unusual dialogue form, its "very loose chronology," its being "the opposite of a lifelike story, a bald epitome," its ambition to analyze "causes and consequences," and the prominent place given to "interpretation," and answered that what characterized *Behemoth* in comparison with contemporary historiography was its "sheer eccentricity."[65] The question that remains unanswered is: why call Hobbes's *Behemoth* a "book of history"?

Hobbes may have himself said something on this issue, depending on how we understand his complaint that the pirated printing of *Behemoth* had "a foolish title set to it"[66]—*History of the Civil Wars of England*. In his correspondence, Hobbes referred to the book as "my Dialogue of the Civil Wars of *England*,"[67] "my booke of the Civill Warr,"[68] "my Book concerning the Civil Wars of *England*, &c.,"[69] and possibly an "epitome" of English "troubles."[70] Except for once, in his *Prose Life*, probably written not much earlier than the cited letters,[71] he never called it a history. Did he, when he complained, mean to say that calling the book "History" was foolish?[72] If that was the case, have most Hobbes scholars read the book "foolishly"? What might they have missed when they read the book as "history"?

2 "A Work of Politics"

In April 1642, Mersenne arranged for the printing of Hobbes's *De cive* and circulated the work through his network, soliciting responses to that "*estrange livre*." He described

---

[62] "The Publick Faith," in Cleveland 1687: 201.

[63] Wootton 1997: 229.

[64] Wootton 1997: 217, 219.

[65] Wootton 1997: 219–221.

[66] To John Aubrey, August 18/28, 1679, in *Correspondence*, 2: 772.

[67] To William Crooke, June 19/29, 1679, in *Correspondence*, 2: 771.

[68] To John Aubrey, August 18/28, 1679, in *Correspondence*, 2: 772.

[69] To William Crooke, August 18/28, 1679, in *Correspondence*, 2: 774.

[70] *Correspondence*, 2: 697. François du Verdus, in his response to a lost letter of Hobbes to him from July 20, 1666, mentioned "votre Epitome de vos Troubles." Verdus to Hobbes, April 3/13, 1668. For the argument that the book we call *Behemoth* was actually entitled by Hobbes as *Epitome of the Civil Wars*, see Schuhmann 1996: 156; 2000: 4; 1998: 198.

[71] When he was about eighty years old, he wrote in English "Historiam Belli Civilis Anglicani, inter Regem Carolum primum et Parliamentum ejus." *Vita*, xx; *Prose Life*, 252. Cf. Terrel 2008: 177 n. 32. On the date of composition: Tricaud 1985: 280.

[72] Seaward (2010: 53) wrote of Hobbes's "reluctance" to call his book on the Civil War a "history."

the book as "moral or political,"[73] but one of his correspondents responded categorically with: "This is not a book of morals, it is of politics."[74] Something similar might clearly, and perhaps more easily, be said about *Behemoth*. But understanding in what sense *De cive* was "a book of politics" may help us comprehend *Behemoth's* political nature, or the nature of *Behemoth's* politics.

De cive was the third section of a large systematic work covering the whole area of philosophy. Why this third and last part of the system was first to appear, and why the whole system was in progress for such a long time are questions that have puzzled Hobbes scholars. I find Jean Terrel's detailed reading of Hobbes's biographies very helpful in looking for answers. Terrel has sought to show how political events—in the first place the English Civil War—and Hobbes's responses to them repeatedly interrupted, and influenced, the execution of the systematic philosophical work.[75] Most notable among Hobbes's responses to political crises were the circulation of *The Elements of Law* in manuscript in 1640[76] and the production of his "Politique in English";[77] that is, of *Leviathan*, about ten years later. Both the production and the publication of *Behemoth*, too, may be considered responses to critical political developments.[78] It appears then that *The Elements*, English and Latin *Leviathan*, and *Behemoth* belong to a different class and have to be dealt with differently than his "whole Course of Philosophy":[79] that is, *De corpore, De homine,* and *De cive.*

Hobbes wrote his political interventions as a political theorist would, using elements of his philosophy. Although these political interventions are, formally, not building blocks of Hobbes's (political) philosophy, they undoubtedly are part of his political thought. Hobbes's political thought was both his political philosophy or science of politics[80] *and* his responses as a political philosopher to political crises.

The unusually political character of Hobbes's political thought may be better understood if we very briefly look at the nature of his philosophy and into the circumstances of his personal life. With regard to the nature of Hobbes's philosophy, I accept Kinch

[73] "[U]n estrange livre . . . *de Libertate, Imperio et Religione,* qui est une morale ou politique d'un Anglois." Mersenne to André Rivet, May 9, 1642, in Mersenne 1970: 151.

[74] "[C]e livre n'est pas des morales; il est de la politique." Baptiste Masoyer-Deshommeaux to Mersenne, September 10, 1642, in Mersenne 1970: 264–265.

[75] Terrel 2008.

[76] On the assumption that Tuck (1988: especially 26–27) was right when he determined that Hobbes had written up his philosophical system in a quite detailed form by 1640, *The Elements of Law* is a good example of Hobbes drawing on his existing philosophical work for a political intervention. Cf. Tuck 1998: xi–xii. See also Baumgold 2004.

[77] Robert Payne to Gilbert Sheldon, May 13, 1650, cited in Tuck 1991: ix. Because Payne reported to Sheldon what he had heard from Hobbes, the "Politique in English" may well have been Hobbes's own designation.

[78] The writing of *Behemoth* may be seen as a response to the introduction of the *Bill against Atheism and Prophaneness* into the House of Commons in 1666, which could have made Hobbes liable to prosecution. See Milton 1993: 509, 512. Nicastro (1977: 1) linked the appearance of *Behemoth* in print to the fears of a new civil war in 1679–80.

[79] *Vita carmine expressa,* lines 143–144; *Verse Life,* 257.

[80] Hobbes took pride in having been the first to lay the foundations for the "science" of politics. See *De corpore:* Epistola dedicatoria. Cf. Sorell 1988; Malcolm 1990.

Hoekstra's argument that Hobbes's conception of philosophy was not primarily alethic, or truth-oriented, and that he did not regard truth as the ultimate philosophical value or aim.[81] For Hobbes, philosophy was practical to such a degree that "practical philosophy" for him was a pleonasm.[82] The aim of philosophy was to work for the public good, to benefit the commonwealth or humanity, or to further human welfare. Hobbes was "keen to claim" that all of his philosophical efforts—not just particular arguments but also the subject of most of Hobbes's work—"should be seen in light of the end of human benefit."[83] His philosophical work, with the "preponderance of political philosophy in his writings," was in this sense an "eirenic project . . . independent of, and perhaps even in tension with, a philosophy with truth as its primary aim."[84]

From when he left Oxford until his death, with only a few interruptions, Hobbes was employed by the Cavendishes, one of the wealthiest families in England. For much of his adult life, he lived in close proximity to English and European high politics. His "practical and personal knowledge of European politics was unrivalled by any English thinker of his generation (and arguably by only one on the Continent, the Dutchman Hugo Grotius)."[85] His job as a secretary, advisor, tutor, and translator, involved him in political thinking. Hobbes had been a political thinker long before he became a (political) philosopher. By the time he became a philosopher,[86] he was a politically formed man. Samuel Hartlib's impression of Hobbes when he first met him in 1639 is telling: he called Hobbes a "fine political brain."[87]

The nature of Hobbes's intellectual pursuits before the translation of Thucydides, the first publication carrying his name, is evidenced by his tutorial work, catalogues of the holdings of the Hardwick library, personal connections, and literary remains. These include Hobbes's translation (with marginal notes) of Fulgenzio Micanzio's letters to William Cavendish;[88] the translations of Bacon's *Essayes* into Latin[89] and Italian (which included the first publication of the essay "Of Seditions and Troubles"), in which Hobbes most likely played a role;[90] the collection of ten essays, a fair copy

---

[81] Hoekstra 2006: 26, 27.

[82] Hoekstra 2006: 32.

[83] Hoekstra 2006: 29, 32.

[84] Hoekstra 2006: 32.

[85] Tuck 1991: xii–xiii; cf. Tuck 1998: ix.

[86] "[T]empore ab illo/ Inter philosophos et numerabar ego." *Vita carmine expressa*, lines 33–34.

[87] "Ist ein Wacker Politischer Kopf." Cited in Malcolm 2007: 89. My suggested translation is: "A fearless political mind."

[88] De Mas 1987; "Introduzione." cf. Gabrieli 1957; De Mas 1987: "Sussidi cronologici"; Malcolm 1984, 2007.

[89] Cf. Aubrey 1898: 1.331.

[90] See "Delle Seditioni, & Turbationi," in Bacon 1618: 96–102. In this essay, Bacon cited *Pharsalia* I.181–82: "*Hinc vsura Vorax, rapidumque in tempora foenus,/ Hinc concussa fides, & multis vtile bellum.* Questo multis vtile bellum, é certo, & infallibil segno, d'un stato disposto alle Turbationi e Seditioni." Bacon 1618: 99. Cf. Bacon 1985: 45. Thomas May's translation of the poem was printed in 1627, dedicated "To the trve Louer of all good Learning, and iust honour of his owne *Ranke*, WILLIAM, *Earle of Deuonshiere*, &c." A point May thought worth bringing to the attention of the dedicatee was how Pompey and Caesar, thanks to their "prosperous atchiuements in forreine warres," were able "to

of which in Hobbes's hand William Cavendish appears to have presented to his father,[91] and the *Horae subsecivae*;[92] and Hobbes's translation of a reason-of-state propaganda treatise *Altera secretissima instructio Gallo-Britanno-Batava Friderico V data*.[93] Much of this evidence, but especially Hobbes's translations of Micanzio's letters, *Altera instructio*, and the *Peloponnesian Wars*, express an unsoothingly realistic and nonredemptory view of politics, to which we commonly refer as *reason of state*. The reason-of-state political culture was "clearly what the young Hobbes was most at home in."[94]

"Reason of state," as defined in Giovanni Botero's very popular *Della ragion di stato*, was "the knowledge of the means" by which the state as "a stable rule over a people . . . may be founded, preserved and extended."[95] The term Botero used for knowledge was "notizia," designating concrete, empirically bound knowledge.[96] Hobbes learned to use such knowledge of the means for founding, maintaining, and expanding the state for analyzing politics. He practiced such analysis well into his old age. He was one of the rare political theorists who were able to look into the abyss of "iniquity" and "folly"—even of "double iniquity" and "double folly"—that is human politics, without blinking. "Iniquity" and "folly" (or the double measure of each) are the words that appear in the opening paragraph of *Behemoth*[97] and designate the subject of the book. *Behemoth* is, indeed, prominently a reason-of-state tract. In no other work of Hobbes is the political culture of his formative years more directly and openly present than in *Behemoth*.

Behemoth, however, is not solely a reason-of-state tract. It is also marked by Hobbes's "science of politics." *Behemoth* thus demonstrates that Hobbes, on turning to "science" or becoming a "philosopher," had not "largely left behind" his "earlier humanist preoccupations."[98] Rather, he continued to work in the humanist reason-of-state tradition while he simultaneously practiced his new science of politics.[99] This duality operates most clearly in *Behemoth*.

---

ruine that state, which before they serued" (May 1627). This book about civil war and the ruin of the state could not have escaped Hobbes's attention. See Malcolm 1984: chap. 8.

[91]   Malcolm 2007: 6. Printed in Wolf 1969: 135–167.

[92]   Anonymous 1620.

[93]   Malcolm 2007.

[94]   Tuck 1993: 282. Cf. Malcolm 2007: 109, on Hobbes's "familiarity with quite a range of literature on 'ragion di stato.'"

[95]   "Stato è vn dominio fermo sopra popoli; e Ragione di Stato è notitia di mezzi atti à fondare, conseruare, e ampliare vn Dominio così fatto." Botero 1606a: 1; cf. Botero 1956: 3.

[96]   See Descendre 2009: 65.

[97]   See *Behemoth*, 107.

[98]   Cf. Skinner 2008: 13. The debate on Hobbes's early humanist "phase" goes back to Strauss (2001) (German manuscript completed in 1935, first published in English translation in 1936), was reintroduced by Reik (1977), and rerun with great erudition and sophistication by Skinner (2002a, 2008).

[99]   Cf. Hoekstra 2006: 27.

3 REASON OF STATE AND THE SCIENCE
OF JUST AND UNJUST

Behemoth has only rarely been read as an exemplary reason-of-state analysis of the English Civil War. It seems to me that the prevailing understanding of the nature of Hobbes's philosophy does not encourage such reading. And there is little in reason of state that may appeal to a philosopher. Meinecke famously complained about the legion of third- and fourth-rate minds and mediocre writers a historian of reason of state has to deal with.[100] The most comprehensive study of reason of state in relation to Hobbes is Malcolm's introduction to Hobbes's translation of *Altera instructio*, and it touches on *Behemoth* only tangentially.[101]

Malcolm looked at "themes and lines of argument" in Hobbes's "mature political writings" that "seem to echo the teachings of 'ragion di stato' theory."[102] Another approach in Hobbes studies has been linking aspects of Hobbes's work with the names of writers associated with reason of state. In this approach, *Behemoth* has figured more prominently. On the assumption that three of the "discovrses" in *Horae subsecivae* were by Hobbes, Richard Tuck, for example, argued that "Hobbes in 1620 was an absolutely authentic Tacitist" and that "this Tacitism of the early Hobbes" persisted in his later work. In *Behemoth*, most notably we can find "a Tacitist account of politics preserved intact."[103] Tacitism is a late form of humanism, the result of the growing interest in Tacitus in the latter half of the sixteenth century. The commentaries on Tacitus, which became very numerous in the early seventeenth century, made clear "the link between the rise of the idea of reason of state and the revival of Tacitus."[104] Tacitus was then regarded as "a master of reason of state," as "the premier writer for the new study of *reason of state*."[105] That was the way of thinking about politics in which the young Hobbes was steeped.

Noel Malcolm was prompted to think of Tacitus by Hobbes's "willingness to sanction extreme breaches of moral norms [that] far exceeded anything in the reason of state tradition (with a possible exception of Naudé's admiring account of 'coups d'état')",

---

[100] Meinecke 1976: 76, 140.

[101] Malcolm 2007: especially 113–123. The same is true of Borrelli 1993: chap. 7. Meinecke 1976: 249–255, is a general discussion of Hobbes's political philosophy on the basis of *De cive* and *Leviathan*. The discussion on Hobbes and reason of state in the 1974 Tübingen conference on *Staatsräson* was overshadowed by the absence of the notion in Hobbes, whereas the papers basically appended reason of state to interpretations of other notions or issues in Hobbes's philosophy. See Schnur 1975: part 3 and 22–23 representing Hobbes's political theory as a "negative answer" to reason of state: "out of reason of state there grew the reasonableness of Leviathan."

[102] Malcolm 2007: 114.

[103] Tuck 2000: 107, 109.

[104] Burke 1991: 485, 486. For the beginning and spread of Tacitism, see Tuck 1991: 39. and chap. 3. For the relation between Tacitism and reason of state, see Baldini 1992: pt. 3.

[105] Burke 1991: 485; Tuck 2000: 103.

an example of which was Hobbes's suggestion in *Behemoth* that killing in time "those seditious Ministers, which were not perhaps a thousand"—whom Hobbes blamed for the outbreak of the Civil War—might have saved the lives of 100,000 people who died "in that Warre." "It had been (I confesse) a great Massacre, but the killing of a hundred thousand is a greater."[106] Malcolm has also discovered a Latin translation of *Behemoth* by a German law professor, Adam Ebert, completed in 1708 and dedicated to Friedrich I of Prussia. Because Ebert read Hobbes in the Tacitist key, the translation—entitled *De Rebus gestis Olivarij Cromwellj*—allowed Malcolm to ask whether there was a basis for such a reading in Hobbes's work itself. Malcolm's answer was a qualified yes.[107]

Behemoth has also been read with references to Machiavelli or Machiavellism. Nigel Smith, for example, saw Hobbes in *Behemoth* adopting "not a Thucydidean or even Tacitean posture but that of Machiavelli in the *Discorsi*, commenting on historical events through his own interpretative framework." The question of why Charles I, crippled by financial problems, "could not keep his 'corrupted' people in line by force," Smith argued, was to be read as a Machiavellian counsel.[108] Bernard Willms, too, identified a Machiavellian counsel in *Behemoth*. He cited the exchange in which Hobbes's character A referred to Henry VII and Henry VIII of England, the first of whom knew how to fill his coffers "without much noise of the people" whereas the second's virtue was "an erly seuerity," and he pointed out that "this without the former cannot be exercised." Speaker B responded that that looked to him "like an aduice to the King" to leave the seditious Presbyterians alone "till he haue gotten ready money enough to leuy and maintain a sufficient army, and then to fall vpon them, and destroy them." A's reply was: "God forbid that so horrible, vnchristian, and inhumane a designe should euer enter into Kings heart."[109] Willms interpreted that reply as an expression of Hobbes's "outrage" at that "Machiavellian" suggestion.[110] What if Willms lacked the needed sense of humor? Even so, he could have read this passage in connection with one later in the book, where Hobbes had suggested the timely killing of 1,000 subversive priests—and understood that it was very unlikely that Hobbes was indeed abhorred by the thought of "so horrible, vnchristian, and inhumane a designe."

Wootton's study has come closer to giving a reason-of-state interpretation of *Behemoth* than any other reading. But let us examine how strong the evidence is for Wootton's claim that *Behemoth* is a "Machiavellian text."[111] In *Behemoth*'s opening paragraph, A invited his younger interlocutor B to the "diuells mountain" to look at "all kinds of Iniustice, and of all kinds of Folly that the world could afford, and how they were produced by their dams *hypocrisy* and *self-conceit*." B's response to the invitation is as follows: "I should be glad to behold that prospect. You that haue liued in that time,

[106] Malcolm 2007: 118; *Behemoth*, 231. On Naudé, see Freund 1975.
[107] Malcolm 2009: especially 58.
[108] Smith 1994: 352.
[109] *Behemoth*, 182.
[110] Willms 1975: 287.
[111] See note 63.

and in that part of your age wherein men vse to see best into *good* and *euill*, I pray you set me ... vpon the [... Devil's] mountaine by the relation of the actions you then saw, and of their causes, pretensions, iustice, order, artifice, and euent."[112] About halfway through the first dialogue, B reiterates this program: "your purpose was to acquaint me with the History not so much of those actions that pass'd in the time of the late troubles, as of their Causes, and of their Councells, and Artifice by which they were brought to passe."[113] Hobbes spelled out, in the words of his character B, that this "method" was what distinguished his telling of the history from other existing histories of the Civil War.[114] Hobbes's distinction was that, rather than relating historical events, he was exploring and explaining how history was made. The publishers of *Behemoth* did not miss the importance of that "method." Those "causes," "counsels," and "artifices" figured on the title pages of the first editions. As Wootton emphasized: "the preeminent authority on causes, counsels, and artifices" was Machiavelli.[115]

A concept central to a reason-of-state understanding of politics was "interest." The term was rarely used by Machiavelli but was crucial in Guicciardini, who thus helped establish it as "the watchword of the late sixteenth and early seventeenth centuries."[116] Botero stated unequivocally that interest is the basis on which princes make their decisions and that interest overrides all other arguments.[117] In the final analysis, he equated reason of state with the pursuit of interest: "In the end, reason of state is no different than reason of interest."[118] In *Behemoth*, Hobbes used the concept of interest as an analytical tool and did so more often in the first two dialogues than in the last—more narrative—two. On the one hand, interest was related to power and helped to explain it. Hobbes thus spoke of the "Kings interest"[119] and of the interests of "forraigne Princes"[120] or simply of the interest "of those that are in possession of the power to hurt" someone else.[121] On the other hand, interest helped explain human nature. Men, as Hobbes described them, were "pursuers of their own interests and preferments."[122] That was true of the "common people," of the dignitaries, and of bodies of men. The "common people" were "ignorant of their duty to the publick" and were "neuer meditating any thing but their particular interest."[123] Bishops acted in pursuit of "their priuate

---

[112] *Behemoth*, 107. Karl Korsch, one of the leaders of the revolutionary left in post-World War I Germany, found in this opening of *Behemoth* the inspiration for coping with defeat by the Nazis. Korsch 1939: 67.

[113] *Behemoth*, 166.

[114] *Behemoth*, 166–167.

[115] Wootton 1997: 222.

[116] Tuck 1993: 39. Guicciardini seems also to have coined the term "reason of state," but the text in which he did so was only printed in the nineteenth century. Cf. Malcolm 2007: 94–95.

[117] Botero 1589: 60; 1956: 41.

[118] "[I]n conclusione, ragion di Stato è poco altro, che ragion d'interesse." Botero 1606b: 68. Cf. Polin 1975: 27; Malcolm 2007: 94. Burke (1991: 482) cited Béthune as saying the same thing.

[119] *Behemoth*, 144, 334.

[120] *Behemoth*, 213.

[121] *Behemoth*, 158.

[122] *Behemoth*, 145.

[123] *Behemoth*, 158.

interest."[124] And "factions" had no interest "of their owne" in the "Common wealth."[125] In both these aspects, interest helped clarify why people acted the way they had and why that had brought about the Civil War.

But actions proceed from opinions. "For the Actions of men proceed from their Opinions; and in the wel governing of Opinions, consisteth the well governing of mens Actions," Hobbes wrote in *Leviathan*.[126] In *Behemoth*, he famously stated that "the Power of the mighty has no foundation but in the opinion and beleefe of the people."[127] These are striking formulations, yet such understanding of the key importance of opinion for the maintenance of power was not unique. It was, in fact, developed by reason-of-state writers. They understood that the power of the prince depended on his "reputation." In *Della ragion di stato*, "riputatione" is a prominent term, and, at one point, Botero defined it as, next to affection, one of the "two foundations on which all authority must be built."[128] In a treatise appended to later editions of *Della ragion di stato*, Botero "developed that argument in a more recognizably Machiavellian way."[129] He now described reputation as one of the three foundations of the principality. The other two were love and fear, which Botero called "simple," whereas reputation was "composed of the one and the other"—and was thus "better" than either of the other two because it contained in itself what was "good" and "useful" (*vtile*) in them.[130] It was a more formidable underpinning of power than force: Tacitus's Tiberius knew that the maintenance of his affairs benefited more from reputation than it rested on force.[131] Now, this foundation of princely power itself rested on nothing firmer than "opinion and belief." As Botero phrased it, "the reputation of a prince rests on the opinion and belief that the people have of him."[132]

Botero's wording here is almost identical to Hobbes's in the *Behemoth*.[133] But other writers of reason-of-state treatises dealing with this issue worded their views differently and also used different terms or concepts (e.g., consensus and esteem).[134] What matters here is the recognition that the maintenance and augmentation of power depended on what people thought or believed about it. Opinion began to be conceptualized in a distinctively political context, in a way similar to the way credit would

---

[124] *Behemoth*, 213.

[125] *Behemoth*, 215.

[126] *Leviathan*, 91.

[127] *Behemoth*, 128.

[128] Botero 1956: 113. This passage is not in Botero 1589.

[129] Malcolm 2007: 103.

[130] Botero 1600: 45^v, 46^r.

[131] Botero 1600: 47^r.

[132] "[L]a riputatione di un Prencipe è posta nell'opinione, e nel concetto, che il popolo ha di lui." Botero 1600: 44^r. Cf. Malcolm 2007: 104.

[133] Hardwick library had "a whole collection of works by Botero." Malcolm 2007: 109. To Kinch Hoekstra I owe the information that "the *Aggiunte* is present in Hardwick, listed in the circa 1630 catalogue MS E. 1. A. as 'Botero. I Capitani.' The only indication of the edition in that catalogue is that it is an octavo volume."

[134] See Malcolm 2007: 104.

be about a century later: as an immaterial thing producing material effects.[135] But that immaterial thing producing material political effects could itself be produced. Botero understood reputation as a product of the prince's behavior, as an effect that the prince's action had on the "multitude." He knew the cause of the effect (*la ragione dell' effetto*)[136] and thus, in principle at least, how to produce the desired effect. Much reason-of-state writing consists in explaining how that could be done, how opinions and beliefs on which rests "the Power of the mighty" may be formed and directed. From Machiavelli's *Prince* well into Hobbes's own time, advice had been given to the ruler by Machiavelli's admirers and adversaries alike on how to "act in order to gain reputation,"[137] and they discussed techniques that would impress the grandees and keep the populace "content."[138]

Hobbes was more interested in capitalizing on the fundamental insight that opinion had the power to shape human action and to conserve or undermine public authority than he was in elaborating the techniques of statecraft. The key importance of opinion informs much of what Hobbes had written on politics. In *The Elements of Law,* he offered "the opinions concerning law and policy," which were beneficial to commonwealth.[139] *De cive's* aim was to dispel "opinions" that clouded the "authentic" understanding of "just and unjust."[140] *Leviathan* targeted "erroneous doctrines" that determined the objects of passion in ways detrimental to the advancement of "Civill Power."[141] Underlying the argument in *Considerations upon the Reputation* were issues of opinion, especially the insertion of improper religious considerations into the discourse of sovereignty.[142] The Latin *Leviathan* was published because Hobbes saw that "men's disagreements about opinions" could not be "eliminated by arms" but "must be destroyed" by arguments, and he took on the task of washing away "that democratic ink," which had fueled "those civil wars concerning religion in Germany, France, and England."[143] But in no other work is the *problématique* of opinion so in the forefront as in *Behemoth.* Especially in the first two dialogues, the key importance of opinion for the maintenance of power is the organizing principle of Hobbes's analysis. In Hobbes's own explanation, the first dialogue dealt with "certaine opinions in Diuinity and Politicks," which were "the seed" of civil war, and the second with "the growth of it" in the warlike exchange of opinions "between the King and Parliament";[144] that is, with "a kind of

---

[135] Malcolm 2007: 104, cited duke de Rohan's comment on reputaton: "C'est vne chose vaine en apparence, mais qui produit de solides effects." On credit, see especially Defoe 1710: 6. Botero 1600: 43^r, distinguished *riputatione* from *credito* in the sense that the former referred to public persons and the latter to private persons. The rise of the public credit made that distinction obsolete.

[136] Cf. Botero 1600: 43^r, 45^r.

[137] Cf. Machiavelli 1988: chap. 21.

[138] On *contentezza*, see Borrelli 2009: chap. 1.

[139] *Elements of Law*, The Epistle Dedicatory: 20.

[140] *On the Citizen*: Preface: 9–10.

[141] *Leviathan*: 2; cf. The Epistle Dedicatory.

[142] *Considerations*; cf. Lessay 1993: 75.

[143] Latin *Leviathan*: 502, 509–510; *Leviathan* (Curley): 476, 488.

[144] *Behemoth*, 106.

Warre between the Penns of the Parliament, and those of the Secretaries and other able men that were with the King."[145]

Hobbes's "method," the principles and key concepts with the help of which he organized his examination and interpretation of the Civil War, and the great many "Machiavellian" counsels, examples of artifice, deception, disguise, disingenuity, hypocrisy, feigning, simulation and dissimulation, and instrumental usages of religion, allow us to characterize the analysis in *Behemoth* as a reason-of-state analysis. But I do not think all that makes *Behemoth* a "Machiavellian text" and the "politics of *Behemoth* ... the politics of *The Prince*," as Wootton argued.[146] Hobbes's politics was not reason of state.

There are two key moments here. The first is Hobbes's dismissal of prudence. *Prudentia politica* was the "category on which the argument in support of *ragion di stato* was founded."[147] From the positive reception of the category in his preface to the translation of Thucydides, Hobbes moved to rejecting it in *Leviathan* and in *De corpore*.[148] In the 1620s, he saw well-written history as teaching men prudence: "the *principall* and *proper worke* of History, being to instruct, and enable men, by the knowledge of Actions *past*, to beare themselues prudently in the *present*, and prouidently towards the *Future*."[149] A quarter of century later, in *Leviathan*, prudence for Hobbes was "but experience" and, as such, could not be the basis for proposing a universally valid standards of just and unjust.[150] Without knowledge of just and unjust, "Force, and Fraud" become "the two Cardinall vertues," which is what happens in "civill Warre."[151] In *De corpore*, prudence was excluded from philosophy. Because Hobbes defined philosophy as "*such knowledge of effects or appearances, as we acquire by true ratiocination from the knowledge we have first of their causes or generation: And again, of such causes or generations as may be from knowing first their effects*"; because "Memory of things" is knowledge "given us immediately by nature, and not gotten by ratiocination" and, as such, "not philosophy"; and because "Experience is nothing but memory; and Prudence, or prospect into the future time, nothing but expectation of such things as we have already had experience of, Prudence also is not to be esteemed philosophy."[152]

In *Behemoth*, Hobbes takes a clear, negative stance against prudence (as taught by reason of state's endless recourse to historical examples) when he comments on "the ground and originall" of the Parliament's claimed right to "the whole [>and absolute]

[145] *Behemoth*, 212.

[146] Wootton 1997: 217, 225.

[147] Borrelli 1990: 149.

[148] See Borrelli 1990: 152–155; 1993: 230.

[149] *Eight Bookes:* "To the Readers."

[150] *Leviathan*: 60; *De corpore*, I.i.2. In *Leviathan*, 34, Hobbes seems to differentiate between "good" prudence—the wit acquired through "much Experience, and Memory of the like things, and their consequences heretofore"—and bad prudence when "you adde the use of unjust, or dishonest means, such as usually are prompted to men by Feare, or want," producing "that Crooked Wisdome, which is called CRAFT."

[151] *Leviathan*, 63.

[152] *De corpore* I, i, 2. See *De corpore*, 2; I cite the translation in *English Works*, 3.

Soueraignty." That "ground and originall" was "a question of things so long past, that they are now forgotten. Nor haue we any thing to coniecture by, but the Records of our own Nation, and some small and obscure fragments of Roman Histories. And for the Records, seeing they are of things done onely, sometimes iustly, sometimes vniustly, you can neuer by them know what Right they had, but onely what Right they pretended."[153] The response to the question of "what light we haue in this matter from the Roman Histories" was the following:

> It would be too long and an vselesse digression to cite all the ancient Authors that speak of the formes of Commonwealths which were amongst our first Ancestors the Saxons, and other Germans, and of other Nations, from whom we deriue the titles of Honour now in vse in England. Nor will it be possible to deriue from them any argument of Right, but onely examples of fact, which by the ambition of potent subiects haue been oftner vniust then otherwise.[154]

If history was of no help in deciding what was right or just in political conflict, Hobbes's denunciations of "democraticall gentlemen" for reading and citing Greek and Roman histories was not merely an expression of his dislike of the "democraticall" bent of the cited authors (among whom neither Thucydides nor Tacitus are ever named). Rather, Hobbes understood that nothing important in political life could be learned from them: they were a source of examples that might have taught prudence, but not the just and unjust. Prudence for Hobbes might have been commendable in private men. It was, for example, all that was needed for tending to the "busines of ... priuate estates ... But for the Gouernment of a Common-wealth, neither wit, nor prudence, nor diligence is enough without infallible Rules and the true Science of Equity and Justice."[155]

This is the other crucial moment in which Hobbes differed from "Machiavellism" or reason of state: the "Science of Equity and Justice," or the "Science of Justice and Equity," or the "Science of Justice," or "the Science of Just and Vniust."[156] These different names all designated the Science that taught "the necessary Rules of Justice" derived from "euident Principles" "and the necessary connexion of Justice and Peace."[157] The lack of that science brought people "into these troubles" (i.e., civil war).[158] However, the science did exist, but no man could "teach it safely, when it is against the interest of those that are in possession of the power to hurt him."[159] "The Rules of *Just* and *Vniust* sufficiently demonstrated, and from Principles euident to the meanest capacity, haue not been wanting;

---

[153] *Behemoth,* 205–206.

[154] *Behemoth,* 206.

[155] *Behemoth,* 198. This differs from the position in *Leviathan,* 34, that "[t]o govern well a family, and a kingdome, are not different degrees of Prudence; but different sorts of businesse."

[156] *Behemoth,* 158, 198, 323.

[157] *Behemoth,* 322–323.

[158] *Behemoth,* 323.

[159] *Behemoth,* 158.

and notwithstanding the obscurity of their Author, haue shined not onely in this, but also in forraigne Countries to men of good education."[160] That "Author" was Hobbes himself, and the science his "science of politics," a science locked out of the universities by his adversaries: "But out of *Vniuersities* came all those Preachers that taught the contrary."[161]

Behemoth is thus a study of reason-of-state politics, which Hobbes understood very well (unlike the King's incompetent counselors, such as Edward Hyde, the future Earl of Clarendon).[162] Hobbes's criticism of them is very telling and gives us an insight into the complexity of his attitude to reason of state. He seems to have preferred reason of state to earlier approaches to politics, he was able to think consequently from the premises of reason of state to often unsettling conclusions, but he gave the science of politics precedence over political prudence. His calling the King's fainthearted counselors persons of "Experience" was the acknowledgment of their prudence. But their ignorance of the science of politics led them to think, for example, that the "gouernment of England was not an Absolute but a Mixt Monarchy."[163] In Hobbes's view, that was a fundamental misunderstanding of sovereignty, so that the "Mixt Monarchy" that they praised was "indeed nothing else but pure Anarchy."[164] They were still absorbed with (ultimately Aristotelian) "forms of government" made irrelevant by reason of state's studious elaboration of techniques of statecraft. The declarations they wrote on behalf of the king were "very long and full of quotations of Records, and of Cases formerly reported."[165] Therein lay a triple weakness, the effect of which was the weakening of the royal position. First, on the basis of records, it was impossible to prove the King's right or justice. Second, they relied on Common Law, which, in landmark state trials of James I and Charles I's reigns, provided arguments against the strengthening of royal sovereignty and modernization of government along the lines of reason of state.[166] (That "legalistic constitutionalism" was one of *Behemoth*'s main targets.[167]) Third, they indulged in polemics when they should not have: "To what end did the King entertaine so many Petitions, Messages, Declarations and Remonstrances, and vouchsafe his answers to them, when he could not choose but clearly see they were resolued to take from him his Royal power?"[168] Instead, the counselors should have endeavored "to procure him an absolute victory in the Warre."[169] Offering "Propositions . . . of Treaty and accommodation" to the King's adversaries and writing and publishing "fruitlesse" declarations was "of great disaduantage to those Actions by which the King was to

---

[160] *Behemoth*, 158–159.
[161] *Behemoth*, 159.
[162] Cf. Seaward 2010: 32–33.
[163] *Behemoth*, 260.
[164] *Behemoth*, 263.
[165] *Behemoth*, 262–263.
[166] See Berkowitz 1975: 178.
[167] Cromartie 2005: lxiii.
[168] *Behemoth*, 242.
[169] *Behemoth*, 260.

recouer his Crowne and preserue his Life. For it tooke away the courage of the best and forwardest of his Souldiers that looked for great benefit by their seruice out of the Estates of the Rebells, in case they could subdue them, but none at all if the businesse should be ended by a Treaty."[170]

In Hobbes's view, the royal party led a half-hearted and consequently self-defeating reason-of-state politics. As such, it failed to conserve the state, which by definition was the primary aim of reason-of-state politics. The Parliamentary party conducted a more daring and consistent—and, consequently, successful—reason-of-state politics. The result was destruction of the state, which is the opposite of the declared aim of reason-of-state politics. Hobbes's history of the Civil War, as an analysis of the "Causes, Councells, and Artifice" that brought it about and shaped its course, was an analysis of reason-of-state politics as practiced by both parties, politics that caused the dissolution of the state.[171] "Machiavellism," for Hobbes in *Behemoth*, was the art of unmaking the state. Hobbes's own politics was countering both royalist and anti-royalist reason of state with "the Science of Just and Vniust." Instructing men in "their duty to the publick"[172] and teaching them the "obedience to the Laws of the Common wealth" (for to "obey the Laws is Justice and Equity"[173]), Hobbesian science was a conservative force: maintaining the public authority in order that peace might be preserved. The "Rules" of that science were Hobbes's response to the opinion-centered politics of reason of state, which either sounded out trivial vanities or pushed people into civil war.[174] As a political theorist, Hobbes worked on both levels: he analyzed reason-of-state politics of civil war and propounded the peace securing "Science of Just and Vniust." *Behemoth* thus shows how history was made and suggests how it may be judged.

REFERENCES

Anonymous. 1620. *Horae Subseciuae: Observations and Discovrses*. London.

Anonymous. 1750. "The Life of Thomas Hobbes, The Philosopher of Malmesbury," in *The Moral and Political Works of Thomas Hobbes of Malmesbury. Never before collected together. To which is prefixed, the Author's Life*. London.

Aubrey, John. 1898. *Brief Lives*, edited by A. Clark. Oxford: Clarendon.

Bacon, Francis. 1618. *Saggi morali del Signore Francesco Bacono, cavagliero inglese, Gran Cancelliero d'Inghilterra. Con vn'altro suo trattato Della sapienza degli antichi. Tradotti in Italiano*. London.

Bacon, Francis. 1985. *The Essayes or Counsels, Civill and Morall*, edited by Michael Kiernan. Oxford: Clarendon.

---

[170] *Behemoth*, 260.

[171] Cf. Fagiani 1981; Carrive 1983; Nicastro 1995 (French translation: Nicastro 1992).

[172] *Behemoth*, 158.

[173] *Behemoth*, 165.

[174] For readings of *Behemoth* as an analysis of the destabilizing effects of doctrinal warfare, resulting from people acting on competing judgments about their transcendental interests, see Kraynak 1982, 1990: chap. 2; Lloyd 1992: chap. 6.

Bacon, Francis. 2000. *The Advancement of Learning*, edited by Michael Kiernan, vol. 4 of The Oxford Francis Bacon. Oxford: Clarendon.

Baldini, A. Enzo, ed. 1992. *Botero e la "Ragion di Stato": Atti del convegno in memoria di Luigi Firpo (Torino 8-10 marzo 1990)*. Firenze: Leo S. Olschki.

Baumgold, Deborah. 1988. *Hobbes's Political Theory*. Cambridge: Cambridge University Press.

Baumgold, Deborah. 2004. "The Composition of Hobbes's *Elements of Law*." *History of Political Thought* 25: 1.

Berkowitz, David S. 1975. "Reason of State in England and the Petition of Right, 1603–1629," in *Staatsräson: Studien zur Geschichte eines politischen Begriffs*, edited by Roman Schnur, 165–212. Berlin: Duncker & Humblot.

Borot, Luc. 1990. "Introduction," in *Thomas Hobbes, Béhémoth ou Le Long Parlement*, edited and translated by Luc Borot, 9–33. Paris: Vrin.

Borot, Luc. 2004. "Hobbes, Rhetoric, and the Art of the Dialogue," in *Printed Voices: The Renaissance Culture of Dialogue*, edited by D. Heitsch and J. -F. Vallée, 179–190. Toronto: University of Toronto Press.

Borrelli, Gianfranco. 1990. "*Ratio status* e *Leviathan*: prudenza, saggezza e disciplina nella formazione della moderna categoria di sovrantà," in *Thomas Hobbes: le ragioni del moderno tra teologia e politica*, edited by Gianfranco Borrelli, 147–164. Napoli: Morano.

Borrelli, Gianfranco. 1993. *Ragion di stato e Leviatano: Conservazione e scambio alle origini della modernità politica*. Bologna: Il Mulino.

Borrelli, Gianfranco. 2009. *Il lato oscuro del* Leviathan: *Hobbes contro Machiavelli*. Napoli: Cronopis.

Botero, Giovanni. 1589. *Della Ragion di Stato Libri Dieci. Con Tre Libri delle Cause della Grandezza delle Città*. Venetia.

Botero, Giovanni. 1600. "Della ripvtatione del Prencipe," in *Aggivnte di Gio. Botero Benese Alla sua ragion di Stato, nelle quali si tratta Dell' Eccellenze degli Antichi Capitani. Della Neutralità. Della Riputatione. Dell' Agilità delle forze. Della Fortificatione*. Venetia.

Botero, Giovanni. 1606a. *Della ragion di stato, libri dieci. Con tre libri delle cavse della grandezza delle città. Di nuouo in questa vltima impressione, mutati alcuni luoghi dall' istesso autore, & accresciuti di diuersi discorsi*. Venetia.

Botero, Giovanni. 1606b. "Discorso della Neutralità," in Giovanni Botero, *Della ragion di stato, libri dieci. Con tre libri delle cavse della grandezza delle città. Di nuouo in questa vltima impressione, mutati alcuni luoghi dall' istesso autore, & accresciuti di diuersi discorsi*. Venetia.

Botero, Giovanni. 1956. *The Reason of State*, translated by P. J. and D. P. Waley. London: Routledge & Kegan Paul.

Brockdorff, Baron Cay von. 1929. *Hobbes als Philosoph, Pädagoge und Soziologe, Erster Band*, 2nd ed. Kiel: Lipsius and Tischer.

Brownley, Martine Watson, 1989. "Sir Richard Baker's 'Chronicle' and Later Seventeenth-Century English Historiography." *The Huntington Library Quarterly* 52: 4.

Burke, Peter. 1991. "Tacitism, Scepticism, and Reason of State," in *The Cambridge History of Political Thought, 1450–1700*, edited by J. H. Burns with the assistance of M. Goldie, 479–498. Cambridge: Cambridge University Press.

Carrive, Paulette. 1983. "Béhémoth et Léviathan," in *Hobbes, philosophie, politique, Cahiers de Philosophie Politique et Juridique de l'Université de Caen*, 3. Caen: Université de Caen.

Catlin, George E. G. 1922. *Thomas Hobbes as Philosopher, Publicist and Man of Letters*. Oxford: Basil Blackwell.

Champion, J. A. I. 2006. "*An Historical Narration Concerning Heresie*: Thomas Hobbes, Thomas Barlow, and the Restoration debate over 'heresy,'" in *Heresy, Literature, and Politics in Early Modern English Culture*, edited by D. Loewenstein and J. Marshall, 221–253. Cambridge: Cambridge University Press.

Cleveland, John. 1687. *The Works of Mr. John Cleveland: containing his poems, orations, epistles, collected into one volume, with the life of the author*. London.

Coates, Benn. 2004. *The Impact of the English Civil War on the Economy of London, 1642–50*. Aldershot: Ashgate.

Collins, Jeffrey R. 2007. *The Allegiance of Thomas Hobbes*. Oxford: Oxford University Press.

Corfield, Penelope. 1973. "Economic Issues and Ideologies," in *The Origins of the English Civil War*, edited by C. Russell, 197–218. London: Macmillan.

Courntey, William Prideaux. 1921-2. "Maseres, Francis (1731-1824)," in *The Dictionary of National Biography*, edited by Leslie Stephen and Sidney Lee, vol. 12, 1292–1294. London. Oxford University Press.

Cromartie, Alan. 2005. "General Introduction," in Thomas Hobbes, *Writings on Common Law and Hereditary Right*, edited by Alan Cromartie and Quentin Skinner, xiii–lxv. Oxford: Clarendon.

Defoe, Daniel. 1710. *An essay upon publick credit: being an enquiry how the publick credit comes to depend upon the change of the ministry, or the dissolutions of Parliaments; and whether it does so or no. With an Argument, Proving that the Publick Credit may be upheld and maintain'd in this Nation; and perhaps brought to a greater Height than it ever yet arriv'd at; Tho' all the Changes or Dissolutions already Made, Pretended to, and now Discours'd of, shou'd come to pass in the World*. London.

De Mas, Enrico. 1987. "Introduzione," in Fra Fulgenzio Micanzio, O.S.M., *Lettere a William Cavendish (1615-1628), nella versione inglesa di Thomas Hobbes*, edited by R. Ferrini, with an Introduction by E. De Mas, 9–29. Rome: Istituto storico O.S.M.

Descendre, Romain. 2009. *L'état du monde: Giovanni Botero entre raison d'État et géopolitique*. Geneva: Librairie Droz.

Dietz, Mary G. 1990. "Hobbes's Subject as Citizen," in *Thomas Hobbes and Political Theory*, edited by Mary G. Dietz, 91–119. Lawrence: University Press of Kansas.

Fagiani, Franceso. 1981. "Leviathan contra Behemoth: Costruzione e dissoluzione dei corpi politici." *Materiali per una storia della cultura giuridica* 11: 2.

Farnell, James F. 1977. "The Social and Intellectual Basis of London's Role in the English Civil Wars." *Journal of Modern History* 49: 4.

Freund, Julien. 1975. "La situation exceptionelle comme justification de la raison d'État chez Gabriel Naudé," in *Staatsräson: Studien zur Geschichte eines politischen Begriffs*, edited by Roman Schnur, 141–164. Berlin: Duncker & Humblot.

Fussner, F. Smith. 1962. *The Historical Revolution: English Historical Writing and Thought, 1580-1640*. London: Routledge and Kegan Paul.

Gabrieli, Vittorio, 1957. "Bacone, la Riforma e Roma nella versione hobbessiana d'un carteggio di Fulgenzio Micanzio." *The English Miscellany* 8: 195–250.

Gooch, G. P. n.d. *Hobbes: Annual Lecture on a Master Mind, Henriette Hertz Trust of the British Academy, 1939*. London: Humphrey Milford.

Hill, Christopher. 1990. *A Nation of Change and Novelty: Radical Politics, Religion and Literature in Seventeenth-Century England*. London: Routledge.

Hobbes, Thomas. 1629. *Eight Bookes of the Peloponnesian Warre Written by Thvcydides the sonne of Olorus. Interpreted with Faith and Diligence Immediately out of the Greeke by Thomas Hobbes Secretary to ye late Earle of Deuonshire*. London.

Hobbes, Thomas. 1640 [2008]. *The Elements of Law*, edited by J. C. A. Gaskin. Oxford University Press: Oxford.

Hobbes, Thomas. 1655. *De corpore*. London.

Hobbes, Thomas. 1680. *Considerations upon the Reputation, Loyalty, Manners, & Religion of Thomas Hobbes of Malmsbvry*. London.

Hobbes, Thomas. 1682. *Tracts of Mr. Thomas Hobbs of Malmsbury, Containing I. Behemoth, the History of the Causes of the Civil Wars of England, from 1640. to1660. Printed from the Author's own Copy: Never printed (but with a thousand faults) before. II. An answer to Arch-Bishop Bramhall's Book, called the Catching of the Leviathan: Never printed before. III. An Historical Narration of Heresie, and the Punishment thereof: Corrected by the true Copy. IV. Philosophical Problems, dedicated to the King in 1662, but never printed before*, London: Printed for W. Crooke.

Hobbes, Thomas. 1723. *The history of the Grecian War ... Written by Thucydides. Faithfully translated from the original by Thomas Hobbes ...* London: printed by B. Motte.

Hobbes, Thomas. 1812. *The History of the Grecian War ... Faithfully translated ... by Thomas Hobbes, of Malmsbury. A new edition, corrected and amended*. London: Longmans & Co.

Hobbes, Thomas. 1822. *The History of the Grecian War ... Faithfully translated ... by Thomas Hobbes, of Malmsbury. A new edition, corrected and amended*. London: G. & W. B. Whittaker.

Hobbes, Thomas. 1823. *The History of the Grecian War ... Faithfully translated ... by Thomas Hobbes, of Malmsbury. A new edition, corrected and amended*. London: G. & W. B. Whittaker.

Hobbes, Thomas. 1824. *Thucydides in English; chiefly from the translation of Hobbes ... With notes and various readings, an analysis, and a collation of other editions with the amended text of Bekker*. Oxford: Munday, Slatter, and J. Vincent.

Hobbes, Thomas. 1830. *Thucydides in English; chiefly from the translation of Hobbes ... With notes and various readings, an analysis, and a collation of other editions with the amended text of Bekker*. Oxford: H. Slatter, and J. Vincent.

Hobbes, Thomas. 1966. *Leviathan*. In *Opera Latina*, edited by Gulielmi Molesworth. London: Bohn.

Hobbes, Thomas. 1966. *T. Hobbes Malmesburiensis Vita*. In *Opera Latina*, edited by Gulielmi Molesworth. London: Bohn.

Hobbes, Thomas. 1994. *The Prose Life in The Elements of Law Natural and Politic, Part I Human Nature, Part II De Corpore Politico, with Three Lives*, edited by J. C. A. Gaskin. Oxford: Oxford University Press.

Hobbes, Thomas. 1994. *The Verse Life, in The Elements of Law Natural and Politic, Part I Human Nature, Part II De Corpore Politico, with Three Lives*, edited by J. C. A. Gaskin. Oxford: Oxford University Press.

Hobbes, Thomas. 1994. *Leviathan*, edited by Edwin Curley. Indianapolis: Hackett Publishing Company.

Hobbes, Thomas. 1997. *The Correspondence of Thomas Hobbes*, 2 vols., edited by Noel Malcolm. Oxford: Clarendon Press.

Hobbes, Thomas. 1998. *On the Citizen*, edited and translated by R. Tuck and M. Silverthorne. Cambridge Texts in the History of Political Thought. Cambridge: Cambridge University Press.

Hobbes, Thomas. 2008. *Thomae Hobbes Malmesburiensis vita [carmine expressa] authore seipso*, edited and translated by Jean Terrel, *Hobbes: vies d'un philosophe*, 132–168. Rennes: Presses Universitaires de Rennes.

Hobbes, Thomas. 2010. *Behemoth, or, The Long Parliament*, vol. 10 of The Clarendon Edition of the Works of Thomas Hobbes, edited by Paul Seeward. Oxford: Clarendon.

Hoekstra, Kinch. 2006. "The End of Philosophy (The Case of Hobbes)." *Proceedings of the Aristotelian Society*, New Series 106: 25–62.

Howell, Roger. 1983. "Neutralism, Conservatism and Political Alignment in the English Revolution: The Case of Towns, 1642–9," in *Reactions to the English Civil War, 1642–1649*, edited by J. Morrill, 67–87. New York: St. Martin's Press.

Korsch, Karl. 1939. "State and Counter-Revolution." *The Modern Quarterly* 11: 2.

Kraynak, Robert P. 1982. "Hobbes's Behemoth and the Argument for Absolutism." *American Political Science Review* 76: 837–847.

Kraynak, Robert P. 1990. *History and Modernity in the Thought of Thomas Hobbes*. Ithaca, NY: Cornell University Press.

Lessay, Franck. 1993. "M. Hobbes considéré dans sa loyauté, sa religion, sa réputation et ses moeurs," in Thomas Hobbes, *Textes sur l'hérésie et sur l'histoire*, edited by Franck Lessay, 75–88. Vol. 12/1 *of Oeuvres de Thomas Hobbes*. Paris: J. Vrin.

Letwin, William. 1972. "The Economic Foundations of Hobbes's Politics," in *Hobbes and Rousseau: A Collection of Critical Essays*, edited by M. Cranston and R. S. Peters, 143–164. Garden City, NY: Doubleday.

Levy, Fritz. 1997. "The Background of Hobbes' *Behemoth*," in *The Historical Imagination in Early Modern Britain: History, Rhetoric, and Fiction, 1500–1800*, edited by D. M. Kelley and D. H. Sacks, 243–266. Cambridge: Cambridge University Press and Woodrow Wilson Center.

Lips, Julius. 1927. *Die Stellung des Thomas Hobbes zu den politischen Parteien der großen englischen Revolution, Mit erstmaliger Übersetzung des Behemoth oder Das Lange Parlament*, with an introduction by Ferdinand Tönnies. Leipzig: E. Wiegandt.

Lloyd, S. A. 1992. *Ideals as Interests in Hobbes's Leviathan: The Power of Mind over Matter*. Cambridge: Cambridge University Press.

Lucan. 1627. *Lvcan's Pharsalia: or The civill Warres of Rome, betweene Pompey the great, and Iulius Caesar: The whole ten Bookes*, Englished by Thomas May Esquire. London.

Macdonald, Hugh, and Mary Hargreaves. 1952. *Thomas Hobbes: A Bibliography*. London: The Bibliographical Society.

MacGillivray, Royce. 1970. "Thomas Hobbes's History of the English Civil War: A Study of Behemoth." *Journal of the History of Ideas* 31: 2.

MacGillivray, Royce. 1974. *Restoration Historians and the English Civil War*. The Hague: Martinus Nijhof.

Machiavelli, Niccolò. 1988. *The Prince*, edited by Quentin Skinner and Russell Price. Cambridge Texts in the History of Political Thought. Cambridge: Cambridge University Press.

Macpherson, C. B. 1962. *The Political Theory of Possessive Individualism: Hobbes to Locke*. Oxford: Oxford University Press.

Malcolm, Noel. 1984. *De Dominis (1560–1624): Venetian, Anglican, Ecumenist and Relapsed Heretic*. London: Strickland & Scott Academic Publications.

Malcolm, Noel. 1990. "Hobbes's Science of Politics and his Theory of Science," in *Hobbes oggi: Atti del Convegno internazionale di studi promosso da Arrigo Pacchi (Milano-Locarno 18–21 maggio 1988)*, edited by A. Napoli in collaboration with G. Canziani, 145–157. Milano: Franco Angeli.

Malcolm, Noel. 2002. *Aspects of Hobbes*. Oxford: Oxford University Press.

Malcolm, Noel. 2007. *Reason of State, Propaganda and the Thirty Years' War: An Unknown Translation by Thomas Hobbes*. Oxford: Clarendon.

Malcolm, Noel. 2009. "'Behemoth latinus': Adam Ebert, Tacitism, and Hobbes," in *Hobbes's Behemoth: Religion and Democracy*, edited by Tomaž Mastnak, 38–72. Exeter: Imprint Academic.

Maseres, Francis. 1812. "A Preface to the Present Edition of This History," in Thomas May, *The history of the Parliament of England, which began November the third, MDCXL; with a short and necessary view of some precedent years.* London.

Maseres, Francis. 1815. *Select Tracts relating to the Civil Wars in England, in the reign of King Charles the First; by writers who lived in the time of those wars, and were witnesses of the events which they describe,* edited by Francis Maseres. London: R. Wilks.

Mastnak, Tomaž. 2009. "Introduction: The Ways of Behemoth," in *Hobbes's Behemoth: Religion and Democracy,* edited by Tomaž Mastnak, 1–37. Exeter: Imprint Academic.

May, Thomas. 1627. "The Epistle Dedicatory," in *Lvcan's Pharsalia: or The civill Warres of Rome, betweene Pompey the great, and Iulius Caesar: The whole ten Bookes,* Englished by Thomas May Esquire. London.

Meinecke, Friedrich. 1976. *Die Idee der Staatsräson in der neueren Geschichte,* edited by Walther Hofer, 4th ed. München: R. Oldenbourg.

Mersenne, Marin. 1970. *Correspondence du P. Marin Mersenne, religieux minime,* vol. 11, edited by Cornelis de Waard. Paris: Éditions du Centre National de la Recherche Scientifique.

Metzger, Hans-Dieter. 1991. *Thomas Hobbes und die Englische Revolution, 1640–1660.* Stuttgart: Frommann-Holzboog.

Milton, Philip. 1993. "Hobbes, Heresy and Lord Arlington." *History of Political Thought 14:* 4.

Nicastro, Onofrio. 1977. *Note sul* Behemoth di *Thomas Hobbes.* Pisa: Felici.

Nicastro, Onofrio, editor and translator. 1979. Thomas Hobbes, *Behemoth.* Bari: Laterza.

Nicastro, Onofrio. 1992. "Le vocabulaire de la dissolution de l'État," in *Hobbes et son vocabulaire: Études de lexicographie philosophique,* edited by Y. -Ch. Zarka, 259–287. Paris: Vrin.

Nicastro, Onofrio. 1995. "Il vocabulario della dissoluzione dello stato," in idem, *Politica e religione nel seicento inglese: Racolta di scritti,* 195–224. Pisa: Edizioni ETS.

Norbrook, David. 2001. "The English Revolution and English historiography," in *The Cambridge Companion to Writing of the English Revolution,* edited by N. H. Keeble, 233–250. Cambridge: Cambridge University Press.

Parkin, Jon. 2007. *Taming the Leviathan: The Reception of the Political and Religious Ideas of Thomas Hobbes in England, 1640–1700.* Cambridge: Cambridge University Press.

Pearl, Valerie. 1961. *London and the Outbreak of the Puritan Revolution: City Government and National Politics, 1625–43.* London: Oxford University Press.

Pearl, Valerie. 1972. "London's Counter-Revolution," in *The Interregnum: The Quest for Settlement 1646-1660,* edited by G. E. Aylmer, 29–56. Hamden, CT: Archon Books.

Pocock, J. G. A. 1999. "Thomas May and the Narrative of Civil War," in *Writing and Political Engagement in Seventeenth-Century England,* edited by D. Hirst and R. Strier, 112–144. Cambridge: Cambridge University Press.

Pocock, J. G. A. 2000. "Medieval Kings at the Court of Charles I: Thomas May's Verse Histories," in *Perspectives on Early Modern and Modern Intellectual History: Essays in Honor of Nancy S. Struever,* edited by J. Marino and M. W. Schlitt, 442–458. Rochester, NY: University of Rochester Press.

Polin, Raymond. 1975. "Le concept de Raison d'État avant la lettre d'après Machiavel," in *Staatsräson: Studien zur Geschichte eines politischen Begriffs,* edited by Roman Schnur, 27–42. Berlin: Duncker & Humblot.

Porter, Stephen. 1996. "Introduction," in *London and the Civil War*, edited by S. Porter, 1–30. Houndmills: Macmillan.

Ranke, Leopold von. 1957. *Englische Geschichte*, edited by W. Andreas. Wiesbaden: Emil Vollmer.

Reik, Miriam M. 1977. *The Golden Lands of Thomas Hobbes*. Detroit: Wayne State University Press.

Richardson, R. C. 1988. *The Debate on the English Revolution Revisited*. London: Routledge.

Robertson, George Croom. 1910. *Hobbes*. Edinburgh: William Blackwood.

Rogers, G. A. J., and Tom Sorell, ed. 2000. *Hobbes and History*. London: Routledge.

Schnur, Roman, ed. 1975. *Staatsräson: Studien zur Geschichte eines politischen Begriffs*. Berlin: Duncker & Humblot.

Schuhmann, Karl. 1996. "Thomas Hobbes, *Oeuvres.*" *British Journal for the History of Philosophy* 4: 1.

Schuhmann, Karl. 1998. *Hobbes: Une chronique*. Paris: Vrin.

Schuhmann, Karl. 2000. "Hobbes's Concept of History," in *Hobbes and History*, edited by G. A. J. Rogers and Tom Sorell, 3–24. London: Routledge.

Seaward, Paul. 2010. "Introduction," in Thomas Hobbes, *Behemoth, or, The Long Parliament*, vol. 10 of The Clarendon Edition of the Works of Thomas Hobbes. Oxford: Clarendon.

Skinner, Quentin. 1965. "History and Ideology in the English Revolution." *The Historical Journal* 8: 2.

Skinner, Quentin. 1991. "Thomas Hobbes: Rhetoric and the Construction of Morality." *Proceedings of the British Academy* 76: 1–61.

Skinner, Quentin. 1993. "'Scientia civilis' in Classical Rhetoric and in the early Hobbes," in *Political Discourses in Early Modern Britain*, edited by Nicholas Phillipson and Quentin Skinner, 67–93. Cambridge: Cambridge University Press.

Skinner, Quentin. 1996. *Reason and Rhetoric in the Philosophy of Hobbes*. Cambridge: Cambridge University Press.

Skinner, Quentin. 2002a. *Hobbes and Civil Science*. Vol. 3 of idem, *Visions of Politics*. Cambridge: Cambridge University Press.

Skinner, Quentin. 2002b. "Classical Liberty and the Coming of the English Civil War," in vol. 2 of *Republicanism: A Shared European Heritage*, edited by Martin van Gelderen and Quentin Skinner, 9–26. Cambridge: Cambridge University Press.

Skinner, Quentin. 2008. *Hobbes and Republican Liberty*. Cambridge: Cambridge University Press.

Smith, Adam. 1978. *Lectures on Jurisprudence*, edited by R. L. Meek, D. D. Raphael, and P. G. Stein, The Glasgow Edition of the Works and Correspondence of Adam Smith. Oxford: Oxford University Press.

Smith, Nigel. 1994. *Literature and Revolution in England, 1640–1660*. New Haven, CT: Yale University Press.

Sommerville, Johann P. 2000. "Hobbes, Selden, Erastianism, and the History of the Jews," in *Hobbes and History*, edited by G. A. J. Rogers and Tom Sorell, 160–188. London: Routledge.

Sommerville, Johann. 2004. "Hobbes and Independency," in *Nouve prospettive critiche sul Leviatano di Hobbes nel 350 anniversario di pubblicazione/New Critical Perspectives on Hobbes's Leviathan upon the 350th Anniversary of its Publication*, edited by L. Foisneau and G. Wright, 167–173. Milano: FrancoAngeli.

Sorell, Tom. 1988. "The Science in Hobbes's Politics," in *Perspectives on Thomas Hobbes*, ed. G. A. J. Rogers and A. Ryan, 67–80. Mind Association Occasional Series. Oxford: Clarendon.

Stephen, James Fitzjames. 1892. *Horae Sabbaticae: Reprint of Articles Contributed to* The Saturday Review, *Second Series*. London: Macmillan.

Stephen, Leslie. 1904. *Hobbes*. London and New York: Macmillan.

Stewart, Dugald. 1854. *The Philosophy of the Active and Moral Powers of Man*, in vol. 6 of *The Collected Works of Dugald Stewart, Esq., F.R.S.S.*, edited by W. Hamilton. Edinburgh: Thomas Constable and Co.

Strauss, Leo. 1936. *The Political Philosophy of Hobbes: Its Basis and Its Genesis*, translated by Elsa M. Sinclair. Oxford: Clarendon.

Strauss, Leo. 2001. *Hobbes' politische Wissenschaft in ihrer Genesis*, in *Hobbes' politische Wissenschaft und zugehörige Schriften-Briefe*, edited by Heinrich Meier and Weibke Meier, vol. 3 of *Leo Strauss Gesammelte Schriften*, 3–192. Stuttgart: J. B. Metzler.

Terrel, Jean. 2008. *Hobbes: vies d'un philosophe*. Rennes: Presses universitaires de Rennes.

Thomas, Keith. 1965. "The Social Origins of Hobbes's Political Thought," in *Hobbes Studies*, edited by K. C. Brown, 185–236. Cambridge, MA: Harvard University Press.

Tönnies, Ferdinand. 1889. "Preface," in *Behemoth or the Long Parliament. By Thomas Hobbes of Malmesbury. Edited for the first time from the original ms. by Ferdinand Tönnies, PhD*, vii–xi. London: Simpkin, Marshall, and Co.

Tönnies, Ferdinand. 1925a. *Thomas Hobbes Leben und Lehre*, 3rd ed. Stuttgart: Frommann.

Tönnies, Ferdinand. 1925b. "Herbert Spencers soziologisches Werk," in idem, *Soziologische Studien und Kritiken, Erste Sammlung*. Jena: Gustav Fischer.

Tönnies, Ferdinand. 1936. "Contributions à l'histoire de la pensée de Hobbes." *Archives de philosophie*, 12: 72–98.

Tönnies, Ferdinand. 1998– . *Ferdinand Tönnies Gesamtausgabe*, edited by Lars Claused et al. Berlin: De Gruyter.

Tricaud, François. 1985. "Éclaircissements sur les six première biographies de Hobbes." *Archives de Philosophie 48*: 2.

Tuck, Richard. 1988. "Hobbes and Descartes," in *Perspectives on Thomas Hobbes*, ed. G. A. J. Rogers and A. Ryan, 11–41. Mind Association Occasional Series. Oxford: Clarendon.

Tuck, Richard. 1989. *Hobbes*. Oxford: Oxford University Press.

Tuck, Richard. 1991. "Introduction," in Thomas Hobbes, *Leviathan*, edited by Richard Tuck, ix–xxvi. Cambridge Texts in the History of Political Thought. Cambridge: Cambridge University Press.

Tuck, Richard. 1993. *Philosophy and Government, 1572–1651*. Cambridge: Cambridge University Press.

Tuck, Richard. 1998. "Introduction," in Thomas Hobbes, *On the Citizen*, edited and translated by R. Tuck and M. Silverthorne, viii–xxxiii. Cambridge Texts in the History of Political Thought. Cambridge: Cambridge University Press.

Tuck, Richard. 2000. "Hobbes and Tacitus," in *Hobbes and History*, edited by G. A. J. Rogers and Tom Sorell, 99–111. London: Routledge.

Vaughan, Geoffrey M. 2002. *Behemoth Teaches Leviathan: Thomas Hobbes on Political Education*. Lanham, MD: Lexington Books.

Willms, Bernard. 1975. "Staatsräson und das Problem der politischen Definition: Bemerkungen zum Nominalismus in Hobbes' 'Behemoth,'" in *Staatsräson: Studien zur Geschichte eines politischen Begriffs*, edited by Roman Schnur, 275–300. Berlin: Duncker & Humblot.

Wolf, Friedrich O. 1969. *Die neue Wissenschaft des Thomas Hobbes: Zu den Grundlagen der politischen Philosophie der Neuzeit*. Stuttgart–Bad Cannstatt: Friedrich Frommann.

Wood, Anthony. 1692. *Athenae Oxonienses: an exact history of all the writers and bishops who have had their education in the most ancient and famous University of Oxford*, etc. London.

Wood, Anthony. 1813–20. *Athenae oxonienses: An Exact History of all the Writers and Bishops who have had their Education in the University of Oxford. To which are added the Fasti, or Annals of the said University*, edited by Ph. Bliss. London: Printed for F. C. and J. Rivington et al.

Woolf, D. R. 1990. *The Idea of History in Early Stuart England: Erudition, Ideology, and "The Light of Truth" from the Accession of James I to the Civil War*. Toronto: University of Toronto Press.

Wootton, David. 1997. "Thomas Hobbes's Machiavellian Moments," in *The Historical Imagination in Early Modern Britain: History, Rhetoric, and Fiction, 1500–1800*, edited by D. M. Kelley and D. H. Sacks, 210–242. Cambridge: Cambridge University Press and Woodrow Wilson Center.

Worden, Blair. 1993. "Ben Jonson Among the Historians," in *Culture and Politics in Early Stuart England*, edited by K. Sharpe and P. Lake, 67–90. Stanford, CA: Stanford University Press.

Yerby, George. 2008. *People and Parliament: Representative Rights and the English Revolution*. Houndmills: Palgrave Macmillan.

CHAPTER 26

....

HOBBES ON THE NATURE AND SCOPE OF POETRY

....

TIMOTHY RAYLOR

1 INTRODUCTION

....

ALTHOUGH we think of him today as a political philosopher, Thomas Hobbes was a man of his age, with wide-ranging intellectual interests. These interests included the theory and the practice of poetry, in both Latin and English. As a Latin poet, Hobbes was precocious. While a schoolboy, he translated Euripides's *Medea* into Latin iambics.[1] When tutor to the Cavendish family, he penned a chorographical poem in hexameters celebrating the several "wonders" of the Peak, his patrons' power-base in the North Midlands.[2] In the middle years of the century or later, he wrote and dedicated to William Cavendish, third earl of Devonshire, a brief astronomical poem expounding his theory of the motion of the Sun, Moon, and Earth.[3] There was talk among his followers in the early 1660s that he intended to turn his entire philosophical system into Latin verse—"in a style," as one of his enthusiastic French disciples put it, "somewhat similar to that of Hesiod."[4] Although nothing came of this extraordinary scheme—the account of which may have been prompted by sight of the astronomical poem previously mentioned—Hobbes nonetheless composed, perhaps as early as 1659 and certainly by 1671, a lengthy satirical history of the church in elegiac couplets: a history that constitutes an expansion and continuation of the anti-ecclesiastical material in the third and fourth parts of *Leviathan*.[5] In his eighties, Hobbes returned to poetry,

---

[1] Aubrey 1898, 1: 328–329.
[2] For the date and occasion, see Malcolm 2007: 10; Martinich 1998.
[3] Hobbes 1973: 439–447; Sergio 2007: 54–56; *The Clarendon Edition of the Works of Thomas Hobbes* (hereinafter *HW*) 7: 625, 628 n. 5.
[4] *HW* 7: 625.
[5] Completed by 1671, but not published until 1688: see Hobbes, *Historia Ecclesiastica*, 84–86.

both Latin and English, with fresh vigor. In 1672 (his eighty-fourth year), he completed in Latin elegaics an autobiography (it was published in 1679). In the following year, he published a translation, in rhymed English quatrains, of the story of Ulysses's voyage home from Troy (i.e., books ix–xii of *The Odyssey*; 1673). It was reissued in 1674. Hobbes was sufficiently pleased with it to press ahead with a translation of the entire *Odyssey*, which duly appeared in 1675. This was followed, a year later, by his translation of the whole *Iliad* (1676). Even this wasn't all. Shortly before his death at the age of ninety-one, Hobbes emerged as a love poet, composing, in rhymed quatrain stanzas, some amatory verses insisting on his continued ability to love "and have a mistresse too."[6] One can only marvel at his stamina, resilience, and optimism.

Hobbes's literary activities were not restricted to verse composition. He made several forays into criticism and theory, contributing short essays in the form of letters to promote "heroic poems" by two of his acquaintances—one, in 1650, on behalf of Sir William Davenant's *Gondibert* and another, in 1668, in favor of Edward Howard's *The Brittish Princes*. He returned to epic theory again in 1675, prefacing his *Odyssey* with a brief critical account of "The Vertues of an Heroique Poem."

Whereas literary scholars have long recognized Hobbes's "Answer," at least, as a major contribution to literary criticism and theory, students of the philosopher have tended, until quite recently, to give little attention to Hobbes's contributions in the field of literature and have displayed nervousness or uncertainty about how to make sense of them. In his classic study of Hobbes, for instance, the moral philosopher John Laird speaks for the quality of Hobbes's literary criticism, but immediately undercuts his own judgment: "In my ignorance of these things, I shall rashly affirm that Hobbes was a very good literary critic."[7] Such writers have taken the cue from Hobbes himself, who adopted a wryly self-deprecating stance with regard to his literary excursions. About his translation of Homer, he was famously dismissive: "Why then did I write it? Because I had nothing else to do. Why publish it? Because I thought it might take off my Adversaries from shewing their folly upon my more serious Writings, and set them upon my Verses to shew their wisdom."[8] Hobbes adopted a similarly offhanded stance with regard to his critical writings. His essay on *Gondibert* was struck by some of the salvos of mockery directed at Davenant's overblown ambitions: ambitions that led him to publish a Preface, complete with commendatory verses by his friends, to a poem that wasn't even half finished. When, eighteen years later, Edward Howard approached Hobbes for a comment on *The Brittish Princes*, the philosopher introduced his remarks by reminding Howard of prior attacks on his critical judgment: "My Judgement in *Poetry* hath, you know, been once already Censured by very good Wits, for commending *Gondibert*."[9] The sense that Hobbes thought little of his poetry and criticism, deploying it merely to draw fire from his controversial forays into geometry,

---

[6] Aubrey 1898, 1: 364–365.
[7] Laird 1934: 41.
[8] *HW* 24: xcix.
[9] *HW* 7: 704.

physics, and political philosophy, has informed and perhaps rather too strongly shaped critical responses to them.

But it is a mistake to take Hobbes's self-deprecation at face value. Despite his insouciance about it, Hobbes nevertheless invested several years of his life in literary endeavor. As Eric Nelson, their editor, notes, the two Homer translations amount to 28,000 lines: taken as a whole, they represent Hobbes's longest single work.[10] And although Hobbes acknowledged the attacks on his praise of *Gondibert*, he nevertheless declined to yield to them, dismissing his attackers as mere "wits" (thereby drawing on the hierarchical distinction between wit and judgment that informs his psychology) and insisting that his critical opinions needed no revision: "they [i.e., the wits] have not, I think, disabled my testimony."[11] As we shall see, neither in his letter to Howard nor in the preface to his *Odyssey* does Hobbes engage in any fundamental revision of his critical stance.

Although students of Hobbes might, over the long term, be charged with neglect of his literary activities, this has been significantly redressed in recent years as growing interest in Hobbes's rhetoric—driven by the linguistic turn in the histories of philosophy and science—has brought new attention to his writings in the field of poetry and literary criticism and a fresh concern with the place of poetry in his thought. Hobbes's major poetic projects—his *Historia Ecclesiastica* and his translations of *The Iliad* and *The Odyssey*—recently appeared for the first time in scholarly editions, and commentators have become increasingly preoccupied with aligning his theoretical pronouncements about poetry with his apparently shifting attitude to rhetoric—a topic that is now, thanks to important work by a number of scholars (above all David Johnston and Quentin Skinner) close to the heart of Hobbes studies.[12] Central to this new concern is the belief that in Hobbes's changing attitude to rhetoric may lie an explanation for the distinctive texture of his philosophical and stylistic masterpiece, *Leviathan*. And poetry has been drawn into this discussion because, if Hobbes's attitude to rhetoric underwent a thaw at the time he was working on *Leviathan*—appearing no longer as a threat but as a potential aid to political philosophy and government—then might not his attitude to poetry have undergone a similar shift? After all, in composing his "Answer," Hobbes was responding to Davenant's bold restatement of the humanist vision of poetry as a necessary adjunct of government.[13] And it was while working on *Leviathan*—in January 1650—that Hobbes composed the "Answer."[14] Hobbes's generous acknowledgment therein that he has turned to Davenant for assistance offers further encouragement for this approach: "I have used your Judgment no lesse in many thinges of mine, which comming to light will thereby appeare the better."[15] Although Hobbes's "many thinges"

---

[10] *HW* 24: xiv.

[11] *HW* 7: 704.

[12] Hobbes, *Historia Ecclesiastica*; *HW* 24–25; Johnston 1986; Skinner 1996.

[13] Davenant (1971): 27–44.

[14] Hobbes dated his "Answer" from Paris [December 31 1649/] January 10 1650, by which time he was probably already at work on *Leviathan*; in May 1650, his friend Robert Payne learned that he had completed thirty-seven of its projected fifty chapters; Malcolm 2002: 19.

[15] Hobbes 1971: 54.

is strategically vague, pointing away from any work in particular, the acknowledgment has encouraged scholars to set about determining Davenant's impact on *Leviathan* and to search for a re-evaluation of poetry in Hobbes's thinking at this time.

That investigation has yet to find a consistent focus or to generate consensus. To Ted H. Miller, Hobbes's "Answer" to Davenant announces nothing less than "an alliance between poetry and philosophy," and *Leviathan* itself is a kind of poem—something approaching, in Miller's view, a court masque.[16] To Conal Condren it asserts that the poet can become "a true philosopher."[17] But not all commentators see poetry as occupying quite so prominent a place in the disciplinary scheme of the "Answer" or in Hobbes's thinking more generally. Eric Nelson agrees that Hobbes is keen to promote a union of poetry and philosophy and sees him so doing in the 1675 essay "Concerning the Vertues of an Heroic Poem." Nelson nonetheless argues that, despite Hobbes's presumed rapprochement with rhetoric at mid-century, the "Answer" presents a restricted account of poetry in which the role of fancy has been "radically constrained."[18] Nor is there agreement on the claim that Hobbes offers, in the "Answer," a clear and unambiguous statement of a revised view of poetry and its relationship to philosophy. Condren suggests that although Hobbes seems to move, in the "Answer," toward a more positive view of poetry than he had previously held—seeing in it a potentially valuable ally of a philosophy in which he had, in the wake of the civil wars, lost confidence—he is nevertheless confused and contradictory about the precise nature of that relationship—drawing, at one moment, a sharp distinction between philosophy and poetry and urging, at another, that the poet can and should be a philosopher.[19] Richard Hillyer goes further, suggesting that Hobbes tries to paper over the gaps between philosophy and poetry while remaining "incoherent" on the larger question of the status of eloquence.[20] There is, in sum, no agreement, either on the precise character of the relationship between poetry and philosophy adumbrated by Hobbes in his "Answer" to Davenant or about its broader significance.

In this chapter, I argue against the view that Hobbes's understanding of the relationship between poetry and philosophy is significantly shifting, confused, or incoherent. I suggest that his understanding of the nature and purpose of poetry, and of its relationship to philosophy, remains fundamentally consistent from the early 1640s through to the mid-1670s. This understanding allows no space for the kind of union in which a poet might take on himself the role of philosopher. From early to late, Hobbes sees poetry as a dutiful servant of philosophy but in no sense as an art or science capable of

---

[16] Miller 2004: 81–82. Like a court masque, *Leviathan* operates as a "mirror for princes" (Miller 2004: 91–102; see also Miller 2011: 193–199). But not all mirrors for princes are profitably seen in terms of the masque, and one might feel that *Leviathan* wants the essential components of a masque: a dramatic fable, music, dancing, singing, and scenic transformations.

[17] Condren 2000: 138.

[18] *HW* 24: xxxiv, xxxvi.

[19] Condren 2000: 102, 111–113.

[20] Hillyer 2007: 38. Hillyer accuses Condren of recognizing such incoherence and attempting to minimize its significance (209 n. 27).

being charged with doing genuine philosophical work. I show that the main evidence in favor of the view that Hobbes was, in the "Answer," attempting to promote poetry as a philosophical art or science lies in the misreading of a crucial and much-quoted passage from that text. Despite local variations in focus and detail, Hobbes's various accounts of the nature and scope of poetry are clear and consistent about the kind of work the poet has to do: that work gives him no authority to act as a philosopher.

2 POETRY IN THE *ANTI-WHITE*

Modern understanding of Hobbes's thinking about poetics is founded primarily upon his "Answer" to Davenant and his Preface to Homer. Although these works afford his most detailed discussions of its nature and characteristics, another important discussion of poetry has yet to be fully integrated into the scholarly conversation. This discussion provides us with a wider disciplinary context for Hobbes's understanding of the nature and purpose of poetry and thus helps us glean the coherence underlying Hobbes's later, better-known, but more narrowly focused remarks. The discussion in question forms part of Hobbes's examination of language in the opening chapter of his lengthy animadversions (late 1642–mid-1643) against Thomas White's *De mundo* (1642)—a work not widely known prior to its publication in 1973, and one that has still not been adequately addressed. Hobbes's discussion of poetry in the *Anti-White* (as it is generally known to English-speaking scholars) predates the "Answer" by the better part of a decade and offers a brief but valuable glimpse of Hobbes's understanding of the relationship of poetry to its sister arts or sciences.

In his animadversions against White, Hobbes examines poetry, along with logic, history, and rhetoric, as one of four legitimate ends of speech. In Hobbes's division, it is that kind of discourse in which we "glorify [certain] deeds and, by celebrating them, . . . hand them down to posterity."[21] As such, poetry differs from logic, which is concerned with demonstrating universal truths in order to produce philosophy; from rhetoric, which aims to persuade people to act in certain ways; and from history, which aims at narrating something.[22] Poetry is closely allied to history in that it works by narrating something; but it differs by virtue both of its metrical form, which is required for remembrance, and its purpose: the glorification of deeds rather than the accurate accounting of things that have happened. Thus, whereas history is concerned with offering full and accurate narratives of events, poetry "relates deeds of great moment, and it deliberately sets aside truth."[23] The focus on glorification implies some proximity

[21] *Anti-White* I. 2: Hobbes 1976: 25; Hobbes 1973: 106 ("volumus facta nobilitare, et celebrando tradere memoriae posterorum").

[22] Hobbes 1973: 106–107; Hobbes 1976: 25.

[23] *Anti-White* I. 3: Hobbes 1976: 26; Hobbes 1973: 107. This definition raises the question of whether Hobbes would regard several of his own verse compositions based on historical events—the account

between poetry and rhetoric: *epideictic rhetoric,* the rhetoric of praise and blame. But poetry differs from rhetoric by occasion—it is aimed at posterity rather than (merely) at contemporaries—and also (in consequence) by form: in order that it can be remembered and transmitted to posterity, it must employ meter.

Despite the fact that logic, history, rhetoric, and poetry are all presented as legitimate forms of speech, Hobbes observes some crucial distinctions between them. Logic aims at demonstrating the truth of universal assertions, which is, in Hobbes's view, the work of philosophy; its intellectual and linguistic procedures must therefore be unambiguous definitions and necessary deductions. Ornamented language and *sententiae* must be avoided. Among ornaments, metaphors are particularly troublesome because, working through double-signification, they are by nature ambiguous, sliding between different categories. Thinking with metaphors is like tallying an account without troubling to keep one's figures in their proper columns. Generalizing aphorisms or *sententiae* must be eschewed because a *sententia* is "an ethical theorem or a universal assertion about manners" that lacks a rigorous logical underwriting of its truth.[24] Although not necessarily true, it nonetheless sounds plausible. Given its aim of memorializing praiseworthy deeds, poetry may legitimately employ metaphoric language for ornament—presumably (although Hobbes is not explicit on the point) in order to glorify and celebrate such deeds. The poet should, however, avoid the use of *sententiae,* except where these are put into the mouths of speakers in order to characterize them: "That part of the poem where the poet speaks *in propria persona* is the relation of a particular fact, whereas every maxim is universal."[25] The poet's concern is with particular facts, not universal truths; his aim is glorification and celebration, not philosophical demonstration. By offering seemingly universal maxims or aphorisms, the poet would be usurping the role of logic without following its proper and rigorous procedures; he would thus be trespassing on the field of philosophy. From this it follows that, as Hobbes puts it, philosophy has nothing to do with poetry.[26]

The function of poetry in the *Anti-White* is thus limited to the celebration and memorialization, in fictional narratives, of glorious deeds, for posterity. And poetry is effectively coterminous with epic or heroic poetry; there is little space if any here for genres like comedy, pastoral, or lyric. If, as recent scholarship has suggested, Hobbes in his "Answer" announced a new alliance between poetry and philosophy according to which the poet might become a philosopher, his views must have undergone a radical transformation in the years between 1643 and 1650.

---

of his tour of the Peak District, his verse autobiography, his history of the early church—as poems. I address the question at the end of this chapter.

[24] *Anti-White* I. 1–2: Hobbes 1973: 105, 106–107; Hobbes 1976: 23, 25.

[25] *Anti-White* I. 2: Hobbes 1976: 25; Hobbes 1973: 107 ("ea pars Poematis quae est ex persona Poetae narratio est facti singularis, at omnis sententia universalis").

[26] *Anti-White* I. 3: Hobbes 1973: 107; Hobbes 1976: 26.

3 POETRY IN *LEVIATHAN*

Did such a transformation occur? Did Hobbes change his mind at the end of the 1640s about the sharp distinction he had articulated around 1643 between poetry and philosophy? Some evidence to support such a view might be found in the table of sciences in chapter nine of *Leviathan*, which places poetry under the general heading of science or philosophy. Poetry is now apparently a species of philosophy. What has changed here, however, is not the understanding of poetry vis-à-vis philosophy but the definition of philosophy itself. No longer concerned with general theorems or universals, philosophy is here defined *"Knowledge of the Consequence of one Affirmation to another."*[27] Under this definition, poetry appears, alongside logic and rhetoric, as knowledge of the consequences of speech. Thus, logic involves knowledge of consequences "In *Reasoning*," rhetoric "In *Perswading*," and poetry "In *Magnifying, Vilifying*, &c."[28] Poetry has gained no sudden competence in dealing with universal truths.

Hobbes's definition of poetry in *Leviathan* represents not a rejection but an amplification and clarification of the definition he had offered in the *Anti-White*. In the earlier work, he had defined poetry by its immediate purpose, which was (as we have noted) to "glorify [certain] deeds and, by celebrating them, . . . hand them down to posterity." In *Leviathan*, Hobbes defined poetry as the knowledge of consequences from magnifying and vilifying in speech. The two definitions intersect at the point of celebration: the earlier definition articulates the immediate goal of celebration—glorification (and, thereby, remembrance); the later one, its means: magnification. Specifying magnification as the means of glorification makes explicit the link implied in the *Anti-White* between heroic poetry and epideictic rhetoric, which, according to both Aristotle and Hobbes, achieves its effects in precisely this manner.[29] Indeed, the link with epideictic rhetoric is strengthened by Hobbes's inclusion of magnification's opposite, vilification: this being the technique by which epideictic rhetoric goes about the work of blaming. Whereas the introduction of vilification represents an amplification of the definition advanced in *Anti-White*, allowing space within the sphere of poetry for satire and comedy, it does not involve any change in underlying principles. Poetry remains the art or science of using language to memorialize, whether positively or negatively. It still has nothing to do with the quest for universal truth and nothing, therefore, to do with philosophy.

The broadening in *Leviathan* of the definition of poetry to admit (by implication) satire and other genres than the heroic squares with the more detailed, systematic overview

---

[27] *Leviathan* 40. This definition is not, in any case, one Hobbes consistently maintains: a very different definition of philosophy as the knowledge of generations by effects, and vice versa, appears at *Leviathan* 367 (cf. *De corpore*, I. 2).

[28] *Leviathan* 40+. Condren cites as proof of Hobbes's confusion about the status of poetry its omission from this table of sciences (Condren 2000: 107); but poetry is not omitted.

[29] Aristotle 1926: I. 9; *Elements of Law* IX. 11.

of the genres of poetry Hobbes offers in his January 1650 "Answer" to Davenant—a text written while Hobbes was working intensely on *Leviathan*. In the "Answer," Hobbes takes what seems on the face of it to be a very different attitude toward poetry from that offered in either the *Anti-White* or *Leviathan*, in which its role was conceived as magnification or vilification. The role of the poet is here more broadly construed than in *Anti-White*: it is "by imitating humane life, in delightfull and measur'd lines, to avert men from vice, and encline them to vertuous and honorable actions."[30] This is, of course, a thoroughly humanist conception: the poet as moral pedagogue.[31] But it does not involve a radical shift from the earlier understanding. In *Anti-White*, Hobbes defined poetry by reference to the immediate end of heroic poetry—that of glorifying certain deeds and (by the use of meter) memorializing them for posterity; in *Leviathan*, he focuses on the linguistic means of such glorification—magnification—and admits its inverse, vilification, thus acknowledging (by implication) the existence of satire as a species of poetry. In the "Answer," he takes his consideration of the causes of poetry a step further back, examining the purpose of memorializing glorious deeds—and, by implication, vilifying ignoble ones. The purpose of celebrating glorious deeds in meter is to encourage men to emulation: "to encline them to virtuous and honorable actions"; the purpose of vilification is "to avert men from vice."[32] In other words, it is difficult to believe that this humanist conception of the function of poetry does not also underlie Hobbes's prior formalist and materialist accounts of its modes of operation.

But the account offered in the "Answer" is not identical with that in *Leviathan*. In regard to the kinds and genres of poetry, it involves an extension or at least a greater degree of specification. In the *Anti-White*, poetry had been treated as, in effect, coterminous with epic or heroic poetry. In *Leviathan*, the definition expanded to allow vilification as well as magnification, thus giving entrance to satire, while its concluding "&c." gestured toward the possible existence of other modes and genres. This nods toward the full generic breakdown offered in the "Answer," according to which there are precisely three kinds of poetry determined by social and physical location: heroic (concerned with the court), "scommatique" (concerned with the city), and pastoral (concerned with the country), each distinguished into two species by manner of representation, either narrative or dramatic. Thus, heroic narrative is epic and heroic drama, tragedy; "scommatique" narrative is satire and drama, comedy; pastoral narrative is simply pastoral and pastoral drama, pastoral comedy.[33] The scheme breaks out of the binary antithesis between magnification and vilification, the heroic and the ignominious or satiric, allowing the introduction of pastoral modes and with them models of conduct neither extraordinarily glorious nor extremely blameworthy.

Despite its greater inclusivity, this remains a highly restrictive definition, one that can recognize as species of poetry neither lyrics, such as sonnets, epigrams, and eclogues,

---

[30] Hobbes 1971: 45.
[31] As noted by Nelson, *HW* 24: xxxiii–xxxiv.
[32] Hobbes 1971: 45.
[33] Hobbes 1971: 45–46.

which are here classed as "Essayes, and parts of an entire Poeme," nor didactic verse, which is improperly concerned with offering general "morall precepts" rather than narrative or dramatic representations of action.[34] A sonnet is not a poem; Lucretius is not a poet. The exclusion of both lyric and didactic verse aligns with Hobbes's rejection of nonepic poetry and universal aphorisms in the *Anti-White*. And both definitional moves rest on the assumption that the poet is engaged in motivating virtue by narrative or dramatic representation: a view that undergirds both Hobbes's conflation of poetry with epic poetry as the magnifier of glorious deeds in *Anti-White* and his view of poetry working by magnification or vilification in *Leviathan*. Hobbes has not, in the "Answer," changed his mind about the nature and scope of poetry; he has simply given us a more expansive and more detailed account of it.

4 THE ROLE OF THE POET

Although moral philosophy is the necessary foundation of an heroic poem, Hobbes does not assert in the "Answer" to Davenant that the poet might furnish an account of ethics that aspires to the level of true philosophy; on the contrary, he maintains a clear theoretical division between the competencies of poetry on the one hand and those of philosophy on the other. Scholars who see Hobbes articulating in the "Answer" a newly authoritative role for the poet within the sphere of moral philosophy find their evidence in a crucial passage concerned with the scope of fancy:

> But so farre forth as the Fancy of man, has traced the wayes of true Philosophy, so farre it hath produced very marvellous effects to the benefit of mankind. All that is bewtifull or defensible in buildinge; or mervaylous in Engines and Instruments of motion; Whatsoever commodity men receave from the observation of the Heavens, from the description of the Earth, from the account of Time, from walking on the Seas; and whatsoever distinguisheth the civility of *Europe*, from the Barbarity of the *American* sauvages, is the workemanship of Fancy, but guided by the Precepts of true Philosophy. But where these precepts fayle, as they have hetherto fayled in the doctrine of Morall vertue, there the Architect (*Fancy*) must take the Philosophers part upon herselfe. He therefore that undertakes an Heroique Poeme (which is to exhibit a venerable and amiable Image of Heroique vertue) must not onely be the Poet, to place and connect, but also the Philosopher, to furnish and square his matter, that is, to make both body and soule, coulor and shaddow of his Poeme out of his owne store: which how well you have performed I am now considering.[35]

The main point is clear enough: where philosophy has failed to establish firm foundations, fancy should play the philosopher's part. In other words, in deploying moral

---

[34] Hobbes 1971: 46.
[35] Hobbes 1971: 49–50.

philosophy in his poem, the poet should follow his own fancy rather than the false pre-cepts of erring philosophers. Scholars who see here a rapprochement between poetry and philosophy construe this passage as a rejection of Hobbes's habitual separation of philosophy from poetry. Condren, for instance, reads it as seeming to suggest that "where philosophy has failed . . . poetry has actually to take its place."[36] But Hobbes's statement does not contradict his habitual distinction of philosophy from poetry because he is here commenting on exceptional circumstances: that is, those in which philosophy has failed. Nor does he claim that "where philosophy has failed . . . poetry has actually to take its place."[37] Even in such exceptional circumstances, there is no question of poetry taking the place of philosophy; rather, where philosophy has failed, *fancy* must fill its place.[38] The suggestion therefore is not that philosophy requires poetry; it is that poetry requires philosophy. Where no true philosophy is to be found, the poet must invent a philosophical framework from his own fancy. But although this is necessary as a structure for his poem, there is no suggestion that it will also be valid as philosophy. Hobbes praises Davenant for having played the role of both poet and philosopher *only* in the composition of his poem. His praise is restricted in both occasion and scope. Only in the exceptional case that philosophy has failed to provide true foundations may the poet's fancy operate independently to furnish a frame for his work. And this will be a merely contingent structure, producing only provisional truths; it does not license a poet to practice philosophy.

What, though, does Hobbes mean when he asserts that philosophical precepts "have hetherto fayled in the doctrine of Morall vertue"? Does he, as Condren infers, express a sudden loss of confidence about the status of his own philosophical endeavors or about the value of philosophy in general, gesturing toward the need for a supplement—a sup-plement that might be furnished by poetry?[39] I think not. Eric Nelson is, to the best of my knowledge, the first scholar to have attended to the impact of the word "hetherto" here. In asserting that the precepts of philosophy "have hetherto fayled in the doctrine of Morall vertue" Hobbes, in Nelson's view, claims that where previous philosophers have failed, he had himself "revealed the true face of moral philosophy": had, in other words, finally set down firm principles for the poet to work from.[40] But where has he done so? Nelson is circumspect on this point, noting parenthetically that it was "pre-sumably in 1640 with the *Elements* [*of Law*]."[41] I am not convinced by this suggestion, and it seems to me that Hobbes's "hetherto" works rather differently.

The most obvious objection to the view that Hobbes is here implying that he had, ten years earlier, in *The Elements of Law*, firmly established the doctrine of moral virtue is

---

[36] Condren 2000: 111, 112.

[37] Condren 2000: 112.

[38] On fancy, its relationship to judgment, and its implications for the relationship between philosophy on the one hand and rhetoric and poetry on the other, see the important discussions in Nauta (2002: 42–48) and Lemetti (2006: 184–185).

[39] Condren 2000: 112.

[40] *HW* 24: xxxvii.

[41] *HW* 24: xxxvii.

that the word "hitherto" means not "until quite recently" but "[u]p to this time, until now, as yet."[42] It does not therefore assert that true moral philosophy has already been definitively established. Although it may be possible to incorporate "ten years ago" (i.e., 1640) within a very broad construal of "this time" or "now," this doesn't seem to be the thrust of the passage. And there is further evidence against it in that Hobbes is, in his "Answer," praising Davenant for doing what poets must do in the absence of correct doctrine: building out of his own store. If he believed that *The Elements* provided an adequate moral philosophical basis for poetry, he could have found some way of saying so: gently chiding Davenant, perhaps, for following false precepts or correcting him, as he in fact chides and corrects him for other errors.[43] What Hobbes says, however, is unequivocal on this point: "He therefore that undertakes an Heroique Poeme . . . must not onely be the Poet, to place and connect, but also the Philosopher, to furnish and square his matter, that is, to make both body and soule, coulor and shaddow of his Poeme out of his owne store."[44] There is no suggestion that the poet can simply follow an existing authoritative theory of moral philosophy.

Nelson is certainly correct that Hobbes believed, by the time he completed the *Elements of Law* in 1640, that he had discovered the true principles of moral philosophy: he implied as much in his discussion of the deficiencies that mar existing accounts of ethics and by gestures to his own use in *The Elements of Law* of the proper method of scientific ratiocination.[45] Hobbes nonetheless shied away from claiming that he had *demonstrated* these principles. The Dedicatory Epistle to the work is guarded about its scope and emphatic about its limitations:

> they that have written of justice and policy in general, do all invade each other, and themselves, with contradiction. To reduce this doctrine to the rules and infallibility of reason, there is no way, but first to put such principles down for a foundation, as passion not mistrusting, may not seek to displace; and afterward to build thereon the truth of cases in the law of nature . . . by degrees, till the whole be inexpugnable.[46]

Hobbes goes on to claim that he has adumbrated to the earl of Newcastle, orally and in private, the foundational principles of a science of justice and policy: principles he has here, at the nobleman's request, "put into method"; but he does not assert that he has adequately demonstrated them. On the contrary, he concedes that he has not, noting that he had no appetite to offer the lengthy series of case studies that would be required to build "the whole."[47] Thus, while he claims to have laid the foundations for

---

[42] *OED* 1.

[43] For an examination of such instances, see Raylor 2010.

[44] Hobbes 1971: 50.

[45] *Elements of Law* XIII. 3. I disagree with David Johnston, who sees in this passage an admission that Hobbes, no less than his predecessors, has "failed to *communicate*" the truths of moral philosophy (Johnston 1986: 90).

[46] *Elements of Law*, Ep. Ded. (Hobbes 1969: xv).

[47] *Elements of Law*, Ep. Ded. (Hobbes 1969 xv–xvi).

an understanding of such matters, he explicitly notes that he has not raised the building; and while he asserts that his doctrine "is not slightly proved," he declines to assert that it is incontrovertibly demonstrated. Nor, finally, is he quite clear for what "science" his discussion of law and policy lays the foundation. He does not give it a name. As we shall soon see, his lack of clarity on this issue does not stop at the Dedicatory Epistle to *The Elements of Law*.

Even in his subsequent development and formal exposition of his philosophical system in the *Elementa philosophiae*, Hobbes is less than crystalline about where, exactly, he has established the true principles of moral philosophy. One might expect such an assertion to appear in *De cive*, which appeared, albeit in a private printing, in 1642, where it was billed as the third section of the *Elementa philosophiae*, one dealing with the citizen.[48] And there is some evidence to warrant such an expectation. In the Dedicatory Epistle to the earl of Devonshire, Hobbes asserts that from two certain principles of human nature—cupidity on the one hand and fear of violent death on the other, he has "demonstrated by the most evident inference in this little work the necessity of agreements and of keeping faith, and thence the Elements of moral virtue and civil duties."[49] Hobbes's reference to these definitively demonstrated "Elements of moral virtue" might seem to allow us to infer that a full treatment of moral philosophy is contained in *De cive*. But, within the text itself, Hobbes is less emphatic. In his discussion of natural law, he implies that he has treated moral philosophy in an ad hoc manner only, focusing on just those aspects of it that pertain to the preservation of civic concord: "The *Lawes of Nature* therefore are the summe of *Morall* Philosophy, whereof I have onely delivered such precepts in this place, as appertain to the preservation of our selves against those dangers which arise from discord."[50] And in the opening lines of the 1642 edition, Hobbes defers treatment of the passions—one of the central concerns of moral philosophy—to the prior, second, section of the *Elementa philosophiae*, *De homine*.[51] That section would not be published for another sixteen years. Hobbes thus saw *De cive*, at the time of its first printing, as furnishing the elements of citizenship, but he was not quite categorical that these entailed a full account of moral philosophy.

There is, in Hobbes's gradual exposition of the *Elementa philosophiae*, some slippage in the scope and placement of moral philosophy within his system.[52] The Preface to the second edition of *De cive* (1647) promises that a full treatment of the subjects traditionally taken to constitute moral philosophy will be forthcoming in *De*

---

[48] *De cive*, title page (*HW* 2: 89 n. 1).

[49] Hobbes, *On the Citizen*, edited and translated by Tuck and Silverthorne, 6 (the translation in *HW* 3: 27 is, unhelpfully here, somewhat looser); *HW* 2: 75–76.

[50] *De cive* III. 32 (*HW* 3: 75, 2: 120).

[51] *HW* 2: 89–90 n. 11; *HW* 3: 41 n. b.

[52] On the shifting placement of moral philosophy, see Tuck 1996: 179–180; Sorell 1996: 50, 54–57; Rutherford 2003: 376–377. Rutherford points out that the boundary between ethics and politics is not clearly drawn in Hobbes's writings. (I am grateful to Juhana Lemetti for bringing Rutherford's article to my attention.)

homine—"imagination, Memory, intellect, ratiocination, appetite, Will, good and Evil, honest and dishonest, and the like."[53]

But the account of moral philosophy given in *De corpore* (the first part of the trilogy, published in 1655) drops the broader discussion of psychology and ethics and retrospectively limits it to the passions: "*appetite, aversion, love, benevolence, hope, fear, anger, emulation, envy, &c.*"[54] In the Preface to *De corpore*, Hobbes boldly claims that he has already established the science of "civil philosophy" (it is "no older . . . than my own book *De Cive*");[55] but it is not clear whether this refers to civil philosophy broadly defined—which, in the division put forth in the opening chapter of *De corpore*, includes both ethics and politics—or narrowly defined, covering only politics, which in this account is also known as civil philosophy.[56] The treatment of moral philosophy eventually offered in *De homine* (the remaining, second, section of the trilogy, issued in 1658) is brief and cursory, addressing, in the course of three short chapters, appetites and aversions, good and evil (chapter XI), the passions of the mind (chapter XII), and the virtues and vices (chapter XIII). And Hobbes implies that some, at least, of such material has already been covered: because virtues and vices have no meaning outside a civil polity, consideration of moral science ("scientia moralia") is only possible within the context of an examination of civil society.[57] Having promised in *De cive* (1642) a full treatment of moral philosophy under the study of the human being in section two of the *Elementa*, Hobbes announces, with the publication of *De homine* in 1658, that moral philosophy in fact falls under *De cive*, its third part, first printed sixteen years earlier.

Not only does Hobbes variously describe the contents and philosophical divisions within his system, he also frequently implies, without quite categorically asserting, his achievement in establishing the true science of moral philosophy. He does so by redeploying the stock phrase already seen at work in the "Answer" to Davenant, which hinges on the word "hetherto" (Lat. *hactenus*).[58] In the 1647 Preface to *De cive*, Hobbes writes that "what hath hitherto been written by Morall Philosophers, hath not made any progress in the knowledge of the Truth."[59] Early in *De corpore* (1655), he notes that "the knowledge of these rules is moral philosophy. But why have they not learned

[53] *De cive*, Pref. (*HW* 3: 35; *HW* 2: 82). The definition of moral philosophy in *Leviathan* is similar: "Morall Philosophy is nothing else but the Science of what is *Good*, and *Evill*, in the conversation, and Society of man-kind"; *Leviathan* 79.

[54] *De corpore* VI. 6–7 (*The English Works of Thomas Hobbes of Malmesbury* [hereinafter *EW*] 1: 72, 73–74; *Thomae Hobbes malmesburiensis opera philosophica quae latine scripsit omnia* [hereinafter *OL*] 1: 64, 65). The account of the scope of moral philosophy offered in the opening chapter ("men's dispositions and manners") seems broader, however; *De corpore* I. 9 (*OL* 1: 10; *EW* 1: 12).

[55] *De corpore*, Pref. (*EW* 1: ix; *OL* 1: xcxv).

[56] *De corpore* I. 9. In *Leviathan*, by contrast, Hobbes distinguishes ethics or moral philosophy from politics or civil philosophy, treating the former as a subsection of a generic natural philosophy which he opposes to civil philosophy (40+).

[57] *De homine* XIII. 8–9; Tuck 1996: 180.

[58] On Hobbes's use in multiple works of stock phrases, see Baumgold 2004.

[59] *HW* 3: 26, 2: 75 ("nihil profuisse ad scientiam veritatis quae hactenus scripta sunt à Philosophis moralibus; placuisse vero non illuminando animum").

them, unless for this reason, that none have hitherto taught them in a clear and exact method?"[60] The use of the term "hitherto" or "hactenus" ensures that the phrasing is imprecise and suggestive, pregnant with implication. Such phrasing does not directly assert that the true face of moral philosophy has already been definitively revealed; it implies, rather, that it has not until now, and we may construe "now" as broadly—"in this age"—or as narrowly—"in this book"—as we like.

Despite some vagueness within his philosophical trilogy, there is one work in which Hobbes comes close to asserting unambiguously that he has established the true principles of moral philosophy. At the end of the second book of *Leviathan*, Hobbes ruminates on the pedagogical potential of his project and writes:

> [W]hen I consider . . . that neither *Plato*, nor any other Philosopher hitherto, hath put into order, and sufficiently, or probably proved all the Theoremes of Morall doctrine, that men may learn thereby, both how to govern, and how to obey; I recover some hope, that one time or other, this writing of mine, may fall into the hands of a Soveraign, who will consider it himselfe, . . . and by the exercise of entire Soveraignty, in protecting the Publique teaching of it, convert this Truth of Speculation, into the Utility of Practice.[61]

The phrasing here is too oblique to constitute a direct assertion that Hobbes has, in *Leviathan*, succeeded where Plato and others had failed. Once again, the handy "hitherto" is put to work. But in its agile skip from pointing out the failure of all prior attempts to put into order and prove "sufficiently, or probably . . . all the Theoremes of Morall doctrine" to its hope that *Leviathan* will be taken up by a sovereign and imposed as public doctrine, it clearly although delicately implies Hobbes's triumph in the field of moral as well as political philosophy.

The conclusion to be drawn from Hobbes's treatment of moral philosophy in his works of the 1640s and 1650s is that in the "Answer" to Davenant (composed in January 1650) Hobbes considered his definitive statement of the principles of moral philosophy to lie in *Leviathan*, on which he was then hard at work. Hobbes made the claim as directly as he ever did at the end of the second part of that work, which he probably composed soon after the "Answer" (he had written thirty-seven chapters by May 1650). In both works, Hobbes registers the view that moral philosophy has been, up until this point, utterly inadequate. His praise of Davenant's construction of an ethics from his own store of fancy does not therefore suggest that Hobbes has lost heart in the value of his earlier writings or has lost faith in philosophy itself. Nor does it imply that Davenant should have followed Hobbes's own moral philosophical system:

> But where these precepts fayle, as they have hetherto fayled in the doctrine of Morall vertue, there the Architect (*Fancy*) must take the Philosophers part upon herselfe.

---

[60] *Concerning Body* I. 7 (*EW* 1: 8); "Est autem hujus regulae cognitio moralis philosophia. Quare autem eam non didicerunt, nisi quod a nemine clara et recta methodo hactenus tradita sit?" *De corpore* I.7 (*OL* 1:7).

[61] *Leviathan* 193.

He therefore that undertakes an Heroique Poeme (which is to exhibit a venerable and amiable Image of Heroique vertue) must not onely be the Poet, to place and connect, but also the Philosopher, to furnish and square his matter, that is, to make both body and soule, coulor and shaddow of his Poeme out of his owne store: which how well you have performed I am now considering.[62]

Seen in reference to the forthcoming *Leviathan*, Hobbes's praise of the poet registers no sense that the poet is the new philosopher. Hobbes praises Davenant as a poet without either endorsing the ethics inscribed in his poem or criticizing him for failing to follow a system of moral philosophy Hobbes had not yet fully expounded.[63] He praises Davenant as a poet for inventing ethical precepts in the absence of philosophical ones. Such praise implies but tactfully averts the explicit articulation of a deeper criticism: that the moral philosophical underpinnings of *Gondibert* were ill-founded.[64] And the word "hetherto" initiates a countermovement, hinting at the imminent obsolescence of its ethical principles. It gestures toward the possibility that the long-felt lack of a valid system of moral philosophy is about to be remedied once and for all with the establishment of a new science: one that all subsequent poets would be obliged to follow.

5 HOBBES AND LITERARY CRITICISM

If, as I have suggested, by the end of the 1650s Hobbes believed that he had not only established but also, within either *Leviathan* or the *Elementa philosophiae*, had demonstrated the true principles of moral philosophy, we would expect his later writings on poetry to reflect this advance by curtailing any philosophical leeway the poet might earlier, in the absence of such a body of principles, have been given. When we turn to Hobbes's later pronouncements in the field of literary criticism this is exactly what we find.

Hobbes wrote two works of literary criticism in later life: a brief commendatory epistle to Edward Howard on his historical poem *The Brittish Princes* (October 24, 1668) and an essay "To the Reader: Concerning the Vertues of an Heroique Poem" prefaced to the second edition (1675) of his translation of the *Odyssey*. Both are consistent

---

[62] Hobbes 1971: 49–50.

[63] Davenant had no doubt read *De cive*; Dowlin presents convincing evidence that Davenant's discussion of love in the Preface is indebted to Hobbes's account in *The Elements of Law*, which he must therefore have read in manuscript (Dowlin 1934: 47).

[64] On this point I am in complete agreement with Nelson, *HW* 24: xxxvii. This is not the occasion on which to explore the moral philosophy of Davenant's poem; suffice it to note that the ethics of *Gondibert* appear to be based on traditional Aristotelian moral principles: in particular, on the doctrine of the mean, a doctrine Hobbes repeatedly repudiated. For the poem's assumptions about the dangers of excess and the desirability of moderation, see, for example, I.iii.32; Gladish's note (Davenant 1971: 296); cf. II.ii.18 and II.iii.15; and Scodel (2002): 172–174. Hobbes attacked the doctrine of the mean in, e.g., *Elements of Law* XVII. 14 and *De cive* III. 32.

with the account of poetry offered in the "Answer" to Davenant: neither raises the possibility that the poet possesses any philosophical liberty.

In his letter to Howard, Hobbes echoes the key criteria for poetic composition Hobbes had adumbrated, almost two decades earlier, in his "Answer" to Davenant. He celebrates the judicious contrivance of the story, the heroism and variety of its matter, the dignity and clarity of its language, and its decorum—its match between character and language: "Your Poem, Sir, contains a well and judiciously contrived Story, full of admirable and Heroick actions, set forth in noble and perspicuous language, such as becomes the dignity of the persons you introduce, which two things of themselves are the height of Poetry."[65] All are aspects of the heroic poem on which he had spoken in the "Answer."

Hobbes does not merely align Howard's poem with such standards; he also defends the poem from three apparent lapses from them. One is the limited scope of the poem's action. Hobbes excuses this by arguing that it's not size that's important, but skill and judgment: Homer, too, wrote on a smaller scale (in the spurious *Batrachomyomachia*) and is not disgraced by that.[66] Another is the poet's use of the fictionalized history of early Britain to celebrate his own ancestors: a strategy at odds with the impartiality Hobbes had celebrated in Davenant's choice of a fictional Lombard for his hero.[67] Here, Hobbes is obliged to engage in some special pleading, arguing *tu quoque* (Virgil did it, too), and discovering in Howard's choice the compensating virtue of ancestral *pietas*. A final and more serious objection—deleted from the printed text of the letter—was to Howard's decision to comment on religion: "I remember a line or two in your poem, that touched upon divinity, wherein we differed in opinion. But since you say the book is licensed, I shall think no more upon it, but only reserve my liberty of dissenting, which I know you will allow me."[68] The lines in question have been identified by Noel Malcolm to be those in which Howard offers a naturalistic account of the origins of religion and glances at the corrupting influence of "Priesthoods pious frauds."[69] Because Hobbes undoubtedly agreed with Howard's critique of priestcraft, his objection was presumably, as Malcolm suggests, to the public articulation of such criticism. His concerns are related to his fears, in the later 1660s, that he might be prosecuted for heresy: concerns that led him to insist that he had never written against the established Church of England and to forgo publication of his satirical verse history of the early church, the *Historia Ecclesiastica*.[70]

On turning to the 1675 essay "Concerning the Vertues of an Heroic Poem," we find similar material organized in a slightly different manner. The components of an heroic

---

[65] *HW* 7: 704; cp. Hobbes 1971: 50–53.

[66] *HW* 7: 704.

[67] Hobbes 1971: 48.

[68] *HW* 7: 705.

[69] *HW* 7: 706 n. 8.

[70] Parkin 2007: 240; *HW* 11: xlv–lviii (for the general concern); Aubrey 1898, 1: 339, Milton 1993: 510 (for the suppression of the poem).

poem remain those we have met in the "Answer" and in the letter to Howard: decorum in choice of words,[71] perspicuity and facility of style,[72] careful contrivance of plot,[73] elevation of fancy,[74] impartiality,[75] clearness of description,[76] and amplitude and variety of subject.[77] But in the 1675 essay, all these aspects of invention, arrangement, and style are subordinated to the master-virtue of "discretion": "The Vertues required in an Heroick Poem (and indeed in all Writings published) are comprehended all in this one word *Discretion*."[78] "Discretion" Hobbes had defined in *Leviathan* as the faculty of discrimination or judgment, especially in social or public affairs: "in matter of conversation and businesse; wherein, times, places, and persons are to be discerned."[79] It is a discriminating faculty, aimed at distinguishing difference as opposed to (like its opposite, wit) similarity. In the context of the heroic poem, it means "That every part of the Poem be conducing, and in good order placed to the End and Designe of the Poet."

But discretion pertains not only to the design and execution; it also concerns the purpose of the poem: "And the Designe is not only to profit, but also to delight the Reader."[80] The goal of heroic poetry is declared to be "accession of Prudence, Justice, and Fortitude, by the Example of such Great and Noble Persons as he introduceth speaking, or describeth acting" actions that may be either true or feigned.[81] Although this Horatian framing ("profit and delight") is new to Hobbes, the definition of the purpose of heroic poetry squares with Hobbes's account of it in the "Answer" as an imitation of a certain kind of human action, written in delightful verse and designed to incline men to "to vertuous and honorable actions."[82] There is no suggestion that, in designing a fable to move his reader to virtue, the poet need or should do more than adhere to an authoritative moral philosophy; it appears to be no part of his responsibility to determine or adjudicate the nature of honor or virtue. As such, then, neither in its stylistic nor in its ethical aspects does the concept of discretion afford the poet room to act as a philosopher. On the contrary, it is in the nature of discretion that the poet should follow authority. This much is implied by Hobbes's earlier contrast, in the "Answer" to Davenant, between modern divines and classical poets, who were the divines of their age. Whereas modern divines sow controversy and discord, "in the Heathen Poets, at least in those whose workes have lasted to the time wee are in, there are none of those indiscretions to be found, that tended to subversion, or disturbance

---

[71] Cp. *HW* 24: xcii–xciii, xcvi; Hobbes 1971: 52–53.
[72] Cp. *HW* 24: xciii–xciv, xcvi; Hobbes 1971: 47, 52.
[73] Cp. *HW* 24: xciv, xcvi; Hobbes 1971: 50.
[74] Cp. *HW* 24: xciv, xcvi–xcvii; Hobbes 1971: 50.
[75] Cp. *HW* 24: xciv–xcv, xcvii; Hobbes 1971: 48.
[76] Cp. *HW* 24: xcv, xcvii; Hobbes 1971: 51.
[77] Cp. *HW* 24: xcv–xcvi, xcix; Hobbes 1971: 51.
[78] *HW* 24: xcii.
[79] *Leviathan* 33.
[80] *HW* 24: xcii.
[81] *HW* 24: xcii.
[82] Hobbes 1971: 45.

of the Commonwealthes wherein they liued."[83] Hobbes was not guilty of dissimulation when he announced in his 1675 essay that Homer was a discreet poet. The suggestion that "all poetry published before 1640 by definition lacked discretion" underestimates Hobbes's historicism.[84] Homer was discreet for his own time, although not for ours. And the consequent claim that Hobbes disingenuously yielded "the first place in Poetry to *Homer*" merely in order to promote his own translation overlooks both the nuanced discriminations by which Hobbes makes his case for Homer's superiority in discretion to both Virgil and Lucan. Homer excels in contrivance; Lucan in height of fancy; Homer and Virgil both in justice and impartiality; Homer in clearness of image and also in amplitude and variety. The claim also ignores his denial that he is elevating his own efforts: "But howsoever I defend *Homer*, I aim not thereby at any reflection upon the following Translation."[85]

6 Poetry versus Philosophy

Hobbes's literary critical writings develop a coherent account of the nature and scope of poetry. That account evolves over time, growing in range and sophistication between its first, brief articulation in the *Anti-White* of 1643 and its full exposition in the "Answer" to Davenant of 1650 and later finding a new organizing principle in the essay "Concerning the Vertues of an Heroique Poem" of 1675. Although not all its expositions are so fully or clearly developed, there are no substantial or significant shifts in the understanding of the nature and scope of the art articulated in any of Hobbes's critical works. The poet's job is to offer fictional narratives, in verse, to magnify and glorify great deeds or to vilify vile acts, whether real or imagined, in order to move men, through emulation of great heroes, to virtuous action. It may be that a poet will, on occasion, lack an adequate moral philosophy with which to frame his narrative; in such circumstances, he may invent ethical precepts to support his poem. There is no suggestion, however, that such precepts will have the authority of philosophy. And even this rather limited space for imitation of philosophical action was only briefly granted to the poet; by the time Hobbes's philosophical trilogy was in print, the true principles of moral philosophy had, ostensibly, been provided.

Recent accounts that have sought to raise the status of poetry in Hobbes's thinking by linking it with his philosophy have overstated the case. Hobbes's understanding of the nature and scope of poetry is not an expansive but a restrictive one, severely limiting

---

[83] Hobbes 1971: 48–49. However disingenuous it may have been, Hobbes's insistence to the king in the Epistle Dedicatory to his *Problemata Physica* of 1662 that he had published nothing to damage the present established order of the church represents another manifestation of the same position: *Problemata Physica* (OL 4: 301–302); *Seven Philosophical Problems* (EW 7: 4–5); Milton 1993: 506.

[84] *HW* 24: xxxvii.

[85] *HW* 24: xxxiii–xlii (for the argument); 24: xcvi–xcix (for the evidence against it).

both its field of operation and its content. In one sense, poetry remains throughout Hobbes's thinking firmly subordinate to philosophy, with no independent philosophical authority.[86] There is no question, even at his moment of greatest latitude, of the poet taking on the philosopher's part. In another aspect, Hobbes's definition of poetry is so narrow as to come close to defining it out of existence. Restricted to verse narratives or dramatic representations of feigned human manners, Hobbes's definition of poetry excludes both philosophical poetry and love lyrics.[87] Such restrictions raise the surprising prospect that few, if any, of Hobbes's original verse compositions are, in his view, poems. His late amatory lyric must obviously be excluded as a fragment. Like the writings of Lucretius, his cosmographical poem, *De motibus solis*, is versified natural philosophy. Whereas several of his other verse compositions engage in glorification or vilification, how many can be said to do so by way of feigned manners and fictional narratives? The Latin verse autobiography, *Thomae Hobbesii malmesburiensis vita*, celebrates the philosopher's life; *Historia Ecclesiastica* attacks the early church: both are histories. *De mirabilibus pecci* celebrates the "wonders" of the Peak and is primarily chorography. It does possess a narrative frame—that of a journey—but this is barely developed and, since it records a journey that Hobbes undertook in the company of his patron, it should probably not be regarded as presenting feigned as opposed to actual manners.[88] That the journey was undertaken by some who were "keen to fully understand the causes of things" ("promptis rerum perdiscere causas") marks it as a philosophical poem, but its efforts to offer natural philosophical explanations of the region's wonders are not satisfactorily developed.[89] In sum, rather than allowing poetry to encroach on the territory of philosophy, much less taking on the role of poet himself, Hobbes severely restricts the competence of poetry and limits its scope so narrowly that it is questionable whether, by his own account and despite his numerous forays into verse composition, he ever wrote an original poem. He was not merely being modest when, in his most important essay into the field of literary criticism, he proclaimed "I am not a Poet."[90]

ACKNOWLEDGMENTS

I thank the Dean and President of Carleton College for their support of my research and my colleagues in the Department of English for their encouragement. A version of this chapter was read at Ghent University in November 2010, as part of the retirement celebrations for Professor J. P. Vander Motten; I thank my host, Sando Jung, for

---

86 Raylor 2010: 70–72.
87 Hobbes 1971: 45–46.
88 Martinich 1999: 76; Malcolm 2007: 10–11.
89 *De mirabilibus pecci*, l. 83 (*OL* 5: 327). For this aspect of the poem, see Martinich 1999: 71–76.
90 Hobbes 1971: 45.

the invitation to present it. I am most grateful to Juhana Lemetti and Noel Malcolm for comments on an earlier draft of this material.

REFERENCES

Aristotle. 1926. *The "Art" of Rhetoric*, edited and translated by John Henry Freese. Cambridge: Harvard University Press/London: Heinemann.

Aubrey, John. 1898. *Aubrey's Brief Lives*, edited by Andrew Clark. 2 vols. Oxford: Clarendon Press.

Baumgold, Deborah. 2004. "The Composition of Hobbes's *Elements of Law*." *History of Political Thought* 25: 16–43.

Condren, Conal. 2000. *Thomas Hobbes*. New York: Twayne.

Davenant, William. 1971. *Sir William Davenant's "Gondibert,"* edited by David F. Gladish. Oxford: Clarendon Press.

Dowlin, Cornell March. 1934. *Sir William Davenant's "Gondibert," its Preface, and Hobbes's Answer: A Study in English Neo-Classicism*. PhD dissertation, University of Pennsylvania.

Hillyer, Richard. 2007. *Hobbes and His Poetic Contemporaries: Cultural Transmission in Early Modern England*. New York/Basingstoke: Palgrave Macmillan.

Hobbes, Thomas. 1971. "The Answer of Mr. Hobbes to Sir Will. D'Avenant's Preface before *Gondibert*," in *Sir William Davenant's "Gondibert,"* edited by David F. Gladish, 45–55. Oxford: Clarendon Press.

Hobbes, Thomas. 1983– . *The Clarendon Edition of the Works of Thomas Hobbes*. 27 vols. Oxford: Clarendon Press. [HW]

Hobbes, Thomas. 1973. *Critique du De mundo de Thomas White*, edited by Jean Jacquot and Harold Whitmore Jones. Paris: Vrin.

Hobbes, Thomas. 1969. *Elements of Law, Natural and Politic*, edited by Ferdinand Toennies. 2nd edn., introduced by M. M. Goldsmith. London: Cass.

Hobbes, Thomas. 1839–45. *The English Works of Thomas Hobbes of Malmesbury*, edited by William Molesworth, 11 vols. London. [EW]

Hobbes, Thomas. 1658. *De homine*. London.

Hobbes, Thomas. 2008. *Historia Ecclesiastica*, edited and translated by Patricia Springborg, Patricia Stablein, and Paul Wilson. Paris: Champion.

Hobbes, Thomas. 1651. *Leviathan*. London.

Hobbes, Thomas. 1998. *On the Citizen*, edited and translated by Richard Tuck and Michael Silverthorne. Cambridge: Cambridge University Press.

Hobbes, Thomas. 1839–45. *Thomae Hobbes malmesburiensis opera philosophica quae latine scripsit omnia*, edited by William Molesworth. 5 vols. London. [OL]

Hobbes, Thomas. 1976. *Thomas White's De Mundo Examined*, edited and translated by Harold Whitmore Jones. Bradford/London: Bradford University Press.

Johnston, David. 1986. *The Rhetoric of "Leviathan": Thomas Hobbes and the Politics of Cultural Transformation*. Princeton: Princeton University Press.

Laird, John. 1934. *Hobbes*. London: Benn.

Lemetti, Juhana. 2006. *Imagination and Diversity in the Philosophy of Hobbes*. Helsinki: University of Helsinki Press.

Malcolm, Noel. 2002. *Aspects of Hobbes*. Oxford: Oxford University Press.

Malcolm, Noel. 2007. *Reason of State, Propaganda, and the Thirty Years' War: An Unknown Translation by Thomas Hobbes*. Oxford: Oxford University Press.

Martinich, A. P. 1998. "Francis Andrewes's Account of Thomas Hobbes's Trip to the Peak." *Notes and Queries* 243: 436–440.

Martinich, A. P. 1999. *Hobbes: A Biography*. Cambridge: Cambridge University Press.

Miller, Ted H. 2004. "The Uniqueness of *Leviathan*: Authorizing Poets, Philosophers, and Sovereigns," in *"Leviathan" After 350 Years*, edited by Tom Sorell and Luc Foisneau, 75–103. Oxford: Clarendon Press.

Miller, Ted H. 2011. *Mortal Gods: Science, Politics, and the Humanist Ambitions of Thomas Hobbes*. University Park: Penn State Press.

Milton, Philip. 1993. "Hobbes, Heresy and Lord Arlington." *History of Political Thought* 14: 501–546.

Nauta, Lodi. 2002. "Hobbes the Pessimist?: Continuity of Hobbes's Views on Reason and Eloquence Between *The Elements of Law* and *Leviathan*." *British Journal for the History of Philosophy* 10: 31–54.

Parkin, Jon. 2007. *Taming the Leviathan: The Reception of the Political and Religious Ideas of Thomas Hobbes in England 1640–1700*. Cambridge: Cambridge University Press.

Raylor, Timothy. 2010. "Hobbes, Davenant, and Disciplinary Tensions in *The Preface to Gondibert*," in *Collaboration and Interdisciplinarity in the Republic of Letters: Essays in Honour of Richard Maber*, edited by Paul Scott, 59–72. Durham Modern Languages Series, FM32. Manchester: Manchester University Press.

Rutherford, Donald. 2003. "In Pursuit of Happiness: Hobbes's New Science of Ethics." *Philosophical Topics* 31: 369–393.

Scodel, Joshua. 2002. *Excess and the Mean in Early Modern English Literature*. Princeton: Princeton University Press.

Sergio, Emilio. 2007. "Thomas Hobbes's *De motibus solis* (1649–1653): Problems of Dating." *Notes and Queries* 252: 54–56.

Skinner, Quentin. 1996. *Reason and Rhetoric in the Philosophy of Hobbes*. Cambridge: Cambridge University Press.

Sorell, Tom. 1996. "Hobbes's Scheme of the Sciences," in *The Cambridge Companion to Hobbes*, edited by Tom Sorell, 45–61. Cambridge: Cambridge University Press.

Tuck, Richard. 1996. "Hobbes's Moral Philosophy," in *The Cambridge Companion to Hobbes*, edited by Tom Sorell, 175–207. Cambridge: Cambridge University Press.

CHAPTER 27

HOBBES AND PARADOX

JON PARKIN

THE thought that Hobbes is a writer of paradoxes might come as a surprise to readers familiar with the idea that Hobbes, perhaps above all other political philosophers, wrote in terms that were designed to expunge ambiguity and vague thinking. Indeed, it is often the case that Hobbes is associated more with a distinctively *anti*-paradoxical mode of writing, a sign of his role as one of the first moderns in reaction against the philosophical ambivalence of Renaissance rhetorical culture. Rosalie Colie's seminal study of paradox cast Hobbes in this light, as a thinker presiding over the demystification of the Renaissance paradox, and others have followed suit; Bryan Crockett argued that Hobbes can be seen "as the prophet of an emerging non-paradoxical order" in response to the epistemological crisis facing early modern England.[1]

However, the thought that Hobbes can be lined up as a characteristically *anti*-paradoxical writer has been undermined in more recent years by historians of philosophy, often those with a more analytical bent, less concerned with situating Hobbes within the wider literary context. In a recent article in *Political Theory*, Patricia Springborg comments that "for a systematic philosopher Hobbes is the most paradoxical of thinkers," identifying the paradoxes in question by what she characterizes as various inconsistencies in Hobbes's work.[2] The suggestion that Hobbes's work contains inconsistencies that might count as paradoxes in some sense is not unfamiliar, and indeed finds its way into the title of several recent books,[3] but it is one that disrupts our view of a thinker who is regarded as *the* systematic philosopher *par excellence*. As Springborg notes, the idea that Hobbes might exhibit paradoxical traits tends to produce strenuous efforts to demonstrate the coherence that is judged to be lacking, either by telling a developmental story about the system, in which Hobbes's later recensions repair defects in earlier versions, or through analytical attempts to eliminate inconvenient *aporiae*. In both of these cases, Hobbes's theory is saved from paradox, but other, more

---

[1] Colie 1966; Crockett 1995, 49.

[2] Springborg 2009, 676–688.

[3] See, for example Kramer 1997, or more recently Parrish 2007.

contextual, writers take a different tack. Deborah Baumgold, for example, sees inconsistency as an unavoidable consequence of Hobbes's serial and layered mode of composition; as the palimpsest is recycled the argument complicates.[4] If Baumgold's position implies that paradox infects Hobbes's work accidentally, others detect more deliberate and subversive motivations; Hobbes's paradoxical *reductios* are aimed at demonstrating the absurdity rather than the coherence of positions. If Hobbes's account of Christian doctrine makes little sense, it is because Hobbes believes that Christianity is really nonsense. Paradox, in this typically, although not necessarily, Straussian reading, becomes a marker of subversion, the sign of stealthy heterodoxy pursued by covert means.[5] Springborg's alternative suggests that the genuine paradoxes are there because they represent the tensions between Hobbes as a philosopher and a courtier's client, forced to apply his ontology and epistemology to political problems whose terms were at odds with the requirements of his metaphysics.[6]

For all the recent awareness of paradox in his work, there have been some surprising omissions in the discussion of Hobbes and paradox, not least a consideration of his own views and those of his contemporaries on the nature and importance of paradox.[7] As we shall see, Hobbes was widely regarded by his contemporaries as a paradoxical writer, and what is more, it was a label that he seemed to accept. He appears to have taken some pride in his paradoxical style and defended a very particular understanding of paradox as an important component of his intellectual project.

In what follows, I examine Hobbes as a paradoxical writer on his own terms and consider what this might mean for understanding Hobbes's work. In the first place, this is to carry out the under-laboring task of establishing what Hobbes and his contemporaries might have meant by the term paradox, and what Hobbes sought to do in defending his distinctive characterization of paradox. I then move on to explain exactly why this understanding of paradox may well be crucial to understanding the complicated nature of the Hobbesian project, in particular the transformative dimensions of Hobbes's political writing, which involved a very distinctive process of reframing individuals' minds. What this inquiry will suggest, to some extent against the commentators cited earlier, is that Hobbes's paradoxes (as he understood them) are not to be simply analyzed away, explained as faulty developmental stages, attributed to his composition process, or exposed as satirical *reductios* or tensions within his work; instead, I argue that paradox was crucial as a means of inaugurating the processes of intellectual transformation that constituted a central feature of Hobbes's general approach. For Hobbes, paradox lay at the heart of a strategy that was designed not simply to tell readers how to behave but also to make them complicit in the process of internalizing a Hobbesian way of thinking.

[4] Baumgold 2008, 827–55.

[5] See for example Curley 1992.

[6] Springborg 2009, 684.

[7] Paradox is not considered as a *topos* in any of the major treatment of Hobbes's rhetorical theory: Johnston 1986; Prokhovnik 1991; Skinner 1997.

1

When Hobbes's contemporaries used the term *paradox* the most common usage referred to the literal meaning in Greek, alluding to a statement that was beyond (*para*) common opinion (*doxa*). An important mediating *locus classicus* upon which such a definition tended to rest was the *proemium* to Cicero's *Paradoxica Stoicorum* which identified the key features of paradox (*quae quia sunt admirabilia contraque opinionem omnium*).[8] The sense in which paradox involved such heterodox movement is captured quite neatly in the titles of two of the most famous sixteenth-century books of paradox, Ortensio Lando's *Paradossi cioe sentenze fuori del comun parere* (1543) and Anthony Munday's *The defence of contraries: Paradoxes against common opinion* (1593), both of which allude to the Ciceronian version of the Stoic paradoxical tradition.[9] Typically this tradition, revived for popular audiences in the sixteenth century by works such as Erasmus's *Moriae encomium* (*In Praise of Folly*) (1511), consisted of the praise of unusual subjects, provocative defenses of propositions officially disapproved, through to the presentation of puzzling theses appearing to offer something like logical contradiction.[10] If these often playful forms were some of the most important literary manifestations of paradoxical writing, paradox as a concept also encompassed ideas that were simply strikingly novel and unusual, as, for example, where new positions in natural philosophy were discussed. In 1616 John Bullokar's *English Expositor* defined paradox as "an Opinion maintained contrary to the commonly allowed Opinion, as if one affirme that the earth doth mooue round and the heauens stand still." Users of this understanding of paradox understood that their paradoxical beliefs might someday be accepted as orthodoxy, and it is in this sense that Robert Boyle referred his *Hydrostatical Paradoxes* (1666). As Hamlet remarks to Ophelia of his own paradoxical opinion, "This was sometime a paradox, but now the time giues it proofe."[11]

---

[8] Cicero 1942, 257: "These doctrines are surprising and they run counter to universal opinion." Cicero's text consists of paradoxes argued against received opinion, although his intention is satirical in that his paradoxes restate Stoic ethical doctrine which in his own hypocritical society had become *contra opinionem omnium*, and therefore paradoxical.

[9] Lando's highly influential work deploys the Stoic mode of reasoning in inverting Aristotle's account of external goods, so life, wealth, fame, health, and beauty are rejected in favor of death, poverty, ignominy, sickness, and ugliness. Munday's later English text is in fact derived from it, via Charles Estienne's 1553 *Paradoxes*. The latter transformed Lando's work into a rhetorical tool for law students learning how to plead cases *a contrario*. Munday's *Defence* translated Estienne's work, with the paradoxically minded denizens of the Inns of Court as its likely audience. John Donne's celebrated *Paradoxes* can be shown to have emerged from this milieu. For discussion see the valuable and detailed work in Pizzorno 2007.

[10] For discussion of these literary forms, see Colie 1966, 3–12; Malloch 1956, 191–203.

[11] I. B. 1616, n.p. referring to what became known widely as the "Copernican paradox"; Boyle 1666; see also Boyle 1661; Shakespeare 1623, 265 [*Hamlet* 3.1.113–16].

That Hobbes was a paradoxical writer was a conclusion that that his readers found hard to avoid. This was so in both the broad sense that the arguments he made seemed to go well beyond accepted opinion and also in some of the more technical senses that Hobbes seemed to take, at times, perverse delight in shocking his readers with the advocacy of provocatively extreme positions, the presentation of profoundly counterintuitive observations, and logically unacceptable or contradictory statements. This tendency is usually associated with the rhetorically more extravagant *Leviathan*, but it is worth noting that Hobbes's readers had the same reaction to his earlier work and particularly to *De cive*. Although widely regarded as the one of Hobbes's clearest and most conservative technical discussions, *De cive* was found by most readers to be a peculiarly difficult book, typically puzzling and hard, but characteristically paradoxical with its teasing, almost aphoristic provocations.

Readers were quick to report the book's paradoxical qualities: The Frenchman Thomas de Martel, after examining the first, limited and anonymous, 1642 edition was moved to comment that it contained "many paradoxes about the state and Religion." Hermann Conring, appalled at Hobbes's conflation of right and power and the thought that animosity should be the basis for government asked, "Would any good man put up with such paradoxes?" Roger Coke in 1662 also abstracted Hobbes's "monstrous paradox" that Hobbes's state of nature in *De cive* was to be cured by laws of nature "of his own making."[12] One critic who saw *De cive* almost exclusively as a book of paradoxes rather than a serious work of philosophy was arguably Hobbes's earliest and most important, John Bramhall, bishop of Derry. Bramhall penned one of the earliest manuscript responses to the 1642 edition of *De cive* (in 1645), the bulk of which found its way into a later published critique of that work and *Leviathan*. What is striking about Bramhall's response to Hobbes is that he treats his work as a "heap of misshapen errors, and absurd paradoxes"[13] on the Stoic model, offering catalogs of exclamation mark-inducing examples. These are mostly captured in short quotations which are then listed, not for detailed refutation, but rather as an exhibition of Hobbesian intellectual atrocity. Some of the more famous Hobbesian paradoxes are identified this way for the first time in the literature: "The civil laws are the rules of good and evil, just and unjust, honest and dishonest; and therefore, what the lawgiver commands, that is to be accounted good; what he forbids, bad."[14] Bramhall also quotes the celebrated formula from *De cive*: "Security is the end for which men make themselves subject to others; which if it be not enjoyed, no man is understood to have subjected himself to others, or to have lost his right to defend himself at his own discretion."[15] Bramhall's commentary leaves it to the reader to make up his mind, "What ugly consequences do flow from this paradox, and what a large window it openeth to sedition and rebellion, I leave to the reader's judgement."

[12] Hobbes, *De cive*, ed. H. Warrender, 300; Malcolm 2002, 474; Coke 1660, 25.
[13] Parkin 2007, 41; Bramhall 1845, 547.
[14] Bramhall 1845, 541; cf. Hobbes *On the Citizen*, trans. Silverthorne, 132 [12.1].
[15] Bramhall 1845, 554; cf. Hobbes *On the Citizen*, trans. Silverthorne, 77–8 [6.3].

If the readers of *De cive* found it to be a book of paradoxes, the same was inevitably true of *Leviathan*. Bramhall naturally found seamless stylistic links between *De cive* and *Leviathan* in this regard, identifying in the later work "hundreds of paradoxes" and adding to his lists of "absurd senseless paradoxes" examples such as Hobbes's inversion of the relationship between natural and civil law (in which the former only become laws when settled by the commonwealth). The paradoxical presentation (typically) prompted indignation from the bishop: "God help us! Into what times are we fallen! When the immutable laws of God and nature are made to depend upon the mutable laws of mortal men."[16] Although Bramhall makes Hobbes's paradoxical style a trademark feature of his critique, he was certainly not alone in identifying Hobbes in this way. William Rand found *Leviathan* "too paradoxicall." Alexander Ross, another early critic of Hobbes, referred to Hobbes's "strange paradoxes." Edward Hyde, Earl of Clarendon, referred to Hobbes's "odious paradoxes," and Henry More to "his wicked *Paradoxes* concerning the word *Church*, and *Power Ecclesiastical*."[17]

Hobbes was thus judged by his contemporaries to be a paradoxical writer; as Leibniz put it, Hobbes was "noted for his paradoxes."[18] It might be possible to write off this characterization as the creation of his critics; after all, they were determined to demonstrate that Hobbes's arguments were riddled with inconsistencies, and "paradoxical" could be taken as an inconsequential term of abuse to that end. However, it is worth noting that Hobbes himself was not averse to the thought that his work was paradoxical. Indeed, he appeared to not only accept that he was a paradoxical writer, but he seemed to also take some pride in the fact.

Hobbes frequently referred to the paradoxical quality of his work. In *The Elements of Law,* he noted that the consequences of his deductions "to some may seem a paradox." They included theories about sound which "must needs appear a great paradox" and the thought, italicized in the printed version, *"That the Command of him who Commands is a Law in one thing, is a Law in every thing,"*[19] as well as the idea discussed in *De cive* that "in a *Monarchy*, the subjects are the *multitude*, and (yet the paradox is) the *King* is the *people*."[20] Hobbes understood very clearly the paradoxical character of *Leviathan*, referring to his "paradoxes of Religion" within the text, a comment he makes again in the appendix to the Latin edition where he comments that in each part of *Leviathan* "there are Paradoxes, both Philosophical and Theological."[21] Certainly in *Leviathan* Hobbes lacks any embarrassment at all about the fact that his work can be construed

---

[16] Bramhall 1845, 544.

[17] Hartlib 2002, 62/30/3b–4a; Ross 1653, 13; Hyde 1676, 310; More 1694, 89.

[18] Leibniz 1988, 46.

[19] Hobbes, *De corpore politico,* ed. Gaskin, 178. This is not the only occasion where Hobbes highlights paradoxical statements typographically, see for example *De cive* 1.10: "Natura dedit *vnicuique ius in omnia.*"

[20] Hobbes, *De cive* 12.8: "Et in *Monarchia*, subditi, sunt *multitudio*, & (quamquam paradoxum sit) *Rex* est *populus.*"

[21] Hobbes, *Leviathan*, ed. Malcolm, iii.1227: "Insunt in singulis partibus Paradoxa quaedam tum Philosophica, tum Theologica."

as a collection of paradoxes, something that is consistent with some of his private correspondence where one can detect a note of pride about what he calls "my paradoxes."[22]

Hobbes's willingness to draw attention to the paradoxical features of his work suggests that his critics were not wrong to identify paradox as a characteristic and intentional feature of his work. However, where they wanted to portray Hobbes's paradoxical approach as at best puzzling and at worst as the sign of confusion and error, Hobbes seemed to take a better view of the paradoxical quality of his philosophy. To understand why this might be, it is worth probing Hobbes's views on paradox a little more closely.

2

Hobbes's most extended discussion of paradox and its role in discussion occurs in *Questions Concerning Liberty, Necessity and Chance* (1656), part of the debate with John Bramhall on the free will question. Hobbes clearly took some pleasure in pressing upon the paradoxical qualities of his compatibilism, which allowed supposedly free actions to be described simultaneously as the products of a material necessity. The tension in the arguments clearly riled Bramhall, who complained that Hobbes's departure from common opinion about free will betrayed the fact that Hobbes was one of a "handful of men, who have poisoned their intellectuals with paradoxical principles."[23] When considering Hobbes's thought that all actions contribute to each action in some way, Bramhall comments, "I can but smile to see with what ambition our great undertakers do affect to be accounted the first founders of strange opinions, as if the designing of an ill-grounded paradox were as great an honour as the invention of the needle, or the discovery of the new World." For Bramhall, influenced by the association of a paradoxical style with the self-indulgence of Stoic philosophy, paradox "is a private opinion of one man, or a few factious men, assumed sometimes out of an error of judgement, but commonly out of pride and vain glorious affectation of singularity, contrary to the common and received opinion of other men."[24] Hobbes was thus a typical Stoic, wrong-headedly obsessed with novelties.

Bramhall's thought that Hobbes was simply indulging in the invention of paradoxes for their own sake irritated the philosopher, who shot back a revealing set of comments about the use and abuse of the term paradox in the debate:

> The Bishop speaks often of Paradoxes with such scorn or detestation, that a simple Reader would take a Paradox either for a Felony, or some heinous crime, or else for some ridiculous turpitude; whereas perhaps a Judicious Reader knows what the word signifies. And that a paradox is an opinion not yet generally received. Christian Religion was once a Paradox; and a great many other opinions which the Bishop now holdeth, were formerly Paradoxes. Insomuch as when a man calleth an opinion Paradox,

---

[22] Hobbes 1994, I.124.
[23] Hobbes 1656, 33.
[24] Bramhall 1657, 285–6.

he doth not say it is untrue, but signifieth his own ignorance; for if he understood it, he would call it either a truth or an error. He observes not, that but for Paradoxes, we should be now in that savage ignorance which those men are in that have not, or have not long had Laws and Common-wealth, from whence proceedeth Science and Civility.[25]

The passage is interesting for a number of reasons, not least of which is the central role that Hobbes ascribes to paradox in the process of bringing mankind from ignorance to a condition in which man enjoys the benefits of science and civility. Hobbes's definition rules out Bramhall's thought that paradox is simply a palpably false or ridiculous position and substitutes instead something categorically interesting about the status of paradoxes as opinions the truth or falsity of which cannot be straightforwardly identified. Paradoxes by their very nature are opinions that not only go beyond common opinion but are opinions that are also not properly understood by a reader, because to understand the paradox would dissolve its paradoxical nature and render the opinion true or false. The distinguishing feature of the paradox here is its indeterminacy for the reader. A paradox signifies the reader's ignorance and also a curious moment of suspension when the reader can judge a statement neither true nor false. It might seem odd to find Hobbes defending this judgemental indeterminacy, but what is particularly interesting is the subsequent link that Hobbes makes between the deployment of paradox and the connection with the process of civilization. Were it not for paradox, men would be in a state of savage ignorance.

The passage offers an important hint about the significance of paradox in his larger political project. Hobbes does not explicitly tell us any more about the function of paradox, but I would suggest that we can reconstruct Hobbes's understanding of the role of paradox by linking it to his general theory of knowledge and in particular by connecting it to the tradition of discussion about the nature and role of wonder.

The relevant ideas here are Hobbes's thoughts on the ways in which men are excited to the discovery of new knowledge. In *The Elements of Law*, Hobbes talks about the ways in which human curiosity is aroused:

Forasmuch as all knowledge beginneth from experience, therefore also new experience is the beginning of new knowledge, and the increase of experience the beginning of the increase of knowledge; whatsoever therefore happeneth new to a man, giveth him hope and matter of knowing somewhat that he knew not before.[26]

To encounter strange forms of novelty thus leads to the development of curiosity, as an appetite for knowledge:

And this hope and expectation of future knowledge from any thing that happeneth new and strange, is that passion which we commonly call admiration; and the same considered as appetite, is called curiosity, which is appetite of knowledge.[27]

---

[25] Hobbes 1656, 239.

[26] Hobbes, *Human Nature*, ed. Gaskin, 57 [9.18].

[27] Ibid., see the similar comments in *Leviathan*: 6.38, 26: "Joy, from apprehension of novelty, ADMIRATION; proper to Man, because it excites the appetite of knowing the cause."

From this beginning, explains Hobbes, comes all philosophy: astronomy from the admiration of the course of heaven; natural philosophy from the strange effects of the elements and "from the degrees of curiosity proceed also the degrees of knowledge among men."

In saying this Hobbes was, of course, being utterly conventional in subscribing to a familiar philosophical trope about the relationship between philosophy and wonder. Both Plato and Aristotle had made the point that philosophy begins with wonder (*thaumadzein*). In *Thaetetus,* Plato comments that "wonder is the feeling of a philosopher, and philosophy begins in wonder."[28] In the *Metaphysics,* Aristotle suggested that it is "owing to their wonder that men both now begin and at first began to philosophize."[29] Aquinas would gloss this thought by commenting that

> wonder is a kind of desire for knowledge; a desire which comes to man when he sees an effect of which the cause either is unknown to him, or surpasses his knowledge or faculty of understanding. Consequently wonder is a cause of pleasure, in so far as it includes a hope of getting the knowledge which one desires to have.[30]

St. Thomas observes that "wonder gives pleasure, not because it implies ignorance, but in so far as it includes the desire of learning the cause, and in so far as the wonderer learns something new, i.e., that the cause is other than he had thought it to be.[31]

The early-moderns followed this argument faithfully in discussing the relationship between wonder and knowledge. For Francis Bacon wonder "is the seede of knowledge."[32] Descartes, in the *Passions of the Soul,* made wonder, for this reason "the first of all the passions." It is "a sudden surprise of the soul which causes it to apply itself to consider with attention the objects which seem to it rare and extraordinary."[33] Wonder, in appropriately small amounts (too much was a bad thing in Descartes's view) "makes us learn and retain in our memory things of which we were previously ignorant."[34] Wonder thus drives us from ignorance toward the search for truth.

Hobbes had signaled his interest in "wonder" as a concept in his early pastoral poem *De mirabilibus pecci,* where the "wonders of the Peak" (as a later English translation styled them) were subjected to poetic scrutiny.[35] He would use the English

---

[28] Plato 1953, 251 [155d].

[29] Aristotle 1933, [982b12–13].

[30] Aquinas 1993, [1a2ae. 32 A8]. See also Aquinas's comments in the *Summa contra Gentiles*: "Man has a natural desire to know the causes of whatever he sees; and so through wondering at what they saw, and not knowing its cause, men first began to philosophize, and when they had discovered the cause they were at rest. Nor do they cease enquiring until they come to the first cause." Aquinas 1993, [III.xxv].

[31] Aquinas 1993, [1a2ae. 32 A8 Rp 1]

[32] Bacon, 1605, 6.

[33] Descartes 1984, 353. For Descartes's view of the the role of wonder see Schmitter 2002, 99–108. See also James 1997, 169–70; 187–9.

[34] Descartes 1984, 354.

[35] For discussion of Hobbes's view of wonder (in comparison with Descartes) see Deckard 2008, 950–955.

word "wonder" in *Leviathan* (a point to which we shall return), but usually he prefers to address the phenomenon using a term he takes to be interchangeable with wonder: "admiration."[36] This was derived from the Latin *admiratio*, with its sense that intellectual activity is suspended under the influence of emotion.

Hobbes's discussion of admiration/wonder in the *Elements* adds a characteristic twist to the traditional usage in making some suggestive comments about the ways that *admiratio* links to *effective* curiosity: His point is that if curiosity is engaged effectively then knowledge will make greater progress. Predictably, Hobbes links effective curiosity to the extent to which the wondrous novelty is connected to human interests. Where there is little obvious connection between the novelty and the usual set of human interests the effect was not likely to be dramatic: "For to a man in chase of riches or authority . . . it is a diversion of little pleasure to consider, whether it be the motion of the sun or earth that maketh the day, or to enter into other contemplation of any strange accident, than whether it conduce or not to the end he pursueth."[37] However, where human interests could be engaged effectively, novelty offered a peculiar form of delight. Where the novelty offered the chance of allowing a man to better his own estate "in such case they stand affected with the *hope* that all gamesters have while the cards are shuffling." Hobbes also refers to this feature of knowledge acquisition in *De homine*, pointing out the essential difference between animals and human beings in this regard. Animals admire something new or unusual so that they can determine if it is dangerous or harmless, but men "when they see something new, seek to know whence it came and to what use they can put it."[38] Man's restless desire to augment his powers makes him fundamentally alert to new ways in which this might be achieved. Wonder-inspiring novelty engages with this basic motivation and generates, even where the outcome is uncertain, the hope that some benefit might result.

Admiration, then, operated to motivate the observer confronted by novelty in distinctive ways, producing delight or joy through the raising of hope. Hobbes made it clear that this process happened naturally when mankind encountered strange natural phenomena, but Hobbes was also interested in the artificial creation of wonder and the effects that it engendered. There were characteristically two sides to Hobbes's interest: a critical interest in the corrupt use of man's susceptibility to wonder, and a parallel constructive interest in reworking that same tendency.

The critical interest emerged from Hobbes's suspicions about those that the Greeks called the *Thaumaturgi*, or the "workers of things wonderfull."[39] Hobbes discusses this issue in chapter 37 of *Leviathan*, where he discusses the nature of miracles—the admirable works of God "also called *Wonders*."[40] Here Hobbes is keen to distinguish the

---

[36] Hobbes uses "admiration" and "wonder" alongside each other in *Leviathan*, but when translating the relevant line in the Latin version collapses them into *admiratio*. See *Leviathan*, ed. Malcolm, ii.684–5 [37.5, 234].

[37] Hobbes, *Human Nature*, ed. Gaskin, 53 [9.18].

[38] Hobbes, *On Man*, ed. Gert, 62 [12.12].

[39] Hobbes, *Leviathan* 37.12, 237.

[40] Ibid., 37.1, 233. For a helpful recent discussion of Hobbes on miracles, which clarifies the purposes of chapter 37, see Whipple 2008, 117–142.

truly miraculous ("*a work of God ... done, for the making manifest to his elect, the mission of an extraordinary Minister for their salvation*") from things that only seem so but which nevertheless generate *admiratio*. Those things include phenomena that are strange, "that is to say, such, as the like of it hath never, or very rarely been produced," and things that cannot be accounted for by natural causes. Hobbes unsurprisingly suggests that not all of these phenomena are properly miraculous. He goes on to argue that many arise from various artificial forms of trickery practiced by deceivers upon ordinary people whose limited knowledge, particularly of natural causes, renders them particularly liable to being deceived. The artificial exploitation or creation of admiration and wonder was thus identified as a major source of the power of Hobbes's priestly confederacy of deceivers. The discussion as a whole nevertheless brings out the peculiar importance of *admiratio* as the often artificial means by which individuals were commonly motivated toward the adoption of particular beliefs.

It was this thought that seems to have driven Hobbes's particular interest in the artificial creation of wonder, which clearly offered a means by which man's natural response to wonder could be enlisted in the service of Hobbesian philosophy. By a neat, and typically Hobbesian reversal, the very same tools deployed by the *Thaumaturgi* could be deployed to effect the destruction of their kingdom of darkness. The means by which Hobbes appears to have pursued this strategy was via his aesthetic theory, in which admiration was to play an important role.

The creation of *admiratio* had long been a topic of some interest within early modern literary theory.[41] Antonio Sebastiano Minturno, who in *De Poeta* (1559) held that poetry should delight and instruct through the mobilization of the passions, suggested that poetry attained the end of instruction through the representation of deeds in such a way as to excite admiration. Whether directly influenced by this tradition or not, Hobbes's own aesthetic theory clearly placed a premium on the creation of *admiratio*, and he referred to it as an important goal of good poetry.[42] One of the main ways that such *admiratio* could be created was through the deployment of novelty, which as Clarence Thorpe has shown, occupies a central role in Hobbes's aesthetic writing.[43] As Hobbes comments in chapter 8 of *Leviathan*, the poet's fancy, or imagination, pleases because of its "extravagancy," and a capacity of expression "easily fitted with similitudes, that will please, not only by illustrations of his discourse, and adorning it with new and apt metaphors, but also by the rarity of their invention."[44] In his *Answer to Davenant*, composed around the same time, Hobbes discusses the relationship between the capacity for novelty in the knowledgeable poet, which "pleaseth by excitation of the minde" and the generation of *admiratio*: "for novelty causeth admiration, and admiration

---

[41] For discussion see Spingarn 1925, 52; Thorpe 1937, 1114–1129; Thorpe 1940, 59ff. See also Skinner 2002, 155–7.

[42] See his comments in Hobbes, *Translations of Homer*, ed. Nelson, i.xciii: "For the work of an Heroique Poem is to raise admiration . . ."

[43] Thorpe 1937.

[44] Note that "but also" becomes "above all" in the Latin edition of 1668. Hobbes, *Leviathan*, ed. Malcolm, ii.107.

curiosity, which is a delightful appetite of knowledge."[45] Here the literary ability of the philosophically-informed poet to generate *admiratio* by literary effects is linked to the development of knowledge. Although Hobbes is writing about poetry here, and specifically about the use of metaphor, this does not, of course exhaust the range of literary techniques associated with the relationship between novelty and admiration. And one of the most important figures for this relationship was, of course, paradox.

The connection between paradox and wonder was well established. Cicero's formulation in *Paradoxica Stoicorum* made clear the link the between the transgressing of common opinion and the creation of wonder (in the words of Robert Whittington's sixteenth-century translation of Cicero, paradoxes were "Maruaylous questions").[46] Indeed, George Puttenham's *Art of English Poesie* (1589) explicitly referred to paradoxical tropes as "wonderers."[47] John Florio's 1598 Italian-English dictionary calls a paradox "a maruellous, wonderfull and strange thinge to heare."[48] When the character of Paradox came on stage at the Gray's Inn revels in 1618, he explained that a paradox is "a straine of witt and invention, scrued above the vulgar conception, to begett admiration."[49] Hobbes would have been no stranger to the connection between paradox and wonder not only within the available literature but possibly also from his personal connections. Margaret Cavendish, the wife of his patron the Earl of Newcastle, composed paradoxical essays in the style of the game of "wonders" played at the Duchess of Lorraine's court.[50] Some of Hobbes's literary associates in the 1650s also appear to have experimented with paradox as a literary form, which they combined with distinctively Hobbesian political theory.[51]

The clear connection between paradox and wonder now starts to make sense of Hobbes's interest in paradoxical styles of presentation. Presenting his theory in a deliberately paradoxical form, Hobbes seems to have adopted a writing strategy that was precisely calibrated to generate a sense of admiration and wonder in his reader, which we know from his reception that it did. Far from providing a straightforward elaboration of his arguments in an appeal to the rational faculties, Hobbes appears to have deliberately sought instead to arrest his reader's rational process with *admiratio*. The general purpose of this strategy appears linked to Hobbes's theory of knowledge, and the manner in which the disruptive moment of wonder at Hobbes's artificial intellectual novelties might resolve itself into some level of excited curiosity into the possibility of new and beneficial knowledge.

---

[45] Davenant 1650, 138; see also the discussion in Reik 1977, 151–3.

[46] Cicero 1942, 256–7; Whittington 1534, n.p.

[47] Puttenham 1589, 189

[48] J. Florio 1598, 257.

[49] Pizzorno 2007, 120–7; Platt 2009, 20.

[50] K. Whitaker 2003, 126.

[51] John Davies, who produced the first edition of *Liberty and Necessity,* was a friend of the occasionally Hobbesian John Hall of Durham, whose Latin *Paradoxes* he would translate in 1653. Hall's work, produced under a pseudonym, begins with the distinctively Hobbesian-flavored paradox: "That an absolute Tyranny is the best Government." De la Salle 1653, 3–30.

3

One very plausible objection to this line of argument is that Hobbes never presents us with his account of paradox and its operation in so many words. However, this is hardly surprising. To explain a strategy that is designed to stimulate wonder clearly runs the risk of compromising the very considerable effects for which he undoubtedly hoped.[52] But we are not left without any clues of Hobbes's thought about the relationship between paradox and admiration in the way that I have suggested. That Hobbes's arguments were intended to work this way is indicated by two significant pieces of evidence. They both describe examples of what seem (for Hobbes) ideal reader responses to paradox. The first is contained in a letter to Edmund Waller dating from 1645. Hobbes was at this point in exile in France. After the informal circulation of the first edition of *De cive* and a growing underground awareness of his work, he found himself confronted by a number of antagonists. On some occasions these encounters took the form of gladiatorial matches, which may have been designed for entertainment as well as for philosophical purposes. The most famous of these was the encounter between Hobbes and Bramhall, engineered by the Earl of Newcastle in 1645, whose household, as we have already seen, took an interest in games of paradox. The paradoxical quality of Hobbes's work took center stage in the discussion with Bramhall, but this may not have been the only occasion where Hobbes's paradoxes were discussed. Writing to Waller, Hobbes comments, "My odde opinions are bayted.[53] But I am contented with it, as beleeuing I haue still the better." One reason for his content involved the evident success of his paradoxical style of philosophy. "When a new man is sett upon me; that knows not my paradoxes, but is full of his own doctrine, there is something in the disputation not unpleasant." What Hobbes finds "not unpleasant" is the way that the unwary reader is forced to respond to the paradoxical style, and Hobbes's description is revealing of his underlying theory of paradox: "He thinks he has driuen me vpon an absurdity when t'is vpon some other of my tenets and so from one to another, till he wonder and exclayme and at last finds I am of the Antipodes to ye schools."[54] Hobbes could be describing the encounter with Bramhall; one of the reasons why the latter identified him with the early Stoa was his frustration at the manner in which Hobbes deployed chained, or *sorites*, arguments

---

[52] This may reflect the generally cautious methodological approach indicated by the remarks recorded by Jean-Baptiste Lantin, who recalled that Hobbes used to say "that he sometimes made openings, but could not reveal his thoughts more than half-way." Malcolm 2002, 542.

[53] Showing some self-knowledge about the character of his arguments, Hobbes presents himself as a bear or wild animal subjected to "bayting," a striking anticipation of a similar metaphor allegedly deployed by Charles II, who, according to Aubrey, upon seeing Hobbes at court, commented, "Here comes the bear to be baited." Aubrey 1898, i.340. This raises an interesting point about how Hobbes's philosophy was sometimes designed as entertainment (either in the gladiatorial contexts arranged by Cavendish or, as the metaphors here imply, the sport of the bear gardens). Paradoxes, as Margaret Cavendish's use of them suggests, were seen as a form of philosophical entertainment.

[54] Hobbes, *Correspondence*, i.124.

composed of linked paradoxes. Hobbes was also evidently pleased with the way that his arguments generated *admiration*, together with the exclamation typical of Bramhall's written response, as his opponent realizes quite how radical Hobbes's connected paradoxical positions might be. Clearly at some level this was enjoyment that came from befuddling someone with strong preconceived ideas, but the process here is revealing of the role that Hobbes gave to paradox. His interlocutor is someone who is convinced of his own position and whose initial response to Hobbes's presentation is that it is an absurdity, but Hobbes's sustained paradoxical performance drives him to a condition in which he is reduced to wondering at the character of Hobbes's argument. Conviction has given way to marveling at the novelty of Hobbes's position, and the interlocutor is clearly not where he was before and is in a condition in which his curiosity could be engaged by the marvel to know more.

If paradox undoubtedly had this "softening up" effect, the question remains what was supposed to happen next. Another important clue comes from one of the most famous stories about Hobbes, the account of his conversion to Euclidean geometry. Although this is a story about Hobbes, told by Aubrey, it seems highly likely that Hobbes himself was the source of the story. Like many stories that Hobbes told, they tended to capture more than simply autobiographical memories and often served to reinforce elements of his arguments. The presentation of the conversion experience here is important because we see the effect of paradox upon a reader:

> Being in a gentleman's library in ... Euclid's Elements lay open, and 'twas the 47 El. Libri I. He read the proposition. "By G___", sayd he, "this is impossible!" So he reads the demonstration of it, which referred him back to such a proposition; which proposition he read. That referred him back to another, which he also read. Et sic deinceps, that at last he was demonstratively convinced of that trueth. This made him in love with geometry.[55]

The impossible paradox generates *admiratio* (signaled, as ever, by exclamation), which in turn raises curiosity, and leads the reader through a chain of connected reasoning with the well-known consequences for the history of philosophy. What the Euclid example brings out quite nicely is the way that the effect of paradox draws the reader into the resolution of the mystery. The paradox shatters the existing frame of reference, and the reader is driven to reconstitute that knowledge under the pressure of the psychological effects of wonder. That this is an active process driven by the reader amplifies the effects when the process works. In the case of Hobbes, the non-rational starting point for the encounter with Euclid engenders nothing less than love for geometry (which might be understood to enhance Hobbes's powers).

It is not hard to see that the pattern of the Euclid example is one that Hobbes adopts again and again in his writings, which are littered with underdetermined paradoxes designed like mines to set off explosions of paradigm-shattering *admiratio*. One of the most obvious is the title of *Leviathan*, where the paradox of a powerful monster, but

[55] Aubrey 1898, i.332.

one which simultaneously demonstrated the power of God, set readers into Hobbes's carefully crafted confusion. The very first reports of the book drew attention to the oddity of the title. Bishop Brian Duppa, writing to Justinian Isham in July 1651, possibly unsure whether the book had received a more sympathetic hearing from the latter, commented that the book had "a title that I wond'red at." The same puzzlement was registered by the English republican William Rand, who had found in Hobbes's work "some things too paradoxicall" but nevertheless found himself meditating on the meaning of *Leviathan* more generally.[56] For most early readers of Hobbes's work, the paradoxical title of the book acted as a kind of wonder, whose indeterminacy was a source of curiosity as to the contents.[57] Naturally, we can also see the famous title page operating in the same paradoxical manner. The purposes of anamorphic art were often paradoxical insofar as they offered simultaneous representations of different objects seen from particular perspectives. The effects that they had were often described in terms of an aesthetic of wonder and delight. The *Leviathan* title page, as Noel Malcolm shows, offers a typically paradoxical puzzle about the rational and nonrational basis of political authority that is certainly not straightforwardly decoded.[58] Every reader who picks up the book (to this day) is affected by *admiratio* upon seeing it, the necessary nonrational prelude to a productive encounter with the contents of the book.

Those contents were also mined with paradox. To return to some of the central paradoxes identified by writers like Bramhall, we can see how the approach was supposed to work. The discussion of the obligatory force of natural law is an interesting example, because it was an argument that many of Hobbes's critics identified as distinctively paradoxical in its apparently provocative inversion of the relationship between natural and civil law. Having laid down an exhaustive account of natural law in chapters 14 and 15, Hobbes sets up the paradox by suggesting at the end of chapter 15 that natural laws are not properly called laws, because laws are properly the word of "him that by right hath command over others."[59] Hobbes's statement here was puzzling to his contemporaries, who tended to trip over the sentence in some confusion; they were rescued shortly afterward in the English edition by the more comforting thought that if the same theorems as delivered in the word of God "then they are properly laws." The suspicion that this solution is not all that it seems is hinted at throughout part II, where, again in a quotable but perennially confusing paradox, the law of nature and the civil law "contain each other and are of equal extent," a suggestion that leads to the very disturbing thought that they become properly laws when commanded by the commonwealth.[60] The previously comforting thought that the word of God, traditionally understood to be Scripture, is doing any serious work in terms of generating obligation is queried in chapter 33, which in itself raises the specter of the paradox that God's word is determined by the magistrate.

---

[56] Isham 1951, 41; Hartlib 2002, 62/30/3b–4a.

[57] It is worth pointing out that this helps explain why the initial response to *Leviathan* was rather muted; readers often weren't clear about Hobbes's meaning, which was not straightforwardly heterodox. See Parkin 2007, 97–103.

[58] Malcolm 2002, 200–229.

[59] Hobbes, *Leviathan* 15.41, 80.

[60] Ibid., 26.8, 138.

Hobbes toys with his contemporary reader's emotions throughout this discussion; the short and shocking aphoristic statements providing the moments of *admiratio* that moved commentators like Bramhall to exclamation. But, having achieved this effect, Hobbes invariably attempts to capitalize on the curiosity thus aroused to get the newly motivated reader to reconstruct and internalize the argument that supports the statement. Intriguingly, when he came to revise the argument in the Latin *Leviathan*, Hobbes did not attempt to flesh out the argument at the end of chapter 15 but simply docked the mention of the word of God. The effect is to deepen the paradoxical character of the discussion. The reader is simply left to puzzle over the paradox that the laws of nature were not actually laws because law properly "is the word of one who commands, whether orally or in writing, in such a way that that everyone who is bound to obey knows that it is his word."[61] The change to the text captures something important about Hobbes's deployment of paradox, in that the reader, having been provoked, now has to discover exactly who or what the commander in this case is.[62] Paradox generates the motivation for the reader to discover the inner logic of Hobbes's argument, a logic that their previous sets of beliefs may have rendered impossible, but which their curiosity, provoked by *admiratio*, now encourages them to investigate for themselves.[63]

4

Hobbes's use of paradox was one of his distinctive writing strategies and is perhaps a surprising feature of what is often supposed to be a supremely rationalist philosophy dedicated to banishing obscure signification. Although it seems a counterintuitive thought, Hobbes crucially relied on the suspension of reason and the cultivation of wonder to motivate the kind of reader engagement that would make his philosophical project successful. Success, looked at from this perspective, lay in the ability to dislodge the reader's existing views by confronting them with artificial wonders, and in such a way that would direct the resulting curiosity toward Hobbes's new perspective.[64] If readers could be thus enticed into internalizing Hobbes's arguments, then this process

---

[61] Hobbes, *Leviathan*, ed. Malcolm, ii.242–3.

[62] This might suggest an alternative reading of the contracted nature of Hobbes's argument as it appears in Latin. The abbreviation in some cases might have been intended to enhance paradoxical literary effects.

[63] It has been suggested to me that these passages admit to more straightforward internal interpretations which appear to have eluded Hobbes. Such interpretations can be (and have been) given, but the simple fact that Hobbes did not give these accounts (and Hobbes was certainly capable of writing clear summaries) combined with the fact that scholars have puzzled over their precise meaning for several hundred years suggests that something else may be involved.

[64] It is worth making the point that Hobbes does seem to have been encouraging a shift of perspective, as opposed to asking his readers to endorse fundamentally counterintuitive ideas. Typically, Hobbesian paradox operates through the presentation of *admiratio*-inducing figures which constitute the prelude to getting the reader to reimagine quite conventional sets of relationships in Hobbesian terms. One of the difficulties with making sense of Hobbesian arguments is that readers

could play a key role in the transformation of passive readers into active, responsible authors of commonwealths. Paradoxically, the apparently anti-democratic use of paradox—a kind of magic—thus becomes a condition for the creation of a responsible and self-conscious citizenry.

Did it work? Clearly this is difficult to assess. Judging by the critical reception given to Hobbes's work, one is tempted to the verdict that the philosopher's interest in paradox was something of a disaster. Hobbes's critics, as rattled as everyone else by the infuriatingly indeterminate puzzles that Hobbes devised, busily got to work "deciding" his paradoxes, exposing them as heresy and error. And yet, as I have suggested elsewhere, the very process of exposing Hobbes's paradoxical theses nevertheless meant that wider audiences became familiar with Hobbes's wonders, which, in spite of the critical storm, retained their capacity to provoke *admiratio* in ordinary readers and thus new ways of thinking about philosophy and politics.[65] Had Hobbes adopted a less compelling mode of presentation, it is probably the case that his work would have been markedly less influential than it was and continues to be.

This last point brings us back to the modern discussion of Hobbes's paradoxes and their broader significance. It would seem that the anti-paradoxical character of Hobbes's theory has been overstated by commentators too keen to make Hobbes's work part of a decisively modern riposte to Renaissance culture. Hobbes was certainly keen to counter the abuse of marvels and miracles, but he was too aware that the psychology of wonder was a persistent and valuable element of the human condition and that any attempt to bring about enlightenment and progress paradoxically depended on it for success.

In terms of thinking about the nature of Hobbes's theory, the arguments pursued here suggest that we should be cautious before we make assumptions about the implications of Hobbes's paradoxical formulae. It may be worth thinking harder about the structural role of Hobbesian paradox within the text and thinking about how the text might have been designed to unfold to his readers. This is certainly not to imply that Hobbes's theory was entirely consistent or that his paradoxical formulae did not contain potentially heterodox consequences or even that contextual tensions were not sometimes apparent in his work. But it is to suggest that that we need to recognize that Hobbes's paradoxical approach to his subject matter may have had as much to do with his distinctive writing strategies and his determined attempts to frame the minds of his seventeenth-century readers.

BIBLIOGRAPHY

Aristotle. 1933. *Metaphysics*, translated by H. Tredennick. Cambridge, MA: Loeb.
Aquinas, Thomas. 1993. *The Collected Works of St. Thomas Aquinas.* Charlottesville, VA: Intelex.

are frequently hung up on the typically shocking paradoxical formulation and fail to graduate to the often rather conventional conclusions that Hobbes reaches. I would like to thank Al Martinich for his insightful comments about this feature of Hobbesian paradox.

[65] See the comments in Parkin 2007, 413–14.

Aubrey, John. 1898. *Brief Lives*, edited by G. Clark. 2 vols. Oxford: Oxford University Press.

B[ullokar]., I [John]. 1616. *An English expositor teaching the interpretation of the hardest words vsed in our language*. London.

Bacon, Francis. 1605. *The tvvoo bookes of Francis Bacon. Of the proficience and aduancement of learning, diuine and humane*. London.

Baumgold, Deborah. 2008. "Difficulties of Hobbes Interpretation." *Political Theory* 36(6): 827–855.

Bramhall, John. 1657. *Castigations of Mr Hobbes*. London.

Bramhall, John. 1842-5. *The Works of . . . John Bramhall*, edited by J. H. Parker. Oxford: Oxford University Press.

Boyle, Robert. 1661. *The sceptical chymist*. London.

Boyle, Robert. 1666. *Hydrostatical Paradoxes*. London.

Cicero, Marcus Tullius. 1942. *On the Orator*, translated by H. Rackham. Cambridge, MA: Harvard University Press.

Coke, Roger. 1660. *Justice Vindicated*. London.

Colie, Rosalie. 1966. *Paradoxia Epidemica: The Renaissance Tradition of Paradox*. Princeton: Princeton University Press.

Crockett, Brian. 1995. *The Play of Paradox: Stage and Sermon in Renaissance England*. Philadelphia: University of Pennsylvania Press.

Curley, Edwin. 1992. "I durst not write so boldly: or how to read Hobbes's theological-political treatise," in *Hobbes e Spinoza*, edited by Daniela Bostrenghi, 497–593. Napoli: Bibliopolis.

Davenant, W. 1650. *A discourse upon Gondibert an heroick poem / written by Sr. William D'Avenant; with an answer to it, by Mr. Hobbs*. Paris.

Deckard, Michael Funk. 2008. "A Sudden Surprise of the Soul: The Passion of Wonder in Hobbes and Descartes." *The Heythrop Journal* 49(6): 948–963.

De la Salle, J. 1653. *Paradoxes*. London.

Descartes, R. 1984. *The Philosophical Writings of Descartes*, vol. 1, edited by J. Cottingham, R. Stoothoff, and D. Murdoch. Cambridge: Cambridge University Press.

Estienne, Charles. 1583. *Paradoxes*. Paris.

Florio, John. 1598. *Worlde of Wordes*. London.

Hartlib, Samuel. 2002. *The Hartlib Papers*, edited by M. Greengrass and M. Hannon. Sheffield: Sheffield University.

Hobbes, Thomas. 1656. *Questions Concerning Liberty, Necessity and Chance*. London.

Hobbes, Thomas. 1984. *De cive*, edited by H. Warrender. Oxford: Oxford University Press.

Hobbes, Thomas. 1994. *The Correspondence of Thomas Hobbes*, 2 vols., edited by Noel Malcolm. Oxford: Oxford University Press.

Hobbes, Thomas. 1994. *Human Nature and De Corpore Politico*, edited by J. C. A. Gaskin. Oxford: Oxford University Press.

Hobbes, Thomas. 2012. *Leviathan*, edited by Noel Malcolm. Oxford: Oxford University Press.

Hyde, Edward, Earl of Clarendon. 1676. *A brief view and survey of the dangerous and pernicious errors to church and state, in Mr. Hobbes's book, entitled Leviathan*. Oxford: Oxford University Press.

Isham, G. 1951. *The Correspondence of Bishop Brian Duppa and Sir Justinian Isham 1650–1660*. London: Northampton Record Society.

James, Susan. 1997. *Passion and Action: The Emotions in Seventeenth-Century Philosophy*. Cambridge: Cambridge University Press.

Kramer, Matthew. 1997. *Hobbes and the Paradoxes of Political Origins*. Cambridge: Cambridge University Press.

Leibniz, Gottfried Wilhelm. 1988. *Political Writings*, edited by Patrick Riley. Cambridge: Cambridge University Press.

Malcolm, Noel. 2002. *Aspects of Hobbes*. Oxford: Oxford University Press.

Malloch, A. E. 1956. "The Techniques and Function of the Renaissance Paradox." *Studies in Philology* 53(2): 191–203.

More, Henry. 1694. *Letters on Several Subjects*. London.

Munday, Anthony. 1593. *The defence of contraries: Paradoxes against common opinion*. London.

Parkin, Jon. 2007. *Taming the Leviathan: The Reception of the Political and Religious Ideas of Thomas Hobbes in England 1640–1700*. Cambridge: Cambridge University Press.

Pizzorno, Patrizia Grimaldi. 2007. *The Ways of Paradox from Lando to Donne*. Florence: Leo S. Olschki Editore.

Plato. 1953. *The Dialogues of Plato*, translated by B. Jowett, 4th ed. Oxford: Clarendon Press.

Platt, Peter G. 2009. *Shakespeare and the Culture of Paradox*. Farnham: Ashgate.

Parrish, John M. 2007. *Paradoxes of Political Ethics*. Cambridge: Cambridge University Press.

Reik, Miriam. 1977. *The Golden Lands of Thomas Hobbes*. Detroit: Wayne State University Press.

Ross, Alexander. 1653. *Leviathan drawn out with a hook*. London.

Schmitter, A. 2002. "Descartes and the Primacy of Practice: The Role of the Passions in the Search for Truth." *Philosophical Studies* 108(1–2): 99–108.

Shakespeare, William. 1623. *Mr. VVilliam Shakespeares comedies, histories, & tragedies Published according to the true originall copies*. London.

Skinner, Quentin. 1997. *Reason and Rhetoric in the Philosophy of Thomas Hobbes*. Cambridge: Cambridge University Press.

Skinner, Quentin. 2002. *Visions of Politics: Hobbes and Civil Science*. Cambridge: Cambridge University Press.

Spingarn, Joel E. 1925. *A History of Literary Criticism in the Renaissance*. New York: Columbia University Press.

Springborg, P. 2009. "The Paradoxical Hobbes: A Critical Response to the Hobbes Symposium." *Political Theory* 37(5): 676–688.

Thorpe, C.D. 1937. "Addison and Some of His Predecessors on "Novelty." *PMLA* 52(4): 1114–1129.

Thorpe, C.D. 1940. *The Aesthetic Theory of Thomas Hobbes*. Ann Arbor: University of Michigan Press.

Whipple, J. 2008. "Hobbes on Miracles." *Pacific Philosophical Quarterly* 89(1): 117–142.

Whitaker, K. 2003. *Mad Madge: Margaret Cavendish, Duchess of Newcastle, Royalist, Writer and Romantic*. London: Chatto and Windus.

Whittington, R. 1534. *The paradox of Marcus Tullius Cicero*. London.

Index